MW01013326

THE HANDBOOK OF IS'

There is growing interest i.
the world. This *Handbook* pro\
tion of political life in Israel from t.
present. The themes covered include:
solved issues that have been left to fester,
(the Knesset, government, judiciary, preside.
and commissions of inquiry); citizens' political p.
political parties, civil society, and the media); the fo.
bedeviled Israeli democracy since its establishment (sec
religion, the status of Israel's Arab citizens, and econom.
with concomitant social gaps); and the contours of the politica.
and its impact on Israel's democracy. The authors skillfully inte
detailed basic data with an analysis of structures and processes, mak
ing the *Handbook* accessible to both experts and those with a general interest in Israel.

Itzhak Galnoor is Herbert Samuel Professor of Political Science (emeritus) at Hebrew University of Jerusalem, and Academic Director at the Chazan Center at the Van Leer Institute. He has been a Visiting Professor at many international universities, and served on the Executive Committee of the International Political Science Association (IPSA) and edited its Advances in Political Science book series, published by Cambridge University Press. He is the author of: *Privatization Policy in Israel: State Responsibility and the Boundaries between the Public and the Private* (with others, 2015). In 2015 Galnoor was awarded the Lifetime Achievement Award of the Association of Israel Studies (AIS) and in 2016 the Scholar Achievement Award of the Israel Political Science Association.

Dana Blander is a senior researcher at the Israel Democracy Institute (IDI) in Jerusalem, the editor of IDI's online magazine "Parliament," and a clinical psychologist. Her research focuses on Israeli politics and political philosophy. She received her degrees in Political Science and Psychology from the Hebrew University of Jerusalem. Her doctoral thesis, "Ambivalence as a Challenge to the Political Order," won the Hebrew University Berger Prize for academic excellence. In 2010–11 she was AICE Visiting Professor at Tufts University.

The Handbook of Israel's Political System

Itzhak Galnoor

Hebrew University, Jerusalem

Dana Blander

Israel Democracy Institute, Jerusalem

Gila Svirsky
Senior Translator

Ira Moskowitz
Translator

CAMBRIDGE
UNIVERSITY PRESS

University Printing House, Cambridge CB2 8BS, United Kingdom

One Liberty Plaza, 20th Floor, New York, NY 10006, USA

477 Williamstown Road, Port Melbourne, VIC 3207, Australia

314–321, 3rd Floor, Plot 3, Splendor Forum, Jasola District Centre, New Delhi – 110025, India

79 Anson Road, #06-04/06, Singapore 079906

Cambridge University Press is part of the University of Cambridge.

It furthers the University's mission by disseminating knowledge in the pursuit of education, learning, and research at the highest international levels of excellence.

www.cambridge.org
Information on this title: www.cambridge.org/9781107097858
DOI: 10.1017/9781316160978

Originally published in 2013 by Am Oved Publishers as *The Political System of Israel*, written in the Hebrew by Itzhak Galnoor and Dana Blander (ISBN 978-9-651-32349-2).

First published in English by Cambridge University Press in 2018. Principal Translator, Gila Svirsky; Translator, Ira Moskowitz.

First published 2018

Printed in the United States of America by Sheridan Books, Inc.

A catalogue record for this publication is available from the British Library.

ISBN 978-1-107-09785-8 Hardback

To my beloved children:

Shaked

Alon

Amir

Klil

Dana

To my beloved grandchildren:

Rotem

Zohar

Maayan

Oren

Ori-Yeela

Itzhak

May they live as equal, happy citizens.

Contents

Figures

Tables

Preface

Politics

In many democracies around the world, including Israel, the reputation of "politics" has been sullied. Surveys indicate dwindling public trust of the authorities, political leadership, media, and political parties. This disenchantment derives both from the high expectations of the state that were never realized as well as the improper behavior of some politicians. Nevertheless, the term "politics" will be used in this book in an entirely neutral manner, even biased somewhat toward the positive, in recognition of the onerous tasks imposed on good, dedicated, and honest politicians.

The tasks that we, the citizens, bring to the political system include problems that have proven intractable in other frameworks – the economic market, social organizations, the community, or even the family. Indeed, the issues we relegate to politics are among the most sensitive (security, environment) and elusive, certainly more than issues addressed in the business world. To carry out these tasks, politicians must build coalitions, mobilize support, conduct negotiations, compromise, postpone decisions, and balance the public good with more narrow, conflicting interests. Without these tools, politicians would find it very hard to set policy or implement it, but because of these tools, the image of the "political" has become synonymous with dishonesty or corruption.

To come up with creative solutions or compromises, the political process has sometimes had to merge disparate elements.[1] Such solutions may appear strange, but are often a function of the complexity of the problem and the fact that no simpler practical solution can be found. Bear in mind also that "engaging in politics" is not

[1] For example, the Gaza-Jericho Agreement between Israel and the Palestinian Authority in May 1994 defied geographical logic, but created a common denominator, allowing for an end to the political stalemate. In another example, the Tal Commission, appointed in 2000 to examine the issue of drafting Yeshiva students into the army, recommended a compromise designed to appease both the secular and ultra-Orthodox communities: Young ultra-Orthodox men who elected to discontinue their Torah studies would be allowed to enter the job market after an abbreviated military service. This proposal met opposition from both seculars (as it allowed for the continued shirking of military service) and the ultra-Orthodox (as it spelled the beginning of apostasy), and failed.

confined to national or local government, but can also be found in public organizations or corporations, as well as universities, hospitals, volunteer associations, and sometimes even families. Naturally most of us would deny that we ever "engage in politics," but prefer to ascribe such behavior to a self-interested other: "They" do dirty politics, while "we" operate out of legitimate interests. A negative approach to politics (a climate of "anti-politics") endangers democracy because it may stir a demand for "rule by experts" – elected or not elected – who will straighten out the politicians.[2] This belief in the need for "experts," like the yearning for "strong leaders," paves the way for a non-democratic regime. In politics, there is legitimate manipulation and sometimes necessary contortions, but these must be done with integrity or risk the loss of credibility. Political behavior must be legitimate, not just in keeping with the law or some code of ethics, but because elected representatives must set a personal example. In short, politics is a social mechanism and therefore not "good" or "bad" in and of itself; note, also, that in some democracies, politics is not perceived as fundamentally bad. In Israel, too, many examples exist of positive politics: a government minister who resigns because a decision conflicts with his world view or conscience; a Knesset member (MK) who tables a bill for the public good despite criticism from her constituents; Knesset members from different parties who make common cause to promote an issue; politicians who turn down an opportunity for an interview on the grounds that they are not familiar with the issue.

For purposes of this book, we will make do with a simple definition of the "political" as compared to the non-political – "the effort to develop and utilize organized social power" (Heller 1933, 301). To which we add that, in democratic politics, cooperative activity to achieve common goals rests upon consensus regarding the rules of the game. The merit of this definition is that politics is defined as a tool for purposeful activity by society. No issue is inherently "political"; it becomes political when it has a common component that requires organized effort (e.g., compulsory education, epidemic prevention, security, law, environmental quality). Issues enter and leave the political system in accordance with the preferences of that society: A decision by society, for example, not to leave it up to a driver to calculate the risk of injury in a car accident led to legislating the mandatory wearing of seat belts. A neutral discussion of politics is intended to restore to it its lost honor, as distinct from the deeds or foibles of specific politicians or dissatisfaction with the political system of Israel (Galnoor 2003).

Political Systems

A political system is not a concrete entity – it is not the ruler or the government, nor is it a state, institution, or organization, but rather an abstract concept – the sum total of political interactions in a specific society (intended, as noted, to enable cooperative activity).[3] This analytical concept allows us to draw from the range of human endeavor those activities that can be defined as "political." The market, for example,

[2] In the 2003 Knesset election, a party ran for office named "A Different Israel – Because We're Fed Up with Politicians." Purporting to engage in "politics without politicians," they even convinced 7,144 people to vote for them.

[3] This definition is drawn from Easton (1965, 49–50), who holds that a political system is a series of social interactions of individuals and groups geared to the "authoritative allocation of values."

is part of the economic system, but the laws and regulations governing it, and their enforcement, are political. Another example: When the state arrogates decision-making about pensions – and makes these payments compulsory – pensions have become political. Note that what is political in one society may not be political in another. Public health services may be the responsibility of the political system in one national or regional government, but not in another. The concept "political system" allows us to think about political activity in terms of interactions within all of society, not just within the governing institutions or nationally. Thus, the analysis also incorporates a discussion of the dynamics of political life, such as the technological breakthroughs of online media and their repercussions on public space; the impact of civil society organizations; the degree of "politicization" of certain issues (such as civil service appointments); or the "politicization" of issues unique to Israel, such as relations between religion and the state.

Steering Capacity and Representation

The role of the political system resembles that of steering a ship: keeping the system steady and guiding it toward common goals.[4] Steering capacity is therefore the ability of the political system to secure its self-survival, to invest in its own viability, to adapt to environmental changes, and, of course, to shape policy and make binding decisions. A political system without steering capacity is a ship with a disconnected rudder. It can drift, but it cannot engage in purposeful movement. The concept of "steering capacity" points to the dynamic of political activity that must navigate in situations of flux, trauma, or crisis. For this reason, we prefer "steering" to other terms, such as "governability," which suggests the ability to govern a specific society; or "capacity to govern," which ignores the fact that political activity requires not just governance, but also the trust of its citizens and their cooperation in the steering process. Our approach in this book is that focusing on the government does not reveal the range of happenings in the political system, which may include some non-democratic elements that reduce the contribution of citizens, social organizations, and the media. In every democratic society, there are multiple centers of power in addition to the government, and no one of them is entirely sovereign (Dahl 1971, 24). The steering mechanism must connect well the helm and the rest of the ship, the political system and society (on profiles of steering capacity in Israel, see Galnoor 1996). And a *democratic* political system is also measured by its responsiveness to the will of the citizens – its representativeness.

"Representation" in a democracy means that citizens authorize those elected to public office to work toward common goals. At the same time, every democracy grapples with questions about the system of representation, how to ensure oversight of elected officials, and conflicts between the general, public interest and partial, vested interests. Added to this is the media revolution, which is transforming personal and public patterns of behavior, and has already brought about dramatic political changes locally and globally.

[4] The original Greek concept of government refers to the art of holding the steering wheel (Deutsch 1963, 182).

In this book, we focus particularly on the tension between steering capacity and representation, and whether the balance between them has been upset. True representation allows citizens not just to cast a ballot, but to influence the political system and sometimes even become involved in policymaking; true steering capacity requires that the government navigating the political system will act not just according to the legitimate interests of individuals and groups, but also mediate between conflicting interests, and work toward achieving goals for the public at large. In other words, steering capacity means that when the government turns the wheel, the ship actually turns with it; and, in the age of media, that this is not just the *image* of movement.

We start from the first two decades following the establishment of the state, when the steering capacity of the Israeli political system was strong in terms of achieving common goals, withstanding crises, and maintaining stability. This is not a value judgment; no claim is made that these goals were worthy, or that the progress was inclusive of all social groups, or that stability is necessarily a good thing. Indeed, in the relevant chapters we suggest that the steering capacity in the early period was achieved largely at the expense of the representation, openness, transparency, and public oversight of policymaking. The balance, in other words, was tipped toward steering capacity rather than representation. Later, the political system became more responsive to public concerns, and could be said to be more representative. But was it? And if so, how did steering capacity fare? And has the result been that Israeli society is more or less democratic? We will try to answer these questions in the final chapter of this book.

Structure of the Book

The book opens with the formative years of the political system around the establishment of the state, and considers its development to this day. A factual description is integrated with an analysis of processes and their significance, and does not avoid presenting the positions of the authors on controversial matters.

The five parts of the book:

- Part I: "Establishing the State" presents the formation of the political system in the early years (1948–53) in the context of the political heritage from the Yishuv period, and the supremacy of politics. The second chapter raises the question "Does Israel have a constitution?" and lists the issues that have never been resolved, but left to fester for future generations.
- Part II: The five chapters of "Institutions Matter" examine the institutional framework – the presidency, legislature, executive, and judiciary – as well as the oversight monitoring mechanisms, such as the state comptroller, with the pitfalls of each and subsequent crises in steering capacity.
- Part III: "Political Society" is about the political behavior of citizens and bodies that are not part of the political system. It tracks the political participation of Israeli citizens in various channels (political parties, elections, civil society, media), and declining public trust in the elected organs.
- Part IV: "Unresolved Policy Problems" probes the four issues that have bedeviled the Israeli political system since its inception (security, the status of Israel's

Arab citizens, economic inequality with concomitant social gaps, and religion–state relations). It traces the sources of these problems and the reasons why they have become political challenges.

- Part V: Finally, "Democracy in Israel" considers the contours of Israel's political culture, its impact on democracy, and the dangers facing it.

The book is based on the course "The Government of Israel" taught for many years by Professor Galnoor in the Political Science Department of Hebrew University, previously published writing, and his experience as Civil Service Commissioner under Prime Minister Yitzhak Rabin (1994–96). Significant insights presented here were developed during his years with the Israel Democracy Institute (1988–93). The book also draws from the publications of Dr. Blander and her work in the Israel Democracy Institute. Above all, this book is the result of seven long years of fruitful work together.

Acknowledgments

First and foremost, we thank our students in the Political Science Department of Hebrew University, whose thoughtful questions and contributions have enriched the chapters of this book. Through the long years of writing, we accumulated many debts and we cannot possibly name them all: the students who served as dedicated research assistants for the course; colleagues who shared their thoughts and advice; participants in the departmental seminar where we presented a chapter from the book; and those whose written and public words affected us. To all, we are grateful.

The authors wish to underscore their deep appreciation to the following people who wrote or helped write the first drafts of several chapters: Dr. Amnon Cavari – the chapters on the judiciary and the elections; Dr. Ofer Kenig – the chapters on the political parties, the elections, and coalitions; and Dr. Yael Peled – the chapter on Israel's Arab citizens.

The work of several research assistants greatly improved the content of the book: Naomi Himeyn-Raisch, Paz Carmel, Elihu Sapir, Eyal Tsur, Yuli Rzaev, Benjamin Schvarcz, and Asaf Sheratzky. We thank them and hold them blameless for any errors that remain or data that slipped through our and their fingers despite our best efforts.

It is a privilege and pleasure to express our deep gratitude to several colleagues who took the time to read parts of the Hebrew manuscript and contributed significantly to its improvement: Prof. Leah Achdut, Ms. Shlomit Asheri-Shahaf, Dr. Ariela Aufir, Dr. Amnon Cavari, Prof. Momi Dahan, Prof. David Dery, Prof. Ruth Gavison, Prof. Reuven Hazan, Prof. Menachem Hofnung, Dr. Hagai Katz, Ms. Anna Kempelman, Prof. Ruth Klinov-Malul, Prof. Mordechai Kremnitzer, Prof. David Levy-Faur, Prof. Yehiel Limor, Prof. Moshe Maor, Prof. Suzie Navot, Dr. Yael Peled, Prof. Leslie Sebba, Dr. Neta Sher-Hadar, Prof. Gayil Talshir, Ms. Efrat Waksman, Prof. Yael Yishai, Atty. Nurit Yisraeli, and Prof. Yitzhak Zamir.

Special thanks to Dr. Rivka Markus, head of the Knesset Archive, for her generous assistance in locating documents and data; and to Prof. Elie Rekhess and Dr. Arik Rudnitzky, who shared with us data used in the chapter on Arab citizens of Israel. These individuals are responsible only for the corrections made and errors avoided; we bear responsibility for the rest.

The entire project was supported by a grant from the Israel Science Foundation and written almost entirely at the Van Leer Jerusalem Institute, which provided a safe harbor for Itzhak Galnoor for many good years. Completion of the Hebrew book was made possible thanks to support for our graduate assistants from the Levi Eshkol Institute and the Bernard Cherrick Center – both at the Hebrew University.

English Version

This *Handbook* was published with the support of the Israel Science Foundation.

In addition, support for the English translation of the book was provided by the Israel Institute; the Van Leer Jerusalem Institute; and the Israel Democracy Institute.

The translation of this book required several tasks at once: make it lucid for English readers; omit details about Israel that would require long explanations; keep within the page limit, given that an English text can be a third longer than the Hebrew; correct omissions and errors; and update it extensively as the Hebrew book was published in 2013. Orchestrating it all was our senior translator, Gila Svirsky, who translated most of the chapters and the Hebrew bibliography, scanned the entire manuscript to ensure uniformity, and made valuable improvements of the content. Alongside her, doing exceptionally good work, was our second translator, Ira Moskowitz. We are greatly indebted to Gila and Ira. We would like to thank our editors at CUP, Lewis Bateman and Sara Doskow, who took over from Lewis in 2016; Daniel George Brown, the content manager; and Julene Knox, our expert copy-editor, for their enthusiastic support, encouragement, and professional handling of such a complicated manuscript. Thanks also to two anonymous readers, whose comments and good suggestions we tried to follow to the best of our ability.

Updating was carried out with great devotion by Guy Freedman, a Ph.D. student at the Interdisciplinary Center Herzliya (IDC), whose work was supported by the Levi Eshkol Institute. In updating we also received valuable help from Adv. Udit Corinaldi-Sirkis, Prof. Aviad Hacohen, Prof. Nissan Limor, Prof. Rafi Mann, Prof. Hillel Nossek, and Adv. Nir Weiner. The long and detailed index was prepared with devotion by Mrs. Fern Seckbach.

In a book of this length, errors are unavoidable. We would be grateful to readers who draw our attention to them and welcome those who wish to respond:

Itzhak Galnoor at the Jerusalem Van Leer Institute (itzhakg@vanleer.org.il) or

Dana Blander at the Israel Democracy Institute (danabl@idi.org.il).

Jerusalem 2017

PART I

ESTABLISHING THE STATE – THE SUPREMACY OF POLITICS

Aren't efforts to personify a state – attributing to it a "personality," age, character, and even territorial limbs – misleading about the essence of this social institution?[1] We would like to start by saying that a discussion of the state and its political systems does not suggest their omnipotence, nor assume that they exhaust the richness of human endeavor. Politics should be the handmaid of society, not vice versa. This does not contradict our view that there is a critical formative period in the history of a state, a period whose impact can be felt in both short- and long-term political patterns.

Political life in Israel in the twenty-first century cannot be grasped without an in-depth understanding of the pre-state (Yishuv) and early state periods. By this we mean that the history of every group contains chapters with formative elements, whose influence abides from generation to generation. For the Jewish public, the Holocaust and the state-making process are such chapters; for the Arab public, the Zionist enterprise and establishment of Israel were formative. Therefore, common to the chapters in Part I is the effort to glean from the pre-state and early state periods those elements that continue to influence the political system in Israel. We omit the historical descriptions during this period, which can be found in other works, and focus only on issues that can help elucidate what took place in later years.

Chapter 1 presents the influence of the political institutions – British, Zionist, and Yishuv – on Israel's post-1948 parliamentary system, and sums up what remains from the pre-state heritage. Retrospectively, despite elements of continuity, 1948 was clearly a watershed for the state and its political leadership: internationally – the attainment of legitimacy for the Zionist movement; and internally – the attainment of exclusiveness for the political system. This chapter discusses the founding of the state and the shaping of its institutions and patterns of political behavior during the first five years. The discussion concludes in 1953, not because of the significance of this year (though it marked Prime Minister Ben-Gurion's first retirement), but because the matters under discussion had stabilized: the founding of institutions, the consolidation of state authority in security and foreign affairs, the holding of democratic elections, and state involvement in new internal areas. Chapter 1 closes with a

[1] On different approaches to the institution of the state, see Galnoor 1995, 8–16.

discussion of the meaning of the state's victory over its rivals, and its emergence as the institution with the greatest influence on society, its groups, and its people.

Chapter 2 describes the events around creating a constitution at the time the state was founded, but extends the discussion to the issue of a constitution in contemporary times. Had the leadership of those years managed to forge a written constitution out of the diverse views, as had many states in their early years, this period would have had an even greater formative influence. Nevertheless, we believe that what exists and what is missing in Israel's unwritten constitution ("the 1949 constitution") are rooted in that early period: the actual constitutional status, the standing of the Basic Laws, recourse to the Supreme Court's constitutional rulings, and the controversial issues that largely remain extra-constitutional. In this chapter we also ask whether a written constitution would have helped surmount the internal divisions in Israeli society, and perhaps even prevented some of the troubles and crises that have beset Israel over the years.

Part I of this book also lays the groundwork for two threads that weave their way throughout the volume: the primacy of politics in Israeli public life; and the ongoing tension between the relatively broad representation in the elected bodies of the political system and its steering capacity.

1 The Formative Early Years of the State (1948–1953)

1.1 The Yishuv Period – The Beginning of Israeli Democracy?

It is encouraging to observe veteran democracies because the longer they maintain a democratic system, the better their chances of remaining a democracy. Does this apply to Israel? How many years before a state can be called a "veteran democracy"? And what do the years of democratic experience imply – in addition to the longevity, is there a qualitative component to this experience?

Efforts to infuse the pre-state institutions with a democratic character – the Zionist Congress elections held from 1897 in Diaspora Jewish communities, the campaigns for these elections, and the functioning of the Zionist institutions – all set a fairly democratic course for the state-in-the-making. This gradual and extended process meant that, by 1948, it was virtually axiomatic that Israel would have a democratic system of governance. But were the obstacles that plague Israeli politics and democracy in the twenty-first century already planted during this period?[1]

The period preceding establishment of the state holds many secrets that could help make sense of Israel's contemporary political system. First, the Zionist institutions of the Jewish community (the Yishuv) continued to operate for a long time: the Histadrut Labor Federation, the Jewish Agency, and some of the political parties began under Ottoman rule, while others – the Chief Rabbinate, the Civil Service, and the courts – originated during the British Mandate. Second, Yishuv patterns of political behavior continued in the state, such as the electoral system and the "religious status quo." Most importantly, the violent conflict between Jews and Palestinians, which affects virtually all aspects of the two nations, was rooted in the historical events of pre-1948 Palestine (E.I.).[2] In this book, we discuss the formation of the Jewish political system, but not the parallel development of the Palestinian political community, because, among other reasons, all efforts failed to establish a

[1] On the formation of the Jewish community's political system during the British Mandate, see Horowitz and Lissak (1978) and Galnoor (1982). On *economics*, see Barkai, Gross, and Metzer. On *institutions, parties, and movements*, see Akzin, Goldstein, Heller, Reuveni, Sager, and Shapiro. On *significant individuals*, see Bilski, Miller, Pappe, Porath, Segev, Shaltiel, Teveth, and Zahor. All the documents from this period have now been made public.

[2] In this book, we use the official British designation "Palestine (E.I.)" to indicate the Mandatory area west of the Jordan River. In referring to the geographical area, we use the term "Land of Israel" (Eretz Israel) or "Palestine," as appropriate.

joint political framework, and the Palestinian institutions had no direct impact on the Israeli political system (Horowitz and Lissak 1977, 19–46; Porath 1974). The discussion below is based on the following assumptions about the period of the state:

- The foundation of the Israeli political system was laid prior to establishment of the state, and well before most of the Jewish population made an appearance after 1948.
- To understand much of Israeli foreign and internal affairs, their roots in the Yishuv must be examined – from the conflict with the Palestinians to issues such as the religious–secular rift, the multi-ethnic structure, the ideological debate over the state, territories and borders, and relations with Diaspora Jewry.
- Political patterns of activity during the Yishuv period are important, whether in the finding of continuity (as in the coalition structure) or discontinuity (as in managing social conflicts).
- The establishment of the state of Israel in 1948 was an historic watershed in terms of the international standing of the Zionist movement. There is a fundamental difference between a national movement striving for independence and a sovereign state. With respect to the political system itself, however, there is considerable continuity (Sager 1971, 29–49; Rubinstein 1976, 284).

The political system of the Zionist movement and the Jewish Yishuv achieved its main goal. Within a relatively brief span of eighty years, from the end of the nineteenth century to the middle of the twentieth, the framework of a state was erected, largely through political activity. Not all nationalist movements that strive for independence ultimately succeed, and not all that succeed accomplish their goal by displaying a rather advanced capacity of their political system.

Thus some seven decades after the founding of Israel, and a century since the beginning of the political system, it can be said that the establishment of Israel did not take place *ex nihilo* because existing political institutions provided vital continuity and context. The implications of this are numerous. Israeli parliamentarism has a long history, for example, dating back to the first Assembly of Representatives in 1920. This history holds out hope for continuity, but also dismay over the faults that remain uncorrected for such a long period.

The issue of continuity is also relevant for the dispute within Israel over the source of the Israeli–Palestinian conflict: Shouldn't the establishment of the state mark the dividing line between how a voluntary national movement conducts itself (e.g., bending the rules) and how the government of a properly run country operates, one that is presumably cautious about the legality of its actions, both domestically and internationally? In any event, one cannot fully grasp contemporary Israeli politics without digging into its roots in the Yishuv period. The political system that evolved during the pre-state period showed exceptional capability (to be called "steering capacity") in achieving its main goals. Under objectively trying conditions, it successfully attained the goal of establishing a state; and its skill at navigation won legitimacy and a willingness to participate from most of the Jewish population, hence its decisions were accepted as binding.

In retrospect, that political system no longer exists in the twenty-first century, even though some institutions and patterns of behavior survived the journey. The Yishuv system showed great vitality in the first decade of the state, but began to wane, institutionally and functionally, in the 1960s, as will be seen. The basis for democratic political participation was laid, but some components – which did not exist or could not be built during the pre-state period – were still missing. On the eve of the Six Day War (1967), the political system had already advanced well beyond the starting point of democratization.

At that point, the "Yishuv period" seemed to be drawing to a close, and an opportunity arose of launching a new stage – of stabilizing the system and filling in the missing pieces. Things, however, worked out differently.

1.2 Establishment of the State

In a seminar of the Dror Zionist youth movement held in a Displaced Person camp in Germany in 1947, youth who had survived the Holocaust met with emissaries sent from Palestine. One of the young women participants described the encounter as follows:

> [We were] convinced that after the atrocities of the war, it would be impossible not to build a new world, one more just and pure, in which all inhabitants would be equal. On this fertile soil of hopes and expectations, the emissaries from Eretz Israel, bearers of the tidings of redemption, were fervently welcomed …
>
> They appeared to be the sons of the gods and were idolized, with no connection whatsoever to whom they were personally, simply because they belonged to the land of dreams – the Hebrew Kibbutz in Eretz Israel, which embodied an image of the Jewish future in its best and most beautiful incarnation, more noble and just than anything imaginable.

And the author adds:

> This was the atmosphere in 1945–1948 … Those who did not experience it would be hard pressed to understand the pathos of the era, life on the ideological edge, lofty words that were real and self-evident, but sound today like a collection of flowery phrases. (Holtzman 2002, 227)

The land of dreams, an image of the future – these are not flowery phrases when one describes, even retrospectively, the yearning for a state. The founding of Israel released a flood of emotion that had been building up since November 29, 1947 with the UN decision to establish a Jewish and an Arab state, and reached a crescendo in the Declaration of Independence on May 14, 1948. The state was born in a turbulent war on the heels of the Holocaust, and was perceived as an era of genesis, the launch of a social and cultural revolution, raising expectations of redemption in all its forms. Even a staid civil servant like Ze'ev Sherf (later cabinet secretary), who oversaw arrangements for the new government mechanisms, writes emotionally more than a decade later (1959): "We were as dreamers. Joy and fear were bound together. Present and past were interwoven; vision and reality intermixed; the messianic era had arrived, the end of subjugation by foreign rulers" (1959, 56).

On May 14, 1948, the five Hebrew-language, morning newspapers issued a joint edition called "Day of the State," which carried the text of the Declaration of Independence and a manifesto issued by the Provisional State Council rescinding the British White Paper that had restricted Jewish immigration to Palestine. Were these the harbingers of redemption? A glance through the newspapers in the early years of the state reveals that all symbols of Israeli sovereignty became the source of enormous pride – the flag of Israel flying at the UN, Herzl's remains brought for reburial in Jerusalem, foreign ambassadors presenting their credentials to the president of the state, Israeli athletes in international competitions, the Hebrew encyclopedia, El Al's first flight, etc. How many speeches were given that began, "For the first time in two thousand years…," an expression so overused it became an example of a stock phrase.

In a meeting of intellectuals with Ben-Gurion in 1949, the question arose of whether creation of the state could be termed – figuratively, of course – "the coming of the Messiah." Ben-Gurion's reply:

> The moment he [the Messiah] arrives, he will cease to be the Messiah. When you find his address in the telephone directory, he will no longer be the Messiah … The Messiah is needed so that he will not arrive. Because waiting for the Messiah is more important than the Messiah himself and the Jewish people lives awaiting him and believing in him. Which is the reason why the Jewish people exists at all. (quoted in Segev 1986)

In a high school civics text from the early 1950s, the author expressed his concerns about education "in a new state such as Israel, whose rules and life are not the product of a long civic or political tradition, and in which many inhabitants come from regions of the world that have no democratic civic tradition." The author was even willing to forego the older generation, writing that civics must be taught in schools "so that a common citizenship framework will be created at least for the younger generation" (Fishman N.d., 7).

What was understood by the concept "state," or at least what did the leaders understand by it? Two issues stand out in the confidential protocols of Mapai's Central Committee as they discuss the longed for sovereignty. The first was the ability to bring immigrants into the country without asking anyone else's permission – hence the rush to cancel the Mandate regulations that forbade immigration, and the concern about control of the ports as soon as the British had evacuated. And the second was the appearance of uniformed Hebrew soldiers and policemen as a symbol and perhaps pledge to withstand external threats (Avizohar and Bareli 1989, 306–7). Ben-Gurion, however, was focused on security matters; after proclaiming the state, he entered two sentences in his journal: "At four in the afternoon Jewish independence was proclaimed and the state was established. Its fate is in the hands of the defense forces" (ibid., 512).

These ideological leaders, who spoke and argued incessantly about everything, provided few details about the meaning of the long desired state. And it was surprising to find – even among seculars – that redemptive, quasi-messianic terms became buzzwords, such as "establishment of the Third Temple" (Sherf 1959, 226). And some humorists managed to capture the trepidations, as well: "For two thousand years the Jews prayed in vain for a state; why does it have to happen in my generation?"

The debates were ultimately channeled into what was then defined as an aspiration for "statism" – giving priority to overall national rather than particularistic considerations. Statism was presented as diametrically opposed to "sectarianism" and factionalism, and a remedy for the social and partisan divisiveness of the Yishuv period (Yanai 1982, 63–66; Yanai 1987, 169).[3] We will return to this at the end of the chapter.

[3] Horowitz and Lissak (1978) emphasize the role of legitimacy in this debate: The statist view is that government legitimacy derives from public support, while the class view asserts that legitimacy is conditional and derived from social movement frameworks.

The definitions of "state" in the twenty-first century differ from those used in the previous century in the era of the territorial nation-states. The state is still the main organizing framework, but alongside the previous exclusive approaches and the continuation of national struggles, global perspectives and even indications of a post-state era have appeared. See, for example, a definition that already carries intimations of transience: "The state is a geographically delimited segment of human society united by common obedience to a single sovereign" (*The International Encyclopedia Social Sciences* 2001, vol. 15, 150). In other definitions, the "state" is one of three institutions, along with "the market" and "civil society" (*The International Encyclopedia Social Sciences* 2001, 14962). In earlier definitions in international law, a state is characterized by a permanent population, a defined territory, a government, and its relations with other states (international legitimacy) (Montevideo Convention 1933). When these components exist over time, a state is considered "sovereign" vis-à-vis other states. A state is also a "nation-state," if it is intended to realize the right to self-determination of a specific group (a nation) that has distinctive characteristics such as ethnic origin, language, religion, history, or other relational qualities. In Israel as a new state that expresses Jewish national aspirations, these common characteristics exist, but unlike other states, it is also a new fusion of nation and territory.

The story of the state of Israel begins with a group of Jews who called themselves "Zionists" and began to see themselves as belonging to a nation that lacked a state of its own. Initially, the main challenge was the need for territory, unlike other national movements that emerged in a struggle against conquest, or strived to overcome an internal schism. The special challenge of the Zionist movement was the very conceptualization and definition of this old-new nation – was it Jewish? Hebrew? Israeli? Over one hundred new states were established after World War II, but the Zionist national movement that created Israel in 1948 was unique from another perspective. It was a movement of national renaissance, European in its world view and concepts, which had come too late for the European "spring of nations" in the nineteenth century, and too early for the Asian and African liberation movements in the twentieth century. As a result, the creation of Israel resembled, but also differed from, those of other new states. Regarding the newborn state as virtually sacred is familiar from other new states (Binder et al. 1971; Geertz 1963). However, the ongoing external threat has made the very preservation of Israel not just its primary challenge, but also a defining feature of Israel's Jewish national identity.

Of the four characteristics of the state cited above, territory and population were still vague in 1948, while international legitimacy was relatively more assured due to the UN approval of the Partition Plan of 1947 and recognition of the new state by the USA and the USSR. The government stabilized very quickly, followed by recognition of the sovereignty of the state. Despite the many internal divisions during the Yishuv period, it was patently clear in May 1948 that the new state would have one government over one army, one police force, and one civil service. Israel was from the outset a "strong state" vis-à-vis the society it served (*The International Encyclopedia Social Sciences* 2001, 14978–82). This strength is apparent in many states at their inception, but it was surprising, considering that most of the early leaders were socialists and, in theory at least, professed a belief in the gradual disappearance of the state. Furthermore, some of its leaders held liberal views, including perception of the state as a social contract rooted in natural rights, i.e., a mere tool for realizing social goals. Even Jabotinsky, who placed the state above all factional interests, including class, was a true liberal who wrote, "I, too, have a blind hatred for the idea that the state is everything" (Bilski Ben-Hur 1993, 30). A weak state, however, was not the predominant concept, and the fact remained that little attention was given to clarifying the essence of the state; and some were fearful of sanctifying statehood or were concerned about its enormous power.[4] An étatist view of the state as the be-all and end-all appeared later in political and security considerations, and heavily influenced Israeli history after 1967. In the period immediately after the founding of the state in 1948, Israel displayed "stateness" according to both Fukuyama's (2004, 7–9) criteria – the scope of its activity and its institutional capacity.

1.3 Transitional Institutions and the Legal Infrastructure

The Partition Plan with Economic Union approved by the United Nations in 1947 included details about the transition arrangements and governance in the Jewish and Arab states to be established. The UN plan even defined the democratic form of governance (parliamentary), the electoral system (proportional representation), and various rights (religious, minority, and women's suffrage). The role of the Constituent Assemblies would be to "draft a democratic constitution."

The Jewish institutions prepared themselves by setting up the transition bodies in accordance with the partition proposal, and in March 1948, the leadership of the Jewish Agency and the Va'ad Leumi (the Jewish National Council) agreed to establish a provisional council. This was preceded by intense negotiations among the parties, concluding in an unwritten "inter-party covenant" in which the existing balance of power would serve as the basis for constituting the council, as follows: twelve Yishuv members of the Jewish Agency executive, fourteen executive members of the Va'ad Leumi, and another nine representatives of parties not included in these two institutions (Avizohar and Bareli 1989, 363–69). On April 18, 1948, the Provisional State Council and the Provisional Government were established, but these names were soon changed to the People's Council and the People's Administration due to the opposition of the Mandatory government. The members of these provisional bodies had not been elected to them, but most had been elected earlier to the Zionist or Yishuv institutions. The Provisional Government was established with an agreed upon political makeup of thirteen members that was not elected or approved by the Provisional State Council, but wielded great power and did not require a vote of confidence by the council (Medding 1990, 14). It was a coalition government, and a threat of resignation by some of its members carried enormous weight, as would become clear to Ben-Gurion and his party during the Altalena affair (see below).

These provisional bodies served for a short period, but were of signal importance as the transition institutions of the new state, established with inter-party agreement. They operated successfully until the first elected government took its place in March, following the January 1949 election. Institutional continuity from the Yishuv period

[4] On messianic expectations, see Segev 1986; on the influence of western liberalism on Chaim Weizmann, see Dowty 2001, vol. 1, 16; on the views of those who negated the state, see Galnoor 1995, 124–129.

was preserved in these temporary bodies, as mentioned, but particularly noteworthy was the effort to be inclusive even of parties not previously represented – for different reasons – in the leadership of the Jewish Agency and the Va'ad Leumi: the ultra-Orthodox, Revisionists, and Communists. Thus the Provisional State Council scored an extraordinary achievement by securing the participation of most of the political groups, with the exception of the Arabs, the Civil Union Party, the Irgun, and Lehi (the small opposition pre-state military organizations).[5] The Provisional Government was a broad coalition, comprising no fewer than eight out of thirteen parties in the Provisional Council. The efforts at inclusion were made primarily at the expense of Mapai, which was left without a majority in the Provisional Government (five out of thirteen including a representative of the List of Sephardim). Mapai's representation in the Provisional Council (some 30%) was just under its proportion in the Assembly of Representatives (1944) and the Zionist Congress (1946). Even the two workers' parties combined (Mapai and Mapam) did not control a majority of the Provisional Council. However, whatever Mapai lost in representation in the provisional institutions, it gained by winning broad public legitimacy. The authority of the provisional institutions was undisputed by the vast majority of the Jewish public, even on sensitive issues like the induction orders issued in April 1948, or administrative matters such as taxes or car licensing.

The makeup of the provisional institutions, though the members had not been elected, also influenced the character of the future parliamentary system. In practice, a division of function emerged between the legislative and executive branches, and the fact was established that the executive branch is based on a coalition.

A. Declaration of Independence

The Declaration of Independence was a moment of jubilation. The governance issues raised by the Declaration and the accompanying documents concerned the international standing of the newly created state and its functioning vis-à-vis its citizens.[6] The Declaration strives to give external, international validity to the sovereign state of Israel by citing the Balfour Declaration of 1917; the Mandate of the League of Nations of 1922, which recognized the right of the Jewish people to rebuild its national homeland; the contribution of the Jewish Yishuv during World War II, which earned it the right to be counted among the founders of the United Nations; and, above all, the decision of the General Assembly to establish a Jewish state. In this brief Declaration, the United Nations is cited no fewer than seven times, the most important being: "By virtue of our natural and historic right, and on

[5] The original decision about membership in the institutions states that a place would be reserved for an Arab representative in the People's Council. See discussion in the Mapai Central Committee dated March 6, 1948 in Avizohar and Bareli (1989, 379). The Declaration of Independence included an appeal to the Arab inhabitants of Israel to "participate in the building of the State" based on "due representation in all its provisional and permanent institutions." The Civil Union Party boycotted the elections to the Assembly of Representatives and the Zionist Congress, and was felt to be represented by the General Zionists. There was no desire to give the Irgun or Lehi leaders direct representation in the provisional institutions – the three members of the Revisionist movement were considered their representatives.

[6] On the legal validity of the Declaration, see *Kol Ha'Am v. Interior Minister* 1953 as well as *Yardor v. Central Elections Committee to the Sixth Knesset* 1965 (Rubinstein and Medina 2005, vol. I, 39–55).

the strength of the resolution of the United Nations General Assembly, we hereby declare the establishment of a Jewish state in Eretz-Israel, to be known as the State of Israel." Note that "Eretz-Israel" is not a territorial term; the Declaration, like other Provisional Government decisions, refrained from defining the borders of the state of Israel.

With regard to gaining internal legitimacy, several sources are cited in the Declaration – beyond the "natural and historic right" – drawn from the actions that led to independence: Jewish settlement in the country; the contribution of the Zionist movement; Jewish efforts in the Diaspora; and the necessity of resolving the problem of the Jewish people in the wake of the Holocaust. Members of the Council who signed the Declaration felt the need to emphasize that they were representatives of the Yishuv and the Zionist movement. The Declaration asserts the responsibility of the state toward its present and future citizens: first, a commitment to immigration and the ingathering of Jews in the Diaspora, which expands the state's responsibility to Jews who are not citizens; second, development of the country for the benefit of all its inhabitants; third, the foundations of freedom, justice, and peace as envisaged by the prophets of Israel; and, fourth, equality of rights to all its inhabitants irrespective of religion, race, or sex, and freedom of religion, conscience, language, education, and culture. This is the credo of the Declaration, and two issues are absent: "equality" as a value in and of itself, as opposed to "equality of rights" – which is surprising considering the socialist ideology of the key leaders; and the terms "democracy" or "democratic regime," which are not directly cited. In the last chapter of this book, we discuss the question of whether democracy was at the time perceived as self-evident.

With regard to the structure of the government, the Declaration adhered closely to the directives of the UN Partition Plan, calling for provisional transition institutions, elections, a constitution drafted by the Constituent Assembly, and elected authorities in accordance with the constitution.

B. Early Legislative Acts

The first legislative act of the Provisional State Council, in parallel with the Declaration of Independence, was to issue a Manifesto in what was then called the Official Gazette, conferring upon itself the role of legislative authority, and even bestowing a measure of legislative power upon the Provisional Government for purposes of emergency legislation (Article 1). This act of circular authorization may be understood because of the need for transition arrangements, which were also explicitly cited in the UN decision. Article 3 of the Manifesto is of particular importance, as it states that the law extant in Palestine prior to establishment of the state shall remain in force, subject to any modifications that ensue from laws and amendments enacted after establishment of the state and its authorities. It thus stipulated that not only would the Mandatory courts continue to function in their previous format, but that the legal norms in Palestine (E.I.) would continue in Israel, unless otherwise decided. In other words, Israel perceived itself to be part of the British legal family (together with the crown colonies) with all this implies about its legal culture and underlying values. This continued for many years until independent Israeli legislation had sufficiently accrued and the legal umbilical cord was finally severed by the Foundations of Law Act (1980) (see Chapter 6).

Although the Law and Administration Ordinance of 1948[7] was meant to be temporary, it was in effect the first constitutional document and determined the division of function between the governing authorities – that the government will operate in accordance with policy laid down by the council and will be accountable to it. Several of its articles remain in force to this day. From the outset, the provisional leadership attributed great importance to having a legal framework for its activities, including the authority to govern, issue regulations, and collect taxes. The Ordinance again cites the intent to include Arab representatives in the council who recognize the state of Israel, but this never came about.

Article 9 of the Ordinance set out the provisions for emergency regulations. On May 19, 1948, the Provisional State Council declared a state of emergency, and this declaration is periodically renewed by the Knesset to this very day. Looking back, one can justify these regulations during the war of 1948–49 and the austerity period that followed. However, continued use of this drastic measure is the subject of intense debate, and the courts have been asked to intervene out of concern that ministers would use emergency regulations for inappropriate purposes.

In this context, we note the Emergency Regulations to Prevent Terrorism issued by the government on September 20, 1948.[8] While the background for this was the Altalena incident (June 1948), the issue of these regulations was directly precipitated by the assassination of Count Bernadotte on September 17 (see below). Based on the regulations and ordinances to prevent terrorism, Lehi, the Irgun, and affiliated bodies were outlawed. The Ordinance defines a terrorist organization and activity, but the most problematic article – perhaps the most undemocratic legislation of the Provisional State Council – states, "If the Government, by notice in the Official Gazette, declares that a particular group of persons is a terrorist organization, this notice shall serve in any legal proceeding as proof that the group of persons is a terrorist organization, unless the contrary is proved" (Article 8). This use of circular reasoning to define a terrorist organization transfers the burden of proof to the accused, and undermines the rule of law. This order remains in force and increasingly stringent amendments have been added to it over the years (Amnon Rubinstein 1991, vol. 2, 814–18).

None of the documents published upon the establishment of Israel delineates the geographic area or borders of the state. In a meeting of the People's Administration on May 12, 1948, Pinchas Rosenblüth (Rosen), Minister of Justice, raised the question of borders, noting that one cannot proclaim a state and applicable laws without stipulating the area of jurisdiction (Bondi 1990, 392). The dilemma was as follows: Should the borders of partition be declared the borders of the state of Israel, in accordance with the UN General Assembly resolution, or should Israel await the territorial outcome of the war? Ben-Gurion and others opposed setting borders on the grounds that if the other side opposed partition and the state had to be established by force, these factors would determine the future borders of the state (Sherf 1959, 105–6). A vote was held, and the majority decision was that the borders

7 Published in the Official Gazette No. 2 on May 21, 1948. The term "ordinance" was taken from Mandatory terminology and used for all legislation enacted by the Provisional State Council. Knesset legislation is referred to as "law."

8 Replaced soon after by the Prevention of Terrorism Ordinance (1948), in force retroactively from May 14, the day the state was established. Official Gazette No. 24, September 29, 1948.

of the state would not be part of the Declaration, leaving another crucial issue unresolved to this very day.[9]

C. Law of Return (1950)

Although the Law of Return was enacted by the first Knesset, not during the transition period, it belongs in this discussion because it shaped the character of Israeli society. The wording of the Declaration of Independence – "the right of the Jewish people to rebuild its National Home" and "establishment of a Jewish State in Eretz-Israel" – is not surprising, because this was the formulation used in the UN partition decision. The new phrase was "the state of Israel," and this did arouse debate among the drafters of the Declaration (Sherf 1959, 100–6). The Law of Return, in comparison with the Declaration, presents a more decisive view of the "Jewishness" of Israel. The law asserts that Israel belongs to the entire Jewish people, whether they are citizens or have not yet immigrated ("ascended") to Israel.[10] This has two far-reaching implications for governance. The first is the argument that a constitution cannot be written – not for (or in the name of) all the Jewish citizens who have not yet moved to Israel. Second, the law assigns a different status to Israel's non-Jewish citizens. The law is a kind of promissory note from Israel to Jews all over the world, one that can be claimed by obtaining citizenship after arrival in Israel. The 1950 formulation stipulates that "every Jew is entitled to immigrate to Israel," and those who arrive receive "immigration certificates" and become citizens. The Citizenship Law passed in 1952 states that anyone who enters Israel under the Law of Return can become an Israeli citizen. Since the "Who is a Jew?" question did not have much political resonance in the early years of the state, little was made of the difference between "Jews" who became citizens through the Law of Return and those who immigrated to Israel, but were not considered Jewish under Jewish law (Halakha).

Within a short time, however, this issue would indeed preoccupy the political system, with no solution in sight despite amendments to the Law of Return and intervention by the courts. The Law of Return did not establish a Jewish-religious identity to the state, and it could be argued that it was originally intended as a form of affirmative action for Holocaust survivors (Kimmerling 2004, 258). In retrospect, however, the Law of Return did forge the perception that Israel is "a Jewish state," with all the differences this implies between Jewish and Arab citizens, such as rights to the land.

In symbolic parallel with the Law of Return was adoption of Jewish content for the flag – the blue and white colors of the *tallit* prayer shawl and a Star of David in the center – and the seven-branched candelabra, based on the one used in the ancient Jewish temple, as the emblem of the state. Similarly, Hatikva, the national anthem, with its Jewish content ("a Jewish soul longing"), expresses the

[9] The UN Partition Plan assigned to the Jewish state 52 percent of the area of Palestine (E.I.). Following the war and the 1949 ceasefire agreements, Israel controlled about 75 percent of the land area (Galnoor 1995, 289).

[10] For the wording of the draft Law of Return and explanations, see *State Records: Bills*, No. 48, June 27, 1950, 189–90. For parliamentary debate on the Law of Return, see *Knesset Records*, First Knesset, Second Session, No. 30, 2094–107.

Jewish character of Israel. The state symbols were anchored in the Flag and Emblem Law (1949). And in 2004, Hatikva was officially legislated as the national anthem.

1.4 Transition Put to the Test

"They say it was fun here before I was born," according to a popular Israeli song, and the Yishuv period is drawn in the vivid colors of unity for a common cause – the national struggle, ingathering of the exiles to Eretz Israel, settlement, opposition to the White Paper, the Independence War (1948–49), and so on. A reminder is in order, therefore, that during the pre-state period, Jewish society was fragmented and factious. There were intense struggles, some of them violent, political assassinations, and clashes that verged on a civil war. While the struggle between Jews and Arabs was the overriding issue, the period was also riddled with internal conflict, primarily between the Labor camp and the Revisionist movement.[11] The internecine feuding within Jewish society reached a peak soon after the establishment of Israel, manifested in three prominent events that all took place in the second half of 1948: the Altalena affair (June), the assassination of Count Bernadotte (September), and the disbanding of the Palmach (starting in November). Thus, within the space of half a year, at the height of the war, the newborn political system faced three internal tests of signal importance. At base, all three revolved around the state's exclusive prerogative to employ force.

A. The Altalena Affair (June 1948)[12]

Upon establishment of the state, the Irgun and Lehi signed agreements to disband their underground organizations and join the Israel Defense Forces (IDF). Irgun activity persisted in Jerusalem, however, which was designated an international city according to the UN Partition Plan. The *Altalena*, an Irgun ship bearing arms and immigrants, reached the coast of Israel on June 20, 1948, during the first lull in the war. What transpired before the ship reached shore is the subject of fierce debate to this day – what had or had not been agreed between the Provisional Government and the Irgun about the distribution of the weapons. The negotiation did not produce a clear understanding, however, and violent clashes continued for three days. On June 22, at the height of the crisis, the ship, anchored off the coast of Tel Aviv, was shelled by the IDF. Sixteen Irgun fighters and three IDF soldiers were killed (though the exact number of casualties is also in dispute). The Irgun responded by announcing that it no longer recognized the Provisional Government nor would its soldiers serve in the IDF; the government began to arrest their commanding officers.

[11] A few examples: the split in the Haganah and founding of the Irgun (1931), the assassination of Arlosoroff (1933), clashes between the Histadrut and the Revisionists over control of the employment bureaus (1934), the resignation of the Revisionists from the Zionist Organization and founding of the "New Zionist Histadrut" (1935), the wrangling over the Peel Commission report (1937), the "hunting season" as the Haganah sought to suppress Irgun anti-British activities (1944), and the debate over the Partition Plan (1947). There were also intense struggles within the Labor camp itself – such as the arguments over the Biltmore Declaration (1942) and the split of Mapai (1944).

[12] Gilead 1963, vol. 2, 971–78; Niv 1965–76, vol. 6, 259–78; Lankin 1974; Brenner 1978; Nakdimon 1978; Yanai 1982, 25–38.

In a meeting of the Provisional State Council on June 23, Ben-Gurion called the incident "insurrection" and asserted that the danger from an internal wrenching was no less than from an external enemy. He insisted on the need for "one army that obeys one government and one supreme command," saying that no state can tolerate individuals or organizations bringing even the smallest amount of private arms into the country. On the previous day, Ben-Gurion had said, "This is an attempt to murder the state. Compromise is not an option."[13] B. Weinstein, who represented the Revisionists in the council, inveighed against Ben-Gurion and the government for their "unbridled lust for power," and demanded a parliamentary commission of inquiry. Effective political opposition came from the representatives of the religious parties (Mizrahi and Ha-Mizrahi), who announced their resignation from the Provisional Government. The threat was not carried out, however, because – together with the General Zionists and HaOved HaTzioni parties – they forced Ben-Gurion to moderate his stance and establish a special committee under the Provisional Council to mediate relations with the Irgun. Yanai notes that the compromise resembled patterns of behavior during the Yishuv period, though Ben-Gurion wanted to assert the exclusive authority of the new state institutions, particularly in matters of security (Yanai 1987, 174; Ben-Gurion 1969, vol. 1, 179–91).

In practice, the Irgun ceased to exist as a military force some three months later, and the government successfully met its first test for imposing authority in the name of the new state. The Altalena affair had been a violent confrontation: lives were lost and bitter feelings remained, surfacing periodically during the early years of the state. Nevertheless, the crisis had been contained and did not deteriorate into a civil war. In retrospect it was evident that both sides had showed restraint. Less than a month old, the political system of the new state could notch a major achievement: Unlike other national movements in similar positions, Israel did not have a blood-drenched struggle over government power (Sprinzak 1979, 95).

B. The Assassination of Count Bernadotte (September 1948)[14]

On September 17, 1948, Count Folke Bernadotte was assassinated in Jerusalem by four members of Lehi, a Hebrew acronym for "Fighters for the Freedom of Israel."[15] Bernadotte, a member of the Swedish royal family, had been appointed by the UN in May to be a mediator for Palestine. Compromises devised by Bernadotte were known as the first and second proposals, and sought to adapt the 1947 Partition Plan to the new situation after the eruption of war. According to Bernadotte's first proposal, an Arab state would not be established, but rather a federation of Transjordan and Israel. Transjordan would include all the territories designated by the Partition Plan to have become the Arab state as well as the Negev, which the Partition Plan had assigned to Israel; Israel would include the entire Galilee, part of which had previously been assigned to the Arab state. Jewish anger focused primarily on Bernadotte's proposal not to internationalize Jerusalem, but to annex the entire city

[13] The People's Council 1948, 4–5.

[14] Nadel 1968; Zameret 1988, 143–56; Ilan 1989; Shamir 1994.

[15] According to the testimony of Meshulam Makover, who participated in the assassination (Zameret 1988, 155–56).

to Transjordan. The proposal met with vehement opposition by both the Israeli government and the Arab League. Under pressure from the superpowers, Bernadotte revised the plan and submitted a second proposal in which he restored the idea of internationalizing Jerusalem.

Lehi continued to operate in Jerusalem after the state was founded with the avowed intent of preventing the city from becoming internationalized. A week before the assassination, Lehi activists had demonstrated against Bernadotte in Jerusalem. The decision to kill Bernadotte was made by the Lehi leadership because they believed his plan "left no doubt that it would pave the way to liquidation of the Jewish state only weeks after it drew its first breath" (Y. Shamir 1994, 97). Responsibility for the assassination was claimed by the National Front, an unknown body understood to be Lehi. The murder shocked the Yishuv and the provisional institutions, primarily because of the damaging international repercussions.[16] Ben-Gurion fumed at a meeting of the Provisional State Council on September 23, 1948, calling the killing "a tragic, horrifying, and shameful act carried out by a gang of good-for-nothings, cowards, and repugnant schemers," and the council held a moment of silence in memory of Bernadotte and his deputy, Col. André Serot, the French UN observer who had been killed with him. In response, the government took the following measures: It arrested 184 Lehi activists in Jerusalem and sixty-two throughout the country, liquidated the Lehi bases and confiscated their weapons, ratified the Emergency Regulations to Prevent Terrorism, and offered a substantial reward for anyone giving information leading to the capture of the assassins. Among those arrested was one of the Lehi commanders, who was convicted and sentenced to eight years in prison. In his remarks to the council, Ben-Gurion did not forget to mention the Altalena affair, which he called "the first attack on the sovereignty and authority of the state of Israel," and he announced that the government had decided to disband the Irgun within twenty-four hours, in Jerusalem as well.[17] Soon after, the Prevention of Terrorism Ordinance was issued.

Lehi elected not to engage in active resistance, preferring to become a political movement – the Fighters' List, which ran in the election for the Constituent Assembly in January 1949. Heading the list was the arrested commander and it won one Assembly seat (5,363 votes). The Fighters' List did not coalesce as a party, however, and dissolved by the time of the second election to the Knesset in 1951.[18] The state institutions decided not to stoke the conflict with Lehi, despite external pressure (primarily from the Swedish government), and most Lehi members under arrest were freed within a few weeks without being brought to trial.[19] After the election, in the transition period prior to the convening of the elected Knesset, the Provisional State Council passed a pardon law that enabled the

[16] The Bernadotte proposal was never implemented, and some attribute this to the assassination. Others claim that the murder almost led to adoption of the plan by the UN General Assembly. See Ilan 1989, 72–73.

[17] The People's Council: The Provisional State Council, vol. 1, Session 19, September 23, 1948.

[18] In his 1994 autobiography, Yitzhak Shamir wrote that the desire to free Friedman-Yellin was among the main reasons for establishing the Fighters' List (1994: 51).

[19] According to Nadel, they weren't really under arrest (1968: 132–50). The Swedish government was furious about the inadequate investigation of the murder, the Swedish Prosecutor General reporting, "It is not clear that the Israeli authorities genuinely wanted to find Bernadotte's murderer" (ibid.: 154).

release in February 1949 of all the Lehi prisoners. Bernadotte's assassins were never brought to trial.

Thus, the second test of the political system was not just about the state imposing its authority over dissident organizations, but also its demand for exclusive control of foreign policy. Using limited force, the state brought about the complete dissolution of the underground organizations and enacted draconian emergency regulations, followed by the Prevention of Terrorism Ordinance. Evident in this incident, too, is a mix of the democratic application of government authority together with partisan considerations of consolidating Mapai's control. In retrospect, the former had primacy.

C. Disbanding the Palmach (November 1948)[20]

The Palmach (a Hebrew acronym for "strike force") was created by the Haganah (the main military arm of the majority) in 1941, thus acrimony around its disbanding bore a different character than the two previously described events – this was more "in the family" of the organized Yishuv – within the framework of the labor movement and the Histadrut (Bar-Or 2003, 239–50). The Palmach was the elite military unit of the Yishuv, and in 1948 it was the force that bore the brunt of the fighting. The Palmach also had a clear party affiliation – its military bases were in the kibbutzim, primarily those belonging to the Hakibbutz Hameuchad movement, from which almost all its senior officers derived. The Palmach had a separate Command headed by the Palmach Commander, who was not directly subordinate to the National Command of the Haganah. When the Ahdut Ha'avoda party (and its affiliate, Hakibbutz Hameuchad) split from Mapai in 1944, the dispute over the Palmach's separate status became a clearly political matter, exacerbated when Ahdut Ha'avoda merged with Hashomer Hatzair to form Mapam (the "united workers' party") in January 1948, shortly before the Constituent Assembly election. The tension between them was also ideological: "The aim of disbanding the Palmach was not to dismantle an undesirable framework," asserted Yigal Allon, one of its leaders, "but to dismantle its values." Allon later also called the Palmach "a legal workers' army under command of the entire labor movement."[21] The issues in contention were not merely authority and subordination, but also the character of the IDF. Ben-Gurion regarded the Palmach as a separatist organization; Mapam saw it as a pioneering, military vanguard.[22]

The first stage began with the dismissal of Yisrael Galili (identified with the Palmach), from his post as head of the Haganah National Command, in late April and early May 1948. Ben-Gurion, who had just taken over the Ministry of Defense in the Provisional Government, argued that there was no need for another layer between him – the government-appointed minister – and the chief of staff. Based on previous arrangements, the National Command was composed of equal representation of the parties – both the labor movement and civilian bodies – but Ben-Gurion

[20] Gilead 1953; Pa'il 1979; Yanai 1982, 38–50; Shapira 1985; Gelber 1986.

[21] Protocol of Hakibbutz Hameuchad Council, Autumn 1948, 83, 87.

[22] Ben-Gurion's personal pattern of leadership also figured in this affair, as Anita Shapira points out (1985, 11–17).

wished to revoke this arrangement and subordinate the Haganah (later the IDF) directly to him. He wrote in his journal (May 12, 1948) that he would not accept the defense portfolio unless "our army is subordinate to the people, only the people. That everyone in the armed forces acts in accordance with his defined authority and an authoritative appointment, that security be the decisive consideration in all security matters" (Ben-Gurion, 1983, vol. 1, 412). Mapam claimed that Ben-Gurion was using subordination and loyalty as a pretext, as there was no doubt about the absolute loyalty of the Palmach to the political leadership and the minister charged with security (unlike the breakaway organizations), hence Ben-Gurion's motivations were personal and partisan. At the same time, Mapam's representatives opposed giving Ben-Gurion absolute control over security matters, and demanded that Mapam be included in leading the battle "relative to its power and importance" (A. Shapira 1985, 26). The dismissal of Galili sent shockwaves through the senior ranks, and four department heads in the General Staff threatened to resign.[23] This stage ended with a compromise forced on Ben-Gurion in which Galili would return, but not as head of the National Command. In September 1948, Galili tendered his resignation.

In the second stage, Ben-Gurion ordered the dissolution of the Palmach Command, which had authority over three Palmach brigades operating independently within the IDF. These brigades had been incorporated into the IDF as soon as it was formed, but they continued to take orders from the Palmach Commander.[24] Ben-Gurion viewed the Palmach as a party-driven, sectoral organization, and compared its separatism to the Altalena and Bernadotte incidents (A. Shapira 1985, 56). Despite the clear differences between them – the Palmach was not a threat to the government – the principle underlying the three incidents is similar: Ben-Gurion's determination to end Yishuv patterns and forge a unified, apolitical military organization that would be loyal to the government. Disbanding the Palmach was also in the self-interest of Mapai and Ben-Gurion, who were fearful of Mapam's threat to their hegemony, more than any threat from the Irgun or Lehi. Ben-Gurion also feared a takeover of the IDF by the Palmach Commanders, who were identified with Mapam. For example, when Yigal Allon was appointed GOC Southern Command in August 1948, he quickly set up a kind of surrogate Palmach headquarters as "the command center for the Palmach team" (A. Shapira 2004, 388, 412). Mapam representatives in the Histadrut added to the fear when they claimed that the Palmach was the only force that did not hesitate to act against the Irgun in the Altalena incident, and the one that would stand up to any threat of "Jewish fascism" (Yanai 1987).

In September 1948, the order was issued from the chief of staff to disband the Palmach Command. The crisis reached a head in deliberations of the Histadrut's Executive Committee in October 1948 – a surreal scene, in the words of Anita Shapira (2004, 409). On one side were the prime minister and minister of defense;

[23] This "generals' revolt" also concerned other matters related to their appointment and management of the war (Avizohar and Bareli 1989, vol. 2, 458–62, 477–79).

[24] It was apparently the National Command that issued orders to the Palmach brigades on May 24, 1948 not to accept direct orders from the IDF chief of staff, but only from the Palmach National Command (Ben-Gurion 1969, vol. 1, 278). On Ben-Gurion's exploitation of this information, see A. Shapira 1985, 51.

and on the other were representatives of the Histadrut parties along with the chief of staff and senior officers – a discussion was being held in the Histadrut Labor Federation about dissolving a military unit! By a two-thirds majority, the decision to disband the Palmach Command was upheld, and the order was carried out in November 1948. These deliberations exposed the differences: the "statist" approach, represented by Ben-Gurion, which demanded a centralized, professional, and apolitical IDF; and Mapam's sectarian approach, which viewed Ben-Gurion as militaristic and étatist, and favored an army with a "labor world view" – pioneering, socially concerned, and "of the people."[25] There were also ideological differences – whether Israel's "orientation" should be toward the east or the west (Bialer 1990); and disputes about the essence of the state. These disagreements were also infused with personal and party interests, as well as campaign considerations as the January 1949 election approached.[26]

All this was preceded by events on the southern front: In August 1948, as noted, Yigal Allon, the former Palmach Commander, was appointed GOC Southern Command, and in late December, the IDF launched a campaign to remove the Egyptian army from Israel. At Allon's initiative, Israeli forces entered the Sinai Peninsula and reached the outskirts of el-Arish. Crossing Egypt's border precipitated an international incident, and the British threatened to invoke the Anglo-Egyptian defense treaty against Israel (Ilan 1983, 82, 84; Ben-Gurion 1983, vol. 3, 914–16). Ben-Gurion quickly responded that the entry into Sinai had occurred "in the heat of battle," and that he would issue an order to the IDF to retreat. The order was issued, but Allon took his time carrying it out, which Ben-Gurion viewed as the final act of defiance (A. Shapira 2004, 356–59). The IDF's retreat from the Sinai was completed on January 2, 1949. The dissolution of the Palmach did not lead to a violent clash, and held no risk of a civil war, as was clear from the last Order of the Day issued by the Palmach Command: "We are leaving our posts while the battle still rages, before our mission is complete. We do not believe that our leaving has strengthened the nation in battle, but we are accustomed to discipline and we accept the order."[27]

Yigal Allon was dismissed as GOC Southern Command in October 1949, and resigned from the IDF shortly thereafter together with other Palmach Commanders. Importantly, the confrontation within the labor movement took place *after* the confrontations with the separatist military organizations, although the labor movement divisions had begun earlier. Ben-Gurion's unequivocal reaction to the Altalena and Bernadotte incidents made it easier for him to dissolve the Palmach – the last

[25] The Histadrut discussion ended with a decision to view the Palmach brigades as an integral part of the IDF, disconnected from a National Command. It also concluded that ways would be explored to introduce pioneering values of the Labor movement into the IDF. See protocol of the Histadrut Executive Committee, October 14–15, 1948.

[26] We note in passing that the Mapai list to the Constituent Assembly carried the names of army officers, and some were even elected (and later resigned) such as Moshe Dayan, Asaf Simchoni, and Moshe Netzer. See *Memo*, Central Elections Committee, February 7, 1949. Other IDF officers, such as Yigal Allon, participated in their parties' election campaigns, but did not run for office. See Shapira 2004, 449.

[27] Published on November 6, 1948 (Gilead 1963, vol. 2, 976).

separate military framework – and to thereby establish the exclusiveness of the IDF and its subordination to civilian authority, even in the midst of war.

In this case, too, the rivalries did not disappear, but were diverted to parliamentary channels. Mapam (with its Palmach veterans) won nineteen mandates in the Constituent Assembly, making it the second-largest party. In retrospect, the third transition test – the disbanding of the Palmach – seemed to extinguish the fear of attempts to establish an alternative political or military center, and decisively established the exclusiveness of the government (Galnoor 1982, 274–77).

D. The Test of Transition

A new state faces the challenge of establishing legitimacy for its central governing structure. When a state comes into being through a violent struggle conducted by military organizations that answer to separate authorities, a monopoly on the use of force (army, police, militias, and armed civilians) is crucial. In the case of Israel, this came to the fore in the three events described above within a brief half year of its founding, yet by the time the elected institutions were in place in early 1949, questions of political legitimacy and the monopoly of the IDF were no longer acute. Many later crises touched upon the issue of legitimacy, such as the dispute over religious education in the immigrant camps, or the violent demonstrations against German reparations in 1952, but the exclusiveness of the elected government was not cast in doubt.

Therefore, let us look again at the three tests of 1948 (Table 1.1) to understand their significance for the regime in formation.

In terms of governance, all three events were significant in demonstrating the exclusive authority of the new government, and this is what made possible the state's monopoly on the use of military force and its conduct of security and foreign affairs. Of the three, the Altalena affair was the most traumatic, leaving in its wake many years of bitterness, hence its importance as a precedent. The disbanding of the Palmach was the longest crisis, and critical for showing consistency in the state's dealings with the various armed groups from the pre-state period, both right and left. The Bernadotte assassination provided an opportunity for the Provisional Government to legislate far-reaching deterrent measures to meet challenges to the state's monopoly on force.

The political significance of these events – consolidating power and promoting the interest of the ruling party and its leaders – was an important factor, but it would be an exaggeration to see it as the main consideration. Mapai headed by Ben-Gurion dominated the political system even before the state was founded, and such far-reaching measures would not have been necessary to preserve its power. Politically, the state leadership simply capitalized on an opportunity.

Despite the intensity of the confrontations, the bloodshed in the Altalena affair, and the animosity that remained, a reflective look back reveals that no "civil war" was ever in the offing, nor was there a violent struggle for taking over the government. The pre-state groups showed restraint in the test of transition. The ideological struggles, organizational rivalries, and clashing personalities were transmuted into a competition for votes, thereby creating the opportunity for a legitimate, democratically elected government.

Table 1.1 *The significance of the 1948 tests for governance and politics*

	Altalena affair	Assassination of Bernadotte	Disbanding of the Palmach
Significance for governance			
Monopoly on the use of force	Great	Minimal	Medium
Control over security and foreign affairs	Medium	Great	Minimal
Demonstration of exclusiveness	Great	Great	Great
Demonstration of the democratic rules	Medium	Minimal	Great
Political significance			
Consolidation of the central government	Great	Medium	Minimal
Promotion of the interests of Mapai and Ben-Gurion	Great	Minimal	Great

1.5 The Elections of 1949–1951

Free and open elections are a necessary condition for democracy, particularly in a newly formed political system. Indeed, societies that continue to be democratic and hold regular elections discover in retrospect that their first steps had a significant impact on what came later. In the first three years of Israel's existence, four elections were held – to the Constituent Assembly, which became the first Knesset (January 1949), the Histadrut Labor Federation (May 1949), the local authorities (November 1950), and the second Knesset (July 1951). Voting for the Constituent Assembly was postponed from October 1948, but the fact that it was held before the war ended, thereby shortening the life of the Provisional Government to a brief eight months, testifies to the desire to place the political system on a legitimate, elected foundation.

Israel carried out its first census on November 8, 1948 and counted a population of 782,000 (within the temporary borders before the war ended), of whom 713,000 were Jewish and 69,000 were Arab (approximately 9%). A total of 506,569 citizens aged eighteen or over were deemed eligible to vote. The census was probably not precise, particularly with respect to new immigrants, many of whom did not yet have a permanent address, and the Arab population. The number of eligible voters was therefore also imprecise.

More important: who was eligible to vote? During the Yishuv period, various groups tried to limit the right to vote of others or gain extra weight for their votes. Such views were heard in the deliberations about the Election to the Constituent Assembly, and some proposed an "adjustment period" before new immigrants could vote on the grounds that they were not yet familiar with life in Israel and would not yet know for whom to vote.[28] Others wanted to drop the ultra-Orthodox from the voting rolls on the grounds that they "don't recognize the state of Israel." But the main debates were waged over the right to vote of the Arab population that remained in Israel. The Declaration of Independence proclaimed "full and equal citizenship and due representation" of the Arab public in all state institutions. How would this be realized? Ben-Gurion's deliberations with his advisers on Arab affairs

[28] Provisional State Council discussion of the elections ordinance, 26th session, 1948–49, pp. 8, 10, 11.

reveal some reservations.[29] Ben-Gurion asked whether it was better that Arabs participate in the election and, if so, in a separate or mixed list? Some thought it better that Arabs not participate at all because the situation was still unclear, because of doubts about their loyalty, and there was fear that the right to vote would only increase their demands as citizens. Also evident in these talks was the desire of Ben-Gurion's advisers on Arab affairs to protect their own exclusive turf, and to prevent other parties – the Communists in particular – from "running around" among the Arabs soliciting their votes. Another proposal was to replicate the arrangement used for the ultra-Orthodox during the Yishuv period – to create for the Arab citizens a *curia* (separate voting for a fixed number of their representatives) that would ensure optimal control over both the voters and those elected. Another adviser explained that the matter had actually been decided because Mapam and the Communists were already courting Arab voters, hence there was no practical way to prevent Arabs from voting, and the Histadrut also supported it. Ultimately a decision was made on principle that the Arabs should not be denied the right to vote, that the number of voters would be determined by the census (which limited eligible voters to only about 40,000), and that Arab lists affiliated with Mapai would be created. Thus, despite the narrow and very partisan considerations, the democratic principle was established almost incidentally that citizens have an intrinsic right to elect representatives, and that it is not up to the representatives to decide who has the right to vote for them.

A. Election to the Constituent Assembly (January 1949)

What were the main issues of this election campaign? Mapai appropriated the battlefield victories, and in its platform advocated for peace agreements with the Arab states based on the boundaries defined by the military achievements. It supported discreet diplomatic negotiations that would ensure the continued support of the two superpowers that had recognized Israel. Ben-Gurion saw the military achievements as delineating the boundaries of Israel's territorial demands, hence his decisions to withdraw the troops from Lebanon and the Sinai Peninsula – where they had crossed the pre-state international borders. In his opinion, crossing an international border jeopardized expansion of the Jewish state's borders within the area of Mandatory Palestine, as asking for too much could lead to renewed discussion about the 1947 Partition Plan borders. The end of the war was already in sight in early 1949 – a ceasefire agreement was signed in February with Egypt, and by July agreements were made with Lebanon, Transjordan, and Syria. This affected the election campaign: Should parties support the ceasefire agreements, which fell short of being peace agreements and might entail the division of Eretz Israel along these borders? Should Israel still support the creation of an Arab (Palestinian) state, or support the de facto possession of the West Bank by the Transjordan kingdom? What should be Israel's foreign policy orientation – pro-west or pro-Soviet? What should the policy be toward Arab refugees? And what about the status of Jerusalem?

[29] See consultation on December 18, 1948 in Ben-Gurion 1983, vol. 3, 882–84.

In disagreements about security and foreign affairs, Mapai found itself on one side of the debate with support from the religious parties, the New Aliya Party (the Progressives), and often the General Zionists. On the other side were the parties Mapam and Herut, and the Communist Party. Mapam viewed the ceasefire as a way to end the fighting, but it opposed signing any agreement with the Emir Abdullah, whom they viewed as a lackey of British imperialism. Within Mapam was the hard-line Ahdut Ha'avoda faction, which opposed agreement with Egypt or approval of the ceasefire lines as the permanent borders, because it viewed the Jordan River as Israel's rightful eastern boundary. Mapam also opposed Israel's initial pro-western overtures. The Herut platform called for continuing the armed struggle until liberation of both banks of the Jordan River. It opposed any accommodation with the Hashemite Kingdom, which Herut viewed as conceding Israel's territorial integrity and reliance on a sworn enemy – Britain. The Communist Party initially objected to the idea of partition, but following the Soviet Union's changed policy, it supported the Yishuv struggle during the War of Independence, and welcomed the ceasefire agreements on condition that an Arab state would also be established alongside Israel.

The platforms of the political parties up for election in 1949 reveal that after the establishment of Israel, differences narrowed on matters of security and foreign affairs in comparison with the pre-state rivalry. This is even more striking during the 1951 election, when ideological differences shifted to internal matters. The rivalry did not disappear, however, and resumed between Mapai and the opposition parties on the conduct of the war and its outcomes, the east–west orientation, and reparations from Germany (1951–52). Internal disagreements were not new, but now tangible, and any one of them could have undermined the stability of the brand new state:

First, ideological differences between the camps: Should socialism be put into practice in our times? What economic policy should prevail in the difficult post-war situation? This was connected to the question of the east–west orientation, and even led to a split in the Kibbutz Hameuchad movement (1951).

Second, differences between veterans and newcomers were evident long before 1948, but immigration then became a major burden both in terms of quantity (a quarter of a million immigrants in 1949) and ethnic makeup (immigrants from Asian and African countries now outnumbered those from Europe and the Americas). How should they be absorbed and, as the pressure mounted, who should be absorbed? And what kind of society should evolve in the new state?

Third, the conflict between religious and secular Jews was not new – it had already appeared at the first Zionist Congress (1897). But suddenly the Zionist movement faced a question it had managed to sidestep for over fifty years: Now that the government was in Jewish hands, would it be "a Jewish state"?

Fourth, when the dust had settled from the 1949 war, approximately 160,000 Arabs remained in Israel, some 14 percent of the total population (J. Landau 1971, 17). How would the Jewish nation behave toward the non-Jews who lived in their newly established sovereign state?

Fifth, although the core mission of the Constituent Assembly was supposed to be drafting a constitution, and this was mentioned in the 1949 campaign and appeared in the party platforms, it is surprising how little the parties, particularly Mapai, discussed the substance of this constitution – a portent of things to come.[30]

On the election campaign itself, evidence comes primarily from the press of that period: rallies in the city squares; assemblies in halls and movie theaters; posters showing political platforms and cartoons; street criers with megaphones; etc. More intimate channels were widely used: meetings at party branches, workplaces, immigrant associations, or immigrant camps led by ethnic and religious group leaders. In these channels, the parties in power – Mapai and the religious – had a significant advantage. The press served as the main channel to disburse election propaganda, because every large party had its own official or semi-official newspaper that carried party announcements and support articles.[31] Radio time was allocated for electioneering: fifteen minutes to an existing party and ten minutes to a new list. The election campaign was fierce, even by the standards of Yishuv politics, which had never been placid. This is because of what had preceded the election – the Altalena incident, Bernadotte's assassination, and the disbanding of the Palmach.

Less is known about what happened on election day itself. The newspapers did not report any unusual incidents, but Asher Tsidon, who served as Deputy Speaker of the Knesset, testified, "The elections were carried out in exemplary fashion with a minimal loss of time … The integrity of the balloting was beyond doubt" (Tsidon 1964, 26).[32] Recall that all this was taking place during wartime, and that during the state of emergency, there were severe restrictions on movement and censorship of all printed material, particularly the daily newspapers. We have no authoritative information about the misuse of these measures by the government during the election campaign (such as limiting the paper ration to newspapers), and no appeals challenged the fairness of the election. Major changes in this regard happened prior to the second Knesset election, as noted below.

As Table 1.2 shows, there were no great surprises in the results of the election to the Constituent Assembly in 1949: Mapai remained dominant (forty-six mandates) as did the whole labor movement (sixty-five mandates); and the two labor parties – Mapam and Mapai, together with their affiliated Arab party and the Sephardic and Yemenite lists – won seventy-two mandates. These were the final days of the war, and the deep fears of 1948 turned into sighs of relief with the military victory, which helped both Mapai and Mapam in the election. Mapam, the second-largest party (nineteen mandates), appears to have surprised Ben-Gurion, who wrote in his journal, "Mapam received much less than I imagined it would" (Segev 1986, 261). Herut

[30] In the Constitution Committee chosen by the Provisional State Council, it became clear even before the election that there was little enthusiasm for drafting a constitution, and a suggestion was made that the Constituent Assembly first decide if a constitution was necessary. Constitution Committee Session, December 23, 1949, State of Israel Archive, File B-3. Quoted by Rozin 2002, 24, footnote 303.

[31] The main newspapers: *Al Hamishmar* of Mapam; *Herut* of the Herut Movement; *Davar* of the Histadrut and especially Mapai; *Haboker* of the General Zionists; *Haaretz* (for a while) of the Progressives; *Hatzofeh* of Mizrahi and Hapoel Ha-Mizrahi; *Hamodia* of Agudat Yisrael; and *Kol Ha'am* of the Communist Party.

[32] On the provisions to ensure fair elections, see the Election to the Constituent Assembly Ordinance (1948), which also stipulated that a Supreme Court judge must preside over the Central Election Committee.

Table 1.2 *Results of the election to the Constituent Assembly (1949)*

Party list	Percentage (rounded)	Seats	Comments
Labor camp			
Mapai	36	46	United Hashomer Hatzair and Ahdut Ha'avoda
Mapam	15	19	
Civil-Revisionist camp			
Herut movement	11	14	Irgun veterans
General Zionists	5	7	Previously the New Aliya Party
Progressive Party	4	5	A women's organization
WIZO	1	1	Emerged from the Union of Revisionist Zionists
Fighters' List	1	1	
United Religious Front	13	16	Hamizrahi, Hapoel Ha-Mizrahi, Agudat Yisrael, and Poalei Agudat Yisrael
Other			
National Unity List of Sephardim	4	4	Openly for the first time
Yemenite Association	1	1	Christians Arabs
Communists	3	4	
Democratic list, Nazareth	2	2	
Nine lists that did not win seats	4	–	
Total	100%	120	

Source: Central Election Committee of the Constituent Assembly, "Memorandum," 5 Shevat 1948–49.

(the fourth-largest party, with fourteen mandates) had hoped for more – at least to become the alternative as the second-largest party – and so had the General Zionists (seven mandates), which had hoped to restore its standing as a key party in the Zionist movement. The United Religious Front had a respectable showing (sixteen mandates). Estimated voter turnout was very high at 87 percent. Some 33,000 Arabs voted – approximately 79 percent of those eligible. Over half their votes went to the Arab party (Democratic List of Nazareth), 22 percent to the Communists, and 10 percent to Mapai (J. Landau 1971, 167).

Twenty-one lists participated in the election, an impressive selection on all counts, of which twelve won seats in the Constituent Assembly – none of them entirely new to Yishuv politics, although the two ultra-Orthodox parties and some other lists participated in the election for the first time. Despite changes in the makeup of the population, the election results reflected the same balance of power that had existed in the Yishuv period.

The big surprise was the coalition, which was presented for Knesset confirmation on March 10, 1949 (Figure 1.1). Left-wing Mapam remained outside the government, both because it was perceived to be a rival to Mapai's hegemony and because of deep disagreements on foreign and internal affairs. There was consensus in this coalition on security matters, foreign affairs, relations with the superpowers, and compromise over what was then called "a mixed economy" between Mapai's

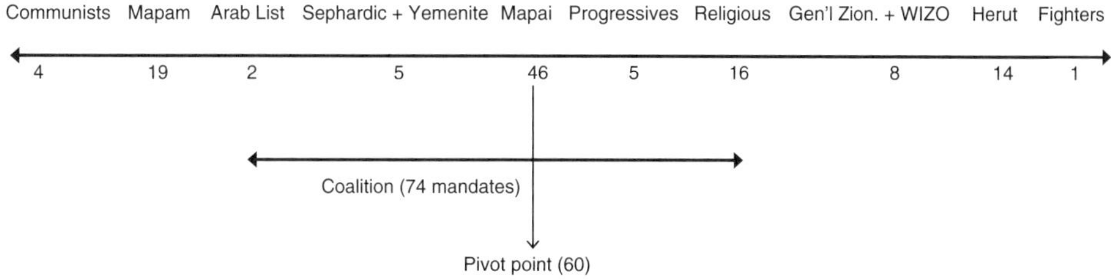

Figure 1.1 The first Knesset (1949): Alignment of parties based on security and foreign policy, and the coalition formed

moderate socialist version and the Progressive's even more moderate liberal or capitalist version. The following issues appeared in the coalition basic principles:

- Foreign affairs shall be based on friendship with all peace-seeking states, especially the United States and the Soviet Union.
- The government shall prepare a four-year plan for immigrant absorption and development based on a planned economy: nationalization of the water sources, natural resources, lands in arid regions and services necessary for state security; encouragement of private capital and adoption of private and cooperative entrepreneurship in the small towns and cities; and special incentives for productive capital investments that foster rapid and efficient development of the country's resources and economic opportunities.

The issue of religion and state was mentioned only in passing: "The state shall provide for the public religious needs of its inhabitants, but shall abstain from intervening in religious affairs; the Sabbath and holidays shall be national days of rest in Israel." Even a kind of core educational curriculum was agreed upon – a list of compulsory subjects to be taught in all schools. However, the government relied on the support of the religious parties, and consented to a "status quo" arrangement on religious matters in the coalition agreement, including extensive concessions in allowing separate school systems for the religious parties. Although the coalition appeared stable – together with the affiliated parties, it incorporated two-thirds of the Knesset members and controlled the balancing point on matters of security and foreign affairs – the first government did not last long. By early 1950, it was already unable to function due to disagreements with the religious parties about education in the immigrant camps. A second coalition government, similarly composed, was formed in October 1950, but this became a transition government as it failed for the same reasons, and early elections for the second Knesset were held on July 30, 1951. Mapai could easily have established a coalition without the religious parties, but Ben-Gurion insisted on excluding Mapam on the left (primarily because of its position on foreign affairs) and the General Zionists on the right (primarily because of its position on internal affairs), and he hoped that Mapai would increase its power in a new election.[33]

33 See Ben-Gurion's announcement to the Knesset on October 16, 1950 (see Horowitz and Lissak 1977; and Zahor 1997, 30).

Election of the Constituent Assembly was a formative event that enhanced the nascent democracy in Israel, adhering to the formal rules of the game under the trying circumstances of an external war and internal dissension. The decision to hold the election during a lull in the war, and refusal to use the state of emergency as an excuse to limit the right to vote, were a badge of honor for the provisional state's leadership. This badge, however, would soon be facing new tests.

B. Election to the Histadrut Labor Federation (May 1949)

Election to the Histadrut was of great importance both for governance and socioeconomic reasons (Barkai 1983, 112–19). Histadrut membership rolls included veterans and newcomers, members of kibbutzim, moshavim (collectivized farming communities), urban communities, and cities, farmers, laborers, wage-earners, tradespeople, secular and religious, members of socialist parties, and also Communists and religious members.[34]

Some 139,000 people voted in the Histadrut election of May 1949, roughly 80 percent of those eligible; this was about 32 percent of those who had voted in the Knesset election. The election was a power struggle between the two rival workers' parties in the wake of the Knesset election four months earlier. Mapai won 57 percent of the vote and Mapam 34 percent. Both parties were happy with the results – Mapai for maintaining its edge and Mapam for growing in power as it chipped away at the hegemony of Mapai. The other votes were divided among the Progressives, Ha-Mizrahi, and the Communists. If we view the Histadrut as a kind of civil society organization, holding regular elections contributed to deepening democratic values. On the other hand, if we view the Histadrut as part and parcel of the ruling power, the election results shored up the dominance of Mapai and the Labor camp (Etzioni 1959, 198). Both perceptions are partially right, because the political system during this period was composed of overlapping organizations (Galnoor 1982, 341).

C. Local Authority Elections (November 1950)

Elections to the local authorities were not held regularly during the Mandate period, and establishment of the state made it necessary to hold them as soon as possible.[35] Election day was postponed more than once because of the need to change some of the Mandate period rules – ensuring voting rights for women, revoking the special privileges of the propertied class and taxpayers, and lowering the voting age from twenty-one to eighteen. Another reason for postponement was the ruling parties' fear of getting the voters' verdict at the height of the economic austerity program. The electoral system was proportional, with the seats in the local councils distributed in accordance with the percentage of votes won by each party, and the mayor was usually elected by a coalition of lists. Most of the parties competing in the local elections, certainly the large ones, were identical to the national parties, and it was the

[34] Arabs were allowed to join the Histadrut only in 1959. By 1965, some 38,000 Arabs had joined and were accorded full voting rights for the first time (Landau 1971).

[35] This section is based largely on the work of Rozin (2002, 135–85).

national party leaders who generally made the decisions about local candidates and the composition of the local coalitions.

Determining eligibility to vote was sometimes difficult because many new immigrants lived in temporary residences in towns and transit camps. Initially some 411,000 names appeared on the voter rolls; this increased by 10 percent to some 450,000 following appeals filed with candidates competing in forty-three local authorities. Two flaws in the democratic process appeared in these elections. First, the new immigrants had no autonomy whatsoever in managing their affairs in the transit camps, which were considered temporary quarters, so it would have been possible to erase them entirely from the voter rolls. Although this ruthless idea was rejected, Mapai and the religious parties, which had considerable clout in the transit camps, gerrymandered the voting districts to incorporate the camps into the veteran town districts, thereby weakening the other parties (Rozin 2002, 135–36). Second, what should be done about the Arab inhabitants? Most lived under martial law, and – without much soul-searching – elections were simply not held there. Arab candidates appeared only on the Mapai list in Haifa and the Communist lists. Upon its establishment, Israel had within its territory two Arab cities – Nazareth and Shfar'am – and the local authority of Kfar Yassif (Maoz 1962, 235). In 1950–52, four new local councils were established, and the first local elections were held in 1954. The Communist list won 38 percent of the votes, but the seven small lists – the Muslim and Christian lists, most of them supported by Mapai – united in a coalition and left the Communists in the opposition. In the following local election in 1955, five Arab local authorities participated, and in 1959, twenty-three participated (J. Landau 1971, 223).

The local elections in 1950 were the first elections that did not necessarily revolve around the large issues of security and foreign affairs, and were only indirectly related to the leadership of Mapai and Ben-Gurion. The context was complex, however, as the economic crisis, rationing, and diminishing confidence in the state authorities cast their shadow over the local voting. Mapai found itself attacked from the right (the General Zionists), who campaigned on the issue of the government's economic policies – the suffering of the citizens, the bureaucracy of the rationing regime, the black market, and corruption (N. Gross 1997, 137–50). They openly touted themselves as an alternative to the Mapai government, or at least able to become partners in the government.

On the left, Mapam also had an interest in undermining the party, which had kept it out of the government coalition. Mapam viewed the government's economic policies as a slap in the face to the workers and capitulation to the right-wing bourgeoisie and religious clericalism (Oren quoted in Rozin 2002, 145). Mapai's response was predictable: It emphasized the remarkable achievements of the state under Ben-Gurion's leadership and sought to soft-pedal the rationing regime by explaining its role in enabling more immigration, state-building, and security (Ben-Gurion quoted in Rozin 2002, 153).

Mapai also responded with several practical measures, some of them effective. First, it decided (illegitimately) to compete on the local level not as Mapai, but under the name and sponsorship of the Histadrut. This was done not just to get around Mapai's negative image and responsibility for the austerity program, but primarily to access Histadrut funds for its election campaign. This incensed Mapam and the Zionist Workers Party (the Progressives), who were also Histadrut members and running in the local elections. Second, Mapai focused its election campaign not just on its natural constituency – workers, laborers, public bureaucrats, the "working intelligentsia," cultural and intellectual figures – but also on the middle-class bourgeoisie: professionals, merchants, and tradespeople. In other words, it tried to appeal directly to urbanites and housewives, who felt burdened by the ongoing lack of goods and believed that the distribution was inequitable.

In October 1950, the government fell, and with it the Ministry of Supply and Rationing was dissolved, a new economic policy was instituted, and the rationing regime was eased. Dov Yosef, the minister who oversaw rationing, was made the scapegoat for all this and became the butt of jokes about austerity, the profiteers, and the black market. Third, Mapai made use of all the tools at its disposal – the government, the Histadrut, and the party – to bring pressure on the voters, especially in the employment offices, workplaces, transit camps, and immigrant communities, as well as Arab voters in the mixed cities. It is hard to know the impact of this activity and how responsive the voters were, especially considering that most voters lived in urban settings, and the newspaper descriptions of "a reign of terror" remain anecdotal.[36]

The first elections for local authorities brought up an agenda that had not previously been part of the public discourse. The party in power was forced to hear out the concerns of the citizens, leaving it fearful of being turned out of office in the coming Knesset election. Social and economic issues were paramount, raising questions about collective goals versus individual needs – what was perceived by many as careerism and the lack of a pioneering spirit. Also intermingled were questions about the regime and the democratic rules of the game, though a serious discussion about the role and standing of the local authority was unfortunately never held.

The parties themselves regarded the cumulative results (in all local authorities) as a reflection of their ability to unseat the government. Voting turnout was high (about 80%) considering that the local elections were held separately from the election to the Knesset. The results were viewed as a resounding defeat for Mapai, which won 27 percent of the cumulative total votes, 80 percent less than it had garnered in the 1949 Knesset election, and as a huge victory for the General Zionists, which took about 25 percent of the votes (compared with 5 percent in the Knesset election), almost bringing it on par with Mapai. The General Zionists demonstrated significant inroads in the three big cities: Tel Aviv – 31 percent; Haifa – 22 percent; and Jerusalem – 16 percent. No significant change was apparent in the strength of Mapam, Herut, or the religious parties, except for the Progressives, who lost votes as partners in the government coalition.

Mapai took immediate steps to contain the damage, and signed agreements to cooperate nationally with Mapam, the religious, and the Progressives, intended to thwart the General Zionists from forming coalitions in many local authorities, or at least to increase the labor parties' slice of these coalitions. These agreements enabled Mapai to take over the mayor's office in Haifa and Petah Tikva (Weitz 1999, 91–99). In the long run, Mapai began to shape its policies to accommodate the opposing

[36] *Haboker* of the General Zionists actually suggests the opposite in an article entitled "Even the pressure didn't work," November 16, 1950.

groups in the 1950 local elections – the urban middle class, merchants, tradespeople, and professionals (Rozin 2002, 161–68).

The General Zionists, Herut, and also Mapam raised hard questions about how the 1950 elections had been conducted. Mapai was universally criticized for using the mechanisms of state and the Histadrut to buy the votes of immigrants and Arabs and to bias the election results (Rozin 2002, 173–75). It is hard to determine the extent of this, especially since the stories appeared in the party-owned newspapers and were not tested in court, but corruption clearly existed and was even worse in the second Knesset election. Above all, these local elections were the first demonstration of the independence of Israeli voters, who made sophisticated use of their ballots, and did not hesitate even then – in the days of Mapai dominance – to split their votes on the local and national levels.[37] These flickers of political freedom made Mapai even more fearful of the autonomy of the local authorities, and it worked vigorously to ensure their utter subordination to the central government.

D. Second Knesset Election (July 1951)

Elections for the second Knesset were held eight months after what was called at the time "Mapai's downfall" in the local elections. The Knesset election was moved up because of disputes within the government about religious education issues, but the local elections had raised awareness – also in Mapai – about the need to regain public confidence.

Disagreements over security and foreign affairs did not evaporate, particularly as tension continued along the borders, but the difficult economic situation shifted public attention to domestic affairs and the ideological rivalry between Mapai and the General Zionists.[38] The General Zionists tried to unseat the dominant party, while Mapai under Ben-Gurion sought an absolute majority in the Knesset to avoid the pitfalls of a coalition. Mapai election propaganda continued to trumpet slogans like the pioneering spirit, mobilizing and educating the nation, but made a great effort to find its way into the heart of a public that had tired of the tension of war, austerity, and having to absorb a mass immigration. Signs of pragmatism were evident, especially in economic matters and in Mapai's willingness to integrate the separate school systems under the aegis of the state – a position the General Zionists had held for years. The General Zionists published a detailed economic and social platform that promised freedom for entrepreneurship, choice of a profession and place of work, reining in bureaucratic intervention and coercion, and preventing monopolies and dependence on party affiliation.[39]

Interparty rivalry degenerated into corrupt electioneering in the transit camps and immigrant communities. The opposition parties accused Mapai, the Histadrut (including Mapam), the religious parties, and the Progressives of dividing up control over the transit camps by an agreed upon key (D. Hacohen 1994, 207).[40] Although

[37] This attitude was reflected in an article in an independent newspaper, which viewed the election results as a longing for more freedom and less bureaucracy (Zilber quoted in Rozin 2002, 169).

[38] Bar-On called the period 1949–53 "four years of grace" on security matters (Zameret and Yablonka 1997, 13–14).

[39] From the platform of the General Zionists to the second Knesset.

[40] Ephraim Kishon (1989) would later satirize these events.

the voting in these places was neither free nor fair, did it affect the overall election result? Mapai and its allies were accused of rigging the election, but it is entirely possible that the new immigrants would have voted for the parties in power anyway. Mapai received an estimated 60 percent of the immigrant vote in the transit camps, and the religious Ha-Mizrahi also won double the support in these camps than it won in the election at large (Weitz 1996, 129). Thus, those new immigrants who recently left the transit camps had "punished" Mapai at the ballot box, as voting for Mapai increased less than 2 percent overall in this election.

The General Zionists had increased their strength from seven to twenty mandates (and another three together with the ethnic parties), and became the second-largest party, though it was still far from threatening the domination of Mapai (which won forty-five mandates and another five from the affiliated Arab parties). The coalition in the first government of the second Knesset resembled its predecessor, with the exception of the Progressives, and had a slightly smaller majority of sixty-five mandates (Figure 1.2). Continued disputes with the religious parties forced Mapai to change its position, and in December 1953, the General Zionists and the Progressives joined the coalition. Thus the ideological "upheaval" of Mapai, which had begun in the local elections, was complete. To wit, a 1955 ideological essay by Moshe Sharett gives up on nationalizing the means of production and expresses support for a mixed economy (1955, 10).

The momentous events in the first three years of the state made the election to the second Knesset formative in terms of its impact on society and democracy, helping shape the future character of the state.[41] For the first time, the "simple man" appeared in election propaganda, as opposed to the collective "we" of the Yishuv and state-building period.

The election to the second Knesset elucidated several important characteristics of Israeli political life, which would last for a decade or more:

- Elections became the only route to power. They were regularly held and the range of parties offered to voters was diverse on all levels.
- A government could not be formed without Mapai, the dominant party, though it did not have an absolute majority (even with its allied parties), and had to govern by coalition.
- The coalitions shared a rather clear ideological continuum to the right and left of Mapai on security and foreign affairs. Nevertheless, the coalition was not stable, and government crises were frequent, especially on matters of religion and state.
- Until the 1960s, as in the first and second Knesset, the coalitions rested on a rather stable alliance of Mapai with the Progressives as well as the uneasy "historic alliance" with the National Religious Party (Gutmann 1961, 18).
- Mapai had no ideological compunctions about choosing coalition partners from the right or left, although all coalitions would be formed "without Herut or Maki [the Communist Party]." This lasted until 1967.
- Mapai sought as broad a coalition as possible to stave off the possibility that the government would fall if one of its partners resigned.

[41] "Public debate in the election campaign for the first Knesset did not focus on the character of the future state, but on the past" (Zahor in Zameret and Yablonka 1997, 31).

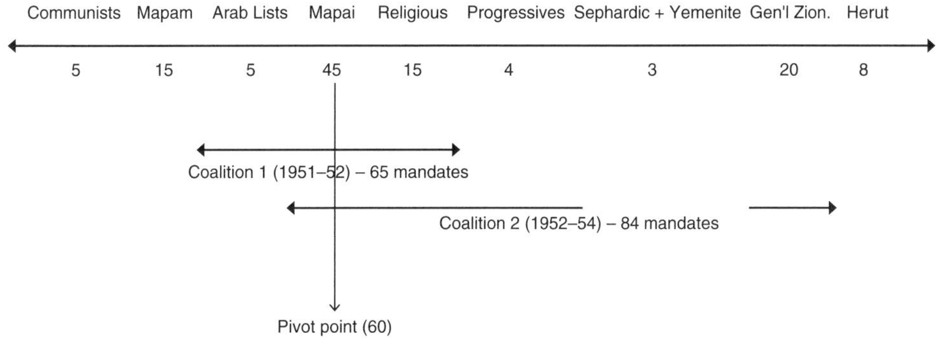

Figure 1.2 The second Knesset (1951): Alignment of parties based on security and foreign policy, and the two coalitions formed

- Mapai was careful to ensure a majority for itself within the government, and retained key ministries – Defense, Foreign Affairs, Finance, Education, Agriculture, Labor – which contributed to coordination, but also created a tradition of centralization within the executive branch.

Though frequent government crises might create the impression of instability, voting fluctuations were relatively small and did not chip away at the dominance of the ruling party (Dowty 2001, 39–44). The elected government in those years was fairly stable in terms of its steering capacity – more stable on issues of security and foreign affairs, less so on internal matters.

1.6 The State and Its Meaning

The permanent and provisional arrangements that emerged during the 1948–51 period shaped the political system in Israel for many years to come. A transition from volunteer and revolutionary groups to political institutionalization invariably brings with it adjustment difficulties, and in this sense Israel's transition period resembles that of other new states (*The International Encyclopedia Social Sciences* 2001, 14975). The profound significance of the political institutions should be emphasized, as their survivability also embodies the history of the nation-building (Fukuyama 2004, 134).[42] Ben-Gurion, who led the transition from Yishuv to state, also found it hard to adjust to the new "normalcy," and tried to inspire youth with his vision of "statist pioneering," encouraging them to join him in settling the Negev when he resigned from the government in 1953 and moved there.[43]

The new state had many tasks and many pretensions. It demanded compliance, a monopoly on the use of force, and exclusive rights to the symbols of state; the state, or more accurately its leaders, aspired also to shape society and educate its members. Israeli citizens, for example, were prohibited from leaving the country without an exit permit, as stipulated in the Emergency Regulations: "An exit permit shall be issued only in exceptional cases if there is justification and a compelling reason."[44] Security

42 On the centrality of institutions, also see Hall and Taylor (1996, 955).
43 See Ben-Gurion's letter to the members of Kibbutz Sde Boker (Yanai 1987, 180).
44 Announcement of the Aliyah Ministry, Emergency Regulations (Leaving the Country), August 25, 1948, Article 7.

was given as the reason for this prohibition, but in a government discussion from 1953, the underlying motivation became clear – to prevent members of this "wandering nation" of Jews from leaving the country (Sharett 1978, A, 255). Similarly, inculcating the use of Hebrew also became a coercive national mission: The Council for the Control of Films and Plays was used to ban plays in Yiddish (Wolfowicz 2004). That same year, the council chair sent an enthusiastic letter to the manager of the Eden Cinema in Jerusalem praising his artistic and cultural taste in choosing "the kind of films that should be shown to the Israeli public" (Sivan 1991, 195). The political leaders, particularly Ben-Gurion, believed that "intellectuals" should be engaged in national missions, and the intellectuals – authors, artists, and academics – were eager to comply (Segev 1986). Underlying the discussions about how to serve the state was a willingness to subjugate everything to "the good of the state."

What did they mean at the time by the term "statism" – the Hebrew word rooted in the term for "kingdom"? Statism originally conveyed the opposite of factionalism, which had typified the Yishuv period, i.e., "statism" came in response to the fear that social and party divisiveness would carry over into the state. There were also doubts about the ability of the Jewish people to work together cooperatively within a state framework: "A vision and emotions are not enough to build a state. They are enough for … surviving in the Diaspora, for running a yeshiva, university, or rabbinic office – but not for building a state" (Ben-Gurion quoted in Yanai 1987, 171).

Together with the soaring expectations at Israel's founding, fears arose about the waning of the revolutionary fervor and volunteer spirit – the very characteristics that had made possible realization of the dream. The question being asked (not by everyone, of course) was, "What will happen to the pioneering spirit?" Thus was born the idea, particularly salient with Ben-Gurion, to do both: to merge the social revolution with political sovereignty; to place the state as the prime symbol of identity without undermining the sense of mission; to hold aloft the symbols of the ancient Biblical kingdom without imbuing it with religious content. The term "statist pioneering" captures the aspiration for this merger – continued pioneering, but with the initiative, encouragement, and guidance of the state. In this plan the IDF was considered the quintessential statist-pioneering institution, as the focus of identification for everyone ("the people's army") and because it was also charged with the role of society-building – absorbing and integrating new immigrants, education, settlement, and even some health services.

Those in opposition viewed statism as little more than an étatist ideology with totalitarian overtones, as it aspired to give spiritual status to the institution called "state."[45] It was Ben-Aharon, one of the leaders of Ahdut Ha'avoda, who – in the course of a debate about disbanding the Palmach – asserted that the culture and values of a nation are not shaped "by ministers and their lackeys" (Ben-Aharon 1977, 60). But Ben-Aharon and his colleagues also asserted the primacy of socialist Zionism, and viewed the state as the only tool for its realization.

The second stratum of statism concerns the division of tasks between the state and the other social bodies. Proponents of statism wished to transfer to the state all the tasks carried out by voluntary bodies in the Yishuv – development, settlement,

[45] Pinchas Lavon, a Mapai leader, Histadrut Secretary General, and government minister, was one of the main articulators of this view (Horowitz and Lissak 1977).

manual labor, immigrant absorption, making the desert bloom, etc. The proliferation of youth movements was also perceived by them as party factionalism, and Ben-Gurion wanted to unite them into one youth movement (Yanai 1987, 179–80). Some organizations in the labor movement, on the other hand, wanted to continue to function, and even justified this in ideological terms. They supported the "nationalization" of security and foreign affairs, and even certain parts of education and employment, but not preparing hearts and minds for pioneering, viewed as an intimate process that should remain with the social bodies. This debate – statism versus "movementism" – had a direct impact on the perception of the state. The statists viewed the state as a completely sovereign, independent institution that derives its legitimacy from the law and the people; the movementers saw the state as the emissary of society, the servant of social movements (Horowitz and Lissak 1978, 278; Medding 1990, 47, 135). The former sought to maximize centralization, while the latter assigned independent functions to civil society.

The third stratum concerns the character of the state itself. Statism is a civic conceptualization of the state, whose task is to forge a common civic culture. But the statists did not go all the way with their civic model because, *inter alia*, they did not want to integrate Arab and other non-Jewish citizens into the state. Moreover, in the framework of Jewish state solidarity, religious people had the option of recourse to Halakhic authority, not state sovereignty (Dowty 2001, 33–34). Liebman and Don-Yehiya see statism as "civil religion," i.e., not just a rival to the movementism of the Labor camp, but a secular alternative to traditional religion, and thus it was also supported by non-socialists, such as the General Zionists and Revisionists (Liebman and Don-Yehiya 1983, 81–85; Kimmerling 2004, 151). In retrospect, it does indeed seem as if the adherents of statism led by Ben-Gurion tried to merge the unmergeable: the pioneering spirit of the revolutionary period with the institution of the state. Because they came from the socialist school of thought, they wished to continue to shape society and its members using the new sovereign toy. In this they were close to the Revisionists for whom "society" and "state" were one and the same. Statists of all types were joined by the national religious Zionists, who could even be considered the main proponents of this view. The state for them was "the beginning of redemption," and after 1967 they advocated in its name to expand its sovereign territory.

The only ones who held a clear, precise view of the meaning of the newly established state were the ultra-Orthodox. Most had boycotted the organized Jewish community during the Yishuv period, but the vast majority agreed to cooperate with the state and its institutions for instrumental reasons. It did not cross their minds to give the secular kingdom or its offices any role in their communal affairs. A small group called the Neturei Karta went much further, boycotting the state entirely. They maintained this boycott for a long time, and four decades after the establishment of Israel, they issued "passports" for themselves, printing in four languages (Yiddish, Hebrew, English, and Arabic): "The bearer of this certificate is a Jew and not a Zionist and does not belong to the national-heretical movement that has taken control of our holy land, called the Zionist state, which abused the name of Israel."[46]

[46] The reason they wanted to forego Israeli passports was the hijacking of passenger planes by Arab organizations and the harm to Jewish passengers suspected of being Zionists. *Davar*, December 2, 1985.

In retrospect, the state defeated its rivals and, as we shall see in the coming chapters, quickly became a powerful institution with a crucial influence on society, its groups, and its members. In "The First Decade Exhibition" held in Jerusalem in 1958, the state displayed its achievements, and most of Israel's residents made a pilgrimage there. Artists were also asked to participate in the "Decade of Hebrew Drawing," including Streichman ("To your seed I have given this land"), Shemi, Danziger, and others. It is eminently characteristic of this period that a large mural by Zaritsky ("Power") was too modernist for Ben-Gurion's taste, and moved to a more obscure location in the exhibition (Shefi 1997, 293–94).

To assess the steering capacity of the political system during this transition period, we must recall the challenges it faced. Heading the list was its success in meeting external challenges: establishing a state, military victory, and international legitimacy that enabled safeguarding of the fruits of that victory. To these should be added Diaspora Jewry's broad support for Israel, even though most did not view it as their country. The internal challenges ranged from "nation-building," i.e., shaping a society that would be completely different from Jewish communities in the Diaspora, to economic, physical, and institutional development. Moreover, they were seen through the prism of the Holocaust and the desire to view Israel as a continuation/contrast/response to the communities that had been wiped out – to provide shelter for the homeless and a new beginning for those searching for a home. In the years 1948 to 1952, some 700,000 Jews immigrated to Israel, triggering an economic crisis that led to austerity policies and the black market, as well as the repercussions for governance that we noted. All these changed Israeli society irrevocably.

The newly established political system met the challenges and successfully made it through the transition period. This is not to assert that the solutions were necessarily the right ones or that the problems were solved or disappeared. On the contrary, the vast majority of the foreign and internal problems would return in the coming years – some to haunt Israel because of the temporary solutions that had been improvised during the transition period. The author of a 1959 book gives high praise to Israel in comparison with other new states on all matters related to governance and political leadership, but low grades on economic planning, work productivity, governing mechanisms, and administrative competence (M.H. Bernstein 1959, 415–17). As for other important questions – were stable foundations laid for a democratic government, for example – we will return to these in the closing chapter.[47] Here we note only that the steering capacity of the political system – the ability to steer society toward common goals – gradually waned. At the same time, it was inevitable that the strong state established in 1948 would change, and the more society developed, the more demands would grow for the autonomy of civil society, the economy, and citizens – as individuals who stand on their own (Ezrahi 1997).

[47] For a different view of the development of Israeli democracy, see Bareli 2014.

2 Does Israel Have a Constitution?

Assume for a moment that the Constituent Assembly elected in 1949 had fulfilled its mission and endowed Israel with a written constitution: Would it be possible to predict the calamities of governance and other misfortunes that could have been averted? Was MK Nahum Nir, chair of the Constitution, Law and Justice Committee, correct when he said in 1950 during the Knesset debate about the constitution, "If we enact a constitution once, the shockwaves will come only once, and not every other day"? And was MK Menachem Begin prophetic when he said that, without a constitution, the government would consider itself above the law, do whatever it pleased, and even act against the will of the majority? On the other hand, perhaps others were right when they said that a constitution should be written at the end of the revolution, not at the outset, and that establishing a state is only the beginning.[1] And some other speculative questions: After close to seventy years of statehood without a formal constitution, was Ben-Gurion correct in saying that principles already established in democratic states do not need affirmation by a special document, hence a written constitution is not essential for the existence of a state?[2] And if a written constitution had been enacted at that time in the spirit of the Declaration of Independence, and had over time been instilled into all strata of society and the elected representatives, would its very existence as a formative document have had an impact on certain matters:

- Would a written constitution have prevented the ***risks to the democratic regime*** in cases such as the decision about the reparations from Germany (1951–52); the Lavon affair (1960/61); postponing the Knesset election until after the Yom Kippur War (1973); the agreement to rotate the prime minister (1984); the disgraceful negotiations to form a coalition after the fall of the Unity Government (1990); the frequent crises since the assassination of Prime Minister Rabin (1995); or the non-democratic bills and laws tabled in the Knesset since 2009?

1 These quotes are from deliberations about the constitution in the first Knesset, respectively: MK Nir – *Knesset Records*, First Knesset, Second Session, No. 4, February 1, 1950, 717; MK Begin – ibid., February 7, 1950, 739; MK Bar-Rav-Hai, ibid., 726–27; MK Ben-Gurion, ibid., February 20, 1950, 813.

2 Ben-Gurion in the Constitution, Law and Justice Committee, November 23, 1949, Israel State Archive, vol. 21, Protocols of the Constitution, Law and Justice Committee.

- Would it have served as a framework for instilling the norms of ***human rights, civil rights, and minority rights***, and would it have deterred the government from violating them?
- Would it have unambiguously regularized ***relations among the branches of government, especially between the judiciary and the elected bodies (Knesset and the Executive)*** – and would it have reduced the political energy that is wasted on this (e.g., the failed attempt to strengthen the executive branch by direct election of the prime minister in 1996–2003)?
- Would it have reduced friction over sensitive issues in Israel, or at least ***forced these conflicts to abide by the democratic rules of the game***, particularly the issues of security and the disposition of the occupied territories, the status of Arab citizens, religion and state, social gaps, and relations with the Diaspora?
- Would it have set the limits of a "***self-defending democracy***" – especially in security-related states of emergency – and also set the boundaries between anti-democratic activity and legitimate forms of participation and protest of citizens, groups, and movements?
- Would it have helped prevent ***political and administrative corruption*** – whether related to political parties in the early years of the state or the personal corruption of recent years – of presidents, prime ministers, ministers, Knesset members, mayors, and senior civil servants?
- Would it have the power to ***educate for democratic values***, or help instill a democratic political culture, especially with regard to respect for the rights of "the other"?

The length of this list and the complexity of the questions speak for themselves – even the most ardent proponents of a formal, meticulously written constitution do not rest their hopes on a constitution for resolving all these problems. Even in the most democratic states, most of which do have a written constitution, these documents have not always prevented mishaps. And yet, could it be that Israeli society would have been in a more advanced stage of its democratic development with a written constitution than without one? And even if the constitution did not resolve some of the most deeply controversial issues, such as religion and state, and on the assumption that the regime did not change, would a constitution have enabled a wiser handling of sensitive matters, one that does not endanger the very foundations of democracy? Can we agree at least that superfluous and often ugly political battles would have been toned down?

In general, postponing the decision about the constitution became detrimental to turning democratic principles into widely accepted conventions that no longer require constitutional support. The passage of time did not resolve the issues that had been swept under the carpet, issues that surface repeatedly and arouse deep divisions. One glaring example is the authority of the elected state institutions versus the political authority of the rabbis (religious leaders); another concerns the definition of a permanent "state of emergency," which enables the government to circumvent some laws and employ administrative detention – incarceration without trial. And, above all, the primary question is whether the constitution has the power to end the obfuscation of some fifty years regarding the status of the occupied territories? It is hard to find a comparable fog in other democracies. These territories are "administered" by the military, but Israeli law is selectively applied to them, while the "Israeli" settlements and their inhabitants are in effect "ex-territorial" local authorities. Is this a constitutional matter, or would a constitution's reach be too short?

At the very least, is it possible that an educational opportunity was missed – that a democratic constitution would enhance respect for the rule of law, the legality of the regime, and the existence of irrevocable human and civil rights? In other words, perhaps the role of the constitution is minimal – the assertion that beyond the legitimate differences of opinion in society, there are common values and agreement to act in accordance with them.

Although Israel has no rigid written constitution universally acknowledged as the supreme law of the land, it does have extended constitutional arrangements: the Basic Laws; the constitutional rulings of the Supreme Court; and the binding norms that have evolved over the years, such as the system of governance. If we add to this the Declaration of Independence from 1948, whose principles were given legal validity in a 1992 Basic Law, it could be said that a constitution does exist in the material (essential) sense (Akzin 1966, 144–50), i.e., "as a combination of principles and arrangements that derive from the existing social reality and the laws of the state" (Rubinstein and Medina 2005, 54). And if Israel does indeed have a constitution, or a quasi-constitution, why has this not contributed more to the stability of the political system, the rule of law, or at least the legality of the regime itself? Could Finer have been correct in claiming (Finer, Bogdanor, and Rudden 1995, 1–3) that constitutions do not, in and of themselves, add or detract without the historical context that actually determines their validity? One cannot claim that democracies are more stable when they rely on a constitution, or on a constitution that is hard to amend. Long experience from many countries indicates that the writing of a democratic constitution contributes more to stability only when there is consensus from the outset about democratic values and the need to anchor them in binding rules. And one more point: While the constitution is the most supreme and binding norm for a political system and its citizenry, the individual qua individual may still hold norms that are paramount, whether they are called "natural rights," ethical codes, or Biblical injunctions.

In this chapter, the central issue is not just why a formal constitution was not written soon after Israel was founded, but what has been the substitute for a written constitution. We will claim that, in practice, a "1949 constitution" has emerged and is the material constitution to this day. Debate over a constitution did not end with the early years of statehood, but continues to the present – concerning the status of the Basic Laws, constitutional areas not covered by Basic Laws, and the constitutional contribution of the Supreme Court. In the conclusion to this chapter, we return to the questions: Is there a constitution in Israel? And what have the citizens lost by taking such a distinctive constitutional route?

2.1 Constitutions

Most states have constitutions, but few have stable constitutions that have lasted for a century or more, and all these are democracies.[3] Yet the order of events – what leads to democratic and constitutional stability – is not clear: Perhaps a stable regime and

[3] Heading the list are Britain (an unwritten constitution), the United States (1787), Sweden (1807–9), Holland and Norway (1814), Belgium (1831), New Zealand (1840 – a Basic Law), Denmark (1849), Canada (1867, an unwritten constitution), Luxembourg (1868), Switzerland (1875), Australia (1900), and Finland (1919). See Bogdanor (1988) and also the website of International Constitutional Law: www.servat.unibe.ch/icl/ (accessed October 16, 2017).

well-established relations between state and society are what make a constitution stable, and not vice versa.[4] Constitutions can be categorized according to diverse criteria, but for our purposes the following distinctions are sufficient:

1. *A formal, supreme, and rigid constitution* – such as that of the United States – is a unified, written document. It is formal, as compared with the collection of conventions in Britain; and it is superior to ordinary laws, both legally and in terms of the values expressed. Its rigidity generally derives from the difficulty of amending a constitutional document, unlike amending ordinary laws (in contrast with a flexible, non-supreme constitution, which can more easily be rewritten).
2. A constitution is *realistic and stable* if it correctly reflects the constitutional state of affairs and political regime, and if the government and citizens act in accordance with it over time. The opposite is a *nominal* constitution, whose content (or a significant part of it) is ignored or frequently modified (often not in keeping with the amendment procedures). Thus the realistic dimension of a constitution exceeds the document itself, and concerns its validity for society and politics.

A constitution strives to reflect the way of life of a specific public and its willingness to act within an agreed political framework, and therefore there is no "correct" constitution, only arrangements whose suitability can be tested over time. The most fundamental difference is between democratic and non-democratic constitutions, as the latter is not designed to perform the vital task of restraining the ruling power. In a true "constitutional regime," the government, as well as the citizens, is subject to and constrained by the constitution. Neuberger (1990) suggests that in the long run and for educational reasons, a dictatorship "that operates by a nominal constitution is a lesser evil than a dictatorship that dispenses with all constitutional pretense" (1990, 17) because such a constitution at least affords an opportunity to those who oppose it to demand some rights in its name. We think, however, that it is preferable that such regimes not pretend to constitutional legitimacy – indeed, in such countries there have been as many constitutions as governments.

A constitution may be born at the very beginning – in the wake of a revolution or establishment of a state; or it may become part of the journey, reflecting the political tradition of public life and guiding it in times of crisis. It is also the expression of a common identity (when one exists), or an attempt to forge that identity, at least in terms of shared values.[5] The British have a live constitution although it is not written, and it expresses the tradition and history of the state. It is not formal, supreme, or rigid, but rather a collection of constitutional conventions, Parliamentary acts, agreements (such as the Magna Carta), common law, laws, and court rulings (Bagehot 1867; Finer, Bogdanor, and Rudden 1995, 40–101). In practice, because this constitution has served for generations, it is formal and fairly rigid; although it can be changed rather easily in terms of procedures, this has happened infrequently and with admirable gradualism. As a result, the British constitution is perhaps the most

[4] The relatively stable constitutions of Germany and Japan after 1945 also demonstrate the importance of a constitution in a particular historical context.

[5] The efforts to forge a European constitution and the crises surrounding its confirmation provide a good example of the multiple roles of the constitution (Habermas 2006, 25–45).

realistic and stable of democratic constitutions.[6] Just before the 800th anniversary of the Magna Carta Libertatum (1215), the British constitution stood the test of Scotland's referendum on independence with democratic robustness and agility (September 19, 2014).

What is the situation in Israel? Supreme Court Justice Alfred Witkon wrote in 1962 that had a constitution been approved, it would have indicated a willingness of those competing for power "to assume the burden of a fundamental legal order that cannot be altered through happenstance" (1962, 75). One can deduce from these words that this burden was never assumed. Amnon Rubinstein spelled it out: "And who knows whether an opportunity was not missed at the time that will not soon return" (1991, 447). Akzin, on the other hand, who supported a written constitution and proposed one of his own, took a more practical approach, believing that a constitution neither helps nor harms, if profound changes occur in the structure or world view of the society (1965, 6–7; 1966, 58). Akzin also speculated (1966, 109–11) about whether Israel has an "English constitution" in the material sense. In sum, Israel has Basic Laws (see below), which constitute a partially material, flexible, nominal, and unstable constitution. And the question is whether such a partial constitution can perform the public educational role (A. Barak 1987, 12–19)?

2.2 Developments upon the Founding of Israel

Constitutions are usually created at historical turning points, at a time of major transformation – the founding of a state, collapse of a political entity because of war and conquest, or a profound change in the political system or social structure. The establishment of Israel was one such milestone – some would say a propitious moment – for writing a constitution. The 1947 UN resolution on partition had enjoined the Jewish and Arab states to enact democratic constitutions.[7] Accordingly, Israel's Declaration of Independence contained a commitment to enact a constitution by a Constituent Assembly elected for this purpose, and for the provisional bodies to operate until a government was so elected. Judging from the preparations and statements made, the leadership appeared to have wanted a constitution, and they immediately ensured the holding of elections not to a regular parliament, but to a Constituent Assembly whose sole mission – as its name implies – was to write a constitution. The plan went awry, however, as will be seen below.

Following the 1947 UN resolution, the Jewish Agency Executive in 1949 entrusted the task of preparing the first draft of a constitution to Dr. Y.P. Kohn.[8]

[6] It is interesting in this context to consider the new constitutions written after the "democratic revolution" with the fall of Communism in 1989 (Thompson 2000, 1–20).

[7] The UN decision specifies a parliamentary system and proportional elections. Friedrich (1949) wrote that this level of detail should be regarded as no more than "authoritative advice." He also enthusiastically praised the draft constitution of Y.P. Kohn.

[8] Dr. Yehuda Pinchas Kohn had studied law in Germany and written his doctoral dissertation on "The Constitution of the Independent Irish Republic." His son, Shlomo Kohn, wrote that, as an observant Jew, his father had incorporated sources from Jewish tradition. See Kohn 1949 and "Material for the meeting of the Constitution, Law and Justice Committee" by MK Eliezer Cohen, Committee Files, May 2003. However, a later study concluded that these were mainly symbolic references and that "Kohn understood that the constitution must be a modern and secular one that refrains from expressing preference for the Jewish religion or assumes any form of religious character (apart perhaps in the Preamble)" (Radzyner 2010, 16).

After the founding of Israel, the Provisional State Council appointed eight of its members to a Constitution Committee in which seven political parties were represented, headed by Zerah Warhaftig from Ha-Mizrahi (hereinafter, "the Warhaftig Committee"). This committee was charged with "preparing a draft constitution and submitting it with minority opinions of committee members to the Constituent Assembly" (quoted in Tsidon 1964, 361). The broad representation of parties in the Warhaftig Committee reflects the intent to prepare a document that would express as wide a range of world views as possible. Four other draft constitutions were submitted to the Warhaftig Committee, which chose Kohn's proposal as the basis for its deliberations.[9]

The Warhaftig Committee deliberations revealed growing consensus. Its work was carried out with transparency (rare in those days) and its proposals and discussion summaries were published in their entirety – stimulating vigorous public debate in the daily press (Rozin 2002, 26). The committee submitted preliminary recommendations to the Provisional State Council in January 1949, on the eve of the Constituent Assembly election. It was already known that the Provisional Government under Ben-Gurion was having second thoughts about the need for a constitution. A majority in the committee proposed that the elected Constituent Assembly enact a constitution and then immediately dissolve, whereas a minority, which included the committee head, proposed that the Constituent Assembly not be obligated to enact a constitution, but become the legislative branch. Looking back at these recommendations, we note that there was broad agreement at the time and no explicit opposition of the religious Zionist parties to the idea of a constitution.[10] Meir Loewenstein, the representative of the Orthodox party Agudat Yisrael, was the only committee member clearly opposed: "Any constitution that is the handiwork of man has no place in Israel. If it contradicts the Torah, it is subversive; and if it is identical to the Torah, it is superfluous."[11]

Elections to the Constituent Assembly, postponed because of the war, were held in January 1949. The Transition Law stated that the Provisional State Council would be dissolved after the election, and its authority transferred to the Constituent Assembly, which would thus have a double mandate: to legislate and to write a constitution. Soon after the election, the Constituent Assembly defined itself as "the first Knesset" and thus explicitly declared that writing a constitution was not its sole task. The election campaign for the Constituent Assembly did not revolve exclusively around the issue of a constitution because the war was still raging and other burning issues demanded attention upon establishment of the state (Galnoor 1989, 31–34; Gavison 1985, 147); but by then it was quite clear that the body elected would also deal with ordinary legislation. Nevertheless, the character of the state and form of government to be established were election issues, and all the parties paid serious attention to the constitutional role of the about-to-be-elected Constituent Assembly,

9 See Provisional State Council, Constitution Committee, five booklets: (A) General Committee Deliberations; (B) A Constitution for Israel – Dr. Pinchas Kohn's Proposal; (C) The Legislative Branch; (D) The Executive Branch; and (E) Organization of the State (Constitution Committee 1949).

10 Committee Chair Warhaftig sought "to give standing to the religion of Israel in the state of Israel," and ensure that the version would not introduce to the constitution "anything in conflict with the religion of Israel" (Constitution Committee 1949, Booklet A: 19).

11 Constitution Committee 1949, Booklet A: 22.

and explicitly addressed the future constitution in their platforms, sometimes in detail. Even parties opposed to the constitution after the elections did not suggest this in their platforms, with the exception of Agudat Yisrael.[12]

The other religious parties did not at the time object to a constitution, nor were they very concerned about its potential harm, on the assumption that "the Torah is above the state constitution," i.e., that the status quo from the Mandate period would be maintained, and the constitution would not set hard and fast rules about religious matters.[13] Discussions in Mapai's Central Committee in August 1948 had also fully backed the idea of legislating a constitution (Shapiro 1996, 28). The proposals for a constitution issued by the parties reflected their ideologies. The General Zionists and the Progressives sought to anchor in the constitution the right to private property and free enterprise; Herut emphasized the right to the entire Land of Israel (Eretz Israel); Maki sought adherence to the UN partition decision, proposing that proportional elections be based on separate Jewish and Arab representation; Mapam advocated nationalizing the natural resources and focused on social rights, preference to cooperatives, and the rights of Arab citizens; and Mapam and Maki together objected to what they called "the religious tone" of Kohn's draft constitution. None of the parties proposed wide-ranging regime reforms, such as instituting a presidential system. Innovative ideas included a proposed bicameral parliament (the General Zionists); reform of the proportional electoral system (the Progressives); and strengthening the power of the president (Herut).[14] All the parties assumed that the political arrangements of the national institutions during the Yishuv period would remain in place, and therefore they accepted the main points of Kohn's draft as the basis for their suggested amendments.

The task of drafting the constitution in the first Knesset was assigned to the Constitution, Law and Justice Committee headed by MK Nahum Nir (Mapam). For half a year (May to December 1949), the committee deliberated whether a constitution was needed at all, rather than the content of the constitution (Tsidon 1964, 363). The issue was brought to the Knesset plenary, and after nine meetings, on June 13, 1950, the Knesset adopted the "Harari Resolution," named for MK Yizhar Harari of the Progressive Party, which stated:

> The First Knesset instructs the Constitution, Law and Justice Committee to prepare a draft State constitution. The constitution will be constructed chapter by chapter in such a way that each will constitute a separate Basic Law. The chapters shall be brought before the Knesset in the event that the committee completes its work, and all the chapters together will comprise the State constitution. (Knesset Records, June 13, 1950, 1743)

In the final vote, the Harari Resolution passed by fifty MKs (Mapai and its affiliated parties – the Progressives, WIZO, and one Maki member) versus thirty-eight MKs (the General Zionists, Mapam, Herut, and one Maki member) (ibid., 1721–22; also see Goldberg 1993, 41 and Shapiro 1996, 31). Most representatives of the United

[12] In the 1951 election to the second Knesset, the need for a constitution or "completion of the Basic Laws" (in Mapai's phrase) also appeared in the platforms of most parties, except Mizrahi, which did not mention it, and Agudat Yisrael, which objected (*United Mizrahi Bank Ltd. v. Migdal Cooperative Village et al.* 1995).

[13] The following description is based on Rackman 1955, 24–44.

[14] See Bader 1950 (?), Articles 100–2.

Religious Front voted for a proposal of their own, which did not mention a constitution at all, but stated, "The principles of government and its division of authority, and the guarantee of civil rights and freedoms, shall be established by the Basic Laws" (Tsidon 1964, 366). All the coalition factions voted in favor of the Harari Resolution or the United Religious Front proposal, and all the opposition parties voted in favor of drafting a constitution at once. The Harari Resolution was seen as a compromise between the advocates of and objectors to a constitution: It stated that a constitution would be written, and extended its preparation over time. Before presenting the arguments of both sides, we note that this resolution led in effect to the squandering of the constitution-writing process, which became clear only in retrospect. Why did the Harari Resolution have this effect?

First, the Harari Resolution states, "in the event that the committee completes its work," but no deadline was set; thus, when the excitement of establishing a state had passed, divergent views resurfaced and the political incentive to bridge them waned. The governments headed by Mapai and the religious parties did not rush to enact Basic Laws in the first and second Knessets, as promised, despite the outcries and protest from the proponents of a constitution.

Second, the vague formulation of the Harari Resolution left open many questions that would continue to haunt the Basic Laws: Should they be enacted in a special proceeding? What is the degree of their rigidity (and that of the future constitution), and do they enjoy supreme status over ordinary legislation (Gavison 1998, 61–62)?

Third, when is a Basic Law considered part of a constitution – upon its passage, or only when all the Basic Laws are completed and consolidated? Just before dissolution of the first Knesset in 1951, a subcommittee of the Constitution, Law and Justice Committee proposed a list of subjects to be addressed in the constitution, but this list was not adopted by the committee at large, and to this day no such authorized list exists. The Law of Return, for example, is not a Basic Law.

Fourth, no decision was made about how to formally adopt and ratify the entire constitution: Does this happen when the Knesset decides that the process has ended, or will it require a special Knesset proceeding, or perhaps a referendum?[15]

Although the Harari Resolution is just a Knesset decision, not a law, and ostensibly can be overturned at any point by decision of another Knesset, it was bolstered by political reality, and therefore proved stable and enduring. Indeed, the vague language of the resolution was not accidental, and it was 1958 before the first Basic Law (The Knesset) was enacted. At this rate, calculated MK Nir, the writing of the constitution would be complete in fifty-four years – 2012 (Tsidon 1964, 369). This prophecy was apparently optimistic since the constitution has not been completed to this day.

2.3 The Debate (1950) – Arguments For and Against

The majority of those engaged in this debate declared that it was the role of the constitution to define and preserve a democratic regime. Some were uncertain, though, what kind of constitution would be appropriate for the young state, and

[15] Much later, the constitution proposal of the Constitution, Law and Justice Committee stipulates that "The draft constitution shall be brought to the Knesset for decision and to the nation for ratification," February 13, 2006. www.knesset.gov.il/huka/FollowUpLaw_2.asp (accessed January 5, 2006).

offered a string of arguments for delaying its writing – on the assumption that the existing arrangements could continue until there was clarity about what kind of constitution would be suitable. Amidst the profusion of influences, the British model was viewed by many as worth emulating. But the greatest influence was the fact that the political system of the new state already had unwritten constitutional arrangements that had crystallized during the Yishuv period. These arrangements, providing a framework for the Zionist institutions, had won broad legitimacy among the Jews in Israel, and shaped Israel's constitutional path from its inception in key areas such as the electoral system and proportional representation (as opposed to the British majoritarian system), a unicameral legislature, relations between the legislative and executive branches, the status of the local government, and more. The debate over the constitution has been extensively described, therefore we summarize only the main arguments for and against an immediate written constitution:[16]

A. Formal Reasons

Arguments in Favor

There is an international, legal, and public obligation to prepare a constitution because –

- the UN resolution calls for a constitution;
- the Declaration of Independence makes explicit note of this obligation;
- the term "constituent assembly" testifies that the sole function of this body is to prepare a constitution;
- the elections in January 1949 were to a "constituent assembly," and the voters cast their ballots based on the platforms of the parties that committed to frame a constitution.

Arguments Opposed

The obligation to enact a constitution will be honored even if the Knesset delays its preparation because –

- the UN resolution was not precisely adhered to in other matters – the sovereign Knesset has the right to change it;
- the Declaration of Independence is not a binding legal document, certainly not with respect to a *date* for enacting a constitution;
- the decision to write a constitution was made by provisional institutions, while the democratically elected body can decide if and how to exercise its authority and frame a constitution;
- the obligation to the public is not breached by composing a constitution chapter by chapter, and anyway this matter should be addressed by the parties and their constituents.

[16] On the debate, see Tsidon 1964, 360–68; Galnoor 1982, 64–66; Shimshoni 1982, 53–97; Negbi 1987, 30–42; Emanuel Gutmann 1988, 290–308; Medding 1990, 37–42; Neuberger 1990, 25–37; Yanai in Pilovski 1990, 23–35; Goldberg 1993, 29–48; Bechor 1996, 35–45; Shapiro 1996, 30–33, 57–91; Gavison 1998; and Rozin 2002, 20–36.

B. Substantive and Political Reasons

Arguments in Favor

- In new countries, the constitution bridges experiences and aspirations for a common future. Democracies, which Israel wants to be counted among, have written constitutions; the so-called unwritten British constitution is well rooted in democratic traditions and rules of governance, unlike the Israeli case;
- a constitution molds the character of the democracy and ensures proper governance and the rule of law (and some added – a separation of religion and state);
- the factionalism and divisiveness in Israeli society make necessary a consensual and common civic infrastructure[17] (some added – to counteract the tendency among Jews to factionalism; and others said – to create a new Israeli identity);
- a constitution is designed to protect human, civil, and minority rights (some added – primarily the minority rights of Arab citizens); and Jews have a deep commitment to human rights;
- a constitution would help stabilize the government, and rein in the legislative and executive branches (some added – by way of judicial review);
- the constitution has intrinsic educational worth for inculcating democratic values, especially in a country of new immigrants.

Arguments Opposed

- Although an agreed upon constitution has many benefits, for contentious issues (religion–state relations and socioeconomic ideologies), a constitution would only exacerbate the rifts or risk being ignored;
- new states adopted constitutions when their revolutions were over, while Israel is only at the beginning, as most Jews have not yet moved to Israel (and some added – the constitution of Israel belongs to the entire Jewish people);
- a democracy can be established without a written constitution as in Britain (or the unwritten, voluntary system during the Yishuv period); in any case, ordinary legislation is sufficient to protect civil rights;
- the dispute about the status of religion in Israel is substantive. It cannot be glossed over by fancy words or formulations, and poses a threat of a rift between the religious and the secular, and between Jews in Israel and the Diaspora. Observant Jews should not be forced to choose between their faith and their loyalty to the state (some would add – time will help create the conditions for resolving this problem);
- the branches of government should not be overly constrained, certainly not at the outset of their assumption of power or during the emergency period. Flexibility must be maintained on open issues such as the status of Arabs in Israel or the question of borders, and on governance issues such as reducing the

[17] Dr. Kohn, the author of the draft constitution, raised this argument in a personal letter to Ben-Gurion: "We have no common language on matters of utmost importance, we must forge a general agreement between us on the basic issues, and this must be done by a constitution" (Shapiro 1996, 31). Proponents of a constitution for the European Union often use a similar argument – the constitution will promote integration and create a "European consciousness" (see Finer, Bogdanor, and Rudden 1995, 21).

number of parties or defining the electoral system (some added – there is no need for judicial review, with its anti-democratic power over decisions made by the elected legislature);

- a rigid constitution means superfluous constraints on governing flexibility; it is preferable to adopt incremental solutions and thereby avoid ideological pitfalls in order to create a common capacity for action.

Much of the public believed it to be a matter of time before a carefully drafted constitution would be enacted, and that the writing was postponed to allow for due deliberations and enable a bridging of differences. An editorial in *Haaretz* (June 15, 1950), for example, expressed satisfaction with the Harari compromise, and full faith in the intent to begin immediately to enact the Basic Laws. MK Pinchas Lavon, on the other hand, believed that the decision to enact Basic Laws meant that Israel would not have a constitution at all (quoted in Shapiro 1996, 53).

2.4 "The 1949 Constitution"

A. What Turned the Tide against the Written Constitution?

It is commonly believed that the main obstacle to framing a constitution was the issue of religion and state – the fear of a Kulturkampf (Lerner 2004, 239) – meaning that the secular majority agreed to postpone a constitution to prevent observant Jews from dropping out of the political system. Meir Loewenstein, an ultra-Orthodox member of the Knesset, made it crystal clear:

> Is it conceivable that a secular constitution would be studied in the religious schools, if one were enacted, God forbid? The pupils might conclude that the Torah is no longer valid in Israel … I am warning you: The attempt to enact a constitution can only lead to an intense war of opinions, fierce and uncompromising, a war over the soul defined by the frightening term Kulturkampf. (Knesset Records, 4, February 7, 1950, 744)

Yet it is entirely possible that the ultra-Orthodox and their Knesset representatives would have ultimately reconciled themselves to the constitution, neither resigning from the Knesset nor isolating themselves from the community completely, just as they had grown accustomed to the idea of Israel as a secular state. This would be conditional upon the constitution not deviating from the vague formulation of the Warhaftig Committee, i.e., not establishing a clear-cut separation of religion from state. The religious Zionists, who were a decisive majority in the United Religious Front, were more moderate – they were willing to go along with the religious status quo and even make a stronger version of it constitutionally binding. It was this religious camp who then changed its mind, preferring to safeguard the status quo through extra-constitutional political agreements. At this stage, their Knesset representatives expressed staunch opposition to a constitution, and supported an alternative to Harari's proposal. Their change of heart can be explained as follows: As long as they assumed that a constitution was inevitable, they preferred to cooperate in order to influence its content, but the moment Mapai, led by Ben-Gurion, retreated from support of the constitution, the entire Religious Front also came out against it (Galnoor 1982; and see Gutmann in Bogdanor 1988, 294; Neuberger 1990, 32–37; and Rozin 2002, 33–35).

The decision to frame a constitution was not defeated because of principled opposition by the religious, not out of fear of a Kulturkampf, and not because of Mapai's coalition considerations (Goldberg 1993, 37). The order of events was reversed: The religious parties took a more extreme view only when they realized that opposing the constitution was consistent with the changed position of the ruling party, as it also served their religious world view. Furthermore, the Mizrahi and Ha-Mizrahi parties were partners and key players in the Yishuv political system, hence, like Mapai, they became convinced that a constitution would undermine the previous political order.

The failure to frame a constitution at that historic junction was a missed opportunity, as agreement could have been reached about everything else in exchange for concessions to the religious – concessions that were ultimately made anyway. If a consensual constitution had been forged, with the exception of religious issues, perhaps the gaps would have narrowed, or at least not increased over time. And even if the gaps had not narrowed, writing and approving a constitution would not have been held hostage to religious issues, as is now the case.[18] It could be argued, on the other hand, that if a constitution in 1949 had dealt explicitly with the separation of state and religion, this part could not have been implemented, and the stature of the constitution would have been compromised from the outset.

The second explanation for the fact that the constitution was not written at that time concerns pragmatic, power considerations of the ruling party, and Ben-Gurion in particular. According to this view, Mapai opposed a constitution because it would have clipped the wings of those already in power – the ruling elite (parties and politicians), and Ben-Gurion (see Neuberger 1990, 37; Goldberg 1993, 29; Shapiro 1996, 33; and Aronson 1998, 11). Surely behind the ideological debate, there were also considerations of power, as the opposition, particularly MK Begin (Herut), did not tire of pointing out:

> If the Constituent Assembly were to enact a constitution, the government would not have a free hand to do as it pleased ... There is a ruling sect here that stands above the law because there is no constitution to restrain it. This is how you want to continue, and it's the real reason for your opposition to the constitution, which you do not admit to the nation. (Knesset Records, 4, February 7, 1950, 740)

MK Ya'ari (Mapam) feared that the desire to maintain the state of emergency, with the powers it gave the government ("it has the authority to dismiss the Knesset"), was the reason for the coalition's opposition to a constitution that would guarantee civil rights (ibid., February 13, 1950, 768). Nevertheless, the pragmatic considerations extended beyond Mapai's immediate desire to preserve the coalition with the religious parties. Had the constitution been a burning issue for Mapai, it would have presumably included it in the coalition agreement (the constitution was not mentioned there at all), or even formed an alternative coalition without the religious parties. More relevant are the arguments that Ben-Gurion supported the Harari Resolution because he hoped to change the proportional electoral system without constitutional obstacles, and he vehemently opposed judicial review. But even these

[18] This was especially evident in the opposition of the religious parties to a Basic Law that would include a declaration protecting human and civil rights (see Karp 1993, 333–37).

matters could have been overcome by framing a constitution that would suit this perception of the state (see discussion in Chapter 1).

Those who point to Ben-Gurion as the main obstacle to a constitution base this on his "statist" approach, which placed the state at the center of collective endeavors in security, the economy, and pioneering activities, claiming that he opposed the constitution as it would be "superior to the state."[19] Some take this a step further and combine Ben-Gurion's "statism" with his placement of the nation's needs over human and civil rights, which the constitution was meant to ensure (Yanai 1990a, 28). These explanations do not quite relate to the main issue because, as noted, Ben-Gurion's statism was primarily a struggle against the sectoralism of the state-in-the-making, and a constitution could have actually helped him impose state authority over the army, the Histadrut, and the parties; or, to define it differently, the division of labor between central government and various pre-state bodies.[20] Is it possible that Ben-Gurion did not understand that the constitution could help unify "the Hebrew nation that has always been deficient in its sense of statism" (quoted in Aronson 1998, 27)? Certainly there is a grain of truth to the claim that Ben-Gurion (and many MKs) objected to the constitution because they feared its constraint of their powers, they did not want human rights to stand in their way, particularly in matters of security, and they did not want the Arab minority to use the constitution to safeguard its rights, as well as other pragmatic reasons. However, this would not explain the *change* in their position, especially after the 1949 election, some six months after the state came into being.

B. The Material Constitution

The change that took place in the coalition parties of the first Knesset was actually no change at all. These parties discovered that despite the momentous arrival of the state, the political system was business as usual, and they quickly decided that there was no point in altering it. The main reason that a formal constitution was not written was that the unwritten "material constitution" handed down from the Yishuv period was already too rooted to be changed. At the time of the establishment of the state and the War for Independence, the Jewish public in Israel and the Diaspora, and its leaders, felt borne aloft on the wings of history; framing a constitution was part of this sense of elation. There was a desire to imbue the document of the constitution with the magnitude of the event, the tidings to the world that, behold, the Jewish people now had a state, and that this state belonged to the family of enlightened and democratic nations.[21] This was an historic moment, appropriate for grand rhetoric and, as we suggest above, the constitution would have been politically possible in exchange for a compromise on the status of religion. This moment of grace

[19] "What motivated him [Ben-Gurion] was the concern that enacting a constitution would weaken the state" (Shapiro 1996, 31).

[20] "Constitutions are codes of norms which aspire to regulate the allocation of powers, functions, and duties among the various agencies and officers of government, and to define the relationships between these and the public" (Finer, Bogdanor, and Rudden 1995, 1).

[21] Enormous importance was attributed to the written word in those days, hence "the document of the constitution." This is based on the discussion in the Constitution Committee headed by Warhaftig (Constitution Committee 1949, Booklet A, 1948) and newspaper articles from that period.

did not last long, however, as the Declaration of Independence met the needs of the public and many leaders for a celebratory and ceremonial historic document.[22] It felt to many as if the "constitution" had already been written, and Ben-Gurion said explicitly in late 1949 that an historic document declaring the intentions of the state already exists – the Declaration of Independence.[23] Meanwhile, Israel had been admitted as a member of the United Nations in 1949, and the constitution became an internal Israeli affair. Subsequent events in domestic Israeli politics reviewed above – especially the familiar procedures of forming a coalition, and the frequent crises that led to early elections in 1951 – actually set in motion the "unwritten constitution" inherited from the Yishuv political system, and led to postponement of the writing of the formal constitution. In addition, the challenges of security issues and foreign affairs only increased the desire of political leaders to adhere to the known ways of doing things. According to this analysis, more than Ben-Gurion wanted to continue the revolution ("statism") without a constitution, he preferred to adhere to the unwritten "constitution" and the mechanisms of the previous system (revolutionary at the time), out of fear that a written constitution would not enable him and his party to conduct the affairs of state in the way to which they had become accustomed. Furthermore, the system seemed to be working – the victory in the War for Independence, success in the tests of transition (Altalena, Bernadotte, and the disbanding of the Palmach – see Chapter 1), and elections conducted for the Knesset and the Histadrut (January and May 1949) – why change it?

Ben-Gurion feared "the artificial strengthening of minorities" (*Knesset Records* 4, 1950, 813), i.e., the need to form "broad coalitions" that would reduce the government's freedom of action. "Minorities" in this context meant not Arabs, but the political camps and parties – primarily Herut and Mapam – but also the many splinter groups in the Yishuv, which, in Ben-Gurion's opinion, "interfered" with collective efforts to realize the larger mission. On these grounds, he managed to persuade most Mapai leaders, thus creating the coalition majority in the Knesset. Precisely because he did not like the system that had evolved in the Zionist institutions, he feared it would become entrenched in a constitution. He and his allies viewed the constitution as an institution that would further reduce the already constrained flexibility of the government. Many in the opposition, on the other hand, believed the constraints were insufficient, and wanted a constitution to prevent the arbitrary exercise of power by Mapai and its domineering majority.

Throughout the pre-state period in his roles in the Zionist institutions, Ben-Gurion complained repeatedly of "the system" – for which his party was primarily responsible – and feared that a constitution would prevent it from being changed and would not allow its replacement by the "English" system – a regional majoritarian electoral system.[24] Ben-Gurion and several Mapai leaders opposed a

[22] Shahar writes about the ambivalence that accompanied the Declaration of Independence – its role as a legal document versus its role as "a poem of the founding prophets" (2002: 523).

[23] Recorded in the Constitution, Law and Justice Committee of the Knesset in November 1949 (quoted by Rozin 2002, 40). Akzin (1966, 136) noted another important point: The Declaration also set some governance matters, particularly the government's subordination to the parliament.

[24] In 1954, Ben-Gurion began his efforts to replace the national-proportional electoral system with a regional-majoritarian system. His resignation from the government in 1953 is sometimes attributed to his disgust with the coalition politics forced on him (Yaacobi and Gera 1975, 47, 55–57).

constitution not because they were not democrats or wanted to limit civil rights, but because they believed these matters could be dealt with by ordinary legislation and the existing customs. They opposed a constitution after the 1949 election because they did not view it as something that would "strengthen the state," i.e., something that would foster a common civic framework. Ironically, in those years, the constitution could have contributed to "statism" – not in the étatist or nationalist sense, but by creating a more direct affinity between the individual citizen whose rights were protected and the state charged with protecting them. Habit prevailed, however, and the Yishuv "constitution" was transferred word-for-unwritten-word to the political system of the newborn state, and even contributed to its stability.

The debate about the constitution in the years 1948–50 and the decision that ensued are a mirror image of the political modes of operation during the Yishuv period that were carried over into the state, where they continued for many years. These included maximal flexibility, ambiguous decisions meant to gloss over differences, adapting previous decisions to changing circumstances, and postponing decisions in the face of deep divisions. Thus, the Constituent Assembly became an ordinary legislative body, its name was changed to "the first Knesset," and a decision was made to write a constitution, but to do so incrementally. In retrospect, this decision epitomizes the political culture of Israel that lasted for many years.[25]

C. The Components of the "1949 Constitution"

The "1949 Constitution" does not exist as a legal entity – there is no document bearing this name. In practice, however, the unwritten components of the "1949 Constitution" are what determined the foundation and institutions of the Israeli regime – above all, that Israel would be a parliamentary democracy. This "constitution" was given effective legitimacy in the first election of 1949 and later in the Harari Resolution of 1950.[26] When did the "1949 Constitution" begin to take shape? It actually began one year earlier when the provisional institutions were established through a process of broad consensual decision-making between the representatives of the Jewish people (the Jewish Agency) and the Yishuv. We note in particular the decision of the Zionist Executive Committee in April 1948 to establish the Provisional People's Council with thirty-seven members. This was an interparty pact that encompassed the large parties and groups in Jewish society at the time (Avizohar and Bareli 1989, vol. 2, 303). Thus the model of Israeli democracy was created, which used political means to mediate social disputes – religious or other. Excluded from this pact were Israel's Arab citizens.

The "1949 Constitution" is a collection of arrangements – both formal (e.g., the Election Law) and informal (e.g., the religious status quo) – that reflect the "consociational democracy" of Zionist and Yishuv politics. The ethos of the "1949 Constitution" is that of flexible, mostly secret arrangements whose purpose was to build consensus and avoid internal rifts by channeling social rivalries into the

[25] As early as 1955, Rackman (47–49, 93) noted that in this decision about the constitution, the political leaders did not manage to rise above the familiar and did not seek profound reform, as needed when founding a state. Rackman proposed in 1958 that a "constitutional convention" be convened, as held in the United States to write its constitution a decade after its own declaration of independence.

[26] For a similar approach, see Elazar 1988.

political system. This was also the essence of the Harari Resolution (1950) – an ad hoc agreement to start a gradual process with no specified content or deadline.

The "1949 Constitution" is based on the Yishuv political arrangements: a parliamentary democracy, the previous political institutions, a unicameral system, a proportional electoral system without geographic representation, a fragmented party map, the necessity of coalitions, mechanisms to mediate conflicts and crises, a division of labor between the political center and secondary centers, weakness of the local authorities, and more. The formal part of the "1949 Constitution" is contained in the official documents subsequent to the establishment of Israel – the Declaration of Independence, the Manifesto, the Law and Administration Ordinance, the Prevention of Terrorism Ordinance, the Law of Return, and the World Zionist Organization-Jewish Agency (Status) Law. Many of these components were granted formal standing in the three governmental Basic Laws (The Knesset, The President, and The Government) enacted between 1958 and 1968.

We conclude this section with three observations that presaged the future. First, the constitutional arrangements of 1949 and later contributed to the stability of the regime, which was no mean feat in a brand new country fighting for its survival. Only in retrospect do we know that the political system was by then already quite stable, and would not have been undermined by a restrictive constitution. The constitutional arrangement chosen in 1949 had clear short-term advantages, especially the prevention of turbulence in a difficult period. On the other hand, the long, drawn-out process of preparing a constitution has exacerbated the disputes and, in the long range, even contributed to instability.[27]

Second, all the large, organized Jewish groups were included in the political arrangements, namely, as noted, the Revisionists, the ultra-Orthodox, and the Communists. Thus an informal constitutional basis was created for the consociational arrangements that will be discussed in Part III of this book. Arab representatives did not take part in the groundbreaking pact of April 1948, they were not partners to the Declaration of Independence, written in the name of "representatives of the Hebrew Yishuv and the Zionist movement," and they were not included, even symbolically, in the provisional institutions (Jabareen 2005). Their exclusion could be explained by the circumstances at the time, but today it is patently clear that whoever was excluded at the time found it very hard to become a partner in the future, and this applies also to some Jewish groups, such as those who arrived in later waves of immigration. The list of participants in the unwritten arrangements of the "1949 Constitution" was then sealed for many years to come.

Third, the agreements at the time were made by parties and organized Jewish groups – the term "political elite" does not apply here, both because of the quite inclusive nature of the arrangements and because the boundaries between "society" and "politics" were blurred. Those absent from the launching of the "1949 Constitution" were "the citizens" – the new private and collective entity that was just created (or that should have begun its life) upon establishment of the state. Their rights were listed in the Declaration of Independence, but the unwritten constitution was shaped primarily by parties and organized groups.

[27] Akzin wrote in 1956 that in a volatile nation with a tendency toward dogmatism, a formal constitution is a vital safety valve for stability (ibid., 338).

In 1949, an opportunity was missed for building a broader base for a democratic political culture in Israel – not just the rules of the game concerning majority politics and elections – but a constitution anchoring these rules in an ethos of equality and liberty. At any rate, the "1949 Constitution" was an expression of the consensual democratic model of the Jewish community in Israel – a democracy of negotiations (Lijphart 1999).

2.5 Developments until the 2000s

Attitudes about the legacy of the 1950 Harari Resolution divide into two partially overlapping perspectives. One focuses on the circumstances at the time, pointing out that compromise was the only practical measure, and that the constitution is indeed being written over the years, chapter by chapter, in accordance with the level of agreement that can be reached. From this perspective, Israel has a constitution today, partial but real in the sense that it exists, has legitimacy, and functions. The other points to the collusion and failed leadership, and maintains that it was clear even then that Israel would still not have a formal constitution many years later. We focus here on the developments in the wake of the Harari Resolution, including the question of the constitutional status of the Declaration of Independence, and the debate over the continued role of the Knesset in enacting a constitution.

Many of those who voted for the compromise decision, including MK Harari himself, believed that the constitution would soon be written, at the latest during the term of the second Knesset. But this opportunity passed, and the circumstances that had created a majority against a constitution in 1949 continued and even strengthened. Soon after the Harari Resolution, the Law of Return was enacted with broad, virtually wall-to-wall, Jewish consensus, yet it does not have the stature of a Basic Law. The proposed bill to entrench the article in the Law of Return that gives every Jew the right to immigrate to Israel also failed to pass (Gavison 1998, 62). The same fate was shared by other constitution-like laws – the Equal Rights for Women Law (1951) and the Citizenship Law (1952). In the first decade of the state, the fact was firmly established that Israel had no formal constitution and that the quasi-constitutional Basic Laws do not require a supermajority and do not enjoy supra-legislative status. A subcommittee of the Knesset's Constitution, Law and Justice Committee prepared a list of subjects that the Basic Laws would address.[28] However, the first draft of the Basic Law: The Knesset was legislated only in 1958 by the third Knesset. In a 1962 article, Pinchas Lavon noted that parliamentary democracy was accepted as a fact in Israel, but that the education system did not instill honor and respect for it. As to the constitution, Lavon (1986) noted:

> Coalition arrangements are not preferable to a constitution that will clarify fundamental issues in state matters … It is better to have one big struggle than endless quarrels and schemes that bring no honor to the state or to religion. (1986, 67–68)

[28] To wit, organization of the state (governance arrangements); local government; individual rights; security services; labor matters; Law of Return; and civil law; as well as two additional suggestions: national minority rights, and the Sabbath and Jewish law (based on Tsidon 1964, 367).

A. The Status of the Declaration of Independence

In the absence of a constitution, what is the legal status of the Declaration of Independence – is it a constitutional or legal document, or something else? Akzin (1966, 128 and 138) asserts that those who regard the Declaration of Independence as merely a legal document miss the point, as it is a formative, historic document. Indeed, a claim was made in 1948 that laws in contravention of the principles in the Declaration of Independence should be declared null and void, but the Supreme Court rejected this view, ruling that the Declaration has no supra-legal constitutional status by which other laws can be measured, but that it expresses the vision and credo of the people (*Ziv v. Gubernick* 1948; *Karbutli v. Minister of Defense* 1949). These rulings were issued when it was still believed that the constitution was about to be written. Subsequently, the Declaration was accorded the status of an interpretive document, whose principles can be used to examine other laws, as noted by Justice Agranat in 1953:

> Indeed, the Declaration does not fall within constitutional law that determines the validity or invalidity of various ordinances or laws, yet insofar as it expresses "the vision of the people" ... it is our duty to pay attention to what is declared in it when we interpret and give meaning to the laws of the state. (*Kol Ha'am v. Minister of the Interior* 1953)

In 1962, the Supreme Court overturned a decision of a local council to prohibit Reform Synagogue services in a municipal hall, citing the affirmation in the Declaration of Independence of freedom of religion for all citizens of Israel (*Peretz et al. v. Kfar Shmaryahu Local Council* 1962). The Declaration thus became somewhat similar to the preamble in the constitutions of other states, whose legal standing could be characterized as "a constitutional compass" (Rubinstein and Orgad 2005, 38, 46). The Declaration of Independence is cited in many court decisions, studied in school civics classes, and has become part of the public discourse on the essence of democracy in Israel. In the 1990s, the tenets of the Declaration of Independence were given formal constitutional status upon enactment of the new Basic Law:

> Fundamental human rights in Israel are founded upon recognition of the value of the human being, the sanctity of human life, and the principle that all persons are free; these rights shall be upheld in the spirit of the principles set forth in the Declaration of the Establishment of the State of Israel. (Basic Law: Freedom of Occupation, Article 1, amended 1994)

B. The Role of the Knesset in Enacting a Constitution

The task of writing a constitution was assigned to the Knesset in the Harari Resolution. Before it dissolved, the first Knesset resolved that the second Knesset would have all the powers, rights, and obligations that the first Knesset members had; and that this resolution would also apply to the third and any subsequent Knessets, so long as no other legislation contravened it (Second Knesset [Transition] Law, 1951, Articles 5 and 10). At first this appears obvious, particularly in light of the fact that all the Knessets have continued the process of legislating the Basic Laws. Nevertheless, a fierce legal debate erupted regarding the "constitutional continuity" of the Knesset, and the two interconnected questions: Was the power of the first

Knesset (the Constituent Assembly) to frame a constitution passed on to subsequent Knessets? And, does the Knesset have unlimited authority to legislate as it pleases, to limit future legislation by restrictive clauses, to legislate a requirement of a supermajority, and the like? (See Rubinstein and Medina 2005, 53–124 on the constitution.) The central issue here concerns judicial review (see Chapter 6), in light of the two Basic Laws enacted in 1992 – Human Dignity and Liberty, and Freedom of Occupation. These laws contain articles that would make amendment difficult (and the latter has a formal entrenchment clause – "This Basic Law shall not be changed except by Basic Law passed by a majority of the members of Knesset").[29]

The questions that arise: Is this constitutional legislation? Does it apply to the other Basic Laws? If so, do the courts have general authority to exercise judicial review on the constitutionality of legislation? These questions were addressed in a detailed decision by an expanded panel of seven Supreme Court justices in 1995, in which the majority opinion written by President Shamgar stated that the Knesset has constituent authority, whether because it continues to wear the "two crowns" (formative constituent authority and ordinary legislative authority), which it inherited from the first Knesset, or because it has this inherent authority (*United Mizrahi Bank Ltd. v. Migdal Cooperative Village et al.* 1995 – hereinafter the "Mizrahi Bank ruling"). Justice Barak entitled these two Basic Laws "a constitutional revolution" because the Knesset, by power of its constituent authority, bestowed upon the state a constitutional human rights charter (Mizrahi Bank ruling, 140–78). Moreover, by virtue of the existence of Basic Laws with constitutional status, Basic Laws are on a higher level than ordinary legislation and the court has the authority of judicial review to determine the constitutionality of Knesset legislation. In the words of Justice Barak, "the Israeli politic became, with regard to human rights, a constitutional politic."[30]

Although the general decision was unanimous, Justice Mishael Cheshin wrote that the Knesset does not have the authority to frame a constitution because constitutions are bestowed in a unique moment of pomp and with the participation of the entire nation – like the thunder and lightning in the giving of the Torah on Mount Sinai – and not by an ordinarily elected Knesset, which itself must be subordinate to the constitution. Basic Laws, in Cheshin's view, are regular legislation with a special name, because the Knesset is not omnipotent nor does it have the authority to be binding upon itself. Furthermore, a special process must be sought to enact a constitution, such as a special constituent assembly or a referendum (Mizrahi Bank ruling, 292). Cheshin's main concern was the abuse of the power of the Knesset to deviate from the principle of democratic majority rule. He maintained that the court has the authority to overturn laws passed by the Knesset when they violate basic rights, but that this authority has existed beforehand, and therefore the two new Basic Laws do not constitute a "constitutional revolution" (ibid., 406–9).[31]

[29] Amendments to the Basic Law: Referendum, passed by the Knesset on March 12, 2014, also require a majority of Knesset members. See Article 5: http://main.knesset.gov.il/Activity/Legislation/Documents/yesod15.pdf (accessed October 16, 2017). Furthermore, some specific articles in Basic Laws require a majority of Knesset members for amendment (see Table 2.1).

[30] From English translation of the Mizrahi Bank ruling: 257 (Justice Barak); 74 (Justice Shamgar); 139 (Justice Barak); 155 (Justice Zamir). See also Barak 1997, 3.

[31] Gavison (1998, 121–47) also believes that these two Basic Laws should not be viewed as a "constitutional revolution." See also Landau 1996, 697 and Bendor 1995, 443.

In this ruling, the court gave legitimacy to the evolving material constitution (the "1949 Constitution"), and moved one step closer toward bestowing a special status upon the Basic Laws. Although the two new Basic Laws introduced to the constitution some important (though partial) elements from a human rights charter, in practice it was the court ruling that gave constitutional status also to the other Basic Laws – even before they were consolidated as a constitution. In the measured words of then President Meir Shamgar:

> against the background of the two new Basic Laws that directly deal with the protection of fundamental rights, this expanded bench now has the opportunity to establish an entire system, adjusted to our present constitutional umbrella ... From now on, it is appropriate that all Basic Laws be governed by a legislative policy that expresses the doctrine of normative hierarchy, by which Basic Laws can be amended only by other Basic Laws. (Mizrahi Bank ruling, 46)

This "normative hierarchy" places constitutional legislation (Basic Laws) at the top, followed by ordinary legislation, which stands above secondary legislation (regulations).[32] Thus, the existing Basic Laws have supra-legislative status, even if not all of them have additional constitutional features such as rigidity and supremacy, and even though the Knesset can change them by a simple majority. The next question then is the meaning of the Basic Laws in terms of the structure and functioning of the political system.

2.6 The Basic Laws and their Significance

Justice Cheshin believed that the Harari Resolution was a "limping" compromise, primarily because the character of the constitution was not established, and the status of the Basic Laws was not resolved (Mizrahi Bank ruling, 326–31).

A. Basic Laws that Were Enacted

From 1958 through 2014, the Knesset passed twelve Basic Laws. Table 2.1 presents the Basic Laws, the year enacted, the main subjects covered, whether there is immunity from Emergency Regulations, articles requiring a special majority for amendment, the level of detail of the law, and the number of amendments.

No agreed list exists of constitutional subjects that are worthy of Basic Laws, and those already enacted were not legislated according to an orderly plan, a particular order, or any unequivocal criteria about why this law is a Basic Law. Moreover, there is no internal connection – in form or content – among the Basic Laws. The Basic Law: The Knesset, for example, defines the essence of that institution ("a house of representatives"), but there is no comparable definition of role in the Basic Law: Government ("the executive branch"), while the Basic Law: The Judiciary does not address this matter at all. The Basic Laws about The Knesset and The Government, which are the most detailed, do not define the authority of the Knesset and the government toward each other. The process of legislating the Basic Laws also

[32] Akzin, inspired by the jurist and philosopher of law Hans Kelsen (1881–1973), called this "the hierarchical structure of norms" and "the pyramid of norms" (1966, Part I, 30–32, 120–28).

Table 2.1 *Basic Laws and their significant features*

Basic Law (year enacted)	Main subjects addressed	Immunity from Emergency Regulations	Rigidity: special majority required for amendment	Level of detail; number of amendments*
1. The Knesset (1958)	Composition, electoral system, right to vote and be elected, reasons for disqualification of parties and candidates, term of office, immunity, Knesset committees, resignation/suspension/replacement of MKs, parliamentary commissions of inquiry, dissolution of the Knesset	Art. 44 (80 MKs to amend)	Art. 4: electoral system (61 MKs to amend); Art. 9A: extension of term of office (80 MKs to amend); Art. 34: dissolution of the Knesset (simple majority to amend); Arts. 44, 45: stability and rigidity of the law (80 MKs to amend)	Very high; 41 amendments
2. Israel Lands (1960)	Status of state land and Jewish National Fund land, legal procedures for their sale, legal prohibition on transfer of ownership	None	None	Low; no amendments
3. The President of the State (1964)	Functions and powers, method of election, term of office, immunity, suspension/resignation/termination of office/replacement	Art. 25 (simple majority to amend)**	None	Medium; 10 amendments
4A. The Government (1968)	Composition, method of formation, change of composition and addition of ministers, acting minister, secrecy, delegation and transfer of powers, deputy ministers	Art. 42 (61 MKs to amend)	None (revoked and replaced by Basic Law: Government [1992])	High; 6 amendments
4B. The Government (1992)	Composition, direct election, special elections and early elections, publication of coalition agreements, change of composition and addition of a minister, budget, secrecy, delegation and transfer of powers, deputy and acting ministers, secondary legislation	Art. 53 (the entire law required 61 MKs to amend)	The entire law required 61 MKs to amend (revoked and replaced by Basic Law: Government [2001])	High; 9 amendments (the ninth repealed the law)

(Continued)

Table 2.1 *(Cont.)*

Basic Law (year enacted)	Main subjects addressed	Immunity from Emergency Regulations	Rigidity: special majority required for amendment	Level of detail; number of amendments*
4C. The Government (2001)	Composition, method of formation, change of composition, addition of ministers, responsibility, eligibility to serve, replacement, secrecy, delegation and transfer of powers, deputy ministers, forming the government, continuity of the government, early elections and dissolution of the Knesset, interrogation of the prime minister, removal from office of the prime minister, other minister, or deputy minister; vote of no-confidence	Art. 41 (the entire law requires 61 MKs to amend)	The entire law requires 61 MKs to amend	Medium; 2 amendments
5. The State Economy (1975)	How to levy taxes, compulsory loans, and fees; state budget procedures and approval; state property transactions; currency notes and coins; audit of the state economy	None	Art. 3B: failure to pass the budget (61 MKs); Art. 3C: amendments to the Budget Law (at least 50 MKs in favor)	Low; 8 amendments
6. The Military (1976)	Subordination to the civil authority of the government; procedures for appointing a chief of staff; mandatory service and recruitment; exclusiveness of the army and its authority	None	None	Low; 1 technical amendment
7. Jerusalem, Capital of Israel (1980)	Jerusalem, complete and united, as the capital of Israel; seat of government and other branches; freedom of access to holy places; development of city	None	Arts. 5 and 6 require 61 MKs to amend	Low; 1 amendment
8. The Judiciary (1984)	Independence of the judiciary; judicial power; appointment of judges; period of tenure; retirement/suspension/re-posting; Supreme Court and High Court of Justice; appeals; the standing of precedents	Art. 22 (can be amended by a simple majority)**	None	Low; 2 amendments

9. State Comptroller (1988)	Functions and powers; election; removal from office; accountability toward the Knesset; role as state ombudsman	None	None	Medium; 2 amendments
10. Human Dignity and Liberty (1992/94)	Right to life, body, dignity, property, personal liberty, privacy, freedom of movement, qualifications to the law	Art. 12 (simple majority to amend)**	None***	Low; 1 amendment
11. Freedom of Occupation (1992/94)	Freedom of occupation; qualifications for licensing; effect on non-conforming laws as of 1994	Art. 6 (the entire law requires 61 MKs to amend)	Art. 7 requires 61 MKs to amend	Low; 2 amendments****
12. Referendum (2014)	Mandates the holding of a referendum if the government decides or signs an agreement that the laws, jurisdiction, and administrative authority of Israel will no longer apply to a specific geographical area, unless approved by 80 or more MKs	Art. 4 (the entire law requires 61 MKs to amend)	Art. 5 requires 61 MKs to amend	Low; none

* Only the substantive amendments were counted.

** Only of those participating in the vote.

*** Does not deal with the issue of the supra-legal status of the law.

**** In 1994 the law was re-legislated with two amendments.

varied. While the first Basic Law was initiated by the Knesset's Constitution, Law and Justice Committee, the body that inherited the mantle of a constituent authority, many Basic Laws were initiated later by the government, and one ("Jerusalem, Capital of Israel") began as a private member's bill. We will now examine the status of the Basic Laws according to the features of constitutions presented earlier in this chapter.

Formality: The status of the Basic Laws differs from that of ordinary legislation, not just in name, but also usually in the attitude of the Knesset toward their legislation.[33] For this reason, the Basic Laws are not just a collection of accepted norms written in formal legal language. On the other hand, it is hard to define them as a formal constitution, because they are indeed separate chapters lacking a constitutional spine with an internal logic.

Supremacy: Upon enactment of the 1992 Basic Laws, all the Basic Laws were accorded supra-legal status by the Supreme Court. This means that if an ordinary law contravenes a Basic Law, the Basic Law prevails. Furthermore, the power of the court to exercise judicial review was established, i.e., the authority to invalidate ordinary laws if they are inconsistent with Basic Laws. Judicial review is a matter of controversy, however, and it was the Supreme Court, not the legislature, that established the supremacy of the Basic Laws.[34]

Akzin wrote that, logically, a Basic Law should not be changed other than by another Basic Law, but he wondered if this logic would apply in "the political climate of Israel" (1966, 119–20). Indeed it did not apply, and Israeli governments have not hesitated to use a Knesset majority to change Basic Laws for random coalition reasons.[35] Moreover, significant changes have been introduced, amendments that a supreme, rigid constitution is intended to prevent or minimize, out of concern that such changes would be based on a fleeting majority or partisan compromises.[36] The redrafting of the Basic Law: Government – twice in one decade – also falls into this category of changes caused by the lack of normative supremacy of the Basic Laws. One might also question the constitutional need for some of the subjects legislated as Basic Laws, and certainly some paragraphs and subparagraphs in Basic Laws are dubious matters for a constitution (Meridor 1993, 387; Gavison 1998, 120). On the other hand, there are subjects that have not yet been addressed in Basic Laws, such

[33] Justice Barak believed the Basic Laws are "of a singular nature … a substantive expression of the process by which the constitution was enacted." In contrast, Justice Cheshin believed that the formal status of the Basic Laws was never established: he noted of the MKs' attitude toward the 1952 laws that "the day of adopting the Basic Laws was just another day"; indeed, the Basic Law: Freedom of Occupation passed by a majority of thirty-two against twenty-one, meaning that most MKs did not even bother to show up to vote (Mizrahi Bank ruling, 206–7, 352, respectively).

[34] The first time the High Court called for a change in primary legislation and the Knesset complied was *Bergman v. Minister of Finance* 1969.

[35] Examples of such changes in the Basic Laws: an amendment in 1979 to appoint Simcha Ehrlich second deputy prime minister in the Begin government; cancellation of the limit on the number of government ministers (1999) in the Barak government; a failed attempt by the Sharon government in 2004 to change the Basic Law so that Shimon Peres could be appointed acting prime minister (he was given the title "deputy prime minister").

[36] After the election of Meir Kahane to the Knesset, for example, an amendment was passed in 1985 to the Basic Law: The Knesset intended to prevent the election of a party that incites to racism. In a compromise with the right-wing parties, the amendment also disqualifies parties that negate the existence of Israel as the state of the Jewish people from running for the Knesset (Article 7A).

as the Law of Return, even though its substance is patently constitutional. The Knesset not only avoided specifically attributing supra-legal status to the Basic Laws, but even rejected attempts to assign them a special legislative process, such as a mandatory supermajority for their approving or for amending a Basic Law; and/or more stringent legislative procedures (such as four readings instead of three); or ratification by the subsequent Knesset. With the exception of the two Basic Laws on human rights, the supremacy of the other Basic Laws is controversial, certainly in terms of their public stature, which differs from their legal standing, as laws that define the rules of governance. The concrete expression of supreme status came when the court, in the wake of the two Basic Laws of 1992, struck down provisions of law that contravened them.[37]

Rigidity: To what extent is it more difficult to change Basic Laws or their articles than to amend ordinary legislation? The requirement of a supermajority touches upon the general issue of the Knesset's authority to entrench provisions that cannot be changed by a simple majority. The stature of a formal constitution rests on it being difficult to modify – an amendment would require special procedures, such as a referendum. Such stringent mechanisms are intended to preserve the rules of the regime, and especially protect the rights of individuals and minorities against the tyranny of a transitory majority. Table 2.1 shows that the Basic Laws as a whole are not characterized by rigidity, which applies only to select articles in several Basic Laws. These articles show varying levels of entrenchment – the majority required to amend them ranges from an absolute majority of sixty-one MKs to a two-thirds majority of eighty MKs. The Basic Law: The Knesset is distinctive, however, for the supermajority required to amend the electoral system, extend the term of office, or dissolve the Knesset. Immunization does exist to protect some Basic Laws against invalidation by the Emergency Regulations: The Knesset, The President, The Government, The Judiciary, Human Dignity and Liberty, and Freedom of Occupation. And yet the Basic Laws cannot be considered rigid because most can be modified by simple legislative procedures. Theoretically, a small majority of MKs could, for example, pass a bill to establish a second house of representatives. This is the situation, ostensibly, in other governments where the parliament is formally omnipotent, as in Britain, but the unwritten constitution there is so powerful this could never happen.

In sum, the Israeli legislature created a legal morass with regard to the status of the Basic Laws. It is sufficient to examine the different requirements of a supermajority or the immunity from Emergency Regulations (in Table 2.1) to understand the "unfriendly" nature of the Basic Laws as a public constitutional document. The Supreme Court needed no fewer than 437 pages in its Mizrahi Bank decision to explain that the Basic Laws are constitutional.

B. Basic Laws and the Political System

Let us now look at the Basic Laws not just from a formal point of view, but in terms of their validity as a working constitution in society and the political system. Such

[37] For a list of these, see Rubinstein and Medina 2005, 99, footnote 171. For later rulings, see footnote # 33 in Chapter 6. The Supreme Court had earlier struck down laws for procedural reasons, such as the Bergman ruling in 1969 or *Derekh Eretz v. Broadcasting Authority* 1981. See discussion of judicial review in Chapter 6, Section 6.8.

tests are less common in legal literature, although lately there is a greater demand to "translate" the constitution into a language that would enable a non-legal discourse by citizens, removing it from the exclusive exegesis of the courts (Tushnet 1999).

Reality: To what extent do the Basic Laws make the constitution a reality, or are they nominal provisions that can be ignored? The Basic Laws do dictate the rules of governance in Israel in the specific areas they address. For key issues – elections, formation of the government, method of selecting judges, duties of the president, subordination of the military to civilian authority, or the role of the state comptroller – the Basic Laws function as constitution in every respect. What's more, because of various Supreme Court rulings, which we shall examine below, the Basic Laws have become more powerful in setting norms that have established the authority of judicial review. Accordingly, the democratic rules of the game in Israel rest primarily on the Basic Laws; with regard to the broader principles of democracy, however, where the constitution (the Basic Laws) is meant to be formative, the Basic Laws as they stand today do not offer much help.

Some lacunae remain in issues such as the division of authority between the Knesset and the government, or the source of the court's authority to exercise judicial review. The impotence of the existing partial constitution was revealed when the Knesset decided to amend the method of electing the prime minister without fully examining the impact this would have on other components of the system, or the relationship between politics and society. With the same casualness that the Knesset changed the law in 1992 (by a majority of fifty-five to thirty-two), it rescinded the change in 2001 (by a majority of sixty-nine to thirty-one), and restored the previous electoral system. Thus in terms of the reality of the material constitution, an unhealthy brew has been concocted of three different components: the formal part, generally observed punctiliously (e.g., the acceptance of majority decisions, the electoral system); the nominal part, sometimes ignored (e.g., the constitutional status of the Basic Laws, or the status of the State Budget Law); and the unwritten, ostensibly "British" part, which is frequently breached in Israel (e.g., norms about coalition discipline, the status of religious judges as civil servants, party funding). One may even argue that the constitutional elements in Israel are not very solid because they are subject to political struggles and too often adjudicated in court.

Stability: This criterion is also circumstantial, because a society might, after all, have a formal, stable constitution and yet frequently amend it, with broad consensus, to suit changing circumstances. Nonetheless, a written constitution that is rigid and supreme is generally more stable, which does not necessarily reflect the degree to which it is realistic, of course – the extent to which there is adherence to it. The Basic Laws in Israel have frequently been amended (see Table 2.1); indeed, with the exception of the Basic Law: Israel Lands, every Basic Law has been amended at least once, including the two Basic Laws from 1992, which were amended very soon after they were enacted, for coalition purposes.[38]

[38] The Basic Law: Freedom of Occupation was changed in 1994 following *Mitral Ltd. v. Prime Minister et al.* 1993. The "override clause" was added due to a coalition agreement between Labor and Shas during the Rabin government, and later two amendments were added. The Basic Law: Human Dignity and Liberty was amended in 1994.

The Basic Law: The Knesset was amended forty-one times as of 2014, including changes both trivial and substantive.[39] This is also true of the Basic Law: Government, in which a very significant change was made – altering the system of election of the prime minister, with all that this entails. Amendments made to the other Basic Laws did not affect governance as profoundly, leading to claims that the Israeli constitution is "stable," since it helped prevent radical amendments such as changing the form of government (to a presidential system, for example), changing the electoral system, or instituting drastic measures to limit the number of parties. Others might claim, however, that the Basic Laws created an "unstable" constitution, because they are not properly implemented. They could point to the gap between what the Basic Laws say and what actually takes place in Israeli politics – the frequent crises and the crumbling consensus about the essence of democracy. Both positions illuminate different, sometimes contradictory, facets of the Israeli political system. What is common to both is a deep dissatisfaction with what exists, whether because of a lack of reform or a failure to ensure the constitutionality of governance.[40]

2.7 Subjects Missing from Israel's Basic Laws

Some Basic Laws include non-constitutional subjects, while others are "framework laws" that leave the details to ordinary legislation.[41] One might also call into question the subjects chosen to be Basic Laws, such as the state economy or a referendum, as opposed to important legislation that was not given the status of Basic Laws, such as the Freedom of Information Law (1998). The most important question, however, is which key subjects are still missing from the Basic Laws, i.e., from the future written constitution, largely as a result of which the constitution has never been completed. The three most important are the status of religion in the state (a subject so contentious that the other two are affected by it, not to their benefit); a human rights declaration; and a Basic Law: Legislation, which would establish the constitutional standing of the Supreme Court and its role in judicial review. Below we list other subjects that have been cited as worthy of inclusion in the constitution.[42]

A. The Status of Jewish Religion in Israel

A written constitution would pose many difficulties with respect to the common contents of Israeli society (Galnoor 1982, 79–110). This issue also concerns, of course, the status of other religions in Israel, but the constitutional hurdle relates to the status of the Jewish religion. If the spirit of the constitution were Jewish-national-religious, non-Jews would find it impossible to see themselves as "Israeli"; if the spirit were civilian-secular, some traditional and most observant Jews would find it hard to identify with this version of "Israel." Many Jews in Israel do not distinguish between their

[39] See the full text of Basic Law: The Knesset and its forty-one amendments in http://main.knesset.gov.il/Activity/Legislation/Documents/yesod4.pdf [in Hebrew] (accessed October 16, 2017).

[40] On dissatisfaction with the political system, see Arian, Atmor, and Hadar 2007. On the status of the Basic Laws, also see Amnon Rubinstein 1991, 452; and Rubinstein and Medina 2005, 123–24.

[41] For example, the Basic Law: Government from 2001 moved some of the details to the Government Law (2001).

[42] For a proposal to consolidate the existing Basic Laws with just a few gaps to fill in, see Bendor 1999.

national identity and their faith, both regarded as cut of the same cloth. Secular Jews, on the other hand, do distinguish between Judaism as a religion and their Jewish, national, and cultural identities; the distinction is sharper among those whose secularism is a firm world view. It is doubtful that a formal constitution, even a consensual one, would be able to unravel this complex knot, which also resonates for Jews in the Diaspora. In any event, delaying the approval of a constitution did not help; on the contrary, the question of the status of Jewish religion in Israel has over time become an albatross impeding completion of the constitution.

We noted earlier that, in our opinion, the religion–state issue is not what prevented legislation of a constitution in Israel's early years. The obstacle created at that time could be described as follows: A constitution would lead to a head-on collision with Halakha (Jewish religious law), because a constitution would define the state as secular, and invalidate the authority of the religious institutions on matters of personal status (Gutmann in Bogdanor 1988, 294–98). The moment the issue was framed this way, the religious issue became an excuse for those who clung to the previous political order, and wanted to suspend all decisions on governance: "Let us build the constitution piece by piece through Basic Laws, just as we built our country dunam by dunam [bit by bit]" (Burg quoted in Tsidon 1964, 366). The draft constitution proposed by Kohn avoided taking a decisive stand on the question of religion, and left the previous arrangements in place, i.e., constitutional formulations were not proposed about the "Jewish character" of the state. The draft constitution prepared by Akzin in 1965 stated that Israel "views its special mission as nurturing the values, culture, and future of the Jewish nation"; his draft calls for freedom of religion in matters of conscience and worship, preservation of the authority of the religious courts, and the obligation of the state to ensure the religious needs of all its citizens. Nothing was mentioned about the status of Judaism in the state, and he explains why:

> It is better not to introduce into it [the constitution] provisions that, even if a large majority would support them, touch upon deep and principled divisions, and harm faiths and beliefs held dear, not to mention that the point of a constitution is to guide and restrain the state, not to establish faiths or beliefs, which, in a free country, are in the individual domain. In the Israeli reality, this means *avoiding principles that relate to religion*, and to the social and economic path to be taken. (Akzin 1965, 9 [our emphasis])

In a draft bill prepared in 1964 by MK Hans Klinghoffer (the Liberal Party) for a Human Rights Declaration, a more explicit formulation was proposed: "There shall be no coercion in the state for reasons of religion or opposition to religion," but nothing specific was said about what the status of religion would be (Klinghoffer 1964, parag. 23). On the other hand, in proposed bills that began to appear in the 1980s, a fundamental change emerged, and the dominant trend was to clearly separate religion from the state.[43] These included, for example, demands to eliminate any prohibitions for religious reasons, instituting freedom of choice for a religious or civil marriage, revoking religious laws (on burial, the raising of pigs, selling of bread on Passover), recognizing the Conservative and Reform streams of Judaism,

[43] On the changed approaches regarding the need for a constitution in the 1980s, see Gavison 2003, 53–70.

eliminating discrimination against Muslims and Christians on religious grounds, and more (*A Constitution for Israel* 1987, parags. 7A, B, 22).

In a proposal prepared by the Israel Democracy Institute, the emphasis was on a "constitution by consensus" and therefore no statement is made about the status of the Jewish religion in the state other than a declaration of principle: "The state of Israel shall guarantee the status and independence of all the religions therein" (parag. 11A); and also that "Every person shall have freedom of religion. No person shall be deprived of rights, and no obligations shall be imposed on a person on grounds that are essentially religious" (Israel Democracy Institute 2005, parag. 22). Nevertheless, it was proposed that certain matters be declared constitutionally "non-justiciable," such as religious conversion, the authority of religious courts, marriage and divorce, and kashrut laws. Thus, this draft proposes that the Knesset, i.e., the political body and not the courts, make these decisions (230–31, parag. 164).[44] In a draft constitution deliberated by the Knesset's Constitution, Law and Justice Committee, it was said, "Every individual has freedom of belief, religion, and worship," and one of the alternatives proposed was that the constitution recognize that "justiciability is also in the hands of the rabbinical courts."[45]

The Basic Laws circumvented the fundamental question of the status of religion in the state, and even obfuscated it, at least verbally, by defining Israel as "a Jewish and democratic state." On the other hand, in the material constitution – the sociopolitical reality of Israel – important developments transpired. Positions taken by the ultra-Orthodox concerning the draft of yeshiva students into the IDF, or by settlers in the occupied territories on obeying Knesset laws and government decisions, led to head-on collisions between the state and religious law, and often undermined the stature of the judiciary. At the same time, the laws that determine the authority of Israel's religious institutions have not fundamentally changed, although their legitimacy is diminishing among the seculars – in matters of marriage and divorce, for example. Even the worst fear of the religious leaders – an end to the exclusiveness of Orthodoxy as the only recognized stream in Israel – is slowly transpiring.

Thus, the leadership in 1949 agreed not to clarify, let alone define, the status of Jewish religion in the state; had some mild form of "status quo" been entrenched in a constitution, written or intimated, perhaps these arrangements might have been more stable today. These days it is almost impossible to frame a consensual constitution without addressing the religious issue and its many ramifications. At any rate, the absence of a constitution has not prevented continued feuding over religion, and in the long run has not enhanced the willingness to reach an agreement. On the contrary, the divisions seem to have become so deep that a Shas MK said that even entrenching the Ten Commandments in the Israeli constitution would meet with their resistance, if the Supreme Court were the final arbiter (Gavison 2003, 64).

B. Declaration of Human and Civil Rights

The framing of the constitution was not put off in 1950 because of human and civil rights issues, although some harsh words were sounded in the Knesset debates

[44] For a critique, see Chazan 2005.

[45] Knesset website.

both from the right (the need to subordinate individual needs to state goals) and from the left (the need to emphasize the collective at the expense of the individual). Representatives of opposition parties who were concerned about their standing emphasized the importance of including a declaration of rights in the constitution, and a few said explicitly that this was needed to protect the Arab citizens of Israel.[46] Why then is there no Basic Law with a full declaration of rights? The two Basic Laws from 1992 ensure the following rights: individual dignity and liberty; freedom from violation of one's life, body, or dignity; the right to property; freedom from restriction of liberty by imprisonment, arrest, or extradition; freedom to enter or leave Israel; the right to privacy and intimacy; and freedom of occupation, profession, or trade. We note that many subjects were left out of the original formulation of the bill. The Constitution Committee of the first Knesset listed almost all the issues that appeared later in the many proposals for legislating human and civil rights (Tsidon 1964, 367; see also Lahav and Kretzmer 1985, 154–72). Unlike human rights declarations in other democracies, absent from Israeli law is a clear constitutional assertion of the principle of equality among people on which universal human liberties and civil rights are based, namely: "All human beings are born free and equal in dignity and rights."[47]

It is customary to present the evolution of a rights discourse by "generations": (1) human and civil rights; (2) social, economic, and culture rights; and (3) quality of life and environmental rights (Bendor 1999). Based on this list, the issues that are missing, either fully or partially, from Israel's Basic Laws are the following: freedom of religion, faith, and conscience; freedom of opinion and expression; freedom of science; the right to personal freedom and security; freedom of movement (as opposed to freedom from deprivation of liberty); freedom of assembly and demonstration; freedom of organization and association; and juridical rights (freedom from arrest and imprisonment, rights of the detainee, right to a fair trial, and the presumption of innocence). Others add: workers' rights (and the right to strike); social rights (education, health, housing, social security, and children's rights); political rights (the right to vote, run for election, organize a party, and pursue collective and cultural activity). And still others would add civil *obligations* to the list of rights, such as a citizen's obligation to obey the constitution and the law, to contribute to the general welfare, to participate in protecting the state, and to pay taxes.[48] We note that few constitutions mention such obligations out of a belief that the constitution (and the laws) confer sufficient authority upon the state, and there is no need to add to it the citizen's

[46] The Arab issue was not central to the Knesset debates about the constitution in 1950, and only two MKs referred to this in their remarks.

[47] The Universal Declaration of Human Rights, United Nations, 1948. See also: "all men are created equal, that they are endowed by their Creator with certain inalienable Rights" (Declaration of Independence, United States, 1776); "Men are born and remain free and equal in rights" (Declaration of the Rights of Man and of the Citizen, France, 1789); "So God created man in his own image, in the image of God he created him" (Genesis 1:27); "based on freedom, justice, and peace" (Declaration of Independence, Israel, 1948).

[48] Akzin (1965) formulated it this way: "to take part in protecting the state, in the burden of taxes, in mandatory payments and work and emergency services as imposed on him by law" (ibid., 192). In his constitution proposal, he also wrote, "Every Israeli citizen must have an affinity with and loyalty to the state of Israel" (ibid., 193).

obligations, not to mention that one of the main objectives of a constitution is to protect the people from its government.

In our opinion, consensus could be reached about most of the human freedoms and civil rights, both among the public and the parties. Thus the reason for not including them in the Basic Laws is not related to any breach of Jewish law, but to the fear of the religious parties that incorporating a human rights declaration in the Basic Laws – especially one declaring the freedom of religion, conscience, and worship – would undermine the existing arrangements and sever the connection between religion and state. Another motivation is the concern that a human rights declaration would lead Israel's Arab citizens to demand equal allocations of land and other resources, as well as recognition of their collective rights.

C. Relations Among Government Branches and the Constitutional Status of the Supreme Court

The Basic Laws concerned with issues of governance (The Knesset, The Government, and The President) are very detailed, and this is not the place to ask if they are in need of change, or whether the more technical provisions should be transferred to ordinary legislation. One should take into account, however, that if the current governance arrangements were anchored in a constitution, the legislator would have less freedom to make changes, and future amendments would be difficult.

Missing in Israel's Basic Laws is a constitutional definition of the authority of the Knesset vis-à-vis the government. What is the standing, for example, of Knesset decisions that are not acts of legislation? Also, the Basic Law: The Knesset does not define a hierarchy among the Basic Laws, ordinary legislation, and regulations. But the primary unresolved issue – *inter alia*, because the Basic Laws related to governance were enacted separately – is the definition of the interrelations among the three government branches, particularly the constitutional authority of the Supreme Court and the High Court of Justice. In the Basic Law: Judiciary (1984), nothing at all is said about the constitutional status of the Supreme Court, its authority to engage in judicial review of legislation, or even its less controversial power to review decisions made by the executive branch.

None of the bills entitled Basic Law: Legislation was passed by the Knesset. The first was submitted by the government in 1976, with the intent of closing some lacunae in the legislative process, and establishing the constitutional status of the Basic Laws and judicial review over them.[49] When Minister of Justice Shmuel Tamir resubmitted the bill in 1978, he emphasized three innovations: bestowing constitutional supremacy upon the Basic Laws by requiring a supermajority (of eighty MKs) for their passage and amendment; explicitly making the Basic Laws the standard

[49] Many proposals for a Basic Law: Legislation were submitted over the years, starting with Minister of Justice Haim Zadok (*Knesset Records*, 76, 8th Knesset, 3rd Session, Booklet 18, February 17, 1976, 1704–12); two by the Constitution Committee, the most recent in March 2001 (*Knesset Records*, 15th Knesset, 3rd Session, Booklet 17, March 19, 2001, 3542–59). The first bill was submitted during an Alignment (Labor) government, and the second during a Likud government in 1978, which refutes the claim that the campaign to establish judicial review began only after the Likud came to power in 1977, meaning it was an effort by the old elites to retain power. It is more correct to see this as reflecting the loss of trust in the political system.

for testing the validity of ordinary legislation; and authorizing the Supreme Court to hold session as a Constitutional Court to rule on the validity of laws or provisions in laws, based on petitions claiming that they contravene a Basic Law (*Knesset Records*, August 2, 1978, 3975–77). Opposition to this bill crossed party lines and exposed diverse views among Supreme Court justices (E. Rubinstein 1980, 191–92). Many MKs objected because they believed that giving the court authority to revoke laws reduces the sovereignty and supremacy of the Knesset. Others, including judges, opposed for fear of politicizing the Supreme Court and appointments to it, and they also feared a flood of petitions about every law passed in the Knesset. Many continued to cling to the disputed, and in our opinion erroneous, approach that struck deep roots after the 1950 Harari Resolution – that the absolute supremacy of the parliament applies also to constitutional legislation.

There is an internal logic in the claim that judicial review should be rooted in a formal, written constitution. When the court is faced with a conflict between the constitution and a law, it has no choice but to apply the more supreme law and revoke the law in conflict with it.[50] Conversely, constitutional flexibility such as that in the legislation of Israel's Basic Laws is consistent with the absence of judicial review, because in both cases the majority refuse to accept limitations imposed upon it (Lijphart 1991, 228). As we shall see in Chapter 6 about the judiciary, the two Basic Laws from 1992 on human rights created a constitutional ranking between themselves and ordinary legislation, and, in the wake of various rulings, also determined in practice the authority of the Supreme Court as a constitutional court.[51] This important constitutional issue needs to be solved – perhaps according to the original 1949 draft constitution of Dr. Kohn, who suggested a framework for the relations among the three branches of government, including establishment of a constitutional court drawn from the Supreme Court with the authority to revoke laws that contravene the constitution.

D. Israel: The Nation-State of the Jewish People

In recent years, various MKs have submitted proposals for a new Basic Law titled "Israel as the Nation State of the Jewish People." The bills define Israel as Jewish, based on the right of the Jewish people to fulfill their historical right to self-determination in the land of Israel. Unlike the previous definition of the state ("Jewish *and* democratic"), this new formula creates a false premise that the state belongs to the Jewish people only, including Jews who are not Israeli, and it implies that democratic values could be overruled by Jewish ones. The bills also elevate existing elements from regular laws – such as the state symbols, the national anthem, and the right of return – to the statute of a Basic Law.[52]

50 This was one reason for the development of judicial review in the United States in *Marbury v. Madison* (1803).

51 This led to many initiatives of private members bills to establish a separate constitutional court, based on a system of political party appointments – for example, MK Zevulun Orlev, "Proposed bill for constitutional court 2009," P 607/18.

52 See bill tabled by MK Ayelet Shaked et al., "Israel as the Nation State of the Jewish People," no. 1550/19/P, July 22, 2013.

Additional subjects remain outside the Basic Laws, and the following list does not suggest that they rightfully belong in a future constitution, only that they are no less important than some subjects about which Basic Laws do exist: the status of Arab citizens of Israel; gender equality and women's rights; the borders of the state; local governments; the civil service;[53] parties; civil society; freedom of expression; and freedom of the press.

We close in the same way we opened: A decision exists to frame a constitution, and twelve chapters of it have already been enacted as Basic Laws. It is fitting therefore to take a broad perspective of the Basic Laws currently present and absent, and the possibility of consolidating them into one constitution that will serve for generations.[54]

2.8 Constitutional Rulings[55]

The constitutional vacuum left by the Harari Resolution, when combined with the sluggishly legislated Basic Laws, posed a practical challenge to the court – how to act, especially in the areas of human rights, civil rights, and governance. Supreme Court rulings concerning the provisions of a law or legal questions that require a ruling are binding precedents referred to as "case law." This is generally the realm of interpretation – a situation covered by law that must be interpreted. Such a ruling becomes a precedent that is binding on the lower courts, but not on the Supreme Court itself, which retains the authority to change it (Basic Law: Judiciary, Article 20A–B). A "constitutional ruling" refers to a ruling that has become a constitutional precedent, such as the Mizrahi Bank ruling on the court's authority to engage in judicial review.

A. Rulings on Human and Civil Rights

The Israeli Supreme Court, in session as the High Court of Justice, has established many rights, and its rulings have constituted binding precedents. Although these rulings do not have the status of articles in a constitution, they can be seen in every sense as "constitutional rulings," which have won legitimacy among most of the

[53] On the constitutional basis for the civil service in Israel, see Galnoor 2011, 30–43.

[54] The coalition agreements of the governments of Rabin (1992), Netanyahu (1996), and Barak (1999) include passages about the intent to complete the Basic Laws. In parallel, the Knesset's Constitution, Law and Justice Committee worked intermittently to complete the constitution. In the coalition agreements of the Olmert government, the parties agreed "to act to complete the Basic Laws in consensus, or to frame a constitution in consensus," April 27, 2006, www.knesset.gov.il/docs/heb/coal2006avoda.htm [in Hebrew] (accessed October 16, 2017). On the other hand, a coalition agreement between the Likud and Labor in the Netanyahu government noted, "Change in the Basic Laws shall be made with the agreement of the coalition factions," March 30, 2009, www.knesset.gov.il/docs/heb/coal2009Avoda.pdf [in Hebrew] (accessed October 16, 2017).

[55] Since the Supreme Court must base its rulings on existing legislation, all its decisions could be seen as part of the material constitution, thus simplifying the issue. This, however, blurs the distinction between constitutional legislation and its interpretive court rulings, on the one hand, and constitutional rulings, which become binding constitutional precedents, on the other. See also Dorner 1999, 1327. In Chapter 6, we discuss "judicial activism" and the disagreements, which have only grown since the 1980s, over the constitutional status of the Supreme Court and its rulings on matters previously considered political.

Jewish secular public in Israel (Barzilai, Yuchtman-Yaar, and Segal 1994; Gavison, Kremnitzer, and Dotan 2000, 29–31).

The ruling that paved the way for this unique process – completion of the "rights chapter" in Israel's unwritten constitution by way of the courts – had already appeared in 1953. *Kol Ha'am*, a Communist Party newspaper, had harshly criticized the Israeli government, writing that it "trades in the blood of Israeli youth." In response, the Minister of the Interior suspended publication of the newspaper on the grounds that the publication might "endanger public safety." The Supreme Court accepted *Kol Ha'am*'s petition against the Interior Minister, revoked the suspension order, and thus introduced into Israel's unwritten constitution the paired concepts of freedom of expression and freedom of the press. Justice Agranat stated in the ruling that freedom of expression constitutes "the precondition for the realization of virtually all other freedoms," and based his decision on the democratic credo in Israel's Declaration of Independence (*Kol Ha'am v. Minister of the Interior* 1953, 878 and 884). This was an extraordinary ruling in light of the context – the state of emergency in the early 1950s, military censorship of the press, the security ethos, the centralization of governmental authority, the unpopularity of the Communist Party, and the notion that the sacrifice of the individual is justified for the good of the collective.[56]

Following this principled decision, the Supreme Court continued to bolster freedom of expression and the press in a series of rulings;[57] and eventually added rulings that in practice instituted freedom of information.[58] Other areas in which the High Court created a basis for constitutional rights include due process,[59] freedom of occupation,[60] freedom of assembly,[61] the right to demonstrate,[62] equal rights for women,[63] and against the privatization of prisons.[64]

B. Rulings on Religion, Arab Rights, and Social Rights

Unlike the above, other human and civil rights and collective rights have not been unequivocally established by court rulings, leaving them with no solid constitutional foundation. These are deeply controversial issues in Israeli society, above all the freedoms of religion, conscience, and worship.

Religious issues: In 1962, the Movement for Reform Judaism petitioned the court when a local council refused to lease a hall to them for worship services. The court, which based its ruling on rights cited in the Declaration of Independence, overturned

56 This last statement is by Justice Agranat (Lahav 1997, 110). The *Kol Ha'am* ruling heads the list of significant precedents cited in later rulings (Shahar, Gross et al. 2004, 248–54).

57 For example: *Israel Film Studios v. Geri* 1962; *Kahane v. Executive Committee of the Israel Broadcast Authority* 1985; *Laor v. the Israeli Film Censorship Council* 1986; *Schnitzer v. the Chief Military Censor* 1988.

58 See the survey in Ostrovsky-Cohen Committee Report 1995.

59 *Al-Khuri v. Chief of Staff* 1950; *Kaufman v. Minister of the Interior et al.* 1953.

60 *Bejerano v. Minister of Police* 1949; *Sheib v. Minister of Defense* 1951; see also Barak-Erez 1999.

61 *G'eris v. Haifa District Supervisor* 1964.

62 *Saar v. Minister of the Interior and the Police* 1979; *Levy et al. v. CO Southern District, Israel Police* 1984; *Levy v. Government of Israel et al.* 2005.

63 *Israel Women's Network v. Government of Israel et al.* 1994; *Israel Women's Network v. Ministry of Labor* 1998.

64 *Academic Center of Law and Business et al. v. Minister of Finance et al.* 2009.

the local council's decision. However, the court dealt specifically with this case, hence the ruling could not serve more generally to accord recognition to the Reform Movement on par with Orthodox Judaism – a recognition that has not been given in legislation or judicial ruling. This is just one example of the court shying away from rulings on the *principle* of religious freedom in Israel. From the perspective of the religiously observant, on the other hand, many Supreme Court decisions are seen as enhancing the character of Israel as a secular society. They would argue that at issue is not the application of Halakhic authority to the laws of the land, its institutions, or the way of life of its inhabitants, but rather a lack of consideration for the customs and special needs of the religiously observant. For instance, the High Court decision that compels a religious council to accept the membership of a woman (*Shakdiel v. Minister of Religious Affairs et al.* 1988).[65]

The most complex issue, and one that has reached the court many times, is referred to as "Who is a Jew?" For the "Shalit case," the Supreme Court convened as a panel of nine judges for the first time in 1968, and the majority decision (5:4) recognized the children of the petitioners (a Jewish father and agnostic mother) as Jews in terms of their nationality, even though the mother was not Jewish and therefore the children are not considered Jewish by Halakha (*Shalit v. Minister of the Interior* 1970).[66] Although this was seemingly a technical case of registration by the Interior Ministry, had this judgment remained in place, it would have set a precedent in placing the freedom of the individual above the accepted definition of his or her national-religious identity as a Jew in Israel. In reaction, however, the government hastily submitted a bill to change the law, and the Knesset amended the Law of Return so that it defines a "Jew" as someone born to a Jewish mother, or who has converted to Judaism, and who is not a member of another religion.[67] In a dissenting minority opinion in the Shalit case, Justice Agranat stated that in his view the Supreme Court must not pass judgment when society and the political system prefer ambiguity: "The problem before us ... does not admit of a judicial solution, but lies entirely in the ideological sphere. Since there are, in my opinion, profound differences of opinion within the Israeli public, I think that we should not intervene" (*Shalit v. Minister of the Interior* 1970, 574).

The Shalit case is instructive for two reasons. First, the fact that the ruling did not last indicates that, in religious issues, the Supreme Court can create a valid, constitutional precedent only when there is sufficient public and political agreement (or apathy). Second, the more petitions that were filed on the subject of religion and state, the less able – and later the less willing – was the court to rule on them. The list of subjects that reached the court and were often not adjudicated includes: kashrut (regulating the certification of Jewish dietary laws), work and public transportation on the Sabbath, conversion to Judaism, and drafting girls into the army. Observant Jews, on the other hand, could point to cases in which the court did intervene: the

[65] Other examples: *Association of Butchers v. Chief Rabbinate* 1986; *Raskin v. Jerusalem Religious Council* 1990; *Horev v. Minister of Transportation* 1997; *Ressler v. Israeli Knesset* 2012.

[66] Six years earlier, the Supreme Court had denied the petition of a Jewish-born Christian to recognize him as of the Jewish nationality and thereby eligible to immigrate under the Law of Return. The ruling stated that the definition of "Jew" includes national and religious dimensions that cannot be separated (*Rufeisen v. Minister of the Interior* 1962).

[67] Article 4B of the Law of Return. The amendment was passed in the tenth Knesset in March 1970.

drafting of yeshiva boys to the army, conversion to Judaism outside of Israel, public transportation on the Sabbath, prayer at the Western Wall, the sale of pork, and the opening of movie theaters on the Sabbath. The fact that two "lists" exist and partially overlap reflects the court's inability to rule on religious matters. For example, the High Court of Justice allowed the opening of movie theaters on the Sabbath, but in response the Knesset passed an amendment to the Municipalities Ordinance (1990, no. 40), which allows the local government to enact its own rules, even rules based on religious tradition – thus reversing the intent of the High Court ruling (*Israel v. Kaplan et al.* 1988 – in the matter of the opening of cinemas on the Sabbath).[68] Although the court from time to time issued specific rulings on religious matters, it largely chose to avoid decisions on matters of principle, thus in practice helping maintain the status quo on religion.[69]

Rights and equality – Israel's Arab citizens: This is another area in which the court did not establish unequivocal rules, certainly not in the early years of the state, while some changes that we mention below have occurred in recent years (see Chapter 15 for a detailed discussion). In general, the Arabs in Israel have not found remedy in the courts in appeals related to their status as "absentees," the restoration of their lands, or their right to return to the villages from which they were expelled. The famous court rulings on Iqrit and Bir'im only confirm this generalization, because even though in this one instance the Supreme Court ordered that the expelled villagers return to their lands, this has not taken place to this day.[70] The court refrained from altering the situation that had existed during the period of martial law that ended in 1966, thus contributing to the perception that the Arabs pose a danger to Israel. In the al-Ard case, the Supreme Court issued a majority ruling that this Arab list was not eligible to run in the 1965 Knesset election because it objects to the existence of Israel as a Jewish state:

> Just as a human being does not have to agree to be killed, a state too does not have to agree to be destroyed and erased from the map. Its judges are not allowed to sit back idly and watch in despair because of the lack of a positive rule of law when a plaintiff asks for their assistance in bringing about the demise of the state. (Zussman in *Yardor v. Chair of the Central Elections Committee for the 6th Knesset* 1965)

From the 1990s, Jewish and Arab rights organizations had begun to petition the High Court of Justice to prevent discrimination against Arabs, which resulted in several victories, such as the ruling that obligated the Tel Aviv-Jaffa municipality, in which an Arab minority resides, to add Arabic to public signage in Hebrew;[71] a ruling that entitled an Arab family to buy a home in the Jewish community of Katzir (*Ka'adan*

68 See also *Ressler v. Minister of Defense* 1988.

69 "The more a state has rifts based on nationality or religion, and the more it has 'chronic' minorities whose chances of becoming a majority and wielding political power are small, the greater the fear that the majority will act against the rights and interests of the minorities" (Gavison 1998, 51).

70 The case of displaced persons from Iqrit has accompanied the legal and political system in Israel since the War for Independence. The residents of this village, ordered to evacuate upon its conquest, were promised that they could return to their homes when the security situation would allow it. To this day, the promise was not kept (*Daoud et al. v. Minister of Defense et al.* 1951). More recently a request was made for another deliberation (*Sabit v. Israel* 2004). See Sheleff 1996, 20–23, 86–88.

71 *Adalah and the Association for Civil Rights in Israel v. Municipality of Tel Aviv-Jaffa* 2002. This specific petition dealt with the towns of Tel Aviv-Jaffa, Ramle, Lod, Acre, and Upper Nazareth.

v. Israel Land Administration et al. 2000); and a ruling that revoked a government decision from 2002 that had allocated national education priority areas to 500 Jewish, but only four Arab, communities (*Supreme Monitoring Committee for Arab Affairs in Israel v. Prime Minister of Israel* 2006 – unpublished). Nonetheless, the cumulative impact of these rulings and precedents is still limited (Barzilai 1999, 45; Haider 2005–10: 2008). Thus, in 2014 the High Court of Justice rejected an appeal against a provision in the 2011 amendment to the Cooperative Societies Ordinance that enables "Admissions Committees" in community settlements to scrutinize candidates on the basis of "incompatibility with the social and cultural fabric" of the community (*Sabah v. the Knesset* 2014), a provision that can easily be used to reject Arab candidates.

The sharpest official statement that the principle of equality applies to Arab citizens in Israel and that discrimination must be prevented does not appear in the Basic Laws, ordinary legislation, or court rulings, but in the 2003 Report of the State Commission appointed after the killing of twelve Arab citizens in October 2000 ("the Orr Report"):

> The Jewish majority must keep in mind that the state is not just Jewish, but also democratic, because ... equality is one of the cornerstones of a constitutional state structure, and the prohibition on discrimination applies to all its citizens. It must understand that the events that turned the Arabs into a minority in the state were a national tragedy for them, and their integration into Israel entailed painful sacrifices for them. (vol. 2, 780)

A constitutional – or legal, political, or administrative – solution to the status of Arab citizens of Israel is still far off. Moreover, when "state security" is at stake, the Supreme Court treads carefully, often more inclined to accept the official version of the security authorities. In the past, for example, the court did not challenge the policy of administrative detentions (based on the Mandatory ordinance), although as early as 1948, it clarified that even during administrative detention, "the authorities are bound by the law as are all citizens of the state."[72] Since then, Israeli law regulates this, and there are few administrative detentions of Arab citizens of Israel.

Social rights: In this area, too, the High Court of Justice sought to avoid entering the lion's den, but was dragged into it in recent years. This subject remains controversial in other democratic countries as well, pitting those who believe that the state should be obliged by law (or perhaps even constitutionally) to ensure its citizens' basic needs – a minimum level of education, healthcare, adequate housing, etc. – against those who claim that these should be left to the priorities of the individual or the policy and budgetary wherewithal of the government.[73] The following social rights are included in a proposed "Constitution for Israel" (1987, 12–13): workers' rights, access to a means of livelihood, and the right to education and medical care. The proposed constitution of the Knesset's Constitution Committee included the right to health and adequate surroundings, and the right to environmental quality.[74] In a discussion of whether the state is obliged to provide free education in the regular

[72] *Al-Karbutli v. Minister of Defense et al.* 1949. Nevertheless, in *Sheib v. Minister of Defense* 1951 (a case dealing primarily with the freedom of occupation), the civilian side prevailed over Minister of Defense David Ben-Gurion. Also see *Bejerano v. Minister of Police* 1949.

[73] See, for example, *Gamzu v. Yeshayahu et al.* 2001.

[74] Knesset Constitution, Law and Justice Committee 2006.

school system for children with special needs, Justice Dalia Dorner noted that given the right to education and the principle of equality, the state is obligated to provide the required minimal budget; only expenses above this amount are discretionary.[75]

C. Governance

Has the court managed not just to strengthen the rule of law, but also the legality of the regime and make it constitutional? Has this been accomplished through the judicial oversight of public administration and legislation? Do the conclusions drawn from these two questions also apply to the territories occupied by Israel since 1967? The answer to the first question is positive: Since the founding of Israel, the judiciary in general, and particularly the Supreme Court, has contributed more than any other institution to ensuring the rule of law and recognition of the principle that governance must have legal underpinnings in a democracy. This is an enormous achievement, particularly considering that one reason for reluctance about a written constitution was disdain for the complicated "legalisms" of jurists as opposed to the flexible pragmatism of politicians (Sprinzak 1986, 64).

Another impressive achievement is the success thus far at leaving the judiciary outside the wheeling and dealing of a party-driven political system. With respect to the legality of governance – having the government itself subject to the law – achievements were also attained here, from broadening the rules of standing in the Supreme Court to include any individual or group that feels harmed by the authorities, to judicial review over decisions made by the president, the Knesset, the government, the ministries, IDF officers, the attorney general, and others (see Galnoor 2004). The development of State Commissions of Inquiry (see Chapter 7) headed by judges also created a monitoring mechanism that allows for an examination of the discretionary decisions of public officials. The judiciary has perhaps done more in practice to preserve the constitutional order of governance in Israel than the Basic Laws themselves, including assurance of the independence of the courts, and this in itself is a major achievement. What's more, the fact that the rule of law in Israel has recently weakened is by no means the fault of the judiciary.

With regard to the judicial review of laws, this began with *Bergman v. Minister of Finance* in 1969, which for the first time tested the clout of a provision in a Basic Law and the authority of the court to nullify ordinary legislation in conflict with it. The petition challenged the Parties Financing Law, which gave preference to political parties in the outgoing Knesset over new parties trying to gain seats and enter the Knesset. The High Court ruled that the term "equal elections" in the Basic Law: The Knesset meant both the right to elect and the right to be elected, and therefore a law favoring parties in the outgoing Knesset is incompatible with this principle. It ruled that the Knesset has the choice of either legislating this inequality by a supermajority, as required by the Basic Law, or correcting the law to eliminate the inequality. The Knesset chose the latter. This significant intervention was presented as a seemingly procedural matter, as were other cases in which the High Court struck down Knesset legislation because it contravened the principle of equality in the Basic Law: The

[75] *Marciano et al. v. Minister of Finance* 2003. See also Ben Bassat and Dahan 2003, 1–38.

Knesset (*Derekh Eretz v. Broadcasting Authority* 1981; *Rubinstein v. Speaker of the Knesset* 1983; *Laor Movement v. Speaker of the Knesset* 1990).

As noted, on the basis of the two 1992 Basic Laws, the Mizrahi Bank ruling (1995) directly established the authority of the Supreme Court to engage in judicial review of legislation. Since then, more than fifty such lawsuits were submitted, but the court declared null and void only a few provisions in laws passed by the Knesset on the grounds that they contravene Basic Laws. The Knesset adhered to these rulings and chose to amend laws accordingly (Rubinstein and Medina 2005, 108). Nonetheless, the subjects on which the court exercised its authority to nullify laws did not touch on issues of values, substantive governance issues, or controversial matters.[76] In this sense, there is a gap between the rhetoric and the implementation of judicial review, and yet bills have been tabled to limit the court's power of judicial review.[77]

D. The Constitutionality of Israel's Control over the "Administered Territories"

We will not discuss here the legal status of the territories, the legality of settlements, or the convoluted laws and regulations underpinning Israeli governance in these areas (Hofnung 1996a). The Basic Laws contain absolutely nothing that might help clarify these issues, and the only question for our purposes is whether the substantial number of Supreme Court interventions in matters related to the occupied territories amounted to constitutional regulation, or at least brought what was happening there under effective judicial review.[78] The right of Palestinian residents of the territories to petition the High Court of Justice was recognized as early as 1969 (*Ravidi and Maches v. Hebron District Military Court, the IDF, et al.* 1970; *abu Hilu et al. v. Government of Israel* 1974), leading Justice Barak to write (A. 1987, 17), "The actions of the military authorities in Judea, Samaria, and Gaza have been brought under judicial review." And indeed in cases from the late 1970s, the court did not summarily dismiss these petitions, and was willing to deliberate the status of the settlements, despite the heated controversy about them domestically and internationally.

In two cases – the Beit El and the Alon Moreh petitions – the High Court, after some hesitation, did pass judgment, but managed to avoid entering the heart of the matter (*Ayoub et al. v. Minister of Defense et al.* 1979; *Dweikat et al. v. Government of Israel* 1979). In neither case did the court take a stand on the substantive (and also the constitutional, in our opinion) issue of the settlements beyond the Green Line

[76] A recent case (e.g., *Eitan: Israeli Immigration Policy Center v. Government of Israel* 2014) concerned the detention of illegal immigrants. In another important case (*Movement for Quality Government v. Prime Minister* 2015), the court annulled a key clause in the government agreement with gas companies and called for regulation via legislation.

[77] Hofnung (1997, 212–14) believes that the "constitutional revolution" has not engendered much change, and that in fact there is regression compared with the legal situation prior to enactment of the two Basic Laws in 1992. Gavison (in Gavison, Kremnitzer, and Dotan 2000, 94–104, 129–32) argues that the two Basic Laws do constitute a significant change in the protection of human rights, but that the discourse of a "constitutional revolution" obscures the fact that there is no consensus in Israel about constitutional objectives. Dotan (Gavison, Kremnitzer, and Dotan 2000, 188–90, 200) believes that the constitutional revolution endowed the court with broad authority to revoke Knesset legislation, but left the politicians the option of responding to judicial review. Nevertheless, in his opinion it did not create real change in relations between the judiciary and the Knesset.

[78] Note, for example, that the French constitution from 1958 regulates the constitutional aspects of the "Overseas territorial communities" (Articles 72–75).

(Israel's pre-1967 borders), but rather examined only the legality of the orders issued by the authorities (see E. Rubinstein 1980, 222–23). These rulings, and others that followed, changed nothing – with the exception of cases in which the courts protected the rights of individual Palestinian residents of the territories. Such individual matters included entrance permission, damages by the IDF, house demolitions, deportation, curfew, etc. Consistently, the High Court refused to adjudicate the general question of the legality of the settlements (*Bargil et al. v. Government of Israel* 1993). This also holds for the rulings issued on the route of the "Separation Barrier": The High Court ruled it legal by international law as it was built in response to security needs (*Mara'abeh et al. v. Prime Minister of Israel et al.* 2004 and 2005), and addressed only the rights of individual Palestinians who live alongside the barrier (Arieli 2011). The question of principle never arose – why hundreds of kilometers of fence needed for security had to be constructed almost entirely on the Palestinian side of the Green Line, not on the Israeli side. It became clear that the fundamental (so-called "ideological") issue of Israeli control of these territories – that are not part of the state of Israel and where several million people reside who are not its citizens – is beyond the authority and strength of the Supreme Court.

2.9 So Does Israel Have a Constitution?

The debates about a constitution encompass issues that have preoccupied Israel since its establishment – from the strength of its democracy, the centrality of security, equality questions, the status of religion, and the rights of Arab citizens to issues of governance and the operation of the political system. We began by asking whether a formal, written constitution would have helped overcome the divisions and perhaps even prevented some governmental calamities, and now is the time to answer. The qualifications that would have to be added to give a positive reply to this question turn the answer into a negative. In the current situation in Israel, a constitution would be able to anchor some agreements, but not create them *ex nihilo*. If there were *broad* consensus (of a supermajority, including a majority of the two large minorities – the ultra-Orthodox and Arab), it would be possible and desirable to give this consensus supra-legal status as a rigid, written constitution that is the supreme law of the land. In the beginning of the twenty-first century, however, this condition does not exist. In this sense, the opportunity in the early years of the state – to utilize the constitution to create consensus and instill democratic values and rules – has indeed vanished.

In comparative terms, one can distinguish between two types of democracies – those built on agreements (of a majority larger than the minimum necessary) and those built on majority rule alone (Lijphart 1999, 2–8). The first type, to which Israel belongs (as do Switzerland and Belgium), is called a "negotiation democracy," and these states generally have overlapping legislative and executive branches, proportional elections, a multiparty system, organized interest groups, and other features in common. The second type, called a "Westminster democracy" (typified by Britain, New Zealand, Canada, and others), is a "majoritarian democracy," characterized by non-proportional elections, a two-party system, and other differences. The difficulty from our perspective is that the second type is generally the one that has constitutional flexibility, the supremacy of the parliament, and limited judicial review. In the negotiation democracy, on the other hand, the category to which Israel belongs, one finds familiar governance patterns in Israel, but also formal, rigid constitutionality and judicial review. Thus Israel is an exception in the consensus democracy group, because it has no formal constitution, and debates still ensue about the supremacy of the Knesset (and its subordination to the Basic Laws) and the formal status of judicial review.

The debate about a constitution for Israel relates both to substantive issues and to the process for deciding these issues. The subjects that are absent from the Basic Laws and the court's constitutional rulings are not at all random. They relate to the controversies around which it is difficult not only to mobilize a majority, but also to achieve broad consensus in Israeli political culture. The subjects missing from Israel's material constitution are those that society and the political system find hard to deal with in the absence of broad consensus: the constitution as the supreme law of the land, the status of religion in the state, a declaration of human and civil rights, minority rights, definition of the form of regime, the constitutional status of the Supreme Court, and the status of the civil service, the local authorities, and the political parties. In retrospect, it turns out that at least one of the claims of those who objected to putting off a decision about the constitution in the early years of the state turned out to be right: "They predicted that temporary arrangements very quickly become permanent, and that time is a tool for establishing facts no less than formal decisions" (Galnoor 1982).

Since the 1980s, the stepped-up efforts to complete the framing of the constitution, including the Supreme Court's "creative" period of precedent-setting rulings, have been rooted in extra-constitutional and extra-legal sources (Shahar, Gross, and Goldschmidt 2004, 288). One explanation for these activist efforts is that completion of the constitution was intended to change the balance of political power, and that the veteran secular, Ashkenazi elites are hoping the constitution will serve as an ally in their weakened status vis-à-vis the new political forces (Gavison 2003, 62). The problem with this explanation is that the missing majority for framing a constitution fluctuates and lacks a clear sociopolitical identity. It frequently changes, almost in accordance with the government coalition at the time. Parties on the left or the right sometimes join the religious hard core who oppose a constitution.[79] Thus, opposition to the Basic Law: Legislation crossed party lines. Arab citizens are ambivalent toward a constitution: They want it to entrench their rights as citizens and a collective group, but they fear it will actually entrench the privilege of the majority in a "Jewish and democratic" state, and undermine their few achievements, such as the official status of Arabic. Jewish settlers in the territories, who generally oppose the constitution and Supreme Court intervention, began to argue that the state is violating their rights, and even turned to the High Court to prevent the disengagement from Gaza in 2005.[80] Moreover, notes Barzilai, High Court rulings that contributed

[79] The Labor–Shas coalition agreement in 1992 contained a section pledging legislation to preserve the status quo on religious affairs, which would have undercut the High Court's authority to intervene in these matters (*Velner v. Rabin et al.* 1995).

[80] *Gaza Coast Regional Council et al. v. Israeli Knesset et al.* 2005; *Gaza Coast Regional Council et al. v. Prime Minister Ariel Sharon et al.* 2005. High Court petitions on the same issue that were consolidated in this case – HCJ 1798/05, HCJ 2252/05, HCJ 2703/05; HCJ 3059/05; a High Court case on the evacuation of synagogues – *Bar Hen et al. v. Prime Minister Ariel Sharon et al.* 2005; *Shimoni v. the Prime Minister* 2005; *Levy et al. v. Government of Israel et al.* 2005.

to some limited social change have always been issued during a national unity government or a narrow coalition that was favorably disposed to the Supreme Court (Barzilai 1998, 45; also see Hofnung 1997, 229–83).

The Constitution, Law and Justice Committee of the sixteenth Knesset published a consolidated draft of constitution proposals, which included the various positions taken.[81] This proposal, like others, offers no fresh ideas, and the divergent views on substantive issues suggest that the obstacles will be difficult to surmount. To some extent this is because the majority now oppose completion of the constitution for reasons not unlike those of the majority who opposed it in 1950: A constitution could in their opinion curtail their freedom of action when in power.

Hence, Israel is a "consensus democracy," which prefers to be a "majoritarian democracy."[82] The paradox is that the fear of a constitution that would give more power to the Supreme Court has led to the absence of a constitution, which only served to strengthen the court in the 1980s, when the power of the elected political institutions (the Knesset and the government) began to weaken. And it was the Knesset itself, more than any other institution, that called upon the Supreme Court for help, even before legislation of the 1992 Basic Laws, and certainly after them.[83] It should be noted that a constitution would have stipulated that not only were the Knesset and the government subordinate to "the constitution regime," i.e., a supra-constitutional framework, but so too would have been the Supreme Court itself.

What the controversial constitutional issues have in common is that no decisive rulings have been issued about them to this day, only a collection of arrangements, agreements, and policies that reflect a majority (at least politically) that are fearful of change. Thus, the "1949 constitution" remains in effect somewhat vague, known to few, but still functioning. And of course changes have been introduced over time, as in relations among the branches of government, to be discussed in the coming chapters.

Over the years, several Basic Laws have been added to the unwritten constitution, most concerned with rules of governance, and a minority with some specific human and civil rights. As a result, rather than having a formal, written constitution, user-friendly and educationally helpful, what exists is a labyrinth of Basic Laws that differ from each other, complex court rulings, and reams of interpretations that even experts find hard to follow. Taken together they do not express fundamental values and aspirations about living together in the state, but reflect arrangements for the allocation of power and distribution of tasks among the government branches; and to a lesser extent, between the branches and the public.[84]

81 http://huka.gov.il (accessed February 2, 2006).

82 This is the spirit in which the minority opinion of Justice Cheshin should be understood: He favored enactment of a constitution, but wanted it to be done by a large majority, not in haste, because "...I cannot agree to enacting a constitution *without consulting the people*" [italics in the original], Mizrahi Bank ruling, 349.

83 The amendment to the Basic Law: The Knesset in 1984, which allowed for the disqualification of a list of candidates to the Knesset, allowed the court in practice to decide on the interpretation of "Jewish and democratic." Also see Avnon 1998, 65.

84 A somewhat different view is that Israel has a "partially formal constitution, but one that fully protects the most critical human rights with excellent and efficient judicial oversight" (Rubinstein and Medina 2005, 124).

A constitution cannot be expected to resolve thorny substantive disputes or prevent governance blunders by virtue of elegant formulations. And yet given the current situation, it would be preferable to reach broad agreement on the maximum possible issues, without pretensions of resolving the irresolvable. It is imperative to forge a broader, formal constitutional structure, one that will contribute to a democratic common denominator and stability, so that in another fifty years, Israeli society will not again regret that it chose to continue with the current constitutional ambiguity.

PART II

INSTITUTIONS MATTER

In Part II, we concentrate on the political institutions themselves, and in Part III, we look at society with its numerous participants – permanent and transient – in the political process. We do not suggest a sharp distinction between institutions (and their formal infrastructure) and the political behavior of voters, elected representatives, political parties, the new media, and civil society organizations. We often venture into what lies beyond institutions, such as the balance of power among them or the dynamics of change over time. Basic information is provided about the institutions, with references to other sources, and then we concentrate on the main issues, such as: the importance of the institution of the presidency; the deteriorating status of the Knesset and its impact on Israeli democracy; the crisis following the experiment in direct election of the prime minister; the importance of the Supreme Court in Israeli society and politics; and the expanding role of the monitoring mechanisms such as the state comptroller and inquiry commissions.

3 The Presidency and the Symbols of Power

> A president is not a ruler, not a judge, not a lawmaker, but he is allowed to dream, to instill values, to act honestly and with compassion, with courage and kindness. Nothing prohibits a president from performing good deeds. He is entitled, and even obligated, to serve his people, to nurture love of the people, of the state, of all human beings. To draw near those who are far, to gaze into the distance, to aid the weak, comfort the bereaved, bring hearts together, increase equality, bridge differences, support spiritual and scientific creativity.
>
> (Peres, inaugural address, 2007)

Thus did Shimon Peres, Israel's ninth president, define the role of the president. In Israel, as in constituent monarchies (Spain, the Netherlands, Norway), the president is the symbolic head of state, not in charge of the executive branch. The Israeli presidency resembles that of Finland, Germany, Greece, India, Ireland, Italy, and Turkey. It does not resemble the presidential systems of the United States, Brazil, Russia, or South Africa, where the president performs both symbolic and executive functions. In his or her personality and stature, the president of Israel represents the state itself and all its various authorities, groups, and citizens. The institution of the presidency is intended to instill a unifying dimension in society and its political system, and to contribute to solidarity. This mission, though not legally defined as such, is its essence. The president is expected to rise above the political fray, parties, and rivalries, and to bridge social cleavages. Hence the democratic significance of the institution; hence its dependence on the personality of the incumbent.

3.1 Shaping the Institution of the Presidency

At the first meeting of the Provisional State Council (Protocols, May 16, 1948), Ben-Gurion proposed, in accordance with a decision of the Provisional Government, that Professor Chaim Weizmann, the veteran head of the Zionist movement, be elected president. At that time, the presidency was obviously not yet anchored in law, nor was the role of president defined. The reasons raised in the council in favor of Weizmann were personal. Ben-Gurion viewed his election as "an historic justice, more than a constitutional change or political statement," noting, "If there is anyone alive who deserves to be president of the Jewish state, it is Dr. Chaim Weizmann." Ben-Gurion viewed the election of a president as something needed by the Yishuv, the Zionist movement, and the Jewish public, which justified "the sin of violating an abstract formality." Dissenting were those who opposed the election of Weizmann on political grounds, in that he represented a specific world view, and also on the constitutional grounds that the council (a provisional body) was not authorized to conduct this election, particularly of someone who was not even a member.

Despite the constitutional misgivings, Weizmann was elected president of the Provisional State Council by a vote of thirteen to two, with ten abstaining. A debate about the powers of the president was held only later in the Constitution Committee of the Provisional State Council, and the legal underpinnings of the presidential powers appear first in the Transition Law (1949), modeled largely after the President of the French Fourth Republic. After election of the Constituent Assembly (the first Knesset), voting for a president was held on February 16, 1949, and Weizmann won by a resounding majority of eighty-three votes, with MKs from Herut, the Communist Party, and the Fighters' List casting votes against him (see Table 3.1). The nature of his task, however, was not clear to the elected president: "The only place the government allows me to stick my nose," said witty President Weizmann in a newspaper interview, "is into a handkerchief" (*New York Post*, September 6, 1951; also see Fischer 1996).

Weizmann found it hard to reconcile himself to a position with no authority and no real political influence. He was the first president and head of state, but nobody had any idea of the job description. The first formal definition of the procedure for the election of the president and some of the official functions appeared in the Transition Law (1949) and provisions added to the State President (Tenure) Law (1951), which were replaced in 1964, by the Basic Law: The President. Nonetheless, lack of clarity remains about several issues, which we discuss below. In retrospect, the institution of president has been largely shaped by those who held that position.

3.2 The Basic Law: The President (1964)

According to the Basic Law, the president is the head of state. Since amendment of this law in 2001, the president is elected for one seven-year term only. Previously, a president had been elected for a five-year term, and could be reelected for a second term. Candidacy requires the supportive signature of ten MKs, and the president must be elected by an absolute majority of sixty-one MKs in a secret ballot held in a special session. If this majority is not attained in the first round of voting, the two leading candidates move to a second round, and the winning candidate is elected by a simple majority.[1] This mode of election has a singular advantage – it enables the MKs and parties to bridge their differences and elect a figure who will win the trust of the public. It also has a clear disadvantage – if the election reflects the existing balance of power in the Knesset, the president will find it hard to win the public trust. This disadvantage is magnified when the elected president is a party activist,

[1] Amendment 9 to Article 8 of the Basic Law: The President passed in 2013. Previously, if an absolute majority of MKs was not attained in the first round, a second round of voting was held for all candidates. If an absolute majority was not attained in the second round either, a third round was held for the two leading candidates, and the candidate with a simple majority would win.

as all the presidents to date had been at the time of their election with one exception (Ephraim Katzir). The disadvantage became evident in the 2014 election of the president, which turned into an ugly, personal feud among, initially, no fewer than seven candidates.

A. Immunity of the President

The law defines two types of presidential immunity – immunity with regard to the discharge of his or her functions and immunity from criminal proceedings. The former means that the president "shall not be amenable to any court or tribunal, and shall be immune from any legal act, with respect to anything *related to his functions or powers*" (emphasis added). When giving testimony, the president is also not obligated to disclose anything learned during the discharge of his or her duties, and this immunity continues after the president's term ends.

Immunity from criminal proceedings is granted only during the term of office: An incumbent president may not stand trial on criminal charges. An investigation into the suspicion of criminal charges, on the other hand, can be conducted about an incumbent president. In 2000, President Ezer Weizman was investigated on suspicion of having accepted large sums of money from a businessman without duly reporting it to the authorities. Due to insufficient evidence and expiration of the statute of limitations on some of the charges, the prosecuting attorney did not issue an indictment against Weizman, but did severely criticize his actions. Several months later, President Weizman resigned from office. In 2006, a criminal investigation of President Moshe Katzav was launched on suspicion of sexual offenses. A year later, shortly before his term of office expired, President Katzav resigned from office, rejected a plea bargain on lesser charges, and stood trial. He was convicted on two counts of rape, obstruction of justice, and other offenses and was sentenced to seven years in prison in March 2011.

B. Removal of a President from Office or Temporary Cessation of Activity

A president can end a term of office by illness, resignation, or because the Knesset removes him or her from office because of "conduct unbecoming his status as president of the state." Removal of a president because of unbecoming conduct is a serious matter, and the law requires that a complaint be submitted by twenty MKs to the House Committee, which – by a three-quarters majority – agrees to recommend to the Knesset plenary that the president be removed from office. The removal must be approved by a majority of ninety MKs, after the president has been given an opportunity to refute the claims. To date, the Knesset has not removed any president from office, but, as noted, two presidents (Weizman and Katzav) resigned near the end of their terms. When the attorney general decided to bring serious charges against President Katzav, some MKs sought to have him removed from office, but President Katzav asked the House Committee to approve a "temporary cessation of activity" (January to July 2007), during which the Speaker of the Knesset served as acting president, after which Katzav tendered his resignation.

The House Committee can also propose to the Knesset plenary – by a two-thirds majority of its members – removal of a president from office for health reasons (based on a medical opinion), which must be approved by a majority of MKs.

3.3 The Functions of the President

The president first and foremost performs ceremonial functions: reception of the public on holidays, official visits to other countries, accreditation of diplomats, award of the State Soccer Cup, etc. The specific duties relate to all three branches of government:

For the legislative branch, the law requires the president's countersignature on every law enacted, except laws related to the president's own powers.[2] The president also signs treaties with foreign states after ratification by the Knesset.

For the executive branch, the Basic Law: Government specifies in detail the role of the president in the formal process of forming a government in the aftermath of an election or upon resignation of the prime minister. The president can exercise real discretion, however, when the prime minister asks to dissolve the Knesset, as we shall see below. To perform his or her presidential duties, the president must be kept informed, and therefore receives government reports of its activities – written summaries of government decisions and oral reports from the prime minister or the cabinet secretary. The president may request and receive information on any subject, including classified data. By virtue of being head of state, the president accepts the credentials of diplomats in Israel, and confirms the appointments of Israeli diplomats abroad. Every signature of the president on an official document requires a countersignature by the prime minister or other minister, with the exception of documents related to the formation of the government or dissolution of the Knesset.

For the judiciary, the president signs the letters of appointment of judges in the civil courts and the (Jewish or Muslim) religious courts. The president has the sole authority to pardon offenders or commute their sentences (see below).

A. Disagreement over the Powers of the President

Periodically, bills have been proposed (though not passed) to limit presidential intervention in public matters not in national consensus. Such bills were tabled, for example, in an effort to prevent President Ezer Weizman from taking stands on controversial issues, on the grounds that presidential involvement in political issues prevents him from discharging his traditional functions.

These disagreements revolve around the extent to which the president has discretion in carrying out his or her duties. "He is a symbol," claim those who oppose presidential discretion, "and should not be deciding or intervening in controversial matters; a symbol should be satisfied with contributing to national unity." "No," respond the supporters, "although the president is generally a symbol, he also has specific powers and is free to use his discretion within the framework of the law." In the complicated political situation in Israel, the use of discretion by the president arouses controversy, and this has increased as divisiveness has grown in society. For example, President Weizman refused on principle to rubber stamp pardon recommendations made by the Minister of Justice. This disagreement became public

[2] On the significance of the presidential countersignature, see Symposium 1995, 16–17.

when he refused to pardon Palestinian security prisoners as mandated by the Oslo Interim Agreements in 1993. Weizman's critics viewed this as interference that was clearly political. In other cases, presidential discretion could lead to a constitutional difficulty: The law stipulates that the president must "sign every law" – what would happen if the president for any reason refuses to sign a law passed by the Knesset?[3]

The following discussion focuses on three key functions of the president: the symbolic role, involvement in forming the government, and the authority to grant pardons. These powers have aroused public and legal debates, which also touch upon the status of and need for the institution of president.

B. The President as a Unifying Symbol

The most distinctive function of the president is to serve as a symbol. Although the law does not define what is meant by "A president shall stand at the head of the state," the accumulated experience points to agreement that the president remain above the political fray, party differences, and internal social divisions. Thanks to the lofty and independent stature of the office, the president can represent shared values and uncontroversial views. This bestows great importance upon the presidency, especially in times of crisis.

However, the president is generally a public figure whose previous views are known and usually associated with a particular political party. The fact that it is the Knesset that elects the president from candidates proffered by the parties or MKs only reinforces this link. To date, the vast majority of presidential candidates (and nine of the ten elected to the post) were MKs or otherwise politically identifiable.[4] The law does not prohibit the president from being a party member, although "the president customarily stands above the parties" (M. Landau 1994, 12). President Katzav continued to be a Likud member, while Shimon Peres canceled his membership in the Kadima Party upon being sworn in as president, as did his successor, President Rivlin, from the Likud Party. The expectation is that, from the moment of election, the president is no longer the emissary of a party.[5]

The non-partisan character of the office is therefore contingent upon how the president chooses to be involved in the public discourse, the content and timing of these pronouncements, and his or her personality. Over the years, criticism has periodically been directed at presidents who expressed their views on controversial issues or attempted to influence political opinion. Most of Israel's presidents have evoked criticism for some utterance or another. After the Yom Kippur War,

[3] Justice Moshe Landau believed that the president's countersignature is a requirement of symbolic value only, and that this function, as opposed to the authority to issue pardons, is not open to presidential discretion (1994, 23). In other countries, creative solutions have been found for this constitutional problem. In Belgium in 1990, for example, the parliament passed abortion laws, which King Baudouin vehemently refused to sign into law. The government declared the king "incapacitated to govern," and the cabinet discharged the function of the head of state and approved the laws. The next day, the government declared that the king was again capable of ruling.

[4] Herut, for example, conditioned its support for electing Yitzhak Ben-Zvi to a second term as president on his resignation from Mapai, if elected; Ben-Zvi refused, and the Herut MKs abstained from voting (Kraines 1961, 128).

[5] This issue came up in the debates of the Constitution, Law and Justice Committee over the future constitution, and opinions were expressed on both sides (Protocol 86, November 9, 2003).

President Katzir aroused ire by saying, "We are all guilty." President Navon threatened to resign if a State Commission of Inquiry was not appointed to investigate the slaughter in the Lebanese refugee camps Sabra and Shatila during the First Lebanon War. President Herzog derided the press as "hostile media," joined the demand to change the electoral system, and criticized the High Court decision to sanction the openly racist Kahane list in the 1984 Knesset election. President Ezer Weizman's term of office was riddled with statements that drew fire: a call for a "time out" in negotiations with the Palestinians after the 1995 terrorist acts; an invitation to Chairman Arafat of the Palestinian Authority to visit him at his home after Netanyahu was elected prime minister in 1996; urging of the government to negotiate with the Syrians in 1999 after formation of the Barak government; support for a national unity government; and insulting statements about women and homosexuals (NRG 2005; Goren and Harnick 1996). President Katzav engaged in several controversial initiatives: In defiance of the recommendation of the Prison Service Release Committee, he shortened the prison term of Margalit Har-Shefi, who did not report Yigal Amir's plans to assassinate Yitzhak Rabin; he supported a ceasefire (*hudna*) with the Palestinians; and he expressed a willingness to visit the Palestinian parliament in Ramallah. President Peres too was criticized for making political statements, beyond those expected of the president; he argued, for example, that Israel should push for a peace agreement with the Palestinians without delay, and asserted Israel should conduct peace negotiations with Hamas (an acronym for the Islamic Resistance Movement).

While the president may be a unifying symbol, he or she cannot be expected to take a vow of silence or avoid issues of concern to the public. Nevertheless, taking a stand that is unacceptable in some circles can undermine the stature of the presidency. Proposals to resolve this problem by legislation are futile, because one cannot legislate what a president may or may not say. It makes more sense to elect a figure who is cognizant of the stature of the office, and whose utterances on controversial matters would not be driven by political aspirations. The vagueness in defining the symbolic function is what enables the president to shape the institution as a figure aloof from day-to-day disputes, yet involved in the current events and aware of public sentiment.

The symbolic aspect of the presidency is also related to the characteristics of Israel's presidents (see Table 3.1). Of the ten presidents Israel has had, eight had been ministers or MKs when elected or in previous years, and one (Navon) returned to political life after his term as president expired. All the candidates elected after Chaim Weizmann were proposed by Mapai or the Labor Party, except for Moshe Katzav and Reuven Rivlin, who came from the Likud, and Shimon Peres from Kadima (formerly of Labor). Two presidents (Chaim Herzog and Ezer Weizman) were military men, and one (Ephraim Katzir) was a scientist. Only two presidents (Navon and Katzav) were of Mizrahi origin, and so far no presidents have been women, Orthodox, or Arab. This profile of partial representation is not significantly different for the list of unsuccessful candidates for the job, although among them are two religious candidates and three women. The presidents have generally been chosen in the first round of voting, except Ben-Zvi, who was elected by a small margin in 1952 in the third round; Peres, who was

Table 3.1 *Presidents of Israel and election support by MKs (number of votes)*

Year	President elected	Number of votes	Other candidates
1949	Chaim Weizmann	83	Prof. Joseph Klausner
1951	Chaim Weizmann	85	None
1952	Yitzhak Ben-Zvi (Mapai)	62 (in the third round)	MK Peretz Bernstein (General Zionists); MK Mordechai Nurock (Mizrahi); Yitzhak Greenbaum
1957	Yitzhak Ben-Zvi	76	None
1962	Yitzhak Ben-Zvi	62	None
1963	Zalman Shazar (Mapai)	67	MK Peretz Bernstein (Liberal Party)
1968	Zalman Shazar	86	None
1973	Ephraim Katzir	66	Prof. Ephraim Elimelech-Urbach
1978	Yitzhak Navon (Alignment)	86	None
1983	Chaim Herzog (Alignment)	61	Prof. Menachem Elon
1988	Chaim Herzog	82	None
1993	Ezer Weizman (Labor)	66	MK Dov Shilansky (Likud)
1998	Ezer Weizman*	63	MK Shaul Amor (Likud)**
2000	Moshe Katzav (Likud)*	63	MK Shimon Peres (Labor)
2007	Shimon Peres (Kadima)	86 (in the second round)	MK Reuven Rivlin (Likud); MK Colette Avital (Labor)
2014	Reuven Rivlin (Likud)	63 (in the second round)	Former MK Dalia Itzik; Justice Dalia Dorner; MK Meir Sheetrit (Kadima); Prof. Dan Shechtman

* Resigned from office.
** This is the first time a candidate ran against an incumbent president.
Source: Knesset website.

elected in the second round as the only candidate; and Rivlin, who was elected in the second round.

Except for Chaim Weizmann in 1949 and Yitzhak Navon in 1978, who were elected by a large majority, all the other presidents were elected to their *first* term by a slim majority of sixty-two to sixty-seven MKs, indicating that the voting in the Knesset followed party lines, which detracts, as noted, from the representativeness of this institution. For a *second* term, however, the presidents were elected by a large majority – an average of seventy-eight MKs in support. The fact that only once did someone run against an incumbent president (Shaul Amor versus Ezer Weizman in 1998) also reveals that serving a term of office expands the base of support of a president among the Knesset factions. This matter has become irrelevant since 2001 when the law stipulated that a president is elected for only one seven-year term, hence a serving president no longer has to recruit the votes of MKs for a second term.

C. Role of the President in Forming a Government

This role is defined by the Basic Law: Government enacted in 1968 (which was in effect until election of the fourteenth Knesset in 1996). It is primarily ceremonial and modeled after the tradition in constitutional monarchies where the elected government acts in the name of the monarch – or, in Israel, in the name of the state that the president represents. The president, after consulting with parties represented in the Knesset, assigns the task of forming the government to an MK, who must complete the task within twenty-eight days. If the MK fails, the task is assigned to another candidate who agrees to accept this task, or to an MK recommended by the parties that constitute a majority in the Knesset. If none of the candidates is able to form a government, the president informs the Speaker of the Knesset, the Knesset is dissolved, and new elections are held.

The now defunct direct election of the prime minister (Basic Law: Government, enacted in 1992) changed the involvement of the president in forming a government: If the prime minister is directly elected, the president no longer needs to choose someone to form a government. On the other hand, the law assigned the president an important new role in the event of dissolution of the Knesset by the prime minister, who, in this system, had the authority to dissolve the Knesset: "should the prime minister ascertain that a majority of the Knesset opposes the government, and that the effective functioning of the government is prevented as a result." However, this must be done "with the approval of the president of the state." From the wording of the law, the president was not obliged to approve the prime minister's initiative to dissolve the Knesset, and had substantial discretionary power to limit or even restrain the prime minister in this matter. This posed a difficulty: If the president were to oppose the prime minister's desire to dissolve the Knesset, a constitutional impasse could ensue – although the government was unable to function under the given conditions, the Knesset could not be dissolved because of the president's opposition. During the period this law was in effect, this dilemma never arose.

The new version of the Basic Law: Government, amended in 2001, restored the previous system and the role of the president in forming the government. The most significant change in the 2001 law relates to the dissolution of the Knesset. Unlike the Basic Law of 1968, and similar to the Basic Law from 1992, the prime minister is empowered to dissolve the Knesset with the consent of the president. Yet, the constitutional complication noted above was corrected – an option was given to a majority of MKs to ask the president to assign the task of forming a government to a specific MK, and only if this fails will the Knesset have to dissolve.

When would the president's role in forming a government be significant? When there is a need to rely on the president's discretion to decide which MK should be asked to form a government. The law offers the president political assistance in this: the obligation to consult with representatives of the parties, meaning that the task must be assigned to the candidate that the MKs indicate has the greatest chance of success. Since all the proposals that would legally require the president to assign this task to the head of the largest party failed, the president can select the MK with the greatest chance of success, even if he or she does not head the largest party.[6]

In the 1984 Knesset election, an unprecedented situation arose. The Alignment Party under Peres won forty-four mandates, but could not form a government without the support of the religious parties, which refused to establish a narrow government that would require the external support of Arab parties. The Likud had dropped to forty-one mandates (from forty-eight in the tenth Knesset), and found it hard to reestablish a right-wing–religious coalition with the required majority. Based on consultations with the parties, President Herzog assigned the task of forming a government to Likud head Yitzhak Shamir, even though Likud was not then the largest party. Shamir was unable to comply, however, because the left and right blocs in the Knesset were of equal size. The solution ultimately found under the patronage of the president was to create a unity government in which Peres and Shamir would rotate as prime minister, two years each (on the "rotation coalition" see Chapter 11). Thus, a two-bloc coalition was formed supported by ninety-seven MKs, which lasted the entire term of office. During this process, another question arose about the obligation of the president to consult with "representatives of the Knesset parties." President Herzog argued that the law did not require him to consult with representatives of *all* the parties, and therefore newly elected MK Meir Kahane was not invited to this consultation.

Another unusual situation was created after the Knesset voted no-confidence in the government in 1990, following a crisis in the national unity government. For a while it seemed as if Shimon Peres, head of Labor, had the support of most MKs, who actually asked President Herzog to assign him the task of forming a new government, though he did not head the largest Knesset party. Peres failed, however, and the president then assigned the task to Likud leader Yitzhak Shamir, who did manage to form a government that lasted until the 1992 elections. More recently, Kadima headed by MK Livni emerged as the largest party (twenty-eight mandates) in the 2009 Knesset election, but President Peres assigned the task of forming a government to Netanyahu, the head of Likud (twenty-seven mandates), because he had a greater chance of success in forming a coalition, which he did.

As noted, the president was rarely called upon to use discretion to form a government or dissolve the Knesset. Nevertheless, in crisis situations, even if they are infrequent, measures should be available to preserve the stability of the political system. One option that exists in similar regimes is to grant the president explicit discretionary power to dissolve the Knesset in order to prevent a stalemate in the event that the Knesset and the government do not see eye to eye. In a situation like this, the president would be a deterrent safety valve in relations between the two branches of government.

[6] This issue had already come up in 1951 after resignation of the Ben-Gurion government. President Chaim Weizmann approached Ben-Gurion requesting that he again form a new government, even though Ben-Gurion had announced that this was impossible in light of the constellation of forces in the Knesset. MK Ari Jabotinsky and others petitioned the High Court on the grounds that the president was violating the Knesset's rights by assigning this task to an MK who refused to accept the job, and he should approach another MK. The court ruled that the authority to assign the task of forming a government is within the executive power of the president, and the court has no authority over this (*Jabotinsky v. Weizmann* 1951).

D. The Power to Pardon[7]

The law states that "The president of the state shall have the power to pardon offenders and lighten penalties by the reduction or commutation thereof." The president is also authorized under the Criminal Register and Rehabilitation of Offenders Law (1981) to reduce the statute of limitations and expungement periods that apply to criminal records (convictions and court rulings without a conviction). The president's power to pardon is a legacy of the High Commissioner's power during the British Mandate. These issues are intertwined with principles of justice, as well as human lives of inmates and their families. Democratic governments grapple differently with the prerogative rulers once had – familiar from folk tales and legends – to sentence or pardon offenders. Some states leave pardon power exclusively up to the courts (by retrial or other means), and others entrust it to a separate authority that can pardon or show clemency (Sebba 1977, 83–121).

Although in Israel a pardon is the joint responsibility of the president and the Minister of Justice, the authority resides with the president, hence their roles are not symmetrical. The request for a pardon usually comes from the convicted offenders and their families, and the Prison Service provides its professional opinion to the Amnesties and Pardons Division of the Ministry of Justice. It is the minister who makes a recommendation to the president, and if the president agrees to pardon, a countersignature is required of the Minister of Justice. Thus the president has discretionary power and is not obliged to accept the minister's recommendation about a pardon, although this rarely occurs. The president, however, is not authorized to grant a pardon without a recommendation.

The law does not define the scope of the power to pardon, the legal criteria for the presidential exercise of discretion, or the need for transparency, and does not address the issue of judicial review of presidential decisions. Based on the content of the law and cumulative experience, the power to pardon does not bestow on the president permission to interpret the law or intervene in any way with the court's considerations. In granting a pardon, the president weighs factors and considerations *beyond* legislation and court decisions – personal, humanitarian, and the public interest. Clemency is related to compassion, and operates beyond the letter of the law.

The type of pardon that has provoked considerable controversy, practical and theoretical, is called a "full pardon," which expunges the punishment and, some believe, also the crime that led to the conviction, thereby creating a "clean slate." A full pardon is clearly intended to endow the recipient with an opportunity for rehabilitation – to turn over a new leaf – and make it easier to get a job, for example. Theoretically, the offense can also be expunged, erasing the mark of disgrace from the offender, either during the sentence or after it has been served, but what does this really mean? After all, the fact that a crime was committed does not disappear, nor does the fact of the conviction. If these are expunged, the pardon ostensibly also erases the court ruling. Thus the facts remain (a crime was committed), the conviction disappears, but a gray area persists in which "a non-offender was pardoned" – which might be relevant, for example, in applying for several civil service positions.

[7] We are grateful to Professor Leslie Sebba for his incisive comments on this subject.

Based on court rulings, a full pardon does not necessarily mean that the conviction is ignored, if the pardon was granted for public reasons (*Eisenberg v. Minister of Housing and Construction* 1993). This High Court ruling reinterprets the assertion that a full pardon granted by the president is equivalent to a conviction that was completely expunged.[8] In other words, the authority of the president in Israel is more restricted than the sweeping royal prerogative that can entirely exonerate someone from the guilt assigned by a court. Thus, the all-encompassing royal benevolence is replaced by democratic clemency moderated by the limits of the public interest.[9] The meaning of the term "offender" in the context of a pardon also came up in the debate about the president's power to grant a pardon *prior to* a conviction, as we shall see below.

The second type is a conditional (or partial) pardon, which leaves the conviction in place, but shortens or lightens the sentence, for example, reduces the prison term, or converts a prison term to a fine or suspended sentence. The president has the authority to commute the terms of criminals sentenced to life in prison, or to change a life sentence to a defined period after completion of seven years of the sentence. In a pardon of this nature, too, the president cannot raise matters that came up in the trial or the sentencing, but may take into consideration changes that took place after the sentence such as the health or family situation of the offender.[10]

Another significant limitation is that the president can grant only individual pardons, and has no general power of amnesty. The power to grant amnesty remains with the Knesset as the legislative authority, which it used to mark the founding of the state in 1948 and victory in the 1967 Six Day War. This was the last of such legislation. Amnesty is an extraordinary act in any democracy, because legislation naturally precedes adjudication, and the legislator has no cause to intervene in this arena. Furthermore, a legislative act of amnesty for a specific group could be carried out for the wrong reasons. As for prisoner exchanges, such as the deal struck with the Palestinian organization of Ahmad Jibril in 1985, the president granted "individual" pardons, so to speak, to those tried in the civil courts (those tried in military courts were granted a pardon by the chief of staff). Since the Ministry of Defense prepared the lists, it is unlikely that the president would have examined each and every name, therefore this act could be seen as a collective pardon, or an amnesty. In a case like this, because a political act is at issue and not a pardon, it is more appropriate that the Knesset, not the president, approve the deal. In 2014, the Knesset amended Article 11 of the law denying the president the power to release those convicted of "murder in extreme circumstances," thereby preventing the use of such prisoners in agreements that include prisoner swaps.

[8] To clear the reputation of an offender by expunging the criminal charges, a separate procedure is defined in the Criminal Register and Rehabilitation of Offenders Law – 1981 (see H. Cohn 1985).

[9] This is narrower than the broad interpretation given to the presidential pardon power in the court decision *Attorney General v. Matana* 1962.

[10] A decline in health was the reason given for pardoning Joshua Bension, who was convicted in 1975 of stealing $47 million, and had been a contributor to the Likud and other groups supportive of the Greater Land of Israel movement. Bension was pardoned by President Katzir at the recommendation of Menachem Begin, then Minister of Justice, based on medical opinions attesting that his life was in imminent danger (Bension died in 2004).

Pardon Prior to Conviction

Is the president authorized to grant a pardon prior to an individual's conviction? How can the authority "to pardon offenders" – in the words of the law – be activated if the individuals have not yet been defined by a court as offenders? The law does not explicitly prohibit the president from doing this, and Justice Berenson's 1962 opinion, in which he wrote in passing that the president is authorized "to pardon any offender even before he is brought to trial," was accepted until the 1986 debate around the "Bus 300 affair." At the conclusion of a complicated and stormy affair (that even had a TV version), then Attorney General Yitzhak Zamir announced that his office had prima facie evidence of criminal offenses by Avraham Shalom, head of the General Security Services (GSS), and three senior officials, and called for their indictment. Prime Minister Peres and Deputy Prime Minister Shamir came out in defense of the GSS head, objecting to the attorney general's view, and they had Zamir replaced as attorney general. Although the GSS head claimed in his defense that all his deeds were carried out "with authority and permission," he was forced to resign. In parallel with his resignation, the cabinet recommended to President Herzog that the four be pardoned in advance, prior to their indictment or even investigation, to prevent the disclosure of state secrets. The president accepted the recommendation and pardoned the GSS head and three senior officials, who were suspected of very serious offenses – involvement in the killing of terrorists who had been captured alive, obstruction of justice, and subornation of perjury. This was the first and only time in Israel that a president pardoned someone who had allegedly committed a crime, but was not yet convicted.

In response to a High Court petition, two of the three judges (Shamgar and Ben-Porat) ruled that the president, like the king of England or US president, has the authority to pardon prior to a conviction, if vital to the public interest or called for by extreme individual circumstances (*Barzilai v. State of Israel* 1986). They stated that such conditions obtained with respect to the GSS figures, and therefore the president's pardon was legal. Nevertheless, they noted, this is an exceptional use of authority, a rare and extreme measure that should be used only infrequently as a "safety valve." In a minority opinion, Justice Barak wrote that the Basic Law: The President is an Israeli law, and therefore parallels cannot be drawn with kings or presidents in completely different political systems, but rather that the intent of the legislation must be examined. Barak agreed with the majority that the authority of the president is residual, and for that very reason he or she has no authority to intervene in other branches of government. The president has no means to investigate the facts or uncover the truth, and therefore must act in accordance with court rulings, not intervening at any stage of the judicial process, and therefore the president has no authority to pardon prior to conviction. Hence a pardon can be applied only after the other authorities have fully performed their roles.[11]

The majority ruling raises serious constitutional issues – beyond the semantic quibbling over the word "offender"[12] – because it indirectly reinstates the non-democratic prerogative of the ruler's grace. Indeed, while a presidential pardon is an

[11] For a critique of the High Court ruling on the Barzilai case, see Kremnitzer 1987, 595–620.

[12] On the meaning of the word "offender" and further opposition to allowing a presidential pardon prior to conviction, see Feller 1987, 691–94.

exercise in clemency after the court has passed judgment, in a pre-conviction pardon the president suddenly intervenes prior to the actions of the police, attorney general, prosecutor, and court, without explicit authority to do so. Though debate continues, as noted, about whether a full pardon expunges the offense, a ruling that enables an advance pardon leaves open the possibility of expunging the very fact that an offense was committed. The use of a pre-trial pardon would also allow for another problematic phenomenon – political pardons to bypass court rulings.

External Review of the President's Pardon Decisions

Should the pardon considerations and decisions of the president be subject to formal scrutiny? Opinions are divided about judicial review because of the president's immunity in the discharge of his or her duties. Some claim that because the president is a symbol, judicial review should not be applied to presidential decisions, except in exceptional cases. The rationale is that if the court reviews presidential pardon decisions, it would be placing itself above the president and interfere in the separate function of pardon-granting. Different opinions were voiced in the Supreme Court about this issue. In the Matana case (*Matana v. Attorney General* 1960), the validity of the president's decision was in fact examined – despite the indirect language – and thus judicial review was exercised over a president's decisions (Rubinstein and Medina 2005, 856–58). In the Barzilai case, the majority ruled that "even if the president erred in his judgment, it is not sufficient to offset the legal validity of his decision" (*Barzilai v. State of Israel* 1986). On another occasion, the court ruled that "The president's action in judicial matters is not above the law and not extra-judicial, hence it is subject to the judicial review of the courts" (*Ronen v. Minister of Education A. Rubinstein* 1999 – unpublished).[13]

With respect to parliamentary supervision of the presidential pardon decisions, the proper address for this is the Ministry of Justice, as the minister's countersignature is generally perceived as an expression of ministerial responsibility. Indeed, one can address a parliamentary question to the Minister of Justice concerning a pardon or ask for it to be discussed in a Knesset committee, hence the deed, not the president, is subject to parliamentary supervision. For example, the decisions to pardon the GSS officials and Jewish underground members were debated in the Knesset (Rubinstein and Medina 1996, 869–70).

Ministerial supervision of pardons is conducted by the Minister of Justice by virtue of ministry involvement in the process. A pardon requires agreement between the Minister of Justice and the president: the former submits recommendations (based on assessments conducted in the ministry) and the latter exercises the authority to pardon. The president usually heeds the minister's recommendations, but is also free to turn them down. According to an official in the Ministry of Justice (personal communication 2006), the president has only rarely requested further clarifications. President Ezer Weizman exercised his right to refuse when he announced in 1995 that he would not pardon those convicted of murder who were given life sentences, thereby altering the custom of automatically commuting prison terms for these offenders. He maintained that he did not have the tools to decide on commuting a life sentence, and transferred this authority to a special professional

[13] See also Symposium 1995; and Israel Democracy Institute 1997.

committee (Ministry of Justice, personal communication 2006). A situation may also arise in which the president wishes to grant a pardon, but the Minister of Justice objects, as happened with Amos Baranes, convicted of murder in 1974 and given a life sentence. Over many years, he maintained his innocence, and President Navon supported a pardon, but Minister of Justice Moshe Nissim opposed it on the grounds that it would undermine the justice system. Finally, in 1983, President Herzog agreed to commute Baranes's sentence to another twelve years until his release.[14] The involvement of the Minister of Justice in the president's decisions on pardons could politicize the process (H. Cohn 1985, 17). There is a concern that the minister will take advantage of his or her role for inappropriate reasons. To prevent this from happening, one proposal is to transfer the Amnesties and Pardons Division from the Ministry of Justice to the President's Bureau, both to prevent the intermingling of governmental branches, on principle, and to uphold the essence of the law, which is the clemency prerogative of the president (Sebba 1977).

The president's reasons in pardon decisions are ordinarily not made public, primarily to protect the privacy of the offenders and their families. As a result, there is almost no media or public critique of the president's pardon decisions. Those who advocate full transparency regarding pardons believe these decisions should be treated the same way as any governmental process, which must be explained to the public, especially to preclude any doubt as to good faith. Suspicions were aired (though never confirmed) that President Moshe Katzav accepted favors for granting pardons – evidence that suspicions grow when decisions are not transparent and made without public scrutiny. Those who oppose publication of the reasons for the decisions argue that they should remain confidential, both to allow the president freedom of action and to safeguard the individual's privacy. One compromise that might balance these needs is to publish the general policy for granting pardons and the reasons in cases of public interest, or when the pardon is granted to offenders of serious offenses.[15]

Transparency relates to the issue of equality. Do all prisoners, regardless of their nationality, religion, class, age, or gender, have access to the pardon process? Every convicted offender may submit a pardon application to the president, and the instructions appear on the website of the Ministry of Justice's Amnesties and Pardons Division. But it is practically impossible to determine if there has been discrimination in granting pardons. The lack of transparency is also reflected in the absence of hard data about the pardons, and the little that exists is insufficiently accessible to the public. The President's Bureau and the Ministry of Justice report on the acts of pardon, but the data are inconsistent and do not enable monitoring of changes in the number of applications, the considerations, and the actual pardons over the years. It is also impossible to examine the question of equality, because demographic and other data do not exist about prisoners who are pardoned versus those who are not.

Table 3.2 presents the inadequate, partial data available about the applications and pardons granted by three presidents in years randomly chosen. Full pardon includes minor sentences such as fines; and commutation of sentences includes

[14] In 2002, Baranes was acquitted of the murder charge (Bana, Kra, et al. 2002).

[15] This was the recommendation of the Knesset's Constitution, Law and Justice Committee on February 7, 1990 (Rubinstein and Medina 1996, 867).

Table 3.2 *Pardon applications and pardons granted*

Year	President	Pardon applications	Full pardons or sentence commutations
1986	Herzog	2,033	221
1996	Weizman	1,785	168
2006	Katzav	1,995	446
2015	Rivlin	1,948	151

Despite extensive efforts, we were unable to obtain complete data about pardon applications and decisions. Full information, including breakdown into the different categories of pardons, was received only for 2014 and 2015 from President Rivlin's legal adviser (personal communication). Other sources include an internal report of the Ministry of Justice, annual government reports, and President Katzav's legal adviser (personal communication).

reducing a life sentence, reducing incarceration of five years or more, reducing shorter sentences including suspended sentences, commutation of a driver's license suspension or fines, and reducing the term of the statute of limitations.

Table 3.2 indicates that those engaged in the task of pardons have much work on their hands. In the period 2011–15, an average of 2,292 pardon applications were submitted each year. The data extant do not enable us to judge whether there were significant differences among the four presidents during this period in exercising their authority to pardon offenders or reduce their prison terms. However, President Katzav granted 446 pardons in 2006, by far a higher percentage of the total applications (22%) than any of the three other presidents (no explanation was given for this figure, received from his legal adviser in a personal communication).

The president's power to pardon is vital and necessary – less to correct a miscarriage of justice and more to introduce other, post-sentencing considerations, contributing compassion and clemency after the legal system has completed its work. Indeed, the court sometimes suggests to offenders that they apply for a pardon in cases where the court is constrained by the law in its ruling. In the case of a young man who killed his abusive father, for example, the court recommended that the defendant apply to the president to commute his sentence to seven years.

Nevertheless, there is ambiguity about how the president exercises this power, and we believe the process should be clarified to safeguard the public interest, ensuring humanitarian considerations and preventing inequality and injustice. The measures required are not revolutionary. First, it must be established that the presidential pardon be exercised only after the other judicial authorities have completed their work. This will prevent interference by the pardoning authority in the work of the judiciary. Second, consideration should be given to limiting the presidential pardon to only those cases recommended by an independent professional committee. This will not diminish the authority of the president, and will leave the Minister of Justice out of the pardon process. An orderly, transparent, and reasoned proceeding with the support of a professional committee will protect against the risk of "benevolence that borders on arbitrariness."[16] Another possibility is to legislate constraints on

[16] Proposed by Prof. Mordechai Kremnitzer at a joint seminar of the Political Science and Law Faculties at the Hebrew University, January 28, 1998.

the pardon of murderers, and set conditions for commuting a life sentence.[17] Third, MKs should be prohibited from lobbying the president about pardons, as happened prior to commutation of the sentence of the Jewish underground convicts and other instances. This practice is untenable, as it introduces political considerations into the pardon, emptying it of its humanitarian content and undermining the presidential stature.

3.4 Does Israel Need the Institution of President?

Many proposals have emerged over the years for changing – expanding or contracting – the duties and powers of the president. Some have even called for eliminating the institution of president. These demands intensified after the scandal leading to the resignation of President Weizman and more so after the imprisonment of President Katzav on criminal offenses. The status of the institution was undermined further during the campaign for the election of the tenth president in 2014. This campaign was held under the shadow of suspicion of corruption and misconduct of several candidates and two decided to withdraw their candidacy.

Those who advocate eliminating the presidency argue that the institution lacks practical purpose or authority and is wasteful. The power of the president is only a sham, they say, because the president's decisions are not independent, but based on the binding recommendations of others: the accrediting of ambassadors, the appointment of judges, pardons, and the signature on laws that have already been ratified by the relevant minister (Polas 1992; Kimche 1992). In this view, the financial cost of the presidency does not justify the symbolic benefit, and if there is a need for such symbolic tasks, the Speaker of the Knesset, the prime minister, or one of the ministers can serve this function and save the expense to the state (the budget of the President's Bureau in 2016 was NIS 58 million [roughly $1.8 million], including ongoing expenses of former presidents). Opponents also claim that the president represents only a fleeting balance of power in the Knesset, and therefore cannot fulfill the presumed unifying function.

Others, however, advocate expanding the symbolic authority of the president, for example, that the president serve as commander in chief of the IDF and appoint – on the recommendations of the government – the chief of staff, chief of police, attorney general, and others. And some want to bestow practical powers on the president – to initiate state commissions of inquiry, or at least appoint its members; to head the Judges' Selection Committee; to head social and economic councils, and more. At the constitutional level, it was proposed that the president be accorded some of the powers given to presidents in similar regimes, such as the power to dissolve the Knesset in extenuating circumstances, to send a law back to the Knesset for further deliberation (so that the president would serve as a kind of "second, restraining house"), or to call for a national referendum.[18] To strengthen the legitimacy of the institution and increase trust in the president, it was also proposed that the president be chosen by direct election of all the citizens. This, in our opinion, is a

[17] A bill to this effect was tabled in the Knesset in 2001, which included a minimum of seven years of incarceration before a life sentence can be commuted (Negbi 2004, 159).

[18] For further examples, see Yaron 1973, 5.

populist proposal, inconsistent with the practice of similar regimes in which the stature of the president is firm even though he or she is elected by parliament. In Israel, we recommend continuation of the current practice – that the president be elected by the Knesset representatives – not only to avoid adding yet another divisive election, but above all to prevent a situation in which the president is chosen by a small number or a tiny majority of the population.

In our view, the institution of the president, which represents the state more than any other political institution, is of singular importance. This is the main reason that it has lasted for so many years and in so many different forms in democratic countries. In Israel, because of the social fragmentation, which is also reflected in the composition of the Knesset, a president is even more important. The presidency serves a bridging function, and therefore the ceremonial and symbolic powers of the institution should be expanded (e.g., choosing the winners of the Israel Prize). At the same time, one should guard against giving executive powers to the president, because this could undermine the essence of the institution and harm its unifying function.

3.5 The Future of the Institution of the President

Over the years, the office of the president in Israel generally fulfilled its function well, especially in comparison with other political institutions, and is worthy of praise. Although the early resignations of Ezer Weizman, the conviction of Moshe Katzav, and the acrimonious personal campaign for the presidency waged in 2014 stemmed from the behavior of individuals, these affairs cast a long shadow on the institution and election to it. Because of its symbolic character, the presidency is largely shaped by the individual in office, perhaps more than other institutions, and comparable to the Speaker of the Knesset. In Israel, the office of the president also comes in for criticism, but the general picture has been of a relatively high level of public trust. In the years 2003–6, for example, the average trust in the president was 68 percent, dropping to 22 percent in 2007 with the revelations of suspicions against President Katzav. It rose to a high of over 70 percent on average during President Peres's term of office (2007–14) and President Rivlin's first year (Hermann et al. 2011–15: 2015, 86).

The stability of the presidency is even more important in the face of the fluctuations in the political system since the 1980s, and the changes in the system of governance – instituting and then repealing the direct election of the prime minister. These shocks to the system changed the constellation of political parties in Israel, the status of the Knesset, and the steering capacity of the government, and they were also felt in the Supreme Court. The stature of the presidency was relatively less affected, perhaps because this institution had become a necessity during times of political turmoil. The presidency is also of singular importance because of the complicated weave of Israeli society. The secret of its power is its ability to be the most "Israeli" in the eyes of all the social groups in Israel – distant from the other branches of government, but still linked to their activity. The president does not take sides in disputes, but is not cut off from events, and may express opinions in a way that is appropriate for the position.

For the presidency to optimally fulfill its symbolic role, it must stand apart from the social and political bickering as much as possible. Therefore, a president should not come to office directly from representing a party in the Knesset, nor return to the political arena at the conclusion of the presidential term. To that end, it is recommended that legislation set a cooling off period *prior to* election as president, so that a serving MK cannot be a candidate for the job. In this respect, the novelty in the 2014 election was the two non-political and the two women candidates. A longer cooling off period should be required for a president before assuming any political role after completion of the presidential term. This will expand the range of candidates, both in terms of their personal background and the life experiences they bring to the role of president of Israel.

4 The Knesset: First among Equals?

4.1 The Parliament in a Parliamentary Democracy and in Israel

Israel is a member of the family of parliamentary democracies. In every democracy the people are sovereign, and what distinguishes one democracy from another is the institution in which the people place their trust for embodying that sovereignty. In a parliamentary system, trust is placed in the house of representatives elected by the people; in a presidential system, it is divided between the president and the house of representatives. To be sure, there is no one "correct" form of government, as the system is intended to suit the political temperament and serve the needs of that society. The form of government also determines the division of functions among the institutions: In a parliamentary system, the separation of powers means three main things: the supremacy of the parliament in the political system, which includes oversight of the executive branch; partial overlap between the legislative and executive branches; and a separation between these two branches and the judiciary. The belief that the three branches are of equal standing is alien to a parliamentary system, in which the government rules by virtue of the trust placed in it by the parliament, and is subordinate to that parliament.

In a parliamentary democracy, the institution of parliament is rife with contradictions. On the one hand, it has tremendous power: Montesquieu feared that a parliament would appropriate all the authority, leaving the other branches powerless. On the other hand, the parliament seems weak and ineffectual, a rubber stamp for the executive branch, which initiates legislation, enacts regulations, and implements policy. These contradictions are more comprehensible if we look at the parliament's main task in a parliamentary democracy – forming the government from within its own ranks and bestowing upon it support – a vote of confidence or no-confidence, as the case may be. It could happen, of course, that the body established by the parliament and endowed with its trust will rise up against its creator and limit the parliament's ability to act independently. Parliaments in western democracies are generally reactive – they do not initiate most of the legislation, and have difficulty opposing specific initiatives of the government. Parliaments deal with larger issues, and serve primarily as an arena for debating bills and clarifying policy, without taking an active role in shaping it. However, there are also proactive parliaments that do take an active role in legislation and policymaking, and this power diminishes the government's room for maneuver (Mezey 1979).

In Israel, the Knesset is the only inclusive, representative body, and therefore it is the Knesset, not any other institution, that embodies sovereignty. The Knesset is a unicameral legislature with 120 members elected by the public in general elections that are national, direct, equal, secret, and proportional. As emphasized in Chapter 2, the Knesset is an incarnation of the institutions of the Zionist movement and of the provisional bodies established at the same time as the state. Its name comes from the "Great Knesset [assembly]" during the period of the Second Temple (approximately 530 BCE to 70 CE).[1] An MK's term of office is four years, although the Knesset has the authority to dissolve itself earlier.[2] The Knesset, because it is elected by and represents the public, is also the institution that gives legitimacy to other political institutions – it shapes the corpus of law by which the judiciary judges; based on the Knesset's vote of confidence, the government is able to govern; the president of the state and the state comptroller are elected by the Knesset; and it is the forum where public political life in the state is conducted. In the absence of a written constitution and as the only inclusive representative body in the state, the Knesset is virtually all-powerful and can enact any law it wishes. In the words of MK Yizhar Harari, "If it wishes, it changes the law; if it wishes, it changes the foundations of the state. If it wants a president, there will be a president, if it wants a government of one type or another, it will have a government of one type or another."[3]

In practice, the power of the Knesset is moderated by the Basic Laws, the courts, the separation of powers, and various political processes. The system of democratic representation prevents the Knesset from being homogeneous, although theoretically the public could elect all 120 representatives from one party even in free elections. Within the Knesset are factions, a coalition and opposition, representatives of diverse views and interests, backbenchers, frontbenchers, MKs who toe the line of those who put them into office, and MKs who follow their own conscience. This mosaic, renewed at every election, is what makes the Knesset the most representative body in Israeli society, though definitely not the only one. The fragmented composition of the Israeli Knesset has led to the (so far) ongoing need for a coalition that can provide a stable majority to the government in power. A parliamentary coalition means consent to party discipline, which limits an MK's ability to act independently. We will expand on this in Chapter 11 when we discuss coalitions.

In Israel, as in many democratic countries, the Knesset is subject to judicial review by the Supreme Court, which, in the absence of a constitution, has over time become the most significant institutional constraint on the power of both the legislative and executive branches, preventing them from doing as they will. The Knesset does not operate in a vacuum, and is influenced by the activity of interest groups, the media, and lobbyists. Nevertheless, by virtue of the elections, it is the public that

1 The number derives from the number of members in the Great Knesset or, according to tradition, 12 tribes × 10 in a *minyan* – the minimum number for communal worship = 120. In the Constitution Committee of the Provisional Government, proposals were considered for having a smaller number of seats in the Knesset (Warhaftig 1988, 94–95).

2 There are also other ways to shorten the Knesset's term. The Knesset can extend its term of office in extenuating circumstances, and this happened twice: The Provisional Government delayed elections from October 1948 to January 1949; and the eighth Knesset postponed elections from October to December 1973 because of the Yom Kippur War. This was anchored in law in 2007 in an amendment to the Basic Law: The Knesset.

3 Knesset Protocols, deliberations of the Basic Law: The Knesset, October 8, 1956, p. 4.

bestows power upon the Knesset, and ultimately judges the deeds and performance of its members. In a democratic system, the most effective sanction on parliamentary activity is public opinion, with the verdict pronounced every election day.

The Knesset elected in 2015 was the twentieth, thus since the first election on January 25, 1949, the average Knesset has lasted about three and a half years. During these decades, the power and status of the Knesset have undergone profound changes.

4.2 Changes in the Status and Functioning of the Knesset

From the very beginning, the Israeli political system managed to channel the major disputes from the pre-state period into the parliament, which became the main forum for public discourse and grappling with the key issues. However, the Knesset was under the hegemony of the labor movement and Mapai, the dominant political party, thus parliamentary discourse was constrained and circumscribed, and Knesset members were bound by party discipline. The government could rely on a stable and disciplined majority in its parliamentary coalition, and in this sense it was the government that kept an eye on the Knesset, not vice versa. The ministers, for example, would show up at Knesset committees in order to set forth the government's position, ensuring that this was the view that would prevail (S. Shenhav 2003, 243–49). A study of Knesset legislation in the first decade reveals that only 11 percent originated as private members' bills (103 in the first four Knessets compared to 932 proposed by the government). No motions of no-confidence were submitted in the first Knesset, and all told only forty-two in the three Knessets that followed.

In the 1960s, the status and scope of activity of the Knesset began to shift, harbingers of the erosion of Mapai's hegemony in the wake of the Lavon affair. During those turbulent days, MKs used the Knesset's Foreign Affairs and Defense Committee to lash out at the party in power and mobilize multiparty parliamentary opposition to it (Yanai 1982, 111–15). This strengthened the Knesset, exemplified by increased oversight of the defense system at the end of the Ben-Gurion era, and later the formation of a unity government on the eve of the 1967 war. In parallel, the number of private members' bills rose sharply to 566 in the three subsequent Knessets (1961–73) – compared to 103 in the first four Knessets; many more no-confidence motions (seventy-six) were also submitted in this period.

The years following the 1967 war dramatically transformed the political system. The 1973 election in the shadow of the Yom Kippur War undermined the standing of the labor movement, whose loss of the 1977 election sounded the final chord of the era of one dominant party. The orderly change of the governing leadership proved that the Knesset was a stable political institution that could both absorb the change and withstand the lurching. This dramatic transformation (the "upheaval") also strengthened the opposition as a viable alternative to the ruling coalition. In the late 1970s, the Knesset was a decisive arena in the historic decision that crossed party lines – the peace agreements with Egypt – and this shored up its position as the body representing the sovereign political power in Israel (Diskin and Galnoor 1990, 710–17).

Since the 1980s, government coalitions have either been very broad (the unity governments in 1984–88, 1988–90, and 1999–2003) or quite narrow (Begin's coalition in 1981–83; Shamir's in 1990–92; Rabin's in 1992–95; and Netanyahu's in 1996–99).[4] These fluctuations left their mark on the Knesset. The parity between the two political blocs as well as the unity governments' ongoing fear of dissolution together served to buttress the power of the small and medium-sized parties, giving every Knesset member critical influence. Unity governments (with two-thirds of the Knesset members in the coalition) also weakened the Knesset as a body since a large number of MKs serve in the government as ministers or vice ministers.[5] There were incidents of members deserting their parties, breaches of faction discipline, and excessive individualism of Knesset members.[6] The eleventh and twelth Knessets (1984–88 and 1988–92) showed a significant increase in parliamentary activity: 314 motions of no-confidence in the government, as opposed to 209 in the ten previous Knessets combined; in the twelfth Knesset alone, 1,491 private members' bills were submitted as opposed to 243 government bills. How the unity government was brought down in 1990 and replaced by a narrow, Likud-led coalition was a low point in Knesset history.

The 1990s saw the beginning of internal primaries in several parties as well as direct election of the prime minister in 1996. The effect on the Knesset of these two developments was paradoxical: Institutionally the Knesset was weakened, while individual MKs – and well-organized factions like Shas (an ultra-Orthodox party) – gained power. Another change, common to many democracies, was the rise of the politics of personality (Rahat and Kenig, forthcoming), reflected in the Knesset by a total smaller than the sum of its parts – individual MKs working frantically to attract media and public attention, with dubious political effectiveness, while the parties struggled to carry out their parliamentary functions. The result: weakening of the institutional impact of the Knesset. The 1990s also saw a huge increase in the indicators of individual parliamentary activity, such as individually initiated legislation, with thousands of private members' bills submitted in each Knesset (over 4,000). Although only a small portion of these were enacted into law (6% on average in the twelfth through seventeenth Knessets), almost half the total bills tabled in the twelfth through eighteenth Knessets were private members' bills (more about this below).

The most troubling phenomenon was the sharp decline in public esteem of the Knesset and its members. In the 1990s and 2000s, the institution of the Knesset was at the bottom of the scale of public trust: Only a third of the public felt it could place its trust in the Knesset, and only one out of ten believed that the Knesset as an institution protects democracy in the best way possible (Arian et al. 2005–10: 2010, 89). In 2014, trust in the Knesset remained low at 35 percent (Hermann et al. 2011–15: 2014, 61).

[4] The coalition formed by Barak in 1999 was broad, but brief. This was also true of Sharon's coalition in 2001, which had originally included the Labor Party, but narrowed after Labor resigned.

[5] In 2014 the Knesset enacted the Governance Law, a series of proposed amendments to the Basic Law: Government and Basic Law: The Knesset. Among other things, the amendments proposed limiting the number of government ministers to nineteen (including the prime minister), limiting the number of deputy ministers to four, disallowing the appointment of ministers without portfolios, and raising the election threshold of parties to the Knesset to 3.25 percent. See www.knesset.gov.il/committees/heb/material/data/H29-08-2013_10-03-05_512.pdf and www.knesset.gov.il/committees/heb/material/data/H29-08-2013_10-05-00_515.pdf [in Hebrew] (accessed September 13, 2014).

[6] This was already evident in the ninth Knesset, 1977, which began with thirteen parties and ended with twenty, primarily because of the splintering of Dash (Democratic Movement for Change).

The gap between the role of the Knesset as the backbone of the political system and its low public stature raises questions about how the Knesset can fulfill its task as a trusted servant of the sovereign.

4.3 The Constitutional Infrastructure

As we described in Chapter 2, a proclamation issued on May 14, 1948 declared that "The Provisional State Council shall be the legislative authority." Its powers were set out in the Law and Administration Ordinance (1948). The Provisional State Council concluded its work upon election of the Constituent Assembly in 1949, which was assigned the task of writing a constitution to be based upon the precepts of the Declaration of Independence. The Constituent Assembly enacted the Transition Law (1949) and converted itself into the first legislature. According to this law, "The legislature of the State of Israel shall be called the Knesset." The first Basic Law, passed in 1958, is The Basic Law: The Knesset, which states, "The Knesset is the legislature of the State." The key articles in this law define the system of elections (which can be changed only by a majority of sixty-one MKs); the right to vote and be elected; persons who are disqualified from running for the Knesset; and the establishment of permanent committees and a parliamentary Commission of Inquiry. Another article bans the participation in elections of party lists and candidates who negate the existence of Israel as a Jewish and democratic state, incite to racism, support the armed struggle of an enemy state or terror organization against Israel, or travel to an enemy state. Articles have recently been added that define the law regarding an MK convicted of a crime involving moral turpitude or sentenced to prison. Other articles seek to prevent changes of the law through emergency regulations and prohibit the Knesset from extending its term of office. Despite this being a Basic Law, it was amended forty-one times until 2014 in response to changing circumstances.

Ever since its founding, Israel has maintained a legal state of emergency. Until 1996, the declaration of a state of emergency was not brought to the Knesset for approval. Now in accordance with Article 38 of the Basic Law: Government, this declaration is within the authority of the Knesset – at its own initiative or the suggestion of the government – and every year the Knesset declares that the state of emergency persists.[7] The Basic Law: Government also defines the power of the Knesset vis-à-vis the government – a vote of confidence upon presentation of the government members (Article 13D) and the authority to express no confidence in it (Article 28).

The Knesset Law (1994) describes the working procedures of the Knesset and its committees, election of the Speaker, the method of setting an MK's wages, rules for dissolving parliamentary factions, and more. In 2000, the status of the leader of the opposition was established by this law – an MK from the largest party in the opposition or one with the support of a majority of opposition MKs. The Statute of Knesset Operations is the formal legal guidebook according to which the daily life of the Knesset and its committees are conducted – the procedures of meetings, setting of the agenda, proceedings in legislation, and ethical rules. Other rules relevant to

[7] In 2004, the Knesset rebelled and extended the state of emergency for only half a year because of the government's refusal to remove several laws and regulations from the list to which the state of emergency applied. *Israel State Records*, Government Notices 5301, May 31, 2004, p. 3006 [in Hebrew].

the Knesset are the Knesset Building and its Compound Law (1968), which secures the place of work of the legislators, and the Knesset Members Immunity, Rights and Duties Law (1951), which will be discussed separately in this chapter.

The aforementioned laws and other laws regulating the work of the Knesset will be discussed below in the context of the three main functions of the Knesset as a parliament: representation, legislation, and oversight of the executive branch.

4.4 The First Role of the Knesset – Representation

A. The Essence of Representation

Representation is the raison d'être of the legislature; without it there is no meaning to the concept of the rule of the people, or democracy. The Knesset is not and cannot be a replica of society. The tapestry of a society comes in many colors – cultural identities, organizational affiliation, geographic distribution, etc. But the *political* weave of the social tapestry must be reflected in the Knesset, so that the diverse world views and public interests are represented there. On the presumption of full political equality, the Knesset is a "true reflection" of the political will of the citizens and groups (or at least those who bothered to vote), as ascertained periodically by the election results. The Knesset is not the sole arena where society's diverse components operate – there is also the economic market or civil society – but it is the only one that can lay claim to the crown of political representativeness, as reaffirmed at every election.

The electoral system in Israel in which the entire state is one electoral district, with an emphasis on proportional representation and party lists, strongly enhances the representativeness of the Knesset. The group photo on election day reflects the political components of society, as even relatively small groups are invited to try their hand at being elected. Most western democracies with a parliamentary system and proportional representation have an election threshold of 4 percent or more (for example, Sweden – 4%; Germany – 5%; New Zealand – 5%). Until recently, Israel had been on the lower end of the election threshold (2%), alongside Denmark (2%) and the Netherlands (0.67%) (Kenig 2007, 2015). In the 2015 election, the threshold was raised to 3.25 percent and a minimum of 136,854 votes were required for entry into the Knesset.

During the period when parties were almost the only institutions in the political system, the composition of the Knesset was considered a snapshot of society, thus a standard for distributing power and resources in social, economic, and professional institutions. Indeed, the composition of bodies vastly different from each other was designed to be fully or partially reflective of the distribution of Knesset seats. These included the Jewish Agency's Board of Governors, the Plenum of the Israel Broadcasting Authority, the Student Union with its elections based on party lists, and even the Trustees of the Israel Soccer Association. In the 1950s, even players for Israel's national soccer team were selected in accordance with their party-affiliated sports clubs – Hapoel, Maccabi, and Beitar. This arrangement – referred to as "the party key" in Israeli political jargon – was born in the pre-state period and suited well the hegemony of Mapai. When the composition of the Knesset is the only "correct" overall division of society, politics reigns supreme and the government has more options for centralizing its control, while glossing over social heterogeneity and discriminating against those not represented by the parties. The party key system continued for about two decades after Israel's establishment, and began to dissipate in the mid-1960s, when Israeli society grew and changed, and Mapai's power began to ebb. Certainly copying the system of party representation into public institutions and organizations hemmed in their ability to operate professionally and deal with issues according to other criteria – such as regional diversity – which could conceivably have been more appropriate.

With the changes in the structure and standing of the parties (see Chapter 9 on parties), especially since the early 1990s with adoption of the primaries and the electoral system change, the perception of representation was also transformed: Although Knesset members are still chosen according to party lists, party representation has diminished, and MKs have begun to see themselves as personal, sectoral, or geographical representatives.

B. Knesset Factions and Knesset Members

In taking the oath of office for the Knesset, the member pledges "to bear allegiance to the State of Israel and faithfully discharge *my mission* in the Knesset." What is that mission? Do MKs represent the party on whose list they were elected, the interests of their constituents, personal considerations, or the larger public interest? Is the MK a public representative or a representative of a specific public?[8] The dilemma rooted in the nature of representation applies not just to members of the Knesset, but also to the party: Is it the mandate of the party to promote the interests of its constituents without taking into consideration the good of all, or must it take a broader view of the public interest? Parties that aspire to be part of the government must weigh the immediate interests of their constituents together with general, long-term interests, if only to widen their circle of supporters. The dilemma is even more acute in the small parties – a kind of interest group with a homogeneous set of constituents – between the specific interests of their voters and broader considerations. Hence members of the Knesset face an ongoing struggle between their mission and loyalties, on the one hand (with potential conflicts between the party line and faction discipline), and considerations of conscience and the public weal, on the other.

In the past, the prime loyalty of most MKs was to their party, and they hearkened to its directives both because of their ideological commitment and their dependence on it, if they wanted to be included again in the list of candidates. The fading power of the parties led to electoral considerations becoming more personal; thus, together with party affinity, the decisive considerations for a candidate are the interests of his or her constituents. Electoral considerations are a legitimate and necessary part of politics – parties or candidates not elected remain outside the political game, and their constituents will not be represented.

In addition to representing specific world views and interests, what determines the behavior of the Knesset faction and the character of the MKs' activity these days is their image in the media and social channels, and the feedback from voters as

[8] The ethical code in the Statute of Knesset Operations states that the Knesset member is "a trustee of the public, and his duty is to represent the public that voted for him in a manner that will serve human dignity, the advancement of society, and the good of the State; he shall assiduously act in accordance with the laws of the State, and shall work to advance the principle of the rule of law."

reflected in opinion polls. Some MKs draw support from voters who do not censure or sanction them for seeing to the interests only of those in their circle; and some win support for their activities on behalf of the general public interest. In either case, party fragmentation and the fact that the government is a coalition tend to moderate (not always, of course) the exclusive representation of narrow interests. Although all parties work for the good of their voters, they find it necessary to compromise when faced with parties that are also working for the good of *their* own voters. So that representing the good of the public is not embodied at the level of parties and individual MKs, but, it is hoped, at the level of the Knesset as a whole.

C. Does Representation Mean Reflecting Certain Groups in Society?

To have a precisely accurate representation of the entire society, each and every person would have to be a member of parliament. Therefore, as noted, the Knesset is neither a replica of society nor a photograph of it in miniature. In politics, a completely accurate reflection of the makeup of the population is not possible, and therefore the Knesset reflects the relative power of groups in society who win representation at a given time. For many years, certain groups were under-represented in the Knesset (women, Arabs, Mizrahim [Jews originating from Muslim countries], while other groups were over-represented (men, Ashkenazim [Jews of European descent], Jews, kibbutz members). An examination of the changes over the years in the representation of various groups in the Knesset reflects the changes in Israeli society. The under-representation of women is the most striking over the years, despite some improvement: From the first to the thirteenth Knesset (1949–92), the number of women MKs ranged from eight to twelve. Since then, a moderate increase can be discerned, and in the twentieth Knesset (2015), women make up over a quarter (27%) of MKs (see Table 4.1). This ratio is among the lowest of parliaments in democracies.

The most significant improvement can be seen in the representation of Mizrahi Jews (first and second generation): The first Knesset had fewer than 3 percent Mizrahim, but a quarter of the MKs were Mizrahim in 2009, and about a third in 2013 and in 2015. The percentage is higher if only Jewish MKs are counted. Some of this change is related to the electoral success of the Shas Party, most of whose voters and members are Mizrahim. The representation of Arabs has also grown, but is still not commensurate with their proportion in the population of those eligible to vote. In 2013 the Knesset had twelve Arab and Druze members (10%) and in 2015 there were seventeen (14%), not all of whom were elected from Arab parties.[9]

Most voters who are Orthodox Jews, Arabs, or immigrants from the former Soviet Union tend to vote for their "own" parties. Hence the growing trend to think of Knesset representation in "tribal" terms: religious-ethnic-nationalist (S. Ilan 2000). Although it is common to count the number of MKs in these categories to test for representativeness, in practice the sectors in Israel do not vote homogeneously – this is true not only of women and Mizrahim, but the religious and Arabs also cast

[9] For information about previous Knesset members, see Brichta 2001; for more recent MKs, see the Knesset website: www.knesset.gov.il/mk/eng/Individual_Find_eng.asp (accessed October 16, 2017).

Table 4.1 *Number of women elected to the Knesset (1996–2015)*

Knesset (year)	Number of women
14 (1996)	14
15 (1999)	17
16 (2003)	25
17 (2006)	17
18 (2009)	22
19 (2013)	27
20 (2015)	32

Numbers alter during the Knesset term because of changes in the MKs.

Source: http://knesset.gov.il/main/eng/home.asp (accessed October 16, 2017).

their votes for diverse parties. The question is whether sharing the same identity as a particular constituency is enough to guarantee that the interests of that group are represented. For example, did the increased number of Mizrahim in the Knesset narrow the gaps between Mizrahim and Ashkenazim? Did the increased proportion of Arab MKs transform them into legitimate partners in a coalition, or improve the situation of Arabs in Israel? Not necessarily. Representation in terms of the presence of members of a specific group in the Knesset does not ensure concern for their interests, because a direct link does not necessarily exist between the identity of the MKs (women, Mizrahim, Arabs, etc.) and their legislative activity (A. Ben-Arieh 2001).[10]

Public opinion also suggests that representation, even when it reflects the makeup of society, does not guarantee that the interests of a particular public will be represented: Over half the public (57%) believe that the distribution of power in the Knesset does reflect – to some or a large extent – the diversity of views in society at large; and yet some two-thirds believe that MKs do not properly represent those who voted for them (Arian et al. 2005–10: 2008).

D. Representation in the Knesset and the Parties

If the aspiration is that the Knesset reflect the makeup of a population as accurately as possible, it would be necessary to set quotas and institute an affirmative action program for those sectors defined as under-represented. Who will define these sectors, and how? Such a system would be arbitrary and contrary to democratic principles, according to which the makeup of the parliament is determined by the choice of the public. It is the voters, not the legislators, who create the mosaic of their legislature. Indeed, a mechanism like this would discriminate against new groups who are not assigned quotas. The belief, for example, that a

[10] The Ben-Arieh study (2001) found no connection between religiosity, ethnicity, or residence in development towns and the activity of MKs on social issues – both on the formal level of legislation and the informal level of responsiveness to personal appeals of citizens. Ben-Arieh found that the MKs most active in social issues were women from left-wing parties.

party representing pensioners would never make it to the Knesset was confounded in the 2006 election.

Therefore, a more effective way to ensure broader representation might be accomplished by ensuring the due representation of women, Mizrahim, new immigrants, Arabs, etc. on the party lists of candidates.[11] This trend is visible in the larger parties, as they guarantee places in the primaries to specific groups, thus aspiring to become an aggregator of diverse interests. Parties are considered aggregators of interests if, in hopes of becoming a ruling party, they compromise and blur their messages enough to avoid identification with particular groups and their interests. Most of the smaller parties became an extension of specific interest groups. In 2006, twelve parties were represented in the Knesset, but only three – Kadima, Labor, and Likud (which together won 46% of the total votes and sixty Knesset seats) – were aggregators of diverse interests. The 2009 Knesset had a similar makeup, though the power of the interest aggregating parties grew (Kadima, Likud, and Labor combined won sixty-eight seats, or 56% of the total). In 2013 the power of the aggregating parties declined slightly (Likud, Labor, Kadima, and Yesh Atid combined won fifty-five seats, or 46% of the total). In 2015 it grew to seventy-five seats (58%) because, in addition to Likud and Labor, there were two parties in the center – Yesh Atid and Kulanu.

The other parties represented specific groups in society – Arabs, the Orthodox, the ultra-Orthodox, settlers, immigrants. One might wonder which Knesset would be more representative: one composed of a party for each group and specific sectors, or a Knesset in which most parties have a broad platform with *internal* representation of sectors and groups. If for a moment we ignore the question of which groups are actually represented – and especially which are not – it can be said that a "sectoral Knesset" is more representative in terms of the specific groups, but less representative in terms of having a broad view and social concerns that cut across the sectors. A sectoral Knesset is also problematic in terms of its steering capacity, as will be seen below. In addition, it is not clear whether sectoral representation moderates the social rifts or exacerbates them. It may well be the case that sectoral parties, which seek to maintain their power among their constituents, may actually prefer to sharpen the differences and increase discord.

E. Over-Representation and Steering Capacity

Steering requires balance between the representativeness of the legislature and the political system's ability to function effectively and discharge its duties. Israel's system of strict proportional representation combined with a comparatively low election threshold (3.25%) leads to fragmented representation in the Knesset. Because of its electoral system, the Knesset, through its parties, can well represent various groups in society and give them voice. This is a valuable asset because the system is well suited for Israeli society, riven by internal social divisions. Having these divisions

[11] In the primaries, for example, the Likud Party reserves spots 10, 20, 24, 29, and 34 for women, spot 25 for non-Jewish candidates, and spot 30 for new immigrants (see www.newlikud.org/#!primaries/c1pck [in Hebrew]). In the 2013 Labor primaries, the reserved spots are 5, 9, 14, 19, 24, 29, 34, 36, 39, 42, and 45 for women, 18 and 26 for minorities (Arabs and Druze), and 20 for new immigrants (see the Labor Party constitution at www.havoda.org.il/wp-content/uploads/2016/03/Constitution.pdf [in Hebrew] (accessed June 4, 2016).

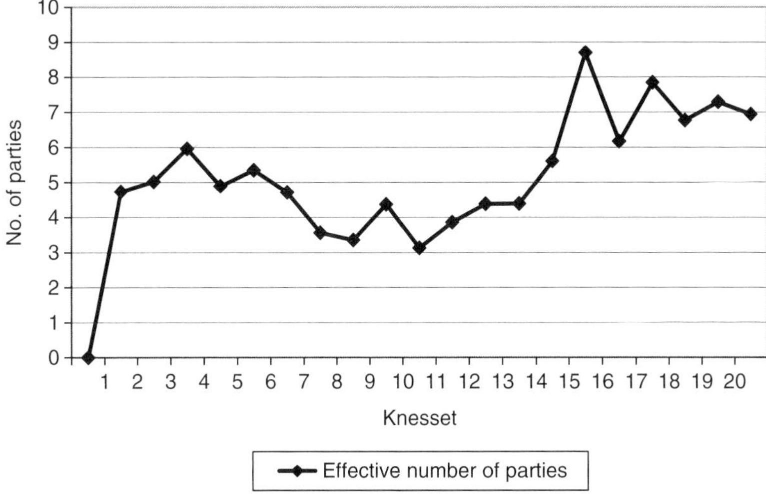

Figure 4.1 The effective number of parties in Knessets 1–20 (1949–2015)
Source: Data provided courtesy of Dr. Ofer Kenig.

represented in the parliament is supposed to channel social tensions into the political system in order to reach compromise and forge consensus among the parties.

The Index of the Effective Number of Parties is an in-depth analysis of the fragmentation of representativeness: Fragmentation decreases with fewer and larger parties, and vice versa.[12] When applied to the Knesset, the Index (Figure 4.1) shows that fragmentation increased over the years, especially during the period of direct election, when voters took advantage of the opportunity to split their vote: one ballot for a party and the other to the candidate for prime minister. Fragmentation was at its lowest in the tenth Knesset (1981) election. Since then, because of the disappearance of the dominant party and the change of governing party, fragmentation again increased and reached a high point during the fifteenth Knesset (1999) election. Over the past decade, many small or medium-sized parties were elected to the Knesset, unlike the first three decades of the state when there was one dominant party, and the 1980s with two large, equally powerful parties. In the sixteenth Knesset election (2003), the fragmentation index decreased after the system of direct election of the prime minister was rescinded, but in 2006, it again rose when the largest party (Kadima) won only twenty-nine seats, the second largest (Labor) won nineteen, and ten small parties won no more than twelve seats each. To prevent parliamentary factions from splitting and MKs from breaking away during the Knesset term, the Knesset Law was amended in 2004 (Amendment 18) to impede such actions. Until 2008, the law allowed faction splitting only if a third of the MKs in the faction were willing to do so (indicating a real crisis within the party). In 2008,

[12] The Index of the Effective Number of Parties [N] weights the number of parties in the parliament and their relative size, and indicates the level of fragmentation in the parliament. The index is calculated according to the following formula:

$$N = \frac{1}{\sum s_i^2} \quad (S_i \text{ is the ratio of Knesset seats of the 1 party})$$

the Knesset Law was amended to allow factions to split even if the breakaway MKs constituted less than a third, provided there were at least seven. The Governance Law, passed in 2014, reinstated the previous method – allowing MKs to form new factions only if they constitute a third or more of the current faction. In 2009, fragmentation somewhat decreased because the five largest parties together won ninety-four seats and the remaining seven parties won three to five seats each, but it still remained high. In 2013, fragmentation increased and in 2015, the effective number of parties decreased somewhat to 6.94.

Greater fragmentation naturally hinders steering ability. When there is fragmentation, the coalition finds it hard to enforce party discipline for votes and decisions, and the government is forced to recruit support for its activities, sometimes from opposition parties. We already noted one result of this situation – the rising power of individual MKs and well-organized factions, while the institutional power of the Knesset wanes. Small, sectoral parties competing with each other for extremist positions also make an appearance in a more fragmented Knesset.

4.5 The Second Role of the Knesset – Legislation

A. The Hierarchy of Legislation

The Knesset is the legislature, and no other governance institution is authorized to enact state laws. Although not explicitly anchored in law, there is a legislative hierarchy among laws, as follows:[13]

- Heading the hierarchy are the *Basic Laws* – the Knesset enacts these according to the "Harari Decision" and by virtue of its legacy as a constituent assembly.[14] The status of the Basic Laws is inferior to that of a constitution, and in some respects superior to ordinary laws. Some Basic Laws (The Government and Freedom of Occupation) are entrenched, while some articles in other Basic Laws are also entrenched, i.e., they can be changed only by a special majority of sixty-one members of the Knesset. Some Basic Laws have a "stability" clause protecting them from emergency legislation, and can be violated only for a purpose deemed worthy.
- *Ordinary legislation* – laws passed in the Knesset with a simple majority that can be changed by a simple majority.
- *Secondary legislation* – regulations set by government ministries. These enable implementation of the law and require only the signature of the relevant minister. Regulations that set criminal penalties require the approval of a Knesset committee.
- *Emergency Regulations* – during a state of emergency as declared by the Knesset, the government is authorized to impose emergency regulations for purposes of defending the state, protecting public security, and ensuring the provision of vital supplies and services. Such regulations can temporarily suspend any law (except laws and articles specifically protected from this) and can impose taxes or levies. They expire within three months unless extended by law.

[13] See Chapter 2 on the attempts to anchor this hierarchy in the proposed Basic Law: Legislation.

[14] Is every Knesset a constituent assembly? See the Bank Mizrahi ruling: *United Mizrahi Bank v. Migdal Cooperative Village* 1995. Also see Rubinstein and Medina 1996, 369–74.

- *The Budget Law* – the Budget Law is unique among laws as it is valid for only one year (or for two years, on and off since 2009), and sets out details of the government's expenditures and estimated revenues. The Budget Law passes with a simple majority; failing to pass it within three months of the start of the budget year is equivalent to a vote of no-confidence in the government.

B. The Legislative Process

A law can originate in one of three sources: the government, a Knesset committee, or a member of the Knesset. A proposed bill comes up in the plenary for three readings, each with a different purpose. A private member's bill – one initiated by an MK – must also go through a preliminary reading. If it passes, it is sent to a Knesset committee to prepare it for the first reading. The first reading is a general discussion about the nature of the law and the need for it, concluding in a vote to accept or reject the bill. Acceptance moves it to the appropriate Knesset committee. The second reading is a specific discussion of each article in the proposed bill as formulated by the committee. At this stage, MKs can submit reservations on which votes will be taken in the plenary. The third reading is the vote on the final text of the bill. Every law must be signed by the minister charged with its implementation and by the president, the prime minister, and the Speaker of the Knesset, after which it is published in Israel's State Records.

C. Legislation Initiated by the Government or by Private Members

In a parliamentary democracy, the vast majority of bills are usually initiated by the government, while a minority are private members' bills. This had also been true in Israel until the late 1980s, when even some private members' bills were initiated by government ministries, which preferred for party-related and other reasons to have them tabled as private members' bills. Since 1992 this dynamic has been reversed, as evident in Table 4.2, and the proportion of laws passed in Israel that began as private members' bills is now the highest of any parliamentary democracy, amounting to virtually half of all the laws. In the first twelve Knessets, an average of 15 percent of the laws passed originated as private members' bills; in 1992–2006, some 50 percent of the laws originated as private members' bills. In the eighteenth Knesset, 281 private members' bills (47%) were enacted into law versus 316 government bills (53%).[15] In the nineteenth Knesset, 112 (42%) of the 265 bills passed originated as private members' bills. The sharp rise in the number of private members' bills is even more surprising in light of the fact that the scope of legislative activity remained stable over the years.

Since the early 1990s there has been a meteoric rise in the number of private members' bills tabled in the Knesset (Figure 4.2). The total number of bills submitted in the five Knessets 1992–2009 was 3,760. As noted, only a tiny proportion (6%, on average) of these private members' bills become law, thus these bills, more than intended to become law, serve the goal of drawing attention to the hyper-activism of the MKs. This is also why, contrary to political reason, many of them are submitted by

[15] Thanks to the Knesset Archive for these data.

Table 4.2 *Ratio of private to government bills out of all bills tabled in Knessets 1–19 (1949–2015)*

Knesset	Private members' bills		Government bills		Total bills tabled
	Number	%	Number	%	
1	4	2.0	200	98.0	204
2	5	1.8	274	98.2	279
3	21	7.4	264	92.6	285
4	13	10.5	111	89.5	124
5	34	12.2	244	87.8	278
6	25	9.7	234	90.4	259
7	40	12.5	279	87.5	319
8	72	20.0	288	80.0	360
9	81	21.0	304	79.0	385
10	30	16.2	155	83.8	185
11	71	24.5	219	75.5	290
12	143	40.7	208	59.3	351
13	250	53.4	218	46.6	468
14	140	51.3	133	48.7	273
15	239	59.6	162	40.4	401
16	199	49.8	201	50.3	400
17	226	49.5	230	50.5	456
18	281	47.0	316	53.0	597
19	112	42.3	153	57.7	265

Note: The data do not include laws that originated with Knesset committees, hence the proportionate amount is based on the total of private members and government bills.

Sources: Blander and Klein 2002, 42; Knesset website and the Knesset Archive.

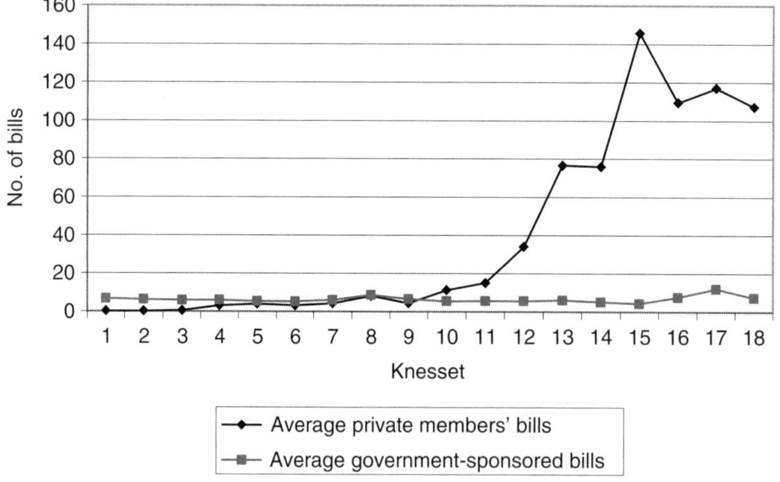

Figure 4.2 Private members' and government-sponsored bills submitted each month on average in Knessets 1–18 (1949–2013)
Source: Blander and Klein 2002. Data for Knessets 16–18 courtesy of Rivka Marcus, Knesset Archive.

members of the coalition.[16] The picture changes, however, with respect to the few private members' bills that do become law: In most cases, it was ideology that motivated the MK to persist through all the obstacles to turn the bill into law (Maor 2008, 93–94).

We have no content analysis of the differences between the two types of legislation, but we note one critical, principled difference. The government initiates legislation it believes to be necessary to advance its policies and manage the affairs of state. Most of these bills originate in ministries, which have at their disposal a large professional staff and advisers able to prepare complex legislation on matters that require expertise and knowledge. Every government bill is then formulated, and often reformulated, in the Legislation Department of the Ministry of Justice and requires the approval of the Ministerial Committee for Legislation. After this extensive process, MKs and committees often find it difficult to cope with the complexity of government bills that reach the Knesset. Neither the committees nor the MKs have adequate in-house advisers or professional support, and therefore they increasingly rely on external experts and advisers. This is especially true for government submitted bills, particularly the Budget Bill and Economic Arrangements Bill, presented to the Knesset as one unit, as the MKs and committees have insufficient time or resources to study them properly. Despite these limitations, Knesset committees do manage to introduce changes into government bills, even the budget proposal. In recent years, MKs and committees have received support from the Knesset Research and Information Center, which reviews data on legislative matters at the request of MKs. Knesset committees consult with their legal staff and receive assistance from parliamentary aides.

In private members' bills, MKs express the desires, needs, and interests of particular groups and the public that government ministries are unaware of, do not support, or do not wish to allocate resources to. These bills provide a channel for MKs to raise a different voice than that of the government, such as a voice advocating for the disadvantaged. Laws passed to ensure equal rights for people with disabilities, to take affirmative action for Arab citizens, to reintegrate the mentally disabled into the community, or the Freedom of Information Law and the amendment to the Women's Equal Rights Law – all began as private members' bills. Note that many private members' bills are initiated by extra-parliamentary groups promoting issues of importance to them. These groups provide information and professional assistance to the MKs preparing the bills, and sometimes lobby in the Knesset for their passage. Accordingly, MKs who operate as independent and responsible political entrepreneurs can enrich the process of legislation.

On the other hand, when an MK is driven only by a desire for publicity, private members' bills can devaluate the work of the parliament. Legislation is a valuable social mechanism entrusted to the legislator to use selectively and responsibly, yet the roster of private members' bills contains issues that do not reflect a seriousness of purpose. Getting into the media is not sufficient reason to submit a private bill, and MKs have many other channels for action and exposure. Knesset members also have the option of "tactical" bills – the threat of private legislation to compel the government to do something it refuses to do or is delaying. When MKs from coalition factions are party to such initiatives, they undermine the principle of collective responsibility and the stability of the government.

[16] Forty percent of the private members' bills submitted in the fourteenth Knesset were from MKs in the coalition (Blander and Klein 2002, 42).

A private member's bill that becomes law can be very expensive for the state budget. On the one hand, this is a logical and natural way for MKs to pressure the government to apply resources to new goals. On the other hand, it is the Knesset that enacts the Budget Law, hence illogical for it to make laws that exceed the ceiling on expenditures that the Knesset itself approved. In practice, these struggles between the two branches of power are familiar in all democracies. The Knesset receives from the government a complete and closed budget proposal prepared by the Finance Ministry, and does not have the ability to redesign it. Thus, budget changes made in the Finance Committee and then the Knesset plenary are usually marginal, and arrived at after extended negotiations with party representatives or sometimes ministers trying to restore lost funding to their ministries. The weakness of the coalition in recent years has forced the Knesset to negotiate over the last crumbs of budget until the very last minute, and even beyond the deadline set by law for the budget to take effect.

Sometimes MKs use private members' bills to advocate for plans that were not included in the budget. This is legitimate, as noted, except for proposals that would cost billions of shekel that are submitted impulsively or to please a narrow group of voters. Thus MKs are required to specify the funding sources for their bills and the impact on the state budget. As a result, the Basic Law: State Economy was amended in 2003 to require the support of at least fifty MKs in each reading for private members' bills that carry a price of over five million shekel a year.

D. Financial Legislation

Financial legislation is one of the most important areas of Knesset legislation. In a parliamentary system, the executive branch prepares the budget bill, the legislature enacts it into law, government ministries are charged with its implementation, and control and audit are performed by the parliament, parliamentary committees, and state comptroller. Ever since a distinction was made between the king's and the public purse, the budget became a piece of legislation, not just a document of intentions. Thus parliaments established the principle that, in democracies, there is "no taxation without representation" (only the elected body of a public is authorized to impose taxes upon them), and no expenditures without legislative authorization. According to the Basic Law: State Economy, no taxes, compulsory loans, fees, or other compulsory payments shall be imposed except by law. The executive branch also has no authority to impose taxes or change the tax rate; it is the Finance Committee, for example, that decides on any changes in subsidy rates or raising the price of electricity or water.

The Budget Law is unique because it is in force for a specified period and includes all anticipated government expenditures and estimated revenues for financing them. The law sets the framework of activity for all government ministries, and also for state involvement in society and the economy. The "budget pie" – the total amount of expenditures and their division into "slices" of fields of activity – is an expression of the order of priorities and actual work plan of the government in power. This is why the Knesset's failure to approve a budget is equivalent to a vote of no-confidence in the government. The Budget Principles Law (1985) describes the structure and content of the Budget Law, sets sanctions for deviating from the budget, and establishes the authority of the finance minister to engage in oversight of the public sector. The law underscores Knesset oversight of the budget by instructing the Finance Minister to submit a report to the Knesset about adherence to the budget and any deviations from it.

In many countries, the Budget Law is often accompanied by supplementary legislation for imposing new taxes or authorizing new economic activity. In Israel, the "Arrangements Law in the State Economy" was first enacted in 1985 during an economic crisis, and was designed to allow the government to take drastic measures to end inflation and stabilize the economy. The Arrangements Law, which was an emergency measure, was never revoked, however, because the Finance Ministry realized what a powerful legal tool it had for instituting policies that the Knesset would not have legislated or, conversely, for nullifying the substance of laws that had already been passed. The Arrangements Law is also the Finance Ministry's solution for private legislation that entails budgetary expenditures, i.e., it is an attempt to rein in the power of the Knesset.

Over time, the Arrangements Law has become a "bypass law," enabling the hasty dispatch of existing laws under cover of passing the budget, or allowing for fundamental changes in the governance of social or economic affairs. On the pretext of saving the state money, this omnibus law contains many legislative matters with little or no connection to the budget. The 2007 Arrangements Law, for example, included sections that amend the Pharmacists' Law, merge local authorities, and make changes in the Electric Corporation. Above all, the Arrangements Law reflects impatience with the slow, orderly democratic legislative process, and therein lies its greatest danger.

E. "Problematic" Laws

Legislation is designed to set general norms of conduct for citizens, society, and the government. The laws of the land regulate collective behavior at all levels and strata, and therefore legislators must be scrupulous about the proper use of legislation, respectful of its purpose, and ensure enforcement. Democracies generally avoid legislation that is not impartial, and violation of this rule can be brought before the Supreme Court.[17] But the law, a well-honed social tool, must not be misused, and the legislator must take responsibility for this.

Labeling a law "problematic" could be interpreted as license not to obey it; a law that passes is a law, however, and reflects the will of the majority at that moment. If the law is truly problematic, it will presumably be later revoked by a different majority vote in the Knesset. Thus what is said below is intended to draw attention to some problems in principle created by the functioning of the Knesset as a legislative institution: the choice of subjects that require legislation, the content of the laws, their enforceability, and purpose. Some problems in laws enacted by the Knesset are a product of the large number of legislative initiatives (to be discussed later) and their hasty passage, while others relate to their content.

[17] Israel's law books do carry laws that are not impartial, as irrelevant criteria were used to allow discrimination in resource allocation to some segments of the population. A National Insurance grant only for "army veterans" was passed, for example, to circumvent Arab citizens (it was later revoked).

"Personal" Laws

These laws were enacted with reference to a specific person because of particular political circumstances. Although laws are supposed to set general norms, not relate to an individual or solve a temporary problem, some laws and amendments have been enacted by the Knesset for reasons extraneous to the essence of legislation:

- *Examples of amending the "Basic Law: Government" for coalition or personal purposes.* A 1980 amendment stating that the prime minister can have more than one deputy was designed to allow Prime Minister Menachem Begin to remove Simcha Ehrlich from his position as finance minister and compensate him with the job of deputy prime minister. In 1999, after formation of a new government headed by Ehud Barak, the paragraph limiting the number of deputy ministers was revoked for coalition reasons. And prior to the special election for prime minister in 2001, the requirement that the prime ministerial candidate be a member of the Knesset was modified so that a candidate can also be head of a party represented in the Knesset – a change designed to allow Benjamin Netanyahu, who was not an MK at the time, to run for prime minister.
- *Examples of personal laws.* The amendment to the Release from Imprisonment on Parole Law from 2001 was enacted to deal with Yigal Amir, the assassin of Yitzhak Rabin; this amendment bars a presidential pardon or commutation of a life sentence for anyone convicted of assassinating a prime minister for political or ideological reasons. Amendment of the Early Release from Prison Law enacted in 2001 allows a special Release Committee to set free prisoners who meet certain conditions after having served half their sentence; this was passed to enable the early release of former MK Aryeh Deri, then serving a prison term.

Laws in Response to Supreme Court Rulings

The Knesset has sovereign power to re-legislate any law, and may do so in response to a court ruling. A problem arises, however, if the only reason for a new law is to bypass a court ruling, or to retroactively allow for something that had been technically legal, but was declared illegal or improper by the court. In 1989, for example, the Knesset passed Amendment 8 of the Party Financing Law, which raised the unit of campaign financing retroactively, after the election was held. The Supreme Court ruled that the amendment contravenes the principle of equality, and invalidated it on procedural grounds – that the bill did not pass each reading by a majority, as required by the Basic Law: The Knesset (*L.A.O.R. Movement v. Speaker of the Knesset* 1990). Thus, to retroactively increase campaign funding for parties elected, the Knesset passed an amendment to the Basic Law that requires a majority of MKs in the three readings, but not in the preliminary reading. This law was designed to bypass the High Court. An example of another kind is the amendment to the Basic Law: Freedom of Occupation following the High Court ruling about the import of non-kosher meat (*Mitral Corp. v. Minister of Commerce and Industry* 1993). Coalition pressure from the religious parties in 1994 led to re-legislation of the Basic Law, introducing an article stipulating that any law that infringes upon freedom of occupation shall be valid if passed by a majority of MKs and if it explicitly states that it is valid despite what is written in the Basic Law: Freedom of Occupation.

As noted, one must distinguish between these examples and other legislation that seeks to address a problem or lacuna raised by the court. In 1984, for example, the High Court of Justice accepted the Kach Party's appeal against its ban by the Central Election Committee, hence the Knesset amended the Basic Law: The Knesset to specify the criteria for invalidating a party that seeks election (Article 7A).[18]

Declarative Laws

These are laws for purposes of making political declarations on controversial issues related to security or foreign affairs. The intent is to legally constrain the Knesset or government from future policy changes. For example, the Law and Administration (Abrogation of Application of Law, Jurisdiction and Administration) Law (1999) was passed in an effort to prevent the government from signing an agreement in which territory would be ceded; such an agreement, according to the law, now requires approval of a majority of MKs and a national referendum. Similarly, a law entrenching denial of the right of return (2001) seeks to thwart future agreements and hamper the government's ability to engage in negotiations about the Palestinian refugee issue. The law states that the Israeli government shall not sign any agreement in contravention of its articles, and requires a majority of MKs to approve government decisions regarding refugees. Declarative laws such as these are a misuse of legislation, and indeed their political validity is questionable.

Laws Passed under the Wire

One recurring phenomenon in the Knesset is the marathon of legislation during its waning days prior to an election. The race is on to pass laws during this fleeting moment of power and without due deliberation. This is true even for important pieces of legislation, such as the Basic Laws (which do not require any special legislative procedure and can be passed by a simple majority). Just before dispersion of the twelfth Knesset, three very important Basic Laws were passed within two weeks in March 1992: Freedom of Occupation (passed with twenty-three votes in favor, none opposed); Human Dignity and Liberty (thirty-two versus twenty-one); and The Government (fifty-five versus thirty-two). This trend includes attempts at legislating laws that are essentially non-democratic. For instance, a bill submitted by the Minister of Justice will pose limitations on non-profit organizations that receive funding from foreign governments (Azulay, Eichner, and Efraim 2015). Another government bill in the twentieth Knesset would amend the Basic Law: The Knesset to allow for suspending, or even firing, MKs who oppose Israel's existence as a Jewish and democratic state, or who support any armed opposition against Israel (Knesset Communications and Public Relations Division 2016).[19]

A large number of the "problematic laws" cited above could also fall under the rubric "superfluous laws," whether because the matter itself is improper, or should have undergone an orderly procedure, or should have been dealt with in a different framework or other means. The attempt to use legislation to compel citizens to be

[18] In this category is also the Deferral of Service for Yeshiva Students Whose Vocation is Torah Law (2002) (the so-called "Tal Law"), passed after the High Court decision and at its request that the legislature address this issue.

[19] See E. Gross 2016.

moral – as in the "Thou Shalt Not Stand Idly by the Blood of thy Neighbor Law" (1998), which transforms the moral principle of helping someone in need into a legal obligation – demonstrates the extent to which legislation can be misappropriated. Moreover, such laws are not enforced – not out of bureaucratic neglect or their cost, but because they were intended not to set norms, but for public relations.

F. The Knesset as the Legislature

According to the Knesset website, the Israeli legislature has enacted 5,623 laws from its founding in 1949 until the close of the eighteenth Knesset in 2013 – a rich harvest of eighty-eight laws annually, on average. But this average is deceptive because a third of the laws were enacted in recent years (1992–2013), and not during the state-building period when no laws yet existed. Clearly the Knesset has enacted an unusually high number of laws in recent years, just at a time when the moral constraints of society and the government have slackened. In Chapter 6, we discuss the judicialization of the public sphere in Israel in terms of the multiplicity of laws and court rulings. A large portion of the laws originated as private members' bills, and this can be seen as a real change in the balance of power between the Knesset and the government. The main reason for the multiplicity of private laws is the declining power of the executive branch and the power struggle between it and the Knesset for political entrepreneurship. In this context, we note the institution of primaries in the parties and direct election of the prime minister, which led to greater fragmentation in the Knesset and the rise of the politics of personality in Israel. One indication of this is the link since 1992 between the high number of private members' bills and the rise in the effective number of parties in the Knesset (Blander and Klein 2002, 63).

The legislative process reflects a paradox: the theoretical power of the Knesset versus its ability to wield this power. On the one hand, despite the Knesset's increased legislative independence vis-à-vis the government, MKs still find it hard to deal with government-initiated legislation, such as the Budget or Economic Arrangements Bills. On the other hand, and perhaps in reaction, MKs submit a large number of private members' bills, now forming more than half the laws enacted, a ratio unheard of in comparable democracies. Private legislation has become one of the main channels for MK activity; such political activism would have been a blessing for citizens, had it not been exploited by some MKs for irresponsible legislation.

This has often had the effect of channeling issues into legislation that had previously been dealt with by other – and more appropriate – parliamentary methods (debates, Knesset decisions, committee recommendations, etc.). And this creates a problem of laws that are not implemented. As we shall see below regarding oversight and control, the Knesset has no mechanism for monitoring the enforcement of laws, or ensuring that ministers enact regulations to implement the law, other than the unsystematic audits of the state comptroller. In other words, passage of a law in the Knesset is not the end of the road, and more than one law is merely gathering dust, which can lead to the devaluation of legislation (S. Ilan 2000).[20]

[20] Laws not implemented are usually laws that give rights or benefits to disadvantaged populations. The privileged ensure that laws important to them are put into effect. For many examples of laws not implemented, see Alon 2004.

4.6 The Third Role of the Knesset – Oversight of the Executive Branch

One of the important, though less glorified, roles of the Knesset is the exercise of oversight and control of the executive branch. Because the Knesset does not conduct a vote of confidence or no-confidence for every government action, day-to-day monitoring is carried out by diverse methods – committee deliberations, plenary debates, motions for the agenda, and parliamentary questions. The effectiveness of these methods depends upon the MKs and the assistance available to them; committee work; the clout of the opposition; and public response to what is happening in parliament. Preference for a specific method also depends upon the political culture. In the British parliamentary tradition, for example, "Question Time," in which the prime minister responds to questions from the opposition, is considered an important method of scrutiny and censure – both because it is the custom to provide substantive (and witty) responses, and because Question Time is broadcast on television and attracts considerable interest. This is not the case in Israel. Parliamentary questions are not well honed for use as oversight, and the attempt to institute a televised Question Time evoked little interest among MKs, the ministers, or the media. And we note the obvious – nowadays the politics of oversight is also subject to the caprices of the media.

What about the debates and decisions in the Knesset plenary and committees? Claims about their effectiveness in the past should not be exaggerated, keeping in mind the dominance of the government in those years and the power of coalition discipline. Nevertheless, until about the 1980s, what went on in the parliament enjoyed considerable public attention, and made a significant independent impact on democratic discourse. There are historic decisions for which the government could not have won public support without the Knesset's approval, such as ratification of the peace agreements with Egypt in 1979–80 (Diskin and Galnoor 1990). The parliament had a public voice of its own, which also enhanced its oversight and legislative functioning. But much has changed since then, and evidence of this is the tendency of MKs to prefer legislation – even its improper use, as noted above – as a way to make political decisions. Enormous changes have also taken place in the work of the Knesset committees, to some extent because their sessions have been opened to the public and the media since 1996. One result has been that discussions in the committees now play to the cameras, while the conscientious legislative work of other MKs remains unseen.

Parliaments find it hard to discharge their oversight duty because of the limited sanctions available to them, and this is also the case with regard to ensuring the implementation of laws by government ministries, as noted. If MKs cannot compel ministers to respond to their parliamentary questions, the oversight function of such questions is diminished, and MKs are discouraged from submitting them. The overall picture of Knesset oversight and control is affected, above all, by the fluctuations in its relationship with the executive branch. Distinctions should also be made between various channels, such as the growing power of the institution of state comptroller.

A. Confidence and No-Confidence

A no-confidence motion is different from other forms of oversight as it embodies a key function of the parliament in a parliamentary democracy – the expression of support in the government. A no-confidence motion is the Knesset's most significant political sanction, and it is naturally submitted by an opposition party on the grounds of opposing a specific government policy or government failure in its actions. A no-confidence motion by opposition parties has some deterrent value because passage would bring down the government and force a new election. Thus, coalition members are not likely to support a no-confidence motion, and the government can usually override it and continue to function. Even though a great many no-confidence motions have been submitted to the Knesset over the years, only once – during the Unity Government headed by Yitzhak Shamir in 1990 – did a government actually fall as a result of a no-confidence vote. The Labor Party, which was then in the coalition, colluded with Shas to bring down the government – a maneuver termed "the dirty trick" in Israeli political parlance – and the no-confidence vote passed by a majority of sixty versus fifty-five. The upshot of that vote, however, was different than Labor had planned: Labor MK Peres was unable to form a coalition with a majority of Knesset MKs, and Likud MK Shamir returned to power with a narrow government that did not include Labor.

According to the original Basic Law: Government, passed in 1968, a simple majority was all that was required to bring down a government in a no-confidence vote. The fall of a government, however, did not bring elections in its wake because the Knesset was not required to dissolve if another government could be formed that had majority support. In 1992, the amended Basic Law: Government raised the threshold, declaring that a majority of sixty-one MKs was required to bring down a government by a no-confidence vote, thereby lowering the risk to the government. The law created a kind of "balance of deterrence" between the Knesset and the government, as a no-confidence vote would automatically dissolve the Knesset as well. The revised Basic Law: Government (2001) reverted to the previous continuity option in that the Knesset does not dissolve if it manages to establish an alternative government, but this law adds a new and powerful tool for increasing government stability: the requirement of a "constructive" vote of no-confidence, as stated in Article 28:

> An expression of no confidence in the government shall be made by a decision of the majority of the members of Knesset requesting that the president assign the task of forming a government to a Knesset member who gave his written consent thereto. If the Knesset has expressed no confidence in the government, the government shall be deemed to have resigned on the day of the expression of no confidence.

Thus a no-confidence motion requires that at least sixty-one MKs support an alternative candidate for prime minister and a no-confidence motion cannot be impulsively submitted and bring down the government. It is not enough to have a simple majority that votes "no," but a constructive majority that says "yes." The theoretical advantage of this measure is that it prevents a vacuum in the political system and reduces the incentive for frequent expressions of no-confidence in the government. In practice, however, the change has had no effect on the frequency of no-confidence votes (Table 4.3), as such motions proposed the name of a fictitious potential candidate. Furthermore, the requirement of an alternative candidate could create a situation in which the government has no majority in the Knesset, but the opposition has not mustered an alternative, agreed upon candidate. In a case like this, a minority government continues to govern, even though it does not enjoy majority support of

Table 4.3 *No-confidence motions in the Knesset (1949–2015)*

Knesset	No-confidence motions
1 (1949)	0
2 (1952)	7
3 (1955)	29
4 (1959)	6
5 (1961)	33
6 (1965)	12
7 (1969)	31
8 (1973)	13
9 (1977)	45
10 (1981)	33
11 (1984)	165
12 (1988)	149
13 (1992)	91
14 (1996)	84
15 (1999)	129
16 (2003)	156
17 (2006)	193
18 (2009)	319
19 (2013–15)	243

Sources: S. Weiss 1998; Knesset website.

the Knesset, as it cannot fall by a no-confidence vote. What works in one political culture (this system exists in Germany) apparently does not work in Israel.

Thus no-confidence motions remain primarily a tool for political rebuke or censure of government policy. Frequent recourse to them, which intensified after 1984, has blunted their edge. To hold back the flood of no-confidence motions, the Statute of Knesset Operations sets down several constraints: A party with fewer than ten MKs can submit no more than three no-confidence motions every session. On certain issues, the government may seek to transform a no-confidence motion into a vote of confidence, often in an effort to prevent coalition members from voting against the government position.

In times of emergency or historic decision, a no-confidence motion is the only political sanction available to the Knesset. Declaring war or signing an international agreement is the prerogative of the government, which is obligated only to notify the Knesset without the MKs having power to prevent or change the decision. If a majority of the Knesset opposes going to war, the only means at its disposal is a no-confidence vote in the government or a decision to dissolve the Knesset. These are far-reaching measures, and MKs would hesitate to take them and appear irresponsible during fateful times, let alone for less momentous issues. As for international agreements, the Knesset has no legal obligation to ratify them, and the Statute of Knesset Operations states only that "The government is authorized to decide that a particular treaty, in respect of its importance, shall also be brought to the

Knesset for approval or ratification." Nevertheless, since the Camp David Accords with Egypt in 1978, the government has customarily brought such agreements to the Knesset for approval. This was done with the Oslo Accords, the Peace Treaty with Jordan, and the Wye River Memorandum (on Hebron), but the government also has the authority not to involve the Knesset in a significant process such as approval of a peace treaty. Under such conditions, the Knesset could express no-confidence in the government and force it to resign. However, the recent Basic Law: Referendum, approved in 2014 (and the 2010 Referendum Law), made this custom mandatory, stating that any peace treaty or government decision to withdraw from territories under Israeli jurisdiction must be approved either by a majority of Knesset members (sixty-one) and a referendum, or by at least eighty MKs. This has changed the formal status of the Knesset with respect to these critical decisions. Another option to vote no-confidence in the government is the budget bill – failure to approve this constitutes a no-confidence vote in the government, but also forces the Knesset to dissolve.

In the following discussion, we distinguish between the oversight mechanisms of the Knesset as a body (in the plenary or committees), and the oversight mechanisms available to parliamentary factions or individual MKs – although there is overlap between them.

B. Oversight Mechanisms Available to the Knesset as a Body

Knesset Decisions

The prime minister and other ministers pledge in their oath of office "to abide by the decisions of the Knesset." What is the standing of Knesset decisions that are neither laws nor no-confidence motions? Some of these decisions have a declarative character and some contain instructions about specific policies; they can relate to the work of the Knesset itself (such as the 1950 Harari Decision) or to the work of the government. But does the Knesset have the authority to tell the government how to act, and are government ministers obliged to abide by Knesset decisions that contain instructions for action?

The separation of powers in a parliamentary system means, *inter alia*, that it is the task of the parliament to express confidence or no confidence in the government's policies, and not to dictate day-to-day decisions. Therefore, if the Knesset passes a decision that carries an implicit instruction, whether or not the minister abides by this decision is a political matter, and the sanction for not abiding by it is also political. The government acts as it wills and does not act as it does not will. This is also true about decisions made by Knesset committees, which constitute recommendations only, and the sanction for ignoring them is political, not legal.

The principle that took root is the same as in other parliamentary systems – the Knesset and its committees do not make decisions that directly intervene in law enforcement or in ongoing executive decisions (Rubinstein and Medina 2005, 746–47). Occasionally, however, the Knesset or its committees do take executive decisions – generally in internal affairs, not security or foreign affairs – with the intent of dictating their implementation to the government. In 2000, for example, the Knesset Education Committee decided that the Ministry of Education must suspend the use of a particular history text on the grounds that important chapters in Jewish history were lacking. The Education Committee also saw fit in 2003 to declare Daniel

Barenboim a *persona non grata* because he conducted a composition by Richard Wagner (associated with anti-Semitism and Nazism by many Israelis) in an Israeli concert hall. A claim could not even be made in the latter case that this was a matter of oversight. But these are exceptions, and decisions of the Knesset and its committees are generally of a declarative nature, intended only to support or censure the government for its policies. They have validity only on the political and public level, but bear no mandatory or legal status. In 1987 a decision was made by two Knesset committees – Finance and Foreign Affairs and Defense – to continue development of the Lavi aircraft, but the government halted the project soon after. One must distinguish, of course, between Knesset decisions that have no legal standing and Knesset decisions in which it discharges its legal mandate, such as election of the state president and state comptroller, or lifting an MK's parliamentary immunity.

Knesset Committees

Most Knesset activity takes place in the committees, not the plenary. Through committees, the MKs perform their tasks of legislation and oversight, because this is where deliberations take place about proposed laws and the actions of government ministries. There are twelve permanent committees, and the Knesset is authorized to create other committees and subcommittees. For instance, the 2009 Knesset established special committees on the rights of children, the problem of foreign workers, and drug abuse. The Committee for the Advancement of Women had been a subcommittee that became a permanent committee. The Ethics Committee is a permanent committee with special standing because it functions on the authority of the Knesset Members Immunity Law, and exercises a quasi-judicial role toward MKs. It is authorized to impose sanctions on MKs for violating the ethical rules of the Knesset, engaging in prohibited activity, or other offenses. Another type of committee is the parliamentary commission of inquiry, which will be examined separately below.

MKs are assigned to committees according to party representation, with the role of chair subject to coalition negotiations. By custom, the chair of the State Control Committee is an opposition MK. Since there are many committees with large membership in them, every MK serves in several committees. In the eighteenth Knesset, for example, thirty-seven MKs were ministers or deputy ministers, so each of the remaining eighty-three MKs was a member of more than two permanent committees, on average, in addition to subcommittees and special committees. As a result, committee attendance is low, and since no quorum is required, the chair is sometimes the only one who shows up.

A committee chair wields great power. He or she sets the committee agenda, is able to promote or bury bills, or can slow their progress through the legislative pipelines. In 1988, for example, MK Micha Reisser was forced to step down as chair of the Knesset Committee because of unreasonable delays in referring a bill to committee about separating the local and general elections. Committee work now has greater transparency: Meetings are open to the public and broadcast live on the Knesset television channel. Committee protocols (except those of the Foreign Affairs and Defense Committee) are open to the public and available on the Internet. Transparency is a positive development in terms of public oversight of the committee work of the MKs, but may have negative repercussions when the deliberations turn into unbridled – and often televised – shouting matches.

Committees discuss bills in their assigned areas, and prepare them for a second and third reading; private members' bills are prepared for a first reading. Committees have the authority to recommend to the Knesset plenary not to deliberate a private member's bill in the first reading and to remove it from the agenda. On the other hand, a committee cannot refuse to move a bill that passed its first reading into the second and third readings, but it can slow down its progress. Committees are also authorized to sponsor bills in the following areas: Basic Laws and laws dealing with the Knesset, Knesset elections, Knesset members, or the state comptroller. Only about 4 percent of the total laws enacted by the Knesset since its founding have originated in committees.

What about oversight and control? Most Knesset committees have areas of responsibility that cover more than one government ministry: The Knesset's Foreign Affairs and Defense Committee can summon the two ministers or their officials to committee hearings; the Labor, Welfare and Health Committee can call for explanations in all three fields. In practice, the Knesset committees find it hard to monitor and oversee the activity of the government ministries, the regulations enacted by ministers, or even, as noted, the implementation of laws passed. According to the Basic Law: Government, the government must provide any information requested by the Knesset and its committees, and assist the committees in discharging their duties. The Knesset committees, moreover, have the authority to summon a minister or civil servant, but no power to apply sanctions to someone who does not show up, or to compel governmental bodies to submit requested documents. The professional assistance provided to committees is limited, and MKs do not invest much effort in the unappreciated job of oversight.

Parliamentary Commissions of Inquiry

Article 22 of the Basic Law: The Knesset allows the Knesset plenum to establish a parliamentary commission of inquiry on matters of concern to it, either by empowering one of the permanent Knesset committees or by appointing committee members from among the MKs. The appointment of committee members is based on their party affiliation, taking into account the balance of forces in the Knesset, and must by law include members of the opposition. In Britain, for instance, a parliamentary commission of inquiry is a sharp oversight tool of which ministries are fearful, but with which they must cooperate, even though its powers differ little from those in Israel. In Israel's political culture, on the other hand, a parliamentary commission of inquiry is weak as it has no formal standing or special powers, unlike a state commission of inquiry headed by a judge, which is authorized to summon witnesses, question them under oath, and subpoena documents. The history of parliamentary commissions of inquiry in Israel reveals no fundamental difference between them and one of the Knesset's permanent committees – inquiry commissions have no additional powers and their political and public clout is identical. Because of the party makeup of parliamentary commissions of inquiry, most of their reports remain unimplemented and fail to elicit broad public support.[21]

The first parliamentary commission of inquiry was appointed in 1951, based on the British model, to inquire into police conduct toward detainees in the Jalami

[21] The procedures of parliamentary committees of inquiry were deliberated by the High Court of Justice, which ruled that they are permitted to take political considerations into account, hence they resemble other Knesset committees (*Kariv v. Knesset House Committee* 1985).

camp. The commission's conclusions were harsh, and so was the reaction of the government, which viewed the report as gross interference in matters that should be off limits to MKs. After publication of the report, MK Yohanan Bader, a member of the commission, quipped that Mapai members visited the grave of party forefather Berl Katznelson and swore they would never again agree to another parliamentary commission of inquiry. Indeed, the 1958 law did not bestow power on these commissions, and only in 1987, after Labor lost control of the government, did the Knesset appoint the next parliamentary commission of inquiry, and this was on a non-controversial topic – the rising number of traffic accidents in Israel.

Since then, opposition MKs have stepped up their efforts to establish parliamentary commissions of inquiry, and the number of those approved by the Knesset has increased: nine in the fifteenth Knesset (1999), three in the sixteenth Knesset (2003), and five in the seventeenth Knesset (2006). By the end of the eighteenth Knesset (early 2009), a total of twenty-five parliamentary commissions of inquiry had been established about a wide range of subjects.[22] Attesting to its low status, the chairs are generally novice MKs and not, for example, former ministers. Some commissions never completed their reports, and most recommendations have never been implemented, so they have not proven to be an effective oversight mechanism. This generalization does an injustice, however, to some parliamentary commissions that did have significant impact or were effective in raising public awareness about an important issue. Among these are the commissions on locating and restoring the property of Holocaust survivors, trafficking in women, social disparities in Israel, and traffic accidents.

The Effectiveness of Knesset Committees: Real and Ideal

Based on the accepted measures for assessing the effectiveness of parliamentary committees – the right to initiate legislation, the power to amend bills referred to them, and autonomy in setting the committee agenda – Knesset committees have considerable power (Strom 1998, 21–59). And yet committees are not perceived as powerful players in the political system, either in the eyes of the government or apparently in the eyes of the MKs themselves, as evidenced by their poor attendance at committee meetings. Exceptions to this are the Foreign Affairs and Defense Committee because of the subject matter, the Finance Committee because of the budget deliberations, and cases in which the committees have managed to force their will on the government. There is a disparity between the formal power of the committees and their exercise of this power, particularly with respect to oversight of the government ministries.

Increasing the number of MKs or passage of the so-called "Norwegian Law," which would appoint replacement MKs for those who serve in the executive branch, would enhance the effectiveness of the Knesset and enable more MKs to devote time and energy to committee work. Other proposed reforms include: limiting the number of committees in which each MK can participate; establishing a quorum for committee meetings and decisions; and improving staff assistance and outside consulting from independent experts. Also proposed is giving Knesset committees

[22] Listed on the Knesset website: www.knesset.gov.il/committees/eng/ParInqCommittees_eng.asp (accessed October 16, 2017).

the power to compel ministers and civil servants to appear for questioning and provide requested documents, and sanctions for those who refuse. The changes are also designed to increase the transparency of deliberations within government ministries and to enhance the oversight function of Knesset committees vis-à-vis public administration.[23] The drawback of this proposal is that summoning officials not through the minister could undermine the principle of ministerial responsibility to the Knesset. An even more far-reaching proposal is creation of separate sources of information and independent staff work for the Knesset, to eliminate the Knesset's dependence on the executive branch, following the example of the independent Congressional Budget Office in the United States. Reducing dependence is a logical measure, but eliminating it entirely could be an artificial implant that does not suit the parliamentary system of Israel.

Budget Oversight[24]

We described earlier the Knesset's role in financial legislation, and here we discuss its role in oversight of the Budget Law.

Budgeting is a tool for decision-making about values, not just with regard to expenditures – such as the share allocated for welfare services – but also with regard to revenues. The burden of taxes, licenses, and duties reflects society's willingness to transfer private resources into the public treasury for purposes of meeting common goals. Moreover, taxation is also a tool used by democratic regimes for redistributing resources among the citizens – making the burden more equitable and reducing social gaps by a system of progressive taxation.

In a parliamentary system, the executive branch has more power in the budgeting process than the legislative branch, in contrast with a presidential system such as that in the United States, where budget authorization is largely in the hands of Congress. In Israel, once the budget proposal has left the Finance Ministry, it will undergo relatively few alterations as a result of negotiations with the ministers and party representatives, government approval, and the deliberations in the Knesset Finance Committee. With the exception of years when the coalition was fragile and the prime minister had difficulties passing laws (e.g., during the Barak and first Sharon administrations), the government usually puts the budget proposal through the Knesset without significant change (no more than 3% of the total expenditures). Based on fifteen years of experience in passing budgets, former Finance Minister Avraham Shochat remarked: "The Finance Ministry is very centralized, the body that actually makes the decisions. Government deliberations generally dabble in the margins, as do the Knesset deliberations. No budget was ever really changed – not by the government nor by the Knesset" (Ben Bassat and Dahan 2006, 29–30).

While this statement is generally true, it could be somewhat modified because the initial budget proposal has already undergone alterations following concessions made by the prime minister and finance minister to coalition parties, especially those in strong bargaining positions. Ironically, during the years of direct election of the prime minister (1996–2003) – a measure intended to increase executive power

[23] For proposed reforms of the Knesset committees, see Hazan 2001, 87–102.
[24] Based on Galnoor 2011, 84, 88–90.

vis-à-vis the Knesset – the small parties acquired much greater bargaining power in the budgetary process.[25]

Deliberations in the Knesset Finance Committee commence after the budget has passed its first reading in the Knesset. Although this committee has almost unlimited power over government policy as expressed in the budget, committee members are not equipped to grapple with the complexity of the budget proposal. As noted, changes are usually marginal: pre-planned additions from the budget reserve designed to respond to specific demands of committee members. These changes generally do not relate to major socioeconomic policies, and they certainly do not touch upon security matters. The budgeting process in Israel is centralized and partially secretive, and the superficial deliberations of the budget proposal in the Knesset Finance Committee are part of this phenomenon.[26] In consequence, government policy, as implemented in practice through the budget, remains largely outside the scrutiny of the Knesset. In 2009 the government managed to get Knesset approval in the form of a Basic Law for a two-year budget (on and off since 2009), further diminishing Knesset control over the budget.[27] However, the one-year budget has since been reinstated.

Passage in the Knesset of the state budget constitutes an overall vote of confidence in the government, as well as a test of the coalition's powers of persuasion. It is not a manifestation of Knesset oversight of the government. Moreover, the fact that Knesset approval for the Budget Law goes hand in hand with approval of the Arrangements Law – containing legislation that is not financial and also the revocation of some laws passed by the Knesset – clearly reveals the Knesset's failure at oversight. This also holds true for the legal provisions, which call for approval of the Finance Committee for budget-line changes above a specific amount – approval that is generally automatic and not the product of increased financial scrutiny. Budget oversight – together with no-confidence motions, which address overall policy – is the single most important tool of the Knesset; in its absence, the Knesset relinquishes its power to affect the steering of the political system.

Oversight of Secondary Legislation

Laws enacted by the Knesset are called primary legislation. Secondary legislation (also referred to as "delegated legislation" or "subordinate legislation") consists of the regulations made by ministers under the power given to them by primary legislation in order to implement and administer the requirements of that primary legislation. Sometimes the law confers the power to make regulations on an authority, statutory body, or specific official. Why are regulations necessary?

[25] An examination of budget allocations among ministries found an increase in the relative portion of ministries headed by small parties, especially religious parties, particularly during the first Netanyahu government (1996–99) and the Barak government (1999–2001). See Arian, Nachmias, and Amir 2002, 118–20.

[26] Israel is ranked second among OECD countries for a centralized budget process (Ben Bassat and Dahan 2006, 32).

[27] The Basic Law: State Budget (Special Instructions) was enacted for the years 2009 to 2012. This was a temporary extension of the Basic Law: State Economy and valid only for those years, not a Basic Law in its own right. For the text of the temporary budget laws, see http://main.knesset.gov.il/Activity/Legislation/Laws/Pages/LawPrimary.aspx?t=lawlaws&st=lawlawsbasic&lawitemid=2002342 [in Hebrew] (accessed June 5, 2016).

Because the law sets a general norm, which must then be translated into individual provisions – customs regulations, for example, that list the thousands of products on which customs duties must be paid. Secondary legislation is voluminous compared to primary legislation, and is what the citizen generally encounters – parking regulations, for example. Secondary legislation calls for expertise and is more flexible to allow for amendments in changing circumstances. In the absence of regulations passed to implement laws, Knesset primary legislation may never become operational. For example, the Prevention of Nuisances Law (1961) was never activated because the regulations on environmental pollution required for its implementation were never put in place. This is not the only instance. During the fifteenth Knesset (1999–2003), for example, regulations were made for only 60 percent of the laws for which ministers had to set regulations, and it took an average of more than eight months before such regulations were put in place (D. Ben-Porat 2002).

New regulations prepared by government ministries must be tabled in the Knesset. Although authorized to discuss these regulations, Knesset committees are not empowered to invalidate them other than through a full legislative process. Exceptions to this rule are regulations whose infringement would incur criminal penalties, and these require approval of the appropriate Knesset committee prior to their publication. For other regulations, a discussion is generally conducted in a committee or the plenum, and these receive passive approval, as Knesset silence in this matter constitutes consent.

Thus the Knesset and its committees provide little oversight of secondary legislation because the Knesset is currently empowered to invalidate regulations not by committee decision, but only through a convoluted legislative process. Having a monopoly on secondary legislation accords enormous power to government ministries because they can translate the Knesset's primary legislation into practice as they see fit, or alternatively neglect to implement the law by failing to issue regulations. In proposals for the Basic Law: Legislation, a mechanism was suggested that would empower the Knesset to invalidate any regulation by decision within thirty days of its publication. This law has not been passed, meaning that the Knesset still has no mechanism to exercise oversight of secondary legislation, despite their importance to citizens of the state.

Oversight of Declarations of a State of Emergency and Government Emergency Regulations

In discussing the legal infrastructure, we noted that the Knesset has the authority to declare a state of emergency either on its own or the government's initiative, which is valid for no longer than one year, but renewable every year without limit. The Knesset also has the authority to repeal the declaration of a state of emergency. In extraordinary circumstances, however, the government too is authorized to declare a state of emergency, which expires within one week if not approved by the Knesset. During a state of emergency, the government may pass emergency regulations for specific purposes (enumerated in the law), and also temporarily suspend a specific law unless that law or articles in it are immune from suspension by emergency regulations. Such regulations must be tabled by the government as soon as possible in the Foreign Affairs and Defense Committee.

Ostensibly, oversight is ensured and the Knesset is even empowered to repeal emergency regulations by law or majority decision of MKs. Nevertheless, because a state of emergency has been declared in Israel since its founding and the Knesset has never failed to renew it, and based on the experience of governments having sometimes used emergency regulations for inappropriate purposes, there is a need to strengthen parliamentary oversight of the government's far-reaching authority to pass emergency regulations. At the very least, ordinary legislation should have priority over emergency regulations and, if this is not possible, the government should be required, when issuing emergency regulations, to table a parallel ordinary bill so that the emergency regulations will be replaced by ordinary legislation or rescinded (Rubinstein and Medina 2005, 948).

Oversight by Monitoring Mechanisms

The Knesset also engages in oversight of government activity through the use of special monitoring mechanisms: the state comptroller and state commissions of inquiry, which the Knesset's State Control Committee is authorized to establish in special circumstances. These will be considered in Chapter 7.

C. Oversight Mechanisms Available to Parties and Individual MKs

Motions for the Agenda

Every MK is entitled to submit a motion for the agenda – to propose a subject to the Speaker of the Knesset for discussion in the plenum. In this way, parties and MKs fulfill their mission to publicly address current issues, whether in response to government actions or to raise awareness about an important subject. This can be an urgent motion – deliberated the same week it is submitted; or an ordinary motion – not to exceed the quota for such motions for each party. The Knesset can decide to discuss the issue, remove it from the agenda, or move it to a committee. Before the motion comes up for discussion, it is submitted to the government, which states whether it wishes to present its position about it. Not all motions are discussed on the Knesset floor, but submitting them draws public attention – to the issue and to the person who submitted it. In the tenth through sixteenth Knessets (1981–2006), an average of 3,000 motions for the agenda were submitted in each Knesset. In the seventeenth through the nineteenth Knessets (2006–15), the numbers grew to 5,713, 8,586, and 3,979 respectively, and the annual average reached 2,075.[28]

Parliamentary Questions

A parliamentary question is a question of a factual nature addressed by an MK to a minister in the realm of the minister's authority. If a motion for the agenda is an ideological tool of parties, a parliamentary question is a parliamentary weapon of MKs as they discharge their duty of oversight. Ministers or deputy ministers must respond in the plenum within twenty-one days to an ordinary question; to an oral question posed in the plenum, within two days; and to a question addressed directly

[28] Data for the nineteenth Knesset from the Central Bureau of Statistics: www.cbs.gov.il/shnaton66/st10_06.pdf (accessed June 6, 2016); for the seventeenth and eighteenth Knessets generously provided by Yossi Dolev and Yehonatan Sari-Levi at the Knesset Archive. For earlier years, see the Knesset website: www.knesset.gov.il (accessed October 16, 2017).

to the minister, in writing to the MK. This last option is the most effective for handling a substantive matter because it takes place away from the spotlight.

Parliamentary questions in the British parliament are a way for the Member of Parliament (MP) to acquire information and deal with specific cases on behalf of his or her constituency. In this tradition, the parliamentary question is a platform for drawing public attention to issues by way of a verbal fencing match between the MP who asks and the minister who responds. The aim of the questioner is to weave into the brief question both a request for information and veiled criticism of the anticipated reply. The aim of the responder is to provide a substantive, witty reply, and anticipate the follow-up question. British ministers have staff who specialize in preparing such responses for the ministers (Chester and Bowring 1962).[29]

In Israel, most parliamentary questions originate in media-raised issues, while a minority are drawn from citizens' appeals or the MK's own initiative (Caspi 1998, 510). As already noted, in 1996, an effort was made to institute a British-like "Question Time," but it evoked little interest among the MKs, ministers, media, or the public. Although some 4,000 parliamentary questions are submitted in every Knesset (www.Knesset.gov.il and Knesset Archive), the institution of parliamentary questions has not taken its place as an integral part of the parliamentary culture in Israel or as an effective oversight mechanism. Neither the prime minister nor the ministers take on these questions as a public challenge, and the Knesset cannot impose sanctions on ministers who do not respond to them.

Political Discussion and Special Sessions during a Knesset Recess

At the request of at least forty MKs, the Knesset is empowered to convene a session on a subject of concern in which the prime minister must participate (no more often than once a month), even during the period of a Knesset recess. However, it is not easy for a multi-faction opposition to mobilize support for such an action, except in rare circumstances. One such example was the "disengagement from Gaza" carried out by the Sharon government in 2005 during the Knesset summer recess. Many factions in the opposition opposed this plan – for entirely different reasons – and forty MKs were successful in compelling the government to participate in two special Knesset sessions about the disengagement and its repercussions.

Media Publicity

A key channel of influence for Knesset members is the media. MKs often issue press releases about their legislative initiatives, motions for the agenda, and parliamentary questions. When these receive publicity – and the competition among MKs for media attention is fierce – they put pressure on the government, which tends to respond to what appears in the media. Media attention is an excellent way to raise public awareness about an issue. MKs, however, tend to make use of the media primarily to publicize their own actions and less as a tool to scrutinize government activity (Cohen, Tsfati, and Sheafer 2008, 331–44). At the same time, the key channels that compete with MKs these days are the new media, which have no need of the Knesset as a public arena. They (together with public interest organizations) are increasingly considered an alternative to the MKs' limited oversight capacity.

[29] Also see UK, House of Commons Information Office on "Parliamentary Questions" 2010, www.parliament.uk/documents/commons-information-office/p01.pdf (accessed June 6, 2016).

Petitions to the High Court of Justice

Submitting a petition to the High Court of Justice is an extra-parliamentary channel of action, one that has been used by MKs increasingly since the 1980s.[30] The broadening of legal standing in the High Court threw open the door to appeals by MKs on issues related to the Knesset, the government, the parties, and more. As will be seen below, the willingness of the High Court to intervene is generally limited to constitutional or procedural questions related to the work of the Knesset, and therefore it is strange to find MKs submitting petitions "against themselves" about subjects that the Knesset can and should resolve of its own accord.[31]

In the period 1986–98, MKs filed 240 petitions to the High Court of Justice on a variety of subjects such as parliamentary procedures, elections, funding allocations, civil service appointments, and political activity. Forty-six percent of the petitions related to decisions made by the executive branch and can be seen as an attempt to exercise scrutiny over its work. Most of the petitions were submitted by MKs and not by parties, which also indicates the waning of the parties and the rising power of the individual member of the Knesset. What motivates MKs to turn to the High Court? These petitions are generally submitted by opposition MKs, i.e., they serve as an extra-parliamentary channel for opposition members to criticize majority decisions in the Knesset or government decisions. But even coalition MKs, particularly backbenchers, submit petitions to the High Court. Another powerful motivation of MKs is their desire to raise their media profile. Some submit petitions even when their chances of success in the High Court are negligible (only 7% of MKs' petitions were fully and 2% partially accepted in the years 1986–98). Nevertheless, petitioning the court has become another avenue of influence for the MK – in a quarter of the petitions submitted in 1986–98, the state changed its position even before the court issued a ruling. MKs who petition the High Court tend not to settle out of court because they prefer the ongoing media coverage of the court case, regardless of the outcome, unlike public-interest non-profits, for example, which are willing to settle out of court (Dotan and Hofnung 2005, 75–103). The many petitions submitted by Israeli parliament members to the High Court of Justice are not a common practice in other parliamentary democracies, and undermine the independence of the legislative branch.

D. The Knesset as Scrutinizer

The Knesset has available to it numerous and diverse methods of oversight and control – the fruit of long years of parliamentary traditions. However, Knesset oversight does not constitute a *replacement* for governmental activity, but rather is meant to scrutinize it in order to correct and improve it. To engender a real change in policy,

[30] This discussion does not pertain to petitions submitted by factions and MKs against the Central Elections Committee because, by law, the High Court is the venue for these matters; and it does not pertain to petitions of MKs (such as Shmuel Flatto-Sharon, Meir Kahane, Mohammed Miari, and Rafael Pinchasi), who believed that their rights as MKs were violated by quasi-judicial decisions made by the Knesset.

[31] For example, the petition against the Speaker of the Knesset and the Chair of the Constitution, Law and Justice Committee to compel them to table the proposed Basic Law: The State Economy did achieve its aim – a settlement was reached between the parties that was given validity as a court ruling (*Poraz v. Speaker of the Knesset* 1991).

a change of government is required. A significant part of the oversight takes place *ex post facto*, after the government has already executed the policy or the minister has made a decision. The role of the Knesset is to criticize and, when it deems fit, express no confidence. But in some areas the Knesset must take action before the deed – scrutiny of the Budget Bill, determining whether secondary legislation is consonant with the primary legislation, and proactive oversight of emergency regulations. The Knesset has more than enough authority in these matters, but does not make enough use of it. Another realm in which the Knesset should exercise its oversight function is to obligate the government to submit all international agreements to the Knesset for ratification. Furthermore, in times of war, there is no reason why the media are full of *Sturm und Drang*, but the Knesset falls silent, a mere spectator of the action. Indeed, this is the time of greatest need for a public forum.

With regard to Knesset oversight of government ministries, this is largely ineffective, with the exception of the state comptroller reports. We noted the objective reasons above, and add here that some MKs have demonstrated a tendency to use irresponsibly the means available to them. The indiscriminate use of parliamentary commissions of inquiry or High Court petitions, and the overuse of no-confidence motions and motions for the agenda, undermine the Knesset's ability to engage in oversight and control. The Knesset – as a group and individually – loses more than it gains when its actions are perceived as phony and media-oriented, and this is sadly evident in the negative attitudes toward the Knesset found in survey research. As noted, the contempt of the government ministries toward the Knesset as an institution also has practical implications: recourse to the Arrangements Law, failure to implement laws that are enacted, lack of cooperation with parliamentary commissions of inquiry, and parliamentary questions left unanswered.

To make the Knesset's oversight and control of the executive branch more effective, the existing mechanisms should first be put to optimal use. Then the addition of other mechanisms might be considered that would allow for Knesset involvement in the early stages of decision- and policymaking. For example, the tabling of Knesset drafts of the government's policy papers, as is common in Britain, would enable debate among the parties and the public before its final formulation. Another area in serious need of overhaul is the parliamentary handling of the Budget Bill and budget revisions during the fiscal year.

E. Overseeing the Knesset[32]

Is the Knesset entitled to do whatever it sees fit because, *inter alia*, Israel has no rigid, written constitution to constrain it? Who oversees the overseer? The most basic level of supervision over the Knesset is exercised by the citizens on election day. Between elections, the courts have authority to oversee Knesset activities, which are also subject to the rule of law. As noted, the judiciary tends not to intervene in the content of legislation, but does scrutinize other matters – the compatibility of legislation with the Basic Laws, internal Knesset procedures, and the Knesset's quasi-judicial

[32] See Chapter 6 on the relations between the legislative branch and the judiciary.

decisions, such as lifting an MK's immunity. Here we discuss only judicial intervention in the internal affairs of the Knesset.

During the 1980s, relations altered between the Knesset and the judiciary, with both sides contributing to the change: MKs frequently turned to the High Court of Justice for legal remedy, and the court was responsive to these appeals, showing a willingness to intervene in internal Knesset matters within the aforementioned limits. The High Court ruled that judicial intervention is an option only when there is a danger to "the web of parliamentary life" or "the foundational values of our constitutional order" (*Sarid v. Speaker of the Knesset* 1981–82). Accordingly, the court dismissed petitions on matters such as setting the date for a no-confidence motion or replacing the chair of a Knesset committee (*Ratz v. Acting Speaker of the Knesset* 1990; *Reisser v. Speaker of the Knesset* 1988).[33] On the other hand, the court ruled to protect the rights of MKs and Knesset factions, beginning with the difficult test posed by the election of Meir Kahane, the head of a racist party, to the Knesset. Kahane's petition against the Knesset Speaker, who prevented him from submitting a bill with racist content, was accepted by the High Court, which ruled that the Speaker or Deputy Speakers exceeded their authority by introducing considerations of content into their decision about tabling a bill (*Kahane v. Speaker of the Knesset* 1985). This ruling led to changes in the law and the Statute of Knesset Operations, establishing that the Speaker has authority to disqualify a bill submitted by an MK if it is racist in essence or rejects the existence of Israel as the state of the Jewish people. A subsequent petition submitted by Kahane was dismissed because the Knesset Speaker could now disqualify the bill based on the amendment (*Kahane v. Speaker of the Knesset* 1986). Kahane kept the High Court busy, and a petition submitted by his faction was accepted by the High Court, which ruled that denying their right to express no confidence in the government was a significant breach of the fundamental values of a democracy (*Kach v. Speaker of the Knesset* 1985).

Other oversight by the judiciary relates to the quasi-judicial decisions by the Knesset to lift an MK's immunity. The court invalidated a Knesset decision to lift an MK's immunity because the process was flawed; in other cases, where an MK's immunity was revoked by the Knesset, the court invalidated the decision because of extraneous considerations or an insufficient evidentiary basis (*Pinchasi v. Knesset* 1995).

Judicial review contributes to Israeli democracy because it provides a constitutional framework that prevents the Knesset from doing as it will and establishes the principle of the legality of the entire political system. More than increased intervention reveals "judicial activism," it reflects the waning institutional authority of the legislative branch. The court can intervene only when a matter is brought before it. The increasing number of petitions brought to the High Court of Justice by MKs reflects the inadequacy of the mechanisms within the Knesset for solving disputes. The Knesset has political mechanisms to reach agreement and compromise, and a statute that specifies the rules of conduct – these should be used before seeking judicial redress.

[33] For other examples, see the Israeli Association for Parliamentary Issues 1988.

4.7 Knesset Factions, Knesset Members

A. The Factions

A "faction" (or "parliamentary group") refers to the members of a party list who have been elected to the Knesset. Factions are the representatives of the parties in the Knesset, and can represent one party or several that have merged. During elections, voters cast their vote for a list, not for individual Knesset members, and therefore factions are a significant factor in forming the government and in parliamentary activity. Factions have many functions: They submit a candidate for prime minister to the president following elections, they select the members of the Knesset committees, and they negotiate with the Finance Ministry about changes in the state budget. Many aspects in the work of the Knesset are determined on the basis of faction membership, such as participation in debates, or quotas for submitting private members' bills. Factions alone, not individual MKs, can table a motion of no-confidence. Party and election campaign funding is also based on a faction key, which – in an era of personal politics – arouses the ire of MKs and candidates who do not want to be dependent upon the party.

Faction Discipline

Until the 1980s, faction discipline in the Knesset was rigid, and members of a faction voted with one voice, except when the faction decided in advance to allow freedom of voting to its members. The decline of the stature of the parties, the institution of primary elections, and the growing politics of personality all led to a significant decline in faction discipline among Knesset members. With the exception of well-organized parties such as Shas, many MKs – from the opposition as well as the coalition – tend to vote differently than their party's position or abstain from voting. For example, in the vote on disengagement from the Gaza Strip in 2005, the vote was split among members of the Likud and the National Union-Yisrael Beitenu. Even in voting on the Budget Bill, which is tantamount to a vote of confidence in the government, coalition MKs have withheld support on the first readings or abstained to protest budget cuts. The easing of faction discipline reflects the increasing stature of MKs as individuals, and allows for greater individual discretion. Nevertheless, faction discipline is an important element in the stability of the political system; undermining it threatens the stability of the coalition as an institution and the steering capacity of the government.

Resigning from a Faction

It is hard to give an unequivocal response to the question, who owns the mandate of an elected member of the Knesset – the MK personally or the party list from which he or she was elected? This question has been asked since the earliest days of Knesset activity in the general context of faction discipline, especially with respect to the resignation of an MK from his or her faction.[34] In 1990, following the so-called "dirty trick" when inducements and personal benefits were offered to several MKs for voting against

[34] This phenomenon is disparagingly referred to as "kalanterism," named for Rahamim Kalanter, who was appointed deputy mayor of Jerusalem in 1956 in exchange for defecting from his faction in the City Council.

their faction, legislation was passed to make the conditions for resignation more stringent. Article 59 of the Knesset Law (1994) seeks to distinguish between resigning from a faction and splitting from it – an MK's resignation is considered a split if at least one-third of the faction members resign, comprising at least two people. This distinction is important because (according to the Basic Law: The Knesset), resigning from a faction entails sanctions, but a split does not: An MK who resigns cannot be a candidate for the coming election in a party list that had been represented in the outgoing Knesset. The same law also establishes that an MK shall be regarded as having resigned if he or she voted against the position of the faction in a no-confidence vote in exchange for the promise of benefits (a job, inclusion in the list of candidates, etc.). An MK who resigns from a faction, but continues as an MK, is not eligible to join another faction in the Knesset, may not serve as minister or deputy minister, and is not eligible for party financing. In 2009 the Likud tried to split the Kadima Party by passing an amendment that recognizes seven MKs who resign as a split, even if this is less than one-third of the faction members, as required by the Governance Law.[35]

The Opposition (see Chapter 11, "Government Coalitions")

B. Knesset Members

The Right to Be Elected

Every Israeli citizen aged twenty-one or over has the right to run for election to the Knesset. Barred from election to the Knesset are the president of the state, rabbis and ministers of other religions, judges, religious court judges, the state comptroller, the IDF chief of staff and senior army officers, and senior civil servants. Also banned from election to the Knesset is anyone who committed a criminal offense defined as one of moral turpitude, was sentenced to actual imprisonment for a term of over three months, and seven years have not yet elapsed since completion of the prison term. The sanction of prohibiting an individual from running for the coming Knesset is also imposed on MKs who resigned from their factions as described above.

The right to serve in the Knesset is delimited by amendments to the Basic Law: The Knesset. According to the first amendment from 1985 (Article 7A), a list of candidates is not eligible to run for election to the Knesset if its goals or actions, expressly or by implication, include any of the following: negation of the existence of Israel as a Jewish and democratic state, incitement to racism, support for armed struggle by a hostile state or a terrorist organization against the state of Israel, or travel to an enemy state. In this law, the Knesset was seeking to protect itself from racist parties such as Kach and – in a compromise with right-wing parties – it added a clause against extremist Arab parties.[36] In a second amendment from 2002, this prohibition was extended to individual candidates. This came about in reaction to a speech given by MK Azmi Bishara in Syria, which could be interpreted as support for terrorism and an enemy state. Changing the law in response to an individual case is problematic, no less because at issue is the basic right in a democracy to be elected to public office. Similarly imposing limitations on a list of candidates is problematic,

[35] Knesset Law (1994), Amendments 23 and 59(1) (enacted in 2009). Nonetheless, the Kadima Party did not split.

[36] On the first formulation of the law, see Bracha 1984.

because it means that the Knesset has assumed the authority to narrow the democratic electoral space of citizens and to constrain their right to exercise their untrammeled judgment at the ballot box.

The Work of the MKs

The media frequently broadcast scenes of a deserted Knesset plenary – one lone member at the podium addressing empty seats and a few sleepy MKs. In a survey in 2000, most respondents ascribed negative characteristics to members of the Knesset – selfishness, laziness, and insensitivity to public feelings – and were of the opinion that MKs do not view their work as a mission, but a source of income and status, and a springboard to entering the government. As of 2015, not much had changed: Most citizens believe Knesset members do not work hard and do not perform their duties well. Only 35 percent feel they can trust the Knesset and most also believe that Knesset members are more concerned with their own interests rather than the public weal (Hermann et al. 2011–15: 2015, 60). Certainly not all MKs are cut of the same cloth, and there seems to be a disparity between their actual work and their public image. In the Rosen-Zvi Report, the job of a Knesset member is thus described:

> An MK is always on duty. Everything he does will be viewed as part of his job. His responsibilities as a public representative constitute a permanent burden of ongoing work: presence in the plenum and Knesset committees, legislative initiatives, submission of motions for the agenda, parliamentary questions, preparation for committee work, speeches in the Knesset, public lectures, participation in meetings, party activity, public activity in various bodies, participation in public and private events throughout the country, response to constituent requests orally or in writing, media contact with the public and daily contact with his constituency. (Rosen-Zvi Committee 1995)

The vital importance of an MK's work to society and the political system demands of them serious attention to their mission and responsible behavior that evokes public respect. Not everyone is up to the task. Nevertheless, there is insufficient awareness of the enormous difficulties in carrying out the work of an MK and the need for professional support to enhance their parliamentary functioning (Galnoor Committee 2000).

To ensure that MKs devote the time required to their parliamentary work, they have been prohibited since 1996 from engaging in any additional work other than unpaid voluntary activity. An MK cannot serve as mayor of a local council, or head a corporation or state institution. This amendment was revolutionary, as MKs in the past had held parallel jobs and were unable to participate fully in parliamentary life. When Ehud Olmert served as MK while also serving as mayor of Jerusalem, for example, he led the Knesset in absenteeism from votes, plenary debates, and committee meetings. In this matter, the Immunity Law states that the Knesset Ethics Committee has the authority to impose sanctions on any MKs who are absent without justification for over two straight months or a third of the Knesset meetings. The Rules of Ethics for MKs also enumerate constraints to prevent conflicts of interest, including a prohibition on representing clients in the Knesset and its committees, and the obligation to submit a declaration of assets to the Knesset Speaker. In addition, formal registration and transparency are now required by law from lobbyists operating in the Knesset.

The Trap of MKs in the Media Age

The transition from party politics, centralized and secretive, to an age of media exposure has had both positive and negative results for the public: A transparency and openness previously unknown are now integrated with superficiality and haphazard behavior, also previously unknown. In discussing the media in Chapter 13, we note this phenomenon in other countries, but the transition in Israel was so fast and abrupt that many MKs found themselves adrift in unknown waters. To be elected to the Knesset, individuals – especially those vying in primaries – must attract media attention or they will remain unknown (Galnoor 1998, 195–214; R. Hazan 1998, 78–84). Media attention, however, is not always flattering, and the public expects politicians to behave responsibly and judiciously, despite the short attention span of the new media. Over-exposure of MKs may have done them a disservice, contributing to their negative public image. It is hard to break out of this vicious cycle of competition, especially when nourished and escalated by political rivalries. The general public is also fickle. In the past it frowned upon faction discipline, which prevented MKs from exercising their own judgment and voting with their conscience; today the public wants stability in the political system, including faction discipline, and is ambivalent about MKs who vote against their parties' positions.

The media are also caught in a trap: They criticize MKs for impetuous, shortsighted decisions, and yet they regularly put the spotlight on spinmeisters, fast-talkers, and extremists. They focus on MKs who submit provocative bills, for example, and report how many bills were submitted by each MK, but the success rate of these bills, which is practically nil, goes unreported.

4.8 Immunity of Knesset Members

In democratic political systems, immunity is designed to allow the legislature to work unencumbered. Immunity exists in many countries as a constitutional arrangement to protect parliament members from interference by the executive branch (such as the arrest of opposition members to prevent them from voting), or to enable elected representatives to express their views and discharge their duties without fear. Thus immunity is not only the interest of those elected, but primarily the interest of the voters who should zealously protect the independence of the legislative branch. Immunity serves all the functions discussed in this chapter – representation, legislation, and oversight of the executive. Hence authority is given to the parliament itself to protect its members and decide when and how to lift a member's immunity.

To Israel's credit, immunity was established early, under the Mapai government, by the Knesset Members Immunity, Rights and Duties Law (1951) (hereinafter, "the Immunity Law"), and was later accorded constitutional standing in Article 17 of the Basic Law: The Knesset. A distinction is made between two types of immunity based on the MK's actions and how they are justified: **Substantive (essential) immunity** applies to an MK's actions related to his or her functioning as a Knesset member; this immunity cannot be lifted and extends to acts committed even after an individual has left office. **Procedural (limited or parliamentary) immunity** applies to all other actions of the MK, and a special procedure, described below, is required to lift this immunity to allow for an MK to be brought to trial.

To complete the picture, MKs also have immunity from search, detention, and wiretapping, and are ensured freedom of movement and the right to leave the country. MKs do not have immunity for traffic violations, penalty offenses, or administrative violations.

A. Substantive Immunity

> A member of Knesset shall bear no criminal or civil responsibility, and shall be immune from any legal proceeding, with respect to a vote, an oral or written expression of opinion or any other act, inside or outside the Knesset, if ... carried out as part of the discharge of his duty as a member of the Knesset. (Immunity Law, Article 1A)

The primary stumbling block in establishing immunity concerns the meaning of "as part of the discharge of his duty." For an MK to have the protection of substantive immunity, a connection must be established between the MK's actions and "the discharge of his duty." Immunity will protect MKs if the act they committed, even in violation of the law, was relevant for performing their parliamentary functions. Knesset members gave much thought to this connection in deciding whether to lift the immunity of various MKs, as did the High Court of Justice to which appeals were submitted. In 1985, for example, the Knesset lifted the immunity of MK Mohammed Miari for participating in a conference of the PLO, defined by law at the time as a terrorist organization. The High Court overturned this Knesset decision, ruling that what Miari said at the conference falls within the realm of substantive immunity, designed to protect the freedom of expression of MKs. A minority opinion contended that statements that appear to be in support of the leader of a terrorist organization are not consistent with the MK's oath of loyalty to the state, and therefore are not covered by substantive immunity (*Miari v. Speaker of the Knesset* 1985). In the case of MK Rafael Pinchasi in 1993, the High Court formulated criteria to determine when an MK's action falls within the realm of "discharging his duties" and is protected by substantive immunity. With respect to Pinchasi, the court overturned the lifting of his immunity on the grounds of an insufficient evidentiary basis (*Pinchasi v. Israel Knesset* 1995; also S. Navot 1998).

The question of what is covered by immunity periodically occupies the political system, more so in the past decade. For example, the immunity of MK Azmi Bishara was lifted by the Knesset in 2001 to allow an indictment against him for violation of the Prevention of Terrorism Ordinance based on the content of speeches he made both in Israel and Syria. The High Court of Justice ruled that Bishara's immunity cannot be lifted because he enjoys substantive immunity (*Bishara v. Attorney General* 2006). In 2002, the Knesset amended the Immunity Law to narrow the scope of substantive immunity, stipulating that immunity does not apply to Knesset members who engage in an action or express an opinion that entails

> denying the existence of the state of Israel as the state of the Jewish people; denying the democratic character of the state; incitement to racism because of color or race or national-ethnic origin; support for an armed struggle of an enemy state or for acts of terrorism against the state of Israel or against Jews or Arabs by virtue of their being Jews or Arabs, in Israel or outside of Israel. (Article 1A1)

Reading this new article in the Immunity Law can only lead to the conclusion that Israel's legislators in the 1950s were more tolerant and self-confident than were its legislators in the twenty-first century.

B. Procedural Immunity

Procedural immunity applies to all other actions of a Knesset member to which substantive immunity does not apply. Its purpose, as noted, is to protect Knesset members from arrest, false accusations, or harassment by the executive branch, and to afford the MKs freedom of action. In 2005, the Knesset revised the law regarding procedural immunity (Amendment 33). Previously, procedural immunity had been automatically granted to Knesset members during their term of office. This was the general rule, and an extensive procedure was needed to lift this immunity. As of Amendment 33, MKs do not have procedural immunity unless they explicitly request it. Furthermore MKs are entitled to procedural immunity against criminal charges only in extraordinary circumstances, as enumerated in the following list: the MK believes that he or she is entitled to substantive immunity (i.e., that the offense was committed as part of discharging his or her parliamentary duties); the indictment was not filed in good faith; the matter falls within the internal jurisdiction of the Knesset regarding disciplinary infractions; the functioning of the Knesset will be harmed by proceeding with criminal prosecution; or the public interest will not be harmed by not proceeding with it. The amendment shifts the burden of proof to the Knesset member, who must justify why an indictment should not be filed as for any citizen.

Lifting procedural immunity: In the process required to lift procedural immunity, the Knesset's House Committee and the Knesset plenum play a quasi-judicial role. Changes were made to the Immunity Law because of the increased number of cases in which MKs are charged with offenses, and also the wrangling between the Knesset and the court. The first time a Knesset member's immunity was lifted was in 1954, then because of traffic violations that were still covered by the Immunity Law. By 2010, a total of approximately fifty MKs had their immunity lifted, some more than once, and two-thirds of these were lifted after 1990. Most requests by the attorney general to the government to lift the immunity of a Knesset member in order to press charges were approved by the Knesset, generally following extensive debate. In some cases, the Knesset turned down the request to lift an MK's immunity, and several times the court intervened to disqualify the Knesset decision (Alon 2003; Solomon 2006).[37]

Until passage of Amendment 33, the procedure was that the attorney general submitted to the House Committee a request to revoke procedural immunity. If a majority in the committee decided that the immunity should *not* be lifted, the matter ended there;[38] if the House Committee *agreed* to lift immunity, the approval of the Knesset plenum was required. In other words, a Knesset member had immunity, and the attorney general had to request its removal.

[37] Our thanks for their help in providing data to Arbel Astrakan, legal adviser to the Knesset House Committee, and to Rivka Marcus and Daniel Rakmistruk of the Knesset Archive.

[38] At the time the House Committee could decide not to lift the immunity of an MK despite a request to do so by the MK, as happened initially with MK Yehiel Hazan. See Alon 2003b.

Today an indictment against an MK will be submitted to the court with the approval of the attorney general and a copy will be sent to the MK, the Speaker of the Knesset, and the chair of the Knesset House Committee. The MK has the right not to request immunity, in which case the matter will be handled like that of any citizen. Or, within thirty days, the MK may ask the Knesset to grant immunity, based – unlike in the past – on one of the reasons given in the aforementioned list. The deliberation about this immunity request will take place in the House Committee with the participation of the accused MK and the attorney general. What happens next was completely changed by Amendment 33: If the House Committee rejects the MK's request and lifts the procedural immunity, the decision is final and the matter goes to the courts; if the committee decides to grant the MK's immunity based on the list of reasons, the Knesset plenum must approve this in an open vote. An MK can appeal a decision in the High Court on the grounds that the House Committee's decision was unreasonable. If the committee lifts the MK's immunity and the MK does not object, only notification of the Knesset is required, not a vote in the plenum.

C. Involvement of the Court in Lifting Immunity

Decisions about immunity are a quasi-judicial power of the Knesset, and the High Court does not hesitate to intervene when appeals are submitted about these decisions. In these rulings, the court primarily examines whether the matter was one of substantive immunity (in which case the immunity cannot be revoked), and whether the Knesset's decision-making about revoking the immunity followed proper procedures, as in the Pinchasi case mentioned above when the court overturned the Knesset decision to lift his immunity. In other cases, the High Court ruled that the Knesset should not be judging MKs on the offenses, as this is not its task and it does not have the tools to do so. The Knesset must be persuaded that the attorney general's request to lift immunity was made in good faith, set on a firm factual basis, and is not discriminatory. For this reason, the court overturned the lifting of MK Miari's immunity on the grounds that the Knesset plenum introduced extraneous considerations and thereby exceeded its authority (*Miari v. Speaker of the Knesset* 1985). The High Court does not hesitate to exercise judicial review over the Knesset's considerations in immunity-lifting procedures.[39]

4.9 The Knesset and the Other Branches – A Balance of Power

This chapter opened with the question, is the Knesset first among equals? In the summing up below, our starting point is that, in the Israeli parliamentary system, the roles and status of the Knesset are shaped by the character of the regime: Institutionally

[39] In 2003, for example, Likud MK Michael Gorlovsky was accused of having voted twice in a Knesset vote. Gorlovsky pleaded guilty to the Knesset's Ethics Committee, which ruled that he had committed a disciplinary offense, and suspended his participation in Knesset debates for four and a half months. When the attorney general sought to have Gorlovsky's immunity lifted, the House Committee refused. In 2005, in response to a petition from a civil society organization, the High Court overturned the House Committee's decision stating that an MK's immunity does not include the freedom to vote twice. In another case, the High Court in 2010 instructed the Knesset to explain why certain rights were denied of Arab MK Hanin Zoabi despite the immunity law and previous rulings on the matter (see Blander 2011).

the Knesset is, above all, the exclusive national "representative branch" and the bearer of sovereignty by virtue of having been elected – from which are derived its mandate to legislate and its political supremacy. The perception of "three constitutionally equal branches" or the Knesset as "first among equals" does not take into consideration the essence of governance in Israel – that the government serves by virtue of the trust placed in it by the Knesset and is subordinate to the Knesset (A. Barak 1999, 129). In the Israeli system, the separation of powers resembles that of Britain, the Netherlands, or Sweden. Overlap of the governance functions does not allow its definition in terms of the American model of "separate branches." In Israel, the primacy of the Knesset as the parliament must be recognized, without detracting in any way from its subordination to the constitution (the Basic Laws) and the absolute independence of the judiciary with its power of judicial review.

When examining the relationship between the Knesset and the other branches, we must first point out that the entire political system has greatly changed from the previous, well-organized, party-dominated democracy. The Knesset's place in society has declined, as has the power of all the branches of government. Indeed, power relations among the branches of the political system are not a zero-sum game. A strong government does not necessarily mean a weak parliament, and vice versa; an active judiciary could be a sign of a weak legislature or of a strong one that must be held in check; and strong legislators do not necessarily reflect the institutional power of the legislative house itself. Has the Knesset gained or lost power compared with the other branches of government? In the past, the Knesset was all-powerful in theory, and barely subject to judicial review, but in practice was almost entirely subordinate to the executive branch (with some important exceptions). Since the 1980s, this balance of power has shifted, making it necessary to distinguish between the power of the Knesset as a body and the power of individual Knesset members.

Changes in the party topography of Israel – the end of the hegemony of one party, parity between two political blocs, the impact of primaries and the direct election, and the ongoing coalition instability – have all left their mark on the power of the Knesset and its relations with the other branches. The Knesset as a body has weakened, primarily because of the decline of the parties as the backbone of parliamentary activity, in parallel with the ascendancy of the individual Knesset member and the politics of personality. The most salient demonstration of this trend is the proliferation in recent years of private members' bills submitted by MKs from both the opposition and the coalition. A weak Knesset, however, is not necessarily a sign of a strong government. The combination of elections that fail to produce a clear advantage for any one party, the fragmentation of the factions in the Knesset, and the slackening of party discipline – all undermined the consensus-contribution of coalitions, and rocked the stability of the government. The complexity of the balance of forces between the Knesset and the government can be discerned during the eras of unity governments or broad-based coalitions. Ostensibly these should be prototypes of a strong government and a flaccid Knesset, but data about parliamentary activity under unity governments in the 1980s and broad-based coalitions in the 1990s suggest that parliamentary activity was then at its height. In the absence of faction discipline, the broad-based coalition was not capable of controlling independent parliamentary activity. Nonetheless feverish Knesset activity does not necessarily indicate power, and may simply conceal the underlying weakness.

Relations between the Knesset and the judiciary also reflect dramatic change and increased tension on a long list of issues, from matters of principle such as judicial review through a series of High Court rulings on the disqualification of party lists or the lifting of immunity. In this area, too, the balance of forces is complex, and a simple statement such as "the court is trying to rule the Knesset" has no basis in reality. On the one hand, the Knesset often recoils from taking a stand about critical and controversial, value-laden issues – matters that must be resolved in the political-public sphere (such as the meaning of "a Jewish and democratic state," the route of the Separation Barrier, and whether to draft yeshiva students into the army) – laying these hot-button issues at the feet of the court. Furthermore, MKs have increasingly turned to the High Court to deal with the Knesset's internal affairs, thus by their own petitions abdicating to the court their responsibility for important decision-making. And of sad note is the large number of MKs who have engaged in criminal activity, some serving prison sentences. On the other hand, the Knesset manages to wield its power by legislation that flies in the face of the judiciary, whether laws designed to circumvent the High Court, or changing laws retroactively following High Court decisions in order to legalize previous Knesset decisions. Occasionally very disturbing proposals can be heard by MKs (and former Justice Minister Daniel Friedmann) to "rein in the High Court" or establish a separate constitutional court. One positive example of the complexity of the relationship: Although the Supreme Court has so far disqualified very few Knesset laws as unconstitutional, the possibility of this happening has sharpened Knesset awareness during the legislative process, leading MKs to craft legislation with an eye toward the question, "Would this pass the Supreme Court?" In this way, the two branches fulfill their roles optimally, without petitions or confrontations.

A responsible and powerful parliament is vital for a stable political system with steering capacity. The institutional vigor of the Knesset as a body that represents, legislates, and oversees is critical for the proper overall functioning of the democratic political process. The strength of the Israeli parliament is that it reflects the palette of colors of Israeli society; its shortcoming is that the representatives do not always handle well the institutional responsibility thrust upon them. The populist tendency of some Knesset members is a two-edged sword in terms of the stature of the Knesset, their own stature, and the necessary balance of power between the legislature and the other branches.

Many elements are required to enhance the Knesset institutionally. We named only a few here, and set aside the electoral system for discussion in Chapter 10. These include passage of the Basic Law: Legislation; strengthening the standing of the Knesset factions; introducing essential changes in Knesset responsibility for the Budget and Arrangements Laws; bestowing on the Knesset Finance Committee responsibility for enforcing the state comptroller's recommendations; and reform of the structure and work methods of the Knesset committees. Above all, none of these proposals will have any impact at all if Knesset members do not conduct themselves as responsible representatives to the voter, the party, and the public – without help from the Knesset Ethics Committee.

5 The Executive Branch and Attempts to Strengthen It

5.1 The Executive Branch in Parliamentary Systems and in Israel

The "executive branch" includes the prime minister, ministers, ministries, and other governmental bodies.[1] The government, composed of the prime minister and ministers (the cabinet), heads the executive branch and is responsible for managing the affairs of state. As emphasized in the previous chapter on the Knesset, the government in a parliamentary democracy is an emissary that governs by virtue of the parliament's confidence in it. This emissary has complex functions, however, and therefore also broad powers – from the moment a government is formed and for as long as it maintains the confidence of the Knesset, it functions as an authority in its own right that is subordinate to the rule of law.

Studies of political systems in democracies often use the terms "governance," "governability," and "executive power." We prefer Karl Deutsch's phrase "steering capacity," which points up the complexity of the government's tasks in operating and managing a political system (1963).[2] This mission includes coping with the challenges of survival, maintaining stability, and guiding the system toward the society's common goals. To that end, the government usually has exclusive authority to enforce the laws, set and implement policies, make decisions, and apply the coercive power of the military and the police. The government is also in charge of the steering mechanism: managing the ministries, statutory authorities, and government corporations.[3] A government and its ministries have many additional responsibilities, such as representing the state to foreign parties, implementing the Budget Law, enforcing court decisions, and supervising the local authorities.

A. The Executive Branch and the Separation of Powers

Democracies differ in the relationship between the executive branch and legislative branch (the parliament). In the British parliamentary system, whose basic

[1] The Basic Law: Government does not distinguish between these, stating that "the government is the executive authority of the state."

[2] For earlier approaches toward governance, see Crozier, Huntington, and Watanuki 1975.

[3] On the structure of public management in Israel, see Galnoor 2011, 27–42.

principles were adopted by Israel, the executive branch is an extension of the parliament. The prime minister is elected by the parliament, must have its confidence, reports to and is accountable to it, and can be dismissed by it, usually, by a majority.[4] The power and stability of the government are drawn from its base of legitimacy in the house of representatives and, in states like Israel, in the parliamentary coalition.

In Israel, the steering capacity of the government and its leader rests on four progressively smaller circles:

- its position among ***the public*** in the election and thereafter;
- its power ***in the Knesset*** based on the size of the coalition, its ideological position, and the effective number of parties;
- its control over ***the coalition*** based on the agreements, the number of participants, and the strength of the main party; and
- the strength of ***the main party*** and the standing of the prime minister within the party.

The more the prime minister's party has larger and stronger circles of support – as had Mapai in its heyday – the greater its power, stability, and steering capacity; conversely, the lesser the circles of support – as with the teetering Barak government in 2001 – the less it is capable of making binding decisions. In reality, the interaction among these four circles is complex and unpredictable. For example, the prime minister needs a strong and homogeneous coalition with a solid parliamentary majority, but to create this base of support in the Knesset, the number and heterogeneity of the parties in the coalition must often be increased. An alternative coalition is not always an option, and when it is, too narrow or too broad a base could limit the prime minister's room for maneuvering. A second example of the complexity concerns cohesiveness within the party. The party strives to impose discipline over its Knesset faction and government ministers, and they strive to be free of party dictates. In sum, the steering capacity of governments requires cohesiveness in all avenues of the political system. A breakdown in any of the circles – loss of public confidence or the resignation of a coalition partner – affects the other circles and impedes the steering capacity of the government and prime minister.

In a parliamentary system, the separation of powers between the legislative and executive branches is not absolute, because the government is derived from and accountable to the parliament (the relationship between the executive branch and the judiciary will be more fully discussed in Chapter 6). In Israel, almost all ministers are also Knesset members, which creates personal overlap between the two branches. Unlike the Knesset, the government does not embody sovereignty, is not a representative body, and does not legislate (though it initiates bills and is responsible for secondary legislation). The Knesset also oversees government activity and supervises the ministries and all budgeted bodies.

[4] In Britain, the prime minister can shorten the term of the parliament by declaring early elections. In Israel, the prime minister can dissolve the Knesset in exceptional circumstances (Article 29 of the Basic Law: Government), but this does not necessarily lead to new elections.

B. Changes in the Responsibility and Authority of the Executive Branch

The expansion of the state into additional areas of activity in the twentieth century strengthened the executive branch. One indicator of this in western democracies is the rise in public expenditures, which approached half the GNP in Israel (Arian, Nachmias, and Amir 2002, 35). The executive branch needed more resources to pay for security expenditures, and was simultaneously taking on new fields such as welfare services and environmental protection. As a result, the civil service expanded, especially into service provision and the regulation of private bodies (oligopolies, air transportation, pharmaceuticals, etc.). When "big government" began to suffer from "overload," it was attacked from both wings: The right accused it of an unbridled expansion of duties, bureaucracy, and procedures that, among other things, encumber the parliament in carrying out oversight; and the left accused it of conservatism and failure to reduce social gaps. Toward the end of the twentieth century, this trend was reversed in the direction of privatization and deregulation, entailing a reduced role for the state and a shirking of responsibility for basic social services (Galnoor 2011, 60, 150–57). Accordingly, the executive branch in most western countries began to shrink, blurring the boundaries between the public, business, and social sectors. This is the broad context for the steering problems of the executive branch, which finds it increasingly difficult to shape policy on key matters in foreign affairs, security, and social issues.

Although the executive branch in Israel was strong from the outset, as it was forced to face a range of challenges, this power was tempered by the need to operate through coalitions and political parties, and to take into account bodies like the Histadrut (the main workers' union), the Jewish Agency, and sectoral groups. Thus, the fading of the parties and other bodies as mediators between government decision-makers and the public also helped strengthen the executive branch. The media, for example, whose political role has grown, excelled at shining the light on government activities, but could not fulfill the roles of oversight or mediation. At the same time, the weakening of the state also affected Israel. Thus two conflicting phenomena are visible in Israel. On the one hand, the executive branch has a broad scope of duties, primarily because of the dominance of security, development needs, immigrant absorption, etc. On the other hand, the public sector has shrunk, and responsibilities that clearly fall on the state in welfare and education have been sloughed off onto others – social agencies and commercial enterprises. The crisis of the executive branch's steering capacity in Israel is paradoxical: The public is dissatisfied with government activity, but also with public services contracted to others – services for which citizens justifiably continue to hold the state responsible.

Israel's first election, held in 1949, led to the formation of the first government that won the confidence of the Knesset. From then until 2015, Israel has had thirty-four governments by official count, all coalitions. In the next section, we briefly present some milestones in the history of these governments.

C. Governments in Israel: A Brief Survey

Government Identified with the Dominant Party (1948–1965)

In the first two decades of Israel's history, the institution of government was stable, even though more than a dozen governments served during this period due to frequent coalition changes. The steering capacity of these governments rested on the unchallenged standing of Mapai as the dominant party – in the public, the Knesset, the coalition, and the government. Coalitions were composed of a small number of parties (the three regulars were Mapai, the religious party, and the Progressives, with another couple from the right or left). Mapai insisted on keeping what it perceived to be the key ministries, in addition to the prime ministry: defense, finance, foreign affairs, education, and agriculture. Political crises led more than once to the resignation of the prime minister and early elections (e.g., because of education policies in 1951 or the Lavon affair in 1960/61), but the new governments always resembled their predecessors – certainly the identity of the dominant party remained a constant. The main personnel changes in this period were the resignation of Ben-Gurion in 1953, the appointment of Moshe Sharett as prime minister for a short period (1953–55), the final resignation of Ben-Gurion in 1963, and the appointment of Levi Eshkol. In retrospect, despite the onerous tasks of the early years, the governments had very impressive achievements. The domination of Mapai reached a peak during the Sinai Campaign (1956) and the 1959 election, but cracks soon appeared during the next years.

End of the Revolutionary Era and the Weakening of Steering Capacity (1965–1977)

Resignation of the founding leader and the placid leadership of Eshkol marked the gradual transition from revolutionary fervor to a more democratic politics. This "normal" development came to an abrupt end in 1967 on the eve of the impending war. During that "waiting period," the public lost faith in the judgment of the leaders, and the government needed reinforcement – the addition of the Rafi and Gahal parties to the "national unity government." Decision-making in the wake of the 1967 war required a government with more steering capacity than had existed since the establishment of the state, but in the critical post-war period, the governments found themselves trapped by a broad coalition drunk with victory and preferring to decide not to decide. In retrospect, it is clear that the Alignment (Labor) was not willing to tackle the big issues, and even if it had wanted to, it no longer dominated the coalition government numbering twenty ministers. Indeed, Golda Meir's government, formed in 1969 after Gahal resigned, did not change the policies, which led straight into the Yom Kippur War. The year 1973 was an earthquake in the chronicles of Israeli governments. It shook the foundations of the unwritten contract between the citizens and their government, the contract that assured Israelis that, in matters of security, they could rely fully on the civilian and military leadership. This upheaval was already reflected in the 1973 election with the growth of Menachem Begin's opposition party as an alternative to the Alignment, and in the public fury that brought down the Meir government in 1974 and finally brought the Likud to power in the 1977 election.

Changing of the Guard (1977–1983)

The election upheaval of 1977 marked the end of an era in which one dominant party was identified with the government, and indeed transformation of the entire political system. It also provided a test – passed successfully – of the first regime change in Israel. At first it looked as if the Likud, which had won over a third of the votes, would inherit the mantle of the dominant party. In the subsequent election of 1981, however, even though the Likud increased its power and formed the government, the Alignment garnered an equal number of votes, launching a two-bloc period in Israeli politics. The first Begin government (1977–81) could record a major achievement in signing a peace treaty with Egypt, which was ratified in the Knesset despite strong opposition within both the coalition and the opposition. Unlike the government's skilled steering of foreign affairs, in internal matters – particularly economic policies – it triggered an unprecedented inflationary spiral in Israel. During this period, the government launched Project Renewal for rehabilitating distressed neighborhoods within Israel proper, and poured vast amounts into the construction of Jewish settlements in the occupied territories. The second Begin government (1981–83) was unable to stabilize the economy and was responsible for the first Lebanon War, leading to Begin's resignation as prime minister.

The Unity Governments: Achievements, Stalemate, and Decline (1984–1990)

The election results of 1984 and 1988 ended in a tie between the two large parties, creating two political blocs in the Knesset; in the absence of a pivot party, two successive unity governments were formed (1984–88 and 1988–90). Steering capacity would have been enhanced had the Likud and the Alignment – which together held about eighty seats after these elections – formed a unity government without the small satellite parties. But these two parties did not trust each other, and as a result formed very large coalitions in terms of the number of MKs and parties. The first unity government invented a new concept in politics – an agreement to have two prime ministers serve in rotation. It also reached three very difficult decisions: partial withdrawal from Lebanon, an economic program ending inflation that had spiraled to over 400 percent, and a halt to development of the costly Lavi aircraft. On the other hand, the periods of the unity government – particularly the second – were marked by stalemate and dysfunctionality in external affairs because of the polarized opinions of the two main partners. This unity ended in shameful political chicanery, marking a nadir in Israeli politics.[5] The government subsequently formed by Yitzhak Shamir did not record any singular achievements or failures.

Instability: Narrow Governments, Assassination of the Prime Minister, Direct Election, and Minor Upheavals (1990–2009)

The 1990s were marked by narrow governments composed of numerous factions, which reflected the increasing fragmentation of the Knesset. Thus was the Shamir government formed in 1990 followed by the Rabin government after the 1992 election with the support of sixty-two MKs. The Rabin government made historic decisions on security and foreign affairs: the Oslo Agreements, back-channel negotiations with Syria, and a peace agreement with Jordan; and several new domestic initiatives such as investing more state funds in education and in Arab communities. These initiatives were abruptly terminated on November 4, 1995 when Yitzhak

[5] In a court ruling in 1991, Menachem Elon, Deputy President of the Supreme Court, expressed his view of what was then called "the dirty trick": "The boundaries have burst between forbidden and permitted political acts" (*Jerzhevski v. Prime Minister Yitzhak Shamir et al.* 1991).

Rabin was assassinated in order to halt the peace initiative. Ever since, a heavy shadow of extreme right-wing terrorism has hovered over Israel.

Following the assassination, the government changed hands many times and became a revolving door for prime ministers and parties. Between 1992 and 2009, seven elections were held and six prime ministers held office, reminiscent of the dizzying pace of political crises in Italy. The main events of this period: The Labor Party, which had returned to power in 1992, lost in 1996 when Benjamin Netanyahu from the Likud won the first direct election for prime minister. The pendulum of power swung back to Labor in 1999, when Ehud Barak defeated Netanyahu in the election for prime minister, but this was short-lived. Barak resigned in 2001, and a special election was held for prime minister, won by Ariel Sharon of the Likud. Labor joined the Likud-led government, but resigned in 2003 and forced an early election (conducted according to the reinstated previous electoral system), in which the Likud headed by Sharon won again (thirty-eight seats). The Gaza disengagement led to a split in the Likud, with Sharon establishing the Kadima Party together with some Labor Party members. When Sharon took ill, the Kadima Party, now headed by Ehud Olmert, won twenty-nine seats in the 2006 election. The Olmert-led government embarked upon two major military operations – the second Lebanon War (2006) and the military campaign in Gaza (December 2008 to January 2009). Olmert did not stand for reelection in 2009 because he was being investigated for corruption.

This long period was marked by instability and inaction in foreign affairs. The attempt to strengthen the executive branch by constitutional means – direct election of a "prime ministerial government" – was a failure, in contrast with the first unity government, which had been fairly stable. Netanyahu and Barak, who had been elected in the direct election system, served relatively short terms (together less than five years), and the governments they led demonstrated neither steering capacity nor stability.

Netanyahu's Three Governments (2009–)

Netanyahu formed the next government in 2009 (a coalition of five parties and seventy-one MKs), even though Kadima, headed by Tzipi Livni, had won twenty-eight seats in the election – one more than the Likud. This period too has been characterized by short-term governments (elections in 2013 and again in 2015), after which the Likud formed the government and Netanyahu remained prime minister. Following the 2009 election, the Kadima Party fell apart. Livni created Hatnuah and in the 2015 election formed a joint list with Labor. In 2013, Yesh Atid captured the center of the political spectrum, becoming the second-largest party, and joined the coalition on condition that the ultra-Orthodox parties would be left out. In 2015, Kulanu, a new center party, joined a narrow right-wing coalition of sixty-one MKs, while Yesh Atid remained in the opposition. During this period, Israel embarked on two major military operations: Pillar of Defense (in November 2012) and Protective Edge (in July–August 2014), both against Hamas in the Gaza Strip.

5.2 The Constitutional Infrastructure

With enactment of the Law and Administration Ordinance in May 1948, the powers, jurisdiction, and administration of the provisional government were set down in law.

The Transition Law from 1949 regulated the changeover from provisional arrangements to the first legitimate government, which won a vote of confidence from the first elected Knesset in March 1949.

A. Basic Law: Government

The 1968 version of the Basic Law: Government primarily organized and consolidated the existing rules. This is the only Basic Law that was replaced twice – in 1992 and 2001. This law defines the composition of the government (the prime minister and ministers), eligibility for holding these positions, the process of forming a government, removal of a prime minister or minister from office, procedures for expressing no confidence in the government, the authority of the prime minister to dissolve the Knesset, the residual power of the government (see below), and other powers such as declaring a state of emergency or war. Some articles that deal with governmental work were moved to a separate law – the Government Law (2001), including the obligation to publish coalition agreements; a cooling-off period for heads of the General Security Service (GSS) or Mossad, IDF generals, and senior police officers prior to their appointment as ministers; establishment of a Ministerial Committee for National Security; the powers of government commissions of inquiry; and other provisions.

The operating procedures of the government are defined in the Statute of Government Operations, which contains a list of the standing ministerial committees and their procedures, procedures for legislative proposals, states of emergency and regulations for states of emergency, policy regarding secrecy and disclosure of information, and follow-up on the implementation of government decisions.[6]

B. Formation of the Government, Termination of Office, and Continuity

In the electoral system of Israel, which returned to its original format in 2001, election results determine the composition of the Knesset, but not who the prime minister will be. The prime minister is the Knesset member who is able to form a coalition that wins the confidence of the Knesset. Chapter 3 describes the procedures by which the president assigns the task of forming the government to one Knesset member. This MK has twenty-eight days to form a government, which can be extended by fourteen days. If these efforts are unsuccessful, two additional attempts can be made by other MKs. Failure in all these efforts will be deemed as if the Knesset chose to dissolve, and new elections will be held. The prime minister-designate presents to the Knesset the proposed "Government Policy" of his or her coalition. This document has political rather than legal standing as an outline of the ideological platform of the partners to the government.[7] In addition, the prime minister-designate presents to the Knesset the ministers, deputy ministers, and distribution of portfolios, and asks for its confidence. The Knesset serves four years, which is the natural life expectancy of the government, whose term should end as the Knesset's term expires. In practice, however, all governments but two were dissolved before the Knesset

[6] See the website of the Office of the Prime Minister: www.pmo.gov.il/IsraelGov/GovDocuments/Pages/default.aspx [in Hebrew] (accessed May 10, 2016).

[7] The government may act in contravention of its declared Government Policy, so long as it continues to enjoy the confidence of the Knesset (*Fuchs v. Prime Minister of Israel* 2004).

term expired, generally due to crises within the coalition.[8] The two exceptions – one Knesset and one government serving out their full term – were under Golda Meir (1969–74), which actually lasted more than four years, as the election was delayed because of the Yom Kippur War, and the Begin government (1977–81). The Rabin government (1992–95) might conceivably have also served out a full term. The term of office of Israeli governments is relatively short: The average term of thirty-three governments (until 2015) was two years, without significant differences between the eras, except for the high turnover of prime ministers since the 1990s.

The prime minister can cause a government to fall by resigning. Ben-Gurion, who resigned seven times over the course of fifteen years in office, brought down the government each time, and usually returned to form a new one. If the prime minister dies or is permanently unable to fulfill his or her duties, this is deemed to be the resignation of the government. The Eshkol (1969) and Rabin (1995) governments ended in this manner. With regard to the Sharon government (2006), after the prime minister was unable to fulfill his duties, the government appointed Ehud Olmert to be acting prime minister until formation of a new government after an election. Most commonly, a government falls when a faction that is a senior coalition member resigns because of ideological disagreements or sometimes personal issues (see Chapter 11 on coalitions). The main instrument to end the term of a government is a no-confidence vote by the Knesset. In practice, this happened only once, in 1990, because prime ministers generally prefer to preempt a Knesset no-confidence vote by resigning or calling for early elections. The Knesset can bring down a government by deciding to dissolve itself and calling for early elections. Other instruments that were not yet used: ending a prime minister's term because of an offense marked by moral turpitude, or Knesset failure to approve the Budget Law.

To ensure continuity, the law states that after a government resigns or a new Knesset is elected, the outgoing government must continue to serve until formation of the new government. A court ruling from 1976 states that a transitional government "incarcerates" the ministers, with "no one coming or going."[9] A transitional government has the same power as any government, but is expected not to launch new policies because it has no majority in the Knesset and a no-confidence vote cannot be taken against it.

C. Additional Powers of the Government

According to the current Basic Law: Government, the government is authorized to rearrange the distribution of portfolios among the ministers, and to transfer areas of authority and responsibility from one minister to another. The government operates via standing ministerial committees. Deliberations and decisions of the government in certain fields (state security, foreign affairs, and other designated matters) are

[8] This was different during the period of direct election of the prime minister because the resignation of the prime minister was linked to dissolution of the Knesset. As for duration, the thirty-second government served four years (2009–13), but the eighteenth Knesset was dissolved beforehand. The thirty-third served two years (2013–15).

[9] After Rabin resigned as prime minister in 1976, two ministers from the Independent Liberal Party asked to resign, but a High Court ruling required them to remain in the transitional government (*State of Israel v. Moshe Kol* 1976, 1977).

confidential. Government ministers are responsible for secondary legislation, i.e., regulations for implementing the laws passed by the Knesset. The Knesset has the authority to declare a state of emergency, but in urgent and exceptional situations, the government has the authority to declare a state of emergency for a set period. The law does not address the question of the formal authority of the government to declare war or sign international treaties, but clearly this is within the purview of the government, and not of any other body.

Article 32 of the Basic Law: Government states that the government has residual power "to perform in the name of the state and subject to any law, all actions which are not legally incumbent on another authority." Residual power originated in the prerogative of the British crown that was transferred to the executive branch in order to prevent a legal vacuum. In the absence of legislation, the government is authorized to act at its discretion but is "subject to any law." The government is not authorized to use its residual power if Knesset legislation covers the matter; the Supreme Court, for example, revoked a 1993 governmental decision about the classification of development towns because Knesset legislation addresses this matter (*Kiryat Gat v. State of Israel* 1993). It is under the rubric of residual power that the government of Israel engages in war, signs international treaties, and ensures the printing of postage stamps.

5.3 The Political Fabric of the Government

A. Coalitions (for a comprehensive discussion see Chapter 11)

In parliamentary democracies, coalitions are the link between the legislative and executive branches, i.e., between the preferences of voters and the composition of a government whose policies will affect their lives. This bridge between electoral politics and the politics of governmental policies is generally necessary when no single party holds a parliamentary majority. A coalition is also a pragmatic compromise among party positions and the groups they represent. It is thus a pact among political parties for a set period, an agreement to cooperate in order to advance the interests of their constituents and the public at large. The parties that participate in a coalition formulate a political program – policies that bridge the gaps between them. Clearly the character, conduct, and stability of a coalition are shaped by the system of government, the electoral system, election results, and the political temperament.

Since 1949, all the governments in Israel have been coalitions, thus a coalition is part of the political culture. This is not a constitutional requirement, but the product of the political constellation of forces and election results. An electoral system that emphasizes proportionality allows for a large number of parties to be represented. Thus, the political system from the outset made room for a diverse range of groups in society as it aimed to achieve broad consensus. Accordingly, a coalition is not negative, nor does it intensify factionalism, but it is a stabilizing mechanism that strives to bridge existing differences in society. The desire for inclusion and creation of the broadest possible consensus were manifested in the tendency to create surplus or grand coalitions. The more divisive society became, the more this tendency increased. On a practical level, the aim was to form a stable coalition that would prevent the government from falling if one party left, meaning that a coalition had to be seventy to eighty MKs (Koren and Shapira 1997, 37). From one perspective, multiple parties in the coalition are a source of instability; from another, they ensure that not every resignation will bring down the government. Since the end of Mapai's domination in Israeli politics, it can generally be said that the more parties in a coalition, the harder for any single party to capture the pivotal position. Until 1967, the dominant party had some room to maneuver within the coalition (which had seventy-five MKs, on average). The national unity government in 1967 was a broad coalition of 107 MKs, but this preceded a new era in which coalitions were either very broad or very narrow ("minority governments"), and most were unstable.

B. Unity Governments

Unity governments are a specific case of a grand coalition in which the two large parties are members, and – in Israel – usually smaller parties as well. The first unity government was formed in June 1967 to cope with the impending war, perceived as an existential threat to the state. The coalition was expanded by two parties – Rafi (Moshe Dayan as the Minister of Defense in place of Levi Eshkol) and Gahal (Menachem Begin and Yosef Sapir as ministers without portfolio). A similar unity government was reestablished after the 1969 election, held during the War of Attrition, despite the success of the Labor Party, which won fifty-seven seats. This time it was a coalition government in every sense, and Gahal had five ministers and three portfolios. Nine months later, the Gahal ministers resigned from the government in the wake of disagreements about the plan proposed by US Secretary of State William P. Rogers to bring the War of Attrition to an end.

The two unity governments in the 1980s were not the product of a national crisis or public demand, but rather of the stalemate produced by the election – the parliamentary draw between the two large parties (and two blocs), which prevented either from forming a coalition. A unity government was also an attempt to respond to the political polarization reflected by the election returns. The coalition agreements of the 1984 unity government contained unique arrangements such as rotation of the prime minister (Prime Minister Peres resigned after two years, when Prime Minister Shamir took over), and the formation of an internal cabinet within the government with parity between the sides and mutual veto power. Despite the ideological differences between the two partners, this unity government made important decisions and served out its full term. The 1988 unity government that followed was also the product of the ongoing stalemate between the two political blocs, and a drifting of some voters to the small, extremist parties. In retrospect, its establishment was an anachronism based on a search for the "least of all evils," but it might have been better to call for a new election immediately. In this unity government, there was no rotation agreement, and this time around the coalition partners paralyzed each other. The ugly denouement of this government in the spring of 1990 marked a watershed in the decline of Israeli politics (see Section 5.1C above).

Another coalition of the two large parties was headed by Ariel Sharon, who won direct election as prime minister in 2001. While the two large parties had held sway in the unity governments of the 1980s, this was not the case in the Sharon-formed coalition because the Knesset elected two years earlier continued to serve, and fewer than 40 percent of the seats were held by the Likud (nineteen) and Labor (twenty-six) combined. This coalition of 2001 added six parties to the two large ones for a total of seventy-seven MKs. The second Intifada broke out during this government's tenure, and internal divisions led to a foreign policy stalemate that brought an end to its term after only two years. Following the 2003 election, Likud and Labor continued together in coalition, though other partners shifted. The disengagement from Gaza catalyzed the resignation of two right-wing parties, as well as a schism in the Likud and Labor parties, and the creation of Kadima. In the 2006 election, no single party garnered more than 25 percent of the Knesset seats, and the size disparities narrowed among the four or five largest parties. As a result, the term "unity government" has been meaningless since the 1990s because the governments have in practice been ordinary coalitions in which the two largest parties at the time participated. Following the 2009 election, the two largest parties combined (Kadima and Likud) did not win 50 percent of the Knesset seats, and did not agree to cooperate in a coalition.[10]

C. Minority and Narrow Governments

A minority government is composed of one party or a coalition of parties representing fewer than half the members of parliament. It can sustain itself by virtue of external support, permanent or ad hoc, from parties that are not in the coalition. When parties outside the minority government provide routine support, they help create a "blocking majority" to prevent the opposition from forming an alternative government.

Minority governments are rare in Israel, and over the years only two governments have had a formal coalition of fewer than sixty MKs. After the resignation of Shas in 1993, the Rabin government was left with only fifty-eight MKs (Labor, Meretz, and another two MKs who joined later), and relied on the routine, outside support of the Arab parties (in a non-formal coalition agreement). This was the first and last attempt at a relatively stable minority government, and – although it had steering capacity – its opponents accused it of lacking legitimacy, which ended in the assassination of the prime minister. The second minority government in the wake of Rabin's assassination was the same coalition under Peres. The Barak coalition (1999–2001) was at first supported by seventy-five MKs from seven factions, but this gradually whittled down to a minority government of thirty-two MKs and became a transitional government on its way to new elections.

The term "narrow government" generally refers to a coalition with a small parliamentary majority. Some examples: the first Rabin government in 1974 (sixty-one MKs); the Begin coalition after the 1977 election was originally a narrow government (sixty-two MKs), which then expanded when joined by the Dash Party; the Begin government after the 1981 election (sixty-one MKs); the Shamir government in 1990

[10] Another short-lived attempt to form a kind of "unity government" took place in 2012, when MK Shaul Mofaz became head of the Kadima Party and joined the Netanyahu coalition. Seven party members headed by Tzipi Livni left Kadima to form a new faction – Hatnuah. Two months later, Kadima withdrew from the coalition and the eighteenth Knesset was dissolved (www.haaretz.com/israel-news/in-surprise-move-netanyahu-mofaz-agree-to-form-unity-government-cancel-early-elections-1.428843 [accessed October 16, 2017]).

after dissolution of the unity government (sixty-two MKs); and the Netanyahu government after the 2015 election (sixty-one MKs).

Theories of coalitions use the phrase "a minimum winning coalition" (see Chapter 11) to refer to an efficient allocation of resources among the partners, i.e., payment of the minimum political benefits to the coalition members. In Israel, the major parties seek to avoid a narrow coalition, because experience suggests that government decisions on controversial issues lead to the resignation of parties and the breakup of the coalition. Narrow coalitions are generally not sufficiently stable in Israel, and, more importantly, not perceived as legitimate by the public or the political system. In Israel, far-reaching policy decisions seem to require a broad consensus.

5.4 The Prime Minister

A. The Role of the Prime Minister and Power Bases

The prime minister is often compared to the conductor of an orchestra, but the metaphor is far from precise: Politics allows for coordination, not harmony, certainly not control, and the instruments keep changing during the performance. Plato's metaphor of a ship captain is more apt because it entails the task of navigation and coping with wind and waves. In Israel, the prime minister's task of steering is particularly difficult because the winds whip, the waves are high, and the passengers are stubborn. In a Knesset debate after the 1976 Entebbe rescue operation, MK Menachem Begin said of Prime Minister Rabin, "All ministers are equal, but the prime minister has one iota more of responsibility."

Prime ministers in Israel must head the party list and be its candidate for the position; to head the executive branch, they need the confidence of parliament, without which they cannot win the public trust. The real candidates for prime minister become apparent only after the election, and sometimes only coalition negotiations determine who will become prime minister. During the period of direct election of the prime minister, there were only two candidates, and it was clear who would be prime minister as soon as the votes were counted. Prime ministers have formal power by virtue of their duties set by law, while their political power, as noted, derives from the support they gain in the widening circles of the party, the government coalition, the Knesset, and the public. By virtue of their position, prime ministers set the agenda not just for the government, but for the entire political system. Formally, government decisions are made by a majority of ministers, and the prime minister votes only in the event of a tie, but it is rare for the government to make a critical decision to which the prime minister objects, and for the prime minister to remain in power.

In Israel, the prime minister shapes policy in matters of security and foreign affairs. For this reason, some prime ministers also served as defense ministers: David Ben-Gurion, Levi Eshkol, Yitzhak Rabin, and Ehud Barak. In many cases, the prime minister took initiatives at his or her own discretion, winning government approval only retrospectively: Ben-Gurion's decision to launch the Sinai Campaign (1956) was presented to the government for approval only on the eve of battle; Begin's decision to respond to Sadat's peace overture (1977) was a personal decision, as was Rabin's decision to approve the Oslo Accords (1993); Sharon's disengagement plan from Gaza (2004) was publicly announced before it was presented to the government. This does not include multiple cases when the government was kept in the dark in the planning stage – for example, preparations to launch an attack on Iran's nuclear sites (Buchbut 2015).

The need for wide circles of support and the necessity of building a coalition are potential pitfalls for the prime minister in Israel, but also a source of power. In Canada, for example, the model is "the government of the prime minister," i.e., a government composed only of members of the prime minister's party, rather than a coalition of parties. Ostensibly the Canadian prime minister would seem to have more political power. The advantage of the Israeli prime minister, however, is that critical decisions supported by the coalition and a Knesset majority have a greater chance of gaining public acceptance and being implemented. One reason for the weakness of prime ministers during the era of direct election was that the new electoral system undermined the sources of their political power, as they did not gain the support of the relevant circles, especially their party and the Knesset.

B. The Prime Minister and the Party

Until the 1970s, prime ministers drew their power mainly from their parties. The prime minister was the envoy of the movement, and to operate in internal affairs, the backing of the party was needed. Even Ben-Gurion, who was fed up with partisanship and advocated statism, and who had the power to force his will on the party in security matters and foreign affairs, could not, despite his clout, dictate the composition of the government. It was the party's internal Nominating Committees that largely decided who would be candidates for the Knesset and who the ministers from Mapai would be.[11] The change began after the Yom Kippur War during Yitzhak Rabin's first term (1974–77). Rabin was the first prime minister whose appointment clearly took into consideration two centers of power: the public (Rabin had not been in the government responsible for the Yom Kippur War) and the party (Rabin won the party's first primary election). Menachem Begin's election posed a new pattern of prime ministership. Begin was the undisputed head of the Herut movement, but his power was drawn from the public that had twice elected Gahal as the main party. There were additional reasons for the rise of personal politics, but this trend peaked in the 1990s, when the electoral system took on a "presidential" model of prime minister based on the public's direct support. The immediate result was the weakening of the parties. The prime minister did not need a party to be elected, nor was the prime minister bound by party decisions. On the contrary, now the prime minister's power within the party was a product of his or her public standing. The personality of the prime ministers, however, did not help win votes for their parties (see Table 5.1). On both occasions that elections were held simultaneously for the Knesset and the prime minister, voters split their ballots, abandoning the parties of those for whom they voted for prime minister.

When the candidates for party head and prime minister were chosen by primaries, the party stopped being dominant. This is also true for the party institutions, which ended their role as a forum for ideological debate or consultation. The most

[11] In 1959, Ben-Gurion appointed three young ministers to his government – Moshe Dayan, Giora Yoseftal, and Abba Eban – in defiance of Mapai veterans, but this was an anomaly and marked the beginning of a schism within the party.

Table 5.1 *Support for the prime ministerial candidate versus support for his party during the period of direct elections*

Year	Elected prime minister	Support for the PM	Support for the PM's political party
1996	Benjamin Netanyahu	51%	25% (32 seats)
1999	Ehud Barak	56%	20% (26 seats)

The 2001 election was only for prime minister. Ariel Sharon was elected with 62% of the vote, and the Likud continued with nineteen from the previous Knesset (14% of the vote).

telling example of this concerned Prime Minister Sharon's plan to disengage from Gaza. In May 2004, Sharon was forced by his party to get approval for this plan through a referendum among Likud members. Although the plan was rejected by the party, the prime minister pressed ahead with it and ultimately quit the Likud, founding a new party named Kadima, and bringing personal politics to new heights in Israel.

C. The Prime Minister and the Ministers

The prime minister and the ministers are not of equal standing in Israel, as stated in the law: "The government is composed of a prime minister and other ministers." Each minister is accountable to the prime minister in his or her domain of responsibility, so the prime minister is indeed the first among equals. Nevertheless, the authority of the prime minister toward the ministers does not resemble that of a presidential system in which the ministers serve as advisers to the president, and the government does not require the confidence of the house of representatives. In Israel, the Knesset expresses confidence or no confidence in the entire government, not personally in the prime minister or individual ministers, and it is the government that is jointly accountable to the Knesset. Kenig and Barnea studied 206 ministers in governments from 1949 through 2007, and found that the prime minister is not generally the one who decides who will be minister from other parties in the coalition. There were several exceptions to this, however, in the history of Israeli politics: Golda Meir vetoed the appointment of Yitzhak Raphael of the National Religious Party (who was indicted on criminal charges) as a minister in her government. On the other hand, party constraints on the prime minister increased as the internal process of choosing Knesset candidates became more democratic within the parties, and there was a clear correlation between an MK's rank in the party list for the Knesset and his or her chances of being appointed minister (Kenig and Barnea 2009, 268). In other words, the prime minister in Israel did not have much room for maneuver in appointing government ministers – either from his or her own party or from other parties.

Over the years, the power of a prime minister over the ministers has increased. The amendment to the Transition Law in 1962 was intended to strengthen the coalition's collective responsibility, stipulating that the prime minister has the power to dismiss a minister if he or she or the minister's party voted against the government or abstained from voting. The significant change came in 1981 with an amendment to the Basic Law: Government stating that a minister is accountable to the prime minister, and authorizing the prime minister to dismiss a minister without having to show cause. This power is one of deterrence, and indeed prime ministers have not had to use this authority because ministers hastened to resign before being dismissed.

The coalition structure means that the ministers are not rubber stamps for the prime minister's initiatives, and can constrain the prime minister's actions, especially in domestic policies. The government is often a federation of ministers and ministries, and the prime minister has to maneuver among them and take them into consideration. Important decisions have been made contrary to the views of the prime minister. Two examples: the decision of the Provisional Government in October 1948 not to attack the Arab Legion or to conquer parts of the West Bank was made contrary to Ben-Gurion's stand; and the decision of the unity government in 1987 to cancel the Lavi aircraft project was made despite Prime Minister Shamir's position. Usually, when prime ministers realize that they have no majority in the government, they exercise their option not to bring such matters to a vote.[12] Or, if they are adamant, they can threaten resignation or even resign, as indeed happened from time to time.

D. The Prime Minister and the Coalition

Governments and prime ministers in Israel are dependent upon the size and unity of the coalition, whose stability is a function of the makeup of the Knesset. The more the Knesset is fragmented into many parties; the higher the Index of the Effective Number of Parties (see Figure 4.1 in Chapter 4); and the more flaccid the party discipline – the less stable the coalition. An unstable coalition means impaired steering capacity of the executive branch and its head, and this can undermine regime stability. Forming a stable coalition is therefore the prime minister's first job, and it means conducting negotiations with other parties even before officially becoming a prime ministerial candidate with the intent of persuading them to recommend one's candidacy to the president. How the coalition is formed and the content of the coalition agreements speak volumes of the future ability of the prime minister to navigate the coalition. In the past, coalition negotiating teams had been composed of senior party figures, but in recent years this task has been turned over to attorneys appointed by the parties.

The prime minister is almost always head of the largest Knesset faction. The exceptions are few: Yitzhak Shamir in 1986 and Benjamin Netanyahu in 2009 became prime ministers because of the size of the political bloc that supported them, even though in both cases their party (Likud) was not the largest in the Knesset. The prime minister's power also depends upon the relative size of his or her own party within the coalition. When the party is small or fragmented, the prime minister's ability to navigate state policy is reduced. This is also true when the coalition contains a large number of parties, which forces the prime minister to invest considerable energy in mediating conflicts among them. Coalition discipline cannot be coerced because it is ultimately the product of agreements and understandings;

[12] In July 2013 Netanyahu postponed a vote regarding the release of 104 prisoners because he realized that most of the ministers would vote against it. www.ynet.co.il/articles/0,7340,L-4410463,00.html [in Hebrew] (accessed May 31, 2016).

hence, the prime minister is cautious about taking action against coalition partners who stray, or using prime ministerial powers to dismiss ministers.

E. The Prime Minister and the Knesset

Prime Ministers Levi Eshkol and Menachem Begin enjoyed appearing in the Knesset and regarded the parliament as the central political forum – Begin presented the peace agreement with Egypt for a Knesset vote, without any assurance that it would pass. Others, such as Yitzhak Rabin and Ehud Barak, disdained the "chatter" of the MKs, viewing Knesset activity as a disturbance to the work of the government. Ariel Sharon was not the only prime minister who preferred to announce an important political initiative (such as the Gaza disengagement) in a public venue rather than from the Knesset podium, and only later did he bring the plan to the Knesset for approval. Since the 1990s, prime ministers have not had an easy time in the Knesset, and they certainly have not had it under their thumb. Currently the prime minister has the authority to dissolve the Knesset – with the consent of the president – if a majority of MKs express opposition to the government, resulting in its inability to function properly. But this does not necessarily mean new elections, because the Knesset majority has the option of announcing its intention to establish an alternative government within twenty-one days. A prime minister can also take steps to dissolve the Knesset and call for early elections, as Rabin did in 1977, but the risk is that the party could appoint an alternative candidate to do the job.

The Knesset has more than one way to give sleepless nights to the prime minister. It can vote no confidence in the government, or enact a law calling for early elections, thereby forcibly ending the prime minister's term of office. In 1999, Prime Minister Netanyahu joined the Knesset's initiative to call for early elections in order to prevent a vote of no-confidence in him. On the other hand, as noted in Chapter 4, the Knesset often fumbles in exercising oversight of the prime minister and government ministries, especially if there is a stable coalition. The parliamentary tools of policy debates or parliamentary questions to the prime minister – in which prime ministers report to the Knesset about their policies and respond to questions from the opposition – have not adequately evolved in Israel. Although the Knesset, at the request of forty MKs, has the authority to convene a session to discuss any matter and to summon the prime minister to appear, it is preferable that this not be accomplished by coercion.

F. Changes in the Status of the Prime Minister

As of 2016, a dozen individuals have served as prime minister in Israel, several in non-consecutive terms (see Table 5.2). Most prime ministers were in their sixties or older when elected to this position for the first time, with the exception of Yitzhak Rabin (52), Benjamin Netanyahu (47), and Ehud Barak (57) – the latter two in direct elections. Only one (Golda Meir) was a woman and none were Arab. Seven prime ministers were born in eastern Europe (Ben-Gurion, Sharett, Eshkol, Meir, Begin, Shamir, and Peres), and five were born in Israel (Rabin, Netanyahu, Barak, Sharon, and Olmert). Those elected prime minister were generally seasoned politicians, with the exception of Rabin and Netanyahu in their first terms of office, and Barak, the latter two serving for short terms (thirty-six and twenty months, respectively). Direct

Table 5.2 *Prime ministers of Israel (1948–2017)*

	Term of office	Previous positions	Country of birth	Age upon election	Party
David Ben-Gurion* (1886–1973)	1948–53; 1955–63	Chair of the Jewish Agency and the Zionist executive	Poland	62	Mapai
Moshe Sharett (1894–1965)	1954–55	Foreign Minister	Ukraine	59	Mapai
Levi Eshkol (1895–1969)	1963–69	Agriculture Minister; Finance Minister	Russia	68	Mapai
Golda Meir (1898–1978)	1969–74	Labor Minister; Foreign Minister	Ukraine	71	Mapai / Labor
Yitzhak Rabin* (1922–95)	1974–77; 1992–95	Chief of Staff; Ambassador to the United States; Labor Minister	Israel	52	Mapai / Labor
Menachem Begin* (1913–92)	1977–81 1981–83	Head of Etzel; Chair of Herut; Minister without Portfolio	Poland	64	Gahal / Likud
Yitzhak Shamir* (1915–2012)	1983–84; 1986–92	Lehi officer; senior Mossad agent; Speaker of the Knesset; Foreign Minister	Poland	68	Likud
Shimon Peres* (1923–2016)	1984–86; 1995–96	Director-General of the Defense Ministry; Defense Minister; Finance Minister; Foreign Minister	Poland	61	Mapai / Labor
Benjamin Netanyahu* (1949–)	1996–99; 2009–13; 2013–15; 2015–	Ambassador to the UN; Deputy Foreign Minister; Finance Minister	Israel	47	Likud
Ehud Barak (1942–)	1999–2001	Chief of Staff; Interior Minister; Foreign Minister	Israel	57	Labor
Ariel Sharon* (1928–2014)	2001–3; 2003–6	Major General in IDF; Minister of Agriculture, Defense, Housing, Infrastructure, and Foreign Affairs	Israel	73	Likud
Ehud Olmert (1945–)	2006–9	Jerusalem mayor; Health Minister; Industry, Trade and Labor Minister; Communication Minister; Finance Minister	Israel	61	Kadima

* Elected prime minister more than once.
Source: Gleaned from multiple sources.

election of the prime minister fostered the entry into politics of media personae, who later had a hard time navigating the labyrinth of political life. Until direct election, prime ministers served five years, on average. Ariel Sharon broke the mold – by not being a media persona and not serving a short term in office. He was elected twice and served over five years in a row until brought down by a stroke in January 2006. Ehud Olmert (May 2006–March 2009) was prime minister for almost three years. Netanyahu served a cumulative total of nine years as prime minister through 2015. Three of the twelve prime ministers had come from the military (Rabin, Barak, and Sharon), two came from security-related fields (Shamir and Peres), and seven had previously held senior positions in the Ministry of Foreign Affairs.

Changes in the Basic Law: Government, twice replaced in its entirety, are indicative of the changes in the status of the prime minister. On the one hand, the formal power of this office was enhanced – a prime minister now has the power to dismiss ministers and dissolve the Knesset. But also evident are the diminishing stature and lowered expectations of the prime minister, once expected to be a paragon of integrity. The 1968 law contains no reference to grounds for removing a prime minister from office by the Knesset. The legislators at the time presumed the personal honesty of the prime minister – indeed, it seemed improbable that the holder of this office would be convicted of an offense. This was put to the test when Prime Minister Rabin resigned in 1977 after revelations that his wife was the holder of a foreign currency account, which was then illegal for Israelis. Thus, in the 1992 version, the law specifies circumstances for removal of a prime minister because of a criminal offense or for political reasons – eighty MKs could dismiss a prime minister even without charges of criminal activity. This was introduced to balance the power of a prime minister who won by direct election. The very existence of a legal provision concerning dismissal for reasons of a crime reveals that it was no longer assumed that the prime minister would have an unblemished record, and the law outlines a scenario in the event that the prime minister is suspected of committing a crime involving moral turpitude. This is also true for the 2001 law with additional details (Article 18): If the prime minister is convicted of an offense that does not involve moral turpitude, the Knesset cannot use this procedure to remove him or her from office, unless a no-confidence vote has passed. The picture is quite bleak: Investigations for various offenses were launched for Israel's most recent four prime ministers, and Ehud Olmert was convicted of bribery, sentenced to nineteen months, and began serving his prison term in 2016.

Prime ministers carry a heavy burden. To date, not a single prime minister in Israel has retired gracefully from this position. Most have not written memoirs, and the few that have reveal very little of the inner workings of the job (Ben-Gurion 1976–87; Rabin 1979; Y. Shamir 1994; S. Peres 1998).[13]

5.5 The Ministers

What do ministers do? Gad Yaacobi, who served as Minister of Transportation in the years 1974–77, wrote that half his time was devoted to ministerial activity,

[13] Prime Minister Moshe Sharett (1954–55) did not write a memoir, but he left a very detailed and intriguing personal diary published in nine volumes (Sharett 1978).

two-fifths to his work as a member of the government, and the rest to the Knesset, the party, and public activity (1980, 173–74). If so, no time is left for thinking, let alone public-media activity, which takes up a significant part of a minister's time in the twenty-first century. Early governments in Israel had few ministers (twelve), but broad-based governments have had as many as twenty-five. The Sharon government (2001–6) and Netanyahu's first government (2009–13) had over thirty ministers. The 1992 Basic Law: Government limited the number of ministers to no fewer than eight and no more than eighteen, but this provision was rescinded because of coalition needs. On the assumption that fifteen executive branch ministries are sufficient, these and a few ministers without portfolio should meet all governance needs. The Governance Law, passed in 2014, limits the number of ministers to nineteen, the number of deputy ministers to four, and does not allow for ministers without portfolio.

Regarding the path to becoming a minister in Israel, the parties were and remain the main recruiting pool – in the years 1974–2007, some 70 percent of the 144 ministers had been party activists at some level, including local authorities, labor unions, and student unions. The remainder had been senior military officers (14%); outsiders from the media, academia, business, etc. (10%); and others (6%). Almost all (92%), however, had been Knesset members prior to their appointment as ministers (Kenig and Barnea 2009, 270–71).

A. The Minister: Responsibilities, Powers, and Sources of Support

Until the Governance Law was passed in 2014, a minister could, for a limited period, have responsibility for more than one ministry. A minister could also be "without portfolio," responsible for a specific issue but not a ministry, or tasked with an assignment that cuts across ministries. The flexibility of this mechanism, however, has often been exploited for coalition purposes. Indeed, the Sharon government (2003) outdid others by appointing two ministers to the Finance Ministry – Netanyahu as the Minister of Finance and Meir Sheetrit as "minister in the Finance Ministry." The Governance Law no longer allows for ministers without portfolio, nor for ministers to be responsible for more than one ministry.

Upon taking the oath of office, a minister pledges "to faithfully discharge my duty as a member of the government." Ministers are accountable to the prime minister, but autonomous in carrying out their duties, setting ministry policy, and representing their ministry to the public, the government, or the Knesset. The minister is obligated to report to the Knesset on ministry activity, to respond to parliamentary questions and motions for the agenda, and to personally appear or send a ministry representative to Knesset committees. A great burden of responsibility rests on the minister's shoulders for enacting regulations to flesh out laws that the ministry was authorized by the Knesset to implement, particularly in light of the Knesset's difficulty in overseeing the ministry's work. By law, ministers have special powers at their discretion, such as the Minister of the Interior's authority to grant Israeli citizenship in cases that fall outside the Law of Return. By an unwritten agreement, ministers refrain from intervening in each other's affairs unless the matter is one of overarching policy or of common concern and debated in the government or a ministerial committee, or related to the budget process.

Are the ministers the ones who set ministry policy, or are they merely titular heads with the real power in the hands of the bureaucrats? The perceived dichotomy between politicians and administrators is far from accurate (Galnoor 2001, 1886–91). First of all, in a democracy, it is the minister only who is accountable to the Knesset and the public for the ministry's activities. Second, decision-making in the ministries is a joint task of the politicians and the civil servants, although the roles change at different stages of the process. And there are constraints: The ability of the ministers to set in motion long-term policy is limited because of their brief term in office and their desire to show "results" to the public. Yet, the ministers are responsible for the broad vista and for revealing blind spots in the expertise of specialists and officials, and the final decision is theirs. More than one minister has had a decisive influence on ministry policymaking, even long term; and more than one civil servant has saved the ministers and the public from egregious errors. The power of an individual minister vis-à-vis the prime minister or other ministers also depends upon his or her personal stature. Some ministers may be able to influence sensitive foreign affairs and security matters, even when these are outside the purview of his or her ministry. After the Yom Kippur War, for example, Golda Meir claimed that she had gone along with the views of the generals in her government – Dayan, Barlev, and Allon. In the Begin government, Minister of Defense Ariel Sharon initiated and pushed for launching the first Lebanon War. In his positions as Minister of Agriculture, Defense, Housing, and Infrastructure, Sharon also expedited the construction of settlements in the West Bank and Gaza.

The personal influence of a minister can be wielded in internal affairs as well, particularly on economic matters, but this is more difficult because of the direct involvement of other ministers, interest groups, and the public. The economic policies of Finance Minister Yoram Aridor (1981–83), for example, are thought to be responsible for the spiraling inflation in Israel of those years; Finance Minister Benjamin Netanyahu (2003–5) together with Finance Ministry officials brought about a drastic change in Israel's social-economic policies in an effort to reduce the welfare state and encourage private enterprise.

Ministers need circles of support and legitimacy. In the past this came from the party, without whose support it would have been almost impossible to become a minister. It was the party that sent representatives to the Knesset and the government, and ministers considered themselves its emissaries. The party remains the main source for recruiting ministers: The ranking of MKs on the party list or the size of their "camps" within the party affects their chances of becoming ministers. Once appointed, however, the ministers aspire to become public figures, so that even the party institutions that selected them cannot ignore them. Sometimes this search for popularity-at-any-price has led ministers into embarrassing media appearances. Another important source of support for ministers is the prime minister: While they are accountable to the prime minister, who has the power to depose them, of greater importance is the prime minister's political support for the minister's policies, especially during budget debates.

B. Who is Eligible to be a Minister?

Only a citizen and resident of Israel can be appointed minister. Not eligible to be ministers are office holders who legally may not run for the Knesset (e.g., senior civil servants), unless they left that position prior to their appointment. On the other hand, senior security personnel (IDF officers with a rank of major general or higher, and the senior officials of the GSS, Mossad, Police, and Prison Service) have had their mandatory cooling-off period extended to three years (from half a year) before being allowed to run for office.[14] Also ineligible to serve as minister is anyone convicted of an offense deemed by the court to involve moral turpitude, for a period of seven years from completion of the sentence or issue of the verdict. MKs who resigned from their parties may not be appointed minister during the same Knesset term, to prevent resignations for purposes of being appointed minister.

A minister need not be a member of the Knesset, which enables the appointment of professionals or others not previously involved in party politics. These are rare, and no common denominator exists in terms of success at the job or their ability to navigate politics. More frequently, the appointment of non-MKs to head ministries has been used to bring specific individuals into politics (e.g., Barak and Mofaz upon their retirement as IDF chiefs of staff); or to compensate party members who did not win election to the Knesset; or – when a minister resigns from the Knesset – to make room in the Knesset for the next candidate on the party list.

C. Deputy Ministers

With the agreement of the prime minister and approval of the government, a minister can appoint an MK to serve as a deputy minister tasked with assigned activities in the Knesset or the ministry. This practice originated with the British custom of training parliament members to be junior ministers, thereby linking the executive and legislative branches. Hence the requirement that deputy ministers, though not ministers, must be MKs. In Israel, however, the position of deputy minister has assumed an entirely different meaning – it has become part of the calculation in negotiating a coalition. As far back as Israel's second government, a deputy minister was appointed and the position was legally established in an amendment to the Transition Law of 1951. The 1992 Basic Law: Government limited the number of deputy ministers to six, and the Governance Law further reduced this to four. A deputy minister's job ends when the minister who made the appointment completes his or her term of office, or following a decision by the prime minister, the government, or the appointing minister.

Many deputy ministers served in various governments, including some who became acting ministers when no minister was appointed. This arrangement of "deputy ministers with the status of minister" who are in fact responsible for all ministry matters does not exist in the law, because deputy ministers have no powers of their

[14] An amendment to the Government Law 2001 (Cooling-off Period for Persons Serving in the Security Forces Law) passed in 2007.

own.[15] Some deputy ministers had defined roles, but others found it hard to be usefully engaged in the narrow space between the minister and the director-general of the ministry. In the Sharon government (2003–6), no fewer than sixteen deputy ministers served at various times. Public criticism of this led the heads of Kadima and Labor to pledge during the 2006 coalition negotiations that no deputy ministers would be appointed in their government, but five months after its formation, two were appointed, one from each party. In the 2009 Netanyahu government, nine deputy ministers were appointed from among the MKs who were coalition partners.

In deliberations about the future constitution held by the Knesset's Constitution, Law and Justice Committee (2006, 119), support was expressed for a clear definition of the powers and duties of deputy ministers. Should this come about, the position would lose its political flexibility and original usefulness – facilitating relations between the government ministries and the Knesset with its committees.

D. Resignation and Dismissal of Ministers

A minister can resign from the government by tendering a letter of resignation to the prime minister. Resignations of this sort usually happen in the wake of a minister's objection to government policies. Moshe Dayan, who served as the Minister of Foreign Affairs in the Begin government, resigned in June 1979 to protest the freeze in negotiations over autonomy for the West Bank. One year later, Minister of Defense Ezer Weizman resigned due to his opposition to the government's policies concerning the Palestinians, the settlements, and cuts to the defense budget. Minister of Energy Yitzhak Berman resigned in September 1982 after the first Lebanon War to protest the failure to appoint a commission of inquiry. Minister Arens resigned in 1987 because the government abandoned development of the Lavi aircraft. And in June 2004, Ministers Effi Eitam and Yitzhak Levy resigned from the Sharon government because of the plan to "disengage" from the Gaza Strip and evacuate the Israeli settlers there.

Until 1981, the prime minister had the authority to dismiss a minister only on the grounds of violating coalition discipline. Rabin used this power in 1976 to dismiss National Religious Party ministers after their faction abstained in a no-confidence vote. Today, the prime minister has the power to dismiss a minister for any reason whatsoever. Following the events at Sabra and Shatila, the Kahan Commission of Inquiry recommended that if Minister of Defense Sharon did not resign, Prime Minister Begin should use his authority to dismiss him. Begin refrained and merely shifted Sharon to the post of minister without portfolio (February 1983). In 1990, Prime Minister Shamir dismissed Shimon Peres, after which the government fell in a no-confidence vote. Until 2002, dismissal of a minister by the prime minister was rare in Israeli politics, because it could lead to a coalition crisis. Nonetheless, Sharon dismissed fourteen ministers in his two terms as prime minister, including one from his own party, for their breach of collective responsibility and to ensure a government

[15] The arrangement of deputy ministers serving as de facto ministers has been used primarily in coalition agreements with the ultra-Orthodox parties, which do not want their MKs to be party to the overall decisions of the government. This arrangement was invalidated by the High Court of Justice, which ruled that Deputy Minister of Health Yaakov Litzman of the United Torah Judaism Party may not be "a 'quasi' deputy minister who fulfills the functions of a minister" (*Yesh Atid v. Prime Minister Benjamin Netanyahu* 2015).

majority for approval of the Gaza disengagement plan. It is hard to say that this set a precedent for future dismissals because Sharon's actions preceded a split in the Likud.

E. Ministerial Committees

A significant share of the government's work takes place in ministerial committees, to which governmental powers are delegated. Some of these are permanent, statutory committees (the Ministerial Committees for National Security, for Economic Affairs, on Legislation, and for Symbols and Ceremonies); and some are ad hoc committees on specific issues.[16] Although the decision of a ministerial committee is as binding as a government decision, a minister can appeal it within two weeks from publication of the decision. The Statute of Government Operations sets out the working procedures of ministerial committees; without the approval of the Ministerial Committee on Legislation, for example, the government cannot table a bill in the Knesset.

The Agranat Commission identified weak links in the government's decision-making process in matters of security and during states of emergency, and recommended creation of the Ministerial Committee for National Security, in addition to a small ministers' team headed by the prime minister, to make urgent decisions on conducting a war. After various bodies were established, a decision was made to anchor the Ministerial Committee for National Security in the Government Law 2001. The size of this committee cannot exceed half the number of ministers, and it includes the prime minister (chair), acting prime minister, and Ministers of Defense, Justice, Foreign Affairs, Internal Security, and Finance. The meetings of this committee are classified, and its decisions are deemed equivalent to government decisions, other than the fact that they are not made public. The Winograd Commission of Inquiry into the second Lebanon War found many flaws in the working of the Ministerial Committee for National Security.

F. Small Decision-Making Forums[17]

Politics takes place in both formal and informal settings. It is not surprising, therefore, that in addition to the official meetings of the government plenary, there have always been small forums of ministers (and advisers) with whom prime ministers consult and deliberate. Decisions are "pre-cooked" in these forums before being brought to the government plenary, and experience indicates that this has both advantages and disadvantages. On the one hand, the smaller forum allows for free and open discussion in a setting that may be more creative and free of time constraints, which could improve the decision-making process; on the other hand, the smaller forum might narrow the range of options by closing the decision prematurely, thereby preventing the government plenary and ministers not in this inner group from reopening it. Furthermore, important decisions are often made covertly in these small forums and not brought to the government for approval.

[16] A listing of the ministerial committees and their statutory status can be found in the appendix to the Statute of Government Operations: www.pmo.gov.il [in Hebrew] (accessed April 29, 2011).

[17] Based on Galnoor 2011, 61–63.

Many of these unofficial gatherings remain unknown, but several have entered the Israeli political lexicon: "our ministers" in the 1950s – the forum of Mapai ministers who sought to create a uniform front in government discussions; or "Golda's kitchen" – the senior ministers and advisers who met in the prime minister's home on Saturday nights prior to the Sunday morning government meetings. In 1996, Prime Minister Netanyahu established his mini-kitchen cabinet that included the Ministers of Foreign Affairs and Defense. A different kind of group was Ariel Sharon's "Farm Forum," which, according to media reports, included loyalists and businessmen, who met in different constellations to advise the prime minister.

Sometimes the government itself creates a more compact decision-making body to deal more efficiently with a specific issue. In the coalition agreements of the unity governments in 1984 and 1988, a "narrow cabinet" was established to include an equal number of senior ministers from both major parties. Some sensitive decisions were then made in the cabinet, although critical decisions were brought for approval to the entire government. At the same time, an even smaller "forum of prime ministers" was created, which included Shamir, Peres, and Rabin.

Should the appointed minister be an expert in the field of his or her ministry, rather than a politician? The question reflects a lack of understanding of the role of the minister. The Minister of Health does not deal with health services, but with health policy. There is nothing wrong with the minister being a doctor, but having this expertise is not necessary; what is required is the ability to see the issue in its broad context and to shape policies. This also holds for the Ministers of Defense, Justice, Finance, Agriculture, Immigrant Absorption, and the others. Too much expertise could be a problem for a minister, because it might increase the tendency to become bogged down in details. For resolving more detailed issues, it would be advisable for the minister to make use of the services of experts.

G. Government Ministries

There is no "right" or "wrong" number of government ministries or employees within them. In 2014, there were nineteen ministries, and our proposal to reduce their number to fifteen is based on an evaluation of the functions of the ministries and their continuity. The number of employees does not reflect the relative power of the ministry or its influence on policymaking. In the informal hierarchy of power, the Ministry of Defense tops the list of powerful ministries, well above the others, because of its critical function and the size of its budget – some 14.4 percent of the total government budgeted expenditures for 2016.[18] The Ministries of Finance and Justice also occupy important, albeit different, spheres of influence. The Ministry of Finance was always very powerful by virtue of its control over budgets, cash flow, and capital import. The Emergency Economic Stabilization Act of 1985,[19] intended *inter*

[18] www.haaretz.com/israel-news/.premium-1.687018 (accessed June 5, 2016).

[19] This economic plan, launched in the summer of 1985, was intended to halt galloping inflation, then in excess of 400 percent annually, and to reduce the budget deficit. The primary measures taken were the reduction of salaries, prices, and credit, and stabilization of the shekel exchange rate. The main objective of the plan was achieved: Inflation was gradually reined in to 20 percent a year, and reduced to a single digit a decade later. The plan was also a landmark in the transition of Israel's economy from a social-democratic state to a more liberal market economy.

alia to allow for closer monitoring of the state budget, transformed the Ministry of Finance into a highly centralized planner of activities in other government ministries.

The increased power of the Ministry of Justice derives from changes in the Israeli legal system. The "judicialization" of the public sphere in Israel and the increased resort to courts to resolve public and political disputes also affected the public management sector (Galnoor 2004, 500–42). Corruption cases involving politicians and public servants in national and local governments have multiplied since the 1980s, while the attorney general and legal advisers increased their influence within the ministries. All these changes affected the number of employees involved in investigations and enforcement – those working for the Ministry of Justice, the police, and the prison system – as well as the number of judges.

The Office of the Prime Minister was originally a random collection of functions. It was not a staff unit aimed at helping the government and its head determine policy. Direct election of the prime minister from 1996 to 2001 strengthened the role of the Prime Minister's Office as coordinator of the other ministries, and the number of employees more than tripled in 2010 from 764 in 1990. However, because of the structure and lack of organizational tools for staff work, the actual influence of the Office of the Prime Minister on the activities of other ministries and the implementation of programs across ministries is still limited. Other powerful ministries have a diverse range of clients, such as the Ministries of Education; Health; Industry, Trade and Labor; Agriculture; and Welfare. The federative structure of government ministries in the Israeli executive branch and the lack of senior civil servants who change positions across ministries inhibit joint programs and coordinated policymaking.

5.6 Types of Responsibility in the Executive Branch

The government and its ministers are accountable to widening circles, from the party to the public at large. We now examine more closely the types of responsibility that have evolved in political activity, legislation, and in the wake of reports by commissions of inquiry.

A. Collective Responsibility

From the moment the government makes a decision, the entire government, by law, is responsible to the Knesset for that decision. This responsibility also applies to the decisions of a minister or a ministerial committee – decisions made by virtue of the authority delegated to them by the government. The principle of collective responsibility means that policies are not attributable to the prime minister or other ministers, but to the government as a whole, and therefore the Knesset expresses confidence or no confidence in the government as a body, not in the prime minister or a specific minister. A minister bears responsibility for the government's decisions, even if he or she did not participate in making them, opposed them, or abstained from voting on them. If the government renounces responsibility for the activity of a minister, he or she should resign, not wait to be dismissed.

The Transition Law from 1949 states, "The Government shall be collectively responsible for its activities to the Knesset, shall report to it on its activities, and shall hold office so long as it enjoys the confidence of the Knesset." This principle appeared in the Basic Law: Government of 1968, was rescinded during the period of direct election, and was restored in 2001. By virtue of this collective responsibility, it is reasonable to expect that a minister will not publicly attack the government or leak information about its deliberations; the reality, however, is quite different. Ministers and coalition parties abrogate their collective responsibility for various reasons, but primarily in an effort to mobilize public opinion against a decision taken by the government despite their opposition. In the media age, with politics so highly personalized, the public has no patience for a minister who does not reveal his position, asserting, "I made my views clear in the government debate," particularly if he or she opposes a government decision but remains in the government. Examples abound of ministers who have criticized the policies of their own government: In 1978, Defense Minister Ezer Weizman publicly chastised the government for "not wanting peace." In a newspaper interview in 1979, Foreign Minister Moshe Dayan decried the government in which he served with the Biblical phrase, "Your destroyers and devastators have issued forth from you" (Isaiah 49:17). Both ultimately resigned from the government. In 2004, Avraham Poraz, Minister of Internal Affairs, reported to the media that he had opposed and voted against the decision to kill Sheikh Ahmed Yassin, founder of Hamas. Public declarations by ministers obligate the entire government, and therefore, in properly run democracies, ministers avoid making such declarations unless the prime minister asks them to do so. It is hard to know whether the blunt statements by Foreign Minister Avigdor Lieberman in the Netanyahu government (2009) were made at his own initiative or at Netanyahu's behest. Ministers who oppose government decisions have only two courses of action: reconcile with the decision because it obligates them, or resign and make their views known. A minister who wants to enjoy both worlds – to remain in the government and shirk responsibility for its policies – will eventually lose credibility.

Collective responsibility includes a minister's accountability to the prime minister for his or her area of responsibility. This is intended not just to enhance the prime minister's status among the coalition partners, but also to contribute to the collective effort for which the prime minister is accountable to the Knesset. The Direct Election Law eliminated this collective responsibility because it found a replacement for it – the prime minister's direct accountability to the public, a concept taken from the presidential system. In consequence, these governments were "a prime ministerial government." However, because only a quasi-presidential system was put in place (see the discussion below), the matter of accountability became convoluted and untenable. The law stated that in addition to the minister's accountability to the prime minister for his or her area of responsibility, the minister "must report to the Knesset on the discharge of his duty" (Article 33F). In other words, an individual minister bears parliamentary responsibility to the Knesset, and a majority of seventy MKs have the power to dismiss a minister. Thus, collective responsibility was replaced by double personal responsibility – first, of the prime minister and, second, of the individual minister in whom the Knesset could vote no-confidence. On the other hand, however, the Knesset did not have the power to enforce collective responsibility by voting no-confidence in the government as a whole. Fortunately, this law was never put to the test while it was in force, as its internal logic is flawed.

B. Faction/Coalition Responsibility

A 1962 amendment to the Transition Law established "faction responsibility," a corollary of collective responsibility: A minister, as a member of the government, is responsible for the vote of his or her faction (party) in the Knesset. A faction that is a member of the coalition is prohibited from voting against the government's position in substantive matters (a no-confidence vote, the state budget, or any subject for which the government calls in advance for coalition discipline), and the ministers of that faction are responsible for how their MKs vote in the Knesset. If a minister or his/her faction vote against a government bill, or abstain from voting without prior consent from the government, it is deemed a resignation from the government by the minister.

Faction responsibility is designed to strengthen the coalition and also help ministers cope with obstructionist MKs in their own faction: Members of a faction in the coalition may not vote in the Knesset against government positions unless "voting freedom" was granted in advance. This amendment was enacted after a series of events in which coalition factions voted against the government, or abstained from supporting it in no-confidence votes. In 1950, ministers from the religious parties engaged in a "ministers' boycott," refusing to participate in government meetings in protest of its education policies. Such coalition crises, some of which even brought down the government, led Mapai to conclude that legal sanction was necessary. The final straw was a vote to ratify an arms deal with Germany in 1959. The Ahdut Ha'avoda and Mapam parties, which were members of the coalition, voted together with the opposition against the government position. Ben-Gurion called upon the ministers from these parties to resign, but the law did not allow him to dismiss them. The first actual use of the 1962 amendment was made in 1976 when Prime Minister Rabin used his authority to dismiss the members of the National Religious Party from the government after two of its three ministers abstained from a no-confidence vote in the government following desecration of the Sabbath during an Air Force ceremony.

The first indications of the demise of faction responsibility appeared during the Begin premiership (1977–81) when the Dash Party was given freedom to vote on the critical issue of establishing settlements in the occupied territories. The broader context, however, was the fading of a dominant party, which had once been powerful enough to impose faction responsibility upon the coalition partners. During the period of the unity governments in the 1980s, faction responsibility was further eroded. The government preferred to ignore violations of coalition discipline by the ministers in order to maintain coalition stability. Since then, examples have multiplied, such as in 1998 when MKs from the National Religious Party voted in the Knesset against redeployment in Hebron, even though they were part of the government led by Netanyahu, who approved the agreement. Faction responsibility remains on the law books, but, like collective responsibility, it has lost all political clout. Knesset members from coalition factions – and sometimes even ministers – vote against government policy or abstain from (or are absent during) critical votes. This is both the result of the weakening of the coalition as a steering mechanism and also a factor causing it.

C. Ministerial/Parliamentary Responsibility

Ministers are accountable to the Knesset and thereby to the public for their own actions and for everything that takes place in their ministries. This is the intent of ministerial responsibility, which is essentially parliamentary responsibility, even though there are subtle differences between the two – ministers in Israel are accountable to the prime minister as well. While both collective and faction responsibility are mandated by law, ministerial responsibility is in essence political – a principle accepted in parliamentary systems. A minister is generally responsible for a specific ministry, but what are the limits? Is the minister responsible only for his/her decisions and policy, or also for the individual decisions, omissions, and failures of every ministry employee? Is a civil servant's action deemed to be the minister's action – for example, should the Education Minister be held accountable for the actions of every schoolteacher? And what is the significance of this responsibility – is the minister expected to resign when the actions of a ministry employee are seriously flawed? Stories abound of Japanese ministers who commit suicide or British ministers who resign after grave failures are revealed in their ministries. The reality is different in these countries as well as in Israel.

Ministerial responsibility is thus defined: "The minister is accountable to the Knesset for all the activities in his ministry, even if he did not know of them in advance or was not involved in them" (Zadok 1974). Since ministerial responsibility is a political norm, the sanction for it is also political – whether a minister can continue in office rests on the extent of his or her political support (Gutmann 1975, 167). In other words, if the minister does not resign and is not dismissed, this means in effect that the entire government takes responsibility for the failure. The principle of ministerial responsibility is recognized in Supreme Court rulings and in the Agranat Commission's report of its investigation into the Yom Kippur War. Ministerial responsibility has two facets: *parliamentary* – the obligation of ministers to report to the Knesset on the activities of their ministries and to respond to parliamentary questions – as mandated in the Statute of Knesset Operations and also, for example, in the law obligating ministers to appear before Knesset committees; and *public* – realization of this political responsibility depends entirely on the minister and the extent of the public criticism.

Can ministerial responsibility be enforced? Because of collective responsibility, the Knesset cannot vote no-confidence in an individual minister, or dismiss a minister from office. The only ones who can translate ministerial responsibility into action are the ministers themselves, if they feel it is appropriate to resign, or the prime minister, who is empowered to dismiss ministers. In the past, lack of support from the party could force a minister to resign. It is difficult to come up with unequivocal examples of an individual minister resigning for reasons of ministerial responsibility (as opposed to the resignation of an entire faction) because motives are often mixed and may include opposition to a general government policy. Justice Minister Yaakov-Shimshon Shapira resigned from the government in 1972 at his own initiative, declaring that he took responsibility for the Netivei Neft affair; after later returning to the post, he resigned again because of the failings of the Yom Kippur War. Minister without Portfolio Moshe Arens resigned in 1987 after the government decision to cancel development of the Lavi aircraft. There are also informal mechanisms to enforce ministerial responsibility. Public and party dissatisfaction can prevent a minister from being reelected to the next Knesset or from being appointed minister, as happened to Yoram Aridor, who served as Finance Minister in 1983.

Should the Knesset be given the power to enforce ministerial responsibility through no-confidence votes in an individual minister? In response to a proposal of this nature made by MK Menachem Begin while a member of the opposition, Justice Minister Haim Zadok said:

> In our law there is symmetry between assuming a position and being dismissed from it, between a Knesset vote of confidence and no-confidence. We do not have a vote of no-confidence in an individual, just as we do not have a vote of confidence in an individual ... It is true that along with the collective responsibility of the government there is also individual ministerial responsibility ... Regarding collective responsibility, there is a constitutional sanction of no-confidence and the government falls, while the sanction for ministerial-individual responsibility is a public, political sanction, not a constitutional one. (Knesset session, December 25, 1974, quoted in Yaacobi 1980, 100)

Commissions of inquiry – both state and other – have significantly contributed to clarifying the issue of ministerial responsibility in the political culture of Israel (see Chapter 7). The Agranat Commission (appointed in 1973) examined the decisions of the military and civilian bodies prior to the Yom Kippur War and whether the IDF was fully prepared for the war; the Kahan Commission (appointed in 1982) investigated the events surrounding the events in the Sabra and Shatila refugee camps during the first Lebanon War; the Winograd Commission (appointed in 2006) investigated the second Lebanon War. These commissions added to ministerial responsibility the dimension of personal responsibility of those in political and administrative power, which we shall discuss below. The Agranat Commission distinguished between ministerial responsibility to the Knesset and a minister's personal responsibility, which is fundamentally a matter of discretionary decisions. With respect to the military echelon, the Agranat Commission asserted that senior officers bear personal responsibility, i.e., they erred in their judgment, and therefore should be dismissed. Concerning the political echelon – Prime Minister Meir and Defense Minister Dayan – the commission did not attribute to them errors of judgment, and therefore did not impose on them personal responsibility or recommend their dismissal. These decisions by the commission are still controversial, but it is important to emphasize that the commission did not exempt the prime minister or Defense Minister from ministerial responsibility. The commission's claim, justified in our opinion, was that accountability on this level should be subject only to political sanction – elections and public opinion. Commission member Yigael Yadin later argued that the commission did not exempt the ministers from parliamentary and public responsibility, and that the voter indeed passed judgment on them. Yadin meant that the Meir–Dayan government fell as a result of the commission report and public outcry, and neither served in the next government. The disagreement over the commission's recommendations concerned exempting the ministers from personal, not ministerial, responsibility.[20]

[20] See debate in the *Knesset Records*, Session 37, Eighth Knesset, on "Announcement by the Prime Minister of her Resignation," April 11, 1974.

The Kahan Commission held Defense Minister Ariel Sharon personally responsible for the events that took place in the refugee camps in Lebanon, and recommended his dismissal. With regard to Prime Minister Menachem Begin and Foreign Minister Yitzhak Shamir, the commission ruled that they bore ministerial responsibility, but like the Agranat Commission, it did not recommend sanctions against them. Prime Minister Begin's resignation half a year after publication of the Kahan report was a way of taking responsibility for what had transpired.

D. Personal Responsibility of Public Officials

Like the Agranat Commission before it, the Kahan Commission distinguished between ministerial (parliamentary) responsibility, which is a political matter, and the personal responsibility of senior political, military, and administrative officials. With respect to ministers, personal responsibility is, of course, part of their overall ministerial responsibility. Given the lessons from the Agranat Commission report, the Kahan Commission explored in depth the issue of responsibility, asking whether decision-makers had acted correctly within the parameters of the information available to them at the time of the decision. In defining personal responsibility, it added an important distinction – direct versus indirect. Direct responsibility pertains to an action performed, whether intentionally or not, while indirect personal responsibility pertains to not having prevented an action from occurring whose consequences could have been foreseen, and over which one had some influence, even if performed by a third party. To be sure, this does *not* refer to the responsibility of public officials for criminal offenses, but rather to actions within the purview of their decision discretion. The Kahan Commission stated that even though it was the Christian Phalange troops in Lebanon who had direct responsibility for the events at Sabra and Shatila, Defense Minister Ariel Sharon had indirect personal responsibility, and it recommended that he resign or be dismissed by the prime minister.

The Winograd Commission, which examined the events around the second Lebanon War (it was not a State Commission of Inquiry), set forth a coherent set of principles on the subject of personal responsibility and the conclusions drawn from it. In contrast with the Agranat Commission, it did not distinguish between the military and civilian echelons, and assigned personal responsibility for the flawed conduct of the war on the prime minister, the Minister of Defense, and the chief of staff, although it refrained from recommending resignations or dismissals. The essence of this approach was formulated as follows in the final report: "We regarded it as more appropriate to present only the facts, conclusions, and systemic recommendations, and to allow the army itself or the court of public opinion to assign personal responsibility for the war" (Winograd Commission 2008, 71, 74).

In retrospect, the approach of the Winograd Commission – that it is up to the public to assign personal responsibility – seems to have proven itself. Within two years of publication of the interim report (in April 2007), the senior officials who had been found responsible for the failings of the war – Prime Minister Ehud Olmert, Defense Minister Amir Peretz, and Chief of Staff Dan Halutz, as well as other senior military officers – were no longer in their positions.

In other democratic countries, there is nothing comparable to the commissions of inquiry used in Israel to determine personal responsibility. This mechanism allows for monitoring the actions of public officials – politicians, senior civil servants, senior security personnel, and senior officers in the military and police force. What is innovative is that a norm was created in which public officials are subject not just to the law and general public criticism, but to specific review of a commission of inquiry, which examines their decisions *ex post facto*.

Notwithstanding the above, surveys indicate that the subjective view of most Israeli citizens is that politicians in Israel are not accountable to the public: This was the view of 39 percent of the Jewish population in 1969, which rose to 70 percent in 2008 (Arian et al. 2005–10: 2008, 51). One often hears Israeli citizens say, "No one takes responsibility," mainly because of those officials who declare, "I take full responsibility" and then continue in office as if nothing had happened. The pervasiveness of this feeling among the public can only undermine the steering capacity of the executive branch.[21]

5.7 Direct Election of the Prime Minister (1996–2003)

Israel is virtually the only democracy that experimented with changing its electoral system, an experiment that ran the course of seven years. Direct election of the prime minister began with enactment of the 1992 version of the Basic Law: Government, and was first implemented in the 1996 election. The experiment failed – the law was changed in 2001, and the subsequent 2003 election was conducted according to the previous system – but its effects can still be felt in the political system. Direct election provides an opportunity to examine the effects of an attempt to strengthen the executive branch by changing the support base of the prime minister, i.e., enhancing the steering capacity by giving the prime minister a personal mandate directly from the public, similar to that of presidential systems. Recourse to this method suggests that its proponents gave up on the possibility of enhancing the power of the executive branch by strengthening the institutions that mediate this power – the Knesset, the parties, public management, and civil society.

A. The Context

Broad public support for changing the electoral system emerged in the wake of the events of spring 1990 with the fall of the second national unity government, which had spent its two-year term in political gridlock, both large parties engaged in relentless rejection of each other's initiatives. We reviewed these events in the previous chapter, and here we cite only the precedents set during this period, most of them negative: a party (Shas) reneging on its promise to support an alternative coalition; MKs switching parties, prostituting their vote in return for the promise of being made a minister; secret coalition agreements with financial allocations to seal them; and the fall of a government by a no-confidence vote for the first time in Knesset history. Three months of political crisis were accompanied by widespread public protest: the public had lost its trust in the political leaders, demonstrations were held expressing revulsion at the corruption, and there was a deep desire for change in the political system. Out of this sense of profound disgust, a solution was born, one whose adherents had been waiting in the wings for an

[21] In a 2010 survey, 50 percent believed that "politicians are in politics only for personal gain" (Arian et al. 2005–10: 2010, 70).

Table 5.3 *Questions for classifying political systems as parliamentary or presidential*

	Head of the executive branch require parliament confidence?	
	No	**Yes**
Parliament elects the executive branch head	Parliamentary system (Britain)	Mixed system (Switzerland)
Not the Parliament	**Mixed system (Israel 1996–2003)**	Presidential system (USA)

opportunity to introduce change in the electoral system. Thus, despite strong opposition from most Israeli political scientists (see, e.g., Galnoor 1992), a private member's bill was submitted by four leading MKs from different parties. The law passed the Knesset in March 1992 – fifty-five in favor and thirty-two opposed (Alon 1995).

B. The System

The system of direct election of the prime minister removed Israel from the family of parliamentary democracies, but did not move it into the family of presidential democracies. The electoral system adopted was unique, unlike any other. In retrospect, it can be said that what emerged from the extended debates in the Knesset combined some of the shortcomings of a parliamentary system with the shortcomings of a presidential system – Reuven Hazan named it "presidential parliamentarism" (Hazan 1996, 21–37). Lijphart classifies parliamentary and presidential systems according to two criteria: Who elects the head of the executive branch? And does the head of the executive branch require the parliament's confidence to stay in power (Lijphart 1984)?

Based on these two dimensions, as shown in Table 5.3, the Israeli system of direct election created a unique governance category: It was not a pure parliamentary system, as the prime minister was not elected by the Knesset, although there was a parliamentary component as the government required Knesset confidence to govern; and it was not a pure presidential system, because although the head of the executive branch was directly elected by the public, mutual dependence with the Knesset persisted. The Knesset could dismiss the prime minister or vote no-confidence in the government, while the prime minister had the power to dissolve the Knesset. The law created a kind of "deterrence balance" between the Knesset and the prime minister: A no-confidence vote in the government could lead to the Knesset being dissolved, unlike a parliamentary system in which a no-confidence vote does not necessarily dissolve the parliament, because an alternative government can be established; on the other hand, the prime minister is also not eager to dissolve the Knesset because this would require him or her to stand for election again.

Splitting the vote for the Knesset and the prime minister yielded two types of elections:

Regular elections, in which the voter simultaneously casts one ballot for the Knesset and a separate ballot for the prime minister. Such elections would be held at the completion of a term of office, or following a Knesset no-confidence vote in the government, or when the prime minister dissolves the Knesset. Regular elections of this sort were held twice in Israel – in 1996 and 1999 – prior to completion of a full term of office.

Special elections to determine the prime minister only, held at the initiative of the Knesset – when it dismisses the prime minister by a vote of eighty MKs or removes a serving prime minister who has been convicted of a crime involving moral turpitude. Prime ministers can also initiate a special election if they resign, stop serving as a Knesset member, or do not form a coalition within forty-five days. Special elections would also be held if the prime minister dies or is permanently unable to fulfill the duties of prime minister. One special election of a prime minister (Ariel Sharon) was held in 2001 after the resignation of Prime Minister Barak.

C. The Dream and the Reality

Proponents of direct election cited several objectives that the new law was designed to achieve: strengthening the power of the prime minister and the executive branch, weakening the bargaining power of the small parties, improving the quality of the political leadership, and increasing stability while enhancing governability. Direct election not only failed to attain these objectives – it was even counterproductive for some. Proponents claimed that the desired results were not achieved because the system was not fully implemented. In their view, had the law not created such a strong dependence of the prime minister on the Knesset, and had the electoral system to the Knesset also been changed, the negative effects of the law would have been reduced or eliminated, and the Knesset would also have been strengthened (Alon 2001). Below we list the main objectives sought by direct elections and the actual results.

Strengthening the Prime Minister and the Executive Branch

The expectation was that direct election of the prime minister by the public would bestow greater legitimacy on this position, which would fortify the prime minister when confronting the Knesset and the parties. In contrast with the previous system in which the person who would be prime minister became clear only after exhausting coalition negotiations, direct election meant that the next prime minister would be known as soon as the vote was tallied, and this would strengthen his or her power and make it easier to form a coalition. It was assumed that a prime minister so elected could set policy from a position of strength and be judged in the court of public opinion every four years.

In practice, however, the prime minister was weakened by direct election. The first coalition during the period of direct election, which was formed by Netanyahu, had only sixty-seven MKs; the Labor Party, which was in the opposition, had more MKs than the Likud, which headed the coalition. Although subsequent coalitions were larger at the beginning of their term (seventy-five MKs in the Barak government and seventy-seven MKs in the Sharon government), they did not last long. The power bestowed upon the prime minister by direct election was only an illusion: The prime minister became a Samson, whose strength could be turned against him. The concern that the election would yield a "contrarian Knesset" with a permanent majority against the prime minister did not materialize. The reality was not far off, however, because the coalitions formed were fragile. Direct election created competition between the prime minister and MKs, who drew their power from the same source – the public. The weakness of the prime minister had consequences – Barak set out for a summit meeting at Camp David with Yasser Arafat, the chair of the

Palestinian Authority, even though a majority of the Knesset did not support him. His claim that his legitimacy was derived from the public who voted for him in direct election was not borne out. Direct election created an illusion among prime ministers that they had the support of the public over the heads of the Knesset, but in practice their political survival depended upon the Knesset. This paradox built into the system became apparent when even the power of the prime ministers in "their own" governments was not enhanced. Parties in the coalition were quick to exploit this weakness and the governments became a revolving door for parties to enter, exit, and return again.

Matching Bargaining Power to the Size of the Party

Direct election was meant to free the prime minister from the pitfalls of a coalition, especially those dug by small parties, because the position of prime minister would not be dependent upon any party, even the party of the prime minister. Proponents of the system failed to distinguish, however, between the prime minister's formal-legal power and political power. Although directly elected, the prime minister in Israel must rely on the political power of other institutions – the party, coalition, or Knesset – to actualize the election and govern. The social structure in Israel continued to dictate the need for a coalition, and being elected prime minister was not enough to sweep the winner's party into a majority of Knesset seats. In fact, the opposite happened as voters "punished" the parties of the prime minister and diminished their power. Popular support for the prime minister did not ensure parliamentary support, which is vital for steering the system. And with regard to the bargaining power of the parties, this only increased with direct elections, and hope dissipated of ending the political extortion of parties disproportionate to their size. Rather than having one lengthy and exhausting round of negotiations to form a coalition, the new system created incentives for two or even three rounds of bargaining:

- *First, prior to the election.* Efforts were made by prime ministerial aspirants to co-opt small, like-minded parties in order to forestall a loss of votes to them, in exchange for guaranteeing their leaders realistic places on the list of Knesset candidates. This happened with Gesher and Tzomet, which joined the Likud prior to the 1996 election, and Meimad, which joined Labor prior to the 1999 election. Efforts were also invested in courting the religious parties prior to the election to have them instruct their voters to support a particular candidate for prime minister.
- *Second, if none of the candidates for prime minister won a majority, a second round of voting would have to be held.* Between these two rounds, unprecedented wheeling and dealing would have taken place to win over the voters of candidates who did not make it to the final round. This did not happen because the two main candidates were able to win the support of potential rivals even before the first round – primarily by promising posts in the new government.
- *And, third, bargaining over formation of the coalition, familiar from the previous electoral system.* Negotiations also took place during the term of office to avert frequent coalition crises, especially during the season of budget deliberations.

Electing a "Non-Partisan" Prime Minister

Those advocating for direct election also tacitly hoped that the person chosen for prime minister would not be a party functionary or politician, but a leader, a statesperson. They were tired of party ideologues. And indeed the new system fostered centrism in candidates in order to win votes from all the camps. Two of the prime ministers who won office via direct election (Benjamin Netanyahu and Ehud Barak) were relatively new faces and lacking in political experience. This is not the place to evaluate their success as prime ministers, but their terms were short, and their careers as first-time prime ministers followed a similar trajectory: they both had a meteoric rise to political power and their terms as prime minister were brief; they both lost the subsequent election, resigned as party heads, resigned from the Knesset, and abandoned politics for several years immediately after failing to be reelected; and both later made a comeback to head their parties. In any event, it is doubtful that the hope for leaders of a different ilk was fulfilled during the period of direct election. It is apparently easier to be elected than to govern. Ariel Sharon, who subsequently won direct election as prime minister, was a seasoned political veteran of the old school, and although he was not young, new, or a media celebrity, he remained in power for five years until a stroke incapacitated him.

Enhancing Governability and Increasing Stability

Direct elections ultimately reduced the power of the institution of prime minister, because they disconnected it from the real political arena, which continued to be the parliament, dominated by parties. Media emphasis on the personality of the candidate became decisive both in electing the prime minister and in his or her conduct in office, and it reinforced the populist dimension of this complex position. During the terms of Prime Ministers Netanyahu and Barak, the political agenda seemed to have been largely set by public opinion polls: Far-reaching plans suddenly popped up whose only purpose was media spin to enhance the stature of the prime minister. Some examples: Barak's initiative to frame a secular constitution, or his highly publicized request for forgiveness from the Mizrahi community on behalf of "all the generations" of the Labor Party for its historical mistakes in integrating these immigrants.

The proponents believed that a prime minister elected directly by and accountable to the public would not need parliamentary tools such as collective and factional responsibility, which they considered a source of weakness of the executive branch in Israel. Prime Ministers Netanyahu and Barak indeed viewed governance as personal policies for which they were accountable to the public only. They interpreted this public accountability to mean that they were to govern alone, without a government or a Knesset. It turned out, however, that undermining the collective responsibility of the government became an obstacle to steering capacity, rather than strengthening it. Indeed, the governments were unstable, coalition membership frequently changed, and the prime minister repeatedly came up against resistance – in the Knesset, the coalition, the government, and ultimately the public.

D. The Status of Ministers in a Prime Ministerial Government

The expectation was that ministers directly accountable to the prime minister would be selected according to their abilities, that there would be more professional expertise among them, and that they would evince more responsibility and discipline. Netanyahu even announced upon election in 1996 that he intended to establish "a government of experts and not politicians," although he ultimately appointed only one minister who was not an MK, and led a government that did not consist of experts (Caspit and Kfir 1997, 314). Prime Minister Barak went so far as to rescind the cap on the number of ministers and deputy ministers in the government, as stipulated by the Basic Law: Government. The proponents of the system had hoped that government ministries would undergo a process of depoliticization, but this did not happen, and neither the prime ministers directly elected nor the ministers chosen by them were free of political considerations when making appointments to the civil service. Prime Minister Netanyahu, for instance, dismissed the Civil Service Commissioner at the government's very first meeting so that the commissioner would not prevent him from making political appointments within the government ministries. With a weak prime minister, the ministers did not become a rubber stamp, and often did not view themselves as obligated by the government's positions. The National Religious Party, a coalition partner, voted in the Knesset against Netanyahu's approval of the Wye Agreement in 1998. The ministers in Barak's government resigned one after another. Although Sharon fired more ministers than any previous prime minister, he did so during his second term of office, which he did not win by direct election. As noted, some wanted the government to be a "professional cabinet," not a "political" one, a futile hope in the first place because the role of minister is fundamentally political.

E. The Big Bang: The Shattering of the Parties

Direct election changed the party system. At the time it was instituted in 1996, the Knesset was no longer dominated by one major party, but two relatively large parties held sway: The Likud and Labor together controlled some 65 percent of the Knesset seats in 1988 and 1992. Direct election further split the parties and led to the creation of many mid-size and small parties. Voting with two ballots – one for the prime minister and the other for the Knesset – inflated the narrow-interest parties and deflated the large parties, which were reduced to mid-size. In 1981, the two large parties held ninety-five Knesset seats (Likud forty-eight, and Alignment forty-seven), in 1988 they had dropped to seventy-nine seats (Likud forty, Alignment thirty-nine), and in 1992 they were down to seventy-six seats (Labor forty-four and Likud thirty-two). A decade later, after two direct elections to the Knesset (1996 and 1999), the power of the two parties had diminished to a mere forty-five seats in the Knesset. In contrast, the narrow-interest parties doubled their power or more: In 1992, they won eighteen seats, and won forty-eight seats in the 1999 election (Kenig, Rahat, and Hazan 2004, 33–61). Thus, the consequences of direct elections proved to be antithetical to the prediction that they would strengthen the major parties, based on the belief that voting for a specific candidate for prime minister would encourage voting for his or her party.

Politically savvy Israeli voters realized at once the opportunity they had been handed by splitting the ballot – one vote for the prime minister, but the other not necessarily for the prime minister's party, but for the party that most closely reflected their sectoral identity. Not only did the major parties lose their electoral clout, but the connection weakened between the prime ministerial candidate and his party. All campaign attention and financing had been focused on the candidate at the expense of the party and its Knesset candidates. As a result, the major party candidates – both those elected to the Knesset and particularly those who failed to get in – felt that they owed nothing to the party head who was elected prime minister. As noted, the split ballot led to split parties: There was no significant change in the number of factions during the period of direct elections, but their relative size changed: The Index of the Effective Number of Parties rose dramatically from 4.39 in 1992 to 8.69 in 1999.[22] Fragmentation continued even after direct election was repealed: In the 2009 election, the two largest parties jointly held only fifty-five Knesset seats. A fragmented Knesset finds it hard to be effective, and this directly harms the steering capacity of the government. Most of the parties turned into ruling versions of interest groups, lacking the ability to fulfill their distinctive function as "aggregators of interests." In Chapter 10, we look at the fact that the weakening of the parties did not begin with direct elections in the 1990s, but ensued from a combination of factors, in Israel as in other democracies. There is no doubt, however, that direct elections exacerbated this trend, with all the negative implications for the stability of the political system.

F. The Status of the Knesset

The designers of the direct election system were justifiably concerned about conferring dictatorial power upon the prime minister, and therefore they also sought to strengthen the Knesset as a legislative and oversight body. To that end, the law granted powers to the Knesset vis-à-vis the executive branch that do not exist in a presidential system: the power to bring down the government by a majority of MKs voting no-confidence in it; the power to dismiss a prime minister by a majority of eighty MKs; and the power to dismiss a minister by a majority of seventy MKs. Another new power granted the Knesset was the authority to declare a state of emergency. In practice, however, the Knesset's status as a legislative and oversight institution was undermined, primarily because it was so fragmented, while the MKs as individuals and those representing narrow interests gained power. Rescinding the collective responsibility of the government toward the Knesset also undercut the Knesset's ability to influence government policies (see Chapter 4).

The attempt to create a "balance of deterrence" between the Knesset and the prime minister was intended to prevent frequent crises. It was hoped that the Knesset would hesitate to vote no-confidence in the prime minister because bringing down the government meant dissolving the Knesset, while the prime minister would hesitate to dissolve the Knesset because that would mean a new election for prime minister as well. These hopes were dashed, however. The three governments during

[22] See Figure 4.1 in Chapter 4.

the direct election era (1996, 1999, and 2001) had short lives – an average of two and a half years. And the balance of deterrence to prevent frequent elections was frequently overturned, once by the Knesset and twice by the prime minister.

G. Political Participation

Direct election is a mechanism of direct democracy that also aims to stimulate public participation. The assumption is that giving voters the opportunity to directly choose their prime minister, without the mediation of parties, would increase political participation. It was meant to be the answer to the criticism of party lists in which voters cannot change the candidates proposed, and which does not foster accountability of the elected representatives to the voters. Proponents asserted that when citizens feel they have direct influence, they will want to exercise their democratic right to vote. Furthermore, unlike the list system, in which a prime minister is determined only after coalition negotiations, in direct election the citizens decide who will be their prime minister, and they know who has the job as soon as the votes are counted.

This assumption was proven wrong, too, as the system did not increase voter turnout in Israel. Having four election campaigns in seven years also did not foster participation. The special election for prime minister, held only in 2001, had the lowest turnout until that date (62% compared with an average of about 80% in all previous elections). Voter turnout was also not helped by the fact that Arab citizens largely boycotted these special elections because they felt they had no suitable candidate, and could not express their preference for a party. With regard to the public learning immediately who would be prime minister, this one certainty provided by the new system did not ensure that whoever was elected prime minister would be capable of governing.[23] What's more, the political culture in Israel is not sufficiently tolerant to allow voters for the losing candidate to view the elected rival as their legitimate prime minister.

H. Returning to the Parliamentary System

Many of the concerns that had been raised by those opposed to the law, particularly the weakening of the parties and the harm to the steering capacity of the entire political system, did in fact materialize.[24] The failure was clear, particularly to the major parties, and by the early 2000s a campaign was underway by the Israel Democracy Institute, both among the public and the parties, to abolish direct elections. Interestingly, Prime Minister Sharon supported their repeal, even though he had this system to thank for his election in February 2001 with a resounding 62 percent of the vote. It was clear to Sharon that he could not govern effectively when his party, the Likud, held only 19 seats in the Knesset and the coalition. Labor also agreed to the change, having lost hope that direct elections would lead to the prime

[23] This was also not certain as another round of voting was required if no single candidate won at least 50 percent of the votes counted. In the 1996 election, the outcome was temporarily unclear because the difference between Netanyahu and Peres was some 30,000 votes (Felsenthal and Machover 1995, 57–68).

[24] On the day the Knesset enacted the law to institute direct elections, articles pro and con appeared (Amnon Rubinstein 1992; Galnoor 1992a).

ministership even if its Knesset bloc did not hold a majority of the seats. Thus, accord between the two large parties made possible repeal of the law.

The Knesset quickly enacted a new Basic Law: Government in March 2001 with a 72-vote majority. Most of the small factions opposed the repeal of direct elections as splitting the ballot had been a windfall for them. The law restored the previous parliamentary system, and the 2003 election was conducted accordingly. Nevertheless, several changes were introduced in an effort to stabilize the political system. The main innovation was institution of a "constructive vote of no confidence" similar to the one used in Germany, designed to prevent threats to the coalition on trivial matters and to prevent a vacuum if the government fell in a no-confidence vote. The constructive element was that MKs could not dissolve the government in a no-confidence vote unless a majority had an alternative candidate for prime minister. Remnants from the direct election law included the prime minister's power to dissolve the Knesset under certain conditions, and the Knesset's power to remove a prime minister from office – but not dissolve the Knesset – if he or she was convicted of an offense that involved moral turpitude. The power of a prime minister to dissolve parliament exists in other parliamentary democracies such as Germany, Spain, Holland, and Britain.

I. Lessons from the Failure of Direct Elections in Israel

The failure of direct elections revealed the complex web of relations between the political system and society. Direct elections had changed the system of governance in a way that was incompatible with Israel's social structure and political tradition. The main lesson learned was the need to be cautious of artificial transplants, because elements that work well elsewhere are not necessarily suitable for governance in Israel. Those who advocated for the change were aware of this, and therefore did not seek a full presidential system for Israel. Had a full presidential system been instituted, the experiment would have been more exact, because a presidential system has its own internal logic reflected in a more distinct separation of powers and usually with a rigid constitution, as well as checks and balances on the power of the central branches of government. Nevertheless, the failure of direct elections also suggests why a full presidential system would not work in Israel:

- First, when the head of the executive branch is elected by a majoritarian system, the winner takes all, even if the victory was by a slim margin. This is incompatible with Israeli political culture, which – ever since the pre-state period – has been based on seeking consensus, inclusiveness, and a coalition government. Introducing a majoritarian component into the Israeli system could be problematic precisely because it gives a decisive victory to one side, creating absolute winners and losers. It was clear how direct elections in Israel, rather than fostering centrist politics, deepened the social rifts, as reflected in the split ballot.
- Second, the failure of direct elections in Israel set off alarms about the hasty introduction of elements of direct democracy. Direct elections and party primaries do not exist in most parliamentary systems. In Israel, these measures exacerbated the damage to parties as democratic representative bodies, and threatened to turn the Knesset into a shareholders' meeting of interest groups.

In parliamentary democracies, parties operate in the constant tension between aggregating interests for the good of all and representing particularistic interests. The cumulative total determines the long-term outcomes, and it is important for the scales to tip toward the good of all. Splitting the vote in direct elections threatened to tilt the balance in the wrong direction. The representatives in the Knesset seemed to have in mind only their particularistic interests, leaving considerations about the good of all to the prime minister. There is nothing wrong with adopting elements of direct democracy (such as holding national referendums), as long as these are adapted to the political culture and add a channel for airing public preferences. However, these methods must not upset the balance between steering capacity and representativeness, which is what happened with direct elections. Strengthening one must not jeopardize the other.

- Third, direct elections gave impetus to the trends in Israel of populism and personalizing politics. These ills also plague other democracies, but the Israeli political system faces critical decisions that require superb steering capacity. The period of direct election of the prime minister did not prove that this system was a more effective one for making difficult decisions. On the contrary, it was hard to implement new policies in those years, because they required broader support of the parliamentary coalition.
- Fourth, presidential systems have not shown themselves to be more stable than parliamentary systems; indeed, the opposite is true if South America is included in the list. According to the aggregate political stability index published by the World Bank (e.g., regime democratic stability, repeal of the constitution, internal violence, etc.), the average positive score of thirty-three parliamentary systems was much higher than of the twenty-seven presidential systems studied.[25] As noted, direct election in Israel did not contribute to stability: For one thing, when the prime minister and the Knesset lay claim to separate public legitimacy, it is not clear who is representing the general good, and who have their own interests at heart.

The failure of direct elections was an important reminder of the limitations on using the law to engineer governance. Proponents of the system appear to have wanted to drain politics from the system – to eliminate the thrust and parry of world views, interests, and social divisions. The image sold to the public was that a professional manager would head the state and organize the affairs of state efficiently and without corruption for the good of everyone. Ultimately politics won in Israel, and that is a good thing, because politics reflects real needs more than the so-called "rule of experts" advocated by the proponents of direct elections. The Israeli political system reflects the complexity of society, and any attempt to "organize it" must be cautious, reflective, and appropriate for the social fabric. The parties, social groups, and coalitions are not superfluous "noise" in the political system, but serve important functions of mediation and interest aggregation. The effort to eliminate the legitimate mediators is not just futile, but puts democracy at risk.

To strengthen the executive branch and its head, other elements of a parliamentary system must also be strengthened – those that provide the basis for legitimacy

[25] World Bank 2005.

and the stability needed for steering. Parliamentary systems function even though ongoing adjustments are needed to help turn the gears of the legislative and executive branches, which partially interlock. Each branch has a purpose and a function of its own, and the tension between them gives the political system its dynamism and ability to be both representative and task oriented. To strengthen the executive branch, one must hearken back to the wisdom of the parliamentary system's principles: strengthen the parliament, which is the basis for the power of the executive branch, its extension. In any case, empowering one must not come at the expense of the other.

5.8 Relations between the Central and Local Governments

Local authorities attend to the welfare, education, health, and quality of life of their residents. In Israel they are responsible for providing national services (education, welfare, health, religion, and immigrant absorption) as well as local services (road system, sanitation, water supply, sewerage, garbage collection, licensing construction, market and slaughterhouse regulation, registration of peddlers and porters, firefighting services, and more). As this list suggests, the selection of functions is arbitrary, and varies from country to country according to the perception of the fundamental role of the local authority. In one approach, local government is seen as the executive arm of the central government – ignoring its representation role and emphasizing the administrative functions. It is this approach that prevails in Israel in keeping with the tendency to concentrate power in the hands of the central government. In another approach, the emphasis is on the representativeness of local government as an elective body and its obligation to the norms of service, transparency, and responsiveness to the needs of the public. The latter approach reflects a partnership between the local and central governments, fostering decentralization and local empowerment (Dery 1994, 9–10; Menuchin 2004).

In the representative approach, which guides us here, local government is an expression of communal and local needs that differ from those in society at large and are as legitimate as national policies. Local government has the advantage of proximity to the citizen – for addressing daily needs, the quality of life, and vital services. This proximity requires citizen involvement, and makes room for the development of a small-scale participatory democracy. In addition, local government is an excellent place to recruit national political leaders and advance those who are responsive to the public's needs (Elazar 2001).

In the centralized approach that prevails in Israel, the local authorities are the subcontractors of the central government, whose role is to follow orders and carry out assigned functions. The ministries view the local authorities as a burden – or, at best, as another pressure group demanding resources and services; at worst, they view it as the site of exaggerated politicization, mismanagement, and corruption. Little recognition is given in Israel to the importance of this middle layer between the central government and the citizens. The absence of strong local and regional government exposes citizens to the arbitrariness of state authorities. The "districts" that do exist in Israel are administrative extensions of the ministries, not even defined the same way by each ministry. District heads are merely the bureaucratic arms of the Ministry of the Interior. And, until recently, local authorities were not the subject of much academic research; the dearth of data is reflected in this chapter.[26]

A. Structure and Activities of Local Government

Background Data

Local authorities are organized into six districts defined by the Ministry of the Interior: Jerusalem District, Haifa District, Tel Aviv District, North District, Central District, and South District. There is also one unusual arrangement – an administrative district outside the borders of the state (the West Bank/"Judea and Samaria" District, and, in the past, the Gaza Strip District). As under the British Mandate, each district has a district head appointed by the Minister of the Interior, whose job is to carry out the policies of the ministry and, formally, also to coordinate the activities of the other ministries in the same district.

Israel has two forms of local government, depending upon the size of the population: cities and local councils. In addition, there are non-urban regional councils: small towns, kibbutzim, and moshavim clustered together by region and governed by regional councils. There are also unrecognized localities lacking any municipal standing. All forms are referred to here as "local government."

The Minister of the Interior has the power to authorize new local authorities – to define their standing and the boundaries of their jurisdiction. For recognition as a city, a locality must have at least 20,000 residents, a high level of development, political stability, sound fiscal management, and an adequate level of services (Shefet and Shefet 2004, 20). The interior minister can also authorize a local council if the number of residents exceeds 5,000.

According to the Ministry of the Interior website, Israel had 257 local authorities in 2015, of which twenty-three were beyond its borders (in the West Bank/"Judea and Samaria" District), compared with 126 in the 1950s. Figure 5.1 shows that the number of cities has steadily grown, particularly after the wave of immigration in the 1990s. The number of local councils doubled through this period, though it shrank to 125 in 2015 following the unification of local councils (see below). The number of regional councils has not changed much since the 1980s.

Table 5.4 shows the population distribution according to the type of local authority. In 2015, most Israelis (75%) lived in urban jurisdictions, a minority in local councils (15%), and fewer (10%) in the 971 localities organized in regional councils. The area of jurisdiction of regional councils extends across 80 percent of the total area of Israel. About half a percent of the Israeli population (40,000 people) live in unrecognized localities, all of them Arab.[27] Most Arab citizens of Israel (54%) reside in local councils. As we discuss later, on average the cities and the localities in the

[26] Shevach Weiss's groundbreaking study (1970) should be mentioned. In recent years, scholars from the Open University, Haifa University, the Floersheimer Institute, the Jerusalem Center for Public Affairs, and the Israel Democracy Institute have begun to engage in research about local government. For recent scholarship, see Levy and Sarig 2014 and Szuster 2014.

[27] See Chapter 15 on local government in Arab localities, and on the unrecognized localities. According to the Association of Forty, the numbers are higher – a total of about 75,000 residents live in the unrecognized Arab localities (65,000 in the south and 10,000 in the north and central regions). www.snunit.k12.il/beduin/docs1.html [in Hebrew] (accessed May 10, 2016).

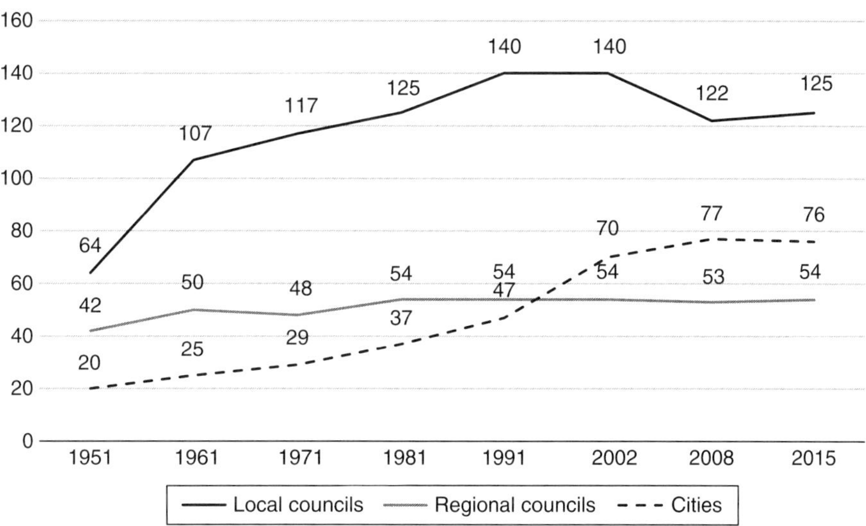

Figure 5.1 Number of local authorities, by type, 1951–2015
Note: Includes twenty-three Jewish local authorities in the West Bank.
Source: Ministry of the Interior website: www.moin.gov.il/OfficeUnits/LocalGovernmentAdministration/Pages/default.aspx (accessed May 16, 2016).

Table 5.4 *Local authorities in Israel – 2015*

Local authorities	Population (1000s)	Population (%)	Demographic distribution*	Total revenues**	Of which, self-revenues**
(A) 76 cities	6,172	75%	86% Jewish and other; 14% Arab	49,847 (74%)	26,469 (79%)
(B) 125 local councils	1,237	15%	41% Jewish and other; 59% Arab	8,259 (12%)	3,003 (9%)
(C) 54 regional councils (971 localities)	828	10%	91% Jewish and other; 9% Arab	9,704 (14%)	3,992 (12%)
(D) localities lacking municipal status	41	0.5%	100% Arab		
Total A+B+C***	8,237			67,810 (100%)	33,464 (100%)

* Out of the 255 local authorities: 172 Jewish; 81 Arab; 2 industrial.
** NIS millions at 2015 prices.
*** The populations in localities lacking municipal status are not listed in the official statistics of the Central Bureau of Statistics, but are part of the total.

Source: Central Bureau of Statistics (CBS), Local Authorities in Israel, updated 2015. www.cbs.gov.il/reader/?MIval=cw_usr_view_SHTML&ID=357 [in Hebrew] (accessed June 1, 2016).

regional councils are wealthier in terms of income and less dependent on the central government for their revenues.

Local Democracy

THE MAYOR. Until 1978, the structure of local government resembled that of the national system, and the mayor was the head of the party list that formed a coalition in the elected local council. Since the introduction of direct elections in 1978, the mayor is elected by secret ballot for a five-year term in direct, general elections that are personal, unlike the party lists that compete for seats in the council. To run for mayor, the candidate must head a party list. The winner is the candidate who garners at least 40 percent of the valid ballots in the first round of voting; if no one wins 40 percent of the vote, a runoff is held between the two frontrunners, and the winner of a majority in the runoff becomes mayor. The mayor-elect does not require a vote of confidence from the council, but in practice establishes a coalition among the lists and council members in order to make it possible to legislate bylaws, gain approval for the budget, and have support for managing the town. By law, any political agreements between the mayor and council members or party lists must be made public.

Mayors serve a dual role: They head the "executive branch," but also chair the council and run its meetings. Mayors have broad management powers: They are responsible for preparing the budget bill, recruiting council approval for it (contingent upon vetting by the Ministry of the Interior's district head); managing municipal employees (except where there is a town manager); and they have the legal power to hire employees without the need for council approval, to reopen debate about a local council vote, and to set in motion the removal of a council member on grounds set by law, such as chronic absence from council meetings. The mayor can be removed from office if convicted of a crime declared by the court to be one of moral turpitude. The council can dismiss a mayor only if his conduct is unbecoming of his position in the eyes of a 75 percent majority. The Minister of the Interior must also vet this decision.

THE COUNCIL. The council is the town parliament, and its size is commensurate with the number of residents – in cities, it ranges from nine to thirty-one members; in local councils, from five to twenty-one. Anyone seventeen years old or over who is registered as a resident can vote in the local election, even non-citizens. The Local Authorities (Elections) Law (1965) states that election to the local council will be based on proportional representation and that the entire town is one election district. In the past, local authority elections were held at the same time as the Knesset election, but since 1978 they have been separate. Council elections are held every five years at the time of election of the mayor: The voter places two slips into the ballot box: one for the mayoral candidate and one for a party running for the council. The number of votes required for a council seat is determined by dividing the total number of valid votes by the number of seats. The threshold for election of a party to the local council is 75 percent of the votes required for a seat in the council, therefore it differs from town to town.

The council is authorized to enact local bylaws. Every quarter, the mayor must present the council with financial and activity reports of the local authority. The council must approve the local authority's policy principles, work plan, and financial matters, including approval of the budget, municipal tax rates, licenses, and fees. The council has to approve the appointment of deputy mayors and various committee members. It must also give approval for the hiring (upon tender) and dismissal of statutory employees (such as the legal adviser, treasurer, secretary, and comptroller). The council discusses the city comptroller report once a year, and provides ongoing oversight to municipal companies and others. Members of the council do not receive wages for their council activity.

B. Problems of Local Government in Israel

Structural Problems

The local authority is accountable to the residents, above all, hence its power to enact bylaws, although these, of course, are subordinate to the laws of the state (Sanbar Committee 1981). Accordingly, the central government must also recognize the local autonomy of the residents, and not treat the local authority as its errand boy for the transfer of money and provision of services. The revenue-generating structure for the local authorities reflects this problematic arrangement.

For years, most local authorities in Israel have carried a heavy burden of deficit and debt because of their income arrangements. From 1990 to 2006, the average annual deficit was approximately 5.5 percent in Jewish local authorities and 6.5 percent in Arab local authorities. Local deficits gradually declined, however, because of the strict rules imposed by the Ministry of Finance – lowering the debt ceiling from 78 percent in 1998 to 54 percent in 2006 (Ben Bassat and Dahan 2008, 8, 13). Diminished income and fewer loans were a recipe for financial distress, even in well-run, uncorrupt local authorities. The recurring problem cited in the state comptroller reports is that the revenues from municipal taxes on local businesses are minuscule in small and poor localities, while the revenues from taxes on households vary with the socioeconomic level of each locality. On top of this, weaker local authorities find it harder to collect municipal taxes and other mandatory payments.

The political culture that evolved in some local authorities has posed further obstacles: First, political appointments – the hiring of incompetent officials: In Israel's early years as a state, appointments were made based on party affiliation; in the 1980s, appointments were influenced by connections – personal, family, or financial. Second, the link between money and power has steadily grown in the local authorities, just as it has in the central government. Third, with town management increasingly difficult and tax collections falling behind, many local authorities have cut back on service provision, while at the same time exceeding their authority in areas such as planning and building oversight. The state comptroller has explicitly pointed out, however, that the responsibility for these failings falls jointly on the local authorities and the Ministry of the Interior.[28] This sorry situation is a reflection of the unclear division of authority and responsibility between the local and central governments, particularly with regard to who covers various budget items. In 2003, 40 percent of the local government expenditures were covered by the national government, compared to 49 percent in OECD countries (Ben Bassat and Dahan 2008, 25).

[28] State Comptroller 1992, 6 and 2000, Report 4, 7.

Subordination to the Ministry of the Interior

The Minister of the Interior has the authority to establish all types of local authorities and set their jurisdictional boundaries. Furthermore, the local authorities must obtain the approval of the minister – via the district heads – for their budgets, loans, guarantees, land use, exemptions from tenders, and formation of municipal companies. Since 1988, the Minister of the Interior's approval is no longer required for each bylaw, but the minister can delay publication of the law in the State Records and even revoke it.

The Budget Principles Law (1985) gave two ministers – Interior and Finance – broad supervisory powers over budget expenditures in the local authorities as well as the power to impose heavy penalties on towns that overspend their budgets. These ministers set the municipal tax rate (with the approval of the Knesset's Finance Committee) and the wages of office holders; they also have the power to halt work not authorized by the budget and to reduce government transfers when the local authority exceeds its budget. This supervision became even more stringent following the 2004 amendment that gave the Minister of the Interior the power to place a local authority "under administration" – to replace the mayor by an appointee – when, in the minister's view, the municipality is not functioning properly.

Budget Sources

The budget of the local authority is divided into the regular budget for ongoing expenses and the development budget for development and investment. The sources of financing for the local authorities are *locally generated revenues* (municipal taxes on households and businesses, licenses, and fees) to finance the provision of local services; *government support* from the budgets of ministries (earmarked grants), primarily to finance state education and welfare services; and *equalization grants* from the Ministry of the Interior to ensure basic services in local authorities with low income or in financial distress. Other sources of revenue are bank loans, grants from the Ministry of Finance, municipal foundations, and donations.

LOCALLY GENERATED REVENUES. The local authority's primary source of direct income comes from municipal property taxes (*arnona*) collected from owners within its jurisdiction, as well as fees for municipal services, levies, imposts, and license fees. Until the 1980s, locally generated revenues covered about a third of the regular budget of local authorities, with the balance coming from the government. In the 1990s, following government cutbacks, the proportions were reversed and now two-thirds are paid for by locally generated revenues. There are significant disparities between local authorities in the amount of revenues they generate. In wealthier towns, locally generated revenues are substantial because of the high socioeconomic level of the residents, while revenues are scant in weaker towns. Here are the extremes: In 2006, locally generated revenues covered 94 percent of the Tamar regional council budget, while they covered only 6 percent in the Abu Basma local council.

The municipal tax (*arnona*) on households is considered progressive because the amount varies with the status of the residential area and size of the dwelling. New research casts doubt on this, however, because the disparities between the local authorities are not truly reflected in the differential tax rates (Horne 2008; Smolsky 2008). The government controls the local tax rate, and local authorities are limited in their ability to give exemptions or discounts at their discretion. In wealthier localities, the municipal tax revenues from commercial firms cover a greater share of the budget; less in poor localities. Because of these differences – particularly per capita income and the presence (or absence) of business – local authorities show dramatic differences in their revenues from taxation as well as their ability to collect the taxes.

GOVERNMENT SUPPORT. Earmarked grants from government ministries finance state-provided services – primarily education and welfare – based on criteria designed to be standard. Since the 1980s, government grants to local authorities – both earmarked and non-earmarked – have been slashed; they were down by an average of 40 percent in the 2000s. Government grants have two objectives: to guarantee basic services to the residents and to equalize, or at least minimize, the gaps between local authorities (Ben-Elia 2004, 33–39). In actuality, government support has often not covered even the earmarked services, leading to further debt and inequality between localities, which reflect their socioeconomic divisions.[29] The purpose of the equalization grant is to ensure basic services to the residents of poor localities, and it is calculated by the difference between an authority's minimum required expenses and its potential revenues. However, support via the equalization grant was withheld as leverage to pressure local authorities to increase their collections. The result was that the proportion of equalization grants in the regular budget significantly dropped in poorer local authorities (Ben Bassat and Dahan 2008, 27–28). Thus, the political patronage of the local mayors by the central government was replaced by bureaucratic patronage.

EXPENDITURES. Data from 251 local authorities underscore the large disparities among local authorities in the type and quality of services they provide. About a fifth of the budget is designated for state services, primarily education and welfare, and a similar amount for local services – sanitation, security, planning and supervision, maintenance of public property, and agricultural services (in the regional councils). The rest is allocated for general expenses, bond repayment, contract services, and subsidies for local companies and non-profits. The non-regular (development) budget finances development work and has issued bonds in recent years to reduce the deficit.

Division of Authority and Responsibility

While policies for education and welfare are set by the government ministries, the local authority is responsible for implementing the programs and direct contact with the residents. To that end, the central government transfers earmarked funds, and the authorities have little say in the matter of how much, how to adapt them to local needs, or the movement of funds from one budget line to another. In the field of education, the official division of labor is that the Ministry of Education sets the content, curriculum, and pedagogical aspects and is responsible for the budget and supervision, while the local authority is responsible for the buildings

[29] Government spending per pupil on education and welfare in the local authorities is set in accordance with the socioeconomic level of the locality, hence this funding only widens the gap (Ben Bassat and Dahan 2008, 16, 26).

and equipment. Although the declared goal is to reach equality in educational services, there are large disparities between localities. Some stem from discrimination in allocating resources, such as less government funding (per student) given to schools in poor Jewish or Arab localities; and some stem from management problems in the local authority itself, including mishandling of funds and corruption.

Approximately two-thirds of the local expenditures on welfare are covered by the national budget. The Ministry of Welfare sets general policy and dictates criteria for whether and how much to fund, while the implementation rests with the welfare services of the local authorities.[30] As for transportation, the local authority is in charge of paving and maintaining public roads within its jurisdiction, but has no power to decide on traffic arrangements. The town cannot even place a traffic sign within its jurisdictional boundaries without the approval of the Ministry of Transportation.[31] Town and building plans that pass the local planning committees also need approval from the district and national planning boards. The involvement and monitoring of the central government – justified on the merits – have turned into a bureaucratic labyrinth (see Bar-Gil 2008).

An example of a government policy that was only partially successful because it was imposed upon the local authorities rather than involving them in the planning was Project Renewal in the 1970s (Shimshoni 2002), in which large sums of state money were invested in urban renewal of low-income, Jewish neighborhoods. The ministries opted for direct contact with "neighborhood leaders," going over the head of the local authority, not even consulting the locally elected leaders. The central government created an image of decentralization and participation, but in practice the approach was paternalistic and weakened the local authority. Another example of such relations between the local and central government was the policy of "direct absorption of immigrants" in the 1990s. The local government was ostensibly given autonomy and an opportunity to demonstrate its ability to carry out a national mission. In reality, however, the local authorities engaged in direct absorption due to the inefficacy of the Absorption Ministry and other ministries, which had no idea how to cope with the challenge. Shifting responsibility to the local government was not accompanied by collaborative planning and the transfer of adequate funds. As a result, wealthy localities took advantage of the policies to attract more established immigrant families, while indigent, elderly, and single-parent immigrants settled in poor localities, becoming a burden there and plunging them into economic distress (Dery 1994, 19–21).

Nevertheless, the pattern of relations between the local and central governments has changed over the years. In the 1980s, unplanned decentralization took place because of several dynamics, mainly the weakening of the central government, and the gradual strengthening of local government in more prosperous areas. At first this was "decentralization by default," in which services were shifted to the local authorities, most of which lacked the tools to handle them. In parallel, the central

[30] The policy of the Ministry of Welfare is to decentralize authority to the social services departments in the local authorities (Dolev et al. 2008).

[31] Ze'ev Bielski, the mayor of Ra'anana, boasted that he put up traffic lights in his city without asking permission from the Ministry of Transportation; approval arrived retroactively (Kfir 2005, 25).

government's ability to monitor the local authority declined, leading to a partial de facto decentralization, particularly among more established towns. Formally, these local authorities remained dependent upon Interior Ministry regulations, the state budget, and the bureaucrats in the central ministries, but informally it paved the way for more independent decision-making and empowerment. However, lack of clarity also fosters arbitrariness and ulterior motives, creating a gray area of relations between the local and central governments. This exacerbates the gaps between localities, so that the strong get stronger and the weak get weaker (Dery 1999).

C. The Crisis in Local Authorities

The situation described above was at the heart of a crisis that saw most local authorities crushed by heavy debt. The central government never had a clear and consistent policy toward local authorities, but its actions – particularly the recurring cuts in funding – articulated an unwritten policy. The local authorities were to be given more responsibility for providing services (although the decision about their scope and quality remained with the ministries), but they would have to make do with less money and adhere to a prescribed recovery program that entailed "streamlining" their services. In this forced deal, the preferred method was to cut back on government funding to the local authorities, both equalization grants and earmarked grants for education and welfare. The inevitable result has been recurring budgetary crises since the 2000s, when onerous municipal deficits ceased to be the exception. A by-product was damage to the public image of the local authorities, as if they were all corrupt and mismanaged (Ben Bassat and Dahan 2008, 6).

State policy was to reduce the national debt, and this was carried out in no small measure at the expense of the local authorities. Earmarked government grants were supposed to be guaranteed income for the local authorities, but they only added to the uncertainty and shortfall – sometimes because the grants were not transferred on time, and sometimes because they were reduced with no prior warning. The local authority found itself between a rock and a hard place – it was being asked to provide state services to its residents, but could not do so because the funds from the government were inadequate. Cutbacks that cause shortfalls followed by grants to cover the deficit do not help a local authority streamline its activities. Such policies do, however, allow for tight central government control.

The severe crisis in which many local authorities found themselves in the 2000s is an example of how irresponsible decision-making can deteriorate a situation. In the context of a national budget crisis, the government made sudden decisions to slash grants to the local authorities by some 40 percent within two years, including reductions in the government earmarked grants and services.[32] Thus, half the local authorities had balanced budgets in 1999, and this dropped to 20 percent in 2004 (Alon Rubinstein 2004, 5). This was a vicious cycle – first an economic crisis, after which the crisis itself was used to prove that the local authorities were not reliable.

[32] Bank of Israel, "The Impact of Government Policy on the Financial Situation of the Local Authorities." Press release, March 25, 2004, on www.bankisrael.gov.il [in Hebrew] (accessed May 10, 2016).

Table 5.5 *Distribution of 252 cities, local councils, and regional councils, by socioeconomic cluster (2008 index) and per capita expenditures (regular budget, 2006)*

Cluster	Number of localities [Arab localities]	Per capita expenditures (NIS, rounded off, 2006 prices)	Examples of localities
1 (lowest)	7 [5]	3,300	Jisr Az-Zarka, Beitar Illit, Laqiya, Abu Basma
2	48 [43]	4,200	Rahat, Umm al-Fahm, Abu Ghosh, Yarka, Elad
3	28 [21]	4,100	Nazareth, Bnei Brak, Beit Shemesh, Tayibe, Shfaram, Netivot
4	26 [8]	4,600	Jerusalem, Sderot, Rameh, Acre, Kafr Yasif
5	52 [2]	5,100	Afula, Beersheba, Eilat, Mi'ilya, Netanya
6	27 [0]	4,900	Rehovot, Rosh HaAyin, Petah Tikva, Qiryat Motzkin
7	23 [0]	5,300	Haifa, Kfar Yona, Ramat Gan, Rosh Pina
8	31 [0]	6,900	Tel Aviv, Shoham, Ra'anana, Kiryat Tiv'on
9	7 [0]	6,700	Ramat Hasharon, Meitar, Kfar Vradim
10 (highest)	3 [0]	7,800	Omer, Savion, Kfar Shmaryahu

Source: CBS, www.cbs.gov.il/publications/local_authorities06/pdf/t01.pdf (accessed June 1, 2016).

The situation began improving in 2009 with increased government allocations to the local authorities and use of the socioeconomic index (see Table 5.5) as a basis for these allocations.

One might have hoped that the deep involvement of the central government in local governance would help reduce gaps and foster greater equality among the localities. In reality, the gap has only grown over the years, as evidenced by the grouping of local authorities into ten clusters based on the socioeconomic status of the residents. This official index is drawn from aggregated data on income, housing, education, employment, and social conditions.

Table 5.5 shows that most local authorities (64%) fall into the lowest five clusters. All seventy-nine Arab localities are in these clusters, with only two in cluster 5. The per capita expenditure in 2006 in the highest cluster was 2.4 times that of the lowest. We do not have more recent data, but there is no reason to assume that this situation has changed much, since only twenty-four local authorities moved up one cluster and sixty-four moved down (see source of Table 5.5). The division between the wealthy and poor localities parallels the division between the center and periphery of the country, and the strong and weak groups in Israeli society. The great majority of localities in the southern district are in the low clusters, 1–5 (with the exception of Beersheba's satellite towns), and most of the northern district localities (86%) are in clusters 2–5. The profile of wealthier local authorities shows them in the center of the country with a Jewish, non-ultra-Orthodox population. With the exception of Jerusalem, which is in the low fourth cluster (because of the relatively large proportion of Arabs, ultra-Orthodox, and poor), and Beersheba (cluster 5), the large cities are in the higher clusters. The ability of the municipal authorities to generate self-revenues also changes, of course, commensurate with their cluster. Locally generated income forms a higher proportion (70%) of the town budget for wealthier localities in clusters 9–10 and a lower proportion (25%) for weak localities in clusters 1–2.

One way to enhance equality among the localities is to change the division of resources – by enlarging the municipal boundaries of weak local authorities, for example, to include land for construction, development, and industrial zones, which would increase local income from municipal taxes (see proposals in Azulai, Widerman-Eliassy, and Dameri-Madar 2009). The land (mostly agricultural) would come primarily from nearby regional councils. The land area of regional councils extends across some 80 percent of Israel, but only 9 percent of the population lives there. The municipal authorities of Arad and Dimona, for example, demanded that the nearby industrial zone of Mishor Rotem, now under the Tamar Regional Council (with a population of 1,300), be transferred to them so they could collect the city tax paid by the factories (where many Dimona and Arad residents work). The decision to divide up the Tamar Regional Council between Arad and Dimona – made by a committee appointed by the Interior Ministry – was never implemented (Alon Rubinstein 2004).

D. The Importance of Local Government

A number of factors have weakened local government: the centralized approach of the national government, lack of a local democratic tradition, ineffective management, political appointments, accumulating debt, and corruption. To break out of the vicious cycle of relations between the central and local governments, the local authority's dependence on government bureaucracy should be replaced by a democratic reliance on its residents. Local authorities and their leaders should be judged on their own deeds, initiatives, and efficacy, not the deeds or intentions of the central government. Strengthening local government will also provide a local component that is important and lacking in Israeli democracy – support for the periphery and involvement of citizens in decision-making that directly affects their lives. Local government has great social value. In the past, it served as fertile ground for the growth of local leaders, some of whom managed to break through to national roles. The proportion of Mizrahim in the leadership of local authorities, for example, rose gradually from 26 percent in 1955 to 47 percent in 1965 and to 51 percent in 1983 (see also Grinberg 1989, 6).

One factor in the Likud's rise to power in 1977 was the local leadership of some who later became government ministers: David Levy, David Magen, Meir Sheetrit, and others. For the Alignment/Labor Party as well, local government became a channel of political mobility for local leaders who later became MKs and ministers – Yehonatan Yifrach, Jacques Amir, Amir Peretz, and Eli Dayan. Recruitment for national leadership later ended, but Mizrahi representation in the local government continued to grow, reaching 60 percent in the 2003 election – higher than their proportion in the Jewish population (Goldberg 2005). When, in the past, mayors were also allowed to serve simultaneously as MKs, they viewed themselves as representatives of the periphery. Some parties such as the Likud and Labor have continued to reserve Knesset seats in their primaries for local representatives. Local government is of critical importance for Arab citizens, as well as ultra-Orthodox residents of cities such as Bnei Brak and Elad. And although the under-representation of women continues, a gradual increase in their numbers as mayors and city council members has been evident (Herzog 2001, 145).

The many changes in local government over the years occurred because of specific needs, not as a result of a consistent and deliberate policy. But local government is in need of thorough and comprehensive reform, starting with recognition of its democratic legitimacy and unique contribution to society and the political system. With the exception of the Sanbar Commission, which advocated structural change, most of the many committees established over the years to examine local government were concerned with funding, and did not get to the root of the problem.[33] This is particularly true of using government grants punitively and, since 2003, the abortive attempts to unify local authorities.

Why did the attempts at reform fail? The central government had no real interest in strengthening local authorities. So long as stopgap measures could be taken to cope with the crisis and allow the authorities to survive, no urgency was felt – until the next crisis. Well-intentioned civil society organizations that came to the aid of weak local authorities allowed the government to shirk its responsibilities, sometimes indirectly causing the inefficacy of local authorities. Reform of local government must recognize the local citizenship of the residents; must take into consideration the uniqueness of local government and diversity among the authorities; and must respond to the special needs of weak authorities (clusters 1–4 in Table 5.5), particularly those in Arab, ultra-Orthodox, and development towns. The main features of the reform needed are known, and therefore we note them in brief:[34]

- Adoption of the principles of the European Charter of Local Self-Government.
- Anchoring the independent, democratic standing of the local authorities in the constitution (Basic Laws) and re-legislating all related laws. Eliminating the current subordination to the Ministry of the Interior and the district heads.
- Devolving power and authority to the local government to allow the central government to concentrate on overall state policy while the local authorities take responsibility vis-à-vis the residents for the autonomous management of local services.
- Fundamental revamping of the financial arrangements, particularly state education and welfare services, with a view toward enhancing the economic

[33] Such as the committee to set criteria for the allocation of equalization grants to local authorities (the Suari Committee) in 1993; the committee to unify local authorities (the Shahar Committee) in 1998; or the committee to examine criteria for allocating equalization grants (the Gadish Committee) in 2001.

[34] The government's proposed Municipalities Bill (2007) goes a long way in the right direction with its declaration that the goal is "to devolve power to the local authorities, which have managed their affairs effectively." Although the bill places too much emphasis on "monitoring and intervention tools," it is clearly intended to change the relationship with the central government and redefine the framework of the local authorities, which will all be called "municipalities." By 2016, the bill had not been advanced.

independence of the local authorities, diversifying their independent sources of income, and creating an objective mechanism to assist weak authorities (Ben Bassat and Dahan 2008, 52–54).

- Redefining jurisdiction boundaries, particularly regional councils, while encouraging residents to decide for themselves about the consolidation of authorities, conurbation of cities, and pooling of services.
- Legislation to ensure the separation of powers within the local government, reducing the number of council members, preventing illegitimate appointments, and ensuring ethical conduct.

5.9 The Executive Branch and the Parliament

In a parliamentary system, the executive and legislative branches partially overlap: the prime minister and most ministers come from the Knesset, and, in terms of functions, both are engaged in legislating and policy design. As for representation, the Knesset is the upper institution in that the government serves by virtue of the Knesset's confidence. As for policymaking, decision-making, and implementation, the executive takes the lead. In Israel, the government's independent leadership and room for maneuvering are particularly salient in matters of security and foreign policy. Each branch naturally tries to encroach on the other's domain. The Knesset seeks to dictate policy details to the government, and not make do with legislation and general debates. The government, on the other hand, wants the Knesset to rubber stamp all its initiatives. The result is a dynamic relationship in which each branch must learn the advantages of cooperation. The government needs the Knesset to bestow legitimacy on its activities, especially in matters of national importance. As noted, Prime Minister Begin asked for Knesset ratification of the peace agreement with Egypt even though the law did not oblige him to do so. Prime Minister Sharon needed the Knesset to enact the law authorizing evacuation from the Gaza Strip. Simultaneously, the Knesset and its committees have tools to monitor and alter the policies of the government and the ministries.

In a parliamentary democracy, it is the government that sets the agenda for the political system and, largely, for the Knesset. This is the context of the often tense relations between the branches, particularly regarding legislation. With the broadening role of government and the growth of the public sector, the Knesset has become increasingly dependent on the government ministries, to the extent that shaping legislation – clearly a Knesset role – is now in the hands of the executive branch. In Chapter 4 on the Knesset, we saw the dramatic rise in private members' bills as a way for MKs to restore lawmaking to the Knesset. And yet the considerable success of government bills – an average of 85 percent since the first Knesset – indicates that the government's legislative prowess has not diminished. Furthermore, ministers have the power to enact regulations. The second problematic area is the Knesset's limited ability to carry out its monitoring and oversight functions. Here, too, Knesset committees are largely dependent upon government ministries as a source of information, although in recent years they have independent information sources such as more parliamentary assistants (three for each MK) and the Knesset Research and Information Center. Had it not been for the existence of monitoring bodies such as the state comptroller, the independent media, and civil society organizations – which serve as watchdogs on ministry activity – it is doubtful that the Knesset could carry out its oversight tasks.

A government is evaluated by its steering capacity – its ability to navigate the political system and implement its policies. To that end, the government needs parliamentary and public support. Direct elections demonstrated how much the executive branch depends upon a stable coalition and a functioning Knesset. Thus, to strengthen the executive branch, it is necessary to strengthen the components of its political power – the Knesset, the coalition, and the parties. Constraining the power of the prime minister by the parliament enhances – and does not undermine – the steering capacity. Reining in the power of the executive branch – without paralyzing it – ensures that government policies that meet the challenge of parliamentary scrutiny will be implemented. This is why the collective responsibility of the government is not an empty slogan, but operationally significant. A government that speaks in contradictory voices conveys instability, and this trickles down to all levels of the political system. Hence political stability must be bi-directional – the government draws strength from the coalition and the Knesset, and the stability it gains in turn enhances the stability of the coalition and the Knesset.

A too-powerful executive branch jeopardizes democracy. It must be kept in check, constrained, and accountable to the parliament and the public. A weak executive branch also jeopardizes democracy by its impotence. The challenge is to shape a parliamentary system that appears at first glance to be impossible – a government with a strong steering capacity and a powerful parliament with effective oversight. On second glance, this is possible – such systems have existed, not without tension, in some periods of Israel's history and in other democratic states as well.

The steering capacity of the Israeli political system was weakened for two reasons: first, the behavior of some elected representatives, which led to a loss of public trust; and second, the institutional developments examined in this chapter. The Knesset lost power as a representative, legislative, and monitoring body, while the personal power of individual MKs grew. The government has considerable formal power, which is virtually unlimited in matters of security and foreign policy; on the other hand, its steering capacity – its ability to make binding decisions – has weakened. Thus what is required is a broad perspective of the state of democracy in Israel, which we take in the final chapter.

6 The Judiciary's Growing Involvement in Public Life

6.1 Rulers and Judges

The two elected authorities "make" democracy, while the judiciary safeguards it. Fixing the world is the job of the first two, while fixing the fixer is the job of the third. To that end, the independence of the judiciary must be vigilantly guarded. In the past, rulers both ruled and judged: "Now Deborah, a prophet, the wife of Lapidot, was judging Israel at that time" (Judges 4:4), and King Solomon was known for being a wise judge who pursued justice. In contemporary times as well, one of the roles of the political system, in the broad sense of that term, is to provide judicial services. Most states have done away with leaders who were in charge of everything, and the first step in democratization is to establish an elected parliament and separate the king's from the public purse. And the second step is to separate the king's throne from that of the judge's. A division of labor thereby evolved, and the public service of judging and doing justice was entrusted to a judiciary. Thus the judiciary encompasses the courts and their judges who seek to enforce the law and administer justice.

6.2 The State and the Role of the Judiciary

In a democracy, the legislature and the executive branch are distinct from the judiciary by a combination of variables: methods of recruitment, mode of activity, and responsibilities. The two "political" branches are elective, use political tools (see Chapter 1) to legislate and make policy, and are accountable to the public. The judiciary (in most countries) is appointed,[1] uses professional tools to resolve conflicts, and is responsible to the public norms embodied by the law. To fulfill its functions, and also to ensure the legality of actions by the regime itself, the independence of the judiciary must be absolute. Another important difference is that the political authorities initiate policies, laws, and amendments, while the judiciary is reactive – it does not initiate, but acts in response to applications of citizens, organizations, and authorities.

[1] The state court judges in the United States are exceptions as most of them are elected. The American system adheres to the principle of representation also in the state courts (ordinary criminal and civil cases that do not involve the federal government), in which a jury represents the public and a judge presides over the trial. The British system has a jury, but the judge is appointed.

From a social perspective, political arrangements are generally more effective than court rulings because they are based on the mobilization of public support, agreements, and compromises. Render unto politics that which is political: As long as the political authorities are operating lawfully, it is preferable that the branches of power remain distinct. The separation of powers and division of function among them is fairly clear, depending on the type of regime, and so are the areas of overlap, such as the role of the courts in interpreting laws based on litigated cases.

In a democracy, the public good delivered by the judiciary rests upon public trust, or citizens will not view the courts as a venue for resolving disputes among themselves, or between themselves and the authorities. Citizens expect the courts to be impartial and administer justice, therefore the foundation of the judicial system rests, above all, on the public's faith in the integrity of the judges; otherwise the principles presented below are worthless.

The basic principles are common to democratic states, and the most important of them is presumed innocence: Everyone is presumed innocent until proven guilty, and does not bear the burden of proof of his or her innocence. Protection from arbitrary law enforcement is so critical, it is commonly held that it is better to allow nine guilty people to go free due to reasonable doubt than to convict one innocent person. In some cases when the crime is punishable by extended incarceration, such as some criminal charges, defense counsel is obligatory, and it is incumbent upon the state to provide a public defender. A citizen in a democracy has the right to a fair trial and, in direct extension, also to a public trial, so that justice will not only be served, but will be seen to have been served.[2]

Another democratic and ethical principle relates to the purpose of punishment – primarily deterrence and not revenge. A democracy defends itself from offenders via the law, and when deterrence does not work, the judges are required to mete out punishments and prison terms. The assumption is that those punished will undergo a process of rehabilitation so that they not repeat their harmful behavior. In an ideal situation, the state would pay judges to be idle – if there are no offenders, the judiciary as a public service would have achieved its goal. Incidentally, this goal might also be achieved by other communal or volunteer-social methods used to resolve conflicts (rabbi, mediator, neighbor, or trusted aunt), which may be preferred to the state's judicial mechanisms. Finally, the wheels of justice turn slowly – efficiency aimed at "closing a case" cannot be a goal if it undermines the (often convoluted) due process, such as the right of every defendant to a worthy defense. In reality, a Robinson Crusoe living in splendid isolation requires no system of courts, but the need to resolve conflicts between individuals or between individuals and the authorities spawns an entire legal system – laws, rulings, and enforcement.

A. Judicial Decision-Making

The law provides a general framework only. Its translation into social and economic rules of conduct requires that the court clarify the law and establish particularistic norms in its rulings. The judiciary thereby participates in the setting of norms in

[2] It is written, "Justice justice you shall pursue" (Deuteronomy 16:20), suggesting that justice within justice shall be pursued – a warning to judges that the process itself must be just (Sanhedrin 10:2).

society, but in so doing is constrained by the boundaries set by the legislator. It is customary to divide the law into three areas: civil law – governing relations between individuals; criminal law – relations between the individual and society; and administrative law – relations between the individual and state authorities, or between two or more state authorities. What sets the judiciary apart from the other branches of government – and is the source of its authority – is legal expertise, which is neither political nor representative. This unique feature of the judiciary is crucial for it to strive for objectivity and neutrality (the "blindness" of the law) in disregard both of public sentiment and the identity or status of those who appear before it.[3] The judiciary does not operate by rallying support or power struggles, which are legitimate tools in the two political branches. Its conduct also differs from the decision-making processes of the bureaucratic civil service (though in some countries like Germany the judges are civil servants), as judicial decisions are individual to each judge, and even the ruling of a panel of judges is the product of individual decision-making.

B. A Litigious Society

In examining the functions of the judiciary in Israel, we must note the demand for its services by society and the citizens. Israeli society has become litigious: When conflict arises, the parties no longer make do with conventional methods such as dialogue, agreed procedures, compromises, or mediation, i.e., the social tools for resolving conflicts extra-judicially are no longer effective. It is hard to say when this began or what its deep-seated roots are, but the data about the number of cases handled by the courts (Table 6.1) reveal that the common course of conflict resolution in Israeli society now passes through the courts. In nearly seventy years, the population of Israel has grown ten-fold, while the number of courts, judges, lawyers, and cases adjudicated has outpaced this exponentially.

When mutual persuasion, mediation with social tools, and internal institutional rules (of the workplace, co-op housing, political parties, etc.) function well, adjudication is the exception. When they do not function – and this is now often the case in Israeli society – the need for an official, authorized mediator – the court – is perceived as the preferable, and indeed the only, option.

C. Caseload

A litigious society places a heavy burden on the courts. A comparative survey (Sulitzeanu-Kenan, Reichman, and Vigoda-Gadot 2007) of the caseload in Israeli courts compared with courts in sixteen other countries carefully chosen for comparison reveals the following:[4]

1. Legal activity per capita: Israel is in first place among the countries surveyed in the number of cases filed proportionate to the size of the population.

[3] As in Jewish law: "Thou shalt not follow the crowd in doing evil; neither shalt thou pervert justice by siding with a crowd: Neither shalt thou be partial to a poor man in his cause" (Exodus 23:2–3).

[4] The countries compared: Australia, Belgium, Cyprus, Denmark, England, Finland, France, Germany, Holland, Ireland, Israel, Italy, New Zealand, Norway, Portugal, Spain, and Sweden. The data are from 2004.

Table 6.1 *Growth of population and caseload – total and Supreme Court (rounded)*

Year	Population (1000s)	Total cases in all courts*	Of which, Supreme Court cases
1950	1,267	91,000	400
1960	2,117	292,000	2,000
1970	2,974	392,000	2,900
1980	3,878	683,000	4,000
1990	4,660	788,000	5,200
2000	6,289	1,093,000	8,200
2013	8,135	1,167,000	8,900
Increase 1950–2013	6.4 times more	12.8 times more	22.3 times more

* Does not include religious or military courts; and does not include minor traffic violations. Total includes cases carried over from previous years.

Sources: CBS *Statistical Abstract* 1950, 1960, 1970, 1980, 1990, 2000; Israel Judiciary 2013.

The average number of cases per 1,000 Israelis was 184, compared with half that (ninety) in the other countries. Even by a conservative calculation (accounting for repeat cases, etc.), every tenth Israeli was legally active in the given year.

2. Judicial workload (the ratio between the number of lodged cases and the number of judges): Israel is in second place with an average of 2,335 cases per judge per year, compared with 1,185 in other countries.
3. Number of judges proportionate to the population: Considering the high level of legal activity, the number of judges in Israel is low: one judge per 12,659 citizens – in sixth place, similar to countries based on a common law judiciary (see below), such as Australia and New Zealand, although the use of jurors in these countries reduces the number of judges.
4. Budget allocation to the judiciary (per capita and per case): Relative to Israel, eight to nine other countries budget the judiciary more generously, and three to four other countries allocate less funding.

Israel removed itself from the family of those using English common law in which there are relatively few judges (some of them lay), a light caseload, and a concomitant small budget. In terms of caseload and legal activity per capita, Israel has also surpassed countries using the continental law system, such as France, Germany, and Scandinavia.

The mounting demand in Israeli society for the adjudication services of the courts has led to an exponential growth in the number of lawyers. Between 1960 and 2014, their number has risen from 2,303 to 57,859 in absolute terms, and, proportionate to population growth, from one lawyer per 919 citizens to one lawyer per 143 citizens by the end of that period (CBS 2014a, table 11.2). In parallel, the role of legal counsel to public organizations and private enterprises has expanded, and separate, specialized courts now exist for municipal matters, domestic matters, small claims, and economic matters.

D. Litigation in the Political Realm

The upsurge in litigation has also left its mark on political life. Politics in Israel, where the norms of governance have been severely eroded and decision-making has been difficult, has brought complex issues into the courtroom for decision, hoping that clear-cut rulings will do the work for them. This has given rise to independent civil society organizations that have turned to the courts to protect rights, even on patently ideological issues. Some examples: The High Court of Justice has deliberated the legality of the settlements and their evacuation (*Duweikat v. State of Israel* 1979 and *Eichenstein et al. v. Sharon et al.* 2004), ruled on the authority of a minority government to conduct negotiations (*Weiss v. Prime Minister* 2001), instructed the state to provide gas masks to residents of the occupied territories (*Morcus v. Minister of Defense et al.* 1991), intervened in the prime minister's authority to dismiss an indicted government member (*Amitai et al. v. Rabin et al.* 1993), and forced the army to open its pilot courses to women (*Miller v. Minister of Defense et al.* 1995). Another issue that we address at the end of this chapter is judicial review by the courts over the executive branch and on the validity of Knesset laws.

6.3 The Sources of Law in Israel

Israeli law is based on the systems that were in place upon the founding of the state – Ottoman law and Mandatory law. The source of Mandatory law is common law used in Britain, which has some codified statutes, but is based predominantly on court rulings and precedents.[5] As early as 1922, the British Mandate authorities decreed that legal interpretations of the civil courts in Palestine would be based on English common law and the doctrines of justice customary in England.[6] Thus, the Mandatory authorities established the principle that would remain valid in Israeli law until 1980 – that the laws set by the British courts would constitute a source of law in Israel.[7]

The founding of Israel forged a new reality. Considering the priority given to political needs over legal niceties by the founding leaders, it is surprising how important it was to them to establish a strong legal foundation (see Chapter 1). To prevent anomie, the Provisional State Council issued a manifesto that gave authority to provisional institutions, including the continuity of Mandatory law and the legal system.[8]

[5] Common law used in Britain and Commonwealth countries is not strictly codified, but consists of layer upon layer of court rulings that evolved with the legal issues that faced the court. Continental law, used in most European countries and based on Roman legal tradition, is highly codified.

[6] See Article 46 of His Majesty the King in Council, Palestine: The Palestine Order in Council (1922): "The jurisdiction of the Civil Courts shall be exercised in conformity with the Ottoman Law ... and such Orders in Council, Ordinances and regulations as are in force ... and so far as the same shall not extend or apply, shall be exercised in conformity with the substance of the common law, and the doctrines of equity in force in England ... Provided always that the said common law and doctrines of equity shall be in force in Palestine so far only as the circumstances of Palestine and its inhabitants and the limits of His Majesty's jurisdiction permit and subject to such qualification as local circumstances render necessary."

[7] On the difficulties of integrating English law with Ottoman law during the Mandate period, see Lahav 1997.

[8] Just months before the founding of the state, a "legal council" was entrusted with the task of clarifying which laws should be revoked upon establishment of the new government and proposing other laws in their stead; suggesting how to establish a Ministry of Justice; critically reviewing laws published; and giving oversight to the court system. This committee prepared a great deal of material, but

This was a practical decision because it enabled the Provisional State Council to define the prevailing law and bestow upon itself the authority to change it as the provisional legislative authority. The Law and Administration Ordinance set out the basic arrangements for establishing the governing institutions and the relations between them, including the judiciary. On matters of law, the Ordinance stated:

> The law which existed in Palestine (E.I.) on the 14th of May 1948 shall remain in force, insofar as there is nothing therein repugnant to this Ordinance or to the other laws that may be enacted by or on behalf of the Provisional State Council, and subject to such modifications as may result from establishment of the State and its authorities.

The process of legislating original Israeli laws and repealing Mandatory legislation has taken years, and is not yet complete. Indeed, elements of the two previous systems can still be found in Israeli law, such as Ottoman land laws (e.g., the "tabu" registry of land ownership) and the Municipal and Tax Ordinances from the Mandatory period that partially remain in force. Other Mandate arrangements were also absorbed into Israeli law such as the status of religious law.

A. The Status of Mandatory Law in Israel

Absorbing Mandatory law as binding precedent had another legal implication – its continued use as a source of legal interpretation in Israel. The assumption was that new legislation and Supreme Court rulings would gradually replace British law. And indeed, the Knesset re-legislated Mandatory ordinances to accommodate them to the needs of Israeli society.[9]

The Knesset also enacted laws that created new legal principles to replace the Mandatory ordinances.[10] Did Israeli law continue to absorb new British rulings after 1948? In a series of decisions, the Israeli Supreme Court revoked the application of post-1948 British law, and then a 1972 amendment to the Law and Administration Ordinance established that "Any provision of a law that requires such law or any expressions of it to be interpreted in accordance with English law or with principles of legal interpretation obtaining in England shall no longer be binding."[11]

the pressures of founding a state prevented the orderly adoption of its proposals. See E. Rubinstein 1980, 33–51.

[9] Some examples: Police Ordinance (New Version) 1971 and Prisons Ordinance (New Version) 1971; Railroad Track Ordinance (New Version) 1972; Physicians Ordinance (New Version) 1976; Penal Code 1977, which is an updated version of a Mandatory ordinance from 1936.

[10] Such as the Contracts (General Part) Law 1973, the Standard Contracts Law 1982, the Companies Law 2000, and others. For a comprehensive review of the evolution of Israeli law since Israel's founding, see Barak 1990, 631.

[11] See extensive discussion in the *Knesset Records*, Seventh Knesset, Session 3, Booklet 3, p. 203, and Booklet 22, p. 1963. On the non-absorption of Mandatory legislation or new interpretations of this legislation, see *Diamant v. Minister of Finance* 1950; *Kol Ha'am v. Minister of the Interior* 1953; and *National Groups v. Minister of the Police* 1970. Regarding deviation from common law precedents, see *Haetzni v. Ben-Gurion* 1957. In a criminal case, Justice Zilberg stated that if, after the founding of Israel, legal innovations made in English courts were to be applied in Israel, "you would find yourself appearing to subordinate Israeli judicature to the constantly changing winds that prevail in the English courts" (*Yakobowitz v. Attorney General* 1952).

B. Foundations of Law Act

The Foundations of Law Act represented the final break from the Mandatory legal system as a source of interpretation:

> Where the court, faced with a legal question requiring decision, finds no answer to it in statute law or in case law or by analogy, it shall decide the issue in light of the principles of freedom, justice, equity and peace of Israel's heritage.

Revoking the binding link to Mandatory law raised the question of its replacement: What would be the new source of interpretation of Israeli law? Shmuel Tamir, Minister of Justice (1977–80), declared when tabling this bill that "after thirty years of legal maturity," the bill is an expression of the desire "to base the legal connection on the rejuvenated spirit of the nation, and to weave within it the treasures of wisdom and ethics of our fathers." Deep divisions erupted in the Knesset over the meaning of "Israel's heritage" with its many diverse layers: How can legal interpretation be derived from this? Is this law an attempt to conceal subordination to the Halakha – the religious law? Similar questions arose with regard to the relationship between universal principles and Israel's heritage: Are these principles a valid legal source, or only as they relate to Jewish law and tradition? Does disengagement from British law also mean renunciation of the implied principles of natural justice, integrity, etc.? Some declared the law to be vague and meaningless, and that it would be preferable to appeal to the principles in the Declaration of Independence, while others demanded that explicit reference to Jewish law be legislated.[12] One way or another, the Foundations of Law Act severed Israeli law from British law, establishing its autonomy. With regard to "Israel's heritage" as a new source of legal interpretation, the concerns raised in the Knesset debate proved exaggerated: The Act did not in and of itself lead to significant changes, nor did it increase the influence of Jewish law on Israeli jurisprudence.[13]

Since the establishment of the state, Israeli law has distanced itself from English common law, and moved more clearly toward codification, i.e., setting norms by statutes. Although there is no written constitution, twelve Basic Laws regulate most of the issues related to state authorities (see Chapter 2).

C. The Legal Foundation

The Basic Law: The Judiciary was enacted in 1984, years after enactment of the Basic Laws that deal with the other branches of government, due to disagreements over the authority for religious matters. The law entrenched the arrangements that had previously existed and established principles for the operation of the judiciary: judicial authority, the independence of the judges, open courts, etc. This Basic Law was preceded by the Judges Law 1953, the Dayanim [Religious Court Judges] Law 1955, and the Qadis [Muslim Religious Court Judges] Law 1961, which established the

[12] *Knesset Records*, Booklet 21, March 12, 1980; Booklet 35, July 23, 1980, 4025–31. See also *Hendeles v. Kupat Am et al.* 1981; Ben-Menachem 1988, 257; Barak 1988, 227–56; Elon 1988, Elon 1987, 227–56; Deutsch 1987–88; Tannenbaum 2003–4, 393–423.

[13] See, for example, *Jerzhevski v. Prime Minister Yitzhak Shamir et al.* 1991 on the use of Israel's Jewish heritage in court rulings.

independence of the various judges, their qualifications, method of appointment, status, term of office, and disciplinary proceedings. The Courts Law 1957 (together with the Sharia Courts Law 1953 and the Druze Courts Law 1962) deals with the structure of the courts and the division of labor among the Supreme Court, the District Courts, and the Magistrate's Courts. The Justice Minister has parliamentary responsibility for the budget and administration of the courts, while the autonomy of the judges and the judicial process are anchored in the law. All judges are professionally subordinate to the Supreme Court president.

The Bar Association Law (1961), which regulates the functioning of the professional lawyers' association, obligates all lawyers to be members and entrusts to the Bar the authority for examining and certifying lawyers, and for disciplinary measures.

D. Additional Laws

In addition to the laws of the state, which ordinarily apply equally to all inhabitants of Israel, there are laws and courts that operate in specific areas. The main ones are as follows.

Religious Law

In matters of personal status, Israeli law adopted the Mandatory system, which gave authority to the religious law of each denomination on personal status issues (marriage, divorce, and other matters to which the parties agree). Religious law in Israel applies to every person in accordance with his or her religion, and jurisdiction over personal status matters is entrusted to the rabbinical, Sharia, and Druze courts. The Jewish rabbinical courts adjudicate according to Torah law, except when a general law applies. As a result, the very same case can be tried in more than one court. Regarding divorce, for example, the religious court has jurisdiction, but for alimony and child custody, general law applies and a civil court, usually the Family Court, might adjudicate these (see below).

Local Bylaws

Bylaws are full-fledged legislation enacted by local democratic bodies. The local authority is authorized to enact bylaws in accordance with the needs and character of its residents, so long as they do not conflict with state law. The bylaws deal with local issues such as the opening of businesses, the demolition of unsafe structures, sanitation, shelters, parking, sewerage, etc. General oversight of bylaws rests upon state laws, which limit the power of the local authority. Local bylaws can reflect the special needs and character of the community: For example, if one side of a street is in Bnei Brak, a religious town, and the other side is in Ramat Gan, neighbors living on opposite sides of the street could reasonably be subject to different bylaws – the Bnei Brak resident might receive a permit to build a ritual *sukkah* on his balcony, and the other might not. Another example is the city of Ra'anana, which has secular and religious residents: The bylaws permit stores to open on the Sabbath only in the industrial and peripheral areas of town, not in the center. Supervision of the bylaws is entrusted to the Interior Minister, who has the authority to prevent a bylaw from taking effect. Municipal bylaws, the Planning and Construction Law, and several additional laws provide the basis for adjudication in the municipal courts of Israel's large cities.

Military Jurisdiction Law

This law, passed in 1955, established a separate military court system that deals with all allegations of offenses by military personnel, whether committed in the regular forces (compulsory or career service) or while on reserve duty (a similar law exists in other countries). The army is a total organization that demands unparalleled conduct, loyalty, and sacrifice. Thus, the military courts do more than just handle internal disciplinary matters, as do the tribunals in other public organizations, but also try serious crimes such as treason, desertion, abuse, unlawful use of firearms, and insubordination. Accordingly, the penalties set by law are more severe, ranging from a reprimand or confinement to base, to life imprisonment or the death penalty (for treason). To support the military courts, the IDF has a Military Police and a Judge Advocate General unit. Military involvement in the daily life of those who serve – whether conscripts or reserve duty soldiers – and the application of martial law to the occupied territories sometimes result in dual jurisdiction. For example, a soldier caught speeding could stand trial in civilian court or military court depending upon who made the arrest – the civilian or military police. This problem becomes much more complex when the offense relates to the personal status issues of military personnel.

Administrative Law

Administrative tribunals are established by a law, regulation, or administrative decision in fields such as taxes and assessments, discipline, labor, property, business licensing and inspection, rehabilitation, and welfare (see Galnoor 2011, 39–41).[14] Examples of administrative tribunals (and the law or regulation that created them): Appeals Committees on Income Tax Assessments (Income Tax Ordinance); National Insurance Tribunal (National Insurance Law); Appeals Committee for Taxicab Registration (Transportation Ordinance); Disciplinary Court in the Civil Service Commission (Civil Service [Discipline] Law); Appeals Committee (Disabled Victims of Nazi Persecution Law); and the Standard Contracts Court (Standard Contracts Law). These tribunals enjoy broad authority, and exercise oversight on the administrative decisions of the government branches.

6.4 Structure and Function of the Judiciary in Israel

The court system in Israel is hierarchical, uniform, and centralized, with various courts specializing in different areas of law. According to the Basic Law: The Judiciary, judicial authority in Israel is given to the courts, religious courts, and other tribunals, i.e., in addition to the general jurisdiction of the courts, the tribunals have jurisdiction over special matters. Specialized courts, such as the Juvenile Court, Family Court, and Municipal Court, are also part of the general court system. At the pinnacle of the system is the Supreme Court, which is also a court of appeals. When the Supreme Court is in session as the High Court of Justice, it seeks to grant "relief in the interests of justice" against the state authorities, or when such

[14] The source of the Israeli administrative courts is the British administrative tribunals. See Government of Britain, "Report of the Committee on Administrative Tribunals and Inquiries," Cmnd. 218, 1957; Tribunals and Inquiries Act 1958.

relief is sought because of a ruling in one of the specialized courts. A ruling by the Supreme Court is binding on every other court (as case law), including all the special tribunals.

A. General Structure

The courts are divided into three hierarchical levels based on their specific jurisdiction and their appellate function.

Magistrate's Court: This court tries criminal cases that carry a maximum sentence of seven years or civil matters up to NIS 2.5 million. In some towns, the Magistrate's Court also serves as a Family Court and Municipal Court.

District Court: This is the court of first instance for offenses that the Magistrate's or other courts are not authorized to try, and it serves as an appellate court for decisions by the Magistrate's Courts. The Administrative Courts Law (2000) transferred to the District Courts, when in session as Administrative Courts, many of the cases that had previously been on the docket of the High Court of Justice. Thus they hear appeals of decisions made by the administrative tribunals.

Supreme Court: The Supreme Court is not the court of first instance for criminal, civil, or administrative matters, but the court of first appeal for District Court decisions and the court of second appeal in rare Magistrate's Court cases (when "permission to appeal" is given). Over time, the High Court of Justice has become a core function of the Supreme Court. The High Court has special authority concerning appeals of judgments made by the Military Court of Appeal, Disciplinary Courts, the Central Elections Committee, and so on. Most Supreme Court cases are tried with a panel of three justices, but over the years more cases have been heard with expanded panels when the Supreme Court deliberates complex issues.

The heavy caseload borne by Israeli courts (Table 6.1) required structural reform of the courts, particularly dividing up areas of jurisdiction. A committee in 1997 headed by Supreme Court Justice Theodor Or recommended keeping the existing structure, but changing the duties so that the Magistrate's Court would become the primary trial court, the District Court would be the appellate court and primary Administrative Tribunal, and the Supreme Court would hear only appeals of District Court decisions or matters of constitutional or exceptional public import (Or Committee 1997). Although the government ratified these recommendations, the main reform implemented was the transfer of administrative cases to the District Courts. Table 6.2 reflects the scope and growth of the law enforcement system.

B. Personal Status Matters

Personal status cases in Israel are under the jurisdiction of two parallel court systems – the civil courts (generally the Magistrate's Court in session as a Family Court) and the religious courts of each faith community: the rabbinical courts for Jews, the

Table 6.2 *Scope of law enforcement system in Israel: Judges, judges in rabbinical courts, lawyers, Israel Police, and Prison Service (1960–2014)*

	1960	1970	1980	1990	2000	2010	2014
Judges							
Supreme Court	8	10	10	11	13	15	15
District Courts	41	56	84	84	100	163	177
Magistrate's Courts*	80	100	123	158	302	389	416
Labor Tribunals	–	10	20	23	42	58	61
Judges in Rabbinical Courts**	63	72	85	99	101	88	85
Lawyers	2,303	4,853	7,254	10,697	23,127	46,515	57,859
Thereof: Newly called to the bar	238	328	349	511	2,589	3,472	3,488
Israel Police	6,794	11,427	17,043	18,021	25,189	27,104	28,382
Prison Service	544	1,470	2,561	3,281	3,756	8,167	8,194

* Including judges in juvenile, municipal, and traffic courts.
** Including the two chief rabbis.

Source: CBS *Statistical Abstract*, no. 65, 2014, table 11.2.

Sharia courts for Muslims, the Druze courts, and the courts of the various Christian denominations.[15] Regarding marriage and divorce, the religious courts have exclusive jurisdiction, while other personal status matters – alimony, custody, legitimation of the status of children, adoption of children, inheritance – can be adjudicated either in a religious court or a Family Court. When there is parallel jurisdiction, the matter will be heard where the case was first lodged – either in the religious court or the civil court. This duality creates a "race for jurisdiction," especially in the Jewish rabbinical court, when each party hastens to open a file in the court that gives an advantage to his or her interests – men prefer the religious court, believing it will be partial to their rights, while women prefer the civil court, believing it is fairer to them. Rulings of religious courts can be appealed in the Religious Appeals Court. Once the religious process is exhausted, it is possible in exceptional cases to appeal to the Supreme Court in its capacity as the High Court of Justice, usually on the grounds that the religious court exceeded its authority.

C. Labor Matters and Social Laws

Since 1969, Israel has made a distinction between the general courts and labor tribunals, which hear cases of employer–employee relations, collective agreements (between labor associations and employers), and strikes (Labor Courts Law 1969).

[15] In personal status cases for people of other religions, or for those "lacking religion" – people of different religions without religious affiliation (such as the child of a Jewish father and Muslim mother) – the Supreme Court president decides which court has jurisdiction.

Under the jurisdiction of these tribunals are social welfare laws such as the National Insurance Law, the National Health Insurance Act, and other labor laws. Labor tribunals in five regions of Israel serve as tribunals of the first instance, and the National Labor Tribunal serves as an appellate tribunal and a tribunal of the first instance in litigation between labor unions and employer associations. Labor tribunal proceedings are adjusted to deal with labor law cases, and the bench includes non-professional judges as representatives of the public.[16] To increase accessibility, labor court proceedings are briefer, take less time, and the parties can appear without legal representation. Strained labor relations, especially in the public sector, have increased the use of labor tribunals – from 10,129 cases in 1974 to over 95,000 cases in 2013, while the number of judges rose from ten to seventy-five (Israeli Judiciary 2007, 131; Israeli Judiciary 2013, 32). Criticism of this institution by both employers and labor unions suggests its importance to both sides. As noted, the High Court of Justice exercises judicial review over rulings by the National Labor Tribunal.

D. Administrative Matters

To exercise oversight of the state's considerable power and to prevent abuse or the violation of individual rights, two types of judicial supervisory bodies came to be established. The continental European model distinguished between administrative and general law, and created a separate legal system for administrative matters. The British model, which was adopted by Israel, does not draw such a sharp distinction, and subordinates administrative authorities to the general law. Dozens of bodies in Israel carry out some form of judicial or quasi-judicial adjudication of administrative cases, and each one specializes in a specific area. There are different names for them: tribunals, appeals committees, petition committees, oversight committees, supervisory judicial authority, and the like. The tribunals almost always operate intra-organizationally with proceedings that are briefer, more informal, and less expensive to the parties involved. Another advantage of these tribunals is their expertise and direct experience in the field.

What kinds of cases do these tribunals try? The best known are the Appeals Committee on Income Tax Assessments, in accordance with the Income Tax Ordinance; and the National Insurance Tribunal, in accordance with the National Insurance Law. Citizens who feel harmed by a decision of the local welfare office are entitled to have these decisions revisited by an Appeals Committee established by the Ministry of Welfare in accordance with the Welfare Services Law (1958). There are also special mechanisms – the Land Registry Supervisor is authorized by the Land Law (1969) to adjudicate conflicts between condominium owners concerning their property borders. This would also be deemed an administrative tribunal, even though the conflict is not between the citizen and a governing authority. In 2006, over one hundred administrative tribunal mechanisms were operating in Israel, distinct from each other with respect to the source of their authority, types of subjects,

[16] The regional tribunals have one professional judge and two public representatives, and the National Labor Tribunal has three professional judges and between two and four public representatives. The public representatives are appointed by the Minister of Justice and the Minister of Labor and Welfare, with equal representation of employers and employees.

degree of separation from the regular role of public servants, the forms of appeal, etc. Decisions made by administrative tribunals can generally be appealed in court, and if no appeal procedure is specified in the law – to the High Court of Justice.

These tribunals have wide-ranging powers and they review administrative decisions in depth, thanks to their firsthand knowledge and expertise in the subject matter. Nevertheless, it could be argued that the very existence of so many quasi-judicial bodies and the lack of central supervision over their operation may be problematic. When flaws are discovered, they usually concern the proceedings because the deliberations in these bodies are internal and fail to safeguard the rights of those filing an appeal. In addition, they are not allocated sufficient resources from the governmental offices and other bodies within which they operate.

The multiplicity of administrative tribunals and the lack of uniformity in their operation led to enactment of the Administrative Tribunals Law (1992), which specifies general rules about how tribunals are established, their authority, the appointment of tribunal members, basic court procedures, the right of appeal, and other matters (Zamir 1999, 90). Although there was a need for such a law, it made the procedures of the administrative tribunals more like those of a regular court, thereby losing some flexibility. To counter this, the law allows the administrative tribunal not to be bound by evidentiary procedures, but instead to function "however appears best to achieve justice." Another limitation is that the law applies only to sixteen types of existing administrative tribunals, but not to others like the City Tax Appeals Committees, which are attached to local authorities. The solution proposed in the law for these problems was to set up a Council for Administrative Tribunals to create a common reference for addressing basic problems that arise during the activity of the administrative tribunals. Although many years have passed since enactment of this law, the council has yet to leave its mark on the field.

In the past, the Supreme Court would hear administrative cases as the court of first and last instance. The burden on the justices led to enactment of the Administrative Affairs Courts Law (2000), which created a Department for Administrative Affairs within every District Court to handle matters such as tenders, planning, construction, and appeals of decisions made in administrative tribunals. Cases that had in the past been adjudicated by the Supreme Court were now moved to the District Court in session as an Administrative Law Court, and using procedures of an administrative hearing, like those common in the High Court. Being in the districts increases their accessibility and shortens the proceedings, as a result of which the number of petitions has increased.

E. Municipal Matters

Municipal Courts have been established in fifteen large cities in Israel to deal with issues under the authority of the local government (construction, business licensing, sanitation, parking, etc.), in accordance with the local bylaws, the Planning and Construction Law, and several other statutes. In several cities – Kfar Saba, Tel Aviv, and Herzliya – the Magistrate's Courts were empowered to also serve as Municipal Courts. The Municipal Courts embody the idea of local democracy and autonomy on matters that are of significance to the daily lives of the residents. They have the advantage of familiarity with the local realities, the needs of the residents, and the problems of enforcing bylaws. These courts should be viewed as the judicial arm of the local government, although they remain subject to the laws of the state, of course, and are subordinate to the state courts. Currently, subordination to the Courts Administration combined with inadequate independence from the local authority impede their functioning, already encumbered by the heavy caseload in these courts as a result of prosecuting more violations of municipal bylaws.

In 1995, a committee headed by Yitzhak Zamir, a Supreme Court justice, recommended enhancing the status of the Municipal Courts without altering their subordination to the Courts Administration. The proposal sought to strengthen the professionalism of the courts – to distinguish between the administrative subordination of court employees to the local authority and their professional subordination to a judge. This was intended to ensure separation of the local authority from the Municipal Courts – a separate building, separate signs, separate stationery, etc. The minority opinion of the committee proposed that the Municipal Courts be disconnected from the Courts Administration in order to gradually strengthen local democracy, and create a clear separation of powers on the local level as well (Zamir Committee 1995).

F. Small Claims Courts

Legal proceedings are by nature expensive and protracted, which deters people from turning to the courts. To ensure that individuals have an opportunity for legal relief regarding ostensibly minor matters that are important to them, Small Claims Courts were established in 1984 within the Magistrate's Courts. These courts hear civil suits brought by individuals up to a maximum amount adjusted periodically (NIS 33,500 in 2016, roughly $8,600). The proceedings are brief, inexpensive, and not bound by the evidentiary rules of regular courts (the sides are generally prohibited from representation by legal counsel), so that the court can exercise flexibility in arriving at a just and quick decision. Small Claims Court judgments can be appealed with the approval of the District Court. Almost 45,000 small claims were deliberated in these courts in 2008, and the judgments generally sought compromise between the sides (Israel Judiciary 2013). These courts can be viewed as institutionalized arbitrators of civil matters.

G. Arbitration and Mediation Mechanisms

Arbitration and mediation can take place outside the courtroom, which can be said to be their natural home. The parties to a dispute may, however, empower the court to deliberate the petition as an arbitrator, in which case the hearings will be briefer and less formal than a court hearing, and the arbitrator – with the agreement of both sides – can dispense with substantive law, court procedures, and evidentiary rules in an effort to reach a just decision. The arbitrator must resolve the matter under the supervision of the court with respect to the proceedings and the outcome. The decision is binding on both parties, who may challenge it only in accordance with the means set by law.

The parties may request a court-appointed mediator to resolve their dispute, though the mediator will have no authority to make a binding decision. Mediation may also be carried out by a mutually agreed arbitrator, and a solution reached by the sides can be given the weight of a court ruling. In contrast with many countries in which mediation is an independent social institution, mediation in Israel rests on the authority of the court and is generally perceived as an extension of the judicial process.[17] Furthermore, even during a regular court proceeding, the court can rule a compromise with the agreement of both sides, or propose that the sides agree on a ruling and avoid continued courtroom confrontation.

6.5 The Status of the Judiciary in Israel

To ensure that justice is both seen and done, and to increase transparency, court sessions are open to the public unless there are special reasons to hold them *in camera*. Constraints are imposed on public discussion and media reports, however, in an effort to prevent them from wielding an influence on – or even appearing to influence – the judges. The prohibition on public discussion of a pending legal proceeding (*sub judice* – "under judgment") is intended to enhance public trust in judges, and prevent the belief – even if mistaken – that such discussions color their judgment. In practice, the media have ignored this prohibition and it remains unenforced, perhaps to protect freedom of expression or simply because it is hard to enforce.[18]

What is expected of a law court in a democracy? That the judges be honest, incorruptible, independent, and have the trust of the citizenry. If the judges score well on these criteria, others may be added with respect to the court proceedings or outcomes. We begin by saying that, in general, the judiciary in Israel satisfactorily meets these tests.

A. Honest and Incorruptible Judges

Even sworn critics of the judiciary in Israel do not cast doubt on the integrity of its judges. Suffice it to say that since the founding of the state and as of 2015, only one traffic court judge was convicted of bribery, and only a small number of judges were tried on other offenses. Indeed, among the thousands of complaints submitted to the Ombudsman for Complaints against Judges (first appointed in 2003), not one was found justified regarding the acceptance of a bribe.

B. Professional and Independent Judges

Upon establishment of the state, Israeli society was highly politicized and party-oriented, which – as indicated in Chapter 1 – also influenced appointments to and patterns of behavior in fields such as the civil service, education, health, and the water authority. In retrospect, it is clear that the Israeli legal system (and a few other systems such as higher education) managed to avoid the partisan politicization of the Yishuv and early state period:

[17] In 1998, the Center for Mediation and Conflict Resolution was established in the Ministry of Justice to encourage use of these mechanisms (Ministry of Justice 2006).

[18] In 2002, the Courts Law was amended and the article on *sub judice* was limited to criminal proceedings or cases in which the intent of the publication is to influence the legal proceeding (see Rubinstein and Medina 2005, vol. I, 146–51).

- During the pre-state period, the Jewish community did not set up its own legal system to parallel that of the British Mandate authorities, as it had in other fields. The reliance on Mandatory courts by both Jews and Arabs in Palestine (E.I.) – except in matters of personal status – fostered a level of trust in the rule of law and professional neutrality.
- In 1948, the newly created courts and legal system were not an extension of the pre-state, party-run institutions, but of the British institutions and legal norms. The Israeli legal system was erected by the Jewish judges and lawyers who had served in the British judiciary in Mandate Palestine.
- Moreover, these individuals zealously guarded the independence of the judiciary as a critical building block of a democracy. The independence of the Supreme Court was not a given, but the product of a determined struggle in the early years led by leading figures in the Supreme Court and Ministry of Justice.[19] One symbolic expression of this was the decision of the Supreme Court justices not just to prohibit party membership for judges, but to prohibit participation in parties, lectures, or events sponsored by political bodies. A fierce battle was also waged to separate the appointment and promotion of judges from political-party considerations, and to establish their autonomy from the executive branch in the matter of their salaries.[20]

On a substantive level, what contributed most to the independence of the judiciary was its insistence on impartiality and its rejection of all attempts to constrain it or subordinate it to the executive branch. A series of early Supreme Court rulings buttressed the legal and regime principles that guide Israel to this day. The principle of the legality of government and the checks on its power was established in the second Supreme Court ruling issued in January 1949, at the height of the War of Independence, as noted by Justice Olshan:

> The authorities are subject to the law as are all citizens of the state. And the rule of law is a bedrock principle of the state. Severe harm would accrue to both the public and the state if the authorities would use the power accorded them by the legislator, even temporarily, in complete disregard of the limitations imposed by the legislator on the use of that power. (*al-Karbutli v. Minister of Defense* 1949)

In a series of other well-known rulings, the Supreme Court established the basic rights of the individual vis-à-vis the authorities (licensing, occupation, and others) as well as the rights of the general public (freedom of expression) (Rubinstein and Medina 2005, vol. I, 159–60). An independent judiciary was not a given, and the Arab citizens of Israel feared that the court would become yet another tool in the hands of the government to impose its authority on them. On the level of individual rights versus the power of the authorities, laws were enacted that applied to all the citizens. In the aforementioned Karbutli case, for example, the High Court of Justice rejected the chief of staff's authority to keep someone in detention based on the Emergency Regulations without a hearing and appeal mechanism. On the other hand, in all

[19] See Olshan 1978, 159–60.

[20] An attempt was made, for example, to give the Knesset control over the appointment of judges. Regarding salaries, someone proposed that they be linked to ministers' salaries, but Pinchas Rosen, Minister of Justice, prevented this from passing (Olshan 1978, 223).

security-related matters, particularly concerning the martial law imposed in Arab-populated areas, the court adopted the position of the state, giving no legal relief to Arab citizens. This was manifested in the expropriation of land from Arab citizens and the policy of "Judaizing" various regions for Jewish settlement there. One exceptional case concerned the Iqrit and Bir'im villagers, who were uprooted from their land during the War for Independence with promises from Israeli officials that they would later be allowed to return. The High Court ordered the state to keep its promise (*Daoud v. Minister of Defense* 1951), but the state has not complied to this day. The fact that a court ruling – usually honored without question – was not enforced in a case related to Arabs led many Arab citizens to lose faith in the Israeli state and legal system.[21] On the other hand, these early court rulings taught the Jewish public about the independence of the judiciary and its determination to safeguard the rule of law.

C. Appointment and Promotion of Judges

The oath of office taken by a judge in Israel: "I pledge to be loyal to the State of Israel and its laws, to judge the nation justly, to rule impartially, and not to discriminate" (the oath of religious court judges does not include the phrase "and its laws").

The Basic Law: The Judiciary states, "A person vested with judicial power shall not, in judicial matters, be subject to any authority but that of the Law." To safeguard this principle and ensure that judges not be beholden to anyone, there was a need to establish as professional and objective a mechanism as possible for appointing and promoting judges. Democracies have a variety of methods to select judges: by the legislature, the executive branch, special constitutional bodies, a combination of authorities, or popular election. From the outset in Israel, a unique system was adopted to appoint and promote judges – the Judicial Appointments Committee – and this was later anchored in a Basic Law. The committee has nine members – three Supreme Court justices, including the president, two ministers, including the Minister of Justice (chair), two Knesset members elected by the Knesset in a secret ballot (customarily one from the coalition and one from the opposition), and two lawyers elected in secret ballot by the National Council of the Bar Association. The Supreme Court president, the Minister of Justice, or three of the committee members can submit nominations. According to an amendment from 2008, a judge must be elected to the Supreme Court by a majority of at least seven committee members.[22] It was customary in the past not to vote, but to try to reach unanimous consensus.

The composition of the committee is designed to combine the professionalism of jurists with the representativeness of Knesset members, the government, and the community of lawyers. The apolitical members of the committee are in the majority (assuming the Bar Association representatives are apolitical), and the coalition or party representatives could thus far not dictate their views. This mechanism affords the five jurists, including the three Supreme Court justices, the ability

[21] As stated in the Or Commission Report 2003, para. 44.

[22] This applies only to Supreme Court judges (Courts Law [Amendment 55] [2008]). The Judicial Appointments Committee selects judges for the Supreme Court, District Court, Magistrate's Court, Traffic Court, and Labor Court. It also selects the president and deputy president of the Supreme Court and National Labor Court.

to have a significant influence on the appointment. In practice, the Supreme Court president and the Minister of Justice have had veto power over appointments, so disagreements that periodically emerge between them may paralyze the process of appointing judges. Criticism of the judicial appointment system focuses on two issues – results and procedures. First, the Judicial Appointments Committee chooses from a limited and unrepresentative pool of candidates, creating homogeneity in the makeup of the courts. And, second, the process lacks orderly preparation, transparency, and the need to give reasons, thereby undermining the quality of the judges appointed. In light of the criticism, a committee was appointed in 2000 to examine the selection methods. Headed by former Supreme Court Justice Yitzhak Zamir, the report of this committee emphasized the qualities of the current system in light of the political realities of Israel:

> [The procedures] have managed to create in Israel ever since its founding a system of judges with a high level of professionalism, honesty, and rigorous independence in their work vis-à-vis the government and other bodies ... It is also viewed by experts from outside Israel as a very good system in comparison with those used in other countries. (Zamir Committee 2001, 85)

The Zamir Committee recommended that neither the makeup nor the authority of the Judicial Appointments Committee be changed, but it acknowledged the need for greater ethical and professional transparency. The committee also recommended improving the nomination process (through the use of a search committee, a detailed questionnaire to each candidate, and a thorough interview), as well as a compulsory training course for new judges. These recommendations were implemented, the circle of those authorized to nominate candidates was expanded, and a procedure was instituted for publicizing the names of candidates to allow for public feedback about them.

Periodically suggestions are raised for changing the makeup of the Judicial Appointments Committee in an effort to increase the influence of the Knesset and government representatives, thereby reducing the influence of the jurists.[23] In our opinion, such changes would politicize the judicial system and introduce patterns that are unsuitable for administering justice. The Judicial Appointments Committee fulfills its tasks fairly well, and if the principle of transparency is maintained, it should not be changed. The judiciary is not a representative body, nor should it be, or it would lose its most important civic quality – absolute independence. An independent judiciary is a cornerstone of democracy, precisely because judges are not required to give a political account of their actions to anyone. Judges in a democracy are accountable to the law, to the basic principles of the society, and to human rights, regardless of the parliamentary makeup at any given moment.

D. Special Requirements of Judges

The special standing of judges and their independence are reflected in it being a permanent appointment (to age seventy) and the prohibition on judges from engaging in

[23] For example, in a bill submitted by MK Michael Eitan, the Judicial Appointments Committee would be expanded to twelve members: three judges, three MKs, three ministers, and three representatives of the Bar Association – to prevent a majority of jurists. *Book of Statutes*, 1983–84, Bills Tabled, 8453803, p. 78.

any other work or public service unless it is of a legal nature or has the consent of the Supreme Court president and the Minister of Justice.[24] A judge can be removed from office in two ways: by a seven-member majority decision of the Judicial Appointments Committee when initiated by the Supreme Court president or Minister of Justice; or as a penalty imposed by the Judicial Disciplinary Court.[25] To ensure the independence of judges from the executive branch, their wages are set by the Knesset Finance Committee. To protect judges from Knesset arbitrariness, the law disallows any reduction in the salaries of judges unless it is part of a wage change in the economy at large. Judges have no immunity such as that enjoyed by MKs, but they do have some protection from criminal investigation and indictment, which requires the consent of the attorney general, who files the indictment. In parallel, disciplinary action against judges takes place in a special disciplinary court.

6.6 Public Trust and Oversight of the Judiciary

A. Public Trust

One of the current, unfortunate characteristics of Israeli democracy is the decline in the public's trust in the political system and its institutions. Moreover, what happens in politics has a significant impact on the courts, including the expectation that they will serve as a "bastion of democracy." This expectation, incidentally, testifies to the vigorousness and independence of the judiciary. The judiciary, however, cannot on its own make up for the "democracy deficit" of a political system, and this decline in trust has also made the court vulnerable to criticism.

And yet the courts in Israel still enjoy considerable prestige, thanks to the integrity and autonomy of the judges. In comparison with the other two government branches and institutions, Israeli courts rank high on public trust in opinion polls. On the other hand, a World Bank index (2006) that includes the "rule of law" (which combines indicators of obeying the law and trust in the law enforcement system) shows a decline in the perceived rule of law in Israel from 89 percent in 1996 to 83 percent in 2014. The level of trust in the Supreme Court is still relatively high, an average of 62 percent in the years 2003–14 – behind trust in the IDF (80%) – far ahead of trust in the elected institutions and parties, which averaged under 44 percent. Nevertheless, trust in the Supreme Court has clearly declined in recent years.[26] This can be attributed to a general erosion of the public trust in institutions; in response to "Which institution best safeguards democracy?," the media and the Supreme Court score far better than the two elective bodies – the Knesset and the prime minister (Hermann et al. 2008, 100). Nevertheless, the Supreme Court has

[24] Judges have served in public roles – commissions of inquiry, elections committees, public committees – and have fulfilled other helpful roles, such as Justice Aharon Barak, who participated in the peace negotiations with Egypt. On the other hand, a judge who signed a Peace Now petition was forced to resign.

[25] The grounds for removal of a judge from office: improper behavior in carrying out the functions of judging; behavior unbecoming of the status of a judge in Israel; conviction of an offense marked by moral turpitude; or the fact that the judge obtained his or her appointment unlawfully.

[26] For an historical discussion, see Barzilai, Yuchtman-Yaar, and Segal 1994; Peres and Yuchtman-Yaar 2000.

been under attack by right-wing and religious groups, as well as government ministers and coalition MKs, who cast doubt on its objectivity and propose curtailing its authority (Hermann et al. 2011–15: 2014, 119–26). These attacks have contributed to the erosion of public trust in the legal system and its value to Israeli society and democracy.

B. Oversight of the Judiciary

Courts exercise oversight over the other branches of government, but are themselves subordinate to the constitution (the Basic Laws in Israel) and the law, as are other public authorities. In addition, the transparency of the court process allows for direct monitoring by the litigants, the media, and the public. There is also internal oversight conducted by the Supreme Court president, the presidents of the various courts, and the Courts Administration. Here we discuss two narrower issues: administrative subordination of the courts and oversight of the work of the judges.

Ministerial Subordination (to the Justice Minister) versus Professional Subordination (to the Supreme Court President)

Politicians are accountable to the public, and periodically put to well-known and effective tests – elections, parties, lobbies, the media, civic organizations, and public opinion. Responsibility for the judiciary is divided: The Supreme Court president has responsibility for the professionalism, objectivity, and integrity of the judges, while the Minister of Justice has ministerial responsibility for administrative matters (budget, management, courthouses, etc.). The boundary line is drawn between the independence of the judges and the administrative subordination of the courts to the Courts Administration – a separation that has existed since the founding of the Ministry of Justice in 1948. Court employees (except judges, whose separate status was established in the Judges Law 1953) are civil servants in every respect, and the Minister of Justice has ministerial responsibility for their work and the services provided by the courts. The actual administration of the courts is handled by the Courts Administration, which is subordinate to the Minister of Justice and the Supreme Court president.

Two Supreme Court presidents, Shamgar and Barak, advocated for an absolute separation of powers, meaning an administrative separation of the court system from the executive branch, to ensure full independence from the other two branches. They proposed the creation of an independent "Judiciary Authority" (to replace the Courts Administration), whose budget and personnel would be determined separately, outside the civil service, as in the American system.[27] The other (European)

[27] See the Committee for the Examination of an Independent Judiciary Authority, *Report*, Jerusalem, April 1996 [in Hebrew]. The majority in this committee recommended creation of an independent body for the judiciary that would integrate the judges and other court employees. This body would be completely distinct from the executive branch of government in its functioning, budget, management of human resources (administrative and judicial), salaries, and the courthouse buildings. It would be headed by the Supreme Court president, who would have exclusive authority for judicial and administrative matters. The committee minority proposed far-reaching reforms and

approach views the courts as organizations providing a public service, not unlike other state services.

In our view, in a parliamentary system, it is the government that should be making these decisions, subject to Knesset approval, such as whether or not to allocate resources to a new building for a courthouse, just as the government decides whether to construct a new school or not. This is why the budget for courts must be deliberated within the framework of the overall budget. The courts are public service providers, and if the Justice Minister were not accountable to the Knesset and the public for these services, it would undermine the principle of parliamentary responsibility. If the minister is not accountable to the public for irregularities in the courts, who would be? Should the president of the Supreme Court be dismissed, as the one proposed to head the administrative apparatus of the courts and bear overall responsibility?

Oversight of the Judges

The trends of openness, transparency, and the public's right to know have slowly penetrated Israel, together with a growing desire to find ways to exercise oversight of judges and the judicial process. The first attempts in this direction, inspired by the ratings fashion, were the judicial evaluations instituted by the Israel Bar Association in 2002.[28]

In a survey by the Israel Bar Association, lawyers were asked to rate individual judges on how they handled cases in which these lawyers appeared. This concept is inherently flawed for several reasons: First, feedback of this kind could adversely affect the quality of the judge's work, and does not exist in courts anywhere in the world, with the exception of several US states. Second, where feedback is given, it should not be of a judge alone, but of the entire judicial process. Third, lawyers are not the "clients" of the court – they represent the direct client (a litigant), while the public is the indirect client, and the more appropriate one to give feedback. Presumably, the ratings submitted by lawyers about a specific judge would be affected by their win/loss record with that judge. Fourth, the feedback should also include an evaluation of the conduct of the lawyers themselves as part of the process.

The judicial evaluations were given wide publicity by the media, blaring the names of judges who scored poorly, and provoking deep resentment among the judges. When all efforts failed to rescind the evaluation, the judges declared institutional non-cooperation with the Bar Association. Judicial evaluations lasted for three years, and were then abandoned. In retrospect, the harm they cause exceeds any benefit, as judges should not have to compete in a popularity contest, certainly not among lawyers. In judicial matters, judges must not have to answer to any authority except the law.

administrative autonomy, but objected to absolute separation from the executive branch. None of these reforms was adopted.

28 The explanatory text for instituting the feedback states:

> The Bar Association sees itself obligated to try to identify both positive features and shortcomings in the judicial system, and to work toward enhancing the one and repairing the other. Only attorneys-at-law, who are the professionals vis-à-vis the courts, can provide this vital service to this important system. Thus, the feedback has come not to defy, but to help.
>
> (www.israelbar.org.il/article_inner [accessed June 13, 2002])

These evaluations had one positive result: They expedited enactment of the (already tabled) Ombudsman for Complaints against Judges Law 2002. The function of this office, launched in 2003, is to evaluate complaints against judges about the discharge of their duty, including how the trial was conducted. (Naturally the ombudsman does not deal with substantive complaints about court decisions.) Out of 882 complaints submitted in 2013 to this ombudsman about judges in various courts, approximately 40 percent dealt with judges in the Magistrate's Courts.

The number of complaints a year seems high, but in 2013 almost a million cases were deliberated throughout the court system by 661 judges, 8 qadis, and 86 rabbinical court judges. Of all the complaints handled in 2013 (898), 36 percent were disqualified as inappropriate for the ombudsman; 85 (9%) were found justified; 395 (44%) were found unjustified; and investigations of the others (11%) were suspended for various reasons (Ombudsman's Office 2014).

Regarding justified complaints, the ombudsman is authorized only to make recommendations, but these carry great weight: a comment, reprimand, or warning recorded in the judge's personal file with a demand to correct the problem; a recommendation to submit the complaint to the Judicial Disciplinary Court; submission of the file to the attorney general, if criminal conduct is suspected; or a recommendation to the Judicial Appointments Committee to remove the judge from office. So far, only two recommendations of the latter two types were made, both regarding rabbinical court judges.

6.7 The Supreme Court

The Supreme Court heads the judicial pyramid in Israel. It is the principal, first, and final judicial instance for rulings of the District Courts or, in exceptional cases, rulings of the Magistrate's Courts. A Supreme Court ruling is binding in every court other than the Supreme Court itself. This is the principle of binding precedent of Supreme Court rulings, which establish obligatory legal norms (case law). Below we will look more closely at the institution of the High Court of Justice, a derivative of the Supreme Court. The Supreme Court has additional, special tasks: It considers appeals on decisions by the Central Elections Committee, the Military Appeals Court, the Civil Service Disciplinary Court, and others. The three Supreme Court justices on the Judicial Appointments Committee have significant influence on the appointment of judges and their promotion through the court system. Whether by law or by virtue of their lofty status and impartiality, Supreme Court justices are from time to time invited to serve on state or public commissions of inquiry, or in other positions such as the Elections Committee. The Supreme Court president is the highest authority with respect to judges, and has broad powers in the judiciary (as a member of the Judicial Appointments Committee, deciding the composition of the Disciplinary Court, etc.), and in the political system (e.g., in the appointment of members of state commissions of inquiry).

A. Characteristics

Most (about 67%) of the sixty Supreme Court justices until 2014 had been judges prior to being promoted to the Supreme Court, some had held senior positions in the Ministry of Justice, and a minority came from academia or the private sector. Initially, most Supreme Court justices had studied law in Europe, particularly in England, but since the late 1970s, more and more have studied law in Israel. Of the ten presidents of the Supreme Court, the first four studied abroad, while the last six studied at least partially if not entirely in Israel – some of these having first served as attorney general or state prosecutor.

By law, the number of justices in the Supreme Court is set by a decision of the Knesset Committee. When first established, the Supreme Court had five justices, and in 2009 the number of positions was set at fifteen – growth that did not keep pace with the increasingly heavy caseload, despite the use of acting justices (see Table 6.1). In 2013, 8,916 cases were lodged with the Supreme Court, most of them petitions to the High Court of Justice. This heavy caseload is reflected in the lengthy term of a "principal case" (adjudicated before three or more judges), which in 2013 was on average thirteen and a half months – ten and a half months for a petition to the High Court of Justice and some nineteen months for a civil appeal (Israeli Judiciary 2014, 13).

In general, Supreme Court proceedings are public and decisions are published in their entirety. A panel of three justices generally presides, or a larger panel for important matters. In light of the controversial nature of the issues brought before the court in recent years and increasing criticism of it, more and more cases are deliberated with an expanded panel of five, seven, nine, or even eleven justices. The appointment of Supreme Court justices is particularly sensitive. In the past, justices were appointed who had held political posts, but in recent years the Judicial Appointments Committee has refrained from appointing candidates who have been politically active, or even those identified with clear political views. In a 2004 amendment to the Courts Law, a cooling-off period of eighteen months was required for attorney generals or state prosecutors before allowing their appointment to the Supreme Court.

A related issue is whether the justices are "representative" of the range of groups in Israeli society. From the outset, an unwritten policy ensured the presence of a "religious seat" on the bench of the Supreme Court, and later an "ethnic seat" (the first Mizrahi incumbent was appointed in 1962). Later came a "woman's seat" (in 1976) and an "Arab seat" (in 2004). In early 2016, out of the fifteen justices – four were women, two Mizrahim, and one Arab.

The Zamir Committee report in 2001 recommended an official policy of appointments that would give weight to the principle of "reflection," noting that primarily Arabs and new immigrants are not "reflected" on the bench (also see Shetreet 2004, 29–43). In our opinion, the judiciary, as opposed to the other two branches of government, is not and should not have to be representative. Positive reflection would entail expanding the pool of nominees to avoid the usual narrow profiles – professionally, regionally, from specific groups, etc. Negative "reflection" would mean foregoing the stringent criteria for judges in order to appoint representatives of specific sectors or political views.

B. High Court of Justice

The purpose of the Supreme Court, when in session as the High Court of Justice, is to provide the citizen with "relief in the interests of justice" vis-à-vis the authorities. The High Court was established by the British government in the Mandate period to avoid entrusting the powers of judicial review to the ordinary courts with their "native judges" – Arabs and Jews. Since then, the High Court has developed – as have the demands and expectations of those who turn to it – both as a unique source of support for citizens and a safeguard for the rule of law.

Who is entitled to seek relief from the High Court? If, for example, a private contractor or the Ministry of Housing is in breach of contract, the High Court is not the venue for litigation, but rather ordinary courts, because this is a matter of contract law, and everyone, including the state, is subject to the law. The High Court becomes the venue when a miscarriage of justice is suspected in the discretionary decision of a government authority; in this sense, the High Court is a tool of citizens not against the government, but on behalf of regulating the authorities and ensuring proper administration. The High Court is a unique institution, one that allows direct access to the Supreme Court for citizens who seek redress from the unjust action of a government authority, after exhausting the other available procedures. To that end, the High Court is authorized by law to issue injunctions ("do" and "refrain from doing" orders) to the state authorities, the local authorities, and anyone performing a public function; to issue a writ of *habeus corpus* to release individuals unlawfully arrested or incarcerated; to prohibit other courts from hearing a specific case, or to overturn a decision made there; to interpret the law; and more. This is the broad and comprehensive meaning of judicial review. The High Court does not initiate a hearing or judicial review about any matter, and does not intervene if a matter is being adjudicated by another court.

High Court of Justice Proceedings

These differ from ordinary court proceedings as they are based on affidavits from the parties rather than in-court examination and cross-examination. It can be said with only some exaggeration that more than the High Court aspires to uncover the truth, it aspires to test the propriety of administrative acts. High Court proceedings are briefer and, in urgent matters, the response is immediate and absolute, even examining a governmental act while it is happening. The ideal of being accessible to citizens is reflected in the low court fees, and theoretically a petitioner can represent him/herself without an attorney. A petition submitted to the High Court is initially heard by one justice, who has the authority to halt the disputed administrative act by issuing a temporary injunction in the petitioner's favor until the petition is deliberated by a panel of at least three justices.

The High Court is overwhelmed by a huge caseload, primarily as the result of the expanded right of standing and the range of subjects brought to it. A court faced with so many cases a year (Table 6.1) is severely overburdened, and this was somewhat alleviated by transferring administrative cases to the District Court. Consequently, the rate of increase slowed down somewhat to 8,916 in 2013. This heavy flow of cases also reflects some misuse of the High Court – by interest groups that submit petitions in order to apply pressure on a public authority (and later rescind the petition), or by MKs who submit petitions to gain publicity. Accessibility is also not a simple matter because submitting a High Court petition requires travel to Jerusalem and overcoming procedural and technical hurdles – few are able to do this without legal assistance. On a substantive level, the High Court does not generally provide financial remedy to petitioners, referring requests for compensatory damages to other courts. The inability to appeal High Court decisions is also sometimes perceived as unfair. The powers of the High Court in Israel are broader than in other countries, but its advantages far outweigh its disadvantages in the context of the Israeli political system, and because it enables citizens and organizations to obtain relief, sometimes immediate, from governmental power.

Right of Standing

A party wishing to submit a petition to the High Court of Justice must first prove actual harm by the governmental authority, i.e., a direct and personal interest in the subject of the petition. In the past, for example, the High Court summarily dismissed a petition of the Hebrew University Student Union in the matter of dormitory construction in Jerusalem, ruling that this was a general plan that did not directly harm the petitioners: "Despite the tendency to expand the right of standing of petitioners, the rule still holds that a 'public petition' is not allowed" (*French Hill Hotel Corporation v. Local Committee for Planning and Construction, Jerusalem* 1973). This has changed, however, and since the 1980s, the High Court has begun to recognize "public petitioners," i.e., the right of standing in matters of general or collective interest. In 1981, a group of Mizrahi academics petitioned the High Court against screening "Pillar of Fire" on the state television channel, on the grounds that the program minimized the contribution of their communities to the Zionist enterprise. The High Court deliberated the right of standing in this case: Although the petitioners could not demonstrate a direct interest, the petition was not summarily dismissed, as the judges stated that the court should not be punctilious about ascertaining whether harm was incurred specifically by these petitioners, as the petition was of prime importance for the rule of law – remedy against a monopolistic body such as the Broadcast Authority. On the substantive claim, the petition was denied on the grounds that a dispute over culture does not justify High Court intervention (*Shiran et al. v. Broadcast Authority* 1981; *Ressler v. Minister of Defense* 1988).

Since then, summary dismissal because of a lack of standing is rare, and many public organizations such as the Association for Civil Rights in Israel, the Israel Union for Environmental Defense, or the National Council for the Child have made use of the High Court to advance their goals. The High Court has become the main address for reviewing government actions, and public officials themselves frequently turn to the High Court regarding Knesset activity, coalition agreements, primary elections, and the like. The expanded High Court activity and its increased power in decision-making are rooted in changes in Israeli society and politics that we discuss below.

Scope of Justiciability

Are there limits to justiciability? Where is the line between matters that are justiciable and those that are not? The search for a clearly defined boundary is futile, beyond the general statements that the Knesset legislates, the government sets policy, and the High Court engages in judicial review. Is there a realm in which judicial review has no power? The answer rests entirely upon the behavior of the public authorities: When they do not break the law, the realm of justiciability shrinks of its own accord, and when they do break the law, the matter becomes justiciable and the realm expands accordingly. And who will judge if an offense was committed? Only the courts, the High Court above all. The dilemma is circular: When demand grows for adjudicated decision-making, more and more issues come to the attention of the court. The court is not obligated to deliberate every issue, but refraining is itself a judgment, and may have social and political implications. The boundary is relative also because some rail against the High Court's over-involvement in ethical and political matters, while others inveigh against inadequate court involvement in security, social, and religious matters (Gavison, Kremnitzer, and Dotan 2000, 37–67). The previous distinction was stated by Justice Zussman in 1960, who noted that the court does not test the wisdom of decision-makers:

> Supervision is restricted to the question of whether the body exceeded its authority … The effectiveness of the discretionary decision or the degree of its wisdom – as distinct from its lawfulness – is not up for examination by this court for the simple reason that the court does not have the tools or instruments for that purpose. (*Miller et al. v. Minister of Transportation* 1961)

This has since changed: Now the High Court of Justice often does examine the wisdom of the decision-maker based on specific standards for review such as the "reasonableness" or "proportionality" of the decision (discussed below). Upon expansion of the fields and scope of judicial review, the High Court found itself in the heart of controversial public issues – questions of foreign policy, security, society, and economics. This expanded role, together with judicial review of the constitutionality of Knesset laws and government actions, has contributed to the relative decline in public support for the Supreme Court that we noted earlier.

6.8 Judicial Review

In this section, we narrow the discussion to the following two subjects: judicial review of the executive branch, primarily the actions of the government and the ministers, and constitutional review of Knesset legislation.

A. Judicial Review of the Executive Branch

In describing the powers of the High Court, we noted its authority to exercise judicial review and enforce norms of proper administration upon government ministries. There is also external legal review of public administration through use of the appeals process in the District Court on rulings of the administrative tribunals. Here we look at judicial review of the decisions and discretionary judgments made by the government and ministers, a power of the court that is in dispute. President Barak thus defined the essence of judicial review of administrative authorities:

> If an action by the executive branch can be implemented in several ways, all of them legal, the judicial branch does not activate its review authority and does not replace the discretion of the executive branch with its own. (A. Barak 1996)

Since the 1980s, the High Court has expanded the judicial review of executive branch decisions by broadening the scope of standing and justiciability. To that end, a set of "review tools" was developed (some had already existed), which constitute a set of criteria to test for lawfulness:

- Does the decision *exceed the authority* of the decision-maker?
- Were the considerations *relevant*, or were there *extraneous considerations or goals*?
- Was an effort made to *balance interests*, and was the decision *proportionate* in terms of harm entailed by it?
- Was the procedure fair, and did it include *the right to a hearing*, etc.?
- And the key question, which partially overlaps the others: Was the decision *reasonable* – put differently, does it fall within the bounds of reasonableness? This means that an administrative action can be invalidated not just because it was "unlawful," but also because it was "unreasonable" in the best judgment of an impartial judge. In other words, the fact that an action is "unreasonable" makes it "unlawful" or "marred by unlawfulness" (Gavison, Kremnitzer, and Dotan 2000, 16–28).[29]

To explain how judicial review operates, the Ginossar case from 1992 is instructive (*Eisenberg v. Minister of Construction and Housing* 1993). Yossi Ginossar was a candidate for Director General of the Ministry of Construction and Housing. A petition claimed that he should be disqualified because of his involvement in two disreputable affairs (Bus 300 and Nafsu), even though he was not criminally indicted (in the Bus 300 case because he received a presidential pardon in advance). Ginossar's appointment had been approved by the Civil Service Commission's Nominating Committee, and when it came to light that this procedure was flawed, the High Court refrained from issuing a show-cause order to give time to the government to reconsider the matter. When the government reapproved the appointment, the High Court did step in and issued a show-cause order. In response, the government appointed a new Nominating Committee, which also vetted the appointment, and the government repeated its decision to appoint Ginossar. Only after this extended process did the High Court agree to review the substance of the government's decision, which it found to be defective:

> The government's decision is flawed. It is clearly unreasonable in the extreme. The government did not properly balance the relevant considerations … and when we concluded that the decision patently deviates from the bounds of reasonableness and is marred by illegality, we have no choice but to declare it invalid.

This is the essence of corrective judicial review. Nevertheless, use of the criterion "unreasonable" is problematic because only a small measure of it is law, while the remainder rests upon the judge's own discretion. Nevertheless, when unreasonable decisions are made by the executive branch, as in the Ginossar case, the court must invalidate them based on its own discretion. In such decisions, it is preferable, in our opinion, that the court use clear language, as did Justice Landau in the Elon Moreh case: "This administrative decision is so patently absurd that it is clearly a case of the decision-making body exceeding its authority" (M. Landau 1989, 5).

The High Court makes use of these review tools to intervene in a range of decisions in the administrative sphere. Note the High Court decision obligating Prime Minister Yitzhak Rabin to dismiss Deputy Minister Deri from the

[29] Hofnung (1997) prefers to call them "formal criteria."

government following Deri's indictment (*Amitai et al. v. Rabin et al.* 1993); obligating the coalition parties to publish political agreements (*Shalit v. Peres* 1990); obligating the Religious Council to appoint a woman member (*Shakdiel v. Minister for Religious Affairs* 1988); and limiting the discretionary power of the Religious Council to issue kashrut certificates (*Raskin v. Jerusalem Religious Council* 1990). Yet another example is the High Court's changed position about intervening in the case of drafting yeshiva students to the army: it had refused to consider the issue on several occasions, but in 1997 the petition was heard and a substantive decision was made.[30] Naturally, expanding the areas of High Court involvement forced it into the domain of controversial issues in Israel, and sometimes into the very eye of the political storm. The High Court's refusal to interfere in the Beit El case set the legal stage for establishment of the settlements (*Ayub et al. v. Minister of Defense et al.* 1979); while its ruling some twenty-five years later altered the route of the "separation fence" between Israel and the West Bank. For comparative purposes, here are excerpts from the majority opinions in these two cases. In the matter of Beit El, Justice Witkon emphasized the importance of settlements for security purposes:

> The main thing is that from the perspective of pure security considerations, there is no doubt that the presence of settlements in the occupied area – even civilian – of citizens of the occupying power makes a serious contribution to the security of that area, and makes it easier for the army to discharge its duties. One need not be an expert in military or security affairs to understand that terrorist elements can act more easily in an area in which a population is apathetic or sympathetic to the enemy, than in an area where people can monitor their activities and inform the authorities about every suspicious movement … We note only that according to the affidavit of the respondents, the settlers are subject to the authority of the army, whether formally or by force of circumstances. They are there thanks to and with the permission of the army. (*Ayub et al. v. Minister of Defense* et al. 1979)

In the matter of the separation fence, Justice Barak stated that the court should intervene in the political and military decision, and that the prioritization of security considerations should be tempered by the proportionality of the action:

> [The key question] of this petition is the legality of the route chosen for construction of the separation fence. This question stands on its own, and requires a substantive answer. It is not sufficient that construction of the fence be motivated by security rather than political considerations. The military commander in a territory under belligerent occupation is not at liberty to carry out every act that is motivated primarily by security considerations. The discretion of the military commander is restricted by the normative system in which he functions, and which is the source of his authority. Indeed, the military commander is not the sovereign in territory under belligerent occupation … He must act within the law that establishes his authority in a situation of belligerent occupation. (*Beit Sourik Village Council v. Government of Israel* 2004)

The court has by and large refrained from intervening in security and foreign affairs. Thus, the High Court denied a petition about conducting negotiations with

[30] *Ressler v. Minister of Defense Ariel Sharon* 1981; *Ressler v. Minister of Defense Ariel Sharon* 1988; and *Ressler v. Minister of Defense* 1988 were denied as the legal standing of the petitioner was not recognized. *Ressler v. Minister of Defense* 1988 was deliberated and denied as not meeting the criterion of unreasonable discretion. While *Rubinstein v. Minister of Defense* 1998 was deliberated and a substantive judgment was made.

Syria and a petition against implementing a prisoner exchange.[31] On the other hand, the High Court did not hesitate to intervene when it believed a policy to be discriminatory. This was true for the Alice Miller case, in which the High Court ordered the IDF to revise its discriminatory policy of not accepting women into pilot training courses (*Miller v. Minister of Defense* 1995), or when it ruled that the Ministry of Defense must take the family's wishes into consideration concerning the text to be written on gravestones in military cemeteries (*Wechselbaum v. Minister of Defense* 1995).

In the current climate of Israeli politics, judicial review helps curb processes that damage or undermine democracy. But what are the boundaries of court intervention? Kremnitzer, who justifies intervention by the court, argues that politics should be constrained, and this might contribute to the legitimization of politics itself (Gavison, Kremnitzer, and Dotan 2000, 231). But if the assumption is that politicians cannot be trusted, there would be no hope of making change in the political system. Therefore, judicial review must be carried out with disciplined self-restraint, or there is no hope that a political culture will emerge that will lessen the need for intervention by the courts and perhaps, with the passage of time, make it superfluous.

B. Constitutional Review

Is it within the authority of the High Court to carry out constitutional review, i.e., judicial review of legislation? Is it within the power of the High Court to nullify a law or a provision of a law if it contravenes a Basic Law? Or contravenes fundamental principles of the system or social values? Or should judicial review be limited to procedural flaws during the legislative process? (On court intervention in internal Knesset affairs, including the issue of immunity, see Chapter 4.) These questions are at the heart of a discussion about the separation of powers in a parliamentary system such as Israel's. In other words, does the legislative branch, in representing the sovereign, have the authority to legislate whatever it wishes, or is it itself constrained so as to ensure the legality of governance, and, in particular, to ensure that the legislator does not change the democratic rules of the game by using these very rules, which has happened more than once in history? If the answer is positive – that there should be oversight of the legislature – the next question is how this is accomplished and by whom. Is any court, for example, authorized to rule that a Knesset law is "unconstitutional," or is this the sole prerogative of the Supreme Court? And what is the implication of giving an appointed judge the power to invalidate a decision made by the elected members of the Knesset?[32]

[31] *Faithful of the Temple Mount and Land of Israel Movement v. Prime Minister* 1993; or *Shalit v. State of Israel* 2008 (unpublished): In June 2008 the High Court denied the Shalit family petition to condition the opening of the Gaza Strip border crossings upon progress toward freeing their son Gilad Shalit from captivity. In *Shahar v. State of Israel* 2008 (unpublished), the High Court denied Shahar's petition against the release of Samir Kuntar, who had killed his brother.

[32] The most common case, which will not be discussed here, is when two laws of equal status conflict with each other, and the court rules by giving preference to the later and more specific law, i.e., the Knesset can change its mind, and therefore a more recent law supersedes an earlier law and a specific law trumps a general law.

In the United States, any court has the authority to nullify legislation; in Canada, the English legal tradition narrowed this to the Supreme Court. In Germany and Italy after World War II, the authority to nullify legislation was given to a special court, whose role was defined as defending democracy. In France, a Constitutional Council was established in 1958 as a separate legal authority with the power to conduct a preliminary review of the constitutionality of bills as part of the legislative process. In England, on the other hand, no institution is entrusted with the authority to nullify acts of parliament, other than acts that contravene obligations to the European Union. In Israel, where no rigid, written constitution imposes constraints on the legislator, review of the Knesset and problematic laws is a particularly charged issue.

C. The "Constitutional Revolution"

Until 1992, the supremacy of the Basic Laws over ordinary legislation was not explicitly established. Thus, articles in the Basic Laws that were not entrenched were equal in status to ordinary laws. The Knesset refrained from clarifying this principle, and put off enactment of the Basic Law: Legislation, which would have established whether the court does or does not have judicial review authority. Even so, the court had already conducted judicial review of several cases, most under the cover of dealing with procedural issues (Mautner 1993, 126–33). In the Bergman case, the High Court deliberated the law that awarded campaign financing only to existing parties, ignoring the needs of new party lists. The formal argument of the petitioners was that the campaign finance law contravenes the principle of equality in the Basic Law: The Knesset, whose amendment would require a majority of Knesset members, but since the law passed without this majority, it should be invalidated. Although the High Court used this argument in its decision, more importantly, it set a precedent that equality of election applies both to the right to vote and the right to be elected. It noted that the Knesset had two options: "It can re-legislate the provisions of the Parties Financing Law, despite the inequality, if it has the necessary majority … or it can amend the law to remove the inequality" (*Bergman v. Finance Minister* 1969).

Also of significance in this case was the fact that the High Court exercised judicial review and the Knesset amended the law accordingly. In other cases, the High Court has not hesitated to hear petitions that challenge the constitutionality of laws, but in the very few instances that it ordered a law nullified, the issue concerned contravention of an entrenched article in a Basic Law (*Derekh Eretz Association v. Broadcast Authority* 1981; *Rubinstein v. Speaker of the Knesset* 1983). In the past, nullifying Knesset laws was a rarity, and the High Court was careful not to intervene in the legislative process or the content of the laws. This was consistent with the British tradition, and – in the political climate then prevailing – it is doubtful that there would have been public support for substantive judicial review of Knesset legislation, hence the emphasis that judicial review be confined to procedural matters. Nevertheless, the precedent was established that the High Court has the authority to intervene and even invalidate Knesset legislation.

The enactment of two Basic Laws in 1992 – Human Dignity and Liberty, and Freedom of Occupation – and the subsequent court decisions changed constitutional review by the Israeli Supreme Court, a change that has been called "the constitutional revolution":

> By virtue of this constitutional revolution, there is a substantive change in the status of some fundamental human rights in Israel, which ceased being merely "unwritten" rights and became "written" rights that enjoy preferential constitutional standing. True, these basic human rights in Israel continue to be part of case law … [but] they have become a normative fulcrum that determines the validity of all legislation. (A. Barak 1992, 12)

The two new Basic Laws contained a number of innovations. First, an entrenchment provision stipulated that amendment requires a majority of Knesset members; second, a "limitation clause" was incorporated, which prevents violation of the Basic Law except by virtue of a law that "befits the values of the State of Israel, is enacted for a proper purpose, and to an extent no greater than is required." Third, and most important, the two Basic Laws anchored a human rights charter, if only partial, that establishes general principles and not just specific arrangements. These changes forged the basis for judicial review by the Supreme Court, both in procedural matters (the need for a majority), and in substantive matters (the supremacy of the entrenched Basic Laws, the limitation clause, and the legislation of human rights). A short time later in the Mizrahi Bank decision, the court explicitly established by precedent its authority to invalidate legislation that contravenes a Basic Law (*United Mizrahi Bank Ltd. v. Migdal Cooperative Village* 1995). Nine judges in an expanded panel agreed that the limitation clause in the Basic Law: Human Dignity and Liberty enables judicial review of the constitutionality of a law, and nullification of any subsequent law that conflicts with a Basic Law. The precedent-setting importance of the Mizrahi Bank decision stems from the general stipulation that Supreme Court authority to exercise judicial review of legislation applies to all the Basic Laws. Thus, the constitutional and substantial supremacy of the Basic Laws was established, and its practical expression was the new legislative procedure whereby every Knesset bill must be examined for conformity to the Basic Laws. Since 1995, the Supreme Court has pronounced the nullification or non-nullification of several legislative provisions in contravention of Basic Laws in the following subjects: arrest of soldiers; investment advice regulations; retroactive licensing of unlawfully operated radio stations; disengagement from the Gaza Strip; the privatization of prisons; guaranteed minimal income for yeshiva students; extending the duration of the law exempting yeshiva students from army service; and amendments to the Prevention of Infiltration Law that would have allowed the extended detention of those entering Israel illegally.[33]

In cases where a law or a provision in a law was nullified, the Knesset generally accepted the Supreme Court ruling and amended the law, avoiding a constitutional clash between the two branches of government. Indeed, clashes were avoided because – despite the rhetoric about a "constitutional revolution" – the Supreme Court rarely used its authority for constitutional review, except in cases that were

[33] *Israel Investment Managers Association v. Minister of Finance* 1997; *Oron v. Speaker of the Knesset* 1999; *Tzemah v. Minister of Defense* 1999; *Gaza Coast Regional Council v. Israel Knesset* 2005; *Academic Center of Law and Business et al. v. Minister of Finance et al.* 2009 (unpublished); *Yekutieli v. Minister of Religious Affairs* 2010 (unpublished); *Ressler v. Israeli Knesset* 2012; *Adam v. Knesset* 2013; *Eitan: Israeli Immigration Policy Center v. Government of Israel* 2014.

not seriously controversial. More commonly, the court refused to nullify laws, both out of respect for the law as reflecting the will of the people, and a desire to avoid clashes with the legislator.[34] There is no disagreement over the Knesset's authority to amend Basic Laws, but the court stipulated that this must be done within the framework of a Basic Law, not as ordinary legislation. The court was also careful to emphasize that the Knesset is not a party to the constitutional dispute, as the ruling is against the law and not the lawmaker.

Nevertheless, the court's authority to exercise judicial review of the "constitutionality" of Knesset laws does not explicitly appear in any law, but was a power assumed by the court in the framework of case law, i.e., by making it a binding court precedent. Proponents contend that the existence of Basic Laws (and, since 1992, even more constitutional Basic Laws) creates an obligation of judicial review and endows the High Court with that power. After all, it would not make sense for the legislator not to be subject to a constitution (Basic Law), and in Israel it is only the High Court that could protect society from the absolute power to the Knesset. Most of those who oppose empowering the High Court with judicial review are generally unhappy with the rulings it issued, and seek to rein it in because they maintain that it represents only a small group of Israelis and their values (secular-liberal). However, there is also substantive disagreement with the court's claim to have this power, particularly its pretension to be able to reflect the fundamental values of society over time. They argue that value-laden issues should be left to the legislators, who are politically elected, and not to appointed judges. They are also concerned that judicial review in general, particularly of laws, will drag the court into the political arena, diminish its impartial status, and undermine its main task of ensuring that justice is done. We will return to this at the end of the chapter in the discussion about judicial activism.

Proposals for changing judicial review range from completely annulling this power of the court, or at least taking it out of the hands of the Supreme Court, to maintaining the status quo. The main proposals that evolved into bills make an effort to establish a separate "constitutional court" – a discrete body that specializes in judicial review – and to increase the influence of elected representatives over who is appointed to this court.[35] A proposal in the spirit of the Canadian model advocates that the court continue to have the authority to rule on the constitutionality of laws, but that the Knesset be empowered to override nullification by a defined supermajority.[36] Another possibility is the model used in several European countries (Norway, for example) in which constitutional review is performed during the legislative process: The court or another body appraises the constitutionality of a bill prior to its final enactment (Kremnitzer 2001). A model proposed by Prof. Shetreet brings together elements of the aforementioned proposals: the Supreme

[34] See, for example, *Hofnung v. Speaker of the Knesset* 1996. From Justice Zamir's opinion in this ruling: "For the Court to invalidate a law, the breach [of a constitutional principle] must be neither negligible nor minor, but glaring and significant."

[35] For example, the proposed Constitutional Court Law 2002 tabled by former MKs Eliezer Cohen and Yigal Bibi, Knesset Bill 3380. See also Dotan 2000, 120–24; Klein 2003, 497–513.

[36] A similar version was proposed by the Knesset's Constitution, Law and Justice Committee in session as the Committee to Prepare a Constitution in Consensus, 16th Knesset, Vol. 2, annotated version of proposed constitutions, Jerusalem: January 2006 [in Hebrew].

Court would have the authority for judicial review when specifically empaneled as a Constitutional Court, which can declare that a specific law contravenes a Basic Law; the Knesset can then choose to amend the law by legislative process to resolve the contradiction, or allow the law to stand (Shetreet 2006, 3, 151). Attempts have been made by members of the Knesset to override judicial review in Israel. A private bill submitted by Justice Minister Ayelet Shaked, for example, would amend the Basic Law: Human Dignity and Liberty to allow the Knesset to pass laws that contravene the Basic Law provided there is approval of sixty-one MKs and a clause that specifies they are aware of the contravention.

In our view, Shetreet's proposal would aggravate relations among the government branches and foment a crisis when the Knesset elects not to resolve a contradiction found by the court. In Israel's current political climate, including some problematic initiatives in the Knesset (see Chapter 4), clearly defined roles with rigid boundaries would be preferable. Furthermore, the court has shown considerable restraint in exercising judicial review, to the extent that some believe its symbolic influence is more significant than its actual impact on Israeli politics (Barak-Erez 2000, 383). At any rate, concern about the overuse of judicial review is unfounded. Hence, the first step is to anchor in a Basic Law the authority of the Supreme Court to engage in judicial review, as was proposed in various drafts of a Basic Law: Legislation. This authority will be exclusive to the Supreme Court in session as a Constitutional Court, and will be activated only after enactment of the law by the Knesset. A court judgment that a particular law is in contravention of a Basic Law will be final and serve to nullify that law, while the Knesset is, of course, entitled to enact another law that is not in conflict with a Basic Law.

D. Judicial Activism

Yitzhak Zamir (1993, 647–58) proposed a neutral definition for "judicial activism": a court's willingness to find a judicial solution for a new problem, and its willingness to set itself as the corrector of the law, i.e., to take advantage of an available opportunity to create a newer and better law (see also A. Barak 1993, 476; Barzilai 1998, 32–34; Maoz 1999, 413). This functional definition correctly ignores the tendency to use the word "activism" in reference to the temperament of the Supreme Court justices or its president. Nevertheless, in political terms, the court is clearly intervening in areas that had previously been within the exclusive purview of the Knesset and the government. Which came first – the growing need of the political system for the adjudication services of the court, or the court's increasing desire to intervene? The demand for judicial services has rapidly grown in other democracies, not just in Israel, hence there is no evidence of "judicial imperialism." Yet why did the court swing its doors open so wide that it came to be called a "society shaper" – was this a case of over-activism?

In the above Ginossar case, politics could not be allowed to continue as usual because the mechanisms designed to prevent an improper appointment had failed, and the corrective involvement of the High Court was needed for providing deterrence and direction. We also gave other examples of the need for High Court intervention when authorities failed to exercise proper judgment. On the other hand, there are also examples of unwarranted court intervention, in our opinion, intervention that overstepped the bounds of judicial authority and entered the explicit domain of politics – policy-making. In the case of the deportation of Hamas members in 1992, the Association for Civil Rights in Israel petitioned the High Court to invalidate the deportation orders on the grounds that the deportees were not given a hearing (*Association for Civil Rights in Israel v. Minister of Defense* 1993). The petition was based on the breach of their rights, and did not address the government policy, leaving the court in a dilemma. Had the justices remained true to their prior decisions concerning the basic right to due process, it would have to halt the deportation; had it ruled that this was not justiciable because it is a political-security issue for which the government is accountable to the Knesset, it would have to ignore its prior decisions and deny its general view of justiciability. In a unanimous ruling, the court chose neither option – it did not invalidate the deportation orders, nor did it summarily dismiss the petition, but rejected the petition after a full hearing. In our opinion, not everything is a matter of law, and the approach that "everything is justiciable" may cause harm.

There have been cases in which the court intervened in areas that called for restraint, but what is called "activism" actually reflects a gradual judicialization of politics. More than this process indicates the over-eagerness of the courts, it testifies to a political system that is faltering to the point where the Knesset, the government, the parties, and the administrative authorities would find it very hard to function were it not for the assistance of the law courts. It would be preferable, of course, for the political culture in Israel to obviate the need to address problems by adjudication, as the courts are not the appropriate venue to resolve ideological disputes or shape controversial policies: This should be the role of the political bodies.[37] Nevertheless, even activist judges eager to grapple with issues best left to politics would not be able to do so without the complicity of the other institutions. When political oversight becomes part and parcel of the political culture, judicial oversight will have less work on its hands. Therefore, the phrase "judicial activism" does not accurately reflect the dynamic: "Activation" of the judiciary would be more to the point, as the process is rooted in the increased judicialization of society and politics that we will now examine.

6.9 Judicialization of Public Life[38]

Judicialization refers to the predisposition to resolve disputes in court that have previously been resolved in social-economic-political frameworks. This definition emphasizes the desire for and reliance on legal remedies, which existed even *before* the jurisdiction of the courts had expanded. Indeed, of concern is not just the intervention of the courts, discussed above, but the judicialization of public life in its entirety. Another aspect of this phenomenon is "legislative judicialization" – the predisposition to regulate the many diverse spheres of our lives through a formal code of laws. The context for this burgeoning judicialization is the inability of Israeli society to function without decrees, through use of the conventional tools of dialogue, agreed procedures, compromise, and decision-making in non-judicial frameworks. This refers not just to the

[37] See consensus among the authors about this matter: Gavison, Kremnitzer, and Dotan 2000, 166.

[38] This section is based on Galnoor 2004, 500–42; also see Avnon 1996, 417–51.

Supreme Court, but to a wide range of phenomena that includes extensive use of the monitoring institutions – commissions of inquiry, the state comptroller (see Chapter 7), the attorney general – and, with increased political corruption, greater recourse to law enforcement authorities and the courts.

The judicialization of politics means that clashing viewpoints and interests have now been shifted into the realm of the judiciary. And this raises questions: Is the assumption well founded that legal decisions will save society from questionable political deeds – and thereby also safeguard the values and democratic rules of the game? Can the judiciary, which is only one branch of the political system (broadly conceived), rescue the other two – parliament and the government – during difficult times? Might the success of the legal system in compelling the other two branches to be more vigilant of the rule of law and the legality of government simultaneously be undermining their steering capacity, which is their primary task? Conversely, if the political system's steering capacity and ability to make good decisions are so erratic, isn't it better to have judicial review to ensure that these branches make decisions that are at least not unreasonable in the extreme?

The political system in Israel is suffering from a "democracy deficit" as political institutions find themselves incapable of coping with both external and internal crises, while public trust is ebbing. Consequently, the general judicialization processes within society have been paralleled and perhaps fed by the judicialization of politics. But the court can merely slow the growth of the democratic deficit, not alone offset it. The "unconventional weapon" of judicial review should be saved for times of crisis, and best left for exceptional cases.

In the parliamentary system of Israel, the judiciary does not have an overall mandate to intervene in the affairs of the other two branches, but only specific, "corrective" authorizations. In this approach, the judge is generally the agent of the legislator; sometimes a partner because of the need to interpret the law in rulings; and, occasionally but rarely, a law enforcement officer to ensure deterrence by corrective intervention in the deeds of the other two authorities.[39] The significance of the corrective role of the judiciary is that it places the court's main sphere of activity outside the political system. This changes during difficult times when there is much to correct governmentally. When rights are not safeguarded and when the other branches do not operate according to the democratic rules of the game – or they change the rules not in accordance with the rules – judicial intervention justifiably increases. These departures should occur only at a time of democratic emergency. Moreover, when public sanctions fail time and again, powerless to deter politicians from corruption or breach of

[39] See the statement by Supreme Court President Aharon Barak (2006): "Can the judge be recognized as a junior partner bridging between law and the public because of his role as the interpreter of legislation? The answer to this question is not at all simple. The main question is whether to accept a model of partnership – albeit a limited partnership – or a model of agency. In the agency model, the judge is an agent of the legislature. He must act according to its instructions, just like a junior officer is bound to carry out the orders of his superior officer. There are many problems with this approach. To my mind, a judge is not an agent who receives orders, and the legislature is not a principal that gives orders to his agent. The two are branches of the state with different roles; one is legislator and the other is interpreter. Indeed, legislatures create statutes that are supposed to bridge the gap between law and society."

trust, the task of the court is to intervene, whether by actual punishment or by invalidating the degraded norms that have taken root. It is futile to assume, however, that judicialization itself can save democracy, or even politics.

The courts in Israel may possibly have already exhausted their valuable corrective contribution to the political system, on several counts. First, the court is not the proper venue to resolve controversial ideological issues that political processes should be forced to address – hopefully Israeli political culture will mature enough to make that possible. Second, the door that had swung open to the judicial review of politics is beginning to close for the wrong reasons, including the irrational reactions of Knesset members and even of the Knesset as an institution.[40] It would be better for this restraint to come from the court itself.

[40] Such as the Knesset decision (December 14, 1999) that calls upon the Supreme Court to refrain from intervening in matters of values, Halakha, ideology, politics, or laws it passes.

7 Monitoring Mechanisms: The State Comptroller and State Commissions of Inquiry (SCIs)

7.1 Guardians of the Public Interest

The two institutions in the title of this chapter are monitoring mechanisms. Despite the differences between them and the additional tasks they have accrued, each is responsible within its legal mandate for auditing, investigating, and scrutinizing the activity of public authorities and their office holders. Democracies also have other watchdogs in the public realm – the media and social organizations, for example – but the tasks of these two "official guardians" are different. The state comptroller is a permanent institution that engages in ongoing oversight in the public sector. A state commission of inquiry (SCI) investigates a specific subject, and disbands upon conclusion of its work. To these can be added the attorney general (not discussed in this chapter), who is legal adviser to the executive branch and also heads the public prosecutor's office, and whose monitoring roles include advising the government and ministries about the legality of their actions. The role of the attorney general is to prevent decisions that violate the law or are improper administratively.[1]

The state comptroller is accountable to the Knesset, which elects him, and through the Knesset to the public; an SCI, on the other hand, is initiated by a government decision and reports to the government, although it is actually accountable to the public. Despite the institutional differences, neither of these two monitoring mechanisms is subordinate to the appointing bodies, as the law affords them independence in discharging their duties. The moment they are duly appointed, "the umbilical cord is cut" from the appointing body (*Ometz v. Prime Minister* 2006), their dependence ends, and they are duty bound by independent, pertinent considerations only.

Over the years in Israel, the need for monitoring has increased, their authority has expanded, and their stature has grown in the political and public arenas. Public attitudes seem to have tipped in opposite directions: The lower the expectations and respect for the branches of government, the higher the expectations and respect for the monitoring mechanisms. Unrealistic expectations often disappoint, of course. The monitoring mechanisms reflect the view that external bodies (or independent ones, such as the attorney general) should be engaged to monitor and supervise the

[1] On the attorney general, see the "Agranat Commission Report" 1962; Gutman 1981; Segal 1988; Barzilai and Nachmias 1997; and Shamgar Committee 1998.

executive branch. These are not elected bodies and therefore cannot replace the Knesset, but they make a substantive contribution to the checks and balances of the political system, enhancing its transparency and operating as emissaries of the public when they investigate events, organizations, and public figures. In Chapter 4 (Section 4.6), we noted that their importance has grown in the face of weak oversight by the Knesset.

In Israel, the monitoring mechanisms enjoy both prestige and judicial authority. State comptrollers usually have a legal background, while SCIs must by law be headed by a judge and their members appointed by the Supreme Court president. Nevertheless, the legal background of those in monitoring roles may serve to limit them to legal review. This reliance on jurists, the increased recourse to monitoring mechanisms, and their growing power reflect the diminished steering capacity of the political system, a growing trend of judicialization, and erosion of the public trust. At the same time, investigations, auditing, and the exposure of failings in the governing authorities might contribute to restoring that trust. A political system that does not shy away from powerful, independent monitoring contributes in the long run to increased trust in it. Thus, monitoring mechanisms can act as a safety valve, if the public does not regard them as revealing only the tip of the iceberg – a fraction of what is still concealed.

In the evolution of monitoring mechanisms in Israel, several events have been turning points, bringing about substantive changes in their functions and power. The state comptroller's role was broadened and even fundamentally altered when it was given the authority to audit the finances of political parties.[2] Another change came with its own decision in the late 1980s to scrutinize political appointments and expand its authority to investigate the ethical conduct of public office holders. The amplified role played by SCIs in politics, public administration, and the IDF came with the Agranat Commission's investigation into the Yom Kippur War (1974). This commission regarded itself as authorized to scrutinize the decision-making discretion of the most senior office holders, and thereby shaped new norms for investigating and monitoring the conduct within all branches of government in Israel. To this should be added the importance and sensitivity of the office of the attorney general, evident during the corruption affairs of public officials in the 1970s and most prominently in 1997 when an attempt was made to take control of this office through a political appointment ("the Bar-On Hebron affair").[3] In the wake of this affair, a

2 Upon enactment of the Parties Financing Law (1973) and expansion of its power in the Local Authorities (Party Financing) Law (1993). In 2005, the state comptroller was authorized to audit the accounts of party candidates in the primary elections (national and local). The amendment to the Political Party Law took effect in 2008.

3 The appointment of Roni Bar-On to the position of attorney general in January 1997 raised concerns due to his membership in a political party (Likud) and reservations about his qualifications for the job. Suspicions also cropped up of a so-called "Bar-On Hebron" deal: As attorney general, Bar-On would be in a position to help MK Aryeh Deri, then facing criminal charges, in exchange for the support of Deri's party (Shas) for the agreement to transfer Hebron to the Palestinian Authority. An investigation was launched against the prime minister, justice minister, director general of the Office of the Prime Minister, MK Deri, and others. Bar-On tendered his resignation one day after starting his new job. The new attorney general, Elyakim Rubinstein, ultimately decided not to bring charges against anyone involved in the affair.

new procedure was instituted for appointing the attorney general in an effort to thwart interference by political or criminal interests.

Following the increase in public dissatisfaction with government performance, the two monitoring mechanisms discussed in this chapter have enjoyed greater independence and been more willing to scrutinize the considerations that went into political decisions. They have gone beyond the original conception of their role and become influential actors in the political system.

7.2 The Institution of State Comptroller in Israel

The office of the state comptroller has unique standing in the Israeli body politic. Some view it as "the long arm of the Knesset" and others see it as an independent entity, a "fourth branch" unto itself. Neither of these views fully captures the essence of this office as it evolved in Israel. In countries that established this institution, the state comptroller is constitutionally an extension of the parliament. Similarly, the comptroller in Israel is elected by and accountable to the Knesset, and submits reports to the Knesset and the Knesset's State Control Committee. Over the years, however, the office of the state comptroller has evolved into an independent monitoring mechanism with its own responsibilities and even enforcement powers, not derived directly from its obligations to the Knesset and not part of its oversight role. In 1988, this office became a constitutional body upon enactment of the Basic Law: State Comptroller. It is regarded as the watchdog of democracy (which leads to the question of its clout, to be examined below), as its revelations of failings help ensure accountability of the authorities to the public.

The tasks of the Israeli state comptroller differ from a classic financial audit. They include monitoring implementation of the Budget Law, scrutinizing expenditures, oversight of operations, and also the legality of activity as well as sound management, efficiency, and savings. The law also authorizes the state comptroller to examine the ethical conduct and "every matter it deems fit." In other words, the state comptroller has broad powers: It scrutinizes a great many bodies and has few constraints on its activity.[4]

A. The Constitutional and Legal Infrastructure

One of the first laws promulgated after the founding of Israel was the State Comptroller Law (1949). An integrated version was enacted in 1958 and subsequently amended many times. In 1988, the Basic Law: State Comptroller was legislated, listing the bodies subject to its audit – ministries, state enterprises, state institutions, state corporations, local authorities, and other entities defined by law as subject to audit. The Basic Law is a framework law, which sets the scope of the audit, establishes that the state comptroller is accountable only to the Knesset, stipulates its independence from the government, gives it authority to access information and other materials for conducting the audit, and establishes procedures for election of the individual to occupy this post. The state comptroller is elected by a majority of Knesset members in a secret ballot (or, in a second ballot, by a majority of those who

[4] For a comparative perspective, see Galili 2005; Schwartz 2005; and Havens 2005.

vote) to serve a seven-year term, which is not renewable. The Knesset is authorized to remove a comptroller from office by a three-quarters majority of its members. No specific qualifications are required, but to date (2016) the eight comptrollers had legal training and, since 1987, have all been retired judges.

The list of bodies subject to state audit is long and includes every institution, enterprise, foundation, or body receiving direct or indirect funding from the state, as well as every entity in which the government has an administrative role. The link to state funding renders many Israeli organizations subject to a state audit (Sharkansky 1995).[5] It should be emphasized that the defense establishment, including the secret services, is subject to audit by the state comptroller, as are public religious institutions, the health funds, universities, government corporations, state funded non-profits, and more. In addition, the comptroller now engages in the oversight of party finances – ongoing party expenditures, the funding of primary elections, and the financing of election campaigns. It is within the comptroller's authority to impose fines on parties that violate the law. In special cases, the law grants the state comptroller all the powers bestowed upon an SCI, including the authority to interrogate witnesses.

Regarding the scope of the audit, the role of the state comptroller is to examine the legality of activities in the audited institutions, and whether those who made the decisions were authorized to do so. When State Comptroller Yitzhak Tunik investigated the banks following the manipulation of their shares, for example, he concluded that the actions taken by the bank directors were illegal. Article 14B of the State Comptroller Law authorizes the Knesset's State Control Committee, given a two-thirds majority of its members, to appoint an SCI regarding a special report of the state comptroller. Under this clause, the Beisky Commission was appointed in 1985, and three other SCIs in 2008 (see below). When the audit raises suspicion of criminal activity, the state comptroller reports this to the attorney general, who decides whether legal action should be taken.

The comptroller examines efficiency and economy. A more complex task is to evaluate the outcome and effectiveness of activities carried out with public funds: Was the purpose of the activity well defined, were alternatives considered, and did the execution match the defined purpose? In 2007, for example, the state comptroller evaluated the effectiveness of dealing with political asylum seekers in Israel and concluded that the handling of this matter was flawed (State Comptroller *Annual Report* 2007, 58B, 112). The law authorizes the state comptroller to examine the ethical behavior of elected officials. This function has earned considerable public attention in recent years because of the criminal investigations against senior politicians and civil servants that emerged as a result of the audit.

The autonomy of the state comptroller is enshrined in law, which is crucial for an auditing body. It is within the authority of the comptroller to decide on the scope of the audit as well as the bodies and subjects to be investigated (unless a request was made by the Knesset, the State Control Committee, or the government for the audit of something within the purview of the state comptroller). Although the Knesset elects the incumbent, the work of the state comptroller is independent of the

[5] It is left to the discretion of the comptroller and the Knesset Finance Committee which bodies to audit among those the state subsidizes or has a role in managing.

legislative branch; it is also independent of the executive branch, which falls under its scrutiny. For this reason, the election of the state comptroller is by a majority of Knesset members in a secret ballot, and he or she can be removed only by a special majority of MKs. This is also the reason for its administrative independence: The office of the state comptroller is not part of the executive branch, nor is its staff in the employ of the Finance Ministry or Civil Service Commission. The budget for this office and salary of the comptroller are set by the Knesset Finance Committee.

B. State Comptroller Reports[6]

The major product of the office of the state comptroller is the annual report, which is submitted to the Speaker of the Knesset and the prime minister. The report is produced by some 590 staff (in 2016) employed by the office of the state comptroller (and ombudsman). With the exception of specific sections dealing with state security and other vital state interests, the report is made public. During the course of the year, the comptroller also publishes separate reports about audited bodies and issues of principle. Prior to publication of the final version of any report, the audited bodies are given an opportunity to respond to the findings, and these responses are incorporated into the report before its submission to the State Audit Division in the Office of the Prime Minister. The report is then submitted to the Knesset together with the responses from the Office of the Prime Minister and other ministries, and the decisions of the Ministers' Committee for State Audit Affairs. The report is deliberated in the Knesset's State Control Committee, which submits its conclusions and suggestions. This committee is authorized to summon state employees and outside experts for a discussion of the findings. The content of the annual report and the discussion of the report's findings in the Knesset's State Control Committee are extensively covered by the media, although interest can wane quickly, depending on the sensitivity of the subject raised.

Which channels monitor the correction of shortcomings? According to an amendment to the State Comptroller Law (2001), the audited body must establish a task force to rectify the failings. The task force will address the problem and report its decisions to the head of the audited body, who then informs the state comptroller and the Office of the Prime Minister of the decisions and measures taken. The Ministerial Committee for State Control monitors the rectification of the shortcomings through the State Audit Division in the Office of the Prime Minister. In addition, the annual report generally reviews the extent to which recommendations from previous years were implemented. Despite all this, monitoring is largely a formality, as audited bodies have ways of circumventing supervision. Thus, the primary tools at the disposal of the state comptroller in Israel – as in other democracies – are political and public, not legal. The comptroller has no formal way to enforce its recommendations. The power of this office is a function of its status and prestige among those audited, particularly the government, the ministries, and those it serves – the Knesset and the public. The most direct contribution made by this office to good governance is its deterrent power, and this takes place far from the limelight and media. This is

[6] For state comptroller reports, see www.mevaker.Gov.il/index.htm/ [in Hebrew, with selected reports in English].

the role of the state comptroller, and it should not be confused with the tools of law enforcement assigned to other agencies.

The state comptroller's recommendations can have a significant impact on legislation and policymaking, as in the following examples: The state comptroller's analysis (1986) of the development of the Lavi aircraft in Israel contributed significantly to the decision to abort the project; also, repeated criticism of defects in the Parties Financing Law led to changes in the law and a limit on the amount any one donor may contribute.[7] Although report findings may not serve as evidence in legal proceedings, they can set legal events in motion: The state comptroller's report in 1991 revealing that funds had been transferred to the educational institutions of the Shas Party by Interior Minister Aryeh Deri triggered an investigation that ended in conviction of the minister. On the other hand, the comptroller can also be ignored, as was the case following the 2003 report, which revealed that the Ministry of Construction and Housing had funded illegal construction and development in the occupied territories (State Comptroller *Annual Report* 2003), and declared that the ministry must stop funding such projects.[8]

C. Special Areas of Oversight

Over the years, the role of the state comptroller has broadened with respect to the types of bodies and subjects audited. Amendments to the law in the 1950s added local authorities and the subsidiaries of audited institutions to the list of bodies subject to audit by the state comptroller; a 1952 amendment gave the comptroller the authority to investigate ethical conduct; and the jobs of ombudsman and monitoring implementation of the Parties Financing Law were later added. The decline of other supervisory institutions and the waning of public faith in the political system enhanced the status of the state comptroller.

The first comptrollers in Israel saw themselves as teachers of sound administration such as the principles of public budgeting, how to organize the financial accounts of the state, and how to prevent mismanagement. Miriam Ben-Porat (1988–98) focused on the ethical conduct of elected officials, struggling to prevent political appointments. During her term, the list of donors to political parties was first published. She did not hesitate to engage in "proactive auditing" and published reports that to some extent intervened in the shaping of policy around issues such as immigrant absorption or preparing the home front for unconventional warfare. Eliezer Goldberg (1998–2005) was known for his wide perspective and willingness to examine issues that cut across institutions, as he sought to improve the overall management culture in a report that dealt with improving staff work in the ministries (State Comptroller *Annual Report* 2004, 55B). Micha Lindenstrauss (2005–12) saw corruption as his primary challenge. And Joseph Shapira (2012–) also dealt with

[7] The *Report on the Parties Financing Law*, June 6, 1989, contained the results of the audit of political parties during the election campaign for the twelfth Knesset. Paragraph 10 recommends that – to avoid the dependence of parties on individual donors – the Knesset should consider an amendment that would limit the size of the donation from a single donor, comparable to the existing prohibition on donations from companies.

[8] For state comptroller reports, see www.mevaker.Gov.il/index.htm/ [in Hebrew, with selected reports in English].

broad issues such as problems in the absorption of Ethiopian immigrants to Israel (State Comptroller *Annual Report* 2013, 63C), or the representation of women in senior public service posts (State Comptroller *Annual Report* 2014, 64B).

D. The Role of Ombudsman

In 1971, the role of state ombudsman was added to the office of the state comptroller.[9] These tasks were combined in Israel due to the perception that good service is key to sound and efficient public management. Another reason was the desire to take advantage of the stature of the state comptroller to improve public services. Thus, a special unit was created under a state ombudsman director. Who is entitled to complain to the state ombudsman? Anyone directly injured (including prisoners) or representing someone injured, or Knesset members regarding injury done to others. Complaints revolve around actions taken without lawful authority, improper behavior, or inflexibility in the bodies audited by the state comptroller. One may not submit complaints to the state ombudsman against the president, the Knesset or its committees, the government, a judicial act, or a judge.

The reports of the state ombudsmen indicate that their services are in great demand, increasing by a hundred percent over a ten-year period. In 2015, for example, over 15,000 complaints were filed, i.e., some 290 complaints a week. According to these reports, the great majority of the complaints are investigated, and some 30 percent are found to be justified. This is a high percentage compared to other bodies that handle complaints. The institutions cited most often for complaint in 2013 were, in descending order, the National Insurance Institute, Israel Police, Ministry of Justice, Ministry of Finance, Ministry of Transportation and Road Safety, Israel Broadcasting Association, and Ministry of Health.[10] Justified complaints are transferred to the ministries for rectification, and the process is generally conducted without publicity. Occasionally the state ombudsman observes a general pattern of complaint and brings it to public notice. The handling of complaints by the state ombudsman is regarded as relatively effective because it is under the aegis of the state comptroller and complaints are handled discreetly; however, data do not exist about the extent to which problems were actually remedied.

As ombudsman, the state comptroller also has the authority to issue protection orders for whistleblowers who reveal corruption at their workplaces or file complaints against the management. In this way, public servants are empowered to speak out publicly and provided protection if they do.

E. Oversight of the Parties Financing Law

The first financial audit of political parties during an election campaign was conducted upon passage of the Election Law of 1969. With enactment of the Parties Financing Law (1973), the state comptroller was given the authority to financially

[9] On the context for establishing an ombudsman (in Hebrew, a "Commissioner for Complaints from the Public"), see J. Tamir 2002.

[10] State Ombudsman, Reports for 2003–10: Report 30, 15; Report 31, 15; Report 32, 19; Report 33, 26, 31; Report 37, 37, 40 [in Hebrew].

audit parties at the time of elections as well as donations to parties and candidates. The law instructs the state comptroller to submit an annual financial audit of the parties and special reports about spending during campaigns. In a striking expansion of its authority, the state comptroller was also given the power to issue a "not positive" report and impose fines on parties that violate the law. In its report for 2003, for example, the state comptroller reported findings that were not positive about seven parties, and sanctions were imposed on them for not fully recording all income and expenditures.

State comptrollers have not been content with auditing party activities alone; time after time, they have noted loopholes in the law that political parties exploited, such as accepting a large donation from a single source. In a controversial move in 1988, the state comptroller published the names of donors who had made political contributions beyond a specific amount and, in 1992, she added a list of donors who contributed to more than one party. In the Party Financing Report of 2003, the state comptroller cautiously noted the positive effect that close monitoring had had on party financing and that the number of activities in violation of the financing law had sharply dropped.[11]

F. The Authority to Establish State Commissions of Inquiry

An amendment to the State Comptroller Law in 1972 (Article 14B) stipulates that if the audit uncovers serious flaws that suggest a broader problem, or to ensure ethical conduct in office, it is incumbent upon the state comptroller to issue a separate report. On the basis of this report, the Knesset's State Control Committee has the authority – at its own initiative or upon recommendation of the state comptroller – to establish an SCI. Expanding the comptroller's authority to include the power to initiate an SCI was intended for cases in which public pressure is insufficient, or if the members of the State Control Committee believe that government opposition to its creation is driven by improper motives. Initially, this powerful mechanism was used sparingly and, in the first thirty-five years since this amendment was passed, only one commission was established under this article: Following State Comptroller Tunik's report on the manipulation of bank shares (and despite government opposition), the Beisky Commission was established in 1985. This self-restraint ended in 2008, however, when the State Control Committee established no fewer than three SCIs (see below). Since then until 2016, no additional committees have been established.

G. Relations between the State Comptroller and Other Bodies

The state comptroller does not "belong" to any branch of government. By law, the office is accountable to the legislative branch and assists it in carrying out its supervisory tasks, but it enjoys absolute independence, particularly when scrutinizing activities of the executive branch. In this sense, the comptroller is "an independent

[11] State Comptroller, *Report on Audit of Party and Candidates' Accounts during the Election Campaign to the 16th Knesset*, November 2003, 4. See state comptroller website: http://old.mevaker.gov.il/serve/contentTree.asp?bookid=399&id=161&contentid=&parentcid=undefined&sw=1097&hw=547 [in Hebrew] (accessed October 16, 2017).

authority in the framework of the parliament" (M. Tamir 2009, 88–91). The State Control Committee is the primary address for the work of the comptroller, but other permanent Knesset committees also deliberate its reports on subjects relevant to their work. The link between the state comptroller and the legislature is vital because the Knesset's attitude to the comptroller reports is critical for the effectiveness and implementation of its recommendations by the executive branch. For comptrollers to properly discharge their duties, they must avoid being identified with partisan positions in the Knesset or the State Control Committee, or their work will be perceived as biased. To date, comptrollers have almost always been successful in this regard.

Government ministries are obligated to provide the state comptroller with all requested information and documentation. Clearly the comptroller's office cannot examine every action of the audited body and cannot repeat the audit year after year. Hence the audit is in some respects a sample and, above all, a deterrent. A very significant limitation on the comptroller's work is the emphasis on documents and correspondence that do not always reveal processes and informal decision-making. The comptroller's dependence on written material could even foster a culture of not recording decisions in ministries to avoid a potentially incriminating paper trail. Nevertheless, the State Control Committee can summon witnesses to fill in the blanks. For example, following a state comptroller report that dealt with a lack of preparation for immigrant absorption, Prime Minister Yitzhak Shamir was ordered to appear before the committee to present his position.

As for the judiciary, the comptroller oversees the management of the courts, but has no authority to engage in review of the judges or their decisions. It is important to emphasize – the state comptroller does not engage in judicial activity, and therefore audit procedures in Israel and other countries must abide by administrative criteria. Comptrollers who had been judges sometimes use judicial procedures in their audits. The audited bodies have the legal right to respond in writing to the findings of the audit. However, when those who were found to fall short by the audit are given the right to a hearing (with representation by lawyers), the boundaries of proper administrative audit have been crossed, as these audits are not intended to focus on private matters or specific people. When the audit raises suspicion of illegality or criminal activity, the findings are transferred to the attorney general.

H. Who Audits the Auditor?

As the state comptroller's role expanded to include the auditing of policies and decision-making, it became more vulnerable to criticism of having become a partner in policymaking. The core argument against this involvement is that the role of the state comptroller is to audit activity retrospectively and therefore policymaking exceeds the authority of this office. Those responsible for the policies are elected officials and the civil servants appointed to implement them. Indeed, if comptrollers were to be partners in policymaking at any level, they would have to be actively involved in it and bear responsibility for the outcomes. Moreover, someone tasked with auditing does not have the tools to weigh policy alternatives either prior to or during their implementation. State auditors in most countries do not have as broad a mandate as the state comptroller in Israel, as this expanded role would upset the balance among the branches of government in a democratic parliamentary system.

The counter-argument is that the decline of the political-administrative system in Israel necessitates expanding the power of the state comptroller. It is better, they say, to prevent serious problems before they occur and resources are wasted, than to audit the damage *ex post facto*. Furthermore, they point out, it is those audited, not surprisingly, who raise the same criticism about commissions of inquiry and the attorney general. State Comptroller Miriam Ben-Porat observed in real time, for example, that a large number of citizens were not given gas masks or other protective equipment during the first Gulf War (1991), and her public declarations did trigger immediate results. Similarly, the audit about the exorbitant costs of developing the Lavi aircraft also affected the decision to scrap this enterprise (M. Ben-Porat 2005, 9–11, 51–57). In an opposite example, had the state comptroller warned prior to the 2001 election about the prohibition on using non-profit funding to finance political candidates, there may not have been a need for the legal measures that followed.

The High Court of Justice does not hesitate to deliberate aspects of the legality and reasonableness of the comptroller's work, but in practice it almost never interferes in the comptroller's administrative audits. This is also why the High Court is not a court of appeals for comptroller reports or opinions, or for the results of ombudsman investigations (see M. Tamir 2009, 54–57).

One exceptional example, which demonstrates the problem of overstepping the bounds of authority, is the investigation by State Comptroller Ben-Porat of the "Turner–Shahal Affair" in 1992, when Minister of Police Moshe Shahal dismissed Police Commissioner Yaakov Turner. Turner claimed to the State Control Committee that Shahal's reasons were illegitimate, an accusation denied by Shahal. The State Control Committee then asked the state comptroller to examine the circumstances of Turner's dismissal. The comptroller stated that in her considered opinion, Turner's version of events was false. Turner appealed to the High Court of Justice, which – after stressing that the court does not serve as an appellate body for comptroller reports and not denying the comptroller's authority to conduct this kind of investigation – ruled to accept Turner's appeal, stating that the comptroller's conclusions were invalid. Although the reason given by the court was a formal one – that Turner had not been given an opportunity to respond to the evidence examined by the comptroller and therefore the rules of natural justice were violated – the practical meaning of this decision was that the comptroller had deviated from the bounds of her authority (*Turner v. State Comptroller* 1995; see also M. Ben-Porat 2005, 338–44).

Another example illustrates a more cautious definition of the role: State Comptroller Eliezer Goldberg was asked in 2004 to examine the government's decision-making in accepting a deal to return to Israel the civilian Elhanan Tennenbaum and the bodies of three soldiers, all being held by the Hezbollah in Lebanon. The proposed deal evoked criticism because Lebanese prisoners were being exchanged for an Israeli who had been involved in criminal activity. The comptroller noted that, prior to the agreement, security had been breached by giving Tennenbaum confidential military intelligence when negative information about him had not been passed on to the IDF. He therefore called for an audit, and submitted a classified report to the prime minister and the chair of the State Control Committee about "Classifying Positions and Jobs and Examining Security Suitability." As for the original assignment, the comptroller found that the decision-making process in returning the Israeli civilian was not improper (Goldberg 2005).[12]

After more than six decades, the boundaries of authority of the state comptroller are fairly clear, and incursions into other branches of governance can be attributed to the excessive ambition of members of the Knesset's State Control Committee or the comptroller himself. The proper arena for activity by the comptroller is the Knesset and public discourse, and the power of this office derives from the public and political support it earns from its reports and recommendations.

I. Does the State Comptroller Have Clout?

The state comptroller is a monitoring mechanism that contributes to the accountability and transparency of the political and administrative systems. The powers of the state comptroller in Israel are very broad in terms of the types of bodies audited and the scope of the audit, defined as "every matter he sees fit." The fact that the state comptroller has become a powerful player is related to two areas: first, expanding the mandate to allow for an audit of the decision-makers and the decision-making process, including scrutiny of policymaking prior to its implementation; and, second, focusing on the ethical conduct of senior officials, including ministers and prime ministers. Indeed, repeated state comptroller reports about improper political appointments have resonated with the public. The state comptroller report with the greatest political clout is attributed to that written by Ben-Porat after the 1992 election, in which she stated that the findings suggest "the buying of power with money."[13]

The growing stature of the institution of state comptroller is further evidence of the diminished steering capacity of the political system. The ongoing erosion of public trust in government institutions transformed the state comptroller into a warrior for ethical conduct. At the same time, the state comptroller audits have become increasingly legalistic, rather than retaining their fundamentally administrative approach to investigation and scrutiny (Dery 2005). When politics looks like a swampland, it is natural to grasp at the high regard for retired judges, but to conduct an administrative audit, there is only the institution of state comptroller.

Can the state comptroller bite or just bark? The answer is yes, there is a bite, but it generally happens out of view. Every time a senior official in an audited body says to himself or a colleague, "We can't do that – it won't get past the state comptroller," the monitoring mechanism has achieved its goal in the best way possible. This impact, however, cannot be proven, while the flaws in the administrative

[12] A third example relating to the issues of boundaries appears in a publication on the ombudsman website from October 2014, which states that even though the mandate of the ombudsman in some countries, such as Israel, does not include safeguarding human rights, ombudsmen should not only be reactive, but also initiate inquiries into human rights matters. www.mevaker.gov.il/he/publication/Articles/Pages/OmbudsmanPortugal.aspx [in Hebrew] (accessed February 19, 2016).

[13] State Comptroller, *Report on Audit of Party Accounts during the Election Campaign to the 13th Knesset*, 1993, 22. The comptroller had audited the Labor and Shas Parties, and quoted Justice Barak (*Jerzhevski v. Prime Minister Yitzhak Shamir* 1991), who had said with respect to the Likud Party having "bought" the support of the Party for Advancing the Zionist Idea, "Government should not be bought with money. A coalition must not be assembled based on the award of material gain to its members."

and political systems are visibly accumulating and repeating themselves, leaving the impression that the audit is worthless. Another reason the impact of the state comptroller is not fully appreciated is that the public demands authoritative decrees, while the findings of an audit percolate slowly and sometimes need repeating until someone pays attention to them. Because these are administrative changes, they cannot be achieved through enforcement, and many administrative corrections take place far from public notice. Thus, in our view, adding more powers to the state comptroller office is unnecessary, as sanctions must take place in the political-public realm. Furthermore, the tried and true ways to apply sanctions against deviant bodies are available to the Knesset. The State Control Committee of the Knesset, for example, can recommend that a budget allocation to a specific ministry be withheld until the problem cited by the state comptroller is corrected. The Finance Committee of the Knesset also has the authority and means to do this. In parallel, it is crucial that implementation of the recommendations made to the audited bodies be monitored by the state comptroller himself, the State Control Committee, other Knesset committees, or the state Audit Division in the Office of the Prime Minister.

A more robust state comptroller is good news for democracy in Israel. Over the years, this auditing body has emerged to make powerful contributions to public administration and stimulate greater caution about the management of public funds by audited bodies. Its power also has educational and deterrent value, especially in the face of weak oversight mechanisms in the Knesset. The impact of the comptroller's findings, however, is commensurate with the prestige of that office, and the audit's effectiveness depends on its perceived legitimacy by the audited bodies, the Knesset, the government, and the citizens. For the state comptroller to fulfill this function properly and maintain the trust of the public and those audited, the comptroller must remain within the bounds of professional auditing, and not be tempted by the burning issues on the agenda of politicians or the media.

7.3 State Commissions of Inquiry (SCIs)

The frequent use in Israel of SCIs has over time created an institution without parallel in other democracies. Although the statutory basis for establishing commissions of inquiry has its source in Mandatory law and was inspired by British tribunals of inquiry, the commissions of inquiry that evolved in Israel are a unique monitoring mechanism in the Israeli landscape.[14]

While reports by the state comptroller address the Knesset, reports by SCIs address the government. It is the government that establishes an SCI (as noted, the Knesset Committee of Control has such authority) and defines its area of investigation in the letter of appointment; when complete, the written report is presented to the government, which is expected to implement the recommendations. The government does not, however, appoint members of the commission or decide on the methods of investigation. An SCI is a special tool used to uncover facts, conduct

[14] For more on British practices see Klagsbald 2001, 21–23; Lindell 2003; Bradbury 2003; and the Inquiry Act of 2005.

investigations, shape policy, and offer recommendations. SCIs deal with issues or events the government wants to keep them out of or which are unsuitable for the usual investigatory or decision-making bodies: Knesset debates, court hearings, a state comptroller audit, or the ordinary decision-making processes of the government or its ministries (Galnoor 1973).

An SCI is external to the three branches of government. It serves as an emissary of the public and is designed to scrutinize a matter of vital public importance. Its members are appointed by the president of the Supreme Court, which bestows the stature and independence of the judiciary upon it. And yet the state commission of inquiry is not a legal entity, nor is its role to do justice, but rather to examine the unfolding of events when the facts are not clear and the subject is unsuitable for the ordinary legal process. A commission is an ad hoc body appointed for a specific aim and is dismantled upon submission of its report. SCIs serve various purposes – sometimes to placate public opinion and sometimes as an external corrective mechanism on decisions made by the executive branch.

A. The Legal Infrastructure

The Commissions of Inquiry Ordinance (1921) conferred broad powers upon the High Commissioner for Palestine to establish commissions of inquiry, define the subject under investigation, and appoint the commission members. These commissions of inquiry had considerable power – to demand any material, issue search warrants, subpoena witnesses to testify under oath, appoint legal representation for the witnesses, impose penalties for perjury, and deliberate *in camera*, if they so choose. During the period of the British Mandate, nine commissions were established under this ordinance, most to conduct factual investigations: the shortage of apartments in Palestine (1921), the Jaffa riots (1921), the certification of slaughterers and burial matters (1922), wages of unskilled workers (1927), and others. Upon the establishment of Israel, the roles of the High Commissioner were transferred to the prime minister, the Justice Minister, and the Minister of the Interior. During the first two decades (1948–68), eighty-six commissions were established under the 1921 ordinance on a variety of matters, some minor and others important: traffic accidents and disasters, exemptions from military service, the conduct of civil servants and soldiers, consulting on issues of public policy, wage demands, reparations for Holocaust survivors, etc. These commissions were established primarily in response to public outcry or to deal with issues that had no other suitable setting. In keeping with the ordinance, the justice minister bestowed investigatory powers on two parliamentary commissions of inquiry: one concerning the black market (1950) and the other regarding police treatment of detainees in the Jalami camp (1951) (*Knesset Records* 1949–50, 5:2246; *Knesset Records* 1950–51, 10:1841).

The Commissions of Inquiry Law (1968)

This law was enacted in the wake of the political turmoil caused by the Lavon affair. One major stumbling block to clarifying this affair was the question of who should investigate it. Many investigations and committees tried their hand over the years and the issue remained open. The Lavon affair played a key role in the 1961 election and then led to the resignation of Ben-Gurion as prime minister in 1963 when his demand to have an inquest was not met. The storm caused by this affair and the twists and turns of the investigation revealed the need for an inquiry mechanism that would be credible, independent, widely accepted, and had statutory powers.

The law gives legal power to establish a commission of inquiry to the government. In addition, the State Comptroller Law (1958) grants authority to the State Control Committee – when passed by a two-thirds majority of its members – to establish a body with all the powers of an SCI in response to a special comptroller report or "under special circumstances and with the approval of the comptroller" on matters included in the annual report (Article 14). This special authority given to a Knesset committee allows for appointment of an inquiry commission even when the government refuses to establish one or for other reasons. By virtue of this article, the Beisky Commission was appointed in 1985 and another three commissions in 2008/9. By 2015, eighteen SCIs had been appointed, including four by decision of the State Control Committee. In addition, two governmental commissions of inquiry were established under the Government Law (2001) (see below), which were granted the powers of an SCI: the Zeiler Commission on the police handling of organized crime (in 2005) and the Winograd Commission on the second Lebanon War (in 2006).

The law states that the government may establish an SCI to examine "a matter of vital public importance at the time, which requires clarification":

- "a matter of vital public importance" indicates a desire to respond to the concerns and feelings of the public. Although it is the government that decides whether a public need exists, appointment of a commission is clearly a response to public opinion.
- "at the time" means that the matter is of current importance. As noted, the law was passed following the Lavon affair, and this formulation was intended to prevent an investigation of those events from being reopened. Eventually the court ruled that even a past event could become of public importance "at the time" (*Alon v. Government of Israel* 1982).
- "requires clarification" – a core role of the committee is to clarify facts about a subject defined in its letter of appointment prior to submission of its recommendations to the government.

An SCI is composed of three or more members appointed by the president of the Supreme Court. It must be headed by a Supreme Court or District Court judge, practicing or retired, hence its judicial gravitas. It should not, however, be identified as a judicial body or court, because the law stipulates that "A commission of inquiry is not obligated to act in accordance with legal procedures." The commission itself sets the work arrangements and schedule for submitting its report. SCIs have broad powers, and can force witnesses to testify or submit documents or other exhibits. They possess the authority of a court, including the power to detain perjurers or impose fines for refusal to testify. Article 9 of the law grants the commission chair the powers of a civil court – to subpoena witnesses, compel testimony under oath, and force a witness to appear. Article 11 imposes penalties – a fine or detainment – for those who fail to show up to testify, or who do not submit the documents demanded or refuse to testify under oath. An SCI is supposed to issue a formal caution in advance to someone called to testify who might be harmed by the commission's conclusions.

The Agranat Commission interpreted this article narrowly, leading to subsequent claims of harm to witnesses who were not cautioned and therefore had no legal representation at the hearings.[15] As a result, the law was amended (Article 15D) to state that a commission of inquiry must caution anyone who might be harmed by its conclusions and give that person access to the relevant evidence. For example, the Or Commission, which investigated the clashes between security forces and Israeli civilians in October 2000, sent cautionary warnings to fourteen office holders who could be harmed by its conclusions, even though the commission made no recommendations about some of them in its final report.

Commission deliberations are generally public, but it may hold them *in camera* if it believes this necessary to protect state security, foreign relations, a vital economic matter, classified methods of the Israel Police, or the moral reputation or well-being of an individual. The Or Commission conducted open hearings, although the testimonies of several members of the General Security Services (GSS) were given *in camera*. During the hearings, the father of one of the Arab civilians who had been killed in the riots attacked a police officer giving testimony, and thereafter a glass cubicle was erected in the hall to protect witnesses from outbursts by spectators, enabling open hearings despite the risk. The commission is responsible for publishing the report and decides whether it should be published partially or in its entirety. A commission of inquiry report may not be used as evidence in a legal procedure, and the recommendations do not have the legal validity of a court judgment.

B. Defining the Subject of the Inquiry

The subject of the inquiry is defined by the government in its letter of appointment. This definition can narrow the commission's investigation to a specific or partial aspect of the matter of "vital public importance." Although the purpose of a commission of inquiry is to clarify factual matters, narrowing the focus could detract attention from the general context and even the important issue itself. The Kahan Commission, for example, was instructed by the government in its letter of appointment to investigate the events in Sabra and Shatila, not to relate to the broader subject of the first Lebanon War or other important issues such as the decision-making process, relations within the political echelon (between the prime minister and the Defense Minister), or relations between the political and military echelons. Similarly, the commission of inquiry appointed in November 1995 upon the assassination of Prime Minister Yitzhak Rabin was intended *inter alia* to allay public concern, but instructed to focus only on the security measures taken by the GSS. Its recommendations were thus limited, and did not address one of the most troubling issues for the public – the incitement prior to the assassination. In contrast, when the Or Commission was asked to investigate the shooting of thirteen Arab citizens in October 2000, this was defined to cover the events on the ground, the police response, and decision-making at various levels, but the commission broadened its lens, devoting an entire chapter to the social and public roots of the events, including the discrimination, deprivation, and distress of Arab citizens of Israel.

[15] Chief of Staff David Elazar and GOC Southern Command Shmuel Gonen were not legally represented. On this issue see Shetreet 1977; Gavison 1976, 548.

C. Status of the Conclusions and Recommendations

Upon conclusion of its work, a commission of inquiry submits a report to the government with the results of its investigation and, if it so chooses, its recommendations. The law leaves unaddressed the question of adoption of the report by the government or implementation of its conclusions and recommendations. Core to the report is factual clarification, and some argue that this should be the sole function of the inquiry commission, as it would be improper for a temporary body appointed in response to public pressure to make decisions on matters of political or public import (Klagsbald 2001, 328–38). We think that making do with factual clarification could harm the public trust in the investigation and even make superfluous the establishment of a commission. A commission that probed and thoroughly investigated a subject is knowledgeable about it and should not get away without submitting conclusions and recommendations. This should be an inseparable part of its task.

The recommendations of a commission can generally be divided into personal conclusions (did the person responsible act properly, use reasonable judgment) and systemic-institutional conclusions (were there problems in the functioning, definition of authority, division of labor, supervision). The Agranat Commission made recommendations on the institutional level (political-military relations) and on the personal level (with respect to the chief of military intelligence, chief of staff, and GOC Southern Command). The Winograd Commission investigating the second Lebanon War was a governmental commission of inquiry, but viewed itself as belonging to the tradition of the SCIs. It noted in its Interim Report that it

> *has the authority* to point out failures in the conduct of any individual (a public servant or elected official from the political or military echelon), criticize this conduct, and draw conclusions about it. *It even has the authority to make personal recommendations*, such as recommending that a specific person not continue in his position. In general, it is not desirable to replace the discretion of those charged with personal decisions with our own discretion. ("Winograd Commission" 2007, 26 [emphasis in the original])

Nevertheless, SCIs are appointed in exceptional circumstances, when the need arises for a special monitoring mechanism:

> *Caution and respect for such authorities does not mean refraining from personal recommendations when such are necessary. In this matter there is no difference between the political and military-professional echelons,* although there are important differences in the nature of the position, the manner of appointment or election, and the source of authority … *In exceptional and outstanding cases, the commission is authorized, and even obligated, not to make do with drawing conclusions; it must also add explicit personal recommendations to these.* (ibid., 26–27 [emphasis in the original])

Is the government obligated to adopt the recommendations of an SCI in their entirety? One view is that the government must accept the findings, conclusions, and recommendations, because the very decision to appoint a commission and make it responsible for ascertaining the truth obligates the government to accept its authority. According to this perspective, the discretionary power of the government about whether to adopt or reject a commission's recommendations is limited and even subject to judicial review. Others would argue, on the other hand, that the government has no legal obligation to heed the commission's recommendations.

After all, a commission of inquiry is not a court, and its status and the validity of its recommendations are in the public realm. Thus, obligating the government to implement the commission's recommendations would contravene democratic principles, and it would be improper for an appointed commission of inquiry to dictate policy and actions to the government. In other words, the sanctions on the government for rejecting the recommendations of an inquiry commission should be political (through the Knesset and the public) and not legal. One might add that obligating a government to accept the recommendations would deter it from appointing such a commission.[16] The practice is that governments are not obligated to abide by the recommendations of a commission of inquiry, but they do not have the right to ignore them or not consider them (*Ganor v. Attorney General* 1990; *Victims' Families v. Public Security Minister* 2006, 8). The stature of SCIs in Israel is such that a government has never entirely disregarded the direct personal recommendations, which have been put into effect immediately. This is not the case for systemic recommendations. Most commissions were thorough and invested considerable thought in their recommendations for systemic change. Inquiry commissions want to ensure that, at the very least, the same error in the decision-making process will not recur, and a foundation will be laid for improved decision-making in the future. Hence, the systemic recommendations are in principle more critical, because they are important for the continued proper functioning of the political system, while the personal recommendations are more like "putting out brushfires." Dismissing someone based on personal recommendations is easier, though, than the long, hard work of systemic reform. Institutional changes also threaten many vested interests, and therefore encounter resistance to carrying them out, or the inability to do so. The Or Commission report is one example. Its recommendations about those responsible were carried out at once, while the conclusions and recommendations about the root causes of the predicament of Arab citizens were neither covered in the media nor implemented.

D. Why Appoint a Commission of Inquiry?

The reason for appointing an SCI is related to the question of whether the government did so willingly or was forced to appoint one due to outside pressure. Several reasons, sometimes overlapping, apply:

- *To assuage public opinion in Israel and restore public trust in the political system.* The cases are the Agranat Commission, appointed in the wake of the Yom Kippur War (1973), the Kahan Commission to investigate the Sabra and Shatila events (1982), and, to some extent, the Or Commission (2000) to investigate the shooting of Arab citizens in October 2000. Central to these inquiries was the question of the role played by the government and its agencies, while the public demand for an inquiry commission reflected its lack of confidence in the government. In all three cases, the government tried to get out of appointing a commission of inquiry, but relented in the face of public pressure. On the other hand,

[16] For the range of views, see Galnoor 1973; Zamir 1983; Segal 1984; Rubinstein and Medina 1996, 840–41.

the government refused to appoint an SCI after the second Lebanon War, but was forced to establish a governmental commission of inquiry (the Winograd Commission 2007) with the powers of an SCI.

- *To placate public opinion internationally*. The cases are the Zussman Commission, which investigated the circumstances of the fire at the al-Aqsa Mosque (1969), and the Shamgar Commission, which investigated the deliberate killing of worshipers in Hebron's Cave of the Patriarchs (1994). The government appointed these commissions for foreign relations purposes, knowing there was no risk that the conclusions would implicate it, as these were individuals acting alone.
- *To alleviate the sense of helplessness of the political system itself and the public.* When the public mood is that the system itself is at risk, the goal of an SCI is to ensure that the threat can be contained. One example was the Shamgar Commission, appointed by the government three days after the assassination of Yitzhak Rabin (1995). This was the only measure available to the government that could reassure the public that the matter would be investigated and not repeated.
- *To scrutinize administrative arrangements where government ineptness has been apparent.* Thus the Witkon Commission examined the management of the oil fields in the Sinai (1972) after administrative failures became public; the Beisky Commission (1985) investigated the manipulation of bank shares after the fall of the stock exchange – a commission established by the Knesset's State Control Committee despite government opposition. And the Landau Commission (1987) scrutinized the interrogation methods used by the GSS, despite the government's displeasure at inviting recommendations about a subject the defense establishment preferred to keep in the shadows.
- *To examine subjects about which the government falters at setting policy or making decisions.* Such issues could have been dealt with through the normal civil service channels or a prestigious public committee such as a British Royal Commission. Instead, the government preferred to turn them over to a commission of inquiry and thereby delay or shed responsibility for addressing it, such as the Kenet Commission to investigate prison conditions (1971) or the Shoshana Netanyahu Commission to study the health care system (1988), an issue of public importance for which there was no need to clarify the facts or formulate policy alternatives, as the matter had been studied many times before. All that was required was a decision by the political system, which happened when it enacted the National Health Insurance Law in 1994. The commissions set up by the Knesset's State Control Committee in 2008 – to examine the assistance given to Holocaust survivors and the water crisis – also belong to this category. In all the above cases, a distinguished public committee would have sufficed rather than convening the special monitoring mechanism of an SCI.
- *To clarify historical events.* The Bechor Commission (1981) was asked to examine the accusation that Abraham Stavsky and Zvi Rosenblatt were party to the assassination of Chaim Arlosoroff in 1933. This killing had stunned the Yishuv almost fifty years earlier, but what triggered renewed interest and led Prime Minister Begin to demand an investigation was publication of a book by Shabtai Teveth that revived these accusations. A petition to the High Court of Justice sought to prevent the inquiry on the legal grounds that it did not meet

the criterion of being important "at the time" (*Alon v. Government of Israel* 1982). The High Court denied the petition, stating that it would not intervene in a government decision and, besides, there is no justification for preventing an inquiry commission from clarifying an historical matter that has public importance at the time the commission is appointed. This interpretation also allowed for creation in 1995 of a commission to investigate the disappearance in Israel of children of Yemenite immigrants in the 1950s, a matter for which public interest had been aroused in the 1990s. The commission was established despite the government's fear of problematic findings, although the fears were not borne out. In our opinion, an SCI is a monitoring mechanism and not intended for such investigations.

- *To examine subjects under the responsibility of non-governmental organizations regulated by the state.* Events that scandalized the public led to appointment of the Etzioni Commission (1971) to investigate corruption in the football league and the responsibility of the Football Association; the Beisky Commission (1985) investigated the events surrounding the stock market crash; the Zeiler Commission (2001) examined the safety of public buildings.[17] In the latter, public outcry forced the government to establish an SCI even though the matter was also subject to a criminal investigation.

The above list is striking for the number and proportion of commissions that investigated security matters and relations between the military and political echelons – the Agranat, Kahan, Landau, Shamgar 1, Shamgar 2, and Or Commissions, and the Winograd Commission. Increased use of SCIs will ultimately blunt their clout.

E. Appointment of State Commissions of Inquiry and Judicial Review

Governments are not eager to appoint inquiry commissions that may expose their failings. They prefer to conduct internal investigations, rather than submit themselves to a public inquiry by an independent body with judicial stature. One example is the Landau Commission, which investigated the interrogation methods of the GSS after their role in the Bus 300 and Izzat Nafsu affairs had caused a public uproar. These affairs had first been investigated internally, without success at uncovering the truth. The Or Commission was also appointed as a result of public pressure, primarily from Arab citizens, after an internal investigation had already been launched by the government. However, public demand to appoint an inquiry commission has not always met with success when faced with vehement government opposition, particularly when security matters are concerned – to wit, the Bus 300 affair, the Pollard affair, and the Mashal affair.[18] Inquiry Committees were conducted about these three matters, and the conclusions were not made public.

Other known cases when pressure was applied on the government behind the scenes: President Yitzhak Navon threatened to resign if an SCI were not appointed to investigate the Sabra and Shatila events; Attorney General Zamir demanded that

[17] The Zeiler Commission was appointed following the "Versailles Hall disaster" – the collapse of a floor in an events hall, killing twenty-three and injuring 380.

[18] In 1997, an Inquiry Committee (the Ciechanover Committee) was appointed to investigate the attempted assassination in Jordan of Hamas leader Khaled Mashal.

an SCI be appointed about the Bus 300 affair, but he was turned down and then forced to resign. After the second Lebanon War, a movement sprang up in Israel with strong media support demanding an SCI. Although the government withstood the pressure, it was forced into establishing a governmental commission of inquiry to which it gave the powers of an SCI – and appointed a retired judge (Winograd) to head it – thereby maintaining the right to appoint its members. This sparked a public outcry and was even challenged in court (see below), but ultimately the Winograd Commission members conducted the investigation as if it were an SCI in all respects.

The Knesset can play an important role in applying pressure on the government to appoint an SCI (and implement its recommendations), whether by threatening a no-confidence vote or by establishing a parliamentary commission of inquiry. The government can also be circumvented by the Knesset's State Control Committee, which has the power, if passed by two-thirds of its members, to establish a commission of inquiry, as happened with the Beisky Commission (see below).

Judicial Review

Although the government has the authority to establish a commission of inquiry, it is not obligated to do so. Is government discretion on this matter subject to judicial review? So far, the High Court of Justice has denied all petitions calling upon the government to establish or disqualify an SCI, primarily on the grounds that this is within the broad prerogative of the government. Thus, noted the court, it will intervene only "in rare and exceptional cases, the like of which have not, and probably will not, come before the court … furthermore, in cases of vital public importance, even those in need of clarification, it is still within government discretion not to establish a commission of inquiry" (*Ronel v. Government of Israel* 1997). This view led to denial of the petition to disqualify the government's decision to establish a commission of inquiry about the 1933 assassination of Arlosoroff.

Petitions to compel the government to establish commissions of inquiry have also been denied.[19] Following the second Lebanon War, the court refused to intervene in the government's decision not to appoint an SCI, but instead to appoint a governmental commission of inquiry. As in the previous examples, the court did not state that government decisions about establishment of a commission of inquiry are not subject to judicial review, but rather that the review is extremely limited.[20] The majority ruled that there is no cause for intervention because the government is not obligated to establish an SCI, and its decision to appoint a governmental commission of inquiry is reasonable. Nonetheless, the court emphasized that the reasonableness of the government's decision does not necessarily indicate that it was a proper one (*Ometz v. Prime Minister* 2006; *Movement for Quality Government v. Prime Minister* 2006). In the minority view, the government's decision to appoint a governmental commission of inquiry was not reasonable: first, because of the conflict of interest

[19] The Arlosoroff affair: *Alon v. Government of Israel* 1982; the Mashal affair: *Amitai v. the Prime Minister* 1997; the Bar-On affair: *Movement for Quality Government v. Government of Israel* 1997.

[20] "Although the interpretation of Article 8A of the Government Law is deliberated for the first time in this ruling, it constitutes yet another link in the chain of rulings issued by this court based on the principle that the scope of judicial review on whether or not to establish a commission of inquiry to investigate a specific matter, and the character of that investigation, is extremely limited" (*Movement for Quality Government v. Prime Minister* 2007).

in the nominating procedure of this committee – that the government appointed those who would be investigating it and submitting recommendations about ministerial decisions; and, second, because the investigatory method is not suitable for the subject of the inquiry – a governmental inquiry commission is meant to examine specific, limited subjects, not large, complex systems like the events of a war. In our view, the minority opinion breached the bounds of government decision-making, and would also interfere in the fabric of relations between the public and its elected officials. And, ultimately, the report of this governmental commission of inquiry (the Winograd Commission) contributed to the resignation of Prime Minister Olmert and the holding of new elections in 2009.

Between a Commission of Inquiry and a Court of Law

Another question that attests to the potential tension between a commission of inquiry and a judicial proceeding: Can the conclusions of a commission of inquiry replace the verdict of a court? Or do they complement it?[21] Some commissions of inquiry have operated in parallel with a criminal proceeding against defendants who had been involved in the event investigated. The Zussman Commission investigated the circumstances of a fire set at the al-Aqsa Mosque in parallel with a criminal proceeding against the individual accused of arson; the Shamgar Commission investigated the assassination of Prime Minister Rabin in parallel with criminal proceedings against Yigal Amir and some others who abetted the murder; the Zeiler Commission examined the Versailles Hall disaster in parallel with the trial against those accused of responsibility for its collapse. In all these cases, the commissions did not address the question of criminal culpability, but rather investigated general aspects – the security arrangements at the al-Aqsa Mosque, GSS security procedures, the licensing of buildings – hence, the inquiry did not constitute intervention in the legal process.

F. Other Types of Commissions of Inquiry

In addition to parliamentary commissions of inquiry established by the Knesset (see Chapter 4), other types of investigations and inquiries can also serve as monitoring mechanisms.

Governmental Commissions of Inquiry

Under the Government Law (2001), ministers are authorized to establish a governmental commission of inquiry to investigate a subject or event within their realm of responsibility. If a retired judge heads this commission, the minister of justice may, at the request of the appointing minister and with government approval, confer

[21] This matter of principle first arose in 1982 in a petition to the High Court of Justice against appointment of the Bechor Commission to investigate the Arlosoroff assassination on the grounds that a Mandatory court had already issued a ruling on it. The High Court rejected the petition, but acknowledged that a commission of inquiry can be disqualified if its assigned task rightfully belongs to a court, such as ruling on the innocence or guilt of someone suspected of a criminal act. But this should not prevent an inquiry commission from clarifying facts about activities that may subsequently be revealed as criminal. The court also recognized that an inquiry commission may overturn a verdict if new evidence of public import was revealed and a retrial cannot be held (*Alon v. Government of Israel* 1982).

upon this commission the powers of an SCI under the Commissions of Inquiry Law (1968). The commission will submit its report and recommendations to the appointing minister, who then presents this to the government and, at the minister's discretion, to the public.

A governmental commission of inquiry differs from an SCI in two key respects: The government appoints its members, not the Supreme Court president, and decisions about publishing the report remain with the appointing authority, not the commission members. As noted, the question of a conflict of interest – that the body under investigation appoints the investigators – has been addressed by the High Court of Justice (after appointment of the Winograd governmental commission of inquiry), ruling that this is not illegitimate. This method is used in countries with parallel institutions – Britain, Australia, Canada, and New Zealand – on the assumption that once the commission is appointed, it conducts itself independently and impartially. Indeed, the concern that the Winograd Commission would be acting "on behalf of the government" dissipated after publication of the report.

The High Court has not been receptive to petitions submitted about the Winograd Commission, and has expressed unwillingness to intervene in the commission's work. Although the court denied a petition to compel the Winograd Commission to publish the protocol of the testimonies, it made clear – in opposition to the stand taken by the commission – that the commission should publish what can be published even before submission of the final report (*Galon v. Governmental Commission of Inquiry* 2007 [258/07]; *Galon v. Governmental Commission of Inquiry* 2007 [1999/07]).

Inquiry Committees

The purpose of an inquiry committee is to examine matters within the scope of the government and its ministries, and it is generally established in the wake of disasters, failures, and the like. A minister may appoint an inquiry committee to examine a matter for which he or she is responsible, as long as an SCI is not already at work on this matter. A minister also has the power to appoint ministry employees to investigate internal affairs. Thus the inquiry committee is not necessarily a monitoring mechanism, but a different kind of tool, one that is fundamentally internal, as opposed to the inquiry commissions discussed above, which are generally public. The inquiry committee has no formal power to conduct an investigation, although it can be granted such powers. The inquiry committee submits its report to the appointing body – generally a minister – who decides what will be done with the findings – whether or not to accept and implement the recommendations, what to publish, and what to keep classified, based on need or public pressure. Inquiry committees have more than once served as a way for the government or a minister to avoid the risk of having an SCI appointed, and its conclusions made public. Inquiry committees are also established to examine sensitive security matters that the government does not wish to be investigated by a public commission. Some examples:

- In 1987, the Tunik–Zamir Committee was appointed to investigate what would become known as "the Shin-Bet affair" or "Nafsu affair."
- Following the "Pollard affair," the government appointed an inquiry committee in 1987 (chaired by Yehoshua Rotenstreich and Zvi Tsur). The report carried no conclusions concerning the responsibility of the political echelon.

- In 1990, the Ne'eman Committee, appointed to investigate the bloodshed at the Temple Mount, stated, "It is not within the purview [of the committee] to deal with or recommend the drawing of personal conclusions by anyone involved in the events."
- In 1997, the government appointed an inquiry committee following Mossad's unsuccessful attempt to assassinate Hamas leader Khaled Mashal in Jordan (the Ciechanover Committee).

G. Commissions of Inquiry with Implications for Governance

The conclusions of several commissions of inquiry have had long-term implications. In their recommendations, they sought to address not just the immediate issue that had led to their appointment, but also to shape norms, point out necessary changes, and improve the decision-making process. These recommendations affected two partially overlapping circles:

- The small, immediate circle – this pertains to the conduct of individuals in the investigated event (e.g., readiness for the Yom Kippur War, the Sabra and Shatila events, the collapse of the bank shares, the October 2000 clashes). The questions they ask: What did those in positions of responsibility know, what should they have known, and to what extent was their decision-making reasonable? Within this circle, the most significant issue concerns the decision-making of those in elective office – the prime minister and ministers in their realms of responsibility. The conclusions regarding those in authority could be personal – recommendations to dismiss or not dismiss them from office, or no recommendation at all. Naturally the investigation in this circle can expand to include the broader work of the government, the ministry committees, and the ministries involved.
- The second, wider circle – this pertains not to individuals, but to patterns of relations: between the system investigated and the ministries and ministers, or between the event and those responsible in the executive branch (relations between military and political echelons, relations between the private and public sectors in the capital market, police functioning and their subordination to the government). The recommendations generally relate to redefining areas of responsibility and authority, changing the process of inter-institutional policy-making, and instituting other legislative and organizational changes.

Examples of recommendations in these two circles made by several of the major commissions of inquiry follow.

The Agranat Commission

The Agranat Commission was appointed in November 1973 to investigate why the Yom Kippur War came as a surprise to Israel: the intelligence about events in the days leading up to the outbreak of the war and the readiness of the military and civilian authorities; preparation for war by the IDF and its activities until "containment of the enemy." The letter of appointment did not authorize the commission to investigate all aspects of the Yom Kippur War.

In its personal recommendations, the commission distinguished between military and political personnel. Concerning the military, the commission placed direct responsibility on the chief of staff, the chief of military intelligence and three of his officers, and the GOC Southern Command, recommending that they be dismissed from their positions. Concerning the political echelon, the commission distinguished between direct responsibility and parliamentary-ministerial responsibility (on types of responsibility, see Chapter 5). It reviewed the conduct of Prime Minister Golda Meir and Defense Minister Moshe Dayan, and concluded that they did not bear direct personal responsibility because they used reasonable judgment considering the information available to them. Concerning parliamentary responsibility, the commission stated, "The question of the possible resignation of a member of the government in this type of case is fundamentally a political issue, and thus we believe that it is not within our purview" ("Agranat Commission" 1975, 44).

In its institutional recommendations, the commission criticized the constitutional deficiencies, particularly the undefined division of authority between the government, the defense minister, and the chief of staff, recommending that these be clarified by law. It recommended establishment of a Ministerial Committee for Security Affairs and a War Cabinet, and the institution of pluralism in intelligence assessment and data-gathering bodies. In retrospect, the Agranat Commission marked a watershed in the governance contribution of an SCI. Despite scathing criticism of its feeble conclusions about the responsibility of the political echelon, it set a precedent in assuming the authority to examine the *judgment* of public office holders – political, military, and administrative – and to recommend their dismissal. Ever since, commissions of inquiry have unflinchingly reviewed the decisions of those in public office. And yet controversy remains ever since, as to whether SCIs tend not to do justice with the political echelon (Ben Ze'ev 1989, 234–44). The Agranat Commission also contributed to improved decision-making on security matters: enactment of the Basic Law: The Military in 1976 and establishment of the Security Cabinet years later.

A precedent then set was that institutional recommendations would be implemented only partially, while personal recommendations would immediately be carried out. The critical importance of systemic recommendations is evidenced by the fact that commissions of inquiry established after the first and second Lebanon Wars again deliberated issues and omissions that the Agranat Commission had already cited.

The Kahan Commission

The Kahan Commission was appointed in November 1982 to investigate the facts and circumstances surrounding the atrocities perpetrated by Lebanese forces against a civilian population in the Sabra and Shatila refugee camps during the first Lebanon War. Only eight years had elapsed since publication of the Agranat Commission report, and the Kahan Commission found itself again deliberating relations between the political and military echelons. Note that the letter of appointment did not assign the commission the task of investigating the war itself and all its aspects. The Kahan Commission was unique in that it saw fit to deal with public and moral aspects of the subject, and formulated norms of behavior concerning a population in an occupied zone because it is important "from the perspective of Israel's moral fortitude and its functioning as a democratic state that scrupulously maintains the fundamental principles of the civilized world" (on the moral aspect, see Zamir 1983, 328).

Like the Agranat Commission, the Kahan Commission also distinguished between ministerial (parliamentary) responsibility, which is a political matter, and the personal responsibility of those in charge, both political and military. Unlike the Agranat Commission, the Kahan Commission did not leave the question of the parliamentary responsibility of politicians to the court of public opinion. It extended the concept, dividing it into direct and indirect responsibility. Indirect personal responsibility means not having prevented an act whose outcome could have been foreseen even if carried out by a third party. Direct responsibility was borne by those who carried out the massacre – the Christian Phalangists – but the commission stated that indirect personal responsibility was borne by Prime Minister Menachem Begin, Foreign Minister Yitzhak Shamir, the Mossad chief, and Defense Minister Ariel Sharon. For the first three, the commission made do with charging responsibility, but for the defense minister, the Kahan Commission recommended that he draw personal conclusions and resign or be dismissed as defense minister by the prime minister. The commission also recommended that the chief of military intelligence be removed, and it charged Chief of Staff Rafael Eitan with direct responsibility, but did not call for his dismissal as he was about to complete his tenure as chief of staff anyway.

The main contribution of the Kahan Commission to the political culture of Israel is in its assertion that an SCI has the authority not just to examine ministerial decisions, but to recommend the dismissal of elected officials. Indeed, subsequent reports of SCIs reflect this escalation: For the first time in the history of Israel, a senior minister was fired based on the recommendation of a commission of inquiry.

The Beisky Commission

The Beisky Commission was appointed in January 1985 following a decision by the Knesset's State Control Committee to investigate the circumstances surrounding the regulation of bank shares that culminated in the stock market crash of October 1983. The gap of more than a year stemmed from government opposition to establishing an SCI. Although the Beisky Commission assigned personal responsibility to Ministers of Finance Yigael Horowitz and Yoram Aridor as well as the ministry director general at the time of the regulation, the commission did not call for their dismissal, as all three had already resigned. The commission did, however, recommend the dismissal of Bank of Israel Governor Moshe Mandelbaum and five senior bank managers whose banks had manipulated the shares.[22] The commission compiled a long list of institutional recommendations about the Bank of Israel, the Israel Securities Authority, the Tel Aviv Stock Exchange, the banks, and the need to limit the banks' activity in the stock market. While the recommendations were not immediately implemented, they have had considerable influence on changes in the banking system over the years.

The conclusions drew criticism from two directions. Should a political legislative body (the State Control Committee) have the power to establish an SCI? Indeed, the

[22] Several banks and their directors petitioned the High Court of Justice prior to publication of the report, contending that a commission of inquiry appointed by the Knesset's State Control Committee was not authorized to deliberate their bank activity, as banks are not audited by the state comptroller. The petition was denied. See *Bank Leumi et al. v. Commission of Inquiry on Bank Share Regulation* 1985.

safety valve set by law – that a special opinion of the state comptroller is required for the Knesset to establish an SCI – held back the flood tides for many years (until 2008, as noted above). The second issue concerns the commission's personal recommendations about the managers of private companies – is the commission a court that rules on guilt or innocence? But this argument is irrelevant as the conclusions relate to their public activity (in cooperation with state bodies), not to criminal offenses that would be tried in a court.

The contribution of the Beisky Commission is that it established that an SCI has the authority to monitor regulatory activities and, in the case of the bank shares manipulation, even to investigate private companies. Its conclusions affirm the principle that norms in the public sector also apply to those responsible in the private sector. This has had positive repercussions on how banks conduct themselves in Israel, as became evident during the global crisis in late 2008.

The Or Commission

The Or Commission was appointed in November 2000 to investigate the clashes between security forces and Israeli citizens in October 2000 during which fourteen civilians were killed, thirteen of them Arabs. Most of the report elucidates the facts and draws personal conclusions regarding the responsibility of those on the political level as well as the police. The Or Commission recommendations also distinguish between elected and appointed officials. With respect to most of those in elective office at the time of the violence, the commission did not make personal recommendations, particularly since the most senior officials no longer held these positions. Concerning Prime Minister Barak, no recommendations were made; regarding Minister for Internal Security Ben-Ami, the commission recommended that he not serve in this ministry. With respect to Arab public figures, no personal recommendations were made, although MKs Bishara and Dehamshe were found to have fanned the escalation and violence. With respect to the police, the personal recommendations were more concrete: the police commissioner – who had resigned by then – not hold any senior position in the field of internal security; and six officers be dismissed or not promoted.

The Or Commission report was notable for its in-depth examination of relations between Arab citizens of Israel and state institutions on issues such as the status of the Arab minority in Israel, discrimination and deprivation, economic distress, radicalization, and relations with the police. For the first time since Israel had become a state, an official report by an independent commission declared that the problems were systemic, rooted in the attitudes of the state and its institutions toward Arab citizens. And, it noted in conclusion, "While the paramount consideration of the commission was its dedication to uncovering the essential facts of the October events, it has not abandoned hope that its work will also ultimately contribute to warmer relations between Jews and Arabs in Israel" (Or Commission Final Report 2003). Accordingly, the Or Commission report also made policy recommendations for the state authorities regarding Arab citizens.[23]

[23] The government adopted the recommendations of the commission and even established a ministerial committee to implement the report, although in practice it all amounted to virtually nothing (Rekhess 2007a, 15–16, 27).

The Winograd Commission

The second Lebanon War (July–August 2006) ended with a ceasefire and a belief among the Israeli public that the war had been mismanaged. As a result, a public campaign began calling for the resignation of those responsible in the government and army. The government refused to establish an SCI; instead the defense minister appointed a committee headed by former Chief of Staff Amnon Lipkin-Shahak to review the conduct of the IDF. As public pressure grew, however, the government replaced this with a government commission of inquiry on which it conferred the powers of an SCI and appointed independent members.

The Winograd Commission's letter of appointment (September 2006) authorized it to examine the full range of issues related to the war in Lebanon: the conduct of the political echelon, the preparedness and management of the defense establishment, the waging of battle and deployment of troops, the problems that emerged on the home front, etc. The importance of the Winograd Commission is that – unlike previous commissions, which had investigated a specific issue during a war – for the first time a commission was asked to examine all aspects of the war, including the events leading up to it. Indeed, the commission carried out a comprehensive investigation and published an interim report in April 2007 and a final report in January 2008, whose unclassified chapters total 892 pages. As for those who played key roles, the conclusions in the interim report were harsh:

> There were serious failings in the decisions made about going to war and how these decisions were made, and the primary responsibility for these falls on the prime minister, the defense minister, and the outgoing chief of staff. Sharing responsibility for these failings are the government and senior members of the IDF general staff, who did not function as they should have. ("Winograd Commission Report" 2007, 26)

The commission emphasized that it had the authority to make personal recommendations for both political and military personnel, but in the final report it merely presented the findings without personal recommendations, stating that it should be left up to the public and political system (Winograd Commission Report 2008 A, 67–71). This approach had a price: Some members of the public, the media, and politicians interpreted the absence of individual "verdicts" in the report as a declaration of innocence, i.e., that those in charge were not responsible for what had transpired. But in fact, during the writing of the report and following its publication, resignations were tendered by the chief of staff, several senior officers, and the minister of defense. Additional factors played into the resignation of Prime Minister Olmert in July 2008, but his role in the failings of the war, as clearly articulated in the Winograd Commission, and the resulting diminished public support contributed to his decision to resign.

The commission believed that its primary focus should be systemic – not just citing past failures, but trying to prevent future failures, and the report contained a very long list of such recommendations in all the many areas of their mandate.

H. Does a State Commission of Inquiry Have Clout?

Located on the seam of the branches of government, an SCI is a unique mechanism that evolved over the years as a response to the need for independent monitoring in the Israeli political system. Increased demand for its services indicates that the public trusts it and believes it has influence over the political system. It is difficult to provide direct evidence of its impact, however, considering there have been eighteen commissions and a long list of purposes for which they were established.

The first question is whether SCIs were successful at clarifying the facts, drawing a reliable picture of what transpired in the event that had stirred up the public. Most SCIs generally succeeded in this, and thereby contributed both to the public's right to know and to strengthening democratic oversight. Removing the fact-finding and conclusion-drawing functions from the government and its arms, or from organizations such as banks or the Football Association, and giving it to an independent investigatory body helped cope with the crisis of confidence that emerged between the public and the government (Ben-Ze'ev 1989, 236).

The second question is whether the commissions that issued personal recommendations about individuals in public positions improved the decision-making of those who followed, or at least prevented them from making the same mistakes. In this regard, a critically important contribution made by the commissions was to define types of responsibility, and set the bar high for assessing it after the event. Commissions of inquiry in Israel thus helped shape the spheres of ministerial and personal responsibility (direct and indirect) that have no such parallel in other democratic countries (see a more detailed analysis in Chapter 5). It may be the case, however, that this type of categorical monitoring is unnecessary in states with a different political culture that has no need of such reports. Furthermore, although the commissions' personal recommendations were implemented, deterrence may not have been achieved, as the failings of public officers (such as the inability to conduct orderly decision-making) are repeatedly cited in other commissions, as seen above.

The third and decisive question is whether the reports improved the process of policymaking and decision-making. Ultimately, this is the aim of this monitoring mechanism – to help shape the norms of both elected and appointed officials in public administration. Although SCIs investigate a specific issue as defined in the letter of appointment, this issue is often a symptom of a more serious systemic disorder – the absence of suitable legislation, established norms, institutional arrangements, or proper procedures.

Commissions of inquiry that addressed relations between the military and political echelons – Agranat, Kahan, Landau, and Winograd – contributed to structuring these relations and clarifying the realms of responsibility, even though many of their institutional recommendations were not implemented. Commissions that dealt with administrative matters – Witkon (Netivei Neft oil fields), Landau (GSS interrogations), Shamgar (Rabin's assassination), and Zeiler (the Versailles Hall disaster) – focused on the questions they were asked, and did not extend the inquiry to systemic questions or proper norms of public administration. Their contribution therefore was limited to the defined area. On the other hand, the Beisky Commission addressed the broad issue of capital markets, and its recommendations were gradually put on track for implementation. This raises the dilemma cited above with respect to the state comptroller: The more specific the conclusions, the more they gain media attention, but not necessarily impact. Conversely, systemic recommendations seep through slowly, but some have been implemented over the years.

Among the many commissions established so far, seven or eight had an impact on shaping the political culture of Israel. The obvious conclusion is that, despite the contribution of commissions of inquiry and their uniqueness in parliamentary democracies, caution should be exercised about their frequent use to avoid diminishing the impact of this institution. Furthermore, the establishment of commissions of inquiry reflects the growing trend in Israel to judicialize politics, as discussed in Chapter 6. The government gives hard-to-handle subjects to a commission of inquiry, rather than using the normal political and administrative channels. As with other trends toward judicialization (e.g., numerous petitions to the High Court of Justice), the overuse of commissions of inquiry could place the judges who serve in them in the eye of the storm.

Another concern for democratic regimes is that a commission of inquiry could serve as a fig leaf for the government, allowing it to avoid coping with problems that demand commitment to a long-term policy. One glaring example of this is the government's attitude, since 2003, to the Or Commission report concerning discrimination against Arab citizens. Governments view adoption of a commission's personal recommendations as the bottom line and do not bother to implement the systemic recommendations. Furthermore, because SCIs have judicial stature, the failure to make personal recommendations about someone can be interpreted by the public as a verdict of "innocent," even if the commission made note of that person's failings or improper conduct. For example, the harsh conclusions of the commissions of inquiry that were not accompanied by personal recommendations had no effect, *mutatis mutandis*, on the continuation of the political careers of Moshe Dayan, Ariel Sharon, Yitzhak Shamir, Rafael Eitan, and Ehud Barak. In other words, the public does not demand severe political sanctions for such individuals because "they were not found guilty." In this way, the distinction becomes blurred between legal and public norms, criminal activity and improper public activity. In this sense, inquiry commissions dislodge the political issue, replacing it with judicial discourse.

Another argument raised against the recommendations of commissions of inquiry is that they encourage the blaming of lower echelon personnel. While elected officials remain in office and await their fate at the polls, which is not always harsh, the personal recommendations against appointed officials are immediately enforced – dismissals, transfers to other posts, promotions blocked, prohibitions on future public employment, etc. In response, it can be said that the public has the democratic tools to punish elected officials, although it does not always choose to use them.

In conclusion, to safeguard the important mechanism of an SCI and its stature as a functioning institution, several reforms are necessary. First, appointment of such a commission should be made judiciously, and only when the subject under investigation is critically important and cannot be effectively handled by existing institutions such as the courts, the state comptroller, Knesset committees, or administrative bodies. And if an inquiry is required, one should consider whether it can be carried out by other investigatory bodies. Many subjects are more appropriately addressed in professional or public committees created to formulate policy proposals, such as the British Royal Commission, provided that the government deliberates the report and announces what it is adopting and what it is not. We have seen that SCIs have not successfully met this test.

The second reform relates to Knesset involvement. The law does not obligate the government to consult with the Knesset or its committees before appointing an SCI and drafting its letter of appointment. But consulting should be done (as in Britain) if only for the practical reason that systemic recommendations are the most important ones, and legislation is usually needed for their implementation. To that end, the law should be changed to require that a commission report be submitted to the Knesset to deliberate it, to give it political legitimacy, and assign one of its committees the task of monitoring implementation of the systemic recommendations. Furthermore, the role of the Knesset's State Control Committee should be reexamined. The goal should be to prevent the overuse of inquiry commissions for unnecessary purposes, as happened in 2008, when three Knesset-initiated commissions were established – on important subjects – which could have been dealt with differently. It is important to reduce the politicization of appointing a commission of inquiry, which could undermine their status and prestige. Authorization of the State Control Committee to establish an SCI (based on a special report of the state comptroller) should be saved for use as a counterweight in cases when the government, for improper reasons, objects to its establishment. Such commissions should be approved only for subjects "of vital public importance," as required by law, and the approval of the Knesset plenary should be required.

SCIs – a rare and effective monitoring tool used in exceptional circumstances – must not be turned into a routine measure by the government or the State Control Committee for subjects that can be investigated, audited, and clarified by other means. Their misuse for political bashing or other irrelevant purposes could fatally harm the stature of an institution that was earned over many long years. It is easy to belittle recommendations of the state commission of inquiry both in the eyes of the public and the government so that they can be ignored more easily. From passage of the Commissions of Inquiry Law in 1968 until 2014, no fewer than eighteen commissions (including Winograd) were appointed – a commission every two and a half years, on average (none in the years 2009–14). The less frequently this monitoring mechanism is used, the more effective it will remain.

7.4 Monitoring Mechanisms: Advantages and Disadvantages

Relations among the monitoring mechanisms are a mix of a division of labor, cooperation, overlap, and competition. When the Knesset's State Control Committee establishes an SCI on the heels of a report by the state comptroller, this is an example of institutional cooperation. Competition, however, also occurs, even in this field. For example, the state comptroller investigated the home front operations during the second Lebanon War, even though the subject was part of the mandate of the Winograd Commission. The commission chose to ignore this subject in its investigation. The comptroller's professional view may contradict that of the attorney general; or the conclusions of an SCI may not be consistent with the comptroller's findings (on the state comptroller versus the attorney general, see M. Ben-Porat 2005, 138–99, 358–69).[24] Ostensibly, the respective turfs are well defined, but in our opinion the purview of the state comptroller is too broad, as are some of the subjects assigned to SCIs. When the monitoring mechanisms are at loggerheads, the reasonableness of the decisions of all monitoring mechanisms is still subject to judicial review. The comptroller is a permanent institution elected by the Knesset, while an SCI is an ad hoc mechanism appointed by the Supreme Court president on the basis of a government decision, and not subordinate to anyone. The Knesset works cooperatively with the comptroller, but has no connection to government-initiated inquiry commissions.

Supervision and oversight in a democratic regime belongs to the legislative branch. The growth of monitoring mechanisms in Israel reflects both the weakness of the Knesset and the lack of public trust in the political institutions. This is why the scope of the work of the state comptroller, originally the emissary of the Knesset in its supervision and oversight roles, increased so much, and why inquiry commissions have become involved in shaping policy. What ties these phenomena together is the expectation of clear "verdicts" on complicated issues, which day-to-day politics cannot provide. The result is the overall judicialization of the supervision and oversight functions – some administrative (the comptroller), some political-public (inquiry commissions), and some purely judicial (the professional opinion of the attorney general). The expectation that monitoring mechanisms can substitute for political decisions is unrealistic. Nonetheless these institutions have often replaced the regular work of elected bodies, such as parliamentary oversight or public sanctions – normative, not criminal – toward officials who behaved poorly. The politicians contribute to this use of monitoring mechanisms and are then alarmed by their independence. The more that monitoring mechanisms take a stand on moral and value-laden issues, the more their quasi-judicial halo will dissipate as public trust ebbs. Thus, the present power of monitoring mechanisms in Israel is another manifestation of judicialization as a result of weak political processes.

However, entrusting such monitoring mechanisms to independent and impartial professionals (usually jurists), beyond the reach of elected officials, is also a reflection of the robustness of the political system. In the absence of other powerful mechanisms of scrutiny, their work should be welcomed as safeguarding the rule of law and standards of proper administration. Although this means that politics gives up the birthright in favor of legal mechanisms, there seems to be no choice in the reality of Israel. Monitoring mechanisms are vital for safeguarding the rule of law and, in the absence of a political culture to protect them, they participate in creating one. The mechanisms presented in this chapter provide a fairly effective arsenal of supervision and oversight. They work, however, only in times of crisis, and are already showing signs of vulnerability.

[24] For example, a dispute ensued between the state comptroller and the attorney general on public housing. The comptroller held that the government is obliged to use revenues from the sale of public housing to purchase more public housing; the attorney general contended that the government could use the revenues as it sees fit (Letter from the attorney general, *Haaretz*, September 18, 2014).

PART III

POLITICAL SOCIETY

In Part III, we examine the political behavior of citizens and bodies that are not part of the political institutions discussed in Part II. By political behavior, we mean activity designed to influence the steering of the political system or, put more generally, the range of relations between individuals or groups and the state. Political relations are only one sphere of an individual's relations, of course, and even these may be partial, such as a social club for the elderly that also lobbies to prevent laws that could adversely affect them. When examining political behavior, we must keep in mind the existence of political non-participation – citizens who do not vote, are not party members, do not participate in voluntary organizations, and are not consumers of political media. Political participation requires resources – mobility, access, information, a sense of efficacy, etc. (Galnoor 1982, 310). These resources are necessary for a society that is political, i.e., whose members play an *independent* role in the political system – a clear reference, as noted, to a democracy.

Non-democratic regimes make no pretense of political behavior that is not dictated from above, while in democracies, a question arises in each of the following chapters about the meaning of representation in a democracy, and the tension between representation and steering capacity. In Israel, as in some other countries, one more question must be asked: What happens to political behavior when the state and its political institutions have become weak? The chapter subtitles in this part suggest some undercurrents of this question:

- Do changes in the direct political participation of Israeli citizens reflect despair of the political system?
- How has the diminished role of political parties affected the government's steering capacity?
- Did splitting the vote in Knesset elections give rise to sectoral representation that hinders the attainment of common goals?
- Have government coalitions, which had once been the main coordinating mechanism in the political system, now changed from an asset to a burden?
- Involvement in civil society is an important component of democracy – do these organizations undermine or enhance the representation of general interests in society?

- Have the new forms of communication – both mass media and social networking – multiplied the channels or is it only an illusion of political participation?

Israelis are unhappy about the functioning of the political system, and the reforms proposed have, as expected, focused on concrete matters such as a constitution, the electoral system, or the power of the political institutions. A discussion of political behavior shifts the spotlight to the citizens: Has the democratic infrastructure set down in Israel's first years as a state (Part I) been internalized? Is the main problem really the institutional crisis (Part II) or policies about critical issues – to be dealt with in Part IV? The answers to these questions are found, we believe, in both the collective profile of political society in Israel as well as the political status of distinct groups (primarily the ultra-Orthodox, women, immigrants, or Arab Israeli citizens), which we examine separately in the coming chapters.

8 Political Participation: Have Israeli Citizens Given up on the Political System?

8.1 Introduction: Patterns of Political Participation

Political participation is the soul of democracy and critical for its existence. Democracy needs citizens who are involved in political life, who know what they want and are willing to work to achieve it. In the absence of public involvement in decision-making, a democracy lacks legitimacy and its driving force (Dalton 1996, 44). Participation therefore bestows legitimacy on a democracy and reflects the trust of the citizenry that the governing institutions are operating on their behalf, and therefore should be obeyed while efforts are made to influence their decisions (Benhabib 1994).

There are two general approaches to conceptualizing citizenship, each leading to a different conclusion about the scope of democratic participation. One approach assumes that in a representative democracy, citizenship is largely passive. A citizen is one who participates in self-governance; in return, he and his property are entitled to protection and the safeguarding of his rights. To realize this passive citizenship, the citizen must fulfill certain conditions that make him a partner in the political framework: He must be present in the territory (at least at a certain stage), obey the law, pay taxes, and in some countries also serve in the military. These obligations are the basic conditions without which political participation is impossible. According to proponents of representational democracy, as articulated by John Stuart Mill, civic participation is realized primarily by the periodic voting for representatives, and it is the representatives who are responsible for making decisions and crafting policy. In short, the citizens express their will primarily at election time, and they must aspire to choose worthy representatives (Mill 2002; Schumpeter 1944).

The other approach assumes active and committed citizenship, which is more wide-ranging than the obligation of elections and involvement in them. Proponents of participatory democracy stress that in addition to obeying the law, paying taxes, and the like, citizens must raise their voices all the time – even between elections – in order to influence the decisions relevant for their lives. For example, besides participating via representatives and parties, citizens organize in groups and lobbies to have an impact. For this participation to take effect, citizens need reliable information, above all, but also access to the centers of governance and decision-making. These processes must be transparent and decentralized, and decision centers must be as accessible as possible to the citizens.

This latter approach is also espoused by those who advocate deliberative democracy. According to this school of thought, public discourse and how groups make their views known are no less important than the parliamentary frameworks. For them, political participation is an ongoing dialogue in which the positions of individuals and policymakers are shaped through the mutual weighing of arguments. Hence this is a participatory process in which decisions (and compromises) are reached between rational individuals with rights and their elected representatives. The deliberative process gives legitimacy to decisions that are taken publicly with the participation of individuals and groups. A process like this needs many diverse channels to enable citizens to speak out on issues of the day (Elster 1998; see also Gutmann and Thompson 2004). We might add that the transition from public discourse to binding political decisions is not guaranteed, as the social protest movements in Israel and elsewhere sadly learned in 2011.[1]

We advocate the second approach, in which political participation is consistent with an active definition of citizenship. Above all, citizenship means rights, but also responsibility, involvement, and even a burden that the citizen must assume by virtue of membership in the political community. A political community is a body of citizens with mutual trust, in which every citizen is a key political actor; the laws, policies, and decisions that affect them are their top priority (M. Walzer 1989).

A. Definitions

The political participation of citizens is expressed in deeds – "activity aimed at influencing the steering of the political system" (Galnoor 1982, 328). This definition does not include all types of citizen participation (such as economic activity), but is deliberately broad enough to include every activity of citizens aimed at decision-makers – politicians, civil servants, and other office holders – with respect to public issues. The purpose of political participation is to directly impact policies and their implementation, and to indirectly impact the election of people who will formulate those policies (Verba, Lehman-Schlozman, and Brady 1995, 38). Participation seeks to transfer critical information to decision-makers about the needs and preferences of citizens, and also to apply pressure in an effort to influence them. Politics is not the profession of political participants, nor do they receive monetary reward for their activism. Democratic political participation is voluntary and autonomous, carried out at the citizen's initiative, unlike the coerced participation of citizens in undemocratic regimes to vote or demonstrate. "Traditional" democratic political participation includes voting, working on an election campaign, giving financial support to candidates, and other activities such as contacting officials, signing petitions, participating in demonstrations, and joining a labor union. "New" political participation (which has increased in Israel since the 1980s) is reflected in civil society activity (see Chapter 12) and the online media (see Chapter 13). There is a link between "traditional" and "new" political participation: Citizens involved in political activity in "traditional" channels are also more involved in voluntary organizations. Furthermore, the more they are active in voluntary organizations – as volunteers, not

[1] See "Occupy movement," *Wikipedia*, https://en.wikipedia.org/wiki/Occupy_movement (accessed February 20, 2016), and Byrne 2012.

just members or donors – the more likely they are to be political activists (Howard and Gilbert 2008).

Thus, all citizen involvement aimed at decision-makers with respect to public issues is considered political participation, even if its goal is personal and seems to have no public or political dimension. The broader definition is necessary because political participation is diverse and multi-faceted, and the public or political significance of any activity may be hard to discern in advance. Activism that may initially not appear political might turn out to be. Membership in a home-owner's association, for example – which does not meet the narrow definition of political participation – could become political if the association appeals to the authorities about a town plan or works to remove a neighborhood safety hazard.

B. Responsive and Initiated Participation

Later we will distinguish between patterns of political participation based on the degree of initiative and effort involved: To what extent does the activity require the citizen to take initiative? Does participation require a significant investment by the individual (in time, resources, or reputation)? Watching political commercials does not require initiative and the investment is minimal. Organizing a group or participating in its activities, on the other hand, does require initiative and effort. We therefore distinguish between responsive participation with low commitment versus initiated participation. These are not dichotomous, as a citizen may be recruited to participate, but later feel committed, take initiative, and show involvement. This is true with respect to social networks in which it is hard to distinguish between responsive and initiated participation.

Responsive participation is generally controlled by political organizations and imposes a passive role on the citizen. It is characteristic of a democracy in which citizens generally trust the political system, or a situation of political calm lacking critical collective challenges. Responsive participation can reflect strong identification with the state and its political system, or a high level of engagement, not necessarily voluntary. A clear example of responsive participation is voting, which requires minimal initiative, resources, or effort. Initiated participation, on the other hand, testifies to the belief of the activists in their ability to make change. Joining a political party or playing an active role in an election campaign are examples of participation out of a sense of commitment. The distinction between responsive and initiated participation is a kind of mirror image of the extent to which the state is involved in the lives of its citizens. When the state is highly involved, political participation is generally responsive – established and centralized, with activism initiated from the top down. When the state is less involved, but functions as an observer or regulator in many areas of life, political participation tends to be initiated – decentralized, autonomous, and not established, with activism arising from the grassroots.

C. Participation in Israel

The role of the state and its influence on mediating institutions (particularly parties and the media) have undergone dramatic changes in Israel. The above distinction between two patterns of participation allows us to examine the state's reduced involvement and to discern the shift in the focus of political participation from the state to society, with the gradual change in participation patterns from responsive to initiated. This change is reflected primarily in the activity of organizations and groups, the center of gravity moving from mobilized, party-sponsored participation during Israel's first decades to voluntary participation in civil society and social networks.

Research about political participation in Israel conducted through the 1980s reveals the paradoxes of political participation in Israel, the core of which was the discrepancy between the avid interest of well-informed citizens glued to political events and the belief that they were unable to influence them, resulting in low involvement (A. Arian 1973, 23–29). Israelis at the time were primarily "interested observers" (Etzioni-Halevy and Shapiro 1977).[2] The paradox is that a politically well-informed citizen generally believes he can make a difference and tends to be active politically. Another paradox is that the two most salient channels of participation in Israel have been the two extremes of the responsive-initiated axis: a relatively high level of established responsive participation, epitomized by voting behavior, and a low level of political activism in parties or contributions to political organizations. Nevertheless, the profile of political participation changed in the 2000s: Established responsive participation (voting) declined while participation in civil society organizations increased. We will return to these below.

The complex nature of political participation can be seen in the phrase "Friday night living room conversations," an image of political debates and discussions. Although lively "public discourse" should lead to political participation, discussion seems to remain in the living room and not lead to action. In Israel the personal is political, but the political does not necessarily become personal. With the progressive disengagement from politics in Israel, this image may have also faded.

8.2 Factors Influencing Political Participation

Political participation is influenced by the political culture, the status of civil society, the degree of trust in political institutions, the institutional structure (such as the party system, electoral system, referendum options, and direct democracy), and the personal resources of the citizens (such as socioeconomic status and education).[3] We briefly present here factors that have an impact and several comparisons with Israel.

A. Factors Related to the Political Culture

Political culture is part of general culture – this is true for a democracy in which the society and its cultural characteristics can influence political activity. In Chapter 18, political culture will be briefly defined as "specifically political orientations – attitudes

[2] Few scholars took a broad perspective of Israeli political participation with the exception of Asher Arian, whose surveys probed a range of participation channels. Others focused on protest activity, such as Etzioni-Halevy 1975, Wolfsfeld 1988, and Lehman-Wilzig 1992a.

[3] The legal and practical underpinning of civil rights could be added to these factors, but we will not address them here. Some studies also suggest a link between economic change and an interest in politics, which leads to political participation, for example Van Deth and Elff 2004.

toward the political system and its various parts, and attitudes toward the role of the self in the system" (Almond and Verba 1963, 12); and more broadly as "the infrastructure of relations between society and its political system … which enables the transition from interpersonal and intergroup relations to joint, organized, political activity." The sum of all the attitudes and traditions in a specific society creates a totality of characteristics that distinguish one political culture from another. Thus, shared political contents and a language of political activity are shaped over time (Galnoor 1982, 79–109). This dimension of political culture determines the depth of the democratic roots and the degree of faith in the democratic way of life; the willingness to believe in political tools such as negotiation, compromise, and agreements; the character and importance of public discourse; and, perhaps most important, the axioms of political ethics – what must never be done, even if not prohibited by law.

Every country has its own political culture with characteristic patterns of political participation. Forms of participation such as joining a party or voting are more common in countries with a collectivist tradition, while protest activity is more common in countries in which individualism is well rooted. In general, there are "country families" having similar patterns of participation, sometimes near each other geographically, which generally resemble each other politically with regard to areas such as the rule of law, level of corruption, government effectiveness, and indicators of democratic behavior. Heading the "participation scale" in Europe, for example, are the Scandinavian countries (Norway, Denmark, and Sweden), while Mediterranean countries (Portugal, Spain, and Italy) cluster at the bottom (Newton and Giebler 2008).

The political culture that evolved in Israel from the Yishuv period is now about a century old – not as young as often believed. Nevertheless, it is quite evident that it is not fully developed, and suffers from internal conflicts and contradictions. This could be attributed to the structure of an immigrant society, in which a common culture and tolerance for diverse subcultures have not yet been realized. In terms of political participation, a strong foundation does not yet exist to safeguard the rules of the game; in other words, the political culture in Israel does not facilitate the democratic management of some matters, for example strict enforcement of the rule of law. With respect to individual attitudes – trust in politics, particularly trust in politicians, has declined and there is no evidence that Israeli citizens are willing to increase their commitment to political participation.

The following are some general characteristics of Israeli political culture that we believe have an influence on political participation:

- Objectively, every society finds it difficult to translate the range of conflicting desires into consensus and common political action. In Israeli society, some deeply held values are in sharp conflict with others. This manifests itself in the absence of clear-cut mandates in election results and the difficulty encountered by government coalitions in trying to function. In addition, inflated expectations of "the state" and its agencies – as if they could resolve all the disagreements – impose a heavy burden. A striking example of this is the government's inability to resolve issues of territory and borders since 1967, which adds to the lack of trust in democratic tools, further encumbering its functioning, and the cycle repeats. Similarly, aborted attempts to write a constitution reflect the difficulty of creating agreed upon rules of the game.

- In the political culture of Israel, opinion polls reveal a shallow grasp of democracy: While the vast majority of Jews express support for democracy, they would – in the same breath – deny political rights to their opponents (Arab or ultra-Orthodox citizens, ideological foes, or others). In a 2008 survey, 83 percent of the respondents agreed that "Every person should have the same rights regardless of his political views," but only 56 percent felt that Arab citizens should have full equality (Arian et al. 2005–10: 2008, 41). A mechanistic view of democracy encourages the yearning for "a strong leader" who will overcome all problems, and even fosters a desire for shortcuts in the democratic process. From here the distance is short to an equivocal view of the law as the foundation of political behavior and thence to illegalism in society and politics (Sprinzak 1986). Another manifestation is slippery political behavior both internally and externally – circumventing the rules with a sly wink (Sasson 2005). These phenomena make it difficult for citizens to participate in politics – in the belief that they understand the rules and, more importantly, that the rules are accepted by all the other players.
- The Israeli public believes strongly that the political system and its public figures are corrupt (see Chapter 18), and this belief has been reinforced by the many acts of corruption that have come to light. It is reflected in the temporary success of parties that held aloft the banner of fighting corruption, and the unwillingness of young people to choose politics as a career. Business people, academics, and other professionals recoil from politics. In this sense, the question is irrelevant of whether politics is more corrupt than in other democratic countries or whether its high rank on the scale of international corruption is justified. The perception of corruption is enough to create a stench that discourages political participation.[4]

The State and Civil Society (for more on this, see Chapter 12)

The level of political participation and its character stand in a complex relationship with the role of the state in the lives of its citizens. When the state is intricately involved in the life of the individual and closely monitors civil society, the possibility of committed political participation diminishes. State involvement then leads to responsive participation, as the individual is in daily contact with the authorities. When the state changes to a non-involved observer, the horizon of activity – of the individual and civil society – expands, but to some extent moves away from politics or serves to replace government policy. In many countries, we see a waning of state power and narrowing of its role in the wake of several developments: the growing emphasis on the community and the individual; globalization with its social and economic effects; and the dynamics of privatization and technological change, particularly in the media, where the state lost its monopoly. The erosion of the institution of state has been accompanied by alternative forms of organizing, particularly civil society and social media, and more diversified channels of political participation (Waxman and Blander 2002, 22).

[4] In 2014, Israel was ranked low (thirty-seven) out of 175 countries in the Corruption Perception Index of Transparency International.

Changes in civil society since the 1980s are evident in the state's withdrawal from many areas of activity and the concomitant strengthening of economic forces and civil society as autonomous arenas. These changes are visible in the proliferation of non-profit organizations, new spheres of activism, the decline of previous organizations (such as the Jewish Agency and Histadrut), the adoption of militant strategies by protest movements and interest groups, easier (though not always effective) access to decision-makers, online channels, and the struggle for legitimacy of social justice organizations. Despite the burgeoning growth of civil society in Israel, the state is still very present in the lives of its citizens, both because of their expectations and because of mobilization around security matters. As a result, political participation in the framework of civil society has, to some extent, a strong institutional affinity (Yishai 1998; Yishai 2008).

Social Capital

Political participation is also affected by the level of accumulated social capital and connections to social networks, which open channels of activism to the individual. By social capital we mean a pool of resources, skills, advantages, and opportunities drawn from belonging to a community and social connections. Other aspects of the social structure are also part of this pool – values, norms, communication networks, interpersonal trust, and trust in the governing institutions – all vital for the proper functioning of society. Robert Putnam (1993), like Alexis de Tocqueville in the nineteenth century, points to voluntary organizations as the source of social capital. These organizations are a crucible for forging social relationships and boosting political involvement because they facilitate communication between citizens and the authorities, establish patterns of negotiation, and confer trust in the system as a whole. As such, they serve as a "school for democracy." Thus, a rich store of social capital contributes to a high level of political participation, and vice versa. Putnam claims that the diminution of social capital in the United States led to a decline in political participation in voting and participation in voluntary channels. Others claim that political participation has not declined at all, but has only shifted in form (Fischer 2005).

Studies about the effect of various components of social capital have found that voluntarism in civil society organizations promotes political participation. Some of these organizations are direct political actors (interest groups and extra-parliamentary groups) that wish to have an impact on shaping policy. Others (e.g., clubs) are not political actors, but also impact the nature and scope of their members' political participation. In the United States, for example, Protestant churches are known to have an influence on the political views of their worshipers and to motivate them to activism. Civil society organizations also impart civic skills. In schools, workplaces, and community organizations, citizens can acquire experience and skills, such as negotiation skills, that will serve them well in the political sphere (Verba et al. 1995). Those who play an active role in their workplace, labor union, or community organization are better informed, more interested in politics, and more willing to engage politically (Hermann 1996, 103–4). Even the degree of interpersonal trust – an important component of social capital – correlates with a higher level of political participation. Those who are less trustful (such as young people) tend to be less likely to engage politically or to formally join an organization.

Since the 1980s, voluntary organizations have flourished (see Chapter 12). Civil society drew strength from the weakening of the state and the growing tendency of citizens to express their political participation in civic channels. Overall, however, participation in civil society is established and passive, and only a minority is active in protest organizations.

Trust in Political Institutions

Trust is one component of social capital; in a larger context, trust is part of the political culture and has a significant effect on political participation. A high level of trust could lead to responsive participation, while a lack of trust could alienate the citizen from the political system and undermine political participation, or alternatively evoke protest activity in an effort to make the institutions more attentive. In most western countries, public trust in the political leaders and state institutions has eroded. This does not necessarily reflect a decline of trust in democracy, but a decline of trust in the political institutions' monopoly on the functioning of the democracy and their ability to cope with challenges. Since the mid-1990s (when studies of this subject first appeared), public trust in political institutions has declined, although in Israel it remained average or higher compared to other democracies. Table 8.1 shows that in the period examined, trust in the institutions changed little (the IDF and Supreme Court ranked highest, the media and the parties ranked lowest), although trust in all the institutions is on the decline (with the exception of the IDF).

In the wake of dissatisfaction with the functioning of the political institutions, which was magnified because of the second Lebanon War (2006) and revelations of corruption at the highest levels of government, responsive political participation diminished, such as voting in national and local elections, while civil society activism accelerated. Research prior to the 2006 election shows the connection between trust in the institutions and voter turnout: 80 percent of those who reported they would not vote stated they have little or no trust in the Knesset; 93 percent feel similarly about parties. Failing to vote is related to a lack of trust in and alienation from government institutions, particularly elected officials. The public places less trust in institutions that it elected compared with non-elective bodies such as the IDF or the courts (Atmor and Hadar 2008).

B. Institutional Factors

The Basic Laws, structure of the political system, and political rules of the game (such as the electoral system) are all institutional factors that affect opportunities for political participation and shape the formal – and informal – channels of participation. A proportional representation electoral system, a high level of candidate competitiveness, and a simple process of voter registration and ballot casting serve to increase election participation.

Elections

The right to vote and run for office: Historically, the process of political enfranchisement in democratic countries – extending the right to vote – accorded political access to many groups (women, minorities, residents of the periphery). Access is a necessary precondition for a sense of political efficacy and participation (Milbrath

Table 8.1 *Surveys of the degree of public trust in the institutions (%)*

	2000	2005	2010	2014	Average
IDF	79	78	71	82	78
Supreme Court	84	72	54	61	68
Knesset	51	40	37	35	41
Government	55	42	33	38	42
Prime Minister	53	48	39	*	47
Parties	32	22	25	*	26
Media	57	50	34	30	43

* Not asked in 2014.
Sources: Arian and Hermann 2010, 77; Hermann et al. 2011–15: 2014, 61.

and Goel 1977). In Israel, the right of women to vote was recognized since election of the first Assembly of Representatives (1920) in the Yishuv period. The principle of general inclusiveness was established in the first election in Israel (1949), and applies to anyone counted in the first census, Israeli natives, and new immigrants who became citizens by virtue of the Law of Return.

On the other hand, constraints on the right to vote and run for office limit access and could reduce political participation or even trigger a counter-reaction – activism in extra-parliamentary or even illegal bodies. One such example came after passage in 1985 of Article 7A of the Basic Law: The Knesset, which disqualifies any lists or candidates that, *inter alia*, incite to racism. Based on this law, the Kach Party was disqualified in 1988 (*Neiman v. Central Elections Committee*). In reaction, Kach members continued to operate in extra-parliamentary and illegal channels, while racist statements from their political platform found their way into other parties that were successfully elected to the Knesset.

Election processes: Scholars attribute the relatively low voter turnout in American elections compared with other democracies to the system of registration – those with voting rights are not automatically listed on the voting rolls. In most democracies, including Israel, eligibility to vote is conferred by citizenship – a citizen is not obligated to specifically register to vote. Other obstacles to voting might be a complicated method of casting a ballot, binding the voter to one polling place, or the absence of clear instructions to the voter. Voting errors or a high number of disqualified ballots could also deter voters in the following election. One successful example was South Africa's first free, post-apartheid election in April 1994. The participation rate was 91 percent, with fewer than 1 percent of the votes disqualified, even though the great majority were voting for the first time in their lives. This was the result not only of a deep desire to participate, but also of intense political education during the pre-election period (Byrnes 1996).

Voting is compulsory in Australia and Cyprus, which guarantees very high voter turnout (90% and higher), but not necessarily political involvement. Another factor influencing participation is the frequency of elections. In the United States, congressional elections are held every other year, and some countries (like Switzerland) conduct multiple referendums, which could cause burnout among voters: In both countries, the average voter turnout is among the lowest in democratic countries (under 60%). The type of electoral system also affects motivation to participate. A proportional electoral system, in which the number of representatives is commensurate with the number of supporting votes, generally encourages participation, while majoritarian systems – in which many votes that are cast fail to win representation – may reduce the motivation to participate. There is also the factor of direct election, which has become magnified in the age of new media: Voting for a person and not for a party list may increase the motivation to participate, particularly if opinion polls report that the candidates are neck and neck. Voter turnout may also be affected by declaring election day a public holiday, which is the case in Israel, rather than holding it on the weekend, as many European countries do.

The structure of the party system and level of competition and polarization also influence participation. In a system that has been dominated by one party for many years, voter turnout is likely to fall, because support for another party is considered hopeless. In a competitive and polarized campaign, on the other hand, voters feel more incentive to participate out of a sense that every vote counts. While a diverse menu of parties representing an array of positions and world views could increase participation – as more citizens may be able to find a party close to their hearts – there is no proof that this is what actually happens, and Israel is a case in point.

In Israel, conditions exist that should foster voter turnout: broad enfranchisement, an electoral system that emphasizes proportional representation, polarized parties, a high level of competitiveness, simple voter registration procedures, and a public holiday on election day. The diverse menu of parties contributed to high voter turnout for many years, but in 2000 voter turnout dropped. From 1949 to 1999, voter turnout had been 80 percent, but mounting repugnance for politics and frequent elections lowered it to an average of 64 percent: Voter turnout for the 2009 Knesset election was 65 percent, though no fewer than thirty-three party lists competed. In 2015, voter turnout rose to 72 percent, with twenty-six party lists competing – ten of whom were able to pass the election threshold.

Mechanisms of Direct Democracy

Referendums: These allow citizens to participate directly in decision-making on public issues (Butler and Ranney 1994; Blander and Rahat 2000; Arieli-Horowitz 2006). A distinction is usually made between a plebiscite or referendum, both a controlled question posed by the government, and a public initiative, which is derived from citizens' action.[5] Participation in a referendum is responsive, while for a public initiative, citizens make use of a mechanism of direct democracy that requires initiative and the investment of resources.[6] In recent decades, the referendum has come into greater use – around the formation of the European Union, for example. In democracies,

[5] Plebiscites originated in Athenian democracy. In modern times, the term is usually used to describe questions put to the public in totalitarian and authoritarian regimes with the aim of legitimizing government measures. In such polls, the participation rate is usually particularly high and the state's position is ratified.

[6] This kind of public initiative exists in several American states and Switzerland, where 50,000 signatures of citizens within a defined period are sufficient to propose legislation for approval of the public at large.

referendums were used to decide territorial questions, constitutional matters, or controversial moral issues (such as abortion). The primary criticism against referendums is that they could weaken the legitimacy of the elected institutions.

A referendum has never been held in Israel, but calls for one have been heard since the 1990s, primarily in the context of political negotiation that would entail territorial concessions. Prime Minister Rabin announced in 1993 that any peace agreement with Syria would be brought to a referendum, and prime ministers have since repeated this pledge on both the right and left. The tendency to seek solutions via referendum only grew in light of the failing trust in political institutions (the government, Knesset, and parties) and their decisions. It is another expression of the decline of parliamentarism in Israel (Barzilai 2006).

Those who advocate referendums claim that for deeply divisive issues, particularly peace agreements, a referendum will not eliminate the rift, but rather produce a definitive decision with broad public legitimacy (Shetreet 2006a). Opponents believe that a referendum is a populist measure that will further lower the status of the elected institutions. The call for a referendum by elected officials suggests that they have internalized the waning of their legitimacy: Sometimes the prime minister wishes to circumvent the Knesset and appeal directly to the public; sometimes the Knesset tries to hold the government back from instituting some policy and turns to a referendum instead of a no-confidence vote and dissolution of the Knesset; sometimes opposition parties demand a referendum in an effort to undermine the government's "mandate" to make decisions. Furthermore, a majoritarian measure such as a referendum could silence the voice of the Arab minority and distance it even further from decision-making. This concern arises in the context of calls to allow only Jews to vote on a referendum regarding territorial issues or the demand to have a special, "Jewish majority" in order to neutralize the Arab vote (Jamal 2006). In a deeply divided society like Israel, a clear, decisive, and majoritarian mechanism could exacerbate dissent, and its results could cause a crisis of legitimacy (Cohen and Rynhold 2006).

In 1999, an amendment to the Procedures of Government and Justice Law stipulated that legislation of a Basic Law: Referendum was required to allow the holding of a referendum about returning territory. In 2010, another amendment to this law was passed that revokes the need for a Basic Law. This law asserts that the government may not sign any agreement that the law, jurisdiction, and administrative authority of the State of Israel shall no longer apply to a specific geographic area unless that agreement is approved by a (regular) majority of MKs and a referendum. Furthermore, Knesset approval by a majority of eighty MKs would render the referendum unnecessary.[7] The law provides a detailed description of the procedures including the question that will be put to the voter in a referendum: "Are you for or against the agreement between the State of Israel and [names of the other parties] that was approved by the Knesset on [date]?" In 2014, the referendum mechanism was entrenched constitutionally with passage of the Basic Law: Referendum in the Knesset. This Basic Law includes the provisions of the 2010 law, and adds a stability clause, meaning that the law can be changed only by a majority of MKs.

7 Procedures of Government and Justice (Annulment of the Applicability of Law, Jurisdiction, and Administration) Amendment 2010.

Party primaries (also see Chapter 9): In the late 1970s, elements of direct democracy began to appear in political parties in Israel, such as members voting for the party chair; in the early 1990s, primaries were held mainly in the larger parties. Besides the merits of direct participation of party members in choosing the candidates, this also had some negative aspects: Primary elections did not significantly improve the representativeness of the lists, and the system in general only strengthened the link between and mutual dependence of power and money. As a result, a channel of political participation was created that is primarily instrumental. Signing up for membership in a party does not necessarily reflect identification with the party or what it stands for, but is mostly intended to support a particular candidate who recruited the new member for purposes of the primaries. The new recruit who joins a party on election eve is not a member in the full sense of the word – he has not been active in its institutions over time and indeed may not even vote for that party in the Knesset election. In the history of Israeli politics, the number of newly recruited members was sometimes higher than the number of votes the party won in a particular region. A survey of Labor and Likud members in 2007 revealed that only 45 percent had joined the party a decade earlier or more, while 24 percent had joined in the last two years, indicating the lack of stability in party membership (President's Commission 2007, 76).

Direct election of the prime minister (see Chapter 5): Direct elections (1996–2003) reflected a desire to adopt a form of direct democracy and strengthen the link between voters and elected officials, as in presidential systems. In practice, it resulted in a split vote between the candidate for prime minister and a party. Those who became prime minister garnered many more votes than their parties in running for the Knesset (see Table 5.1). In this format, participation was an expression of support for the personality of a particular candidate, almost unrelated to his or her world view, and with a much lower level of commitment to his party or its ideology. Furthermore, direct election did not boost voter turnout, but did undermine the balance of the branches of government and force frequent elections – three in five years. The goal of heightening the citizen's trust in the political system and increasing the likelihood of him voting out of commitment to the candidate was not achieved.

Mediating Institutions

Parties: A democratic system based on universal suffrage and elected representatives operates via mediating institutions – parties, in particular (see Chapter 9 following). The status and power of the parties as a bi-directional unit – mediating between society and politics, and between politics and society – shaped the form and intensity of political participation. The parties and affiliated organizations play an important role in expanding access and motivating citizens to participation and activism. Through parties, citizens could realize their political ambitions, learn who could help them, participate in choosing the leadership, and help shape the political agenda. The decline of parties in western democracies narrowed these options while alternatives – primarily the media and civil society organizations – replaced them.

As a result, the parties, particularly those in western Europe, were transformed. In the early twentieth century, most parties had been distinct political communities based on a loyal, homogeneous constituency and they fulfilled significant social and political functions; by the end of that century, they had become skeletal parties that lacked a clear platform, distinctive social profile, or loyal constituency. Their social functions were replaced by interest groups, and parties chose to focus on their narrow political role – selecting the leaders. As a result, the parties and their voters grew apart (Mair 1998). Since the late 1970s, party membership in Europe has sharply fallen: In Italy, which had been a country with exceptionally high party identification, the ratio of membership to total electorate is a third what it had been thirty years earlier (Scarrow 2000; Mair and Van Biezen 2001, 15–16). The change in Israel, which had also been a country of strong party identification, is even more extreme: Parties are no longer the main channel of participation for citizens, leaving a vacuum in the political system that other channels are hard pressed to fill.

The media: In the twentieth century, the mediating role of the parties was inherited – or purportedly inherited – by the media, primarily television (see Chapter 13). Unlike parties, which are capable of bringing together and representing people with diverse interests, forming coalitions, and contributing to political stability, media as a mediating channel do not have these capabilities. Their strength lies in the public attention they receive and their ability to quickly disseminate a large amount of information. The media are not fundamentally representative channels, and their public is a "mass" comprising individuals who are directly informed by the messages transmitted to them, generally from establishment sources: government authorities, commercial firms, or the media corporations themselves. This communication creates the illusion of breaking down the walls – users can "see" politics, the leaders, and office holders "up close," and feel themselves part of the activity. In reality, however, they are spectators who are the recipients of carefully crafted messages, and their participation is virtual. Democracy via TV has become a quasi-democracy, and despite its huge latent potential, the direction of information flow is still one-way – from the leaders to the masses (Galnoor 1998). This is not to ignore the important service that the electronic media perform: transparency, information transmission, stimulating involvement, placing issues on the public agenda, and allowing citizens to address public office holders.

Online media: The above picture was entirely changed with the emergence of ICT (information and communication technologies) and the widespread use of the Internet in electronic channels and social networks. A new arena rapidly evolved for political participation together with new patterns of "public activism." The channel itself is virtual, does not require face-to-face or actual activity, and is increasingly a source of deep social involvement and even active political participation and mobilization. The Internet has penetrated some 46 percent of the global population, with 74 percent penetration in Europe and 88 percent in North America (Internet World Stats 2015).

The uniqueness of online communication in influencing patterns of political participation rests in its being a channel that is interactive, dynamic, horizontal (among surfers), and bi-directional (between political organizations and surfers). The interactivity of the Internet can strengthen social and political relationships and expand the exchange of views and opinions. It contains the potential to develop into channels that will strengthen the deliberative dimension of the democratic political culture. In contrast with the traditional mass media, such as television and print journalism, in which the citizen is a passive consumer, the citizen is an active user of the Internet who can transmit and receive messages from all directions. The citizen-surfer does not merely acquire political information that enhances her participation, but also allows her to express her views instantly on a range of issues. Internet networks have the potential to become a modern *agora*, a political space in which citizens exchange views and influence each other (Lehman-Wilzig 2004). In Chapter 13 we present the online channels that are open to the citizen for political activism.

Although these new channels are just starting out in terms of honing their potential political clout, it is already clear that they are entirely different; comparison with the old channels would be anachronistic. Although the social networks may completely change the character of political participation and oust the traditional channels of participation, a creative merger could ensue, though this may be an illusion. The successful election campaign of Barack Obama for the American presidency in 2009 – in which far-reaching use was made of the Internet to raise funds, mobilize members of social networks, activate supporters, and spread videos and text messages on interactive websites – suggests the potential of this tool for political participation. This also holds true for using the Internet to recruit citizens for mass demonstrations in non-democratic regimes, as happened in 2011 in several Arab countries ("the Arab Spring").

In Israel, a revolution has not yet taken place in the use of online channels for political participation. Political organizations and individuals are still not exploiting the profound potential of the new technology to augment the deliberative arena and transform political culture. So far they have been used primarily to reproduce the existing patterns of participation and make them cheaper and more accessible. In the social protest in the summer of 2011, the first attempts were made to exploit the potential of online communication, and these buds may yet flower. In any event, the decline in participation opens the door to parties who see ICT as an opportunity to recruit and mobilize activists, and to convert commitment into involvement for citizens who had not previously participated in politics.

Laws that Obligate Citizen Involvement in Decision-Making

Recognition of the importance of political participation has prompted the enactment of laws designed to keep citizens informed about events in the political system and to provide opportunities to influence decision-making. The Freedom of Information Law, which recognizes the public's right to know – adopted in most democratic countries (and in Israel in 1998) – is a prime example of a fundamental change of approach from periods when the government had a monopoly on public information (Galnoor 1977; Menuchin 2003). Some laws require inclusion in the decision-making. Planning and building laws, for example, state that the authorities must inform the public about town plans, and interested parties have the right to appeal the decisions of planning and building committees. Opposition to town or national plans has triggered vigorous activism, reflected not just in the submission of formal appeals, but also in protest demonstrations and petitions to the court.

C. Individual Factors

Political Awareness

One factor motivating participation is political knowledge and understanding the rules of the political game. We have no way to measure the "political IQ" of a particular society, but any index would surely point to a bi-directional link between political awareness and political participation. Taking an interest in politics and an in-depth knowledge of events are a precondition and even motivator of political participation: the more the citizen participates, the more his political knowledge grows. Israeli citizens are knowledgeable about and take a daily interest in politics – indeed, an appetite for politics has characterized Israeli society for many years because of the critical role it plays in the life of the citizen. In a 2003 survey, 76 percent of the respondents said they take some or a great interest in politics; 87 percent said they update themselves daily; many added that they often converse with their family or friends about political matters. The proportion of those taking an interest in politics dropped to 62 percent in 2010, while those who update daily fell to 76 percent. These figures are high, but the Israeli citizen's knowledge of politics could also lead to disengagement from it out of repugnance at that knowledge. In parallel, interest has dropped among young people (Arian and Hermann 2010, 62–63). The lack of interest in politics could lead to avoidance of political participation. In a survey on the eve of the 2006 election, for example, 56 percent of those who said they would not vote declared they have little or no interest in politics at all (Atmor and Hadar 2008).

The paradox, as in other countries, is that Israelis head the list in terms of interest in politics and conversing with their friends and family about political subjects, but are at the bottom in terms of political participation from a sense of commitment. In other words, despite the avid interest and involvement of Israeli citizens in politics, they tend not to participate in actual political activity. Based on self-reporting, only 6 percent (in 2003) reported that they were members of a political party; 16 percent said they belonged to an organization or non-profit and were involved in public activity; while 37 percent (in 2008) said that they had volunteered at some point in a social organization (Arian et al. 2003a, 135–42; Arian et al. 2005–10: 2008, 87).

A Sense of Efficacy

Another paradox concerns the high level of (passive) political involvement among Israelis and their sense of inefficacy. It is commonly thought that subjective feelings of efficacy correlate with participation levels; indeed, reason tells us that someone who does not believe in his ability to make change would not be motivated to participate, and that the perception of efficacy, even if not realistic, fosters participation. Yet studies of the sense of efficacy among Israelis found that they generally do *not* believe in their ability to have an impact. The average sense of efficacy between 1973 and 2003 was 34 percent, but this has fallen steadily in the surveys, and only a fifth of Israeli respondents during this period believed that they and their friends can affect government policies to some or a great extent. Although these findings are consistent with the sense of efficacy prevalent in other democracies, political interest and voting turnout are both lower there than in Israel (Arian et al. 2005–10: 2008, 35; Arian et al. 2005–10: 2010, 64). Surveys also show fluctuation in the citizen's sense of efficacy, which apparently alters with changing political events and moods. Nonetheless, despite the many political vicissitudes – the dramatic changes in the ruling party, the political stalemate in the 1980s, the decline of the parties, changes in the electoral system, the signs of direct democracy – only a minority of Israelis consistently believe that citizens are capable of having an impact. Moreover, the higher the Israeli on the socioeconomic scale, the less likely he is to believe that he can make a difference. Like interest in politics, the sense of inefficacy is closely related to voting patterns. Some 90 percent of those who said they would not vote believed that they and their friends can have no impact on government policy, and 70 percent believed that MKs do not care what the public thinks (Atmor and Hadar 2008).

The combination of being well informed politically and a sense of inefficacy is also manifested in the telling of political jokes. While these jokes give some relief for political cynicism and a feeling of inefficacy, they are also a reflection of involvement, interest, and political knowledge. Though political jokes are passive "participation," familiar from totalitarian regimes, their relative frequency in Israel suggests the gap between intense political involvement and waning hope about making a difference.

Demographic Variables

Education and socioeconomic status: Political participation requires resources such as leisure time, money, reputation, social networks, and political skill. There is a positive correlation between civic involvement and levels of education and income: The higher the education and income, the greater the likelihood of participation (Verba et al. 1995, 522–26). Indeed, the more educated an individual, the more likely that he will be aware of the effect of politics on his life, hence the more likely he will participate, particularly since his education may instill in him self-confidence (Hermann 1996, 114).

The link between socioeconomic status and political participation is also reflected in differences between the center and periphery, with citizens in the periphery characterized by a lower socioeconomic level and less political participation. The relationship between socioeconomic status and participation can be explained not just in terms of disparities in the resources required, but also socialization processes that instill a more secure sense of citizenship among those well to do. Conversely, frustration and distrust of the political system undermine the motivation to participate among the disadvantaged.

A direct relationship exists in Israel between political participation and, on the other hand, levels of education and income. The lower the education and income, the lower the participation. A higher proportion of non-voters have little education or income. Since lower education and socioeconomic status overlap with ethnic origin, Israelis of Asian or north African origin tend to vote less than those of European or American origin, who have a higher proportion of well to do and well educated. In addition to the link between participation and levels of education/income, there is another troubling trend: Some 70 percent of those who said they do not intend to vote in the 2006 election reported that they belong to the middle class (Atmor and Hadar 2008). Education and income also affect the channels of participation: Those with higher education and income are more likely to engage in protest activity (Lehman-Wilzig 1992a, 88). Party membership, on the other hand, is a relatively egalitarian channel, as it does not directly correlate with education (Wolfsfeld 1988,

64). Activism in non-profits and the tendency to volunteer and contribute are also related to income: Among those who earn more than the average wage, voluntarism and contributing are more common than among those with lower income (Katz, Levinson, and Gidron 2007).

Gender: Despite the expectation that women and men participate "in a different voice," studies in the United States and Europe indicate that gender differences in political participation are negligible (Inglehart and Norris 2003). In general, women participate less than men, but the gap is small and can be explained by differences in resources: leisure time, income, and education (Verba et al. 1995, 251–63, 265–66). In Israel, too, women are less involved in politics and tend to participate less. While more women prefer non-establishment channels such as protest activity, they were under-represented even among protest activists (Wolfsfeld 1988, 45, 67). The profile of politically active women is different in Israel than in other democracies, where participants were younger, educated, and had more income. Women participants in Israel are older, married, and have a lower income. In other words, the more educated and/or well to do the woman, the more likely to avoid political participation (Yishai 1997). On the other hand, women in political office – MKs, mayors, city council members – are generally better educated, well off financially, and Ashkenazi (Herzog 1999, 112–32). In the 2000s, the gender gap began to change in Israel on voting behavior – not with respect to voter turnout, but in views (more hawkish) and preference for parties (social justice issues). Three women headed parties in the 2013 election – Shelly Yachimovich, Tzipi Livni, and Zehava Galon – and this affected the voting of women.[8]

Age: In most democracies, citizens under the age of eighteen do not have the right to vote for parliament. Young people generally have little interest in politics. If young people do participate, particularly university students, they tend to choose protest channels (Hermann 1996, 116–19). Until a certain age, the life cycle sets the rules: Interest and involvement increase for citizens who have established themselves at work, have families, are property owners, and carry a tax burden. Political participation peaks among forty- to fifty-year-olds. In Israel, as in other democracies, the political involvement of young adults resembles or is slightly lower than that of the general population. We pointed out the drop in voter turnout among young people. In a 2006 survey, almost half the respondents who planned to skip voting were thirty-five years old or younger (Atmor and Hadar 2008). In Israel, too, the young are over-represented in protest activities, but no "student revolution" ever took place, and political activity in the past has been establishment and strongly linked to a political party (Wolfsfeld 1988, 46, 66).

Religiosity: In a 1980s survey, religiously observant Israelis were found to take less of an interest in politics, although their political activism resembled that of other citizens and was carried out primarily in the framework of religious parties (Wolfsfeld 1988, 46, 48). Later, this radically changed: The Israeli settlements in the occupied territories became a focus of identity and political activity for most religiously

[8] Conference on "The Gender Gap in Voting Patterns in Israel," Center for Advancement of Women in the Public Sphere, Van Leer Jerusalem Institute, October 23, 2014. For a comparison with previous elections, see S. Shamir 2009.

observant Israelis, particularly those in the national-religious camp, but also for a significant number who voted for Shas and ultra-Orthodox parties. Settlers and their supporters became highly influential in Israeli politics, both as an organization making inroads in government agencies and as a vocal and effective protest group in the political discourse – in response to the Oslo Accords, for example. By contrast, secular Israelis have become increasingly disengaged from politics. Of those who declared they would not vote in 2006, 54 percent defined themselves as secular – higher than the proportion of seculars who reported they would vote in the election (Atmor and Hadar 2008).

Values: An individual's value system plays a critical role in her willingness to participate politically. In Inglehart's comparative research (1989), he found that respondents with "post-material" values (non-economic concerns such as environmental protection, gender equality, gay rights) were willing to play a greater role and to engage more in protest activity than materialistic respondents. Differences in values also largely reflect class differences. Ideological identification raises a citizen's interest in politics, and encourages him to identify with a party and participate. This is also true for a secular world view or identifying with democratic values that foster political participation. Internalizing democratic values encourages citizens to be more assertive, critical, and involved (Inglehart 1999).

The conditions seem right in Israel – the standard of living and level of education – for the flourishing of post-material values. Studies in the mid-1990s found that concerns about environmental protection and gender equality were just beginning to emerge (Yishai 1999). Changes in the value preferences of Israelis can be seen in several channels of civic activism: the proliferation of feminist, environmental, and LGBT organizations; petitions to the High Court on social justice cases; and environmental activism. The relative success of the "green" parties in local authorities was also a harbinger of change. Support for post-material values is just emerging, however, and inroads into national politics are still being sought, as took place with the social change protest in the summer of 2011.

Many factors affect a citizen's willingness to take part in political activity, but the issue of political participation is still puzzling, especially if examined through a rational lens of cost-benefit. It is hard to explain political participation solely through the "rational player" theory, which assumes that an individual's choice reflects preferences and intent to achieve a return based on beliefs and cognitions about the activity. A rational player operating according to cost-benefit considerations would predict no political participation, since there are many forms of political participation – especially voting – in which the rational actor can "hitch a ride" on other people's participation. The correct assumption would be that the benefit from personal participation is negligible. Studies by Verba et al. conclude that it is hard to explain political participation in narrow terms of self-interest, as people have a range of motivations. Nevertheless, the factors that predict a citizen's participation are the resources at his disposal (education, income, time, and civic skills) and the costs of this participation. As to motivation, many claim that they participate primarily to discharge their civic duties, which reinforces the contention that political participation is altruistic (Verba et al. 2000). Indeed, even though various channels have little impact, political participation may still be high because it is done for its own sake – making an anonymous donation to a party or standing on a street corner holding a sign.

8.3 Changing Routes of Political Participation

In the first two decades of Israel's existence, participation was primarily mobilized and responsive. This suited the political system at the time, which was well organized and centralized, with participation almost exclusively through political parties. The political system and central government, dominated by the labor movement, did not encourage separate or autonomous political activism away from the watchful eye of the political center. Protest activity during this period – the demonstrations in the 1950s of the jobless in the transit camps, the seamen's strike in 1951, or the Wadi Salib events in 1959[9] – met with a forceful government response. Most participation was responsive, with high voter turnout for elections, reflecting both deep identification with the new state and trust in the institutions, as well as well-honed political machinery under the control of the Mapai Party. There was also considerable voluntarism in the party's social organizations, whether out of choice or compulsion. Participation was marked by a sense of unity among the small Jewish community (two million in 1965) and shared contents symbolized by the political system.

In the second period of the state, from the 1970s, the first buds appeared of an autonomous civil society in which civic participation was born of a sense of commitment. The wildcat strikes against the government and the Histadrut during the economic crisis of the mid-1960s had been followed by increased protest activity. The estrangement of politics from society and its citizens, inchoate until then, became clearer following the trauma of the Yom Kippur War and the first Lebanon War. Dissatisfaction with the political leadership intensified during this period, manifested as a desire to "change the system," i.e., the political system and the party map. The feeling deepened that there were no opportunities for real participation or impact, while at the same time interest in politics grew, leading to the founding of new parties such as Ratz, Shinui, and Shas, as well as extra-parliamentary movements.

The third period, from the mid-1980s, was characterized primarily by the decline of parties as the main mediation channel in the political system, deepening political instability, the rising power of commercial interests, and the growth of civil society – organizations, groups, and movements. In the 2000s, most avenues of participation (with the exception of voting, lobbying, and judicial channels) required initiative and commitment. The general level of participation did not rise, but changed its form – a citizen with a desire to participate had to be active and committed, unlike the responsive participation of the past when voluntarism, though authentic, had mostly been mobilized from above.

Table 8.2 compares participation patterns in Israel and several European countries. In general, the form of responsive participation that requires the least effort – voting – is the most common; while least common is the conventional form of political activism – working for or donating to a party or political organization.

[9] Demonstrations against economic inequities that broke out in July 1959 in the low-income Wadi Salib neighborhood of Haifa, whose residents were primarily north African immigrants.

Table 8.2 *Rate of participation by channel – Israel compared with Europe 2010–2012 (%)*

	Channel of participation	European average	Israeli average
Political participation in conventional channels	Voting	76	78
	Political discussion	66*	75*
	Political interest	43	51
	Contact with politicians	12	11
Political participation in an election campaign	Distributing election material	7	4
	Donating	6*	12*
	Working for a party or political organization	4	2
Participation in protest activity	Petition signing	19	13
	Acquisition of a product for moral reasons	24*	18*
	Boycott of a product	16	22
	Demonstrating legally	7	11
Participation in civil society**	Average participation in voluntary organizations	24	26

* Newton and Giebler 2008 (based on the European Social Survey 2002–3).
** Percent of the population who volunteer at least once every six months.
Source: European Social Survey 2010 and 2012.

The frequency of protest activity such as signing a petition or going to a demonstration is also related to the effort required. Thus, responsive activity like signing a petition is much more frequent than participating in a demonstration. A comparison of twenty-two countries, including Israel, found that the level of political participation in Israel is lower than in northern European countries, but higher than countries in eastern Europe or the Mediterranean basin. Note that political participation in Israel is average or higher in traditional channels such as voting and also higher in two types of protest activity – legal demonstrations and consumer-related protests (e.g., boycott of a product) (Newton and Giebler 2008). The analysis below considers responsive and initiated participation separately, each having different levels of initiative and dedication.

A. Responsive Participation

Voting (see discussion on elections in Chapter 10)

Free elections are a necessary condition for democracy; without representation, it is doubtful that other forms of participation are truly possible. Through elections, citizens wield considerable influence – they are able to convey information about their preferences and replace the leadership. The information transmitted in an election is general, however, and voting is responsive – a form of participation that requires little individual initiative. Until the 2000s, the average voter turnout in Israeli general elections was 80 percent. Since then, it has fallen sharply to 67 percent, which removed Israel from the roster of countries with high voter turnout. The voter turnout for local elections has also dipped. Ever since the 1978 change in the electoral system, which separated local and Knesset elections, local turnout has been 56 percent on average. Until the 1980s Histadrut elections were also an important channel of political participation as a large proportion of Israclis were Histadrut members. In the period 1949–65, some 80 percent voted in the Histadrut elections, but since then voter turnout has dropped, even compared to the fall-off in voting for the Knesset; by the 1990s, Histadrut membership declined as did the proportion of members who exercise their right to vote in that election, leaving about one-third of the members making election decisions. This is further evidence of the general decline in establishment participation.

Until the 2000s, when national elections recurred with some frequency, voter turnout was high and stable. This stability prevailed when the political system was dominated by one party; during elections that expelled the party in power – in 1977, 1992, 1996, and 1999; and for the electoral ties of 1984 and 1988. Israelis voted during war and peace, before and after waves of immigration, and during direct election of the prime minister in the 1990s. This began to change in the 2000s. The election held to elect only a prime minister in 2001 was boycotted by most Arab voters following the events of October 2000 (see Chapter 15), but this low voter turnout was a harbinger of things to come. In the 2003 Knesset election, in which the parliamentary system was restored, voter turnout was just 68 percent and this trend continued – unlike the voter turnout in other democracies, Israel ranked twenty out of thirty-two countries in 2006 (Arian et al. 2005–10: 2006).[10] The main reason for the change was the deepening alienation between citizens and their political leaders, who were regarded as self-serving and corrupt.

Voting is a channel for responsive participation, but Israeli voters take full advantage of their ballot. First, the vote is split among many parties. Second, individual voters will also split their vote when given the opportunity to cast two ballots. This option first appeared in local elections: A vote for a specific individual for mayor did not necessarily entail voting for that person's party for the town council. During the time of direct election of the prime minister (1996 and 1999), a high percentage of voters, well beyond the expected, split their support between the prime ministerial candidate and his or her party. In the 1996 Knesset election, the Likud won only 25 percent of the valid votes (thirty-two seats) compared with twice as many garnered by Netanyahu who was elected prime minister; the gap in 1999 was even larger, when Labor won 20 percent of the valid votes (twenty-six seats), while Barak won 2.7 times that number in running for prime minister. As noted, the Israeli is a sophisticated voter, and creatively makes use of a relatively passive channel such as elections to make clear his views and preferences.

When voting was considered a paramount civic obligation, few abstained, hence refusal to vote or an organized boycott of elections was a clear expression of protest. Even during the Yishuv period, various groups boycotted the elections, but casting a "white ballot" as protest became more prevalent only recently. Unmarked ballots are invalid votes, and there is no way of knowing how many of these are an expression of protest by voters who made a point of going to the polls to file their protest, or ballots declared invalid for other reasons. Nevertheless, the proportion of invalid

[10] If voter turnout is calculated as a ratio of the adult population, Israel moves up in rank slightly, and falls into the upper third of voter turnout.

votes grew significantly in the direct elections of 1996 and 1999 to some 2 percent of the ballots for the Knesset and 5 percent of the ballots for prime minister. Some were invalid because of the confusion among voters about the new system of voting, while others were a protest vote by Arab citizens (Jamal 2002, 89). The Arab public boycotted the special election for prime minister in 2001 in protest of the October 2000 events, with only 18 percent of them voting.

In the 2009 election, the proportion of invalid ballots in all the ballot boxes returned to its previous average of about 1 percent. What stands out about the 2000s is that the interest of citizens in politics did not translate into voting, as it had in the past: A third of eligible voters for the Knesset and half of eligible voters for the local election did not bother showing up to vote.

Approaching Public Officials

This channel of political participation – citizens appealing directly to public officials about personal matters – was common in Israel until the 1970s, as it conformed to the political culture. Both private citizens and those in power preferred this system because it is discreet, does not create a precedent, and allows for the conveying of information without applying pressure. A politician or bureaucrat generally prefers private appeals rather than universal criteria because personal contact enhances the power of those in office and allows them to use their status selectively. The system is also convenient for the citizen because she takes the initiative and sets the timing and pressure required to achieve results (Galnoor 1982, 336). This is essentially a form of responsive participation because it comes in reaction to an act or failure to act by a government authority. It shows little autonomy and the initiative or effort required of the citizen is minimal (though interaction with bureaucratic authorities can be exhausting). This form of participation is not carried out on a regular basis, the motivation is usually personal, and it does not entail a clash of views or a need to involve others.

The purpose of the appeal: Personal or public? Approaching an official on a public matter is intended to convey information, express dissatisfaction about a matter of more general interest, or demand relief, such as changing a regulation or eliminating a public nuisance. It belongs to the category of initiated participation, because it constitutes public "organizing" of an individual or group, and indicates political involvement and awareness of the rules of the democratic game. Approaching an official for a private matter is usually in the realm of complaints and reflects a social skill – a demand to actualize rights. On the other hand, appealing to a public official could also constitute "proteksia" – a request for a personal favor – a pattern that suits a paternalistic political system in which the citizen bangs on doors of the bureaucracy in order to get something or complain about a personal matter. Appealing for a personal need is responsive participation, limited to specific cases, and generally has no broader public interest.

To whom to appeal: Elected or appointed officials? Approaching elected officials is more common in countries where voters have direct contact with them. When the elected official represents a district or specific group, the probability of having a successful outcome increases because the representative is obligated to her constituents and directly dependent on their votes. In the United States, for example, about a third of the respondents said that they have initiated contact with public officials, and the proportion is higher for elected officials rather than bureaucrats. Most appeals were made to local or state authorities, and a minority to those on a federal level (Verba et al. 1995, 56).

In Israel, appeals to officials are generally made for personal reasons, not because of good citizenship, and some sort of personal connection is often mentioned – family, ethnicity, military service, etc. – to encourage special treatment. The increased sectoral division of the Knesset into interest groups has created distinct places to turn to for the religious, Russian immigrants, settlers, and others. Another common method is to use go-betweens or "fixers" – people with influence – to get to the officials. In the past, the most common address for appeals was the senior appointed official, who was also politically affiliated, and this remains prevalent. Over time, and with party primaries and the increased personalization of politics, personal appeals to MKs multiplied, even though Israel has no election districts and one votes for a list, not an individual. Some MKs have public interest bureaus funded by the Knesset for these appeals.

Appealing directly to officials is characteristic of the bureaucratic culture that evolved in Israel. Eleven percent of Israelis acknowledged that they have appealed to politicians (Table 8.2 above) and one can assume that more went unrecorded. Britain has a similar percentage (11%), but because of the electoral district system, most appeals are presumably to district representatives. We found no data about discreet appeals to public officials, but one sign of the extensiveness of personal appeals is the growing number of locations to submit complaints. Since 1971, the state comptroller has also served as the state ombudsman, and since 1980 has received in this capacity an average of 6,700 complaints a year – and no fewer than some 14,000 in 2013.[11] Other bodies whose job is to deal with complaints from the public exist in virtually every ministry and the large municipalities, and the IDF has an ombudsman for soldiers. The printed press and other media run columns for consumer complaints. Technology increased the public's ability to access officials: Ministries have websites with a wealth of information, including web-based contacts, to which the citizen can turn directly or with a small investment, avoiding lines or even phone calls. Politicians today, especially during elections, make a point of communicating with their constituents through their Facebook page or Twitter account, using them not only as a broadcasting tool.

It can be argued that not every appeal by a town resident for a discount on her city taxes or by a parent to the school principal is a form of political participation. We think differently. Such activism, despite its narrow purpose, indicates that the citizen understands the rules of the political game in a democracy, files a complaint to attain her rights, and thereby implicitly expresses trust in the political system and its ability to make change. Israeli citizens were always quick to complain, but awareness of rights rose sharply within the last few decades together with a willingness of individuals and groups to appeal to officials to address specific issues. The Freedom of Information Law gave official imprimatur to the right of the citizen qua citizen to request and receive information from public authorities. Although implementation of this law often takes place in the shadows, the number of demands to ministries based on this law and requests for information by citizens are on the rise.

[11] State Ombudsman, Reports for 2003–10: Report 30, 15; Report 31, 15; Report 32, 19; Report 33, 26, 31; Report 37, 37, 40 [in Hebrew].

Table 8.3 *Cases adjudicated by the High Court of Justice 1950–2013*

1950	1960	1970	1980	1990	2000	2007	2013*
86	333	381	802	1,308	–	2,136	1,461

Sources: CBS, *Statistical Abstract* 1997, table 21.6; Directorate of Courts 2008, 16; Israel Judiciary 2013, 13 [in Hebrew].

* The decrease is due to delegation of cases to a lower court.

Appealing to the Court (see Chapter 6)

The difference between turning to the court as a channel of participation and approaching public officials as described above is that the former entails recognition of the judicial system and a larger investment of resources. Furthermore, petitions to the court do not have to go through political or bureaucratic channels. The citizen can directly file a complaint against the authorities to the court and be assured of its impartiality and independence. Here too a distinction must be made between appeals about personal or public matters, the latter usually requiring some organizing and fitting better into the category of initiated participation.

Seeking judicial remedy had been less common in the past, not only because greater resources and patience were required, but also because access to the courts was limited. With the right of standing in the High Court of Justice expanded in the 1980s, the larger role of the administrative courts, and the increased judicialization of politics, applications for judicial redress have multiplied and become an acceptable and powerful channel of participation. Citizens, groups, organizations, and even noncitizens (Palestinian residents of the territories) who feel injured by an arbitrary act of the government or who wish to correct its ways seek out the High Court of Justice (Table 8.3). Particularly salient are the petitions by groups whose voices are not heard in other establishment channels, such as women and Arabs. Organizations like the Association for Civil Rights in Israel, the Israel Women's Network, and Adalah have frequently petitioned the High Court in an effort to influence government policies, safeguard rights, and quash discrimination.

A unique phenomenon in Israel is the petition to the High Court of Justice by public office holders, both elected and appointed, who seek court intervention in order to force a ruling on controversial political or administrative issues. While a large proportion of High Court petitions had once concerned administrative matters, citizens and social justice organizations in the 1980s who felt that the authorities were not responding to their needs stepped up the number of petitions to the High Court, if only to bring the matter to public attention. Petitioning the court also serves as a channel of protest: Citizens and groups submit petitions to the court even when it is clear that the court may refuse to adjudicate the matter, or may demand withdrawal of the petition, or may rule against the petition, all for the purpose of publicizing the issue and voicing their protest. In this sense, legal suits have sometimes taken the place of activism on the ground, as a petition to the High Court might have more value than thousands of demonstrators. In the 1990s, petitions were filed on foreign affairs and security matters even though the probability of having the court intervene to prevent, for example, secret negotiations with Syria, implementation of the Oslo Accords, or the Gaza disengagement was virtually nil (Dor and Hofnung 2006).

B. Initiated Participation

Activity in Parties and Affiliated Organizations (see Chapter 9)

Israel has been described as "a political party country," not just because of the power of the parties, but because large memberships of parties and their affiliates were taken for granted. Party membership is considered deeply committed political participation, but in the reality of the early years of the state, membership was actually responsive because parties were at the heart of political-social-economic power, hence membership in them and their affiliates (the Histadrut, youth movements, immigrant associations) was a means to other ends (Galnoor 1982, 165–71). The fabric of public life was determined by a "party key," with the distribution of resources based on the relative strength of each party. Connection to a party gave citizens access to workplaces, health funds, public housing, sports clubs, and more. Estimates of party membership in the late 1950s ranged between a quarter to a third of all those eligible to vote, which is high compared to other democracies. In Europe in the early 1960s, the average proportion of party members out of eligible voters was 15 percent, which dropped to 10.5 percent in the late 1980s (Katz and Mair 1992). The decline of political participation in this channel was evident in Israel as well. In the early 1990s, the two largest parties (Labor and the Likud) had some 130,000 members, which is fewer than 4 percent of eligible voters. In 2001, this number climbed to some 170,000 members (about 4% of eligible voters). In the primaries preceding the Knesset election of 2015, the number of members registered for the major parties (Labor and the Likud) totaled about 190,000, approximately 3.5 percent of eligible voters, though only half actually voted in the primaries (see Table 8.4).[12]

In the mid-1980s, party membership moved in two contrary directions. Regarding access to resources, the parties declined in status, hence the importance of party membership also declined. At the same time, the influence of party members expanded as they determined party leadership and the list of candidates. In the past, the parties had a highly reticulated hierarchical structure, with four or five bodies interposed between the party member and the leadership (in Mapai these included the conference, the council, the center, the secretariat, and the bureau), and a small number participated in the internal democratic process. Primary elections in which all party members participated were first introduced by the Movement for Democratic Movement for Change ("Dash") in 1977, followed by the Labor Party in 1992, and thereafter the Likud and other parties. Today in most large parties, the leaders and candidates are elected by the membership in primaries or in voting by wider circles, such as the "party center."

Is this why committed participation increased? The primaries created a new type of party member – one who registers for membership right before the primaries and abandons party participation after the vote. The commitment of these members is so short-lived that some even vote for other parties in the general election. These voters are recruited and registered by so-called "vote contractors," who are loyal to a specific candidate or group of candidates, and not to the party itself. As a result, an essentially positive democratic process was corrupted, and internal party elections

[12] "Registering [for a party]," www.mitpakdim.co.il/site/ (accessed February 20, 2016).

Table 8.4 *Primary voting in the two largest parties before the Knesset elections 2013; 2015*

Election cycle	Party	Date of primaries	Registered party members	Voter turnout %	Voted in the primaries
2013	Likud	Nov. 26, 2012	125,000	58	72,367
	Labor	Nov. 29, 2012	60,000	58	35,027
	Total	–	185,000	58	107,394
2015	Likud	Dec. 31, 2014	96,600	55	53,160
	Labor	Jan. 13, 2015	48,000	59	28,367
	Total	–	144,600	56	81,527

Data are based on party reports as reported in the daily press (validity unknown) (see www.haaretz.co.il/news/elections/1.2527295 and www.haaretz.co.il/news/elections/1.2538745 (both accessed June 23, 2016) and the "Registering [for a party]" website www.mitpakdim.co.il/site/# (accessed February 20, 2016)).

take place in an atmosphere of horse-trading. The democratic participation in shaping party leadership now happens in a way that empties party membership of all meaning. What's more, participation in choosing candidates does not come with the ability to influence the party platform or its policies in the Knesset or government.

Enlarging the circle of eligible voters within a party did not, as had been hoped, increase the number of party members. Figure 8.1, based on self-reporting, reveals that, over the years, the percentage of citizens who claim to be members, activists, or supporters of a party has dropped. In 1969, only 38 percent of the public stated that they were *not* a member, activist, or supporter of any party, and this number rose to 50 percent in 1984 and 67 percent in 2014 (Hermann 2014).

Activities in bodies affiliated or identified with parties also changed over time. Prior to the founding of Israel and during its first decades, most organizing was connected to a party, and organizations were linked with parties and used existing political channels. Although collective voluntary activity was vibrant during this period, it was limited to the party and ideological bodies, with political participation taking place in frameworks such as kibbutzim, moshavim, the Industrialists Association, and the like. The Histadrut – the General Federation of Labor – was a key channel for broad-based political participation. As a voluntary federation of workers and wage-earners, the Histadrut had a complex network of financial, social, and cultural organizations as well as activities in labor unions, workers' councils, and workers' shop committees. In the 1950s, the Histadrut had some half a million members who were eligible to vote in it, a million and a half in the 1980s, and only half a million in the 2000s. The kibbutzim were voluntary associations affiliated with political movements. The political participation of kibbutz members was wide ranging and powerful, including over-representation in the Knesset. This organized pattern of participation was characteristic primarily of the Labor camp, and to some extent also the religious-nationalist camp.

So long as Mapai (Labor) was the dominant party of the state, and the state was dominant in all areas of life, few groups operated autonomously. Public space for civic development was constricted, hence social organizations that were not under

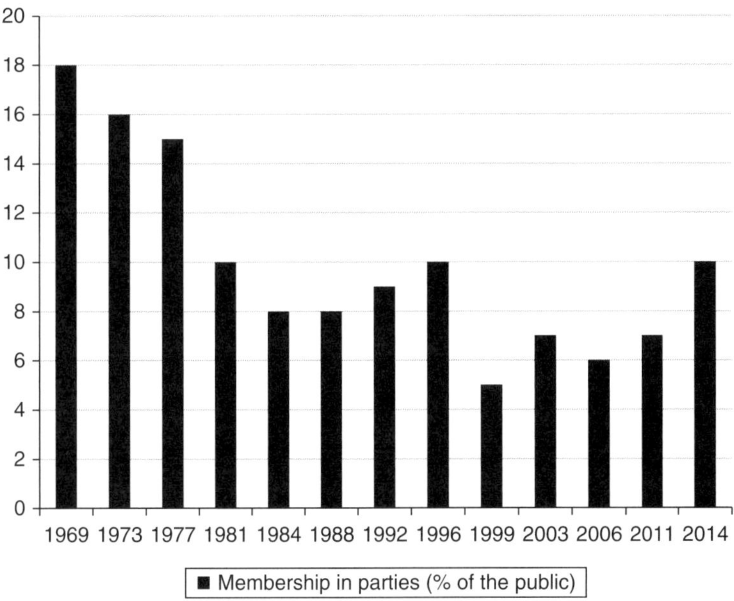

Figure 8.1 Self-reported party membership, 1969–2014
Sources: Arian et al. 2005–10: 2006, 72; Hermann et al. 2011–15: 2014.

the aegis of a political movement or party were few and far between. During this period, it was political power that shaped public space. By the late 1960s and particularly after the Yom Kippur War with the unraveling of public consensus, the loosening of the party grip, and the rising voices of protest from Israelis of Asian and north African ethnicity, groups not part of the party system embarked upon independent organizing. The first to appear were extra-parliamentary movements such as Gush Emunim and Peace Now, who appealed directly to public opinion, and later, in the 1980s, social protest organizations emerged on many issues, which we will make note of in the coming section and discuss in greater depth in Chapter 12. Organized party participation faded in Israel as the institution of state weakened and retreated from many areas of activity. This vacuum slowly began to fill with civil society, as the center of gravity shifted from participation in parties and their affiliates to more committed participation in the third sector.

Participation in Civil Society (see Chapter 12)

This channel of participation requires that an individual work together with others to achieve a common goal. The group might operate on a permanent or temporary basis, and its members actively participate on the assumption that personal inputs will achieve results. This is independent organizing of citizens in non-profits and other organizations that are not in the governmental or business sector, hence their name – the "third sector." Voluntary activity in civil society groups demands intense commitment, public identification with a specific goal, and the willingness to invest effort, time, and money. However, not all third-sector organizations engage in political work. Membership in leisure-time or recreational organizations – a country club, for instance – does not necessarily fall under the rubric of political participation, though membership in the Society for the Protection of Nature could be political and involve participation in campaigns about environmental quality. Activism in third-sector organizations is a cornerstone of a democratic society. In the 1990s, for example, about a third of United States citizens engaged in some form of voluntary community activity. This is lower in Europe – 17 percent in Britain and 18 percent in Holland, for example (Verba et al. 1995, 70). Israel resembles Europe in this respect: In 2003, 16 percent of Israeli citizens stated that they are members of a group, organization, or non-profit that engages in public activism in fields such as education, the environment, or charity (Arian et al. 2003, 136). In 2014, 27 percent said they had volunteered at a social welfare organization on a regular basis (Hermann et al. 2011–15: 2014, 69).

During the early state period, there was little autonomous organizing, as noted, and what did exist was regarded with hostility by the organized political system. The revolution of civil society in public life, which began in the 1980s, turned third-sector organizations into the main channels of political participation for citizens. As these organizations proliferated, their legitimacy also gradually took root as a result of the higher standard of living, changes in the political system, sectoralization in the representation of political parties, and the dissolution of the welfare state. In several fields, civil society organizations came to replace state institutions. Since the 1980s, an average of 1,500 organizations have been founded each year, and in the late 1990s, some 30,000 were registered, 81 percent of them "civil society organizations" and the rest non-profits integrated into the state welfare system (Gidron, Bar, and Katz 2003, 157, 204). As of 2011, over 49,000 organizations were registered. These organizations are active in the fields of religion, education, welfare, philanthropy, culture and leisure, social change, and politics.

Addressing the Media (see Chapter 13)

The growing role of the media in the political system has transformed them into a mediating body between citizens and the government, and a culture has evolved of political participation via the media. Common channels for citizen complaints are newspaper or magazine columns as well as radio or TV programs. Some media outlets have become arenas for voicing opinions about current events – letters to the editor or programs like *You've Got Someone to Talk to* on the IDF radio station. Third-sector organizations make an effort to publicize their views through the megaphone of the media, particularly if they are engaged in public interest issues, such as the National Council for the Child. The media are the main vehicle for protest activity because public awareness of the protest derives from the media attention it receives. In one case, a citizen named Vicki Knafo, by virtue of her long-distance march and media attention, managed to shine a spotlight on the economic policies of the government in 2003, walking from her home in Mitzpe Ramon to Jerusalem. The intense media coverage of her journey encouraged other women to join her protest, and culminated in public discourse and government decisions regarding single-parent families.

Political participation by appealing to the media on public matters requires skill and considerable investment because of the fierce competition for free publicity among all the sectors – governmental, non-profit, and business – as well as the self-interest of the media, most of which are commercial. As will be seen in Chapter 13, the online social networks abruptly shifted participation patterns in the media to multi-directional.

Active Participation in Election Campaigns (see Chapter 10)

Playing an active part in an election campaign on a voluntary basis entails a personal decision to invest in political work for purposes of persuading others. This is how a citizen attempts to magnify his impact beyond the single ballot he casts. Such activism can be in the framework or a party or on behalf of a particular candidate; it can be energetic – such as organizing political gatherings, holding parlor meetings, distributing campaign literature – or random – donating to a party, writing talkbacks on the Internet, or sporting a bumper sticker. Unlike the casting of a ballot, which is a simple and private act, participating in an election campaign requires a willingness of the citizen to expose his views. It demands commitment, initiative, cooperation with others, and deep belief in the value of the free exchange of views in a democratic society.

This kind of participation, although limited to election periods, places a heavy burden on citizens, particularly those with limited leisure. In Israel, as in other democracies, citizens tend not to participate actively in election campaigns. To illustrate, in the 1980s, only 8 percent of Israelis reported that they had participated in an election campaign – less than the proportion in the United States, but higher than in European countries. In the 2000s, 12 percent of Israelis generally stated that they had participated in an election campaign – proportionately fewer than in Britain, but double that of European countries such as Germany, Denmark, and Holland (European Social Survey 2010 and 2012).

In the period when party organizations dominated the state, election campaigns were almost entirely party-oriented, and citizens who participated in them did so by virtue of being a member of a party or its affiliate, such as a workers' council or an employers' association. Most citizens were passive participants: They read campaign propaganda and participated in political gatherings. Over the years, the forms of participation and type of election propaganda changed, both because of the changed status of the parties and also technological developments. Instead of party-organized, mass rallies or parlor meetings, election campaigns were turned over to professional PR people, who diverted them to channels of mass propaganda: slogans, billboards, radio and TV programs, and the Internet. In recent years, for example, a "battle for the intersections" has been waged on the streets during election periods, in which party activists, almost all paid workers, fight for control of intersections by blanketing them with banners and handing out stickers. It has yet to be proven that this visibility of the candidate or party is as important as myth would have it, other than its value to voters who have already made up their minds and draw encouragement from it. The parties, unlike extra-parliamentary movements, are no longer successful at recruiting committed activists or significant donations during the election period, and make do with paid ads funded almost entirely by the election budget provided by the state.

Data about the viewing of campaign commercials on TV indicate that most citizens remain indifferent, despite the enormous investment. In the 2015 Knesset election, the ratings of election commercials on channels 2 and 10 combined were 11.4 percent on the first day and 10.2 percent on average. This averages to over a quarter million citizens daily who bothered to watch the political messages despite the inconvenient broadcast hours, suggesting that despite the competition from the online news channels, many citizens still have a lively interest in this type of political campaign. In parallel, the parties significantly increased their campaign presence on the Internet. The cost has been estimated at one million shekel, with roughly two million views combined (all data from Rosen 2015). One way or another, public interest in the campaigns has greatly declined over the years in all channels, and with it the active participation of citizens in the election efforts.

Making a personal donation to the election campaign of a candidate or party is an accepted channel of participation in many countries. In those with no state funding for campaigns, such as the United States, donations are a form of political commitment that can be called "checkbook participation." In the past in Israel (based on undocumented testimony), employees at some workplaces were forced to donate a specific percentage of their salaries to the party with which the workplace was affiliated. Prior to the Parties Financing Law (1973), some funding for election campaigns came from economic institutions linked to the parties. State funding for the parties reduced their dependence on private donations to finance election campaigns, so donating to parties is no longer a significant channel of participation for Israelis, with the exception of donations to candidates running in the primaries of large parties, which are regulated by law. In the 2013 election, the ceiling for an individual donation was NIS 2,300, and data published by the state comptroller (which mandates publication of every donation over NIS 1,000) reveal that only a small number of citizens participate in politics via donations and that parties do not rely on these donations for their income. In the 2013 election, the total collection by all parties was some NIS 1.3 million from several hundred donors. Many of these donations came from MKs themselves, and some came from payments received by the ballot box monitors, who passed them on to the parties as a donation (State Comptroller 2014).

When citizens in democracies are asked whether election propaganda affects their vote, they tend to respond in the negative for obvious reasons. This may be even more applicable to the well-informed Israeli voter, who claims to already know for whom he intends to vote. The impact of election propaganda is relatively minor, certainly during the era when the party affiliation of citizens was clear-cut and fixed. But this changed, and now the proportion of voters who remain undecided until the last minute has grown substantially, estimated at some 15–20 percent of eligible voters in 2015. To this should be added the spreading disinterest in election propaganda and the election itself, suggesting alienation and disengagement from politics. The Israeli public continues to take no active role in election campaigns, though previously the reason had been the preeminence of the parties and today it is because of their weakness.

Protest Activity

By protest activity we mean action taken by citizens to change the law or government policy. More than actively participating in an election campaign, protest activity demands commitment, initiative, and usually cooperation with others. This activity falls into two categories: protest under the accepted rules of the game in a democratic regime (petitions, strikes, demonstrations); or illegal forms of protest (violence, assassination, terrorism). The former is carried out by citizens who are committed to the political system and its laws, while the latter reflects a willingness to cross the line and not recognize the legitimacy of the prevailing system. The fact that there are borderline cases (e.g., demonstrations that deteriorate into violence) does not obviate the need to distinguish clearly between them.

In Israel, one finds waves of political protest connected to specific events: wars (Yom Kippur, the Lebanon campaigns), the peace process (Oslo Accords in 1993, disengagement from Gaza in 2005), and social and economic crises (austerity in the 1950s, recession in the 1960s, the economic policies of the 2000s, the social protest in 2011). Protest seems to lurk beneath the surface with seasonal fluctuations. At times, protest seems to be a routine event; at other times, there are breaks – the public refuses to leave home for a demonstration. Israel's political history contains several major demonstrations for which it is hard to find a common denominator, other than that the subject was sensitive and that they were mass events or violent. The organizers of demonstrations in the 1950s were primarily opposition parties – Mapam on the left and Herut on the right. Some examples: violent demonstrations by the jobless in transit camps against the government and Mapai; or the "seamen's strike" in 1951 (Hermann 1995, 108). The most serious demonstrations in the early years were the aforementioned Wadi Salib events in 1959 and the violent demonstration against the reparations agreement with Germany, organized by Herut and its leader, Menachem Begin, in 1952. In the latter, some 15,000 people took to the streets, threw stones at the Knesset building, and were dispersed by tear gas. At the time, the government viewed these demonstrations as a direct threat to its rule, unable to see them as a legitimate channel of political participation. Demonstrations were often suppressed with a heavy hand, or led to provisional solutions to appease the demonstrators or to recruit them to the party in power.

During the recession prior to the 1967 war (1965–66), protest spread and the number of strikes hit a record high. Some were organized by the Histadrut against government policy, and some were spontaneous. Figure 8.2 shows that over the course of forty years, the number of strikes decreased and the number of strikers rose – the strikes had become better organized and larger.

Political protest escalated in the 1970s in the wake of the Yom Kippur War, and took on more of a political and social character. In 1974, demonstrators called for the resignation of Prime Minister Golda Meir and Defense Minister Moshe Dayan, and a protest movement of tens of thousands of civilians and reserve soldiers directly contributed to the fall of the government (Ashkenazi, Nevo, and Ashkenazi 2003). This was followed by extra-parliamentary movements – the largest being Gush Emunim and Peace Now – which advocated alternatives to government policy. The most notable social protest in the early 1970s was the "Black Panther" movement of Mizrahi Jews (see below). Until 1966, Arab citizens were under martial law, and the constitutive event in terms of autonomous Arab political activism was Land Day in 1976 (see Chapter 15). The peace agreements with Egypt leading to the evacuation of Israeli settlements in the Sinai Peninsula raised protest to often violent levels previously unknown in Israel, organized by the Movement to Stop the Retreat in Sinai (1982) founded by Gush Emunim and the Tehiya Party. This evacuation saw violent clashes between the IDF and protesters, most notably in the Sinai settlement of Yamit (Sprinzak 1995, 81). Also during this period, a Jewish underground terrorist organization was formed (1980–84), most of whose members were settlers. After attacking and severely wounding Palestinian mayors in the occupied territories and later murdering students at the Islamic College in Hebron, the perpetrators were

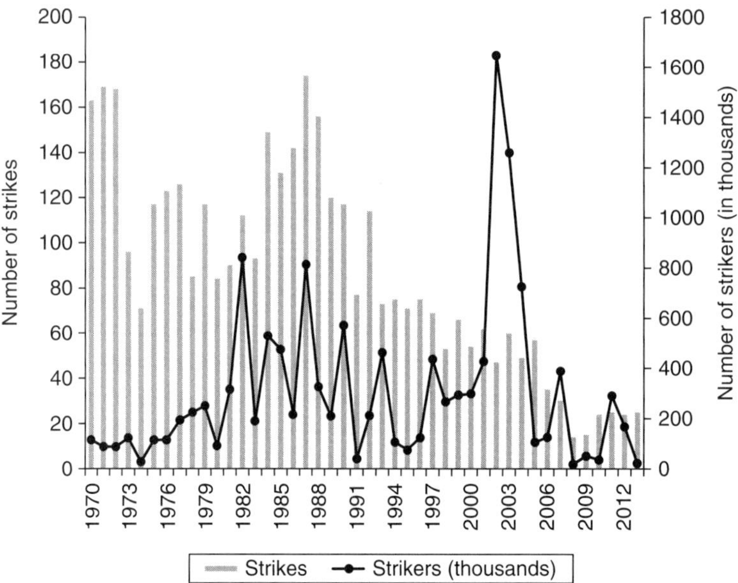

Figure 8.2 Strikes and strikers (1970–2013)
Source: CBS *Statistical Abstract* 2014, table 12.50.

convicted and given lengthy prison sentences, which were later commuted by the president (Sprinzak 1995, 78).

The first Lebanon War aroused unprecedented protest, including a mass rally regarded as the largest in Israeli history until that point – the "demonstration of the four hundred thousand" in Tel Aviv in September 1982, demanding that a state commission of inquiry be established to investigate the events in the Sabra and Shatila refugee camps. The Kahan Commission was appointed and, upon publication of its conclusions, a demonstration organized by Peace Now in February 1983 called for the resignation of Ariel Sharon as Defense Minister. At that demonstration, a hand grenade was lobbed at the crowd by an Israeli right-wing extremist, killing one participant, Emil Grunzweig, and injuring several others. In January 1988, a group of women in Jerusalem began a weekly protest vigil against the occupation. Dressed in black as a sign of mourning for the victims of both sides, this weekly vigil has continued for almost four decades and spawned other vigils across Israel and then an international movement of Women in Black, as these vigils came to be known. Political protest escalated in the early 1990s, and we note the huge demonstration in 1990 of the Movement for a Constitution in Israel under the slogan "We're fed up with corrupt leaders!" in protest of the shady deals by parties and politicians following the fall of the National Unity Government. Progress in the peace process and signature on the Oslo Accords of 1993 brought thousands into the street for and against the agreement. In Jerusalem, a large demonstration was held with right-wing MKs in which "Rabin is a traitor" was chanted, and a picture of the prime minister was displayed in a Nazi SS uniform. On November 4, 1995, a large demonstration in support of the peace agreements was held in Tel Aviv, at the end of which Prime Minister Yitzhak Rabin was assassinated. One week later, a rally in the same plaza, now named for Rabin, was held in his memory in which half a million people reportedly participated. In 1996, 12 percent of the respondents said they had participated in one demonstration or another related to the peace process and 10 percent in demonstrations and rallies related to the assassination of Rabin (A. Arian 1997, 341).

Another type of protest takes place in a religious-ethnic context, such as the rallies that followed the conviction of Interior Minister Aryeh Deri in early 1999 on charges of bribery, fraud, and violation of trust. This time the target of protest was the judicial system: A quarter of a million ultra-Orthodox, by some estimates, participated in mass demonstrations in Jerusalem to protest the court's denial of Deri's appeal. Outbursts of nationalist protest – in the occupied territories and Arab towns within Israel – followed on the heels of Ariel Sharon's visit to the politically sensitive Temple Mount. In reaction, protests took place in Arab towns in October 2000, resulting in the killing of thirteen civilians by Israeli security forces. A state commission of inquiry headed by Justice Or was appointed to investigate the events (see Chapter 7 on commissions of inquiry). The evacuation of Israeli settlers from the Gaza Strip in the summer of 2005 (called "the disengagement" by the government) triggered a wave of demonstrations, some illegal and violent, such as blocking major roadways and using force to resist. The evacuation itself, however, passed almost without violent incident.

The Israeli public generally tends to go along with government decisions, and when it does not, it takes to the streets in organized, non-violent demonstrations. In a 2003 survey, respondents were asked what they would do if the government made a decision about the occupied territories and security to which they objected: 49 percent responded that they would respect the decision; 44 percent said they would legally demonstrate against it; and 6 percent said they would vehemently protest, even beyond what is legal, but without the use of force (by methods such as blocking traffic or demonstrating illegally); only 1 percent testified that they would use any means, including violence (Arian et al. 2003a, 180). The majority that objects to internal political violence is fragile, however, and Israeli society does not have sufficiently strong antibodies to refrain from political violence under trying circumstances. A study in the late 1980s reported that Israelis tend to engage in protest activity such as petition-signing, demonstrations, and strikes more than their counterparts in western democracies: 16 percent of Israeli citizens stated in 1984 that they took part in such forms of protest (Wolfsfeld 1988, 16). This rose to 20 percent of Israelis in 1996 who said they had participated in a demonstration (A. Arian 1997, 341). As for the 2000s, evidence from different sources is contradictory, ranging between 10 percent and 25 percent. In any event, Israel's ranking relative to other countries is medium or high.[13] In the 2011 social protests, about 20 percent of the population participated – the biggest protest in years (Hermann 2014).

The Israeli public does not routinely engage in protest, although it tends to do so during times of political turmoil, when there is willingness to cross the line and commit offenses such as violence, terrorism, and even assassination. In 2003, most Israeli citizens (82%) believed that "under no circumstances is violence justified to

[13] According to Newton and Giebler (2008, based on the European Social Survey), 10 percent claimed to have participated in a demonstration in Israel the previous year. In data from the World Values Survey, on the other hand, 25 percent report they had participated in a demonstration in the past year. We have no way to evaluate these two statistics.

attain political goals"; following the disengagement from Gaza, only 74 percent (in 2007) and 73 percent (in 2013) agreed with that statement (Arian et al. 2003a, 180; Hermann et al. 2011–15: 2013, 148). The social protest demonstrations in the summer of 2011 were unusual: They were mass, cut across traditional sectors, took place throughout the country, and were completely non-violent. As a result of the protest, a group of young citizens banded together to systematically monitor the activities of MKs.[14]

Civil Disobedience as Political Participation (see Chapter 14)

Citizens of a democracy are obligated to the state and its laws. Those unwilling to accept the system as a whole may consider the option of leaving. One of the dilemmas confronting a democracy is the following: What should be done about a citizen who recognizes the legitimacy of the government and the law, but objects to a specific law for reasons of conscience and morality? For this discussion, it is unimportant if the objection is to paying taxes or to service in the military. And let us assume that this citizen has exhausted all legal avenues: He voted for a party that supports his view, petitioned the High Court of Justice, participated in a public campaign to rescind the law, held a hunger strike, etc. – do the rules of the democratic game include his right to refuse to comply with a law as a means of changing it? A positive answer could be interpreted as an invitation to undermine the rule of law, beyond which lurks the threat of violence and political terror. However, citizens who reject the entire system or refuse to recognize the overall legitimacy of the laws of the land are not inclined to undertake nonviolent resistance (civil disobedience) against a specific law.

In contrast, those who accept the system, but wish to change a specific law, claim that as long as they are willing to pay the price for violating it, their activity actually strengthens democratic rule.[15] This dilemma will not be solved here in the context of a discussion about political participation, but we point out that in the Israeli reality where there is a legal obligation to serve in the IDF and its reserve forces, the context for this form of protest – refusing to serve – is an ideological refusal to participate in maintaining the occupation.

In terms of gaining public notice, the roots of the refusal-to-serve movement are generally identified as the "High School Seniors' Letter" written to Prime Minister Golda Meir in 1970 during the War of Attrition by a group of Jerusalem twelfth-graders. They protested the fact that the government was not doing enough to promote peace with Egypt, adding that this made it hard for them to be drafted into the IDF. The protest was understated, but it gained widespread attention because it broke a taboo with its intimation about being drafted. Since that time, there have been many cases of individuals refusing to serve in the IDF, particularly after the first Lebanon War, and several organizations emerged that called for refusal to serve in the occupied territories: on the left, Yesh Gvul and others (with well-respected supporters like Yeshayahu Leibowitz); and, on the right, Jewish Leadership (supported

[14] For example, the website "Jewish Pluralism Watch," Monitoring Report of the Second Session of the Knesset, March 2014.

[15] For a general discussion, see Walzer (1967); I. Menuchin and D. Menuchin (1985), particularly Raz and Walzer; and Weinstein (1999), particularly Avineri.

by various rabbis), who called for refusing to obey orders to evacuate settlers.[16] The major movements on both sides of the political spectrum were careful not to support refusal to serve, because, among other concerns, they feared it would legitimize the other side's refusal to serve.

Data about the scope of military refusal in Israel are not definitive, but we note two related points: In terms of numbers, refusal to serve is a marginal phenomenon, although it has grown over the years and the IDF, which had once ignored it, now does open battle with those who refuse, including bringing them to trial (Sheleff 1989, 134–39). Is there awareness that disobeying the law might be deemed a form of political participation? The surprising statistic is that, in the 2000s, about a third of Israeli citizens believed it legitimate to refuse an order for ideological reasons, whether for serving in the occupied territories or evicting settlers (Arian et al. 2003a, 182–83). In 2013, about a third of Israel's Jewish citizens and nearly 60 percent of its Arab citizens felt this way (Hermann et al. 2011–15: 2013).

Online Participation – A New Pattern of Political Participation?

Israeli society is increasingly cyber and wired: In 2000 only 18 percent of the population reported that they use the Internet, but this soared to some 71 percent in 2014.[17] Nevertheless, Internet use is not uniform among all population groups: There is still less usage among Arab citizens (50%) and the ultra-Orthodox (43%).[18] Some 90 percent of Israelis use the Internet to search for information or data or to access news portals. The proportion of users among the young and mid-age levels (18–49) is 80 percent, and reaches 90 percent among youth (13–17) (Pereg 2009).

As to the subject at hand, to what degree are online media used as a new channel of political participation, not just during election periods? Election forums and party websites create new arenas for political participation. During the primaries prior to the 2003 Knesset election, discussions took place in these forums on a variety of topics such as party ideology, corruption, candidates, and predictions of the outcome. These discussions were described as generally having a civil, rational tone, not aggressive or hysterical. Nevertheless, the number of participants (some 5,000) was negligible in terms of impact on the election results (Lehman-Wilzig 2004, 242–62).

Party websites have the potential to change the character of political participation by creating a shadow mechanism to participation in the field. Research suggests, however, that a real revolution has not yet taken place in Israel. So far most party websites have been conservative: They did not provide channels from the bottom up, opened no interactive discourse, and drew participants primarily from party stalwarts, not the public at large. In the election campaigns of 2006 and 2009 as well, party websites focused on disseminating information – operating mainly as propaganda channels – although they were mainly preaching to the choir. They did not,

[16] See "Clarification of the Obligation of Disobedience," Jewish Leadership Publication, 2004 (pamphlet).

[17] Central Bureau of Statistics, *Statistical Abstract* 2015, Table 9.7, www.cbs.gov.il/reader/shnaton/templ_shnaton_e.html?num_tab=st09_07&CYear=2015, and World Bank, http://data.worldbank.org/indicator/IT.NET.USER.P2 (accessed February 20, 2016).

[18] This is one reason for the inconsistent data about the percentage that uses the Internet. Another stems from contradictory data about ages (from thirteen or from eighteen years old) and from data reflecting the proportion of households or users.

for example, use these media for fundraising. Here and there new forms of participation appeared: Prior to the 2006 election, visitors to the Kadima Party website were invited to propose bills that Kadima should table in the Knesset. It was a populist move, with no real hope of implementation, but the idea of involving citizens in legislative initiatives is innovative. In the 2009 election, the Strong Israel Party (which did not pass the threshold for entering the Knesset) held primaries on the Internet with a high proportion of participation (93% of 1,200 members); members of the Jewish Home Party were invited to use the website to recommend candidates, which served as the basis for the party committee's ranking of candidates; this party also had an online survey to choose a name and logo for the party (Atmor 2009). In 2009, signs were already evident that the online media were being used by candidates and parties for political discourse, but this still cannot be described as a revolution (Atmor 2008, 24). In the 2013 election, many Israeli politicians used their Facebook page to reach out to voters and gain popularity (Samuel-Azran, Yarchi, and Wolfsfeld 2015). In parallel, most third-sector organizations also used the new media in traditional ways, and their websites show little interactive discourse, fundraising efforts, activist recruitment, or strategic use to achieve organizational goals (Zarkawy and Blit-Cohen 2008).

Table 8.5 shows a drop in responsive channels of participation, those that require initiative and resource investment, and a rise in participation out of initiative and commitment. However, the table ignores the fact that the overall proportion of political participants among Israeli citizens is declining in all channels. We shall return to this at the end of this chapter.

The previous discussion points to the changing trends in participation patterns in the Israeli political system – a transition from organized participation to autonomous patterns, as well as a drop in participation, which also characterizes other democracies (see Civic Voluntarism Model (CVM); Verba et al. 1995, 522–24).

8.4 Political Participation of Specific Groups

A democracy aspires to give equal participation opportunities to all its citizens. As with the individual, for groups, too, the level of participation depends on the resources available to them (such as education and income) as well as their access to the political system, i.e., whether its members have the practical opportunity to participate in order to influence policy. High access means there are formal and informal channels that lead to the arenas where policy is set.

Although there may be an expectation that disadvantaged groups in a democratic society will be highly motivated to participate politically, in actuality they participate less. The reason for this is the overlap between status and group belonging: The lower the socioeconomic status of a group, the less social capital they have and therefore they tend to participate less. In the United States, status and ethnic origin overlap. Disadvantaged ethnic groups lack the resources required for political participation, such as education, income, and the experience acquired in voluntary organizations. Another reason for their failure to participate is a lack of trust in the system.

We chose to look at this issue in Israel by examining three groups that are clearly distinct and whose participation patterns are different for various reasons: Arab

Table 8.5 *Changes in patterns of political participation in Israel*

	Initiative required	Resources invested	Commitment	Change
Responsive participation				
Voting	Little	Few	Low	Decreased
Contact with office holders	Moderate	Few	Low	No change
Litigation	Moderate	Moderate	Low	Increased
Initiated participation				
In parties and affiliated organizations	Little to considerable	Moderate	Low to considerable	Decreased
In civil society organizations	Considerable	Considerable	Considerable	Increased
Use of media	Considerable	Few	Considerable	Increased
Use of Internet & social channels	Little to considerable	Moderate	Low to high	Increased
In election campaign	Considerable	Considerable	Considerable	No change
Protest activity	Considerable	Considerable	Considerable	Increased
Refusing military service	Considerable	Considerable	Considerable	Increased

Israeli citizens, the ultra-Orthodox, and new immigrants. One possible common denominator of these groups is that their political participation is driven by the desire to attain political resources from the state – direct allocations for education, health, and welfare services. Thus, the main participation channels of these groups are responsive in the hope of enlarging their political representation. Since their voting public is relatively homogeneous, establishing a sectoral party and winning ongoing support for it from most members of the group is an indicator of success, as in the example of the ultra-Orthodox. Our assumption is that despite significant differences within each group, their level of representation in politics is a true reflection of their level of participation in established channels. We will also note the political participation of the group in civil society and protest activity.

A. Arabs (for a full discussion, see Chapter 15)

Arabs in Israel are caught in a trap: As citizens, they aspire to full and equal rights in all matters, including the allocation of resources, and to that end they must participate in the political system and influence decision-making. At the same time, political participation would mean giving legitimacy to a political system defined as a "Jewish and democratic" state, which is not acceptable to them. This internal contradiction affects their participation patterns, but the trend is fairly clear – Arab society in Israel is undergoing a process of politicization, which means growing awareness of its rights and attempts to realize these rights in various channels, some of them contradictory. The following are the main points on the subject of participation, disregarding the deep cleavages within Arab society.

- Since the 1980s, Arab society has experienced autonomous organizing at all levels – local government, political parties, demonstrations and protest activity, grassroots self-help organizations, but also isolation from the rest of civil society, influenced by the growing Islamic Movement in Israel.
- In 1984, Arab parties that had been affiliated with Jewish parties disappeared and were replaced by parties holding aloft two banners: civic equality and support for the nationalist aspirations of Palestinians in the occupied territories. Gradually, the number of MKs elected from Arab and Arab-Jewish parties (Hadash) increased: From eight members in 1996 to sixteen in 2015.[19] Based on the proportion of eligible voters among Arab citizens of Israel (some 15 percent of the population), Arab representation in the Knesset could reach sixteen to seventeen seats. Since the mid-1990s, however, there has been a tendency to boycott the election in protest of the attitudes of the state, its institutions, and the Jewish majority toward Arab citizens (Rouhana, Saleh, and Sultany 2004). The double ballot during the period of direct elections allowed Arab voters to cast an unmarked ballot for prime minister without hurting the representation of Arab parties. In 1996, 12 percent of Arab voters reported that they had cast an unmarked ballot for prime minister (Kaufman and Israeli 1999). The rupture in relations between the Arab and Jewish public in Israel came in the wake of the events of October 2000: As a result, 82 percent of Arab voters boycotted the 2001 election of prime minister to protest the conduct of the security forces toward Arab citizens, and also because neither candidate (Barak or Sharon) was acceptable to them (Rouhana et al. 2004). Since then, Arab voting rates continue to fall: 53 percent in Arab towns and 58 percent in mixed Jewish-Arab cities in the 2009 election. In the 2013 elections, 57 percent of the Arab population turned out to vote, but the turnout increased to 64 percent in 2015 with the appearance of the Joint List. While most Arab towns have low voter turnout, in some it is particularly high – Kfar Kasem, for example, with 80.2 percent (Atmor 2013).
- Participation rates for Arabs in local elections are particularly high and have remained high over the years. They are much higher than Jewish voting turnout in local elections, and also higher than Arab voter turnout in Knesset elections. Voter turnout in Arab local elections range between 75 percent and 90 percent, higher by an average of 17 percent than Jewish voter turnout in local elections (Atmor 2013; Ben Bassat and Dahan 2009). Local government, unlike the national government, represents Arab society (with the exception of those who live in mixed cities), and is a center of autonomous political power. Its two main institutions are the Council of Arab Mayors, founded in 1974, which represents Arab citizens of Israel not just on a local level, but also on other issues; and the Higher Monitoring Committee of Arab Citizens of Israel, founded in 1982 as an umbrella organization for most groups active in Arab affairs in Israel – Arab

[19] Twelve Arabs in the Joint List and four in each: Meretz, the Likud, the Zionist Camp, and Yisrael Beitenu.

MKs, the National Committee of Arab Local Authorities, members of the Histadrut leadership, student representatives, etc. This committee operates in social areas such as education, welfare, health, and national politics (Al-Haj and Rosenfeld 1990, 130–54).

- Increased political participation among Arab citizens in third-sector organizations is a relatively recent phenomenon, partially due to social changes (Zeidan and Ghanem 2000a; "Galnoor Committee" 2003, 47–50). There were 1,163 Arab third-sector organizations registered in 1998, which increased to over 3,000 in 2007. However, Arab organizations account for about 12 percent of all organizations in the third sector, which is considerably below their share of the total Israeli population (about 20%) (Balbachan 2008a). In addition to Arab organizations, there are some joint Arab-Jewish organizations: Sikkuy working to promote equality for Arabs in Israel; B'Tselem monitoring human rights in the occupied territories; Neve Shalom/Wahat al-Salaam – an Arab-Jewish village; and Ta'ayush addressing issues related to Israeli control over the territories. The Islamic Movement is an important anchor for Arab third-sector organizations, reflecting religious identification and protest against the government, as well as providing welfare and educational services to the working class (Gidron et al. 2003: 138, 156–57, 166–67).

The political participation patterns of Arab citizens of Israel have largely been shaped by the attitude of the state establishment, which is suspicious of any independent organizing by Arab citizens. During the early years of the state, efforts to establish independent bodies were suppressed, after which attempts were made to disqualify Arab parties from running for election. In recent times, opinions have been expressed seeking to delegitimize the right of Arab citizens to participate in elections or referendums on the patently anti-democratic grounds that Arabs should not have a voice in important state decisions (Neuberger 2000). This came to a head in 2013 with the campaign slogan of the Yisrael Beitenu Party, "No citizenship without loyalty," directly targeting the civil rights of Arab citizens of Israel. Vis-à-vis the state, participation focuses on the parties; vis-à-vis the local authorities, the emphasis is on litigation and protest; but the predominant feeling among Arab citizens of Israel is that none of this is effective, as evidenced, for example, by the failure to implement the recommendations of the state commission of inquiry that examined the clashes of October 2000. Internally, there is a wide range of communal and social non-profits, but these do not have the power to close the inequality gap or to compete with the solutions offered by the Islamic Movement. Thus, among Arab citizens of Israel, the process of politicization, increased awareness of rights, and efforts to realize these rights have all coalesced into a sense of inefficacy. The Arab public is slowly acquiring legitimate political power, but this power seems to lead nowhere, which increases their frustration, discourages their participation, and keeps them estranged from the political system.

B. Ultra-Orthodox

The ultra-Orthodox community in Israel is composed of many different dynastic groups, some with branches in other countries, and it includes a small group called the Eda Haredit (or Neturei Karta), which does not recognize the state of Israel or wish to participate in its political system. Most ultra-Orthodox have an instrumental approach to political participation – their avowed goal is to ensure their interests as a group. The ultra-Orthodox parties are thus interest groups that use the Knesset almost exclusively to advance the interests of the public they represent. Ultra-Orthodox participation is mobilized, but unlike the Arab citizens of Israel who had been recruited by the authorities and political parties, recruitment of the ultra-Orthodox is carried out by their own community institutions and rabbis.

The main channels of participation of the ultra-Orthodox are as follows: In the political sphere – via ultra-Orthodox parties; in the community – via extensive activity in voluntary organizations; among the general public – via occasional protest activity in matters of religion and state that they consider vital. These patterns of participation reflect the instrumental attitude of the ultra-Orthodox toward Israel – they do not share its Zionist values. Although the hollow slogan "No citizenship without loyalty" theoretically applies to and threatens them as well, being Jewish protects them from the ethnophobia in Israel, especially as they see themselves as charged with protecting Israel's Jewish character. Political participation thus becomes limited cooperation for purposes of protecting the ultra-Orthodox and imbuing the Israeli public with Jewish content. In 1984, the appearance on the political stage of Shas – an ultra-Orthodox-Mizrahi-social party – caused a revolution, creating a new pattern of involvement in more general affairs of state, and the ultra-Orthodox-Ashkenazi parties also followed suit to some extent. The following are the main points of its participation, setting aside the internal differences that fragment ultra-Orthodox socicty:

- Until 1984, the ultra-Orthodox parties together (Agudat Yisrael and Poalei Agudat Yisrael) could count on five to six seats in the Knesset, on average. The meteoric rise of Shas, which claimed a high of seventeen seats in 1999, testifies to a circle of voters beyond the ultra-Orthodox public. In the elections of the 2000s, all the ultra-Orthodox parties together won an average of sixteen seats, and were able to wield political power beyond their relatively small Knesset faction, particularly Shas, because of their importance to the coalition. This translated into significant achievements on behalf of their constituents: continued exemption from the draft for yeshiva students, the allocation of funds to their institutions, an independent school network, increased allowances for child-support, etc.
- Until 1984, voter turnout among the ultra-Orthodox was slightly lower than the national average (S. Ilan 2000, 74), but the increased influence of the ultra-Orthodox parties contributed to a higher turnout. In the 1996 Knesset election, for example, the voting turnout of the ultra-Orthodox was 10 percent higher than that of the general population (Weiss 1996, 27). In the 2015 election, two ultra-Orthodox parties entered the Knesset – the Ashkenazi Torah Judaism Party (six seats), and the Sephardic Shas Party (seven seats). Together they garnered 451,756 votes – plus 125,158 votes for Yahad (headed by Eli Yishai), which split from Shas, but did not pass the electoral threshold. Accordingly, the vote for the ultra-Orthodox parties was some 14 percent of the total, the same as in the 2013 elections. One can assume that this includes all the ultra-Orthodox who voted, as they usually do not vote for other parties (and excludes small

ultra-Orthodox groups who boycotted the elections). However, this high figure exceeds the total number of actual ultra-Orthodox voters, because Shas gets the support of many voters who are not ultra-Orthodox.

- In municipal elections, ultra-Orthodox voter turnout is also higher than the national average. In 2003, for example, it was higher in the ultra-Orthodox neighborhoods of Jerusalem (Tesler 2005). In some ultra-Orthodox towns and Jerusalem neighborhoods, voter turnout was almost 90 percent. In 2013, voter turnout in Bnei Brak was 67.2 percent and in Rechasim, 79 percent (Atmor 2013).
- The extensive communal organizing of the ultra-Orthodox continues the tradition of autonomous organizing that was once (and still is) characteristic of Jewish communities in the Diaspora. There are no disaggregated statistics for ultra-Orthodox organizations; we only note that, in 1998, religious organizations comprised 43 percent of all the registered non-profits in Israel, well beyond the proportion of observant Jews in the population. In 2007, some 40 percent of the newly registered organizations were religious (Balbachan 2008a). These groups are active in education (after-school programs, yeshivot [religious schools], and educational institutions funded by the state, such as the independent network of the Torah Judaism Party and El Hama'ayan of Shas), welfare, culture, synagogues, *mikvaot* (ritual baths), and charities (Gidron et al. 2003, 61–62). Most of the funding for third-sector organizations in ultra-Orthodox society comes from state coffers, and a small portion from donations.
- Another channel of committed participation in which the ultra-Orthodox have been active (or activated) since Israel's founding is protest activity – sometimes violent – on issues such as the violation of the Sabbath, obscene publications, kashrut, and the desecration of graves.[20] These campaigns take place on two parallel fronts. On the political level, the religious parties work to preserve the status quo; in ultra-Orthodox neighborhoods, they stage protest activities, demonstrate, and block roads to challenge decisions that, in their view, undermine the Jewish character of the state. In the 1990s, for example, a violent and protracted struggle was waged around cars using Bar-Ilan Street in Jerusalem on the Sabbath; the High Court of Justice, asked to rule on the matter, recommended that a compromise be found. The court itself turned into a target of ultra-Orthodox protest in the wake of decisions taken on religious matters, particularly following the conviction of Aryeh Deri. A demonstration by the ultra-Orthodox against the Supreme Court in February 1999 was regarded as one of the largest ever held in Jerusalem.

These patterns of political participation reflect efforts by the ultra-Orthodox camp to protect its communal autonomy in order to preserve its faith and way of life, and this has been successful. To that end – and particularly to preserve its independent school system – the leaders have made a choice to take part in the formal political system in exchange for state resources. Such participation exacts a price – contact with those outside the community. The Ashkenazi ultra-Orthodox have managed

[20] Since 1949, the ultra-Orthodox have demonstrated against the violation of the Sabbath, throwing stones at cars traveling on the Sabbath and clashing with the police at a Jerusalem intersection that has become known as Sabbath Square (Hermann 1995, 109).

with great effort to maintain an autonomous civic system, a kind of federation of the dynastic groups, built on absolute obedience – not always successful – to the religious leaders. The Sephardic ultra-Orthodox remained organized around one party as long as Rabbi Ovadia Yosef was alive. He died in 2013, and in the 2015 election they split into two opposing parties.

The state has recognized the special needs of the ultra-Orthodox, but this policy has encountered mounting opposition among the secular public, particularly in two areas: exemptions from military service for yeshiva students, and allocations to ultra-Orthodox institutions without oversight of the authorities (on relations between the state and a cultural minority, see Margalit and Halbertal 1998). In terms of political participation, the Israeli ultra-Orthodox are an interesting case of "inclusion without assimilation." The state scored a victory by bringing the ultra-Orthodox into the political system in exchange for leaving them out of the social system. This is a source of tension between the sides, and it is too early to say if political participation encouraged the isolation of the ultra-Orthodox community from Israeli society or vice versa – that its isolation led to political participation.

C. New Immigrants

Upon their arrival into Israel, Jewish immigrants are given citizenship and the right to vote, irrespective of their knowledge of the language or political system, or their acculturation into society. Unlike Arab or ultra-Orthodox citizens of Israel, new immigrants do not remain one defined bloc of political participants, unless ethnicity is held constant, and in this sense they have not left a clear and lasting imprint on the political system. This generalization, though true, ignores the many efforts to establish a party of immigrants, new and veteran. The country of origin of Jewish voters has had a marked influence on their voting patterns, and also on the character and composition of the candidate lists in all the parties. This was reflected in the Likud rise to power in 1977 thanks to the strong support of immigrants from north African and Asian countries, and the appearance of Shas as an avowed Sephardic party. But if the emphasis is on *new* immigrants – up to twenty years in the country – their political influence has been relatively limited. This was the case, as we shall see below, until the wave of immigration from the former Soviet Union beginning in the early 1990s. We present below the main points of political participation for three groups – Mizrahim, "Russians," and "Ethiopians."

- The mass wave of immigration following the establishment of Israel did not change the balance of power among the parties, with the new immigrant votes only reinforcing the existing political structure, then dominated by Mapai. With the exception of several examples (the New Immigrant Party, eventually becoming the Progressives in 1948, and the Union of North African Immigrants, which almost entered the Knesset in 1959), the new immigrants did not establish their own parties. As elsewhere in immigrant countries, they were beset by the hardships of absorption, generally identified with the system that took them in, and their political participation was primarily recruited and responsive. This, however, does not contradict the growing sense of deprivation and frustration among north African and Asian immigrants, which intensified over the years and led to the emergence of the Black Panther protest movement in the early 1970s – a milestone in the history of non-establishment political participation in Israel.[21] The votes of the second and third generation of north African–Asian immigrants in the elections of the 1970s led to the toppling from power of Labor and the legitimation of party representation on an ethnic-religious basis with the appearance of Tami, in 1981, and Shas, above all, which has survived since 1984, unlike most other new parties. Along with party participation, civil society activism also thrived. For example, the Mizrahi Democratic Rainbow (see Chapter 16) operated with noteworthy success against the institutional discrimination of Mizrahim in Israel.

- Since the late 1980s, approximately one million immigrants have entered Israel from the former Soviet Union ("the Russians"), constituting some 15 percent of the Israeli population in 2012. The immigrants came from disparate regions and reflected stark differences among them, but the Russian speakers clung to their language and culture, and developed a fairly autonomous social system. Accordingly, they took a different approach to participating in the political system: They wanted to participate, not assimilate, and become a meaningful, independent, political force. The reasons for this were related to the massive size of this immigrant population, their brief but intense relocation, and the resources available for political participation (education), which they brought with them. From the outset, the voter turnout and political involvement of "the Russians" were high. In the 1992 election, they had not yet organized independently, and most voted for the Labor Party, contributing to the election of Yitzhak Rabin as prime minister. In 1996, an independent immigrant party was founded – Yisrael B'Aliyah – headed by Natan Sharansky (which grew out of the Zionist Forum organization); Yisrael B'Aliyah won seven seats in the Knesset and contributed to Benjamin Netanyahu's assumption of power. In the 1999 election, most of their votes for prime minister went to Ehud Barak, while their votes for the Knesset were split between two Russian parties – Yisrael B'Aliyah (six seats) and Yisrael Beitenu, headed by Avigdor Lieberman (four seats). In the 2003 election, some 40 percent of the Russian voters said they would vote for Russian or partially Russian parties (Yisrael B'Aliyah and Yisrael Beitenu, which joined the National Union Party). Many of the other voters also showed hawkish views (about a quarter voted Likud) and anti-religious views (about a fifth went to Shinui) (Goldstein and Gitelman 2004). In the 2006 election, their distinctive voice dissipated as most settled into the right side of the political map, but even then Yisrael Beitenu headed by Avigdor Lieberman became the main "Russian party," collecting eleven seats – about half the Russian immigrant vote (Constantinov 2008). In the 2009 election, the "Russian" sectoral vote was particularly strong: An estimated two-thirds of the Yisrael Beitenu votes (fifteen seats) came from Russian immigrants. In the 2013 election, Yisrael Beitenu joined the Likud and held thirteen of the thirty-one seats won by the joint faction and separately six seats in 2015.[22] In addition to their unique and rapid integration into the political system,

[21] Stenographed protocol from a meeting of the prime minister with the Black Panthers, April 13, 1971 (Jerusalem, 1971).

[22] Yisrael Beitenu left the Likud in 2014. On the voting patterns of immigrants, see Chapters 9 and 10.

immigrants from the former Soviet Union were also distinctive in founding voluntary organizations, particularly in culture and leisure (see Chapter 12 on civil society). They left their mark on the political system of Israel, certainly considering that, since 1992, a significant portion of them voted for the political leader, party, or camp that rode into power, and their representatives have generally been part of the government coalition.

- In contrast with the "Russians," the "Ethiopians" have won virtually no political representation. Their numbers are much smaller: The large waves of immigration from Ethiopia (1980–90) brought in 56,000 people, some 50 percent of all immigrants during those years.[23] This group did not have the resources required for political participation such as education and political skills, hence, despite their efforts, not one Ethiopian immigrant party has won a seat in the Knesset.[24] A handful of Ethiopian immigrants were placed on the lists of other parties. In 2006, 268 voluntary organizations were registered as belonging to or working on behalf of Ethiopian immigrants (Balbachan 2008). (Also see Chapter 12 on the political participation of Ethiopian immigrants.) Their characteristic pattern of participation was repeated demonstrations calling upon the government to bring to Israel family members still in Ethiopia and in protest of discrimination and absorption policies. One matter that incensed the Ethiopian immigrants and many others concerned the fact that the medical authorities were dumping blood donated by Ethiopian immigrants out of fear that it was contaminated with AIDS. In a 1996 demonstration outside the Prime Minister's Office, some 10,000 Ethiopian immigrants held signs saying, "Our blood is just like yours." Clashes with security forces ended in injury to person and property (following which a public committee was appointed to study the event; see Navon Committee Report 1996). This incident clearly captures their sense of being outsiders to Israeli society, and they continue to endure discrimination in every aspect of their lives.

The groups discussed above are very different from each other, but reflect some general findings about political participation. First, efforts at inclusion have been made with the goal of preventing these groups from being left out of the political system. These have taken several forms: co-optation of the Arabs and new immigrants, and significant concessions to the ultra-Orthodox. Indeed, during the early years of the state, the responsive participation patterns of these groups, particularly voting, resembled participation patterns of the general population. Second, as time passed, the democratic system gradually opened up to these groups, enabling them to assume autonomous and more committed channels of participation, including vehement protest of government policy. Third, in the 2000s, each of these groups as well as others not mentioned here have feelings of inefficacy and deprivation – for

[23] Central Bureau of Statistics, *Statistical Abstract* 2007, table 4.4, website of the Ministry of Aliyah and Immigrant Absorption.

[24] Such as Atid Ehad: A Good Future for Israel, headed by Avraham Negusa, which ran for the seventeenth Knesset on a platform of improving the lives of Ethiopian immigrants and bringing the Jews still left in Ethiopia into Israel.

various reasons and at different levels of intensity – that could engender alienation and thwart efforts to include them in the political system.

8.5 Have Israeli Citizens Given up on the Political System?

Political participation in Israel has changed its face. In the early years of the state, participation was extensive, but primarily recruited, responsive, and sponsored by the parties. This pattern gradually lost hold, with voter turnout falling in both the general and municipal elections; on the other hand, the political activism of civil society organizations has intensified, including demonstrations and protest about political and social issues. Israeli citizens are goal-oriented: knowledgeable about politics, closely following events, and looking for ways to participate based on needs and where they believe they can make a difference. Citizens do leave home when something affects them personally, or when a critical decision is imminent (e.g., the future of the territories or socioeconomic matters). Another factor that plays a growing role and we shall examine in the chapter about parties is activism based on identity politics – participation in accord with a group characteristic such as ethnicity, religiosity, gender, or age (Yishai 2001). Table 8.6 indicates that this redefined the party map and composition of about half the Knesset, and has remained strong for a decade or more.

In the early 2000s, catch-all parties accounted for about half the MKs, fewer in 2015. In their place came sector-identity parties – parties whose constituents have a defined collective characteristic – creating a pattern of participation previously unknown. While direct election of the prime minister accelerated this process, the main reason was that a third of the voters in Israel could not find a party to vote for, and disengaged entirely from party politics, or found other channels for civic activity. Voters who had not disengaged chose a distinctive sectoral representation. In parallel, reduced trust in state institutions contributed to the decline in participation by agreement, and to more protest activity and extra-parliamentary activism.

A. Changes in the Channels of Participation

The diminished role of the parties as a mediating agent was integral to this process. On the one hand, the parties became more open and added elements of direct democratic participation, such as holding primaries and election of the party chair. On the other hand, the participation of those recruited for membership is instrumental and mobilized – they have no commitment to the party or its vision, and signed up for membership solely for the purpose of influencing the list of candidates. We mentioned the referendum conducted among Likud members on the plan to disengage from Gaza in May 2004 – an innovation in the democratic life of parties – in which members were to determine the party's position before the government or Knesset makes a decision. The outcome, however, was the opposite: Those who voted in the referendum rejected the plan proposed by their leaders, but this had no effect whatsoever on government policy led by Ariel Sharon. The referendum outcome did expedite Sharon's departure from the Likud and establishment of the Kadima Party.

One alternative to political participation via parties or elections was to shift this participation to voluntary organizations, which contributed to the accelerated

Table 8.6 *Identity parties in the fifteenth and twentieth Knessets*

	1999 (15th Knesset)		2015 (20th Knesset)	
	Number of parties	Total seats	Number of parties	Total seats
Religious/Ultra-Orthodox	2	10	2*	14
Ethnic religious (Shas)	1	17	1	7
Arab, Arab-Jewish	3	10	1	13
Russian	2	10	1**	6
Secular	1	6	1***	11
Settlers	1	4	****	-
Total	10	57	6	51

* Torah Judaism + Jewish Home (NRP).
** Yisrael Beitenu.
*** Yesh Atid.
**** Within Jewish Home.

growth of civic society in Israel. This was related to changes in the standard of living: Population groups that enjoy a higher standard of living have more resources for participation, but perhaps also a tendency to escapism; others who experience a lowering of their standard of living and even poverty may show increased passivity as a result of despair and alienation from the political system, although more protest may also result. Another option is the reflection of "participation" in the media, which is actually passive participation. Nevertheless, the media enhance the chronicling of protest activity, and thereby leverage political participation. We also mentioned technological developments, which create a virtually limitless range of social channels for the political participation of citizens – recruited and not recruited. These channels expand access to information and to unorganized horizontal media, and can provide a means to trigger social activity or protest. They also allow for manipulation, the spread of misinformation, and intemperate language.

Violence

Israel also has citizens whose political participation may involve illegal activity, and some do not shun violence.[25] The assassination of Rabin was a warning of the thin line that separates protest, incitement, and assassination. Political protest (and with some qualifications also refusal to serve in the military) is a legitimate democratic tool for citizens who believe in democracy. It is not legitimate when conducted violently by those seeking to undermine the rule of law and democracy. In this sense, political participation in Israel does not always reflect the internalization of democratic values, but sometimes quite the opposite: the unwillingness of citizens to accept the rule of law and majority rule. Acts of extremism harm not just governance, but also the

[25] For instance, acts of vandalism carried out by religious settlers known as "price tag" actions (Byman and Sachs 2012).

rights of other citizens to participate legitimately in the political process. Violence is beyond the pale in a democracy. It can also lead governments to suppress political participation: to muzzle the media, restrain freedom of expression, broaden the definition of incitement, and narrow the freedoms of assembly and demonstration.

"Anti-politics"

In many democratic countries, including Israel, citizens have an aversion to and even revulsion from politics and politicians. This is manifested as changes in the participation patterns, as noted above, from a drop in voting rates to a search for alternative channels such as civil society activism. One also finds a disdainful tone among political commentators in the media, support for a "government of experts" rather than elected politicians, an unwillingness of talented people to enter politics, etc. On the ideological level, there is a search for alternatives – not just alternative politics and parties, but even another country. We note briefly some of these different phenomena in Israel:

- neoliberal views, which seek to reduce the role of the state and transfer some of its functions to the private sector;
- pronouncements of non-state loyalty – to religion, universal values, global values;
- the community as the main object of loyalty;
- holding the individual and his rights as the sole or main sense of identity.

In and of themselves, these approaches are not a threat to the democratic political system, as long as they do not seek to replace democracy itself. A democratic government, for example, does not attempt to prevent loyalty to religious precepts – it allows the individual to declare that for them, "Thou shalt not kill" is above all a religious or moral precept before it is the law of the land. However, a democratic regime does not allow violation of the law in the name of a religious precept. Thus, the danger to democratic political participation stems from two related phenomena: One is the demand for depoliticization – the removal of as many collective issues as possible from the political system. In Israel this could be a constitution that does not prescribe equality between citizens but gives religious or national priority to the Jewish community, or obedience to leaders who call for breaking the law or placing the Land of Israel above all other commitments.

The second threat to democratic participation has been called "anti-politics" (Hay 2007). It is dangerous to democracy, but less so than depoliticization because it is more about feelings than a world view. Citizens with these feelings – which now encompass most Israelis – have despaired of politics, but not of the political system. Anti-politics is still politics. Citizens loathe politicians and their behavior, but they organize, demonstrate, and protest to change it from within. It is still political participation that does not convey indifference; even those who do not vote and are completely passive do not deny the importance of collective politics. They simply feel that they have no influence over it whatsoever. The border is thin, and anti-politics could easily deteriorate into a search for non-political and even non-democratic alternatives. These voices in Israel have grown louder in recent years, particularly in light of the belief that citizens cannot effect change and politicians are corrupt (Hermann, Zaban, and Lebel 2008). Nevertheless, Israeli citizens still have many expectations of the state and want it to be more involved, not just because of the security situation, but also as a player in the socioeconomic arena – an expectation that increased as a result of the world economic crisis of 2008–9.

B. Does Participation Make a Difference?

Despite lower participation in channels such as voting, most Israeli citizens still vote; indeed, participation in channels that require initiative and commitment has even increased. But does participation have an impact? There is no unequivocal answer, not just because of the constraints of measuring "impact," but also because the impact of participation is closely related to the steering capacity of the political system. When steering capacity is high and stable, as it was during the first two decades of the state, political participation was recruited and reactive, and had less concrete effect. The weakening of the steering capacity actually increased the impact, or at least the potential impact, of citizens, particularly when organized. Some milestones in the political history of Israel serve as indicators. The Lavon affair in the early 1960s undermined the hegemony of Mapai and marked the rise of the media as an independent source of political information; the transfer of power in 1977 showed the ability of voters to change the government; the political stalemate between the two camps in the elections of the 1980s and the National Unity Governments accelerated the organizing of extra-parliamentary groups; the weakening of the political system in the 1990s led to the flourishing of civil society and voluntary organizations. The many election campaigns in the 2000s and the pendulum swings between the parties indicate that an Israeli citizen who chooses to participate in politics can have considerable impact on the elections and the periods between them.

Is the political system responsive to citizens – does it reward political participation? Or is it elitist and manipulative, channeling the participation of citizens as it wills? Most Israeli citizens would say that the latter is correct – that they raise their voices, but the politicians turn a deaf ear. There is a pervasive feeling among citizens that they have no influence. In our opinion, however, the answer is more complex. Israel is an example of a dynamic political system that encourages deep political involvement and a high level of participation. The Israeli citizen does not feel influential because of his goal-oriented temperament and high level of expectation. He derides the culture of political debate, which he considers vacuous when results are not immediate, rushing to the conclusion that he is unable to bring about real change (Ben-Eliezer 1993). The influence of Israeli citizens is indeed small in matters of foreign policy and security, but not negligible in matters of domestic policy, within the constraints of participatory channels noted above. We therefore conclude this chapter by noting that democracy requires alertness, participation, and continuous scrutiny, and there is no guarantee that it will survive other than through the autonomous participation of informed citizens who act out of a sense of responsibility and stick to the rules of the game (Galnoor 1982, 87).

9 Political Parties: Can We Get Along Without Them?

...modern democracy is unthinkable save in terms of the parties.

(Schattschneider 1942)[1]

9.1 The Institution Called a "Party"

Parties, in the classic definition of Almond and Powell (1978), aggregate and represent the interests and views of groups. Parties are organizations that mediate between citizens and the government, and between the government and citizens. Unlike other organizations and mediators, parties aspire to take power and exercise it. As a social organization, they create space for deliberating political ideas and a framework for the political involvement of citizens. At the government level, they are the standing bodies that organize parliamentary work, form coalitions, and coordinate among the various authorities in power. These two functions coalesce in the central event of representational democracy – elections. The parties sort through, aggregate, and represent the various public positions and interests, and mold them into a common platform. They recruit and select candidates, pose ideological alternatives to the voters, and translate these desires into political power through the election process (R. Katz 1996, 108). They also play a vital role between elections – as a channel of communication between voters and elected officials, and mobilizing support for the party in power. Although parties seek to create a common ideological and practical platform for people whose views are similar, the term "parties" evokes associations of parting and divisiveness.[2] Parties are a modern invention – the first institution to create opportunities for mass participation in politics – and yet they have lost their charm for the public. This incongruity stems from the fact that parties are an entirely political channel: The decline in their status relates to the rise of anti-politics in democratic states, discussed at the close of the previous chapter.

[1] Schattschneider was preceded by Hans Kelsen, who wrote in 1929, "Only **self-deception** or hypocrisy can maintain that democracy is possible without political parties ... Democracy is necessarily and inevitably a party state" (Kelsen 1929, 127).

[2] In English the word "party" derives from the Latin *partiri*, to "divide into parts." In Middle English, this evolved into denoting a body of people united in opposition to others. In Hebrew, the root PLG evokes associations of split, separation [פילוג].

The origin of modern political parties is commonly set in the context of nineteenth-century American parties, although the founders of the American republic were wary of them: James Madison, for example, saw parties as divisive, and therefore a threat to the abiding and collective interest of the community. Over time, as the growth of mass democracy made impractical a direct link between the state and masses of citizens, the need arose for mediating institutions, such as parties. The growth of parties as mediators is related to two other parallel events: the establishment of legislatures and the enfranchisement of broad swaths of the adult population. At first, parties grew gradually, commensurate with the activities of the legislators; only in the late nineteenth century did parties rooted outside parliament begin to evolve. The best-known of these were the workers' parties: Labour of Britain and the Social Democrats of Germany. Although parties became indispensable, their relationship with democratic principles continued to be amorphous into the twentieth century. Parties are not mentioned, for example, even in the oldest of democratic constitutions. In new constitutions written after World War II (Germany and Italy), the critical role played by parties began to emerge, and they were included in constitutional documents. It became clear that strong (democratic) parties not only provide an open, civic framework for political participation and electoral competition, but also contribute to the stability of a democratic regime. By the mid-twentieth century, parties were already regarded as an inalienable part of modern politics.

A. Types of Parties in Modern Democracy

The first modern political parties were *elite parties*, founded and run by propertied social elites. Their sphere of activity was local, and they were composed of a small and exclusive circle of members from which parliament candidates were elected or appointed. Elite parties operated in Europe in the nineteenth century, but were not a role model for the parties founded in Israel during the Yishuv period.

Mass parties began in Europe in the late nineteenth and early twentieth centuries, founded by social groups not among the propertied class from which the elite parties drew members. Initially these were the parties of the "unrepresented" and often disenfranchised, and therefore most of them were first extra-parliamentary movements. Mass parties were identified with the working class and labor unions, but they also organized and acted on the basis of religious-cultural identity. A mass party that views itself as the exclusive spokesperson of a defined social group seeks to isolate its members from outside influences and respond to their needs in all areas of life. This meant creating a network of party-affiliated organizations – at the workplace, the residence, for health services, culture, leisure, and sport. Party loyalty therefore derived from a combination of factors – from ideological commitment and personal/group identification to dependence on party services. The large parties during the pre- and early state period – the workers' parties, Mizrahi, and Ha-Mizrahi, and to some extent also later Herut – were mass parties. Ben Aharon, former Secretary General of the Histadrut, described the "battery power" of the workers' parties as follows: At one pole is the ideology and at the other pole, the movement – the organization (Ben-Aharon 1977, 54).

Cadre parties have a narrow base. There are few registered members, and they are headed by a small group of leaders and politicos. In cadre parties, ideology is of secondary importance, as party activity is mainly and narrowly focused on the election period, with a decentralized and rather loose formal organization (Duverger 1972, 63–71; Neuberger 1997, 18–29). Cadre parties are more characteristic of presidential democracies, but are also currently active in parliamentary regimes. As they declined, the veteran mass parties turned into cadre parties, which encouraged the rise of new cadre parties that come to life primarily at election time. In Israel of the 2000s, the Likud and Labor parties still registered members, but they were focused on elections and functioned as cadre parties.

Catch-all parties strive to create a platform with positions and solutions that address all the key issues in society, or those of importance to main groups. They are the mirror image of one-issue or sectoral parties. Catch-all parties (which had once hoped to become mass parties) flourished during the golden age of parties, but soon vanished, to some extent because of increased social mobility and the growth of the middle classes at the expense of the working class. Establishing and maintaining political parties based on separate identities or social class has become increasingly difficult because fewer voters are joining parties, the link between parties and their affiliated organizations has weakened, and parties are finding it hard to preserve their distinctive social profile.

Thus, we see a transition from mass, ideological parties to pragmatic ones, whose virtually only goal is to increase their electoral edge. The ideological component of these parties has faded, and their messages are deliberately vague so they can attract as broad a constituency as possible (Kirchheimer 1966). Catch-all parties are not funded by dues (membership has gradually fallen) or self-generated income, but tend to raise funds from people of wealth or the state coffers.[3] The party leadership is more autonomous, shirking accountability to the party members or institutions, which had characterized the age of mass parties (Mair 1998, 23–32). The process undergone by Mapai is typical of the transition from a mass to a catch-all party, and the turning point was state funding for political parties as of 1969. Based on the 2015 election results, catch-all parties in Israel were the Likud and Labor, though neither won more than 25 percent of the vote, despite their "catch-allness."

B. The Decline of Parties

Toward the end of the twentieth century, political parties in democracies began to decline. The somewhat romantic image of smoke-filled rooms where leaders sit up all night debating the fate of the nation has been replaced by dark visions of corrupt politicians who are interested only in benefiting themselves. Surveys reflect the low trust of citizens in parties. The main criticism is that parties no longer serve an ideological or social function – shaping ideology, educating politically, bridging social

[3] A new model that appeared together with the catch-all party has been called a "cartel party," which resembles them in the vagueness of their messages. The cartel party is an unofficial agreement among party elites designed to preserve their power. As in a business cartel, rivalry is set aside and constraints are instituted to reduce competition. The elites cooperate among themselves to keep out new players who could undermine their monopoly on the party system. When a party cartel is created, none of the member parties is considered illegitimate, and because competition has not entirely disappeared, citizens believe they still have a choice – generally from a list of long standing parties that periodically trade positions of power (Katz and Mair 1992).

gaps, and even being representative – but serve only as a springboard for politicians to land public jobs. Another aspect that we address below is the organizational failure of parties as democratic institutions. The currently unclear status of parties stems to a large extent from the tension between their perception as institutions that are essential to a modern democracy and their growing inability to carry out tasks that are vital to strengthening democracy.

At the conclusion of this chapter, we examine the question of whether a democratic regime is possible without parties. From the perspective of the early twenty-first century, we note that an alternative to parties has not yet been found that can fulfill the same vital role of aggregating and representing interests and views. Civil society organizations and the media, like business organizations, are a critical component of every democracy, but they are not designed – and do not have the legitimacy – to represent citizens (Webb, Farrell, and Holliday 2002). A fascinating question in this context is whether the online social media have opened up new possibilities, i.e., can parties be organized and activated in virtual channels based on online affiliations (and perhaps even membership)?

9.2 Parties in Israel

At the time of the Yishuv and early years of the state, party politics was the essence of the democratic system. The state of Israel emerged from a political system controlled by parties that drew their power from a fairly well-honed ideology, an effective organizational infrastructure, extensive socioeconomic activity, a large membership base, and generous support from public resources. Mapai, the dominant party, together with parties that joined the government coalitions, also took control of other governmental systems: the civil service, the Histadrut, the Jewish Agency, and the local authorities. From the Yishuv period until the mid-1960s, Israel was to a large extent "a party country" (Akzin 1955). The parties served as the main coordinating agents of the political system and performed the role of a clearing house – they gathered, coordinated, and regulated the many opposing demands. The parties succeeded at this task thanks to their control over the main political resources: organizational power, information, funds, jobs, etc. Their power (particularly of those who took part in governance) was drawn from the fact that the struggles over political resources took place primarily through party channels.

The ability of the parties to coordinate among opposing interests was reflected in an agreement reached in internal party forums that obligated their representatives in the Knesset, government, local authorities, Histadrut, government corporations, and other organizations (Galnoor 1985, 161–63). The parties operated a kind of "organizational supermarket" during this period, dividing up political assets via the "cash register" that kept the accounts and allocated resources (Galnoor 1977a, 17). This was carried out in accordance with the "party key" – arrangements between the dominant party and the other parties on the division of funds, jobs, and other resources. Mapai, the dominant party during the first decades, maintained a network of branches through the Histadrut workers' councils and the large workers' committees. The political networks of Mapai and several other parties encompassed diverse areas such as youth movements, health funds, sports clubs, housing companies, welfare services, and even banks. In the mid-1950s, Mapai had more than 400 local branches and some 150,000 members (Medding 1972, 89).

This party system has been variously characterized by scholars of the period as "democracy by an alternative method"; the omnipotent control of party mechanisms by Bolshevik means; governance based on negotiation, compromise, and coalition; and parties as "coordinating agents" (Etzioni 1959; J. Shapira 1977; Horowitz and Lissak 1978; Galnoor 1982). In any case, all agree that parties were the key factor in crafting the steering capacity of the political system. The decline in their power began in the 1960s, and the changes in Israel resembled changes among the mass parties in western democracies, particularly upon the entry of mass media, which reduced the citizen's dependence on information filtered through the parties. The rigid social stratification also began to crumble – mobility increased and class loyalty decreased, which took a toll on the parties. New interest groups began to appear on stage, and they created for themselves alternative channels of access to government centers. The change was even more profound in Israel, and began to undermine both the party hegemony over the political system and internal party cohesion.

This became apparent in Mapai as early as the 1960s. The Lavon affair caused ruptures that culminated in the resignation of Ben-Gurion and other party stalwarts in 1965. Since the Six Day War (1967), the political system has been unable to resolve the key problem (peace and security), which climaxed in the Yom Kippur War (1973). Since then, public trust in the government and, in particular, in the parties and their political wheeler-dealers has begun to fade. The parties gradually lost their ability to function not just as coordinating agents, but even as forums for public discourse. The large parties turned into cadre parties – a loose framework that comes to life for elections, when political positions are at stake. The disappearance of the party link between society and politics means that tension in sensitive social areas like religion, the status of Arab citizens of Israel, or inequality are no longer mediated through parties and now exert direct pressure on the political system. The aggregation of interests is no longer carried out by parties in a way that enables political stability (Galnoor 1998, 196–97).

The Likud and Labor of the 2000s demonstrate the skeletal nature of party activity, as do newer parties such as Kadima (2009), Yesh Atid (2013), and Kulanu (2015). Local branches, if they exist at all, are not a focus of party activity; the involvement of party members is solicited only for events such as election of a new party congress or leadership; and members disappear from view for long periods. There is no longer an omnipotent mechanism, and the party organization is primarily used to run the election campaign. The parties are mired in debt, and generous state funding (see below) does not cover the shortfall. Organizations that had once been linked to parties have disappeared or been unlinked from them – party newspapers,[4] health funds, welfare services, the kibbutz movement – and even the link between parties and sports clubs dissolved after most were sold to private owners. Personalizing politics also hurt the party mediator function: Election campaigns in Israel, as in most

[4] In 2015, the remaining party daily newspapers belonged to religious parties – *Hamodia* and *Yated Ne'eman* – and the Communist Party (the weekly *Yom LeYom* and *al-Ittihad*). The freely distributed *Israel Today* is considered a daily mouthpiece of Netanyahu and the Likud.

democracies (including parliamentary systems), now focus on individual leaders rather than policy or ideology (King 2002), and clear signs of presidentialization are evident (Poguntke and Webb 2005).

During the period in Israel of direct election of the prime minister (1996–2003), those who were elected – Netanyahu, Barak, and Sharon – conducted their campaigns from "above the party," demonstrating its insignificance to them. Although they won, their victory did not sweep their party into the Knesset with a large majority. This trend continued after repeal of the direct election law, when PR experts replaced politicians in designing the campaign and turned the spotlight on the candidates; the media followed suit. This was reflected in the official names of the parties, as in 2015: "The Likud led by Benjamin Netanyahu for Prime Minister"; "The Zionist Camp led by Yitzhak Herzog and Tzipi Livni"; "Yesh Atid led by Yair Lapid"; "Kulanu led by Moshe Kahlon."

The parties active in Israel in the 2000s can be divided into two groups. The first includes the veteran parties, whose roots are in the Yishuv and had in fact originated in eastern Europe at the turn of the twentieth century. They do not bear their original names, but these are clearly veteran parties in terms of historical continuity. Six continued into the twentieth Knesset (2015): Labor (the heir of Poalei Tziyon and the historic Ahdut Ha'avoda, later Mapai); Likud (Revisionist movement and Herut); Torah Judaism (Agudat Yisrael); Jewish Home-National Religious Party (Mizrahi and Ha-Mizrahi); Hadash, part of the Arab United List (Palestine Communist Party and the Israeli Communist Party); as well as Mapam within Meretz. The second group is composed of "made in Israel" political parties. Most parties formed after the establishment of Israel were short-lived; among the relatively veteran parties that continued into the Knesset were Meretz, the heir of Ratz (first elected to the Knesset in 1973); Shas (since 1984); Degel Hatorah (since 1988, today part of Torah Judaism); and the Arab Democratic Party (since 1988, today part of the United Arab List).[5] Thus, the oldest native Israeli party was forty-two years old in 2015.

9.3 Legal Underpinnings

In addition to changes in the functioning of the parties, whose frameworks became looser and more open, their legal status also changed from voluntary non-profits to organizations regulated by two specific laws – the Parties Financing Law (1973), discussed below, and the Parties Law (1992), which altered the constitutional status of the parties, though it is not a Basic Law. Regulating party activity by law poses a dilemma: Isn't it better to allow the parties to run their own affairs as they see fit without intervention from a legislator? After all, voluntary civic organizing could wither if the laws governing them are too formal.

What are the arguments *against* legally regulating party activity? First, it is yet another attempt to judicialize politics, i.e., to fix problems in the political culture by recourse to legal avenues – and past experience has not always turned out well. Second, damaging the voluntary nature of party organizing could curtail the freedom

[5] The Shinui Party founded in 1974 is not the same Shinui Party created prior to the 1999 election that disappeared in 2006. With regard to the other parties in 2015 – Yesh Atid; Kulano; Yisrael Beitenu; and the Joint Arab List – it is too early to say whether they will be short-lived.

of political assembly of social groups. Third, for these very reasons, the law in most western democracies does not regulate party activity.[6] The Parties Law in Israel should be examined on these arguments in the context of the reality in Israel – the need to defend democracy from parties with non-democratic goals, and the desire to ensure the internal-party democratic structure, including procedures for electing party leaders and Knesset candidates (Rubinstein and Medina 1996, 568).

A. Parties Law (1992)

In the wake of the Parties Law, parties entered the constitutional framework of Israel upon enactment of an amendment to the Basic Law: The Knesset (Article 5A): "A list of candidates for the Knesset shall be submitted only by a party; the means of association and registering of parties and the conditions for submitting a list of candidates shall be determined by law." Until that point, organizing as a party was not a condition for participating in the Knesset election or being eligible for public funding. This amendment stipulates that lists of election candidates may be submitted only by registered parties, thereby preventing the spontaneity of independent lists entering the race at the last minute.

According to this law, a party is "a group of persons who joined together in order to promote in a legal way political or social objectives and to express them in the Knesset by their representatives."[7] The law regulates how a party can be founded: At least 100 adult citizens must register with the Party Registrar. To register, applicants must submit the name of the party, its goals, information about the founders, and the party's articles of association. The Party Registrar has the authority to refuse to register a party for formal reasons, such as its name, or for substantive reasons, such as its goals or deeds. Article 5 of the Parties Law, which lists the goals and deeds for which the Party Registrar is authorized to deny a party's application for registration, parallels Article 7A of the Basic Law: The Knesset, which deals with the legitimate grounds for disqualifying lists of candidates.[8] Because refusing to register a party could be a violation of the freedom of assembly, disqualifying a list requires confirmation by the Supreme Court.

Another purpose of the law is to regulate the internal order of the party – how it is managed, the proper spheres of activity of its institutions, the election of party candidates to the Knesset, and the conditions for party membership. The law mandates that there must be rules, but does not set uniform rules for all the parties. Article 14, for example, states that the party must have articles of association under which it operates, and that these articles must include the conditions for party membership, the rights and obligations of members, the establishment of party institutions, rules for choosing candidates for election, etc. The law does not set the specific terms or structure of the institutions.

6 Laws regulating parties are common in countries that have experienced non-democratic regimes – Germany, Austria, Spain, Poland. Other countries (France, Italy, Sweden, Greece) have no law regulating parties, although constitutional articles deal with parties. Britain, Canada, Australia, Holland, Belgium, and Switzerland do not mention parties in their constitutions.

7 This definition excludes local authority elections.

8 When Article 7A was expanded to include more grounds for disqualification, Article 5 of the Parties Law was also amended (see Chapter 11).

In the course of writing the law, legislators disagreed vehemently about whether a party should be forced to institute internal democratic procedures. This has significant implications: Can a democratic political system rest on non-democratic parties? The subject is particularly sensitive in Israel because the ultra-Orthodox and several other parties[9] do not have internal democratic practices, even for the sake of appearance. As a result, the Parties Law does not mandate internal democracy and does not define the method for selecting candidates. It makes do with stating that party candidates for the Knesset shall be elected "by one of the party institutions in accordance with the articles of association."

B. Parties, Factions, and Lists of Candidates

A *party* is an organizational entity that works to promote common goals. Every party operating in Israel is registered in the Party Registry. A list that does not aspire to parliamentary representation and is active only locally is not considered a party.

A *faction* is the parliamentary arm of the party and is composed of the Knesset members who represent it. The faction is the main organizer of parliamentary activity in the Knesset. Membership in the standing Knesset committees, for example, is determined by factional representation. Financial allocations to parties are also given to the factions.

List of candidates: Prior to the election, every party submits a list of 120 candidates for the Knesset, using various methods of selection.[10] After the vote is counted, a party that has won X seats receives that number of representatives in the Knesset, installed in accordance with their ranking on the list of candidates submitted. The individual voter cannot change the order of candidates on the list, nor can the party change the order after the election. Prior to an election, several parties will sometimes band together to create a "bloc" or alignment and submit a joint list of candidates. Table 9.1 presents some of the noteworthy party alignments in Israel's political history.

9.4 Characteristics of a Multiparty Regime

A. The Party System

A party system in a democracy can be examined along several parameters – the number of parties, their relative size, the degree of competition between them, the ideological distance between them, their link to social cleavages, etc. We thereby eliminate from discussion the single-party systems of non-democratic states. Two-party systems are identified with the Anglo-Saxon tradition and the majoritarian system of election: Two parties win a decisive share of the votes, and these two are the only ones that effectively compete for power. In multiparty systems, three or more parties compete – a moderate multiparty system has three to five parties and a prolific multiparty system has six or more parties. Another important distinction,

[9] Prior to the 2015 elections, primaries were held in the Likud, Labor, and Meretz. No democratic elections of candidates were conducted in Yesh Atid, Kulanu, or Yisrael Beitenu.

[10] The list of Flatto Sharon in 1977 had only his name on it, which prevented the party from winning two Knesset seats in keeping with the election results. Large parties usually submit a list with 120 names, in which famous people close out the list as a way of expressing their support for the party.

Table 9.1 *Notable party alignments*

Name of the bloc of parties	Component parties (in various combinations)	Election in which it participated
Mapam	Ahdut Ha'avoda, Hashomer Hatzair	1949, 1951
United Religious Front	Mizrahi, Hapoel Ha-Mizrahi, Agudat Yisrael, Poalei Agudat Yisrael	1949
National Religious Front	Mizrahi, Hamizrahi	1955
Religious Torah Front	Agudat Yisrael, Poalei Agudat Yisrael	1955, 1959, 1973
Liberal Party	Progressives, General Zionists	1959
Herut–Liberal Bloc (Gahal)	Herut, Liberal Party	1961–69
"Small Alignment"	Mapai, Ahdut Ha'avoda	1965
Alignment	Labor, Mapam	1969–84
Likud	Herut, Liberal Party, Free Center, State List	1973–88
Hadash	Rakah, Black Panthers, Hadash–Balad, Hadash–Ta'al, Democratic Front, Maki	1977–2013
Meretz	Ratz, Mapam, Shinui, Meretz: Israel's Left	1992–2015
Torah Judaism	Agudat Yisrael, Degel Hatorah	1992–2015
Likud–Gesher–Tzomet	Likud, Gesher, Tzomet	1996
One Israel	Labor, Gesher, Meimad	1999
National Union	Yisrael Beitenu, Tekuma, Moledet	2003
Likud–Yisrael Beitenu	Likud, Yisrael Beitenu	2013
Jewish Home–National Union	Jewish Home, National Union, New NRP	2013–15
The Zionist Camp	Labor, Hatnuah	2015
The Joint (Arab) List	Hadash, Ra'am, Balad, Ta'al	2015

proposed by Sartori (1976), takes into consideration the ideological distance between the parties in order to distinguish centralized multiparty systems from polarized multiparty systems.

B. The Party System in Israel

Israeli has a prolific multiparty system based on the number of parties and their strength relative to each other. Another characteristic during the first twenty-five years of statehood, which later disappeared, was having one dominant party at the center of the multiparty system – Mapai (Labor). One characteristic that does not appear in the list below, as there are no data to substantiate it, is that party life takes place with considerable friction and little control of impulses. The main characteristics are as follows.

A Multiplicity of Parties

The pluralist social structure in Israel is reflected in the multiplicity of parties, with the proportional electoral system easing the representation of small groups. In the 2015 election, a party list required 136,859 votes to pass the 3.25 percent electoral threshold and enter the Knesset. As a result, a large number of lists – twenty-six on average

Table 9.2 *Number of parties in the Knesset with different electoral thresholds (1984–2015)*

Election year (electoral threshold)	Parties in the Knesset	Parties falling short of threshold	Votes lost (rounded off)	Percentage of lost votes	Lists in Knesset given a 1% threshold	Lists in Knesset given a 3.25% threshold	Lists in Knesset given a 5% threshold
1984 (1%)	15	11	59,000	2.8%	15	13	2
1988 (1%)	15	12	55,000	2.4%	15	11	2
1992 (1.5%)	10	15	131,000	5.0%	11	10	6
1996 (1.5%)	11	9	79,000	2.6%	11	11	6
1999 (1.5%)	15	16	197,000	6.0%	18	15	7
2003 (1.5%)	13	14	131,000	4.2%	15	13	6
2006 (2%)	12	19	182,000	5.8%	14	13	7
2009 (2%)	12	21	131,000	3.9%	12	12	5
2013 (2%)	12	20	76,000	2.0%	15	13	7
2015 (3.25%)	10	15	190,000	4.5%	12	10	8
Average (rounded off)	13	15	123,000	3.9%	14	11	6

from 1949 to 2015 – vie for the voter's favor. Until 1992, the electoral threshold was 1 percent, which is only slightly higher than the "natural threshold" into the Knesset – with 120 Knesset members, every party would need 0.83 percent of the votes to win the first seat if there were no set threshold. Raising the electoral threshold to 1.5 percent in 1992 and to 2 percent in 2006 did not fundamentally change the picture. Pushing it up to 3.25 percent, however, did bring about a reduction of two or three parties, as indicated in Table 9.2.

Table 9.2 reveals that raising the electoral threshold moderately did not affect the incentive to run for the Knesset nor did it deter voters from voting for parties that, in retrospect, had no chance of entering the Knesset. This can be seen as a positive aspect of party pluralism in Israel. Had the threshold been 5 percent in 2009, only five parties would have made it into the Knesset, assuming that voter behavior did not change, although seven parties would have made it in 2013. Raising the electoral threshold to 3.23 percent in 2015 still allowed ten parties into the Knesset, but raised the number of lost votes above the average. With a 5 percent threshold, eight parties still would have entered the Knesset.

The Parties Law, which makes prior registration mandatory to run for election, has also not affected the average number of competing lists, and lately their number has grown – to an average of thirty parties in the elections between 2006 and 2015. Most parties do not win representation, and only a dozen parties have entered the Knesset since its inception (thirteen since 1984). The multiplicity of parties means parliamentary divisions – the number of factions in the Knesset (after the election) has never been fewer than ten parties and reached a record fifteen.[11] In this sense,

[11] This refers to fifteen lists of candidates, some of which are composed of several parties: During the course of a Knesset term, more factions are usually formed than had been elected, due to splits within parties.

the Knesset is very representative and a true reflection of the main groups in society. These divisions dictate coalition governments, which have repercussions for the steering capacity of the government, as can be seen in Chapter 11.

Fragmentation

The multiplicity of parties is not unique to Israel. Many democratic countries have ten or more parties in the parliament, but the number of parties alone is an unreliable index to the nature of the party system – for comparisons or to see change over time. Counting parties ignores the relative size of the parties and accords each an equal weight. In 2004, for example, there were ten parties in the British parliament, while Israel at the time (in the sixteenth Knesset) had thirteen. The difference appears small, but is enormous, because Britain has a two-party system, while Israel's is multiparty.

A more accurate measure is the Effective Number of Parliamentary Parties (ENPP).[12] The index weights the number of parties in the parliament and their relative size. In Figure 4.1 in Chapter 4, we presented the ENPP in Israel since the first election in 1949, and the index clearly reveals that Israel is a fragmented multiparty system. The average ENPP between 1949 and 2015 was 5.6, an unusually high value compared with other democracies (Kenig et al. 2004). Even in 1981, when the two largest parties together won ninety-five of the Knesset seats (almost 80% of the vote), the ENPP did not dip below three. On the other hand, when the two big parties fell sharply in the 1999 election, the ENPP climbed to a record of almost nine, meaning unprecedented fragmentation of the party system. In the five elections in the 2000s, fragmentation returned to an average of seven, still unusually high.

Party Dominance

"Party dominance" is a concept that combines measurable data about size with value judgments about identity and symbols (Duverger 1955). A party is dominant when it has an ongoing numerical advantage over the others, and a coalition cannot be formed without it. It can be dominant even if it does not have a parliamentary majority, if the second-largest party is much smaller. While some criteria relate to coalition arithmetic, to be dominant a party must also be the object of strong identification: This was the case with Mapai (Labor) until 1973 (Goldberg 1992, 34–40). Mapai never had a majority in the Knesset, but was the dominant party not only because it was the largest, but also because of the significant difference in size between it and any other party over a prolonged period. This advantage enabled the party to be continuously in power, though it needed the support of other parties and the other parties could theoretically form a coalition government without it. Another reason it was the main component of every coalition was that it occupied the political center in terms of its positions. However, Mapai was a dominant party also because it was identified with the epic historical era of establishing the state and shaping its values, style, and political discourse. After the founding of Israel,

[12] The Effective Number of Parliamentary Parties (ENPP) weights the number of parties in the parliament and their relative size. This index is used in comparative political studies to examine changes in the number of parties (Laakso and Taagepera 1979), and is calculated according to the formula given in footnote 12, Chapter 4, about the Knesset.

Mapai kept its role as the "natural" ruling party and standard bearer of social goals in general. Until the 1960s, this was helped by the status of Ben-Gurion as a founder, a relatively cohesive political leadership, an extensive network of affiliated organizations, and control over the economic and personal resources of the state (Arian and Shamir 2004). Israel was not the only example of a western democracy dominated by one party. The Christian-Democrats in Italy (until the early 1990s), Japan's Liberal Democrats, the Swedish Social Democratic Party, and the Congress Party in India are other examples of such party systems.

In Israel, the dominant party disappeared in 1977 with the dramatic change of government, but Mapai's power had been eroding for some time. Creation of the "Little Alignment" in 1965, the founding of the Labor Party in 1968, and establishment of the "Big Alignment" in 1969 were all symptoms of Mapai's growing problems and the need to create a broader political framework in order to maintain its dominance. In 1973, after the Yom Kippur War, the Knesset gap between the Alignment and the Likud narrowed to twelve seats, and in 1977, the right overtook the left and brought about an historic transfer of power. Despite its victory in the 1977 election and again in 1981, the Likud did not inherit the mantle of dominance that the Labor Party had worn, because it did not win a much larger number of votes than the other parties over a prolonged period. Since then, there have been many changes of government and the central axis in the government coalition has not been the same party more than twice in a row, and even fell to several transient centrist parties upon occasion (see Chapter 11). During the period of direct election of the prime minister (1996–2003), not only was there no dominant party, but the party system reached record heights of fragmentation as a result of the low combined power of the two major parties. The appearance of Kadima as a large party (2006 and 2009) did not make it dominant because it won less than 25 percent of the seats. In 2013, the Likud–Yisrael Beitenu bloc won thirty-one seats, twelve more than the second-largest party (Yesh Atid), but split into its two components about a year later. In the 2015 election, again, no dominant party emerged.

Another way to present the degree of dominance of a party in the Knesset is through an index of competition based on the ratio between the largest and second-largest parties. When the difference between the parties is small, the index is higher, and competition for political dominance increases. A high index approaches parity at 1; a low index indicates greater party dominance and less competition for power because of the significant gap between the two parties. Table 9.3 shows that the era of Mapai (Labor) dominance and low competition ended in the 1970s; since then, the competition has been acute, with the exception of 2003, when the Likud under Sharon increased the gap to nineteen Knesset seats.

Two-Party and Two-Bloc Systems

Table 9.4 shows that following the dramatic rise to power of the Likud in 1977, Israel appeared for a while to be moving toward a two-party system.

The two largest parties reached the height of their combined power in the 1980s; in the 1981 election, they won a record total of ninety-five Knesset seats (79%). The difference between the two largest parties was small in those years (no more than three seats), and thus the National Unity Government was formed in the years 1984–90. However, this two-party system did not last long – it declined by 1992, continued

Table 9.3 *Index of competition between the two largest parties in the Knesset*

Election year	Difference in mandates between largest and second-largest parties	Index of competition*
1949	27	0.4
1951	25	0.4
1955	25	0.4
1959	30	0.4
1961	25	0.4
1965	19	0.6
1969	30	0.5
1973	12	0.8
1977	11	0.8
1981	1	1.0
1984	3	0.9
1988	1	1.0
1992	12	0.7
1996	2	0.9
1999	7	0.7
2003	19	0.5
2006	10	0.7
2009	1	1.0
2013	12	0.6
2015	6	0.8

* 1 = high competition; 0 = low competition. The ratio between the second-largest and the largest party.

to fade during the period of direct election, and reached a nadir of forty-five seats in the 1999 election. Since then, the two largest parties combined have not garnered 50 percent of the vote. In this situation, the gap between the two largest parties ensures power, but not superiority. Furthermore, it has not been a two-party political system – not in the 1980s nor afterwards – because the large parties were actually blocs of smaller parties, and the small parties remained relevant for coalition purposes.

The political map was therefore characterized by two blocs – a center-left bloc and a right-religious bloc – and the relative weight of these blocs is what determines the coalition structure. In the 1992 election, the center-left bloc edged out the right-religious bloc, making Yitzhak Rabin prime minister. This was followed by a period of direct election, in which the influence of the blocs declined to some extent because of the independent status of the prime minister. The 2003 election gave the Likud, the largest party, a relatively large advantage for the first time, and allowed Ariel Sharon to form two coalition governments without fear of the opposition. The first configuration (February 2003 to December 2004) included center-right parties (Likud, Shinui, the National Union, Yisrael Beitenu, and the National

Table 9.4 *Election results: The two largest parties (1965–2015)*

Election year	Number of seats of largest party	Number of seats of second-largest party	Total seats of two largest parties	Percentage of 120 seats
1965	Alignment 45	Gahal 26	71	59%
1969	Alignment 56	Gahal 26	82	68%
1973	Alignment 51	Gahal 39	90	75%
1977	Likud 43	Alignment 32	75	62%
1981	Likud 48	Alignment 47	95	79%
1984	Alignment 44	Likud 41	85	71%
1988	Likud 40	Alignment 39	79	66%
1992	Labor 44	Likud 32	76	63%
1996	Labor 34	Likud 32	66	55%
1999	Labor 26	Likud 19	45	38%
2003	Likud 38	Labor 19	57	48%
2006	Kadima 29	Labor 19	48	40%
2009	Kadima 28	Likud 27	55	46%
2013	Likud–Yisrael Beitenu 31	Yesh Atid 19	51	43%
2015	Likud 30	Labor 24	54	45%

Religious Party); in the second configuration (January 2005 to February 2006), Sharon switched partners for a more centrist configuration, which included Labor and Torah Judaism.

The election to the seventeenth Knesset (2006) became a three-way race (Kadima twenty-nine, Labor nineteen, Likud twelve), and the coalition that initially formed included the center-right – Kadima, Labor, Shas, the Gil Pensioners' Party, and Yisrael Beitenu (which joined after five months). In January 2008, Yisrael Beitenu left the coalition, which narrowed it again to sixty-seven members. After Prime Minister Olmert resigned, elections for the Kadima chair in September 2008 led to a win by Tzipi Livni, but she was unable to form a coalition and a date was set for elections. The decisive importance of the blocs was again apparent in the 2009 election: Kadima won one more seat than the Likud, but the formation of the coalition was determined by the size of the right-religious bloc (sixty-five seats) versus the center-left bloc (fifty-five seats). In 2013, there was no realistic alternative to a coalition headed by Likud–Yisrael Beitenu (thirty-one seats), with members from Yesh Atid, Jewish Home, and Hatnuah (for a total of sixty-eight seats). In 2015, the Likud advantage of six seats over Labor enabled it to form a minimal right-religious coalition of sixty-one MKs.

Polarization

Another characteristic of the party system in Israel is ideological polarization – a large distance between the two endpoints on various issues, differences that cannot be bridged to reach agreement – to work together in a coalition. Nevertheless, parties polarized on one issue can be close allies on another.

Foreign affairs and security: "Right" and "left" in Israel are usually labels for "hawks" and "doves" in foreign affairs and security. At the right pole are parties that adamantly reject territorial concessions for achieving a permanent accommodation in the Israeli–Arab/Israeli–Palestinian conflict. In the past, these parties included the Likud, Tehiya, Moledet, and, in 2015, the Likud, Jewish Home, and to a lesser extent the ultra-Orthodox parties. At the left pole are parties that believe in compromise to resolve the conflict, oppose Israel's hold on the occupied territories, reject the settlement enterprise, and call for withdrawal to the Green Line. In 2015, Meretz, the Joint Arab List, and Labor's left wing held this view. The ideological positions of Meretz and Jewish Home are two opposing poles, for example, and cannot be bridged.

Religion and state: Along a different axis, the ultra-Orthodox parties at one pole aspire to a state based on Halakha, Jewish religious law (Agudat Yisrael, Degel Hatorah, and to a lesser extent Shas). At the opposing pole are parties with a secular world view, which call for a separation of religion from state and "removing religion from politics": In the past, this included Yisrael B'Aliyah, Shinui, and, in 2015, Yesh Atid, Meretz, Hadash within the Joint Arab List, and to a lesser extent Yisrael Beitenu.

Society and economics: This was a divisive issue in the early years of the state, and of great significance in the party platforms. At one pole were the Communist Party and Mapam, which advocated for socialism, and at the other pole were the General Zionists and, to some extent, Herut, which called for a free market economy. The early 2000s saw no ideological polarization on issues of society and economics, and most parties held similar positions. Polarization exists between parties that advocate a welfare state (Meretz and to some extent Labor) or Marxism (the Communist Party within Hadash) versus neoliberal parties that advocate reduced state intervention, privatization, and a free market (the Likud, Yisrael Beitenu, and Yesh Atid). To some extent, the social protest movement of 2011 restored socioeconomic issues to public discourse in Israel.

National identity of the state: On this issue, the Arab parties are at one pole, aspiring to an egalitarian, civil definition epitomized by "a state of all its citizens," or alternatively recognition of the national collective rights of Arab citizens of Israel. At the opposing pole are Jewish parties such as Jewish Home, Yisrael Beitenu, and a majority of Likud members, who view Israel as an exclusive state for Jews. In the past, the parties at these extremes, both right and left, were usually not members of the governing coalition. This has changed in the three coalitions formed by Netanyahu since 2009, with or without Yisrael Beitenu.

9.5 Mapping the Parties

Parties reflect and represent the social mosaic of a state. Mapping the parties is a tool that helps identify the significant internal political divisions during a given period. In a stable system, such as Israel until the 1970s, the mapping of parties could predict quite accurately party behavior and possible coalitions. In an unstable system, such as Israel afterwards, the mapping is short-lived, with low predictability, because of the flux in principled positions taken by most parties.

The party map in Israel is highly dynamic. From Israel's first election in 1949 until 2015, more than a hundred parties have entered the legislature. Few have survived over time, some morphed into other parties, and new parties have tried their luck in every election. Some parties appeared on the scene as the bearers of new tidings and turned out to be ephemeral. Among those that disappeared after one or two terms are the following (the date of their first Knesset term in parentheses): Rafi (1965), Dash (1977), Yahad (1984), Tzomet (1988), Third Way (1996), Center Party (1999), Shinui (1999), Gil Pensioners' Party (2006), and Kadima (2006).

A. Parties: The Left–Right Security Continuum

The disagreement that shapes the political system more than any other concerns security and foreign affairs. Notwithstanding the fluctuation, this subject continues to preoccupy Israeli citizens and parties, and is reflected in the election campaigns. With several exceptions in recent years, coalitions formed since the founding of Israel were dictated by the stance of the parties on this issue. Although these positions are complex, including subdivisions and tactical stances, the principles can be summarized in terms of their positions about Arab intentions and territorial integrity, particularly the status of the territories conquered in 1967. Right-wing (or hawkish) parties perceive the conflict to be insoluble, forever or in the foreseeable future, and advocate a policy of "managing the conflict" on the basis of forceful deterrence. According to this perception – or because of a religious belief that is independent of it – the right wing rejects territorial concessions as the basis for peace agreements with Arab countries or the Palestinians, and supports settlement in the occupied territories. This was the approach of those on the right who objected to the peace agreements with Egypt, even though the vote in the Knesset crossed party lines. In the Knesset elected in 2015, the most right-wing party is the Jewish Home (formerly the NRP), in close proximity to Yisrael Beitenu and a majority of Likud members. When Shas and Torah Judaism are added, the political right in Israel (including Kulanu, headed by ex-Likud Kahlon) has a majority of sixty-seven MKs.

The more left on the political-security axis, the stronger the view that Israel can achieve peace agreements with the Arab countries and the Palestinians, and the greater willingness to negotiate about the future of the territories and withdraw from all or most of them in exchange for a real peace. The Labor Party supported this position during Rabin's premiership as well as all the parties to the left of Labor. On the left in the 2015 Knesset are the parties that advocate withdrawal to the Green Line, including Meretz, the Joint Arab List, Labor with qualifications, and several MKs from Yesh Atid. But it would also be possible to place Yesh Atid and Kulanu (together twenty-one MKs) at the center of the political continuum, as in Figure 9.1, thus changing the ratio of right to left parties to 57:43. The switch of several party heads who had previously been right wing Likud members should be noted: Ariel Sharon, Ehud Olmert, Tzipi Livni, Likud members, and Dan Meridor.

B. Parties: The Religious Continuum

In this section, we look at the religious cleavage within the Jewish population of Israel, even though religious rifts also occur within the Arab Israeli population.[13] Over the

[13] Although Arab parties can also be located on a religiosity continuum (Hadash as the most secular), placing them on the same continuum with the "Jewish parties" would be misleading.

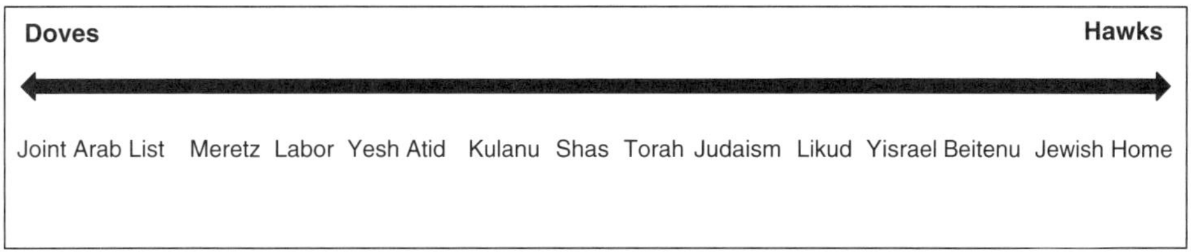

Figure 9.1 Map of the parties on security issues after election of the twentieth Knesset (2015)
Note: Differences between the parties at the center of this continuum are small or non-existent, i.e., the location of Torah Judaism, Shas, Yesh Atid, and Kulanu could shift slightly left or right.

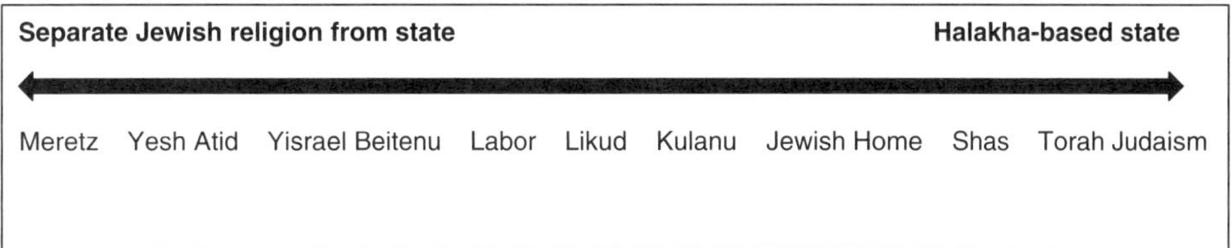

Figure 9.2 Map of the parties on religion–state issues after election of the twentieth Knesset (2015)
Note: Differences between the parties at the center of this continuum are small or non-existent. Location of Yesh Atid can shift to the right.

years, the importance of this issue has fluctuated, and may have been most intense in 2006 because of the presence of a combative secular party (Shinui) as well as the evacuation of the Gaza Strip, which accentuated the connection between religiosity and the territories. In the flux of Israeli politics, the religious issue was consigned to the sidelines in the 2009 election, but returned to the spotlight with the rise of a new party in the 2013 election – Yesh Atid. The rift is not between observant and unobservant Jews, as the levels of observance are many and varied, but relates to the role of religion in the state, as seen in the continuum of Figure 9.2. Ultra-Orthodox parties express a desire for a state based on Halakha. Their instrumental approach to political institutions does not obligate them to recognize the state or its secular laws. Thus, the ultra-Orthodox parties usually refrained from taking an active role in the secular institutions, such as serving as government ministers. This position changed when Agudat Yisrael joined the Begin government in 1977[14] and with the appearance of Shas in 1984.

Although ultra-Orthodox parties joined the coalition, this did not distance them from the ideological endpoint on the religion–state continuum. In contrast, the religious Zionist parties view themselves as part of the state, actively participating in all its institutions, including military service, and their position on basing state law on the Halakha is restrained. In proximity to them is a party like the Likud, which defines itself as "traditional" and supports religious positions such as opposing non-Orthodox streams of Judaism, while Labor advocates compromise on issues of religion and opposes religious coercion. The secular or "free" parties oppose a Halakhic state, and their location

[14] In August 2015, the High Court of Justice ruled that MK Litzman from the Torah Judaism party may not continue as a deputy minister with the authority of a minister, and he became a minister (*Yesh Atid v. Prime Minister* 2015).

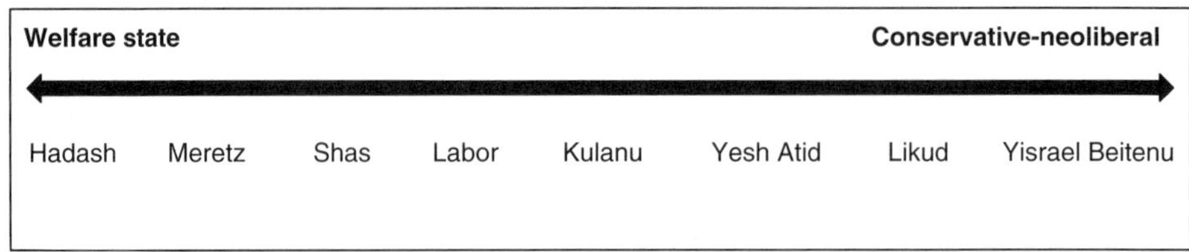

Figure 9.3 Map of the parties on socioeconomic issues after election of the twentieth Knesset (2015)
Note: Parties that did not have a clear position on socioeconomic matters were not included.

on the continuum is determined by their attitude to religious tradition. At the other endpoint are parties with a secular world view, such as Shinui in the past and Meretz today, which support a complete separation of religion and state. Near them are the parties that represent secular Russian immigrants, such as Yisrael B'Aliyah in the past and Yisrael Beitenu in the present, but which are not blatantly anti-religious because of their nationalist views and desire for support from veteran voters.

C. Parties: The Left–Right Socioeconomic Continuum

In most industrialized democracies, the main parties line up along a left–right axis on socioeconomic issues. In Israel, this division is no longer as significant as it once had been, and is not as critical in the political orientation of the parties. There is a gap here between the party's position and the profile of its voters. The Likud, for example, espouses a right-wing economic world view, but attracts more voters who are "workers" and salaried employees than the Labor Party, which defines itself as social-democratic. This makes it difficult to position most of the parties on this continuum, or to define the divisions in ideological terms: capitalism versus socialism, free market versus social welfare, bourgeoisie versus workers. Even newer terms such as "thin government" versus "big government" or views about Israel's privatization policy do not help locate Israeli parties on the socioeconomic continuum. In Figure 9.3, the endpoints are defined by their positions in the 2000s: conservative-neoliberal versus a welfare state ideology.

At the right end are parties that advocate smaller government and more limited involvement (except in security matters), lower taxes, massive privatization, unregulated competition, autonomy of the free market, etc. Representing this conservative view were Shinui in the past, and currently Yisrael Beitenu, most Likud members, Yesh Atid, and some Kulanu members. Moving left are parties supportive of social justice, equality, welfare state services, and full employment and opponents of privatization. Left of center on these issues are some Likud members and some Labor MKs, with the left socioeconomic endpoint occupied by Hadash and, not far away, Meretz, Shas, and several Labor MKs.

D. Jewish and Arab Parties

Unlike the previous axes, the differences here are not necessarily ideological and are virtually dichotomous – a party can be "Arab" or "Jewish" as defined by three parameters: its positions, its constituents, and the composition of its candidate lists.

A "Jewish" party defines Israel as a state for Jews only, and therefore advocates transfer of Arab citizens of Israel to Arab countries, or proof of loyalty as a condition for citizenship. Such was the Moledet party led by Rehavam Ze'evi and now Yisrael Beitenu. Arab parties, on the other hand, call for an egalitarian definition of citizenship – equality for all citizens of Israel and recognition of the collective national rights of Arab citizens of Israel. The dilemma of the Arab parties is between having influence, which would require discreet interaction with government authorities, and public protest (Kenig 2004).

A more flexible definition applies to Arab-Jewish parties – in the past, the Progressive List for Peace and today Hadash, within the Joint Arab List; as well as mixed parties – Mapam in the past and Meretz today. A mixed party does not refer necessarily to a mixed voting constituency, but to a party whose institutions and Knesset candidates include both Arabs and Jews. Parties considered "Arab" according to all three parameters (platform, majority of voters, and all its MKs) are a relatively new phenomenon, which began with the appearance of the Arab Democratic Party in the late 1980s and grew with the formation of Balad and Ra'am-Ta'al, and the decline of the Jewish wing of Hadash. Some Jewish parties have Arab voters, but these numbers have fallen over time to a low of 18 percent (in Arab towns) in the 2009 election (Rouhana et al. 2010, 145) and remain low. In addition to the twelve MKs from the Joint Arab List, four Arabs and Druze were elected to the 2015 Knesset, one from Meretz, Labor, Likud, and Yisrael Beitenu.

E. Ethnic Jewish Parties

Here, too, there is no clear continuum, and no dichotomy; it is hard to find a party that is entirely ethnic in all three parameters: views, majority of constituents, and all elected officials. Ethnic parties (of Sephardim and Yemenites) did run for office in the pre-state period and were represented in the first and second Knessets. Afterwards, despite many attempts to form ethnic lists, they did not pass the electoral threshold and disappeared from the Knesset until the early 1980s. Ethnic parties are the standard bearers of equality among ethnic groups, claiming that ethnic discrimination justifies their separate political organizing. Nevertheless, they remain "Israeli," for example they do not advocate separatism (Herzog 1986; Neuberger 1997, 209). Among the parties that were ethnic on the three above parameters are Tami (1981, 1984), Shas (since 1984), Yisrael B'Aliyah (1996–2003), and Yisrael Beitenu (since 1999). Shas is striking among these because of the ethnic messages in its platform, its fairly well-defined ethnic constituency, and the fact that its Knesset list has only Mizrahim and refuses to include women candidates. Torah Judaism has a well-defined Ashkenazi constituency, but has no blatant Ashkenazi message. All the other Jewish parties oppose the very idea of an ethnic party for reasons of "national unity." Nevertheless, the base constituents of some of these parties have an ethnic profile of their own: In the past, a majority of Likud voters were Mizrahi, just as Labor voters were mostly Ashkenazi.[15] Parties with a clear majority of Ashkenazi voters were Shinui (1999, 2003), Torah Judaism, Yesh Atid, and Meretz (2013, 2015).

[15] This pattern may have returned in the 2015 election, according to initial surveys in which the Likud won a majority of the votes in towns in the periphery.

F. Mapping of Parties and Structural Changes

The above mapping of parties along several axes has changed over time, reflecting flux in the political system and shifts in the importance of each parameter. Although security and foreign affairs remained paramount, the issues changed, as did the focus on them: Security, for example, was less dominant in the quiet decade between the Sinai Campaign (1956) and the Six Day War (1967). Although it was the most important issue in the early days of the state, dissension between the parties focused not only on relations with Arab countries (the Palestinian issue was then a marginal one), but on Israel's so-called international "orientation" – toward the east or the west. These were the early years of the Cold War, and countries such as Israel had to choose to side with the United States and western Europe, or with the Soviet bloc, or later with the "unaligned" bloc of countries. Divisions emerged primarily in the workers' camp when Mapam and the Communist Party chose to identify with the Soviets and Mapai with the west. The socioeconomic cleavage was also a prominent issue during that period – the socialist workers' parties versus the free market parties of the "civil camp." See Figure 9.4 on the positions of the parties along these two axes.

The gap between Mapai and Mapam, both workers' parties, suggests one reason why Ben-Gurion refrained from including Mapam in the first government coalition. Despite their proximity on social issues and alliance in the Histadrut, Mapam's pronounced pro-Soviet orientation created a barrier on matters of foreign affairs and security. Figure 9.4 may seem to suggest that the failure to include Herut in the government coalitions was based on socioeconomic issues. However, Herut was less bourgeois and conservative than the coalition partners – the General Zionists and the Progressives. Excluding Herut is better explained by the ideological distance and bitter rivalry that lingered from the Yishuv period and Herut's hawkish stands on the greater Land of Israel.

In the 1970s, the picture was different. Israel's pro-western orientation had already been established, and the main issue was the fate of the territories conquered in 1967. Ever since, security and foreign affairs beliefs and positions concerning the territories have largely, though not exclusively, determined the identity of parties in Israel.

The position of the Alignment in Figure 9.5 so near the meeting point of the axes is no coincidence: As the party in power until 1977, its views were hawkish (even initiating the settlements); afterwards it glossed over the issues and vacillated between opposing positions, driven mainly by its desire to return to power. The stances it took on socioeconomic issues were also equivocal. The two-bloc party structure described above reflected well the division of parties into doves and hawks. In the 2000s, Labor and Likud drew closer on issues of security and foreign affairs, as evidenced in the establishment of Kadima (2005) with leaders from these two parties. They wished to placate the center, and sometimes it was hard to distinguish between them. This was also true of the socioeconomic divisions. Until the global crisis in late 2008, distinctions between the main parties diminished; and they inhabited the right wing of the socioeconomic ideological axis in terms of what they wanted for the Israeli economy. Since then, Labor has moved slightly to the left on socioeconomic issues, for a short period under Yachimovich's leadership (2011–13).

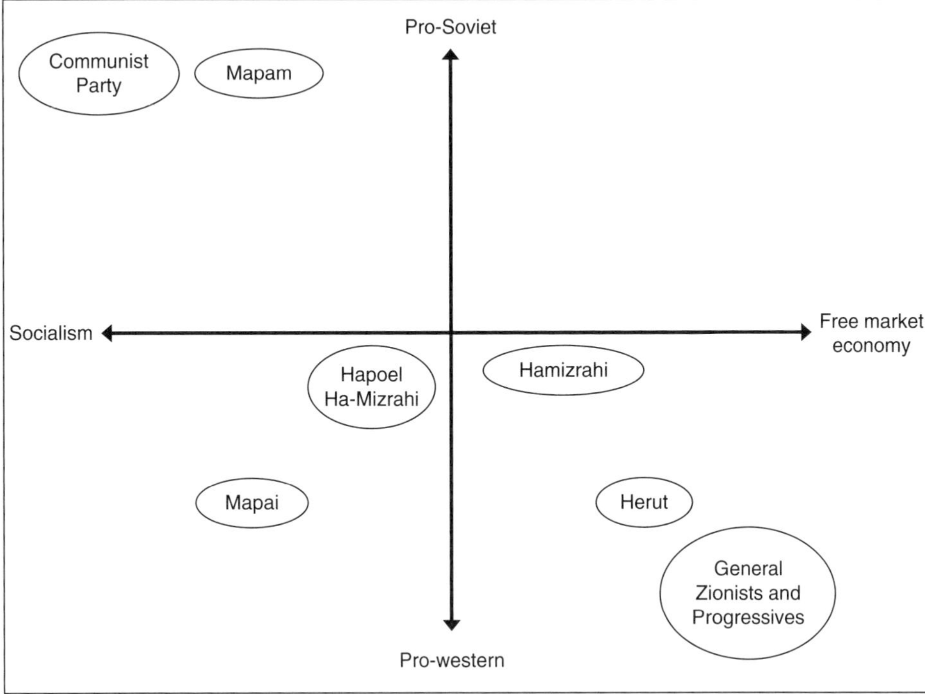

Figure 9.4 Map of the parties in the 1950s – international orientation and socioeconomic ideology

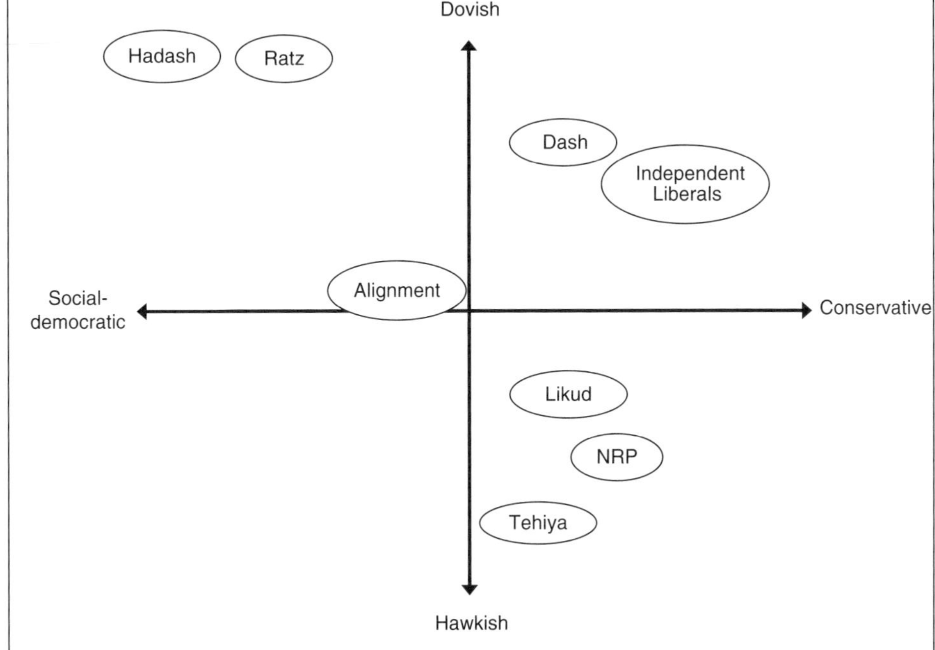

Figure 9.5 Map of the parties in the late 1970s – positions on the territories and socioeconomic ideology

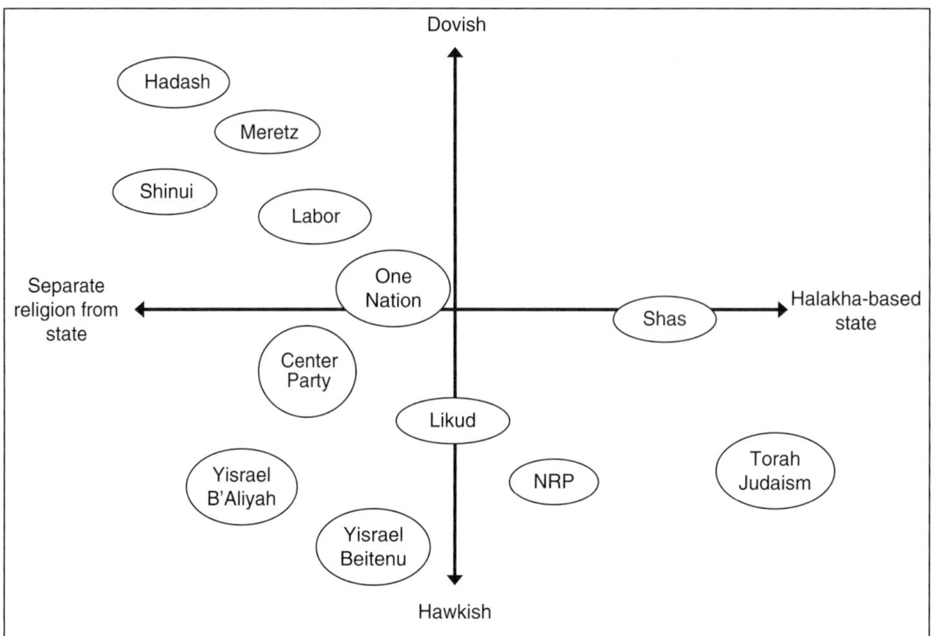

Figure 9.6 Map of the parties in the late 1990s – positions on the territories and religion–state relations

A key phenomenon, whose roots were visible soon after the 1967 war, was the correlation between foreign affairs/security views and the religious–secular rift. Figure 9.6 reveals the growing extremism of the NRP – from moderate to hawkish. At the time, the ultra-Orthodox parties, including Shas in its early days, were at the dovish end of the continuum. Radicalization grew in the 1990s, when all the religious parties moved to the right and are now located on the hawkish end of the continuum.

While Labor was in power, until the mid-1970s, religious–secular dissension was relatively mild. The rifts deepened after the religious parties adopted hawkish views, and following the growth of the ultra-Orthodox parties with the appearance of Shas and its key position in the government coalitions. These developments yielded many achievements to the religious parties in two areas – expanding the settlement enterprise and winning state budget allocations – but they also triggered growing opposition among the secular population and the first extreme secular party – Shinui in 1999 and Yesh Atid in 2013. In terms of the stability in the political system, the radicalization evident in Figure 9.6 is dangerous because of the close correlation between hawkish views and religiosity, and the reverse – dovish views and secularism. This was manifested in the positions taken about the disengagement from the Gaza Strip in 2005: Only the Likud (hawkish, but secular-traditional), early Shas (ultra-Orthodox and a bit dovish), and the Russian immigrant parties (hawks and seculars) could somewhat cross these lines.

Other structural changes in the mapping of parties, mentioned already, are summarized here:

- The ideological differences in the socioeconomic positions evaporated over time, and it is hard to distinguish between the major parties on these issues.

- The national cleavage deepened because the conflict with the Palestinians escalated, particularly since the failure of the Oslo Agreements and with the appearance of independent Arab parties.
- Direct election of the prime minister contributed to ongoing parliamentary fragmentation; in the last three Knessets (2009–15), MKs of sectoral parties outnumber MKs of inclusive parties.

Mapping the parties according to their positions on foreign policy and security, religion and state relations, and policy toward the Arab citizens of Israel reveals fundamental differences in the 2000s. However, mapping the election results since 2009 on these axes has become almost impossible, particularly because of contradictory views even within the same party.

G. Further Changes

Single-issue parties do not offer a comprehensive platform that addresses all areas of life as they focus on one major issue. Many single-issue parties have vied for Knesset seats and most fell far short of the electoral threshold. The few of them that managed to enter the Knesset in the past did not last long, such as WIZO (1949), Haolam Hazeh (1965, 1969), Flatto Sharon (1977), Tehiya (1981–88), and Tzomet (1988–96). Parties representing retired people tried their luck several times and failed until the Gil Pensioners' Party in 2006 won a surprising seven seats, but then disappeared in the 2009 election. Other parties that vied and lost: Panthers, Greens, Women's Party, Men's Rights Party, Has-Mas (against income tax), Green Leaf (legalization of "soft" drugs), Law of Nature (for meditative living), Negev, New Country (against big money), Strength for Israel (a settlers' party), and Ultra-Orthodox Women.

Parties of individuals are parties focused on a candidate, not a world view. Some arose after a key individual quit or was ejected from his or her party and managed to be elected to the Knesset: Rafi (Ben-Gurion), Ratz (Shulamit Aloni), Telem (Moshe Dayan), Shlomtzion (Ariel Sharon), Yahad (Ezer Weizman), and others. Some arose after an individual decided to enter politics on his own: Haolam Hazeh (Uri Avnery), Tzomet (Rafael Eitan), Yisrael B'Aliyah (Natan Sharansky), Shinui (Yosef Lapid), Yisrael Beitenu (Avigdor Lieberman), Yesh Atid (Yair Lapid), and Kulanu (Kahlon). Most of those mentioned used the party they established as a springboard to other parties. Some began as parties of individuals, but became established parties in their own right, such as Ratz. Most parties of individuals do not survive in Israeli politics.

Anti-corruption parties have entered the Knesset with a platform that does not represent ideology or an interest group, but a promise of "clean politics," "changing the system," "cleaning the stables," etc. Such parties claim to be "non-political," are vague on foreign affairs and security, religion, and socioeconomic issues, and aim for the center of the political map. The absence of an ideological backbone prevents them from surviving for long, but their transient and recurring success is an indication of a political (or anti-political) trend in Israeli society since the 1970s. The most prominent example of this was Dash in 1977, followed by Tzomet, Third Way, and the Center Party. All ultimately vanished. In the 2003 election, a party appeared that called itself "Another Israel – Because We're Fed Up with Politicians," offered "politics without politicians," and even found 7,144 people to vote for it.

The dynamics of mapping parties testifies to the many changes in Israeli society: the waves of immigration, international changes, wars, security tensions, economic crises, the emergence of new elites, individual competition, the centrality of the media, social tension – all these play a role in the relentless reshaping of the political system.

9.6 Parties as Organizations: Internal Democracy

Parties are fascinating, complex organizations whose internal behavior raises significant questions for every democratic political system. For a democracy to be sustainable, must its political parties be internally democratic? Does state funding for parties transform them from a voluntary organization into a governance institution? Do party members have a real influence, or do they merely provide legitimacy for the party elite, or leader? What is the difference between a party of many members and one with few? Are parties still representative; if so, whom do they represent – people with shared views or specific sectors? Do internal processes of participation, such as primaries, contribute to the democratization of the party? We address below only some of these questions: different types of parties, party institutions, their organizational structures, and the emergence of candidates and leaders.

A. Party Institutions and the Hierarchical Structure

In mapping the party system and using different typologies, we refer to a party as if it were one uniform player. A party, however, is not monolithic – not in its organizational structure nor in its power distribution – so the time has come to look inside. The actors in a party differ from each other: members versus functionaries, professional politicians versus amateurs, office holders versus volunteers, local or regional versus national members, etc. To simplify the discussion, we distinguish three tiers in the party organization:

Elected officials: In the top tier are elected officials, who are publicly identified as representing the party. These are usually the party's professional politicians, who achieved their rank in some form of election or internal appointment. Elected officials are inevitably faced by a conflict between representing their constituents and party platform and their responsibility to the public at large.

Organizational officials or functionaries: In the second tier are those holding official tasks in the party – referred to as "apparatus." Among these are elected officials who also hold organizational positions, as well as activists from the third tier, such as representatives of groups affiliated with the party (workers' organizations, regional branches, students, women groups). Although this tier is seemingly not autonomous because it draws its power from the leadership and party members, in practice it usually controls the human, material, and organizational resources, meaning it controls the party. Michels's "iron law of oligarchy" ([1911] 1962) does not hold without the effective control of the apparatus.[16]

[16] According to the "iron law of oligarchy," a party is ultimately controlled by a small group in which authority is concentrated, and it is difficult to change the composition of this group.

Activists and members: In the third tier are party supporters throughout the country, the region, or a relevant group, and these are mainly volunteers – the "activists" – with the exception of office holders in the branches. Unlike elected officials and functionaries, the activists are motivated primarily by collective incentives, and therefore they adhere more avidly to the party principles and its distinctive identity, even at the expense of electoral advantage.

What is the status of party members? Someone who joins a party takes on obligations, such as signing on to the party platform and paying membership dues; in exchange, he or she is granted rights within the party organization, such as the right to influence its direction and positions, and the right to vote for its nominees for public office and for its organizational officials. In parties with a large roster of members, a higher body (the congress, the general assembly, or the conference) makes decisions about issues of principle. In the practical life of a party, the leaders and officials control the agenda and sometimes the composition of the higher body, turning it into a vacuous arena. Nevertheless, even if the higher body is a rubber stamp for decisions of the leadership, holding a public discussion and bestowing legitimacy on party actions are important for a party committed to democratic principles.[17]

A dynamic conflict exists between the party tiers. Party voters and activists tend to berate the elected officials for deviating from the party principles and platform; the functionaries want to have a more direct influence on national policymaking; elected officials and office holders frequently declare that the state comes before the party. To what extent should the party dictate the policies of its elected officials serving in parliament or government? Did Prime Minister Sharon have to resign when his party voted against the Gaza Strip disengagement plan of 2005? In fact, this took place somewhat later when he resigned from the Likud and founded a new party – Kadima.

B. The Organizational Structure of Parties in Israel

If parties are the pillars of a democratic regime, then, logically, the parties themselves should function democratically, at least in how they choose their leaders. The more stringent would say that parties should abide by democratic tenets even more strictly than any organization, political or non-political. Practically, at stake are the relations between the elected officials and the two lower tiers in the party organization – party members, above all. In parties democratically run, members have a real influence on the process of choosing the candidates for election, formulating the party platform, and shaping its ideology. In such parties, organizational tools ensure a democratic process in choosing the candidates and party institutions oversee them. In parties run democratically, an elected official, even a prime minister, who loses the confidence of party members, must resign. On the other hand, the main loyalty of elected officials, from the moment of their election, is to all the voters, not just the party they represent. The tension is inescapable, but the guiding principle in a democracy is that

[17] An example of the importance of such a higher body: the turbulent decision of the Labor Party conference in March 25, 2009 to join the Netanyahu government: 680 representatives voted in favor of the chair's proposal to enter the coalition and 407 voted against.

elected officials, despite being the emissaries of a party, have some freedom in their efforts to balance their partisan mission and the common good. Party members, like the general voting public, can punish "wayward" officials in the election that follows.

A political party's broad base consists of the total constituency of citizens who voted for it in the Knesset elections. Beyond this, there is an internal hierarchy – in the Israeli big parties, rank and file members are generally registered, and they choose a broad and representative higher body, called the "party conference," which meets infrequently. The conference authorizes or changes the party constitution and bylaws, sets policy and principles, and decides on mergers with other parties. The party conference is responsible for selecting the party's central committee, which meets more frequently and is entrusted with decisions about ongoing party matters. Between conference meetings, the central committee is the highest party echelon and, in some cases, responsible for electing the party head and Knesset candidates. Heading the party hierarchy is the party leader, generally referred to as the chair.

Over the years, central committees have swelled. Mapai had some 300 members in the central committee in the 1960s. In the 1970s, Mapai – then called the Labor Party – had more than 800 central committee members, and this grew to 1,300 in the late 1990s. Likud had a similar dynamic. The Herut central committee had some 600 members in 1977, which expanded to 900 in 1984 and some 3,000 in 1988 following its merger with the Liberal Party. As for membership, in 1996, Labor had approximately 163,000 members (about a third of its voters), and the Likud had about 179,000 (about a quarter of its voters). In 2013, Labor had approximately 60,000 members (about 15% of its voters), and the Likud had about 125,000 (less than a quarter of its voters). Thus, the primary elections in these parties did not raise the participation level of its registered members.

Smaller bodies are in charge of the ongoing running of the party and its decisions, sometimes referred to as "the apparatus." There are also smaller forums, informal or semi-formal, the most famous of these being the "kitchen cabinets," in which decisions are pre-cooked. In addition, the "faction" – the MKs who represent the party in the Knesset – is a key coordinating body because the MKs are usually members of other party institutions. In some parties, such as the Likud, there is also a professional CEO, who is not necessarily a politician.

C. Choosing Candidates for the Knesset

Article 16 of the Parties Law states that "Party candidates for the Knesset shall be determined in a procedure defined by the bylaws." The law refrained from obligating parties to have internal democratic governance, leaving it up to the bylaws of each party. When this law was passed in 1994, Labor and Likud, as well as other parties, were already democratizing their internal processes. The trend was to expand the body that elects the candidates to the party's list for the Knesset. In 2015, registered members of the three largest parties (Likud, Labor, and the Joint Arab List) had rights they did not previously have in selecting the party's candidates to the Knesset. Prior to the 2015 election, however, internal democratic elections were not held in Yesh Atid, Kulanu, Shas, Torah Judaism, and Yisrael Beitenu. These forty or so MKs tend to be rather submissive to their party leaders.

In the past, the "arranging" and nominating committees reigned supreme in most parties – a small group of senior officials who put together the list of candidates and brought it to the conference or the central committee for ratification. The committee members were not elected but chosen on the basis of behind-the-scenes understandings. The nominating committees generally did not include the leader of the party, who could thereby remain "above personal matters" while exerting a decisive influence on the list of candidates. Shraga Netzer, a prominent activist in Mapai and permanent member of its nominating committees, stated that Ben-Gurion did not hesitate to rearrange the order of the list submitted to him by the committee (Netzer 1980, 142–43). In retrospect, it is surprising that these one-sided committees, who were aware of the internal power relations and would take into consideration the factions composing the party, would also consider factors of representation and include candidates from weaker groups. The Labor Party did this, obviously, to placate these voters, but it did so also because it regarded itself as the all-inclusive mass party. Clearly this "arranging" process was not democratic – inclusive, transparent, and competitive – but it had the advantage of not being affected by media images, and constructing the list to achieve balance and representation as well (Medding 1972; Yanai 1981).

Party procedures began to change in the 1970s – moving up through the party ranks is no longer the only way to get elected to the Knesset. Democratization by holding primaries to elect the party's Knesset candidates began with the new Dash Party in 1977, when voting rights were given to all party members. In that year, Herut elected its candidates to the Likud list by members of the central committee using a system of "sevens." First, the central committee would elect by secret ballot a panel of thirty-five from among all the candidates. Then, these candidates would be ranked through several election rounds, with seven candidates elected and ranked in each round. Each candidate would present himself to one of the sets of seven, and if he failed to be elected to this group, he would automatically move on to the next. This procedure served Herut in four elections and the joint Likud Party in 1992. The concept behind this innovative and democratic system was to open the list to every candidate who wished to run, and at the same time to hold several rounds to give voters a chance to correct the under-representation of groups as they moved from one set of sevens to another. In addition, it allowed initial screening of candidates by electing a panel, and a chance to correct the balance in the party's list to the Knesset (Bar 1996). Over time, however, the participants discovered its weak points and began to distort the outcome by forging alliances in advance between some candidates and excluding others. In the end, the method fostered "deals" and factionalism within the party, leading to a change in 1996.

The Labor Party followed Herut's lead and in 1988 adopted a similar method, using sets of ten, for central committee members to select candidates for the national list (Doron and Goldberg 1990). In 1992, Labor was the first large party in Israel to allow all its members to vote for Knesset candidates in primary elections. The advantage of primaries is democratization, while the disadvantage is the party's inability to control the composition of the list, which could lead to under-representation and harm its chances in the general election. To reduce this risk, mechanisms were introduced to the primaries to ensure representation of geographic districts and population sectors – kibbutzim and moshavim, Arabs, women, and young people. The process of internal democratization peaked in 1996 when the four large parties – Labor, Likud, Meretz, and Tzomet – selected their Knesset candidates by holding primaries among all the party members (Rahat and Sher-Hadar 1999). Labor continued to select its Knesset candidates by this method, but the Likud was not happy with the process or its results, and in 1999 selected its candidates by the vote of some 3,000 central committee members in one round, with mechanisms to ensure the representation of women, immigrants, and young people (Rahat 2001, 10). However, prior to the election of the seventeenth Knesset (2006), the Likud reinstituted primary elections and has since continued electing its candidates by this method, as have the Labor and Jewish Home parties (Kenig 2014).

What are the systems for selecting a party's candidates to the Knesset? If we examine this along an axis of the inclusiveness of the body that makes this decision, we find many possibilities (Rahat and Hazan 2001, 301). The most inclusive one, in which all eligible voters in the country may participate in the election of the party's candidates, does not exist in Israel, and is rare too in other democratic countries on the logical grounds that this should be the business of the party members. Parties in several American states allow this, but candidates in most states are selected in primaries conducted within the party. So too in European countries. For example, the Social Democratic Party in Denmark has its party candidates elected directly by party members (Bar 1996, 71). In Finland, candidates are elected by party members within the electoral districts. In France's Socialist Party, party candidates are selected in special conferences in which all party members in the district branches are allowed to vote. In Britain's Liberal Democratic Party, members select the party candidates directly. In Belgium, all party members have been allowed to vote for the party candidates since the middle of the nineteenth century (Bar 1994, 42–43). As noted, this system was adopted by some parties in Israel at the height of the democratization period, but by the 2015 election it was retained only by the Labor, Likud, and Jewish Home parties.

The next level of inclusiveness is selection of the candidates by an *elected* party institution, and this is common in many parties. This means large elected bodies such as a congress, conference, or central committee, or more limited groups such as a council or an assembly. This method of selecting candidates is no less democratic than others, provided that the selecting body is itself elected democratically and regularly, and its membership cannot be changed by one leader or another. Despite the democratization process within the Herut movement, for example, the central committee, which selected the candidates, did not stand for election for eight years (1978–86). Having an *elected* party institution select the candidates is not common among Israeli parties. Prior to the 2009 Knesset election, only a few parties (Hadash, Balad, and Meretz) thus nominated its candidates, while Kadima, Likud, and Labor held primary elections among those registered. In 2013 and 2015, selecting the Knesset candidates by elected party institutions was not the preferred method.

Closer to the non-inclusive endpoint are parties that select, or rather appoint, their candidates by a *non-elected* party institution, such as a nominating committee. Some adopted this system to avoid internal conflict, such as the NRP in 2009, which gave the authority to determine its Knesset list to a public council of forty people not active politically, though this did not prevent the split in the party. At the non-democratic end are parties that make a pretense of a democratic facade, but in practice it is the decision of one leader or a small group of leaders. Yisrael Beitenu was strict about holding a formal election of the party head, but Avigdor Lieberman, like Rafael Eitan in Tzomet in its day, ran unopposed, and once elected also decided the list of candidates on his own.[18] In Shas and the Torah Judaism components, on the other hand, there is no pretense whatsoever, and Knesset candidates are selected by leaders with religious authority who are not elected. In the 2013 election, party leaders in the religious parties, Yesh Atid, Yisrael Beitenu, and Hatnuah decided on the candidates for the Knesset. Approximately half the MKs in the nineteenth Knesset were appointed this way by their parties. In 2015, as noted, the number of leader-appointed MKs was reduced, but still sizable.

D. Party Leaders – Status and Method of Selection

Some parties have more than one center of leadership power, and some parties, such as those in the United States, have no official definition of the "party leader." In the two largest parties of Germany (CDU and SDP), there is a distinction between the party chair and the candidate for chancellor.

Israel did not always have an official designation of "party leader," though generally it is clear who the leader is. When in late 1953, however, the party appointed Moshe Sharett to replace Ben-Gurion as prime minister, the latter was still considered the undisputed leader of Mapai. In the first three decades, competition in the ruling party was for "the prime ministerial candidacy" or "first on the list of candidates," not party head. The party principal made do with the title "general secretary" – the one responsible for the party organization. The official post of Labor chair was created after the 1977 change of government, when Labor first took to the opposition. Today the elected chair of the large parties, as in the British tradition, is also the party's candidate for prime minister.

The methods by which the party leader was selected also underwent a gradual process of democratization, mainly expanding the pool of those with the right to vote. No longer does the party elite or a small caucus of kingmakers nominate the leader, but he or she must compete for the votes of a broad-based body or of all the party members in a primary election. The first race in the Alignment/Labor for the post of leader (actually then for prime minister) took place in 1974, after Golda Meir resigned the premiership in the wake of the Yom Kippur War. There were two candidates – Yitzhak Rabin and Shimon Peres – and the central committee chose Rabin. In retrospect, this event was a point of no return, entrenching the understanding that the legitimacy of a party leader (and the nominee for prime minister) requires a mandate from the party members, as can be seen in Table 9.5 with respect to Labor, Likud, and Kadima (2005–12). The Likud leader continues to stand for election by all party members. In contrast, the leader of Yesh Atid did not stand for election in either 2013 or 2015.

The change in how party candidates to the Knesset and the leaders are selected led to side effects that cast doubt on the quality of that democratization. The greater openness of the parties and the involvement of members in decision-making did

[18] This was also the case in the Kadima Party, founded just four months before the 2006 election. The list of candidates for the Knesset was decided by Ariel Sharon and a small group of leaders, based *inter alia* on how candidates scored in popularity polls.

Table 9.5 *Methods of selecting leaders in the largest parties (1949–2015)*

Party	Leader	Party leader (years)	How position was achieved
Mapai/Labor	David Ben-Gurion	1948–63	"Natural leader"
	Moshe Sharett	1954–55	Informally selected in party institutions
	Levi Eshkol	1963–69	Informally selected in party institutions
	Golda Meir	1969–74	Ratified by party's Central Committee
	Yitzhak Rabin	1974–77	Elected by party's Central Committee
	Shimon Peres	1977–92	Elected by party's Conference
	Yitzhak Rabin	1992–95	Elected in primaries
	Ehud Barak	1997–2001	Elected in primaries
	Binyamin Ben-Eliezer	2001–2	Elected in primaries
	Amram Mitzna	2002–3	Elected in primaries
	Shimon Peres	2003–5	Elected (Acting Chair) by Central Committee
	Amir Peretz	2005–7	Elected in primaries
	Ehud Barak	2007–11	Elected in primaries
	Shelly Yachimovich	2011–13	Elected in primaries
	Itzhak Herzog	2013–17	Elected in primaries
Herut/Likud	Menachem Begin	1949–83	"Natural leader"
	Yitzhak Shamir	1983–93	Elected by Party's Central Committee
	Benjamin Netanyahu	1993–99	Elected in primaries
	Ariel Sharon	1999–2005	Elected in primaries
	Benjamin Netanyahu	2005–	Elected in primaries
Kadima (defunct)	Ariel Sharon	2005–6	"Natural leader"
	Ehud Olmert	2006–8	Stand-in deputy & "natural leader"
	Tzipi Livni	2008–14	Elected in primaries

not yield the desired results. First, the entrance requirements for party membership were lowered to allow for the "seasonal" registration of people who could vote in the primary elections. These new registrees are not real party members, but recruited by "vote contractors" prior to the election to vote for a specific candidate. It is not clear who pays their membership dues, but vote contractors are suspected of doing so on their behalf. A large number of these newly registered members do not remain in the party, as they do not pay membership dues after the primary election is over. Some individuals have been found to register as members of more than one party at once. Absurdly, parties in some locales had more registered members than votes for it in the general election (Rahat and Hazan 2003).

Second, the primary elections for the Knesset candidates weakened the discipline of MKs. An MK who had in the past been chosen by the leadership or central committee had to demonstrate loyalty and party discipline in order to be reelected. When the selection was transferred to all party members, the positive outcome was empowerment of the MKs to act in accordance with their conscience without being dependent on the party apparatus. The negative outcome was that the MKs were no longer constrained in their behavior as representatives of their party. To be reelected, they now need to be noticed and reach a broad audience, in the party and publicly, leading many MKs to display flamboyant and sometimes irresponsible parliamentary behavior. It also adversely affected their Knesset work: MKs who would defy faction discipline or submit private members' bills that had no chance of passing just to win media notice (Hazan 1998, 78–90; Blander and Klein 2002).

Third, the primaries caused distortions in the representation of geographic areas or social groups, particularly among women and Arabs, so that most parties required corrective action (districts, quotas) to ensure that their lists of candidates would be more representative.

Fourth, a very serious outcome was reinforcement of the link between money and political power, and the many cases of corruption revealed since primary elections were instituted. Candidates exchanged their previous dependence on the party machine with a dependence on patrons to finance their campaigns, or they offered benefits to central committee members to win their support.

9.7 Party and Campaign Financing

For a party to function in a democracy, it needs adequate funding. Public activity is the lifeline of a party, and for this it needs an apparatus, organizational skill, and channels to enable ongoing discourse with its constituents and other groups in society. To mobilize and retain the support of members and voters, parties hire employees and advisers, activate volunteers, acquire services, and maintain their own media. A party with substantial financial resources has an edge over a party strapped for funding. In the past, as part of the conception that a party is a voluntary organization, the expectation was that it will finance activities on its own from membership fees and donations. The changed status of the parties noted above led to a dwindling of these sources and recognition of the need to find alternative income without harming the independence of parties, which are crucial to a democracy.

In many democratic countries, including Israel, recognition of the threat to the *institution* of parties due to inadequate resources led to the allocation of state funds to finance ongoing party activity and election campaigns. Until 1969, Israeli parties ostensibly financed their own activity, as the state was not involved in any direct allocations nor did it exercise oversight of the donations to parties or their financial matters. In practice, however, parties even during that period relied on public moneys channeled through the Jewish Agency, the Histadrut, voluntary organizations, tax easements, etc. In the past, most parties also engaged in some economic activity – business, health services, sports clubs, newspapers, employment offices, etc.

A. The Scope and Limitations of Funding

Campaign financing by the state was a temporary measure at first, allocated for the 1969 elections (to the Knesset, the local authorities, and the Histadrut), but in 1973 the Parties Financing Law was enacted, which regulated state support for the parties' ongoing expenses as well as their campaigns. Following a High Court ruling (*Bergman v. Finance Minister* 1969), the law was amended to ensure greater equality of opportunity for new parties vying against veteran parties. Since then, the Parties Financing Law has been amended dozens of times, but the two purposes of state funding remain: annual ongoing expenses and election campaign expenses. The basis for calculating public funds given to parties for these two purposes is their size in the Knesset – one "funding unit" is given for each MK and another funding unit for every faction to cover their basic expenses.[19] For example, a faction with five MKs would receive six funding units to finance its election campaign in addition to a monthly payment of 5 percent of the funding unit per MK. A public committee headed by a judge, and linked to the cost of living, sets the amount of the funding unit periodically.

In addition, every party has the right to receive private donations, subject to certain legal restrictions. One is the absolute prohibition on receiving donations from a business, whether in Israel or abroad. Another restriction is the maximum amount that one person or his family can donate to a party. In 2015, that maximum was NIS 1,000 annually and NIS 2,300 in an election year. Donation to a candidate in primaries begins at NIS 11,480 and is based on the electorate size. Anonymous donations are prohibited, and the parties are legally obligated to keep detailed records of their accounts and donations. A third restriction prohibits donations from any individual not entitled to vote for the Knesset, i.e., a foreign citizen. A fourth is the ceiling on total expenditures allowed per party – both for ongoing expenses and an election campaign – commensurate with its funding from the state. A party that chooses not to accept state funding for election expenses is exempt from some of these limitations.

Thus, public funding brought close supervision to the party's financial records and, above all, obligated it to transparency. Supervision, control, and enforcement of the Parties Financing Law fell to the state comptroller (see Chapter 7), who, after each election, publishes a detailed report of every party and imposes fines on those with irregularities. Proposals were also made to establish a separate and independent authority, as is common in democratic countries, to supervise the elections and the financial activity of the parties between elections. Another complicated issue concerns how to divide up the funds if a faction splits or merges with another faction. This has implications for the establishment and stability of coalitions, and has been deliberated more than once in the courts (Rubinstein and Medina 2005, vol. II, 777–80).

B. Developments

The transition to regulated funding for parties was difficult because party expenditures generally exceeded their income, creating large deficits. Following the state comptroller's exposure of the proportion of private donations in the election

[19] To avoid short-changing parties that sought election, but failed, the law stipulates that one funding unit shall be given to a party that did not pass the electoral threshold, but won at least 1 percent of the valid votes. In the 2015 election, only two parties that failed to enter the Knesset garnered enough votes (1% = about 42,000 votes) to win a funding unit.

campaigns of the 1980s, and the post-election efforts made by parties in 1981 and 1988 to raise the funding unit retroactively (this amendment was invalidated; see *Rubinstein v. Speaker of the Knesset* 1983 and *Cohen v. Shilansky* 1991), in 1994 the funding method was changed by a deal between the parties: In exchange for a significant increase in the funding unit, the ceiling of legal donations was lowered from NIS 55,000 and limited to Israeli citizens only. State funding then allowed parties to repay their large debts, and the parties almost entirely stopped fundraising from the public. According to state comptroller reports, private funding in the 2000s covered just 1–2 percent of all campaign expenses. Still, some parties plunged into deep debt because of incorrect predictions of their success. Shinui, for example, which had won fifteen seats in the sixteenth Knesset, did not pass the electoral threshold in the seventeenth Knesset in 2006, racking up a NIS 7 million debt; the Gil Pensioners' Party, surprised by winning seven seats in the 2006 Knesset election, earned more than NIS 9 million in party funding, leaving them with a large balance (State Comptroller 2014). As of December 2014, the Likud is in debt for NIS 12 million, Labor for NIS 12.5 million, and the Jewish Home for NIS 20 million, while Yesh Atid had a surplus of NIS 20–30 million and Yisrael Beitenu had a balanced budget (Zarhia 2014).

The Parties Law (1973) had to address three new problems that arose over time. One, which is no longer valid, is the financing of candidates standing for direct election as prime minister; a second concerns the financing of the campaigns, party activity, and donations to local elections as regulated by the Local Authorities (Election Financing) Law (1993); and the third is the financing of primary elections within parties, regulated by law only in 2008, though limits on the total income and expenditures of each candidate were set in 1993 (Levine Committee 2000, 35–48).[20] Some of the public's discontent with the parties and the candidates in Israel is related to the methods they have used to enhance their chance of election. Even though, compared to other countries, Israel allocates very large sums to funding parties and campaign finance,[21] suspicions were raised of election fraud, gross violations of the funding rules, and bending the rules of democratic competition.

In 2000, a public committee appointed by the justice minister proposed a number of reforms in party financing to help them carry out their function while correcting the existing distortions. The recommendations, few of which were adopted, included gradually reducing public funding; raising the ceiling on the amount an individual may donate to a maximum of twice the average wage; transparency of the party accounts and public access via the Internet; clear and unchanging rules for calculating the funding unit, particularly in light of the splits in parties; regulating campaign finance in the local authorities; enforcing the rules about extra-parliamentary activity in the election campaigns; and legislation of an integrated law – campaign finance for the Knesset, the local authorities, and the primary elections (Levine Committee 2000, 68–76).

[20] The law was amended several times – see the Parties (Primary Elections) Law (Temporary Order) (2007). On primary elections, see Hofnung 2004; Hofnung 2006.

[21] The accepted index is the total state allocation to parties divided by the number of eligible voters. In the 1999 election to the fifteenth Knesset, state funding exceeded NIS 193 million, meaning about NIS 45.2 (roughly $11) per eligible voter (this does not include NIS 250 million spent on managing the campaign or in-kind funding – free TV and radio broadcasts, transport of voters to the polls, etc.). By comparison, the spending of other countries per voter: Australia $0.88; France $0.54; Germany $2.91; Italy $1.12; Japan $3.2 ("Levine Committee" 2000, 79).

9.8 Can We Do Without Parties?

In Chapter 8, we compared various channels of political participation and concluded that, despite the extensive social and technological changes, representative democracy cannot function without parties. However, we now add, the parties must adapt themselves to the age in which everything seems accessible, but the individual is more exposed than ever to misinformation and disinformation. The parties have a social role to play when the "masses" are actually composed of disjoined molecules vulnerable to the manipulation of leaders, governments, and special interests. In this context, the party has become even more important – a "hot medium," in the words of Marshall McLuhan. Despite the image of a political machine composed of wheeler-dealers and bureaucrats, a party is a more human channel than the mass media. Its singular advantage over other channels is that a party must be in touch with people, groups, and organizations in order to discharge its functions and win elections (Galnoor 1998, 198). A real party knows not just how to represent, but also how to aggregate interests over extended periods (unlike the social networks), and therefore it remains without rival (Dalton and Wattenberg 2000, 3–18). This, however, has not been the case in most democracies: One index that reflects the low status of parties at the beginning of the twenty-first century is the public's lack of trust in them. In surveys about the degree of trust in various institutions, Israeli parties take last place: Only 24 percent of the respondents trusted parties in 2010, compared with 32 percent in 2003 (Arian et al. 2005–10: 2010, 144). The level of trust the Israeli public places in the parties continued to decline in 2015, with a marked difference between Jews (only 15%) and Arabs (40%, due to the appearance of the Joint Arab List). It remains the lowest compared to all other institutions (Hermann et al. 2011–15: 2015, 59). In a comparative study of twenty democracies, citizens were asked whether parties are necessary. Most answered positively, particularly in Holland, Norway, and Sweden – countries with multiparty systems; fewer responded positively in the United States. In this survey, Israel is in the higher range (73%) of countries that believe in the necessity of parties (Diamond and Gunther 2001).

Early in this chapter, we asked whether parties could be organized and run based on affiliating with (and perhaps even "membership" in) the new media channels and social networks. Online communication creates fascinating opportunities that did not previously exist, particularly for young people, allowing them to belong to, identify with, and operate a virtual political party, whose organizational or legal status is of no interest to them. For such individuals, this kind of organizing seems to constitute a "hot channel" no less than the branches and conferences of parties in the past. Although connecting is carried out privately via a screen, the media possibilities are endless. Virtual organizing was one of the key factors in Barack Obama's two successful bids for the American presidency. The website operated on his behalf reportedly raised vast amounts of personal donations and was used to convey multidirectional information, activate volunteers, and above all penetrate voting groups in society. The 2011 mass protest in which leaders were overthrown in several Arab countries (the "Arab Spring") is largely attributed to the messages conveyed through the social media.

If so, does this constitute a mass, inclusive party unlike any we have seen before? This form of organizing – within civil society as well – is highly individualistic with a strong element of randomness. Still unknown is the degree of commitment and steadfastness of those who connect. And a troubling question is whether the new media reinforce the personification of politics, meaning commitment to a "leader," not a world view. It is still too early to say whether we are seeing a new type of party, an online party, or just a technological tool that still requires old-style organizing. In any event, research about parties and political participation cannot ignore this intriguing and revolutionary development.

In Israel, the future of the parties is shrouded in fog. The fading public trust, drop in active membership, and unraveling identification between voters and parties suggest a future of ongoing decline. What can be anticipated of parties?

- One possibility, called "the end of parties," is that parties will continue to decline until they disappear. According to this prediction, the era of parties is over, and some believe they are no longer necessary. On the assumption that the public no longer needs parties as a channel connecting society with politics, other bodies will take over these functions. The new media are the candidates to inherit the mediation function of parties, as they enable direct and daily "connection" with elected officials, government ministers, and administrators. A corresponding possibility is that interest groups and civil society organizations will inherit the representation functions of parties and undertake the role of directly influencing policymaking. In this scenario, the voters will continue to focus on candidates and their personalities, and will choose "leaders" only, not parties or ideologies. Another theoretical possibility, which unfortunately has supporters, is a "government of experts" (elected or not) that will replace politicians. Because this is a non-democratic solution with no public accountability, we will ignore it. None of the above options addresses the question of what will take over the roles of democratic parties, except those who believe that a new type of representative institution will gradually emerge.
- Another possibility is that the parties will undergo an overhaul on the assumption that they were simply slow in responding to political and social changes, and to the democratic opportunities offered by emerging technologies. According to this conception, the parties are already engaged in adapting to the changes – primarily in their democratization processes – and ultimately will create new avenues of action and organizational structures. In other words, the transformed parties will survive – provided that they decide to play a central role at the heart of the democratic process and adapt to the new political, social, and technological environments.[22]

In our opinion, initial signs are apparent that Israeli parties are adapting to some changes – the internal democratization of the main parties (holding primaries) is an example of this, despite the flaws noted above. The appearance of new parties, the politicization of issues such as environmental quality, the politics of rights, the increased use by parties of a range of new media in their campaigns (Caspi and Lev 2009) – all demonstrate that parties are still a significant institution in social

[22] Dalton and Wattenberg argue (2000, 125) that the Internet will not create a democratic utopia and that virtual party membership lacks the social and educational capital found in face-to-face participation (ibid., 268).

organizing, disseminating new ideas, and the internalization of these ideas. The growth of social movements also breathes new life into the parties and could expand the circle of voters (Yishai 1998a). The strengthening of interest groups is not necessarily a threat to parties, and could even enhance their status if these groups begin to perceive the parties as targets for lobbying. Extra-parliamentary groups such as Gush Emunim and Peace Now have already proven that cooperation between them and parties can have a concrete effect on policymaking.

Common to both forecasts – that the parties will wane or that they will adapt – is recognition of the changes they experienced in the twentieth century. Indeed, the resemblance between a party in the 1950s and the same party in the early twenty-first century is minimal in terms of its activity, organizational structure, and role in society. In this sense, the parties in Israel are no different than their counterparts in the democratic world, although it seems that Israeli parties were even slower in adjusting than parties in other countries, and are now at a crossroads. The reason for this might be the precipitous fall from their all-powerful role in the past, and perhaps, too, they have not yet fully recovered from the seven lean years during direct election of the prime minister, and the ongoing party-less personality cult. Thus, the election campaign in 2015 – some dozen years after abolishing direct elections – was still being waged by advertising agencies as if there were no parties, but only leaders. In spite of the common belief, the public does not blindly follow the media's efforts to personalize politics: Leaders or no leaders, only 3.6 out of five eligible voters went to the polls, and not a single party head won even 24 percent support.

Nevertheless, Israeli parties are not exempt from direct responsibility for their plight. In addition to their inability to renew themselves in a timely manner, corruption has stained the ranks of many parties. It is said "politics costs a lot of money," although there are democracies in which political life did not lead to a corrupt link between government and big business. In Israel, state funding is relatively generous, as noted, and therefore the dependence of candidates on hidden stashes of money can be prevented if the parties would determine to finance their activity differently. It was also not necessary to loosen the rules for party membership and create a loophole that has been exploited by interested persons to recruit members in exchange for favors.[23]

As noted, splitting the vote so that in the 2000s a dozen parties on average served in the Knesset is not itself the source of the problem, because the voting patterns of Israeli citizens are a mirror image of the social mosaic of the country. The disappearance of large, inclusive parties – the backbone of the political system – creates instability and problems for the steering capacity, but the reason for their disappearance lies with the parties themselves, which no longer attract large constituencies. Thus the attempt to reduce the number of parties artificially, by raising the electoral threshold to 3.25 percent in 2015, has failed (as it led to only two fewer parties – see Table 9.2). The social structure and range of world views have for years ensured that the MKs in any Knesset will come from *at least* seven or eight parties. And even if

[23] Examples of corruption among parties are not lacking: donations to non-profits established by Ehud Barak prior to the 1999 election; forged ballots in the internal election for Labor head in 2001 (Burg versus Ben-Eliezer); revelations of corruption in the Likud primaries of 2002; the Cyril Kern affair, revealed weeks before voting for the sixteenth Knesset in 2003, allegedly benefiting Ariel Sharon illicitly; and others.

an electoral system is instituted that arbitrarily creates two parties in Israel, they will fragment into their components after election day. This does not deny the need to reduce the fragmentation and the Effective Number of Parliamentary Parties (see Figure 4.1), so that big parties will be also elected to the Knesset.

There can be no democracy without political parties. Israeli parties do not have to return to the omnipotence of the early years of the state, but rather to establish an organization with an ideology that is internally democratic, makes good use of the new media, holds fair elections to its institutions, and regards itself as accountable to its members, voters, and the public at large.

10 Elections: The Vague Verdict of the Israeli Voter

10.1 Several Principles of Democratic Elections

A group of people who come together to achieve a common goal need some sort of mechanism that will allow them to make decisions and take action. If the point of departure is that all members of the group are equal, the decision-making mechanism must be democratic. It can be based on full consensus – trying to reach a shared understanding and decision by all the relevant actors – or on decision-making by only some of the members. The decision-making group can be rotated among all the members, or it can be chosen by them. The chosen leadership can be one person or more, but an agreed upon mechanism is needed for choosing them, i.e., a system of election. This system will reflect the social structure and values of the group, whether it be a country, a labor union, or a club for retirees. The system most common in democracies is an election in which the leadership is chosen by majority vote.

There are many non-democratic systems for decision-making. In some, people agree – or generally are forced to agree – to follow a powerful leader, an emissary of God, a wealthy individual, or a small group (an oligarchy). Between the democratic and non-democratic methods are the quasi-democratic systems in which the group selects its leader in accordance with set criteria: The stronger, older, or experienced one becomes the leader, or an heir inherits the mantle of leadership. Incidentally, non-democratic regimes also differ in how they select the leadership. How is a kingdom inherited, for example, and who decides on the heir? Or how does one make it into the ruling aristocracy?

The test of whether an election is democratic is fairly simple: Do the voters have the right to change their leader periodically and non-violently? Another important test of a democratic election concerns the extent to which voting rights are inclusive, i.e., not discriminatory against any adult group in that society. After voting rights are established, electoral systems can be categorized by type and subtype, which, as noted, reflect the values of the society and those who compose it. Questions that must be asked about the many democratic electoral systems concern who stands for election – an individual or a party? How are the elective offices divided up among those who ran – is the one who received the largest number of votes elected, or are the votes distributed proportionally among the candidates? What is the term of office of those elected? These and other questions allow us to classify electoral systems.

Democratic elections must strictly adhere to the principle that the votes of all eligible voters must carry equal weight. The principle of equality has two meanings: equality of the votes cast and equal opportunity to be elected. In free elections, this principle allows all individuals and groups in society to give political expression to their views and interests.

Definition: Democratic elections are meant to translate the will of the voters into steering capacity, i.e., governance – leadership with the authority to act in the name of and on behalf of the citizens.

Democracy is not just a form of governance, but also a political culture, and free elections are necessary for democracy – necessary, but not sufficient, because an election must meet tests in addition to equality and inclusiveness of voting (Dahl 2000, 41):

- effective participation – equal opportunity to express views and persuade others;
- well-informed understanding – opportunity for every voter to learn about possible alternatives;
- control of the agenda – the opportunity to decide on the issues to be deliberated.

To determine if this is material democracy, not just procedural, we must also ask: Do other forms of participation exist? Is there freedom of expression? A legislative process? Are the rights of minorities protected? Elections are the heart of the democratic process because they turn citizens into political participants and link the success of political actors to public support. However, the democratic system also requires the ongoing political involvement of citizens. In a democracy, the public has the right to know what its elected officials are doing for them, and public discourse must be open to a range of divergent views. Complementary to the public's right to choose its leaders and replace them, the public must also feel capable of having an impact and must be able to participate in decision-making between elections.

A. The Difficulty of Aggregating Voters' Views and Converting them into a Shared Preference

Whoever has experienced decision-making in a group of people with a variety of views requires no explanation about why the democratic process is arduous and complicated. People have different preferences, and that's a good thing, but when working together, they find it hard to agree on a common goal or how to achieve it. Nevertheless, the other option – imposing a non-democratic decision – is far worse and also immoral. The problematics of creating a rational process of aggregating preferences was shown by Kenneth Arrow in the "impossibility theorem," also known as "the Arrow paradox."[1] Arrow demonstrates the difficulty of consistently aggregating the preferences of different voters into a common preference, moving from the individual's order of priorities to the common denominator of the group's desires (the collective welfare). Thus, we can show the lack of internal consistency when

[1] Arrow ([1951] 1963) was preceded by Condorcet (1785). See Maschler, Solan, and Zamir 2013.

aggregating the preferences of voters, and this is all the more difficult when decisions are made in conditions of uncertainty or when the voters are not offered clear alternatives. Democracies strive to aggregate a range of views of citizens and groups into binding majority decisions. The mission, though complex, is definitely possible and appropriately opens this chapter: There is no ideal or even "correct" electoral system. Democratic elections are part of the dynamic relationship "society–politics–society," i.e., representation.

B. General Remarks about Israeli Elections

The political system in Israel is highly centralized, and the Knesset is the only body determined by direct, general election. The distribution of votes for Knesset seats is considered the sole accurate political profile of Israeli society, and the distribution of power in other institutions derives from it. Although this pattern has diminished over the years, in 2015 one can still find the Knesset party composition replicated in the Jewish Agency, the boards of directors of government corporations, and the plenary of the Israel Broadcasting Authority.

The first election to Israel's Constituent Assembly (the first Knesset) took place in January 1949, even before the war had ended (Weitz 2001, 10–31). Until March 2015, Knesset elections have been held twenty times, of which two elections included the direct election of the prime minister (1996, 1999) and one (2001) was a special election of the prime minister only. In comparison with well-developed democracies, Israel's elections are considered democratic, free, and relatively uncorrupt. Elections have taken place in the midst of a war (1949) and in the immediate wake of wars (Yom Kippur 1973; the Gaza operation in January 2009). The electoral options are numerous, and the voters' verdict is final. The question of the legitimacy of election results successfully passed the test of "political upheavals," particularly in 1977 when the defeat of the dominant party, which had been in power for decades, transpired without tremors to governance. The transitions to direct election in 1996 and back to the previous electoral system in 2003 were also smooth. In the 2015 election, Israel's population was 8.4 million, of whom 5.9 million (70%) were adults with the right to vote, who determined by their vote (or failure to vote) the composition of the 120-member Knesset.

10.2 Elections and Electoral Systems

The electoral system in a democracy connects three elements: the citizen, the party or candidates, and the government. Every electoral system is beset by tension between the desire for broad representation and the need for steering capacity. Representation without steering capacity means the inability to merge a range of views into binding majority decisions. Steering capacity without representation means decisions lacking in social legitimacy, i.e., undemocratic ones. The more a society is fragmented and complex, the more difficult to balance these. Democracies have proven, however, that this can be done, and that they can last. Elections in democracies are meant to link the will of the voters with the composition of the elective bodies, and to enable changes of government at defined periods. Without all these characteristics, elections could take place – such as those in Spain and Portugal during the periods of dictatorship, or in Cuba today – but they cannot be considered democratic.

A. Classifying Democratic Electoral Systems on Three Dimensions

Size of the constituency – the number of representatives elected from each district (not the number of eligible voters). The more elected representatives from one constituency, the greater the chances of achieving more proportional representation. In Israel, Holland, and Slovakia, the entire country is one constituency (the "national" system), from which all the representatives are elected to parliament. Most democracies are composed of several constituencies. Sometimes constituencies have an equal number of representatives: In Britain and Canada, only one representative is elected from each district. In other countries, the representation of constituencies is not uniform: In Sweden, between two and thirty-four representatives are elected in each constituency; and in Finland, from six to thirty-three representatives are elected in each constituency.

For whom you vote – for people, party lists, or some combination of these. In personal electoral systems, the citizen votes for a specific person for president, parliament member, or mayor. A pure personal electoral system is generally identified with the principle of majority rule (see below) and with constituencies in which one representative is elected, such as most British Commonwealth countries. In strict party list systems, the citizen votes for a slate of candidates from one party, and cannot change the list by expressing a preference for one candidate over another. This system is used in Israel, Norway, Spain, Portugal, and Sweden – the voter casts a ballot for a slate of candidates – the ballot shows no candidate names or ranking on the list. In mixed systems, such as those used in Austria, Belgium, Denmark, and Finland, the voter can influence the order of candidates in voting for a party, and has the opportunity to rank or change the order of candidates within the list.

The electoral formula – the mechanism by which votes are converted into representatives and parliament seats, which can be majoritarian, proportional, or mixed. In majoritarian systems, the candidate who receives the most votes in the constituency wins election, even if he or she did not win an absolute majority. In this system, also called "first past the post" (FPP) or "winner takes all," votes given to candidates who lose go to waste.[2] In a proportional representation system such as that used in Israel, on the other hand, the number of representatives on a list is commensurate with the percentage of votes garnered by that list in proportion to other lists. A mixed system combines both, for example the party receiving the most votes wins representation in the constituency, but votes received by the other parties are transferred and integrated into the national list of those parties.

The above three elements can function independently of each other, and the combinations yield a variety of electoral systems. In practice, however, the combinations are limited, and over the years three main types have evolved in most democracies. The first combines single-representative constituencies, a majoritarian electoral system, and personal preference candidates – such as the system used for election of the

[2] In keeping with the coalition agreement after the 2010 election in Britain, a referendum was held on amending the electoral system so that the voters could rank their preferences; if no candidate won more than 50 percent of the vote, the voters' secondary preferences would be taken into account and the proportion of wasted votes would diminish. The proposal was rejected.

US Senate or British parliament. This reduces the number of parties and strengthens steering capacity at the expense of representation. The second type combines a proportional electoral system, generally based on candidate lists, with a small number of constituencies. This system is used in Israel as well as Holland, Luxembourg, Slovakia, South Africa, and Russia: It enlarges the number of parties and strengthens representation, sometimes at the expense of steering capacity (Atmor et al. 2009). The third type is a mixed electoral system, sometimes applied to the same elective body, and is designed to balance out the shortcomings of each system. These can be found in the electoral systems of Germany, Italy, Japan, New Zealand, and France (Y. Levy 2005). In addition, each country customizes the electoral system to suit its distinctive social structure and political culture.

B. The Principle of Proportionality

Another approach to analyzing the electoral system is to assume that all democratic representation ultimately rests upon the principle of proportionality – because this is the link between the voters and the representatives – and thus electoral systems can be classified by the extent of their proportionality. At one extreme are systems that seek to reflect the voters' preferences as closely as possible, and therefore are more proportional. At the other extreme are systems that seek to establish conclusively who won the election, and therefore make do with majority rule and less proportionality, which leaves a larger number of voters without representation. Table 10.1 uses the Gallagher Index[3] to show a correlation between the electoral system and the degree of disproportionality of the election results.

Majoritarian systems clearly yield less representative results than proportional systems. Yet variety exists even within the more proportional systems. The proportional system in Spain produces disproportional results because of the large number of small constituencies. In Holland and Israel, on the other hand, each with one national constituency and low electoral thresholds, the systems produce results that are highly proportional. The electoral system is a subject of controversy in every democracy because each system gives an edge to one group or another. Therefore, in the ongoing debate about the desirable electoral system, governance principles and political interests are intertwined (Diskin and Diskin 1988, 3). To convert the will of the voters to steering capacity, the electoral system must take into consideration the social structure and internal rifts of the voting public as well as the degree of consensus around the common political language – the "common contents" (Galnoor 1982, 9–12). The two endpoints are as follows:

- In a society with a high level of common contents concerning its collective goals and the democratic rules of the game, and with few social rifts, the tendency will be to strengthen steering capacity over representativeness.
- Conversely, in a society in which there is little agreement about common contents and considerable social fragmentation, the tendency will be to prefer representativeness at the expense of steering capacity.

[3] The most commonly used measure of the disproportionality of an electoral system is the Gallagher Index (Gallagher 1991), calculated as follows: The percentage of seats received by each party is subtracted from the percentage of votes that it received; the difference is then squared and divided by two. The square root of the result reflects the disproportionality.

Table 10.1 *Average electoral disproportionality and type of electoral system in twelve democracies, 1945–1996*

	Electoral system	Disproportionality (%)
Netherlands	Proportional	1.30
Denmark	Proportional	1.83
Sweden	Proportional	2.09
Israel	Proportional	2.27
Austria	Proportional	2.47
Germany	Proportional-Mixed	2.52
Finland	Proportional	2.93
Greece	Proportional	8.08
Spain	Proportional	8.15
New Zealand	Majoritarian	10.33
Britain	Majoritarian	11.11
Canada	Majoritarian	11.72

1 = more proportional
Source: Lijphart 1999, 162.

Between these two extremes are many permutations, and the electoral systems enable a variety of options for linking social structure with representation or steering capacity. Majoritarian electoral systems generally enhance the steering capacity of the executive branch of government; more proportional systems allow for a fuller representation of the range of public opinion. Neither will achieve its goal in a democracy, however, if they are not anchored in the social structure.

The proportional electoral system used in Israel combines a fairly high degree of common contents and a fragmented social structure. Direct election of the prime minister sought to emphasize common contents at the expense of the social structure, and failed (see Chapter 5, section 7). On the other hand, coalition governments seek to bridge the gap between social fragmentation and the critical need for steering capacity (see Chapter 11). This is not always possible – when agreement about common contents diminishes, the steering capacity is undermined, sectoral representation is strengthened, and the electoral system has a very hard time bridging the gap. At the end of this chapter, we note several options for reform of the system of election to the Knesset, which take the social structure into account.

10.3 The Electoral System in Israel

Since 1920, elections in the Yishuv were held to the Assembly of Representatives, the Histadrut, the local authorities, and smaller frameworks such as the Hadassah workers' committee, the Dan bus cooperative, workers' councils, the Agriculture Union, and the Farmers' Federation. Thus a tradition of elections evolved and the character of those elections continues to this day (see first two sections of Chapter 1). The first Assembly of Representatives was elected in April 1920 when 22,000 of the Jewish population of Eretz Israel, then numbering 67,000, voted (some 80% of eligible voters). Such a high turnout in a voluntary society reflects political awareness and recognition of the importance of democratic elections. Three more elections were held for Yishuv institutions (1925, 1931, and 1944), the delays caused by external events. The principle of inclusiveness – granting the right to vote to all members of the Jewish community, including women – was established in these elections, despite strong pressure against allowing everyone to vote. The fourth election of the Assembly of Representatives (1944) was held in the format that continues to this day – inclusive, direct, equal, secret, and proportional.

Elections to the various Yishuv institutions gradually laid the foundation for a tradition in which democratic elections are used to determine political leadership and policies are set by majority rule. This is important for understanding the political culture of Israeli elections: The tradition of democratic elections, which began in 1920, will mark its centennial in 2020.

A. The "Philosophy" of the System

The strong connection between social structure and electoral system requires an understanding of the "philosophy" of the system before studying its technical details. As noted, the more fragmented a society, the more likely to have a proportional system of elections. This is not a hard and fast rule, of course, as there are heterogeneous societies with majoritarian systems and homogeneous societies with proportional systems. Israeli society is highly fragmented as its sphere of common contents diminished after the first two decades of Israel's existence. Throughout the years, the Knesset had a fairly constant political configuration of about four ideological groupings, particularly on foreign affairs and security matters, and another four or five socioethnic groups (Arabs, ultra-Orthodox, religious Zionists, and immigrants). This mosaic is the product of the main issues on the agenda – security and foreign affairs, socioeconomic conditions, and the distinct social and religious communities – which creates at least eight groups demanding political representation and capable of realizing it. We wrote "at least" because these groups are also fragmented internally, and every so often another party or group will appear in the Knesset election.

We saw in Chapter 9 that four types of parties have appeared over the years along the main axis of security and foreign affairs: extreme left, moderate left, moderate right, and extreme right. Parties that could be clearly located on the socioeconomic axis were common in the first decades of the state, but these differences blurred over time and began to overlap partially with parties on the security continuum.[4] Throughout the life of Israel, social-oriented and religious groups gave birth to sectoral parties (National Religious Party, Agudat Yisrael, Tami, Arab Democratic Party, United Arab List, Yisrael B'Aliyah, Yisrael Beitenu, and others), adding to the party mosaic. This overall division of parties reflects the makeup of the Knesset through most of the political history of Israel. Moreover, parties that did not fit this division and tried to locate

[4] Parties on the socioeconomic right (Progressives, General Zionists) merged with the hawkish security parties (Herut), while a socialist party (Mapam) became part of the left-wing bloc on security (Labor) and then merged with Meretz. Remnants of parties clearly belonging to the secondary socioeconomic axis can be identified as Hadash, Shas to some extent, Meretz, and some members of Labor.

themselves "in the center" or to offer a new approach did not last even a decade – Rafi, Dash, Tzomet,[5] Third Way, Center Party, Shinui,[6] the Gil Pensioners Party, and Kadima (which dropped from twenty-eight seats in 2009 to eight in 2013, and none at all in 2015). In short, the electoral system must be responsive to the mosaic of groups and views, and with only some exaggeration can it be said that regardless of the electoral system, the Knesset will always have seven to eight parties. By which we mean that even if the system artificially narrowed Knesset membership to two parties, these would soon begin to subdivide. Hence it is better that the electoral system reflect the representational needs of the heterogeneous society in Israel.

The emphasis on high proportionality in the electoral system is not coincidental. It is designed to enable broad social representation, allowing even small groups a voice in the Knesset. The electoral system achieves this by having one state-wide constituency with 120 seats; an electoral formula that underscores proportionality in converting votes to seats; and a relatively low electoral threshold. This combination places Israel at the lower end of countries with proportional representation systems, though the system in some of these countries yields greater disproportionality (Table 10.1). The impact of raising the electoral threshold on the multiparty system or coalition-based governance is yet unclear.

B. Laws and Principles of Election to the Knesset

The following laws regulate Knesset elections and related matters: The ***Basic Law: The Knesset*** sets out the principles of the system, the right to vote and be elected, and when elections must take place. Article 4 states, "The Knesset shall be elected by general, national, direct, equal, secret and proportional elections," thereby ensuring that the principles of the electoral system are anchored constitutionally, protecting it from demands by a relative majority of MKs to amend this article. The ***Knesset Elections Law*** regulates the election process: It stipulates that voting will be for a list of candidates, divides the country into voting districts, creates supervisory election committees, and oversees voter rolls, procedures, and counts. The ***Parties Law*** states that a party must be registered in order to run for election. The ***Election (Campaign Methods) Law*** regulates and places limitations on election campaigns.

General elections: Every adult Israeli citizen has the right to vote in Israel. In other words, citizenship confers this basic democratic right, without conditions or other qualifications. During the Yishuv period, an unsuccessful attempt was made to limit voting rights to those residing in Israel during a given period, to Hebrew speakers, and the like. Those who seek limitations are trying to prevent someone else from voting, such as women, the indigent, Arab citizens, the ultra-Orthodox, or new

[5] Although Tzomet was a party with hawkish views, its messages during the campaign focused on the issue of political corruption.

[6] When Dash disbanded, some of its members, led by Amnon Rubinstein, founded Shinui. Shinui, together with Ratz and Mapam, established Meretz in the 1992 election. For the 1999 election, Avraham Poraz resigned from Meretz and reconstituted Shinui as an independent party. Under the leadership of Yosef Lapid, Shinui was revitalized as a new, secular, middle-class party that railed against religious coercion. It had resounding success – six seats in the 1999 election and fifteen seats in the 2003 election, making it the third-largest party. In the 2006 election, Shinui was erased from the political map.

immigrants, as in the above examples. At the polls, a citizen is required to prove his right to vote and nothing more. Any additional requirement such as a "loyalty oath" is a distortion: It is an attempt by those elected to dictate to the voters – a page taken from the playbook of non-democratic regimes.[7]

In keeping with the principle of inclusiveness, Israel gives the right to vote and makes special voting arrangements for soldiers, the ill, sailors, prisoners, and Israeli diplomats abroad. Although Israelis who live abroad have the right to vote, they must do so in Israel on election day. The principle of inclusiveness is also protected by there being no technical barriers to exercising the right to vote, as in other democracies. In Israel, for example, there is no need for prior voter registration, and the onus for ensuring the right to vote is on the state. Voter rolls are updated annually and voters receive notice of their right as well as the location of their polling station in proximity to their residence. Whoever does not appear on the voter roll may appeal to the Interior Ministry.

Country-wide: For purposes of counting the votes, the entire country (including settlements in the territories) is considered one constituency. The division into 9,263 ballot boxes (in the 2009 election) is for administrative convenience only and has no electoral significance, because the calculation of Knesset seats is based on the total votes received by the party list in voting stations throughout the country. Party lists for the Knesset are national, although their voters might live in a defined area. In several parties, the list of candidates reflects internal geographical distribution, but only for electoral purposes.

Direct: The voter casts a ballot directly for a party list, and the party wins representation in the Knesset proportional to the electoral support it received. There are no intermediaries between the ballots cast and the parties (such as the electoral college in the American presidential election). Direct election does not necessarily mean a direct connection between the voter and the person elected (with the exception of internal regional elections in several parties to determine composition of the list), but between the voter and the list of party candidates. Election of Israel's president is indirect, however, as it is the public representatives in the Knesset who vote for the incumbent of this office.

Equal: This principle has two meanings. First, every vote carries the same weight as every other vote. Second, as ruled by the Supreme Court (*Bergman v. Finance Minister* 1969), equal elections also mean an equal opportunity for each person to be elected (see Chapter 6).[8] The electoral thresholds and the surplus votes agreements are minor deviations from this principle because they lead to votes being "wasted," thereby giving greater weight to other votes (see below). There are also limitations on the right to vote – age, felony convictions, and others – which do not undermine the validity of the principle of equality.

Secret: Voters vote with their conscience and for their beliefs. Democratic elections zealously guard the privacy of voters to protect them from making a coerced choice

[7] For an example of an attempt to undermine the right to vote by adding conditions or declarations, such as a loyalty oath, see the proposed Citizenship (Amendment – Declaration of Loyalty) Bill (2009).

[8] The court ruled in this case that equal opportunity in elections also entails the equal financing of elections, and therefore it invalidated the amendment to the Parties Financing Law that had given an advantage to incumbent parties.

out of a sense of dependence, pressure, or undue influence. In Israel, after the individual has been identified as having the right to vote, voting takes place behind a screen as the voter chooses a ballot and places it into an empty, unmarked envelope. From the moment the voter drops the envelope into the ballot box, the ballot joins the other ballots inside and there is no way of knowing which ballot belonged to any individual. Some interested parties wish to eliminate secrecy in order to control the vote. In the early years of the state, rumors circulated that new immigrants who were unaware of their right to privacy were vulnerable to pressure due to their dependence upon party institutions. Another claim was that residents of small locales – transit camps, Arab villages, kibbutzim, and moshavim – were threatened that how they voted would become known. These days, too, the media report claims of fraud, particularly among ultra-Orthodox and Arab voters, in which pressure is applied to voters or members of the polling station committee, as well as claims that some people cast multiple ballots by posing as others who may be abroad, too ill to vote, or even deceased.[9] Members of the polling station committee, comprised of representatives of various parties, are responsible for preventing election fraud. Only if they themselves collaborate can the voting result be distorted in that polling station. Hence, this is a fairly marginal phenomenon, and it can be said that, in general, the principle of secrecy is protected in Israel and the election results reflect the will of the voters, as in a properly functioning democracy.

Proportional: The distribution of the 120 Knesset seats adheres closely to the percentage of valid votes cast for each party. In other words, the Israeli system, with one constituency and a low electoral threshold, yields results that are very proportional. Nevertheless, to prevent excessive fragmentation, an electoral threshold was set: A party must receive a minimum percentage of votes in order to share in the distribution of Knesset seats. Note, first, that because 120 elected officials represent the entire voting public, there is a natural or mathematical electoral threshold – a list must receive at least 0.83 percent of the vote to win the first seat (100% divided by 120). Prior to the 1951 election, the electoral threshold was set at 1 percent; in the 1992 election, it was raised to 1.5 percent; in 2006 it was upped to 2 percent; and in the 2015 election, it was further increased to 3.25 percent. The aim is to reduce Knesset fragmentation and, as seen (Table 10.2), that goal was only partially achieved by not admitting parties represented by only one MK.[10]

9 Another claim made was that the heads of large clans in Arab villages could ensure the voting loyalty of clan members by using ballots of a particular color, so that the percentage of support from each clan would be known when the ballots were counted.

10 When the electoral threshold was set at 1 percent in 1951, the number of party lists vying for election decreased by four: Two decided not to run and two did not pass the electoral threshold, but would not have entered the Knesset anyway because they did not win enough votes for even one seat. When the electoral threshold was raised to 1.5 percent in 1992, the number of parties contending decreased by only two. Fifteen lists did not pass the electoral threshold, but only Tehiya did not win a seat as a result of the higher threshold. Further raising the threshold to 2 percent in 2006 did not prevent the entry of any parties that would not have entered the Knesset based on the previous threshold (1.5%). In 2006, the Green Party and the Green Leaf Party would have been represented in the Knesset with a 1 percent electoral threshold (they received 1.5% and 1.3% of the votes, respectively), but remained out with a 2 percent threshold. In the 2009 election, no additional list would have been prevented from entering the Knesset if the electoral threshold had been 1 percent or 1.5 percent, while the Green Movement–Meimad was on the border of entering had the threshold been 0.83 percent. If the electoral threshold had been 3.25 percent in 2013, Hadash, Balad, and Kadima would not have been represented, and the number of parties would have dropped from twelve to nine.

Table 10.2 *Comparison of two methods of distributing surplus votes to the largest parties from the seventeenth through the twentieth Knesset elections (2006–2015)*

Party list	Knesset	Votes won by the party list	Seats after Bader–Ofer distribution method	Change in seats using the "largest surplus" calculation
Kadima	17th	690,901	21	–1
	18th	758,032	28	–1
Hatnua	19th	189,167	6	same
Labor–Meimad–the Zionist Camp	17th	472,366	19	same
	18th	394,577	15	–1
	19th	432,118	15	–1
	20th	786,313	24	–1
Shas	17th	299,054	12	same
	18th	286,300	11	–1
	19th	331,868	11	same
	20th	241,613	7	+1
Likud	17th	281,996	12	–1
	18th	729,054	27	–1
	19th	885,054	31	–1
	20th	985,408	30	–1
Yisrael Beitenu	17th	281,880	11	same
	18th	394,577	15	–1
	19th	–	–	–
	20th	214,906	6	same
Yesh Atid	19th	543,458	19	–1
	20th	371,602	11	same
Jewish Home	18th	96,765	3	same
	19th	345,985	12	–1
	20th	283,910	8	+1
Joint List	20th	446,583`	13	+1
Kulanu	20th	315,360	10	same

– = did not participate
same = no change
Source: Results of the seventeenth–twentieth Knesset elections from Knesset 2015.

Election date: The Basic Law: The Knesset states that election day shall be held on the Tuesday of the Hebrew month of Heshvan in the year that the term of the outgoing Knesset expires. Had each Knesset completed its term of office, elections would have been held on a set date once every four years. In reality, most Knessets dispersed prior to completing their term, and elections have been held on various dates (see Chapter 11 on coalitions).[11] Only four elections were held in the month of Heshvan, and since 1977 only one was held upon completion of the Knesset term.

[11] The average term of the nineteen Knessets until 2015 was 3.4 years.

The ninth Knesset served four years and one month, the eleventh Knesset served four years and three months. In all other cases, elections were held early, and the term of office of the nineteenth Knesset that dispersed in late 2014 was particularly short – twenty-five months – resembling the fourth Knesset (1959–61), which served for twenty-three months.

C. Conducting the Election

The Central Elections Committee is charged with conducting the election, and it is ready to do so from the moment the new Knesset takes office, in the event that an election is called early. The committee is composed of faction representatives, relative to their size in the Knesset, and headed by a Supreme Court justice. Subordinate to the Elections Committee and also composed of factions are regional elections committees and local polling station committees (in which at least three factions are represented). The Central Elections Committee has considerable power: It can authorize or disqualify candidate lists, a party nickname, and its letter symbol; it is responsible for preparing for the election, scrutinizing campaign messages, ensuring the legality of the process, and ratifying the results; and it sets the procedure for special voting in double envelopes by soldiers, diplomats abroad, and others. The committee also has a judicial function – it has sole jurisdiction regarding claims of misdeeds or failure to act in accordance with the Knesset Elections Law (1969), although its administrative and judicial decisions can be appealed to the District or Supreme Court, as appropriate.

The most sensitive issue for the Central Elections Committee is its authority to approve or disqualify party lists and, since the 2003 election, candidates on the list as well, in keeping with Article 7A of the Basic Law: The Knesset. Disqualification of a list eviscerates the right to run for office, and therefore should be applied with caution to ensure that the case is exceptional. Until 1985, the law stated that the Elections Committee shall authorize party lists unless procedural criteria are not met, such as submitting invalid signatures. And yet in 1965, the Elections Committee had disqualified the Socialist Party (linked to the al-Ard movement, which had previously been outlawed) on the grounds that "its founders seek to undermine the existence of the state, or its territorial integrity" (*Yardor v. Central Elections Committee* 1964). In an appeal to the High Court of Justice, a precedent-setting decision by a majority ruled that the committee has the authority to disqualify a list of candidates even though it is not explicitly empowered to do so by law. In 1984, the committee disqualified two parties – Kach and the Progressive List for Peace – but this time the High Court ruled that the committee has no authority to invalidate a list without an explicit legal provision to that effect, thereby overturning the previous decision.[12] The two parties ran in the election and both entered the Knesset.

In consequence, the Basic Law: The Knesset was amended, and Article 7A was formulated to authorize the Central Elections Committee to disqualify a list if it negates Israel as the state of the Jewish people, repudiates the democratic character of the state, or incites to racism. Based on this article, the committee disqualified Kach

[12] This decision (*Neiman v. Central Elections Committee*, 1984) severely limited the Yardor decision to cases in which there is a clear and present danger of harm to the state.

in 1988, a decision that was not overturned by the High Court. Over the years, the article was further amended and expanded, and today it allows for the disqualification of lists or candidates if their aims or actions include any of the following: denial of the existence of Israel as a Jewish and democratic state; incitement to racism; or support of armed struggle by an enemy state or terrorist organization against the state of Israel. High Court rulings on decisions of the Central Elections Committee greatly narrowed this article to cases in which there is "imminent certainty" that these conditions obtain (*Central Elections Committee v. Tibi, Bishara, et al.* 2002). As a result, the High Court has not accepted the disqualification of a candidate or a list ever since, overturning decisions by the Central Elections Committee, and rejecting appeals submitted regarding the approval of candidates or lists.[13] In setting stringent criteria for disqualifying parties and candidates from running for office, the High Court of Justice established the right to vote and be elected as guiding principles for safeguarding democracy.

D. Calculation of Results and Distribution of Surplus Votes

Calculation of the election results to determine political representation is done according to the Bader–Ofer method,[14] taking into account the surplus votes agreements reached by the parties. Two parties that signed a surplus vote agreement are considered one list for purposes of dividing up the surplus votes. The allocation of surplus seats between two parties that signed an agreement is calculated by the same method: The list with the greater number of votes wins.[15]

The method of distributing surplus votes slightly favors larger parties, because the relative price of a seat is somewhat lower; however, the overall impact is marginal, since the number of surplus seats is small: three to seven. The advantage to the large parties would be one more seat, at most. This could be important when the gap between the two large parties is small, as happened in the 2009 election, but it does

[13] Prior to the 2003 election, for example, the Elections Committee disqualified MKs Ahmad Tibi and Azmi Bishara from running for the Knesset (*Central Elections Committee v. Tibi, Bishara, et al.* 2002 and 2003); it approved the candidacy of Baruch Marzel for the Knesset (*Pines-Paz v. Marzel* 2003); and it disqualified Balad (*Balad: National Democratic Assembly v. Central Elections Committee* 2003). Upon petition, the High Court overturned the Elections Committee decision concerning Tibi and Bishara, dismissed the appeal on Baruch Marzel's candidacy, and accepted the appeal to overturn the disqualification of Balad. In 2006, the court was not required to address this issue. The Central Elections Committee rejected a request to disqualify the Ra'am-Ta'al list from running for the Knesset. In 2009, the court overturned the decision of the Central Elections Committee to disqualify Balad and Ra'am-Ta'al (*Balad and Ra'am-Ta'al v. Central Elections Committee* 2009). In 2013, the court overturned the decision of the Central Elections Committee to disqualify MK Haneen Zoabi from running for the Knesset (*Central Elections Committee for the 19th Knesset v. MK Haneen Zoabi* 2013). In 2015, once again, the court overturned the decision of the Central Elections Committee to disqualify the candidacies of both MKs Haneen Zoabi and Baruch Marzel (*Central Elections Committee for the 20th Knesset v. MK Haneen Zoabi* and *Central Elections Committee for the 20th Knesset v. Baruch Marzel*).

[14] Since the 1977 election, the distribution of surplus votes has been allocated by the D'Hondt rule, called the Bader–Ofer method in Israel, after those who proposed it – MK Yohanan Bader from Herut and MK Avraham Ofer from Labor. The system gives a small advantage to larger parties, because surplus seats are allocated to the party that "pays" the higher average price per seat, not necessarily the party whose surplus is larger in absolute terms.

[15] For the calculation of election results and distribution of surplus votes, see the official post-election publication of the Central Elections Committee in the State Records.

not determine the composition of the coalition. When the surplus votes were distributed in 2009, each of the following parties received one more seat: Kadima (without having a surplus agreement), Yisrael Beitenu, Labor, Shas, and the National Union. For a small party, on the other hand, adding or losing a seat is significant. Table 10.2 shows the difference between distributing the surplus votes according to the Bader–Ofer method and a simple calculation in which the party with the largest surplus receives an additional seat.

Table 10.2 indicates that in the elections examined, the Bader–Ofer method gave a marginal advantage of one additional seat to the large parties. In 2009 and 2013, almost all the five large parties won an additional seat thanks to the method of distributing the surplus. According to the large surplus method, the large parties would have lost a total of up to five seats, and this would have fragmented the Knesset even more. On the other hand, using the larger surplus method, the following small parties would have received one additional seat in 2013: Kadima, United Arab List, Balad, and Hatnuah, which would have been very significant from their perspective. In 2015, the two largest parties, Likud and Labor, as well as Kulanu and Shas each won one additional seat, while Kulanu, Meretz, the Jewish Home, and Shas would have won one each had the large surplus method been used.

E. Computerized Elections

The system of elections used in Israel is convoluted and expensive – the voter is individually identified by the polling station committee and inserts a ballot into the ballot box; later the ballots are manually counted. The near final results are made public the morning after election day, and the official results are issued several days later. With over four million ballots to be counted, the chances of errors and inaccuracies are manifold. The advantage of this system, on the other hand, is its simplicity, the ease of supervising it, and the ability to conduct recounts if required down to the level of the individual ballot box. Over the years, proposals were often made to switch to a computerized system – for maintaining voter rolls, the actual voting, and tallying the vote. The goal was to simplify the system, publish the results sooner, and prevent double voting, voter error, and vote rigging. Enthusiasm for a computerized system diminished, however, after serious problems turned up in Florida during the American presidential election in 2000. In Israel, technical problems in the Labor primaries in 2009 led to the cancelation of computerized voting, though the experiment went well in the Kadima primaries. There were also serious problems in Likud's computerized primaries in 2012. A bill prepared by the Ministry of the Interior proposed that elections be computerized, first as a pilot program in local authority elections and then for Knesset elections.[16] The bill states that the system will ensure secrecy, credibility, and advanced systems to secure the data. Opponents, including computer science experts, claim that there are problems in securing the data (Hirschauge 2009). The 2015 election was conducted using the old system.

[16] Ministry of the Interior, Memorandum on Local Authority (Computerized) Elections Bill (2008), September 23, 2008. See also MK Meir Sheetrit's private member's bill: Local Authorities (Elections) (Computerized Elections Amendment) Bill 2013, P/19/468 (March 13, 2013).

10.4 Election Campaigns

A voting public that understands the importance of democracy tries to cast a well-informed vote, to learn about the platforms, positions, and candidates of the parties, and to reflect upon previous action and future intentions. The voters have available to them the campaign propaganda of the parties and candidates, as well as media coverage of the election (news and analysis), which is perceived to be more objective and balanced. Election propaganda can shape the public agenda and stimulate involvement in the election process (Galnoor 1982, 344–46). It enables parties and candidates to raise subjects for discussion and gives voters an opportunity to study their positions and arguments. And yet voters tend to deny that election propaganda has any effect on them (as opposed to its effect on others), and this is particularly true of the know-it-all Israeli voter. In a survey conducted as early as 1949 by the Institute of Public Opinion Research, 94 percent of the respondents claimed that "had they voted prior to the election campaign, they would not have voted differently." And, incidentally, they noted that it was the past *actions* of the party that were the main factor in their decision to vote for it, followed by the party platform, with the candidates a distant third.[17]

The Election (Campaign Methods) Law (1959) lists what is allowed and disallowed, and defines the supervisory role of the Central Elections Committee. The nature and style of election campaigns have changed over the years because of changes in society. The following are examples of the style of campaign slogans for election of the first and second Knessets:

- *Mapai:* The historical compass of the workers' party of Eretz Israel is the Zionist-Socialist vision. Two choices: the golden calf or the coming of the Messiah! Kremel [Kremlin] or Jerusalem!
- *Mapam:* For peace, not war; for independence, not subjugation; for stability, not inflation; for pioneering, not profiteering.
- *General Zionists:* Government for the people. No to one class, no to one party, but all the government for all the people. Enough of Mapai rule.
- *Herut:* Jabotinsky followers – loyal service to the entire nation all their lives. [They will] liberate you from Mapai oppression and establish a government of the hoped for fulfillment.

The slogans in the 1990 and 2000 elections were, of course, shorter and simpler, such as: "Peres will divide Jerusalem" (Likud 1996); "I trust a peace made by Sharon" (Likud 2003); and "No citizenship without loyalty" (Yisrael Beitenu 2009). The slogans are personal, promoting party leaders. So, too, the slogans of the 2009 election, though parliamentary, conveyed personal messages such as: "Tzipi Livni – a new kind of leader" (Kadima); and "Barak – at the moment of truth" (Labor). And in the 2013 election: "A strong prime minister – a strong Israel" (Likud–Yisrael Beitenu); "Bibi's good for the rich, Shelly's good for you" (Labor); "Where's the money?" (Yesh Atid); and "Leftists, come home!" (Meretz). In 2015, slogans revolved around the competition between left and right. The Zionist Camp (the joint list of Labor and Hatnuah) issued the slogan "It's either us or him" – "him" referring to Prime Minister Netanyahu. The Likud party responded with: "It's either us or them."

[17] The Institute of Public Opinion Research (May–July 1949), "Attitudes to Elections and Parties among Israeli Residents," Archive of the Institute of Applied Social Research.

A. Changes in Election Campaigns

Over the years, ideology and platforms diminished in importance as the emphasis shifted to emotional and personal propaganda (Marmor and Weimann 2001). However, ideology still plays an important role in Israel compared to other countries, and the pendulum seems to swing between two sets of issues – the emphasis is often on security and foreign affairs and sometimes reverts to socioeconomic issues, as it did in the 2013 election in the wake of the social protest of 2011. The most significant change in the electioneering style is the reduced direct involvement of parties and citizens in the campaigns, and the increased role of the media, advertising, and PR professionals. Election campaigning has become marketing (Caspi and Leshem 2007).

The direction of change is clear: From face-to-face communication in party frameworks, public rallies, and group meetings to mass communication via television, radio, mail, telephone, the Internet, and online channels. In Israel's early years, parties primarily made use of organizational channels, with support from the party newspapers.[18] The ads placed by parties in the newspapers and on public notice boards focused on the party platform and cited the failures of other parties; they included slogans and highlighted the ballot letters of their parties. In the early 1960s, state radio was the main campaign channel. Following enactment of the Election (Campaign Methods) Law in 1959, each party was allocated a specific amount of radio time for its election campaign, and these ads became a hit in the 1961 and 1965 election campaigns. Gradually, with the fading of the mass party and party newspapers and with the introduction of television to Israel (in 1968), the center of gravity shifted to these mass channels.

Television campaign ads were broadcast for the first time in 1969, and at first they resembled speeches at election rallies. Only in 1977 did the parties begin to exploit the unique qualities of television, and non-party people became involved – media and advertising experts – in designing the messages (Caspi and Leshem 2007, 114–19). Election campaigns were no longer direct, but mediated: Public rallies in the town square were replaced by television, and the leader's speech to thousands now appeared in the living rooms of hundreds of thousands. The content also changed: The long-winded speeches (that still offered some sort of political view) now gave way to slogans, images, and stickers; ideological content was converted into messages that suited mass media technology (Galnoor 1982, 253–57). From the late 1970s, the politics of elections became television broadcasts, and until the 1990s, television became the principal medium through which parties and candidates presented themselves to the public. The prohibition at the time on screening candidates in regular television and radio programs as election day approached created absurdities that sometimes made it impossible to convey the news.[19]

[18] The voting public was relatively small and could be brought to public gatherings in city squares, movie theaters, and coffee houses, or they could be expected to study the notice boards on the streets that carried the party platforms, its planned activity, pictures of the leaders, the ballot letters of the lists, and caricatures of rival parties. This system gave an advantage to organized parties that had control over institutions and workplaces. Most newspapers were party-affiliated, and served both to ensure support and coordination for the campaign, and to reach out to those not yet committed to a party.

[19] In television coverage of a meeting between Anwar Sadat and Menachem Begin in 1981, only Sadat was shown on camera because of the prohibition on showing Begin, who was a candidate in the approaching election; half an hour later, the full picture of Sadat and Begin was broadcast in the Likud campaign ads (Caspi and Leshem 2007, 120).

Political campaign ads on television, particularly when only one television channel was broadcast in Israel, increased interest in the election campaign, placed issues on the public agenda, and even contributed to voter turnout. Debates between the main candidates were televised, enabling the public to scrutinize them and their positions, and weigh the differences between them (for a skeptical view of the contribution of television debates, see Galnoor 1980). Americanization of the election campaign in Israel called for heavy financial resources, reduced the chances of candidates without means, and fostered corrupt ties between big business and government (Caspi and Leshem 2007). As to the content of the campaign, we note only the move to negative messages (Weimann and Wolfsfeld 2002). Although in Israel's early years parties had published caricatures of their opponents, these had been intended to sting, not to besmirch.

Over the years, changes were introduced to the election campaign laws: In the late 1990s, the prohibition on the television appearance of candidates prior to election day was rescinded; less time was allocated for television campaign ads, and the period to show these ads was shortened from three weeks to two. Despite increased public funding for election campaigns, the audience for them has diminished, and few look to them for shaping their political choices (Wolfsfeld 1995). The audience for television campaign ads is fading: In the years of only one television channel, some 60–70 percent viewed the ads. In the 1990s, though campaign ads were also broadcast on commercial television channels, viewership steadily declined: For the elections held in the 1990s, just one out of every five Israelis said they never watch television campaign ads, while in 2006, some 60 percent said they never watch them.[20]

Are the television ads and the heavy spending on election campaigns really necessary? The high costs of advertising give an advantage to large parties and increase the problematic dependence on private donors. Nevertheless, the contrary consideration holds sway: This is an opportunity for small or new parties – and candidates with a small budget – to get public exposure. However, considering the declining viewership of the television campaign ads, a very small number of voters still watch them: On the first evening in which election ads were broadcast prior to the 2009 election, some 21 percent of all Jewish households in Israel viewed them on one channel or another (Gaoni 2009). This declined to 6 percent in 2013 and 5 percent in 2015 (Averbach 2015).

Table 10.3 summarizes the changes in the channels of election campaigns. It does not show the impact of these channels or the investment in them, but only the gradual transition from personal and group messaging to mass media channels, and more recently to online communication. Television and some other campaign channels continued to be used, such as parlor meetings organized on the basis of neighborhood, income level, or profession. In the 1980s and 1990s, "complementary" channels appeared such as billboards, leafleting, and bumper stickers. Some of these come and go, such as the car stickers, which have since been replaced by the Internet and social networking. Party-run websites first appeared in the 1996 election campaign. The advantage to using the Internet for campaigning is its relatively low cost and exposure to a large number of users (Caspi and Leshem 2007, 125). Nevertheless, research

[20] From election survey data, Gutmann Institute Archive, Israel Democracy Institute.

Table 10.3 *Use of media channels in Knesset election campaigns*

	1949, 1951	1970s	1980s	1990s and 2000s
Public channels				
Open-air rally	++	+	–	–
Rallies in public halls	++	++	+	+
Street notice boards	++	+	+	++
Street loudspeakers	++	–	–	–
Billboards on roads	–	–	–	++
Party and movement channels				
Ethnic group meetings	++	+	–	–
Workplace meetings	+	+	–	–
Parlor meetings	–	++	++	+
Mass media				
Daily newspapers	++	++	++	++
Local newspapers	–	+	++	++
Radio	+	++	++	++
Television	–	++	++	++
Other				
Direct mail	–	++	++	++
Stickers	–	–	+	++
Phone calls	–	+	++	++
Home visits by volunteers	–	–	+	++
Audio recordings	–	–	+	+
Online communication	–	–	–	++

++ Widespread use
+ Limited use
– Sparse or no use
Sources: Galnoor 1982, 254; Caspi and Leshem 2007, 126.

about the use of websites by Israeli parties in the election campaigns of the 2000s indicates that most were used conservatively – they did not create multi-directional or interactive channels – and if they did create forums, most participants were already party supporters and not the public at large (Lehman-Wilzig 2004). Signs of change appeared in 2009 when politicians and parties used the Internet for political discourse, and some parties claimed a central role for their online election campaign. Likud, for example, reported 12,000 "Internet volunteers" who disseminated messages, transmitted announcements, raised money, built social networks, etc. (Yuval Dror 2009a). In 2009, fifteen of thirty-three parties running for the Knesset made use of at least four Internet platforms: websites, YouTube, Facebook, and blogging sites (Caspi and Lev 2009). By the 2013 elections, most Internet-based campaigning focused on the use of Facebook, especially the pages of various party leaders, though most communication with the constituency remained one-sided, as a broadcasting mechanism of political messages (Haleva-Amir 2014). Although "cyber-politics" is in its infancy in Israel, the growing use of the media at election time increases the direct involvement of citizens in politics as they participate in discussion forums or respond to issues. And it is possible that the decline of previous human channels of communication explains the rise of the new social media.

B. Surveys

Surveys have become an integral part of the election campaign in Israel; they frequently appear at the initiative of the media, the parties, the candidates, or, lately, social justice organizations. Media coverage of the election campaign, public discourse, and the ad campaigns of candidates are based almost entirely on data from these surveys. The surveys impact both the election results as well as politics in general, in several ways: First, surveys not conducted professionally could bias the results. To that end, the Election (Campaign Methods) Law was amended and rules were set (size of the sample, sampling error, identifying the party that ordered the survey and who conducted the survey), though not all surveys abide by these rules. Second, survey findings and the timing of their publication could impact the willingness to vote and the decision for whom to vote, which may also bias the results. With respect to the timing, a 2007 amendment stipulates that surveys and forecasts must not be made public on the three days prior to election day – a shorter blackout period for surveys than that used in many European countries.

10.5 Election Results

A. Voter Turnout

The centralized structure of politics in Israel focuses most of the attention on the Knesset election, and less on the important elections to local authorities, the Histadrut, and other organizations. Knesset elections are very competitive, and until the 2000s, voter turnout was high compared to other western democracies, at about 80 percent (see Figure 10.1). The special election of the prime minister in 2001 saw an unprecedented drop with only 62 percent of eligible voters showing up to vote.

One may have expected that the low voter turnout in the 2001 election was an isolated incident due to the lack of a party ballot and the blatant absence of Arab voters. However, the voter turnout rate did not return to its previous level in the 2003 Knesset election and averaged only 67 percent thereafter. These low voter turnout rates for the Knesset election indicate a general decline in election participation (Figure 10.2). Until the election immediately following the Yom Kippur War in 1973, the average voter turnout for Knesset elections was 82 percent; until the end of the 1990s, it was 79 percent. This relatively high rate of voting declined to an average of 66 percent (for the elections in 2003, 2006, 2009, 2013, and 2015). Although the number of parties vying for election is high (some thirty in the 2000s), voting for party lists that did not pass the electoral threshold was low (on average some 4% of the valid votes since 1949 and 4.5% in 2015) – not a high price for a democracy to pay in terms of strengthening the sense of opportunity for representation in the Knesset (see Table 10.4).

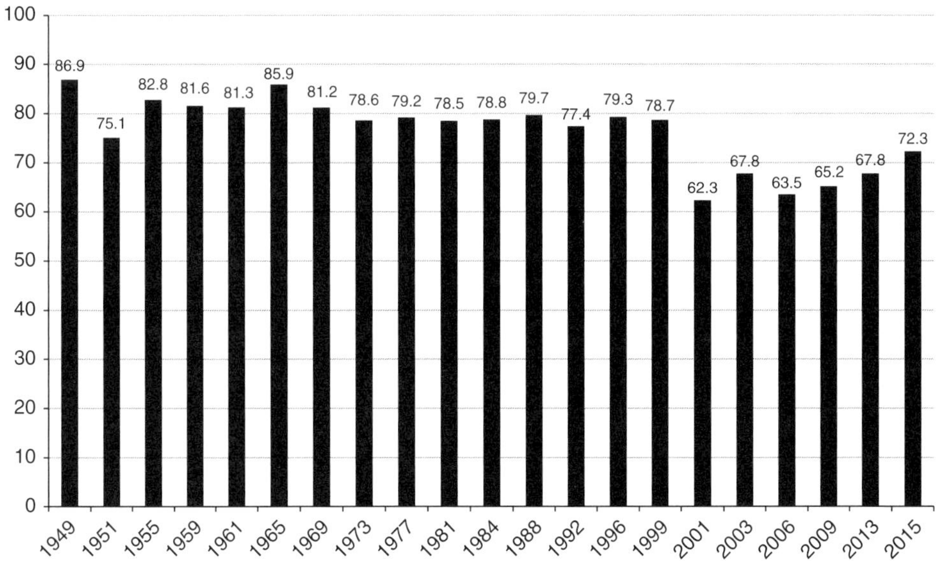

Figure 10.1 Voter turnout 1949–2015
Note: The data for 2001 include the special election for prime minister.

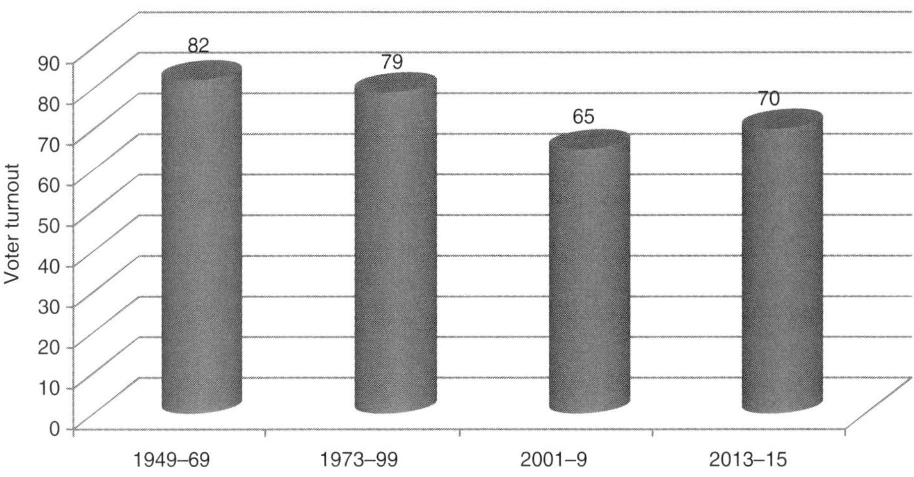

Figure 10.2 Average voter turnout for Knesset elections by period

B. Honest Election Procedures

In the above discussion about secrecy in the Israeli elections, we presented our view that the will of the voters was protected on election day, as in other properly run democracies. More generally, it can be said that elections in Israel are generally fair and not corrupt. Except for isolated incidents and the urban legends that evolved around them of widespread vote rigging, throughout the electoral history of Israel there were only two clear cases of election fraud. One was the conviction in 1981 of Flatto Sharon, a member of the ninth Knesset, for bribing voters, i.e., buying votes.

Table 10.4 *Knesset elections: Residents, eligible voters, parties contending, parties entering Knesset, voter turnout, and invalid ballots (1949–2015)*

Knesset	Residents (in 1,000s)	Eligible voters (in 1,000s)	Parties contending	Parties entering Knesset	Voter turnout (%)*	Invalid ballots (%)
1st (1949)	1,059	507	21	12	**87**	1.2
2nd (1951)	1,494	925	17	**15**	75	1.1
3rd (1955)	1,750	1,058	18	12	83	2.6
4th (1959)	2,062	1,218	24	12	82	2.7
5th (1961)	2,189	1,271	**14**	11	83	2.9
6th (1965)	2,562	1,500	17	13	86	3.1
7th (1969)	2,884	1,749	16	13	82	**4.2**
8th (1973)	3,278	2,037	21	**10**	77	2.1
9th (1977)	3,613	2,236	22	13	79	1.3
10th (1981)	3,948	2,490	31	**10**	79	0.9
11th (1984)	4,159	2,655	26	**15**	79	0.9
12th (1988)	4,441	2,894	27	**15**	80	1.0
13th (1992)	5,123	3,409	25	**10**	77	**0.8**
14th (1996)	5,685	3,933	20	11	79	2.2
15th (1999)	6,125	4,285	31	**15**	79	1.9
16th (2003)	6,690	4,720	27	13	68	1.6
17th (2006)	7,054	5,015	31	12	**64**	1.3
18th (2009)	7,181	5,279	**33**	12	65	1.3
19th (2013)	7,891	5,657	32	12	68	1.1
20th (2015)	8,297	5,882	26	**10**	72	1.0
Range			**14–33**	**10–15**	**64–87**	**0.8–4.2**

* There are differences of up to 2% in various publications concerning the voter turnout until the 1970s.

Note: Bold-faced numbers in columns 3–6 show the extremes in all elections since 1949.

Sources: CBS *Statistical Abstract*; and the Central Elections Committee reports in the State Records (Israel).

In the second, irregularities were found in two ballot boxes (in Bnei Brak and Ramat Gan) after election of the twelfth Knesset (1988). Petitioned to revoke the results, the District Court ruled that a re-vote should take place in these two polling stations.[21] The results of the re-vote did not lead to any change in the allocation of Knesset seats. Rumors exist about the integrity of polling stations where the ultra-Orthodox and Arab citizens of Israel vote, but this has never been brought to court. On the other hand, irregularities have frequently been found in election to the local authorities.[22]

21 The Supreme Court affirmed the decision of the District Court (*Ravitz et al. v. Dayan et al.* 1991) and therefore re-votes were held in these two polling stations in April 1991.

22 On December 27, 2013, for example, the High Court of Justice ordered a re-vote for the mayor of Beit Shemesh after evidence of vote rigging was found.

10.6 Direct Election of the Prime Minister

The system of direct election legislated in 1992 was used in three elections between 1996 and early 2003. In this system, voters would cast two ballots – one for the prime minister and the other for a party. Election of the Knesset and the prime minister would be conducted in parallel, except when a "special election" was held for the prime minister only – as in 2001. For a description of the reasons for the reform and its results, see Chapter 5. Here we look only at the electoral system and its repercussions.

Direct election was introduced to Israel in an effort to strengthen the steering capacity of the executive branch; it was a system borrowed from presidential regimes where the head of the executive branch has a separate political base that provides democratic legitimacy. In Israel, however, direct election did not transform the government into a presidential system, as the Knesset and the government remained interdependent. Table 10.5 shows the gap between support for a candidate and support for his party, which ultimately reduced the power of the two largest parties – the candidates' parties on whose size the stability of the coalition rests.

The election results of 1996 and 1999 reveal that Israeli voters took full advantage of their freedom to split the vote for several reasons. First, the option of choosing a prime minister separately eliminated the previous "strategic vote," meaning the desire to influence the composition of the government. Second, voting separately for a prime minister, even one from a different party, fostered an "honest" vote – a reflection of one's world view or true preference – in the vote for the Knesset. Third, having two ballots allowed voters to distinguish between supporting a "personality" for the prime minister and one's world view or self-interest for the Knesset, thereby encouraging the split vote. Fourth, the focus of the large parties on promoting their candidates for prime minister led them to neglect the party slate and assume vague positions in order to attract more voters. The parties thereby lost some voters who preferred parties with clear stands on issues (see Kenig et al. 2004 on why the vote was split). A split ballot, incidentally, was already familiar to voters from local elections. In short, splitting the vote led to a political split, which weakened coalitions and destabilized the political system. Moreover, the inclination to vote for sectoral parties continued in the 2000s, even after the direct election system was rescinded.

Low voter turnout (62%) in the special election for prime minister in 2001 revealed that groups of voters ascribed greater importance to the Knesset election. What's more, having two ballots enabled some to vote just for the Knesset or just for the prime minister, paving the way for voters to cast a protest vote – a blank ballot – without affecting their ability to influence the outcome.

In these three direct elections, the percentage of invalid votes for prime minister (4.4% on average) was higher by 3 percent than the invalid votes for parties (1.6% on average). Some attributed this to the confusion of voters moving to a two-ballot and two-envelope system. If this were the case, the confusion should have also yielded a high number of invalid votes for the Knesset, but this did not happen; in addition, the "confusion" grew the next time around in 1999. Furthermore, the 2001 election in which there was only one ballot also saw a relatively high proportion of invalid votes (3%). It is more reasonable to assume that the high number of invalid votes for prime minister reflects a protest vote, primarily of Arab citizens, who

Table 10.5 *Results of direct election of the prime minister – votes for the candidate versus votes for the party (%)*

	1996		1999		2001	
Votes for candidate for prime minister	Shimon Peres 49.5	Benjamin Netanyahu 50.5	Ehud Barak 56.1	Benjamin Netanyahu 43.9	Ehud Barak 37.6	Ariel Sharon 62.4
Votes for the candidate's party	Labor 27.5	Likud–Gesher–Tzomet 25.1	One Israel 20.2	Likud 14.1	no election to the Knesset	–
Gap between candidate and his party	22.0	25.4	35.9	29.8	no election to the Knesset	–

Source: Knesset 2015.

cast blank ballots to show a lack of support for both candidates. The rate of invalid votes among Arab voters in the special election of 2001 was particularly high (15%), clearly suggesting a protest vote (Jamal 2002, 89).

In an effort to strengthen the executive branch, this system created two sources of democratic legitimacy. The behavior of the voters, however, produced the opposite effect, because splitting the vote undermined the coalition-governing ability of the two largest parties (see Chapter 11).

10.7 Main Considerations of the Voters

Although voter considerations are varied and complex, voting in Israel ever since its founding has generally been influenced by three main groups of variables: a world view interwoven with party loyalty; the social cleavage between religious and non-religious Jews; and the national cleavage between Jewish and Arab citizens of Israel. In the discussion below, we present the first two groups of factors followed by the effect of demographic variables – ethnicity, age, socioeconomic status, gender, and area of residence.

A. World View and Party Loyalty

According to theories about the acquisition of cognitive and behavioral patterns from the social environment, the primary agent of socialization that influences world views and political values is the immediate family. In Israel, political socialization in the family is composed of parents "bequeathing" to their offspring identification with an ideological approach in terms of "left" and "right" on geopolitical issues, and parties that represent that approach. A study of voting similarity between parents and their offspring indicates that two-thirds of the offspring vote for a party for which the parents had voted at least once, and that almost 75 percent of voters vote for the same political bloc as their fathers or mothers (Ventura 1997). Thus, to a large extent, voting patterns are already acquired in the family, and they foster party loyalty. In the early years of the state, identification was based primarily on belonging to political camps – workers, religious groups, civic groups. Since 1967, however, identification has been related mainly to views on security and foreign affairs, which do not overlap with views on socioeconomic issues. The distribution of views on security and foreign affairs cuts across variables such as income, education, or housing density. Until 1977, election results largely reflected loyalty to a party, and there were no major changes in the size of the camps. A significant change in party loyalty took place in 1977 with the appearance of Dash as a centrist party.

Party loyalty can be measured by the volatility of voting from one election to another – the extent to which voters "switch parties." This indicator has obvious shortcomings, particularly in a political system like Israel's in which parties split and re-form so frequently, but it allows for identifying general trends in party loyalty.[23] Until 1977, for example, volatility did not exceed 16 percent. In 1977, volatility climbed to 23 percent when traditional Mapai voters shifted loyalties and cast votes for Dash. High volatility was again evident in the 1981 election (21%), when Dash disappeared and many voters returned to the Alignment. The virtual tie between political blocs in the 1980s strengthened party loyalty, and there was little shifting of votes in the three elections (1984, 1988, 1992). Since 1996, volatility is on the rise again, reflecting the waning of party loyalty, a process enhanced by direct election, which invited voters to shift their support from the two largest parties to sectoral parties (Kenig et al. 2004). This trend continued and even intensified in the 2000s.

B. Religiosity (Level of Religious Observance)

Until the "upheaval" of the 1977 election, there was no strong correlation between religiosity and voting intention. Although the observant population voted consistently for religious parties, supporters of Mapai/Alignment were hardly distinguishable from supporters of Herut/Gahal/Likud on the variable of religious observance. And being more traditional did not significantly increase the probability that someone would vote for a party on the right or left. As of 1977, however, religious observance (together with ethnicity) became the strongest predictor of the non-Arab Israeli vote (A. Arian 1997, 200). The convergence of the two variables – religious observance and geopolitical views – which has continued ever since, means that the more a Jewish Israeli voter feels an affinity to religion, the more likely that individual will vote for a right-wing party. This generalization encompassed even ultra-Orthodox voters in the 2000s, who had in the past voted for ultra-Orthodox parties that had been more moderate on foreign and security issues.

[23] The Pedersen Index (1979) measures the movement of votes between parties from one election to another. Its advantage is that it is based on real election results, consistently and long term. The index ignores changes in the voting of individual voters, as they cancel each other out. It is calculated as follows: The percentage of votes each party received in the previous election is subtracted from the percentage of votes it received in the current election; the absolute change (whether positive or negative) is totaled, and the sum is divided in two, as every increase in power of one party means a decrease in power of another party.

C. Ethnicity

The link between ethnicity and voting decisions also strengthened in the mid-1970s and is the main factor, though not the only one, in the 1977 upheaval. Until then, Mapai/Labor had won the support of all population groups, including Mizrahi immigrants, because of their dependence on the state bureaucracies, the Jewish Agency, and the Histadrut, and also because of their deference to those who had brought them to Israel from their home countries. The movement of Mizrahi voters away from Mapai/Labor was gradual, and is related to the improved socioeconomic status of many of them, particularly the second and third generation. Their alienation from the former establishment intensified in the mid-1970s and peaked in the early 1980s. The election campaign of 1981 took place in the shadow of ethnic tension, and by the 1984 election, ethnicity was an accurate predictor of the average voter's preferences: Ashkenazim were more likely to vote for the Alignment while Mizrahim for the Likud in the proportion of 1:3, respectively.

This link weakened in the 1990s for several reasons: ethnic tensions eased, Shas came on the scene and merged Mizrahi ethnicity with tradition and ultra-Orthodoxy, and the patterns of the growing "Russian vote" did not easily conform to the traditional ethnic divisions of Israel. In 2003, the voters of Labor and Meretz were largely Ashkenazi, while Shas was predominantly Mizrahi. Shinui attracted very few Mizrahim, but a quarter of its voters were "Russians" (another quarter voted Likud and another quarter voted the National Union). Likud as the catch-all party was the most balanced ethnically, but in any case, it attracted two Mizrahi voters for every one Ashkenazi voter (Shalev and Levy 2004, 253). The change in the party map of 2006 – the appearance of Kadima headed by Ariel Sharon and an independent Yisrael Beitenu led by Avigdor Lieberman – transformed the "Russian" vote, as will be seen below.

D. Age

Age is an elusive variable, and the effect of age on voting choices can usually be discerned only through surveys. The election process in Israel, however, allows for an examination of the actual voting of young people by analysis of the "soldiers' votes" in double envelopes.[24] Two qualifications should be noted about this analysis: First, most but not all of those voting in double envelopes are young people – more than 70 percent until the 2000s; and, second, "soldiers' votes" are not representative of the entire younger population because the ultra-Orthodox, Arabs, and a significant

[24] The double-envelope procedure enables some groups of citizens, including polling station workers, to vote in special ballot boxes wherever they find themselves – IDF bases, hospitals, prisons, the merchant marine, or Israeli representations abroad. In the 2003 election, more than 160,000 double envelopes were cast, most from soldiers in the standing army. One envelope contains the ballot placed by the voter (inserted behind a curtain in full privacy). The polling station committee then places this envelope into a second envelope and the details of the voter are recorded on it. The system is intended to prevent vote rigging and double voting – casting a ballot once in the polling station of one's residence and once in the special polling station. The double envelopes are conveyed to the Central Election Committee, which determines whether the voter voted twice, while ensuring the confidentiality of the vote. If the voter did cast two ballots, the double-envelope ballot will be disqualified. The number of double-envelope votes disqualified has been minuscule: Only 450 such ballots were discarded in the 2003 election.

Table 10.6 *The 1984 election: Distribution of votes in the general population compared with votes in the "double envelopes"*

Party	In the general population (%)	In the double envelopes (%)	Difference (%)
Likud	31.9	32.0	+0.1
Alignment	34.9	26.4	–8.5
National Religious Party (NRP)	3.5	1.8	–1.7
Tehiya	4.0	9.7	+5.7
Shinui	2.6	4.2	+1.6
Ratz	2.4	3.3	+0.9
Kach	1.3	3.0	+1.7
Ometz/Telem	1.2	3.4	+2.2

Sources: Galnoor 1984, Galnoor 1984a.

proportion of religious girls do not serve in the army. Nevertheless, the "double-envelope" votes are a good indicator, and the only one available, of the actual votes cast by 18- to 21-year-old voters.

Is the claim correct that young people are consistently more right-wing? An analysis of the "soldiers' votes" in 1981 and 1984, compared with the general vote, proves that this is not necessarily true. In 1984 (Table 10.6), the proportion of Likud support from soldiers was identical to the support for Likud in the general population; the National Religious Party received less support from soldiers (because fewer women serve in the army), while the more extreme parties – Tehiya and Kach – garnered double or more the support from soldiers than they won in the general public. The Alignment received 8.5 percent fewer votes from soldiers, but the decline was offset by half because of greater support for left-wing and centrist parties (Ratz, Shinui, and Ometz/Telem). The numbers are small; rather than indicating a right- or left-wing voting bias of soldiers, they demonstrate that the veteran parties scored less well or held steady among young people, while new or "lone wolf" parties were more enticing to the young.

Direct election of the prime minister did not alter the general picture, and there is no conclusive evidence that young people tend to be more right-wing. In 1996, Netanyahu received 53 percent of the double-envelope votes, compared with 51 percent of the general public votes; and in 1999, Barak received 55 percent compared with 56 percent of the general public; however, in the special election of 2001, the opposite occurred: Support for Sharon was only 59 percent compared with 62 percent among the general public. Thus the winners did not necessarily earn more support from the young. On the other hand, more young people tended to vote for "trendy" parties. Table 10.7 indicates that, in 2003, the double envelopes held more support for the Likud led by Ariel Sharon, for Shinui (5% more than among the general public), and for the Green Leaf party (3% more than the general public). Green Leaf, which did not pass the electoral threshold, would have earned some five seats in the Knesset if only double-envelope ballots were counted. On the other hand, the proportion between the right + religious versus the center + left, as indicated in

Table 10.7 *The 2003 election: Distribution of votes in the general population compared with votes in the "double envelopes"*

Party	In the general population (%)	In the double envelopes (%)	Difference (%)
Shinui	12.3	17.3	+5.0
Likud	29.4	33.9	+4.5
Green Leaf	1.2	4.0	+2.8
Meretz	5.2	6.4	+1.2
Herut	1.1	1.3	+0.2
National Union	5.5	5.4	–0.1
Labor	14.5	13.5	–1.0
One Nation	2.8	1.7	–1.1
Yisrael B'Aliyah	2.2	0.9	–1.3
United Arab List (Ra'am)	2.1	0.5	–1.6
Balad	2.3	0.5	–1.8
Hadash–Ta'al	3.0	0.8	–2.2
Torah Judaism	4.3	1.8	–2.5
Shas	8.2	5.4	–2.8

Source: Alon 2003a.

Table 10.7 (without Torah Judaism and the Arab parties, which are not represented in the army), reflects a balance between the blocs.

In the past, the delayed tally of the double-envelope votes was fraught with tension because these results could add or subtract a mandate to some parties, even though the results of the general vote had already been made public. In the 1999 election, for example, the double envelopes generated an additional mandate for Meretz and one for the National Union; in 2003, Likud and the National Religious Party (NRP) won additional mandates (*Haaretz*, May 20, 1999 and January 31, 2003). Since the 2006 election, the discrepancies between the double-envelope voters and the general public vote have been negligible, particularly for technical reasons.[25] Of note in Table 10.7, the Green Leaf party received three or more times the vote of the general public; Shinui, Meretz, and One Nation were strengthened; and the ultra-Orthodox, ethnic, and Arab parties were weakened, for understandable reasons. But the figures are small, and therefore the general conclusion is that, despite the prevailing Israeli view that age is a reliable predictor of voting or that young people tend to vote for right-wing parties, the election results reveal no evidence of this. The vote of young people resembles that of older adults, except for the tendency of younger voters to support trendy parties.

[25] The relative proportion of soldiers voting in double envelopes decreased to 68 percent on average in these years, and thus the dominance of young voters using this procedure diminished. Data for 2006 and 2009 were provided courtesy of the Secretariat of the Central Elections Committee.

E. Socioeconomic Status (Income, Education, and Household Density)

Socioeconomic status as a predictor of the voting behavior of Israeli Jews is also elusive (Arab voting behavior will be examined separately). Average income, the natural variable to use for measuring socioeconomic status, does not directly correlate with voting patterns in Israel. Although socioeconomic status (based on average income) is significantly correlated with party preference in western Europe, socioeconomic status in Israel plays a role, but the correlation is neither consistent nor strong. Although it can be said that economically advantaged Jewish voters (the middle and upper classes) have a tendency to vote "left" while lower-income voters tend to vote "right," research consistently indicates that when other factors that correlate with socioeconomic status (ethnicity and religiosity) are held constant, income alone has no significant bearing on voting behavior (Shalev and Levy 2004, 248).

Two other components of socioeconomic status – education and housing density – are more effective predictors of voting. The number of years of schooling, for example, correlates highly with voting: In direct election of the prime minister in 1996, voters with more than twelve years of schooling voted 2:1 for Shimon Peres, while those with little schooling were more likely to vote for Benjamin Netanyahu. Similarly, Labor was more successful among the better educated, while Likud won more votes among those with twelve or fewer years of schooling (A. Arian 1997, 200–1). The education variable is a good indicator of the party for which one votes: In the 2003 election, for example, 55 percent of Meretz voters had an academic education, as did 37 percent of Labor voters, but only 26 percent of Likud voters (Shalev and Levy 2004, 252). At the time a gap prevailed between parties advocating free market capitalism (Likud, Kadima, and Yisrael Beitenu), which together had seventy MKs, though only about a third of the public advocated a capitalist approach (Arian and Shamir 2011, 31). In 2013, as a result of the social protest of 2011, many parties advocated free market capitalism with social sensitivity (Likud–Yisrael Beitenu, Jewish Home, Yesh Atid) (Shamir 2015), and these together won sixty-two MKs, though, again, only about a third of the public advocated a capitalist approach (Israel National Election Studies 2013).

F. Gender, Area of Residence

Western democracies show gender differences in voting patterns, with women more likely to vote for parties that take left-wing positions on social issues. Gender, however, has not been a reliable predictor of voting patterns in Israel, where men had been slightly more likely to favor right-wing parties than women, but the differences were negligible (Arian and Shamir 2004; Shamir 2015). Since the 2009 election, however, some changes have become apparent, with women voters showing greater support for social welfare policies, but preferring more hawkish stands on security issues (Gedalya, Herzog, and Shamir 2009, 165–93). In 2009, significantly more Jewish women voted for Tzipi Livni and Kadima; and in 2013 there was a significant gender gap of 9 percent between men and women in voting for parties headed by women: Labor, headed by Shelly Yachimovich, Hatnuah headed by Tzipi Livni, and Meretz headed by Zehava Galon. As in other western democracies, women in Israel in recent years have voted more than men for center-left parties and parties in which women are visible. The main reasons for this are economic and social changes such as the entry of women into the labor market, increased education, and more feminist consciousness. Area of residence is not correlated with voter preference in Israel.

10.8 Voting Patterns of Certain Groups

A. Arab Citizens of Israel (see Chapter 15 for a more extensive discussion)

Since the founding of Israel, Arab citizens have continuously participated in the Knesset elections; from the 1980s, most voted for Jewish parties – Mapai above all, and the Arab parties affiliated with them.[26] Representation in the Knesset was attractive to the various elites in the Arab population because it brought them closer to the center of resource distribution, and therefore also became a focus of internal rivalries as well as control by the authorities. Matters escalated to the point of political assassination when MK Hamad abu Rabia was murdered in 1981 for not carrying out the rotation agreement with the Druze candidate in his party, Jabr Muadi, i.e., refusing to resign from the Knesset.

The 1977 election was a turning point when Hadash received about half the Arab vote; ever since, the voting patterns of Arab citizens of Israel have been distinct from those of Israeli Jews, and unrelated to the variables surveyed above – age, income, gender, etc. New and independent Arab parties entered the Knesset, such as the Progressive List for Peace (two seats in 1984) and the Arab Democratic Party, (one seat in 1988), and gradually political representation grew (to eight to ten seats), as did competition (three to four main parties). The competition, based on internal divisions among the Arab population (religion, clans, political views, region, etc.), fragmented the Arab parties and undermined their relative strength in the Knesset. Arab MKs (including those elected in Jewish parties) are still under-represented in the Knesset proportionate to the Arab population, also because some Arab citizens choose to vote for Jewish parties. The special election of the prime minister in 2001 was particularly contentious along nationalist lines. The two candidates (Ariel Sharon and Ehud Barak) failed to recruit support among Arab citizens, and only some 20 percent turned out to vote. In parallel the number of blank ballots increased as an expression of protest. The immediate triggers for this were the events of October 2000 and the deep disappointment with the policies of the Barak government, for whom most Arab citizens had voted in 1999 (Jamal 2002, 58). The fragile web of relations did not recover after the special election in 2001, and another decline in Arab voter turnout was evident in the 2003 election. The 2006 election saw not just failure to vote, but an open boycott, with the northern wing of the Islamic Movement calling upon Arabs not to participate in the election. In February, a manifesto put out by the Popular Committee for Election Boycott called for creation of a separate parliament for Arabs in Israel. Despite attempts in the Arab media to convince Arab voters to go to the polls, such as the Manifesto against Election Boycott and for Supporting Arab Parties, voter turnout for the Knesset election in 2006 was 56 percent in Arab towns,

[26] In the first fifty years, the voter turnout of Arabs resembled that of the public at large. In the first Knesset elections, it was slightly higher; as of the sixth Knesset, voter turnout dropped somewhat; in the 1980s, with the entry of independent Arab parties, voter turnout again resembled that of the general population (Jamal 2002). Change began with the special election of the prime minister in 2001.

which was 8 percent lower than the general population; in 2009, 53 percent voted, compared with 65 percent in the general population; in 2015, voter turnout rose to 64 percent (Raday and Rudnitzky 2015), compared with 72.5 percent in the general population. These figures do not include Arab voting in the mixed cities, where turnout is usually even lower (Rudnitzky 2013, 3).

In the elections held between 2009 and 2015, a number of issues affected the Arab vote: Israel's military operations in the Gaza Strip; attempts to disqualify the Arab parties Balad and Ra'am-Ta'al; the law prohibiting citizenship to Arab residents of the territories who are married to Arab Israeli citizens; and the extremist election campaign conducted by Yisrael Beitenu, which cast aspersions on the loyalty of Israel's Arab citizens. A number of contentious issues could be added to this list: the IDF assault on activists sailing on the MV *Mavi Marmara* seeking to break the siege of Gaza, anti-democratic initiatives in the Knesset, the proposed law "Israel is the nation-state of the Jewish people," the Protective Edge military operation in Gaza in 2014, and in 2015 a six-month suspension from the Knesset of Haneen Zoabi, an MK from the Joint Arab List.

The fear was that Arab voters would now entirely boycott the elections; in actuality, voter turnout was lower and more worrisome compared to previous elections: About half the Arabs in Israel did not vote, thereby choosing not to exercise their right to participate in Israeli democracy. This stemmed from their pervasive feeling that they were unable to participate equally in shaping the political agenda because it was being dictated by a Jewish majority that did not take them into account. The growing boycott is a warning that a democratic society cannot afford to ignore (Schafferman 2009; Rouhana et al. 2010). In Chapter 15, we will examine the deeper reasons – normative, cumulative, and instrumental – for changes in the political behavior of Arabs in Israel.

B. The Nationalist-Religious Camp

The voting patterns of the nationalist-religious public are no secret. Since the merger of Mizrahi and Ha-Mizrahi in 1955, the National Religious Party (NRP) has been the exclusive representative of the nationalist-religious camp in Israel. Until 1977, the NRP regularly won eleven to twelve seats in the Knesset (Asher Cohen 2004). This began to change in the late 1970s, and two related explanations have been offered for this. First, the young guard of the NRP sought to free itself from the veteran leadership with its historical and, in their view, confining covenant with Mapai/Labor. They considered Herut, which had begun to gain ground prior to 1977, to be a worthier ally, both because of its affinity to religious tradition and because of its nationalist views. In retrospect, this seems to have severed the bond between NRP voters and their party. Some moved to the Likud, which was not perceived as threatening to observant Jews, and later even to ultra-Orthodox parties because of their staunch religious positions. Second, when the future of the occupied territories and settlements became the defining quality of the NRP, some of its voters found more attractive alternatives – some turned to more hawkish parties such as Tehiya and later the National Union; some went to ethnic parties (Tami, Shas); and others sought religious Zionism with a peace orientation in a party like Meimad.

The NRP's messianic agenda did not recruit new voters, and its power in the Knesset dwindled to four to six seats during the 1980s and early 1990s. In 1996, the NRP advanced to nine seats due to the disappearance of Tehiya (in 1992) and direct election of the prime minister, which allowed many voters to support Netanyahu for prime minister and the NRP for the Knesset. Recovery, however, was a one-time affair. In subsequent elections, the NRP again fell back to six seats, and in 2006 the letter "B," which had been the party's trademark letter since the 1950s, did not appear on a ballot because the NRP had joined the National Union, which won nine seats. The New NRP was a short-lived product of the 2008 merger of the (old) National Religious Party and the National Union. In 2009, the party was renamed the National Home-New NRP, and won only three seats (fewer than 100,000 votes). This was an indication that a significant portion of the nationalist-religious public, as it had been known, no longer felt that the NRP represented it.[27] Indeed in the 2013 election, the name was again changed, this time to the unwieldy and extended moniker "Jewish Home headed by Naftali Bennet – founded by the New NRP and the National Union," but it worked.The combination of hawkish views and appeal to seculars brought many Likud voters to migrate to the National Home + the National Union, which won twelve seats in 2013, though it lost them back to the Likud and dropped to eight in 2015.

C. Ultra-Orthodox Communities

Even during the pre-state period, the ultra-Orthodox were distinct from the nationalist-religious in their way of life, attitude toward Zionism, and political organization. It should be emphasized that the common denominator of ultra-Orthodoxy is absolute rejection of secular culture and the modern Jewish (Zionist) nationalism that is part of it; but besides these key issues, the ultra-Orthodox are divided among themselves into many dynastic communities. For example, only small extremist sects like Neturei Karta completely repudiate the existence of the state of Israel. Other ultra-Orthodox groups changed their extremist views toward the founding of Israel after the Holocaust.

The ultra-Orthodox are distinct from the rest of Israeli society religiously, socially, culturally, geographically, and politically. In the first Knesset election, the religious and ultra-Orthodox parties merged into one list for the first and last time – the Religious Front. By the 1951 election, this had split into two ultra-Orthodox lists – Agudat Yisrael (three seats) and Poalei Agudat Yisrael (two seats). These parties sometimes ran separately (1961, 1965, 1969), sometimes as part of a joint list called Torah Front (1955, 1959, 1973), and since 1992 as Torah Judaism (Agudat Yisrael and Degel Hatorah), which together usually win six seats. Since 1984, there have been separate ultra-Orthodox parties for Ashkenazim (Agudat Yisrael, Degel Hatorah) and for Mizrahim (Shas), the latter also winning voters who are not ultra-Orthodox. Shas reached a high point of seventeen seats in 1999 and fell to eleven to twelve seats in the elections of the 2000s, which lasted until 2013. In 2015, after an additional split, which broke Shas into two

[27] The drop in support for the National Union-New NRP in 2009 happened throughout locales with high concentrations of nationalist-religious voters – cities, kibbutzim, moshavim, and settlements (Asher Cohen 2011).

separate parties – Shas headed by Aryeh Deri and Yahad headed by Eli Yishai – Shas fell back to seven seats and Yahad did not pass the election threshold.

The most salient aspect of ultra-Orthodox voting patterns, particularly among Ashkenazim, is their electoral discipline – intense party loyalty and high voter turnout due to full recruitment on election day. Thus, it can be said that the ultra-Orthodox are fully represented in the Knesset.

D. New Immigrants

Most democracies bestow citizenship upon new immigrants only after they have resided in the country for a certain period of time; Israel, however, confers citizenship and the right to vote to new (Jewish) immigrants immediately upon their arrival. Until the 1990s, the waves of immigrants from the former Soviet Union left their mark on the political system, but not by having separate parties. During the Yishuv period and soon after the founding of Israel, many new immigrant parties were formed, but they did not attract much support or pass the electoral threshold, with the exception initially of the Progressive Party. "Separatism" by new immigrants was not regarded favorably by Israelis, particularly when practiced by Mizrahi Jews, and most immigrants lent their support to existing parties. Two ethnic Mizrahi parties almost won Knesset seats – the Union of North African Immigrants in 1959 and the Black Panthers in 1973.

The mass wave of immigrants from the former Soviet Union that began in the late 1980s changed these patterns. The political system had become more open, and the Russian speakers, many university-educated and white-collar professionals, quickly grasped how the system worked and began to organize to win seats and become an independent political player. First came the Soviet Jewry Zionist Forum headed by Natan Sharansky, founded in 1987 as an umbrella group for immigrant organizations, and this turned into the Yisrael B'Aliyah party in 1996. Even before that, large numbers of Russian-speaking immigrants tended to vote in blocs. In the 1992 election, their vote helped propel Labor back into power on the heels of their dissatisfaction with the absorption process under the Shamir-led Likud government.[28] In 1996, Yisrael B'Aliyah ran for election and won 5.7 percent of the votes, which gave it seven seats in the Knesset.[29] An analysis of voting in areas with high concentrations of Russian-speaking immigrants revealed that more than 40 percent of these votes went to Yisrael B'Aliyah. Right-wing parties – Likud and Moledet – received about a quarter of their votes; religious parties won 13 percent; and Labor with Meretz together, less than 12 percent. In the election of the prime minister, the immigrants gave decisive support (approximately 70%) to Benjamin Netanyahu (T. Horowitz 1999). Since then, two clear patterns have become evident about the voting of these immigrants to Israel: They extensively support a sectoral party, reflecting their desire for political representation; and they are more likely to support the hawkish ideology of right-wing parties, as left-wing parties represent foreign and military weakness to many of them.

[28] According to Epstein (2006, 8–10), "Paradoxically, the mass support of Russian-speaking Israelis for left-wing parties in 1992 and 1999 did not indicate their identification with these parties' positions on the conflict, but rather reflected their rejection of the Likud more than their attraction to Labor."

[29] A second party, Unity for the Defense of New Immigrants, which ran in 1996, received 0.8 percent of the votes and therefore did not pass the electoral threshold.

In the 1999 election, the power of "the Russian vote" became crystal clear: One out of every six eligible voters had immigrated to Israel from the former Soviet Union during the decade prior to the election. Avigdor Lieberman established the Yisrael Beitenu party as a political framework that was not overtly "Russian," bringing general issues to the platform and veteran Israelis into the list of candidates. Nevertheless, the extremist views of this party placed it at the right endpoint of the party continuum, with most of its voters and candidates from the former Soviet Union. In direct election of the prime minister in 1999, the Russian-speaking voters again reversed direction and supported Ehud Barak, the left-wing candidate, in the same proportion as had the general population, while for the Knesset they continued to give definitive support to the sectoral parties and avoided the left. Yisrael B'Aliyah won six seats and Yisrael Beitenu took four (one of its MKs was not a new immigrant). In the 2003 election, the Russian-speaking immigrants seemed to step back somewhat from their separatism. Yisrael Beitenu joined other right-wing parties in establishing the National Union headed by Lieberman, which won seven seats, three of these to Russian-speaking immigrants; the other Russian party, Yisrael B'Aliyah, headed by Sharansky, won two seats and merged with the Likud soon after the election. Some saw these developments as a harbinger of the assimilation of the immigrants and their transformation "from Russians to Israelis" (Goldstein and Gitelman 2004). In the 2006 election, however, Yisrael Beitenu again struck out on its own and increased its power to eleven seats as most Russian-speaking Israelis voted for it (Epstein 2006). In the 2009 election, it soared to fifteen seats and became the third-largest party in the Knesset; in 2013, it joined the Likud (and won only eleven seats), parting from the Likud in 2015 to run on its own, and then winning only six seats – it did not join the Likud-led coalition. Yisrael Beitenu is a catch-all ethnic party (Bagno 2011): It presents itself not as a party of immigrants (though most of its voters are Russian speakers and some of its platform is sectoral), but primarily as a hawkish party that combines secular nationalism with a militaristic approach; indeed, about half its MKs elected in 2013 did not immigrate from the former Soviet Union.

E. Mizrahim (the Ethnic Vote)

In the above discussion about ethnic voting, we also looked at the voting of Mizrahim as a group. Party lists with an ethnic platform that were formed by the veteran Sephardic and Yemenite communities won seats in the first and second Knessets, but then disappeared. The ethnic Mizrahi identity of voters strengthened during the 1980s and 1990s – Tami in the 1981 election and the transformation wrought by Shas since 1984. On the other hand, the ethnic identity of other parties, including Likud and Labor, have in parallel diminished.

10.9 Upheavals and Trends

A. Competition and Fragmentation

The elections held between 1949 and 2015 testify to stability, continuity, and general adherence to the rules of the democratic game. The index of competition, based on the ratio of the largest to the second-largest parties with respect to their seats in the Knesset, indicates that competition has only increased since the 1960s.

Table 10.8 *The share of the two largest parties in the election*

Election year	Largest party (seats)	Second-largest party (seats)	Factions with five or more seats	Two largest parties (%)	Ratio between two largest parties	Index of competition
1949	46*	19 (Mapam)	6	54	2.4	0.4
1951	45*	20 (G. Zionists)	7	54	2.3	0.4
1955	40*	15**	10	46	2.7	0.4
1959	47*	17**	9	53	2.8	0.4
1961	42*	17**	7	49	2.5	0.4
1965	45*	26**	6	59	1.7	0.6
1969	56*	26**	3	68	2.2	0.5
1973	51*	39**	4	75	1.3	0.8
1977	43**	32*	5	63	1.3	0.8
1981	48**	47*	3	79	1.0	1.0
1984	44*	41**	3	71	1.1	0.9
1988	40**	39*	6	66	1.0	1.0
1992	44*	32**	6	63	1.4	0.7
1996	34*	32**	7	55	1.1	0.9
1999	26*	19**	10	38	1.4	0.7
2003	38**	19*	8	48	2.0	0.5
2006	29***	19*	9	40	1.5	0.7
2009	28***	27**	6	46	1.0	1.0
2013	31**	19****	8	50	1.6	0.6
2015	30**	24*	10	54	1.3	0.8

Key:
Dominant party – Period 1 (1949–61)
Organized blocs – Period 1A (1965–69)
Two-bloc system – Period 2 (1973–92)
Political fragmentation – Period 3 (1996–)
Index of competition between the largest and second-largest parties: 1 = high competition; 0 = low competition

Notes: In 2006, the two largest parties were not Labor and Likud, for the very first time, but Kadima and Labor; in 2009, Kadima and Likud; in 2013, Likud and Yesh Atid; and in 2015, Likud and Zionist Camp/Labor again.

* Mapai/Alignment/Labor.
** Herut/Gahal/Likud.
*** Kadima.
**** Yesh Atid.

Source: Knesset 2015.

The years 1949–2015 can be divided into several periods with respect to changes in the voting patterns for parties (Table 10.8):

- In the first period, 1949–69, Mapai was the dominant party; other parties were mid-sized and did not challenge its hegemony. Until 1961, Mapai held two or more times the number of seats won by the second-largest party. In 1965 and

1969 – largely in the wake of the Lavon affair – Mapai's dominance ebbed, reflected in the organizing of a right-wing bloc and Mapai's formation of the Alignment together with Ahdut Ha'avoda and Mapam.

- In the second period, 1973–92, a two-bloc system emerged, right and left, culminating in the political stalemate of the 1980s and "unity governments" – a coalition of the two largest parties. The gap between the two largest parties shrank or completely disappeared, and a significant proportion of the Knesset seats (seventy-six to ninety-five) were divided between them. The number of mid-sized parties significantly dropped, which fueled the rivalry between the two largest parties.
- The third period, which has continued since 1996, is one of party fragmentation, with the two largest parties initially holding 55 percent of the Knesset seats and later fewer than half the seats – 46 percent on average in the 1996–2015 elections (Table 10.8). A small gap remained between the two largest parties, while mid-sized parties proliferated and their coalition importance was enhanced. In the 2006 and 2009 elections, the largest party was a newcomer to the political map – Kadima. And in 2013, the second-largest party was new – Yesh Atid; while in 2015 the third and fourth places were taken by the new Arab Joint List and by a new party, Kulanu, respectively. The appearance of these parties increased the trend toward fragmentation, and competition remained high.

B. Upheavals

The smooth transfer of power from one ruling party to another is a sign of the public legitimacy accorded elections as the democratic form of decision-making. In Israel, a political upheaval means that the entering prime minister is from a different party than the departing one, and this did not happen in Israel's history until 1977. Since then, Israeli voters have brought about another six upheavals: Labor in 1992; Likud in 1996; Labor in 1999; Likud in 2001; Kadima in 2006; and Likud in 2009 (not including the rotation between Peres and Shamir in 1986). In other words, every Knesset election since 1992 brought about a change in government with the exception of Sharon in 2003 and Netanyahu in 2013 and 2015, who both regained their position as prime minister. The transitions have been completely orderly and helped strengthen the democratic rules of the game, with the exception of attitudes toward the Rabin government in 1992, regarded as illegitimate by some of those who opposed his policies.

Except for the change in party of the prime minister, only some of the upheavals significantly altered governance because of the formation of grand coalitions, referred to as "unity governments," in which the largest parties share governance. The upheaval of 1977 was a sharp turning point that ended the historic Mapai era. Thus, too, the 1992 upheaval in which Labor returned to power under Rabin without a senior coalition partner. Later changes of government were less dramatic, as no single party managed to entrench itself as the ruling party. In the 1996 election, Benjamin Netanyahu defeated Shimon Peres, but Labor remained the largest party. In 1999, the premiership again shifted to Labor, but despite its seven-seat edge over the Likud, the Labor government lasted only half a term. In the 2001 special election for prime minister, another upheaval ensued when Likud candidate Ariel Sharon was elected. The next upheaval occurred in 2009 when Kadima won a plurality of the

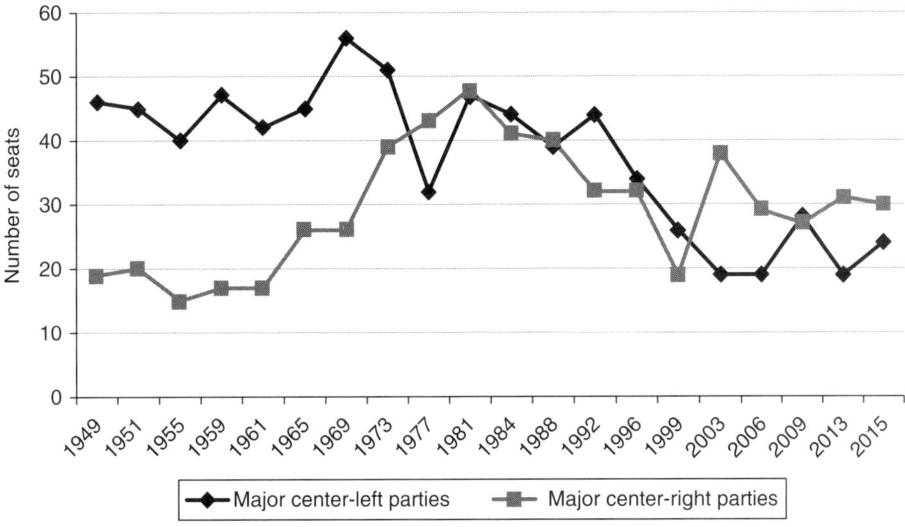

Figure 10.3 Number of seats won by the major political blocs 1949–2015

votes, but it was Likud that formed the government by creating an obstructionist bloc of right-wing parties. In 2013, the ratio between the largest party (Likud with Yisrael Beitenu) and the second-largest party (Yesh Atid) was 1.6, but the Netanyahu-led coalition collapsed in 2014, and the Knesset moved up the election.

During the period of party fragmentation and the waning of the large parties (Figure 10.3), the terms "upheaval" and "unity government" lost their original meaning.

C. Proposed Knesset Electoral Reforms

Electoral reform is an extremely important process in the life of a democracy, but one for which it is hard to mobilize consensus. To change the electoral system, one of two conditions must prevail: recruitment of a parliamentary majority in favor of the change (sometimes even a special majority is required); or transfer of the authority for this decision from the legislature to another arena, such as a special assembly or referendum. The first option sets a very high bar because Article 4 of the Basic Law: The Knesset calls for an absolute majority of sixty-one MKs to amend the electoral system. But this would mean recruiting at least some of the parties in the coalition government, which won their government positions thanks to the old electoral rules. Such parties generally prefer to maintain the status quo rather than risk the uncertainty of change that could topple them from power. In other words, the key to reform is in the hands of those with a vested interest in preserving the status quo. As for the second option, even if there were agreement about the need for reform, the path to change is complex and strewn with obstacles (Rahat 2000). It is therefore not surprising that electoral systems are one of the most stable institutions in veteran western democracies. If changes are made, they are usually minor, such as correcting the formula of the electoral calculation, altering the electoral threshold, or changing the size of the legislature.[30]

[30] Despite the obstacles, significant electoral reforms were instituted in four veteran democracies in the first half of the 1990s – New Zealand, Italy, Japan, and Israel (Norris 1997).

Three main shortcomings beset the Knesset electoral system. First: over-proportionality. As noted, this is singularly advantageous for representing the complex social structure of Israel, but it also fosters a multiplicity of parties, creating fragile coalitions and challenging the steering capacity, which could lead to unstable governments, multiple changes of ministers, and too frequent elections. A second shortcoming is that the rigid list of party candidates prevents voter influence on its composition or the ranking of the candidates, thereby blocking their views about the quality of the nominees. The third shortcoming is that the system is national and does not allow for regional representation, leading to geographic under-representation. Combined with the rigid lists, this constitutes a barrier between the voter and the elected official. Over the years, a number of proposals have been made to reform the electoral system, which can be grouped into the following three categories.

Minor Proposals

These proposals have left in place the building blocks of the existing system – proportionality, rigid lists, and national representation – with only minor changes. One example is the Bader–Ofer amendment in 1973, which altered the formula for dividing up the surplus votes, a change that slightly favored large parties. This amendment did not shake up the political system or alter the election results. Another change was to gradually raise the electoral threshold to 3.25 percent in the 2015 election. Until then, raising the electoral threshold had not drastically reduced the number of parties in the Knesset. In the 2009 election, for example, 67,470 votes (2%) were needed for entering the Knesset. If the electoral threshold had been just half of this (1% or 33,735 votes), no additional party would have entered the Knesset. And if the electoral threshold in 2013 had already been 3.25 percent, only three small parties would have remained outside the Knesset (Table 9.2 in Chapter 9). Despite raising the threshold from 2 percent to 3.25 percent in 2015, a new party – Kulanu – entered the Knesset in 2015, and only two parties who were part of the Knesset in 2013 did not make it into the Knesset in 2015: Yahad, which split from Shas, and Kadima, which by that point had completely dissolved and did not run in the election. Nevertheless, raising the electoral threshold did lead to the merger of small party lists and halted the further proliferation of parties.

Far-Reaching Proposals

One proposal was based on the existing system, but could have significantly affected the behavior of parties and voters, and perhaps even redrawn the party map. This Ben-Gurion initiative formed part of the coalition agreement between Mapai and the General Zionists (December 1952) in which the two parties agreed to seek an electoral threshold of 10 percent.[31] This change never came about because of vigorous opposition from the other factions (Rahat 2001). From time to time, proposals are made to raise the electoral threshold to 5 percent or more. To illustrate some of

[31] How would a 10 percent electoral threshold have changed the outcome? Only three parties would have made it into the second Knesset – Mapai, the General Zionists, and Mapam; similarly, only the two largest parties would have entered the sixth through the eighth Knessets, as well as the tenth to the fourteenth; in 2009, the only parties that would have entered the Knesset would have been Kadima, Likud, Yisrael Beitenu, Labor, and possibly Shas. This is a hypothetical exercise, of course, because a high electoral threshold would have led parties to merge prior to the election in order to pass the electoral threshold.

the effects: If the electoral threshold had been 4 percent in 2009, the following six parties would not have entered the Knesset: NRP, Balad, Meretz, United Arab List, Hadash, and the National Union. Had the threshold been 5 percent in 2013, Kadima, United Arab List, Balad, Hadash, and Meretz would not have entered the Knesset. If the threshold had been 5 percent in 2015, Torah Judaism and Meretz would not have entered the Knesset. Reducing the number of parties by such artificial measures could harm the representation of important groups in society (the ultra-Orthodox and Arabs, for example), who would not find themselves adequately represented in the large parties, and this would undercut the legitimacy of the Knesset as a representative cameral body.

On another plane, initiatives were already afoot in the 1950s to introduce some degree of regional representation into the electoral system, i.e., to do away with the national lists and instead choose some MKs by districts. In the late 1980s, Minister Gad Yaacobi headed a committee that proposed that half the MKs be elected from twenty constituencies having three representatives each, and another half in national elections, without undermining the overall proportionality of the election results. A similar proposal suggested adoption of a mixed system like that used in Germany – combining regional constituencies with proportionality by using a compensatory national pool of towns, which corrects any distortions to proportionality created by the constituencies (Brichta 2007).

Revamping the System

The first such initiative was that of Ben-Gurion in the early years of the state, who wished to institute the British majoritarian electoral system of constituencies with one representative. This would have led to a two-party system, the disappearance of small and mid-size parties, and a transformation of Israeli politics. Although Mapai would probably have been the big winner from this system, Ben-Gurion did not gain his party's support for it because the party leaders understood that it did not suit Israeli society. Other initiatives that are occasionally put forward call for converting the entire system of governance from a parliamentary to a presidential model, generally following the American prototype. The goal is to improve governance by strengthening the executive branch. We have already noted our view about this, i.e., that steering capacity breakdowns are not related to the type of government, but caused by other factors, and that what suits Israel is a form of representation that allows for a parliamentary system.

Attempts to emulate the United States evolved into a drive to conduct direct election of the prime minister, which was adopted in 1992 and applied in the 1996–2003 elections (see Section 10.6 above and discussion in Chapter 5). The reform, however, was a mongrelized presidential system or, more accurately, a quasi-parliamentary, quasi-presidential system that exists nowhere else (Hazan 1998a). The system for electing MKs was not altered, but voting behavior during the period of direct election changed so much that some of these changes continued even after the previous electoral system was restored.

In the 2009 and 2013 elections, slogans reappeared about "changing the system of governance," and this became part of the coalition agreements of the Netanyahu governments. Experience suggests that it would be better – both on principle and for practical reasons – to focus on improving the existing parliamentary system, with corrections to proportional representation, rather than to artificially transplant systems that do not suit Israel. For example, more than a decade since the direct election failure, a partial regional representation system could be considered, while preserving the overall proportional representation of the population.

D. The Indecisive Decision-Making of the Israeli Voter

We opened this chapter by saying that democratic elections are designed to translate the will of the voters into governance with steering capacity, i.e., into leadership that has the authority to act in the name and on behalf of the citizens. The electoral system connects three entities – the citizen, the party/candidates, and the government – and all these systems are marked by tension between the desire for broad representation and the need for steering capacity. Representation without steering capacity means the failure to aggregate a spectrum of opinions into binding majority decisions. Steering capacity without representation means decisions without public legitimacy. Democratic governments in many countries have proven that these two can be balanced. In Israel, too, the elections successfully connect the will of the voters and the composition of the elected bodies, and even make regime change possible. And yet voters continue to express their dissatisfaction with politics, which affects their attitude toward the electoral system. In a 2007 survey, for example, roughly half the respondents thought the system should be changed, and they attributed this to the quality of the political leadership (President's Commission 2007, 3). We believe that the system of election is being confused with the results of those elections and their repercussions for steering capacity. The problem is not the electoral system per se.

Until the 1980s, voting made possible the formation of strong governments, for better or worse, governments that made fateful decisions on matters of war and peace: But the peace agreement with Egypt forged under the Begin-led government may have been the last government decision to have won broad public support. Ever since, most decisions have been controversial, to some extent because voters find it hard to make up their minds about their preferences in critical matters. For a decade or more, for example, a majority of Israelis have expressed support for a Palestinian state and withdrawal from most of the territories, and yet a majority also does not believe that peace is possible and it supports harsh security policies. In the 2003 election, this equivocation led to solid voter support for Ariel Sharon, who the voters believed epitomized a combination of security and territorial compromise. Can one then "blame" the voter for the failure of the electoral system?

The average Israeli understands politics and knows what he or she wants. The average Israeli is a sophisticated voter, exploiting all the options when handed two ballots. The problems are indeed complicated, but the reason the votes are vague and end up changing the leadership so often ("upheavals") has to do with the nature of the alternatives offered. It is the job of the election to reflect society, and the job of the parties and their leaders to present the voter with clear alternatives. Leadership is not a weather vane that spins with the winds of public opinion, but must offer concrete solutions and put them to the democratic test. In this sense, the elected officials have failed dismally, and this is the main reason that voters find it hard to make clear decisions, ideological and electoral, and why they change their minds so often. If we add to this the lack of public trust in the political institutions, wrath over the corruption of some senior politicians, and the adulation of politicians catapulted to transient media glory – one can understand the vague verdicts of the Israeli voter. Manipulating the electoral system will not improve matters, and there is no need for radical change. On the other hand, the need is urgent for parties and leaders to stake out a clear path and offer the voters real alternatives.

10.10 Local Authority Elections

From the first local election in 1950 until 1973, local elections were held in the shadow of national party politics. With the change in the electoral system in 1978, local parties were strengthened and national parties, weakened.

A. Voter Turnout in Local Elections

Until 1978, local elections took place on the same day as the national Knesset election. Once local elections were separated from the Knesset election, a sharp drop was recorded in voter turnout (Figure 10.4). In the first six elections (except for 1950), local and national elections were held concurrently and the average voter turnout was 79 percent; in the following eight elections (1978–2013), voter turnout dropped to 56 percent, on average, where it has remained. In 2003, it dipped below 50 percent for the first time, rising to 52 percent in 2008 and 51 percent in 2013.[32]

In a politically savvy society like Israel, a voter turnout rate under 50 percent in local elections is low in absolute terms and low relative to the Knesset election as well. How can this be explained when quality of life issues and improved local services have only become more important for Israeli citizens? Matters of state, particularly foreign and security issues, are of greater concern to the Israeli citizen, and therefore separating local elections from the Knesset election and canceling the national holiday on local election day (since 1993) contributed to the decline in voter turnout locally. And there is apathy – Israeli voters are aware of the weakness and poor image of the local authority, hence their disinterest and reluctance to invest democratic energy in local affairs.

Nevertheless, voter turnout differs dramatically from place to place. Local intimacy has an effect: In smaller and more remote communities as well as Arab towns, the turnout is markedly higher and resembles that of Knesset elections. In general, there is an inverse relationship between voter turnout and the size of the community: The larger the local authority, the lower the voter turnout. In big cities, particularly in secular neighborhoods, voter turnout is remarkably low. In small Jewish towns (less than 10,000 residents), 65–70 percent of the citizens voted in the 2003 local election; in larger towns (over 65,000 residents), just over 40 percent voted (Ben Bassat and Dahan 2008, 37). All the locales where the voting rate was particularly high (over 90%) were Arab towns. In the 2003 election, half the eligible voters

[32] Ministry of the Interior, election results: www.moin.gov.il/Subjects/Bchirot/Documents/chvreymoatza.pdf and www.moin.gov.il/Subjects/Bchirot/Pages/default.aspx (accessed September 29, 2017). Voter turnout in Arab towns (not including mixed towns) was much higher – approximately 80 percent (Lavie and Rudnitzky 2010, 23; Rudnitzky 2014).

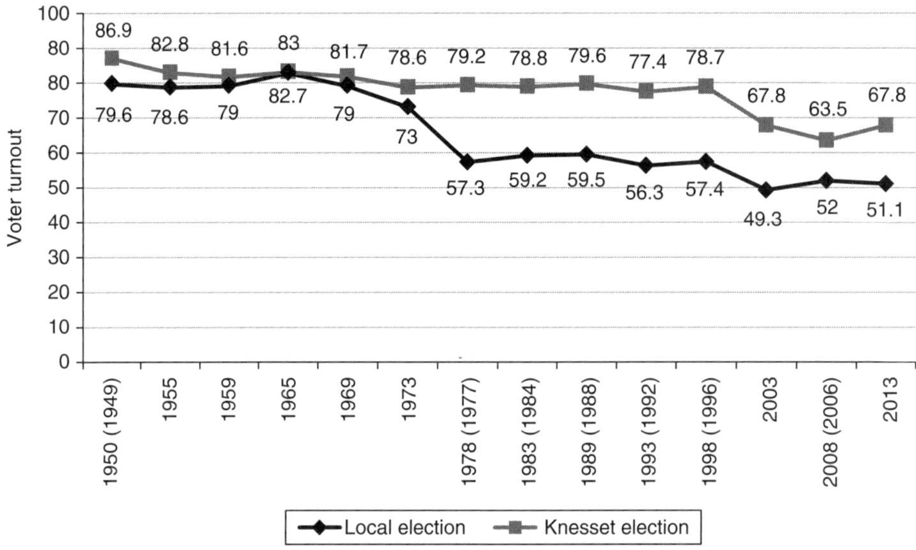

Figure 10.4 Voter turnout for Knesset and local elections 1949–2013
Note: The year of the Knesset election appears in parentheses when local elections were not held the same day. The 2003 and 2013 elections were held the same year, but not the same day.
Sources: Ministry of the Interior website; National Supervisor of Elections.

did not show up at the polling stations even though some 80,000 new, young voters were added to the voting rolls upon the enfranchisement of seventeen-year-olds for local elections. In the 2008 and 2013 elections, the decline of voting was halted, though it remained of concern in terms of the commitment to local democracy and the legitimacy of the local authority.

Figure 10.5 shows the growth of the local party lists until 2003. No data exist for the following years because the national parties almost entirely disappeared from local elections, where campaigns focus on local issues. Local campaigns (with the exception of Jerusalem) are conducted with almost no discussion of foreign or security matters, and certainly not socioeconomic ideology of the left or right. Election propaganda in these campaigns is local, particularly in well-to-do towns, addressing issues of quality of life, education, and transportation. In poor towns, on the other hand, more emphasis is placed on the basic needs of the residents – welfare, housing, and employment.

B. Results of Changing the Electoral System for Mayor

Direct election of the mayor generally managed to stabilize the status of the mayor and prevent the frequent crises that had marred the pre-reform years. The winner of the mayoralty contest who serves a five-year term is known immediately after the election, and the mayor can be forced to resign only by an overwhelming majority (75% of the council members and approval of the minister of the interior). Nevertheless, the stability of the municipal government depends on the strength of the coalition the mayor forms. This can be challenging because changing the electoral

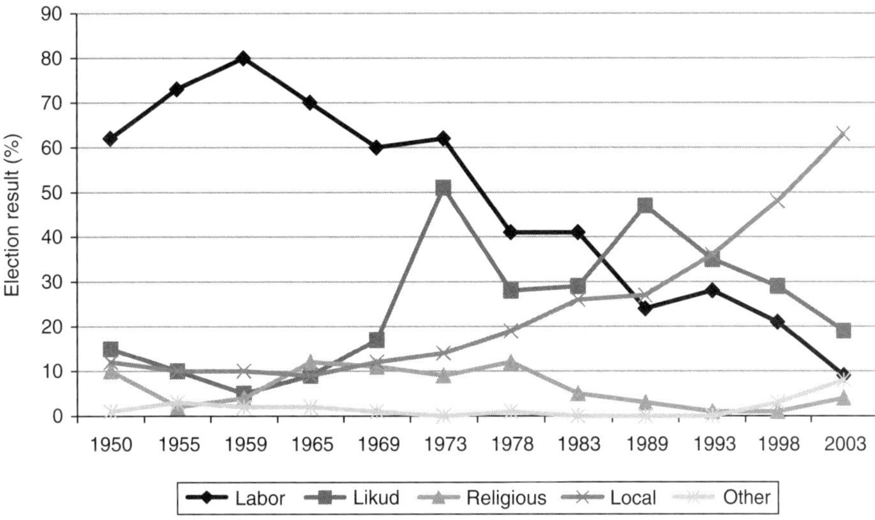

Figure 10.5 Local election results for mayor in Jewish and mixed towns by political bloc 1950–2003 (%)
Source: Brichta 2005, 979.

system in 1978 also affected local voting patterns, which increased the tendency of voters, familiar from the 1960s, to split their vote – sometimes voting for different parties for the Knesset and the local election and sometimes splitting their local vote between the mayor and the council.[33]

The gap widened as independent local parties flourished, and the mayor's party became less significant. In the 2008 election, no fewer than a dozen parties were elected to the Tel Aviv City Council, and Mayor Ron Huldai's local party received only 14 percent of the vote (five out of the thirty-one council seats); in Netanya, incumbent Mayor Miriam Feinberg won by a large majority, but the party she headed took only 25 percent of the council seats; in Ramle, Likud candidate Yoel Lavie won for mayor by a wide 60 percent margin, but his party won only 26 percent of the votes.

A gap between the electoral strength of the mayor and the weakness of his or her party increases the likelihood of a contrarian council, in which the mayor does not have a majority and finds it hard to function. There were also cases of a mayor elected by a majority of residents who could not cobble together a coalition, leaving a dysfunctional council that was incapable of approving a budget, ultimately leading to appointment by the interior minister of a committee to run the municipal affairs until the subsequent election. In more established cities, the mayor has considerable power, and stability prevails in local politics. Vote splitting further fragmented the parties in the town councils, as it increased the chances of small parties being elected. In 1978, an average of 4.8 parties nationally vied for council election, and this doubled to ten in 2008 (Brichta et al. 2010, 7, 66).

[33] A similar pattern – voters who weigh different considerations when two ballots are placed in their hands – was also apparent during direct election of the prime minister. See Chapter 5.

Direct election of the mayor, focus on the personality of the candidate, and the institution of primary elections in several parties all contributed to the trend to personify politics in Israel. And yet research into voters' considerations in the 1993 and 1998 elections found that when an incumbent mayor runs for reelection, local voters also take into consideration how the mayor functioned in budget affairs (Diskin and Eden 1999). The local focus on the rivalry of candidates, not parties, made election financing particularly problematic. Direct election of the mayor led candidates to replace party affinities with a growing dependence on funders who have economic interests. Links between government and big business solidified, and many mayors came under scrutiny. Fifty-three investigations were opened against local authorities in 2004–7; twenty-four mayors were investigated on environmental issues alone. In 2009, forty investigations of elected municipal officials were conducted (O. Tal 2008, 2; D. Navot 2010, 131–51). Athough little research has addressed the financing of local elections, we note that spending is heavy and state comptroller supervision cannot cope with the many problems (Levine Committee 2000, 40; Friedberg 2005).

The declining role of national parties in the appointment of local candidates and in coalition agreements expanded the independence of mayors. Mayors are active in recruiting candidates from the major parties for local election, and this can add to their power if their candidate wins (Razin 2004). On the other hand, it is conceivable (no studies exist about this yet) that this independence narrowed their maneuverability in the corridors of national government, particularly mayors of smaller and poorer municipalities.

C. Link Between Knesset and Local Elections

In the early years, local and Knesset elections were closely linked, until the ebbing of Mapai's power, which was evident in the local elections even before the 1977 upheaval. The shifting balance of power locally was gradual and only a decade later (in the 1989 election) did the upheaval occur in local elections, when most of the mayors were elected from right-wing parties. But even this change was short-lived, because the growth of local parties unlinked local and national elections. That connection between the party power on both levels was generally indirect, particularly when voter turnout declined in the local election.[34] Nevertheless, one trend is common both locally and nationally: the decline of large parties and the rise of special-interest parties. This can be seen in the changed election results in Tel Aviv, Jerusalem, Haifa, and Beersheeba, which had been regarded as the acid test of the national party machine.

The election of Shlomo Lahat as mayor of Tel Aviv in 1973 foreshadowed the Likud's rise to power nationally, but Lahat came from the General Zionist (liberal) wing of the Likud, which had controlled Tel Aviv even previously. The upheaval in the cities began in Beersheeba in 1989 with the election of Likud candidate Yitzhak Rager, but in 1998 an independent candidate won the mayoralty there. In Jerusalem, Ehud Olmert led the Likud to victory in 1993, but the power then shifted to an

[34] Only under certain conditions can the local elections be viewed as a kind of test of party power, particularly of the larger parties (B. Shapira 2005, 1194).

independent ultra-Orthodox contender. In Haifa, Mapai/Labor dominance was preserved until 2003, when Yona Yahav from Shinui took over as mayor, declaring himself an independent candidate. In short, the large parties lost their grip and the mayors of Israel's major cities have largely come from independent lists. An interesting question is whether instituting regional representation in the Knesset election would influence the local elections.

11 Government Coalitions: A Steering Mechanism in the Political System

11.1 Definition: Coalitions as a Steering Mechanism

> The literature [on coalitions] has long suffered from one of the traditional Hollywood biases: much more attention has been given to identifying the right match, and to the process of courtship, than to the actual process of sharing a life (political or otherwise) and working out the concomitant issues. (Strøm and Muller 1999, 278)

A coalition is a temporary alliance between two or more parties collaborating to form a government that can win a parliamentary vote of confidence in order to promote their world views or interests. Coalition parties formulate a political program – policy guidelines designed to bridge the gaps between them. The reason for coalition formation is usually because no single party has a parliamentary majority.

In multiparty parliamentary democracies, the coalition is the link between the legislative authority (the parliament) and the executive authority (the government). It also links electoral politics – the arena in which voters exert influence via their votes – with governmental-bureaucratic politics, where the public's influence is indirect. A coalition is also a pragmatic compromise on the various ideological positions of the member parties. The key players in coalition politics are the parties, which conduct coalition negotiations in keeping with the mandate they received from the citizens who voted for them. This mandate generally includes implicit authorization for taking a seat at the government table and serving as government ministers.

Since the establishment of national institutions in the pre-state era, and throughout Israel's existence, government has always been based on coalitions. In 1933, Ben-Gurion explained his view of what a coalition means:

> A coalition does not mean "how good and pleasant it is for brothers to sit together." It means action and responsibility. The first condition of a coalition is a joint plan of action. A coalition is not a goal, but a means. Only if there is a joint plan that everyone can faithfully serve – then it is a coalition. And a second condition for a fruitful coalition is authorized leadership – a group of people who represent not only their own parties, but have mutual respect and trust and can work together. Without these two [conditions], a coalition has no real value. It is nothing but an illusion. (quoted by Yaacobi 1980, 71)

No party in Israel has ever received enough votes to form a government without other parties. The government coalition has almost always been led by the largest party, with the head of the party's slate of Knesset candidates serving as prime minister. In Chapter 10, we noted the connection between the proportional-national electoral system in Israel and the high likelihood of forming government coalitions. Nonetheless, the electoral system in itself does not preclude a majority party, and the Labor Alignment in its heyday came close to this. While proportional elections do not create a multiparty system, they definitely foster this system, thus increasing the likelihood of forming coalitions. To achieve a parliamentary majority that supports the government, an alliance of several parties is needed. This requires agreements, concessions, and compromises on both the ideological level (charting government policy) and the practical level (allocating ministries among the partners). These agreements are a political-public commitment, and their written expression in what is called a "coalition agreement" does not fundamentally change their political character. For many years, the coalition agreements were primarily political documents, rather than formal "contracts." As such, they were considered outside the purview of the court. In the wake of the political crisis of 1990, the validity and content of political agreements were examined by the High Court of Justice, and have since been viewed as judiciable (Galnoor 1993).

This chapter will examine the central role of the coalition in the Israeli political system and the changes this institution has undergone – transitioning from Lijphart's "consociational" to a more pluralistic model (Lijphart 1984, 215–22; see also Susser and Cohen 1999).

11.2 The Legal Foundation and Political Practice

A. Coalition Agreements

A coalition agreement signed among Knesset parties defines the government's policy guidelines and operating principles, the allocation of ministerial portfolios and functions in the Knesset, and it sometimes also specifies issues on which a party is granted freedom to vote against government policy. In some parties, it is customary to submit the agreement to the party institutions for approval. The coalition agreement can be one document signed between the prime minister's party and all the parties in the coalition, or several documents between the prime minister's party and each partner separately. For example, the coalition agreement signed in June 1977 was of the first type – a single document signed by Likud, the National Religious Party (NRP), and Agudat Yisrael. The coalition agreement signed in July 1999 was of the second type: In addition to one document signed between One Israel (Labor, led by Ehud Barak) and Yisrael B'Aliyah, Meretz, NRP, United Torah Judaism (UTJ), Shas, and the Center Party, separate agreements were signed between the prime minister's party and each of its six coalition partners. The fact that the coalition agreements have become separate has important repercussions: A single agreement among all the coalition partners indicates a good chance of cohesion and is usually authored by politicians, whereas multiple agreements and appendixes create complex bilateral relations within the coalition and lawyers are assigned to formulate them.[1]

[1] The coalition agreement in 2009 was signed between Likud and five parties separately with two additional appendixes. Similarly, the coalition agreement in 2013 between Likud–Yisrael Beitenu and Hatnuah, Yesh Atid, and the Jewish Home included separate detailed appendixes with the latter two. See the Knesset website.

A coalition agreement is a special case of a broader group – "political agreements" – that also includes the formation of a parliamentary bloc, a party platform, and even a campaign speech (Galnoor 1993). In short, a political agreement is a commitment that political entities and elected officials undertake vis-à-vis the electorate and each other. The formal part of the agreement is not necessarily the essence, because political understandings are involved. The public validity of the agreement is determined by the political culture – the public norms and the behavior of political institutions and leaders. The fact that political coalition agreements in Israel had been secret in the past, and included illegal agreements, led to the intervention of the court (Barak-Erez 1999). The court examines political coalition agreements according to two main criteria: whether the agreement is in the public interest and the public official's trustworthiness. The main questions defined in legislation and jurisprudence regarding coalition agreements concern the obligation to make them public, their legal status, and judicial review of their content.

Obligation to Make Public Coalition Agreements (i.e., Submit to the Knesset)

For many years, the practice was that coalition agreements were secret and it was not in the interest of the parties to expose them to public scrutiny in part or in their entirety. Although the public norm of transparency strengthened over the years, it was not clear whether parties that signed a coalition agreement were required to publicize its details. In 1990, the High Court ruled that parties that sign a coalition agreement to establish a government are obligated to publish its details, noting that "it is impossible to maintain the public's trust based on what is concealed from it" (*Shalit v. Peres* 1990). Following this ruling, the Basic Law: Government was amended to require parties entering into a coalition agreement to submit the complete text to the Knesset prior to conducting a vote of confidence on the new government. A similar directive was included in the later version of the Basic Law: Government, enacted in 1992, which extended the publication requirement to agreements pertaining to the election of the prime minister, no-confidence motions, and the appointment of additional ministers and deputy ministers. In 2001, this article was moved from the Basic Law: Government to the Government Law.

Legal Status and Judicial Review of Coalition Agreements

Is there a public or legal obligation to implement the commitments in a coalition agreement? In what circumstances is it permissible to refrain from fulfilling the commitments, and what sanctions can be imposed if the commitments are violated? Will the court enforce implementation of the agreement? Since the crisis following the collapse of the National Unity Government in 1990, a growing number of High Court petitions have asked the High Court to rule on the content and status of coalition agreements. The court is wary of intervening in the political content of the agreements; its main ruling with respect to the justiciability of coalition agreements are as follows:

- The coalition agreement is a binding agreement from a legal perspective, but is not an ordinary contract. Therefore, the usual contract statutes do not apply – i.e., the court will not usually order its enforcement.
- As a political agreement, the main sanction for violation is political, primarily a threat to quit the coalition.

- Political dynamics could lead to non-implementation of a coalition agreement; thus, parties that demand the inclusion of a particular article in the agreement do not always insist on its implementation.

In the past, the court refrained from exercising judicial review of a coalition agreement's content, based on the view that an agreement of this type does not always obligate the sides. Over time, the court changed its approach, and it may examine the agreement even before the parties begin acting upon it (Rubinstein and Medina 2005, 787). Judicial review does not, however, entail the obligation to implement the commitments stipulated in the agreements. Instead, it focuses on the government actions that are likely to ensue from the agreements. Thus, it is possible to declare an agreement invalid even before it is implemented if the agreement itself violates the basic principles of Israel's constitutional structure (*Velner v. Rabin et al.* 1994). The court also recognized the right of a citizen who is not a party to the agreement to petition the court to examine its validity.

In April 1990, the High Court of Justice asserted its authority to invalidate illegal clauses in a coalition agreement that were contrary to the public interest. Following a petition filed against the coalition agreement between Likud and the party led by Yitzhak Moda'i, the court invalidated a clause in the agreement that provided monetary benefit (erasing a debt) in exchange for a political commitment (*Jerzhevski v. Prime Minister Shamir* 1990). In other cases, clauses in agreements were invalidated that included a commitment to job appointments in the civil service or guaranteed spots on the list of candidates for the next Knesset election; the court ruled that such commitments constitute personal gain and do not serve a legitimate public interest. The same applies to a commitment given in one Knesset for a quid pro quo in the next Knesset, because this violates the voter's freedom of choice.

On the other hand, a commitment in a coalition agreement to enact a law is not inappropriate, because this is one of the legitimate objectives of a political alliance. Doubts are liable to arise if the commitment prevents MKs from exercising their own judgment. This issue arose in a coalition agreement in which the Labor Party promised to support a legislative initiative by Shas if the latter agreed to a change in the status quo on religious affairs. The court viewed this as a sweeping agreement between the parties in advance that might compromise their judgment, but the court's majority opinion refrained from invalidating the commitment (*Velner v. Rabin et al.* 1994). And what about financial commitments to promote objectives that appear in coalition agreements? This is a complex question, because parties join a coalition in order to realize objectives that involve budget outlays, and the court is liable to find itself involved in politics if it scrutinizes the purpose of the commitment and the anticipated use of funds.

B. Basic Guidelines

The Basic Guidelines of Government Policy is a document that outlines the principles of the joint plan of the incoming government, the plan for which it seeks the Knesset's vote of confidence. According to the Basic Law: Government, these guidelines must be presented to the Knesset, whether or not it is a coalition government.[2]

[2] A new coalition, unlike a new government, is not required to rewrite basic guidelines. For example, the coalition formed in January 2005 (Likud–Labor–UTJ) adopted the basic guidelines of the previous coalition from February 2003 (Likud–Shinui–National Union–NRP).

The basic guidelines are a political document for all intents and purposes, and not legally binding. Thus, a deviation from the guidelines does not constitute grounds for petitioning the court. Nevertheless, a party can regard a renunciation of what is written in the basic guidelines as justification for quitting the government. Basic guidelines are different from coalition agreements in the level of detail and thus are not considered justiciable. However, there should be no contradiction between the two documents that establish the coalition. The basic guidelines of the government can be found on the Knesset website.

C. Coalition Discipline

"Coalition discipline" entails the responsibility of a coalition partner for the government's decisions, including the responsibility of ministers for how their party votes in the Knesset. This discipline is designed to ensure that government decisions will be translated into a majority in the Knesset, a majority that rests on the MKs from the coalition parties. If coalition MKs vote against a government decision, the prime minister has the authority to fire the ministers who represent the rebellious faction because they are responsible for how their party colleagues vote. In the early days of the state, the prime minister did not have the authority to dismiss ministers, which is a deterrent in enforcing coalition discipline. This led prime ministers to sometimes take the extreme step of resigning, prompting resignation of the entire government to enable formation of a new government without the ministers from the wayward party.

This situation came to an end in 1962 with amendment of the Transition Law, stipulating that ministers are responsible for the Knesset votes of their party colleagues: "A member of the government will be responsible to the government for his voting in the Knesset plenum and for the voting of the faction to which he belongs, in the Knesset plenum." The amendment authorized the prime minister to dismiss ministers if members of their party violated coalition discipline in the following cases: supporting or abstaining from a motion of no-confidence in the government; and opposing or abstaining from a vote on a government proposal pertaining to the state budget or security, foreign affairs, and other matters on which the government decided in advance to impose coalition discipline. Examples of the use of this authority include the dismissal of the NRP ministers by Prime Minister Yitzhak Rabin in 1977 after they abstained in a no-confidence vote to protest desecration of the Sabbath; and the dismissal of Ministers Livni and Lapid by Prime Minister Netanyahu in December 2014 over personal disagreements, which led to early elections in March 2015.

In 1981, the Basic Law: Government was further amended to give the prime minister complete political authority to dismiss ministers at his or her discretion. This established the prime minister's constitutional status vis-à-vis insubordinate ministers; the prime minister no longer had to rely solely on the parties' collective responsibility to enforce coalition discipline. Enforcement of coalition discipline is primarily a matter of political dynamics that are not necessarily connected to violating coalition agreements. The prime minister weighs broad political considerations in deciding when to exercise the authority of the office to dismiss a minister, and the court is not expected to intervene. In some circumstances, the prime minister will ignore a violation of coalition discipline or only threaten to dismiss ministers to achieve a goal and deter them.[3]

Coalition discipline has weakened over the years, mainly due to the erosion of party discipline, and it even declined during the period of direct election of the prime minister, contrary to what advocates of that change had predicted. Governments rose and fell more frequently (see Chapter 5); the coalition became a revolving door for parties that came and went; ministers in the coalition spoke publicly against government decisions without resigning or being dismissed; members of coalition parties did not support the government in Knesset voting, and so on.[4] In a parliamentary regime, the lack of coalition discipline hinders the government's ability to function and therefore makes it difficult for the coalition to serve as a mechanism for bridging disagreements in Israeli society and for ensuring that government decisions are implemented in practice.

D. The Politics of Coalition Agreements

Coalition agreements are political in the sense that their validity is determined by the extent of support they receive from the coalition partners. Lack of party and coalition discipline has turned the agreements into negotiations that continue even after the government is formed, and culminate in new compromises and sometimes in disbanding the partnership. Parties no longer view the coalition agreement as a firm framework for keeping promises or even for setting policy. The political rhetoric is full of statements like "they violated the agreement they signed with us" and, indeed, coalition agreements are regularly violated, as in the following examples:

- 2003: The NRP suspended its partnership in the government, citing a blatant violation of a coalition agreement to maintain the status quo vis-à-vis Sabbath observance.
- 2008: Prime Minister Olmert lashed out at Defense Minister Barak, who charged that a proposal by Justice Minister Friedman contravened the coalition agreement.
- 2014: Foreign Minister Lieberman and Economics Minister Bennett harshly criticized the prime minister during the military operation in the Gaza Strip and espoused positions that conflicted with government policy.

11.3 Types of Coalitions

Governments in parliamentary systems can be categorized by the number of parties in them, and by the extent of government support in the parliament. According to these two criteria, there are five types of governments (Lijphart 1984; Laver and Schofield 1990; Woldendorp, Keman, and Budge 2000):

[3] In March 1990, Prime Minister Yitzhak Shamir dismissed Shimon Peres; Ariel Sharon dismissed five Shas ministers in May 2002 after they voted against the government's stance. Less than a week after the dismissals, the Shas ministers returned to serve in the government. In June 2004, Sharon dismissed National Union ministers Avigdor Lieberman and Benjamin Elon, even before they had violated coalition discipline. In October 2004, Sharon dismissed Ministers Landau and Ratzon, members of his own party, for voting against the disengagement plan; in December 2004, five Shinui ministers were dismissed for voting against the government's budget bill. In December 2014, Netanyahu sacked Ministers Lapid and Livni and the government fell.

[4] For example, the Labor Party joined the coalition following the 2009 election, but five Labor MKs did not consider themselves obligated to support the government, including the vote on the budget bill.

- **Single-party majority government:** One party has an absolute majority in the parliament and does not need a coalition. Governments of this type can be found in states with a majoritarian electoral system, like Britain, which increases the probability of a single party with an absolute majority; however, states with a proportional electoral system, such as Spain and Greece, have also had single-party majority governments. In Israel, there has never been a government of this type.
- **Single-party minority government:** The single party in the government does not have a parliamentary majority, yet there is still no coalition government. This is ostensibly an anomalous situation, but it occurs primarily in states with no tradition of coalition governments. In Canada, for example, most of the governments are single-party majority governments, but sometimes the largest party does not win a parliamentary majority in the election and forms a minority government. This type of minority government, of a single party, has never existed in Israel.

The following three types are coalition governments:

- **Minimal winning coalition:** The coalition is composed of two or more parties, all of which are essential for maintaining a parliamentary majority in support of the government. There are no spare partners in this type of coalition; if only one party leaves, the government will lose its majority and become a minority government (Riker 1962). In Israel, there have been several governments of this type (see Table 11.2). For example, the coalition Sharon formed in 2005 was composed of three parties (Likud, Labor, and UTJ) with a majority of sixty-four MKs; the departure of any one of these parties meant losing the majority in the Knesset. Similarly, Netanyahu formed a minimal coalition of four parties in 2013 (Likud, Yesh Atid, Jewish Home, and Hatnuah), with sixty-eight MKs.
- **Surplus/oversized coalition:** This is composed of two or more parties, but the government does not lose its majority and become a minority government if just one of the parties quits the coalition. Most of the coalitions in Israel have been of this type, and the reason for this is political. First, there is a tradition of inclusiveness that dates back to the Yishuv period, whereby coalitions serve as a coordinating mechanism among social groups. Second, the leading party fears that its partners will wield excessive power, and prime ministers seek to protect themselves from losing the majority if one of the parties quits – a phenomenon that is quite common in Israel. The average coalition majority in governments formed after elections, from the state's inception through 2015, is seventy-five MKs. Surplus coalitions are also formed during times of "national emergency." The main parties join in collective responsibility to confront the challenge, whether internal or external. Examples include the Coalition Government in Britain during World War II and the National Unity Government in Israel formed prior to the war in 1967.
- **Minority coalition:** This is composed of two or more parties that together do not form a parliamentary majority. Coalitions of this type are sometimes formed in Scandinavian multiparty systems. In Israel, no minority coalition has ever been formed after an election, but there were majority governments that became minority governments during their terms. Such governments found it difficult to function and did not last long, operating during a transition period leading up to early elections. For example, the Barak government was a minority government from the summer of 2000 until the election in February 2001.

Table 11.1 *Types of government in twenty-one parliamentary democracies (as at November 2008)*

Type of government	Country
Majority government / one party	Australia, Britain, Turkey, Greece, Portugal
Minority government / one party	Spain, Canada
Minimal winning coalition	Austria, Ireland, Belgium, Germany, Holland, Hungary, Japan, Israel, Norway, Sweden
Surplus coalition	Finland, Switzerland, New Zealand
Minority coalition	Denmark

Source: Israel Democracy Institute 2008.

11.4 Theories of Coalition Formation

Is it possible to formulate rules to help accurately predict the type of coalition likely to emerge, based on the balance of power among the parties? The size of the parties and their ideological views are the principal factors in models developed for predicting a coalition. The basic assumption is that the players are rational and seek to maximize their gains in terms of jobs (ministerial and other appointments) and political achievements (ideology). According to this assumption, the players try to form a minimal winning coalition – a parliamentary majority with as few partners as possible.

In this type of coalition, the negotiations are perceived as a zero-sum game with fixed returns and, consequently, the players seek to form a coalition without surplus parties. The problem is that in a multiparty system there are many permutations of minimal winning coalitions, and it is impossible to reach an unequivocal prediction. For example, Figure 11.1 shows seven potential minimal winning coalitions (Model A) in a simplified system with just five parties (Riker 1962). To narrow the possibilities, Model B is proposed: it assumes that, of the possible minimal winning coalitions, the one with the smallest number of seats will be formed. In the example below, this assumption narrows the potential coalitions from seven to two.

In Models C and D, we add the ideological dimension and ask how the parties' views and positions on the ideological axis affect the likelihood of joining a particular coalition. Model C, which examines the "smallest ideological distance," takes into consideration not only the parliamentary majority and size of the parties, but also their views. The assumption is that among the possible minimal winning coalitions, the coalition with the smallest ideological distance between its most disparate parties will have the greatest chance of materializing (Diskin 2000; Atmor et al. 2009, 1). Of the seven minimal winning coalitions in Figure 11.1, the distance between the extremes is smaller in three of them than in the other four.

Model D further refines Model C, distinguishing between a "closed" coalition, in which there is a continuum of ideologically proximate parties, and an "open" coalition, which skips over one of the parties in the continuum of ideological views (De Swaan 1973). The model assumes that if there is an open (non-continuous) coalition among the potential coalitions with the "smallest ideological distance," then it is reasonable to assume that a party or parties that fall within the ideological span of the coalition partners will join the coalition. In other words, there will be a tendency

Left-wing parties	←――――――――――――――→					Right-wing parties
	Far left 6	Left 51	Center 8	Right 47	Far right 8	
Model A Minimal winning	Seven possibilities: Far right–right–center (63); far right–right–far left (61); far right–center–left (67); far right–left–far left (65); right–left (98); center–left–far left (65); right–center–far left (61)					
Model B Smallest minimal winning	Two possibilities: Far right–right–left (61); right–center–far left (61)					
Model C Smallest ideological distance	Three possibilities: Far right–right–center (63); right–left (98); center–left–far left (65)					
Model D Distance and ideological continuity	Three possibilities: Far right–right–center (63); right–center–left (106); center–left–far left (65)					

Figure 11.1 Coalitions according to the four models – hypothetical distribution of 120 Knesset seats

to create a "closed" coalition, even if the additional party or parties are *not essential* for a parliamentary majority. In Figure 11.1, two of the coalitions in Model C are closed in any case, but the additional possibility of a left–right coalition is not likely because of the lack of ideological continuity. Model D assumes that a centrist party will be brought into the coalition despite the fact that it is "superfluous" – that it would create a "surplus coalition" of 106 MKs, which is more parties than necessary for achieving a parliamentary majority.

If we examine the coalitions formed over the course of Israel's parliamentary history according to Figure 11.1, it appears that only Model D of ideological continuity would usually (but not always) predict the type of coalition. Why are the other models generally unsuccessful at predictions? Most of the coalitions in Israel have been "surplus," including superfluous partners. During the period of the Yishuv and the early years of the state, the tendency to form surplus coalitions could be attributed to the principle of inclusiveness: The political leaders aspired to include a large number of parties in the government as part of consociational politics in an effort to prevent parties from boycotting the political system (see Chapter 1).

Mapai could afford surplus coalitions because of its dominant role as the ruling party and core of the coalition, and it continued to prefer this option even after the principle of inclusiveness began to crumble due to the instability of coalitions and the many crises that led to the frequent departure of parties from coalitions. Prime ministers learned from this experience, and after 1977 they sought to strengthen the stability of their government by forming a surplus coalition; such coalitions allowed greater room for maneuvering because they did not automatically lose their parliamentary majority if one party quit the coalition. Consequently, minimal winning coalitions are rare in Israeli politics, and generally came into being during the course of a Knesset term. Immediately after the election, the clear tendency is to form a broad coalition. Only a few coalitions started out as minimal winning coalitions after Knesset elections – the coalition headed by Menachem Begin[5] in 1981 and the one led by Yitzhak Rabin in 1992. The coalition formed after the 2013 election came close to being minimal with three parties out of four in a position to dissolve the majority.

Another explanation for the failure of the models to forecast coalitions in Israel is that, in most countries, it is relatively easy to place the parties on a single ideological axis (usually left–right), while in Israel the ideological continuum is not clear and unequivocal, and the parties can be placed on at least two ideological axes: security–foreign policy as one axis and religion–state relations as the other. This complexity can explain exceptional cases such as the participation of religious parties in coalitions that are not closed ideologically. Still, in the overwhelming majority of cases, until recently, the positions of the parties on security and foreign affairs and their location on the ideological continuum of hawkishness–dovishness were the determining factors in forming coalitions. Thus, the coalitions in Israel were closed in regard to issues of security and foreign affairs, except for a few cases of "skipping" over parties like Agudat Yisrael and Shas (which are difficult to pin down, or whose views changed on matters of security and foreign policy).[6] Since the mid-1990s, the coalitions have no longer been closed, particularly due to the strengthening of the ultra-Orthodox parties and their frequent control of the balancing point on the axis, the growing role of narrow-interest politics, and the weakness of all of the parties. The coalition formed after the 2009 election was not closed because it left out a centrist party like Kadima and included parties that were very distant from the others ideologically – on foreign policy and security issues as well as religion–state relations. Similarly, the coalition formed after the 2013 election left out the two more right-wing ultra-Orthodox parties, and included Yesh Atid and Hatnuah – more centrist ones. Conversely, the 2015 coalition (see Table 11.2) is right wing and closed.

11.5 Data on Coalitions in Israel

The heterogeneous Israeli society and the proportional system of election engenders a multiparty political system in which a single party has never held a majority in the Knesset. To achieve a parliamentary majority that ensures relative stability, large parties that are capable of forming a government seek to create a coalition based on a surplus majority (see Tuttnauer 2013). Table 11.2 shows that, in most cases, the large parties do not make do with a minimal winning coalition. Instead, they aim to form broad coalitions that include "superfluous" partners that are not required for a parliamentary majority. This practice, which contradicts the theory of minimal winning coalitions, was rooted in the aforementioned principle of inclusiveness – the desire to include as many political movements as possible in the national consensus.

[5] Begin's first coalition (1977) started as a minimal winning coalition for tactical reasons on the assumption that Dash would eventually join and enlarge its parliamentary majority.

[6] Diskin (2000) describes four types of parties that are difficult to place on the ideological continuum and "ruin" the closed coalition model: religious parties, one-person parties, single-issue parties, and ethnic parties. If these are removed from the ideological continuum, the predictive ability of the closed coalition model improves significantly.

Table 11.2 *Coalitions in Israel 1949–2015*

Knesset	No.	Date formed	Prime minister	Coalition partners*	Knesset majority	Type of coalition	Ideology
1st	1	03/49	Ben-Gurion	Mapai + Sephardi affiliates, Progressives, Religious Front	73	Surplus	Center-religious
	2	11/50	Ben-Gurion	Mapai + Sephardi affiliates, Progressives, Religious Front	73	Surplus	Center-religious
2nd	3	10/51	Ben-Gurion	Mapai + affiliates, Hapoel Ha-Mizrahi, Mizrahi, Agudat Yisrael, Poalei Agudat Yisrael	65	Surplus	Center-religious
	4	12/52	Ben-Gurion	Mapai + affiliates, Hapoel Ha-Mizrahi, Mizrahi, Progressives, General Zionists	87	Surplus	Center-religious-right
	5	01/54	Sharett	Mapai + affiliates, Hapoel Ha-Mizrahi, Mizrahi, Progressives, General Zionists	87	Surplus	Center-religious-right
	6	06/55	Sharett	Mapai + affiliates, Hapoel Ha-Mizrahi, Mizrahi, Progressives	64	Minimal winning	Center-religious
3rd	7	11/55	Ben-Gurion	Mapai + affiliates, NRP, Progressives, Ahdut Ha'avoda, Mapam	80	Surplus	Center-religious-left
	8	01/58	Ben-Gurion	Mapai + affiliates, NRP, Progressives, Ahdut Ha'avoda, Mapam	80	Surplus	Center-religious-left
4th	9	12/59	Ben-Gurion	Mapai + affiliates, NRP, Progressives, Ahdut Ha'avoda, Mapam, Religious Front	86	Surplus	Center-religious-left
5th	10	11/61	Ben-Gurion	Mapai + affiliates, Ahdut Ha'avoda, NRP, Poalei Agudat Yisrael	68	Surplus	Center-religious
	11	06/63	Eshkol	Mapai + affiliates, NRP, Ahdut Ha'avoda, Poalei Agudat Yisrael	68	Surplus	Center-religious
	12	12/64	Eshkol	Mapai + affiliates, NRP, Ahdut Ha'avoda, Poalei Agudat Yisrael	68	Surplus	Center-religious
6th	13	01/66	Eshkol	Alignment + affiliates, NRP, Poalei Agudat Yisrael, Independent Liberals, Mapam	75	Surplus	Center-religious / ultra-Orthodox-left
	14	06/67	Eshkol	Alignment + affiliates, NRP, Poalei Agudat Yisrael, Independent Liberals, Mapam, Gahal, Rafi	107	Surplus	Unity
	15	03/69	Meir	Alignment + affiliates, Gahal, NRP, Mapam, Independent Liberals, Poalei Agudat Yisrael	107	Surplus	Unity
7th	16	12/69	Meir	Alignment + affiliates, Gahal, NRP, Independent Liberals	102	Surplus	Unity
	17	08/70	Meir	Alignment + affiliates, Independent Liberals, NRP	76	Surplus	Center-religious

8th	18	03/74	Meir	Alignment + affiliates, Independent Liberals, NRP	68	Surplus	Center-religious
	19	06/74	Rabin	Alignment + affiliates, Independent Liberals, Ratz	61	Minimal winning	Center-left
	20	10/74	Rabin	Alignment + affiliates, Independent Liberals, NRP	68	Surplus	Center-religious
9th	21	06/77	Begin	Likud + Moshe Dayan, NRP, Agudat Yisrael	62	Minimal winning	Right-religious
	22	10/77	Begin	Likud + Moshe Dayan, Dash, NRP, Agudat Yisrael	77	Surplus	Right-center-religious
10th	23	08/81	Begin	Likud, NRP, Tami, Agudat Yisrael	61	Minimal winning	Right-religious
	24	10/83	Shamir	Likud, Tehiya, Telem, NRP, Tami, Agudat Yisrael	64	Surplus	Right-religious
11th	25	09/84	Peres	Labor, Likud, NRP, Shas, Agudat Yisrael, Yahad, Shinui, Morasha, Ometz	97	Surplus	Unity
	26	10/86	Shamir	Labor, Likud, NRP, Shas, Agudat Yisrael, Yahad, Shinui, Morasha, Ometz	96	Surplus	Unity
12th	27	12/88	Shamir	Likud, Labor, Shas, NRP, Agudat Yisrael	95	Surplus	Unity
	28	06/90	Shamir	Likud, NRP, Shas, Degel Hatorah, Tehiya, Tzomet, Moledet, MKs Peretz and Mizrahi	62	Minimal winning	Right-religious
13th	29	07/92	Rabin	Labor, Shas, Meretz	62	Minimal winning	Center-religious-left
	30	09/93	Rabin	Labor, Meretz	56	Minority	Center-left
	31	11/95	Peres	Labor, Meretz, Yiud	58	Minority	Center-left
14th	32	06/96	Netanyahu	Likud–Gesher–Tzomet, Shas, UTJ, NRP, Yisrael B'Aliyah, The Third Way	67	Surplus	Right-religious
15th	33	07/99	Barak	Labor, Center, Shas, NRP, UTJ, Yisrael B'Aliyah, Meretz	75	Surplus	Center-religious-left
	34	03/01	Sharon	Likud, Labor, Shas, Yisrael B'Aliyah, National Union–Yisrael Beitenu	77	Surplus	Unity
16th	35	02/03	Sharon	Likud, Shinui, NRP, National Union	68	Surplus	Center-right-religious
	36	01/05	Sharon	Likud, Labor, UTJ	64	Minimal winning	Unity

(*Continued*)

Table 11.2 (*Cont.*)

Knesset	No.	Date formed	Prime minister	Coalition partners*	Knesset majority	Type of coalition	Ideology
17th	37	05/06	Olmert	Kadima, Labor, Shas, Gil	67	Minimal winning	Center-religious
	38	10/06	Olmert	Kadima, Labor, Shas, Gil, Yisrael Beitenu (the latter quit in 1/2008, and the government returned to its previous makeup)	78	Surplus	Center-religious-right
18th	39	03/09	Netanyahu	Likud, Yisrael Beitenu, Labor, Shas, New NRP, UTJ**	74	Surplus	Right-religious-center
19th	40	03/13	Netanyahu	Likud–Yisrael Beitenu, Yesh Atid, Jewish Home, Hatnuah	68	Surplus	Right-center-religious (without ultra-Orthodox parties)
20th	41	05/15	Netanyahu	Likud, Kulanu, Jewish Home, Shas, UT	61	Minimal winning	Right-religious-ultra-Orthodox-center

Notes: The Knesset website lists only thirty-four "official governments" for the reasons cited in the text. This table does not show coalitions as new if the changes were short-lived (e.g., the departure of the General Zionists in May–June 1953 or the resignation of Shas in May–June 2002), or parties that joined the coalition within a month after its formation. Also not included are coalition changes between the dates listed, or that stem from electoral considerations near the end of a Knesset term (e.g., the resignation of Labor from the first Sharon government in 2002).

* In calculating "coalition partners" we included parties or MKs that were not official members of the government, such as the Arab lists affiliated with Mapai in the years 1949–73. The support of Arab parties given to the Rabin Coalition (1992–95) was excluded because it was partial.

** In January 2011, sixty-six MKs remained in the coalition after the Labor Party resigned from it; the five remaining Labor MKs constituted themselves as the Independence Party.

Therefore, the coalitions formed immediately after an election have usually been surplus coalitions or, less frequently (a total of nine through 2015), minimal winning coalitions. In the few cases in which minority coalitions were formed, they were difficult to function and did not survive long.

The number of governments Israel has had is defined by the criterion of whether the prime minister presented a government to the Knesset and asked for its vote of confidence. Thus, between the elections for the first Knesset (1949) and the twentieth Knesset (2015), thirty-four governments have served in the state of Israel (see Knesset website). The composition of the coalition can change during the course of a government's term, thus there have been more coalitions than governments. On the one hand, it is possible to treat each change in the government's lineup as a "new coalition," but this would yield a large number of coalitions and would not contribute to understanding the real changes in the government. On the other hand, if we only examine the thirty-four cases in which the prime minister asked for the Knesset's confidence, we would miss significant changes in the composition of the government. In Table 11.2, the count is functional and lists forty-one coalitions through the end of 2015 based on the considerations described in the notes.

The surplus coalition has been the most common type in Israel. Though eleven of the forty-one coalitions in Table 11.2 were not of this type, this percentage is misleading because minimal winning coalitions and minority coalitions were of very short duration (the longest of them were the Begin government of 1981–83; the Shamir government of 1990–92; the Rabin government of 1992–95; and the Sharon government of 2005–6).[7] The number of parties participating in coalitions ranges from two to nine; most often, there were four to five parties. On average, a coalition was based on a parliamentary majority of seventy-five MKs. However, many coalitions (nineteen of forty-one) relied on a majority of sixty-one to sixty-nine MKs; nine relied on a majority of seventy to seventy-nine MKs; and five on a majority of eighty to eighty-nine MKs. The six national unity government coalitions each comprised over ninety MKs. Two coalitions formally numbered fewer than sixty MKs, but they relied in practice on parliamentary support from Arab parties. Coalition governments survived for less than two years on average, completing only about two-thirds of their maximum term (Nachmias and Arbel-Ganz 2005). Nonetheless, the average duration of the Knesset term was more than three years; governments came and went for various reasons, not necessarily because of a coalition crisis.[8]

Coalitions have a bad reputation in Israeli society because of the undignified haggling that sometimes accompanies their formation. On the other hand, Table 11.2 indicates that most of the time the coalitions fulfilled their role as a mechanism for creating consensus among social groups. As noted in Chapter 9, the coalition problems since the 1990s are attributable to a decline in the status of political parties, and are not derived from the need to form a coalition.

7 Netanyahu's coalition of 2013–15 was surplus because the resignation of Hatnuah (six seats) would not necessarily dismantle it. In practice, however, it was a minimal winning coalition and indeed quickly dissolved.

8 Such as early elections due to a "crisis of the fourth year" – as the end of term approaches, parties quit the coalition, assuming they will derive greater electoral benefit from not being a member of the coalition (Atmor et al. 2009, 21).

11.6 Coalition Negotiations

The formation of coalitions in Israel is a complex and complicated political task. Coalition negotiation is a process in which representatives of the parties negotiate to forge collaboration and establish a government that will win a vote of confidence from the Knesset. Coalition partners formulate a political program – basic policy guidelines designed to bridge the gaps between them, as well as coalition agreements defining the division of executive positions. Negotiations begin immediately after the election, but the formal process starts only after the president of the state consults with representatives of the parties to determine who has the best prospects of forming a coalition, and assigns the task to that MK (see Chapter 5).[9]

A. Duration of the Negotiations

The MK given the mandate to form a coalition holds discussions with the other parties. While all parties could theoretically become coalition members (as they duly represent the wishes of their voters), this is not the case in reality. Ben-Gurion made a practice of not inviting two parties he regarded as outside the consensus ("without Herut and Maki" became one of his catchphrases); Hadash and the Arab parties have never been considered candidates for a coalition, and the same applied to the National Union when it formed (1999).[10] As noted, ideological proximity is usually a criterion, especially on issues of security and foreign policy, which once largely determined coalition membership. Still, talks are also held with unlikely political bedfellows, in an attempt to strengthen the bargaining position of the party forming the coalition vis-à-vis its "natural partners."

Until the 1977 election, coalition negotiations were long and drawn out – lasting an average of sixty-six days after the election (or about forty days after receipt of the mandate to form a coalition). Since 1977, the negotiation period has shortened to an average of thirty-six days after the election (twenty-three days after the assignment to form a coalition).[11] How do we explain the 55 percent decrease in the average amount of time required to form a coalition? In the initial years after the founding of Israel, it was clear which party would rule and, more or less, which parties would be its coalition partners. The hegemonic status of Mapai/Labor Alignment until 1977 allowed for a comfortable bargaining position vis-à-vis its partners, and it was in no hurry to conclude coalition deals. Moreover, the extended period from the election until assignment of the role was used by the parties for coalition negotiations, and only after the joint platform of the future coalition partners began to emerge did the president announce the designated prime minister. Prolonged coalition negotiations after the 1961 election led to an amendment of the Transition Law in 1962 to shorten this period. The MK tapped to form the government was required to do so within fourteen days, with the option of a 45-day

[9] This description does not apply to the three coalitions formed during the period of direct election, when the prime minister-elect cobbled together a coalition without the need for formal appointment by the president.

[10] President Chaim Herzog did not invite MK Meir Kahane to coalition talks in 1984 because Kahane's racist views were inconsistent with democratic partnership.

[11] Through 1973, the president assigned the task of forming a government an average of twenty-five days after the election. Since 1977, the average is about fourteen days after the election.

extension granted by the president. In the Basic Law: Government 1968, the time period was limited to twenty-one days, with the option of extension. Under the Basic Law: Government 1992, no consultation with the president was required because the prime minister was elected directly, and the period of coalition formation was shortened to the net time between the election and presentation of the government to the Knesset. In the current Basic Law: Government, a period of twenty-eight days is granted from the time an MK is assigned this task, with possible extensions of fourteen days each. After the 2015 election, fifty-seven days were needed to form the government.

After 1977, the identity of the ruling party was no longer obvious, and negotiations sometimes centered on who would be the prime minister. Furthermore, there was no longer one pivotal party – the status of being the coalition axis shifted from one party to another, and the variety of coalition permutations increased significantly. In these fluid conditions with ideological proximity no longer the sole consideration and many parties willing to join a coalition, the president had incentive to quickly assign the task of coalition formation to the MK with the best prospect of success.

B. Negotiation Topics: Ideology and Benefits

Coalition negotiations are conducted in two channels that partly overlap. First, a common denominator for disparate world views must be found, and agreement must be reached on the main policy guidelines of the future government regarding general public matters as well as specific issues that are important to one of the partners. Second, the parties must agree about the allocation of ministerial portfolios, other executive positions, budgets, and so on. In politics, agreement on ideological matters is vague, certainly compared to the allocation of portfolios. However, ideology may be woven into tangible benefits, such as a party's demand to receive a particular government ministry. In recent years, less weight has been given to ideological considerations in coalition negotiations, even on matters of security and foreign affairs, while bargaining over benefits has intensified. An indirect way to examine the ideological "achievements" of a party is to compare the coalition agreement it signs with its platform, election propaganda, and demands prior to joining the government.

Coalition benefits include the allocation of appointments as ministers with or without portfolio, deputy ministers, other civil service positions (e.g., ambassadors), and positions in statutory authorities or government corporations. There are other titles to allocate – "acting prime minister," "vice prime minister," "deputy prime minister," chairs of parliamentary committees, and sometimes positions in the Jewish Agency, the Jewish National Fund, the United Jewish Appeal, and Israel Bonds. In the past, these benefits also included agreements on local government coalitions, but this ended in 1978 when the direct election of mayors was instituted. Concerning government ministries, an informal hierarchy of "portfolio weight" evolved. The heaviest – the Ministries of Defense, Finance, and Foreign Affairs; in the second tier – Education, Economics (industry and commerce), Justice, Housing, and Infrastructure; in the third – the remaining ministries; and in the fourth – ministers without portfolio.

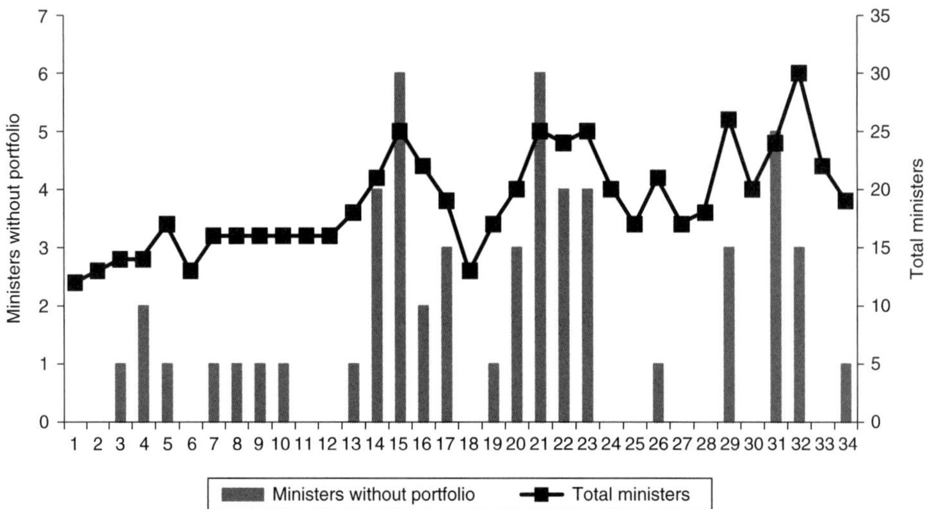

Figure 11.2 Ministers without portfolios in new governments (1949–2015)
Note: Only official government formations are listed – those presented to the Knesset for a vote of confidence by the prime minister.
Source: Knesset website.

C. Number of Ministers

Over the years, coalition pressures have led to an increase in the number of ministers (Felsenthal 1979). Governments in Israel, from 1949 to 2015, were formed with an average of nineteen ministers. The number of ministers in Israel's first governments did not exceed fifteen; the 2009 government, headed by Netanyahu, topped the list with thirty ministers; and the 2015 government, also led by Netanyahu, numbered nineteen ministers and eight deputy ministers. An amendment to the Basic Law: Government in 2014 stipulates that the number of ministers cannot exceed nineteen, but allows for additional ministers if approved by a majority of seventy MKs.

Figure 11.2 shows that the sharp rise in ministers began with the National Unity Government (number 14) formed in June 1967. Subsequently, the number of ministers was limited by law during the period of direct election of the prime minister (1996), and climbed again after an amendment initiated by Prime Minister Ehud Barak in 1999 to inflate the number of ministers in his government to twenty-three. On average, each new government had 1.7 ministers without portfolio, and some governments had no ministers without portfolio. The fifteenth government (under Golda Meir) and the twenty-first government (under Shimon Peres) hold the record for most ministers without portfolio – six. The number of deputy ministers ranges from none to nine.

11.7 Notable Coalition Negotiations

We review here some coalition negotiations in the political history of Israel that marked significant ideological change, or had other unique characteristics. We describe the background (the election, coalition crises); the political balance of power among the participants; the size of the parties and position of pivotal control;

the dynamic of the coalition talks; and the agreement itself. We also discuss the ideological concessions forced upon the large party and the coalition benefits of the partners. In each of the figures below, the parties are on a left–right continuum *according to their positions on security and foreign affairs*. It is difficult to place the ultra-Orthodox parties, some of the small parties, and some of the short-lived parties.

A. 1952: A Turn to the Right – General Zionists Join

Until the 1961 election, which was moved up because of the crisis over the "Lavon affair," the dynamic of coalition formation was similar each time. Mapai, the dominant party in the multiparty system, held the pivot position, and even though it never won a parliamentary majority on its own, a government could not be formed without it. Mapai's political rivals – from left and right – could not cobble together an alternative government in light of the ideological gaps between them. In fact, the bloc of workers' parties (together with the Arab parties affiliated with Mapai) constituted an absolute majority in the Knesset. Thus, Ben-Gurion could have formed a "natural" center-left coalition from an ideological viewpoint, but he chose not to. Mapai distrusted Mapam, the second-largest party in the first Knesset (nineteen seats), and was wary of its pro-Soviet orientation. Negotiations between the two parties were conducted in a way that allowed no chance of success. Consequently, the first three coalitions were based on cooperation between Mapai (and its affiliated parties), the religious parties, and the Progressives. This collaboration and the surplus coalitions they produced would continue until the 1970s (see Table 11.2). Nonetheless, they were unstable because of the fierce dispute over the status of religion in the new state. The frequent coalition crises and its failure in local elections in 1950 led Mapai to turn rightward in the second Knesset and form the coalition shown in Figure 11.3.

In December 1952, Ben-Gurion resigned from the government and Mapai again preferred to rule out Mapam, this time turning to the General Zionists (twenty MKs in the 1951 election and another three who joined them) as a counterweight to the religious parties. During the coalition talks, Mapai accepted several of the General Zionists' ideological demands:

- Economics: freezing wages for workers for one year; limiting the income tax ceiling to 50 percent; cutbacks in public expenditures.
- Government: examining the possibility of raising the Knesset electoral threshold to 10 percent (not practical in light of opposition from the Progressives).
- Education: canceling the different streams within two years (practicable, despite opposition from the religious parties).
- Coalition benefits: the General Zionists received important ministries – Industry and Commerce, Interior, Transportation, and Health.

The Progressives joined the coalition after the demand to raise the electoral threshold was formulated in vague language and the Justice Ministry was returned to Pinchas Rosen. After the government won the Knesset's vote of confidence, Mizrahi and Ha-Mizrahi also joined, based on a promise that religious education would continue to operate separately within the state education system. There were eighty-seven MKs in the new coalition (including support from Mapai's affiliated parties), and sixteen ministers in the government. Mapai retained all the first-tier ministries

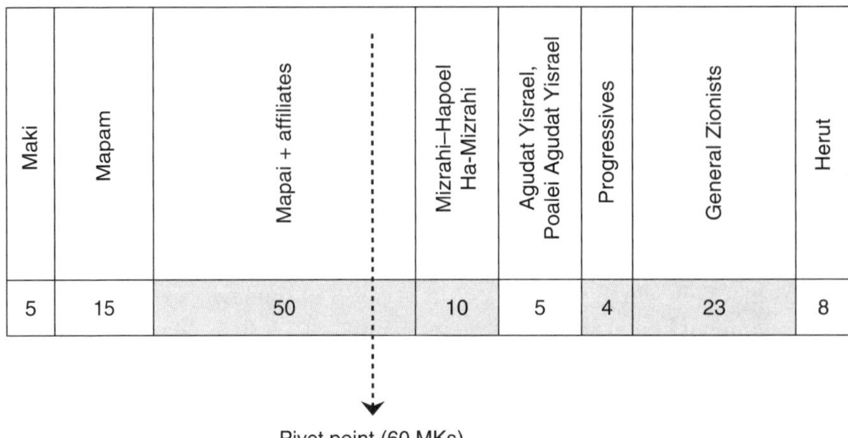

Figure 11.3 The fourth coalition (December 1952) by the parties' positions on security and foreign affairs
Note: The parties in the coalition are shaded gray.

(Defense, Finance, and Foreign Affairs) and secured a majority for itself in the government with nine ministers. Like its predecessors, this was also a surplus coalition that was closed ideologically on security and foreign policies.

B. 1955: First Coalition of the Entire Labor Movement

The collaboration between Mapai and the General Zionists ended after two and a half years. In the 1955 election, the General Zionists dropped to thirteen seats and preferred to remain outside the coalition. Mapai (40+5) still held the pivot position, but since it only had a minimal majority of sixty-one MKs (with eleven MKs from the NRP and five from the Progressives), it turned to the left for the first time, to the two other workers' parties: Ahdut Ha'avoda and Mapam. After the former broke away from Mapam, there was less of a threat from the left against Mapai's hegemony, especially as their Soviet orientation weakened during that period. Difficult birth pains accompanied this change, and the coalition negotiations were the longest in the history of Israel's governments – no fewer than 100 days passed from the election until the new government was presented.

Profound disagreements were resolved through compromise: Ahdut Ha'avoda was forced to settle for a deputy minister in the Agriculture Ministry; the religious parties demanded the Education Ministry and made do with a deputy minister in charge of state-religious education; a formula was found to resolve differences with the Progressive Party over the wages of public sector employees. The coalition was formed soon after the arms deal between Czechoslovakia and Egypt, and the government's basic guidelines emphasized military readiness, foreshadowing the ensuing events (the 1956 Sinai operation). The government declared that it would continue to adhere to the armistice agreements with its neighbors. Israel's foreign affairs, the government stated, would be based on security needs, Jewish immigration, economic development and independence, the needs of the Jewish Diaspora, and allegiance to the principles of the UN Charter (Knesset Protocols, Knesset 3, session 19, November 2, 1955, 229).

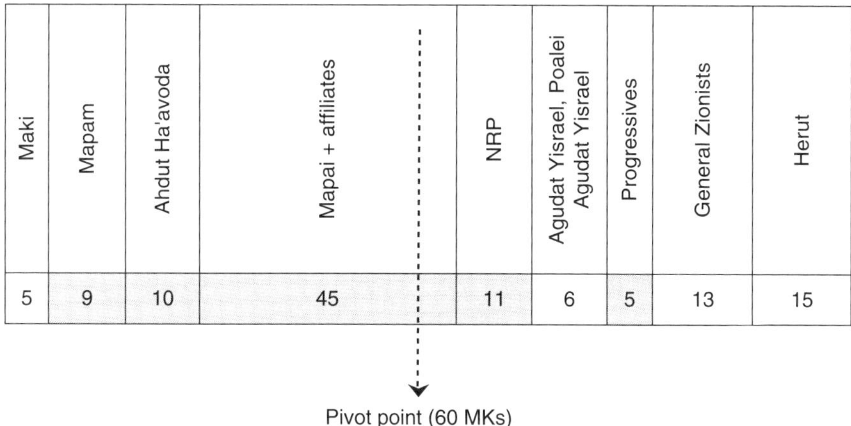

Figure 11.4 The seventh coalition (November 1955) by the parties' positions on security and foreign affairs
Note: The parties in the coalition are shaded gray.

The coalition included five partners and a majority of eighty MKs. Mapai had a majority in the government, composed of seventeen ministers, and continued to hold the most important portfolios. The Progressives retained the Ministry of Justice; the NRP kept the Religious Affairs portfolio and received the Ministry of Postal Services in addition; Ahdut Ha'avoda was assigned the Interior and Transportation Ministries, while Mapam had the Development and Health portfolios. It was a surplus coalition, and, with the exception of the ultra-Orthodox parties (which ceased to participate in the coalition after the crisis over the conscription of women into the IDF three years earlier), it was a closed coalition in its ideological continuum on security and foreign policy.

C. 1961: The Short-Lived Rebellion of the "Club of Four"

The early election in 1961 was held in the wake of the Lavon affair and saw Mapai drop from forty-seven to forty-two seats. The decline in public support compelled Mapai to conduct negotiations from a position of relative inferiority for the first time. While it still played the pivot role, the combined strength of the four parties that Mapai considered "suitable" (the NRP, Ahdut Ha'avoda, Mapam, and the Liberals) totaled forty-six seats, the same number as Mapai and its affiliated lists. These four parties formed a tactical front (the "Club of Four") for jointly conducting coalition talks (Galnoor 1961). They insisted on entering the coalition as a single bloc and demanded half the portfolios in the government and half the important ministries. Theoretically, the Club of Four could have formed a coalition of sixty-eight MKs with Agudat Yisrael and Herut, but in those days this was impossible because of the parties' disparate world views. Ben-Gurion was unable to drive a wedge between the members of the club, gave up in exhaustion, and turned the negotiations over to Levi Eshkol. This had significant repercussions, because Ben-Gurion sought to build a coalition with the Liberals, while Eshkol preferred Ahdut Ha'avoda.

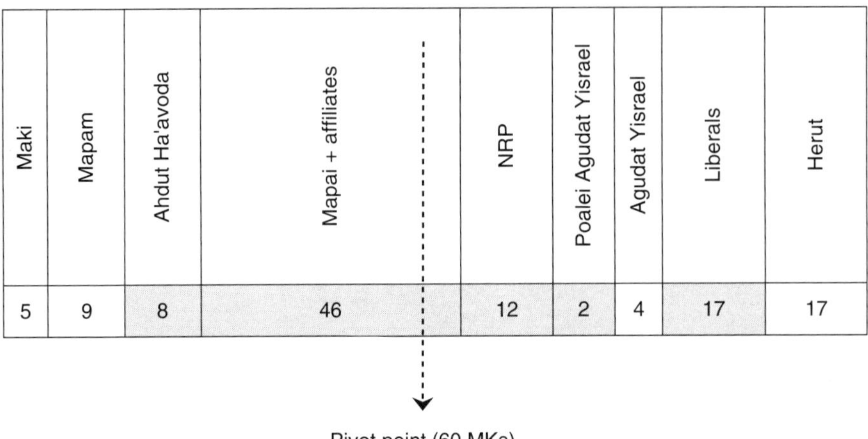

Figure 11.5 The tenth coalition (November 1961) by the parties' positions on security and foreign affairs
Note: The parties in the coalition are shaded gray. Liberals: General Zionists + Progressives

Eshkol succeeded in persuading the NRP to quit the Club of Four and join Mapai's coalition in exchange for three government ministries – Interior, Religious Affairs, and Welfare. Ahdut Ha'avoda was the next to join and received two portfolios – transportation and labor (the first time that Mapai relinquished the labor portfolio). Mapam and the Liberals remained outside the coalition.

This was a coalition of only sixty-eight MKs, the narrowest in six years. Despite its electoral weakness, Mapai managed to increase its number of ministers in the narrow government – from nine to eleven. It retained its monopoly over the Defense, Finance, and Foreign Affairs Ministries. Poalei Agudat Yisrael joined the coalition and made do with deputy minister in the Education Ministry. Another price was raising the number of deputy ministers to six. The coalition is categorized as surplus (the departure of Poalei Agudat Yisrael would not have jeopardized the majority), but it was potentially unstable because the resignation of the NRP or Ahdut Ha'avoda would have toppled the coalition. From an ideological perspective, the coalition was closed, and it lasted, with minor changes and despite Ben-Gurion's resignation in 1963, until the election in 1965.

In retrospect, the decision to leave the Liberals outside the coalition was a catalyst for the formation of Gahal and the subsequent changes in the map of parties in Israel. The struggle to form the coalition in 1961 marked the beginning of the decline in Mapai's hegemony, which accelerated with the departure of Ben-Gurion from the political stage two years later.

D. 1967: The First, Hastily Formed, National Unity Government

Following the 1965 election, Levi Eshkol formed a broad coalition of seventy-five MKs. However, the deteriorating security situation in early June 1967 and the public campaign that undermined confidence in the prime minister and his government led to the expansion of the coalition by bringing two more parties into the

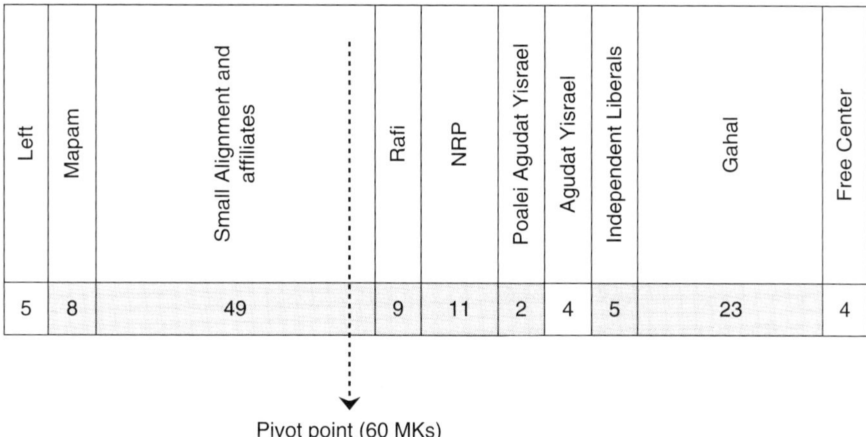

Figure 11.6 The fourteenth coalition (June 1967) by the parties' positions on security and foreign affairs
Note: The parties in the coalition are shaded gray. Gahal: Herut + Liberals bloc; Rafi: Workers of Israel List led by Ben-Gurion; Small Alignment: Mapai + Ahdut Ha'avoda; Left: Rakah (three), Maki (one), Haolam Hazeh (one).

government: Rafi (with Moshe Dayan as defense minister) and Gahal (two ministerial positions without portfolio, one for Menachem Begin). After hasty negotiations, the National Unity Government was established, whose main goal was to boost public morale during the tense days prior to the war (A. Arian 1990). The emergency situation prevented discussion of ideological questions or changes in the ministerial assignments, except for the defense portfolio. The coalition relied on a wide and unprecedented base of no fewer than 107 MKs, with a record twenty-one ministers.

This government was a harbinger of things to come in Israeli politics. First, it set a precedent for a National Unity Government whose strength lies in its ability to mobilize most of the political forces in Israel, and whose weakness is its inability to make decisions during times of peace. The unity government continued to serve for about three years, until 1970, and created an unsound situation from a democratic perspective: There was no significant opposition in the Knesset. Second, this coalition broke the taboo against including Herut in the government and paved the way for the so-called "upheaval" ten years later. Third, it facilitated the return of Rafi (except for Ben-Gurion, who refused to join the coalition) to Mapai/Alignment and the subsequent addition of Mapam. Fourth, it broke Mapai's monopoly on the most important government portfolios.

This was a surplus coalition, of course, which was also closed ideologically, with the usual exception of Agudat Yisrael; the far left and the Free Center Party, which split from Gahal, remained outside the coalition. However, the ideological distance between coalition partners was greater than ever. Consequently, the government was unable to decide on the critical issue of the future of the territories conquered in 1967.

E. 1977: The "Upheaval" and a Right-Religious Coalition Takes Over

The Likud victory in the 1977 election completely transformed the political system that had existed for over thirty years, since the Yishuv period. Israeli democracy successfully withstood this turnover in power, and the labor movement led by the Labor Party lost its hegemony over state affairs. Signs of this had appeared with the Lavon affair in the 1960s, the Unity Government in 1967, and particularly the aftermath of the Yom Kippur War in 1973, but the unequivocal change and the electoral gap between Likud (forty-three) and the Alignment (thirty-two) came as a shock to most pundits. Likud took over the pivot position and, with the addition of Ariel Sharon's Shlomtzion party and the religious parties, had a majority bloc of sixty-two MKs. The fifteen seats of the newly formed Dash party were not enough to make it the power broker, and the NRP's decision to join the Likud government thwarted the Alignment's efforts to form a government under its leadership.[12] Nonetheless, the process of forming the Begin government was complex and Likud made far-reaching commitments to its religious partners (the NRP and Agudat Yisrael). On the other hand, Dash's main demands – changing the electoral system and recognizing the principle of territorial compromise – were not accepted, and Dash remained outside of Begin's initial coalition, which numbered sixty-two MKs. Tactically, the quick formation of a narrow coalition proved itself, and Dash joined four months later, accepting most of Likud's conditions.

The 1977 coalition agreement:

- Thirty-two of the forty-three articles in the coalition agreement addressed issues of importance to the religious public: substantial easing of the IDF's conscription of women; amendment of the Law of Return; amendment of the Anatomy and Pathology Law; a stricter process for granting Sabbath work permits; increased financial support for religious institutions; giving the education portfolio to the NRP.
- Agudat Yisrael, which joined the coalition after many years in the opposition, was allowed freedom to vote in the Knesset on religious matters. It turned down a ministerial appointment in exchange for chair of the Knesset Finance Committee (always chaired previously by an MK from the ruling party) and chair of the Welfare Committee.
- On security and foreign policy, the appointment of Moshe Dayan (who was elected to the Knesset on the Alignment slate) as foreign minister was considered an ideological concession by the prime minister. Dash was allowed freedom to vote with regard to the Jewish settlements.
- Herut's partners from the Liberal Party received key portfolios – finance, housing and construction, and industry and commerce; and the NRP, in addition to the Ministry of Education, received the Ministries of Interior and Religious Affairs.

The original government of sixty-two MKs was a minimal winning coalition, while the coalition shown in Figure 11.7 was a surplus – it would not lose its majority if one of its components quit. It was a right-wing-religious closed coalition from an ideological perspective, with the exception of the ultra-Orthodox parties, which were difficult to pin down ideologically on the security and foreign policy axis. The

[12] Theoretically, Shimon Peres could have formed a government of sixty-six MKs: Alignment (thirty-two), Dash (fifteen), NRP + ultra-Orthodox (seventeen), Ratz (one), and Independent Liberals (one). However, the NRP's ideological decision (in light of the growing strength of Gush Emunim and the Young Members party) to jettison its historical alliance with Mapai prevented this, and the NRP ever since has placed itself in the right-hawkish wing of the party map.

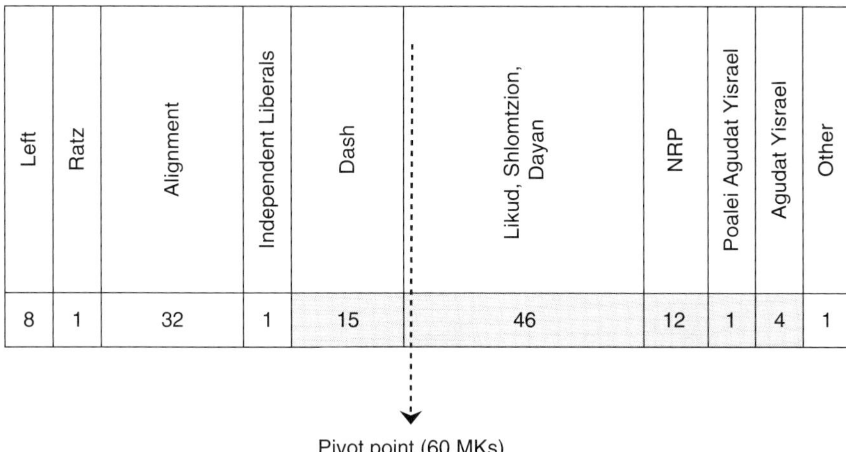

Figure 11.7 The twenty-first coalition (June 1977) by the parties' positions on security and foreign affairs

Note: The parties in the coalition after Dash joined are shaded gray. Regarding the location of the NRP, see footnote 12 in this chapter. Other: Flatto-Sharon; Dash: Democratic List + Shinui; Left: Sheli (two), Hadash (five), United Arab List (one).

decision to join the government led to a schism within Dash that eventually led to its disappearance in the 1981 election.

F. 1984: The Rotation Governments – a Two-Headed Centipede

Election of the eleventh Knesset ended in a tie between the two blocs. The Alignment won forty-four seats, but Likud (forty-one) together with the right-wing and religious parties garnered sixty MKs, which prevented formation of a left-wing government. For the first time in Israeli political history, no large party held the pivot position. Shimon Peres was given the mandate to form a government, but failed.[13] Since neither of the two large parties desired a new election, they agreed to form a grand coalition or National Unity Government.

After thirty-nine days of negotiation, a detailed and precedent-setting agreement was signed that focused mainly on the functioning of the coalition rather than its political content. Central to the agreement was the rotation of prime ministers: Peres would serve for the first half of the term and Yitzhak Shamir for the second. The number of ministers of the Alignment and Likud, and of the left and right blocs, would be identical, for a total of twenty-five ministers and seven deputy ministers – the largest Israeli government until then. Parity was maintained in the allocation of senior portfolios – defense to the Alignment, finance to Likud, and foreign affairs in rotation (Yanai 1990; Donald Horowitz 1990).

[13] More precisely, the Yahad Party, led by former Likud member Ezer Weizman, could have played the role of power broker. Had Weizman agreed to collaborate with Likud (in exchange for the senior position offered him), a unity government would not have been necessary. Weizman supported the Alignment and later joined its ranks.

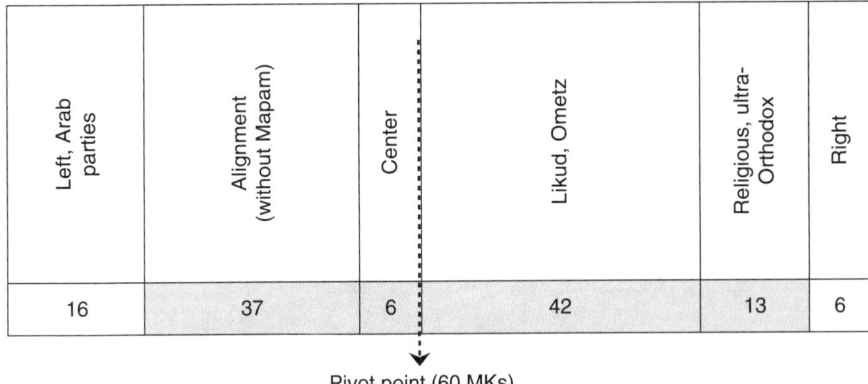

Figure 11.8 The twenty-fifth coalition (September 1984) by the parties' positions on security and foreign affairs

Note: The parties in the coalition are shaded gray. Right: Kach (one), Tehiya-Tzomet (five); religious and ultra-Orthodox: NRP (four); Agudat Yisrael (two), Poalei Agudat Yisrael (two), Shas (four), Tami (one); Center: Shinui (three) and Yahad (three); Left and Arab: MKs who broke away from Alignment (Mapam and Yossi Sarid – seven), Ratz (three), Hadash (four), and the Progressive List for Peace (two).

It was a multiparty, rather than a two-party, coalition, even though the Alignment and Likud held enough seats together (eighty-five) to form a minimal winning coalition without any junior partners. However, the lack of trust between the two large parties made them wary of abandoning their partners. Thus, each surrounded itself with allies from its own bloc – the Alignment with Shinui and Yahad; Likud with the NRP, Shas, Agudat Yisrael, and Ometz. The agreement stated that an inner "cabinet" of senior Alignment and Likud ministers would be formed to deliberate important decisions. The National Unity Government had ninety-seven MKs, and was a closed, surplus coalition ideologically. Only the political "extremes" remained on the outside: on the right (Kach, Tehiya–Tzomet) and on the left (Ratz, Mapam and Yossi Sarid, Hadash and the Progressive List for Peace). The coalition agreement was fully implemented and the unity government completed its term, making several critical decisions, such as the partial withdrawal from Lebanon, the economic plan to curb inflation, and cancelation of the Lavi aircraft project. In the subsequent election of 1988, the bond between the two parties led to the formation of a second National Unity Government, but without rotation due to the edge held by the right-wing bloc.

G. 1990: The Corruption of Coalition Politics

Six years of broad unity governments ended when it became necessary to decide on the future of the territories. Prime Minister Shamir refused to respond to the American peace initiative, and the Alignment (in coordination with Shas) toppled the government in a no-confidence vote. The president asked Peres to form a government because the left-wing bloc, with a pledge of support from Shas and Agudat Yisrael, had sixty MKs and lacked just one for a majority. MK Sharir, who had resigned from Likud, agreed to support the new coalition in exchange for a promise to be appointed minister. The festive Knesset session that convened to present the new government with its coalition of sixty-one MKs turned into a fiasco. Two Agudat Yisrael MKs never showed up and, without the requisite majority, the government could not be formed.

After Peres failed to form a government, the task was assigned to Yitzhak Shamir and the courting continued, this time designed to entice MKs to help Likud reach a majority. MK Sharir was persuaded to return to Likud, and another MK from Agudat Yisrael and one from the Alignment defected to Likud in exchange for promises of appointment as deputy ministers. Shamir managed to put together a narrow government of sixty-two MKs with no fewer than eight parties and splinter groups, and this required many concessions: to the right-wing parties (Moledet, Tehiya, and Tzomet) on foreign affairs; to the religious parties (Shas, NRP, Agudat Yisrael, and Degel Hatorah) on religious matters; and to the individual MKs who joined – jobs. The fragile coalition was a minimal winning one, but it lasted until the election in 1992, perhaps because it was closed ideologically – including Likud and all the parties further to the right. To this day, the events that preceded its formation, coined "the dirty trick," gave a bad name to politics, parties, and the coalition as an institution.

H. 1992: Meretz and Shas under One Roof

In the 1992 election, Labor (forty-four), led by Yitzhak Rabin, recaptured the pivot position by one seat, and formed a bloc with Meretz (twelve), Hadash (three), and the Arab Democratic Party (two), which was sufficient to prevent the formation of a right-wing-religious coalition.[14] Rabin quickly reached agreement with Meretz and, after unsuccessful efforts to enlist Tzomet and United Torah Judaism, he turned to Shas – the most pragmatic of the ultra-Orthodox parties and the most dovish too at the time. The bone of contention was Rabin's promise to appoint Shulamit Aloni minister of education. To reel in Shas, whose six seats ensured a coalition of sixty-two without Hadash and the Arab parties, Labor made a significant ideological concession and agreed to establish an ultra-Orthodox Education and Cultural Division, headed by a deputy minister from Shas. This matter continued to threaten the stability of the coalition until Aloni was replaced as education minister. Another significant concession was the commitment to Shas that any change in the status of the territories would be submitted to a referendum or decided in a general election.

The Labor Party was able to keep the most important portfolios – defense, finance, and foreign affairs. In exchange for the Arab parties' external support for the coalition, agreements were signed on changes in government policy toward the Arab citizens and larger budgetary allocations, and these agreements were implemented. As a minimal winning coalition, it faced a crisis when Shas quit in September 1993 following the indictment of Interior Minister Aryeh Deri. Several MKs who left Likud joined the coalition, but it continued to function as a minority

[14] In terms of the number of votes cast, the right-wing-religious bloc had a slight majority, but since many of the lists in this bloc did not pass the electoral threshold, the pivotal position shifted to the center-left bloc.

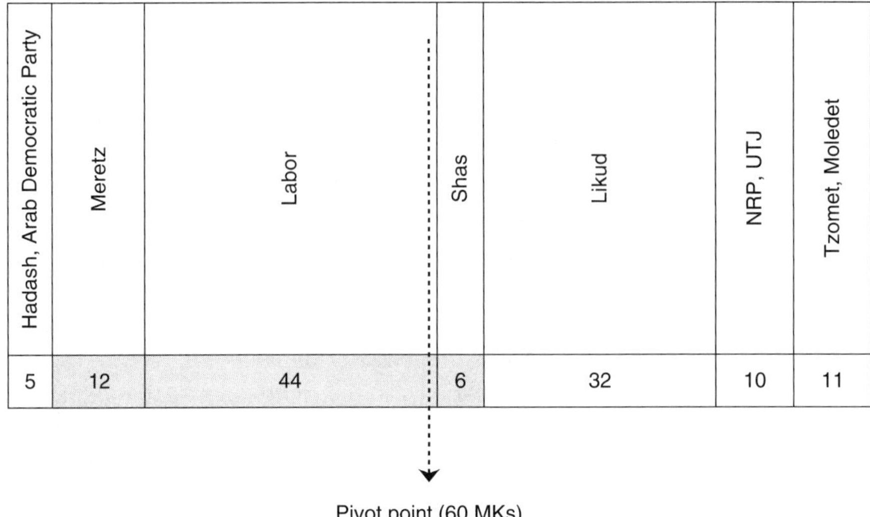

Figure 11.9 The twenty-ninth coalition (July 1992) by the parties' positions on security and foreign affairs
Note: The parties in the coalition are shaded gray, while Hadash and the Arab Democratic Party provided outside support for the coalition. Meretz: Mapam, Ratz, Shinui; Hadash: The Democratic Front for Peace and Equality.

government (with support from Hadash and the Arab Democratic Party) and mobilized a Knesset majority (sixty-one for, fifty against, and eight abstentions) in favor of the Oslo Accords in a vote held on September 21, 1993.

After Rabin's assassination, the government, now led by Shimon Peres, remained intact until the 1996 election. In Figure 11.9, the coalition could be considered closed, because Shas is to the left of Likud in light of its then moderate positions and statements by Rabbi Ovadia Yosef on security and foreign policy. In any event, the combination of Meretz and Shas did not yield long-term results and was to fail again in the Barak government of 1999.

I. 1996: Dividing up the Spoils even before the Election

Under the Direct Election Law that took effect in 1996, there was no question about who would become prime minister. Under this system, however, the prime minister needed a coalition not only to govern, but also to help get elected in the first place. This completely upended coalition politics. The candidates of the two major parties started to conduct coalition negotiations *before* the election, and the right-wing bloc formed a joint Likud–Gesher–Tzomet list that may have tipped the scale in favor of Netanyahu's narrow election victory. Substantial benefits were bestowed upon the two junior partners in this pre-election coalition, including slots for many of their candidates in the joint list, beyond their electoral power, and promises of the foreign affairs portfolio to David Levy (Gesher) and the agriculture portfolio to Rafael Eitan (Tzomet). Netanyahu was elected prime minister, but Likud won only thirty-two Knesset seats, compared to thirty-four for Labor; the right-wing-religious bloc, together with The Third Way, totaled sixty-eight MKs.

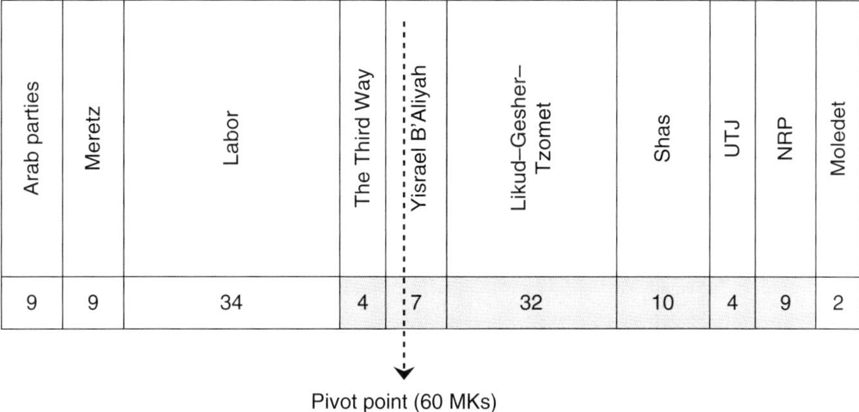

Figure 11.10 The thirty-second coalition (June 1996) by the parties' positions on security and foreign affairs

Note: The parties in the coalition are shaded gray. Arab parties: Hadash (five), Arab Democratic Party (four).

Likud did not hold the pivot position this time, which was held by Yisrael B'Aliyah or The Third Way. The negotiations did not encounter ideological difficulties because, as Figure 11.10 shows, it was clear that the coalition would have a right-wing and traditional orientation. The disagreements centered on the allocation of portfolios because the new Basic Law: Government limited the number of ministers to eighteen and deputy ministers to six. Shas and the NRP each received two ministerial appointments (each responsible for more than two ministries) and The Third Way received one. Yisrael B'Aliyah demanded and received two ministries – Industry and Commerce, and Immigrant Absorption. United Torah Judaism made do with a deputy minister of housing (who functioned as a minister) and chair of the Knesset Finance Committee. Despite the ideological cohesiveness and the ostensible power of the directly elected prime minister, the Netanyahu government ended its term after two and a half years due to internal dissension.

J. 1999: Barak Glues Together a Coalition in a Fractured Knesset

Here, too, coalition negotiations began prior to the election and Ehud Barak formed One Israel (Labor + Meimad + Gesher). His decisive victory in the prime ministerial election appeared to give him flexibility in forming the coalition, but the voters had again split their votes and elected a fractious Knesset of fifteen parties, eleven of them having six or fewer MKs. Barak won with a majority of 56 percent, but his party garnered only twenty-six seats. Thus, the ruling party was a minority within the new coalition. Likud (nineteen seats) was not a candidate for the coalition and preferred to recuperate in the opposition. The Labor Party found itself far from the pivot point – together with its natural partners Meretz (ten), the Center Party (six), and One Nation (two), Labor had only forty-four MKs. Barak did not want to rely on the support of Hadash and the Arab parties (ten), which, combined with Shinui, would have given him sixty MKs. He was wary of leading a minority government and preferred to formulate basic guidelines that were broad enough to allow Meretz and

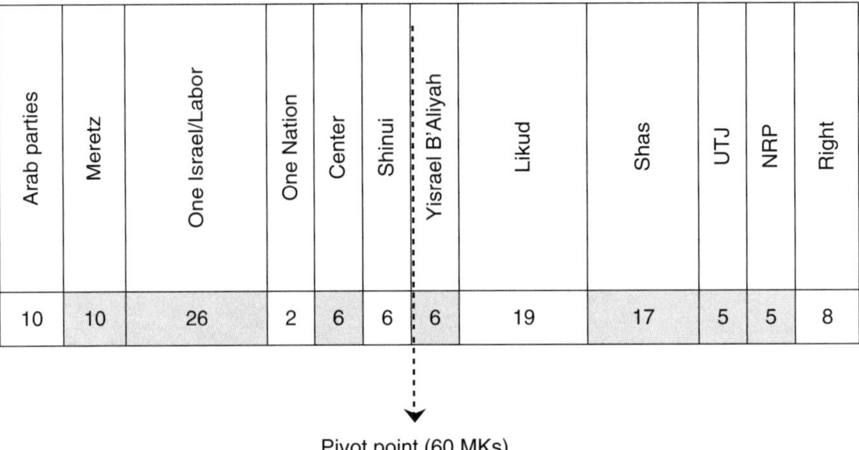

Figure 11.11 The thirty-third coalition (July 1999) by the parties' positions on security and foreign affairs
Note: The parties in the coalition are shaded gray. Right-wing parties: Yisrael Beitenu (four), National Union (four); Arab parties: Hadash (three), Balad (two), United Arab List (five).

the Center Party to serve in a coalition with the religious parties (which held a total of twenty-seven seats). In retrospect, the approach of forming a patchwork government turned out to be a mistake.

Shas joined the coalition, with UTJ and the NRP following suit. The coalition comprised seven parties with seventy-five MKs. Shinui stayed out because of its refusal to cooperate with the ultra-Orthodox parties (Alon 2009). The large number of coalition members, and the lack of a continuum of views on security and foreign policy, made the coalition unstable from the outset. The allocation of coalition benefits was also complicated due to the constitutional limit on the number of ministers (eighteen). And, indeed, the Basic Law: Government was quickly amended in order to solve the coalition problems, and the number of ministers was raised to twenty-three.

Although it was a surplus coalition, Shas enjoyed a strong bargaining position because its resignation would have precipitated the loss of a majority. As noted, the coalition was an ideological hybrid because on foreign affairs and security issues (the settlements, negotiations with the Palestinians and the Syrians), there was a huge gap between the leftmost and rightmost coalition partners: Meretz versus the NRP. The centrist parties Shinui and One Nation were missing from the continuum and Labor was distant from the pivot point. This government, more than any previously, abandoned the tradition of maintaining an ideological continuum in the coalition on security and foreign affairs. Disparities were also evident on religion–state matters between UTJ and Shas, on the one hand, and Meretz and Yisrael B'Aliyah, on the other. Indeed, Barak's patchwork coalition soon collapsed with defections from left and right. Within a year, Meretz quit the coalition (June 2000), and Yisrael B'Aliyah and the religious parties left soon after (July 2000). On the eve of the critical summit meeting between Barak and Arafat at Camp David, the coalition became a minority government of thirty-two MKs. Barak's government of non-contiguous ideology fell in under two years.

K. 2001–2005: Sharon's Various Coalitions

Ariel Sharon won the special election for prime minister in 2001, but inherited from Barak a Knesset in which the parliamentary divide continued to widen as the parties splintered. Sharon's situation resembled that of his predecessor: His Likud had shrunk to nineteen MKs, and the pivot position was controlled by fragments of parties in the center of the political spectrum (Figure 11.12). Sharon chose a sort of "unity government" based on the three largest lists – Likud, the Labor Party (after Barak resigned from the Knesset), and Shas, which together totaled sixty MKs. To gain a majority, Sharon brought four other parties into the coalition: Yisrael B'Aliyah, One Nation, National Union–Yisrael Beitenu, and the Center Party. Together, the seven parties totaled seventy-three MKs.

The government was the largest yet: It had twenty-six ministers, a dozen deputy ministers, and four deputy prime ministers. The small contingent of Likud MKs forced Sharon to make numerous concessions – Likud was a minority in the government, and two senior portfolios (defense and foreign affairs) were given to Labor. It was a surplus coalition, and since Shinui and the NRP were not part of it, the coalition was not closed and left a substantial ideological gap between its leftmost and rightmost partners. During this period, the Direct Election Law was revoked, and the 2003 election were held in the previous format. Likud, led by Sharon, gained considerable strength in this election (forty seats after the merger with Yisrael B'Aliyah) and held the pivot position; the left-wing camp shrank to thirty-six seats; the small centrist parties disappeared and were replaced by Shinui, a centrist party that won fifteen seats. Likud's dominance enabled Sharon to conduct negotiations from a position of power, with the option (like that of Mapai in the 1950s) of forming several coalitions of different ideological bents, as shown in Figure 11.12.

The completely different composition of the two coalitions in the sixteenth Knesset can be seen as reflecting the different objectives Sharon set for himself as prime minister. The first coalition (Likud, Shinui, NRP, and National Union – sixty-eight MKs) was of a conservative centrist nature. This coalition, which served for about two years, focused primarily on socioeconomic issues, instituting neoliberal reforms in the economy and cutting transfer payments and child allowances. This was possible due to the absence of the ultra-Orthodox and left-wing parties. When the prime minister's main objective shifted to the issue of the occupied territories, he brought Labor (January 2005) and UTJ (March 2005) into the coalition, replacing National Union (quit in June 2004) and the NRP (quit in November 2004). The new makeup of the coalition enabled Sharon to carry out the disengagement from the Gaza Strip and northern Samaria, despite opposition from some Likud MKs. In October 2004, two Likud ministers – Landau and Ratzon – were fired after voting against the disengagement plan in the Knesset. Following approval of the plan, opposition intensified from Likud MKs, who sought to conduct a plebiscite on the plan and vote against the state budget. Netanyahu resigned from the government about a week prior to implementation of the disengagement.

Sharon's three coalitions shared common characteristics. First, they were not ideologically closed coalitions. The first (National Union–NRP–Likud–Shinui) can be described as closed on the socioeconomic axis, but this was secondary in Israeli politics. The second coalition was open, because it was missing parties that were

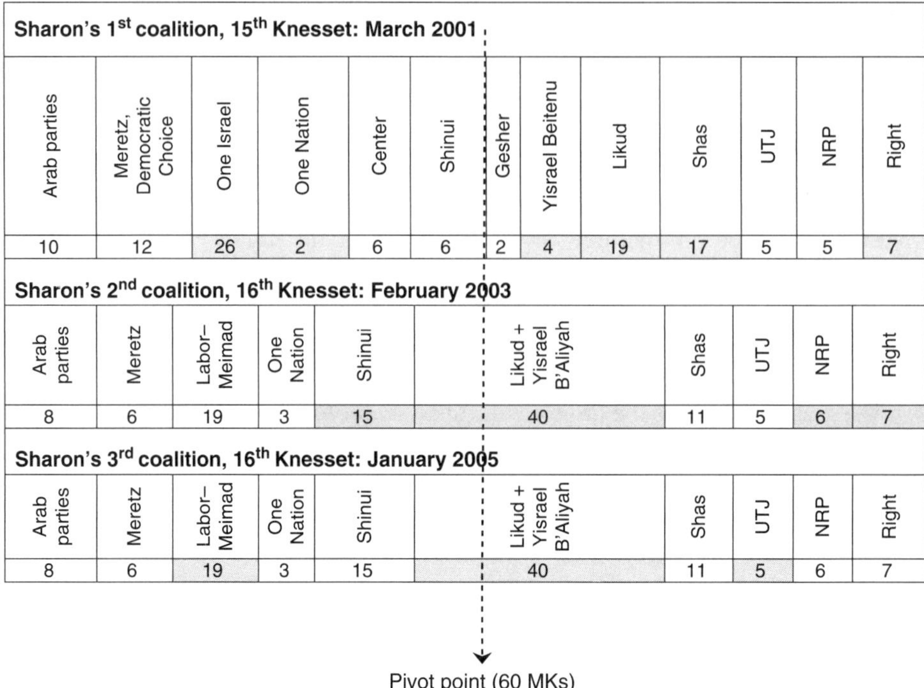

Figure 11.12 Ariel Sharon's coalitions (2001–5) by the parties' positions on security and foreign affairs

Note: The parties in the coalition are shaded gray. Right-wing parties: Yisrael Beitenu, National Union; Arab parties: Hadash, Balad, United Arab List.

relatively more dovish, such as Shas. Likud enjoyed a powerful position in the coalitions of the sixteenth Knesset (2003 and 2005) with fourteen ministers and all of the most important portfolios. The lack of a continuum in Sharon's coalitions reflects the ideological vagueness that has characterized Israeli political parties since the beginning of the twenty-first century. Negotiations focused on the coalition benefits and not on questions of world view. Nevertheless, changes in the makeup of the coalitions and the factors that led to creation of the Kadima party prior to the 2006 election reflected the continued centrality of foreign affairs and security issues.

L. 2006: Olmert's Coalition

Ehud Olmert's coalition following the 2006 election marked the first time in Israel's political history that a coalition was headed by a new party, Kadima, which with twenty-nine seats was also the largest party in the Knesset. Olmert initially built a minimal centrist coalition of sixty-seven MKs from four parties: Kadima (twenty-nine), Labor (nineteen), Shas (twelve), and the Pensioners (seven). This coalition was designed to continue the disengagement, but the second Lebanon War disrupted the plans. After the war, Yisrael Beitenu (eleven seats) joined the coalition, turning it into a surplus coalition that lacked ideological continuity on security and foreign affairs.

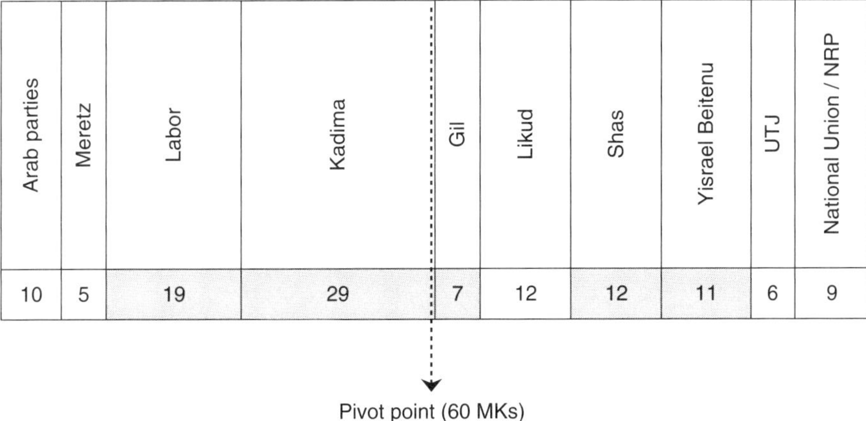

Figure 11.13 Olmert's coalition (2006) by the parties' positions on security and foreign affairs
Note: The parties in the coalition are shaded gray. Gil: The Pensioners' Party; Arabs: Hadash (three), Ra'am-Ta'al (four), Balad (three).

M. 2009, 2013, 2015: Netanyahu's Coalitions

The eighteenth Knesset was elected in February 2009. Kadima won the largest number of seats (twenty-eight), followed by Likud (twenty-seven) and Yisrael Beitenu (fifteen). Benjamin Netanyahu was given the task of forming the government after he managed to forge a majority bloc of sixty-five MKs from the right-wing and religious parties.

In 2009, a center-right coalition was formed together with the Labor Party. On paper, the Netanyahu coalition comprised seventy-four MKs, but it actually had less support because some Labor MKs did not back the government in a Knesset vote of confidence. On security and foreign policy, the coalition was open because for the first time in the history of Israeli coalitions, the largest party – Kadima – was left out. However, the views of Ehud Barak, the head of Labor, were closer to those of Likud. After Barak left Labor with several MKs to form a splinter faction, prompting the remaining Labor ministers to quit the government, the coalition became closed and had sixty-six MKs.

To form a majority bloc, Likud had to make far-reaching promises to its partners, in particular to Yisrael Beitenu. Consequently, the largest ever government was formed with thirty ministers and nine deputy ministers. The coalition started to falter and nearly fell in May 2012 after a motion to dissolve the Knesset passed its initial reading. The entrance into the coalition of Kadima, led by Shaul Mofaz (though Kadima left it two months later), enabled the government to survive almost to the end of its term, finally collapsing in late 2012. Despite the fragility of this coalition, it lasted for four years.

In the 2013 election, the right-wing-religious parties (Likud–Yisrael Beitenu, the Jewish Home, Shas, and the Torah Front) won a majority of sixty-one MKs. The addition of one of the centrist parties – the new Yesh Atid (led by Yair Lapid) or Hatnuah (led by Tzipi Livni) – would have ensured a coalition of eighty

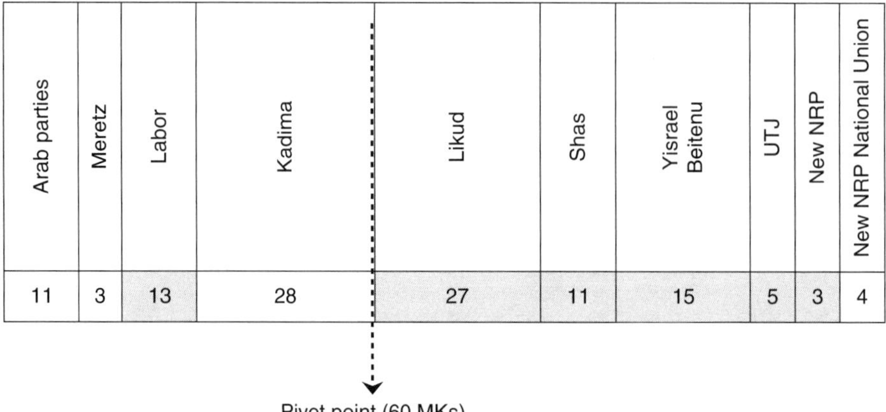

Figure 11.14 Netanyahu's coalition (2009) by the parties' positions on security and foreign affairs
Note: The parties in the coalition are shaded gray. Arab parties: Hadash (four), Ra'am-Ta'al (four), Balad (three).

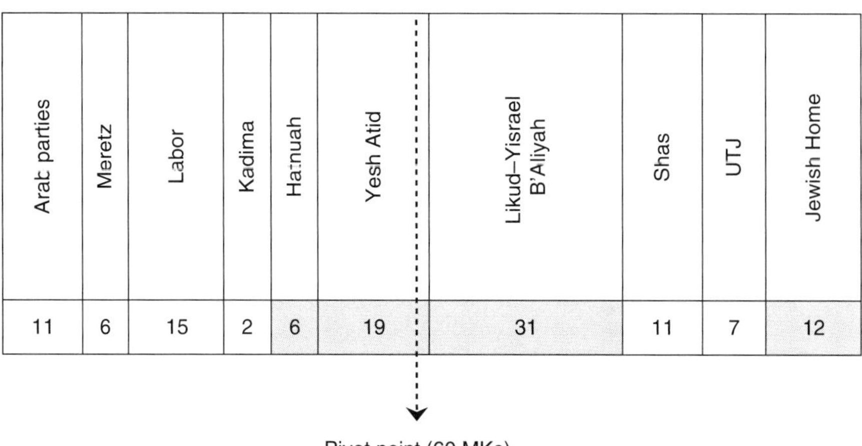

Figure 11.15 Netanyahu's coalition (2013) by the parties' positions on security and foreign affairs
Note: The parties in the coalition are shaded gray. Arab parties: Hadash (four), Ra'am-Ta'al (four), Balad (three).

to eighty-six MKs. And indeed, Hatnuah quickly signed a coalition agreement with Likud. However, an unexpected alliance between the secular Yesh Atid and the religious Jewish Home, committing them to enter the coalition in tandem and leave the ultra-Orthodox parties outside, forced Netanyahu to form a coalition that lacked ideological consistency and was rife with internal contradictions (Figure 11.15).

The internal contradictions in the coalition were not limited to foreign affairs, security, the lack of negotiations with the Palestinians, or different world views about

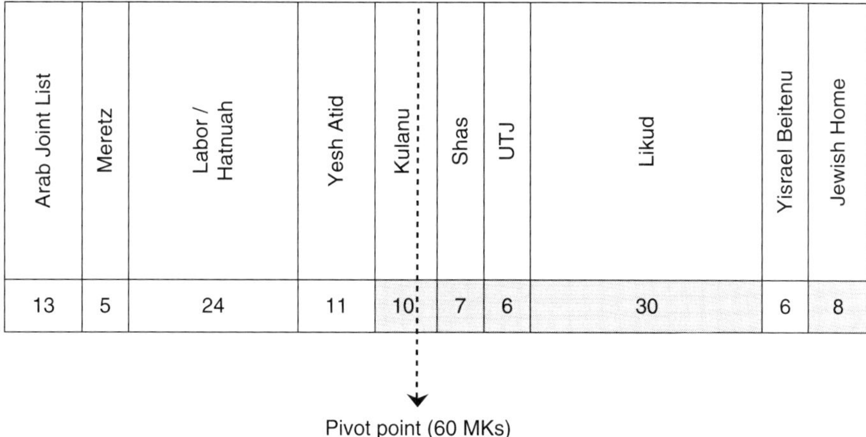

Figure 11.16 Netanyahu's coalition (2015) by the parties' positions on security and foreign affairs
Note: The parties in the coalition are shaded gray.

the essence of the state of Israel; they were particularly salient on matters of economics and society. Each party pulled in a different direction in an effort to cater to its constituency, and there was also a split between Likud and Yisrael Beitenu in early 2014. Serious disagreements arose among the partners during the prolonged military operation in the Gaza Strip (July–August 2014) and the government fell in December 2014 due to profound distrust among the partners, manifested in disputes over legislative proposals and the 2015 budget.

The coalition formed after the 2015 election (Figure 11.16) was closed and right wing, similar to the Netanyahu coalition of 1996 (Figure 11.10). It ranged from the new center party Kulanu all the way to the Jewish Home on the far right. It was initially a minimal winning coalition of sixty-one MKs, and it became stable when Yisrael Beitenu joined and raised the majority to sixty-seven.

This review of coalition negotiations highlights some key points. First, the process of political bargaining is in itself legitimate and necessary, particularly when the voters' decision is equivocal. We noted in Chapter 9 that the multiplicity of parties in itself does not create unstable coalitions. Second, in the past, positions on foreign affairs and security have had a decisive impact on the composition of the coalition. However, since the mid-1990s their effect has declined and coalition negotiations ignore policy issues and turn into haggling about partisan benefits only. Third, when a coalition is closed ideologically, the government can function better, if it is not a minimum winning coalition. Fourth, in recent years, and certainly in the wake of the social protest of 2011, economic and social considerations have become more important; the new center parties (Yesh Atid, Kulanu) became pivotal in the Knesset with a platform and slogans focused on the economy. Fifth, and finally, what weakened the coalition as an institution, more than anything else, was that the power of all the parties diminished: In the 2015 election, no single party won more than thirty seats (i.e., 25%) of the Knesset.

11.8 Decision, Indecision, and Coalition Crises

The coalition structure of Israeli governments ostensibly weakens their ability to operate as a cohesive policymaking entity because the government resembles a federation of bodies with competing political interests. The assumption is that deficient governance is inherent to a multiparty coalition. According to this argument, a coalition government is, at best, a coordinating committee and not an executive body capable of implementing comprehensive policy. This argument, however, is not based on a factual analysis of the reality in Israel or other democracies. Even in democracies where a single party rules, the party itself is usually a federation of diverse interests. Moreover, the parties in a coalition have a strong interest in ensuring that the government survives, makes decisions, and takes action. The extensive experience in Israel proves that coalitions can decide and act in critical arenas, such as going to war or implementing social and economic policies, even when their internal structure is not particularly stable.

Coalitions do not create the social divide; they reflect it. A coalition is designed to increase the probability of consensual policymaking and its implementation. On the other hand, when no clear majority exists for a particular decision, the coalition dynamic forces the government to refrain from sweeping initiatives, and there is a positive side to this. A coalition will often prefer to defer contending with substantive and controversial questions unless it has no alternative. The negative side is that a coalition makes it more difficult to reach decisions amidst uncertainty and to engage in long-term planning. We present below examples of decision and indecision in various Israeli coalitions.

A. Important Decisions Suspended or Deferred

A number of fateful decisions in Israel's history entailed indecision or "a decision not to decide." A coalition government has an aversion to clear-cut decision-making without a solid public majority of support, and the tendency is to defer the decision. We illustrate this with two controversial issues that are fiercely disputed: relations between religion and state, and the status of the territories.

The first coalition after 1948 was marked by collaboration between Mapai and the religious parties, and this led to suspending several decisions because of the great value attributed to the inclusion of religious Jews in the young political system. In Chapter 2, we discussed whether it was the opposition of the religious parties that caused the government to defer writing a constitution for Israel; their voices undoubtedly had an impact. In any case, the nascent state made no new decisions about defining relations between religion and the state. Instead, it decided to continue with the compromises of the status quo arrangements, and these were included in the basic guidelines and coalition agreements. Most of these arrangements were not yet legislated – there was no Sabbath Law and no ordinance prohibiting the sale of non-kosher food. More important in the long run, the defense minister was allowed to defer the military service of full-time yeshiva students. In the 2000s, efforts have been made to increase the number of ultra-Orthodox men serving in the army.

The second example of a "decision not to decide" pertains to the status of the territories captured by Israel in 1967. In retrospect, this turned into a decision to retain most of the territories, excluding Sinai and the Gaza Strip. The deferral of this decision suited the National Unity Government coalition (1967 to 1970), but even after the right-wing Gahal party quit the coalition, the Alignment government led by Golda Meir was in no hurry to decide. It even refrained from discussing the matter due to profound internal disagreements within the ruling party itself, in the government, and in society at large (Beilin 1985). After the third Sharon coalition (2005), which decided on the Gaza Strip disengagement plan, the coalitions led by Olmert and Netanyahu were unable or unwilling to decide on the question of the future of the territories and negotiations with the Palestinians.

B. Important Decisions in Coalition Frameworks

Many important decisions – primarily about security and military matters – were made by coalition governments, some without disagreements among the partners, while others required ideological compromise. The coalition decision that shaped the political system for a long time was the "Harari Decision" compromise in 1950, which stipulated that the constitution of Israel would be written one chapter at a time. Another example is the compromise among the major parties to refrain from embarking on new peace initiatives in the unity government formed in 1984.

On the other hand, in the same unity government led by Shimon Peres, two important decisions were made with virtually the full consent of all the partners – implementation of a comprehensive economic recovery and anti-inflation plan, and the IDF withdrawal from Lebanon to a narrow strip adjacent to Israel's northern border. Netanyahu's coalitions also made noteworthy decisions despite internal difficulties: freezing construction in the settlements for ten months during negotiations with the Palestinians (September 2010); an agreement with Hamas to swap some 1,000 Palestinian prisoners for captured IDF soldier Gilad Shalit (October 2011); and raising the electoral threshold to 3.25 percent (March 2014).

C. Important Non-Partisan Decisions

Until the political upheaval of 1977, important decisions were usually made along the lines of coalition versus opposition, with the exception of emergency periods when the government enjoyed broad public support. On the other hand, the peace accords with Egypt were a salient example of a decision that not only spanned the coalition–opposition divide, but also crossed party lines. In 1978–79, when the Camp David Accords and peace treaty were brought before the Knesset for approval, many Likud MKs voted against the agreements or abstained even though it was Likud leader Menachem Begin who had forged these agreements. Without the support of the overwhelming majority of opposition members, including most Alignment MKs, the Knesset would not have confirmed the agreements (Diskin and Galnoor 1990).

Another example is the Basic Law: Jerusalem Capital of Israel (1980), which states: "Jerusalem, complete and united, is the capital of Israel."[15] The Likud government

[15] In 2000, an article was added stipulating that no legal authority pertaining to Jerusalem may be transferred to a foreign political or governmental body.

adopted the private member's bill, and most members of the Alignment, who did not want to be accused of being unpatriotic, supported the legislation. The peace treaty with Jordan (1994) also won broad support among the opposition parties.

The reforms in the government's structure – direct election of the prime minister (March 1992) and its revocation (March 2001) – are also examples of decisions that crossed coalition lines. This was true for the decision to disengage from the Gaza Strip and northern Samaria. In Knesset votes in 2004 and 2005, many MKs from Likud, the prime minister's party, voted against the plan, while opposition parties Meretz, One Nation, the United Arab List, and Shinui voted for it. More recently, crossing the lines on social and economic issues has become common because of the blurring of ideological differences between the parties. An early example of this was broad support for the National Health Insurance Law (1994).

D. Important Decisions that Led to Coalition Crises

Most of the coalitions ended because of crises between member parties usually due to ideological disagreements – a party felt it could no longer share responsibility for the government's decisions, or one or more partners concluded that their political fate would improve in a new government formed prior to or following an election.

Education for new immigrants in the transit camps (February 1951): Mapai wanted to send the children of immigrants to the religious subdivision of its education system, while the United Religious Front insisted that they be sent to the religious systems affiliated with the Mizrahi or Agudat Yisrael parties. In early 1951, the religious affairs minister resigned, and when the United Religious Front's demands were not accepted, it declared a coalition crisis. Mapai lost a Knesset vote on approving the Education Ministry's policy and Ben-Gurion viewed this defeat as a vote of no-confidence and called for early elections. In the state's short political history, the fact was recorded that a crisis between coalition partners led to dissolving the first Knesset and holding early elections.

"Who is a Jew?" (1958): Interior Minister Yisrael Bar-Yehuda (Ahdut Ha'avoda) instructed ministry officials to register as Jewish anyone who so declared, unless it could be proven false. NRP ministers maintained that this directive conflicted with religious law, demanded its cancelation, and rejected a compromise proposal to completely remove the "nationality"[16] line in Israeli identity cards. The NRP left the government, but because it was a surplus coalition, it did not lose its parliamentary majority and remained in power until the scheduled election in December 1959.

Approval of the Rogers Plan (summer of 1970): The National Unity Government was based on a very broad parliamentary majority, but a severe coalition crisis between Gahal and the Alignment over the peace initiative of US Secretary of State William Rogers brought an end to the coalition that had served (in various configurations) since June 1967. The Rogers Plan was designed to end the War of Attrition in exchange for Israel's willingness to accept UN Security Council Resolution 242,

[16] The Hebrew term *le'om* here refers to ethnic affiliation – Jew, Arab, Druze, etc.

which called for an Israeli withdrawal in exchange for peace. Gahal, led by Begin, threatened to quit, and all of Prime Minister Golda Meir's efforts to dissuade him, including releasing the party from collective responsibility, were to no avail. Begin argued, correctly, that his party must resign because it could not remain in the government without sharing responsibility for its policy.

The peace process (1990): The second unity government between Likud and the Labor Party, inaugurated in 1988, weathered many crises between the two senior partners. The primary dispute was over continuation of the peace process. The Labor Party supported the initiative of US. Secretary of State James Baker. Prime Minister Shamir had reservations about the plan, but was willing to discuss it. The senior Likud ministers – Ariel Sharon, Yitzhak Moda'i, and David Levy – were opposed to any initiative. In early 1990, Labor gave Shamir an ultimatum to accept the Baker initiative, and when the prime minister refused, the party decided to support a no-confidence motion. On the eve of the vote, Shamir fired Peres, in response to which all the Labor ministers resigned. The no-confidence motion passed by a majority of sixty to fifty-five, and the government fell.

Continuation of the Oslo Process (2000): Yisrael B'Aliyah, Shas, the NRP, and Gesher left the Barak-led coalition as a result of Barak's statements about his willingness to compromise with the Palestinians and engage in peace negotiations with Yasser Arafat, the head of the Palestinian Authority.

The disengagement plan (2004): Prime Minister Sharon fired Ministers Avigdor Lieberman and Binyamin Elon (National Union) due to their opposition to disengagement from the Gaza Strip. The NRP ministers gradually followed suit.

Compulsory IDF service for yeshiva students (2012): This had been on the public agenda since the High Court's 1998 ruling that the issue must be resolved. Despite the Conscription Law of 2014 (see Chapter 17), which made arrangements for enlisting yeshiva students, as of 2016 the issue is still rather open.

11.9 The Opposition

The opposition represents tacit assurance that it is possible to replace the government. Therefore, without an opposition, a democratic regime cannot exist. The role of the opposition is, first, to present an alternative to the government's policy, and to criticize and monitor its activity. The opposition is a partner in the parliamentary work of legislation and the process of decision-making. In Britain, the importance of the institution of the opposition is recognized in an expression at least two hundred years old: "Her Majesty's loyal opposition." The British opposition forms a shadow cabinet – an alternative government of ministers assigned to various portfolios in order to set forth different policies than those of the government, and to monitor the activity of the ministries. The opposition leader, the head of the second-largest party in parliament, heads the shadow cabinet.

In Israel, the status of the opposition is not firmly established in the political culture – in part because a dominant party ruled until 1977 and, in part, because the opposition is composed of many Knesset parties and this makes it difficult to present a clear alternative to government policy. Furthermore, most of the coalitions in Israel have been surplus coalitions and some have been unity governments, which left a relatively small opposition. Nonetheless, some important practices have taken root over the years: opposition MKs chair several Knesset committees (such as the State Control Committee); one of the Knesset representatives on the Judicial Selection Committee is from the opposition; periodic meetings are conducted between the prime minister and the head of the largest opposition party, especially during times of emergency; and the head of the opposition addresses the Knesset after the prime minister at special events, such as President Anwar Sadat's visit.

A. Oppositions of Different Types

Over the years, many changes have ensued in the identity, composition, size, cohesion, and political power of the opposition. Clearly, the power of the opposition is commensurate with the number of its members, and it is more powerful when it includes a large party that can be viewed as an alternative to the ruling party. Moreover, the less divided the opposition, numerically and ideologically, the greater its strength.

In the era of Mapai as a dominant party, the opposition was weak because it was relatively small (forty-four MKs on average), divided into right (Herut) and left (Mapam), and lacked a large party that could be regarded as an alternative. The opposition parties were not reticent about criticizing government policy (for example, opposition to reparations from Germany and the Lavon affair), but they did not pose a threat to overthrow the government. Mapai's freedom to choose its preferred coalition partners enabled it to ignore some parties and even disqualify two out of hand ("without Herut and without Maki") because Mapai viewed them as extremist and irresponsible. The significant achievements of the opposition parties were few in number: In 1958, they managed to entrench Article 4 of the Basic Law: The Knesset, which stipulates that any change in the electoral system requires a majority of sixty-one MKs. One year later, the opposition was able to defeat a Mapai candidate and elect an opposition MK, Nahum Nir (Ahdut Ha'avoda), to serve as Knesset Speaker.

While the National Unity Government in 1967 weakened the parliamentary opposition, it was a milestone for Gahal, the primary opposition party, which joined the government for the first time and began to emerge as an alternative to the ruling party. Significant reinforcement of the opposition as an institution occurred in 1977 following the first turnover of power in Israel. This trend strengthened in the 1980s when the party system evolved into two blocs centered around two large parties. In the ninth and tenth Knessets (1977–84), a strong opposition was led by the Alignment and left-wing camp, which presented itself as an alternative to the ruling party. The opposition succeeded in electing its candidates, Yitzhak Navon and Chaim Herzog, as president of Israel. In the first Begin government (1977–81), the opposition led by the Alignment supported the peace agreements with Egypt; and in the second Begin government (1981–83), a large majority of opposition MKs heeded the government's call to be "a responsible opposition" and supported the decision to launch the first Lebanon War (1982). This support eroded during the course of the war, particularly after the events in Sabra and Shatila, and the opposition forced the government to establish a state commission of inquiry to investigate the events.

Though the opposition was divided at that time, it united in 1982, on the eve of the Sinai evacuation, in supporting a no-confidence motion by Tehiya from the right and Hadash from the left, and nearly toppled the government.

During the period of the unity governments (1984–90), the opposition, which initially included a dozen MKs split between right and left, nearly disappeared from the Knesset. However, an "opposition" actually existed within the government itself. Indeed, during the second unity government, the two main partners were just waiting for the right moment to bring down the government, as indeed occurred in the spring of 1990. Accordingly, an "in-house opposition" can exist within the executive branch, as was demonstrated in the 2013–15 coalition headed by Netanyahu.

During Yitzhak Rabin's narrow government (1992–95), the opposition from the right became militant in its personal attacks on Rabin in an effort to thwart the approval of the Oslo Accords in the Knesset. After the murder of Rabin, many argued that the mudslinging campaign against the prime minister conducted by the opposition, with Likud and the NRP in the lead, paved the way for the assassination, but the opposition completely rejected this accusation.

In the years 1992–2001, there were four turnovers of power. Thus, the transition from seats in the government to the opposition benches and back again became a common phenomenon. The Direct Election Law, in effect in the 1996 election, led to a paralyzing balance between the two authorities: The government could not change the Knesset, and the opposition could not topple the government without triggering a new election. The weakening of the major parties, along with the proliferation of splinter parties in the Knesset as a result of the direct election, gave rise to a divided and fragmented opposition. The directly elected prime ministers tended to form broad coalitions at the outset, bringing the opposition into the government. Consequently, government coalitions also became revolving doors, with parties entering and exiting at an unprecedented frequency.[17] Therefore, the decline of the large parties led to an unstable coalition as well as a weaker opposition. The weakening of party discipline and coalition constraints engendered new situations, with MKs from the coalition collaborating with the opposition on some issues. And though this did not suffice to topple the government, it bolstered the strength of the Knesset.

B. Change in the Formal Status of the Opposition

The main change was official recognition of the opposition's status as an *institution*, which previously was not even mentioned in the Statute of Knesset Operations. The Knesset Law amendment (2000) anchored the status of the opposition leader by assigning this position to the head of the largest opposition party, or whoever has support of more than half the opposition MKs. The status of the opposition leader was recognized in state ceremonies and his salary was raised to that of a minister. The law requires the prime minister to update the head of the opposition on matters of state at least once a month.

[17] Four parties quit the Barak government (1999–2001); four parties left the Sharon government (2001–3) while Shas quit and returned; four parties left the second Sharon government (2003–6); and two parties quit the Netanyahu government (2009).

The Basic Law: Government (enacted in 2001 and in effect since 2003) introduced a mechanism of "constructive no-confidence," according to which a government falls only if sixty-one MKs vote for another candidate to form an alternative government. In fact, this innovation considerably reduced the importance of the no-confidence vote, the main parliamentary instrument available to the opposition. In practice, the coalition does not worry about no-confidence motions as long as sixty-one MKs are not lined up against it. There have been cases in which the coalition lost no-confidence votes, but except for a blow to its prestige, this had no impact on the government's status or policies. No-confidence votes do not compel the coalition to mobilize the presence of MKs to thwart the threat, and they have become ceremonial and nothing more than an annoyance.

The test of the opposition in Israel is during national emergencies and war, or in moments of historic decisions. At such times, the opposition is expected to display responsibility and refrain from trying to topple the government and precipitate new elections. On the other hand, this is the fateful hour of the opposition, which should offer an alternative to government policy, strive to replace it, or at least try to prevent it from making grave mistakes.

11.10 The Centrality of the Coalition in Israeli Politics

When coalition partners are motivated by a *political* commitment to the coalition agreement, the coalition mechanism has two great advantages. First, it creates broad consensus in the government, bridging disagreements in society; and second, it increases the likelihood that government decisions will actually be carried out.

In the consociational period in Israeli politics when there was a dominant party (through the mid-1970s), the coalitions were relatively large and based upon broad consensus in Israeli society. After the election, it was clear who would lead the state and, more or less, who would sit in the coalition. Since then, Israeli society has become more pluralistic: citizens' preferences have changed, the party map is completely altered, the power of the large parties has declined, and the party affiliation of the next prime minister is no longer clear prior to the vote. We also noted that the cohesiveness of the coalition has weakened, and the prime minister has been forced to invest considerable energy in its maintenance, not always successfully.

The ideological continuum on issues of security and foreign policy, which characterized the closed coalitions, has blurred, and the allocation of benefits and personal gain has become the primary coalition currency. The ideological ambiguity was manifested in the large size of the coalitions (e.g., the unity governments of 1984–90; the Sharon government of 2001), or their narrowness (since 1974 and up to 2016, nine of the twenty-one coalitions were minimal winning coalitions). In the reality of Israel, this means a high likelihood of instability. The instability is reflected in the flux of parties holding the pivot position of power broker, especially when this position is not controlled by a large party as coalition leader. It is customary to assume that a government's steering capacity improves as a function of several features of the coalition:

- the larger the size of the prime minister's party in the coalition;
- the higher the percentage of ministers from the prime minister's party;
- the greater the number of senior portfolios (defense, finance, foreign affairs) held by ministers from the prime minister's party;
- the smaller the number of parties in the coalition.

Table 11.3 *Indicators of steering capacity in various coalitions*

Coalition	% of prime minister's party in coalition	% of ministers from PM's party	Senior portfolios held by PM's party	Number of coalition partners
Eshkol 1/1966	65	67	3/3	5
Eshkol 6/1967	46	57	2/3	7
Rabin 6/1974	83	84	3/3	3
Shamir 12/1988	42	42	1/3	5
Rabin 7/1992	71	76	3/3	3
Barak 7/1999	35	50	2/3*	7
Sharon 3/2001	26	35	1/3	8
Sharon 2/2003	59	61	3/3	4
Netanyahu 3/2009	36	46	2/3	6
Netanyahu 3/2013**	46 (28)	59 (37)	2/3 (1/3)	4 (5)
Netanyahu 5/2015	49	58	2/3	5

* Foreign affairs minister was David Levy from Gesher, affiliated with the Labor Party.

** Data in parentheses refer to the Netanyahu government after Likud/Yisrael Beitenu split into its two components.

But as Table 11.3 indicates, the steering capacity of a government is not the direct product of simply combining these four indicators. Eshkol's first government scored high on the indicators, and is indeed seen as having high steering capacity. But Rabin's first government (1977) scored even higher on three of the indicators, and is not regarded as having high steering capacity. Other examples: Barak's government (1999) was indeed weak, but Sharon's government (2001), although it appears weaker, was not. Like Barak's government, Netanyahu's 2009 government was weak, and unable to make decisions on many issues, but it survived. On the other hand, Netanyahu's 2013 government was even weaker, and survived only briefly.

In short, the indicators reveal a partial picture and should not be considered foolproof criteria for assessing coalitions. Steering capacity is not only a function of the government's structure and parliamentary majority. Moreover, many coalition governments in which the prime minister was relatively "weak" were still able to make complex and important decisions. Steering capacity depends on the ability of all layers of the political system to implement the decisions made by the elected bodies. Coalitions are one of the important mechanisms in creating and exercising steering capacity.

12 Civil Society: The Third Sector that Grew Unnoticed by the State

12.1 Civil Society, Social Capital, and the Third Sector

What is civil society? There is a wooden bridge northwest of Oxford over a stream flowing south to the Thames River. On the railing is a faded sign explaining that the bridge was built in 1822 with the sweat and money of the residents after the district authorities refused to build it.

The construction of the bridge and the sign are the work of civil society. But this is only a partial answer, because civil society is not only a substitute for government authorities or a means of influencing them. In contemporary usage, civil society exists in its own right, operating in the space between the state, the economic market, and primary frameworks such as the family. Parts may overlap with other frameworks; and state, market, and family activities are also likely to enter and exit from this social space. Civil society is thus a conceptual rather than an institutional system. Its organizations "march to the beat of an infinite range of drums and not necessarily in the same direction" (UK, National Council for Voluntary Organizations 1996, 15). To understand civil society, one must accept the boundless diversity of its components and this may be frustrating for those who seek clear-cut definitions. Indeed, a jumble of terminology defines the organizations that operate in civil society, reflecting the many types of missions and activity: third-sector, social, non-profit, volunteer, charitable organizations, NGOs (non-governmental organizations), and others. In this chapter, we use the more theoretical term "civil society," a broad umbrella that also covers the more organized components – third-sector organizations.

Civil society is an arena of social interaction in which volunteer activity aimed at achieving the goals of the individual, the group, and the public at large takes place. This arena is characterized by shared values, independence vis-à-vis the state and the economic market, and autonomous activity that is usually intended to achieve social benefits (Cohen and Arato 1992). The sum of these cumulative interactions over the years and this civic activity is called *social capital*. According to Putnam, social capital is the collective "product" of maintaining social networks, norms of reciprocity, and trust in others. Social networks contribute to a sense of commitment, belonging, and solidarity, and reinforce cooperation, communication, and trust for the common good of the citizens (Putnam 1995, 67). The term *third sector* denotes organizations that do not belong to the two other sectors – government and business – and we define it here in a reductive manner as organizations that operate in civil society without governmental aspirations or a profit motive, and which have the following characteristics:

- ***formal*** – some level of institutionalization and organizational structure;
- ***private*** – outside the domain of state and local government institutions;
- ***non-profit*** – do not distribute profits to their founders, and budget surpluses are invested in the organization itself;
- ***independent*** – not controlled by an entity external to the organization;
- ***voluntary*** – include a significant component of volunteerism and donations;
- ***open*** – freedom to join and leave at will. (Galnoor Committee 2003, 21–22)

In Israel, third-sector organizations are registered as non-profits, endowments, and public benefit companies. They contribute to developing civil society, work for social change, and create mechanisms of monitoring and control over state and local government, and, in a different way, commercial organizations. However, civil society and its organizations do not always or necessarily constitute a "public opposition" to the state, the government, or businesses. Many organizations in the third sector are service providers similar to government ministries (such as providing services for people with disabilities), while others are frameworks for recreational, sports, or artistic activities, not for revolutionary or oppositional activities. As noted in Chapter 8, civil society, wherever it is alive and kicking, epitomizes democratic participation alongside the ordinary politics of elections, parties, and public bureaucracy. At its best, civil society formulates agreements and disagreements, and grants or denies legitimacy to the government's use of political power (M. Walzer 1977). It enhances the performance of government authorities closest to the citizen, and may expand the circle of partners for setting policy (Putnam 1993). Researchers of civil society particularly emphasize its contribution to public discourse and the addition of subarenas of deliberation and activity (V. Shiffer 2003, 8–34).

In this chapter, we ask what occurs in the overlapping areas of political and civil systems, and how changes in the state's function relate to the activities of civil society.

A. Civil Society in the Modern State

Civil society as a distinct field began to coalesce in the early modern era as the distinctions sharpened between family, society, and state. Civil society was perceived as the space for individuals to exercise their wishes, freedom, and self-expression, and where they aspire to gain property and happiness. In this approach, there is no distinction between the social and economic spheres; for Adam Smith, they are both part of civil society, which should be separated from the political sphere of the state (Islamoglu 2001). Friedrich Hegel also placed civil society between the intimacy of the family and the totality of the state: Within civil society, there is mutual dependence between the individuals in order to fulfill their needs, including needs addressed by "the free market" (Hegel [1821] 1969, 122–33).

Alexis De Tocqueville emphasized the link between a strong civil society and a stable democracy. In his travels in America in the nineteenth century, he was impressed by the abundance of volunteer organizations and believed they play a key role in protecting democracy, especially in boosting equality, because they enable groups and individuals to participate independently in public life. In his view, they also serve as a shield against government tyranny in that they encourage individuals to organize to promote their objectives. Thus, participation in volunteer organizations not only contributes to the development of social connections and mutual reliance among citizens and strengthens interpersonal trust, but it also generates social experience and increases political involvement. Thus, volunteer organizations serve as "a school for democracy" (De Tocqueville [1835] 2003, 32–42). In this arena, people acquire skills for functioning as active citizens, and adopt norms of conduct that are essential for democracy. The contribution of civil society is not only to forge community and achieve collective goals, but also to improve the individual's ability to carry out plans. Civil society organizations contribute to strengthening democracy by providing information to decision-makers, and activity in these organizations is not a substitute for democratic elections, but rather a vital addition to representation. Volunteer organizations can help promote equality in society by representing the interests of groups whose voice is not heard in formal frameworks (Cohen and Rogers 1993). De Tocqueville's argument about the contribution of civil society organizations has been verified empirically in studies that show a positive correlation between participation in volunteer organizations and political activity, greater satisfaction in life, and stronger faith in other people (Howard and Gilbert 2008).

Civil activity, including the establishment of volunteer associations, existed in democratic states prior to the era of globalization and the weakening of the institution of the state.[1] Nonetheless, these two phenomena boosted the strength of civil society and helped create an international civil community that works to protect human rights, women's rights, workers' rights, and environmental quality, to combat poverty and disease, and more. Organizations such as Amnesty International, Physicians without Borders, and Greenpeace mobilize activists around the world to protect the interests of all human beings. The international media and social media networks reinforce global civil society: For the first time in human history, geographic and political borders are not an impenetrable barrier to the dissemination of information and ideas, or the recruitment of activists. Do these trends combine to increase social capital? Putnam argued that social capital is diminishing in the United States and that civil involvement in community organizations has declined (1995). Others, however, point to a decline in participation in formal channels (such as voting), accompanied by increased membership in community organizations and other patterns of participation (Verba et al. 1995, 26). Norris and Davis (2007) show that social capital is not diminishing in most European states.

In parallel to globalization, local affinity has also grown as citizens sought to foster relations within the community in response to alienation, loss of values, commercialization, and the disintegration of binding frameworks in modern society. Localization is reflected in the strengthening of local politics, communal and interpersonal media, and local recreational and cultural activities. Local organizations aim to improve the quality of life and level of services, and to protect common interests

[1] A comparative study by Johns Hopkins University in thirty-five countries identified a trend in the second half of the twentieth century of the expansion of third-sector organizations in all countries – developed nations, developing nations, and those "in transition" – and all regions (Salamon, Sokolowski, and List 2003).

in one's apartment building, neighborhood, and community. These two trends – globalization and localization – express both the weakening of the state's grip and the strengthening of civil society. Another factor is the decline of the welfare state and skepticism about its ability to protect the citizens' interests and respond to their needs. The cutbacks in state welfare services engendered the creation of third-sector organizations that fulfill these roles, on their own or on behalf of the state and the local authorities. The vacuum resulting from the state's retreat also led to the inability of government authorities to cope with natural disasters and civilian injuries in wars, while civil society organizations tried to fill this gap and were sometimes the only ones in the field.[2]

In Israel, most third-sector organizations are active in fields that were previously the responsibility of the welfare state – education, health, and welfare services. The growth of these organizations is also the product of the vacuum created by the weakening of mediating institutions, primarily political parties. Organizations and groups that operated in the past under a government ministry or party aegis (such as the Histadrut Labor Federation, women's organizations, sports clubs) gradually acquired independence and contributed to the strengthening of civil society.[3] At the same time, the state's shirking of its responsibility for providing services in specific fields and the trend toward privatizing them, whether directly or through outsourcing, expanded the state's involvement in regulating social, economic, and ecological policy.[4] The rise in the standard of living freed resources – in certain social strata – for political participation via new independent organizations working to promote equality, individual rights, and environmental protection. Examples include women's and environmental organizations that challenged existing values and policies, and in so doing, contributed to strengthening civil society (Gidron, Bar, and Katz 2003, 10).

In addition to the values of individualism, new needs emerged that the state did not address. For example, the weakening of traditional family connections created social groupings and support networks that were not based on kinship, but rather on a shared fate, such as self-help groups of people with disabilities, patients with particular illnesses, parents of children with learning disabilities, and so on. People tend to participate more in volunteer organizations as their standard of living and education levels rise, and their leisure time increases. As in global organizations that transcend borders, virtual social networks are created to forge connections among people with a common interest regardless of geographic, social, or class-based divisions. In Israel, third-sector organizations are still in the first stage of utilizing such channels as their main strategy (Zarkawy and Blit-Cohen 2008).

2 For example, the earthquake in Cairo in 1992; the floods in New Orleans in 2005; the shelling of northern Israel during the second Lebanon War in 2006.

3 Broadly defined, political parties are part of civil society in that they are volunteer organizations. In Israel, however, the parties are unique organizations whose status is defined in a separate law. They are subject to separate tax arrangements and receive funding from the state budget according to the Parties Financing Law. Therefore, they will not be discussed here as part of civil society (based on "Galnoor Committee" 2003, 22).

4 The Health Law, for example, mandated establishment of a public committee in the Ministry of Health to define a "healthcare basket" that would monitor, *inter alia*, the medications provided by the health funds. In reaction, regulation encouraged the organization of groups to monitor the committee's policies. Such organizations represent people with various illnesses and lobby for the inclusion of specific medications in the healthcare basket (Rosenbloom and Schwartz 1994).

B. Types of Third-Sector Organizations

The third sector is a mosaic of organizations that operate in diverse fields. In the discussion below, we list five types of organizations based on their roles and operational characteristics:

- ***Service providers:*** Some of these organizations are part of the public system, such as universities, health funds, and some religious institutions. Their activity is anchored in legislation or long-term agreements, with primary funding and oversight provided by the state. Some deliver services on a contractual basis and serve as a sort of substitute for government ministries – they provide education, welfare, and cultural services with partial government funding, under periodic contracts with the government or local authorities.
- ***Community organizations:*** These provide a platform for local or general social and civic activity such as sports clubs, cultural and recreational organizations, federations of immigrants, and membership clubs. They are often a reflection of existing social frameworks – place of residence, income, vocation, etc. – and sometimes represent common interests such as regional associations. The principal funding is from membership fees.
- ***Organizations for political and social change:*** These advocacy organizations operate in two forms: They represent the interests of particular groups in society, usually weak groups, or they represent a common cause or public interest, such as environmental protection.[5] These groups and organizations seek to pressure decision-makers to redistribute public resources, or at least to raise political awareness. They differ from regular interest groups in that they aspire to make significant changes in priorities, even when they work to promote the specific interests of poor people, women, or children (Alimi 2008). The difference between social change and political change is a question of definition, as is the distinction between social movements, public interest groups, advocacy organizations, and extra-parliamentary movements.[6] The primary source of funding is

[5] The distinction does not always hold. An organization for social change such as Yedid: The Association for Community Empowerment provides support services for disadvantaged groups through consultation and assistance in realizing their rights. In light of its extensive activity – branches in sixteen cities and assistance for some 400,000 families during the two decades since its inception – it is also an organization that indirectly advocates for the general public interest of social solidarity.

[6] *Interest groups:* The goal of the members is to influence public policy in a particular field – for example, to promote the interests of car owners. Organizations for social change include groups that work for general political and social change, usually with a particular ideological label, hence they are called *public interest groups*. For example: animal protection or anti-pornography groups. Most public interest groups prefer to avoid any connection with the government in order to maintain their freedom of action. *Advocacy organizations* are formed to protect and promote the rights of disadvantaged populations and to influence the decisions of government authorities that affect them. *Extra-parliamentary movements* are similar to political parties in their political essence, but differ from them in that they do not seek representation via election to parliament or aspire to be direct partners in governing. Their activity is usually conducted "in the street," in town squares, and via social networks. Many can be characterized as protest movements. Their modes of operation are direct, emotional, and heated, such as demonstrations, strikes, sit-ins, petitions, and sometimes disruptions of public order. Examples include the student movements in the 1960s and the social protests in the early 2010s. For a different breakdown, see Yishai 2003, 28–33.

contributions and not public budgets, though sometimes they receive assistance from public organizations or political parties.

- ***Professional associations:*** The accepted distinction is between organizations whose objective is to promote the interests of salaried workers (trade unions, such as the Histadrut Labor Federation) and membership organizations of professionals, merchants, business owners, or industrialists (e.g., the Israel Medical Association, the Federation of Israeli Chambers of Commerce, the Manufacturers' Association of Israel). In general, these large-interest groups seek to protect and promote the economic, professional, and class interests of their members. The principal source of funding is membership fees.
- ***Social enterprises:*** A social enterprise uses business strategies to pursue its social objectives (Young 2012). The results of the business activity, all or most of the profits, are earmarked for a social or community objective or reinvestment in the enterprise. This phenomenon is relatively new in Israel and elsewhere. There is disagreement as to whether these should be regarded as third-sector organizations (Gidron and Abbou 2014, 196).

C. Changes in Civil Society in Israel

Since the early 1970s, changes have occurred in Israel that can be described as a transition from a state-dominated society to a more autonomous one. With the establishment of Israel, there were great expectations from the new political system and onerous demands upon it. As years passed, citizens learned from their experience that the state alone could not meet these expectations, and autonomous activity began – first in the business sector, and later in third-sector organizations in civil society. Gradually, politics lost some of its power, as well as its monopoly on managing the lives of the citizenry. Two arenas took root alongside politics: the private economic market, whose autonomy was previously limited due to intensive government involvement; and civil society, which had already existed, but began to acquire independence only in the 1980s. While all eyes were on the change of the ruling party in 1977 and subsequent changes in the political system, an array of thousands of autonomous organizations, interest groups, protest movements, and others sprouted almost unnoticed under the state's nose, changing the character of Israeli society. At the same time, the steering capacity of the political system started to weaken, and this reinforced the establishment of organizations that openly declared that government authorities could not be relied upon to make the right decisions or take the proper action to meet the citizens' needs.

The development of civil society in Israel and the proliferation of third-sector organizations are related, as noted, to global changes and parallel developments in other democratic states.[7] This phenomenon is also connected to the decline of the Histadrut Labor Federation, the kibbutz movement, the general dominance of political parties, and the ideology of social solidarity. Therefore, it is impossible to understand the new political system in the twenty-first century and the nature of

[7] On funding of third-sector organizations in Europe, see Gidron et al. 2003, 57. On funding the third sector in Switzerland, see Nollert and Budowski 2009, 1–3. On patterns of funding in Israel, see Katz, Levinson, and Gidron 2007, 13–15; and Central Bureau of Statistics 2014c, 2–5.

democracy in Israel without emphasizing the roles of the business sector and civil society. This transformation also raises disturbing questions, which we will discuss in the conclusion of this chapter, about a possible contradiction in civil society's contribution to democracy; about the welcome participation of citizens that could go astray; about civil organizations whose contribution is harmful; and about the independence versus dependence of third-sector organizations.

The system of government in Israel is the consensus model, based on coalition agreements and a democracy of negotiation, as opposed to majoritarian democracy, based on the decisions of a single party. Consensus-model regimes tend to maintain a corporatist democracy in which large-interest groups regularly participate in setting policy, rather than a pluralistic democracy in which many interest groups work separately to influence policy in their fields (Schmitter 1989). Is the change in Israel only relative and is its civil society still more corporatist than pluralist as suggested in the past (Lijphart 1999, 177–83), or has Israel joined the democratic states in which policymaking inclines toward a "winner takes all" approach?

12.2 Legal Underpinnings, Funding Sources, and Support

The third sector includes organizations considered corporate entities by law (non-profits and public companies), philanthropies, and public endowments not considered corporations. In addition, there are unincorporated entities.

A. Definitions

A *non-profit organization* (*amuta*) according to the Nonprofit Associations Law (1980) is "two or more persons who wish to incorporate as a body corporate for a lawful purpose not aimed at the distribution of profits to its members." Prior to the law, non-profit organizations were registered under the Ottoman Associations Law of 1906 (Bar-Mor 1999, 3; N. Limor 2010, 14–16; Limor and Brindt 2014).[8] In order to form a non-profit organization, a request must be submitted to the Registrar of Nonprofits, who has the authority to decide not to register an organization if one of its objectives negates the existence or democratic character of Israel, or if it serves as a cover for illegal activities. The decision to deny registration to an organization is subject to judicial review. This review was exercised even prior to the law, as in the petition by the al-Ard Association, whose request to register under the Ottoman Associations Law was rejected (*G'eris v. Haifa District Supervisor* 1964). The court reviews the considerations of the Registrar and tends to interpret narrowly the prohibition on establishing non-profits in order to protect the freedom of association. A non-profit registered under the Nonprofit Associations Law is obligated to adhere to regulatory procedures, including the establishment of institutions for managing the organization and monitoring its activities. An amendment of the 1996 law expanded the authority of the Registrar of Nonprofits and

[8] The Ministry of Justice drafted a new Nonprofit Associations bill in 2014 with a different classification of types of nonprofits, primarily for purposes of regulation. It divides them into publicly or privately financed nonprofits. See the document of principles from February 17, 2014: http://index.justice.gov.il/Pubilcations/News/Pages/newamotot.aspx (accessed October 4, 2017).

increased transparency. Correspondingly, a non-profit that receives public support is required to present a certificate of "sound management" from the Registrar. In 2005, the Registrar of Nonprofits became part of the Israel Corporations Authority in the Ministry of Justice. It is estimated that over 90% of non-profit organizations in Israel are incorporated under the Nonprofit Associations Law (Katz, Levinson, and Gidron 2007, 17).

Non-profit companies: According to the Companies Law (1999), which replaced the Mandatory ordinance, a company for public benefit can register with the Registrar of Companies and declare that it was established for public purposes and not for profit. The Registrar of Companies is authorized to exercise judgment and deny registration of an organization, subject to judicial review. In all other matters, a non-profit company is similar to a commercial one.

Public endowments are trusts designed to promote a public interest. An endowment is not registered as a corporation and operates under the Trust Law (1979) and Trust Regulations (Methods of Investing Public Endowment Funds – 2004). The establishment of a public endowment does not require approval, only the submission of a document to the Registrar of Endowments that specifies its purposes and assets. A trustee of a public endowment is required to submit an annual report detailing financial records and activities.[9]

Philanthropic funds do not have a special legal status and are not subject to different rules of taxation.[10]

B. Funding and Support

We will focus on third-sector organizations that are registered non-profits and have three sources of funding: public allocation (state or local government), private contributions, and self-revenues (see Figure 12.1). In Israel, most third-sector organizations are supported by funds from a public budget, and few – mainly organizations that work for social change – rely solely on private contributions and self-generated income.[11]

Public funding is allocated in three channels:

- Statutory support – a budget transfer anchored in legislation. Examples: the funding of higher education institutions at a level of 60–70 percent of their budgets; collection of the health tax by the government that is transferred to the health funds.
- Support and grants based on criteria set by government ministries to organizations or non-profits in the ministry's area of responsibility. This method replaces the channel known as "special funds" – support allocated in accordance with

[9] Guide to Forming, Registering and Managing Public Endowments. Ministry of Justice, Registrar of Endowments. http://index.justice.gov.il/Units/RasutHataagidim/Guidelines/PublicEndowmentManagement.docx (accessed March 2, 2016).

[10] Government Decision No. 2190 (February 24, 2008) established a committee to examine the subject (N. Limor 2008). In 2011, the Ministry of Justice tabled an amendment to the Companies Law to regulate the activity of philanthropic funds, but this has not yet been enacted.

[11] www1.cbs.gov.il/www/hodaot2014n/08_14_217b.doc (accessed October 4, 2017). Data from the Accountant General (which includes direct allocations) from the government website: www.tmichot.gov.il/irj/portal/anonymous?guest_user=awf_user (accessed January 5, 2006).

coalition agreements (De Hartog 1999). According to the Budget Principles Law (1985), government ministries are required to publish criteria for granting support, as well as a list of public institutions and the amount of support approved for each. In 2014, this support totaled about NIS 1.7 billion, awarded to some 3,000 organizations.[12]

- Payments by the state for services rendered by organizations in accordance with contracts and other arrangements. In 2002, NIS 3.2 billion was transferred from the state budget to organizations to provide various services (Office of the Prime Minister 2008, 10). For example, the Ministry of Social Welfare bought services from non-profits (and also from business organizations) to operate shelters for people with intellectual development disorders; and the state participated, on a contractual basis, in funding 8 percent of the budget of Yad Sarah, a non-profit helping the ill and injured (www.yadsarah.org).

Income Tax Exemptions

According to the Income Tax Ordinance, tax exemptions are granted only to a public institution that is

> a group of people that exists and works for a public objective and whose assets and income are used solely in pursuit of the public objective ... [namely, objectives] pertaining to religion, culture, education, science, health, assistance, or sport, and any other objective approved by the minister of finance as a public objective.

Over the years, finance ministers have added other objectives, including some with a political hue.

Tax Credits for Contributing to a Public Institution

Article 46 of the Income Tax Ordinance grants a credit to someone who contributes to a "public institution" recognized for tax credits by the finance minister and the Knesset Finance Committee. That is, not every public institution offers tax benefits, only those for whom a credit has been explicitly approved. The involvement of the minister and the committee makes the decision vulnerable to political pressure. In 2005, benefits were given to 3,936 taxpayers who contributed to organizations classified as "public institutions." These organizations make up only about 16 percent of the active organizations (Katz, Levinson, and Gidron 2007, 29). The maximum tax credit in 2010 was 35 percent of the contribution, to a limit of NIS 7 million and up to 30 percent of the contributor's income (N. Limor 2010, 161). The cost of the tax benefits to contributors in 2009 was estimated at NIS 170 million, less than 0.5 percent of the total benefits in the state budget that year (Office of the Prime Minister 2008, 10; N. Limor 2010, 161). Among the organizations recognized as "public institutions" are primarily large service providers, while the percentage of organizations in the geographic periphery or Arab organizations is much lower (Katz, Levinson, and Gidron 2007, 41).

Over the years, government support for third-sector organizations has become one channel for mobilizing political support for parties. In the past, the practice was

[12] Data from the Accountant General (which includes direct allocations) from government website: www.tmichot.gov.il/irj/portal/anonymous?guest_user=awf_user (accessed January 5, 2006).

to earmark a general sum from the state budget to support public institutions, and the sum would be allocated according to internal directives of the government ministries, without transparency and without oversight. Only in the 1980s did the High Court of Justice intervene when it ruled that the principle of equality must guide the allocation of state funding for public institutions, and that clear, relevant, and equitable criteria must be made public (*Tomkhei Temimim Yeshiva v. State of Israel* 1983). However, the government circumvented the High Court ruling by adopting transparency in appearance only – the ministries did indeed list the institutions that received support in the Budget Law, but they were still selected in accordance with coalition accords. The listing of institutions did not contribute to the principle of equality; instead, it created a reality in which, in addition to direct support from government ministries, "earmarked funds" were allocated in the Budget Law for political reasons. In 1988, the High Court ruled that funding earmarked for a purpose the state has an interest in supporting should also be examined (*Tzaban v. Minister of Finance* 1988). An amendment to the Budget Principles Law in 1992 prohibited the inclusion of support for "special" institutions in the Budget Law and stipulated that state support for public institutions must be allocated only according to criteria of equality set by the government ministries.[13] Indeed, progress has been achieved in regulating government support for public institutions, but there is still room for deceit and discrimination by defining the types of public institutions, or tailoring criteria for institutions that the ministry wishes to fund. For example, the Ministry of Education conditioned its support for a training center on the candidate having at least thirty years of experience in the field, and that the candidate operate at least 500 classes (De Hartog 1998, 29).[14]

In principle, Israel is among the democratic states that recognize the importance of third-sector organizations and utilize the tax system to encourage their activity. To encourage contributions by citizens, the state is willing to relinquish income (regarding taxation and indirect aid, see the Galnoor Committee 2003, 50–56; Gidron et al. 2003, 103–9). Nonetheless, in comparison with other states, this willingness is limited, primarily because of the restrictions on tax exemptions. Furthermore, Israel is considered the world's largest importer of philanthropic funds – in 2009–13, about 47 percent of the total contributions to the third sector came from overseas (CBS 2014c).

Sources of Funding

Figure 12.1 shows that in 2013 most funding for the third sector (50%) still came from the public coffers. In 1995, however, state funding amounted to 63 percent of all sources. The share of private funding increased as a result of contributions by individuals, businesses, and foundations, as well as self-revenues – the sale of services and membership fees (Katz, Levinson, and Gidron 2007, 13). In fact, most of the public funding (86%) goes to organizations working in health, education, and research

[13] See the criteria for awarding support and the list of public institutions receiving support of the Ministry of Labor and Welfare, *State Records* 5101 (August 12, 2002) and 5117 (October 3, 2002), respectively. The amendment did not include the ultra-Orthodox religious institutions, whose support is based on the criteria of educational institutions.

[14] In 2014, the Ministry of Finance was revealed to have collaborated with the Knesset Finance Committee to distribute so-called "coalition funds" to political parties (e.g., see Zrahiya 2015a).

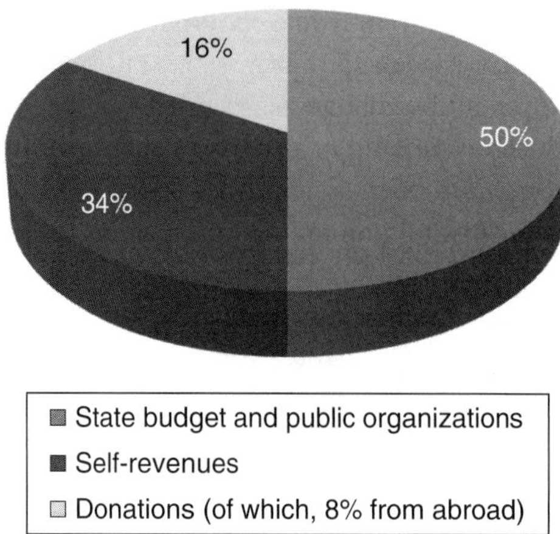

Figure 12.1 Funding sources of third-sector organizations by field (% in 2013)
Source: CBS 2014c.

(primarily the health funds and institutions of higher learning) – areas for which the state is responsible. In all other fields, government transfers account for less than 5 percent of the total funding, and less in social change organizations.

Contributions constitute a small part of overall funding for the third sector, but they increased from 9 percent in 1995 to 16 percent in 2013 (CBS 2014c; Schmid and Rudich 2009, 2), which is a relatively large share compared to other countries. In 1995, for example, contributions accounted on average for only 7 percent of the funding of third-sector organizations in western Europe (Galnoor Committee 2003, 30). The reason for this, as noted, is the high level of contributions from abroad (Shye et al. 1999). In 2007, about two-thirds of the Israeli public stated that they had donated to organizations, and it is estimated that total contributions in Israel reached almost NIS 11 billion in 2013, and an additional NIS 9.5 billion from overseas (CBS 2014c).

12.3 Development of the Third Sector in Israel

During the pre-state period, volunteer organizations, including political parties, made up the institutional skeleton of the state-in-the-making. During the "state corporatism" period, from statehood through the mid-1970s, third-sector organizations were subject to government authorities, political camps and parties, and the Histadrut Labor Federation. In the "pluralistic period" from the late 1970s, independent organizations began to proliferate (this description is based on Yishai 1998; Silber and Rosenhek 1999; Gidron et al. 2003, 119–71, 199–220).

A. The Period of Subordinate Volunteer Organizations

From the outset, the Zionist enterprise has relied on Jewish philanthropy. Generally speaking, it can be said that "civil society" in pre-state Israel and the Diaspora built the political institutions that established the state. From the perspective of the Yishuv and the Jews in the Diaspora who mobilized in support of the Zionist enterprise, the national institutions – the World Zionist Organization, the Jewish Agency, and the Jewish National Council – were voluntary entities of Jews in the Diaspora and later in Palestine, and lacked the formal authority to demand compliance or impose taxes. In 1901, the Jewish National Fund (JNF) was formed to purchase land in historical Israel; and in 1921, the United Israel Appeal was founded to raise money in order to finance the Zionist project. During the Mandate period, the national institutions became, in practice, governance entities in terms of external international recognition and internal legitimacy. They gradually assumed responsibility for social services such as education, culture, employment, and welfare, partly in an effort to create autonomy and independence from the British Mandate authorities. These voluntary entities became the institutions of the state-in-the-making, thereby merging the identities of state and civil society. That is, there was no independent civil space, and institutions such as political parties controlled nearly all areas of life, including the activity of volunteer organizations (Galnoor 1982, 94).

The *General Federation of Workers in the Land of Israel* (hereinafter: the Histadrut), established in 1920, symbolizes the beginning of what would later be called "the third sector." The Histadrut was an umbrella organization of the labor movement that developed a comprehensive system of social and economic services for most of the Jewish population. It was funded by the Zionist institutions and became a small-scale model of a welfare state that provides its members with health services, education, culture, sports, housing, and assistance for the unemployed, pensioners, and the elderly. The Histadrut served as the core organization of other volunteer organizations (labor councils, kibbutz movements, the moshav movement, the workers' stream in education, the Noar Ha'oved youth movement, Hapoel sports clubs) and of economic organizations (Bank Hapoalim, Tnuva, Solel Boneh, and transportation cooperatives).

Members of the two other camps, the civil and religious, maintained their own community organizations in parallel, but the level of organization and ability to mobilize members could not be compared to that of the workers' movement. The civil camp included the National Labor Federation, professional associations (merchants, craftsmen, farmers), youth movements (Maccabi, Beitar), and defense organizations (Etzel, Lehi). The religious camp also controlled organizations and groups such as the Hapoel Ha-Mizrahi federation, the religious stream in education, and the Bnei Akiva youth movement (Horowitz and Lissak 1978, 123–37).

During this period, most of the services were provided via channels with a political identity, and the allocation of national resources was made according to a party-based formula. The purview of political parties stretched beyond the role of political representation and dominated most areas of life for party members – from birth (sectoral hospitals) almost to the grave (the burial societies did not have a political orientation), including education, culture, employment, and welfare. There were, however, a few independent, non-partisan organizations, referred to as "civic," such as Hadassah. Established by Jewish women in America to work in the field of health, Hadassah also served Arabs as well as non-Zionist, ultra-Orthodox Jews. The organization sought to remain voluntary and independent, rejecting an initiative by the Jewish Agency to bring it under its wing. Another example is the Hebrew Scouts, founded in 1919 as the first Hebrew youth movement. As part of the global Scouts movement, it was non-partisan and the only youth movement to include both secular and religious Jews; its activity was later anchored in legislation – the Scouts Ordinance (New Version) 1978.

During the Yishuv period and early years of the state, numerous volunteer organizations and groups were active, but they operated in a well-organized party network with close ties to the authorities. A group that sought access to resources and political influence had to be affiliated to the parties, and through them to the political camps or their organizations. Consequently, the widespread volunteer activity that took place during that period was neatly bound political frameworks (Galnoor 1987, 1–10). However, a new study shows that during the Yishuv period there were many small independent associations (Rozin 2011).

B. The "Statist Corporatism" Period

Until the 1970s, two contradictory trends were prevalent: the "statism" of Ben-Gurion (*mamlakhtiyut*), which aspired to combine all the social functions, including volunteering and pioneering, under the aegis of the state, as opposed to the movement orientation (or class ideology), which sought to keep most of the social roles in the hands of the pre-state volunteer organizations. During these formative years, individualistic approaches were also an antithesis to the state, but they held relatively little sway. These trends shaped the transition crises of the years 1948–52, including the debate over a constitution (see Chapter 2). The resulting compromise can be called "state corporatism." On the one hand, areas such as security, foreign relations, development, and finance became the responsibility of the state; on the other hand, religion, education, health, housing, and other fields operated under arrangements of cooperation and resource allocation between the state and "the political camps," i.e., the large-interest groups in society. The salient examples of corporatist arrangements are the agreements forged among the state, the Jewish Agency, and the Histadrut, which left the responsibility for many services in the hands of these non-state entities, even after the establishment of Israel. In addition, the Histadrut retained a leading role and almost a monopoly in the field of health and the Jewish Agency in the absorption of immigrants, while the political parties sponsored newspapers, sports associations, and immigrant societies.

At the same time, independent organizations had begun to emerge from the grassroots to respond to special needs populations or to address issues neglected by the authorities. Examples include the AKIM (1951) and ILAN (1952) organizations for the disabled, and the Israel Cancer Association (1952). Some of these also received government support. During the first decade, a few protest groups and extra-parliamentary groups also formed, though in retrospect they had a marginal impact. Such groups, for example, advocated against religious coercion and nuclear armament, and in favor of government reforms and a change in policy vis-à-vis the Arab citizens. One of these groups was Shurat Hamitnadvim (the Volunteers' Rank) (1951) – students and teachers from Hebrew University who organized to help teach Hebrew to immigrants in transit camps. Confronted with the conditions in these camps, they sharply criticized the government's policy of immigrant absorption and the corruption of the authorities (Galnoor 1982, 183). On the extremes, terrorist groups such as Brit Hakanaim (Covenant of the Zealots) (1950) sought to impose religious laws on the state using violent methods; while Malkhut Yisrael (Kingdom of Israel) (1953), composed of former Lehi members, used stolen weapons against targets they perceived as anti-religious, pro-Communist, or unpatriotic. This included an attempted bombing of the Knesset during a session on the education system, and a bomb set off in the Foreign Ministry to protest reparation payments from Germany in 1952 (Hermann 1995).

In the 1960s, changes began to undermine statist corporatism – a rise in the standard of living expanded the sphere of activity of the independent organizations in civil society, and of business organizations in the economic market. In the areas of welfare and education, an effort was made to integrate volunteer organizations in addressing social disparities, poverty, and crime, and "self-help" organizations were formed. Organizations later emerged to address social and political issues, such as the Association for Civil Rights in Israel (1972). After the Six Day War, ethnic-based social protest also began, such as the Black Panthers, discussed below. There were also independent philanthropic foundations, some of which had begun in the pre-state period (e.g., the America-Israel Cultural Foundation, founded in 1939), as opposed to the Jerusalem Foundation, which Jerusalem Mayor Teddy Kollek formed in 1966 to circumvent the national and local government bureaucracy and raise funds for the city's development.

During this period, most of the volunteer organizations did not voice strong opposition to government policy, and in exchange they received funding – grants and deficit reduction. There was no transparency because the common practice, then in the relations between the state and third-sector organizations, was not based on reporting, monitoring, and oversight. When independent political and social organizations began to appear in the 1970s, state authorities made an effort to apply the previous co-optation methods to ensure patronage over them, or at least blunt their critiques. And when these methods failed, an effort was made to delegitimize the protest and social change groups, dismissed by the politicians as irresponsible "street movements" (Yishai 1998).

C. The Pluralistic Period

Since the late 1970s, political parties have become less dominant and the steering capacity of the political system has weakened. In parallel, third-sector organizations proliferated and civil society grew. The Yom Kippur War (1973), which undermined the citizens' trust in state institutions, was also a catalyst in this gradual process. Other developments in this period include a rise in the standard of living parallel with growing inequality; the gradual shrinking of the scope of the welfare state; a decline in the preeminence of the Histadrut, eroding the protection of wage-earners; the beginning of privatization; and intensified internal conflicts in Israeli society with growing awareness of discrimination and demands for equal rights. As a result, some new organizations arose to fill the gaps left by the shrinking welfare state and to serve the public's unmet needs. Other organizations expressed dissatisfaction with the status quo and a lack of faith in the political system. The dissolving agreement among the large and institutionalized groups led to a decline in corporatist arrangements and the remnants of collectivism, and to the strengthening of social pluralism, expressed, *inter alia*, in the multiplicity of independent organizations (and in terms of their funding). The Nonprofit Associations

Law of 1980, which gave a legal framework to the process of forming the organizations, also helped encourage their growth.

During the pluralistic period, some of the media became politically independent, and the organizations used them to reach elected officials and government ministries, as well as the hearts and minds of the public. The public arena became a key area of activity for third-sector organizations. And another change occurred: the shrinking role of the state led the government and local authorities to expand their use of third-sector organizations as subcontractors for service provision. However, the most substantive change in the nature of Israeli civil society during this period was the proliferation of organizations that were both independent and "anti-establishment." Their aim was to wage a political battle to improve environmental quality, ensure sound government practices, and promote equal rights for groups such as Arabs, women, the disabled, pensioners, and others. The new organizations influenced the older ones, which also were imbued with an anti-establishment spirit. For example, the veteran Society for the Protection of Nature in Israel was spurred by green organizations like the Israel Union for Environmental Defense, and began to fight for the protection of nature in opposition to government policy (Yishai 1998, 160–61). The Histadrut-affiliated Na'amat: Movement of Working Women and Volunteers, founded in 1921, was influenced by independent women's organizations and began advocating on behalf of women's rights.

The status of civil society in Israeli political discourse was strongly affected by the emergence of protest organizations and extra-parliamentary movements such as Gush Emunim (1974), advocating settlements in the Greater Land of Israel, and Peace Now (1978), advocating a return to the pre-1967 borders.

Since the 1980s, independent organizations, including protest groups, have won public and political legitimacy in Israel. However, in this pluralistic period, most of the funding for the older groups and service-provision organizations still comes from public budgets. Third-sector organizations working for social change have adopted new methods of funding, primarily due to the changed objectives of overseas philanthropic foundations. Previously, donations by world Jewry via the United Jewish Appeal and United Israel Appeal were transferred to the Jewish Agency and directly to universities, hospitals, the philharmonic, and so on. In contrast, the New Israel Fund (NIF), founded in 1979, created a new model of partnership between Israel and Diaspora Jews, and set as its goal the strengthening of democracy and progressive values, promoting pluralism, justice, and equality in Israel; Shatil, a subsidiary of NIF, provides technical assistance to thousands of social change organizations. Its declared objective is to create a sustainable civil society in Israel (see www.nif.org). Other philanthropic foundations, most foreign-based, operate in Israel. According to surveys, the public views this new phenomenon in a positive way (Schmid and Rudich 2008, 33), while parties on the right have tried to curb these foreign donations through legislation.

D. The Involvement of Business in Third-Sector Funding and Activity

The social involvement of businesses has grown. This is reflected in managing businesses in a way that contributes to society, or at least does not violate shared values; funding and assisting social organizations; and direct social action, including social enterprises, as defined above. According to a survey conducted by the Ministry of Industry in 2006, only 9 percent of companies were involved in community activity, and they contributed an estimated NIS 1 billion in donations, products, and services (N. Limor 2010, 43). This is low in comparison to other developed countries, but in Israel these contributions were made with no tax incentives for the philanthropic activity of corporations. A number of companies created funds such as the Israel Venture Network, and businesses have partnered with third-sector organizations to implement programs. In 2011, just over 11,000 businesses contributed NIS 652 million (CBS 2014c).

The social involvement of the business sector in Israel has been influenced by the concept of "social responsibility" in other countries, including the assumption that it is good for businesses. And there is greater understanding that the deteriorating socioeconomic situation in Israel is not only a matter for the government, but that the growing disparity between rich and poor threatens society as a whole. In addition, the cutbacks for social services, and the willingness of third-sector organizations to fill the vacuum in areas from which the government retreated, put public pressure on business people to contribute their part, such as making donations to non-profits that provide food to the poor. In 2005, an annual index of social responsibility was launched by the Tel Aviv Stock Exchange and the organization Maala: Business for Social Responsibility, which ranks Israel's leading companies according to corporate social responsibility. While community involvement is good for the public image of business corporations, it also strengthens the employees' sense of belonging and satisfaction.[15] The state too decided to encourage social involvement: It significantly raised the maximum contribution eligible for tax credit; made it mandatory for companies to make public their policy of contributions to public institutions; and established a joint forum (see below) for the government, the third sector, and the business sector (Office of the Prime Minister 2008).

E. Government Policy

The accelerated growth of the third sector and the large allocations from public budgets did not lead to the formulation of a comprehensive, explicit, transparent, and consistent government policy. The transfer of funds from the taxpayers to third-sector organizations requires regulation by the state, but also recognition in principle of the importance of this sector's independence, no less than that of business. The stance adopted by government authorities was not usually aimed at encouraging the development of the third sector, but rather at tightening supervision. Thus, over the years, restrictions were applied to these organizations, such as legal constraints on the right to form an association and intervention in the internal management of non-profits via the Registrar of Nonprofits, the Accountant General, the tax authorities, government ministries, and others. While this administrative intervention partly stemmed from concerns about the abuse of public funds and was partly a result of bureaucratic impulses, the government's vague

[15] In a survey conducted in 2001, more than 70 percent of the respondents said they would prefer to buy a product from a company that contributes to the community (Katz, Levinson, and Gidron 2007, 21).

policy was largely attributable to a fear of the political implications of the sector's growing strength, particularly the independence of social change organizations. Consequently, concern grew among third-sector organizations that any government policy would interfere in their internal affairs and further restrict their independence and activity.

Nonetheless, the third sector became an influential factor and this required the government to reexamine its policy toward it – whether due to pressure from the organizations, which demanded a new definition of relations between the state and civil society, or to demands for oversight by the government ministries.[16] A practical need also arose to define criteria for policy, taxation, and donation incentives, and to distinguish between service-providing, community, and advocacy organizations working for social and political change. However, what really influenced the change in the government's approach was the tangible contribution of third-sector organizations to the residents of northern Israel during the second Lebanon War. In 2008, for the first time, the government announced a policy reflecting the state's recognition of the legitimacy of civil society and its organizations (Office of the Prime Minister 2008, 7):

- The government of Israel views civil society organizations and businesses acting for the benefit of public objectives that are not merely economic as partners in the effort to build a better Israeli society. The government believes that these organizations have always played an important role in shaping the character of society and strengthening the democratic foundations of the state.
- The government of Israel sees great importance in supporting non-profit organizations based on values of voluntarism and giving, and aimed at advancing the common good.
- The government of Israel recognizes the knowledge and experience of civil society organizations, and will endeavor to include them in policymaking processes.

The government decision charted a comprehensive policy for relations among the government, civil society, and the business sector, and roundtables were convened for ongoing discourse and formulating a joint covenant that would include local government. The operative part included expanding tax breaks for contributions, revising reporting requirements for organizations that receive government funds and those that do not, encouraging entrepreneurship through "social incubators," granting special status to philanthropic foundations, and more. The decision addresses both greater transparency in reporting by civil society organizations as well as government policies for support. The government's declaration of policy was put to test when the economic crisis erupted in 2008. The three-sector "interface roundtable" (government, civil society, and business) discussed ways to help social organizations that faced difficulties in the wake of the crisis. Temporary orders were issued to raise the ceiling for tax-deductible contributions to NIS 7.5 million, and the minimum amount for tax credit was lowered to encourage contributions from

[16] This is the context in which the Galnoor Committee was established with a strong representation of social organizations ("Galnoor Committee" 2003), and the appointment by the government of the Aridor Committee (2006).

the general public. The government later created an assistance fund for third-sector organizations, though the sums were small and the process was cumbersome.[17]

During Israel's first decades, most of the social organizations were affiliated with political-party camps and created the structure of "statist corporatism." This initial model continues to influence civil society in Israel, particularly the view that does not recognize the independent status of third-sector organizations. For example, "volunteering" is still considered the role of the state, and the National Council for Volunteering has operated in the Office of the Prime Minister since 1972. The change that began in the pluralistic era is still in its early stages, and many questions remain about the direction civil society is taking: Is pluralism a result of political changes, or is it rooted in a social divide that adds to the difficulties in shaping a consensual policy, not only in socioeconomic fields, but also in foreign affairs and security? Can civil society contribute to strengthening democracy in Israel? What is the real impact of third-sector organizations on policymaking in their fields of activity? Will new models of "collaborative governance" be created in Israel, a new type of cooperation and coordination among the three sectors, similar to developments in other democratic countries (Bogdanor 2005; Emerson, Nabatchi, and Balogh 2012; Rhodes 2012)?

12.4 The Third Sector in Israel: An Overview

A. Number of Organizations and Scope of Economic Activity

Since the early 1980s, the number of third-sector organizations has burgeoned – non-profits and public benefit companies registered with and reported by the Registrar of Companies. Commensurately, their fields of activity and economic clout have expanded. At the end of 2013, there were 35,974 organizations (68% of the 52,910 registered since enactment of the Nonprofit Associations Law). Table 12.1 shows the number of new organizations registered between 1981 and 2013 – an average of 1,600 annually, most non-profits and a smaller number of public benefit companies. As in the business sector, there is constant turnover in the third sector, as new organizations are created and others cease to operate. Of the registered organizations in 2013, only about 14,000 submitted annual reports to the Registrar and 17,000 had a certificate of sound management, including about 8,000 old Ottoman associations.

Based on these data, approximately 16,000–18,000 are active organizations, i.e., about half the registered organizations. The reasons for this have not been studied, but we know that the overwhelming majority became inactive within ten years of their formation (Gidron and Alon 2007).

Table 12.1 shows an upward trend in the annual average until 2001, with a peak in 1998, when 2,075 new organizations registered. The growing presence of the third sector has economic significance. According to the Central Bureau of Statistics, annual revenues and spending by non-profits in 2011–13 were about NIS 111–12 billion. GuideStar estimates only NIS 42–46 billion, because it excludes all the

[17] In 2013, the Finance Ministry updated the procedures for state budget support for third-sector organizations (Ministry of Finance 2014).

Table 12.1 *New organizations registering with the Registrar of Companies 1981–2013*

	New organizations	Total organizations	Annual average
1981–91	16,467	16,467	1,503
1992–2001	17,619	34,086	1,762
2002–11	15,830	49,916	1,583
2012–13	2,994	52,910	1,497

Source: N. Limor 2014.

statutory bodies, government-affiliated non-profits, and, in particular, institutions of higher learning and health funds (N. Limor 2014).[18]

The number of people employed by non-profits has risen over the years and peaked in 2011 at 430,000 full-time salaried positions, which constituted about 13 percent of all salaried jobs in the economy. Almost half (49%) of these non-profit jobs are in the field of education, 23 percent in health, 12 percent in culture and sport, 7 percent in social welfare, 4 percent in religion, and 1 percent in advocacy. The number of volunteers in 2011 was estimated at 412,000 (equivalent to 58,000 full-time salaried positions) – 35 percent in the field of welfare, 25 percent in education, 8 percent in health, 8 percent in culture and sport, and 8 percent in advocacy.[19] The inclusion of health funds and higher education institutions in the category of the third sector in Israel makes it one of the largest, in monetary terms, relative to other countries (Gidron et al. 2003, 52–55). In reality, it is smaller, and its financial situation is weak and vulnerable. For example, the economic crisis in 2008 and the decline in the dollar–shekel exchange rate at that time had an adverse effect on the amount of contributions, and many organizations suspended or cut back their activity. In a 2008 survey of 220 organizations, 25 percent reported a shortage of funds, 20 percent said they planned to lay off workers, and 10 percent believed they would be forced to stop their activity (Katz and Yogev 2009, 3, 5).

B. Areas of Activity

Of the 36,000 registered non-profits in 2012 (not including Ottoman associations and public endowments), 25 percent were categorized as religious organizations. The next largest category was education and research (20%), followed by culture and recreation (17%), welfare (15%), civic organizations (promoting public issues) (6%), philanthropy (5%), health (2%), and environmental protection (1%). The data relate to the *number* of organizations in each field, not the scope of their activity or their economic importance (e.g., of 899 health organizations). Some areas have undergone accelerated growth, such as welfare in the 1990s as a result of the government's policy of privatization; or educational organizations for children and teenagers in response to the crisis in the education system (Gidron and Alon 2007). The privatization policy reinforced the perception that the primary role of the third

[18] Also see Central Bureau of Statistics 2014c.
[19] Central Bureau of Statistics 2014c.

sector is to provide services, filling the vacuum created by cutbacks in social services (Galnoor, Paz-Fuchs, and Zion 2015).

In parallel, there was natural growth of 50 percent in the number of organizations in the field of culture and recreation – 6,265 sport clubs, youth movements, community centers, and culture organizations (Gidron, Alon, and Ben-Nun 2004, 18, 20). The years 1998–2012 also witnessed 40 percent growth in the number of organizations working for social and political change, environmental protection, and animal rights. The number of these organizations reached 2,535, despite the fact that almost none of them receives state funding. And while their number increased, their activity still accounted for only a small share (7%) of the burgeoning third-sector activity (ibid., 20). On the other hand, the relative number of philanthropic organizations decreased: 5 percent of the third sector in 2012, down from 20 percent in 1985. The data, however, provide no indication of the scope and objectives of the activity (Gidron and Alon 2007).[20]

Third-sector organizations in Israel are mainly service providers, and most of them function like branches of government ministries or local authorities. Accordingly, autonomous civil society is still weak, despite the larger scope of its activity. The third sector has grown and expanded, but there is no evidence of commensurate growth in social capital in Israel – social networks that contribute to a sense of commitment, belonging, and solidarity, and strengthen the cooperation, communication, and trust among citizens. The assumption that membership in social organizations serves as a "school for democracy" also still awaits confirmation.

C. Public Affinity for Third-Sector Organizations

How do citizens perceive the third sector and to what extent are they aware of and willing partners in the activity of these organizations? To examine this question, we will exclude service providers such as the health funds and focus on community and social change organizations. In the Israeli Democracy Index, 19 percent of the respondents reported that they were a "member or participant in the activity of a social organization working for the general good" (Arian et al. 2005–10: 2007, 101). In the 2008 Democracy Index, 80 percent of the general population reported a donation. The average contribution to organizations was NIS 750 a year per household. The scope of volunteering in 2006 was estimated at 400 million hours, and the total value of volunteering, based on the minimum wage, was about NIS 7.5 billion. The data show growth in the reported scope of volunteering and donations particularly vis-à-vis formal organizations. However, the overall percentage of contributors remained stable (Katz, Levinson, and Gidron 2007, 8–9).

Wars and natural disasters provide a test for the public's willingness to contribute via third-sector organizations, and highlight the question of civil society's role during times of emergency. In these situations, non-governmental organizations are sometimes the first on the scene, when the response of government authorities can be slow and unfocused (see Pipa 2006, for example). A survey of the public's

[20] Little research has been conducted on the philanthropic organizations in Israel; see Silver 2008; Schmid and Rudich 2008.

contribution and voluntarism during the second Lebanon War (2006) found that 43 percent contributed money and equipment and 11 percent volunteered practical assistance to residents of northern Israel (Katz, Levinson, and Gidron 2007, 50). The contributions and volunteering were channeled primarily through third-sector and business organizations, or were provided directly by the citizens. Despite this spontaneous mobilization, the citizens of Israel believe that it is the government's duty to respond to social needs in times of crisis. Indeed, during the wars in Gaza in 2008 and 2014, lessons were learned from the non-functioning of government and local authorities, and the role of third-sector organizations on the home front was limited and more coordinated (Bavly et al. 2007; Gidron 2009, 2; Elran and Altshuler 2014).

12.5 Spheres of Third-Sector Political Activity

Spheres of activity have changed since the 1970s. Previously, most activities were institutional, within the political-partisan camps, and conducted in a discreet manner with government ministries. There was little direct lobbying in the Knesset at the time and few appeals to the courts. Here we examine more recent activity: As the organizations became more independent, relations with government ministries became more complex and visible; lobbyists (including party members) deployed in the Knesset corridors; and organizations and groups turned more frequently to the courts. Relations with the media, a central sphere of activity of the third sector, are discussed in the next chapter.

A. Relationship with Parties

We can identify at least three types of relationship between organizations and parties: organizations that function like party branches or are subordinate to parties in some way; organizations that turned into parties; and organizations that collaborate with parties and are identified with them.

First, organizations that are like or subordinate to parties. In Israel's early days, the main social groups were integrated into parties while volunteer organizations were likewise affiliated and identified with "subcenters" of the political parties and camps (Horowitz and Lissak 1978). Organizations that continued to operate in later years include the Histadrut, kibbutzim and other collective settlements, and immigrant societies of the Labor camp; as well as organizations of industrialists, merchants, and citrus growers of the "citizens' camp." Since the parties during the state's early years were also social movements, they subsumed most of the third-sector organizations. This model waned over the years, but did not completely disappear. Since the 1990s, Shas has been an example of this type of party – it became a social movement with a network of volunteer organizations that provide services to ultra-Orthodox Sephardim and needy populations (Yishai 1998a, 165–66; Y. Peled 2001). In addition, non-profits were formed to circumvent the Parties Financing Law and help parties during elections. However, this phenomenon has receded in the wake of reports by the state comptroller and court rulings.

Second, groups and organizations that tried their luck as parties. Some won seats in the first Knesset, though their tenure was short-lived – the WIZO women's organization, the Yemenite Association Party, and the Union of North African Immigrants (Yishai 1987, 115–19). Interest groups running for the Knesset are a recurring phenomenon in Israeli politics: immigrant organizations, pensioners, women, and the disabled, as well as parties advocating for men's rights or tax cuts. The overwhelming majority have failed to win Knesset representation.[21] On the other hand, a small number of movements have turned into parties. The most prominent of these are: the Movement for Civil Rights and Peace, headed by Shulamit Aloni (1973) (later Ratz and Meretz); Shinui, elected to the Knesset in 1977 as one of the founding partners in Dash (Amnon Rubinstein 1982; Urieli and Barzilai 1982; Aloni 1997); the Zionist Forum, led by Natan Sharansky, which formed Yisrael B'Aliyah, was elected to the Knesset in 1996, and merged with the Likud in 2003; and the Greens, who ran for the Knesset continuously after 1999 and did not pass the electoral threshold.

Third, social movements that are identified with or maintain an organizational connection with political parties. They prefer to operate as extra-parliamentary movements – sometimes because they are dissatisfied with the positions of the parties close to them, and sometimes because they opt for direct political action. For example, Gush Emunim, which emerged from the NRP, chose to establish a separate framework identified with the settlers, but they collaborated with MKs from the right-wing and religious parties; Peace Now, whose world view was close to that of Labor or parties to its left (e.g., Mapam, Meretz), was disappointed with these parties, but collaborated with them. Cooperation between a social movement and party can pave the way toward stronger influence by the movement, but can also make it redundant and lead to its demise. This happened to the Black Panthers: Several of its members were integrated into other parties after it failed in elections. Another example is the social protest movement of the summer of 2011: A few of its leaders became MKs, but the movement disappeared from the public stage.

Every social or political movement that seeks to have a real impact faces this dilemma in Israeli politics – to operate outside or within parliament. Experience shows that groups and movements that joined existing parties were swallowed up by them. Others formed independent parties that were short-lived. Most movements opted to remain outside – some independent, some identified with a particular party, and some unknown to the public.

B. In the Labyrinth of the Public Bureaucracy

As noted, the lion's share of third-sector organizations in Israel are service providers and, despite their autonomy, they sometimes constitute a sort of branch of government ministries and local authorities for implementing policy. Here too they face a dilemma with regard to the degree of their independence from the public bureaucracy. Organizations and groups that seek to promote a specific issue and change existing policy might adopt different strategies (Galnoor 1975). One way is to be anti-establishment, criticize government policy, point out flaws, and offer alternatives. For example, the National Council for the Child monitors government policy,

[21] An exceptional case of an interest group that won representation is Gil: The Pensioners' Party, which won seven seats in the seventeenth Knesset, but failed to pass the electoral threshold in the eighteenth Knesset (2009).

presents its own proposals, and does not receive support from the state. The same is true of non-profit organizations of parents and teachers that founded "democratic schools" as an alternative to state institutions; or the Ta'ayush and Adalah organizations, which work to change discriminatory government policy toward Arab citizens of Israel.

Another option is to try to influence from the inside, to step back from an oppositional approach that criticizes policy, and instead seek to involve the organization in government activity – to attain a status whereby the government consults with the organization in advance when formulating policy, as when the Association for Civil Rights in Israel is invited to the Ministry of Justice for consultation on proposed legislation. A third way is when an organization becomes a service provider funded by a government ministry. For instance, democratic schools are recognized by the Ministry of Education and shelters for battered women have gradually won recognition and funding from the local authorities. An example of this type of relationship is the Fidel Association for Education and Social Integration of Ethiopian Jews in Israel, founded in 1996. Its mission is "to end the ongoing failure in absorbing immigrants from Ethiopia by intervening in the process of absorbing Ethiopian children in the education system." Fidel's activity in schools was external and voluntary at first, but the Ministry of Education later took it under its wing and Fidel became its outsourced arm (V. Shiffer 2003, 96, 102, 109, 114).

Organizations are more successful at influencing the public bureaucracy when they win its confidence and are integrated into its activity. On the other hand, integration comes with a price, and these organizations are liable to lose their independence and ability to challenge the system. Many independent organizations discovered only in retrospect that they had entered into an "access in exchange for secrecy" deal. In contrast, organizations that prefer to remain outsiders continue to shout "the emperor has no clothes" – but no one hears them, unless they find other channels to influence policy. Many organizations try to do both: They are involved in the processes of policy formulation, participate in internal discussions in the government ministries, provide information and expertise, and promote their views; at the same time, however, they try to maintain the option of opposing proposed policies, though this could harm their chances of being invited to the next round of consultations.

One way an organization can maintain its independence and avoid such conflict is to ensure that governmental and public committees are required by law or custom to invite their representatives to discussions, or even include them in formulating policy. The law recognizes the need to stipulate an "obligation to consult" with certain entities – for example, in the Antiquities Law. In 1981, the High Court overruled a decision by the minister of education to halt archeological excavations after graves were found at the site because the minister had failed to consult with the Council for Archeology (*Archeological Institute v. Minister of Education* 1981). In another example, the Equal Rights for People with Disabilities Law (1998) states that the ministers responsible for formulating regulations (e.g., mandating access to public transportation) must consult with organizations that work to promote the rights of the disabled. From the government's perspective, the growing strength of third-sector organizations means they cannot be ignored, and government ministries invite them to participate in formulating policy, even when this is not required by law, in an effort to avoid public and legal conflicts at a later stage.

C. In the Knesset Corridors

During Israel's early years, political parties served as the main channels for the activity of volunteer organizations in the Knesset. The parties or MKs were the direct representatives of the most powerful groups in Israeli society – the kibbutz and moshav movements, the Egged transportation cooperative, the Farmers' Association, the Leumit Health Fund, and others. Consequently, the Knesset was a secondary arena for outside lobbying. Change began during the pluralistic period, when the organizations' activity in the Knesset became independent and significant in terms of impact on legislation, the budget, and decision-making in Knesset committees.

The initiative for legislation regarding a particular subject is often the result of efforts by third-sector organizations or commercial companies that directly lobby MKs – and wealthier organizations use paid lobbyists to do this. In the past, lobbying was not a profession; it was based on personal relationships, an MK's interest in a subject, or affiliation with certain interest groups (the agricultural lobby, the industrialists' lobby, the religious lobby) (Yishai 1987, 145–46). With the growing independence of MKs and the proliferation of private members' bills, the organizations – particularly the most powerful and wealthy ones – looked for a direct way to promote their interests, sometimes regardless of the MK's party affiliation. Lobbying in the Knesset became a profession for all intents and purposes, and organizations that could afford it hired lobbyists to promote their interests in the Knesset. Lobbying can be ongoing and long-term – to protect private interests (e.g., in the fields of banking or pharmaceuticals), or to safeguard public interests (e.g., in defense of civil rights). It can be narrowly focused – to promote or block a particular law or policy, as in the case of the many lobbyists hired by the gas exploration companies to fight the Sheshinski Committee recommendations (2011–15) to tax their profits at a higher rate. In 2008, an amendment to the Knesset Law set rules for Knesset lobbyists – restrictions on granting permits for activity, greater transparency by publishing their names, and a requirement to wear an identification badge in the Knesset.[22]

Organizations with specific expertise are invited to hearings held by Knesset committees and even draft legislative proposals for MKs. For example, the Equal Rights for People with Disabilities Law (1998) was the product of collaboration between the Bizchut organization and legislators.

Think tanks also operate in the Knesset through position papers, expert opinions, and participation in processes of legislation and policymaking. In 2014, some fifty-six independent think tanks operated in Israel, including research institutes at universities and others not university affiliated.[23] A 2008 study listed eleven think tanks in the field of social policy; the oldest five being the Van Leer Jerusalem Institute (1959), the Jerusalem Institute for Israel Studies (1978), the Taub Center for Social Policy Studies in Israel (1982), the Israel Democracy Institute (1991), and the Adva Center (1991) (Bensimhon-Peleg 2008). Their activity ranges from basic research to advocacy without research. Each has experts and professionals working for them to promote particular issues, usually in the public sphere.

[22] Knesset (Regulating the Activity of Lobbyists) Law (Amendment 25), 2008. According to the Knesset website, 224 lobbyists were registered at the end of 2016 (http://main.knesset.gov.il/About/Lobbyist/Pages/Lobbyist.aspx [accessed October 22, 2017]).

[23] McGann 2015, 66.

The distinct advantage of involving third-sector organizations in the Knesset work is their contribution of knowledge and expertise, especially in the legislative process. Nonetheless, like the lobbying in the Knesset of private commercial companies, non-profits sometimes represent the interests of particular groups, which could generate inequality, excessive power of strong interests, and discrimination against other groups. The activity of third-sector organizations is not a substitute for the responsibility of MKs for legislation and policymaking.

D. In the Courtroom

The court is the venue of choice for civil society organizations pursuing the protection of rights and prevention of discrimination (Dotan and Hofnung 2001). Since the right of standing was broadened in the 1980s, the High Court of Justice has been more open to petitions by minority groups that have limited access to other channels, and is considered an effective channel for overturning decisions made by the authorities. While in the past an appeal to the court was regarded as a last resort, today many organizations view it as an initial step toward achieving their objectives. A petition to the court itself enables organizations to protest, draw the authorities' attention to the problem, express their desire to participate in decision-making, and place an issue on the public agenda (Dor and Hofnung 2006). Decisive support from the court is a great achievement, and is relatively quick compared with due process in other channels. Furthermore, the price of the petition's rejection (and most are indeed rejected) is relatively low.

Consequently, there has been an enormous rise in the number of petitions filed by groups with a public agenda. In 1980, only 1.5 percent of High Court petitions were submitted by third-sector organizations, compared to 13 percent in 1995. We assume that this has further increased, but data are not available. The petitions pertain to nearly all fields of public policy, and about 40 percent were submitted by organizations whose primary or only mode of action is to file petitions – such as the Association for Civil Rights in Israel, Adalah, the Movement for Quality Government, and the Israel Union for Environmental Defense.

One of the salient examples of reliance on the High Court of Justice is in the fight for equal rights for women. The ruling that mandated affirmative action for women on the directorates of government corporations and the ruling that paved the way for women to join the Air Force pilots' course – two landmarks in the struggle for equal rights – were the result of petitions submitted by the Israel Women's Network and the Association for Civil Rights in Israel (*Israel Women's Network v. Government of Israel* 1994 and *Miller v. Minister of Defense* 1994, respectively). Such organizations succeed more than other petitioners because of their professionalism and familiarity with the legal aspects of policy in their field, and thanks to their ability to reach accords with government authorities outside the courtroom. One of the important consequences of legal success is the enhanced willingness of the authorities to consult with the organizations beforehand out of concern that the decision might ultimately be tested in court (Dotan and Hofnung 2001, 11–12).

Yet there are two sides to the coin. Success is not measured only by acceptance of the petition, or by reaching an accord, because this does not guarantee implementation in practice. For example, the court ruled that the decision to prevent an

Arab family from purchasing land in the town of Katzir constituted discrimination. In practice, even after the court's decision, it took nine years until the family managed to buy land and build their home there (*Ka'adan v. Israel Land Administration* 1995; Yoaz and Ratner 2004). Sometimes the victory of the civil organizations is temporary because the Knesset enacts legislation to circumvent a High Court decision or defer its implementation. The Public Housing Law initiated by MK Ran Cohen (Meretz) and two advocacy organizations (Mizrahi Democratic Rainbow and Community Advocacy) was approved by the Knesset in 1998, but the government annually deferred putting it into effect via the Arrangements Law.[24] In this case, which is not an isolated one, even legislation by the Knesset and a High Court ruling did not guarantee implementation of the achievements of civil society organizations. The main question is to what extent the legal battle is only a fireworks display at the expense of ongoing, incremental civil activity that produces sustainable results. The argument is that a ruling can effectively pave the way – as in the case of women's rights – only if preceded by groundwork conducted by civil society organizations.[25]

The presence of third-sector organizations in the political system is closely felt in party channels, government ministries, the Knesset, the courts, and the media networks, and some of them have achieved recognized status in internal consultations. Their activity has also resonated with the public. Naturally, their influence is greater in critiquing and during policy formulation and legislation, and less in policy enforcement and implementation. There is also a democratic difficulty: The strengthening of the organizations comes largely at the expense of the parties. For example, the struggle to prevent disengagement from the Gaza Strip in 2005 was waged mainly by settlers' organizations (and the heads of local government in the territories), while the voice of parties that opposed the disengagement played a secondary role. Democracy needs the inclusive and effective representation of parties, as well as the range of voices of a strong civil society.

12.6 The Third Sector among Groups in Israeli Society

The distinct groups examined below are not "representative" nor are they in "the majority" (we ignore their numerical weight – of women, for example); and these groups have limited access, for various reasons, to the political centers of power. Despite the substantial differences between the groups, including at the organizational level, and the difference in the policies adopted toward them by the government, the common denominator is that they are fighting for their rights, a struggle conducted in part via political parties and in part via civil society organizations.

[24] See *MK Ran Cohen v. Prime Minister Netanyahu* 1999. In 2008, it was stipulated that the law would take effect in 2011 (Amsterdamski 2008; R. Cohen 2008).

[25] Such thoughts also exist in regard to the famous success of the equal rights movement in the United States:

> The combination of all these factors – growing civil rights pressure from the 1930s, economic change, the Cold War, population shifts, electoral concerns, the increase in mass communication – created the pressure that led to civil rights. The court reflected that pressure; it did not create it.
>
> (Rosenberg 1993, 169)

A. Arab Citizens of Israel

The 1948 war left Palestinian society devastated, without institutions or overall organizations except for a few local authorities and the community structure in the villages.[26] The organizations that had existed during the Mandate period collapsed, and the Waqf (Islamic endowment) institutions and volunteer organizations stopped operating, including those that provided welfare assistance and other services. The Arab political parties that participated in elections starting in 1949 were branches of the Jewish parties (see Chapter 9), with the exception of the Israeli Communist Party (Maki), which became a national-social home for some of the Arab public. Maki's spheres of activity resembled those of the Jewish parties in those days – culture, journalism, youth clubs, sports, welfare, and the like (Nahas 1976).

The military government imposed on the Arab localities until 1966 limited the freedom to organize autonomously because every effort to organize was seen as a threat to the state. Only in 1965 were the Islamic Waqf funds released for education, welfare, and religious services. After the Six Day War, a national and social awakening began among the Arabs in Israel and the first autonomous organizations appeared, most in the form of political and social-cultural groups. In 1974, the National Committee of Arab Local Authorities was formed, the central political organization that not only represents the local authorities, but also operates vis-à-vis state authorities to protect Arab rights. In 1982, the Higher Monitoring Committee of Arab Citizens of Israel was founded – an umbrella group of Arab organizations and political movements as well as representatives of various sectors, Arab MKs, heads of local authorities, members of the Histadrut central committee, and representatives of volunteer organizations such as Ibnaa al-Balad (Sons of the Village), Association of the Forty, and the Arab Students Association. The Monitoring Committee is not an elected body, but considered a representative entity that works to promote the interests of all Arab citizens (see also Chapter 8 on political participation).

The great surge of third-sector activity among the Arabs in Israel began in the 1980s. In 1998, there were already 1,009 Arab non-profits – 4 percent of all registered non-profits in Israel. This percentage is lower than the proportion of the Arab population in Israel, but in 2007 the number of Arab non-profits grew by over 170 percent to 2,767, and 12 percent of the new non-profits registered in 2007 (202 out of 1,713) were Arab, Bedouin, or Druze organizations. The average number of active Arab organizations per 1,000 Arabs is still a quarter that of Jews (Balbachan 2008a, 3). Moreover, only 4 percent of the Arab organizations were granted the status of "public institution," compared to 12 percent of Jewish organizations. Without this status, contributions are not tax deductible in Israel, making fundraising more difficult. Two-thirds of the registered Arab organizations are younger than twenty years old. They focus on the socioeconomic and cultural advancement of the Arab population, and on services the state fails to provide, such as preschool facilities, scholarship funds for students, preventive medical services, and the like. As in the Jewish sector, many Arab organizations (about 25%) are religious.

[26] See a more extensive discussion of Israel's Arab citizens in Chapter 15. The description here is partly based on Zeidan and Ghanem 2000; and Gidron et al. 2003, 156–57, 166–67.

Another cluster includes organizations that fight discrimination and promote equality; for example, they work to preserve the Palestinian cultural heritage, provide legal assistance, defend the rights of Bedouin in the Negev, advocate for recognition of unrecognized villages, and conduct research on Palestinian society. In 1995, an umbrella group – Itijah – was formed to pool the efforts of organizations working to protect the human and civil rights of Arabs, including the Association for Protecting and Defending Bedouin Rights in Israel, the Committee for the Protection of Arab Land, and the Arab Organization for Civil Rights. The Association of the Forty, founded in the 1980s, recorded some success when the state recognized a number of Bedouin localities in the north. Organizations working for equal rights include the Mossawa Center, which fights racist legislation and promotes laws and a constitution that would anchor the full and equal rights of Arabs in Israel; Adalah, which represents Arab civil rights in the courts; and Sikkuy, a Jewish-Arab organization that works for equal status and rights for Arabs in Israel (see the organization websites).

One factor that has contributed to the growth of volunteer activity and services in Arab society is the strengthening of the Islamic Movement since the 1970s. The movement developed a network of welfare, educational, and health services for weak populations to fill the void created by discrimination in the services delivered to the Arab citizenry. The movement devoted special attention to neglected areas, such as early childhood and welfare institutions, as well as subjects that were not spoken about in Arab society, such as juvenile delinquency, alcoholism, drugs, and prostitution. These services give the movement a political power base in the local authorities and the Knesset (the United Arab List – Ra'am, which ran as part of the Joint List in the 2015 election). The Islamic Movement is a non-profit organization funded by contributions and volunteers. The fact that it maintains organizational autonomy enables it to present itself as a state in miniature that can meet the needs of the Arab citizens (Gidron and Alon, 2007, 167). The movement is also involved in the Palestinian national struggle and offers primarily humanitarian assistance, though some of its leaders have been convicted of incitement and hostile activity against Israel.[27] The Islamic Movement adopts practices that are typical of civil society, but it does not share the values of a liberal world view (Rabinowitz 2001).

Extensive volunteer activity, which generally is not organized, occurs in Arab communities and villages in the fields of religion, welfare, education, culture, and development initiatives. The scope of Arab organizations grew as a result of higher education and improved economic conditions, and they can potentially play a central role in self-assistance, social integration, and representation of the community vis-à-vis the authorities. Their growth can also be attributed to the weakening of the state, which more severely affected the Arab population, in part due to the weakness of the Arab local authorities. However, Arab third-sector organizations encounter obstacles inherent in the Arab social structure, which does not clearly distinguish between family, clan, tribe, civil society, local government, and state. The blurring of borders undermines the independence of the volunteer organizations, making it

[27] Sheikh Ra'ed Salah, leader of the northern branch of the Islamic Movement, was arrested in 2003. In a plea bargain, he admitted to having "contact with a foreign agent" and providing service to an "unlawful association" and was sentenced to prison. In March 2015, after a first appeal, Salah was sentenced to eleven months in prison for inciting violence and racism in a sermon given in 2007 (Khoury 2015).

difficult for them to be a center of attraction and identification for the entire Arab population (Sa'di 2001, 345–47).

Philanthropy and volunteerism began to develop only recently in Arab society in Israel: In a 2009 survey (Haski-Leventhal, Yogev-Keren, and Katz 2011), 19–44 percent of the Arab public (including Christians, Druze, and Muslims) said they gave contributions to both formal and informal frameworks; and 9–23 percent reported that they volunteered in both formal and informal frameworks (18–27% reported volunteering only in informal frameworks and 9–21% in formal ones). This is attributable to a low average income, the small number of Arab organizations whose operation is based on contributions, and the deep-rooted perception in the Arab public that the state should finance service provision. Nonetheless, the respondents noted many informal channels for volunteering and contributing directly to the community based on the tradition of charity, which is one of the pillars of Islam (Zeidan and Ghanem 2000, 59–60).

B. The Ultra-Orthodox

Even before the establishment of Israel, ultra-Orthodox society in the Yishuv had long maintained an array of volunteer communal organizations that relied on contributions from Diaspora Jewry. Most of the groups in ultra-Orthodox society adopted a pragmatic approach toward the Zionist institutions, in part to access resources. When the state was founded, the ultra-Orthodox sought a way to benefit from public services without integrating with the secular public. The ultra-Orthodox third sector is composed of a broad network of autonomous and very distinct rabbinical dynasties (*hatserot*) (Friedman 1991, 154–55). These clans, which are also communal organizations, were able to restructure themselves as political parties and successfully fulfill this mission – preserving autonomy while relying on state support. Ultra-Orthodox education, including yeshivas, were primarily funded by the state, but other services – welfare, health, etc. – were provided in volunteer frameworks that relied on contributions. These are third-sector organizations; though, in our assessment, most of them are not registered as non-profits (with the exception of those that receive support from public budgets) and we have no data on their number or activity. The religious third-sector organizations (not necessarily ultra-Orthodox) account for 43 percent of all registered non-profits, a percentage that far exceeds their relative share of the population. Their main fields of activity include religion (57%), education (22%), and welfare (14%) (CBS *Statistical Abstract* 2008, table 7.4).

When Israel was founded, there were two ultra-Orthodox political parties – Agudat Yisrael and Poalei Agudat Yisrael. They recognized the state, and their representatives signed the Declaration of Independence. Since then, they have participated in Knesset and local elections, and even sometimes joined government and municipal coalitions. However, these parties, like all the other Ashkenazi ultra-Orthodox parties, continued to maintain a separate lifestyle and did not allow the secular institutions to interfere in their affairs. The organizations of the ultra-Orthodox are separate – yeshivas, Talmud Torah elementary schools, ritual baths, kashrut institutions, charities, banks, newspapers, wedding halls, and so on. This is a separate community that constitutes about 8 percent of the population and is autonomous in managing its internal affairs; within this autonomy are smaller autonomous units – the rabbinical clans.

Internal collaboration within the ultra-Orthodox community and with the religious camp has had its ups and downs. After the establishment of Israel, the Agudat Yisrael and Poalei Agudat Yisrael parties displayed an ability to maneuver in the coalition structure and forged ad hoc partnerships with both the NRP and Neturei Karta (which does not recognize the state). In 1959, all the ultra-Orthodox parties joined together in violent demonstrations against the opening of a mixed-gender, public swimming pool in Jerusalem. The combined power of the religious parties has been substantial, and resulted in concessions by the secular majority – ongoing draft deferment for yeshiva students (1949) and draft exemptions for religious girls (1951); recognition of an independent ultra-Orthodox education network funded by the state (1953); and establishing the Agudat Yisrael bank from public funds (1965) (Galnoor 1982, 354). Later, the ultra-Orthodox community split into more than two parties, and the most significant change was the separation between Ashkenazi and Sephardic Jews. The emergence of Shas (in the Knesset since 1984), and control by the ultra-Orthodox parties (jointly and individually) of the balancing point in most of the government coalitions since the 1980s, reshaped the allocation of resources for ultra-Orthodox organizations. The schools, Shas's new educational network in particular, received generous public funding. The Shas network offered the public (and not only the ultra-Orthodox) free education, including meals and transportation. In addition to state support, ultra-Orthodox community organizations are still based on contributions from Diaspora Jews and the local community, but no data exist about this. The ultra-Orthodox organizations work within the frameworks of ultra-Orthodox society, with some exceptions like Yad Sarah, which lends medical equipment to anyone in need, and Zaka, which helps locate and rescue people in emergency situations.

According to universal indexes of economic status, nearly 60 percent of ultra-Orthodox society live beneath the poverty line (Bank of Israel 2007; Dattel 2014). This statistic could be misleading, not only because of their different perspective on standard of living, but also because it does not take into account the tight networks of support from volunteer organizations that are characteristic of the ultra-Orthodox communities. Voluntarism among the ultra-Orthodox also differs from the typical pattern in civil society. Ultra-Orthodox activists are not from the upper-middle class and do not have higher education. Nonetheless, volunteer rates are higher than among secular Israelis. In 2009, 34 percent of the ultra-Orthodox reported volunteering in an informal framework, compared to 19 percent among the secular; and 15 percent volunteered in formal frameworks, compared to 16 percent among secular Israelis (Bank of Israel 2007). If the government's policy to integrate the ultra-Orthodox (and Arabs) in the labor market is implemented, a change will also occur in the community structure.

C. Immigrants

Israel is a country of immigrants, and this is also reflected in the organizational fabric of the third sector. During the pre-state era, parties based on country of origin were seen as illegitimate by all the Zionist camps. The exceptions that participated in election of the Constituent Assembly, and subsequently for the Knesset, were immigrants who arrived prior to most Zionist immigrants – the Union of North African Immigrants, founded in Jerusalem in 1920, and the Yemenite Association, founded in 1923. Another exception was the Association of Central European Immigrants, from which the New Aliyah Party emerged in the 1940s, with German immigrants who would later be among the founders of the Progressive Party in 1948.

In the early years of the state, "ethnicity" (*adati-ut*) was a derogatory term used to criticize opponents of the melting pot policy and to prevent the separate political organizing of immigrants by country of origin. However, the desire of the immigrants to maintain their culture, language, connections, and interests led to the establishment of immigrant associations. Almost all were affiliated with parties and the Histadrut, and were formed as a means of political recruitment. Immigrant associations by country or region of origin (e.g., the Association of Latin American Immigrants) were affiliated with Mapai/Labor until the mid-1980s. But the status of these associations began to diminish over time – the immigrants became veteran Israelis, ethnic ties loosened, society changed, the parties weakened, and the immigrants of the 1990s formed organizations of a different type. Nonetheless, the state's attitude toward immigrants in the early stages left a long-term impact on the fabric of ethnic relations. Here we examine four groups of immigrants.

Mizrahim

For the first generation of immigrants from Asia and Africa, no separate and autonomous organizations were created, such as the many associations of immigrants from western countries. The Mizrahi ethnic group was viewed as a single entity rather than numerous diverse communities by country of origin. With the exception of organizations of Iraqi immigrants and the older organizations of the Sephardi and Yemenite Jews, the Histadrut-affiliated Association of North African Immigrants was supposed to represent the Mizrahim who arrived in Israel after 1948. Consequently, no prominent independent organizations were formed, with the exception of the unsuccessful attempt by the Union of North African Immigrants to win election to the Knesset in 1959 in the wake of the Wadi Salib incidents. The change occurred in the 1970s, with the emergence of the second generation of Mizrahim. The Black Panthers constituted a social protest movement of young people of North African origin (mainly Morocco) from impoverished neighborhoods in Jerusalem who came together to protest neglect and discrimination. The movement, which organized mass demonstrations that sometimes boiled over into violence and clashes with the police, surprised the establishment of the labor movement, which failed to understand the protestors and tried to dismiss them as a nuisance (the prime minister at the time, Golda Meir, said disparagingly of them "they're not nice") by resorting to the old methods of delegitimization and cooptation (Black Panthers 1971, 22). Despite their rapid demise, the Black Panthers had a clear impact on the emergence of an independent Mizrahi voice in the public arena in Israel. The Panthers movement failed in the 1973 elections that were held in the shadow of the Yom Kippur War, and its activists dispersed to various parties. Nonetheless, it contributed to the Labor Party downfall in 1977, which shifted the social protest of the Mizrahim to political tracks via the Likud, and later to the meteoric rise of Shas, starting in 1984.

A new stage began in the 1990s, influenced by the discourse of rights, and the Mizrahi social protest movement became a struggle for a fair distribution of resources in society. The Mizrahi Democratic Rainbow, established in 1996 by second and third generation immigrants from Arab countries, sought to rectify past injustices in terms of both awareness and practical action. It aimed to expose the mechanisms that perpetuate the economic disparity and suppress Mizrahi culture, while also fighting to reallocate the resources. The movement worked to enact the Public Housing Law and petitioned the High Court of Justice against the Israel Lands Administration's decision to grant moshavim and kibbutzim rights to land that it claimed belonged to all Israeli citizens. Did the identification of an ethnic (Mizrahi) struggle with a social struggle contribute to advancing the status of Mizrahim in Israel? The answer largely depends on the ability of these organizations to exert pressure, stir public opinion, and influence policy. It also depends on the long-term agenda of Shas, which defined itself as the spearhead of the "Sephardim." The likelihood of advancing this agenda diminished following the split in Shas in the 2015 elections after the death of its rabbinic leader Ovadia Yosef.

"Anglo-Saxons"

Immigrants who arrived from countries with a tradition of civil activity and voluntarism (the United States, Canada, Britain, South Africa) contributed to strengthening the third sector in Israel. We mentioned Hadassah, founded in 1912 by Jewish women in New York, which continues to operate today (see their website). Other organizations, such as the Association of Americans and Canadians in Israel, established in 1951, worked to encourage Jewish immigration and to help immigrants integrate into Israeli society (see their website). The feminist movement that developed in the 1970s was initially identified with women who brought these ideas from North America and encouraged the formation of women's organizations that helped strengthen civil society. The activity of philanthropic funds that raise money overseas also greatly strengthened civil society and the status of third-sector organizations in Israel.

"Russians"

The changes in Israeli society also engendered a different attitude toward the state's ethos of unity, which called for the mixing of groups from different countries of origin. The state's hegemony weakened in the 1990s, and under the influence of ideas about multiculturalism, ethnic-based organizations were no longer stigmatized. This applied to the immigrants from the former Soviet Union and, to a lesser extent, the immigrants from Ethiopia. Following their lead, organizations of "veteran immigrants" were also founded or revived, primarily to keep the communal embers burning. Immigrants from Russia showed a high level of political awareness, despite coming from a non-democratic tradition. In 1988, they established the Soviet Jewry Zionist Forum, an umbrella group for immigrants and immigrant groups from the former Soviet Union, which evolved into the Yisrael Beitenu party elected to the Knesset in 1996. Many immigrant organizations today focus on culture, art, and leisure. For example, the Forum of Immigrant Cultural Organizations in Jerusalem, founded in 2008, includes about thirty immigrant organizations in the field of culture.

"Ethiopians"

Like immigrants from the former Soviet Union, immigrants from Ethiopia also lacked experience in democratic participation. Unlike their Russian counterparts, however, they also lacked the social resources for autonomous community activity. Nonetheless, some young Ethiopian immigrants (including some veterans who had arrived in the first wave of immigration) created self-help, volunteer frameworks to support immigrants from Ethiopia and integrate them into Israeli society. The organizations received initial assistance in administration and funding from the New Israel Fund, and were later funded by the Jewish Agency as well. One of the leading organizations is the Union of Organizations of Ethiopian Immigrants (established in 1990), which served as an umbrella group in social and cultural fields, representing the community vis-à-vis the public, government authorities, and the absorption institutions. The organization helped lead the Ethiopian immigrants' fight against discrimination and the demand for full recognition of their Judaism and the rights of their priests (*kessim*). It organized a demonstration for changing the racist policy regarding blood donations (see Chapter 8). The umbrella group recorded some successes – after a long battle, for example, the state recognized the members of the Ethiopian community who died en route to Israel, and a memorial was built in Jerusalem. The activity areas of the Ethiopian immigrant organizations have changed: At first, most focused on culture and religion in an effort to preserve their tradition. In the 1990s, welfare and absorption organizations were also established, followed by a growing number of advocacy and educational organizations, which try to provide the community with tools to integrate into Israeli society (Balbachan 2008). However, the pace is slow, and a festering sense of discrimination, arrant racism, and police brutality erupted again into violent protest in May 2015.

Immigrant organizations are a unique framework in immigrant countries like Israel. The transition from pressure group to a cultural-heritage organization demonstrates the effect of time, as the newcomers become old-timers regardless of whether their absorption was successful. Despite repeated incidents that threaten to "unleash the ethnic devil," the process of absorbing immigrants in Israel continues. From the perspective of civil society, there are still demands by veteran Mizrahi immigrants who suffered discrimination and seek to exercise their rights, who were not integrated into society or who are working to preserve their heritage. Immigrants from the former Soviet Union and Ethiopia still face problems that pose a difficult challenge primarily due to the size of these groups – together they constitute about 15 percent of Israeli's citizens in the 2010s.

D. Women

Women's organizations have been part of the fabric of Israeli society from the outset, and the changes that took place in these organizations reflect the evolution of the third sector (Yishai 2003, 111–13). During the period of organized and state-affiliated voluntarism, women's organizations, like other groups, were affiliated with parties. Na'amat, for example, operated in the framework of the Histadrut, while WIZO was identified with the General Zionists. Both these "establishment" entities provided essential services such as day care centers, assistance for families in distress, and professional courses for women. They were "establishment" in the sense that they accepted the status of women in society as a given and did not struggle for changes in rights or the distribution of resources. In the early 1970s, a feminist movement evolved in Israel, but it was organizationally and financially weak, primarily due to a lack of public response (including women) to its ideas. Attempts by women's political parties to be elected to the Knesset failed until the Movement for Civil Rights and Peace was founded in 1973 by Shulamit Aloni, who was identified with women's rights.

Feminist women continued to work for recognition of the woman's right to her body (the liberalization of abortion) and for protection against violence, and the struggle gradually bore fruit. For example, the No to Violence against Women organization (founded in 1977) won recognition, and government funds were allocated for treating female victims of violence. The Israel Women's Network (established in 1984) adopted a moderate strategy: It did not call for a feminist revolution, but mainly used legislation and court rulings to improve the status of women, gain equal opportunities, and prevent gender-based discrimination. One example of a groundbreaking petition they filed (*Israel Women's Network v. Government of Israel* 1994) resulted in what is known as the Directorates Supreme Court ruling, which, for the first time, mandated appropriate representation for women on the boards of government corporations and paved the way for the legislative amendment that introduced a policy of affirmative action in the civil service (Galnoor 2003, 361–70). In parallel, other organizations independently established rape crisis centers and shelters for battered women, and later received funding from the local authorities and support from WIZO and Na'amat, which began to assist women who were victims of violence. Many women's organizations fight against religious coercion on divorce-related issues (including cases of women whose husbands disappeared or women refused a divorce).[28] These organizations are relatively powerless with regard to the rabbinical court, which wields exclusive authority on matters of marriage and divorce for Jews. As will be seen in Chapter 17, the High Court's ability to penetrate the realm of the religious status quo is limited, and its intervention sparks friction with the rabbinical establishment and the religious public.

Another important field is the emergence of women's organizations advocating on behalf of a general public interest, such as Women in Black (since 1988), which advocates for ending the occupation; MachsomWatch: Women Against the Occupation and for Human Rights (2001); and Women in Green: Women for Israel's Tomorrow (1993), which supports the continued occupation of the Greater Land of Israel. One group that combined political protest with a female-maternal identity is the Four Mothers Movement established in 1997, which called for withdrawing the IDF troops from Lebanon. The organization – headed by mothers of soldiers – had a strong influence on public opinion and eventually pressured the government to redeploy the IDF – the withdrawal from Lebanon was carried out in 2000.

[28] For example, Mavoi Satum (1995); Kolech: Religious Women's Forum (1998); Achoti (Sister): For Women in Israel (1999); Women's Parliament (1999); Granit: Association for Aid to Women Before, During and After Divorce Proceedings (2000); Center for Women's Justice (2004) (see the organizations' websites).

There is duality in the women's organizations, as in other fields of civil society in Israel. On the one hand, most of the organizations that operated under the auspices of political parties have vanished, and independent organizations have arisen that offer a message of change. On the other hand, most of these organizations work on issues that are not controversial, such as preventing violence against women, while a smaller number work on radical issues that challenge accepted conventions.

In addition to the groups presented above, the third sector includes organized groups of disabled, retirees, environmentalists, and others, which have a significant political presence. Organizations of disabled people demanded their rights in an angry protest in 2002; pensioners were briefly represented in the Knesset; and the environmentalists try time and again to cross the electoral threshold in Knesset elections and increase their representation in local authorities.

12.7 The Third Sector in Israeli Democracy

At the beginning of the chapter, we raised several issues about the third sector in Israel and we return to them now:

- The strengthening of civil society contributes to more democratization, openness, and transparency; at the same time, it promotes narrow interests at the expense of the general public interest.
- The activity of citizens in volunteer organizations is the lifeblood of democratic political participation; but it also opens the way to abuse, corruption, and violence.
- The objectives of most third-sector organizations reflect virtuous motives and seek the common good; some, however, encourage violence, fanaticism, racism, and patronage.
- Third-sector organizations must be independent; in Israel, as in many countries, they depend on self-interested funders that may have their own agenda (business organizations, philanthropic funds), while the service providers continue to depend on government budgets and dictates.

A. Democratization

The activity of third-sector organizations, the organized part of civil society, reflects the strength of Israeli democracy, which is able to contain and internalize their activity – in particular, those advocating social and political change. Third-sector activity contributes to democracy – for instance by protecting civil and women's rights, combating discrimination, and charting environmental policy. The organizations stimulate and influence public opinion via the media, social networks, court appeals, and advocacy in the political-administrative system. They contribute to improving public decision-making by presenting new information and considerations that can prevent erroneous decisions. This involvement helps make procedures more democratic, or at least more transparent, though public officials regard this as "noise" that complicates and delays decision-making. An organization like the Movement for Quality Government is indeed a "nuisance" to the government in its fight against corruption and flawed political norms, but not a nuisance to the public. Petitions against coalition agreements and MKs who switch parties in exchange for political payoffs led to legislation that regulated these matters. Similarly, an appeal that led to the revocation of an unsuitable appointment of a director-general in a government ministry (the Ginossar ruling) helped establish norms of public ethics. In addition, we note the contribution of thousands of community organizations that foster reciprocity and solidarity within society. From this perspective, civil society in Israel meets expectations in its contribution to a more participatory and responsive democracy.

At the same time, the multiplicity of social organizations in itself does not necessarily contribute to equality and representation. First, not all segments of the population participate equally in these organizations. Most participants come from the upper-middle class – more educated and prosperous. They are able to influence public policy thanks to their organizational skills. Second, many of the organizations promote narrow interests, sometimes at the expense of the general public interest. Organizations for social and political change contribute to equality by voicing the concerns of groups that suffer from discrimination and poverty. However, these organizations form a small percentage of third-sector organizations, while the others focus solely on promoting the interests of the groups they represent. Moreover, service organizations function as a substitute for services provided by the state in the past – welfare, education, health, job training, etc. They allow the state to shirk its responsibility for providing equal service, and since these organizations do not see themselves as bound to equality, they are liable to widen the disparities in society. Civil society in itself is not a guarantee of equality and representativeness.

Third-sector organizations are no substitute for representation in parliament and political parties. Parties that seek to gain power aspire to aggregate diverse interests in order to create a broad common denominator. Many organizations, on the other hand, represent narrow interests, which shape their contribution to decision-making. The pluralist model assumes that there is a "social market" in which narrow interests offset each other, but power is not distributed equally and the strong and well-organized groups succeed more than the weak groups, whose access to the political system is limited. Third-sector organizations are not elected by nor accountable to the public and do not represent all segments of society. Naturally, they – and the lobbyists who operate on their behalf – promote the issues that are highest priority for them. Therefore, the Knesset is where most parts of the social mosaic achieve representation, thereby allowing for periodic renewal. The role of the Knesset, the parties, the government, and its ministries – each in its own field – is to examine the diverse (and sometimes contradictory) demands raised by third-sector organizations, and to weigh them through the broad prism of public interest.

B. Participation: Lights and Shadows

The theoretical assumption is that third-sector organizations help boost political participation and generate increased social capital. Activity in such organizations develops a civic identity, strengthens the civic abilities of the participants, and equips them with political skills. Organizations for social and political change recruit activists, conduct protests, stimulate public opinion, and thus contribute to increasing the political involvement of the public. Israeli citizens are quite outstanding in their extensive activity in volunteer organizations with their contribution to their communities and society at large. An example of such activity is the broad coalition that supported the successful initiative to enact the Freedom of Information Law in Israel in 1998 (Menuchin 1999; Galnoor 2003, 153–54).

On the other hand, some organizations abuse the freedom to organize by failing to adhere to democratic values. Fanatic and racist groups have arisen in Israel that sought to harm other groups, such as Kahane's Kach movement, which was later outlawed. There are also groups and organizations that engage in violence, break the law, and are corrupt. These represent a small percentage of third-sector organizations, but sully the name of the entire sector. They abuse the special legal status of non-profit organizations to pursue goals that are not for public benefit. For example, political parties have exploited legal vagueness to form fictitious non-profits to circumvent the Parties Financing Law. Another example are non-profits that have no intention of pursuing their declared objectives, but are designed to camouflage illegal activity, misuse public funds and contributions, or pay high salaries to senior officials or family members. It only takes a few such cases to undermine public trust in all non-profits, dampen the willingness to contribute, and spur the state to overregulate the organizations, thus diminishing their independence (Brauner 2003).

C. Independence

Since the 1980s, civil society has burgeoned in Israel as never before. Organizations have proliferated in number, areas of activity, and scope of involvement. Is the large number of organizations also indicative of a strong and independent civil society, with a civil agenda? In this chapter, we noted two related problems. First, the vast majority of third-sector organizations are dependent on state funding; second, organizations that provide services account for most third-sector activity. Some of these organizations were even established at the government's initiative, and serve as privatized substitutes for state services. This reflects the structural weakness of civil society in Israel, which is still unable to stand firmly on its own feet and maintain organizations free of state intervention. (On "strong" and "weak" civil society, see Taylor 1985.) From this perspective, Israeli civil society does not yet meet the definition: "By civil society, I mean that texture of our lives with others which does not need governments to sustain it because it is created by grass-root initiatives" (Dahrendorf 1997, 77–78). Civil society in Israel has yet to release itself from the bear hug of the state.

Reality, as usual, is more complex: The government supports "responsible" organizations, and makes them dependent on the state, thus diminishing their ability to influence or even criticize the prevailing policy. At the same time, this support nurtures the organizations that may eventually free themselves from the state's patronage and become independent. As noted, many service organizations serve as an extension of government bureaucracy (via contracts). Some operate as business enterprises, with economic considerations taking precedence over the quality of service, such as health services within schools, which have been privatized. On the other side of the coin are non-profits that receive funding from the state (e.g., the health tax that is transferred to the health funds) and are supposed to provide equal service to all. In addition to the service organizations, there are independent organizations for social and political change that promote general public interests and protect the rights of weak groups in society; in a number of cases, these organizations have succeeded in changing the political and social agenda in Israel. They have also created a deterrent effect vis-à-vis the political system, which sometimes prefers to cooperate with them and avoid criticism. Third-sector organizations also succeed in influencing the state's policy and agenda via protest and demonstrations.

The third sector grew under the nose of the state, and if the state had paid attention to the process, perhaps it would have restrained it and not allowed its relative independence. From the perspective of civil society, the dilemma is now: Instead of the collection of laws, tax regulations, and other specific decisions that have accumulated over the years, should civil society demand that the state issue "a declared, explicit, consistent, and transparent policy vis-à-vis the third sector"? (Galnoor Committee 2003, 5). The concern is that this might be a centralized policy with monitoring and regulating mechanisms that would harm the sector's independence, diversity, and creativity. A policy that does not recognize the pluralism of the volunteer sector (which is essentially similar to that of the business sector) could weaken the contribution of civil society, which developed independently from the grassroots, and lead it back into the bear hug of the state.

The desirable solution is indeed to formulate a consistent and transparent policy, but one that does not interfere beyond the necessary regulation of public funds. This means a clear definition of channels of support, equality in gaining recognition as a "public institution" and providing tax benefits to donors, and similar changes in the oversight measures applied by the Registrar of Nonprofits. Third-sector organizations, on their part, should develop effective mechanisms of self-monitoring and regulation in order to close the loopholes that invite abuse and prevent corruption. The umbrella organizations of the third sector are indeed working toward this (N. Limor 2005). On the positive side, we note the important declarative steps the government has taken in recognizing the contribution of civil society and creating mechanisms for collaboration.[29] A new Nonprofit Associations Law is also on the agenda and will need to contend with these challenges (Limor and Brindt 2014).

The starting point for our discussion about the independence of civil society is the assumption that it must exist separately from the state. For neoconservatives, this is the "apolitical area" that includes the economic market, religion, community, and family. However, this distinction is not realistic and largely collapsed in the economic crisis of 2008, at least in regard to the financial market. That crisis dragged the state into intervening in the holy of holies of the business world – the banks. In our opinion, civil society can be political, apolitical, and sometimes anti-political, and it represents another dimension of creating norms that are not the domain of the other two sectors – they are not representative like the institutions in the state political system, and not business-oriented like firms in the economic market. Civil society

[29] Government Decision 3190 (February 24, 2008), "Relations among the government, civil society, and the business sector that contribute to achieving public objectives."

does not operate in a vacuum, and its organizations work collaboratively with others in the diverse arenas of the political system. In what might be regarded as a paradox, a functioning political system – a representative legislature, strong political parties, an impartial judicial system, and, in particular, a government with steering capacity – is vital for the existence of an independent, strong, and influential civil society. And a functioning political system, with a fruitful and diverse cluster of community, social, and political organizations, is vital for democracy.

13 The Media in Israel: Do They Strengthen or Weaken Democracy?

13.1 Media and Politics

To whom does a large part of the Israeli public assign the following roles: protecting human rights, mitigating internal tensions in society, facilitating less inflammatory public discourse, ensuring that promises made to the public are kept, instilling Zionist values, and convincing citizens to support government policy? One might assume that a democratic public expects such activities from its elected officials. However, surprisingly, it designates these roles to the media.[1] Why? Because most of the public believes that politics is conducted primarily on the pages of newspapers, the airwaves, television screens, the Internet, online channels, and social networks – even more than in the corridors of government. An enormous change gradually took shape after the middle of the twentieth century: The media became the link that mediates, reflects, pressures, and also distorts the political reality.

We focus in this chapter on the media's role in Israeli democracy. In the past, the more common term was "mass media," because "they can transmit more information more quickly to more people" (Galnoor 1982, 218). The technology determined the radius of the "mass" – starting with those who could read a notice posted at the gate of the city, and eventually including anyone within the range of television antennas and smartphones. Mass media were characterized by a "broadcast" – usually from a few to many people. Since the Internet revolution, there is no "broadcast" because the media have become interactive – everyone can potentially converse with everyone, all the time. The new media changed the face of society and will also change politics (Dahlgren 2004; McLuhan 1966). For convenience, we distinguish between written media (mainly print and online journalism) and electronic media (primarily radio, television, cable, satellite, and Internet), though this distinction is obviously a technical one and in reality there is a convergence of media infrastructure for communicating messages and content of all types and by a variety of means (Grant and Wilkinson 2008). The new media accelerated the trend of globalization and really did transform the world into a "global village," at least from the perspective of a shared experience of watching the same events at the same time (Dayan and Katz

[1] The percentage of respondents who cited these roles as the media's proper function: 66 percent, 62 percent, 53 percent, 50 percent, 43 percent, and 37 percent, respectively (Arian et al. 2005–10: 2005, 18).

1992; McLuhan and Powers 1989). Mann and Lev-On (2014, 23) also found a correlation in Israel between current topics in print journalism, the Internet, and various web channels.

A. Political Communication

Political communication refers to the multi-directional channels that connect the different parts of society to the political system. In the past, the media primarily played a mediating role – transferring information, demands, and support between various segments of the public and the government, and also among the different branches of government as the bureaucracy expanded. The media developed alongside the traditional arenas of public discourse (parliament, political parties, trade unions, and interest groups), but its independent weight grew and soon supplanted the other arenas and became a mediating channel for them too. At first, the media operated primarily as one-way channels for the top-down transfer of information, from the leadership to the masses, even in democratic regimes. In undemocratic regimes, the government-bureaucracy-media combination created totalitarian systems. As a result of changes in the attitude toward accountability in democratic politics and, in particular, thanks to technological developments, the channels became multi-directional and also served to transfer information, claims, and criticism from the public to the government. Karl Deutsch described the political systems in terms of "a nervous system" – dependent on processes of communication (1963, 145). Accordingly, they combine all the social interactions and flow of information pertaining to collective efforts and power relations. In short, politics, communication, and the media are intertwined.

The media not only mediate between the public and the political system, but serve as a "fourth estate" (see discussion in Schultz 1998), monitoring and critiquing the political system. The media provide a platform for public discourse, but also appear on this stage as an actor, helping set the agenda and sometimes even participating in the decision-making. The relationship between politics and the media is circular: politics needs the media, which gives it a powerful tool for transferring information and messages to the public; the media need politics as a principal supplier of news and events. The political system has other channels – bureaucratic, party, and others – but these are limited in their real-time access to large audiences. In addition, many politicians (and journalists too) believe that the media are capable of shaping the views of the citizens, and this belief acts as a self-fulfilling prophecy, reinforcing the status of the media in politics. On the other hand, politics in many (though not all) countries is the media's lifeblood of information, which creates dependence on political sources. The politics–media–politics circular alliance is strong thanks to the interactions among the systems, based on conflicting interests and mutual stimulation, sometimes collaborating and sometimes competing to expose or conceal information.

The media's reputation as a central player on the political stage derives from the belief that it can shape views, change opinions, and determine the fate of candidates. This view is held strongly in the United States, where private donations to political candidates play a major role. No doubt, the media have "publicity" power, in the broad sense; the media can shape the agenda in the political domain and focus attention on particular people or events. However, is there proof to support the common perception that "you can sell politicians like you sell Coca-Cola"? There are two opposing views vis-à-vis the media's impact on citizens in regard to political issues. According to one polar view, the media are entirely propaganda and can be used to do anything, as in Orwell's *1984* – i.e., they can control people, program their way of thinking, and certainly influence how they vote (see Ellul 1973). A diametrically opposed view is that the media's impact on people and their opinions is only marginal (Mughan and Gunther 2000, 16). This view is primarily based on empirical studies of election propaganda showing that the media are not a key factor in determining how people vote; the media generally reinforce existing views, but do not change them (Elihu Katz 1969). Without resolving this question, we note that the media usually appear behind the scenes on the political stage; they are not responsible for building the set for political theater, but they operate the stage lighting.[2] In addition, the intensive use of social networks creates new possibilities for unmediated and direct politics and for election propaganda – on Facebook, Twitter, and YouTube, for example.

The media exercise substantial influence in setting the agenda of political discussion through what they choose to highlight and emphasize: The press "may not be successful much of the time in telling people what to think, but it is stunningly successful in telling its readers what to think about" (B. Cohen 1963, 13). Topics the media choose to ignore remain in the shadows and it is very difficult to drag them into the light, while other subjects, whether minor or major, become headlines and receive great attention. This shapes the character of the media's influence: Because of its dynamic nature, the media's agenda changes frequently and cannot be long term or farsighted. Topics that were headlines yesterday do not make the back pages or receive airtime. The media lack the patience to follow up developments in events that have played themselves out and are no longer on the agenda. This is clearly the case with the breathless pace of the new media. The media also usually determine the criteria for examining and assessing a particular issue (media priming). In the political arena, the media decide whether to focus on the candidates' world views, character, or personal and family issues. The way the media frame and choose to present a particular matter influences the nature of the discussion. For example, if the media portray poverty as a problem of individuals who are unable or unwilling to work, they generate a psychological and apolitical discussion focusing on the motivation of people and their hard luck. If they portray poverty as a social problem stemming from government decisions or structural inequality, they stir a critical discussion of policy (Mughan and Gunther 2000, 17–18).

The growing power of the media has changed the face of politics; instead of the smoke-filled backrooms of the past, politics is now conducted on television screens (Galnoor 1998, 195) and online channels. However, it appears that media transparency, which sought to remove the mask from politics, in fact created something completely different – it turned politics into a soap opera. If what we see "in front of the cameras" is indeed what is happening, then this exposure has helped create a politics of appearance and sound bites, with catchy slogans whose depth and lifespan are like those of the flashing headlines on news websites. It is a politics of gesture

[2] On political influence, see Axford and Huggins 2001; McCombs and Shaw 1972; McQuail 1977; Robinson 2001.

rather than action, of images instead of meaningful words, of staged reality instead of reality itself (Ezrahi 2006). The immediacy and the directness that media outlets offer reinforce the trend of personifying politics. Television and cyber channels create the illusion that citizens are well-acquainted with the politicians, who visit them frequently. This exposure can be positive if politicians know how to exploit it to present ideas and plans in addition to "marketing one's personality." However, many politicians heed the advice of public relations consultants and choose "to sell" themselves and leave "non-photogenic content" outside of the picture. This results in a negative selection process that promotes shallow politicians and deters others; the exposure then adds to their demystification, and so on. The decline of politics and distrust of politicians is connected to this phenomenon.

B. The Media's Contribution to Democracy

In what way are the media essential for a democratic regime?

- They embody and protect the fundamental values of democracy – the public's right to know, freedom of expression, and freedom of the press.
- In the role of "the watchdog of democracy," free media guarantee the transparency of the political system and help monitor the institutions of government and their activity. Therefore, the media should be protected against arbitrary control and intervention, political or commercial, while competition and pluralism in media channels should be ensured (Mughan and Gunther 2000, 1–27).
- The media as an agent of political socialization can contribute to the knowledge and skills of citizens, raise awareness of political processes, and educate an interested, skeptical, critical, and involved citizenry.
- The media are a platform for open public discourse, which is vital for strengthening the deliberative dimension of democracy.
- Technological innovations help the media boost political participation. For example, mobile video cameras, smartphones, and social networks can serve as online channels of discussion between citizens. Ostensibly, it is possible to conduct direct and immediate democracy – to ask citizens their opinions on any topic in the world (Barber 2003, xiv–xv).
- The media can advance social and cultural pluralism via a range of channels, but also accelerate processes of social isolation. They can also contribute to a common denominator and social cohesion by serving as a sort of "tribal campfire" (Dayan and Katz 1992) to which the public is exposed and from which it draws shared values.

The media have contributed to the demystification of politics, exposing its backroom wheeling and dealing, its inclination to distort facts, and uncovering cases of corruption. However, certain aspects of the new media do not add tranquility to politics or contribute to instilling democratic values. For example, the news – primarily, on television and online journalism – is prone to excessive dramatization: an incident is a "crisis," differences of opinion are a "confrontation," a "fierce battle" is waged on every issue, and too many news items are "exclusive." Quite often they sow panic via inflammatory, multi-colored, banner headlines, news flashes on websites, large pictures, or ostensibly "scientific" revelations. The populist tendency is also salient in the use of language. In the past, the media in Israel, particularly the print media and the radio, were meticulous in using high-level and correct language. Now they seem to have moved to the other extreme: The language is not only slang, but sloppy and inaccurate, cliché-ridden, and – most disturbing – rife with violent metaphors taken from the battlefield and sporting competitions (Caspi and Limor 1998, 86–89). Politics is presented in the media as if it were a war, a boxing match, or a market of hagglers. This is particularly evident when information is reported directly "from the field," unedited.

Is this what citizens want? The media are measured by the circulation of newspapers, the ratings of television programs, the number of radio listeners, page visits to sites, talkback responses, and so on. These indexes, and the ratings in particular, can be seen as an expression of the citizens' free choice and preferences, but this is not the ultimate purpose of ratings. They do express the preferences of viewers at a given moment, but the preferences are mainly supply driven (for example, the supremacy of certain entertainment programs) and influenced by the media's self-publicity. Thus, a television program promoted in a well-publicized campaign is likely to receive a higher rating. The rating is an economic index indicating the value of each advertising moment during the program's broadcast, and does not necessarily reflect the public's real preferences or its assessment of the program's quality. Therefore, the critics say, the culture of ratings is not a democratic expression of the citizens' preferences, but rather a means of imposing commercial codes (Bourdieu 1996).

As long as the media's channels are one-directional, its contribution to political participation is doubtful; there is only an illusion of access because in practice not every person can use it to communicate messages. Long ago, Lazarsfeld and Merton (1948) identified the "narcotizing dysfunction" of the modern media – which creates passive readers/viewers/listeners (and now web surfers) who are caught in the illusion of being politically involved. For example, public opinion surveys and polls give citizens a sense that they influence decision-making processes, when actually oversimplifying complex questions and allowing for only yes/no answers. On the other hand, today's multi-directional media offer real democratic potential because they enable citizens to adapt the various channels to their own needs. Thus, the media's impact on politics has more than one dimension: The media do feed politics and are fed by it, but they also contribute to the dying interest in it and to its negative public image.

C. The Media in Israel: An Overview

Israelis are very connected to the media. The use of media technologies in Israel (television, cable/satellite, computers, mobiles, and smartphones) is among the most widespread and fast paced in the world. According to the 2009 ICT (Information and Communications Technology) Development Index, which measures access to and use of telephony and the Internet, Israel is ranked 29 out of 154 countries. Between 2002 and 2007, there was a sharp increase in the use of cellular phones and the Internet, primarily broadband (Table 13.1).

Israelis are also enthusiastic consumers of media. In the past, this primarily meant the daily newspaper and the radio, then television (88% in 2012), and now,

Table 13.1 *Access to and use of media channels in Israel – 2002, 2007, and 2013*

	2002	2007	2013
Landline telephone lines (%)	47	44	76
Mobile phones (one or more) (%)	99	129	95
Smartphones (%)	–	–	64–72 (2014)
Households with computers (%)	54	62	81
Households with Internet (%)	24	45	71
Internet users (in millions)	1.6	4.1	5.4
Social network use (WhatsApp) (%)	–	–	80

Source: International Telecommunication Union 2009, 91, 93; for 2013, CBS *Statistical Abstract* 2014, table 5.33; Mann and Lev-On 2014, 24; Mann and Lev-On 2015, 70, 78.

as Table 13.1 shows, the online channels. In the past, there was a clear preference among viewers for news, but with the diversification of offerings, the demand for entertainment programs increased.[3] Political issues receive great attention, and in the print media politics is still accorded top priority, though its status has diminished in recent years and more "news" focuses on crime and personal stories. Israelis are "addicted to the news" – 78 percent reported that they follow news updates frequently (daily or several times a week). In 2010, 70 percent of the adult public in Israel watched the news on television or the Internet, a high percentage among western countries (Arian, Philippov, and Knafelman 2009, 44–45; Ariel and Carmel 2011). However, the interest in news has declined in all channels and the percentage of viewers of television news broadcasts dropped to 36 percent in 2016 (Mann and Lev-On 2016, 31).

During Israel's first two decades, the media were linked primarily to the government and political parties. Nonetheless, private independent newspapers had already appeared prior to 1948 (*Haaretz*, *Yediot Aharonot*) and gradually became popular among the Jewish public. From the mid-1960s, the media became more independent and critical. The Lavon affair can be seen as a turning point with the establishment media becoming more critical of the government. At the same time, party-affiliated journalism declined and the status of the private newspapers strengthened. As described below, establishment of the Israel Broadcasting Authority (1965) marked an effort to develop media that would be both public and more independent. The Yom Kippur War exposed the helplessness of the media in Israel – subject to manipulation, censored (willingly or under coercion), and remorseful for letting its guard down during the post-1967 period of euphoria. The crisis of confidence between the media and the government contributed to the development of new rules for their interaction that reflected growing skepticism and mutual suspicion (Caspi and Limor 1992, 230–49).

The revolution in broadcast journalism began at the end of the 1980s: the monopoly of the state media – Channel 1 television and Kol Yisrael (Voice of Israel)

[3] The earlier data come from research conducted in 1990 on consumption of leisure, culture, and media in Israel (Katz and Haas 1995). For 2013, see TGI survey on exposure to newspapers and radio: www.ice.co.il (accessed October 23, 2017).

radio – came to an end as cable television was introduced (1989), as well as a commercial television channel (in 1993, which later became Channel 2), regional radio stations (1995), satellite broadcasts (2000), and Channel 10 (2002). The "open skies" policy engendered a multi-channel media system and new regulatory institutions, though it also created commercial monopolies of a new type. The media grew in power as a key economic branch and many associated industries developed in its wake, most prominently in the advertising and public relations field (Y. Limor 1997). In 2013, NIS 3.646 billion was spent on advertising in the Israeli economy, divided as follows: television (42%), print journalism (29%), Internet (18%), radio (7%), and the rest on billboards and in movie theaters.[4] The new technology created new facts – the emergence of Internet journalism at the expense of print journalism, and the takeover of the media by computers and mobile phones.[5]

This has been a fascinating process of parallel changes in the society and the media that feed into each other: the mobilized and ideological Jewish society of the state's early years had collectivist and patriotic journalism; the individualistic society that subsequently developed has pluralistic media that meet the demand for multiple options and for increasing the proportion of entertainment at the expense of political content. Concurrent with the greater number of media outlets, the political center weakened, large political parties declined and splintered, and features of direct democracy were adopted. The transition from statism to pluralism occurred in parallel in society, politics, and the media.

D. Dilemmas

Technological changes only intensified the dilemma that arose with the emergence of mass media in democratic countries: Are the media a public service that should be entrusted to the state or subject to strict public regulation, or are they a private good to which the rules of the commercial-economic market apply, with minimal public regulation? Or are they a hybrid creature as described by former Supreme Court President Barak concerning a private newspaper – on the one hand, a private entity with vested economic interests, and on the other hand, playing a public role on the stage of democratic discourse (A. Barak 2002, 294)?

The perception of the media as a *public service* is the foundation of public broadcasting, or at least its perception as a balancing and restraining factor vis-à-vis the commercial media. In Israel and some other democratic states, public broadcasting is in crisis for three main reasons (Ezrahi, Ben-Shachar, and La'el 1997): politicization that undermined the credibility of public broadcasting, casting doubt upon its essentiality; public broadcasting's attempts to compete with commercial entertainment programs and its inability to do so; and privatization policies designed to "save" on public spending. The answers to the following questions will determine the character of the media in Israel: Is it an institution with social responsibility or a purely commercial enterprise?

[4] According to data from the Israeli Marketing Association and Ifat Advertising Monitoring published by the Israeli Marketing Association (January 13, 2014): www.ishivuk.co.il/message/1111 (accessed March 22, 2016).

[5] On the influence of online journalism upon print journalism, see *Panim* 2009, 31–37.

- ***Dependence versus independence:*** Will the media become an independent institution that promotes the public interest, or will political dependence be replaced by commercial dependence? Instead of the previous political centralization, will the media be controlled by centralization in the hands of a few tycoons? The media in Israel, which often served in the past as the government's mouthpiece, have become mainly private and decentralized. This change enables the media to be critical in all areas of life, and thus strengthens social pluralism. However, if the media are controlled in practice by a small group of plutocrats who own multiple media outlets, can they reflect the diverse reality in economics, society, and politics? When the media are subservient to a commercial entity and profit is their only interest, does this introduce extraneous considerations of a new type, and conduct no less secretive than that of the political authorities (Ezrahi, Goshen, and Leshem 2003)?
- ***Unity versus multiplicity:*** Does the abundance of channels reflect social diversity or does it foster divisiveness, with the splintering of the media encouraging the atomization of society? Does this abundance enable real pluralism of content, or does it actually create homogeneous content (entertainment) and strengthen the lowest common denominator, lowering the level and quality of the broadcasts?
- ***Journalism (profession or a "gig"?):*** The multiplicity of channels, the new technology, and the so-called economic flexibility (personal contracts, part-time and temporary employment) have affected the status and identity of journalists. The erosion in their status is reflected in the lack of suitable professional training and lower salaries (which is also a side effect of the feminization of the field) (Caspi and Limor 1999, 49–56). With the development of non-establishment channels, the status of journalists is further eroded due to the emergence of bloggers who write opinion columns and commentary on various sites, including online newspaper sites, thereby competing with professional journalists (see Baltatzis 2006; Lowrey 2006; Johnson and Kaye 2004).
- ***Secrecy versus unrestrained publicity:*** The dilemma is between self-restraint with the concomitant danger of political exploitation by the government in the guise of national security considerations and, on the other hand, unrestrained exposure that could constitute a security risk.[6] Some regard the collaboration between the media and the government – security authorities in particular – as one of the chronic childhood diseases of the Israeli media, which do not readily air publicly all the facts that come to their attention, and are unable to monitor the security establishment; conversely, some believe that in Israel, because of the security threat, self-restraint beyond the legal constraints is a reflection of the media's maturity.
- ***Real versus ostensible political participation (citizens or consumers?):*** Do the media support democratic values such as the public right to know and the freedom of expression, and do they encourage democratic processes such as political

[6] See for instance the case of Edward Snowden, a CIA employee, who copied and published classified information from the US National Security Agency (NSA) in 2013. The information revealed a large number of classified documents, including global surveillance programs. *New York Times* editorial, "Edward Snowden, Whistle Blower," www.nytimes.com/2014/01/02/opinion/edward-snowden-whistle-blower.html (accessed March 22, 2016).

participation, or do the media create an illusion of active participation by the citizens when in fact they contribute to turning them into passive "customers" caught in their net?

13.2 The Legal Infrastructure: Formal and Informal Arrangements

Legislation in Israel allows the government to directly oversee the media by ministers via regulatory bodies (such as the Second Authority for Radio and Television), which are usually run by political appointments. The government is also responsible for granting licenses, awarding media franchises, and allocating broadcast frequencies. Two of the central problems are, first, a lack of consistent and clear policy, as reflected, for example, in the large number of supervisory bodies; and, second, a significant gap between the legal prohibitions (some dating back to the British Mandate, including non-democratic sanctions) and actual enforcement. If the legal prohibitions were applied according to the letter of the law, the media in Israel would be among the most restrictive of democratic states. In reality, the media have broad freedom of action because the boundaries of freedom of expression were developed thanks to public norms, court rulings, and arrangements between the political and media elites (Galnoor 1999). We now briefly review the laws according to their purpose (not by date of enactment), as well as the informal arrangements and voluntary media institutions.

A. Laws Regulating the Media

An extensive body of legislation outlines the authority of the media's regulators, but the laws are not grouped together and the regulatory agencies do not operate under a single roof. Therefore, the laws and the media policy based on them are not consistent.

Communications (Telecommunications and Broadcasting) Law (1982)

This law (referred to as the Bezeq Law until 2001) addresses various aspects of regulating the media (technical infrastructure, media organizations, content, and transmission). By law, the Ministry of Communications is responsible for regulating most of these areas – from Internet services to content issues such as original productions. The amendments to the law reflect the effort to keep pace with the technological developments, for example expanding broadcasts and fast Internet. There are also clauses on filtering information – a prohibition on broadcasting pornography or sending junk mail over the Internet or via text messages.

The Communications Law also regulates the work of the Council for Cable and Satellite Broadcasting. The council represents the public's interests in multi-channel television for cable and satellite subscribers. The subscription rate in Israel is one of the highest in the world at about 62 percent of households in 2013 (CBS *Statistical Abstract* 2015, table 5.33). The council has thirteen members, including seven representatives of the public and six representatives of government ministries. The council chair is the representative of the minister of communications. The council serves as a tenders committee for awarding licenses for cable and satellite broadcasts. Its primary roles include setting policy on types of broadcasts, their subjects, content, level, scope, and time; regulating community broadcasts; and encouraging production of original, local productions. The council monitors broadcast performance, compliance with the rules of classification and signaling, prohibition of harmful broadcasts, and the rules of ethics in broadcasting. It also serves as an address for consumer complaints.

Wireless Telegraphy Ordinance [New Version] (1972)

The electronic media use frequencies that are limited in number and belong to the public. Thus, there is a need to regulate the distribution of frequencies and wireless activity. This law stipulates the conditions for granting a broadcasting license and sets the frequencies. The Ministry of Communications is responsible for allocating frequencies and assigning their purpose, and for registering wireless equipment. The law also includes a prohibition on pirate broadcasts. At times of emergency, the minister of communications is authorized to impose supervision on telegraphic transmission and use it for emergency purposes.

Public Broadcasting Law (2014) (Replaced the Israel Broadcasting Authority Law, 1965)

The new law of 2014 established the Public Broadcasting Corporation (PBC) – replacing the previous Authority – which is designed to regulate television broadcasts (Channel 1, the channel for children and youth, and the channel in Arabic) and the national radio (Kol Yisrael), and to monitor the army radio station (Galei Zahal). The law redefined the objectives of public broadcasting as follows:[7]

> The content provided by the PBC shall be independent, address all the citizens and residents of the State of Israel, reflect and document the State of Israel's existence as a Jewish and democratic state, Jewish values and heritage, and give fair, equal, and balanced expression to a range of viewpoints and opinions prevalent among the public in Israel.

The law later states that the corporation shall act: "to expand education and knowledge; promote Israeli culture, high-quality original creative work, and Israeli music; promote innovation in broadcast content and distribution and in broadcast technologies; foster and promote the Arabic language" (Sections 7[B] and 7[F], respectively).

A mandatory license fee imposed on all owners of television sets and automobiles funded the previous broadcasting authority; additional funding came from radio commercials and sponsorship messages on television. Under the new law, the previous fee (which covered about 50% of the authority's budget) will be canceled

[7] The objectives designated in the previous law were: to reflect the life, struggle, creativity, and achievements of the state; to foster good citizenship; to strengthen the connection with Jewish heritage and its values and enhance knowledge of it; to reflect the life and cultural assets of all tribes of the nation from different countries; to expand education and disseminate knowledge; to reflect the life of Jews in the Diaspora communities; to advance the goals of state education; to promote Hebrew and Israeli creative work; and to conduct broadcasts in Arabic for the needs of the Arabic-speaking population and broadcasts to promote understanding and peace with the neighboring countries.

and instead the Ministry of Transportation will collect an additional sum in car licensing fees to be transferred directly to the PBC. The balance will continue to be funded from radio commercials and television sponsorships. The previous system of appointments led to complete politicization and a severe crisis in the broadcasting authority (see below).[8] Until 2014, no fewer than thirteen committees were formed to address this problem, but all attempts to institute reforms in public broadcasting failed.[9] The new law tries to contend with the crisis through a council (directorate) of twelve members, to be formed by a search committee chaired by a judge. The committee will be responsible for recommending suitable candidates for the council to the responsible minister. This mechanism does not completely sever the PBC from politics.[10]

In 2016 Prime Minister Netanyahu changed his mind about the advantages of the law, causing a near crisis in his coalition. Consequently, its implementation and establishment of the new Public Broadcasting Corporation was postponed. The political compromise was that the news division would be separated from the PBC.

Army Radio (Galei Zahal)

The army station began broadcasting in the 1950s at the initiative of the Communications Corps. It is still a military unit subordinate to the chief of staff and funded by a Defense Ministry budget. Its official status was recognized in the Israel Broadcasting Authority Law (Section 48). The station broadcasts on two frequencies: *Galei Zahal* – news and current events programs, and special broadcasts for soldiers; and *Galgalatz* – popular music and traffic reports. It is a subject of controversy: Some argue that a military radio station (which also broadcasts news) has no place in a democratic state, and attempts were made over the years to close down the station or convert it to a civilian framework. Nonetheless, the station continues to operate because of its public popularity and pressure from media figures whose careers began there. The law subordinates the station to partial supervision of the PBC (only in regard to non-military programs), in accordance with rules to be approved by the designated minister and the minister of defense.

The Knesset Channel: Television Broadcasts from the Knesset Law (2003)

The objective of the Knesset Channel, which began broadcasting in 2005, is "to enable access to the discussions and work of the Knesset, foster civic awareness, and reinforce the values of democracy." A committee of five, including representatives of the Knesset and the public, is responsible for the channel's broadcasts and monitors coverage from the Knesset. According to sporadic surveys in 2009, 1–2 percent of Jewish households watch the channel (Izikovich 2009).

[8] Ministers competed for the responsibility of "implementing the Israel Broadcasting Authority Law" and it was one of the coalition perks. Six ministers, including Prime Minister Netanyahu, filled this position from 2001 to 2015.

[9] See Ezrahi, Ben-Shachar, and La'el 1997; Ezrahi 2007. The new law was based on recommendations of the Landes Committee (2014).

[10] However, the law eliminates the separate existence of Educational Television – established in 1963 by the Rothschild family as a unit in the Ministry of Education under the minister of education. In the new PBC, it will be integrated into the channel for children and youth.

The Second Authority for Radio and Television Law (1990)

This law regulates the status of commercial radio and television channels, and defines their purpose: broadcasts "in the fields of learning, education, entertainment, and information on topics of social and economic policy, the economy, culture, science, art, and sport." The Second Authority represents the public interest in commercial channels that are solely funded by selling time slots for commercials; it issues tenders for television and radio broadcasts, and awards media franchises. A public council of fifteen members appointed by the government oversees the authority. The council supervises Channel 2, which began to officially broadcast in 1993; Channel 10, which started to broadcast in 2002; and fourteen regional radio stations (since 2011). It is authorized to oversee the content of the broadcasts and demand compliance with the conditions of the media franchise (e.g., a certain percentage of original productions), and to reject advertisements and programs that offend public sensibilities. The commercial broadcasting channels operate under the tension of regulation by the council, whose members are usually politically appointed, and the economic interests of the commercial franchisees. In 2012–14, Channel 10 faced closure due to serious financial debts. The RGE group eventually bought the majority shares of Channel 10 in 2015, allowing for extension of its license for fifty years (O. Dor 2015). The law also prohibits media cross-ownership (see below).

B. Laws and Regulations on Monitoring, Censuring, Banning Publication, and Freedom of Information

The Press Ordinance (1933)

This ordinance, dating back to the British Mandate, is still in effect today, with several important amendments. According to the ordinance, publishing a newspaper requires a permit from the district commissioner. It also authorizes the minister of interior to halt publication of a newspaper if the minister deems that an article in it may endanger public safety, or could incite panic or despair. In addition, the court is empowered to order the closure of a newspaper if it publishes libelous incitement. The sanctions included in the Mandate-era ordinance usually remain on paper only, but they have been applied in a number of cases. For example, in 1953, the minister of the interior twice ordered closure of the Communist Party's *Kol Ha'am* newspaper because of specific articles. The first time, the High Court of Justice affirmed the closure, noting that the article could have indeed incited panic and despair (*Kol Ha'am v. Minister of Interior* 1953). In the second round, known as "the Kol Ha'am ruling," the High Court overturned the interior minister's decision, ruling that he had overstepped his authority because the article posed no immediate and tangible threat to public safety. The court thus introduced freedom of expression into the Israeli code (*Kol Ha'am v. Minister of Interior* 1953). In the 1990s, the authority to close newspapers was still exercised, primarily against newspapers in Arabic, particularly those published in East Jerusalem (Negbi 1995, 25–26). In recent years, the Ministry of Interior has not enforced the formal requirement to obtain a permit in order to publish a newspaper, and the Press Law, proposed in 2008, sought to revoke this requirement.[11]

[11] The bill passed its first reading in the Knesset in March 2008 (T. Dahan 2008, 45).

The Military Censor

The State of Israel adopted military censorship from the British Mandate's Emergency Regulations 1945. Section 87 stipulates that "The Censor may by order prohibit … any publication … which, in his opinion, would be, or liable to become, harmful to Israel or to the public safety or to public order." The IDF censor's unit is headed by a brigadier general, a high-ranking officer appointed by the minister of defense, whose task is to prevent publication of information on the grounds stipulated above. Under the law, and in accordance with an understanding between the military censor and newspaper editors, censorship is not applied to political topics or expressions of opinion, commentary, or assessments.

How does the military censor operate? The unit notifies media institutions in advance which topics require its approval. The list is updated from time to time, but has always included security affairs and immigration of Jews from hostile countries. Similar to the Press Ordinance, the legislation is draconian, but in practice the military censor operates under a cooperative arrangement between the media and the defense authorities. The "Censorship Agreement" was originally signed in December 1949 and the current version is from 1996. In practice, the agreement transferred punitive authority from the censor to the "Committee of Three" – one representative each of the IDF, the Editors' Committee (see below), and the public.[12] The Committee of Three discusses the censor's complaints against the media organization in question, and hears the latter's appeals on items quashed by the censor. In the past, appeals of committee decisions were sent to the IDF chief of staff, but today they are referred to a judge. Through the period 1950–98, the media submitted only eighty-three appeals against the censor to the Committee of Three and only six in the period 2005–15 (Vaaknin-Gil 2015). Only 15 percent of the appeals were approved in full, while 43 percent were approved in part. Thus, the committee sought to find a compromise between the censor and the media (Nossek and Limor 2002, 89).

One of the salient cases of the use of censorship for political purposes was the prohibition on publishing news of the Kafr Qasim event in 1956, without any real security justification. Even earlier, a comprehensive gag order had been imposed on the details of what was termed "the rotten business" in Egypt in 1954–55 (and later became known as the Lavon affair). The media in Egypt and internationally reported extensively on this, and when two of the Jewish agents were executed in Egypt, the Israeli newspapers published Israel's official version, contending that the charges were fabricated. In 1960, when the Lavon affair began to emerge, the question of responsibility for the "rotten business" appeared in the media under code names: "the affair," "the reserve officer," "the third man," etc. (Galnoor 1982, 230). The Israeli public became aware of these events, which convulsed the political system at the time, more than a decade after they occurred.

Another example is the closure of the *Hadashot* newspaper in 1984 – by administrative order under the Emergency Regulations – after it published a news item

[12] Before the agreement with the Editors' Committee was signed, the censor exercised its authority under the Emergency Regulations to halt the printing of newspapers. For example, *al Hamishmar* was closed for one day in 1948 after publishing a picture of Yigal Allon, commander of the Palmach, contrary to a directive not to publish the pictures of army commanders. After signing the Censorship Agreement, this authority was exercised in only a few cases.

about the formation of a committee to investigate the killing of two terrorists in the "Bus 300" incident. It was easier to shut down this newspaper because it was not a member of the Editors' Committee and hence not protected by the Censorship Agreement (Caspi and Limor 1992, 167–69). Over time, the military censor became less relevant as the political system and defense establishment grew more open. In 1988, the censor rejected an article in the *Ha'ir* newspaper that criticized the head of the Mossad and disclosed the timing of personnel changes at the Mossad. The newspaper petitioned the High Court of Justice, arguing that censoring the article violated the freedom of expression and the public's right to know. The court ruled that the article did not pose a threat to state security and that freedom of expression should take precedence in this case:

> There cannot be a free government without a free press; therefore, the press should be allowed to fulfill its role and only in exceptional and special cases (real harm to security) is there room for prohibiting the publication of news items in newspapers. (*Schnitzer v. Chief Military Censor* 1988)

This ruling restrained the censor's authority to cases in which a real danger to state security could be demonstrated. And indeed, a decade later, the prohibition on publishing the identity of the heads of the Mossad and the General Security Service was revoked.

In the era of global media, military censorship is often irrelevant and sometimes ridiculous. State secrets were also published in the international media in the past, but there was some significance in the fact that the Israeli authorities withheld confirmation, and this also served the goal of preventing the public in Israel from knowing whether the reports were true. Today, when the international media publish an item that is censored in Israel, the Israeli media can make it public, citing foreign sources not subject to the censor's restrictions: "Sophisticated media consumers (whose number is growing) quickly switch to CNN and other foreign sources of information to hear the truth" (Kotev 1999). The online channels broke through nearly all of the barriers and made censorship almost impossible. Accordingly, the IDF prefers to be proactive – to publish information in order to disseminate its version and define the frame of reference. It is true that undemocratic governments have proven that it is also possible to oversee online channels, but ways have been found to circumvent the prohibitions. In Israel, Internet content is regulated under the Communications Law, which requires a special license for broadcasting to the public. However, the definitions in the law do not include explicit reference to Internet broadcasts, and the special nature of the social network does not allow enforcement of this type of requirement vis-à-vis each user, thereby indirectly and in practice recognizing the individual's freedom of broadcast (Karniel 1999).

Civilian Censorship: Council for Review of Films and Plays (Regulation) (1979)

There was also civilian censorship in Israel, exercised under the Mandate-era censorship ordinances (on cinema films and public performances). The council, comprised of fourteen public figures, was assigned the task of restricting or prohibiting plays and films that include violence, pornography, and incitement to racism, or that offend public sensibilities. Even earlier, an Inter-ministerial Committee for Approval of the Importation of Foreign Artists decided in 1965 to prevent the Beatles from performing in Israel. The reason was its "likely negative effect on the youth." In 2008, Israel's ambassador in London wrote a letter of apology to John Lennon's sister on the "historic missed opportunity" (O'Loughlin 2008).

In 1986, the council banned the play *Ephraim Returns to the Army*, claiming that it portrays the Israeli military government in the territories in a distorted way and compares it to the Nazi regime, and therefore offends public sensibilities and disturbs public order. The High Court of Justice ruled that the harm is not severe and does not justify interfering with freedom of expression (*Laor v. Council for Review of Films and Plays* 1986). This ruling led to elimination of the censorship of plays.[13] Nowadays, the council exercises censorship only on films, and its main activity is rating films for age groups. Still, the council occasionally bans films, as it did *The Last Temptation of Christ*, for example, arguing that the film might offend the sensibilities of Christians in Israel. The ban was overturned by the court, which again asserted that this violation of freedom of expression was not justified (*Universal City Studios v. Films and Plays Censorship Board* 1989). In 2003, the council banned *Jenin, Jenin,* a film by Mohammed Bakri that depicts the Palestinian perspective on events in a refugee camp during the Defensive Shield Operation (spring 2002). The council contended that the film is one-sided, distorts facts, and severely offends public sensibilities by portraying IDF soldiers as war criminals. The court overturned the decision, ruling that screening of the film should be allowed and that the public should have a chance to judge for itself (*Bakri v. Film Censorship Board* 2003). Hopefully, this ruling, which transferred the decision-making from the censor to the viewers, will mark the end of the censorship of films, an anachronistic institution that does not exist in other democratic countries.

Laws to Protect Privacy and Prevent Defamation

The media may violate an individual's rights in the name of "the public's right to know" and freedom of expression; the citizen needs to be protected. The relevant laws are the Protection of Privacy Law (1981) and the Prohibition of Defamation Law (1965). In libel suits against journalists, the court must weigh these basic civil rights versus freedom of the press. In general, defamation law in Israel tends to favor those who claim to have suffered libel: they only need to prove that an allegedly libelous article was harmful, while the publisher bears the burden of proving that the article was not false (the "I spoke the truth" rule). In its rulings, the court tends to balance the spirit of the law, while recognizing the need to protect freedom of expression. For example, in his libel suit against *Haaretz* correspondent Uzi Benziman, Ariel Sharon (at the time minister of defense during the first Lebanon War) claimed that the journalist's contention that "Menachem Begin knew very well that he had been duped by Sharon" was a damaging falsehood. The court rejected Sharon's arguments and accepted Benziman's view that it was a case of "truth in publishing."[14] Another case (*John Doe v. Ilana Dayan-Orbach* 2010) illustrates the tension created by the need to balance the values of freedom of expression and a person's reputation. Here, the Supreme Court overturned a district court ruling and

[13] Repeal of the censorship on plays came with Amendment 35 to the Penal Code, 1991; in 1989, the Public Performances (Censorship) Ordinance was lifted.

[14] Sharon filed two lawsuits against Benziman: *Sharon v. Benziman* 1993 and *Sharon v. Benziman* 1998.

found that a report on the *Uvda* television program on Channel 2 complied with the rule of "the truth as known at the time," and that journalists are entitled to a "bona fide" defense (reheard by the Supreme Court in September 2014).

In 2001, the Defamation Law was amended to increase the amount of compensation that can be awarded without proof of damage. This tipped the scale in favor of those who might be harmed by defamation, at the expense of narrowing the boundaries of investigative journalism. This amendment has come under criticism for having a muzzling effect, not only on media reports, but also among citizens, who may choose to refrain from making comments, even when they are true and of public interest, due to the cost in the event of a libel suit.

Freedom of Information Law (1998)

The dilemma of government secrecy versus the public right to know challenges every democracy, and is particularly acute in Israel due to the centrality of security (Galnoor 1977, 178; Galnoor 1989a). However, this dilemma took on a completely new form with the new information technology and the appearance of organizations such as WikiLeaks, which aim to expose all state secrets.[15] In Israel, Article 35 of the Basic Law: Government states that the deliberations and decisions of government ministries and ministerial committees on security matters and foreign relations are classified. The government is empowered to issue an order declaring any matter to be privileged information, and violation of the gag order is a criminal offense under the Penal Code (1977). Secrecy is intended to protect a public interest, but the public's right to know is also a public interest, and secrecy orders have been used more than once for reasons unrelated to the public interest.

This tension inevitably creates the phenomenon of "leaking information" in the political system. Leaking information is a deliberate attempt to use privileged information to promote particular interests (Galnoor 1975a, 67). Leaks pertaining to security or foreign relations are a proven way to gain media exposure, and politicians leak information to promote their political interests. In democracies, however, leaking often serves as a "pressure valve" to release information in response to an overdose of secrecy. In Israel, too, the previous curtain of secrecy was raised with the help of politicians and officials of all ranks, so there is little that is not ultimately exposed in the media. Prime ministers have adopted various measures in an effort to eliminate leaking: Golda Meir preferred a small forum of "the kitchen cabinet," based on personal trust; Menachem Begin was reticent in reporting to government ministers on sensitive matters; others declared cabinet meetings to be sessions of the ministerial committee on security affairs, thus requiring any publication of the discussion to be approved by the military censor. There are also leaks by civil servants for political or ministry-related reasons, but these are less frequent (Caspi and Limor 1992, 221–29). Prior to the 2003 Knesset election, for example, Attorney Liora Glatt-Berkowitz, a civil servant in the State Attorney's Office who was involved in investigating Prime Minister Ariel Sharon and his sons, passed on confidential material

[15] Founded by Julian Assange in 2006, WikiLeaks publishes confidential information, news leaks, and classified documents from anonymous sources. Its website claims a database of over a million documents. www.wikileaks.org/wiki/Wikileaks:About#Wikileaks_has_1.2_million_documents.3F (accessed March 23, 2016).

from the investigation to a journalist from *Haaretz*. The court ordered the journalist to reveal his sources, but he refused; despite this, the attorney was indicted and convicted of "disclosure in breach of duty."[16]

In most democratic countries, freedom of information laws reinforce the public's right to know. In Israel, this law was enacted only in 1998, after a long period of opposition by the government and, particularly, the defense establishment. Section 1 of the law states that every Israeli citizen or resident has the right to receive information from a public authority in accordance with the directives of the law. Establishing the principle of this right completely turned the tables: Whereas all public information was previously privileged unless explicitly permitted for publication, now everything is open unless publication is explicitly prohibited. The main restrictions in the law enable the authorities to withhold information if it could harm state security, foreign relations, public safety, a person's wellbeing, privacy, or commercial interests. The law transfers the burden of proof to the public authorities, who must explain why they are not providing information requested by citizens. In practice, however, long after enactment of the legislation, it remains largely unenforced because of the obstacles to receiving information, the law's limited purview, non-compliance with the law by many public authorities, a lack of resources, and cumbersome proceedings (Arbel and Shwartz-Altshuler 2008, 61).[17]

From enactment of the law in 1998 and through 2006, there were 119 court rulings that directly or indirectly pertained to freedom of information. Of these petitions, the court approved only 39 percent in full and 15 percent in part, and rejected 46 percent (ibid., 98–99).[18] The petitioners were private (74%) and public, addressing broader issues (26%) (ibid., 106–8). The state comptroller's report for 2007 (185–88) notes: about half the authorities did not post the procedures for requesting information; most did not publish accessible and up-to-date information on how to submit requests; those responsible for implementing the law were not suitably briefed on its implementation; and 44 percent did not publish reports on their websites, as required by law. In 2014, 5,548 requests were submitted to various government ministries – 51 percent by private persons – and 57 percent were approved without petitions to the court (https://foi.gov.il). The rulings seem to have encouraged the development of a culture of petitioning the court on public issues.

The review of legislation above shows that, in Israel, oversight and regulation of the media are in many different hands. Public television and radio broadcasts will be the responsibility of the Public Broadcasting Corporation, which is subject to the designated minister and government policy; the Council for Cable and Satellite Broadcasting, appointed by the minister of communications, is in charge of infrastructure; the Second Authority for Television and Radio, whose members are government appointees, oversees the commercial television channels and regional radio stations; the IDF chief of staff and minister of defense are also involved in the media

16 Glatt-Berkowitz claimed, "I did not breach the trust of the public, but acted in the service of the public" (Lubitsch 2005).

17 See the proposed Freedom of Information (Amendment) Bill 19/879/P, 2013.

18 In the United States, 63 percent of the petitions are rejected (Arbel and Shwartz-Altshuler 2008, 102).

with Army Radio under their command. In addition, Israel remains one of the only democratic countries that still exercises censorship every day of the year.

C. Arrangements and Voluntary Institutions in the Media Field

The Editors' Committee

This committee of editors of newspapers and media in Israel is a voluntary arrangement that reflects the willingness of the media to cooperate with the government out of a sense of "public responsibility" for the state's security. It originated as a "Response Committee" of Hebrew newspaper editors during the period of the British Mandate, and continued with the Censorship Agreement. The Editors' Committee only included newspaper editors at first, and the state's leaders would disclose privileged information to them in exchange for a commitment to refrain from publishing it. This was a deal that enabled the political system to ensure the cooperation of the press in exchange for sharing state secrets with the editors. For example, on the eve of the Sinai operation in 1956, the newspaper editors (and the poet Natan Alterman) were invited by Ben-Gurion to observe the unloading of French weapons from a boat in Haifa port in exchange for a promise to conceal this information. Clearly, the newspaper editors agreed not to publish sensitive information because they identified with the security concerns and believed they were protecting a vital public interest. The editor of *Davar* newspaper, Yehuda Gotthelf, articulated this perspective:

> Freedom of the press … is a fundamental institution for democracy. However … what if freedom of information endangers, for example, the possibility of immigration and saving Jews from danger of destruction? Or what if it entails a danger to the security of the State of Israel? After all, if the existence of the state is not secured, there will be no democracy and there will be no freedom, because we won't exist at all. (quoted in Z. Lavi 1998, 338)

The editors' cooperation with the government continued until the 1960s, and gradually the sense of conflict between responsibility to the state and journalistic responsibility intensified. This was particularly true vis-à-vis the editor of *Haaretz*. In 1966, *Haaretz* refused to withhold publication of a news item about Prime Minister Eshkol's visit to Iran, and in 1969, the newspaper published – contrary to the censor's directive – news about the arrival of Phantom jets in Israel, a decision that led the editor to quit the Editors' Committee for a short time. The general mistrust following the Yom Kippur War weakened cooperation between the media and government authorities. In parallel, the technological revolution and changes in the political system accelerated the leaking of information considered to be secret, and eroded the exclusiveness of the information revealed to the Editors' Committee. The committee's status further declined after the election "upheaval" in 1977 and the lack of communication between Prime Minister Menachem Begin and the editors, which peaked during the first Lebanon War.[19]

In the 1980s, the rules of the Editors' Committee were changed, its membership grew from twelve to thirty, and the newspaper editors were joined by representatives of other media, which made it more difficult to function as a discreet forum.

[19] Nevertheless, several secret affairs were disclosed to the editors on a confidential basis, such as the "prisoner exchange deal" (1983–84) and "the Vanunu affair" (1986).

The media representatives were also less willing to obey, and the editors preferred to rely on independent sources of information and to exercise their own discretion instead of following instructions. In 1992, *Haaretz* and *Yediot Aharonot* withdrew from the arrangement, making it no longer viable. The Editors' Committee still formally exists, but it has become irrelevant and is no longer a voluntary mechanism for protecting "state secrets."

Israel Press Council and Code of Professional Ethics

The council was founded in 1963 as the supreme body of the media in Israel. Its members include representatives of the Journalists Association, publishers, editors, and the public. The president of the Journalists Association is usually a prominent jurist. The council is responsible for protecting the values of freedom of the press and the public's right to know, and for maintaining high-quality journalism. Accordingly, it defines the rules of ethics that apply to the media and journalists via the "Codes of Professional Ethics of Journalism" and monitors their practice and enforcement (see the website of the Israel Press Council). This code constitutes a voluntary arrangement that defines the professional creed of journalists, describes the limitations that apply to the media, and sets broad standards for the work of each journalist. For example, it states that journalists should carry out their work with an awareness of their public mission and strictly uphold reliability and accuracy in publication.[20] Other sections stipulate that a newspaper is not compelled to disclose sources of information, must be cautious in publishing details about suspects and criminals, and should clearly distinguish between content and advertisement. In 2007, in the wake of the second Lebanon War and criticism leveled against the media for unprofessional coverage during the war, the Press Council recommended rules of ethics for journalism during times of armed conflict: sections were added about the need to obtain the military censor's clearance before publication, when appropriate; the obligation to provide fair, reliable, and balanced reporting on developments on the home front as well as the battlefront; the obligation to respect human dignity and refrain from close-up photographs of the injured and dead, and implicit reports on casualties prior to notification of their families; and the need for ethical and professional training for military reporters.[21]

The Press Council discusses complaints filed about violations of the code of journalistic ethics. It operates a court of ethics empowered to impose penalties on a journalist or media organization. The penalties range from a warning and publication of an apology to publication of the decision against it in the media. The number of complaints submitted to the council has increased over the years, but it is not considered a strong, authoritative body capable of enhancing the ethical behavior of journalists.

[20] The journalists' first code of ethics was the "Nakdi Document" at the Israel Broadcasting Authority, which defined the rules of ethics – reliability, fairness, balance, and professionalism. The document states that the journalists' role at the authority is to provide reliable information, distinguish between information, commentary, and analysis, and refrain from emphasizing their own opinions in interviews.

[21] Website of the Israel Press Council. Report of the Committee for Defining Rules of Ethics during Armed Conflict. http://moaza.co.il/BRPortal/br/P102.jsp?arc=26627 [in Hebrew] (accessed May 25, 2016).

There is no shortage of laws related to the media in Israel, but it is an assortment from different periods, not an orderly or consistent body of legislation. In general, freedom of the press and freedom of expression are protected in Israel, and the media's freedom exists in practice more than it is anchored in legislation. The boundaries of this freedom have been emphatically demarcated in Supreme Court rulings that reined in draconian and anachronistic legislation such as the Press Ordinance. This freedom also relies on informal arrangements such as the rules of ethics that journalists have taken upon themselves. However, the annual Freedom of the Press index places Israel among the countries whose freedom of the press is limited because of three main factors: freedom of expression and freedom of the press are not anchored in basic laws; some laws restrict freedom of expression, such as the Emergency Regulations; and, above all, freedom of the press is violated by restrictions imposed on the media and journalists in the occupied territories.[22]

Legislation has yet to resolve two dangers facing the media in Israel: the status of public broadcasting and its politicization; and the lack of effective monitoring of commercial broadcasting to prevent conflicts of interest.

13.3 Media Development in Israel – Print Media

The social and political developments (more pluralism and a weaker political center) also largely determined the path of change in the field of media. From the 1990s, technological developments have reshaped the nature and status of traditional print journalism, and possibly tipped the scales in favor of online journalism.

A. The Early Days – Statism

The pioneers of Hebrew journalism in the Land of Israel, *HaLevanon* and *Havatzelet* (1863), appeared during the Ottoman period, but most newspapers published after the establishment of Israel originated during the British Mandate. Journalism in the pre-state and early state period was primarily party-based; it was ideological and mobilized primarily on behalf of the Zionist enterprise. Nearly every party had its own publication: the Histadrut had *Davar* (founded in 1925); Mapai had *HaDor* (1948); Mapam had *al-Hamishmar* (1943); Hamizrahi and Hapoel Ha-Mizrahi had *Hazofeh* (1937); Herut had *Herut* (1948); the General Zionists had *Haboker* (1935); and Maki had *Kol Ha'am* (1937) and *al-Ittihad* (1944). Only *Haaretz* (1918), *Yediot Aharonot* (1939), and *Maariv* (1948) were non-affiliated private newspapers. Private journalism was considered inferior because it was a business that lacked ideology: "MK Begin brought an argument from *Haaretz* newspaper. But what is a newspaper? Someone with money opens a business, hires workers, and writes what he wants to write. I worked at a newspaper and I know what a newspaper is" (Ben-Gurion in the Knesset, April 1951, quoted in M. Naor 1997, 217).

22 Freedom House's Freedom of the Press index assesses journalism by the legal situation in the state, the political and economic influences and pressures on journalism, and actual violations of freedom of the press. In this index, Israel improved from "partly free" to "free" because in 2013 there were no serious legal charges and fewer reported cases of physical attacks or harassment against journalists, marking the lowest rate of violence since 2010. https://freedomhouse.org/report/freedom-press/2014/israel (accessed March 23, 2016).

Print journalism played a key role in the public life of the small Jewish community, thanks to the relatively high education level of the citizenry and, in particular, its high level of political involvement. The multiplicity of languages, which might have hindered the development of journalism, generated a large number of newspapers relative to the size of the population. Spurred by the waves of immigration, additional newspapers were published in various languages. In 1950, seventeen dailies were published, including eleven in Hebrew, and the public regarded the broad array of newspapers as a positive phenomenon (Israel Institute of Applied Social Research 1949). Party-affiliated journalism served as a platform for establishing the party's position on the questions of the day, and as a channel for communicating messages to members, voters, and the public at large. The newspaper was an integral part of the party, so much so that "a party without a newspaper is a mute party" (Y. Limor 2003, 1027).

During the pre-state period, the press played a role in the struggle against the British, and after 1948, it assumed national and educational roles such as instilling the Hebrew language among new immigrants. The newspapers regarded themselves as responsible for national solidarity – preventing the publication of sensitive information, toeing the line of government announcements, and preferring what was defined as collective interests over the public's right to know.[23] Journalism was "statist" and saw itself as a partner in the struggle to reinforce the collective Hebrew identity in the new state via content and symbols such as immigration, the Land of Israel, the Bible, the Jewish holidays, the Hebrew language, the IDF, and the Knesset (Galnoor 1982, 244–45). Cooperation between journalism and government was also a product of the affinity between the political and media elites, which was expressed, as noted, in the activity of the Editors' Committee. Berl Katznelson, the first editor of *Davar*, and Peretz Bernstein, the editor of *Haboker*, were political leaders. Gershom Schocken, the editor of *Haaretz*, was a Knesset Member on behalf of the Progressive Party in the third Knesset, and Herzl Rosenblum (Vardi), who signed Israel's Declaration of Independence on behalf of the "Party of the State," became the editor of *Yediot Aharonot* (Caspi and Leshem 2007, 139; Elizur and Salpeter 1973).

Alongside "statist" journalism, there was also "oppositional" journalism. The salient example during Israel's first decades was the *Haolam Hazeh* weekly, whose editors Uri Avnery and Shalom Cohen scathingly criticized the Mapai establishment, especially the security services, which they called "the apparatus of darkness."[24] There were also newspapers of opposition parties: *Herut* and *Kol Ha'am*; and the ultra-Orthodox *Hamodia* (founded in 1949) and *She'arim* (1951). The control

[23] An example of the media's conduct during that period can be found in the Qibya affair of 1953. In a reprisal raid by the IDF following a killing committed by infiltrators, about sixty Arab civilians were killed, including women and children, and about forty-five homes were destroyed in the West Bank village of Qibya. The loyal media exercised self-censorship, even though journalists were fully aware that the government's official version – that "inhabitants of border villages" did the killing and not IDF soldiers – was false. The Communist Party newspaper *Kol Ha'am* was the only one to call the operation a "massacre" and denounced the government, while the other newspapers focused on denouncing those who were condemning Israel (Morris 1996).

[24] *Haolam Hazeh*, a weekly founded in 1937, was purchased in 1950 by Uri Avnery and Shalom Cohen, and published for another forty years, until 1990. It was a combative opposition newspaper, which boosted its circulation through sensational advertising, gossip, and nude pictures – very unusual in Israel in those days. Ben-Gurion tried to ignore *Haolam Hazeh* in public, calling it "that particular weekly." However, Mapai tried to fight private journalism and established competing newspapers: in

of government authorities was not absolute for an additional reason: Freedom of the press benefited from the tension between the statist line and the party line. The newspapers' adherence to the party interest was not always consistent with the interests of the ruling party, and they occasionally published information that the government was interested in concealing. When the government tried to prevent publication of internal matters that might tarnish its image, this was leaked; and in light of the government's monopoly on information, the leaks became a democratic valve through which freedom of the press developed over time. One of the leaks was about the visit by IDF chief of staff Moshe Dayan to Germany in 1957, when relations with Germany was a highly charged topic. Ben-Gurion accused ministers from Ahdut Ha'avoda of leaking this information to their newspaper, *Lamerhav*; when they refused to resign, he himself resigned and the government fell.

Accordingly, print journalism and state radio during this period operated on two levels. On the national level, they strived to create consensus and deepen the common denominator in Israeli society; on the party level, they expressed the views of their political movements and served as an intermediary between the citizens, the parties, and the leadership.

B. The Decline of Party-Affiliated Journalism

The Lavon affair can be seen as a milestone, marking the end of the era of dogmatic party loyalty and the beginning of the period of journalistic autonomy. The reporting of the Lavon affair broke the taboo on public discussion of security and foreign policy issues. While most of the material remained privileged, the press coverage and leaks from the Knesset Foreign Affairs and Defense Committee were unprecedented. The newspapers themselves took a stance: Some sided with Lavon (*Haaretz*), some supported Ben-Gurion (*Maariv*), and others vacillated between the two (*Davar*). The government, on its part, tried to rein in the media, as it had always done:

> *Davar* does not need to be restrained. *Lamerhav* does not need to be restrained. *Herut* will shut its ears. *Haboker* is restrained in any case by Rokach's promise. In this case, there is actually no need to be concerned about *al-Hamishmar*. In order to influence *Zmanim*, there is no need for a press conference. Only *Haaretz* remains, and it is the main candidate for a criminal act in this situation. Therefore, we must direct efforts toward it, and again there is no need for an Editors' Committee for this. On the contrary, a direct approach, privately, is more likely to succeed.[25]

However, the times had changed, and journalism, including party-affiliated journals, gradually became more independent and critical. The heyday of party newspapers was over: Their circulation declined and they became a heavy economic burden for the parties. Their preeminence as political intermediaries eroded as a result of social and economic changes, and in the wake of political developments following the Yom Kippur War. The public had needs that party-affiliated journalism could

1949, it founded *Hador*, which tried unsuccessfully to compete with *Maariv*; in 1956, the weekly *Rimon* began publication, with support from the General Security Services, to compete with *Haolam Hazeh*, but was discontinued after several months due to a lack of readers (Weitz 2002).

[25] This is how Moshe Sharett (1978, vol. 3, 735), prime minister at the time of the Lavon affair, described the effort to prevent the dissemination of information about Lavon's role in the "rotten business."

not meet, and awareness grew of freedom of expression, as well as a demand for an independent press. The demise of party newspapers was slow, but expected, and happened in parallel with the decline of the parties (Caspi and Limor 1999, 65–72). *Herut* and *Haboker*, owned by the two components of the Herut–Liberals bloc (Gahal), merged in the *Hayom* newspaper in 1965, which shut down in 1969. *Davar* and *al-Hamishmar* lasted much longer (through the mid-1990s), despite economic difficulties. However, their circulation was limited and sectoral. The religious and Arab parties continued to publish affiliated newspapers: *Hazofeh* of the National Religious Party (shut down in 2008), *Hamodia* of Agudat Yisrael, *Yated Ne'eman* of Degel Hatorah, *Yom Leyom* of Shas, and *al-Ittihad* of the Communist Party (see discussion of the Arabic press below).

The privately owned newspapers – *Haaretz*, *Maariv*, and *Yediot Aharonot* – soon outpaced the party newspapers: In the late 1980s, *Haaretz* had an estimated 60,000 subscribers, and the weekend editions of *Yediot Aharonot* and *Maariv* reached about 800,000 households (CBS 1998). The daily newspapers became the main arena of media activity and sometimes functioned as opposition to the government. Growing competition with the broadcast media spurred the daily newspapers to focus more on opinion pieces and commentary, and to change their graphic design to large headlines and pictures (Caspi 1990, 19).

Three of the veteran newspapers are still in business, but their circulation is generally falling due to online journalism and the emergence of newspapers distributed free and financed by advertisements. At the end of 2015, the share of newspaper circulation was as follows: *Yediot Aharonot* 35 percent, *Haaretz* 5 percent, and *Maariv* 3 percent. Free newspapers appeared in Israel starting in 2006; the most successful one is *Yisrael Hayom*, owned by Sheldon Adelson, an American citizen, which reached a circulation of 38–39 percent on weekdays (Averbach 2016; Mann and Lev-On 2016, 34). The prevailing view is that although *Yisrael Hayom* runs at a considerable financial loss, Adelson operates it to support Benjamin Netanyahu. Indeed, *Yisrael Hayom* is reminiscent of a party newspaper from the 1950s. On page two, a list of presumably journalistic "our principles" declares "to remember that we are Israelis."[26]

C. The Growth of Local Journalism

The leaflet *Erev-Erev in Eilat* was distributed free in the southern city from the early 1960s. Local newspapers, which began to appear in the 1970s as advertising broadsheets in outlying cities, were harbingers of decentralization and localism. In the 1980s, they emerged as full-fledged newspapers (usually weeklies) in the big cities, and their overall weekend circulation surpassed that of the daily newspapers. In addition to offering advertising space to local businesses, local journalism became a platform for local politics and a voice of community cohesion. At its peak, it was influential in shaping the local agenda (Caspi 1998a).

[26] The other principles: "to tell the truth, straight and to the point; to support the rule of law; to be fair and balanced; to examine the facts, and if we make a mistake, to correct it." In 2014, the Knesset approved a preliminary reading of a bill designed to limit the free distribution of *Israel Hayom* because of "unfair competition" (*Haaretz*, November 21, 2014). The law was tabled after the 2015 election.

Since the late 1980s, local newspapers have continued to develop in parallel directions: Many became a local branch of national media networks and about two-thirds are now owned by daily newspapers. Others continue to appear as independent newspapers, in part because the new technology enables printing at relatively low cost. Local newspapers are exposed to economic crises that lead to reduced distribution and a decline in the quality of journalism, because they depend almost entirely on local advertising. Consequently, their content shrinks to allow for a disproportionate space for advertisements, which fill about half the newspaper (Y. Levy 2005). In 2014, exposure to local newspapers continued to decline to 20–23 percent among 18- to 44-year-olds and up to 47 percent from age 65+ (Mann and Lev-On 2015, 30). The dependence of these newspapers on local government as a primary advertiser compels them to sometimes serve as a political mouthpiece.

D. Online Newspapers

From the mid-1990s, online newspapers became the public's primary source of information. In 2009, about 75 percent of those polled reported that they surf the Internet, and approximately 80 percent of these Internet users said they use various news websites (*Panim* 2009). The large daily newspapers have online editions (*Yediot Aharonot* – Ynet, *Maariv* – nrg, *Haaretz* – haaretz.com). Nonetheless, despite the rates of Internet usage, a majority of the users said they do not read newspapers on the Internet. In parallel, exposure to the print media did not grow, and averaged 61 percent in 2007–13, but only 55 percent in 2016 (Mann and Lev-On 2014, 36; Mann and Lev-On 2016, 35). On the other hand, exposure to economic journalism, both print and online, is on the rise: In 2014, the aggregate exposure to economic journalism stood at about 20 percent (in descending order: *Calcalist*, *The Marker*, and *Globes*) (Mann and Lev-On 2015, 32). In Israel, as in other countries, the share of print journalism in the advertising market is shrinking: It dropped to 23 percent in 2014 (not including local newspapers) compared to 41 percent for television and a steady increase (22%) for the Internet. Five years earlier, the corresponding figures were 35 percent for newspapers, 40 percent for television, and 14 percent for the Internet (*The Marker*, January 28, 2011, 18; Mann and Lev-On 2015, 41). Does the combination of new media channels and Internet journalism signal the end of print journalism? In 2009, about 50 percent of the public in Israel believed that within a few years they would read news only on the Internet and that print newspapers would disappear (*Panim* 2009).

In our opinion, it is too early to conclude whether print journalism has reached the end of its road; online journalism is competing not only with print journalism, but also with other media channels like television because of their salient advantages – immediacy and collaborativity (Yuval Dror 2009). *Immediacy*: the ability to report on events in real time without the need to await the technical means required for other media. In addition, technological innovations such as apps on mobile devices increase the accessibility of information, which further shortens response time. Such sites publish news from the field, without any censorship or other restrictions (see Michael Dahan 1999 on circumventing censorship via the Internet; also E. Hacohen 2004), and they are updated twenty-four hours a day, including news bulletins. The headline in the morning print edition is yesterday's news compared to the speed at which the main headline changes on the Internet site. *Collaborativity*: the interactivity of online journalism enables consumer-readers to participate in the process of creating the news. Online journalism sites create opportunities for users to express their views on the articles in talkbacks, which also serve as a tool (albeit a problematic one) for assessing the public's interest (for more on this, see A. Cohen and Neiger 2007). Online journalism invites citizens to contribute content through blogs, photographs, news tips, and even news items (Singer et al. 2011). At the same time, immediacy and collaborativity are accompanied by amateurism, deception, and distortion, as well as impulsive and unbridled vilification. It is difficult to apply filtering and editing mechanisms to control the talkbacks. Moreover, in all channels of online journalism, the distinctions between news items, opinions, blogs, and advertisements are completely blurred.[27]

E. Independent Journalism?

On the eve of the 1973 Yom Kippur War, the media fed the public information and official assessments received from government and military authorities without challenging or casting doubt upon them. Members of the Editors' Committee willingly practiced self-censorship, despite the reports of Syrian and Egyptian troops massing along the borders, and acceded to the IDF chief of staff's request to refrain from publishing this information to avoid panicking the public. Journalists who tried to publish news items that crossed the official line were censored (Negbi 1991). When the war broke out, the media again faced a dilemma: In times of crisis, are the media part of the national effort tasked with maintaining public morale, or should they stick to the job of providing reliable information? The great majority were inclined to choose the first option, usually through inner persuasion, following the pattern of mobilized journalism that predated the founding of Israel.

After the 1973 war, the soul-searching began, which gradually led to more independent relations between the press and the political system, accompanied by more skepticism. Journalism became more investigative, and occasionally allowed itself to criticize even the defense establishment (see Chapter 14), as in the General Security Service affair in 1984. Nonetheless, in times defined as "emergencies," the media in general tend to serve, at least initially, as a mouthpiece for the government in its effort to shape or reassure public opinion. These two facets of the media – mobilized and critical – were manifested in the second Lebanon War (2006). At the outset, the media adopted a patriotic stance and did not question the necessity of the war, a view that reflected and also contributed to the public euphoria. At some stage, some media, primarily the press, shifted to harsh criticism of the war and its objectives to the point of portraying it as a failure. This also during the military operation in the Gaza Strip in the summer of 2014 ("Protective Edge") – initial media support, which later ebbed. At first, for example, the media reported 90 percent success of the Israeli defense system against artillery rockets (the Iron Dome). Such changes in the

[27] There is a growing concern about Internet wrongdoing, such as the need to protect minors, to ensure copyrights, to prevent its use for plotting terrorism, to prevent economic monopolies, etc. The dilemma is how to ensure that regulation does not clip the wings of the new media's unprecedented freedom. In western countries some high-quality, online newspapers do not allow talkbacks at all.

media's attitude exact a price in public opinion, as many view its criticism as a blow to morale and proof of "hostile media" (Weimann 2007; Elbaz and Bar-Tal 2016).

The media revolution led print journalism to a crisis – in Israel and other democratic states – because of competition from the new channels and free daily newspapers. Consequently, the future of print journalism is still unclear (R. Rosner 2008; Rolnik 2009). One of the solutions proposed to mitigate the decline of print journalism is to subsidize it (e.g., by granting tax exemptions), but this might allow politicization to return through the back door.

13.4 Media Development in Israel – Broadcast Journalism

In the beginning, there was the radio. Television arrived in Israel only in 1968, and these two outlets enjoyed exclusivity among the Jewish and Arab populations until the 1990s.

A. Kol Yisrael – The Voice of the State

Radio broadcasts in Hebrew began during the pre-state period, and Radio Jerusalem came on the air in 1936 under the patronage of the British Mandate government. The number of licensed radios rose sharply from 836 in 1932 to 42,600 in 1939 – about 80 percent owned by Jews. The British prohibited independent stations, Hebrew or Arabic, but in 1937 the first underground broadcasts of the Irgun began, followed by those of the Haganah (1940) and Lehi (1941). The underground radio broadcasts, primarily of the Haganah from 1946 to 1948, were not only used to communicate information that was censored from Radio Jerusalem broadcasts, but also as a means of mobilization for the national struggle. Broadcast of the Declaration of Independence on May 14, 1948 marked the end of the underground broadcasts and the beginning of state radio – Kol Yisrael, the "Voice of Israel" (E. Almog 2003). The station, which originally operated as a department in the Office of the Prime Minister, enjoyed exclusivity in broadcasting the news, and its main role was to meet the needs of the government. The radio station regarded itself as the voice of the new state. The government saw it as a political instrument and means of educating the public, especially the new immigrants about culture, pioneering, Hebrew-language learning, and more. The government's grip on the radio was consistent with the perspective of statism, political centralization, and the emphasis on government secrecy. A survey in 1950 showed that half the Jewish population listened to the radio regularly, most (42%) to Kol Yisrael and the rest to BBC broadcasts in Hebrew or foreign stations. In 1955, the share of Kol Yisrael listeners rose to 58 percent, and the most popular program was the news (Gratch 1973, 111).

Radio broadcasts were strictly supervised until the mid-1960s, to the point of denying airtime to members of the opposition, as reflected in the accounts of Kol Yisrael employees from that time. Zvi Zinder, the director of Kol Yisrael (1955–60), told how the director-general of the Office of the Prime Minister, Teddy Kollek, and the prime minister's secretary, Yitzhak Navon, instructed him, advised him, and even reprimanded him for broadcasting or failing to broadcast a particular event (Mishal 1978, 41–42). However, there was also a large degree of self-supervision based on the party-ideological identification of Kol Yisrael's leaders with the government. The only visual mass medium during that period was the cinema, where newsreels were broadcast prior to screening the movies. During the years 1953–67, the Geva studios had a monopoly on screening newsreels in theaters throughout Israel. The newsreels were produced by a private company, and there is no evidence that representatives of the government interfered directly with their content. In practice, however, they served as a powerful channel in the government's hands to publicize its version of current events and photographs of the leaders (Galnoor 1982, 226–29).

B. Establishment of the Israel Broadcasting Authority (IBA) and Israel Television

The establishment of an independent public broadcasting authority (IBA) in 1965 (modeled after the BBC) and the transfer of Kol Yisrael from the Office of the Prime Minister during the term of Levi Eshkol were important steps of democratization, but more than anything they were engendered by the changes in society and politics. The previous model lost its hold and the public began to demand reliable information, but they did not necessarily find it on Kol Yisrael, despite the station's serious official tone. In addition, the internal rift in Mapai paved the way for neutralizing Kol Yisrael.

Israel Television was founded in 1968, long after television was introduced in other countries, due to resistance from most of the political parties – coalition and opposition alike. Mapai and Ben-Gurion were concerned about the impact of television and argued that it was a cultural hazard that could undermine the integration of Israeli society; opposition parties feared that Mapai would use it as a powerful mouthpiece for the government's views. When state television was founded, it was made subordinate to the IBA and it has yet to free itself from the government–party connection, reflected mainly in political appointments, despite the many efforts to institute reforms (see the crisis in public broadcasting below). Kol Yisrael (together with Army Radio) enjoyed exclusivity in radio broadcasting until 1995, and Channel 1 television was a monopoly until the 1990s, when 70 percent of the population watched the Mabat nightly newscast:

> It serves as a sort of stage on which every evening, in front of the entire society, the significant discussions were conducted, a stage that serves a range of streams and ideas. It is as if the monopolistic Mabat broadcast gathers the entire Israeli public in a sort of "kibbutz conversation" or agora (market square) of the Greek city-state. (Caspi 1990, 22)

C. The New Map

The IBA's exclusivity could not last, if only because of technological developments. In the early 1990s, the media map in Israel changed drastically. Within a decade, starting with the establishment of cable television (1989), a series of developments transformed the media from monopolistic to pluralistic: the launching of a commercial television station, Channel 2 (on an experimental basis in 1986 and regular broadcasts in 1993), the creation of regional radio stations (1995), satellite broadcasts (2000), the franchise for an additional commercial station (Channel 10, 2002), the appearance of specialized channels in 2002–3 (e.g., Channel 9 in Russian and the Judaism channel Tkhelet/Moreshet – since 2014 the commercial Channel 20), and the Knesset channel (2005). According to Caspi and Leshem (2007, 121–22), the "media revolution" is a result of parallel processes: First, there was a fundamental change in the media itself, shifting from a social to an economic orientation, which relies on the rating culture of market forces. Second was the "open skies" policy, which led to breaking up the monopoly of public broadcasting, the entry of entrepreneurs and private investors, and creation of the capital–government–media nexus. Telecommunications underwent a rapid process of liberalization that also included technological pluralism and competitiveness in private ownership. The state's direct role in providing communication services diminished, and it became primarily an entity that regulates (or tries to regulate) the market (Levi-Faur 1999). Third, decentralization of the media encouraged the growth of local journalism and the creation of media channels that respond to sectoral and local needs (including illegal radio stations). Fourth, the crisis in public broadcasting and the growth of commercial media corporations initially led to centralized control by "media barons" who have cross-ownership. Later, a more complex structure of the media market began to develop, in which each "screen" – at home, at work, or in one's pocket – has overlapping connections to various owners on the media map (see discussion below).

The major changes were first evident when television was introduced:

> We departed from the era of public television as a national experience, and are now in the midst of a post-modern era characterized by segmentation, individualization, and commercialization. Once, we had a national forum for which we paid an entry fee; today, we have a giant video store. (Katz and Haas 1995, 80)

The multiplicity of channels reflected the preferences of the public, which chose to watch fewer news programs on television (also broadcast on Channel 2 and Channel 10), and more entertainment, game shows, and reality programs. The percentage of viewers who watched the news declined for all the channels, certainly in comparison with the Mabat newscast during its period of monopoly. In 2014, the average rating of all the newscasts was about 24 percent for Channel 2, 11 percent for Channel 10, and 5 percent for Channel 1 (Y. Walzer 2015).

Pluralism was supposed to engender variety and strengthen the media's independence, on the assumption that commercial channels, whose revenues do not depend on government favors, would feature bold critiques of the political system. This assumption has not materialized; there is no evidence that the commercial media (the dominant Channel 2 in particular) are more independent of a political perspective. First, the commercial channels are subject to a regime of media franchising and oversight by entities such as the Council of the Second Authority, which are not free of politicization. Second, the fact that they depend on advertisements, and that viewing ratings are the economic oxygen they breathe, leads them to be less daring. They aim to stay within the consensus and not irritate anyone, especially politicians and big business. Preference is given to profitable programs that win high ratings, compared to news and "serious" programming, and it has become clear that consensus is sought not only by the public channels (which depend on the government), but also by the commercial channels because of economic dependence. Self-censorship of the media for economic motives is liable to be more problematic than censorship imposed for political motives, because the former is not transparent and it is harder to demand accountability from a private company. Nonetheless, a study of news coverage in the main broadcasts in 1998 found that the state's Channel 1 (the director-general was Uri Porath) tended to favor the government, the coalition, and the prime minister, and used fewer critical journalistic tools in comparison to Channel 2 (Keshev 1999). The commercial channels are sometimes critical of the government, especially Channel 10, but in general their criticism is implicit and often reserved for satirical programs.

Since the 1980s, changes also began concerning the airwaves. Kol Yisrael expanded its range of activity and added networks, Army Radio broadened its target audience, and regional radio stations were launched. In parallel, pirate radio stations emerged; the first was Abie Nathan's "Voice of Peace," founded in 1973 and broadcast from a ship at sea. Channel 7 ("Arutz Sheva"), a station of Greater Israel adherents and the religious sector, was established in 1988.[28] Most pirate stations were local, commercial, and served defined audiences, including ultra-Orthodox Jews, Arabs, and fans of Mizrahi music. There were about 200 such stations in the 1990s and nearly 300 in the first decade of the twenty-first century (Limor and Naveh 2007). Not only did the pirate stations operate in violation of the law and use frequencies without a license, but they also disrupted other wireless communication (of aircraft and the army, for example). The pirate stations are also not bound by the rules of ethics of the IBA or Second Authority for Radio and Television. In the absence of a legal address for lawsuits on libel, defamation, and violation of privacy, it is difficult for injured parties to sue them. Following several court decisions, however, radio piracy declined and eventually lost its sting with the coming of Internet broadcasting, which required no frequencies or license. In 2015, a few such stations operate from time to time.

Despite the technological developments and proliferation of new media channels, overlapping radio listening in 2014 remained high among the general population: 70 percent on weekdays – 54 percent listened to Army Radio stations, 44 percent to Kol Yisrael stations, and 32 percent to regional radio stations.[29] The primary reason for this is that the radio and mobile devices are means of communication that accompany Israeli drivers on the road.[30]

[28] Channel 7 was an ideological pirate radio station identified with the political right. The funding came from a British donor and the Beit El yeshiva. In 2003, the Jerusalem Magistrate's Court convicted the owners, managers, and editors of the channel for illegal broadcasts (*State of Israel v. Katz et al.* 2003). The government tried to circumvent the court ruling and authorize the illegal channel by amending the Bezeq Law to stipulate that any pirate radio station that broadcasts for five consecutive years (without a license), and whose broadcasts reach most of the country, is authorized and legal. On March 26, 2002, the High Court of Justice ruled that this amendment to the Bezeq Law authorizing pirate radio stations was unconstitutional (*Oron v. Knesset Speaker* 1999). The station shut down and the channel began broadcasting via the Internet.

[29] The data exceed 100 percent because respondents listened to more than one station. From a TGI survey on exposure to newspapers and radio, 2014. www.ice.co.il (accessed October 6, 2017).

[30] In 2014, the average private vehicle traveled 39,222 km annually (Central Bureau of Statistics press release, September 10, 2015). Using a rough estimate of 50 kph and maximum listening time, this averages to 784 hours of annual listening per driver.

D. From Cross-Ownership to Cross-Centralization

When the state's grip on the telecommunications market loosened, cross-ownership emerged, i.e., control by a company or person of several entities that operate in the same or related commercial fields (Ezrahi et al. 2003). Wealthy individuals and groups of investors dominated the main media channels via corporations that controlled more than one media outlet. The three leading corporations in the early 2000s were controlled by three families referred to as "media barons" (Mozes, Schocken, and Nimrodi) (Y. Limor 1997). The concern is that a citizen who was once at the mercy of government- and party-affiliated media driven by political motives would now be at the mercy of the commercial interests of private media organizations – in the morning, reading a newspaper owned by one of the wealthy families, on the train, surfing websites they own, after work, watching a television channel they control, listening to music produced by their subsidiary, reading a book from a publishing house they own, and even buying life insurance, health services, and vacations in hotels under their ownership.

Cross-ownership endangers the free market of information and ideas, and limits the competition among media organizations and the possibility of criticizing them. The danger is that the handful of people who depict reality for the public will do so out of political and economic motives. Cross-ownership could lead not only to the filtering and uniformity of content, but also to the narrowing of free competition and the development of cartels that collaborate at the expense of the citizen. Those who oppose restrictions on cross-ownership argue that in the current era of convergence of diverse media channels, the messages are communicated simultaneously via radio, television, Internet, and cellphones and there is no need for restrictions that are still based on the (erroneous) assumption of a clear distinction between different media. In addition, the transition from analog to digital technology eliminated the need to strictly allocate the scarce public commodity of frequencies, and the consumer can be exposed to a range of almost unlimited channels (Shwartz-Altshuler 2002).

To contend with the phenomenon of cross-ownership, legislation in Israel now sets limits on the percentage of control and prohibits a single entity from holding different media organizations. For example, the Second Authority for Television and Radio Law (1990) restricts cross-ownership by newspaper owners and Channel 2 franchisees,[31] and places restrictions on franchises for regional radio broadcasts, television franchisees, and newspaper owners. The law also limits, albeit less strictly, cross-ownership of print journalism and Channel 10. In addition, there are restrictions on cross-ownership by franchisees for television broadcasts of the Second Authority and owners of satellite television. The Communications Law completely prohibits cross-ownership of print journalism and a national news channel, in addition to the prohibitions in the Antitrust Law designed to prevent the creation of a monopoly in one field.

An example of the danger posed by centralization of the media in the hands of tycoons became apparent in the mid-1990s. In the heat of the competition between the two evening newspapers, illegal wiretapping was conducted: Ofer Nimrodi, the

[31] An owner of a controlling share in a newspaper may not hold more than 24 percent of the voting rights of a Channel 2 franchisee and may not benefit from more than 30 percent of the profits of a corporation seeking to participate in a tender.

board chair, publisher, and editor-in-chief of *Maariv*, was convicted of illegally wiretapping senior personnel at the rival *Yediot Aharonot* and for obstructing justice (*State of Israel v. Ofer Nimrodi* 1995; *Nimrodi v. State of Israel* 2000). The trial also exposed the secret alliances and deals spun between the "media barons," who were not particularly attentive to the public's right to know. A fierce competition subsequently erupted between *Yediot Aharonot* and *Yisrael Hayom*, and cast its shadow over the 2015 Knesset election campaign.

The Seventh Eye began publishing in 2006, first as a bimonthly and since 2008 as an online newspaper.[32] In 2006, it published the Map of Media Ownership in Israel – a complex diagram showing owners with their direct and indirect links to the various media channels. The conclusion from this mapping is that nearly all the media channels are under centralized control, and the previous structure has transitioned into one of multiple cross-ownerships of business interests. In addition, there is regulatory uncertainty vis-à-vis public and private broadcasting. Thus, in 2014, the media map reflected "an X-ray of eclectic uncertainty" (www.the7eye.org.il/50534).

The assumption was that in the transition from institutionalized journalism to pluralistic journalism, a new model of "media-social responsibility" would emerge whereby the government would relinquish control over the media and the media would apply standards of truth and reliability out of a sense of social responsibility. The road to implementing this model in Israel is still long, but cybermedia have clearly introduced unprecedented pluralism (see the final section of this chapter).

E. The Crisis in Public Broadcasting

The status of public broadcasting has declined in all western countries.[33] In an information era of multiple channels and entertainment media, there is ostensibly no longer any reason to maintain a somber public broadcasting channel funded from public coffers. In our view, the opposite is true. Precisely in this era, public broadcasting is vital as a balancing, reliable, and quality-setting channel, free of the stifling restrictions of political and business considerations. When culture is shaped by ratings, it is increasingly important to have a media channel whose standards of quality are different. This is also part of pluralism.

Public broadcasting in Israel, as in many other countries, does not successfully fulfill its mission due to the inherent difficulty of shaping an agenda of worthy broadcasts, and the challenges posed by new technologies and commercial competition. Since the 1990s, the IBA has been unable to make the transition from a monopolist status to a multi-channel era in a multicultural society, and is caught in a mortal crisis. The many public committees formed to study the IBA's structure and operations, and the fact that the government has consistently ignored their recommendations, testify to its dismal state.[34] The ongoing threat to public broadcasting in Israel is a

[32] In its news print form, it was published by the Israel Democracy Institute. The online version, www.the7eye.org.il (accessed October 6, 2017), as of mid-2015, is in danger of closing for economic reasons.

[33] Even the BBC, regarded as the paragon of reliable and quality public broadcasting, has long been criticized for excessive conservatism and commercialism, and some voices are calling for it to close, privatize, or have reduced public funding (Economist 1998, 36).

[34] Including the Committee to Study the Structure and Functioning of the Broadcasting Authority (Livni Committee), 1993; Committee to Study the Structure of Public Broadcasting (Zuckerman

combination of external and internal factors: the government's desire to continue with politicization, as well as serious flaws in management at the IBA, particularly blurring its identity due to capitulation to the culture of the commercial channels.

Party politicization beset the IBA from the start. The 1965 IBA Law stipulated that the plenum, the executive committee, the chairperson, and the director-general be appointed by the government. However, the law did not mandate the appointment of people who are affiliated with a political party. If those making the appointments had adhered to the BBC model, the members of the plenum would be primarily writers, teachers, artists, academicians, and other public figures.[35] In practice, the plenum appointments were made on a party basis in accordance with the ruling coalition at the time. The politicization of the appointments was overt: The parties negotiated their share of representatives in the plenum and executive committee, and in some cases the parties' representatives were selected by vote in their institutions. As a result, IBA plenum membership became a political payoff for party activists, and most of the members regard themselves as representatives of their parties (Caspi 2005, 27, 45–55). All the committees that studied the IBA recommended ending the politicization and transforming the system of appointing IBA officials. However, the recommendations were not implemented, and the IBA's politicization was reflected in decisions about broadcast content, particularly the newscasts. In 1982, for example, the IBA's executive committee decided to ban interviews with public figures who recognized the PLO as an exclusive or legitimate representative of the Palestinians. The High Court of Justice ruled that the decision was unlawful because the only consideration justifying such a ban is a clear and immediate danger to state security (*Zichroni v. IBA Executive Committee* 1982).

Other examples of politicization that border on corruption were cases of politicians who directly interfered with content in order to promote a particular interest, the appointment of cronies to jobs as broadcasters, and instructing members of the plenum how to vote. This also included "screen bribery" – not only acceding to a request by a politician to be interviewed, but also granting a platform for politicians in exchange for promoting the personal interests of IBA officials (Caspi 2005, 78–129). The politicization continued even after public broadcasting lost its exclusivity, and this is apparently the main reason for the crisis – the loss of faith in public broadcasting, and belittling its essential contribution to society and culture. When there is nothing unique about public broadcasting, the many other channels create the feeling among consumers that there is no justification for funding it in addition to their subscriptions to cable, satellite, and online channels.

In our view, public broadcasting should have different objectives than those of commercial broadcasting (Galnoor 1998a). For public broadcasting, the viewers and listeners are first and foremost citizens, while commercial broadcasting sees

Committee), 1997; Committee for Public Broadcasting (Vardi Committee), 2000; Committee to Study the Future of Public Broadcasting (Bresheeth Committee), 2000; Committee for Reform of Public Broadcasting (Dinur Committee), 2005; and the Committee to Study the Plan for Future Public Broadcasting in Israel (Landes Committee), 2014.

[35] The IBA Law (1965) required the government to consult with public entities before appointing members of the plenum, but in practice it did not always comply with this directive. In 2000, the High Court ruled against the government, which had not conducted the mandated consultation, and ordered dispersal of the plenum (*Documentary Filmmakers Forum v. President of the State* 1998).

them as consumers. Public broadcasting should be guided by general societal values that cannot be demanded from commercial channels: reinforcing democracy and equality, encouraging political participation, and creating a platform for balanced political conversation, rather than shallow, tempestuous discourse and ranting. The attempt of commercial broadcasting to please everyone makes it more homogeneous and leads it to ignore unique voices in society, particularly if these voices are not significant consumers. Public broadcasting, on the other hand, aspires to give a platform to diverse groups in society, especially those deprived and peripheral. Public broadcasting must not fall into the trap of ratings or measure itself in terms of the economic market because it is guaranteed to fail in competition with commercial channels. In countries with successful public broadcasting (and there are many examples), one sees high-quality programs, documentaries, original productions, and even good entertainment. In Israel, competition with commercial channels led public broadcasting to suffer double jeopardy: it became a twilight zone in which news, entertainment, and advertising are jumbled together, with excessive public funds invested in broadcasting sporting events; and its popularity nevertheless dwindled.

The guiding principle for public broadcasting is that it should not disregard anyone in the audience of viewers and listeners, not only because they are citizens who pay the fee, but because its considerations when addressing them are free of political and commercial bias. It must meet the unique needs of groups that are of no interest to the commercial channels, and it must also ensure reliable information and be the guardian of quality broadcasts as well as entertainment.

The interaction between the media and the political system has changed over the years. The days of a mobilized media, which subordinates freedom of the press to the state's unquestioned authority, are gone, never to return. The voluntary arrangement of the Editors' Committee, which operated consensually through the mid-1970s, cannot exist in an era of media pluralism and a weak political center. The new mode that developed has pretensions of investigative journalism and oversight, but journalism has also become vulgar and vitriolic, unbridled, lacking in style, and very commercial. However, the picture changes radically in times of emergency. On the eve of the Yom Kippur War, most journalists subscribed to the political "conception" and regretted this later. Yet subsequently, at the onset of wars and military operations, the media are again mobilized and trapped in the security discourse created by the authorities (U. Benziman 2005). In times of emergency, the government does not hesitate to utilize its means of supervision, not unlike the censorship on the eve of the Yom Kippur War. In the first Gulf War (1991), the public became a well-disciplined "captive audience," ready to sequester itself in rooms sealed with plastic wrap and breathe via gas masks in accordance with the IDF's assessment of the Iraqi threat. The media supplied the means for this, and did not ask questions.

Since the 1980s, the trend in Israeli media is from monopoly to decentralization and multiplicity, and from uniformity to diversity. Evidence abounds in the alternative media – the Internet, social channels, and even pirate radio intended for particular social groups. The wealth of channels also has great potential for reflecting social pluralism; however, the decentralization, multiplicity, and diversity can be limited, and even illusory. As noted, there are many newspapers in Israel, but the great majority have limited circulation, while *Yediot Aharonot* and *Yisrael Hayom* reach more than half the households. Multiple channels also do not guarantee diversity because if they all aim at a low common denominator, they become similar. This phenomenon is prominent in newscasts, where there is no real difference between the channels.

Is it possible to characterize the media in Israel in the twenty-first century? On the one hand, they investigate and criticize, reinforce democratic values, and help the public exercise its right to know. Many cases of corruption in government and business in Israel would have remained concealed, had they not been exposed by investigative journalists. The media have deterrent power: public officials ask themselves if a decision or action they take will meet not only the scrutiny of the High Court or state comptroller, but also, and perhaps primarily, whether it will meet the test of media exposure. Ministers, MKs, public managers, and mayors often find themselves in the eye of a media storm and are held accountable for their actions. On the other hand, the media also contribute to undemocratic phenomena, from the corruption of crony capitalism, to pressuring public officials to comply with "newsmaking" codes that are not consistent with the public interest.

13.5 The Media and Groups in Israeli Society

The transition from an ideology of the "melting pot" to the pluralistic era in Israeli society was reflected in the development of media organs among various groups in the society. Even during the period when the media were centralized and party affiliated, some distinct groups were (and still are) able to maintain independent media organs that express their values and world views and are adapted to their needs. Members of these groups are usually consumers of both the general media and sectoral media, reflecting a hybrid identity in some fields (Adoni, Caspi, and Cohen 2006). The group's internal media primarily fill the traditional role of communicating information, and serve as a means of shaping the separate identity.

Accordingly, these media organs present unique content to the community, and create a platform for emphasizing internal matters, as well as protecting the group's interests vis-à-vis society. The exposure to sectoral media may also reflect the lack of confidence in the general media among parts of the public. Such skepticism, including accusations of bias, leads 30 percent of Israelis to look for alternative, sectoral, and external media channels (Peri and Tsfati 2007). Yet, the new technologies make it impossible to maintain complete exclusivity and prevent exposure, as we will see in regard to the most insular community in Israel – ultra-Orthodox Jews.

A. The Media in Arabic

During the Ottoman period, the first Palestinian Arab newspaper appeared in Jerusalem – *al-Quds al-Sharif* (1876). Under the British Mandate, Arabic journalism played an important role in developing Palestinian identity, and its influence peaked during the "Arab Revolt" (1936–39). Since the founding of Israel, the development of the media in Arabic has largely reflected the status of the Arabs in Israel and the extent of their freedom and political equality (Kabha 2006; Caspi and Kabha 2001; Adoni et al. 2006, 57–88).

The First Period: 1948–1967

After 1948, the Arabic press nearly came to a halt, mainly because most of the leading journalists did not remain in Israel. During the period of the military government, Arabic newspapers were published under the auspices of the government or Jewish political parties, with the exception of Maki's *Kol Ha'am*. Typical "sponsored" media included the daily *al-Yom* (1948–68) published by the Histadrut Labor Federation and Kol Yisrael broadcasts in Arabic. The content was official, shaped and censored by the government authorities, and was also of a propagandist nature vis-à-vis the Arabs in Israel and neighboring countries. Mapam, which regarded itself as a Jewish-Arab party, published the weekly *al-Mersad* (1952) and the literary monthly *al-Fajr* (1958). Arabic newspapers of other Jewish parties had low circulation and did not last long.

Kol Ha'am, the newspaper of the Communist Party in its various incarnations, also had a bilingual edition, in Hebrew and Arabic. It first appeared in 1937 as a monthly and later became a daily until 1967. In addition, *al-Ittihad* (1944) survived over the years and became a daily in 1985. Its Hebrew counterpart since 1965, *Zo Haderekh*, continues to operate as a weekly with an online edition (Gozansky 2008). Naturally, these newspapers in Arabic did not have a large circulation in Israel, but they were read by their target audience and offered them the only alternative to the media that acted on behalf of the government. During that period, these newspapers (and *Haolam Hazeh*) were the only ones to strongly criticize the military government and condemn discrimination against Arab citizens. Consequently, the minister of interior imposed restrictions on them from time to time. At the end of the 1950s, an attempt was made to launch a Palestinian national publication (*al-Ard*), but it was shut down after a few issues. Those that appeared were widely circulated and stirred great interest among the Arab public.

Kol Yisrael's broadcasts in Arabic were shaped by the authorities (the Office of the Prime Minister) and the security organizations. Most of the radio executives and presenters were Jewish immigrants from Arab states, and the few Arabic editors and reporters were meticulously selected. In 1965, Arabic broadcasts were also subordinated to the IBA. Even though these broadcasts were under government auspices, they were considered relatively more reliable than the propaganda broadcasts from neighboring states, led by the Sawt al-Arab radio station, which has broadcast from Egypt since 1954.

The Second Period: 1967–1983

The abolishment of the military government (1966) and the conquest of the territories in 1967 posed a challenge for Arabic journalism in Israel, which had to reexamine its national identity and contend with competition from Palestinian newspapers. During this period, three types began to operate in parallel: journalism under the auspices of the government authorities; journalism sponsored by Jewish parties; and newspapers of the Communist Party and other Arab movements. Over the course of this period, government-linked journalism declined and the daily *al-Yom* shut down. The *al-Anbaa* newspaper, sponsored by the prime minister's adviser on Arab affairs and also intended for *hasbara* (propaganda), first appeared in 1968 and barely survived through 1984. When Israel Television was established in 1968, a department for Arabic broadcasts was created. Television broadcasts in Arabic include mainly news and programs on culture, sports, and entertainment. The propagandistic tone that characterized them changed over the years to an agenda of coexistence, with an attempt to bypass the difficult issues in dispute.

The Third Period: since 1983

Changes in Arab society and politics also stirred an awakening of the media (see Porath and Mansour 1990). We chose 1983 because of the emergence of private, independent journalism such as the weeklies *al-Sinara* (1983) and *Kul al-Arab* (1987), published in Nazareth, and *Panorama* (1987) in Taybeh. Their appearance reflected processes of "Palestinization" among the Arabs in Israel (which strengthened after the first Intifada erupted in 1987) and the blurring of the Green Line, as these publications expanded their circulation to include the Palestinian territories and paved the way for additional ones. The rise and growth of commercial journalism came at the expense of party-affiliated journalism, but they continued to appear side by side: the veteran Communist newspaper *al-Ittihad*; a new weekly with nationalist orientation such as Balad's *Fasl al-Maqal* (1996); and publications with the religious orientation of the two branches of the Islamic Movement. However, the two independent commercial weeklies, *al-Sinara* and *Kul al-Arab*, won the greatest popularity. The Arabic-language media also reflect the political divisions and jockeying in Arab society. It is still too early to assess the impact of the merger of parties in the 2015 Knesset elections in the Joint List (Hadash, Ra'am, Balad, and Ta'al), which received very broad support among Arab voters. Some 80 percent of the Arab public is exposed to Arabic journalism: Most read the commercial weeklies and a small number (9%) read a newspaper in Arabic on a daily basis; 17 percent read a daily newspaper in Hebrew, primarily *Yediot Aharonot* (Rekhess and Rudnitsky 2009, Chapter 8, 1–25). In 2016, 82 percent of Arabs owned mobile phones (72% of them owned smartphones) and many, particularly the young, use these and television as sources for news (Mann and Lev-On 2016, 35).

The emphases in Israel's Arabic media are on forging Palestinian identity as part of the Arab and Muslim identities. This journalism has filled an important role in the life of the Arab citizens, fiercely criticizing the way the Hebrew media cover key events such as the killing of protestors by the police in October 2000.[36] As a rule, the Arabic media focus on Palestinian topics and show relatively little interest in "Israeli" issues; i.e., there is a clear tendency toward seclusion and separatism (Barel 2005). In addition, since the mid-1990s there has been growing viewership of Israeli television (82%) and of satellite and cable broadcasts from the Arab world, as a link connecting the Arabs in Israel with Arab countries. Nearly a third of the population of Arab citizens of Israel watches the al-Jazeera television network, which broadcasts news live from Qatar twenty-four hours a day. For example, al-Jazeera raised subjects that the Israeli media seldom address, subjects that are close to the hearts of Arabs in Israel such as the refugees of 1948, Deir Yassin, and Kafr Qasim (Shalata

[36] A study of the coverage of the October 2000 events (*Haaretz*, *Yediot Aharonot*, Channel 1, and Channel 2) found that the Hebrew media saw themselves as representing the Jewish majority, not all the state's citizens; that the events were mainly covered by military, police, and defense correspondents; and that the violent protest by Arab citizens was portrayed as an existential threat to the state of Israel. See, for example, *Yediot Aharonot*'s headline (October 2, 2000): "Intifada in the Galilee and Jaffa" (Keshev 2001).

2001). Over half of the Arab public (58%) listen to the radio; 25 percent listen to Kol Yisrael in Arabic, 19 percent tune in to Radio al-Shams – the only station broadcasting in Arabic in northern Israel – and 17 percent listen to Reshet Bet in Hebrew (Rekhess and Rudnitsky 2009, Chapter 8, 15–16).

Radio al-Shams, which began broadcasting in 2004, targets the young generation as a competitor to Kol Yisrael in Arabic, whose listening audience is primarily older. There were also local pirate radio stations. Arabic-language Internet sites have been launched, such as Panet and al-Arab, the very popular site of *Panorama* weekly, but there is still a digital gap among Arabs in Israel in terms of access to the new technologies. In 2005, only 14 percent of the Arab population used the Internet, as opposed to 48 percent of the Jewish population (Ganayem, Rafaeli, and Azaiza 2009, 177). However, this is changing – in 2015, the rate of Internet subscription was over 60 percent, compared to about 76 percent in the secular Jewish population (Mann and Lev-On 2015, 84).

"The media revolution" in Israel has not fully occurred in the Arabic media. Despite many changes, there is still little print journalism compared to the pre-state period, the Hebrew press, or the flourishing Russian-language press, which has a target audience of similar size. In the period 1983–2005, a total of fifty-six dailies, weeklies, and magazines appeared in Arabic, most lasting only a few years (Kabha 2006).

B. New Immigrants and Foreign-Language Media

Israel is an immigrant state, and new immigrants were a target for political mobilization, education, and propaganda. However, there was ambivalence toward foreign-language media, with ups and downs, and a renaissance (Caspi and Limor 1999, 72–76). In Israel's early years, foreign-language publications (nearly all of which were party affiliated) and radio broadcasts in foreign languages were a means of communicating messages to various groups of immigrants. But these were considered a temporary measure that would decline once the immigrants were assimilated into the melting pot of the new society. Thus, great efforts were made to "impart the language" to the immigrants, including newspapers in basic and vowelized Hebrew, such as the *Omer* daily newspaper (1951–80), published by *Davar*. According to a 1949 survey, 57 percent of the public opposed non-Hebrew journalism, and 53 percent opposed Yiddish journalism in particular (Weimann 2015, 91–93). Nonetheless, foreign-language journalism flourished and in the 1960s nine dailies appeared – in Yiddish, English, Bulgarian, German, Hungarian, Polish, French, Romanian, and Russian. Significantly, there were no newspapers in Arabic intended for Arabic-speaking Jewish immigrants. Arabic was perceived to be the language of the enemy, and newspapers and broadcasts in Arabic were propaganda tools directed toward non-Jews. In the 1960s and 1970s, as Hebrew became the spoken language of most Jews in Israel and it grew more difficult economically to operate party newspapers, the foreign-language publications dwindled. Against this background, the English-language *Jerusalem Post*, which began as the *Palestinian Post* in the British Mandate period (1932), is exceptional in its relative stability. Its readers in Israel are primarily English-speaking Israelis, tourists, foreign businesspersons, and the diplomatic community. Its weekly edition, distributed to English readers abroad, served as an important source of information on Israel (Caspi and Limor 1999, 65, 72–78). In the 2000s, the English edition of *Haaretz/International Herald Tribune* took over this role to a large extent.

Immigration from the former Soviet Union led to a renaissance of Russian-language journalism. In 1998, these included about 120 media organs, including dailies such as *Nasha Strana*, *Novosti Nedeli*, and *Vesti*, as well as Reka radio on Kol Yisrael, and Russian-language channels on Israel Television, and on cable and satellite television. The Russian print media are mainly produced by the immigrants themselves, supported financially by the private sector and social and political organizations. On the other hand, broadcast journalism, primarily radio, is operated by the government for the immigrants (in both Russian and Amharic), and reflects the government's aim to help integrate them into Israeli society (Adoni et al. 2006, 107–26). The consumption patterns of Russian-language media indicate a dual role: the immigrants' connection with the culture of their lands of origin together with acclimation to Israeli society. In the Russian-language media, there is visible tension between cultural separatism and the desire to adapt. Yet clearly the immigrants learn from these media about the political, social, and economic life in Israel. During election periods, for example, the Russian-language media in Israel served as an intermediary between the "Russian" parties and their constituency (Caspi and Elias 2000). A substantial percentage of the immigrants receive information from Russian-language media, and watch significantly more television in Russian than in Hebrew. However, the relative share of Hebrew television and other channels is continually growing because the younger generation's daily life is conducted primarily in Hebrew. For example, according to data from 2006, a large majority (60–70%) of immigrants from the former Soviet Union mainly watched television channels in Russian, particularly Channel 9 (Israel Television's Russian channel) and Russia's state TV channel (ORT). Only about 20 percent watched channels in Hebrew, primarily the news. Just 1 percent of these immigrants above the age of fifty read newspapers only in Hebrew, compared to two-thirds of young people twelve to twenty-four years old. The data on radio listenership was similar (Brandman Institute Research 2006).

The immigrants from the former Soviet Union arrived in Israel when the melting pot concept was no longer dominant in absorption policy, and when there was, at least partial, legitimacy for a pluralistic approach. In addition, the state was no longer able to control media content due to the multiplicity of channels, and this facilitated the growth of more independent journalism in languages other than Hebrew. This could make absorption easier, but it also allows for cultural separatism by the first generation of immigrants. In Israel's early years, as noted, the foreign-language media were expected to gradually disappear. Today, however, the immigrants and many veteran Israelis have come to terms with the existence of a social mosaic.

C. The Media in the Ultra-Orthodox Community

Ultra-Orthodox society, in all its branches and clans, is acutely aware of the importance of the media, but their channels reflect the community structure, and the content is derived entirely from codes hidden from outsiders (Caspi and Limor 1998, 47–49, 75–76; Michelson 1998; Caplan 2006). The media are designed to serve the internal needs of ultra-Orthodox society. In the 2000s, we find in ultra-Orthodox society nearly all forms of media except television – dailies, weeklies, monthlies, local newspapers, street bulletins, leaflets distributed in synagogues, audio cassettes, pirate radio stations, and satellite broadcasts. In a 2009 survey, 58 percent of ultra-Orthodox Jews said they read newspapers (Rosenthal 2009). Many listen to ultra-Orthodox radio, which was once primarily pirate (e.g., "Radio Kol Chai"), and are also exposed to advertisements. The use of mobile phones has spread, subject to the restrictions set by the rabbis.[37] Internet use was initially very limited and channeled to ultra-Orthodox websites, thus controlling the content to which the user is exposed. Nonetheless, a reliable survey indicated that 62 percent of ultra-Orthodox Jews used the Internet in 2011, under certain restrictions (Mann 2014, 34).

In general, the guiding principle in the media of the ultra-Orthodox is not "the public's right to know," but rather what is appropriate to know in the opinion of the rabbis. The ultra-Orthodox press does not publish pictures of women, information on sports, entertainment, pop idols, crime, and the like. The symbols of the state are nowhere to be found in them, or references to Independence Day, secular memorial days, or even photographs of soldiers. The "editors" are "spiritual committees" acting on behalf of rabbis. They determine the content and carefully adhere to the rules of Jewish law, including refraining from defamation and gossip. Thus, the tensions in ultra-Orthodox journalism are completely different. First, instilling faith takes precedence over reliability in reporting. The committees also serve as censors and enforce the rule that the broadcasters and writers are primarily men. Second, they reflect internal disputes of which the general public is usually unaware.

Ultra-Orthodox journalism pre-dated the establishment of the state. The *Hamodia* newspaper (from 1949) of Agudat Yisrael, together with *Hazofeh* of the National Religious Party, are the only two party-affiliated Jewish dailies that survived into the twenty-first century, though *Hazofeh* was shut down in 2008. *Makor Rishon*, which defines itself as "an independent newspaper of a Jewish and patriotic character," was launched in 1997, targeting the same audience as *Hazofeh*, but ended its activity in 2014. Following the resignation of Rabbi Shach from the Council of Torah Sages in 1982, the *Yated Ne'eman* newspaper (1985) was founded and became the mouthpiece of the parties that supported Rabbi Shach – Shas and Degel Hatorah. The newspaper's "spiritual committee" is known for its strictness: It rejects not only news items but also advertisements that contain, in its view, a violation of religious values or a Zionist message. These party newspapers continue to serve as an intermediary between the parties and their constituents, as a mouthpiece for rabbis and politicians who lead the parties, and as an instrument for attacks against rivals. Discussion of the non-ultra-Orthodox media's views of the ultra-Orthodox can also be found in these newspapers (Caplan 2006, 17–21). Shas also publishes *Meyom Leyom*, which began in 1993 as a daily newspaper and became a weekly. One should also mention the ultra-Orthodox weekly *Yom Hashishi* (1983), which targets the wider religious public, not only the ultra-Orthodox, positioning itself as an alternative to the national publications that are "unsuitable" for observant Jews; and commercial weeklies such as *Mishpaha* (1987) and *Bakehila* (1997). More

[37] Under pressure from the rabbis and ultra-Orthodox public, the cellphone companies began to sell "kosher cellphones" that are open only to ingoing and outgoing calls, but block all content applications and charge exorbitant fees for conversations during the Jewish Sabbath (Levi 2009).

recently, due to internal disputes within the Ashkenazi ultra-Orthodox community, *Hamevaser* (2009) and *Happeless* (2012) appeared, using a new distribution technology – free copies sent via e-mail (E. Cohen 2015). In serving its internal needs, the media play a central role in the ultra-Orthodox community. Toward the external world, it is isolationist, reflecting alienation from Israeli society and often seeking to widen the distance. Within the Israeli ultra-Orthodox community, however, strong winds of change are noticeably blowing (see Chapter 17).

13.6 The Media and the Political System

During the period of statism, the political system wielded considerable control over the flow of information to the public, and it could regulate content, primarily through news items in the newspapers, on the radio, and in the cinema newsreels. When changes began in the political system, the media reflected and even intensified these changes. For example, the "Americanization" of the political system – expressed in adopting party primaries (late 1980s) and direct election of the prime minister (1996–2003) – was also evident in the media reports on politics and politicians (Caspi 1996). Prime ministers changed from being leaders to television figures, political parties turned into commercial brands, and the elections became "campaigns" run by public relations and advertising personnel. MKs began to act like entertainers rather than elected officials, while serious politicians were pushed off the stage because they were not seen to be photogenic. The cumulative outcome is that the media purport to directly and immediately fill the roles of political mediation between "the leadership" and "the public," and to skip over the elected representatives or intermediaries such as political parties and third-sector organizations. The media ostensibly offer direct connection between the elected and the voters, but the connection they create is actually between the leader and the masses, thus encouraging populist tendencies. Never have the media been so close to politics, but politics is too complex to relegate it to catchy text messages and tweets, just because they are easy to transmit.[38] Indeed, candidates who prefer to communicate their messages (usually prepared by a copywriter) to meet the dictates of the new media are able to reach a broad audience, but turn themselves into tradable and replaceable commodities. The high turnover of MKs (33%) between the election in 2013 and 2015 is evidence of this.

A. The Parties

In May 2005, *Maariv* launched a campaign against corruption under the headline "Where is the Shame?" and explained, "The political parties are not fulfilling their role properly." In this case, which is not exceptional, the media dared assume a new role – not only to reflect reality and express an opinion on appropriate policy, but also to serve as an alternative to the parties, inheriting their function and directly influencing the setting of priorities and the decision-making process (U. Benziman 2005a). The strengthening of the media occurred in parallel with the weakening

[38] During the 2013 and 2015 elections, party leaders updated their Facebook pages twice a day (Kabir 2012; Social Media Branding 2015).

of the parties, which no longer filled key social roles – mobilizing public support for their views and representing the public's interests. The change is evident in the interactions between the two institutions: While in the past the parties controlled the media and used them to further their needs, today the media wield much greater power than the parties, especially in dictating the political agenda. Will the media (including the online channels) inherit the traditional roles of the parties as intermediaries? The media fill some aspects of these roles with greater efficiency, largely due to their ability to quickly communicate information to large audiences. On the other hand, the parties have a role that the various media channels cannot fill – to aggregate interests, create structured coalitions, and contribute to political stability. More importantly, the parties, as mechanisms of coordination, acted in the past as shock absorbers in political crises (Galnoor 1998, 199–203). Not only are the media channels unable to fill this role, they sometimes even accentuate the shocks and widen the disagreements. For example, not every disagreement between government ministers is "a crisis of confidence," "an unbridgeable gap," or "the end of the road" – unless the dramatic portrayal of every incident as a personal (rather than ideological-political) battle makes it such. The vitriolic rhetoric on social networks is an example of the unbridled incitement that accentuates disagreements in the political system.

The introduction of party primaries transferred the competition between candidates to the media, and the candidates' need to advertise themselves brought the capital–government–media connection to the fore: primaries demand financial resources that are not always available to the candidates. "Direct democracy," which ostensibly operates with transparency via the new channels, turns politics into a market of personal interests that leaves no room for world views or representation of the common good. The lead-up to elections, like a new product launch, stirs great interest that quickly dissipates afterwards. Such relations between voters and those elected pose a danger to democratic representation.

B. The Media's Role in Elections

Election campaigns and the reporting of results are among the peak moments of the media's involvement in politics. "Election fever" grips all the media channels because there is great public interest and, of course, advertising budgets. This close connection is positive, because it stirs the citizens' interest. In Israel, television and radio stations also have an official role, and the Election (Campaign Methods) Law stipulates how the parties can use the channels in election propaganda (see Chapter 10). Without again discussing the question of whether election campaigns have much impact on voter preferences, we note that the candidates regard them as important and act accordingly. In a survey on the eve of Israel's first election in January 1949, some 94 percent of the respondents said that election propaganda does not influence them and that they had decided how to vote before the election campaign began. According to the respondents, the most influential factor determining their choice was the party's record. They cited the party's platform as the next most important factor, and the candidates' personality was ranked only third (Weimann 2015, 94). This was a period of party loyalty, clashes of ideologies, and strong faith in leaders. Until the mid-1960s, election campaigns were conducted primarily via party channels – party newspapers, radio broadcasts, billboards, and direct contact with the voters in public rallies, assemblies, and meetings at the workplace (Galnoor 1982, 253–54).

As in other democratic states, the media revolution in Israel gave television, and later the Internet, a more central role in election campaigns. The mass media, which reach broad audiences with identical messages, turned the campaigns into an effort to control the agenda and topics for discussion, especially topics that will not be discussed. A "successful" candidate is one who identifies the issues that capture media interest and steers the media to address them (Wolfsfeld and Weimann 1999). This approach removed election campaigns from the hands of the parties and candidates, shifting the emphasis from world views to "messages" and the "professionalization" of election management in Israel and many countries. The professionals turned the election into marketing (or public relations) campaigns and the candidate's personality into commercial advertisements (Caspi and Leshem 2007). Commercialized election campaigns also have a significant impact on the image of politics – the emphasis on personal rivalry not only removed ideology from politics, but also crippled some of its principal virtues – the ability to bridge differences, find compromises, and forge stable coalitions. These virtues are often denounced in the media as "a betrayal of values," and if politicians mention "values" in election campaigns, the media belittles them. Since election campaigns managed by media professionals do not focus on content, formulation of the party's platform for voters and party members is perceived as unimportant. In the 2015 elections, the Likud and several other parties did not even bother presenting a platform. Instead, the following played a starring role:

- ***The campaign:*** a marketing strategy based on polls, focus groups, etc., designed to broadcast to relevant "segments" of the voters what they want to hear.
- ***The slogan:*** a catchphrase that deliberately lacks content ("peace and security"; "security and peace") and aims not to annoy anyone.
- ***The jingle:*** a simple, catchy tune with meaningless words, sung repeatedly, preferably by well-known performers, at campaign rallies and in election broadcasts.
- ***The election poster:*** the slogan with the leader's name in the right colors, posted on billboards, the balconies of activists, and plastic banners at road intersections as conclusive proof that "we've conquered the street."
- ***The sticker:*** a short slogan with an awkward rhyme (e.g., "Ha'am [the people] are with the Golan"), pasted alongside similar stickers with simplistic messages on the rear bumpers of cars and prominently on the candidate's website.
- ***Online propaganda:*** the above content, but even shorter, distributed on websites, blogs, e-mail lists, social media, mobile phones, and tablets – circumventing the restrictions of propaganda laws that do not apply to the electronic media.[39]

This list reflects a continuum of gradual development, and the unasked question is, would these campaigns have succeeded without such advertisement? Since there is no proof regarding the impact of the campaign and its components, the label of success is attached in retrospect, while all the slogans and jingles that failed are

[39] In the 2013 elections, an estimated 50 percent of the advertising budgets for election propaganda went to the Internet (Tucker 2013).

forgotten. The viewership rating for election broadcasts on Channel 1 (at that time exclusively on this channel) was 60–70 percent in the 1970s and 1980s (Weimann 2008). Despite the great investment of public funds in election propaganda on television, their ratings have dropped sharply: In the 2003 and 2006 elections, the combined viewership rating on Channels 1, 2, and 10 was only 14–15 percent, far below the ratings for the leading entertainment programs.[40] Nonetheless, the public showed interest in the general media coverage of the election campaign in 2006: 45 percent reported following it to a great extent, but only 38 percent were satisfied with the coverage (Weimann, Tsfati, and Tukachinsky 2006, 3–4). On the first evening of election campaign broadcasts in both 2009 and 2013, there was a combined viewership rating of about 21 percent of Israeli households including all the channels (Gaoni 2009). In 2013 and 2015, there was an average viewership of 5.9 percent and 5.1 percent respectively of all Israeli households, including all of the channels.[41]

The "television debate" was imported to Israel from the US presidential election campaigns (see discussion in Chapter 10). The first debates were held in the 1977 and 1981 elections between the party leaders, Menachem Begin and Shimon Peres (Caspi 1986; Druckman 2003). The television debate introduced new criteria for assessing the leaders' qualifications – appearance, rhetorical ability, body language, and so on, with almost no connection to their views, experience, and ability to lead. According to the experts, the "television personality" determines the candidate's chances, and that is why young and photogenic leaders like Netanyahu and Barak defeated their opponents. This explanation soon changed when Sharon won – this time, because of his "grandfatherly" look, experience, and personality. The television debate is nothing more than a ritual. Its impact on voters' decisions and changing their preferences is limited. It does not provide an opportunity to get to know the candidates and their views because it is a show staged from start to finish by media advisers (Galnoor 1980; for conflicting findings, see Grabelsky-Lichtman, Blum-Kulka, and Shamir 2009).

The television debate can supplement an election campaign that focuses on substantive issues, but cannot replace it. In the past, prime ministers and ministers were party leaders with vast political experience. In the media era, they are judged first of all by their media talents. In Israel, direct election reinforced this trend and turned the media into the exclusive intermediary between the public and its leaders (Peri 2004). Despite the heavy investment in election campaigns, studies show that few voters are directly influenced by this propaganda when it is almost exclusively conducted via the media.[42] With the exception of those who hold no opinion whatsoever, propaganda in the media primarily reinforces existing views. Its important contribution is in stimulating political discourse and stirring political interest among the citizens, particularly during election periods. However, despite the limited impact, when the movement of a few Knesset seats from one side to another is critical, election propaganda takes on greater importance. For example, in the 2015 election, gaps in the polls between the two major parties were small (±3 seats) and within the

[40] Data on viewership of election broadcasts: The Israeli Audience Research Board. www.midrug-tv.org.il/election.htm [in Hebrew] (accessed October 6, 2017).

[41] www.globes.co.il/news/article.aspx?did=1001017292 (accessed March 29, 2016).

[42] The common assumption regarding the sweeping "influence" of television is not taken for granted in research (Liebes and Katz 1986).

statistical error. The polls in the main media channels predicted a tie and thus influenced the election campaign in the final days, which apparently gave the Likud an advantage over Labor/Zionist Camp and the ability to form a government.

C. Polls

The first election poll in Israel appeared in the 1969 elections, and great enthusiasm has developed for them ever since; polls are ostensibly the precise and "scientific" part of the election campaigns. Already in the 1990s, the polls became a focus of news reports and headlines in newspapers, as if these were the arena for the real contest. After the election, candidates explain their failure or success compared to what the polls predicted, not in comparison to past results or their expectations. Obviously, polls are an important tool in many fields when they are conducted properly and when their users know how to interpret them. However, when the polls turn the election contest into a horse race in which there is tension, entertainment, and interim results of winners and losers, they are liable to mislead the voters and contenders alike. Reporting on polls in the media is not sensitive to the complexity of the findings. For example, there are no explanations about validity, or the significance of the bounds of statistical error. Invalid findings receive reams of unsubstantiated media commentary, as if the rise or fall of 1 or 2 percent in a poll is what *always* determines the next coalition.

Publications do not always cite the pollster, sample size, or whether the party or the candidate commissioned the poll. The lack of an "ethical code" for conducting and publishing polls leaves considerable room for manipulative use. Furthermore, Israeli respondents exhibit a tendency to deceive the pollsters in order to sway the results, thus undermining the reliability of the polls (Arian et al. 2003a). There is also a structural problem: The probability of error in Israeli polls seems to be higher because there are relatively large groups of voters (primarily ultra-Orthodox Jews, Arabs, and immigrants from the former Soviet Union) who are more reluctant to cooperate with pollsters or respond honestly. The numerous polls published almost daily,[43] and the publication of unreliable polls, give the public the impression that the election campaign has already been decided, which could decrease the motivation to vote.

In 2002, an important amendment was made to the Election (Campaign Methods) Law, which set rules for conducting polls and how to publish them in the media. A 2007 amendment stipulated that poll results cannot be published within three days of the election to prevent their influence on the election at the last moment. However, the law cannot resolve the other problems cited above, and in the 2015 election, the polls not only missed the actual results, they also had a misleading effect on the public.[44]

The polls contribute to the trivialization of the political process by narrowing it down to contests between candidates with no viewpoints. Most of the public does

[43] Israel Democracy Institute 1999; see also Weimann 1996; Asher Cohen 1999; Weimann, Tsfati, and Tukachinsky 2006; Saidov 2009.

[44] One of the most widely respected polls conducted just before the 2015 election gave Labor twenty-six seats (it actually won twenty-four); and Likud twenty-two (it actually won thirty) (Mako 2015).

not realize how critical the wording of the questions is or how complicated it is to analyze and interpret the results. In addition, because of how the polls are presented in the media, they are often wrong in predicting the election results (though this is not their role). This further contributes to the drop in public confidence in the media in general, which fell to 30 percent in 2014, its lowest point since 2003 (Hermann et al. 2011–15: 2014, 123).

D. At the Knesset

The media agenda determines the parliamentary agenda to a great extent. MKs rely on the information they draw from the conventional media and the social networks for their parliamentary work – submitting legislative proposals, motions for the agenda, or discussions in the committees. For example, already in the 1990s, the media, and the print media in particular, were identified as the primary agenda-setting source of MKs for submitting parliamentary questions (Caspi 1998). The political standing of MKs, which used to be a function of their standing in their party, now largely depends on their media exposure. The level of media exposure of MKs is not directly related to their parliamentary activity, bills tabled, parliamentary questions submitted, or presence in the Knesset. Instead, it depends on their "charismatic skill" – their media initiative and creativity, articulateness, screen appearance, and ability to collaborate with journalists (Sheafer 2001). Consequently, the media give a platform to elected officials who know how to play (or manipulate) the media, and they serve to thin the ranks of MKs who excel in the unglamorous nitty-gritty of legislation in committees or overseeing government ministries. It seems that MKs, especially those fearing the specter of party primaries, must find a way to stand out in the media – any way possible and almost at any price. This is detrimental to collaborative parliamentary and party work because MKs prefer to play starring roles as individuals. Evidence of this is the dramatic increase in the number of private bills and the numerous High Court petitions submitted by MKs (see Chapter 4).

Television has brought the faces and work methods of elected officials into public view since the doors of plenary debates were opened to cameras and, since 1996, to Knesset committee sessions as well. The presence of cameras has affected the conduct of MKs: for the better – because of transparency, and the public's ability to monitor what occurs via the Knesset Channel and to evaluate the work of elected officials; and for the worse – because MKs appear for committee discussions only when they are televised, and insist on speaking whether or not they have something relevant to say, in order to gain exposure. The exposure also contributes to lifting the veil of mystery from politics and politicians, in particular, especially when we see them excoriating each other or dozing during Knesset debates.

E. Government Ministries

There is mutual suspicion between the media and government ministries rooted in a struggle over information. Government ministries are not eager to publish information that is sensitive or could hurt them, though such information may be of special interest to the media. At the same time, the ministries need publicity and seek out the media for this. The institution of spokesperson reflects this tension.

Every government ministry has a spokesperson or communications expert whose role embodies the desires of government ministries and their ministers to control information and win support, and also to "spin" or conceal information. To fill this complex role, the spokespersons are usually journalists who have crossed the lines.

The diametric poles of media–ministry relations are conflict and boycott, on the one hand, and cooperation to the point of identification, on the other. Most journalistic work is conducted between these two poles. Nowadays, journalists generally do not want to be tools in the hands of government spokespersons, and they seek to expose what the government is trying to hide. The daily work in the ministries does not interest the media, which tends to report problems, mistakes, and failures, and this bias contributes to the negative image of the public sector (Vermeer 2003). Still, most of the scandals of political and administrative corruption that reach the courts or the state comptroller are first exposed in journalistic investigations. Thanks to the critical media, the public has become increasingly skeptical of announcements by government spokespersons.[45]

Conversely, there are journalists who become dependent on information provided to them by government ministries – sometimes to the point of blind loyalty. This is not only likely to dull their critical faculties, it is also a disservice to the public, which believes it is receiving an objective report. In Israel, this accusation is often leveled against military correspondents and commentators on defense matters, who are fed exclusively by sources in the security establishment and the IDF. They tend to adopt the establishment versions (and even identify with them unquestioningly) in all things related to state security (Matsik 2009). We previously noted the lack of reporting on the eve of the Yom Kippur War (1973) and later in the Gulf War (1991): An alliance was formed between the IDF Spokesperson's Office and the media, and the public was forced to accept the official version because most journalists did not bother to ask questions or challenge the likelihood of the Iraqi threat and the necessity of gas masks and sealed rooms. These dependency relations are particularly prevalent in times of war, when it is difficult for journalists to know what is happening on the Israeli side, but impossible to know what is happening on the other side, where there is no freedom of the press. The importance the IDF attributes to *hasbara* (literally "explanation" but in fact propaganda) – domestically and abroad – is reflected in the fact that the IDF Spokesperson's Office employed 300 soldiers and seventy officers during the operation in Gaza in the summer of 2014 (Darom 2015). The IDF has its own website in several languages (www.idf.il), and conducts extensive activity on Facebook, YouTube, and other sites.

Problematic media coverage also results when the views of senior ministry officials converge with the general outlook of a particular newspaper, leading to sympathetic coverage of the ministry's policy and denunciation of the policy's opponents. A salient example of this was the ideological affinity in the past between the Finance Ministry's policy and most of the journalists writing for the business section of *Haaretz*, who supported neoliberal economic measures such as budget austerity,

[45] The situation was different in the past: In a 1970 survey, 55 percent of the respondents said that government spokespersons are "always" credible and another 40 percent believed they are "usually" credible (Israel Institute of Applied Social Research 1970, 14).

reduction of government allowances, privatization, and, in particular, condemnation of labor strikes.[46]

The Freedom of Information Law (1998) was cited above as a key turning point in the government's relations with the public and the media, which represents the public's right to know. During its first decade, the law did not meet expectations because the authorities had yet to internalize the change and clung to the law's grounds of confidentiality, or adopted bureaucratic foot-dragging in order to refuse to release information, and also because the public found it difficult to use the law.

F. Interest Groups and Political Protest Groups

The media in Israel are predominantly commercial and funded primarily by advertising. In 2016, a total of NIS 3.9 billion was spent on advertising. Television accounted for 37 percent, print journalism 18 percent, Internet 30 percent, radio 7 percent, and others 8 percent (Mann and Lev-On 2016, 37). This affects the professional independence of all the media channels. Here we discuss groups that do not belong to the business sector.

Relations between the media and interest groups, particularly protest groups, are characterized by "competitive symbiosis" – each side is dependent on the other, but each has its own interests and demands (Wolfsfeld 1991). Accordingly, a calculated collaboration usually develops that enables the two sides to promote their interests: The interest and protest groups need a media platform in order to influence public opinion as a means of influencing a third party, usually the government; the media need news events that the groups generate in their activity.

Strong and well-organized groups such as large labor unions that can organize strikes or mass demonstrations, or powerful organizations like Israel Military Industries that can exert direct influence, do not need to court the media. Often, even the *threat* of a strike creates enough media attention to eliminate the need to actually strike. On the other hand, weak groups depend on the media, and sometimes their very existence is conditional upon the extent of media coverage. The public would have known nothing about demonstrations by immigrants from Ethiopia, or about public housing woes, if the media had not reported them. Internet sites also feed extensively from the institutionalized media. In the case of small or extreme groups, the media are likely to ignore them or cover them negatively, as an esoteric phenomenon. At the same time, the media tend to encourage extreme action and often attribute excessive importance to marginal groups. Such groups might be entirely virtual – i.e., the media coverage is what proves their ostensible presence and even boosts their power. Groups that do not succeed in entering the media via the front door, protest groups in particular, make an effort to enter via the back door by orchestrating disturbances and employing violence (Wolfsfeld 1991, 4–10).

The influence and success of a group or protest action are largely determined by the media framing of an issue. The media may adopt the position of protest groups,

[46] A study of the coverage of labor relations in Israel in four newspapers (*Haaretz*, *Davar*, *Maariv*, and *Yediot Aharonot*) found that *Haaretz* editorials carried the most negative views of strikes. The other newspapers offered more balanced coverage (Peleg 1981, 265–66; see also Herzog Institute 2004). Things changed and, in 2011, *The Marker* (owned by *Haaretz*) enthusiastically supported and encouraged the social protest movement.

emphasize certain aspects, report positively on their struggle, or present them in a negative light. In 2003, for example, the media sympathetically covered Vicki Knafo's march from Mitzpe Ramon to Jerusalem to protest the economic program of the finance minister at the time, Benjamin Netanyahu, and the budget cuts in allowances that hurt single mothers. Despite the sympathetic coverage and presentation of the struggle in terms of "good and bad," the economic program was not revised. Knafo won a few moments of glory, but did not make any real impact. Similarly, the social protest in 2011 enjoyed media support, but was forced to subsequently pursue other paths, with partial success. Third-sector groups and organizations are aware of the power of the media, and many of them employ communication professionals. They seek to influence the information content published in the media, to be identified with their issue, and to serve as an address when response on the issue is required.

The media and interest/protest groups usually benefit from their cooperation. Media coverage puts the groups' issues on the agenda and may help in obtaining information from the authorities, influencing public opinion, and sometimes (more rarely) influencing policy. The media, on their part, gain news events that stir public interest and boost their influence or profits. Interest groups and third-sector organizations are also targets of criticism for the media, which exposes irregularities and corruption in some non-profits, thus carrying out its monitoring role.

G. Legal Defense of Freedom of Expression and Judicial Review of the Media

Freedom of expression is the media's bread and butter. According to the UN's Universal Declaration of Human Rights: "Everyone has the right to freedom of opinion and expression; this right includes freedom to hold opinions without interference and to seek, receive, and impart information and ideas through any media and regardless of frontiers." In Israel, the freedom of expression and freedom of the press are not anchored in basic laws, but court rulings have established these rights, and the connection between these rights and the free activity of the media:

> In Israel, there is a tradition of freedom of expression. It is well connected to our social culture ... It is based on the perception – formulated initially in the *Kol Ha'am* case – according to which public law in Israel recognizes the individual's freedom of expression. However, the state (the government) is authorized to restrict this freedom – and this is the formula of balancing between the individual's right and the interest of the public at large – if, and only if, there is near certainty that the use of freedom of expression will lead to a harsh, serious, and severe blow to public peace and security. This approach aptly delimits the individual's freedom of expression vis-à-vis the government. (A. Barak 2002)

Already in the *Kol Ha'am* (1953) High Court ruling, Justice Agranat ruled that freedom of expression is a supreme right and precondition for exercising other freedoms (*Kol Ha'am v. Minister of Interior* 1953). Thus, to limit freedom of expression, one must prove the near certainty of real damage to important interests such as the existence of the state and public safety. The court also intervened against the military censorship of an article that criticized the Mossad head and noted that he was about to be replaced. The court stated that the article did not pose a real threat to state security and that "information should not be withheld from the public except in exceptional and extraordinary circumstances" (*Schnitzer v. Chief Military Censor* 1988). On the other hand, the court accepted the censor's stance and approved the cessation of publication of the *Hadashot* newspaper for four days due to violation of a gag order about the formation of a committee of inquiry on the "Bus 300" incident (*Hadashot et al. v. Minister of Defense* 1984). Another ruling pertains to the decision of the Israel Broadcasting Authority not to interview MK Meir Kahane or give him a platform for his racist ideas, but only to broadcast items about him that have news value. The High Court overturned the decision, stating that freedom of expression also applies to the IBA and it must provide a platform for diverse viewpoints and opinions, even if these are reprehensible and extremist, as long as they do not cause real damage to public order (*Kahane v. Israel Broadcasting Authority* 1985).

Changes to the media map in Israel also led the court to rule on regulatory issues such as the allocation of frequencies, pirate radio stations, and cross-ownership. The salient example is the attempt by a number of MKs to legitimize pirate channels via an amendment to the Bezeq Law. The High Court ruled that the attempt to legalize broadcasts by the Channel 7 radio station *ex post facto*, a station that had operated without a license or media franchise as required by law, constituted a severe violation of the rule of law and the freedom of occupation of potential competitors (*Oron v. Knesset Speaker* 1999). The court also intervened in cases involving a journalist's right to immunity and the question of restricting freedom of expression on grounds of defamation or libel.[47] The question of freedom of expression in online networks raises difficult problems due to the absence of obligatory journalistic ethics, and the courts in Israel and other countries have yet to find an answer to these problems (Roth 2007; Shwartz-Altshuler 2014, 53–78; see also www.netlaw.co.il).

In summary, while the law in Israel remains draconian, the court's rulings have, in general, protected freedom of expression and stood on the side of the media and journalists. On the other hand, some argue that freedom of expression exists primarily within the four walls of the courtroom and has yet to extend to legislation and public norms (Salzberger and Oz-Salzberger 2006).

13.7 Democratic Politics and the Media

On the Shavuot holiday in 2004, *Yediot Aharonot* (holiday supplement, May 21, 2004) published a list of the "100 Culture Leaders in Israel" in all fields – music, literature, theater, painting, sculpture, cinema, and dance. Most of those on the list, including the first four, were television celebrities. The team that composed the list wrote that they were surprised to find that most of those people on last year's list did not make the new list. There are two interesting points here: First, the culture "led" by those on the list – like the beauty of a beauty queen – was temporary and, in their case, lasted only one year. Second, the team did not distinguish between media and culture, and assumed that whoever leads one *ipso facto* leads the other. If "everything is media," then so is culture. Thus, as most people believe (politicians and media people, in particular), politics too is only what appears in the media. Many Israelis also hold this belief, but their approach is more clear-eyed: In the early 2000s, half

[47] Later, the High Court refrained from intervening – see *Im Tirtsu v. Roi Yellin et al.* 2013 and *Roi Yellin et al. v. Im Tirtsu* 2015.

the public had faith in the media, and more than half also believed that the media are an institution that defends democracy more than the political institutions do (the Knesset, the government, and the parties).[48] And yet, as noted, there has been a steep decline in public confidence in the media in subsequent years, falling to 30 percent in 2014 (Hermann et al. 2011–15: 2015, 123). Do the media "deserve" public confidence? We do not have an answer because the question is worded like questions that often appear in media surveys and which lead to bias and lack of trust. Instead, we present two forces, open and hidden, that each threatens the institution of the media in Israel in its own way – politics and commercialization. The combination of the two is liable to be destructive to democracy. Finally, we discuss the "new media," especially social networks.

A. Politics

Direct control of media content by the political system is not possible in Israel nowadays. Nonetheless, there is still a threat that media organizations might promote the interests of private patrons because they depend on them for funding, subscribers, media franchises, and licenses. From this perspective, an open map of political-party journalism whose views are known is preferable to secret business connections whose biases are not transparent to the public. The concern is that the media serve as an additional arena for political power struggles unrelated to the role of journalism. This can come about through indirect funding, self-censorship, disinformation, leaks, "screen bribery," and other means.

To ensure the independence of the media in Israel and allow them to fulfill their essential role for democracy, measures are needed to protect the media from the scourge of politicization. First, the existing laws are draconian and inappropriate for a democratic state. Israel must close the gap between the legal frame, which enables drastic intervention by government (e.g., shutting down newspapers), and the reality in which freedom of expression usually prevails. Although the restrictive laws are not often put into practice and remain a dead letter, their existence poses the potential threat of deterring and muzzling freedom of expression. Government involvement poses a danger in particular for small media organs and those espousing unconventional opinions, which is the lifeblood of democracy. Second, the government's direct involvement in appointing entities that administer the media (the previous IBA, the Second Authority, and the Council for Cable and Satellite Broadcasting) should be entirely eliminated; we recommend accepting the proposal to establish a public committee to select personnel for these entities without government intervention and in accordance with relevant and transparent considerations. As noted above, the new public broadcasting law does not completely eliminate politicization or dependence on state funding. And yet, the state's overall responsibility for regulating the media, both public and commercial, should remain unchanged.

It boils down to the professional responsibility of the media itself and the journalists, including the responsibility to defend zealously the independence of those seeking to promote particular political or commercial interests. If journalists do not

[48] From 1999 to 2005, the level of confidence in the media was 50–57 percent (Arian et al. 2005–10: 2005, 13–14, 16–17).

maintain their independence, serving instead as a mouthpiece – for government, security, economic interests – the steps recommended above will not generate any change. In our view, greater responsibility falls upon the print media, which carries the tradition of journalistic ethics, especially in light of the transition from print to online channels. Since politics and the media need each other, they must be autonomous. For the good of democracy, each of these two institutions should focus on its role as if the other does not exist: the political system should set the agenda according to the public interest and not in accordance with the media potential of a particular issue; the media must ensure the public's right to know, increase the political system's transparency, oversee policy, and expose failures – regardless of the government's political makeup.

B. Commercialization

The presence of commercial interests in the media, old and new, is inevitable. In Israel, there were private newspapers even in the era of party domination. Commercialization in itself does not preclude the possibility that private media channels can fulfill their public role as trustees of the marketplace of knowledge, information, and democratic opinions. The obstacle is the tension generated between economic and public considerations because the media platform is in the hands of a very few whose economic interests seem to include no incentive to act as guardians of the public, responsible for an asset that is vital for democracy. Commercialization has led to a situation in which the question is no longer about the accuracy of what is written or broadcast, but rather: What has been hidden and omitted, and why? Commercial considerations upset the checks and balances, and muddy the transparency that is so essential for the media. The competition in the "free market" (among the various media channels) did not provide a suitable response to the problem of monopoly because, instead of control by party and governmental interests, there is now control by corporations that own more than one media organ, as well as direct involvement by commercial companies in the media. Despite the multiple media platforms, ownership has narrowed. Unlike the party-affiliated journalism that was openly ideological, citizens are now unaware of the personal and economic interests lurking behind the screen and newsprint.[49]

It is neither possible nor desirable for control of the media to return to the government or political entities. Therefore, the question is one of proportion – creating a regulatory system that can ensure a balance between the conflicting interests. Thus, when economic entities dictate priorities, choosing ratings and circulation over content and quality, control is still in the hands of the users, who can force the commercial owners to change their attitude of disparaging the intelligence of the "customers." For this, it is essential to have high-quality, independent, and stable public broadcasting alongside the commercial channels in order to set high standards for the other media organs. Public broadcasting also serves as a democratic anchor, and assures citizens that they have a reliable and unbalanced source of information *even if they*

[49] One way to minimize this damage is to increase citizens' awareness of the economic connections and alliances underlying the media organizations. When a particular item goes unreported on a television channel, for example, we should ask why and which interests are being served (Lachmann-Messer 1998).

do not exercise their right to view it. The dangers of commercialization demand the development of a media culture that defines the professional conduct of journalists. When economic entities threaten to interfere with content in order to promote a particular agenda (political or economic) or to support politicians, this is corrupt, crony commercialization. Media regulation must be independent and have the capacity to oversee and enforce (Lachman-Messer 1998, 189). Currently, in light of the hodgepodge of laws, and with regulatory and oversight authorities spread among a large number of entities, there is a need for an integrated legal infrastructure for the media, and a consistent regulatory policy in the hands of an independent agency.

C. Cybermedia

There are many ways for a citizen to be politically active via the new media. One can, for example, send a talkback to news items and commentary, join discussion groups and forums, write a blog, or respond to the blogs of others (Atmor 2008). The online channels create countless opportunities for political participation by citizens, including public opinion surveys, electronic discourse with elected officials, feedback on legislative proposals, building websites for political organizations, activity in civil society organizations, signing petitions, organizing demonstrations, and even – its true believers claim – carrying out revolutions.

Despite the potential of these channels, the question arises: What is the nature of this political participation? Some believe that it is a swift and efficient technological tool for expanding existing patterns of participation, making citizens (those who are connected) more accessible. For example, it is easier to sign a petition or solicit donations via the Internet than to go door to door. How cybermedia are used determines the nature of the participation. For example, many political parties still use the online channels as if they were just another way to disseminate knowledge and propaganda, a sort of billboard, a one-way channel similar to the traditional media. One of the sharpest criticisms is that these are not egalitarian channels because certain groups (the poor, the uneducated, and the elderly) have limited access. Those who downplay the revolutionary nature of the new channels, and are skeptical about whether they make a substantial contribution, cite the lack of "quality" in this type of political participation. In their view, the new channels transform political participation from an action that requires presence, investment, and effort into "push-button participation." It is usually conducted individually, remains virtual, and is not translated into organization and action. The investment involved in such participation is low in terms of time and money, which expands the circle of participants, but does not ensure quality participation – real commitment. This can be seen when comparing a talkback to a letter to the editor in a newspaper. The talkbacks are impulsive and often shallow, insulting, and in most cases anonymous, while letters to the editor (selectively chosen for publication) have limited exposure, but demand an investment in writing and argumentation, and are backed by committed people who sign them by name.

Who are the political participants in the new channels? Studies indicate two main populations. The first group comprises politically active citizens who use these channels to increase their involvement, resulting in greater "participation per participant." The second group is the opposite of the first – young people who distanced themselves from politics and would not be active in traditional channels of participation (such as voting or party membership), but now tend to return to politics (Norris 2003). If these findings are broadly valid, then the skeptics are right only about the group of previously involved, older citizens. On the other hand, the fact that younger people find cybermedia to be an attractive channel for political participation suggests that it is something new and effective, and that the skeptics are dismissing it too quickly. The connection emerging from such interaction is indeed virtual, but for the new generation this is nonetheless a human and real connection, which would not have existed before. For them, the advantage of these channels is the fact that there is no central control, no geographic border, no time constraint, and one can choose to remain anonymous. Concerning political connection, for many, these new media seem to be "hot" channels in every way, and they become active and activate others with an intensity that would not shame a party branch or demonstration in the city square.

Of course, the new channels are still in an early stage, and thus the comparison to the old channels is anachronistic. It is too early to establish the scope and depth of their impact. They may indeed completely change the nature of political participation and supplant the traditional channels, or perhaps lead to a creative combination of them. It might also be an illusion. The successful presidential campaigns of Barack Obama in 2009 and 2013 – which made extensive use of social networks to solicit contributions and recruit new members, mobilize supporters and activists, disseminate video clips and text messages via interactive websites, and more – indicated the vast political potential of this new media. This was the prevailing assumption in regard to the revolutions of the "democratic spring" in Arab countries in 2011, which were also called "Facebook revolutions," though this assumption has not been proven.

The media revolution that began in Israel in the 1990s was concurrent with changes in the political system, which shifted the center of gravity from the parties, and to some extent from the elected bodies, to media-focused politics. In summary, we should reemphasize that the media are not a substitute for other mediating entities in the political system. The media themselves are incapable of aggregating and representing a range of views, and cannot translate them into shared and binding political action. It may, however, contribute to "atomized" individual acts, forge commitments, and influence the choice of political leaders. The use of online channels to mobilize political communities is still in its infancy, and appears to have complementary rather than independent potential. There is also the problem that the current use of commercial media channels is based on the assumption that only messages of a particular type (extreme, catchy, superficial) "come across well." Thus, complex messages must find a different medium, which further limits the ability of the media to engage in constructive politics – to formulate compromises and generate agreements. In addition, there are also fabricated "social movements" that exist only on the virtual cybermedia.

For this reason, we should recognize that online technologies cannot be used to transform Israel into a "teledemocracy" in which everyone not only speaks with everyone all the time, but also continually participates in setting policy. In practice, this could become a mass society where no one actually speaks with anyone, and it could fall prey to populists of various sorts. In the foreseeable future, democracy in Israel and elsewhere will remain a *representative system* whose decisions would not be improved by establishing a direct democracy with immediate, daily feedback from citizens on every Knesset and government decision. Nevertheless, real feedback from citizens between elections is vital for democracy, and this is the role of the media channels together with other entities – political parties, social organizations, and the like. The media can strengthen democracy if they communicate unbiased information to the citizens, create a platform for a range of opinions, ensure a wide discussion of views, keep a critical eye on the political and social system, participate in setting the agenda, and encourage citizens to be involved (Gurevitch and Blumler 1995, 97–108).

PART IV

UNRESOLVED POLICY PROBLEMS

In the previous three parts of the book, we presented the components of the Israeli political system: the frameworks that were shaped, in theory and practice, during the first years of the state; the still evolving "1949 Constitution" (and what it lacks); the institutions of the parliamentary system; political society with its individuals, groups, and organizations, and how these participate in the political system (via political parties, elections, coalitions) and outside it (via civil society and the media).

But our description of the political system has yet to address the *results* of the political activity. Israel has complex problems of security or social disparities, for example, and we can trace how the political system addresses them, but this does not tell us the result – to what extent these thorny issues have been treated, or ignored, or deferred. To examine results, we turn to the field of *policy* in the broad sense of action (or inaction) and its effect. We have chosen four critical problems that have accompanied Israel since its inception: security, the status of the Arab citizens of Israel, socioeconomic gaps, and religion–state relations. All four are key issues that have remained unresolved, posing an ongoing policymaking challenge to the political system. In the final chapter of the book, we will also ask whether the inability to contend with these issues stems from difficulties inherent in the problems themselves, or from the political culture of Israel.

What is the source of these politically challenging problems that have remained open and unresolved? Not all the world's problems merit the title "open," and many do not breach the sphere of politics. In some western European countries, for example, church–state relations are no longer considered an acute problem that requires the intervention of the political system. We do not have a convincing answer to the question of how such issues arise or the role of politics in creating them, but one possibility is to view democratic politics as the handmaiden of society, of the communities and individuals it comprises. Then one could say that if a particular society has an open, unresolved issue – an external threat, inequality, competition for resources, environmental damage, etc. – society assigns the task of coping with it to the political system. In the model proposed by Easton (1965), society and its components present "demands," which become input for the activity of the democratic political system. The political system processes these demands (and drops or reshapes some along the way) and turns them into output – policy. In this approach, politics has a great impact because it translates needs into policy. Furthermore, regardless of whether politics changes, moderates, or exacerbates open issues, it does not create them, as they spring from within society.

A second possibility is to assume that in democracies as in undemocratic regimes, the agenda is set almost exclusively by the political system, which also defines the problems and how they unfold. Thus, the political system bears responsibility for making these issues open or not resolvable. Such views, which portray the state or politics as virtually omnipotent, can be traced back to the writings of Machiavelli. A more moderate and dynamic version of this view (e.g., in writings about deliberative democracy) argues that unresolved problems are generated by the interaction of politics and society. So here we have two approaches that are worlds apart: politics as a dominant and even totalitarian social mechanism, versus politics as an arena of discourse and deliberation.

The third possibility is to attribute a fundamental (innate) intractability to the problems themselves. Here, the assumption is that the problems dictate the open agenda, and that efforts to resolve them made by society and politics are futile – this approach has many adherents, especially in Israel. In the literature on policymaking, problems that are difficult to define conceptually, or whose definition is highly controversial, are referred to as "wicked problems" (Churchman 1967, 142; Rittel and Webber 1973). Some would add that we can resolve to address them, but the problems are not resolvable. Hence the difficulty of developing agreed upon criteria for tackling these problems.[1] One characteristic of wicked problems is that although society ascribes great importance to them, they have remarkable staying power and remain open for a very long time. "Wicked problems" in democracies usually relate to social issues such as crime, drugs, alcoholism, impoverished neighborhoods, racial tensions, disparities in education, chronic unemployment, foreign workers, and refugees. The approaches to overcoming these problems are as numerous as the number of problems themselves (Roberts 2000).

[1] Dery 2000. See also "joined-up governance" designed to develop comprehensive policy in order to overcome wicked problems, Bogdanor 2005, 6.

14 Security Reigns Supreme

14.1 The Meaning of Security and Security Policy

> Today I made a pilgrimage to Dhauli, the place where King Ashoka, after a great military victory, looked out at the battlefield where tradition has it 150,000 bodies lay dead, and actually felt shame and remorse and converted to Buddhism. Since by that stage Ashoka controlled virtually all of India, he was able to proclaim an era of peace and nonviolence. This was a little before 300 BCE, and was, I believe, the first and last time in human history such a thing occurred. Ashoka had an edict carved in stone with his proclamation, and above it, at the top of the same large stone, he had carved a small, front half of an elephant (representing Buddhism) emerging from the uncarved rock. If any site in the world is sacred, surely this stone is it. (Personal communication, David Curzon, poet)

A. State Responsibility for Security: Protecting the Population and Sovereign Territory

"Everyone has the right to life, liberty and security of person" appears in Article 3 of the 1948 UN Declaration of Human Rights. Security for its citizens is also the first article in the unwritten covenant between citizens and their state, hence the paramount responsibility of every state. If physical survival takes precedence over all other matters, then failure to ensure survival renders meaningless all other state functions. In the past, rulers imposed taxes, drafted soldiers, and procured weapons to engage in wars or defend against them. Soldiers fought and civilians covered the cost, but these battles raged far from the daily life of most citizens, unless one of these adventures happened to end in defeat or occupation.

In modern times, wars are no longer the pursuit solely of rulers and soldiers, as they have become total – labeled "world wars" in the twentieth century. Nuclear weapons and recourse to them in 1945 instantly transformed the geographic concept of security, turning it into a matter not just between states, but for all denizens of the earth, even after the Cold War drew to a close. Nevertheless, security still remains the most critical test of a political system and its leaders; systems that fail this test are destined to change or disappear (Galnoor 1982).

To achieve security in our era, states must also foil terrorism, a form of violence that puts democratic political systems to a supreme test – challenging their ability to protect the collective while maintaining democratic values. Meeting this challenge accentuates the dilemma facing democratic governments: Do the demands of security undermine democracy (i.e., are the rights of citizens harmed in protecting them from terrorism) or does democracy undermine security (i.e., is the performance of security agencies constrained by the demand for closer civilian oversight of them)?

Defining security as a test of the political system rests on the assumption that a state's citizens or territory are under external threat. The absence of security, however, might result not from external threat, but from threats made by one's own state against another, or from foolhardy policies that are made without – and sometimes with – the support of its citizens.

B. Security Policy

Security policy refers to the overall conception and practical measures taken by the political system of a state to defend its population and sovereign territory. Is security policy inherently more complex and problematic than welfare or economic policies? The citizens of Iceland would probably not think so, while Israeli citizens would say "yes"; and within the same country, the response would be different during times of war or peace. When security becomes fateful, citizens are called upon to be willing to sacrifice their lives – a demand that does not exist in other policy areas. And security policy has some other unique characteristics:

First, security policy is no different in principle than other policies – because its "clients" are not the enemies of the state, but its citizens. Nevertheless, the fact that external actors affect security policy amplifies the uncertainty and forges a different dynamic about security matters between the public and the political system. In democratic countries, for example, public opinion responds differently when confronted by an external threat: paradoxically, despite the significantly higher risk, it is easier to mobilize support for acting against one's enemies than for changing education or taxation policies. In another example of differences, while interest groups also lobby about security issues, they operate more discreetly due to the sensitivity of these matters, unlike lobbying about domestic issues.

Second, security policy is "wasteful"; like insurance, success is measured by the lack of need to set it in motion. The state establishes an army, the army drafts soldiers and acquires immensely expensive arms, the soldiers need training – and all this in the hope that none of it will ever be put to use. Security is a very expensive insurance policy: underspending could end up costing dearly; while overspending comes at the expense of important social goals, and might even increase the temptation to try out military options.

Third, because the results of security policy are intangible, one might confuse deterrence, which is the ultimate success, with a loss of deterrence, which might then require a military act. In consequence, the investment in security could increase or decrease for the wrong reasons. Even if preparations for danger (political, military, or economic) are successful and the threat is averted, perhaps one should not let down one's guard, but rather step up efforts to prevent the next threat. On the other hand, victory in battle can restore deterrence, thereby avoiding the hasty acquisition of arms, the replenishing of inventories, and so on. The problem is that it is difficult to measure the success of security policy or to market deterrence, while victory on the battlefield is crowned with glory.

In the twentieth century, international rivalry and the lethalness of modern weaponry were two important reasons for the globalization of security, which led *inter alia* to creation of the League of Nations after World War I and the search for "collective security" arrangements. International terrorism then posed a new kind of threat, because conventional measures, designed for confrontations and agreements between states, could not address "asymmetric confrontation" between states and irregular forces. International organizations and countries, including Israel, are still searching for ways to cope with this new threat.

C. Diverse Approaches to Israel's Security Policy

The general security issues noted above are even more applicable in Israel, where the turbulent environment is the overriding factor in almost all aspects of life:

> When we are hiking, we are three –
> You, me, and the war to be;
> When we're asleep, we are three –
> You, me, and the war to be. (Levin 1988)

The political, social, and economic history of Israel is checkered with battles, military campaigns, raids, reprisals, redeployments, and other military operations, as well as complex foreign relations, which include boycott, sanctions, confrontations in international organizations, and the like. Since 1967, Israel has been involved in a war of attrition, a war against terror, repression of uprisings, peace treaties, peace negotiations that went nowhere, and preemptive strikes. Wars provide "before" and "after" milestones in the chronology of a state and reference points for internal events (Y. Benziman 2010; Sheffer and Barak 2013). Security policy, as defined above, also entails foreign policy (which will not be discussed separately), because security considerations in Israel largely dictate Israel's foreign policy.

We noted that countries may have to cope with "open issues" that remain unsolved for an extended period, some of them "wicked" problems that are hard to conceptualize or resolve. Is the question of security in Israel "a problem searching for a policy" and does the absence of security for such a long time reflect a failure of the political system? Alternatively, is the problem intractable and the political system is doing its best to cope with factors beyond its control? It is possible, of course, that security policy is both – Israel does face genuine external threats, but it also contributes to the duration of the problem by not coming up with a solution. On the assumption that Israel is sincerely searching for a way to end or contain the conflict with the Palestinians and other Arab rivals – a problem that has festered since the birth of the Zionist movement – we can define the opposing poles of this open issue as follows:

Proponents of Pole 1 contend: The source of the conflict is Arab unwillingness to recognize Israel's existence. Regarding the Palestinians, the source of the conflict with them is their unwillingness to accept the 1947 UN Partition Plan, their disregard of the outcome of the 1948 war and subsequent establishment of Israel, and their desire to reclaim all of Palestine. According to Israeli adherents of this view, the problem is an irresolvable, wicked one.

Proponents of Pole 2 contend: The source of the conflict is Israel's unwillingness to accept definite borders and its intransigence on other issues. Regarding the Palestinians, the source of the conflict is Israel's unwillingness to recognize their right to self-determination within the Land of Israel, and its desire to retain, or at least maintain control over, most of the territories conquered in 1967 (in the West Bank and Golan Heights). According to adherents of this view, the problem for Israel is amenable to policy resolution.

Presenting the issue in this polarized way might anger proponents of either side, or those who argue that the issues are far more complex. For purposes of this chapter, however, these definitions help elucidate the differences in approach and allow us to focus on their challenge to shaping "correct" security policies. According to Pole 1, the conflict has been and will continue to be a permanent feature of the foreseeable future, hence security policy should be based on deterrent capabilities – military (including nuclear) and political (international support) – as well as success in the "wars of necessity" (including preemptive strikes). According to Pole 2, the conflict should be contained while efforts are underway to resolve it, therefore policies should strive for mutually agreed concessions, in the model of the peace treaties signed with Egypt (1979) and Jordan (1994); similarly, the Golan Heights will be returned eventually to Syria in exchange for peace.

Proponents of Pole 1 contend that Palestinian animosity is implacable and will not alter with territorial or other concessions, hence Israel's hold of the occupied territories is irrelevant, as it is not the root of the problem. The derived policy is entrenchment through control by the Israel Defense Forces (IDF), establishment of settlements, repression of Palestinian uprisings, and coping with terrorism. It also requires deflecting international pressure to withdraw from the territories, engage in serious negotiations, agree to accommodations, unilaterally withdraw, freeze settlement expansion, refrain from reprisals, etc.

Proponents of Pole 2 shift the responsibility for solving the problem to the Israeli side, which leads to various political combinations – a declaration, for example, that Israel will relinquish all claims to territories conquered in 1967 and is willing on principle to return (all or most of) this territory gradually in exchange for a definitive peace agreement (similar to the Oslo Accords of 1993). At the heart of such a policy would be Israel's willingness to delineate a permanent eastern and northeastern border of the state.

Presenting the polarized views can be useful for delineating the range of options; it is not an attempt to identify the root of the conflict or determine whether the security policies assumed by Israel were the "correct" ones (G. Golan 2015). At the conclusion of this chapter, we will state our view of this problem. Meanwhile, we simply note the complexity of the issue and the critical role security plays because of the human, social, and economic prices exacted by its dominance in Israeli life. From the beginning of the conflict through Memorial Day 2015, a total of 23,320 soldiers were killed; and since the establishment of the state an additional 1,723 civilians were killed in acts of hostility and terror.[1] To these can be added the emotional burden of insecurity on Israelis and non-Israelis, and the repercussions in other areas of life, from the dangers to democracy to tension and violence in society (Rachamim and Bar-Tal 2006; Bar-Tal 2007). The burden of military service, reserve duty, and bereavement are integral to the lives of Jewish citizens of Israel.[2]

D. A Security-Driven Economy

For many years, Israeli policymakers paid scant attention to the economic implications of defense spending, and it is only a mild exaggeration to say that allocations were first made to security, then to everything else (Patinkin 1959). Compared with other countries, Israel's standing army is large relative to its population (3–5%); and maintaining a reserve duty force adds more expenses (Yaari 2004, 71). Only after the 1967 war did the Israeli public gradually begin to discuss the costs of defense, asking questions like, "What comes at the expense of security?" (Y. Lifshitz 2007, 79–84). The end of the Cold War, for example, cut in half the amount spent on defense by developed countries: In 1995, defense spending constituted an average of 2.8 percent of their GNP, and only 9.2 percent of all government expenditures. In Israel that year, on the other hand, defense spending was 9.7 percent of the GNP and 17 percent of all government expenditures (ibid., 148, 170, 178).

Figure 14.1 reveals the sharp rise in defense spending since 1967 and how this amount rose again in the 2000s. However, the growth of the Israeli economy enabled a gradual reduction to 5.2 percent of the GDP in 2014. Yet, the actual figures are much higher, if one adds indirect expenses such as the alternative cost of the standing army and reserves, pension payments, construction of public shelters, investments in the settlements in the territories, and security expenditures by other government ministries. In comparison with twenty other developed countries, Israel ranked first in 2004 in defense spending as a percentage of the GDP (Tov 2005; Z. Shiffer 2007) and moved down to fourth in the world in 2014 (Even 2015).

The Defense Ministry's budget in 2015 was NIS 52.6 billion (roughly $13.5 billion at 2015 exchange rates), some 13.5 percent of the state budget (Israel, Ministry of Finance 2014). This hefty slice of the national pie is not deliberated in the same way as the expenditures of other ministries – most of it is classified for security reasons. It is a "framework budget," i.e., a global sum whose internal allocations and line-item changes are carried out with minimal external supervision by the Finance Ministry. The details of the Defense Ministry budget are not published in the proposed Budget Bill, nor are they deliberated and approved by the Knesset Finance Committee plenum, but only in a joint subcommittee of the Finance and the Foreign Affairs and Defense Committees. As of 2007, an important change was made – the non-classified line items of the defense budget are published in a separate booklet.

The special status of the defense budget is recognized in the Budget Principles Law (1985), which relaxed the rules for approval and management of this budget.

[1] Israel Foreign Ministry, Media Center, Memorial Day. April 21, 2015. http://mfa.gov.il/MFAHEB/PressRoom/Pages/Rememberance_Day_and_Independence_Day_210515.aspx [in Hebrew] (accessed May 2, 2016).

[2] In the 2010s, discussion began about the possibility of changing the mandatory draft (Y. Levy 2015).

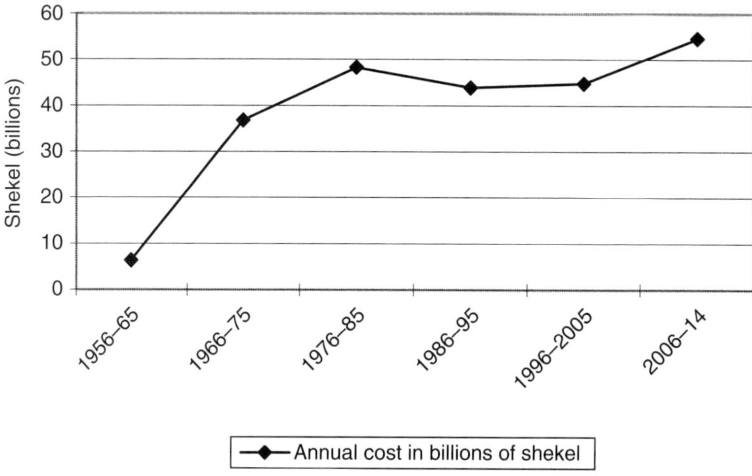

Figure 14.1 Security expenditures in Israel 1956–2014
Sources: CBS 2011, "Table 2 – General Government Defense Consumption Expenditure" and World Bank N.d.

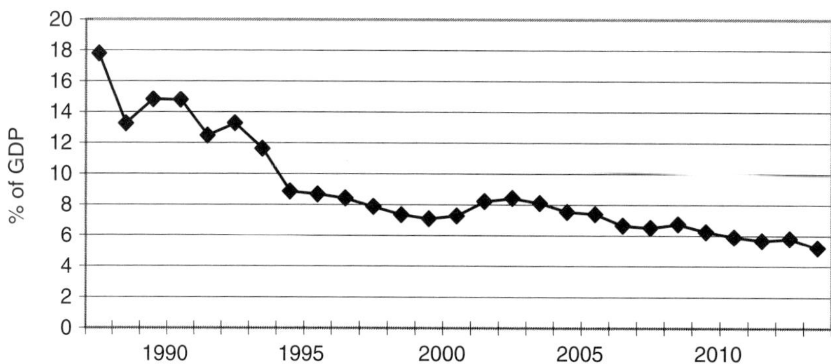

Figure 14.2 Security expenditures in Israel 1988–2014 (% of GDP)
Source: World Bank N.d.

To enable flexibility, for example, the Knesset Finance Committee is informed of changes, but does not have to approve them. The Brodet Committee, which proposed reform of the defense budget, warned, "Civilian oversight of the defense budget by civilian bodies and authorities (outside the Defense Ministry) is inadequate" (2007). Internal Defense Ministry supervision of IDF expenditures is also inadequate because, among other things, the head of the Defense Ministry's Budget Division also serves as financial adviser to the chief of staff. This job is usually held by a senior IDF officer who is a member of the General Staff and subordinate to the chief of staff (Y. Lifshitz 2007). Yehezkel Dror describes the predominance of security in Israel:

> in the percentage of national resources directly or indirectly allocated to security; in the amount and involvement of citizens' service in the military; in the quantity of security-related research; and other quantitative measures. Moreover, both in the national

consciousness and government considerations, security plays a key, qualitative role, which sets it apart from what takes place in other democratic countries. (Yehezkel Dror 1989, 25; see also Wald 1992)

E. The Threat to Democracy

External threats have fostered a "culture of security" with its relentless emphasis on security. While the threat is real, feelings also play a role, and as we shall see in the concluding section, most citizens are willing to subordinate democratic principles, such as human and civil rights, to security considerations. The main victims of the supremacy of security in Israel are Arab citizens and Palestinians in the occupied territories. In the name of security, Arab citizens were placed under a military regime (1949–66) with severe constraints on their basic rights (see Chapter 15). The main long-term damage was the state appropriation of Arab-owned land on various legal grounds, usually defined as "security needs."

The daily life of Palestinians who live in the territories controlled by Israel since 1967 is particularly grim, driven by Israeli security interests. The military regime in the territories operates under the Defense (Emergency) Regulations enacted by the British Mandatory authorities (see below), which allow for measures such as the sealing of homes, curfews, administrative detention, and security justified deportation. Palestinian terrorism, particularly the suicide bombers, further tipped the scales toward security considerations as a justification for human rights violations. Efforts to prevent terrorism were used to justify deeds such as the killing of captured terrorists in the "Bus 300 affair" (Lahav 1988) or giving false testimony to the courts or public commissions of inquiry. Counterterrorist activity also raised new questions, such as the right of a democratic state to use measures like "targeted killings" – taking the lives of people suspected of involvement in terrorist activity without due process and in disregard of civilian casualties (Enoch et al. 2007). This is also true of military actions in response to indiscriminate shelling from the Gaza Strip. According to IDF figures, in Operation Cast Lead (December 2008 to January 2009), 1,166 Palestinians were killed, and in Operation Protective Edge (July–August 2014), 2,125 were killed – most apparently civilians in both cases.[3] Figures from other sources are higher.

Sometimes security measures entail actions that abrogate human rights in order to save lives. Thus, restricting Palestinian freedom of movement in the Israeli held territories is a severe violation of their fundamental rights and dignity, but freedom of movement of terrorists and arms into Israel would be patently dangerous; checkpoints are designed to prevent this from happening.[4] At the same time, the High Court of Justice ruled more than once that security reasons do not justify violating the dignity of a human being, and do not confer sweeping power to prevent residents from access to work, school, medical services, or meetings with their families (Barsela 2007).[5]

[3] For 2008/9, see YNet 2009. For 2014, see Ministry of Foreign Affairs N.d.

[4] In one case, a Palestinian ambulance driver from the Balata refugee camp attempted to deliver an explosive device in an ambulance for purposes of a suicide attack in Israel (Frish and Weiss 2002).

[5] *Mara'abe v. Prime Minister* 2005; *Head of the Village Council al-Zawia v. Minister of Defense* 2006.

The belief that Israeli democracy must defend itself not just from external enemies but from internal ones as well has resulted in legislation and norms that undermine fundamental civil liberties. The perception that the country is in a perennial state of emergency fosters the belief among some that democratic values are a luxury.[6]

14.2 The Institutions of the Security System

The "security system" is the inclusive term for several interrelated systems. The first is *the civilian-political system*, which includes the defense minister, the minister's advisers, the Ministry of Defense, subsidiary units, and defense-related government corporations such as the Israel Aerospace Industries and the Rafael Advanced Defense Systems Ltd., which are subject to the authority of the defense minister. The second is *the military system* – the IDF headed by the chief of staff and General Staff, under the authority of the government and subordinate to the defense minister. And the third is *the intelligence system* – the Mossad for special operations and the General Security Service (GSS), both subject to the authority of the prime minister. We add here the National Security Council, which – although it is a civilian body – operates primarily as an arm of the security system.

A. The Ministry of Defense

The Ministry of Defense is a civilian body with responsibility for the defense budget, approximately $11 billion in 2015, in addition to the equivalent of about $2.5 billion in US aid (made available to Israel for the acquisition of US-manufactured military products), for a total of some $13.5 billion annually (Israel, Ministry of Finance 2014). The Ministry is also responsible for the defense industries and their research and development, defense-related relations with foreign countries, and security exports. It mediates between the military and external bodies, especially concerning military acquisitions. Based on this division of labor, the IDF defines its operational needs and the budget required, while the Defense Ministry handles contacts with manufacturers, vendors, and contractors. The ministry also attends to security-related welfare matters – support for veterans, memorialization of casualties, aid to bereaved families, rehabilitation of disabled veterans, and similar.

B. Defense Industries

Israel Military Industries Ltd. IMI has been in operation since 1933 when it was set up to supply weapons to the Haganah, the pre-state paramilitary organization. Upon founding of the state, IMI became a subsidiary of the Defense Ministry, and it was converted into a government company in 1990. Its areas of activity are research,

[6] Yitzhak Zamir, upon his resignation as attorney general, stated:

> If we allow the needs of the hour ... to justify breaking the law on the grounds of state security or the public good, we could find ourselves moving from the rule of law that protects civil rights into another type of state.
>
> (Negbi 1987, 10)

development, and manufacture of arms, weapons systems (such as the Uzi submachine gun), ammunition, and other military supplies for domestic use and export, as well as civilian activity in the field of metals and chemistry. Company turnover in 2015 was $1.7 billion, and it has 3,200 employees.[7] IMI has not been profitable lately and is a candidate for privatization.

Israel Aerospace Industries. IAI was founded in 1953 for the maintenance of Israeli aircraft in cooperation with the Air Force. Later it began to provide technological solutions for Air Force needs, and engage in manufacturing for domestic use and export. Its products include military and civilian aircraft, unmanned aerial vehicles (UAVs), space technology, missiles, weapons systems, and the upgrading and maintenance of aircraft and engines for Israel and foreign clients.[8] Company sales in 2015 were $13.7 billion, net profit was $89.4 million, and it has 16,000 employees (Israel, Ministry of Finance 2014).

Rafael Advanced Defense Systems Ltd. Rafael originated in the Science Corps in 1948 and became a government corporation in 2002. Rafael is responsible for R&D of security systems, and focuses on final assembly, inspection, simulations, and engineering solutions. It markets its products to the IDF and other countries. Sales in 2015 were $7 billion. It has 7,700 employees (Israel, Ministry of Finance 2014).

C. The IDF

The IDF evolved from paramilitary forces in the pre-state period, especially the Haganah. The Law and Administration Ordinance (1948) authorized the Provisional Government to establish armed forces, and by virtue of this ordinance, it enacted the Israel Defense Forces Ordinance. The Basic Law: The Military was enacted as a result of the Yom Kippur War (1973), and established that the IDF is subordinate to the civilian authority of the government. The chief of staff, who is the supreme commander of the IDF, is subordinate to the defense minister. The General Staff is composed of five branches with three regional commands and the home front command: the air force and space, the navy, ground forces, the armored corps, and the professional corps. IDF personnel include the professional army – mainly officers in command and staff positions; the regular army of soldiers in compulsory service; and reserve duty forces.[9]

D. The National Security Council (NSC)

The NSC was established in 1999 in the Office of the Prime Minister, and serves as an advisory body to the prime minister and the security-policy cabinet, providing analyses and assessments, and tracking performance and implementation of government decisions (Yaari 2006, 7–14).[10] Creation of the NSC was a delayed response to the

7 "Ratings of Security Systems," Dun's 100, *Globes*. http://duns100.globes.co.il/rating?did=1001061336&cid=1000856442 [in Hebrew] (accessed May 3, 2016).

8 Israel Aerospace Industries: Profile. www.iai.co.il/2013/10285-en/CompanyInfo-CompanyProfile.aspx [in Hebrew] (accessed May 3, 2016).

9 Israel Defense Forces. www.idf.il/1498-en/Dover.aspx (accessed May 3, 2016).

10 National Security Council. www.nsc.gov.il/he/About-the-Staff/Pages/default.aspx [in Hebrew] (accessed May 3, 2016).

Agranat Commission's recommendations (1974) about the need for an independent body to advise the government about security-related policies. The need to establish this body appeared in Section 7 of the Government Law (2001); in 2007, following the conclusions of the Winograd Commission about the second Lebanon War, the government decided to establish the NSC as a staff body to the prime minister and the government. It became law in 2008. The mandate of the NSC is to coordinate the staff work of the government on matters pertaining to national security, formulate assessments and recommendations about policy to the prime minister, express its views on the defense budget proposal, and operate a center for crisis management and national emergencies. The prime minister appoints the NSC director with the approval of the government. Thus far, all directors have come from the security organizations, and the actual impact of the NSC and its director is debatable.

E. Intelligence Services

AMAN. Acronym in Hebrew for the Military Intelligence Branch. AMAN is in charge of intelligence gathering and provides the defense establishment with ongoing evaluations and the national intelligence assessment, which serves as the basis for government security policy. It is also responsible for military censorship.[11]

GSS. The General Security Service (known colloquially as the "Shabak" or "Shin Bet") was separated from the IDF in 1949 and placed in charge of internal security, counterespionage, and protection of leaders and vital facilities in the state and abroad. Until 1966, the GSS was instrumental in operating the military regime over the Arab population in Israel, and after the 1967 war, it became responsible for preventing hostile activity in the occupied territories.[12] Its role in protecting Israeli bodies overseas was upgraded following the hijacking of an El Al plane to Algeria in 1968 and the murder of Israeli athletes in Munich in 1972. Since 2002, the GSS has operated by virtue of the General Security Service Law, which states that it is responsible for ensuring the security of the state and the democratic regime and its institutions from threats of terrorism, sabotage, subversion, espionage, and exposure of state secrets (see below). GSS activities are classified, and public oversight is carried out by the Knesset Foreign Affairs and Defense Committee, the Supreme Court, the attorney general, and the state comptroller. By law, the GSS head must submit a quarterly report to the Ministerial Committee for Security Affairs or the Knesset Foreign Affairs and Defense Committee, and respond to their queries.

The Mossad (The Institute for Intelligence and Special Operations). Founded in 1949 to coordinate and centralize the intelligence services of Israel, initially as part of the Foreign Ministry and since 1952 in the Office of the Prime Minister.[13] The Mossad is in charge of clandestine intelligence gathering and special operations outside the borders of Israel; thwarting the development of non-conventional weapons by hostile countries; preventing the sabotage of Israeli and Jewish targets abroad; the

[11] The chief military censor proposed making it a civilian body (Vaaknin-Gil 2015).
[12] Israel Security Agency. www.shabak.gov.il/english/pages/default.aspx (accessed May 3, 2016).
[13] The Mossad. www.mossad.gov.il/eng/about/Pages/default.aspx and www.mossad.gov.il/eng/history/Pages/default.aspx (both accessed May 3, 2016).

discreet fostering of political ties; and assisting the immigration of Jews to Israel from places where this is not allowed.

The boundaries between the intelligence services are not well defined, and their respective spheres of authority are not anchored in law (despite the GSS law of 2002), leading to overlap in activity and friction between them.[14]

14.3 The Legal Infrastructure

A. Legislation Defining the Security Organizations and their Functions

The ***Law and Administration Ordinance (1948)*** stated that "The Provisional Government is authorized to establish armed forces on land, sea and air, which shall be authorized to engage in all legal activities required to protect the state." By virtue of this ordinance, the ***Defense Army of Israel Ordinance (1948)*** was enacted, declaring, "The Israel Defense Forces composed of land, sea, and air forces is hereby established." Article 4 intended to ensure that only one military apparatus would be established, which would supplant the rival underground forces from the pre-state period. The ordinance also formulated the oath of allegiance of IDF soldiers "to the State of Israel, its laws, and legitimate authorities."[15] The Basic Law: The Military (1976) also establishes the IDF exclusivity: "No armed force other than the Israel Defense Forces shall be established or maintained except under law."

Since its establishment, the IDF has discharged national tasks that are not strictly military. In fact, military activities unrelated to state security lacked legal grounding until passage of an amendment in 1995 to Article 18 of the Law and Administration Ordinance, which authorized use of the military for national missions such as education, immigration and absorption, health, home front security, and the welfare of IDF soldiers (Drory 2005). This amendment also broadens the definition of military service to include "recognized service" in the Defense Ministry, other ministries, and public bodies regulated by the government in the fields listed above.

The Mossad and the GSS are subordinate to the prime minister. There is no special law regarding the Mossad and it operates by virtue of the Basic Law: Government, according to which the government has "residual power" to carry out any activity that is not the province of another body or law. The General Security Service Law (2002) asserts that "The General Security Service is accountable to the government" and the prime minister has responsibility for the GSS on behalf of the government. In addition to the functions cited above, the law states that the GSS shall act on behalf of the state, not on behalf of any political-party interests, and it lists the oversight bodies: The Ministerial Committee for GSS Affairs, a subcommittee of the Knesset Foreign Affairs and Defense Committee, and an internal auditor. The most controversial article in the law states that the GSS is responsible for ensuring "the security of the state, the democratic regime, and its institutions from threats of

[14] On cooperation and coordination among the intelligence services, see Knesset. Foreign Affairs and Defense Committee 2004, 37.

[15] Article 4 of the Amendment to the Law and Administration Ordinance (Additional Directives) (1948) retroactively ratified the ordinance that had been passed by the Provisional Government as if the Provisional State Council had accepted it (Kremnitzer and Bendor 2000, 28).

terrorism, sabotage, subversion, espionage, and exposure of state secrets"; and the most problematic and vague term in this list is "subversion," which does not appear in any other Israeli law and can encompass almost any act of which the government does not approve.[16]

B. Legislation Regulating Military–Civilian Relations

The subordination of the IDF to civilian authority, and the government's authority over security matters, were never put to a real test even prior to passage of the ***Basic Law: The Military (1976)***. This law passed in the wake of the Yom Kippur War and the Agranat Commission report that criticized the absence of

> a clear division of authority, obligations, and responsibilities in matters of security among ... the government and prime minister, the defense minister, and the IDF chief of staff, and definition of the relationship between the political leadership and senior IDF officers. (Agranat Commission 1975, 25–26)[17]

The Basic Law stipulates that:

- the army is subject to the authority of the government;
- the minister responsible for the army on behalf of the government is the minister of defense; and
- the chief of staff is appointed by the government at the recommendation of the defense minister, and is subordinate to the defense minister and subject to the authority of the government.

According to the accepted interpretation, although the chief of staff is subordinate to the defense minister, in the event of conflict between the views of the defense minister and the government, the chief of staff must obey the government (Kremnitzer and Ben Dor 2000, 47–48). This matter, however, still requires more elucidation (Even and Gross 2008) (see below). The law does not establish a civilian commander for the army, nor does it detail the authority of the prime minister in the field of security. According to the ***Government Law (2001)***, the prime minister chairs the Ministerial Committee for Security Affairs, whose members include his deputy and the ministers of defense, foreign affairs, justice, internal security, and finance. The Basic Law: Government states that a government decision is needed to declare war, but not to take military action to protect the state and public security.

The Knesset role in these decisions is taken *ex post facto* – notification by the government to the Foreign Affairs and Defense Committee "at the earliest possible time" and notification to the Knesset plenary upon declaration of war. The law gives the government authority to declare a state of emergency and enact emergency regulations in times of need. The Knesset and its committees may provide oversight to government actions during a state of emergency, but the law allows the government considerable leeway: It is authorized to declare a state of emergency even without

[16] See the letter from GSS Director Yuval Diskin to the attorney general concerning the newspaper *Fasal al-Makal*, in response to a letter from the Association for Civil Rights in Israel dated April 26, 2007 (Yoav Stern 2007).

[17] See more extended discussion below about military-political relations.

Knesset approval, and to extend the term of the emergency if the Knesset does not convene (details below).

C. Additional Security Related Legislation

The ***Security Service (Consolidated Version) Law (1986)*** stipulates the obligation of conscription to the IDF in the regular army and reserves. This law gives the defense minister the authority to issue exemptions from regular service or reserve duty, or to reduce or defer regular service at the minister's discretion "for reasons related to the size of the IDF's regular or reserve forces, or for reasons of education, security settlements, the national economy, family, or other reasons." In addition, the law specifies the circumstances in which a woman is exempt from compulsory service: if she is married, a mother, pregnant, or "for reasons of conscience or religious family life that prevents her from serving in the security forces." The ***National Service Law (1953)*** applies to women who do not serve in the IDF for religious reasons, and requires these women to serve in civilian organizations. However, only in the 1960s did girls in the religious youth movements begin to volunteer for national service. Government decisions intended to encourage volunteerism for national service did not significantly increase the numbers; nor did the recommendations to institute compulsory national service for yeshiva students (Tal Committee 2002) and Arabs (Ivri Committee 2005).[18]

The ***Military Jurisdiction Law (1955)*** defines the standing of internal orders within the IDF (High Command and General Staff Orders). The law accords far-reaching authority to the chief of staff to issue orders to the army and those subordinate to him, in effect giving "autonomy" to the army to manage its own affairs (Yehuda Ben Meir 1995, 34). This law applies to conscripts, reserve duty soldiers even when not on active duty, civilians employed by the army, and employees of the military industry. By law, the Military Court has the power to issue sentences: from warnings, fines, and demotions to life sentence and even the death penalty (for treason during wartime).

Penal Code (1977) – Part II, Section 7 specifies offenses related to state security, foreign relations, and classified information: treason, causing harm to the armed forces, espionage, transmitting state secrets or negligence in safeguarding them by a public official, and undermining foreign relations.

Release of Prisoners Based on State or Security Reasons (Amendments 9, 10, Government Law), 2014. The government would not be allowed to release prisoners who committed murder "in aggravated circumstances." This aimed to tie the hands of the government and prevent negotiations on the release of such prisoners in exchange agreements.

D. Emergency Legislation

Defense (Emergency) Regulations (1945) originated in the British Mandate period and confer extensive powers upon the military commanders to curtail individual

[18] On the Tal Committee, see the Knesset website: www.knesset.gov.il/docs/heb/tal.htm [in Hebrew] (accessed May 3, 2016); also see Mei-Ami 2007. On the Ivri Committee, see H. Greenberg 2005.

rights, including the authority to detain an individual for an unlimited period, deport from Israel, prevent the publication of newspapers and books, take possession of or demolish houses, and impose a curfew. Some regulations that had allowed for unlimited administrative detention without judicial review were replaced by the ***Emergency Powers (Detention) Law (1979)***, which limited the power to impose administrative detention, transferring it from the military commanders to the defense minister, with an obligatory judicial review.

The Defense Regulations are imposed primarily against Palestinians in the military-ruled occupied territories, and allow for punishment and deterrence without due process. Based on these regulations, houses belonging to suspects or those convicted of serious security offenses have been destroyed or sealed, residents of the territories were expelled (e.g., Hamas members in 1992), curfews were imposed, and stores, offices, and educational institutions were shut down (Hofnung 1991, 316–25; Benvenisti 1993, 441–70). The most frequently used measure is administrative detention, and the number of those detained reached thousands during tense periods.[19] Infrequently, such detention is imposed against Jewish settlers, for instance after Jewish terrorist attacks on Palestinians in 2015 (Dvori 2015). Despite the many attempts to do away with these Mandatory era regulations on the grounds that they are extra-judicial procedures and not part of Israel's legal corpus, they remain in place.

Emergency Regulations. The authority to declare a state of emergency is conferred upon the Knesset; once declared, the government, prime minister, or any minister so authorized may enact emergency regulations that can change, suspend, or set conditions upon any law, provided that the purpose of the regulation is to ensure state defense, public security, and vital supplies and services. A state of emergency was declared in May 1948 and has continued uninterrupted ever since.[20] Nevertheless, emergency regulations may not prevent an appeal to the courts, impose a punishment retroactively, or violate human dignity. Some laws or articles in laws are immune from emergency regulations, such as the Basic Law: The Knesset, or the Basic Law: Government. The Basic Law: Government (2001) states that it is the authority of the Knesset to renew annually the declaration of a state of emergency (Article 38B). Attempts have been made to use emergency regulations for matters other than security, such as preventing strikes, but these were rejected by the High Court of Justice (see more in Chapter 4 on the Knesset).

E. Legislation and the Borders of the State

Israel's borders were not set in the Law and Administration Ordinance of 1948 because the government and notably Ben-Gurion opposed this, pending the outcome of the war (see Chapter 1). Accordingly, the state borders, or, more accurately, the borders of control of the state, were delineated by wars, ceasefires, and peace

[19] According to B'Tselem, 1,794 administrative detainees were held in Israel in November 1989, 12 in December 2000, 1,007 in January 2003, and 584 in December 2015. See www.btselem.org/administrative_detention/statistics (accessed May 4, 2016).

[20] This first appeared in the Law and Administration Ordinance (1948); later in the Basic Law: Government (1968); and now in Basic Law: Government (2001), Article 38.

agreements. The ***Jurisdiction and Powers Ordinance*** of September 1948 allowed the defense minister, by declaration, to apply Israeli law to the territories occupied by the IDF, even if these were outside sovereign state territory (Rubinstein and Medina 2005, 931–32). After the occupation of territories in 1967, a different approach was adopted: The Law and Administration Ordinance was amended to read, "The law, jurisdiction, and administration of the state shall be in effect throughout the area of the Land of Israel that the government so established by order" (Paragraph 11b). Furthermore, explicit legislation was enacted to apply Israeli jurisdiction to two specific areas. First, east Jerusalem was annexed according to a Law and Administration Order by the government in June 1967, and this was reinforced in 1980 by the Basic Law: Jerusalem. An amendment from 2001 attempts to thwart all future efforts to return parts of Jerusalem:

> No authority related to the Jerusalem domain that is stipulated in the law of Israel or the Jerusalem municipality shall be transferred to a foreign body, whether political, governmental, or a similar foreign party, whether permanently or for a defined period.

Second, the ***Golan Heights Law (1981)*** applied Israeli law, jurisdiction, and administration to the Golan Heights (which is outside the "Land of Israel" as understood in the Jurisdiction and Powers Ordinance) to prevent the return of that territory to Syria.

In the absence of a law to the contrary, the government is not obliged to seek Knesset approval for covenants, agreements, or decisions such as withdrawal from occupied areas. According to the ***Statute of Government Operations***, the government may bring covenants to the Knesset, and this has become the custom over the years. On the other hand, as early as 1999 an amendment to the Government and Law Arrangements Law stated that a Knesset majority of sixty-one members is required to legislate withdrawal from the territories, and that this decision must be brought to a referendum. In 2014, the ***Basic Law: Referendum*** was enacted, which states that any agreement in which the law, jurisdiction, or administration of the state of Israel shall cease to apply to a territory shall require a Knesset majority of sixty-one MKs and approval by referendum (unless it has been approved by eighty MKs).

F. Legislation Pertaining to the Occupied Territories

On principle, Israeli law does not apply to the territories conquered in 1967 (Blum 1971, 315; Dinstein 1971, 5; Benvenisti 1993; Sheleff 1993, 757–809; Kretzmer 2002; Rubinstein and Medina 2005, 926–35; Cohen and Cohen 2014, 105–20). Since then, some territory (the Sinai Peninsula) was returned as part of a peace agreement with Egypt or by unilateral withdrawal (the Gaza Strip), or following the Israel–Syria Disengagement Agreement of 1974. Israeli law was applied in some areas (Jerusalem and the Golan Heights) following legislation, and some areas were transferred to the Palestinian Authority in keeping with the Oslo Accords and other agreements.

The occupied territories are under military rule, and the military commander is sovereign there, albeit subject to Israeli administrative law and international law, in keeping with the Hague Convention (1907) and the international humanitarian provisions of the Geneva Conventions (1949), which Israel agreed to apply without conceding that these are occupied territories (Kretzmer 2002; Shamgar 1971, 264).

Since the occupied territories do not fall under Israeli jurisdiction, the Knesset has practically no oversight power there, and this has created a complex and distorted legal duality. One law applies to the Palestinian residents while Israeli law applies to the Jewish residents of the same area. For Palestinians, for example, the 1945 Emergency Regulations are often applied, but these are rarely invoked for the Jewish settlers. In another example, Israeli law applies to the Jewish municipalities in the territories by order of the military commander, and in most matters they are not ex-territorial and their Jewish residents are treated as if they live inside Israel. Non-Israeli residents of the territories have the right to appeal to the Supreme Court, even though Israeli law does not apply to them, and the court engages in judicial review of decisions made by the military commanders. This entangled situation is hard to unravel: Although non-Israelis of the territories have the right to appeal to the Israeli Supreme Court against the Israeli authorities, most prefer not to exercise this right, as it would accord legitimacy to Israeli rule over them. This duality creates inequality before the law, which only intensifies with selective law enforcement (Karp 1984) on Jewish and non-Jewish residents of the territories. Most scholars of international law – certainly outside Israel – are of the opinion that all the Jewish settlements in the territories, without distinction, are illegal. The Fourth Geneva Convention prohibits an occupying power from transferring citizens from its own territory to the occupied territory. The Hague Regulations prohibit an occupying power from undertaking permanent changes in the occupied area unless required by military needs in the narrow sense of the term.[21]

14.4 Wars and Peace Agreements

The basic guidelines of the first government established after the Knesset election in 1949 declared that freedom of expression must be preserved "while safeguarding the security of the state." The state of Israel was founded three years after the Holocaust amidst a bloody war. A subjective sense of existential danger has gripped Jewish citizens of Israel (and Arab citizens as well, for entirely different reasons), whether well founded or not. Neuberger defined this as a "mental state of emergency" that affects the perceptions and feelings of the citizens, the public, and the apparatus of state (Neuberger, Ben Ami, and Gross Rophe 2007, 7). In its wake has come a willingness to mobilize for emergency efforts, hence the images of "an army of the people," "a nation in uniform," "a mobilized society," and the like. The ramifications of this are reflected in the degree to which Israeli society is "militarized" or "civilian," hence the terms "a garrison state," "an army that has a state," "military democracy," etc. (Lissak and Kimmerling 1984, i; Lasswell 1941, 455–68). The leadership in 1948, led by Ben-Gurion, also viewed the IDF as a tool to foster social cohesiveness and a means to mold the new Israeli (Horowitz and Lissak 1989, 195–230; Y. Greenberg 1991, 40–41; Kadish 1996, 53; Pedatzur 2003, 103). Even in the twenty-first century, the IDF still performs educational functions and has socialization mechanisms, though fewer than in the early years (Lissak 1971, 325–40).

[21] For the position of Israel's Supreme Court, see *Dawikat et al. v. State of Israel et al.* 1979.

The fact that in Israel most men and a significant proportion of women serve in the army, and that this is extended by reserve duty, has a major impact on the social ethos of the country. The "Spirit of the IDF" ethical code, for example, states that

> The discharged serviceman may make use of his military status, including his reserve or retired rank, or may grant permission to others to do so, only in civilian contexts that do not compromise the IDF's values and basic principles, or its honor and the trust it enjoys among the public. (Israel Defense Forces 1994, 11)

Another example is the centrality of the army and security issues in Hebrew literature, theater, art, and many other areas of life (Urian 2004, 221–22; Ben Eliezer 2003, 29–76). This context will be particularly salient when we examine below developments since the founding of Israel.

A. A Chronology of Wars and Hostilities

The expression "a hundred years of warfare" has been used to describe the ongoing conflict since the birth of Zionism, but this term fails to capture periods of relative quiet as well as major changes in the nature of the conflict, its players, and scope. Nevertheless, as noted, the history of Israel is a chronology of wars and hostilities, as well as direct and indirect agreements with adversaries, from the Armistice Agreement in 1949 through the peace treaties with Egypt and Jordan and the ongoing costly hostilities in southern Lebanon and the Gaza Strip.

As Table 14.1 indicates, wars and military operations are an integral part of the experience of life in Israel. The longest period of relative calm extended for ten years – from 1957 to 1967. Hence, the first question is whether 1948 – the year of Israel's founding and the War for Independence (what the Palestinians refer to as the Nakba – the disaster) – should be regarded as the historical watershed, i.e., a critical turning point.

Proponents of Pole 1, as presented above, would argue that the pre-state struggle continues unabated, and that the reasons for the 1948 war are the same as the reasons for all the military clashes that followed. According to this approach, the conflict remains an open issue because it is rooted in the enduring unwillingness of Palestinians and the Arab countries to recognize Israel's existence. Therefore, the flare-ups of hostilities are interlinked as one ongoing defensive war, and the question of who started them is irrelevant because Israel poses no threat to the neighboring countries. Furthermore, the conflict with the Palestinians is not the crux of the matter, because a Palestinian state could have been established in the West Bank and Gaza Strip before Israel took control of them in 1967. Objectors to this approach say that a sharp distinction should be made between the struggle for establishing a state, carried out primarily in the international arena, and how the sovereign state of Israel conducts its affairs. They point to the peace agreements with Egypt and Jordan, two countries that had previously refused to recognize Israel, and the attempts (unsuccessful so far, but not abandoned) to forge an agreement with the Palestinians, suggesting that the conflict with the Palestinians and Syria is also not intractable.

According to Pole 2 proponents, the source of the conflict is Israel's unwillingness to reconcile itself to the partition borders of 1949 (or 1947), as evidenced by the various wars. Accordingly, the 1956 and 1967 wars were part of an Israeli expansion

Table 14.1 *Wars and military operations, Arab states (1948–2015)*

	Years	Initiated by	Adversaries	Outcome
War for Independence	1948–49	Palestinians, Arab states, the Arab League	Egypt, Syria, Lebanon, Transjordan, Iraq	Armistice agreements; partition of the land
Sinai Campaign	1956–57	Israel, France, Britain	Egypt	Evacuation of Gaza Strip; restoration of previous border; international guarantees; UN force in the Sinai
Six Day War	1967	Egyptian escalation in the Sinai, Israel	Egypt, Jordan, Syria	Occupation of the Sinai, Gaza Strip, Golan Heights, West Bank
War of Attrition	1969–70	Egypt	Egypt	The Rogers Plan (ceasefire)
Yom Kippur War	1973–74	Egypt, Syria	Egypt, Syria	Separation of forces agreements in the Sinai and Golan Heights
Gulf War	1991	Iraq	Iraq	Two dead, about 300 wounded, property damage (in Israel)

Landmarks in the ongoing conflict with the Palestinians since 1967

Attrition in the Jordan Valley	1968–70
The first Intifada	1987–91
The second Intifada	2000–5
Gaza Strip operation (Cast Lead)	2008–9
Gaza Strip operation (Pillar of Defense)	2012
Gaza Strip operation (Protective Edge)	2014
Uprising in the West Bank (on and off)	Oct. 2015–

Military operations and wars in Lebanon since 1978

	Year	Adversary
Litani Operation	1978	Palestinians
First Lebanon War	1982	Palestinians
Operation Accountability	1993	Hezbollah
Operation Grapes of Wrath	1996	Hezbollah
Second Lebanon War	2006	Hezbollah

plan, which suffered setbacks because of Arab resistance. As a result, the plan is now revised and limited to maintaining Israeli control over the remaining territories from the 1967 occupation – in the West Bank and the Golan Heights (Y. Shenhav 2001, 204–11; Azulay and Ophir 2008, 445–50). Objectors to this approach contend that the feeling of existential threat in 1956 and 1967 was real for both the public and decision-makers, and that, ever since, Israel has proven its willingness to give up territory in exchange for peace. What continues is the refusal of most Palestinians (and Syria) to recognize Israel, as evidenced by the Hamas victory in the 2006 Palestinian parliamentary election.

Between these two approaches are others, but this brief description foregrounds the issues that affect security policy from a broad perspective, beyond the strict military aspects.

Looking at the chronology of Israel's wars, we find a striking difference between what preceded and what followed the 1967 war. During the earlier period, all Israeli wars and military operations were perceived as defensive (including the questionable Sinai Campaign of 1956, viewed as a necessary preventive action); further, they were considered successful from the Israeli perspective. This was a period of widespread consensus about security policy. Military victories were attributed to the political leaders, and enhanced the stature of both the political and the security systems (Galnoor 1977a). Thus deterrence was achieved, and arguably a resounding victory, as the 1967 war appeared in the euphoric aftermath.

Portents of a grayer future were evident in the ongoing resistance after June 1967, such as the sinking of the destroyer *Eilat* by the Egyptians in October 1967; and the onset of Palestinian resistance, which led to the failed IDF reprisal in Karameh, Jordan, in March 1968. These shadows only darkened during the War of Attrition, first under PLO shelling from Jordanian territory into Israel in the Jordan Valley, and later under Egyptian shelling of Israeli military outposts across the Suez Canal in 1969–70. During the War of Attrition along the canal, which continued for a year and a half, 721 Israelis were killed, 594 of them soldiers, and another 2,659 were wounded. Some 5,000 Egyptian soldiers and civilians were killed and injured, and heavy damage was inflicted on the cities along the canal (Carmel 2001, 671).[22] The War of Attrition was the first war since the founding of the state that Israel did not win and that the situation afterwards was worse than before from an Israeli point of view. Since that time – all of Israel's wars, without exception, have been controversial within Israel. Victories were not achieved as in previous wars, results were equivocal, and some wars were perceived as not defensive at all, but launched to achieve political ends.

The major rupture came with the Yom Kippur War in October 1973. In retrospect, the essence of this failure was not the surprise attack or intelligence lapse, but Israel's foreign and security policy in general, which caused the war. As we shall see below, after the 1967 victory, these policies were left in the hands of the defense system, headed then by Defense Minister Moshe Dayan, even more than previously. The civilian leadership under Prime Minister Golda Meir willingly consented to the defense monopoly on policy about the occupied territories, and so did most of the public, the political parties, and the mass media. In this sense, the "conception" that

22 For different figures, see Small and Singer 1982.

failed in 1973 was giving the defense system a monopoly on security policy (Galnoor 2008, 263–81). This is the essence of the earthquake that followed: Previously most Israeli citizens would contend with their leaders in domestic affairs, but relied on and trusted them in foreign affairs and security. The Yom Kippur War shattered that trust in the civilian and military leadership, and in the political system as a whole. In the wake of the Agranat Commission report (see Chapter 7), the chief of staff, head of intelligence, and other senior officers were dismissed. Although the commission cleared the prime minister and defense minister from personal responsibility, public pressure forced the government to resign. Ever since, as was the case after the War of Attrition and after the Sinai Separation of Forces Treaties in 1974–75, Israel has found itself worse off after the wars than before them. What's more, the economic burden of security doubled after 1967, and continued to grow until the peace agreement with Egypt in the late 1970s.

The peace treaties with Egypt in 1979 and Jordan in 1994 moved events into the eastern and northern borders of Israel (and later the Gaza Strip), and forged a new security reality – an easing of the strategic threat to Israel's existence by its neighbors across the border, and a growing need to address the Palestinian issue and its spread into Lebanon. Even the firing of missiles from Iraq into Israeli territory in 1991 was indirectly related to the Palestinian issue (at least as pretext). Negotiations and agreements with the Palestinians that began during Rabin's term (1992–95) continued sporadically afterwards, but took a hostile turn after Hamas (an acronym for the Islamic Resistance Movement) took control of the Gaza Strip in 2007.

B. The Palestinian Issue after 1967

How did the defense system cope with the Palestinian problem? After the 1967 war, the occupied territories were entrusted to the IDF, and military rule was imposed in the West Bank and Gaza. Defense Minister Moshe Dayan was "prime minister of the territories," for all intents and purposes, governing through the military commanders (Gazit 1995). The names used for the military regime changed periodically, and even "Civil Administration" was used for a while in 1981 (Eldar and Zertal 2007). The reality in these areas was dictated primarily by two factors – the defense system and gradually the Jewish settlement enterprise, with a population of approximately 421,000 in 2016 (some 80,000 families).[23]

Israeli policy vis-à-vis the Palestinian issue after the 1967 war was an implicit decision not to decide. Thus Israel followed in the footsteps of the Khartoum Resolution of September 1967 in which eight Arab heads of state declared that until Israel withdrew from Arab lands conquered in 1967, there would be "no peace, no recognition, and no negotiations." Israel operated on the assumption that time was on its side, and that a solution would present itself to the complex dilemma: on the one hand, it was apprehensive about annexing the territories and did not want to grant political and civil rights to the Palestinian inhabitants; and, on the other hand, it was unwilling to return the territories for various reasons – emotional, religious, and security-related. In effect, no policy was formulated because Israel itself was not

[23] Excluding Jewish settlers in the Arab neighborhoods of east Jerusalem (Levinson 2009 and Central Bureau of Statistics *Statistical Abstract* 2016).

clear about its goals following the 1967 victory, which left it in control of some 90,000 square kilometers from the Suez Canal to the outskirts of Damascus. The main question was what to do with the West Bank and Gaza Strip. Various governments, including the Likud, which came to power in 1977, refrained from taking a decisive stand (such as legally annexing the territories), and retrospectively it became clear that time was not on Israel's side, and many opportunities were missed. Reality, as is its way, did not come up with a solution, and in the absence of clear goals, the policy was reactive, and usually further complicated matters.

After the 1967 war, Israel missed an opportunity for negotiating the future of the West Bank with King Hussein of Jordan. In September 1967, the government of Israel privately conveyed to the United States its willingness to return territory to Egypt and Syria in exchange for peace agreements. The West Bank and the Gaza Strip were excluded from the offer, not by chance, because the Israeli government had adopted Dayan's approach that there was no need for haste, not even with King Hussein, but instead to strive for a "functional solution" – Israeli territorial control in exchange for a pledge of normalcy (and eventually autonomy) for the Palestinian inhabitants of the territories. Even prior to this, Deputy Prime Minister Yigal Allon had outlined his "Allon Plan," which would annex to Israel a 15-km-wide strip along the Jordan River and provide a corridor to Jericho, with autonomy to the Palestinians in the remaining areas (Yeroham Cohen 1973). Like the "functional solution," the Allon Plan too was not officially adopted by the government, but served as the basis for Jewish settlement in the Jordan Valley. The governments of Israel decided not to decide, but all the plans and actions were unilateral, not based on negotiations with Jordan or the Palestinians, nor was an effort made to find any partner. This approach became a dead end rather quickly, however, upon resumption of Palestinian resistance in 1968, Hussein's relinquishing of claims to the West Bank in 1974, terrorism, and escalation into the first Intifada in 1987.

Prior to this, in 1978, Israel and Egypt had signed the Camp David Accords, in which Israel agreed to give full autonomy to the Palestinians (the Hebrew version refers to them as "the Arabs in the Land of Israel"), to recognize their legitimate rights and just needs, and to enter into negotiations over the final status of the territories, to be finalized within three years. The Palestinians were neither party to these Accords nor were they consulted. In any event, nothing came of the "autonomy talks," with the exception of Moshe Dayan's resignation from the government due to its foot-dragging, and the fact that even the Begin government did not annex the territories (Bar-Siman-Tov 1994, 195–211). The first Lebanon War (1982), in which the PLO fled Lebanon for Tunis, did not fundamentally change the situation in the territories, but increased the motivation of the Palestinians within the territories to take fate into their own hands. Israel's National Unity Governments (1984–90) were by and large paralyzed on issues of foreign affairs and security, and the only significant initiative was the London Agreement of April 1987 forged between then Foreign Minister Shimon Peres and King Hussein of Jordan. This agreement called for an international conference to launch negotiations on the future of the territories based on recognition of the legitimate rights of the Palestinian people. Prime Minister Yitzhak Shamir opposed the agreement; it was not approved by the government.

The first Intifada, which broke out in late 1987, took Israel by surprise because it was a popular, locally driven uprising, lacking clear ties to Palestinian leaders outside the territories (Kimmerling and Migdal 2003). Activists organized strikes, stone-throwing, and Molotov cocktails, which escalated to stabbings, execution of collaborators, and terrorist acts against civilians within Israel. The IDF of the post-Lebanon War was unprepared for this kind of resistance, and its first reaction was to instruct the soldiers to harshly beat the demonstrators and stone-throwers. This was followed by arrests, closures, sealing of homes, shooting of demonstrators with rubber-coated bullets, infiltration by undercover units, and mass expulsions. This outbreak of widespread revolt after twenty years of occupation should not have come as a surprise, because it was clear by now that Israel's policy to "decide not to decide" – and meanwhile establish settlements – was a failure. According to the IDF, during the first Intifada (1987–91), 66 Israeli soldiers and 157 civilians were killed, while 4,918 soldiers and 4,195 civilians were wounded. On the Palestinian side, 808 were killed by Israeli security forces, and 985 at the hands of other Palestinians, with 16,824 wounded.[24]

The six years of Intifada dissolved consensus in Israel around several previously held beliefs: the occupation was no longer regarded as "enlightened"; the border between Israel and the territories again became palpable, not only because of the closures; several organizations such as the Association for Civil Rights in Israel and B'Tselem began intensive documentation of events in the territories; and soldiers and officers were being brought to court for violating the human rights of Palestinians in the territories. Voices could now be heard in the IDF asserting "there is no military solution to the Intifada, we need a political solution" (Chief of Staff Dan Shomron quoted in Grinberg 2009). The Palestinians from within the territories and the PLO, which had begun to support the Intifada from its headquarters in Tunis, could now record achievements: indirect recognition of them by the Shamir government at the 1991 Madrid Conference (formally as part of the Jordanian-Palestinian delegation), even though the conference bore no tangible fruit. Meanwhile, change was also evident in the PLO's Declaration of Independence in November 1988, which laid the basis for a Palestinian state within the West Bank, side by side with Israel.

The next milestone was mutual recognition by Israel and the Palestinians (or the PLO, more accurately) in the Oslo Accords' Declaration of Principles, signed in Washington in September 1993. As part of this series of agreements, which were approved by the Knesset, responsibility for designated areas in the territories was transferred to the Palestinian Authority.[25] The IDF was not party to the talks that led to the Oslo Accords, yet they marked a dramatic shift in Israeli policy. It was the political echelon who reached these agreements with the Palestinians, like the other peace agreements and unilateral withdrawals, some with the active opposition of top military figures. Yitzhak Rabin, then prime minister and defense minister, made sure to neutralize the opposition, and negotiations with the Palestinians on implementing these accords were

[24] IDF Spokesperson. Other sources claim more casualties among the Palestinians: www.btselem.org/statistics/first_intifada_tables (accessed May 4, 2016).

[25] The "Oslo Accords" were signed on September 13, 1993 and later ratified by the Knesset: sixty-one in favor, fifty opposed, eight abstentions. "The Cairo Agreement on the Gaza Strip and Jericho Area" was signed on May 4, 1994, and the subsequent "Law Implementing the Agreement on the Gaza Strip and Jericho Area" was passed by the Knesset in December 1994. The "Interim Agreement on the West Bank and the Gaza Strip," often referred to as "Oslo 2," was signed in Taba in September 1995 and ratified by the Knesset on October 5, 1995: sixty-one in favor, fifty-one opposed.

conducted primarily by IDF and General Security Service officers. Because security officers were also leading the Palestinian side, critics of the accords later claimed that Oslo was no more than a deal between the intelligence services of both sides.

On the ground, however, an implicit confluence of interests emerged between Jewish and Palestinian extremists to subvert the Oslo Accords and any political solution based on the principle of partition. On the one hand, a "Jewish underground" that used terrorism against the Palestinians appeared in the early 1980s. The political power of the settlers grew after the Oslo Accords, and intimidated Rabin from proceeding with their evacuation from Hebron in February 1994 after the massacre of Muslim worshipers there at the hands of a settler. On the other hand, the agreements did not put an end to attacks by Palestinian terrorists from the Hamas and Islamic Jihad movements, which came to a head in 1995. Terrorism led to a tougher military response, both executed and planned, as demonstrated at the outbreak of the second Intifada in 2000. Israel's changed policy toward the territories and the reduced military monopoly in policymaking both ended abruptly with the assassination of Rabin and subsequent vicissitudes in relations with the Palestinians. Neither side adhered to the Oslo Accords with the detailed timetable of stages.

The next milestone was the failed effort to reach a comprehensive agreement at Camp David in July 2000. Many conflicting interpretations have been written about the reasons for the failure, but here it is sufficient to note that Ehud Barak had been elected prime minister in 1999 with the active engagement of the security elite (Peri 2006, 77–90) and that, following the political failure of Camp David, he resumed a strategy based entirely on security considerations. The failure to implement the Oslo Accords, which brought frustration and mutual suspicions, left both sides unwilling to seek a comprehensive and permanent solution to the conflict. When the Palestinians renewed the Intifada in 2000 with the goal of achieving by force what had not been accomplished at the negotiating table, they discovered that the Israeli side had learned the lessons of the first Intifada, and the IDF was well prepared for renewed hostilities. The IDF's first reaction was an open-fire policy on demonstrators, and 129 Palestinians were killed in the first month of Intifada (Harel and Issacharoff 2004; Eldar and Zertal 2007, 534). The IDF was determined to prevent the revolt from spilling into Israel from across the Green Line, but terrorist activities evolved into suicide bombings within both Israel and the territories.

The second Intifada, which began in October 2000 and waned in 2005, differed from its predecessor in scope, with a large number of casualties on both sides. According to the IDF Spokesperson, 1,115 Israelis and foreign citizens were killed by the end of September 2006, of whom 785 were civilians and 330 security forces. Estimates of Palestinian casualties range from 3,333 (according to the IDF) to 3,861 (according to the Palestinian Authority). Barak's minority government was already at the end of its tether, so these decisions were made almost exclusively by the defense leaders – the minister of defense and the chief of staff – as in the previous model.

Following the prime ministerial election of 2001, the main actors changed: Ariel Sharon as prime minister, Binyamin Ben-Eliezer as defense minister, and Shaul Mofaz as chief of staff (and defense minister from late 2002) initially continued the previous policy. Indeed, it could be said that, in the early 2000s, an all-out war in terms of scope and casualties was waged for the first time between Israel and the Palestinians, a war that raised the frustration level on both sides. The Palestinians turned toward suicide missions and brought Hamas to power in the January 2006 election, while a civil war in June 2007 removed the Gaza Strip from the control of the Palestinian Authority. In parallel, the Sharon government undertook unilateral measures: first, the decision in 2002 to construct a separation barrier between Israel and the territories, a "you're there and we're here" policy; and, second, the disengagement and evacuation of Israeli settlers from the Gaza Strip, carried out in August 2005.

C. The Separation/Security Barrier

The separation barrier between Israel and the West Bank was planned to be about 717 km long (some 34 km of which were to be wall segments and the remainder a fence).[26] By 2012, about 500 km (70%) were completed and, since then, the main construction stopped. In addition, a 240-km fence along the border between Israel and Egypt in Sinai was completed in December 2013. Another fence is planned for the Golan Heights along the ceasefire line with Syria, thus surrounding Israel from all directions. The West Bank barrier was an incarnation of the separation concept envisioned by Prime Minister Yitzhak Rabin following the terrorist attacks in 1994–95, and in practice continued the policy of closure that had begun during the first Intifada. The "separation plan" along the route of the Green Line was not implemented during the Rabin administration, and also not during Netanyahu's first term of office in 1996–99, but was again raised by Prime Minister Barak after the 2000 Camp David summit collapsed. The official rationale for constructing the barrier was security: preventing the infiltration of terrorists and the entry of Palestinian laborers.

Construction of the barrier was controversial from the outset: In the IDF, some objected because they viewed it as an ineffectual defense measure and exorbitantly expensive. Others cast doubt on its effectiveness in the face of high motivation on the other side. Prime Minister Sharon, who was originally opposed to the barrier, changed his mind after a series of murderous attacks, and the government approved its construction in June 2002. Public opinion polls in 2005 registered a clear majority of support (some 80%) (Ben Meir and Shaked 2007, 64). The route of the barrier ("the seam zone") was planned by the National Security Council, the Defense Ministry, the IDF, and other defense-related bodies, and the estimated cost, according to the Brodet Committee, was approximately $3.3 billion (at 2007 prices) (Brodet Committee 2007). The planned route of the barrier generally follows what had been the Green Line until 1967, but leaves, with the exception of Jerusalem and several other areas, some 9 percent of the West Bank on the "Israeli" side of the fence. In February 2005, the route of the barrier was modified as a result of Supreme Court rulings that security needs must be balanced with considerations for the fabric of life of the area residents.[27] Dozens of petitions were filed about the fence, some by Jewish landowners, and the route was modified several times.

[26] Data from Israel, Ministry of Defense, "Israel's Security Fence," www.securityfence.mod.gov.il/Pages/ENG/operational.htm (accessed May 4, 2016), and Shaul Arieli, "Data about the Barrier, 2012," www.shaularieli.com/77951/%D7%92%D7%93%D7%A8-%D7%94%D7%94%D7%A4%D7%A8%D7%93%D7%94-1 [in Hebrew] (accessed May 4, 2016).

[27] *Beit Sourik Village Council v. Government of Israel* 2004; and *Zaharan Yunes Mara'abe et al. v. Prime Minister of Israel et al.* 2005.

The Jewish settlers objected to the barrier because of its proximity to the Green Line and the fear that its route would ultimately delineate the eastern border of Israel, leaving them outside it. If the border were drawn according to the planned route of the barrier, 48 of the 122 Jewish settlements in the West Bank would remain west of the barrier (inside Israel), incorporating 76 percent of all the settlers outside greater Jerusalem. This would leave only 74 settlements for evacuation with a population of 65,000 in 2007 (Shragai 2007). On the left, opposition to the barrier was based on the fear that it was intended to annex to Israel the areas surrounding the settlements, hence this unilateral initiative would preempt negotiations with the Palestinians. The Palestinians object to the barrier because it is an Israeli unilateral action that predetermines, even if not explicitly, the borders of the future Palestinian state. Furthermore, construction of the barrier required the expropriation of their property and in many places the barrier separates farmers from their lands, and severely disrupts the fabric of life of those who live on both sides of it. The International Court of Justice in the Hague ruled that construction of the barrier beyond the border of Israel is illegal.[28]

Israel claims that the barrier was erected purely for security purposes. However, the twists and turns of its route, and the fact that for hundreds of kilometers there was no security reason to construct any segment of the barrier west of the Green Line (i.e., inside Israel), lend credence to the claim that there were also political motives. Decisions made about the barrier exemplify the poor decision-making process in matters of security – alternatives were not seriously studied, and facts on the ground were created without considering their legal, international, or humanitarian ramifications (Arieli and Sfard 2006; Galnoor 2008, 268). The use of high-trajectory weapons from southern Lebanon and the Gaza Strip has raised profound questions about the barrier's effectiveness for security. In 2012 the government decided not to allocate additional funds for continued construction of the barrier's missing segments. Another reason was that, in comparison with Gaza, the level of hostilities in the West Bank subsided, despite the fact that since the 2009 Netanyahu government was elected, no serious negotiations have taken place between Israel and the Palestinian Authority.

D. Disengagement from the Gaza Strip

The disengagement plan from Gaza was formulated by Prime Minister Ariel Sharon, presented to the public in December 2003, first approved by the government in April 2004, and implemented by the IDF in the summer of 2005. Underlying the disengagement was the assumption that despite agreement in principle that the conflict will be resolved by "two states for two nations," there was no credible Palestinian partner for negotiations, and therefore to prevent burnout of the IDF and perhaps end the political stalemate, Israel must take unilateral measures independent of Palestinian cooperation. The plan called for evacuation of settlements and military facilities from the Gaza Strip and a minor area in the northern West Bank. Some 13,000 Israeli civilians were moved out within two weeks by 42,000 soldiers and

[28] International Court of Justice, "Legal Consequences of the Construction of a Wall in the Occupied Palestinian Territory" (July 9, 2004). www.icj-cij.org/docket/files/131/1677.pdf (accessed May 6, 2016).

police officers, at a cost, including compensation to the evacuees, of some NIS 9 billion (roughly $2.3 billion) (State Comptroller *Annual Report* 2006, 1104). This unilateral withdrawal did not bring about the desired results, and security within Israel adjacent to the Gaza Strip deteriorated, particularly after Hamas took control of Gaza in June 2007. In June 2006, the Israeli soldier Gilad Shalit was taken hostage, and in the years 2000–7, no fewer than 2,383 Qassam rockets were fired from Gaza into Israel.[29]

Consequently, a blockade was imposed on the Gaza Strip by Israel and Egypt and a series of Israeli military operations followed the shelling of rockets on Israeli civilians (see Table 14.1). The goal of Operation Cast Lead (December 2008 to January 2009) was "to strike hard at the Hamas regime for purposes of improving security adjacent to the Gaza region for a prolonged period, while enhancing deterrence and reducing rocket attacks to the extent possible."[30] The operation consisted primarily of airstrikes, with limited ground action. According to IDF publications, 1,166 Palestinians were killed in the operation, of whom 871 were members of Hamas or other terrorist organizations (YNet 2009). According to human rights organizations in Gaza, some 1,300 Palestinians were killed, more than half of them civilians (Greenberg and Waked 2009). The operation caused widespread destruction and 100,000 people were left homeless.

Within Israel, Operation Cast Lead won broad public support, including most political parties with the exception of the Arab parties and to some extent Meretz. Internationally, however, the operation led the UN Human Rights Council to appoint a fact-finding mission headed by Judge Richard Goldstone to investigate violations of international law by Israel and the Palestinian forces. The Israeli government decided not to cooperate with the inquiry. The report was published in September 2009 and contained harsh criticism of Israel's actions as a deliberate, disproportionate assault intended to terrorize the civilian population. The report also condemned the Palestinian rocket attacks on Israeli civilians (UN Human Rights Council 2009). In November 2009, the UN General Assembly endorsed the Goldstone Report (114 in favor, 18 against, and 44 abstaining), and called upon Israel to investigate the "war crimes" it committed. The operation and the Goldstone Report also provoked public debate in Israel about the limits of force against a civilian population (Margalit and Walzer 2009; Shalom 2009).

Subsequently, the war between Hamas and Israel continued with intervals of *tahidiyye* (periods of calm), causing casualties and disruption on both sides. Since 2009, Israel has launched two additional major attacks inside the Gaza Strip. In Operation Pillar of Defense (November 2012), Israeli airstrikes lasted seven days during which rockets fired from the Gaza Strip reached Tel Aviv and Jerusalem. Israel launched Operation Protective Edge (July and August 2014) after three boys were kidnapped and murdered. The initial goal was to destroy the tunnels constructed by Hamas leading from Gaza into Israel, but the operation grew more involved and lasted fifty days. According to IDF publications, Israeli casualties inside and outside Gaza were 67 soldiers and 5 civilians killed, and 620 soldiers and 837 civilians wounded; Palestinian

[29] The Intelligence and Terrorism Information Center, Israel Intelligence Heritage and Commemoration Center, "Rocket Threat from the Gaza Strip 2000–2007," December 2007.

[30] *BaMachaneh*, January 2, 2009 [in Hebrew]. This is an IDF-published journal.

casualties were 2,125 killed (about half of them civilians) and about 11,000 wounded (Ministry of Foreign Affairs N.d.). Palestinian figures are not much higher, but a majority of those killed (70%) were civilians (Palestinian Center for Human Rights 2014). The operation destroyed sizable portions of the Gaza Strip cities.

E. Lebanon

Until the 1970s, it was said that Lebanon would be the second country to sign a peace treaty with Israel. All this changed after the PLO redeployed in Lebanon after fleeing Jordan in 1970. The presence of hostile forces nearby in a country with limited military capacity transformed Israel's northern border into a serious security liability. During the first Rabin government (1974–77), Israel was wary of direct military involvement in Lebanon's internal war, preferring to give support to the Christians in the south (the "good fence" policy). Israel's first protracted action inside Lebanon was Operation Litani, launched in March 1978, and the IDF remained in southern Lebanon for three months. When the IDF withdrew, a UN Interim Force in Lebanon (UNIFIL) was created to oversee the truce, but in effect the region became a state-within-a-state controlled by the South Lebanese Army (SLA), with Israeli backing. This was the beginning of Israel's entanglement in Lebanon. Syrian involvement and continued attacks on Israel's northern communities provided the impetus for the first Lebanon War, launched in June 1982. This was a "political war" for all intents and purposes because the political goals were no less important than the military aims: expelling the PLO from Lebanon and ending terrorist raids; installing a friendly government headed by Christian allies; and forging a peace treaty between Lebanon and Israel. To accomplish these objectives, it was deemed necessary to get the Syrian army out of Lebanon (Schiff and Ya'ari 1984).

The mandate of the State Commission of Inquiry (Kahan Commission 1983) was to investigate only the events in the refugee camps of Sabra and Shatila, not to examine how the decision was made to embark upon a war in Lebanon. Nevertheless, many testimonies since then have indicated that although this was a political war, the initiative, planning, and execution were entirely entrusted to the defense system – Defense Minister Ariel Sharon and Chief of Staff Rafael Eitan. Indeed, not even Prime Minister Menachem Begin, let alone the government and the Knesset, were privy to the larger plan and goals: While they had endorsed a limited action of up to 40 km inside Lebanon against PLO terrorism, the IDF had for the first time conquered the capital of a neighboring country, proving again that when a defense minister and the IDF are of the same mind, especially if the minister is a former general, the civilian leadership is helpless.

Thus, nine years after the Yom Kippur War, the first Lebanon War led again to the dismissal of a defense minister, Ariel Sharon (following a commission of inquiry), with Prime Minister Begin resigning soon after, in October 1983. This was the second time that a "conception" forged by the defense system was a total failure, and it mired Israel for many long years in what came to be known as "the Lebanese swamp." The PLO was forced to retreat to Tunis, but eventually regained its power and the Syrian army remained in Lebanon. Subsequently UNIFIL was reinforced and Israel gradually retreated to the security zone, but continued to operate in Lebanon via the SLA. The massive retreat to the Awali River was carried out in September 1983, when

Moshe Arens was defense minister, and the IDF did not object. Another withdrawal in 1985 marked the recreation of a "security zone" in southern Lebanon, from which the IDF retreated in 2000.

Meanwhile, Hezbollah, a Shiite terrorist organization, began to entrench itself in southern Lebanon in the 1980s as a result of domestic Lebanese politics, but also in reaction to Israeli control of the south. Attacks on UNIFIL and the IDF in Beirut and Tyre after 1982 were attributed to Hezbollah, as well as raids into the security zone, rockets fired into northern Israel, and the hostage-taking of Israeli soldiers. Hezbollah activity led to a renewal of the tit-for-tat cycle of violence with Israel and cross-border reprisals lasting a week or two: "Operation Accountability" (July 1993) and "Grapes of Wrath" (April 1996).

The realization that the IDF presence in southern Lebanon was not effective took a long time to dawn, eighteen years to be precise. The loss of life and political pressure from parties and protest movements all finally led Israel to withdraw unilaterally from southern Lebanon in May 2000. Hezbollah took over the area and sporadically engaged in raids into Israeli territory, such as the hostage-taking of three soldiers in October 2000 and rocket attacks on civilian communities. The relative quiet was interrupted in July 2006 when Hezbollah attacked an IDF patrol, killed three soldiers, and captured two. Israel launched a massive military response that, like the one in 1982, inflicted major damage on the civilian population and the physical infrastructure throughout Lebanon. Unlike 1982, however, this was primarily an air bombardment, with the ground operation more limited to specific areas in the south. During this war, Hezbollah shelled northern Israel and caused severe damage and many casualties. The second Lebanon War ended after thirty-four days, in which 119 soldiers and 43 civilians were killed in Israel, with 1,187 killed across the border in Lebanon. It ended in a ceasefire based on a UN Security Council resolution (UN Security Council 2006).

Despite public pressure, the Israeli government refused to establish a state commission of inquiry, but ultimately agreed to a government commission of inquiry (the "Winograd Commission"), and this time, unlike the commissions after the Yom Kippur War and the first Lebanon War, the mandate was to investigate the war itself and not just one aspect of it. The commission's interim and final reports sharply criticized the "failings and flaws" of a process in which the prime minister and defense minister approved unchallenged the plan that had been presented by the chief of staff:[31]

- The plan was brought to the government only after the decision had been predetermined elsewhere; although the ministers asked questions, they were unable – and perhaps unwilling – to examine other alternatives.
- Overnight on July 12, and in great haste, the government endorsed the recommendations of the defense system as presented, and authorized a small team of ministers ("the forum of seven") to approve the specific military operations, without these being presented again to the decision-makers and without

[31] For a detailed description of the decision-making process on the first day of the war, see the Winograd Commission's *Interim Report* (2007, 103–31); on the two other points, see the commission's *Final Report* (2008, vol. II, 250 and 517).

consulting additional bodies such as the Ministry of Foreign Affairs or the National Security Council.

- Even after it became clear during the course of the war that the original military objectives were not being achieved, and the need arose to evaluate how to continue, the IDF equivocated for an extended period "before bringing the decision clearly and sharply to the political echelon."
- None of the civilian forums – the government, the forum of seven ministers, or the Ministerial Committee for Security Affairs – convened with the requisite frequency to remain abreast of the changing dynamic of the war.

To conclude the subject of the wars, the events in Lebanon are not isolated, but raise the question of whether the ongoing recourse to military force has not kept potential political solutions at bay, or even made matters worse. Being bogged down in Lebanon for so many years – is this not a case of what happens when security monopolizes strategic thinking in foreign affairs and defense?

F. Withdrawal from Territories and Peace Agreements

During the long years of conflict, the IDF occupied territories beyond Israel's international or provisional borders, and then withdrew for various reasons. For the subject of this chapter, the relevant question is whether the decisions about withdrawal, like most of those about war, were also monopolized by the defense system. We will then ask the same question about the peace agreements.

Withdrawal from territories is of military significance, of course, and carried out by the army, which is usually not very keen about it. During the Ben-Gurion era, unsuccessful attempts were made by IDF commanders in 1949 (and again in 1957) to prevent the withdrawals from Sinai. However, even then the IDF had been a senior partner to the armistice agreements negotiations. This changed in 1967, from when it can be said that the initiative for every territorial withdrawal noted in Table 14.2 came from the civilian leadership. The IDF was sometimes not privy to early contacts (as in the peace agreements with Egypt or the Oslo Accords), sometimes opposed to them (as in leaving Lebanon in 2000), and sometimes a full partner (as in the partial pullback from southern Lebanon in 1988, the exchange of territory with Jordan, and the disengagement from Gaza in 2005). For example, the decision to withdraw the IDF from Lebanon in May 2000 was taken by the political leaders, while the IDF, as noted by Chief of Staff Shaul Mofaz, "carried out the orders of the political echelon," even if the decision, in the opinion of the military, was a mistaken one. The decision to disengage from Gaza in 2005 was made without military involvement and executed over the objections of Chief of Staff Moshe Ya'alon, who claimed it would "give a tailwind to terrorism." As a result, Ya'alon's term was not extended for an additional year (Peri 2006, 137–53). In all these withdrawals, a civilian leader with security credentials was involved: Dayan, Rabin, Barak, and Sharon. This relates to the peace treaties and other agreements that appear in Table 14.3.

Israel has valid peace treaties with two Arab countries, the fruit of efforts by civilian leaders – Menachem Begin and Moshe Dayan's efforts led to a peace treaty with Egypt in continuation of the Separation of Forces Agreement regarding Sinai in

Table 14.2 *Withdrawals from territories*

Withdrawal	Year	Event
First withdrawal from Sinai	1949	IDF reached al-Arish in the Sinai and withdrew to the international border under international pressure and orders from Ben-Gurion.
Armistice agreements	1949	Ceasefire lines set with Transjordan, Syria, and Lebanon including territorial exchanges and demilitarized zones.
Second withdrawal from Sinai and the Gaza Strip	1957–58	The US and USSR forced Ben-Gurion to order the IDF to retreat from the Sinai and Gaza Strip.
Third withdrawal from Sinai	1982	Peace treaty: Sinai gradually returned to Egypt, pre-1948 line restored as the internationally recognized border.
Withdrawals from Lebanon	1983; 1985	Partial withdrawal to the Awali River and creation of a "security zone" in southern Lebanon.
Oslo Accords*	1994	Transfer of control over most areas in the West Bank to the Palestinian Authority.
Transfer of territory to Jordan	1994	Peace treaty: parts of the Arava returned to Jordanian sovereignty; pre-1948 line became the internationally recognized border.
Withdrawal from Lebanon	2000	Unilateral withdrawal from southern Lebanon to the international border.
"Disengagement" from Gaza	2005	Unilateral withdrawal from the Gaza Strip and evacuation of Israeli settlements there.
Withdrawal from Lebanon	2007	Withdrawal from southern Lebanon following the Second Lebanon War.

* Actually a series of agreements in the years 1993–98.

Table 14.3 *Direct agreements between the sides involved*

	Year	Adversary	Outcome
Armistice	1948–49	Egypt, Syria, Lebanon, Transjordan	Lasted nineteen years until 1967.
Separation of forces in Sinai and the Golan Heights	1974	Egypt and Syria	Lasted with Egypt until the peace agreement; still valid with Syria.
Camp David Agreement	1978	Egypt	The basis for the peace agreement.
Peace agreement	1979	Egypt	Valid.
Declaration of Principles (Oslo Accords and other agreements)	1993–95	Palestinian Authority	Only sparsely and partially implemented.
Peace agreement	1994	Jordan	Valid.

1974; and Yitzhak Rabin and Shimon Peres forged the treaty with Jordan. A peace agreement was also signed with the Christian government installed in Lebanon after the 1982 war, but it was not ratified by the Lebanese parliament and went down in history as an Israeli attempt to dictate an agreement by military force.

Agreements with the Palestinians – from the Oslo Accords on Rabin's watch, their sparse continuation under Netanyahu's first government, and the effort to revive them under Barak – only ended in disappointment. Subsequent Israeli leaders began to explore unilateral solutions – under Sharon, construction of a separation barrier and disengagement from the Gaza Strip – while prolonged negotiations between the Olmert government and the Palestinian Authority yielded nothing. No serious negotiations took place after Netanyahu returned to power in 2009.

In sum, the IDF played no role in initiating these peace agreements and sometimes opposed them. On the other hand, it supported construction of the separation barrier as a way to fight terrorism, and backed evacuation of the Gaza Strip once Halutz took over as chief of staff.

14.5 Attitudes about Security

Public opinion carries relatively little weight in security policymaking, with one important reservation. When policies are unequivocal and initiated by charismatic leaders, the Israeli public tends to go along with them (Kies 1975, 36–53). Two examples: In 1976, 40 percent of the Israeli public objected to returning the Sinai Peninsula to Egypt, but by late 1977, after President Sadat's visit to Israel, only 16 percent continued to oppose it (Guttman 1978, 8–14). Also in 1998, most Israelis (56%) opposed a unilateral withdrawal from Lebanon, as 64 percent believed that the security zone makes a positive contribution to Israeli security (A. Arian 1999, 81), but when the government carried out a unilateral withdrawal in 2000, 74 percent were in favor (A. Arian 2001). On the other hand, public opinion has greater impact when policies are vague, tentative, or partial. Indeed, uncertainty among decision-makers decreases support: The Oslo Accords, for example, did not win comprehensive public support, compared to *post facto* support for other policies (Hermann and Yuchtman-Yaar 1997, 191–222).

A. Public Opinion

Relations between political leaders and public opinion changed radically in the age of multiple media. Until the early 1980s, the public was almost never exposed to security policy as it was being formed, learning about it only during implementation. After 2000, the process of policymaking on security issues had become fairly visible: The public knows when an emergency political meeting is convened, what the subjects under discussion are, what was said, and usually what decisions were made. Being able to look behind the scenes demystifies policymaking on security issues, sharpens public opinion, and gives it greater weight (Hermann 2005, 194–96). Correspondingly, political leaders take pains to survey public opinion, and the results often influence their behavior. Almost every weekend, for example, surveys appear in the Israeli media reflecting public opinion about key political matters, including security issues. In general, the Israeli public shows intense interest and involvement in security matters, and pollsters rarely encounter respondents claiming "I don't know" or "No opinion" (Hermann and Yuchtman-Yaar 1997, 207).

A prime characteristic of Israeli-Jewish public opinion on security issues is the tendency to cluster around the middle: In a 2006 survey, some 50 percent took centrist views, 22 percent were moderate right, and 16 percent moderate left, while 10 percent were extreme right and 3 percent extreme left. Notably, the combined right is 12 percent stronger than the combined left. Six years later (2012), the pattern had not changed much, with a marginal gain (4%) for the moderate right (Ben Meir and Shaked 2007; Ben Meir and Bagno-Moldavsky 2013, 30). The existence of a solid center on security issues has marked Israeli-Jewish public opinion for many years, and indicates a potential consensus. Nevertheless, public opinion is far from static, so that one can say that the center has "moved right" or "moved left" in accordance with events and policies. A good example of this is the public's view of an independent Palestinian state: In 1977, 80 percent of Israeli Jews believed that "another independent Arab state in the West Bank will not arise" (Guttman 1978, 8–14). Thirty-five years later, in 2012, 69 percent supported the solution of "two states for two nations" and 59 percent supported the establishment of a Palestinian state (Bagno-Moldavsky and Ben Meir 2014).

An analysis of the changes in the survey questions indicates a transition from general formulations ("territory in exchange for peace") in the period between the Six Day War and signing of the peace treaty with Egypt, to questions about specific policies (autonomy for the Palestinians, a Palestinian state, population transfer, full/partial withdrawal, etc.). Another characteristic of the questions concerning the public's perception of security is the absence of reference to "partners": Israel is portrayed as the side that takes the initiative and has the capacity to act, while the Arab states, particularly the Palestinians, play a passive role (Shamir, Ziskind, and Blum-Kulka 1999, 353–77). Public attitudes on security matters are also characterized by contradictions and inconsistencies. For example, while public opinion supports establishment of a Palestinian state – a solution that entails return of the territories – these same respondents often oppose the return of territories when specifically asked. Thus, it is possible that the Israeli-Jewish public indeed holds these two incompatible views, while the political leaders take ambiguous stands, such as proposing a solution that – at the same time – annexes territory, opposes population transfer, gives rights to the Palestinians, and ensures a Jewish majority in the state of Israel (A. Arian 1999, 103–4). Finally, a good part of the Jewish majority that supports a Palestinian state have become skeptical since the end of the second Intifada (2005) and only 30 percent believe there is a possibility of achieving peace with the Palestinians (Bagno-Moldavsky and Ben Meir 2014), blaming the other side for the volatile and suffocating deadlock.

We indicated above that the surveys cover Israeli Jews only. On security matters, most opinion surveys ignore the Arab population, hence the views of about 20 percent of Israeli citizens are not represented at all. Since the opinions of Arab citizens are radically different from those of Jewish citizens, the impression given by these figures is distorted. For example, the figures above about the size of the left in Israel, or about those who support a two-state solution, would change dramatically with the addition of Arab citizens of Israel. Failure to include Arabs in the surveys reflects the predominant view in Israel (over 75%) that Arab citizens should not be partners to "national decisions" such as the future borders of the state (Ben Meir and Shaked 2007, 14, 80).

B. Feeling under Threat

The feeling of being under threat is an important contextual variable for understanding Jewish public opinion in Israel with regard to security. Most Israelis believe that both their personal and national security is at risk. These feelings are intensified by wars and threats of annihilation and weakened by progress toward peace.[32] Underlying the sense of threat is a siege mentality nurtured by the Jewish-Israeli ethos of "behold, a people who lives alone, set apart from other nations" (Numbers 23:9), an ethos that the world is hostile. This perception of being a nation that must face enemies bent on its destruction comes through clearly in the famous statement by then Prime Minister Yitzhak Shamir, "The sea is the same sea, the Arabs are the same Arabs, and the goal is the same goal – destruction of the state of Israel." Such declarations have impact on the ranking of threats by Israeli Jews, and in 2012, they assessed security threats to Israel in the following (descending) order: nuclear weapons in the hands of Iran, chemical and biological weapons in the hands of enemy countries, the widespread renewal of terrorism, shelling of missiles and rockets. The assessment of Arab intentions is a reflection of that sense of threat: During the 1980s and 1990s, between a quarter and half of the Jewish population of Israel believed that Arabs "seek to conquer Israel and destroy most of the Jews who live there." There is a link between feeling threatened and views about security/foreign affairs: The greater the sense of threat and lack of faith in the other's intentions, the more likely to seek hawkish solutions (war, the refusal to return "a single inch" of territory); conversely, the lesser the sense of threat, the greater the willingness to negotiate and make territorial concessions (A. Arian 1999, 58 and 197–99).

While Israelis have generally experienced a sense of *personal* security over the years, this has declined following the suicide bombings since the 1990s, which has increased the sense of vulnerability: Some 80 percent expressed anxiety that they or family members might be hurt by a terrorist. Personal insecurity increases hawkish views and support for aggressive countermeasures. Paradoxically, when the public is asked about its personal and national affairs, Israelis in the 1980s and 1990s assessed their personal situation as better than the national situation: They expressed pessimism on national matters, but optimism on personal affairs. This attitude is confirmed by later surveys in 2004–12, despite the increased Iranian nuclear threats and the shelling by Hezbollah in the north and Hamas in the south (on the 1990s, see A. Arian 1999, 40–48; on the 2000s, see Bagno-Moldavsky and Ben Meir 2014).

The sense of vulnerability is also affected by confidence in the IDF's ability to cope with threats. In the late 1980s and 1990s, some 40 percent of Israelis felt that the IDF had weakened. After the second Lebanon War, half said their confidence in the IDF had declined because of the war, which had undermined Israel's deterrent capacity. Nevertheless, in 2012 a substantial majority of the Jewish respondents

[32] The data that follow are from A. Arian 1999, 32–56 and 87–205; Ben Meir and Shaked 2007, 21, 48; Bagno-Moldavsky and Ben Meir 2014, 49–53.

expressed confidence in Israel's ability to cope with external threats.[33] They also had more confidence in the IDF than in any other state institution.

C. Mapping Attitudes in Society

Until 1967, foreign affairs and security were not highly controversial issues in Israel. Public opinion was fairly homogeneous, and most people supported, or did not question, the policies of the Mapai Party leadership. The War for Independence led to a closing of ranks but a number of issues arose in the wake of the war – the Arab refugees, the status of the ceasefire agreements with the Arab countries (the Rhodes Agreements) – and their implications for the borders of Israel. There was the issue of Israel's "orientation" toward the superpowers – would it join the eastern bloc or the western bloc in the Cold War that had just begun? Surveys conducted by the Institute of Social Research in 1949 found that 73 percent of Israelis objected to allowing the Arab refugees to return, and 80 percent thought the Rhodes Agreements with Egypt were a political achievement. A similar percentage viewed Israel's acceptance into the United Nations as a major victory (Gratch 1973, 195). The military operations across the borders in the early 1950s and the Sinai Campaign in 1956 were also widely supported by the public.

Change set in after 1967, and a deep cleavage has riven Israeli society ever since, dividing the hawks (on the right) and doves (on the left) with regard to the future of the occupied territories. These positions correlate with views about peace agreements with Arab countries, and attitudes toward the Arab citizens of Israel. Put schematically, the unequivocal hawkish position is that territories should not be returned in exchange for peace, opposition to the formulation "two states for two peoples" and establishment of a Palestinian state in any territory, and refusal to evacuate settlements (Rott 2014). The supreme value is the Greater Land of Israel. The unequivocal dovish position is that the occupied territories should be exchanged for peace, acceptance of "two states for two nations," agreement to establishment of an independent Palestinian state in the West Bank and Gaza, and consent to the evacuation of settlements. The supreme values are peace and democracy.

Surveys indicate that dovish views have gained ground over the years. From 1967 until the 1980s, most Israelis expressed hawkish views about returning the occupied territories. Almost 90 percent were not willing to return any part of this territory, or willing to return just a small portion, in exchange for a peace agreement (Yishai 1985, 393). Although the first Intifada (1987) hardened views toward Palestinians in the short run, it contributed in the long run to an approach identified with dovish views – that there is no choice but to enable establishment of an independent political entity in the territories. Events like Palestinian support for Iraq during the first Gulf War, and suicide bombings in the second Intifada, have temporarily halted this trend, but as the years pass, an increasing number of Israeli Jews support dovish views (Figure 14.3). In 1987, only 21 percent supported a Palestinian state, rising to 50 percent in 1997 and 59 percent in 2012. Nevertheless, as noted above, a majority have become rather skeptical about the chance of peace.

[33] Though some 10 percent fewer than in 2006 (Bagno-Moldavsky and Ben Meir 2014, 52).

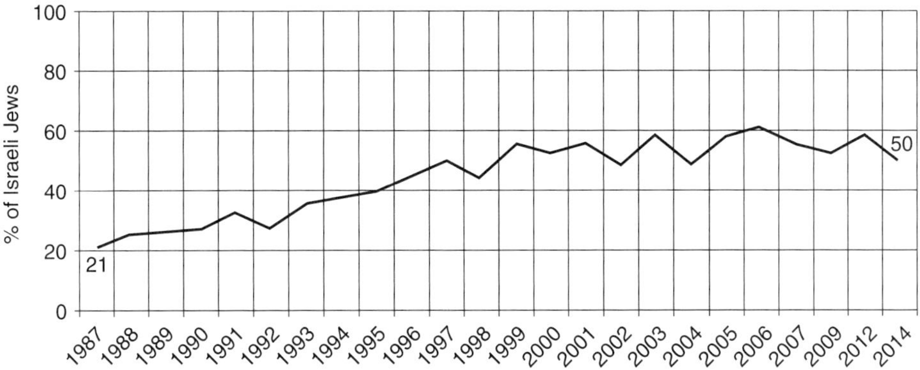

Figure 14.3 Support for establishment of a Palestinian state 1987–2014 (% Israeli Jews)
Source: Bagno-Moldavsky and Ben Meir 2014.

Successful military operations and the early days of war generally lead Israelis to close ranks and increase support for the government. For example, the airstrike against Iraq's nuclear facility in 1981 enhanced support for the government and its security policy (Yishai 1985, 393). During the first Lebanon War, 93 percent of Israelis believed that it was justified, and 70 percent approved the launching of the second Lebanon War, half supporting the notion that the IDF should continue until Hezbollah is destroyed or has returned the captive soldiers (Ben Meir and Shaked 2007, 21). The various Gaza campaigns also won support from Jewish Israelis: Six days after the battles began in late 2008, the vast majority (96%) applauded the operation, and three weeks later, 78 percent defined it as "a success."[34] As for the 2012 operation, a majority (54%) supported the ceasefire with Hamas and 40 percent supported a military operation should Palestinian fire recur (Hebrew University 2012). At the start of the 2014 operation, 91 percent expressed approval (*Mako* 2014); and toward the end, a majority (51%) felt Israel had won the battle as opposed to 45 percent who felt it was a draw (Ben Meir and Einav 2015).

Unilateral measures taken by Israel are also widely endorsed – up to 80 percent supported construction of the separation barrier. Responses to the disengagement from Gaza, on the other hand, were mixed: When originally implemented in 2005, a majority endorsed it; but by 2007, support had fallen to 36 percent, after Israeli civilians continued to be the target of shelling from the Gaza Strip (Ben Meir and Shaked 2007, 21).

In 2012, Iran with nuclear weapons was considered the highest threat to Israel, but a majority of 80 percent supported continuation of the policy of opacity and ambivalence concerning Israel's nuclear capability. An Israeli military attack? Jewish public opinion was split in the middle (Bagno-Moldavsky and Ben Meir 2014). Table 14.4 summarizes the main changes in Israeli public opinion.

[34] Channel 2 news, January 2, 2009. http://reshet.ynet.co.il/9127.aspx and www.haaretz.co.il/hasite/spages/1055752.html [in Hebrew] (accessed June 24, 2010).

Table 14.4 *Changes in consensus since 1967*

Issues on which public opinion has become more dovish
- Return of territories for peace agreements (including returning Sinai for peace with Egypt and land in the Arava for peace with Jordan)
- A two-state solution; establishment of a Palestinian state
- Equal rights for Arab citizens in Israel (which will remain a "Jewish State")

Issues on which public opinion has become more hawkish
- Chance of a peace agreement with the Palestinians
- Israel as a "Jewish State" (or the "national state of the Jews")
- Democracy and civil rights as fundamental values (when in conflict with Jewish values)

Issues about which there is broad public support (around 80%)
- The separation barrier
- Demand for Arab/Palestinian recognition of Israel
- Demilitarization of the Palestinian state

Issues about which there is broad public opposition (around 80%)
- A peace agreement with Syria in exchange for returning the Golan Heights
- Right of return for the 1948 Palestinian refugees
- "Dividing Jerusalem" (i.e., relinquishing East Jerusalem)

No up-to-date data are available on the extent of support or opposition regarding past unilateral withdrawals from Lebanon and the Gaza Strip.
Source: Based on opinion polls of Israeli Jews in Ben Meir and Shaked 2007; Bagno-Moldavsky and Ben Meir 2014.

D. Mapping the Party Positions

Until the 1967 war: In the early years of the state, the differences between political parties revolved around the issues of borders and orientation in foreign affairs – should Israel be pro-west or pro-east? Mapai supported the 1949 ceasefire agreements and shaped pragmatic policies that would allow for retaining the support of both superpowers. Despite the military success, Ben-Gurion refused to allow the IDF to entrench itself beyond Israel's international borders with Lebanon and Egypt. The Mapai position generally won support from the religious parties, the Progressive Party, and the General Zionists. Opposed to these policies were Mapam and the Israeli Communist Party (Maki), on the left, and Herut, led by Menachem Begin on the right, each for different reasons. Mapam opposed a pro-western orientation of foreign affairs and the "Palestinian parts" of the ceasefire with Transjordan and Egypt, because of its support for a binational state in the entire Land of Israel, and its opposition to partition. The Herut movement demanded that the military battle continue, and in its election platform of 1949 it demanded the "liberation" of both banks of the Jordan River. Maki first opposed the idea of partition, but later – backed by the USSR – it supported establishment of the state of Israel and welcomed the ceasefire agreements on condition that an Arab state be established beside the Jewish state. From the early 1950s, Maki adopted an anti-Zionist line (Galnoor 1989, 204). During the 1950s and 1960s, disagreements arose over various issues of foreign affairs and security, such as the reparations from Germany (1951–52), but the serious differences between these parties were mainly on internal matters.

From the 1967 War to the 1993 Oslo Accords: The outcome of the Six Day War divided political parties along a hawk–dove axis, which in Israel is regarded as right–left division. In the years 1967–77, the hawkish view that was espoused by Herut (eventually Gahal and the Likud) and the National Religious Party (NRP) focused on opposition to returning the territories conquered in 1967 – the West Bank, Gaza Strip, Golan Heights, and Sinai. During that period, the ultra-Orthodox parties did not hold hawkish views, and even opposed settlements. Dovish views were less resolute than hawkish views, supporting negotiations with the Arab countries and "territorial compromise" for peace. This was the vague position of the Labor Party, in power until 1977, which had support from Mapam and the Civil Rights Party (Ratz), with important differences over whether *all* the conquered land had to be returned, or only part of it. The election platforms of the Alignment/Labor Party (1968–88) stated that Israel would not return to the pre-1967, armistice "Green Line." All the Zionist, left-wing parties announced support for a "united Jerusalem." The Communist Party (Rakah) and the other Arab parties called for withdrawal to the 1967 Line and for establishment of a Palestinian state, even unilaterally and under PLO control.

In the decade after 1967, the number of Knesset members with hawkish views rose from thirty-seven to sixty-two – those who opposed any territorial compromise and viewed the Jordan River as Israel's eastern border (Yaniv and Pascal 1980, 260–67). Nevertheless, the Likud government signed a peace treaty with Egypt and it was ratified by a large majority in the Knesset. This revealed an inconsistency between the 1977 election platforms of the parties, and the views and votes of their Knesset members as they ratified this peace treaty. From 1977 on, party membership was not the exclusive indicator of views about foreign affairs and security, and MKs sometimes crossed party lines on these issues (Diskin and Galnoor 1990, 710–17). The exception was and still is that religiosity is a predictor of views about foreign affairs and security, and support or opposition to the Oslo Process, for example, was closely correlated with religious self-definition (Hermann and Yuchtman-Yaar 1997, 203).

Since the mid-1990s: The main issue dividing the parties revolved around the conflict with the Palestinians and the future of the territories, and often focused on the Oslo Accords (1993), which affirmed that most of the West Bank would fall under the aegis of the Palestinian Authority. The extremist parties on the right supported population transfer and annexation of the territories, without giving citizenship or civil rights to the Palestinian residents. Right-wing parties – the Likud and the NRP – continued to support the idea of the Greater Land of Israel, opposed negotiations with the PLO, and harshly criticized the Oslo Accords. Left-wing and Arab parties supported the Oslo Accords, negotiations with the PLO, and territorial compromise. The Arab parties and Rakah supported return of all the territories, including East Jerusalem, and restoration of the 1967 line; while the Labor Party and Meretz were in favor of returning most of the territories.

The Oslo Accords reshuffled party platforms with respect to negotiating with the Palestinians. The Likud platform now affirmed the conducting of negotiations, but conditioned them upon reciprocity and the implementation of previous agreements. Under Netanyahu, the Likud government signed the Wye Agreement in 1998, which included scheduled stages for implementing the Oslo Accords, although other right-wing and religious parties continued to oppose the peace initiative with its far-reaching concessions. Subsequently, the NRP, Shas, and the Yisrael B'Aliyah Party resigned from the Barak government in opposition to the Camp David Summit in

2000. Many Likud members opposed the disengagement from Gaza in 2005, which led Sharon to form a new party, Kadima, and win the 2006 election. Events since then – particularly the emergence of Hezbollah and Hamas as security threats, the stalemate in the West Bank, and the changes in the Knesset parties – have blurred the left–right division. In 2015, the Arab party and Meretz support unconditional negotiations with the Palestinians and establishment of a Palestinian state. The position of the Labor Party and particularly the new center parties (Kulanu and Yesh Atid) is rather equivocal, while the Likud and the religious parties are opposed.

Fluctuation in public opinion and party positions reveals the potential for flexibility in security policy. Events and policy decisions create a new reality around which public opinion and the parties reorganize themselves. While public opinion is not the primary shaper of security policy, its impact has somewhat increased in comparison with the past, and is a factor that decision-makers take into account (Hermann 2005).

14.6 Civilian–Military Relations

The military is subordinate and accountable to civilian authority. This is a democratic commandment also anchored in Israeli Basic Law. The elected officials are responsible for setting security policy and strategy, and for the decisions derived from them (Erez 2006, 9–13). The military provides professional expertise to the elected representatives in shaping and setting policies and implements the decisions made. In this sense, there is no difference between security and other areas in terms of the division of labor between the political and professional echelons, including the inevitable overlap in the decision-making process. Indeed, in all countries the voice of the military is very influential in security policy decisions. General MacArthur gave an example of the spirit that subverts the supremacy of civilian authority in the United States – a democracy that has never been under threat of military coup:

> I find in existence a new and heretofore unknown and dangerous concept that the members of our Armed Forces owe primary allegiance or loyalty to those who *temporarily* exercise the authority of the Executive Branch of Government rather than to the country and its Constitution which they are sworn to defend. (quoted in Spanier 1959, 235 [emphasis added]; also see Finer 1962)

According to this approach, the military has a better understanding of what is meant by loyalty to the country and the constitution than those who are "temporarily" elected to office. Had MacArthur made do with "loyalty to the Constitution," one could argue that he was only saying that the military should not obey unconstitutional orders. However, he believed that, even in a democracy, the military is not merely a tool in the service of decision-makers. Ben-Gurion took the opposite view:

> The military does not determine policy, governing, laws, or the conduct of the government and state. The military does not even decide the structure, arrangements, or guidelines of its own action, and obviously does not decide about peace or war. The military is only the implementing arm, the defense and security arm, of the government of Israel. The military organization and its character are shaped solely by civilian authorities: the government, the Knesset, and the voters. The military is subordinate to the government in every sense. (Ben-Gurion 1955, 141)

In Israel, the involvement of the IDF and other security services in setting defense policies is rather substantial compared to other democratic countries. Most scholars agree that this is "a symbiotic relationship" between the defense and civilian systems (Lissak and Kimmerling 1984, i). The disagreement is about the reasons for this phenomenon, its scope and significance, the risks, and its effect on the quality of the defense policies.

A. Government/Ministry of Defense (MoD)/Israel Defense Forces (IDF), Mossad, General Security Service (GSS)

These bodies together determine security policy. Although they are separate institutions that often compete with each other, their systems are intertwined, as we shall clarify below. Also, the senior civilian and military echelons are formally separate, but not with regard to the policymaking process.

Government: In Israel, neither the government nor the prime minister has the staff capacity to engage in an independent analysis of the issues on the agenda, and both rely on the professional staff work of the relevant ministries. The attempt to transform the National Security Council (NSC) into a planning and involved body, whose recommendations are seriously deliberated has not yet been successful. Israel's Foreign Ministry has not carried much clout in setting policies about foreign affairs or security. On the other hand, two bodies directly under the prime minister – the Mossad and the GSS – do wield great influence. Although these are operational bodies, they often provide the only alternative views to those presented to the government by the IDF.

Ministry of Defense (MoD): According to its official site, its main activity is on behalf of the IDF, its "principal client." It is not responsible for military policies or strategy, but is in charge of procurement, finances, property, and the like. The minister of defense, on the other hand, has considerable and sometimes decisive influence on security policy. The prime minister's weight in setting this policy was more significant when he also served as defense minister (as did Ben-Gurion, Eshkol, Begin for short periods, Rabin, Peres for a short period, and Barak); similarly, the prime minister's influence was enhanced when the defense minister lacked clout with the army (as happened with Lavon and Peretz). This pattern was set by Ben-Gurion who removed the defense ministry and the IDF from coalition-party politics, but at the same time created almost total overlap between the defense ministry and the army. The Ben-Gurion pattern also sowed confusion about civilian authority: From its inception, the IDF was indisputably subordinate to the civilian Ben-Gurion, who headed the government and the defense ministry, but the IDF still maintained almost exclusive powers to influence his decisions. This pattern of giving exclusivity to the IDF, which may have been reasonable in the early years of Ben-Gurion, who was a civilian in fact and outlook, and who did not hesitate to oppose IDF recommendations (or accept the resignation of Chief of Staff Yigal Yadin), was already dysfunctional when Sharett was prime minister, Lavon the defense minister, and Dayan the chief of staff (1954–55). This dysfunctionality reached a crisis in relations between Prime Minister Eshkol and the General Staff on the eve of the Six Day War, and severely undermined state security during the Golda Meir–Moshe Dayan–David Elazar era, who were responsible for the Yom Kippur War.

Israel Defense Forces: The IDF is in charge of strategic and tactical planning, and military operations. The assumption is that security policy – from which strategy is derived – is set by the political echelon, which relies heavily on professional military planning, but also takes into account the broader national considerations as well as international relations, economic factors, political constraints, and so on. Research about security-related decision-making in Israel indicates that the IDF has a monopoly not just on staff planning and the formulation of alternatives, but also on the actual shaping of security policy. The government and prime minister rely *almost always* on the exclusive recommendations of the IDF, and *always* when they are acceptable to the defense minister and chief of staff, or when the other security services voice no opposition (Pedatzur 2003, 108; Rosman-Stollman and Kampinsky 2014). By virtue of his office, the chief of staff also plays a special role in policymaking about security matters, and is a regular participant in meetings of the cabinet and the Ministerial Committee for Security Affairs. Nevertheless, his actual power still depends on his relationship with the defense minister and prime minister.

The Mossad and the GSS: These two intelligence agencies are directly accountable to the prime minister, and constitute an independent and sometimes alternative channel for policy evaluations and recommendations. Their importance increased because most of Israel's wars and military confrontations after 1973 concerned entities that are a focus of activity of these two agencies (Palestinians and Lebanese). Nevertheless, neither the Mossad nor the GSS have the capacity for staff planning that the IDF has, and they also lack its official standing (Halevy 2006).

B. Options for Relations among the Government, MoD, and the IDF

In examining the relationship among these three spheres, let us set aside two unrealistic options – a rigid, hierarchical chain of command or an absolute monopoly of one of the spheres. Rather, let us focus on the areas of overlap, their significance, and the dynamic of change. Naturally during times of war or emergency, military considerations override all others, while during times of peace, civilian considerations gain more attention. What are the dominant considerations in Israel in each of these spheres? For the military (including here the Mossad and GSS), the considerations pertain almost exclusively to operations and intelligence. The government – the supreme democratic authority – cannot lose sight of overall civilian, strategic considerations in favor of the other two. But what about the Defense Ministry – is it an independent sphere – more civilian in some situations and more military in others? Is the Defense Ministry the military's emissary to the government, or the civilian emissary to the military? From 1948 to 2015, sixteen defense ministers held office (for no less than a year, some for multiple terms), and seven did not come via the IDF. Is the background of the defense minister critical? Until 1967, all the defense ministers were civilian; the turnabout came with the appointment of Moshe Dayan in early June 1967. This was the first time the office of prime minister was separated from defense minister, and friction immediately developed between Eshkol and Dayan, leading to the need for an agreement to divide up the functions (Yehuda Ben Meir 1995, 101–2; Peri 1983, 136–38). Ever since, with the exception of fewer than ten aggregated years under Peres, Begin, Arens, and Peretz, all subsequent defense ministers came from the military.

We present below four schematic options for relations among the government, the Ministry of Defense (MoD), and the IDF (plus to some extent the Mossad and GSS). For each option, examples are given of wars or military operations. During the Ben-Gurion era, the division of function among the three spheres was entirely different, therefore most of the examples are from subsequent years (examples based on Peri 1983; Yehuda Ben Meir 1995; Galnoor 1996, 156–75; Erez 2006; Peri 2006).

Option 1: The Government Imposes Absolute Authority

This is ostensibly the formal situation, but because of the weight of the defense system, it is rare for the prime minister and government to impose decisions opposed by the defense minister and chief of staff, or without their knowledge. This has been more common for peace initiatives (e.g., contacts between Foreign Minister Moshe Dayan and Egyptian leaders, which preceded Sadat's visit to Jerusalem in 1977), or decisions about territorial withdrawal (from Lebanon in 2000, or the Gaza Strip in 2005).

The most enlightening example of civilian supremacy is the almost single-handed stand taken by Levi Eshkol, then prime minister and defense minister, against extremely heavy pressure from the General Staff during the "waiting period" leading up to the 1967 war. The hesitation of Eshkol and a few ministers to the immediate launch of a preemptive strike, and their intent to first exhaust diplomatic channels, was met with a breach of discipline from the top military officers (later called "the Generals' Revolt"), and derisive comments in the media about Eshkol. Facing the IDF with its halo of victories stood a government that did not inspire confidence and a prime minister with an image of weakness and indecision. The confrontation was also that of a personal ethos: the young, native-born generals, brimming with self-confidence, facing off against the elderly political hacks in government, holding onto a bumbling and fearful diaspora mentality. And in the center for two long and bitter weeks, Levi Eshkol stood firm, mobilizing diplomatic support for the military operation, without which the victory of the Six Day War would not have had such resonance (for better and worse). This was democratic civilian primacy in the full sense of the term, as a result of which the "Generals' Revolt" did not materialize. Some view this event as proof that a military coup in Israel is highly unlikely, if not impossible (Gluska 2007). Eshkol paid a high price for this, however: He was forced to step down as defense minister and was replaced by Moshe Dayan, and the 1967 victory was not attributed to him. He died a short time later. The crisis of the "waiting period" did not detract from the power of the military or its dominance vis-à-vis the political leadership, *inter alia* because the military operation was successfully executed, while the government had no strategic policy whatsoever and no non-military goals for the war (Yehuda Ben Meir 1995, 145).

A different example is Menachem Begin's decision to destroy Iraq's nuclear reactor in 1981 (Nakdimon 1987). According to available sources, the initiative came from the political leadership – Prime Minister Begin and several other ministers – while the IDF and Mossad harbored serious reservations about the operation, even opposition. This raises an interesting question: Can the government dictate a military operation that the military opposes for professional reasons, in the same way it can order the Ministry of Transportation to pave a road? This is highly doubtful, and indeed the indecision continued for a year and a half, dividing MoD, the Ministerial

Committee for Security Affairs, and the government. The final decision was taken in the wake of changed circumstances (the Iran–Iraq War), Prime Minister Begin's assumption of the MoD after Ezer Weizman's resignation, and Chief of Staff Rafael Eitan's mobilization of military support.

The disengagement from Gaza in the summer of 2005 was ostensibly a contrary example – a measure initiated by politicians and executed by the military, despite the disagreement between them (Misgav and Label 2008). Disengagement was a political move, however, and not a military operation. The dearth of examples in which the civilian authority commanded the army and other security bodies to embark upon a military operation they opposed should not be surprising, because of the obvious reluctance to take responsibility for a deed that endangers lives. Nevertheless, this reasoning should apply in the reverse situation as well: when the IDF tries to dictate a military action to the government. Here the experience is different, as we shall see, but first we present a common intermediate option in which the defense minister is the key player.

Option 2: The Defense Minister Dictates Policy (and Its Execution) to Both the Civilian and Military Echelons

To isolate a real instance of this option, we look only at cases in which the prime minister was not also serving as defense minister. In these cases, the defense minister managed to exclude the government and military from real involvement in the decision-making process. Experience suggests that, to accomplish this, the defense minister must be a former military figure with security credentials respected by civilian and military leaders alike, as well as the public. The most common precondition for this is a dominant defense minister with a prime minister who has not come up through the IDF ranks: Dayan during the terms of Eshkol and Meir (1967–74); Sharon during Begin's term (1981–83); and to some extent Rabin during the terms of Peres and Shamir (1984–90). In each of these periods, as illustrated below, significant events happened in which the defense minister's conception largely dictated the overall policy to the government and the IDF. It did not happen, for instance, in the Gulf War (1991) when Arens was defense minister and Shamir prime minister, both of them with no IDF background.[35]

In 1967, Defense Minister Dayan was in effect also "Minister of the Occupied Territories" – his views about relations with the Palestinians became unofficial government policy, and the basis for the operation of the military government. Some examples: the open border with Jordan, non-intervention in the daily lives of the Palestinians, the cultivation of local leadership, the transfer of IDF camps to the territories, etc. (Gazit 1995). All these evolved from Dayan's approach that there was no need to act in haste and find a solution to the occupation, because time was on Israel's side and a "functional compromise" would eventually emerge based on Israel's military control over the territories and full autonomy for the Palestinians. Dayan's approach did not change despite Palestinian resistance to the Israeli occupation soon after the 1967 war, which gradually escalated. This was also true for

[35] During the second Intifada (2000–5), three ex-IDF officers served as ministers of defense – Barak (also prime minister), Ben Eliezer, and Mofaz, but the latter two did not dictate policy to Prime Minister Sharon.

Dayan's views about Egypt and Syria, which were based on two assumptions proven false by the 1973 war and thereafter: first, that the Khartoum resolutions (no to peace with, recognition of, or negotiations with Israel as long as the occupation lasts) proved that none of the Arabs were potential partners for Israeli concessions; and, second, that the Arab states were incapable of, or would not dare to start, a war with Israel. Until 1970, the unity government in Israel was incapable of deciding one way or another, and, even afterwards, Dayan's approach was accepted by most government ministers, few challenging the conduct of the military government in the territories.

Another example of policy dictated by the defense minister was the first Lebanon War (A. Naor 1986). Ariel Sharon became defense minister in August 1981 in the second Begin government, and shortly thereafter he presented the government with his Oranim Plan for fighting terrorism in southern Lebanon. Although the plan was not approved, Sharon instructed the IDF to continue surreptitiously working on a grand plan (Oranim-B) that included strategic goals vis-à-vis Lebanon and Syria. This grand plan was not known to the prime minister, the Ministerial Committee for Security Affairs, or even the Mossad (Yehuda Ben Meir 1995, 152). After the attempted assassination of Israel's ambassador to London, the defense minister and chief of staff presented the limited Oranim Plan to the government. The government approved a 72-hour military operation that evolved into a full-scale war with Lebanon and Syria, continued for four months, and took the lives of 650 Israelis and an estimated 18,000 Palestinians and Lebanese.[36] Following this war, the IDF remained in Lebanese territory for eighteen years. Without entering the debate about what government ministers knew, what exactly they had approved, and to what extent the chief of staff was dragged along or was leading the campaign, the policy objectives were those of Defense Minister Sharon, and when the plan won the chief of staff's support, the politicians could not stand up to them: "The Lebanon War was a colossal failure of civilian oversight of strategic planning" (Yehuda Ben Meir 1995, 156).

The first Intifada (1987–91) illustrates another type of role of the defense minister (Schiff and Ya'ari 1990; Mitzna 2006, 55–60). This popular uprising, which began twenty years after the conquest of the territories, surprised the government and the IDF, but the Israeli reaction was the opposite of what was expected: Many ministers demanded that severe measures be taken against the Palestinian civilian population, but Chief of Staff Dan Shomron staunchly opposed this. Peri thinks that the IDF reached the conclusion before the political leadership that there was no military solution to the uprising, and that Israel should negotiate with the PLO (Peri 2006, 34–35). Between them stood Defense Minister Rabin, who – with the full support of Prime Minister Shamir – directly supervised IDF operations against the Palestinians, and protected the army from the over-involvement of the politicians. This policy, more military than political, was primarily that of one man until, under American pressure, Shamir agreed to participate in the Madrid Conference of 1991, which paved the way for recognition of the PLO. The question of whether Rabin's change of heart began

[36] Different sources give different figures: 19,000 (AP, March 5, 1991); 17,825 (*Washington Post*, September 3, 1982); and 12,000, including those killed in 1978; see also http://necrometrics.com/20c300k.htm (accessed May 5, 2016).

during that period or later does not alter the fact that as defense minister he dictated the policy during the first Intifada – for the government and the IDF both.

Option 3: The Defense Minister and the IDF Dictate to the Government

This option overlaps the previous one to a large extent, as evident in the above examples. What is distinctive here is that, from the outset, the defense system (the IDF and defense minister) cooperate to dictate to the government or even force a specific policy on it. The most salient instance was mentioned above – the decision to go to war in 1967 after Dayan was appointed defense minister. Another example concerns not military action, but refraining from it – in 1975 when Chief of Staff Mordechai Gur, with full backing from Defense Minister Shimon Peres, refused to execute Prime Minister Rabin's order to evacuate settlers from an attempted settlement (Sebastia). Rabin later remarked that backing down was the biggest mistake of his first term as prime minister (Rabin 1990). As noted, the combination of the clout of the army and the stature of the defense minister leaves little room for the government to exercise its policymaking power.

Questions about the excessive influence of the defense system first arose in the Lavon affair. As a result, the Ministerial Committee for Security Affairs – founded in 1953 as a way for the government to oversee the IDF – was bolstered, and the issue faded from public attention during the relatively quiet Eshkol premiership. The question of the committee's authority was swallowed up in the crisis preceding the Six Day War, and eclipsed altogether in the euphoria that followed. Before and during the Yom Kippur War, however, Defense Minister Dayan was responsible not just for shaping security policy, but also for operational decisions, and questions arose about the division of responsibility with the chief of staff.[37] The Agranat Commission seems to have finally established the principle that the defense minister is a civilian office and not the super-chief of staff or the IDF supreme commander who directs the chief of staff in field operations (Agranat Commission 1975, 25). This principle was formulated in the Basic Law: The Military, and became part of Israel's constitution. Prime Minister Begin expressed this clearly when he said that the defense minister does not represent the army to the government, but rather represents the government to the army (A. Naor 2006, 42).

However, Begin did not manage to apply this rule to Sharon during the first Lebanon War. He was more careful after Sharon's dismissal, appointing Moshe Arens, a civilian, the next defense minister. This phenomenon of the defense minister and chief of staff joining forces to dictate to the government has not disappeared, however, but taken a new form. From 1996 through 2015, six out of eight defense ministers who followed Arens were military men: Mordechai, Arens (for several months before the 1999 election), Barak, Ben-Eliezer, Mofaz, Peretz, again Barak, and Ya'alon. Consequently, the relationship between the defense minister and chief of staff has become less complex, as evidenced in the agreements between them about the various military operations in Gaza (2008–14; see Table 14.1). Yet, the question of the relevance of military experience came up again with the appointment of Amir

[37] Chief of Staff David Elazar claimed that Defense Minister Dayan interfered in operational matters and hence had responsibility for the decisions then made. See Elazar's letter to the prime minister quoted in Peri 1983, 140.

Peretz as defense minister in the Olmert government in May 2006. What seemed at first to be an important milestone in the appointment of a civilian defense minister – who was "neither general nor admiral," in the words of Peretz himself – turned into a debate after the second Lebanon War about the credentials required for this office. Peretz's resignation after publication of the Winograd Commission's Interim Report stemmed from the fact that, in his few months on the job, he had little influence on either going to war or how to conduct it (Winograd Commission 2007, 179–80). Opinions about Peretz's functioning as defense minister are contradictory: Some criticized him for a lack of military experience; others for unwillingness to exercise civilian judgment.

Option 4: The IDF Dictates to the Government and the Defense Minister

During the pre-state period, the principle was established that the underground military organizations were subordinate to their respective civilian leadership (Bar-Or 1998, 267; Horowitz and Lissak 1978, 242–46; History of the Haganah 1954, 1018; Lissak 1983, 53). In Chapter 1, we presented the Altalena affair, the assassination of Bernadotte, and the dismantling of the Palmach as constitutive events in defining the authority of the government over the armed forces during the formative period of the state. Nevertheless, as early as Moshe Sharett's premiership (1954–55), the IDF carried out cross-border retaliatory raids without government approval, while the intelligence disaster in Egypt and its aftermath revealed the poorly defined interface among the government, the defense minister, and the chief of staff. Over the years, especially after the Yom Kippur War, civilian oversight of the IDF gradually increased, partially in response to pressure from the media and public opinion, so much so that it is hard to imagine a military coup in Israel. Nevertheless, questions do arise periodically about whether the IDF is too dominant, whether it is the IDF that in practice dictates government policy – whether Israel is "an army that has a state" (Sheffer and Barak 2013).

In the discussion here, we look at the IDF's role in government policymaking, and the impact of recommendations made by the chief of staff. The Agranat and Winograd Commissions pointed to over-reliance of the political echelon on the IDF status reports – the government's dependence on the exclusive assessments and recommendations provided by the chief of staff. Of course, the government may rely on any sources it chooses, but reliance on the military evolved many years ago, and the IDF has thwarted all efforts to bring in additional, outside sources of information, analysis, and recommendations to the government. The absence of alternative sources has taken its toll on the construction of reality. Some claim, for example, that Israel missed an opportunity for negotiating with Egypt prior to the Yom Kippur War because of "the conception" instilled in the government by the defense minister and the IDF (Galnoor 2008, 263–81). This monopoly of the government's ear by the IDF brings up other questions: To what extent should the chief of staff narrow his professional military assessment to exclude political issues and positions?[38] Is it possible and practical to demand that this distinction be made? At the very least, is

[38] An example of blurred boundaries can be found in Chief of Staff Dan Halutz's words to the government prior to the second Lebanon War, noting that the purpose of the operation was not to achieve military victory, but that Israel's reaction must be sufficiently harsh to stimulate international pressure (Winograd Commission 2007, 120).

the chief of staff obliged to present other views held by IDF personnel to the government? And if there is a conflict between the views of the defense minister and those of the government, whose orders should the chief of staff follow?[39]

Examples are sparse in which the IDF entirely dictates policy because of the stature of the defense minister, especially if the minister had been a high-ranking military officer. Sometimes perplexed politicians turn to the IDF to help them make decisions. It was the IDF's idea to start the Six Day War, for example, and the government had no plan of its own. In other words, the IDF is not generally faced with the problem of whether it should obey the policy of the government, as the IDF is often asked to initiate this policy (Benjamini 1983, 67). To date, no chief of staff has been directly dismissed by the government, and in the few cases that the chief of staff was forced to resign, the circumstances were different: Yadin resigned in 1952 because of differences with Ben-Gurion about budget cuts; Elazar resigned in 1974 because of the Agranat Commission report; Ya'alon's term was not extended by a year (2005) because of his opposition to the Gaza disengagement (Ya'alon 2008); and Halutz resigned in 2006 in anticipation of publication of the Winograd Commission report. In the two examples below, the IDF did not engage in a coup, but dictated its own approach, leaving a very narrow margin for independent, civilian judgment.

First – the military conception dictated the policies in Lebanon from the outbreak of the civil war there in 1975. Following Operation Litani in 1978, a security zone was established in southern Lebanon under the control of the IDF. Defense Minister Sharon used this involvement to embroil Israel in Lebanese politics in 1982, and later, in keeping with the IDF's demand, the withdrawal from Lebanon did not include the expanded security zone, which was turned over to the South Lebanon Army (the SLA). The IDF remained in the security zone and opposed another withdrawal in 1985, even though the enemy in this zone had changed – it was now Hezbollah instead of the Palestinians: "The conception that the security zone was a strategic asset that served Israel's needs went unchallenged until the late 1990s" (A. Sela 2007, 26–27). Eventually, it became clear that Israel's military presence in southern Lebanon was a liability; by spring 1998, the government declared its willingness to withdraw in exchange for suitable security arrangements. Chief of Staff Mofaz objected, however, and continued to object even when the government under Barak ordered the IDF to carry out a full withdrawal from Lebanon in May 2000, hoping it would still be able to protect the security zone and the SLA (Shelah 2006, 69–71; Peri 2006, 94–95). This retreat from Lebanon up to the international border appears prima facie to be a good example of a government decision duly executed by the IDF, but it was accompanied by a defiant declaration by the chief of staff that "The IDF does not decide on its own missions," implying that he does not take responsibility for the results. Indeed, the retreat seems to have had a traumatic effect on the

39 The formal answer to this last question is clear: Although the chief of staff is subordinate to the defense minister, in the event of conflict between the positions of the defense minister and the government, the chief of staff must accept the authority of the government (Kremnitzer and Bendor 2000, 47–48). During the Yom Kippur War, for example, the "kitchen cabinet" authorized the chief of staff to decide about launching an assault, despite the opposition of Defense Minister Moshe Dayan (Gazit 2006, 40). The court also ruled that government decisions obligate the chief of staff, even if opposed by the defense minister (*Dawikat et al. v. State of Israel et al.* 1979).

IDF, as evidenced by its determination to return to Lebanon in July 2006 to take care of the "unfinished business" with Hezbollah.

Second – the second Lebanon War is another example of the IDF's virtual monopoly of policy decisions. Although here, too, the defense minister and prime minister made the recommendations, and the government's endorsement means that it bore full responsibility, nevertheless the pattern remained identical – thirty-three years after the Yom Kippur War, and twenty-four years after the first Lebanon War. Who actually initiated, planned, and presided over the second Lebanon War? The Interim Report of the Winograd Commission does not draw an explicit conclusion, but it does point out serious flaws in the decision-making process: The government hastily embarked upon a broad-based military action that escalated into a war without having a clear plan or defined objectives. The political leadership, and the prime minister in particular, relied too heavily on the chief of staff and the military, without consulting independent sources. During the first days, no serious discussions were held by the political or military echelons or jointly about the operation, its objectives, and how to achieve them. No alternatives were presented to the decision-makers, and no attention was paid to other bodies that sometimes participate in such deliberations (e.g., the heads of the Mossad, the GSS, and the National Security Council) (Winograd Commission 2007, 1 and 199–200). In short, the second Lebanon War demonstrated once again a flawed pattern in which senior military officers wield influence beyond the bounds of their expertise.

Within the broad category of the IDF's ability to oppose the prime minister and defense minister, we should mention the case of Israel's policy toward Iran. According to Barak, Prime Minister Netanyahu, himself as defense minister, and other ministers supported an attack on Iran's nuclear installations. But the strong opposition of two chiefs of staff, the heads of the Mossad and the GSS, and several ministers prevented the military operation in 2010 and again in 2012 (as testified by Barak in Kfir and Dor 2015, 317–31).

C. Is the Military in Israel Subordinate to Civilian Authority?

As for the "proper" relations between the military and political leadership, some believe that a security (and security-obsessed) system operates in Israel – an interwoven complex of civilian and military agencies rooted in a society that educates for militarism.[40] Others hold that the military and political echelons fulfill roles that are separate, but unavoidably overlapping – not ideal, but reasonable cooperation. Ben Meir suggests that civilian authority not be rigidly defined, but seen as a balance that fluctuates with social needs or along the axis of emergency–non-emergency. As examples of proper balance, he cites the decision to cancel development of the Lavi aircraft and the decision to refrain from responding to the Iraqi Scud missiles that struck Israel during the 1991 Gulf War, both decisions taken after intense debate and disagreement among the government, defense ministry, and the IDF. In the conclusion to his 1995 book, Ben Meir wrote that IDF–civilian relations are basically positive, healthy, and balanced. In 2003, he wrote that the military echelon has deeply internalized the democratic principle of subordination to the elected civilian

[40] For a survey of various approaches, see Peri 1996, 94–112.

representatives (Yehuda Ben Meir 1995, 12, 114, 161–68, 178; Yehuda Ben Meir 2006, 19–21). Ehud Barak holds a similar view: "Relations between the military and political echelons in Israel are fundamentally healthy, though not perfect" (E. Barak 2003, 29).[41] Peri believes that military–political relations in Israel are indeed complex because even though the IDF views desired policies through a security lens, it has also supported peace initiatives. Nevertheless, Peri writes (2006, 22, 253–55) that the military does shape defense policy in Israel, and tends to exert a militaristic and conservative influence.

What can be learned from the options presented above? Had it not been for the second Lebanon War, it could have been said that the process of civilian leadership taking the reins of security policy has been slow and drawn out, but heading in the right direction. The Lavon affair dissolved the Ben-Gurion ethos of security policy being ostensibly "above" politics and legitimate differences, and brought external oversight to the defense system. The Yom Kippur War shattered the myth that the IDF must not be publicly criticized. Just as the defense budget is no longer entirely confidential, so too public discourse about security issues has become more prevalent, with the glaring exception of Israel's nuclear policy. By now the government has taken some independent security initiatives, whether leaving Lebanon in 2000 in response to public pressure, or evacuating the Gaza Strip in 2005. The media too became somewhat more critical after having mistakenly held its tongue prior to the debacle of the Yom Kippur War. Over the years, there have also been fewer cases of the IDF unilaterally dictating policy to the government.

And yet the 2006 Lebanon War demonstrated that these changes were apparently superficial. The moment the IDF was bent on comprehensive military action – whether justified or to erase the humiliating retreat of 2000 – alternative solutions were not raised or seriously debated. The question was not whether military action should be taken against Hezbollah, but how and when; and it became evident that the prime minister, and coincidentally the defense minister, did not exercise independent judgment, and when the chief of staff convinced both of them, the government seems not to have had a mind of its own. Thus in many respects, the situation in 2006 returned to the previous pattern of government/MoD/IDF relationships.

In sum, the IDF's influence over defense strategy and overall national policy is too powerful, often exclusive, and decisive. Other bodies with entirely different perspectives should balance it. Why this has not happened thus far is related to the broader issue of militarism.

14.7 On Militarism

> We, a group of feminist women and men, are convinced that we need not live in a soldiers' state. Today, Israel is capable of a determined peace policy. It need not be a militarized society. We are convinced that we ourselves, our children, our partners, need not go on being endlessly mobilized, need not go on living as warriors … We now realize that the words "national security" have often masked calculated decisions to choose military

[41] For a similar view – that the IDF should be a full partner to the political echelon in shaping policies – see Ya'alon 2006, 17.

> action for the achievement of political goals ... We will not go on being mobilized, raising children for mobilization, supporting mobilized partners, brothers, fathers, while those in charge of the country go on deploying the army easily, rather than shaping other solutions. (New Profile 2007)[42]

The view presented above, regardless of how many people hold it, exemplifies a profound shift among Jews in Israel. While mobilization for security purposes was in the past perceived as necessary and unavoidable to ensure the existence of Israel, today the voices heard are more diverse. The broad consensus around the ethos of security no longer exists, and questions are being raised about the degree of militarization of Israeli society.

Militarism is defined as "The prevalence of military spirit and ideals among the people. The political condition characterized by the predominance of the military class in government and administration. The tendency to regard military efficiency as the paramount interest of the state."[43] In a militaristic society and culture, the army is the foremost symbol, wars are at the heart of the collective experience, and security issues top the public agenda (Kimmerling 1993, 123–40). Militarism also means the tendency to overuse violent means to resolve political problems (Ben-Eliezer 1998).

Phrases used in Israel such as "the people's army" or "a nation in uniform" are attempts to gloss over the thorns of militarism: The army is important only as a tool, and citizens are willing to mobilize only because self-defense is at stake. These phrases, however, suggest a blurring of boundaries between the individual, society, and the state, and the primacy of military needs. Horowitz tried to overcome the difficulty of this duality, and in his 1982 article he offered a somewhat vague definition: The IDF is "a civilianized military in a partially militarized society" (1982, 77–106). Later, Horowitz and Lissak described the dual challenge posed by security in Israel: On the one hand, militarization of the civilian sector is expressed in widespread mobilization for security needs; on the other hand, the military sector has been "civilianized," expressed in the army's openness to civilian influence.[44] Ben-Dor noted the two levels in the IDF – career officers in the standing army, and soldiers and reservists doing compulsory service in the army – a duality that, in his opinion, prevents militarization and creates open borders between the military and society (1977, 421–22).

Some maintain that this may have been the case until the 1970s, but that changes occurred later, while others claim that research about civil–military relations was biased from the outset and did not expose the militarism in Israeli society (Kimmerling 1993, 129–30). The harshest critic of militarism in Israeli society was Hebrew University professor Yeshayahu Leibowitz, a highly regarded intellectual and outspoken social critic, who warned right after 1967 that this war would turn the IDF into an occupation army, and Israel into "a Shabak state" (the Hebrew nickname for the General Security Service). Recent research suggests a new direction of developments: Israeli militarism is no longer characteristic of the entire society, but only of specific groups that had once been defined as marginal: the nationalist religious, Mizrahim (Jews originating from Muslim countries) in lower and middle

42 Also see Ben-Eliezer 1998.

43 *Oxford English Dictionary* 1970, VI: 438.

44 Referred to as "the porous borders between the military and civilian sectors" (Horowitz and Lissak 1989, 106).

socioeconomic classes, and immigrants from the former Soviet Union. According to this hypothesis, younger and middle-class Jews, primarily Ashkenazim (Jews of European descent), do not contribute their share anymore, and so the previous, all-inclusive "citizens' army" is gradually being replaced by something else – perhaps de-militarism coupled with re-militarism. Accordingly, it is not only Arab citizens and ultra-Orthodox Jews who do not ascribe intrinsic value to army service, but middle-class Israelis as well (Kimmerling 1993, 129–30).

These issues provide the context for three specific subjects that we discuss below: the effect of the security situation on Israeli society; the militarization of politics; and the politicization of the army.

A. The Militarization of Society

The feeling of most Jews in Israel, and many outside it, is that the existence of the State of Israel provides them greater security from a world hostile to Jews. This fear is so deep-seated among Jews that it is beyond the ability of leaders, whether civilian or military, to uproot it. When the civilian David Ben-Gurion and the general Yigal Allon warned (1960, 228) of the danger of "the destruction of the Third Temple," Jews were shaken to the core, as the fear of the Holocaust emanated from these words. Thus, a discussion about the militarization of Israeli society must begin from these deep layers, because if militarism does characterize Israel, it may be rooted not in the army, but in the community itself. The same fear could be observed in Israel in the 2000s from possible Iranian nuclear weapons, despite Israel's alleged nuclear deterrent ability (Pedatzur 2007). And yet it is possible that, over the course of time, the existential fears that gripped Israel on the eve of the 1956 Sinai Campaign and the 1967 Six Day War may have evolved into a reverence for military force (Barzilai and Inbar 1996, 19–50). Perhaps those glorious battlefield victories paved the way, making it possible for society to place military matters at the top of its priorities for a long time, whether by force of circumstance or habit, and be just a step away from militarism. In what follows, we consider militarism in this sense of the danger of going overboard, not the assumption that Israeli society is under the boot of its security/military leaders or that Israel is a "military democracy."

The data about the centrality of security in Israeli life have already been presented. In addition to compulsory military service, long years of reserve duty, enormous state expenditures on defense, and more, is there a subjective layer? What is the effect on Israeli men of spending five years of their adult life in uniform – three years in compulsory service and another aggregate twenty to thirty months in reserve duty – not to mention call-ups at times of emergency? And what is the significance of the fact that every adult Israeli has personally experienced at least one war? Are militaristic factors an organizing principle of Jewish-Israeli culture? A foreigner to Israel who observes the number of civilians walking around with weapons, the security inspections at the entrance to every public facility, the pre-draft pep talks in high schools, the expertise of average citizens about military matters, and so forth could easily conclude that life in Israel is indeed militaristic. In addition, there is the tendency of citizens to believe that there is "no alternative" to military means for coping with the conflict and terrorism (Stein 1990). But after terrorist attacks in other countries in recent years, the situation in Israel is no longer exceptional, even in terms of the impact of security on the lives of its citizens. And still many countries, including Israel, tend to favor military solutions to political problems.

Clearly the long years of conflict and ongoing tension have left their mark on Israeli citizens, as individuals and as a society. Israelis are exposed to a military environment even before they are conscripted – in schools, para-military (*Gadna*) training, Memorial Day ceremonies, war stories told by family members, and many other ways. "The situation" or "the conflict" has cast its spell over Israeli culture, from army entertainment troupes and the use of military language in civilian life to architecture and the practices of bereavement (Shamgar Handelman 1986; M. Ben-David 1990; Handelman and Handelman 1991, 3–17; Sivan 1991; Miron 1992; O. Almog 1993, 179–210; Levinger 1993; Lomsky-Feder and Ben-Ari 1999; Lomsky-Feder 2003, 366–68; Yossi Katz 2014). Some have called it "the culture of security," whether describing the pervasive security-political norm or society as a whole (Horowitz and Lissak 1989; Pedatzur 2003, 87–117).

And there are other questions: Has the security situation led to emigration from Israel? Or rising intolerance, violence, or corruption? We noted that the results of all the post-1967 wars were controversial – did this affect the atmosphere of trust within society, or the distrust of politicians? Hofnung points to another result: "Over time and wherever it exists, maintaining a state of emergency while safeguarding democracy is possible, but it takes a heavy toll" (1991, 346). In the concluding chapter of this book we raise a related question: What is the effect of the "culture of security" on the democratic values of Israeli society? When most citizens believe that democracy "interferes with" security, and that democratic values can be set aside to allow the army to get the job done (as in the slogan, "Let the IDF Win!"), is this not already a militaristic society?

On the other hand, there is also evidence of diminished militarism. Since the 1973 war, an inside debate has ensued about the character of society, including the dangers of militarization. Security rationale no longer remains unchallenged, as evidenced by the changed rhetoric for justifying the settlements in the territories occupied in 1967. They were originally founded under Labor Party rule and were justified by security reasons – in the Golan Heights, the Jordan Valley, and even in the so-called "land barrier" between the Gaza Strip and Sinai. With the rise to power of the Likud in 1977, the justifications for settlements remained mixed until the Elon Moreh case in the High Court, when the IDF's formal legal response to a Peace Now petition put an end to the claims that the settlements were necessary for security.[45] Ever since, distinctions are commonly made: between "political" and "non-political" settlements, "authorized" and "unauthorized" settlements, "legal settlements" and "illegal outposts," etc. The evacuation of settlements from Gaza in 2005 – which had previously been considered necessary for security – was justified because, *inter alia*, they were considered a security liability.

Another possible symptom of diminished militarism in Israeli society is the lower motivation to serve in the IDF – this is true for both the regular army and the reserves – and the growing number of young men and women who refuse to serve.[46] Until the early 1980s (the first Lebanon War), avoiding the draft was not

[45] *Dawikat et al. v. State of Israel et al.* 1979.

[46] On the link between lower motivation and refusal to serve, see Epstein 2003, 215–39.

considered an option because military service was regarded as a key component of one's citizenship as well as an entry ticket to Israeli society. Being graded "profile 21," meaning exempt from military service, was regarded as a mark of Cain, limiting one's ability to integrate in society (Galnoor 2003). However, several converging processes contributed to lowering the proportion of those drafted: A population growth spurt meant that the IDF did not need the entire age cohort for compulsory service, especially not the young women, but also not as many young men. However, the IDF was reluctant to apply a selective draft, preferring to be more lenient about exemptions, and thereby helped create a category of "draft dodgers." Some fear that if this becomes widespread, there will be an insufficient supply of suitable candidates for the IDF.

Because of changing values, as noted, draft dodging has taken a toll not only on marginalized social groups, but also on educated, middle-class young people from the urban center.[47] A different view is held by Stuart A. Cohen, who argues that the source of change is the diminished status of the military as a profession because of the penetration of economic market considerations, its need to rely on civilian technologies, and the post-modern zeitgeist in Israel (2006, 769–88). In 2013, about 26 percent of young men were not drafted (Pesso 2013), compared with about 12 percent in 1990. Some of this can be ascribed to demographic change: The largest group among those not drafted were those who declared that "Torah study is their profession," i.e., ultra-Orthodox young men, who were fewer than 4 percent in 1980, but rose to 14 percent in 2013. In 2008, 11 percent were not drafted on various other personal grounds (such as disability, a criminal record, living abroad). And 5 percent were not drafted because of "incompatibility with army service" – this is the category branded "shirkers" (Barda 2007). Among the draftees, a slight decline in motivation is perceptible, and this is more evident with regard to service in combat units (70% in 2013). In 1974, two-thirds of young respondents said they would serve even without a compulsory draft. This number was cut in half within two decades. Those who said in 2008 and 2009 that they would try to avoid service (23% and 14%, respectively) or serve only in non-combat roles (13% and 12%) seem to be responding to the events of the moment, such as the Gaza campaign in late 2008 (Arian et al. 2005–10: 2008; Arian, Philippov, and Knafelman 2009). In parallel, motivation to do reserve duty has declined. This was already evident during the first Lebanon War, and is related to conscientious objection for specific political reasons, both left and right (see below) (Ben-Eliezer 2003, 40–50). The drop in motivation also reflects rising individualism in society. Many young people are no longer willing to sacrifice a long and significant period of their lives to military service, and many reserve duty soldiers do not want to be perceived as "suckers" who abandon their jobs and families for the sake of reserve duty. On the other hand, there has been an increase in the willingness to do military service that offers incentives, such as serving in elite units or learning high-tech skills that can be used in civilian life. And participation in the military of the ultra-Orthodox has increased in recent years. Equally interesting, fewer religious women choose the option of not serving and decide to be drafted – from 935 in 2010 to 1,830 in 2014 (*Haaretz* Supplement, September 25, 2015, in Hebrew).

[47] Yagil Levy calls this a class-related "motivation crisis" (2003, 236–63).

Another manifestation of diminished militarism in Israel resulting from the demystification of the army is the increasing criticism of parents about how the army is treating their children. Until the 1990s, parental involvement was confined to visiting the base on weekends and attending ceremonial events (e.g., course graduations). Parents, like the rest of society, had been full partners to the security ethos. Since then, however, parents have played a more critical role in what happens to their drafted children. The army is tolerant of the PTA-type involvement that relates to the IDF as if it were school and the commanders, the teachers. Parents may have the private phone number of commanding officers or approach them to prevent abuse of their children or to defend a "soldiers' revolt."

The IDF is more troubled by criticism from parents whose children died in uniform. Many bereaved parents no longer play a passive role. In the early 1980s, a group of parents organized to protest the first Lebanon War. By the early 1990s, the criticism of bereaved parents over failed operations and training accidents had gained increased visibility. Media attention to military failures also contributed to the process of demystifying the army in the eyes of the public. Bereaved parents as well as others criticized the army's tendency to whitewash, conceal, conduct only internal investigations, and issue official versions of events that evaded the real questions. The struggle of bereaved parents about how to memorialize their children symbolizes the transition from collectivism to individualism. In the late 1980s, families of the fallen soldiers started to add personal expressions on the tombstone, as well as objects, photographs, etc. (Yossi Katz 2014). Thus the military tombstone and the military cemetery became one of the expressions of a transformation, from a society that emphasized the importance of the collective, to a society that recognized the significance of the memorialized individual. When the IDF stubbornly insisted on a uniform inscription on the gravestones in military cemeteries, the parents petitioned the High Court of Justice, which ruled in 1995 that when the Defense Ministry makes a decision about an inscription, it must take into consideration the personal need of the family to express its sense of loss.[48]

The waning standing of the IDF and the Defense Ministry in the eyes of some soldiers' parents was epitomized in the struggles to have missing and abducted soldiers returned to Israel. Sometimes the families wage their battle from within the system, but sometimes they criticize the government's lack of action, conduct public campaigns, and take matters into their own hands, often in defiance of the official position.[49] When Hamas abducted the soldier Gilad Shalit to the Gaza Strip in June 2006, his family, supported by a public organization, conducted a major campaign in Israel and abroad and influenced the government decision to obtain his release (October 2011) in exchange for 1,027 Palestinian prisoners.

The debate that arose during the first Lebanon War about whether Israel should be engaged in a "war of choice," i.e., using military force to advance political ends, raised questions about militarism. It was during this war that cases appeared of refusal to follow orders, and these have continued in small numbers for diverse reasons over three decades. The withdrawal from Lebanon in 2000 also bore the markings of a

[48] *Wechselbaum v. Minister of Defense* 1995.

[49] The families of three Israeli soldiers missing in action during the first Lebanon War took direct action, running an international network of volunteers (Azulai 2007).

civilian challenge to the IDF's claims that remaining in southern Lebanon's "security zone" was critical: "This move [withdrawal] represented civil society's success at bending the will (and above all the logic) of the military-security establishment, despite the monopoly of this body on shaping security policy" (A. Sela 2007, 21).

One would assume that military failures, which reveal the limits of force, should have the effect of reducing militarization. It is commonly believed that ever since the first Lebanon War, the IDF would not launch a war for which broad consensus does not exist in Israel, and this appears to be true, at least with respect to the opening stages of subsequent military operations. Reality is more complex, however. The first Intifada and the failed efforts to reach an accommodation with the Palestinians led to escalation of the violent struggle. As a result, the IDF prepared for a "low-intensity war," and when the second Intifada erupted, the IDF struck with full force, even civilian targets. On the opposite side, the Palestinians opted for terrorism and suicide bombings against civilians and military persons alike. The long years of struggle with the Palestinians, and later with Hezbollah in Lebanon and Hamas in Gaza, did not reduce militarism in Israeli society. Indeed, it even intensified in the 2000s, which may explain the widespread support among Jewish citizens for launching the second Lebanon War in 2006, or the numerous military operations in response to the shelling of Israeli civilians from the Gaza Strip.

How would the debate about making the IDF a volunteer, professional army fit in with the conflicting dynamics within Israeli society? On the one hand, the army itself would probably support such a move because it is hard to rely on conscripted soldiers and reservists, who are ultimately civilians; better to invest in well-compensated professionals with high technical skills. The concern is, however, that a professional army would indeed be militaristic, especially if it attracts soldiers with extremist views. And some fear that a professional IDF will not feel subordinate to the political leadership, or will take orders from religious leaders, or even stage a coup. On the other hand, a professional army and a militaristic society are not necessarily compatible. Sparta had a universal draft because in a society that sanctifies a military way of life, people want to be involved personally and directly. In our view, ending the compulsory draft and the reserve service in Israel would mark a revolutionary change in the security ethos of "the people's army." A professional army would, for economic reasons, primarily attract individuals from disadvantaged groups. As for militarism, it is not expected that a professional army would increase the tendency to use military force, or reinforce the supremacy of security.

B. The Military-Industrial Complex

We pointed out earlier the large proportion of defense-related expenditures in Israel; here we ask whether this has led to the emergence of groups with a vested interest in promoting the use of military force. Those who make a living from security-related professions would naturally want to see a large defense system, but this is a small proportion of the total work force, and there is no reason to assume that they are necessarily militaristic. Let us assess therefore the influence of the Israeli defense industry – the so-called military-industrial complex.

After 1967, the Israeli defense industry experienced major growth, striving to maximize Israel's independence from foreign suppliers of arms and ordnance. Other motivations included the desire to develop home-grown technology that would be secret, innovative, and power-enhancing; to contribute to the local economy – research, development, and high-tech; and to enhance Israeli power and its deterrent capabilities (Y. Lifshitz 2007). These efforts have been influenced by two developments. One was the generous security aid from the United States, which obligates Israel to purchase American-made arms and supplies. And the other was the increasing importance of security-related exports, which have become a significant part of the Israeli economy, with billions of dollars of defense contracts annually. Israel exported approximately $7 billion of security-related products in 2008, making up 85 percent of the defense industry's sales (ibid.). In 2015, Israel exported approximately $5.6 billion worth of security-related products (G. Cohen 2015; CBS 2016).

Israel's defense industry is composed of three government corporations (Israel Aerospace Industries, Rafael, and Israel Military Industries Ltd.) and two private corporations (Elbit Systems Ltd. and Elisra Electronic Systems Ltd.). Four of these (all but Elisra) are ranked among the 100 leading defense contractors in the world (Tishler and Shefi 2005, 20–23). In addition, another 150 small companies manufacture for both the civilian and military markets. Among the weapons manufactured by Israel for the IDF: the Merkava tank, the Arrow anti-ballistic missile system, satellites, missiles, and unmanned air systems. To this should be added the "anti-terrorism industry," which grew by leaps and bounds after September 2001, and in which Israel has a significant international presence. Thus a substantial military-industrial complex exists in Israel, and until recently it operated in secrecy with only loose public oversight.[50] Nevertheless, the Israeli case differs from the American one, as the Israeli military industry is largely publicly owned (Mintz 1985, 623–39).

Is the Israeli military-industrial complex a powerful pressure group? Lifshitz believes it is (Y. Lifshitz 2007), and that this group worked to expand the military-industrial system and had an advantage over others in its ability to influence public policy. Were they dominant – capable of dictating militaristic policies to the political system? The military-industrial complex in Israel has declined over the years for economic reasons (competition and market instability), but also for other factors. Canceling development of the Lavi aircraft in 1987 marks a turning point: Open debate within the defense system, the introduction of economic considerations, the involvement of civilian bodies and public debate, the reluctance to fire thousands of workers – throughout all this, there was no sign of the defense-establishment monopoly that had encouraged the government to embark upon this megalomaniac project seven years earlier. Another example was the reform forced on Rafael, again in a relatively public debate and drawn out process (1994–2002), which led to Rafael's downsizing and transformation from a classified, insular unit in the Defense Ministry to a government-owned corporation (Galnoor 2003, 167–82). This trend may continue if there is a willingness to evaluate the economic feasibility of the defense industries on parameters such as their monopolization of the technological labor force, or the effect of their preference for government investments in research and development.

[50] The Supervision of Defense Exports Law 2007 regulates Israel's export of security-related products, expertise, and services for reasons of national security, foreign policies, international commitments, and other vital state interests. The Defense Export Controls Directorate in the Defense Ministry is in charge of implementing this law.

Such criteria were not used in the past, and broader considerations may arise such as the significance of defense-related exports to Israel's foreign relations, or even the social and moral implications of the global arms trade.

C. The Militarization of Politics

Has a militaristic world view taken over Israeli politics in terms of the issues; who is elected or nominated to public office; and who bears the responsibility for results? We noted that in Israel it is generally the IDF that defines the security reality, which then shapes the options for action. Another element in the militarization of politics is the blurred distinction between political and military leadership, as military men (and subsequently also senior GSS officials) move directly into high political office, often immediately after shedding their uniform.[51] Former career officers do not necessarily have a narrow military perspective; examples can be brought in both directions. Indeed, politicians who come from the military do not have identical views and are distributed among various political parties in Israel.

Nevertheless, the strong presence of senior military officers in politics, beyond what is usual in democratic countries, suggests that the public wants them there, or at least this is the thinking of the parties that rank them high on their election lists. In the Labor Party, for example, many party heads were former generals: Rabin, Barak, Ben-Eliezer, Mitzna. Having a significant number of senior political figures who have spent twenty to thirty formative years of their lives in the military no doubt influences the substance of a country's policies. Someone whose entire adult life is shaped by a system designed to cope with threats might find it hard to make the switch to a world view of opportunities and cooperation. Furthermore, those who enter politics are senior officers who come from the same organization, drilled in the same methods and modes of operation, and – despite the age differences between them – are familiar with each other. Barak and Sheffer (2006, 235–61) suggest that there is an "old boy security network" in Israel – a web of security forces alumni – who have common values, perceptions, and interests. They estimate several thousand in this informal network, who maintain contact among themselves to influence policymaking.

Is there proof that such a network operates? There is evidence to the contrary, from the open political rivalry between former IDF officers to conflicting views about security matters, such as whether or not to continue development of the Lavi aircraft, the reform of Rafael, or disagreements about the need for a separation barrier. What does appear to be a common denominator of military men in politics is their absolute backing of the IDF and their tendency to see the IDF as the only, or at least the primary, instrument for policymaking in foreign affairs and security. Furthermore, the fact that the IDF has been a central source for recruiting top political officials has had far-reaching implications for the behavior of officers in uniform who have political aspirations. Indeed, high-level IDF officers have negotiated with party representatives shortly after (and some say before) leaving active duty, and some parachuted directly into senior political office: Chief of Staff Shaul Mofaz, for

[51] The Cooling-Off Period for Members of the Security Forces (Amendments) Law (2007) extended the cooling-off period for senior officers from half a year to three years.

Table 14.5 *Former senior military officers in the Knesset*

Knesset	Year elected MK	Former senior officers
1st	1949	4
2nd	1951	1
3rd	1955	2
4th	1959	3
5th	1961	3
6th	1965	5
7th	1969	4
8th	1973	8
9th	1977	10
10th	1981	8
11th–16th*	1984–2003	12–14
17th**	2006	15
18th	2009	12
19th	2013	13
20th	2015	9

* In the eleventh to sixteenth Knessets, there was little fluctuation.
** From the seventeenth Knesset, former GSS and senior police officials are included.
Sources: Sources differ significantly in defining "a former senior officer" and, until 2006, they excluded those who served in the GSS, Mossad, or Police. Through the tenth Knesset, data are based on Peri 1983, 103 (who includes career army officers ranked lieutenant colonel and higher); for the eleventh to sixteenth Knessets, based on Barak and Sheffer 2006, 248; from the seventeenth Knesset, based on the Knesset website.

example, was appointed defense minister in November 2002, just four months after he left the army.

In discussing Israeli society, we noted internal contradictions and signs of demilitarization, but no such trend is visible in Israeli politics. The picture that emerges from Table 14.5 is clear and stable over time. In the election to the First Knesset, a blurring of boundaries was understandable, as members of the pre-state military organizations became candidates. However, IDF officers on active duty ran for the first Knesset on the Mapai and Mapam lists, revealing a failure to understand the principle of separating the military from politics; these officers were not elected, and later this was prohibited by law. Until the Seventh Knesset (1969), all former senior military officers elected to the Knesset belonged to left-wing parties (Mapai, Ahdut Ha'avoda, and Rafi) and only since 1973 have they been elected to the Knesset in parties on the right.

Until the 1970s, there were fewer than five former senior military officers in the Knesset at any one time. This did not change even in the 1969 election, when one might have expected more military men to be elected following the 1967 victory. Indeed, this is what happened in drawing up the lists of candidates for the 1973 election, which were prepared prior to the Yom Kippur War and not altered afterwards. After 1973, the proportion of former senior military officers in the Knesset doubled or more (eight to fifteen MKs), constituting about a tenth of all Knesset members. This is high by any measure, and raises the question of why it happened, in light of the fact that none of the post-1967 wars was considered a clear-cut victory. One explanation is that former military officers are relatively young, perceived as successful leaders, and enjoy public confidence. Another is that senior military commanders get more public exposure than potential civilian leaders, and in the communication era, this paves their way into politics. A more substantive explanation, in our opinion, is that when security deteriorates, the public searches for salvation among those with a security background – whether for purposes of imposing an iron-fist policy or for ensuring that security will be an integral part of any peace agreement. The parties seem to know what they are doing because former military officers not only entered the Knesset, but assumed senior positions – prime minister, defense minister, other ministers, mayors, etc.

Until the 1970s, not a single former general headed a political party in Israel. The first was Yitzhak Rabin, former chief of staff, and this was after the Yom Kippur War. Later Yigal Yadin was chosen to head the Dash Party in 1977, but this was years after he had served as chief of staff, and the party he headed was a new one that pledged to change Israeli politics. Another five of the fifteen Dash candidates elected to the Knesset were former military men. This was a trend – that same year, Ariel Sharon was elected to the Knesset as head of a new party, and soon other military men headed new lists, such as Moshe Dayan, Ezer Weizman, Rafael Eitan, Rehavam Ze'evi, and others. After a period of security tension, chances rise that the prime minister will be a former general: Rabin after 1973 and again in 1992 after the first Intifada; Barak and Sharon after Palestinian terrorist attacks in the territories and Lebanon. This is also true for defense ministers – since 1967, most have been military men.

This picture repeats itself for ministers. Between 1955 and 1967, only one or two former officers served as ministers. This increased to three before the Six Day War, six or seven in subsequent governments (1984–90), seven in the Barak government (1999–2001), five or six in the Sharon and Olmert governments (2001–9, including former GSS and Mossad officers), and six, four, and three in the Netanyahu governments (2009, 2013, 2015, respectively). Of particular interest is that some 75 percent of former officers elected to the Knesset ultimately became ministers. Such a high percentage is unparalleled in other sectors represented in the Knesset – kibbutz or moshav members, former mayors, and certainly women, as only about 15 percent of female MKs became ministers. It is important to emphasize that the retired officers who became ministers joined a variety of parties: From among the thirty-six ex-security officials who became ministers through 2015, fourteen were in left-wing parties, fifteen in right-wing parties, and seven in centrist parties (Goldberg 2006, 380; Knesset website).

Party loyalty is not strong among former military men, and there is a tendency to search for "the center" – no fewer than eleven changed parties over the years (Dayan, Sharon, Weizman, Ben-Eliezer, Mordechai, Kahalani, Eitam, Mofaz, Mitzna, Barak, and Dichter), and they or others (Yadin, Amit, Yariv, Eitan, and Lipkin-Shahak) searched for their political home in centrist parties. There is no way to determine whether Israeli governments with an abundance of military men tend to resort more to force of arms or an iron-fist policy, but one can assume that the large number of

Table 14.6 *Former senior military officers who served as prime ministers, defense ministers, party heads, or mayors of large cities (1949–2015)*

Years	Prime ministers	Defense ministers	Party heads	Mayors of large cities
1950s				
1960s		Moshe Dayan (Alignment)		
1970s	Yitzhak Rabin (Labor)	Ezer Weizman (Likud); Moshe Dayan (Alignment)	Yitzhak Rabin (Alignment); Meir Pa'il (Moked)	Shlomo Lahat (Tel Aviv)
1980s		Ariel Sharon (Likud); Yitzhak Rabin (Labor)	Moshe Dayan (TELEM); Rehavam Ze'evi (Moledet); Yigal Yadin (Dash); Rafael Eitan (Tzomet); Yitzhak Moda'i (Liberals); Asaf Yaguri (Ya'ad); Ezer Weizman (Yahad)	Shlomo Lahat (Tel Aviv)
1990s	Yitzhak Rabin (Labor)	Yitzhak Rabin (Labor); Yitzhak Mordechai (Likud); Ehud Barak (Labor)	Yitzhak Rabin (Labor); Ehud Barak (Labor); Rehavam Ze'evi (Moledet); Yitzhak Mordechai (Center); Amnon Lipkin-Shahak (Center); Avigdor Kahalani (Third Way); Rafael Eitan (Tzomet); Yuval Ne'eman (Tehiya)	Shlomo Lahat (Tel Aviv); Amram Mitzna (Haifa); Yitzhak Rager (Beersheba); Ya'akov Turner (Beersheba); Ron Huldai (Tel Aviv)
2000s	Ehud Barak (Labor); Ariel Sharon (Likud, Kadima)	Binyamin Ben-Eliezer (Labor); Shaul Mofaz (Likud); Ehud Barak (Labor)	Ehud Barak (Labor); Binyamin Ben-Eliezer (Labor); Amram Mitzna (Labor); Ehud Barak (Labor); Ariel Sharon (Likud, Kadima); Effi Eitam (NRP)	Ron Huldai (Tel Aviv)
2010s		Ehud Barak (Atzmaut); Moshe Ya'alon (Likud)	Shaul Mofaz (Kadima)	Ron Huldai (Tel Aviv)

Source: Collected from various sources.

ministers with a security past in the government since 1984 (most of them senior ministers) had the effect of prioritizing a security perspective in policymaking.[52]

Among the civilian positions filled by former officers, the relatively high proportion of mayors stands out. The number who served as mayor in Israel's four large cities (Table 14.6) increased in the 1990s. This is especially surprising for Tel Aviv, the most "civilian" city in Israel, most of whose mayors were military men after 1973, as opposed to right-wing Jerusalem, which never had a military man as mayor. Since local authorities are not in charge of security matters, having former generals serve as mayor seems to stem from the system of direct election for the office of mayor, which tends to favor known figures, such as ex-generals, who are also considered skilled administrators.

There is no evidence that parties headed by or featuring military men have been more or less successful in election campaigns. There does, however, seem to be public support for former military figures – in internal party elections as well as in competitions for prime minister or minister. In the 2001 and 2003 elections, Ariel Sharon was elected prime minister because, among other reasons, he had the stature of a military leader, who could attain both "security and peace," as he pledged in his campaign. The fact that Sharon was elected prime minister, despite the shadow on his reputation from the first Lebanon War, suggests that Israeli voters do not punish military leaders for their military failures. Sharon took ill before the 2006 elections, and since then the major parties have been headed by civilians (Olmert, Livni, Peretz, Yachimovich, Herzog, and Netanyahu).

Despite the differences between events, Table 14.7 shows that the political careers of prime ministers who had been involved in controversial security events were harmed more than the careers of defense ministers or chiefs of staff, most of whom remained unscathed. Indeed, those directly criticized by state commissions of inquiry – Dayan, Sharon, and Eitan – were reelected to the Knesset and served in senior ministerial posts.

D. Politicization of the Army

Of the twenty chiefs of staff who served Israel from its founding until 2015 (not including Chief of Staff Eizenkot), eleven – the majority – entered politics, were elected to the Knesset, and with the exception of one (Tsur) served as ministers.[53] This is a very high proportion, and does not include senior officers from the GSS, Mossad, and Israel Police, who more recently have started political careers. This phenomenon is not positive or negative in and of itself, unless the functioning of these senior officers was affected by their future political plans while still serving in the security system, or toward the end of their service. Israel's legislators saw fit to be strict about this, and extended the cooling-off period of army officers from half a year to three years before allowing them to enter politics. Hence the first question about the politicization of the army is whether promotions in the IDF or other security forces are affected by party or personal interests. The danger, of course, is the

[52] The very short and unsuccessful career of the civilian Amir Peretz as defense minister (2006–7) may have strengthened this effect.

[53] Since 2007, however, the last three chiefs of staff have not entered politics as of 2015.

Table 14.7 *Reward and punishment in Israeli politics*

Security event	Prime minister	Defense minister	Chief of staff
1973–74 Yom Kippur War	Golda Meir – resigned	Moshe Dayan – resigned; returned in 1977 as foreign minister	David Elazar – dismissed
1982–83 First Lebanon War	Menachem Begin – resigned	Ariel Sharon – dismissed, remained in government; elected prime minister 2001–6	Rafael Eitan – completed term; MK 1984–99, agriculture minister 1991–92
1987–91 Intifada I	Yitzhak Shamir – not reelected in 1992	Yitzhak Rabin – elected prime minister in 1992	Moshe Levy – completed term
2000–5 Intifada II	Ehud Barak – not elected in 2001. Ariel Sharon – elected in 2003	Ehud Barak. Binyamin Ben-Eliezer – resigned (party left government)	Shaul Mofaz – completed term, defense minister 2002–6
2006–7 Second Lebanon War	Ehud Olmert – did not run for reelection in 2009	Amir Peretz – resigned	Dan Halutz – resigned

appointment of unqualified people. The second question is whether extraneous considerations – unrelated to the optimal operation of the IDF or other security forces – affected these appointments. The danger here is the potential harm to operational effectiveness.

The IDF and other security forces are part of "politics" in the large, public sense of the word, and it is a political system that steers them. They also engage in "political activities" by virtue of the missions imposed on them, such as military government in the occupied territories or the Israeli presence in south Lebanon. The question we pose is whether appointments are "political" in the sense that those making them expect the appointees to conform to their ideology or opinions? Although no proof exists, it is fairly clear that appointments in the IDF and other security forces during the early state period – almost all made by Ben-Gurion – were political, but not necessarily party-related. Although Ben-Gurion kept supporters of other parties away from senior IDF positions, he did not give his party Mapai a foothold into the army itself. In Ben-Gurion's lexicon, the IDF was a "state mission" above party politics, although there was no proper constitutional or parliamentary oversight at the time. Since the officers appointed by him were generally suitable for their positions, one can be somewhat forgiving in retrospect, certainly in comparison with the armies of other new states, or considering the politicization of Israel's civil service at the time. Ben-Gurion managed to bend the defense system to his civilian will, no mean feat in light of the confrontations with the pre-state military organizations in 1948–49 (see Chapter 1), and the fear of the army seizing control. This is not to say that senior officers were completely cut off from the ruling parties, as illustrated by Mapai's Recruitment Division, which held meetings and information days for IDF commanders and even arranged jobs for them after their discharge (Hofnung 1991,

261). This pattern of politicization continued after the Ben-Gurion era, reflected in cases in which political leaders invoked the security issue without cause, for example before the formation of Golda Meir's new government in March 1974.[54]

The political upheaval of 1977 did not immediately lead to the appointment of right-wing military men. However, the rift within Israeli society over the future of the territories was bound to affect the politicization of the IDF sooner or later, not necessarily in terms of party loyalty. The appointment of the chief of staff is generally based on an agreement between the prime minister and the defense minister, but the choice of the prime minister prevails in the event of disagreement. Although the defense minister has more power over other senior IDF appointments, the recommendations of the chief of staff carry the day. Ben Meir concluded in 1994 that the military system in Israel is not characterized by political appointments (Yehuda 1995, 125). Peri, on the other hand, asserts (1984) that, after 1967, compatibility between the chief of staff and ruling party could be more easily discerned, and he gives the example of Rafael Eitan's declaration soon after his commission as chief of staff in May 1978 that Israel should never return the territories. Does someone check into the political views and party loyalties of senior officers, especially before they are sent to serve in the territories? This is hard to imagine, but the danger exists. One example was previously mentioned – the struggle between Prime Minister Netanyahu and the chief of staff and other generals, who were too left-wing for him. This confrontation led to "the democratic putsch of 1999," according to Peri, when former senior military officers organized to back the candidacy of Barak (Peri 2006, 77–90; Peri 2003, 125–44). Another example of appointing a chief of staff because of his willingness to support the prime minister's policy took place in 2005, when Prime Minister Sharon and Defense Minister Mofaz refused to extend the term of Chief of Staff Moshe Ya'alon because he opposed disengagement from Gaza, appointing Dan Halutz, who supported it, in his place (Peri 2006, 284). Another reported conflict was the disagreement between Defense Minister Barak and Chief of Staff Ashkenazi regarding military operations against Iran (Kfir and Dor 2015, 317).

The aforementioned examples do not indicate politicization of the IDF, but they do suggest that the possibility exists and should not be ignored in light of the sometimes strained relations between the civil and military echelons. On the other hand, the danger of declining professional military capabilities relates to a broader problem. The ongoing occupation has made the IDF the ruling power in the territories, and for nearly fifty years it has been preoccupied with policing and the battle against terrorism. These functions are not the bread and butter of any army: They affect its operational readiness and proficiency, dragging it into the political maelstrom. For instance, announcements by the IDF Spokesperson were once considered accurate and judicious, but over time its credibility has been undermined in the media and the public, especially its reports about the territories. After the second Lebanon War, four out of five Israeli civilians asserted that they have no faith in statements made by the IDF Spokesperson (Weimann 2007, 26). The report submitted to the government by Talia Sasson about "unauthorized outposts" (2005) found that senior military officers collaborated in illegal activities. Politicization was also manifested in

[54] Based on an investigation of *Maariv* from February 10 through March 12, 1974, conducted by Meir Nitzan for the author as a research assistant at Hebrew University, 1982.

the direct involvement of senior officers in negotiations over political or security matters. This tradition began as early as the Armistice Agreement in 1949, but that was a time of broad consensus in Israeli society, which did not exist by the time of negotiations with Egypt after the 1973 war, not to mention negotiations with the Palestinians over the Oslo Accords, in which IDF officers directly affected the substance of the agreements.

To return to the opening definition of militarization, the fact remains that wars are the heart of the collective experience in Israel, and security affairs top the list of the public agenda. Consequently, the military still wields great influence over the political and administrative leaders. What has significantly changed is that military perceptions and ideals are no longer so core to the identity of most civilians as they had been in the past.

14.8 External Oversight of the Defense System

The army is a unique organization because of its totality and the critical role it plays. In democratic countries, questions arise about supervising the armed forces, and examples abound of military officers who have acted in defiance of their civilian superiors. On the one hand, the problem is exacerbated in Israel because of the centrality of security and the tendency to view it as an enclave that "outsiders" have no right to scrutinize. On the other hand, Israel has never had a military coup, and ever since the military was subordinated to the civilian provisional government in 1948, the democratic principle of civilian authority has never been seriously challenged.

Below we focus on different forms of oversight and control mechanisms of the defense system: political (the Knesset and government); economic and administrative (the Finance Ministry and other ministries); legal (the courts); commissions of inquiry; and public (political parties, interest groups, the media, and public opinion).[55] The discussion will focus mainly on the IDF, but occasionally on the Mossad and the GSS.

A. Political Supervision and Control

The defense system in Israel is under the supervision and control of the elected representatives. In practice, does its level of autonomy deviate from what is desirable in a democratic society? Yaari describes well the two extremes: When supervision is absolute, political commissars control the army; when supervision is absent, the army controls the political system (2004, 10). The civilian body that should have the task of preventing the army from dominating politics is, first and foremost, the parliament – through its own mechanisms or the government. The Knesset, however, has no formal authority in the field of security, and is not even mentioned in the Basic Law: The Military, which defines the forms of civilian authority over the military. The Knesset also has no tools for supervising and controlling the defense system, and it fulfills this role only generally, indirectly, and sporadically.

55 A similar classification appears in Key 1959, 312–36.

Although Ben-Gurion centralized the authority for all defense-related institutions into his civilian hands, by so doing he excluded the Knesset and often even the government from dealing with security affairs. For instance, the decision to wage the Sinai Campaign in 1956 was made by the government only one day before launching the operation, and the Knesset merely rubber stamped it (Galnoor 1996, 172). Knesset involvement in declaring wars was also minimal, as opposed to the more drawn-out decisions about withdrawal from territories, for which it was harder to mobilize public support, thereby providing involvement and sometimes even decision-making to the Knesset, such as the decision in 1978 to evacuate the Sinai. The law does not require Knesset approval for the government to declare war. The government did not bother to inform the Knesset that it had launched the first Lebanon War, which the Knesset did ratify two days later in the wake of a proposed no-confidence vote. By the same token, only on the sixth day of the second Lebanon War (July 17, 2006) did the prime minister present the government's goals to the Knesset; in the following no-confidence vote submitted by the Arab parties, seventy Knesset members supported the government. The lack of supervision and control is particularly evident with regard to the occupied territories – these were defined by government order as "administered territories held by the IDF" and subject to military command. Ever since, the ability of the Knesset and its committees to find out what is going on there has been limited.

In two important areas, the Knesset has formal supervisory powers: declaration of a state of emergency (Basic Law: Government) and emergency mobilization of reserve duty soldiers.[56] These powers are intended to prevent or at least moderate rash decisions by the government or prime minister, but so far the Knesset has never turned down a government request in these two areas. The role of the Knesset in approving or ratifying international agreements has also not been anchored in law, but since 1974, there is a prevailing custom of bringing agreements of political or military import to the Knesset.[57] Although there is no constitutional requirement to obtain Knesset approval to declare war or ratify peace agreements, this approval is still critical for providing legitimacy to government policies. The Knesset vote to approve the Camp David Accord and peace agreement with Egypt is an example of a decision made in the Knesset (Diskin and Galnoor 1990, 710–17). The sole body that can perform a supervisory role is the Knesset Foreign Affairs and Defense Committee, especially through its subcommittees: Intelligence and the Secret Services; Security Strategy and Enhancement of IDF Forces; Readiness and Ongoing Security; Personnel in Security Forces; Foreign Relations and Information; and the Security Budget Subcommittee, staffed jointly with the Finance Committee. Deliberations in this committee and its subcommittees are held *in camera* and with the participation of the prime minister, senior ministers, the chief of staff, and directors of the intelligence agencies. The General Security Service Law (2002) states that the GSS director must submit a quarterly report of GSS activities to the Subcommittee on Intelligence and the Secret Services, and also report to it as requested.

[56] Security Service Law 1986, parag. 29 (7), 29 (2), 34 (2); Emergency Employment Service Law 1967, parag. 11.

[57] Para. 6 (4) of the Statute of Government Operations. Also see Shetreet 1985–86; Rubinstein and Medina 2005, 918.

Relative to the situation prior to the Yom Kippur War and compared with other civilian frameworks, Knesset members in the Foreign Affairs and Defense Committee have a unique opportunity to look behind the curtain of security, and even influence it every so often. Some examples: a subcommittee was established to monitor implementation of the Agranat Commission report (1974); Prime Minister Rabin consulted with this committee before the Entebbe operation in 1976; a committee headed by Abba Even investigated the Pollard affair (1984–88); and the classified report in 1987 of the Subcommittee on Security Affairs headed by MK Dan Meridor had an impact on the IDF. Also worthy of mention: the investigation by the Committee on Foreign Affairs and Defense of the intelligence failure prior to the 1991 Gulf War; the committee that investigated the second Lebanon War; and the subcommittee of the State Control Committee that examines reports on the IDF and the security agencies (Yaari 2004, 23–25). Although these matters are classified and it is difficult to gauge the overall scope of supervision, from the work of the joint Security Budget Subcommittee it can be seen that in practice the Knesset exerts little control. A kind of agreement exists: "The defense establishment satisfies the curiosity of the legislators, while they in turn rubber stamp the budget" (Yehuda Ben Meir 1995, 47). Accordingly, the defense system was from the outset defined as an enclave, and it lacks adequate, effective parliamentary supervision (Hofnung 1996, 244; Rubinstein Committee 2004).

With respect to supervision by the government and the Ministerial Committee for Security Affairs – is the defense system also off limits for these bodies? The government plenary has no tools to assess recommendations made by the security services, especially if these recommendations are supported by the prime minister and/or defense minister. The IDF commands excellent staff work, which produces well-reasoned recommendations from the military perspective. Sometimes the government makes use of this experienced, responsible, and confidential apparatus to produce position papers on non-military matters as well, such as preparations for peace negotiations or strategic policy and planning. The prime minister too lacks separate tools for this kind of staff work, and he usually relies on the military secretary, who comes from the IDF and returns to it at the end of his term of office. In this sense, a prime minister who also serves as defense minister is in an even worse position, because the second role may limit the range of considerations of a prime minister. The National Security Council has not managed to fill this vacuum: If it operates outside the security enclave, its chance of having an impact is limited; if it operates from within, its analysis will be coordinated in advance with those on the inside. Thus, the situation has not fundamentally changed since the Agranat Commission pointed out the pitfalls of the military monopoly, and recommended that the government create alternative sources of information and analysis for security policymaking (Agranat Commission 1975, 32).

The importance of the Ministerial Committee for Security Affairs (the MCSA) has changed over the years. It was established in 1953, but Defense Minister Ben-Gurion made sure it would not have independent decision-making powers. After the election in 1961, held in the shadow of the Lavon affair, the coalition agreement stipulated that control over the defense system would be tightened and the MCSA would have more power, such as the right to submit recommendations directly to the government. In practice, the MCSA became an important advisory body only during the term of Prime Minister and Defense Minister Levi Eshkol, and faded away during Golda Meir's "kitchen cabinet" era. During the National Unity Government of 1969, for example, the MCSA was composed of seventeen out of the twenty-four government members, and took no part in the decisions leading up to the Yom Kippur War. The MCSA was reconstituted as a smaller body in 1974, as recommended by the Agranat Commission, but another commission recommendation to establish a "war cabinet" of no more than five ministers was not implemented. Prime Minister Begin did not often convene the MCSA, not even before or during the first Lebanon War, and the unity governments of 1984 and 1988 created the "cabinet," a new body with the same authority.

The formal change took place in 1991 when the Basic Law: Government was amended, and the MCSA became a statutory body that must be formed when a new government is installed, and has a specific configuration of ministers not to exceed half the total number of government ministers.[58] According to the Statute of Government Operations, the MCSA has the authority to deliberate the following subjects: security goals and policy; IDF-related matters including the army structure, deployment, preparation, matériel, and research and development; the annual intelligence assessment and monitoring of events; intelligence reports; political issues; military and security operations; and coordination of government activities in the occupied territories. The list is lengthy, and the deliberations are classified – the decisions of this committee are not circulated even to other ministers (who can examine the meeting records only in the government secretariat). Despite all this, the influence of the MCSA is limited, as in the past, both because of its unwieldy size and because it functions at the initiative of the prime minister and the needs of the defense minister. Before and during the second Lebanon War, the MCSA was not convened at all, but replaced by an ad hoc group of senior ministers ("the forum of seven"), which made decisions, while occasionally the Political-Security Cabinet met to approve the call-up of reserve troops or expand the ground war. The Security Cabinet did not provide a counterweight to "the relative power of the planning, staff, intelligence, and the IDF assessment apparatus, versus the weakness of the political apparatus" (Israel, Winograd Commission 2007, 172, 238–45).

B. Economic and Administrative Supervision and Control

So far we have used the term "the defense system" to include the Defense Ministry, the IDF, and the other security agencies in Israel. The Defense Ministry, however, is fundamentally a civilian body, which in theory should be supervising the IDF. Indeed, attempts were made to separate the two as early as the Ben-Gurion era: The IDF was responsible for training and fighting, while the Defense Ministry provided a support system, including procurement and budgeting (Perlmutter 1969, 80). In practice, the IDF is also involved in procurement, weapons export, research and development, and definitely in budget decisions (U. Eilam 2007; Brodet Committee 2007, 70). The Defense Ministry has no mechanism for supervising the IDF, and

[58] In the 32nd government, headed by Benjamin Netanyahu, the MCSA grew to fifteen ministers and another five "observers," out of thirty government ministers all told.

the defense minister has no civilian staff – neither for strategic planning nor for evaluating the IDF intelligence assessments, which are transferred directly to the government. "Over the years, mainly as a result of the many wars Israel had to fight, the IDF has slowly but surely encroached on MoD's domain" (Yehuda Ben Meir 1995, 88). Similarly, the Office of the Prime Minister has no tools to supervise the security agencies subordinate to it: the Mossad, the GSS, Nativ,[59] and the Atomic Energy Commission.

The other government ministries are also limited in their ability to supervise the defense system. The Finance Ministry, particularly the Budget Division and the Accountant General, hold sway over all the ministries, with the exception of Defense. Until recently, the defense budget was classified, and the overall amount was decided in closed session of the prime minister, the defense and finance ministers, and the chief of staff. Setting the ceiling of the security budget was not left to the Budget Division, because the security slice of the budget pie did not compete with other slices. Furthermore, the Finance Ministry was not involved in preparing the defense budget, and had no control over its internal divisions (Tov 2003, 56–59). These days, the overall amount of the defense budget is deliberated in the government, as are major defense purchases, and this is a significant, positive achievement of the Budget Division. In parallel, deliberations in the Knesset and the Finance Committee subcommittee have become more substantive, but still lack the ability to control the real size of the defense budget.[60]

C. Legal Supervision and Control

In reply to the question "What is more important – security or the rule of law?" most respondents lean toward security (A. Arian 1995, 112). Although the question itself implies a problematic bipolarity, responses indicate that in the Israeli world view, security reigns supreme. It also suggests the problem in the legal system: "Do the courts give no priority to national security? Yes, the courts do give priority to national security," which is an existential interest (Zamir 1989, 27). In other words, from the outset, courts in Israel tried to balance security interests and individual rights, and leaned toward the former.

The Rule of Law and Security Needs

Since the early years of the state, the Israeli Supreme Court took the view that security considerations do not necessarily trump human rights considerations in every case. In *al-Karbutli v. Defense Minister*, the High Court in 1948 ordered the release of a detainee held in accordance with the Defense (Emergency) Regulations (1945) on the grounds that the arrest had been illegal. In the famous *Sheib v. Defense Minister* case (1951), the court criticized the interference of the Defense Ministry

59 Nativ (officially called "the Liaison Bureau") is a secret unit in the Office of the Prime Minister. It was established in the 1950s to encourage Jewish immigration from the Soviet Union, but has since moved on to other tasks, including the recruitment of Jonathan Pollard (1985) for espionage in the United States.

60 See attempts to make the budget more transparent: Workshop for Public Knowledge; and Locker Committee 2015.

with granting a teaching permit to a former Lehi activist.[61] The ruling of the District Military Court about the Kafr Qasim massacre, a ruling that defined "a patently illegal order," was a milestone in establishing norms of conduct for IDF soldiers and judicial review over security bodies.[62]

The rule of law in Israel is on a constant collision course with security demands, if only because a state of emergency has existed in Israel since its founding, one that enables the government to circumvent the Knesset and issue Emergency Regulations, carry out administrative detentions, enforce military censorship on security-related subjects, and more. In retrospect, the courts have come a long way in establishing the norm of civilian, judicial supervision over the defense system, yet the duality remains and oversight has been limited because the courts generally accept decisions made by the security authorities and refrain from intervention. On the one hand, the High Court has intervened in several military decisions – forbidding the use of "human shields";[63] preventing the promotion of commanders;[64] protecting individual rights; and other issues. An instructive example was the expansion of judicial authority on issues of privileged information. In the past, it would have been sufficient for representatives of the security forces to inform the court that revealing the facts of a particular case would harm state security, and this would obligate the judge; today the judge is authorized to demand that the evidence be presented to him (not in the presence of the petitioner) before rendering a decision.[65] On the other hand, judges tend to accept what is presented to them as "security considerations" without further ado, such as the decision to expel Hamas activists in 1992, or the virtually automatic rejection of petitions by those who refuse to do military service.[66]

The Occupied Territories

Since 1967, the territories have posed a singular challenge to judicial review. From the outset, the Supreme Court ruled that it has jurisdiction in the territories, even though they were not annexed to Israel (Gazit 2003). The goal was to protect the rights of the Palestinian residents, and indeed in the few cases in which Palestinians in the territories turned to the court, they occasionally won redress. But an Israeli court clearly cannot serve as a neutral arbiter of Palestinian claims against Israel,

[61] Dr. Yisrael Sheib, formerly an activist in Lehi, applied to be a schoolteacher in 1950, but was rejected on the grounds that the Defense Ministry objected to his appointment. The court ruled that it is not within the purview of the Defense Ministry to interfere in educational considerations, which are at the discretion of the Education Ministry.

[62] Court-Marshal MR 3/57 *Military Prosecutor v. Shmuel Malinki et al.* 1957. Also see Eilam 1991, 53–70; Rosenthal 2000, 225–44.

[63] This refers to a situation in which security forces wishing to arrest a wanted person order a neighbor or acquaintance to lead the way into the house to avoid harm to the soldiers.

[64] *Anonymous v. Chief of General Staff* 1999. In March 1999 the High Court ruled that the promotion of an officer would be permanently blocked following his conviction for unbecoming conduct in the wake of sexual relations with a subordinate.

[65] Amendment to parag. 5a of the Evidence Laws 1968. See Zamir 1989, 28. Section 46a of the Evidence Ordinance (New Version) (1971) states that if the prime minister or defense minister declares in writing that revealing specific evidence could harm state security, the authorities are exempt from the obligation to produce the evidence in court. The law does not apply, however, "if a Supreme Court Justice finds, based on the petition requesting that the evidence be revealed, that the need to reveal the evidence in order to ensure justice overrides the reason not to reveal it."

[66] *Association for Civil Rights in Israel v. Defense Minister* 1993; *Algazi v. Defense Minister* [unpublished]; *Zonshein v. Judge Advocate-General* 2002. Also see Barzilai 1999, 229–49.

especially when security matters are involved. Thus, the court generally accepted the views of the security bodies, and most petitions from Palestinians – in cases of administrative detention, land expropriation, demolition of houses, and deportation of suspects – were denied.

As a result, some claim that the courts, perhaps unwittingly, contributed to legalizing the occupation – protecting the individual rights of petitioners, but not challenging the conduct of the state in the territories defined by international law as occupied (R. Shamir 1990, 781–805). An elaborate legal structure was created for these territories that are controlled by Israel, but not a part of it: They are defined as "administered" and Palestinians live there under a military government that is subordinate to the defense minister, while another set of laws applies to Israeli civilians (the settlers) who live in the territories. A particularly difficult problem is enforcement of the law on Israeli settlers, as described in the Karp Report as early as 1984. In addition to all of this, there is the enormous legal complication of Israel annexing East Jerusalem (see Section 14.4 above). This situation did not fundamentally change even after some territories were transferred to the Palestinian Authority and Israel withdrew from Gaza in August 2005. The courts did not, and perhaps could not, alter this reality, which is often legally untenable.

The High Court of Justice ruled that security considerations applied to the territories are subject to judicial review, to prevent violations of the rights of the Palestinian residents (Hofnung 1996, 249). In the view of David Kretzmer (2002, 196), the cumulative effect of applying the Supreme Court's standing and prestige to the judicial review of events in the territories is not positive: "The mere existence of this review has had a significant restraining influence on the authorities. However, in the actual decisions themselves, especially those dealing with substantive questions of principle or policy, the legitimizing function of the Court has been dominant." This dual role became strikingly clear when the High Court did not hesitate to examine the precise route of the separation barrier whose construction began in 2002, including security considerations, and even forced alterations of the route in specific areas.[67] At the same time, the need for a barrier and the legality of placing it on land beyond the borders of Israel were accepted by Israel's High Court, and used in international circles to defend Israel's position. Nevertheless, in July 2004, the International Court of Justice in the Hague issued an advisory opinion that Israel must cease and desist from constructing the barrier on the grounds that it cannot claim the right to self-defense beyond the 1949 ceasefire line.

Rulings Related to Security

The High Court of Justice increasingly extended its intervention in "security considerations," especially after 1973, and set limits on the IDF's almost total autonomy in decision-making, and even more so on the intelligence agencies, which had operated until then in complete secrecy – the GSS, Mossad, and Nativ. With respect to the IDF, the Agranat Committee Report could be considered precedent setting, though it was a state commission of inquiry, not a court. During that period, the High Court of Justice was not yet willing to intervene in military matters, which

[67] *Zaharan Yunes Mohammed Mara'abe, Association for Civil Rights in Israel et al. v. Prime Minister of Israel et al.* 2005.

were regarded as professional and not justiciable, exemplified by its decision to deny the petition of Motti Ashkenazi, who wanted the court to compel the IDF to investigate the Yom Kippur War and make public its findings. The turning point was the High Court's 1979 ruling on Elon Moreh, which rejected the professional opinion of Chief of Staff Rafael Eitan, who claimed that a settlement in that location is important for security. Another landmark was *Alice Miller v. Defense Minister* (1994), when the court intervened in a decision with operational implications, forcing the Air Force not to automatically reject women as pilot candidates. These examples suggest that the High Court intervenes in security matters only when it believes that the claim of security considerations is abused or overused to justify violations of the law.

The Bus 300 affair (1984–86) was a landmark in oversight of the GSS, when the High Court explicitly stated that security is subordinate to the law, and therefore not all means, such as perjury, are justified in protecting state security. Although a majority decision of the High Court sanctioned the "pardon in advance" issued by the president of Israel to those involved, a precedent was set that external inquiry committees and the court can openly intervene in decisions made by the GSS. Soon after, in the Nafsu affair, the Supreme Court ruled that the GSS had perjured itself in court and used torture to elicit a confession.[68]

The first open, judicial review of the Mossad was in the ruling on *Schnitzer et al. v. Chief Military Censor et al.* (1988), which voided a decision made by the military censor to ban publication of an article in *Kol Ha'Ir* that criticized the Mossad director and noted that he would soon be replaced. In the wake of this decision, the names of the Mossad and GSS directors were declassified. However, criticism of the Mossad came not necessarily from a court ruling, but following a series of botched operations that evoked public outcry.[69] Also worthy of mention is Nativ (the Liaison Bureau), which became infamous for its responsibility for the Jonathan Pollard affair

[68] **The Bus 300 affair:** In April 1984, Israeli security forces stormed Bus 300, which had been hijacked by terrorists. Israel subsequently announced that all four terrorists had been killed in the operation, but the *New York Times* reported that two of the terrorists had been taken alive and were later killed by Israeli security forces. The Israeli newspaper *Hadashot* published a photo showing one of the apprehended terrorists walking away from the bus. Following investigation by two commissions of inquiry, the fact that the GSS had given false information came to light. Great efforts were made to keep the matter from the public, including Prime Minister Shamir's dismissal of Attorney General Yitzhak Zamir, who refused to call off the investigation. When the GSS director resigned, he and three senior officials were pardoned "in advance" by President Herzog before an indictment against them was filed. This pardon was approved by the High Court in a majority opinion.

The Nafsu affair: Izzat Nafsu, a Circassian-Israeli intelligence officer, was convicted of treason and collaborating with the enemy. After seven and a half years in prison, Nafsu was exonerated on the grounds that the conviction was based on false evidence and perjury by GSS agents. *Nafsu v. Chief Military Prosecutor* 1987.

[69] These included assassination of the wrong man in Lillehammer, Norway (1973); its role in the first Lebanon War (1982); and the unsuccessful attempt to assassinate Khaled Mashal in Jordan (1997), which led the Knesset Subcommittee on Intelligence and Secret Services to declare that there were problems with the Mossad's functioning. Other mishaps: the death of two Mossad agents in a traffic accident in Vienna while tailing Dr. Majid Abaspour, Iran's Deputy Defense Minister and contact person for Nahum Manbar, later convicted of selling arms to Iran (1993); a failed operation in Bern in 1998 in which Mossad agents tried to bug the apartment of Abdullah Zein, a Hezbollah operative in Europe; and the capture of Mossad agents during operations in Switzerland (1998), Cyprus (1998), and New Zealand (2004).

(1985) – it continues to operate despite repeated internal investigations, and with no apparent judicial review. In the words of General (res.) Aviezer Yaari, former head of the Security Audit Department in the State Comptroller's Office, "The role of civilian courts in oversight of the military, as important and improved as this may be, remains sporadic and limited" (2004, 66).

D. Monitoring Mechanisms

Mechanisms to monitor and supervise security bodies are not self-evident in Israel. Until the early 1970s, a veil of secrecy surrounded security policy, and security bodies enjoyed full immunity for their actions and conduct. Since 1973, however, the mechanisms for monitoring the security bodies have gradually gained in stature. For each, a constitutive event helped buttress its standing as a supervisory mechanism for security issues: state commissions of inquiry began investigations of security mishaps with the Agranat Commission's inquiry into the Yom Kippur War (1973); the state comptroller became a legitimate and effective auditor of security bodies and policies in the wake of two reports – one on decision-making about the Lavi aircraft (1987) and the other on the distribution of gas masks to the public during the Gulf War (1991); and the attorney general took on the role of human rights defender when he stood firm against abuse of security considerations in the Bus 300 affair (1986). The discussion below will be limited to commissions of inquiry.

Commissions of Inquiry on Security Matters

Until 1973, when confronted with a crisis, the government would appoint an independent commission or one that reported to it. These commissions and their reports were not made public, or they were selectively published as warranted by political needs. For what later became the Lavon affair, for example, Prime Minister Sharett appointed a commission of two, who reported directly to him, and subsequently a committee of seven government ministers, who were under obligation to report to him, but not to the Knesset or the public.

Following the inadequate investigation of the Lavon affair, the Knesset enacted the Commissions of Inquiry Law (1968), which enabled the creation of state commissions of inquiry that are entirely independent once initiated by the government. In the wake of the Yom Kippur War and the loss of public confidence, the government was forced to appoint the Agranat Commission, an independent state commission of inquiry. This commission and its methods were milestones in the investigation of security failures. The Agranat Commission report was the first to examine security matters, making a significant contribution to civilian oversight by stating that civilian authority over the military must be explicitly stipulated by law. Indeed, five of all the fifteen inquiry commissions appointed until 2015 (see Table 14.8) dealt with security events or bodies. The two government commissions of inquiry that were empowered as state commissions also examined security entities: the Zeiler Commission investigated the Israel Police, and the Winograd Commission investigated the IDF during the second Lebanon War. However, when there is no public pressure within Israel for investigation of an event, the government avoids the appointment of a state commission of inquiry, as in the case of the public Turkel

Table 14.8 *State commissions of inquiry and government commissions of inquiry on security matters*

Commission (year of appointment)	Subject of inquiry	Entity investigated
Agranat Commission (1973)	Events of the Yom Kippur War	IDF and the political echelon
Kahan Commission (1982)	Events at Sabra and Shatila refugee camps (first Lebanon War)	IDF and the political echelon
Landau Commission (1987)	GSS interrogation methods	GSS
Second Shamgar Commission (1995)	Assassination of Yitzhak Rabin	GSS (Personal Security Unit)
Or Commission (2000)	Killing of Arab citizens by the police	Israel Police and the political echelon
Zeiler Commission (2005)*	Organized crime	Israel Police and the State Attorney
Winograd Commission (2006)*	Second Lebanon War	IDF and the political echelon

* A government (not a state) commission of inquiry.

Commission – appointed because of international pressure – to "examine the maritime Incident of 31 May 2010."[70]

The Agranat Commission was the first to demonstrate how powerful a commission could be in the fields of security and political-military relations, and contributed to demystifying security issues and increasing transparency in security affairs. Chief of Staff David Elazar resigned after publication of the interim report, and later the prime minister and defense minister were forced to step down as a result of public protest, even though the commission did not find them directly responsible for the failures. The Agranat Commission recommended the regulation of civil-military relations, and in 1976 the Knesset enacted the Basic Law: The Military. This commission also proposed that an alternative body be established to provide the government with independent position papers and intelligence assessments, hence the National Security Council was created in 1999. And still, more than thirty years after the Agranat Report, the Winograd Commission pointed out that the IDF has retained exclusivity in providing information, assessments, and proposals to the political decision-makers.

The Kahan Commission (1982), charged with investigating events in the Palestinian refugee camps during the first Lebanon war (and not the war itself), also looked at the decision-making process and the military-political interface. This report set a precedent by calling for a political dismissal – it recommended that Ariel Sharon step down as defense minister for "indirect personal responsibility." The Winograd Commission (2006) examined the conduct of the political leaders

[70] In an attempt to enforce the naval blockade imposed by Israel on the coast of the Gaza Strip, nine activists were killed on board the Mavi Marmara ship and a number of Israeli soldiers were injured. See Israel, "Turkel Commission" and discussion in Cohen and Cohen 2014, 279–83.

and the entire defense system on all aspects of the second Lebanon War. It refrained from suggesting dismissals, but assigned personal and ministerial responsibility to Prime Minister Ehud Olmert, Defense Minister Amir Peretz, and Chief of Staff Dan Halutz:

> The prime minister is responsible, ministerially and personally, for the flawed decisions and faults in the decision-making process. The prime minister made decisions without having a detailed plan ... He did not demand to see and weigh other options, and did not show the proper skepticism about views presented by the military. This was his failure.
>
> The defense minister's lack of knowledge and his inexperience led to his failure to discharge his task in its entirety.
>
> [The chief of staff] failed in not being prepared for this foreseeable event, not presenting the complexity of the operation to the political leadership, and thus not providing information, assessments, and plans ... that would have enabled them to meet the challenges better. The responsibility of the chief of staff is all the more serious ... because he gave [the prime minister and defense minister] the impression that the army was fully ready, and that operational plans for this situation were prepared. (Winograd Commission 2007, 115–16)

The interim report contained institutional recommendations: improvement of the decision-making on political-security issues by weighing alternatives and considering recommendations of bodies other than the IDF and the security services; strengthening the National Security Council to enable the prime minister to make reasonable and independent decisions that do not rely exclusively on military assessments; and establishing a national crisis management center in the Office of the Prime Minister (Winograd Commission 2007, 145–49).[71]

A commission headed by Supreme Court Justice Moshe Landau (1987) investigated the interrogation methods of the GSS, censured their practice of perjury in court, and prohibited harsh interrogation practices (though it granted permission to use "moderate physical pressure" under unusual circumstances). This report evolved into the General Security Service Law (2002), which states that in addition to the oversight of the attorney general, other mechanisms of control and supervision would be strengthened: a Ministerial Committee for General Security Service Affairs, a subcommittee of the Knesset Foreign Affairs and Defense Committee, and appointment of an internal comptroller within the GSS. After the assassination of Yitzhak Rabin, the Shamgar Commission examined the Personal Security Unit of the GSS and the procedure for protecting senior officials. Police conduct was the subject of an inquiry by the Zeiler Commission, which revealed a dangerous link between a number of police officers and some underworld figures (Zeiler Commission of Inquiry 2007).

These commissions have had an impact primarily through enforcing the dismissals or resignation of senior officers of the IDF, Police, and GSS – and occasionally political leaders too – whether before or after publication of the report. Commission reports also generally contain institutional recommendations, but the impact of these on security policy or the conduct of security bodies has been limited.

[71] This center was created in August 2007 under the National Security Council.

Other Monitors

The state comptroller is the only external body authorized to conduct ongoing audits of all the governmental security organizations – the IDF, defense ministry, defense industries, intelligence agencies, and the civil administration in the territories. From 1987 to 2002, for example, it published an average of thirty security-related audits annually, about half dealing with the military (Yaari 2004, 56).

Is the comptroller's audit of the defense organizations effective? What is investigated is usually the process of decision-making, not the content of these decisions. It does not ask whether a particular weapon system should be developed or acquired, but how the decision was made. The impact of this kind of secret audit is limited (Hofnung 1991, 125–26), though it sometimes extends beyond these limitations. Thus, the 1986 report about the Lavi aircraft influenced the decision to cancel the project.

The fact that such an audit exists establishes civilian supervision of security bodies. It exposes the decision-making process to the Knesset and sometimes also to the public, and highlights problem areas, thereby increasing transparency of the defense system and requiring that the audited bodies correct the shortcomings. However, there is no systematic audit of security bodies because of the multiplicity of subjects requiring examination and the limited access to these bodies.

The attorney general, charged with protecting and representing the public interest, is at the heart of the debate about human rights versus security needs. The event that gave the attorney general the role of oversight into security organizations was the Bus 300 affair (1984–86) and the resolve of then Attorney General Yitzhak Zamir to conduct an investigation. This affair and another led to partial lifting of the veil of secrecy, and turned the GSS into a legitimate object of scrutiny by the other monitoring mechanisms, including the Landau commission of inquiry mentioned above, which investigated the interrogation methods of the GSS.

The attorney general serves not only as guardian of the rule of law in the face of security demands, but is sometimes called upon to help shape policies in foreign affairs and security (Shamgar 1971, 262–66; Gutman 1981, 236–39; Gordon 1998, 83).

Once a security matter is scrutinized by one monitoring mechanism, it becomes a legitimate target of investigation by the others. This was the case after the second Lebanon War: As the Winograd Commission was doing its work, the state comptroller conducted an audit about home front activities during the war. One concern, however, is that the monitoring of security-related activity could constrain military commanders in fear of a future investigation, and would prevent them from taking decisive action based on their professional judgment. This may also be true of political policymaking – the fear that a decision could be retroactively challenged by oversight bodies might foster a reluctance to take decisions and a tendency to avoid responsibility. In some circumstances, monitoring mechanisms could be abused for finding scapegoats to blame for failures, rather than as an audit or oversight mechanism for the public good. So far, the positive outweighs the negative, because – despite the drawbacks – there is public legitimacy for oversight and auditing of the defense system for purposes of protecting the public interest, safeguarding the rule of law, and improving the process of decision-making.

14.9 Public Oversight of the Defense System

As long as Israeli society gave automatic approval to government policies in foreign affairs and security, public involvement in security affairs was not regarded as legitimate. Until the early 1970s, security issues were considered outside the pale of public involvement, and therefore protest activity was minor and few civil society organizations advocated about public policies. Indeed, politicians and the public alike expected unity and solidarity about security actions taken by the government. This taboo against civilian involvement began to crumble with the Lavon affair, which exposed the flaws in decision-making with regard to security issues. The waiting period prior to the Six Day War, with its image of Levi Eshkol as a vacillating figure, had evoked public protest, but these were secondary factors in the developments leading up to the war.[72] However, since the Yom Kippur War, foreign and security affairs have been subject to vigorous internal debate, and public intervention is considered legitimate, even by the concerned families on prisoner exchange. Nevertheless, during wars or military operations, the public is still expected to show unity and a common front (Hermann 2005).

The channels that enable public involvement in security matters include the media; grassroots groups or organizations that seek to affect security policy or monitor military activity (especially in the occupied territories); protests within legal bounds (e.g., demonstrations, petitions); non-violent, illegal protests (e.g., refusing to serve in the army); and political violence and terrorism (e.g., violent opposition to evacuating settlements, underground terrorist activity, and political assassination).

A. The Media

In discussing the media in Chapter 13, we listed the tools available to the state to prevent the publication of information defined as classified. We reviewed the developments from when the press and radio were largely tools of the government, until the aftermath of the Lavon affair, when this began to change. We also noted that the independent newspapers had on several occasions served as opposition to the government, gradually liberating themselves from dependence on government sources (Galnoor 1982, 247–48). One illustration of the nationalist stance of the media in the early 1970s was its report of a plane hijacking in Leningrad in May 1970 by a group of Jewish refuseniks (Mendelevitch 1985, 43–53). The Israeli press downplayed the hijacking itself and highlighted the persecution of Jews by the Soviet regime. The facts about the attempted hijacking, which appeared in the foreign media, were not objectively presented in the Israeli media, and the story was framed as an event about anti-Semitism. This was self-censorship; the press did this without any formal request to do so by the authorities (Skorbianski 1972).

Prior to the outbreak of the Yom Kippur War, the media extended full cooperation to – and were perhaps in the thrall of – the political and security perceptions of the government, even serving as its spokespersons. Only rarely were news items excised by the military censor; during the war itself and immediately following, the

[72] For example, a group of wives of military officers, dubbed "the merry wives of Windsor," who demonstrated for Moshe Dayan's appointment as defense minister before the Six Day War.

media voluntarily participated in the national effort to avoid undermining public morale (Cohen-Almagor 2007, 73).[73] Much has changed since the trauma of 1973, but the dilemma remains: Is it the task of the media to investigate and supervise the defense system, making public everything it knows, or should the media, in light of Israel's special security needs, demonstrate self-control beyond the legal constraints? Criticizing without restraint could jeopardize the security of Israel's citizens; self-censorship could turn the media into a tool of the defense system in the guise of security concerns. Aspiring to "balance" the two on a case-by-case basis is often suggested, but it is not attainable because relations between the media and the defense system in Israel have historically been marked by obedience and cooperation. One might reasonably ask, shouldn't greater demands be made of the Israeli media, which – although they are now more open and critical – during times of intense security concerns again become the voice of the official authorities for mobilizing and placating public opinion?[74] This duality marks the Israeli media in general, except beyond the Green Line, where it can be said that there is governance, but no free media (Haaretz 2003). Lahav presents the two sides of the picture – an activist and energetic press protected by the court, and a press subject to constraints, censorship, and sometimes even sanctions (1993, 173–95).

The security system has a method more effective than censorship for preventing publication – a monopoly on military and security information. This allows them to set the agenda about the security discourse in Israel, which is accomplished primarily through military correspondents who have no independent sources and rely almost exclusively on the IDF. Whether through natural selection or necessity, these military correspondents and commentators – for the press, radio, and especially television – have often become messengers for the IDF. And these correspondents find themselves in a trap – forced to choose between cooperation, which gives them access to classified information, and freedom of the press (Weimann 2007, 22; Negbi 1995, 80–82; Nossek and Limor 2006, 484–510). The pool of military correspondents in the Journalists Association is regarded as a fiefdom of the IDF. Additional channels for influencing public opinion include Galei Tzahal (the IDF radio station), military periodicals, the Defense Ministry publishing house (closed in 2009), control of access to the archives by the History Branch of the Defense Ministry, and the media's security commentators, who are virtually all former military men. The IDF's Spokesperson Unit is now greatly expanded to include public relations functions, international and cyber branches, and a communication school to train spokespersons.[75] The IDF has joined the era of the new media, and in the context of the oversight issue we are addressing here the question is, what has happened to the IDF's credibility?

In the past, Israelis have generally had full confidence in IDF pronouncements, especially by comparison with the distorted information that appeared in the Arab,

[73] During the first Gulf War (1991), the Israeli public and media became a captive audience to the assessments of Israeli intelligence and security services about the Iraqi threats, the need for gas masks, and the importance of remaining in a sealed room.

[74] For a critique of how the media functioned with regard to the 2005 disengagement from Gaza, see Lebeau 2005.

[75] Israel Defense Forces. IDF Blog. www.idfblog.com/about-the-idf/idf-spokespersons-unit [in Hebrew] (accessed May 6, 2016).

media-controlled states. Indeed, it was understood that Israel's release of inaccurate information was directed primarily at foreign audiences, not for Israeli consumption. For example, an announcement in 1953 reported that Israel's reprisal in Qibya in which sixty-nine Arab civilians were killed was carried out by irregular forces from border communities, not the IDF. The assumption was that Israeli citizens, who are closely tuned in to what is going on in their country, would understand this to be *hasbara*, a euphemism in Hebrew for propaganda. Cracks appeared in this credibility during the Yom Kippur War, and since then it is put to a daily test, especially because of the international "media war" that accompanies security-related events, above all when there is injury to civilians.

Following the first Lebanon War, the Israeli public had become more skeptical of announcements issued by the IDF Spokesperson (Peri 2001, 242). During the first Intifada (from late 1987), a duality was already evident in the media reports about security events. Correspondents, especially in the print media, did not make do with the official versions, and exposed what was happening in the occupied territories, sometimes based on the reports of foreign correspondents, including Palestinian sources. Upon outbreak of the first Gulf War (1991), on the other hand, the media aligned itself with the government, while radio and television news were virtually controlled by the IDF (Barzilai 1991, 38). The second Intifada (from 2000) exposed the dilemma even more starkly because of the suicide bombings and the IDF's harsh response to Palestinian civilians in the territories. In an era of commercial competition, a common interest emerges between the media's desire to show the battleground and the security official's desire to release information that reinforces the Israeli version of events for both domestic and foreign consumption. For example, when Israeli TV showed horrifying pictures of the wounded that had been broadcast by the other side, it added a security interpretation, so that "The [Israeli] viewer sees pictures of the injured child, but he also does not see them. He sees them as enemy propaganda, i.e., from the outset he sees them as pictures that someone else will be seeing" (Yuran 2001, 88).

Another question that often arises in Israel is whether the media perform any oversight functions or whether they only report. In the age of the multi-channel, online commercialized media, the dilemma has not been resolved, as illustrated by the harsh public criticism of the media as "hostile" during both Lebanon Wars separated by twenty-four years (Negbi 1985, 50–53; Barzilai 1991, 26; Yadgar 2002, 18–30; Weimann 2007, 10–16). Succinctly put, public criticism of the media during and after those two wars accused them of undermining the war effort, showing inconsideration for the feelings of soldiers at the front and civilians in the rear, and rendering aid to the enemy (e.g., by reporting the sites of rocket hits during the second Lebanon War). At the same time, the Israeli government was accused of making its case poorly in the international media compared with the sophisticated efforts of the other side in what was called "the first really 'live' war in history" (Kalb and Saivetz 2007, 43–66). With respect to the media's failure to be more critical, the Ethics in Times of Conflict Committee of the Israeli Press Council stated: "...journalists must maintain the basic rules of a free press in a democratic country – all the more so in times of emergency." Concerning the media's role in stirring up patriotic fervor, one recommendation was to avoid the pitfalls of live coverage, especially by playing up failures and mishaps (Israeli Press Council 2007, 20–22).

The military operations launched by Israel in the Gaza Strip (2008, 2012, 2014 – see Table 14.1) again evoked questions of Israeli media coverage.[76] Because of the news control, the media would publish official military-government statements without seeking independent confirmation, especially with regard to the IDF policies on opening fire. Thus, even after the Gaza operation, when the IDF made public (April 2009) the military investigation of five events during the operation – *Yediot Aharonot* and *Maariv* accepted the IDF version virtually unchallenged, which pinned sole responsibility for civilian casualties on Hamas and presented failures as one-off errors, not deliberate or systematic. On the other hand, *Haaretz* coverage was much more critical, asking tough questions about the direct and indirect messages given to soldiers and commanders, the problematic and permissive open-fire orders, and the fact that the IDF was investigating itself.[77] In other words, most Israeli readers of the printed news were not aware of the conflicting reports about how the IDF had conducted the operation. The government and the IDF managed to stifle public debate about the operation, hence when the Goldstone Report appeared in September 2009, accusing the IDF of war crimes and demanding an investigation, most Israeli media and citizens supported the official government stance, which dismissed the Goldstone Report as baseless propaganda (UN Human Rights Council 2009). Six years later, during the Gaza Operation in 2014 (Protective Edge), the conflict was as alive as ever. More than six hundred citizens complained to The Second Authority about the news on TV Channels 2 and 10, the majority accusing them of not being patriotic enough. Similarly, readers of *Haaretz* threatened to cancel their subscriptions because Gideon Levy's articles severely criticized the IDF conduct against civilians (Avraham 2014; *Globes*, July 21, 2014).

Israeli journalists are repeatedly exposed to the anguish that afflicts the lives of Jews in Israel, but because they lack a tradition of independent journalistic reporting about security issues, they do not handle it well, especially in times of war and tension. Before and during a war, the media, like most citizens, take refuge in the emotion-laden corner of mobilizing against an enemy, fear of undermining the common effort, identification with IDF soldiers, and pulling together in the struggle for world opinion. Israeli-Jewish citizens have a profound need and desire to rely on the IDF, and the media identify with these feelings and express them. Only afterwards, in realization that the wars fought since 1973 have all been controversial or even failures, do public opinion and the media wake up and voice their disappointment in and censure of the politicians and – indirectly and less incisively – the IDF. The "messengers," i.e., the media, also do not emerge unscathed from this convoluted process.

[76] In 2009 it was characterized as initially "inflammatory, militant, and jingoistic," and downplayed stories about civilian casualties (Keshev Center for Protection of Democracy in Israel 2009).

[77] Note the headline: "The IDF: 'Operational errors' led to the killing of the innocent," *Haaretz*, April 24, 2009. Another example is the Breaking the Silence report on July 15, 2009, "Soldiers' Testimonies from Operation Cast Lead," in which field soldiers reported on the use of human shields (in defiance of High Court rulings), the wholesale demolition of homes, and permissive open-fire regulations, which sometimes led to the killing of innocent bystanders. The strident media attack against this report and the fact that Israel's two largest newspapers ignored it, as opposed to *Haaretz* (see July 15, 2009), is documented in Keshev Center for Protection of Democracy in Israel 2009.

And yet public critique of the media does not usually accuse it of not having discharged its duty of scrutiny and oversight. After the second Lebanon War, for example, critics were not asking why the media had ignored the growing missile armament of Hezbollah, the lack of fortifications of homes in the north, or the IDF's failure to prepare for a war against terrorist organizations and guerilla fighters (Weimann 2007, 32). Military correspondents who had known these problems chose not to address them; those who were unaware of them were equally derelict in their professional duty. In Peri's words, "The pattern of oversight of the Israeli media over the military and security is instrumental, partial, and not substantive" (2008, 221–22).

In Israel, because the enduring security crisis is perceived as existential, the media have long had a hard time discharging their duty to report and thereby respect the public right to know. In other democracies, too, the balance has been upset in the face of the terrorist attacks in the 2000s. Nevertheless, what happened elsewhere cannot serve as an excuse for Israel, because terrorism is relatively new in those countries, and it is hoped they will return to safeguarding human rights, and not just focus on preventing terrorism. We reiterate that Israel has undergone significant change over the years – from almost total media mobilization for the national cause to willingness to keep at least one eye open and criticize even when the security issue is sensitive. But on balance, especially for the electronic media with its visual presence in security matters, the media serve more as an instrumental voice of the Jewish collective and the state than an oversight mechanism for the public.[78]

B. Civil Society Groups and Organizations

The turning point for independent, civilian advocacy on foreign policies and security was the Six Day War and its aftermath. The lack of a clear-cut government policy about the future of the occupied territories created a vacuum that was filled by groups seeking to shape policy: on the right, Gush Emunim with its vision of the Greater Land of Israel, and on the left, Peace Now, with its vision of peace.

Gush Emunim was founded in 1974 for purposes of settling throughout the Land of Israel in an effort to redraw the borders of the state. Its supporters, mostly religious, put themselves completely at the service of this agenda, and with the tacit support of the government, they established settlements throughout the territories. Their success in these settlements created facts on the ground that governments could not ignore. When government policies changed, and appeared to be heading toward political compromise, Gush Emunim and other groups engaged in protest activities against the government, and sometimes these became violent, such as in their resistance to the evacuation of the Sinai settlements, the Oslo Accords, and the disengagement from Gaza (Shafat 1995; Eldar and Zertal 2007; Hoverman 2008; Aran 2013). Some of the settlers engaged in terrorism against the Palestinian population in the territories, either for ideological reasons or as a strategy – to exact a vicious "price tag" from Palestinian civilians and undermine Israeli government

78 For the view that the media have become intrusive and harmful of the IDF, see S.A. Cohen 2006.

policy. Other Jewish right-wing organizations emerged, such as the Faithful of the Temple Mount (1967), the Elad Association to promote Jewish settlement in Jerusalem (1986), Women in Green (1993), Israel's Media Watch (1995), the Israel Academia Monitor that engages in surveillance of Israeli academic activities (2004), Human Rights in Judea and Samaria (2002), and Im Tirtzu to strengthen Zionist values (2007).

Peace Now was founded in 1978 to promote peace with Arab countries and the Palestinians, to halt the settlements in the occupied territories, and to advocate for their evacuation. It was established by IDF reservists, and in the early years emphasized the security credentials of its members (Bar-On 1985; Reshef 1996; Feige 2002). Peace Now engaged primarily in demonstrations, rallies, petitions, and formulating an alternative policy ("territories for peace," "occupation corrupts") that would challenge government thinking. The movement supported the peace agreement with Egypt and opposed the 1982 war in Lebanon. A hand grenade thrown at a rally by a right-wing activist (February 10, 1983) killed a Peace Now activist and injured several others. Its most important strategy, considered extremist at that time, was to accord recognition to the PLO and meet with its members in the 1980s when this was illegal. Its success was in changing public opinion, and the fact that, since 2000, most Israelis support the concept of two states for two nations. Other organizations against the occupation and its effects were Yesh Gvul (1982), Women in Black (1988), B'Tselem (1989), Gush Shalom (1993), Four Mothers Movement for Israeli withdrawal from Lebanon (1997), the Coalition of Women for Peace (2000), Machsom Watch, to monitor the military checkpoints to prevent harm to Palestinian civilians (2001), and Breaking the Silence to assemble testimonies on IDF conduct in the territories (2004).

Some civil society organizations critique Israeli security policy and present alternatives or channels of dialogue with Palestinians, such as the People's Voice ("the Ayalon-Nusseibeh Initiative") or the Geneva Initiative. Others engage in civilian monitoring of military activities, particularly those in the occupied territories. Organizations such as B'Tselem, the Association for Civil Rights in Israel, and the Public Committee against Torture in Israel seek to prevent human rights violations or arbitrary acts carried out on the pretext of security. Other groups that have an impact on the IDF: women's organizations that demand equality for female soldiers or fight sexual harassment in the IDF, and green organizations that oppose IDF plans viewed as harmful to the environment such as the campaign in 2007 to prevent construction of a huge IDF training base in the Negev.

Civil society activism on security matters helps raise public awareness about specific issues, and mobilizes public support for new ideas. When security policy is ambiguous – either deliberately or not – movements with a security agenda can have an impact. For instance, Gush Emunim forced the Labor-led coalition under Rabin (1974–77) to agree to settlements in the territories even though they were built illegally, and opposed the security policy of the government at the time; Peace Now and other organizations legitimized negotiations with the PLO in the 1980s; and the Four Mothers Movement expedited withdrawal from Lebanon in 2000. In contrast, opposition from settlers' organizations was unsuccessful when faced with determined political action such as the withdrawal from the Sinai (1982) or the disengagement from the Gaza Strip (2005).

C. Public Protest

The vehement and bitter public protest that followed the Yom Kippur War (1973) heralded the beginning of legitimacy for direct citizens' involvement in foreign affairs and security policy. And indeed, that protest bore fruit – it brought about the resignation of the government headed by Golda Meir. During the first Lebanon War, public protest was led by Peace Now, groups of reserve soldiers, and bereaved parents – even as the battles raged – and climaxed in a confrontation between the Likud government and the extra-parliamentary left. This protest did not target the conduct of the war or an intelligence failure, as had been the case during the 1973 war, but the very decision to embark upon a "war of choice" and its objectives (Yishai 1985, 390–91). The first such anti-war demonstration took place as the first ceasefire was declared in Lebanon, and protesters were joined by reserve duty soldiers who came directly from the frontlines. This demonstration marked the first time in Israel that civilians had publicly come out against a war declared by the government. Later, the "demonstration of the 400,000" took place – regarded as the largest rally until then – in the wake of the events in the refugee camps Sabra and Shatila. This massive public protest led Prime Minister Begin to appoint a state commission of inquiry to investigate the events and was a factor in his subsequent resignation. In a rally in support of the Oslo Process organized by the peace movements and left-wing parties on November 4, 1995, Prime Minister Yitzhak Rabin was assassinated.

At the launch of the second Lebanon War (2006), the public expressed unqualified support for the government's decision. When rocket fire on the northern towns did not halt, however, and the feeling that the war was not achieving its aims intensified, protest against the government began to surface. After the war ended, sentiments multiplied that it had been conducted poorly, which fanned the flames of public unrest. A protest movement of reserve duty soldiers quickly formed, which called for the resignation of the prime minister, the defense minister, and the chief of staff, and demanded a state commission of inquiry. This movement had partial success when a governmental commission of inquiry was established (the Winograd Commission), and then accomplished its aim when the chief of staff and defense minister both resigned, and the prime minister did not run in the next (2009) election.

D. Non-Violent, Illegal Protest – Refusal to Serve

Conscientious objection to military service as the expression of a pacifist world view was rare in the early years of Israel's history, appearing only in isolated cases.[79] After 1967, "selective refusal" on ideological grounds first appeared – the refusal to serve in the occupied territories, rather than conscientious objection to military service in general – and this became an important and sensitive subject in public discourse. In March 1978, a letter signed by 348 reserve duty officers was delivered to Prime Minister Begin with a demand that the government pursue a peaceful path.

[79] Particularly among members of the Israeli Communist Party, the New Israeli Left Movement, and Matzpen. Amnon Zichroni is considered Israel's first conscientious objector (1954) and a symbol of pacifist refuseniks (Sheleff 1989, 134–39).

Those who signed this "Officers' Letter" (which triggered the founding of Peace Now) did not mention refusal to serve, far from it, but rather implied that motivation to serve was linked to Israel's peace policies. In 1979, another important letter appeared – a declaration signed by twenty-seven Jerusalem high school seniors that they are unwilling to serve in the occupied territories. This trend slowly gathered momentum, and during the first Lebanon War, Eli Geva, an IDF colonel, requested a release from duty as brigade commander because he refused to carry out an order to invade west Beirut. Since then, refusal to serve in the territories and draft resistance became forms of public protest, and these triggered the founding of Yesh Gvul (1982), which openly supported draft resistance and encouraged others not to serve in Lebanon and subsequently the occupied territories (Menuchin and Menuchin 1985). Conscientious and political objection increased during the first Intifada in late 1987. The clubbing of Palestinians, the use of rubber-coated bullets, and the killing of young men throwing stones or civilian demonstrators motivated some soldiers to refuse orders on the grounds that they were illegal.[80] Subsequently, there were cases of refusal during the second Intifada and later among reserve officers in elite units such as pilots, commandos, and intelligence officers.

Originally selective refusal to serve in the territories was motivated by the left – to express opposition to the occupation, the government's policies in the territories, and IDF operations against the Palestinians (Epstein 2003, 215–39). Gradually selective refusal appeared on the right – in opposition to evacuating occupied territories, settlements, or outposts, and often based on calls of rabbis to refuse such orders. It began with the founding of the Movement to Stop the Retreat in the Sinai (1982) after the signing of a peace treaty with Egypt and the violent opposition to evacuating those settlements. The Oslo Process was accompanied by threats of refusal to serve, but since no settlements were actually evacuated, the struggle evolved into violence in other arenas, as we shall see below. The next wave of right-wing refusal to serve took place during the disengagement from Gaza in the summer of 2005. According to one estimate, sixty-three Orthodox soldiers refused to participate (Bender 2005; Weinstein 1998), but the evacuation of Gaza settlements led to a growing sense of alienation among settlers and some rabbis, who threatened to refuse IDF evacuation orders and "to disengage from the State of Israel."

It is difficult to estimate the number of refuseniks on the right and the left, but they have been increasing over the years. In the past, the IDF preferred to ignore the defiance of individuals and opted for quiet agreements with them. When the number grew and the media took an interest, the IDF stepped up enforcement and incarcerated those who refused to serve. Several appealed to the High Court of Justice, which ruled that selective refusal, i.e., refusal to serve in specific areas or carry out

[80] From a statement of principles by Yesh Gvul:

> The uprising in the territories and its brutal repression by the army prove the terrible price of continuing the occupation with no political solution in sight. We, IDF reserve-duty soldiers, declare that we can no longer carry the burden of participating in and being responsible for this moral and political decline. We hereby declare our refusal to take part in repressing the uprising and revolt in the occupied territories.

The original Yesh Gvul website from which this quote was taken was hacked, but more information is available on the Yesh Gvul Facebook page: www.facebook.com/Yesh.Gvul.1982/info/?tab=page_info (accessed May 10, 2016).

specific orders, is illegal. Nevertheless, the High Court did recognize the legitimacy of conscientious objection to military service in general.[81]

Despite its spread, only isolated cases of refusal appeared during the second Lebanon War, and the Winograd Commission praised the high motivation of the reserve duty soldiers. The threat to the IDF from open and illegal refusal to serve remains limited, but symptoms are visible in the decreased motivation to do army service. Public opinion surveys indicate that the vast majority of Israelis oppose illegal forms of protest (Hermann 2005).

E. Political Violence

Right-wing protest over foreign and security policies evolved into political violence after critical events – in the years 1978–84 following the peace treaty with Egypt and subsequent evacuation of the Sinai settlements; and after the first Lebanon War.[82] Radical right opposition to the Camp David Accords was vehement, and also evident in the rise of the Kach movement headed by Meir Kahane, who linked racism against Arabs and opposition to returning territory. The "Jewish underground" arose during this period, a covert group of mostly settlers who were exposed in 1984 after five years of terrorist activity that included murdering students of the Islamic College in Hebron, maiming Palestinian mayors, and more. They were planning to blow up the primary Muslim holy place in Jerusalem (the Dome of the Rock) because they believed that for the redemption of the Jewish people, Muslims must be removed from the Temple Mount and – in the meantime – the peace treaty with Egypt must be annulled. Three underground members were sentenced to life in prison, and others to extended terms, but all were released early after a presidential pardon. In parallel, the Movement to Stop the Retreat in the Sinai was being organized with support from rabbis of Gush Emunim, whose goal was to prevent Israeli withdrawal and the evacuation of Jewish settlements. Movement activists, including Kach members, engaged in violent confrontations with the IDF during the evacuation in April 1982. Similar scenes, but without violence, took place twenty-three years later in 2005 during the evacuation of the Gaza Strip settlements.

The protest of the left against the first Lebanon War and for appointment of a state commission of inquiry was interpreted by the right as a "knife in the back of the nation," and it had tragic consequences. Emil Grunzweig, a Peace Now activist, was killed in February 1983 outside the Office of the Prime Minister in a demonstration that called for the resignation of Defense Minister Ariel Sharon in accordance with the Kahan Commission recommendations.

Political violence escalated again in 1992–95 to protest negotiations with the Palestinians and the signing of the Oslo Accords. In 1994, the massacre of twenty-nine Muslim worshipers in the Tomb of the Patriarchs in Hebron by settler Baruch Goldstein was also an attempt to use political terrorism to disrupt the process and undermine the negotiations. The right-wing demonstrations against the Oslo Accords,

[81] *Algazi v. Minister of Defense* [unpublished]; *Zonshein v. Judge Advocate-General* 2002. On the involvement of the High Court, see Sheleff 1993, 757–809; on the history of refusal to serve, see Epstein 1999, 319–54; Reznik 2003, 520–29.

[82] The following is based on the work of Sprinzak 1995, 78–88.

this time co-sponsored by the Likud Party under Benjamin Netanyahu, bore violent fruit – incitement against the "Oslo criminals," which culminated in November 1995 with the assassination of Prime Minister Yitzhak Rabin. Although the assassin, Yigal Amir, acted alone, his ideological-religious motivations reflected the view of those who believed that government policy was a desecration of God's name. Did the assassination change the course of Israeli policy or the future of Israeli-Palestinian relationships (Grinberg 2000, 123–51)? No one knows whether the process might have been derailed or kept on track. Nonetheless, the bold steps taken by Rabin required charismatic leadership and rested to a large extent on the trust the public felt for Rabin as "Mr. Security." Assassination of the leader who guided the complex Oslo Process left the chance of making peace with the Palestinians in grave doubt.

The impact of the media, civil society, and non-violent protest on shaping security policy is marginal with the exception of the few cases noted above. These channels are primarily effective in creating a critical public climate. Such pressure sometimes impels the government to turn to other monitoring mechanisms, such as commissions of inquiry, and sometimes forces those in office to take responsibility and resign. Such mechanisms, public oversight included, are generally activated *ex post facto*, and their ability to influence the shaping of security policy is limited. Compared with these democratic measures, in the Israeli reality after the assassination of Rabin, political violence has been more successful.

14.10 Security Policy and Democracy

This chapter began with the question of whether security policy in Israel is an "open issue" – unresolved over an extended period; hard to conceptualize; or whether it poses an intractable dilemma. We presented the two extremes, from those who believe the security problem is intractable to those who believe that change is in Israel's hands (Efrati 2003). In concluding this chapter, we address this question and the link between security and democracy.

A. Does Democracy "Get in the Way" of Security in Israel?

On the one hand, for a state to exist and for its existence to be democratic, its survival and continuation must be ensured, i.e., security needs must be met and threats to the citizens or borders must be averted. Meeting security needs sometimes raises the possibility of limiting (or entirely rescinding) democratic rights such as freedom of expression (by censorship), freedom of movement (by curfews), the right to a fair trial (by administrative detention), and the right to choose how to lead one's own life (by the obligation of army service). On the other hand, meeting democracy requirements may sometimes require reining in security considerations, because it is too easy to cross the line between temporary constraints and the retraction of democratic rights; there are many historical precedents for this.[83]

[83] On the US reaction to the terrorism in 2001, see United States, National Commission on Terrorist Attacks upon the United States 2003.

The tension between collective security and human and civil rights exists in every democracy. In countries such as Israel where a state of emergency is legally in force continuously and where the public mood is that of a constant emergency, the balance generally tips toward security (Neuberger 2007, 5–10). In government decisions and court rulings, the assumption is that national security takes priority over other considerations because it is a matter of survival, and therefore when an intractable dilemma arises, security interests generally hold sway. A democracy can withstand this so long as it is absolutely clear that this is a temporary and exceptional situation, but the concern is that temporary measures pave the way for extended use or abuse of the security argument. Thus it becomes easy to undermine the principles of democracy and civil rights on the grounds of security needs (Zamir 1989, 20).

In the twentieth century, democratic governments demonstrated their clear superiority to non-democratic regimes in ensuring the security of their citizens, and yet the subjective belief has not disappeared that a democracy is constrained from fully protecting its citizens. Now in Israel, and in other democratic countries afflicted by terrorist threat too, a belief is common that non-democratic regimes and terrorist groups have an edge in the battle.[84] In Israel, no military coup was ever necessary for security to appropriate the field of policymaking:

> In the case of Israel there would hardly ever be the need for the men on horseback to take over, for their solutions to the major challenges were either integrated into the political system when they were still in uniform, or they themselves enjoyed a peaceful, perfectly natural move to the highest political positions once they left the army. (Ben-Ami 2005, 15–16)

And yet the Israeli case is regarded as unique because of Israel's ability to maintain reasonable, democratic institutions and uphold the rules of the game (within the Green Line), despite the ongoing security threat. In discussing militarization, we examined some of the implications of this for Israeli society. Since the first Intifada, awareness has grown in Israel about the repercussions of a security culture on human values, such as prohibiting the torture of terrorists or even recognizing the harm caused to civilians by construction of the separation barrier.[85]

Yet the dilemma is usually presented as: how to ensure that security does not "get in the way" of democracy versus how democracy does not "get in the way" of security. Correspondingly, there is a search for "the right balance," "proportionality," or a case-by-case solution. In our view, on the assumption that we want to preserve democracy, we should be more concerned about the zealous promotion of security considerations than the zealous promotion of democratic values. Security means deterrence, the ability to win wars, and also the daily protection of citizens' safety. But democracy also protects its citizens; it is crucial to point out that, in the long run, no state has the right to exist if its citizens do not enjoy democratic freedoms and equality. In this sense, the High Court of Justice, B'Tselem, and other monitoring

[84] Of the constraints on Israel's security, Prime Minister Yitzhak Rabin said that the Palestinian Authority has the advantage of fighting Hamas "without a High Court of Justice or B'Tselem" (TV Channel 1, March 1994).

[85] Conversely, in the Palestinian uprising of October 2015, Israeli civilians were encouraged by the government to "counterattack terrorists," resulting in the indiscriminate killing of Arabs and Jews, mistaken as terrorists.

organizations do safeguard the state precisely as the IDF does. The fact that one's adversary does not have such democratic institutions that tie its hands is utterly irrelevant, because a democratic society does not aspire to behave like a non-democratic regime. In democracies, the burden of proof for breach of any freedom always falls upon the state. When the state acts against a citizen's rights in the name of security, it is not the citizen who must defend his or her rights, but the state that must prove its action will enhance public security, just as the state must justify the expropriation of property for public interest or must maintain the innocence of every individual until proven guilty.

And now we reach the heart of the matter: Democracy *never* interferes with security, because it has developed tools to cope with states of emergency and measures to ensure that these are temporary. As long as such legal arrangements are within the rules of the democratic game – from an emergency government to temporary, limited constraints on civil liberties – there should be no fear of the special provisions required by a state of emergency. Israeli society, because of its long experience with the ongoing security threat, should by now have internalized the fact that democracy and security are not incompatible.[86] In a state of emergency, the pendulum will usually lean toward security measures, but democratic states, Israel among them, should by now have learned the lesson: In retrospect, security considerations tend to be used to excess.

B. Security Policy: Is the Issue Irresolvable?

It is very hard to draw up a credible balance sheet about what was done or not done by Israel in order to ascertain who is to "blame" that security has remained an open issue for so very long. By the late 1950s, Israel had already begun to try to escape the trap of external threats by developing a nuclear option (Avner Cohen 1998). According to unofficial reports, the nuclear option was considered by Israel twice – in the early days of the 1973 war and as a deterrent threat against Saddam Hussein in the Gulf War of 1991. Moreover, Israel's policy has been to prevent other regional countries from obtaining nuclear capability, demonstrated in the attack on Iraq's nuclear reactor in 1981; the alleged attack on a Syrian reactor-in-the-making in September 2007; and the preparation for an attack on Iranian nuclear installations since the early 2000s.

Some changes have significantly reduced the immediate strategic threat – peace treaties with Egypt and Jordan, the Beirut Declaration of the Arab League of 2002 (reaffirmed in 2007), which proposes recognition of the state of Israel in return for all territories conquered in 1967; the upheavals in many Arab countries since 2011. On the other hand, the conflict with the Palestinians has become more difficult to disentangle, and flare-ups in the West Bank, Lebanon, and Gaza have become more frequent. Simultaneously a new adversary, and one bearing a nuclear threat, has emerged in Iran.

Here we return to the polarized views with which we began this chapter: Is the source of the conflict the unwillingness of Arab countries and the Palestinians to

[86] Indeed, some measures taken by the United States to ensure "homeland security" after 9/11, such as detention without civilian oversight, would be illegal in Israel.

recognize the existence of Israel, or the unwillingness of Israel to live within specific borders and/or its intransigence on other issues? In our view, even if the former were more correct, Israel cannot allow itself to assume that the same model of transition from warfare to peace that worked so well with Egypt and Jordan would not be applicable on other fronts. The price of continuing the policy of "managing the conflict" is so steep (above all morally) that Israeli society has no choice but to seek a way out (Bar-Tal 2007, 25).

In this sense, the risk of delineating a final border for the state of Israel along the 1949 lines with agreed changes is smaller than the risk entailed by continuation of the conflict. Democracy in Israel is not stable, if only because through most of its history – since 1967 – Israeli citizens have not made up their minds, even among themselves, about the future of the territories then conquered. The decision must be a democratic-political one – by the government and approved by the Knesset – exactly like the decisions to launch a war in 1967, to build settlements in the occupied territories, and to evacuate Sinai and the Gaza Strip. In democracies, such strategic policies are not left up to religious leaders. Viewing the situation as "an intractable conflict" is not just fatalistic, but terrifying for the future of Israel.

15 Arab Citizens of Israel

My country is at war with my people.
(Arab MK Emil Habibi)

15.1 The Challenge to the Political System of Israel's Arab Citizens

In the previous chapters, we examined the political behavior of Israel's Arab citizens with respect to various subjects (participation, elections, civil society, and the media). Here we present Israel's Arab citizens as a separate national group within the political system.

Israel's political system, which had been based on broad consensus in the past, has become more pluralistic (see Chapter 8). Does the greater pluralism also embrace the Arab citizens[1] who live in a state defined as "Jewish and democratic"? Israel's Declaration of Independence proclaims full equality for all Israel's citizens and calls upon members of the Arab nation "to participate in the upbuilding of the State on the basis of full and equal citizenship and due representation in all its provisional and permanent institutions." This solemn pledge has not been kept. The aforementioned consensus has been characteristic of the Jewish citizens of Israel, most of whom even believe that Israel would be better off had the Arabs remained outside the state, though they could remain as tolerated "subtenants" (Benziman and Mansour 1992) – a "hollow presence" is how author David Grossman defined the status of Israel's Arab citizens (1994). With respect to representation, too, Israel's Arab citizens had little influence on events in the political system or Israeli society. They remained outside the circles in which the "1949 constitution" was formulated and took root (Chapter 2). And after some seventy years, the Arabs are still not regarded as equal and legitimate partners for shaping the future of the state and society.[2] Suffice it to say that the Arab parties have never been considered full

[1] The terms commonly used are controversial semantically and symbolically. Israeli Jews generally refer to "the Arab minority," "Arab Israelis," and "the Arab sector"; many Arabs say "Palestinian Arabs in Israel," "the 1948 Arabs," or "the 1948 refugees." In this chapter, we generally refer to "Arab citizens of Israel" or "the Arabs in Israel."

[2] In a Knesset session on June 24, 2015, Deputy Minister of the Interior Yaron Mazuz said, "The Arab MKs should return their ID cards … we are doing you people a favor by even allowing you to sit here."

members of government coalitions,[3] and that the Arab public generally does not participate in the social and economic discourse about issues claimed by Jewish Israelis to be relevant only for Jewish society, such as housing, education, employment, poverty, drug use, etc.[4]

Nevertheless, the growing pluralism of the political system has strengthened the foothold of Arabs in Israeli society and politics. This can be seen in their shedding of Jewish political patronage and the rise of a generation of proud Arab intellectuals – aware, knowledgeable, and determined to win for the Arab citizenry their fair share of resources and rights, political and social, in both public life and the political system (Rabinowitz and Abu Baker 2002). This change led to the writing of the "Vision Documents" (2006 and thereafter) in which prominent Arab citizens outlined their aspirations and plans as citizens of Israel. We shall return to these documents at the chapter end, but provide here a short quote from the most representative of these, written under the aegis of the National Committee of Arab Local Authorities in Israel:

> We are moving toward a new era of self-recognition, where it is necessary to create our future path, crystallize our collective identity, and draw up our social and political agenda ... "Who are we and what do we want for our society?" (2006, 5)

These documents do not in and of themselves challenge the democratic order. Nation-states are not generally mono-ethnic, if only because the approximately 200 sovereign countries that populate the globe in the twenty-first century do not allow for the expression of all aspirations for territorial self-determination (Galnoor 1995, 24–28). The fact that the Jewish and Arab communities in Israel are distinct from each other nationally, religiously, culturally, linguistically, and geographically makes integration difficult, but the situation is not unique. What is distinct to Israel is that the problematic inter-ethnic relations are exacerbated by the Israeli–Arab conflict and the territories occupied in 1967. The small circle of Jewish–Arab relations within Israel overlaps the larger circle of conflictual relations with Palestinians, Arab countries, and the Islamic world; separating these emotionally is almost impossible (H. Ghanem 2009). Furthermore, each of these nations is struggling with questions of its own identity. Jewish citizens are still wondering "Who is a Jew?" and "Who is an Israeli?"; Arab citizens are asking "Who is a Palestinian-Arab-Muslim (Sunni or Shia)/Christian/Druse?" These struggles over individual, communal, religious, and national identity and the tensions among them do not foster rapprochement, compromise, or concessions (Al-Haj 1997). And these struggles only intensified after 2011 following the convulsions of the Arab Spring and the bloodshed between Sunnis and Shias in the Muslim world. Into this cauldron with its mix of Jewishness and Arabness, Islam and Judaism, Israeliness and "Cana'anism," ingredients are often added that can be toxic to achieving a common civil identity. Among Jews, for example, Arabs are often perceived as a "fifth column" or "demographic threat," and there is an obsession with maintaining a "Jewish majority"; among Arabs, perceptions exist of "colonial Israel"

[3] During the Rabin administration (1992–95), an agreement was reached between the Labor Party and two Arab parties – Hadash and the Arab Democratic Party – to support the coalition without being a member of it.

[4] In the social protest of the summer of 2011, Arab citizens minimally participated, erecting several tents in Arab towns.

or a "secret transfer plan." The situation is not symmetrical, of course, as the majority has the moral obligation to meet the minority more than halfway.

In short, these perceptions have affected policymaking about Israel's Arab population, and have fed the unwillingness and perhaps even inability to resolve the issue for so long. We asked in the introduction to this part of the book, is this an "open" policy issue, like the security issue discussed in the previous chapter? Or is it a "wicked problem" (Rittel and Webber 1973), hard to conceptualize and resolve? Alternatively, is it perhaps a problem in search of a policy?

First, we present (with some inevitable reductionism and over-simplification) the two opposing poles on this open question, poles representing approaches that have been around since Israel's creation:

- One pole: Although Arab citizens of Israel are legal citizens, they are loyal not to Israel, but to the hostile neighboring countries. They pose security threats (Palestinian, Arab, Muslim) as well as the threat of territorial irredentism.
- The opposite pole: Israel's Arab citizens are citizens like all the others, with rights and obligations as individuals and with a distinct national, religious, cultural, and linguistic identity as a group.

These two approaches can either lead to "external" solutions – territorial division, population transfer, autonomy, a binational state, etc.; or to ideological solutions – an alliance of Semitic nations (Jews and Arabs), Cana'anism, class solidarity, secular Israeli multi-nationalism, and others. If one rejects the immoral solutions (such as "transfer" – forcing Arabs and Arab towns out of Israel's borders), and setting aside solutions that are not currently practical (such as a binational state),[5] two political alternatives remain from the perspective of the Israeli political system. In one, the fear of a "fifth column" Arab minority would lead to a policy of absolute control, i.e., the resumption of martial law over Arabs in Israel; while the other may engender a policy never before attempted in Israel – accepting Arabs as full-fledged, equal citizens, ensuring they have the same status and rights as Jewish citizens, and accepting them as partners in a new Israeli, civil consensus. The latter alternative would pose two questions:

- Would Israel, whose very existence embodies the Zionist vision of Jewish self-definition and independence, allow for non-Jewish citizens in its midst, in particular the indigenous Arab minority?
- Can the Arabs in Israel, who have been estranged from their own homeland, accept minority status in a country defined by the Zionist vision?

15.2 The Historical Context

With the end of World War I and establishment of the British Mandate for Palestine (Eretz Israel), the Arab and Jewish communities found themselves living side by side. The former was an indigenous community, many having lived there for generations, some coming from nearby, but with a national identity yet inchoate. The latter, a community of Jewish immigrants inspired by the national Zionist awakening in

[5] On the "one-state" or "binational state" solutions, see Rekhess 2008; A. Ghanem 2009; Bashir 2011.

the nineteenth century, was determined to establish a state for the Jewish people in the historical Land of Israel. When the UN voted in 1947 to partition the land into two states, one Jewish and one Arab, fewer than two million people were living in Mandatory Palestine according to the report by UNSCOP (United Nations Special Committee on Palestine), two-thirds of them Arab and one-third Jewish. According to the partition resolution, some 800,000 people would reside in the designated Jewish state, two-thirds of them Jewish and one-third Arab, while the designated Arab state would contain fewer than 2 percent Jews.

The partition proposal was enthusiastically accepted by the Zionist movement and the Yishuv, but rejected by the Arab leadership of Palestine, the Arab countries, and the Arab League (Galnoor 1995, 286). In May 1948, the state of Israel was established, while the Arab state that was supposed to arise in parallel did not come into being. Controversy aside about how many native Arabs fled and how many were driven out, as of 1949 some 160,000 Arabs remained within the ceasefire borders of the new state of Israel. Upon the cessation of hostilities, some of the Arabs who remained in Palestine – or who returned during the ceasefire – became "internal refugees" (residents of destroyed villages who now lived elsewhere in Israel) or "present absentees."[6] This definition includes all the refugees that remained within Israel prior to the census taken on November 8, 1948. Some resided in villages near their hometowns, and some were sent to absorption villages in accordance with IDF orders. The precise number of internally displaced Arabs during this period is not known (though it is between 20,000 and 50,000, of whom 90 percent were Muslim and 10 percent were Christian).[7]

The policies concerning Israel's Arabs that were put in place by the Provisional Government during the war and the state-in-the-making period were based on the aspiration that as few Arabs as possible would live in Israel, and on the assumption that those who remained would be a security risk. (On the Ministry of Minority Affairs, abolished in July 1949, and the military government, see Osatzky-Lazar 2006, 16–20.) The martial law imposed in September 1948 represented a clear security orientation, of course, and became the main instrument for dealing with Arab minority affairs (Benziman and Mansour 1992).

Martial law, pursuant to the 1945 Mandatory Defense (Emergency) Regulations, was imposed over the areas inhabited by the Arab population for purposes of control and the provision of basic services. First imposed on the territories intended to be the Arab state according to the Partition Plan, it was later extended to all the Arab towns in the Galilee, the Triangle region, the Negev, and the mixed cities of Ramla, Lod, Jaffa, and Ashkelon. A separate military government was installed in Jerusalem because of its special status in the Partition Plan. The military administration was

[6] The term "present absentees" was created in the wake of the Absentee Property Law (1950), which transferred the property left in Israel by Palestinian refugees to the state-appointed Custodian for Absentee Property. Because many of those absent were not living in their hometowns, but living in Israel (and counted as residents of other Arab towns), the oxymoron "present absentees" was born.

[7] Kabha and Barzilai 1996. According to Morris (1988), 102,000 Arabs lived in Israel in November 1948 (based on the census), and the Foreign Ministry claims that another 30,000–40,000 Arabs infiltrated into Israel after the census. According to Hillel Cohen (2000, 22), the Jewish National Fund archives and the State Archive count 23,000 internally displaced Arab refugees in Israel in the early 1950s.

adjunct to the General Staff and directly subordinate to the minister of defense. The role of the military governors appointed by the minister was to ensure control over the Arab citizens by imposing limitations on movement, expulsions, travel permits, administrative detention, curfews, and blocking entry to some areas. The Ratner Commission appointed in 1955 to review the need for maintaining martial law recommended continuing it, and listed the following among its non-security goals: preventing the entry of Arab refugees to Israel, preventing Arab residents from returning to their homes in conquered areas, and keeping immigrant towns in the periphery separated from the Arab population (Osatzky-Lazar 2006, 48–50).

The imposition and broad scope of martial law drew fire from many in Israel. Those in favor of the military government cited the hostility of the Arab population and their proximity to the border zones; those who disapproved – Mapam, Maki, and the Council for Abolishing the Military Government – opposed use of the Mandatory Defense Regulations, decried the danger of political-party manipulations, and cited government intervention in the elections on behalf of the ruling parties. The Kafr Qasim events in 1956 intensified public debate because the killing of Arab citizens (including women and children) who were unaware of the curfew and returned late to their village took place in the area under military rule. The incident laid bare the problematic relationship between the state and its Arab citizens. Despite proposed legislation, public petitions, and recommendations by a ministerial committee headed by Justice Minister Pinchas Rosen, the security establishment under Ben-Gurion staunchly objected to rescinding martial law. It was Levi Eshkol, heir to Ben-Gurion as prime minister and minister of defense, who engineered the easing of the military government in late 1966. In practice, the new circumstances created by the 1967 war and the imposition of martial law in the occupied territories are what led to the final termination of the system within the borders of Israel.

The outcome of the 1967 war further exacerbated the problematic status of Arabs in Israel. First, the occupation of the territories strengthened the bond between Palestinians in Israel and those in the territories. Second, the war fueled nationalist and hawkish views among Jews in Israel. The liberation/conquest of the holy places evoked national and even messianic irredentism among Jews and frustration among Muslims, which intensified the tension between the individual, communal, religious, and national identities within Israel. Israeli control over more Palestinians seems to have further raised the level of "wickedness" of the open Arab issue in the political system.

This tension erupted into confrontation and bloodshed on March 30, 1976, which came to be known as Land Day. Arab anger at the Israeli government's policies of land expropriation was not new, but the government decision to expropriate 20,000 dunam in the Sakhnin region triggered calls by Rakah leaders and affiliated council heads to hold protest marches and a general strike. The demonstrations boiled over into stone-throwing and blocking roads; in clashes with the police and IDF troops, six demonstrators were killed and some thirty were injured. Ever since, this day is commemorated by Arabs in Israel with strikes and protests against the expropriation of their lands.

A similar event, though in a different context, occurred in October 2000. After MK Ariel Sharon's provocative visit to the Temple Mount and subsequent eruption of the second Intifada, violent clashes broke out in Israel between Arab demonstrators and security forces. Police fire resulted in the killing of thirteen Arab citizens who were demonstrating, and one Jewish citizen, who was killed by a thrown rock. The October events shredded the fabric of relations between Jewish and Arab citizens, and deepened the mutual distrust: Jews felt threatened, fearing that the Arabs were joining the Intifada in the territories; and Arabs viewed the willingness of the police to open fire and kill demonstrators as proof that the state cared little about shedding the blood of its Arab citizens. The extent to which this event evoked Arab fury and frustration cannot be overstated. The government headed by Ehud Barak tried to dodge responsibility by appointing a low-level inquiry committee, but pressure from Arab leaders as well as other factors forced the government to establish a state commission of inquiry to investigate "the clashes between the security forces and Israeli citizens" (see discussion of the Or Commission in Chapter 7).

The Or Commission report, issued in 2003, explored the context of these events in depth – the ongoing discrimination against Arab citizens of Israel. It also described the flawed conduct of the police during the clashes and recommended that the evidence be examined for bringing charges against several police officers. The report also noted growing extremism among Arabs in Israel generated by their identification with the Palestinian struggle, rising religious fanaticism, and the irresponsible actions of several Arab leaders, including incitement to violence. For Arab citizens, the events of October 2000 continue to symbolize their betrayal by the state, epitomized by the fact that the legal adviser to the government chose not to intervene in the decision of the Police Investigations Unit not to indict anyone involved, and the fact that the ministerial committee established by the Sharon government to implement the report's conclusions accomplished nothing.[8] Five years later, Shimon Shamir, a member of the Or Commission, wrote that notwithstanding the efforts made by several ministries in the Olmert government of 2007 to reduce the gaps (such as the appointment of MK Raleb Magadele, the first Arab minister, to the post of minister of science, culture, and sport), "in the general situation of the Arab sector, change was meager and the sorry state of affairs depicted in the report has not fundamentally altered" (S. Shamir 2009, vii).

The status of Arabs in Israel is linked to the future of the territories and resolution of the Israeli–Arab conflict. The statement by Emil Habibi, renowned Arab author and Knesset Member, that "My country is at war with my people" is a reflection of the fact that this conflict is not "external" to the state and not in the realm of ordinary majority–minority relations. Israel's inability to resolve the conflict with the Palestinians casts a dark shadow over Israeli society, including relations between its Jewish and Arab citizens. Deepening this shadow are the two nation's very different historical memories of the 1948 events and what preceded them: The war of liberation of one side is the Nakba – the disaster – of the other.[9] The pendulum has swung erratically over the years: from hope and willingness for conciliation in the wake of the peace treaty with Egypt, the Oslo Process, peace with Jordan, and the Engagement Plan; to despair and confrontation in the wake of the two Intifadas,

[8] In October 2008, the Higher Arab Monitoring Committee submitted a petition to Prime Minister Olmert signed by some quarter of a million people demanding that those responsible for the events of 2000 be indicted (Jerusalem Post 2008).

[9] On how the Jewish public in Israel constructs its perceptions of the Nakba as reflected in the five major newspapers, and on the "Nakba Law" enacted in 2011, see Jamal and Bsoul 2014.

the terrorist attacks, the wars with Lebanon, the rise of Hamas in the Gaza Strip, the firing of rockets from Gaza, the frequent military campaigns, and the internal wars in the Muslim world. And these have been reflected in the two paths traveled on the open issue of the place of Arabs in Israeli society – social and political exclusion in parallel with integration and equality.

15.3 Legal Underpinnings

Of the 160,000 Palestinians who remained within the borders of Israel at the close of the War of Independence, some 60,000 accepted Israeli citizenship and the remainder were eligible for citizenship as stipulated by the Citizenship Law (1952). Citizenship and its limitations as defined by this law were premised upon their residence or birth in Israel. The civil status of Arabs in Israel is linked to the issue of Israeli citizenship in general; for our purposes, we make do with a concise summary: While citizenship policies with respect to Jews are remarkably flexible – citizenship is granted immediately upon immigration to Israel by virtue of the Law of Return – the ability of non-Jews to obtain citizenship is highly circumscribed. The most severe limitation (absolute refusal to consider the granting of citizenship) is imposed on Palestinians on the grounds of security and ensuring a Jewish majority (Rubinstein and Medina 2005, vol. II, 1072).

The conditions stipulated by law for becoming a citizen prevented many Arab residents of Israel from becoming citizens until amendment of the Citizenship Law in 1980, which stated that anyone born in Israel shall be an Israeli citizen. The broad powers bestowed upon the interior minister in this matter were exploited to prevent the granting of citizenship to Palestinians married to Israeli citizens. This policy is anchored in the Citizenship and Entry into Israel Law (Temporary Provision) (2003), which states that residents of the occupied territories shall not be given a permit to remain in Israel if the interior minister or area commander declares them to be a security risk; this law also states that Palestinians from the territories who are married to Israeli citizens (usually Arab citizens) are not eligible for citizenship or residency. A 2007 amendment asserts that citizens of an enemy state who are married to Israeli citizens are not eligible for any residency or citizenship status.[10] Although a temporary provision is not forever, the validity of this law has been extended time and again since 2003, even though the High Court of Justice issued an order nisi in July 2008 instructing the state to explain why this law should not be invalidated as it undermines the fundamental right of an Israeli citizen to choose a spouse and establish a family there (*ACRI v. Minister of Interior Affairs* 2008). In 2012, the High Court rejected the petitions (six judges versus five), accepted the state's position about security concerns, and, between the lines, accepted the demographic considerations (*Galon v. Attorney General* 2012). Another amendment in 2010 obligates the non-Jew requesting Israeli citizenship to declare loyalty to Israel as "a Jewish and democratic state." This requirement is not imposed on Jews.

Following repeal of the military government in 1966 – which had abrogated many rights of Israel's Arab citizens – the status of Arabs in Israel can be assessed

[10] The following are defined as "an enemy country" in Amendment 2 (2007) of the Citizenship and Entry into Israel Law (Temporary Provision): Iran, Lebanon, Syria, and Iraq.

through the lens of the large body of relevant laws passed by the Knesset. Several of these explicitly cite Jewish national origin as the basis for the legislation, such as the Law of Return (1950) or the Basic Laws that define Israel as a "Jewish and democratic" state (Kretzmer 1990). Other laws imply a distinction between Jewish and non-Jewish citizens, such as the laws and regulations that seek to preserve the Jewish character of Israel. From this large corpus, we examine here the most salient laws in three groupings – those that set the symbolic and practical status of the Arab versus the Jewish community, property laws, and laws related to resource allocation.

A. Civil and Symbolic Status

Citizenship laws have important symbolic functions: they determine the status of the Arab community in Israel, they establish the Jewish nation-state, and, in practice, they give priority to the Jewish over the Arab community. Indeed, the struggle between Jews and Arabs for the same territory is riddled with attempts to monopolize the symbols, not just through law. Hebraicizing the names of Arab places is one example. The most striking law of this nature is the Law of Return, which transforms every Jew in the world into a potential citizen of Israel. The right to citizenship is also bestowed upon any Jew's spouse, as well as his or her children and grandchildren and their spouses. Another example is the Law and Administration Ordinance (1948), which establishes the Jewish character of Israel in which the Jewish Sabbath and holidays are national days of rest. The Flag and Anthem Law (1949) accords formal status to Jewish religious and national symbols, which are not meaningful to Israel's non-Jewish citizens. Other legislation gives special status to Jewish institutions: The World Zionist Organization – Jewish Agency (Status) Law (1952) gives these two institutions special standing in Israel. The Jewish National Fund Law (1953) awards it special status, and half the governing council of the Israel Land Administration must be composed of JNF representatives. These institutions are not Israeli, but designed to serve only the Jewish population, and this has many practical implications for the Arab population with respect to lands, settlement, public services, and other critical issues.

The Foundations of Law Act (1980) states that if the court is confronted by a legal question that it cannot decide by recourse to statute law, case law, or precedent, "it shall decide it in the light of the principles of freedom, justice, equity and peace of Israel's heritage." Notwithstanding the vagueness of the law and the difficulty of applying it to rulings (see discussion in Chapter 6), the law recognizes the Jewish basis for jurisprudence in Israel. Amendment 7 to the Basic Law: The Knesset prohibits political parties and candidates from running for the Knesset if their goals or activities deny the existence of Israel as a Jewish and democratic state. We note that this clause would disqualify not just advocates of "a state of all its citizens" or a binational state, but also those whose goal is to make Israel a Halakhic state that is not necessarily democratic.[11]

[11] In 2014, an amendment to this Basic Law was tabled that would have given the Knesset authority to remove an MK from office because of his or her expressed support for an armed struggle against Israel. The bill was intended to target Arab MKs, since such matters can be dealt with by existing criminal law.

The question of the status of the Arabic language alongside Hebrew also belongs to the sensitive realm of symbols. Israel did not change the Mandatory regulation that made Arabic one of the three official languages together with English and Hebrew (English as an official language was rescinded by Article 15(B) of the Law and Administration Ordinance) and the official status of Arabic was given judicial weight by a Supreme Court ruling (*Adalah et al. v. Municipality of Tel Aviv-Jaffa* 2002 – see Section 15.9 of this chapter). On the other hand, the proposed constitution of the Knesset Constitution, Law and Justice Committee attempted to downgrade the status of Arabic: "Hebrew is the language of the state … Arabic has special status as the language of the Arab residents of Israel" (2006, Articles 7 and 7B).[12] Fostering the Hebrew language is official policy anchored in the Supreme Institute for the Hebrew Language Law (1953) and the Broadcasting Authority Law (1965); only in 2007 was the need recognized to also foster Arabic language and culture in Israel with passage of the Supreme Institute for the Arabic Language Law (2007).

Other laws explicitly prioritize the majority Jewish community: The State Education Law (1953), which defines the goals of education, establishes that elementary school education shall be based upon the values of Jewish culture as well as loyalty to the state and the Jewish people. Although Article 4 notes that in "non-Jewish" institutions the curriculum shall be adapted to the special conditions there, it does not define the goals of education of the non-Jewish population of Israel (Al-Haj 1996, 69–82). Similarly, the Broadcasting Authority Law (1965) and the Second Authority for Television and Radio Law (1990) list among their roles "strengthening ties with the Jewish heritage and its values"; with regard to Arabic, the law states, "to have Arabic language programs that meet the needs of the Arabic-speaking population and broadcasts to promote understanding and peace with the neighboring countries in accordance with the foundational trends of the state." The Chief Rabbinate of Israel Law (1980) gives legal standing to the rabbinate, but not to any parallel Muslim, Christian, or Druze religious institutions.

B. Land

The most egregious discrimination against Arab citizens of Israel relates to land ownership. The Absentee Property Law (1950) expropriated the lands of those defined as "absentees," a term applied only to Arabs. Similarly, the Land Acquisition (Validation of Acts and Compensation) Law (1953) states that when certain conditions are met (conditions that would apply only to Arab – owned "absentee property"), the land becomes the property of the Development Authority. These two laws were the main tools for expropriating land from Arab citizens. In addition, articles in the Basic Law: Israel Lands (1960), the Israel Land Administration Law (1960), and the Jewish National Fund Law (1966) formulate arrangements that prohibit the leasing of JNF-owned lands to non-Jews. This prohibition was not put to a judicial test; when the issue arose, the Land Administration prevented judicial review by transferring the disputed plot from the JNF to the Israel Land Administration, which has no prohibition on leasing land to non-Jews (*Kadan v. Israel Land Administration* 2000).

[12] The Israel Democracy Institute proposal would also downgrade the status of Arabic: "Hebrew shall be the language of the state; Arabic shall be an official language" (Israel Democracy Institute 2007).

Another example is the Agricultural Settlement (Restriction on Use of Agricultural Land and of Water) Law (1967), which prohibits the subletting of Jewish-owned JNF property or the transfer of water quotas on that land by subletting.

Against this background, it is clear that

> The question of the ownership and management of land in the state is a key question in the fabric of relations between Jews and Arabs in Israel … Large tracts of land lost by Arab citizens of Israel (beyond the property of Palestinian refugees who were forced to live outside Israel) as a result of expropriations, legislation that works to reduce land ownership by Arabs, and discriminatory policies weigh heavily on the Arab public in Israel. (Schnell, Biger, and Rosenberg 2013, 7)

The authors recommend that Arabs be accepted as full partners in managing the land resources of the state and be partially compensated for their loss of property as a result of the 1948 war and its aftermath. To that end, they set forth recommendations that differ from the tough policies currently in place, but "all this without putting at risk the character of Israel as a Jewish state" (ibid., 10). They place the land problem within the category of majority–minority relations, not as a matter of equal citizenship in a state.

C. Resource Allocation

Although discriminatory policy against Arab citizens is not explicit, some laws continue to make a distinction between allocations for Jews and Arabs by defining military service as a criterion for eligibility. Thus, without explicitly citing them, Arab citizens can be excluded as they do not serve in the military, while Jewish citizens who do not serve (such as the ultra-Orthodox) can be included through regulations that circumvent the law. For example, a 1970 amendment to the Discharged Soldiers Law (1949) made eligibility for special child allowances contingent upon military service, while the Discharged Soldiers Law of 1984 gave discharged soldiers priority in acceptance to schools of higher education – both laws discriminatory against Arab citizens. The law also affirmed that discharged soldiers – even if they served for only three weeks – would be entitled to larger mortgages. The state, of course, has the authority to reward those who serve in the military (such as a discharge grant), but must not discriminate against groups that are not drafted for military service. A High Court of Justice ruling from 1991 (*Gross v. Ministry of Education*) and the Discharged Soldiers Law of 1984 more clearly delineate the legitimate remuneration for actual service versus using the "army veteran" label as a way to discriminate against Arab citizens (Saban 2000, chapter 7).

Other discriminatory laws: The Encouragement of Capital Investments Law (1959) offers grants and tax exemptions to industrial enterprises in priority areas, but the proportion of Arab towns in the priority areas is minuscule. The Income Tax Regulations (1985) award tax benefits to sixty-five localities along the northern border, including one Druze (Hurfeish) and one mixed (Ma'alot Tarshiha) town, but four Arab localities were added to the list following a High Court petition (Benziman and Mansour 1992, 131–36).[13] Meanwhile, another way was found to give priority to

[13] The towns that won inclusion in the Income Tax Regulations (1985) were Hosen, Gush Halav, Hurfeish, Mi'ilia, Ma'alot-Tarshiha, Safsufa, Avdon, Aramshe, Fassuta, and Rehaniya (Me'ona) (Income Tax Authority 1995, 28–29).

Jewish towns: The Development Towns and Regions Law (1988) aims to "encourage settlement, development, and social and economic progress of development towns and regions and their inhabitants," but the law was never implemented because of its high cost. In 1993, the government decided to award benefits in education, housing, and industry to towns in "National Priority Areas" (Decision 721), but the priority map was initially drawn to include only Jewish towns. Druze and Circassian towns were added in 1998. In 2002, the government agreed to redefine the priority areas and benefits (Decision 2288), but only four Arab localities were included among the 535 entitled to education benefits. Adalah and the Higher Monitoring Committee of Arab Citizens of Israel petitioned the High Court of Justice against the discrimination of Arab towns. The High Court accepted their basic arguments – that the government decision is discriminatory as it contravenes the principle of equality – and stated that a decision like this requires Knesset legislation (*Adalah et al. v. Israel Land Administration et al.* 2006; T. Rosner 2006). In 2007, the government tabled a bill entitled "Setting National Priority Areas," declaring in 2008 that "the periphery is a national priority area" (Decision 3960). This was eventually incorporated into the Arrangements Law enacted for 2009–10.[14]

The Jewish Religious Services (Consolidated Version) Law (1971) allocates state money to Jewish religious councils only. Laws provide state funding to faith-based institutions and non-profits for Jews only, such as the Yitzhak Ben-Zvi Institute Law (1976), intended to deepen public awareness of the continuity of Jewish settlement in the Land of Israel and to promote research about its history; or the Mikve Israel Agricultural School Law (1976), among whose goals is the education of young people according to the Jewish heritage. Such support is not new, but there is a glaring absence of support for parallel Arab institutions. Israel as the state of the Jewish people is a legal fact, and the Knesset Law even authorizes the chair to disqualify any bills that deny the existence of Israel as the state of the Jewish people (Kretzmer 1990, 27), but this does not entitle the state to discriminate against non-Jews in allocating state resources.

Another law that ostensibly deals with the allocation of resources is Amendment 40 to the Budget Principles Law (2011), which authorizes the finance minister to withdraw funds from a state-supported institution if it rejects the existence of Israel as a Jewish and democratic state; incites to racism, violence, or terrorism; supports the armed struggle or terrorism of an enemy state or terrorist group against Israel; marks Israeli Independence Day or the day of Israel's establishment as a day of mourning; or engages in an act of destruction or desecration of the state flag or other state symbols. This amendment has been dubbed "the Nakba law" because of the section intended to deter Arabs from marking Israeli Independence Day as a symbolic day of mourning.

D. Laws that Ignore the Existence of Arab Citizens of Israel

The laws cited above reflect the privileging of Israel's Jewish over its Arab community; they are designed to shore up Jewish primacy in society and the state. In

[14] Government Decision 130, May 12, 2009, "Promoting and Encouraging the Periphery," was included in the Budget Bill for 2009–10. www.mof.gov.il/BUDGETSITE/ECONOMICPLAN/Pages/EconomicPlan20092010.aspx (accessed May 13, 2009).

addition, a diverse variety of laws either ignore the very existence of Arab citizens in Israel, or discriminate against them. They can be grouped into three categories: first, discriminatory laws clearly aimed against Arab citizens, such as property laws, laws encouraging capital investment, and income tax regulations; second, laws that give precedence to the Jewish over the Arab community, but do not formally contravene the principle of civil equality – they are a reflection of the fact that Jews are the majority in Israeli society, for example the Law and Administration Ordinance, which designates the Jewish Sabbath and holidays as the official days of rest, and the Foundations of Law Act, which instructs the court to look to Jewish heritage for difficult to resolve legal issues. And the third category are laws that harm Arab citizens "unintentionally," i.e., bills drafted or laws passed without considering the problems that may result to Arab citizens. This lack of thought testifies that Arab citizens are not counted among groups whose needs and desires must be taken into account during the legislative process. Laws and regulations that ignore the needs of Arab citizens exist in many areas, and later in this chapter we cite several with respect to local authorities, non-profits, and others.

The most important legal-constitutional statement in this matter is the declaration in the Basic Laws that Israel is a "Jewish and democratic" state. This statement was not made without forethought, of course, but it is doubtful that its full impact on Israel's Arab citizens was considered. The byline "Jewish and democratic" under the official name of the state of Israel has created conceptual and practical complexities for the political and legal system as well as the citizenry. It probably does not even deepen the "Jewishness" of Israel (Avnon 1996; Galnoor 2003/4, 515). When the state itself, not the society or culture, defines itself as Jewish, non-Jewish groups justifiably feel left out of the civil collective. Bestowing constitutional status upon a statement that lacks consensus or fails to accommodate a fifth of the citizens creates severe problems in defining the status and role of Israel's Arab citizens. Their reaction appears in the Vision Documents:

> Defining the Israeli State as a Jewish State and exploiting democracy in the service of its Jewishness excludes us and creates tension between us and the nature and essence of the State. Therefore, we call for a Consensual Democratic system that enables us to be fully active in the decision-making process and guarantees our individual and collective national, historic, and civil rights. (The National Committee of Arab Local Authorities 2006, 5)[15]

Various demands appear in the Vision Documents, from general recognition of the collective and individual rights of Arab citizens, to recognition of their cultural autonomy, to recognition of them as a separate national minority, which would mean governmental reorganizing as a binational state (Y.T. Jabareen 2006; Smooha 2013).

[15] The formulation in Mada al-Carmel's "Haifa Declaration" (May 2007):

> Our vision for the future relations between Palestinian Arabs and Israeli Jews in this country is to create a democratic state founded on equality between the two national groups. This solution would guarantee the rights of the two groups in a just and equitable manner. This would require a change in the constitutional structure and a change in the definition of the State of Israel from a Jewish state to a democratic state established on national and civic equality between the two national groups, and enshrining the principles of banning discrimination and of equality between all of its citizens and residents.
>
> (Mada al-Carmel 2007, 16)

15.4 Arab Society in Israel

Data about Arab society are difficult to interpret because of methodological inconsistencies in defining the terms or samples, and because these are relatively new research categories. Some data, for example, do not include the Druze or Bedouin populations of Israel; in some studies, the category "other non-Jews" includes Christians who are not Arab. And there are political biases and demographic sensitivities about including the Druze of the Golan Heights or the Arabs of East Jerusalem. On the other hand, there is a tendency to treat "Arabs" as if they are a homogeneous group, without distinguishing between Muslims, Christians, Druze, or Circassians, or noting differences between residents of the Galilee, the Triangle, mixed cities, and Negev Bedouin. Hence, the statistical profile of Arab society in Israel will be subject to some critique, primarily with regard to the political aspects of the definitions.[16]

A. Population

According to the Central Bureau of Statistics, the Arab population of Israel at the end of 2016 was 1.8 million, approximately 21 percent of the total population of Israel; if the residents of East Jerusalem and the Golan Heights are excluded, the population is 1.35 million (some 18%). Distribution by religion: approximately 83 percent are Muslim, 9 percent are Christian, and 8 percent are Druze.[17] In recent years, the proportion of Christians in the Arab population has declined because of the reduced mortality rate of Muslims, the lower fertility rate among Christians, and the higher emigration rate of Christian Arabs leaving Israel. For the first two reasons, the proportion of Druze has also somewhat declined. The high growth rate of the Arab population in Israel (2.2% compared with 1.8% among Jews) almost entirely stems from natural population growth, but this is declining, except for the Bedouin in the south. As a result, Arab society is very young, particularly the Muslim population, with a median age of only 21.0, compared with a median age of 31.6 in the Jewish population (CBS *Statistical Abstract* 2014).

Most of the Arab population lives in the north of Israel: 717,000, constituting 55 percent of the total northern population (2013). In all other regions, Arabs constitute a minority. Most Arabs (54%) live in local and regional councils; the others live in the thirteen urban areas (34%), the seven mixed cities (8%), and other localities (4%).[18] The most common community is rural with a population

[16] Haider (2005–10: 2005) as well as Gharrah (2015, 14) include the permanent residents of Arab, mixed, and Jewish localities in the category "Arabs," though, unlike the CBS, they do not include the Arab residents of East Jerusalem or the Golan Heights nor the Circassians (a total of over 300,000 people in 2013). The data that follow are mostly drawn from publications of the Central Bureau of Statistics and the National Insurance Institute because the aforementioned distinctions, while important politically and symbolically, are not significant for the overall comparison of Jews and Arabs. Nevertheless, more refined data will also be presented, and will be explicitly noted.

[17] CBS website (the religious distribution is based on the 2014 *Statistical Abstract*). CBS defines "Arabs" to include Muslims, Arab Christians, Druze, residents of East Jerusalem, and the Druze population of the Golan Heights. According to Gharrah (2013, 18), the Arab population of Israel in 2010 was 1.2 million, which does not include East Jerusalem or the Golan Heights, approximately 83 percent of them Muslim, 9 percent Christian, and 9 percent Druze.

[18] The seven mixed cities in which Arabs live, in order of population, are Haifa, Jaffa, Lod, Ramla, Acre, Nazareth Illit, and Ma'alot Tarshiha for a total of approximately 100,000 residents in 2010. "Other" primarily includes Bedouin localities in the south (Gharrah 2015, 16, 28).

Table 15.1 *Education among Arabs and Jews (2010–2011)*

	Arabs	Jews
Average number of children per classroom – primary school	27	24
Average number of children per classroom – secondary school	27	25
Attendance in preschools of two-year-olds	8%	40%
Men with 13 or more years of schooling	25%	53%
Women with 13 or more years of schooling	27%	60%
High school seniors who passed matriculation exam	50%	58%
High school seniors who passed matriculation exam and meet university entrance requirements	36%	50%

Sources: Haider 2005–10: 2010, 48–54; Gharrah 2013, 113–14; Rudnitzky 2014, 55.

of 20,000 or less: Some 55 percent of the Arabs in Israel reside in villages with 5,000 residents or more; and 6 percent live in hamlets with fewer than 2,000 residents. Approximately 35 percent live in urban areas (Arab or mixed). The Bedouin population numbers approximately 100,000, only 4 percent still nomadic (Himeyn-Raisch 2008).

In all the areas examined, great progress has been made in the situation of the Arab population, yet major gaps remain with the Jewish population.

B. Education

As Table 15.1 shows, gaps begin early, with a low proportion of Arab two-year-olds attending preschools, compared to Jewish two-year-olds. The marked difference between the two populations in educational investment is evident in several areas, including more crowded classrooms in Arab schools, though this has improved over the last decade. The gap in secondary school education is also closing: About half the Arab population attends high school compared to a fifth in 1975. The proportion of those matriculating is similar for Jewish and Arab students, but a gap of 14 percent remains between Arab and Jewish high school seniors who meet university entrance requirements.

At the other end of the spectrum, the high proportion of Arabs who have not studied at all, most of them women, is striking. According to Abu-Asba (2006, 185), two main types of obstacles impede schooling for Arabs in Israel: the first relates to infrastructure and crowded classrooms in Arab communities, particularly in preschools and elementary schools, which directly affect achievement (as measured by scholastic tests), the dropout rate, matriculation scores, acceptance to schools of higher learning, and other education indicators. The second obstacle concerns Arab identity – policies that do not take into consideration the national and religious distinctiveness of the Arab-Palestinian minority in Israel, failing to offer cultural-educational autonomy and collective rights. In general, the education of Arab citizens has improved over the past decade, as have scholastic achievements, and gaps between men and women have closed, though the levels are still significantly lower than in the Jewish population (Khamaisi 2011, 182).

Table 15.2 *Standard of living indicators: Arabs and Jews (2009–2012)*

	Arabs	Jews
Infant mortality rate per 1,000 live births (2010)	5.6	2.7
Home ownership (2009)	93%	70%
Persons per room (2009)	1.4	0.8
Civilian labor force participation rate – men aged 15+ (2012)	66%	70%
Civilian labor force participation rate – women aged 15+ (2012)	27%	64%
Unemployment rate – men (2010)	6.7%	6.6%
Unemployment rate – women (2010)	10%	6.3%
Employed as academics, professionals, or managers (2009)	21%	40%
Unskilled workers (2009)	12%	7%
Poverty rate among families before transfer payments and direct taxes (2012)	58%	23%
Poverty rate among families after transfer payments and direct taxes (2012)	52%	15%
Poverty rate among children before transfer payments and direct taxes (2012)	68%	16%
Poverty rate among children after transfer payments and direct taxes (2012)	60%	15%
Life expectancy (in years) (2010)	78	82

Sources: Haider 2005–10: 2010, 83–86; Gharrah 2013, 18, 46; Rudnitzky 2014, 59.

C. Standard of Living

With regard to health, significant gaps prevail between Jewish and Arab citizens of Israel, though these have greatly narrowed – reflected not just in the improved infant mortality rate, but also in extended life expectancy, better health services, changes in nutritional patterns, and other health indicators. Life expectancy had been about four years longer for Jews in 2010 (both men and women), but this was reduced from a gap of fourteen years in the 1950s (Haider 2005–10: 2010, 25). Standard of living and education are intervening variables for health. Among those in need of prescription drugs, for example, financial constraints led 42 percent of Arabs to pass on the purchase of medicine compared to 11 percent of Jews; for dental care, 42 percent of Jews and 66 percent of Arabs did without dental care for financial reasons.[19]

On housing, some gaps stem from cultural differences, but overcrowding is also evident. Although 93 percent of Arab families live in a home they own, compared with 70 percent of Jewish families, the average price of a home in an Arab locale was some 30 percent less than a Jewish home in 2007 (Haider 2005–10: 2010, 37). Disparities in overcrowding are reflected in the average number of persons per room – 75 percent higher among Arabs. In household size, Arabs had an average 4.6 persons per household in 2008, compared with 3.5 persons in Jewish households (CBS *Statistical Abstract* 2014, 7). Ownership of durable goods (refrigerator, washing machine, TV, mobile phone) was similar in Jewish and Arab homes, but a gap favoring Jewish ownership is evident with respect to cars, landline phones, cable and satellite TV, and connection to the Internet.[20]

[19] Central Bureau of Statistics 2008, 7–8.
[20] Central Bureau of Statistics 2013a.

D. Income and Employment[21]

The gross average income of an Arab household in Israel was approximately 59 percent that of a Jewish household in 2012.[22] In 2014, the gross monthly income of an Arab wage-earner was approximately 67 percent of a Jewish wage-earner.[23] The proportion of welfare payments (most from the National Insurance Institute) in the income of Arabs is one and a half times higher than among Jews.[24] Then again, income sources available to Jewish households – capital and property, other institutional payments and stipends, help from other households, and non-work income from abroad – are not generally available to Arab households.

With regard to employment, 47 percent of Arab citizens of Israel participated in the civilian labor force in 2012 (compared to 61% of Jewish citizens), though about a quarter are part-time employees (Rudnitzky 2014, 57). There is a significant gap between men and women: While the labor force participation rate among Arab men (66%) resembles that of Jewish men (70%), the participation of Arab women, though on the rise, is still very low: 27 percent of Arab women compared with 64 percent of Jewish women. Unemployment among Arab men resembles unemployment among Jewish men in 2010 (6–7%). Distribution by occupation, however, reveals a very high proportion of Arab citizens in construction jobs and the like (40%), and fewer holding academic, white-collar, or management jobs – 21 percent compared with 40 percent among Jewish Israelis (Haider 2005–10: 2010, 85).

E. Poverty Indicators

The Arab population of Israel is poorer than the Jewish population, and poverty is severe among Bedouins in the south. In the decade 1995–2006, poverty deepened among Arab families, even relative to the increased poverty among Jewish families. According to the poverty index of the National Insurance Institute, families categorized as "non-Jewish" constituted 13 percent of the total population, but 24 percent (almost double) of the poor population; this rose to 35 percent after receipt of transfer payments and tax payments, i.e., welfare allowances manage to pull more Jewish families out of poverty.[25] In 2012 (Table 15.2), the incidence of poverty among Arab families was 58 percent, falling to 52 percent – a decrease of only 6 percent – after transfer payments and taxes. Even those who question the accuracy of poverty indicators cannot ignore the large income gap between Jews and Arabs, which further exacerbates the tension between the two groups (Momi Dahan 2007, 67).

The gaps are clearly evident in the socioeconomic ranking of Arab local authorities. *All* are in the five lowest clusters (out of a total of ten clusters). Table 15.3 presents

[21] Data from the National Insurance Institute, *Annual Report 2008*, June 2009, unless noted otherwise.

[22] CBS 2012.

[23] CBS 2014. According to Gharrah (2013, 80), 53.8 percent of Arab wage-earners earn less than the minimum wage.

[24] The monthly income of Arab citizens of Israel comes from the following sources: 79 percent from work; 18 percent from transfer payments; and 3 percent from other sources (Gharrah 2013, 98).

[25] Data are from Endeweld, Fruman, and Gottlieb (2008, 13–14, 43), and apply to the general category of "non-Jews." According to Haider (2005–10: 2010, 86), the incidence of poverty among Arab families in 2009 was higher: 58 percent versus 29 percent among Jewish families (a gap of 29%). After transfer payments and taxes, the gap rose to 33 percent (46% and 13% respectively).

Table 15.3 *Ranking of Arab localities in the socioeconomic clusters of Israeli localities (2008)*

Cluster	1	2	3	4	5	6–10
Number of Arab localities in each cluster	5	43	21	8	2	0
% of Arab localities in each cluster	71%	90%	75%	31%	4%	0

Cluster 1 is the lowest socioeconomic ranking.
Source: CBS, www.cbs.gov.il/publications/local_authorities06/pdf/t01.pdf

the data on the Arab local authorities and their percentage of the total authorities in that cluster.

The low ranking of Arab localities in Table 15.3 is a reflection of the low public investment in Arab towns, compared with Jewish towns. The picture is even bleaker than in the previous decade. Notwithstanding some internal shifts, every Arab local authority is ranked in the five lowest clusters. In fact, the three regional councils composed only of Arab localities are ranked in the two lowest clusters of the regional council index (Haider 2005–10: 2010, 116). This is a reflection of inadequate service provision, from water and sewerage to medical clinics, fire trucks, and post offices.

F. Equality

The Equality Index, published since 2006 by the organization Sikkuy, aggregates data from the fields of education, health, welfare, employment, and housing within the Jewish and Arab populations, combining and weighting them into one value.[26] The underlying assumption is that under conditions of equality, the share of the Jews and Arabs in the overall resource pie will correspond to their share of the population. Over four years, the index has been negative, indicating that there has been no progress, and in fact inequality has gotten somewhat worse – from an index of 0.34 to 0.36 (in the range of values between –1.0 and +1.0, with zero indicating full equality). The report puts it this way: "Overall, the government's output for a single Jew is the same as its output for 1.56 Arabs in the population" (Haider 2005–10: 2010, 86). More distressing is the 16 percent increase in overall inequality between Jews and Arabs during this period in four of the five areas, with the exception of education. The greatest disparity is in social welfare outlays.

Differences can be found between groups within Arab society. Christian Arabs, for example, are much better off than Muslim Arabs or Druze as a result of modernization and secularization. On the other hand, the Bedouin in the south and Arab women are much worse off than Arab men (particularly in the areas of education and employment). In general, although most of the gaps between Jews and Arabs have narrowed since the founding of Israel, they had been so wide at the outset that they remain quite severe. To illustrate, two-thirds of Arab households in 2010 are in the

[26] The index weights each group relative to its size in the general population. The weight of each of the five areas in the weighted index is based on the share it receives out of the total national expenditure in these five areas (Haider 2005–10: 2010, 16).

three lowest income deciles, with only 6 percent in the three highest income deciles (Gharrah 2015). Thus, compared with Jewish households, the gaps remain wide.

15.5 Political Participation

In Chapter 8, we described three periods of political participation and the link between participation patterns and the Israeli government's attitude toward the independent organizing of Arab citizens. Here we examine participation through parties, voting, and election campaigns, followed by participation in local government. We also note that parties are not the only or even the primary arena of Arab political participation in Israel.

A. Political Parties

The participation of Arabs in Israeli political parties changed significantly with the shift from "affiliated" lists operating under the aegis of Jewish parties to independent Arab parties. A third type of party activity – a joint list of Arabs and Jews – could be found in Maki (the Israeli Communist Party) in the 1950s and 1960s. Maki split prior to the 1965 election, however, as ideological disagreements surfaced between the Jewish and Arab members, and between those who embraced pure Communism and those with more Arab nationalist views. The Jewish offshoot (which retained the name Maki) under Shmuel Mikunis and Moshe Sneh won just one Knesset seat, while the Arab-Jewish offshoot that emerged (Rakah – the New Communist List), headed by Meir Vilner and Emil Habibi, won most of the Arab votes and three Knesset seats. A later incarnation of the Arab-Jewish partnership was the Hadash party (the Democratic Front for Peace and Equality, founded by Rakah), which won about four seats in each Knesset from 1977 to the 2013 Knesset election (one seat was usually held by a Jew).

In the 1950s and 1960s, approximately 50 percent of Arab voters cast ballots for the affiliated Arab parties, about 20 percent voted for Maki/Rakah, and some 30 percent voted for Jewish parties, even right-wing and Orthodox religious parties. Change began in the 1970s, though some 30 percent of Arab votes are still cast for "Jewish parties," even during elections in the 2000s. The affiliated parties that were active until 1977 were founded by Jewish parties using the co-optation method – drafting Arab leaders to support a Jewish party in exchange for representation in the Knesset. Mapai, however, designed a system to win the support of Arab voters without pledging them a role in the party institutions. Ever since the 1950s, on the other hand, Mapam ensured that an Arab representative would have a realistic place in its list of candidates. The Arab MKs in the affiliated parties were almost all traditional leaders – heads of hamulas (clans) or clergy, whose constituents were rewarded for their political support. Candidates on the affiliated lists had to be vetted by the mother parties, and the MKs so elected played a political role primarily in local matters.

In the 1981 election, the Labor Party (in the Alignment) dropped sponsorship of its affiliated party and called upon Arab voters to cast their ballots directly for Labor. They took this step because of the increasing difficulty of maintaining the system of political patronage, the decline of the affiliated party in the 1977 election,

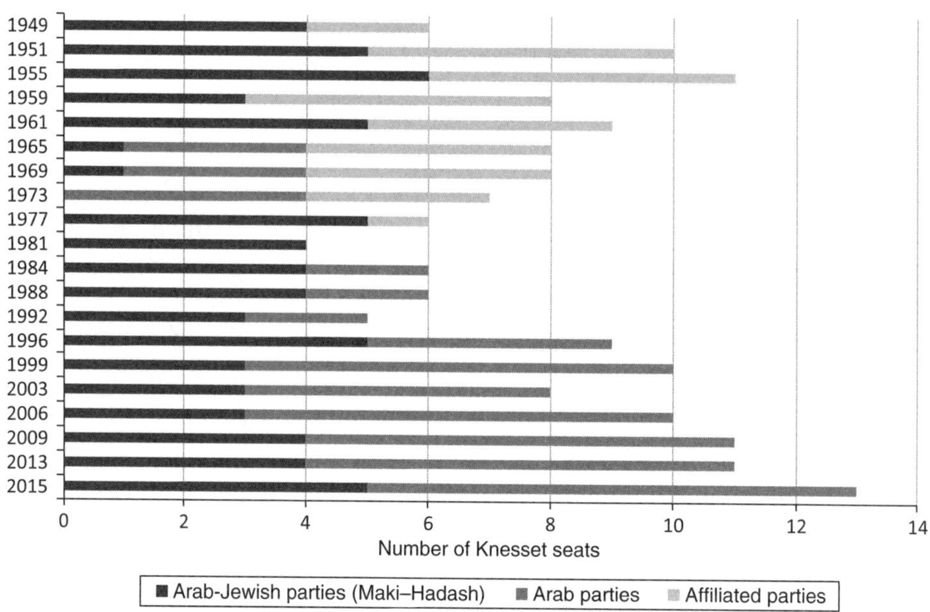

Figure 15.1 Distribution of Knesset seats following elections (1949–2015): Affiliated parties; Arab-Jewish parties; Arab parties
Notes: In 1965 and 1969, Rakah won three seats and Maki won just one. In 1984, the Progressive List for Peace, a joint Arab-Jewish party, won two seats. In 2015, the Arab parties Balad, Hadash, and Ra'am-Ta'al ran together under the name the "Joint List."
Source: Knesset website.

and the hope that more Arab voters would choose to support Labor directly (see Figure 15.1). Later, the Labor Party also created a separate Arab electoral district and reserved places on its Knesset list for an Arab and a Bedouin candidate. Other parties followed suit and established "district primaries" to guarantee Knesset seats to Arabs, Druze, and Bedouin.

The disappearance of the affiliated lists opened two possible tracks for Arabs who wished to be elected to the Knesset from a Jewish party: competing in the sectoral districts for a reserved slot on the Knesset list; or vying for a place on the national list, with no guaranteed slot for Arabs. Although the second alternative was less common than competing for a reserved slot, it turned out to be a viable option. In 1996, for example, Nadia Hilu, a Christian Arab woman, was elected to a realistic slot in the fourth grouping of the Labor Party primaries, and then won a slot in the second grouping in the 2006 primaries. Her election by tens of thousands of Jewish party members to an unreserved, realistic place in the national list suggests that a route does exist for the political integration of Arab citizens of Israel – not just the political elites but rank and file party members (Neuberger 2000, 136).

Since the 1980s, independent Arab parties have been the main vehicle for the participation of Arab citizens in Israel's parliamentary politics. The first "pure" Arab party – in terms of its positions, voters, and representatives – was the Arab

Democratic Party (Mada) formed in 1988 by MK Abdulwahab Darawshe after his resignation from the Labor Party. This party won a seat in the 1988 Knesset election and two in 1992. Since 1996, it has run for election as the United Arab List (Ra'am) and, despite its various reincarnations, maintained an average of four seats in the elections between 1999 and 2009. Prior to this, a joint Jewish-Arab party had been formed – the Progressive List for Peace headed by Mohammed Miari and Matti Peled – which initially won two seats, dropped to one in 1988, and did not pass the electoral threshold in 1992. In 1996, groups of Arab academics came together to found the Balad Party – the National Democratic Assembly – headed by Azmi Bishara. That year, Balad partnered with Hadash and together won five seats. Since 2003, Balad has run on its own and won two to three Knesset seats.

The move to direct election of the prime minister strengthened the independent parties and affected the participation and influence of the Arab electorate. The 1996 election saw a proliferation of new Arab parties and movements: the Arab Unity for Progress and Renewal Party, Balad – the National Democratic Assembly, the Progressive Covenant, and the Arab-Islamic Bloc (Osatzky-Lazar and Ghanem 1996). Some of these were centered around one individual – Dr. Ahmad Tibi, Mohammed Zeidan, Atif Khatib, or Dr. Azmi Bishara – and some later folded into other movements. In sum, since 1996, Hadash and the Arab parties have provided the main framework for party organizing of Arabs in Israel, and won a combined total of nine to ten seats every election, reaching eleven MKs in 2009 and 2013 (9% of the total Knesset seats).

In March 2014, the electoral threshold was raised to 3.25% – supposedly to enhance governance by reducing the number of parties in the Knesset, but more likely motivated by the desire to reduce or even eliminate Arab representation in the Knesset. This law means that a party must win at least four mandates to pass the electoral threshold, jeopardizing the parliamentary life of two Arab parties (with three MKs each) and Hadash (with four MKs), which they had won in the 2013 Knesset election. While unifying the parties was an obvious solution, it was not easy to bridge the ideological differences between, for example, the Islamic Movement and the secular arm of Hadash, or between the nationalist views of Balad and the moderate positions of the Arab Movement for Renewal. Further complicating this were the long-standing personal rivalries between the leaders and voters of the parties, as well as the fear that setting the rivalry aside would reduce the turnout of Arab voters.

The pressure of three months until election day conjured a political miracle, and a coalition was formed of all four parties that preserved their separate identities. The coalition stood for election under the non-committal name "the Joint List" and was headed by one person – Ayman Odeh, the secretary general of Hadash. (The ideological platform is discussed in the following section.) Defying expectations, voter turnout among the Arab population rose to 64 percent and the Joint List won thirteen Knesset seats in the 2015 election (the thirteenth is Jewish), becoming the third-largest party in the Knesset (Raday and Rudnitzky 2015). Haider lists several reasons that contributed to its formation: the trend of declining votes for these parties; the rise of civil society organizations, which were displacing the parties; fierce and sometimes violent rivalries between the parties, which had paralyzed the work of the Higher Monitoring Committee; and the urgent need for unity in the face of the racism and anti-democratic legislation in Jewish society. He notes that creation of the Joint List signified the choice of civic discourse and support for the two state solution (Haider in Raday and Rudnitzky 2015, 13–15).

B. Ideological Platform

The platforms of the main Arab parties have diverse ideological roots – Marxism, pan-Arabism, pan-Islamism, Palestinian-Arab nationalism, etc. Nevertheless, two main issue areas dominate the Arab parties – the Israeli–Arab conflict and the place of Arabs in Israeli society and state. Since the 1990s, most Arabs in Israel have been in agreement about these two subjects – resolving the Palestinian problem by establishing an independent, sovereign Palestinian state beside the state of Israel, and, within Israel, absolute equality of rights between Arabs and Jews (Reiter and Aharoni 1993, 14).[27] Since 2011, they have also had to address the revolutions in Arab countries and the Sunni–Shia divide in the Muslim world, although this was noted only obliquely in the joint 2015 election platform.[28]

Synthesizing Marxism and Nationalism

Over the course of many years, Maki/Rakah worked hard at bringing these two ideologies together, and the synthesis still exists to some extent in Hadash (whose official, full name is the Democratic Front for Peace and Equality – the Israeli Communist Party and Arab and Jewish Groups). The synthesis also prevailed in Mapam, with some modification. In Israel's early years, Arab MKs in the affiliated parties distanced themselves from ideological issues or from expressing a view about the Jewish–Arab conflict. In contrast, the MKs from Maki recognized the legitimacy of Israel as early as the 1950s, though they objected to its Zionist identity; they adopted the Soviet line in their criticism of Israel's foreign policy, and gave representation to the disadvantaged Arab citizens. Rakah's position, and later that of Hadash, is that the Arabs are a Palestinian national minority in Israel, hence the demand to establish a Palestinian state on the 1967 borders and give full equality to Israel's Arab citizens. The Arab-Jewish partnership was based on this platform, and prior to the 1977 election, the Hadash tent was broad enough to accommodate the Black Panthers headed by Charlie Biton as well as "the academics of Nazareth." The party rejects the solution of a binational state and supports recognition of the national rights of the Arabs in Israel. In the 1980s, Hadash won broad support – an average of 34 percent of the Arab public – as it was perceived as the only party capable of representing their national aspirations. At the same time, it created a solid base in the local authorities and became a kind of establishment party, capable of rewarding its activists and voters with municipal jobs, scholarships, and the like.

[27] According to survey research conducted in June 2009 by the Truman Institute and the Palestinian Center for Policy and Survey Research, 63 percent of the Arab citizens of Israel and 60 percent of the Palestinians in the territories support the solution of "two states for two nations." A Pew Survey from 2015 indicates that 50 percent of Israeli-Arabs believe a two-state solution is possible, a 24-point drop since 2013. See Pew Research Center 2016.

[28] Paragraph 7 of the platform: "The Joint List rejects imperialist intervention in the affairs of the countries of the region and the world, the policy of 'divide and rule,' ethnic and religious sectarianism, and the dissolution of states and nations."

But changes in the mid-1980s adversely affected Hadash: The power and influence of the Christian-Arab and Jewish party members waned, as the Muslim-Arab membership grew; changes in the Soviet Union under Gorbachev triggered heated internal debates, leading to the departure of intellectuals such as the writer Emil Habibi and others. The collapse of the Communist regimes further weakened Hadash, and members began to hemorrhage to other parties. In the 2000s, Hadash won just 25 percent of the Arab vote. Its relatively moderate positions were its downfall, even though the main points of its platform were largely adopted by the other Arab parties (as well as Jewish left-wing parties), absent the element of an Arab-Jewish partnership. Some Hadash voters were deterred by the decline of Communism; some were put off by its adherence to the democratic rules of the game; and others rejected the view that a Palestinian state should emerge side by side with Israel. The more radical found a home in the new parties formed since the 1990s (J. Landau 1993, 84). Nevertheless, with the 2009 Knesset election, Hadash renewed its vitality, added some Jewish voters, and grew from three to four Knesset seats. Hadash is the lead member of the Joint List, whose platform includes support for an independent, sovereign Palestinian state beside Israel on the June 4, 1967 borders. The Joint List's eight-point platform represents the common denominator of the parties, though Hadash, maintaining its tradition, continued to publish a separate, detailed platform.[29]

Two States for Two Peoples

Resembling Hadash in its positions, but without the Marxist component, was the Progressive List for Peace, a new Arab-Jewish party formed in 1981 in response to the changes in Arab society as well as the need to reformulate a position on foreign affairs. The Progressive List for Peace was created by a group of Hadash members from Nazareth who were jockeying for power in the local authority, and it focused on local politics. Encouraged by its success in Nazareth, the Progressive List turned to national activism, and made common cause with other movements, such as Arab academics from Umm al-Fahm and a group of Jews who had split from Sheli, a small, left-wing party. In its platform for the 1984 election (it won two seats), the Progressive List demanded full equality for Arabs and Jews; mutual recognition of the right of both nations to self-determination; Israel's withdrawal from all the occupied territories including East Jerusalem; negotiations with the PLO as the Palestinians' sole legitimate representative; and the immediate withdrawal of the IDF from Lebanon. Rivalry with Hadash over the Arab vote led the Progressive List to radicalize, as it expressed support for the right of return of Arabs to their homes in Haifa, Acre, and Ramla. The chief figures in this party were Atty. Mohammed Miari, who had previously been with the al-Ard group, Major General (Res.) Matti Peled, and the journalist Uri Avnery (J. Landau 1993, 86; Reiter and Aharoni 1993, 22). Although the Progressive List was short-lived (1984–92), it played a role in the change of heart of the Rabin government and Israeli public opinion, leading up to the Oslo Accords.

[29] Both platforms can be found on the Hadash website: http://hadash.org.il (accessed October 11, 2017).

Emphasis on Muslim-Arabism

The Arab Democratic Party, formed prior to the 1988 election by Abdulwahad Darawshe (previously a Labor Party MK), was the harbinger of a new type of independent Arab party and the first to define itself as an Arab party with a clear Muslim voice. Unlike the parties that had preceded it – Rakah/Hadash and the Progressive List for Peace – the Arab Democratic Party refrained from openly appealing to Jewish voters or expecting their support. Darawshe had resigned from the Alignment primarily because of its refusal to recognize the PLO, but he adopted a relatively moderate platform ideologically (unlike the platform of the Progressive List for Peace), and emphasized that Arabs are loyal to the state and its laws, which does not conflict with support for a sovereign Palestinian state alongside Israel. Between the two issues – the national struggle and the struggle for integration and equality – the Arab Democratic Party focused more on equalizing the civil and economic rights of Arab citizens of Israel, and it expressed its willingness to participate in a government coalition to achieve these goals. At the same time, the party presented itself as an independent, Muslim, nationalist Arab party, one that aspires to realize the demands of Arabs in Israel and Palestinians in the territories (J. Landau 1993, 87). In the 1988 election, MK Darawshe won one seat in the Knesset, and in 1992 it ran together with the "southern wing" of the Islamic Movement and won a second seat for MK Taleb el-Sana, a Bedouin representative. From 1996 on, the party ran together with the United Arab List as Ra'am-Ta'al, winning four seats. In the 2006, 2009, and 2013 Knesset elections, the combination of Ra'am–Mada–Ta'al won four seats and joined the Joint Arab List in 2013.

The Arab Movement for Renewal (Ta'al) was founded in late 1995 by Ahmad Tibi as a movement that brings together professionals and academics. In the 1999 election, Ta'al ran together with Balad, and in the 2003 election, it forged a union with Hadash, which won three seats. Ta'al advocates full civil partnership for Arabs in Israel, recognition of Arabs as a national minority, with all this entails in terms of collective rights, and eliminating the Zionist character of the state of Israel – leading to attempts to disqualify the party, but the Supreme Court voided the decision (Rekhess and Rudnitzky 2009, chapter 6, 14–15).

A State of all its Citizens

Opposition to the parties mentioned above – personal and to some degree ideological – led to the formation of Balad: National Democratic Assembly by Azmi Bishara prior to the 1996 election. Unlike the Arab Democratic Party, which sought equality and integration for Arabs in Israel, Balad did not recognize the legitimacy of defining Israel as a Jewish-Zionist state, and sought to replace it with a slogan that quickly caught on – "A state of all its citizens." Balad sought a definition for Israel that accorded no preference to any of its component communities, and demanded autonomy – cultural, educational, and other – for the Arab community (Bishara 1993). Its approach has elements of the pan-Arabism that took hold in Egypt under Gamal Abdel Nasser. As for foreign policy, Balad was no different than the other Arab parties: It demanded an independent Palestinian state and the right of return to Israel of Palestinian refugees. Balad was the only party, however, to vehemently object to the Oslo Accords, as it considered them subversive of Palestinian interests. In the 1996 election, Balad ran with Hadash, winning five Knesset seats. Prior to the

1999 election, the two Balad MKs (Bishara and Mahameed) split from the joint list and ran as an independent party, winning two seats. In the four elections between 2003 and 2013, Balad won three seats. In 2007, an investigation of MK Bishara on suspicion of aiding the enemy during the second Lebanon War was made public; Bishara fled Israel and resigned from the Knesset. In 2015, three Balad MKs were elected as part of the Joint List.

Emphasis on Islam

The Islamic Movement, with its emphasis on Islam, is not a political party (with the exception of the southern wing, which joined the United Arab List, as noted above), so it will be examined separately as part of civil society. Nevertheless, the political aspects of the rise of the Islamic Movement among Arabs in Israel should not be ignored. The reasons for its growth (according to Rekhess and Rudnitzky 2009, chapter 8, 26–31) are the failure of secular Arab nationalism; the rise of religious fundamentalism in the Muslim world under the influence of Iran; disillusionment with modernization and the changes it wrought in traditional society; and discrimination by the Israeli government against Arab economic development and social services. Its views are drawn from the Muslim Brotherhood in Egypt with its slogan "Islam is the solution." Nevertheless, the early leaders of the Islamic Movement in Israel took a pragmatic approach – accommodating Islamic ideology to the forces of reality – seeking a political solution to the Palestinian problem and leaving the permanent solution to future generations. Since 1983, the Islamic Movement has successfully competed in local elections, and its candidates have become mayor of several local authorities – Umm al-Fahm, Jeljulia, Rahat, and Hura. A key component of the Islamic Movement is its stance toward the Israeli political system. The "southern wing" headed by Sheikh Abdullah Nimar Darwish believed in participating in Knesset elections; its representatives were elected to the Knesset as part of the United Arab List in 1996, and have served in the Knesset ever since. The "northern wing" headed by Sheikh Ra'ed Salah boycotts the elections and calls for Arab separatism in Israel.

Overlapping and Contradictory Trends

In the 2013 election, three "Arab parties" won election to the Knesset – Hadash (four seats), Balad (three seats), and Ra'am-Ta'al (four seats). Altogether, eleven MKs were elected from these parties (of which one was a Jew – Dov Khenin from Hadash). Another two Arabs were elected from "Jewish" parties (Esawi Frej from Meretz and Hamad Amar from Yisrael Beitenu), i.e., Arab representation of thirteen MKs in the Knesset (11%). In 2015, thirteen MKs were elected from the Joint List (one of them a Jew) and four from other parties: Meretz (Esawi Frej), the Likud (Ayoob Kara), the Zionist Camp (Zouheir Bahloul), and Yisrael Beitenu (Hamad Amar) – a total of sixteen Arab MKs in the Knesset (13%), which approaches their proportion of eligible voters in the total population (only about 15% because of the young age of the Arab population). The common denominator of most Arab representatives in the Knesset is the aspiration to promote Arab interests within Israel and Palestinian interests outside it. It should be emphasized that the Arab parties represent a range of ideological views and a mosaic of social groups, despite the decision to run as one political bloc in 2015. In the past, the variation between

Arab parties was notable in the configuration of power in the Knesset and the coalitions formed within it: The United Arab List, for example, stood together with the Torah Judaism party on certain communal and religious matters. An Arab party has never been a fully official member of a government coalition, yet Balad and the Progressive List for Peace, which opposed political cooperation, were clearly distinct from the Arab Democratic Party and Hadash, which allowed for such cooperation, even with the coalition, on specific issues. A change in attitude of the political system – and of the Jewish parties in particular (except for Meretz) – toward the Arab representatives in the Knesset could strengthen their integration in parliamentary and governmental activity.

As noted earlier, party activity is not the main political framework of the Arab population in Israel. Other channels of activity are the local authorities as well as the movements and organizations of civil society. One segment of the population has no interest in participating in the national political system, and boycotts it. Another segment, such as the National Committee of Arab Local Authorities, takes a more practical approach and is willing to make demands of the government and negotiate for them.

C. Voting in the Knesset Elections

In Chapter 10, we noted the increased representation of Arabs in the Knesset and the intensifying competition among Arab parties until the 2015 election. Table 15.4 presents an overview of these dynamics: first, the rise of independent Arab parties; second, the gradual decline of joint Arab-Jewish parties; third, fluctuation in the support of Mapai/Labor; fourth, ongoing, though inconsistent, support of Arab voters for the Likud and Jewish religious parties (NRP and Shas); and, fifth, support for Jewish parties such as Meretz on ideological grounds.

Voting for Mapai and the affiliated lists had instrumental, not ideological, motives, and was part and parcel of the government's political patronage of Israel's Arab population during the first two decades of the state. Thus, in parallel with the decline of the affiliated lists from almost 60 percent of the Arab vote at their peak in 1959 was the waning of support for workers' parties and the Histadrut among Arab voters after 1973, which reached a low of 4–5 percent for the Labor Party in 2013 and 2015. Joint Arab-Jewish parties experienced an ebb and flow in support from a high of 52 percent of the Arab vote in 1977 to a low of 23 percent (for Hadash) in 2013. The ideological Communist component of this partnership almost entirely disappeared – Maki had 22 percent of the Arab vote in the 1949 election, 23 percent at its height in the 1961 election, and did not make it into the 1973 Knesset at all. The proportion of Jewish votes given to parties defined as Arab-Jewish is very limited. Nevertheless, Rakah, the Progressive List for Peace, and later Hadash continued to affirm this partnership, and Hadash is an ongoing and influential presence in Arab politics. In the 2015 election, the Joint List won only several thousand Jewish votes.

Since the late 1980s, Knesset elections have seen the rise of independent Arab parties. Together with Hadash, support for these parties reached approximately 60 percent in 1988 and 70–80 percent in the 2000s. Disappointment with the achievements of Hadash and the Arab Democratic Party as well as the events of October 2000 strengthened the Arab parties, which (without Hadash) won 54 percent of the

Table 15.4 *Arab vote distribution in Knesset elections 1949–2015 (rounded %)*

Knesset	Year	"Affiliated list"	Jewish-Arab party (Maki/Hadash)	Arab parties	Mapai/Labor/Mapam	Herut/Likud + NRP + Shas	Other parties*
1	1949	52	22	–	10	1	15
2	1951	55	16	–	17	1	11
3	1955	58	16	–	25	1	1
4	1959	59	11	–	24	6	–
5	1961	46	23	–	25	4	2
6	1965	44	24	–	24	7	2
7	1969	41	31	–	17	10	2
8	1973	36	37	–	13	12	2
9	1977	21	52	–	11	8	8
10	1981	12	39	–	29	14	6
11	1984	–	32	18**	26	9	16
12	1988	–	34	25	17	10	14
13	1992	–	23	24	20	19	14
14	1996	–	37***	25	17	5	16
15	1999	–	21	49	7	8	16
16	2003	–	28****	41	9	8	14
17	2006	–	24	48	13	4	11
18	2009	–	28	54	5	6	7
19	2013	–	23	54	4	8	11
20	2015	–	–	83	5	6	6

* Other parties: From 1992, primarily Meretz; in 2015, Meretz, Kulanu, and Yesh Atid.
** Progressive List for Peace.
*** Ran jointly with Balad.
**** Ran jointly with the Arab Movement for Renewal.
Sources: Various sources provide somewhat different data. We chose to rely on Lavie and Rudnitzky (2009, 16), which is based on Neuberger (1998, 121); Osatzky-Lazar and A. Ghanem (1999, 45); and Rekhess (2007). Election data for 2003 and 2006 do not include the votes of Arabs who reside in the mixed cities. For 2013 and 2015, see Rudnitzky 2013; Raday and Rudnitzky 2015.

Arab vote in 2009 and 2013, ensuring their representation in the list of candidates for the Joint Party in 2015.

Arab support for the ruling party did not disappear with the decline of Labor. In the 1981 election, following the political upheaval of 1977, 7 percent of the Arab vote went to the Likud and another 7 percent to the National Religious Party (NRP); the rise of Shas brought it 5 percent of the Arab vote in 1992 and Shas has continued to win several percentage points of the Arab vote ever since. The absence of Shas from the government prior to the 2015 election reduced its support among Arab voters to under 2 percent. Arab votes for the Likud, Yisrael Beitenu, and the Jewish religious parties is surprising, considering the positions of these parties on foreign affairs, security, the occupied territories, and internal affairs (a Jewish state, citizenship, religion and state). This support can be assumed to be instrumental – a demonstration of loyalty to the parties in power in an effort to advance the interests of the Arab public, realize the goals of Arab interest groups, and bring benefits to the Arab leadership. The Interior Ministry, for example, was under the control of the NRP and Shas for many years; and some parties, such as the Likud, established Druze electoral districts, virtually guaranteeing a Knesset seat to a Druze candidate. The Arab vote for all the Jewish parties combined was 19 percent on average: 18 percent in the 2009 election, 23 percent in 2013, and 17 percent in 2015.

Some Arab voters cast a ballot for Jewish parties for ideological reasons, mostly having to do with dovish positions about the occupied territories. The increased support for Labor under Yitzhak Rabin in 1992 (20%) and Shimon Peres in 1996 (17%) are cases in point. Ratz/Meretz, though not a ruling party, also attracted Arab voters, primarily the better educated, because of its support for equality within Israel and its dovish stand on foreign affairs. Support for Meretz reached a high of 11 percent in 1996, but plummeted to 3 percent in the 2013 and 2015 elections.

Although the potential Arab vote in 1949 was 10 percent of the population at large, Arab voters have generally not been able to translate their votes into political power. This refers not to the representation of individual Arabs in the Knesset – their representation has gradually grown to a total of sixteen MKs (13%) in 2015, and also some Arabs vote for Jewish parties – but rather to their ability to influence politics in Israel, as do Jewish groups that are smaller than the Arab population. The main reason for their lack of political clout is *external*: Arabs in Israel are outside the Jewish-Zionist consensus, and their ideological, collective, and individual needs are accorded only partial recognition. Proof of this is that their representatives are excluded from the government coalitions, with the exception of a short period and only partially in the governments of Rabin and Peres (1992–96). Another reason is *internal*: the ability of Arabs in Israel to score political victories via elections has been undercut by ideological, political, and social divisions within the Arab community, not unlike that of the Jewish public.[30] The key factors in their inability to formulate a common ideological and political agenda are the gulf between those who would maintain tradition versus those who call for change in Arab society, the absence of a dominant Arab party, and the inability to agree on leadership that would be acceptable to most Arab voters. It is too early to assess whether the Joint List (2015) marks a fundamental change in this reality.

The growing conviction among Arab voters that they are unable to effect change is reflected in the fluctuating gap between Jewish and Arab citizens in voter turnout for Knesset elections. In the elections held between 1951 and 1973, proportionately more Arabs voted than Jews because of the political patronage system noted above; as of the 1977 election, this gap greatly narrowed and voter turnout among Arabs fell below the Jewish turnout, which had also declined. In the elections between 2003 and 2013, the gap widened to an average of 9 percent – a very significant spread in terms of the representation of Arabs in the Knesset as well as the size of the center-left

[30] A number of Arab groups that sought election did not pass the electoral threshold, meaning that their votes were wasted (Kaufman and Israeli 1999, 86). In the 2013 election, this included 3,546 votes for the Daam Workers Party; in 2015, less than 1 percent of the total votes (3,905) were cast for two new Arab parties that did not pass the electoral threshold.

Table 15.5 *Voter turnout among Arabs and Jews for Knesset elections 1949–2015 (rounded-off percentages)*

Knesset	Year	Arabs	Jews
1	1949	80*	87
2	1951	85	75
3	1955	92	83
4	1959	89	82
5	1961	86	82
6	1965	88	83
7	1969	86	82
8	1973	80	79
9	1977	76	79
10	1981	70	78
11	1984	75	79
12	1988	73	80
13	1992	70	77
14	1996	77	79
15	1999	75	79
15**	2001	18	62
16	2003	62	68
17	2006	56	64
18	2009	53	65
19	2013	57	68
20	2015	64	72

* A very rough estimate. Rekhess and Rudnitzky (2009, chapter 6, 22) give a low estimate of 69 percent.

** Direct election of the prime minister only.

Notes: Voter turnout among the Arabs is estimated because of the difficulty of isolating Arab votes in the mixed cities. Data differ markedly between scholars.
Sources: For 1949–92 election data, see J.M. Landau 1993, 96; for 1996–2006 election data, see Schafferman 2009; for 2013 and 2015 election data, see Raday and Rudnitzky 2015, 4; for Jewish turnout, see CBS *Statistical Abstract*; and the Central Elections Committee reports in the State Records (Israel).

political bloc. The defiantly low turnout of Arabs (18%) who showed up to vote in the prime ministerial election of 2001 was a reflection of their alienation from the national political system as well as protest against the state following the October 2000 events (Rouhana et al. 2004, 326; A. Ghanem 2004, 330). Other explanations for the drop in voter turnout for Knesset elections were the boycott by members of the Islamic Movement; internal changes in Arab society that weakened the recruiting ability of traditional leaders; and the fact that the increasing level of education of the Arab men, and particularly the Arab women, was not channeled into support for new candidates or independent parties.

Nevertheless, Table 15.5 reveals that voter turnout had already risen by 3 percent in 2013 (similar to the increase among Jewish voters), while the 2015 election saw a dramatic increase of 7 percent (compared to 4% more Jewish voters). The voter turnout gap between Jews and Arabs dropped to 8 percent, and were it not for the low voter turnout among Bedouins in the south (47%), the gap would have shrunk even more. One hypothesis, not yet researched, is that raising the electoral threshold triggered a counter-reaction – the opposite of what had been expected by those who wished to lower Arab Knesset representation by raising the electoral threshold. Voting was perceived as an act of defiance against those who promoted this legislation, and this directly contributed to formation of the Joint List headed by a new leader and the highest voter turnout since 2003. Another possible factor is the exhortation to Likud voters by Prime Minister Netanyahu to vote because "Arab voters are going in droves to the polls" – which raised the overall voter turnout significantly in the last two hours compared to 2013 – presumably of voters for both Likud and the Joint List.[31]

In Section 15.6 below, we examine political participation on a local level, but here we note that voter turnout for local elections in Arab towns is very high, indicating the importance attributed to local politics by Arab voters (see Table 15.6). At the same time, voter turnout among Jews for local elections fell to just 51 percent in 2013 (and even less in previous local elections), leaving a large gap with Arab voters in local elections.

Among Arab citizens, a voting gap also exists between municipal and Knesset elections, with local turnout 14 percent higher in the elections held between 1999 and 2006, the gap rising to 17 percent in 2013, a year in which elections to the Knesset and the local authorities were held within nine months of each other. Local elections are often marked by heated family and clan feuds, suggesting that local politics was largely a reflection of internal feuds. Traditional frameworks hold sway in these local elections, with candidates representing big clans or the coalition of several clans. In the local elections of 2003, for example, forty-two of the fifty-three mayors were elected based on the allegiance of voters to the candidates' families (Amara 1998; Mustafa 2005). Running for mayor in 2013 was so contested that, in about a third of the Arab localities (twenty-five out of seventy-three), no candidate received the requisite 50 percent in the first round, necessitating a second round.

D. Arabs as a Campaign Issue and in Coalition Negotiations

The status of Israel's Arab citizens is not a key issue in the campaigns of the Jewish parties, but can be read between the lines when party platforms include phrases

[31] At about 3 PM on election day, Prime Minister Benjamin Netanyahu posted a video on his Facebook page in which he urged Likud supporters to vote:

> The right-wing government is in danger. Arab voters are going in droves to the polls. Left-wing nonprofits are bussing them in. We don't have V15 [a group that mobilized against the reelection of Netanyahu]; we have Order 8 [an IDF emergency draft order], we have only you. Go out to the polls, bring your friends and family, vote Likud to close the gap between us and the Labor Party.
>
> (https://www.youtube.com/watch?v=Q2cUoglR1yk [accessed October 13, 2017])

With respect to the time of voting, Atmor and Friedberg report that voter turnout increased by 9.4 percent in the final two hours that the polls were open. This late surge could explain the gap between the media's exit polls and the official results announced the next morning. See Israel Democracy Institute N.d.

Table 15.6 *Arab voter turnout for the local and the Knesset elections, 1977–2013 (in percentages)*

Knesset elections		Local elections	
Year	Voter turnout	Year	Voter turnout
1977	76%	1978	84%
1981	70%	–	–
1984	75%	1983	89%
1988	73%	1989	89%
1992	70%	1993	89%
1996	77%	–	–
1999	75%	1998	91%
2003*	62%	2003	75%
2009	53%	2008	78%
2013	57%	2013	83%

* The sharp drop in 2003 is attributed to protest against the merging forced on several Arab localities, particularly Druze towns, without asking residents for their views. Several mergers were rescinded.

Notes: Voter turnout among the Arabs is estimated because of the difficulty of isolating Arab votes in the mixed cities. Data differ markedly between scholars.
Source: Brichta and Pedahzur 2001, 74. On Knesset voting, see Table 15.5 above. On local voting in 2003, see Mustafa 2008; on local voting in 2008, see Rekhess and Rudnitzky, 2009, chapter 6, 33; on local voting in 2013, see Rudnitzky 2014, 13–15.

such as "Land of Israel," "People of Israel," "Jewish state," "Jewish heritage," or "national unity." The shaky civil status of Arabs in Israel can also be seen in discourse about the legitimacy of "the Arab vote" in policymaking. Questioning the right of a national minority to participate in decision-making in a democracy about issues regarded as existential by the majority is not unique to Israel.[32] Actually, it was the relative ideological integration of some Arab parties (Hadash, the Progressive List for Peace, and the Arab Democratic Party) within the left-wing and their linguistic, cultural, and political "Israelization" (acceptance of the democratic rules of the game) that catalyzed mounting challenges by right-wing parties about the right of Arab citizens to participate in critical political decisions, such as the peace agreements with the Palestinian Authority. Such delegitimization has been around since Israel's early years, and was then not limited to the right wing. However, denying the right of Arab citizens to participate in important decisions was accelerated by the two-bloc era created by the elections of the 1980s. On the one hand, the election stalemate raised the value of the Arab vote, particularly since the Arabs in Israel largely agreed with the political left on foreign affairs. On the other hand, Arab parties were not recognized as partners. In 1984, for example, when it appeared as if a

[32] See Neuberger (2000, 139) for other examples: the right of the Russian minority in Lithuania, Latvia, and Estonia to participate in decision-making that led to the independence of these states; the right of the minorities in Quebec, particularly the Anglophones, and sometimes specifically Jews, Indians, and others, to participate in decision-making about the independence of Francophones who constitute the majority in this part of Canada.

left-wing government would incorporate Arab parties, Yitzhak Shamir announced that under no circumstances should a government lean on the votes of non-Jews; and, in 1987, Ariel Sharon blamed the Arabs for Likud's inability to form a government, and even believed after the 1992 election that Arabs should not be allowed to participate in a referendum about existential matters, as their first loyalty was to the Palestinian national interest.

In the 1992 election, the Labor Party returned to power with a slim edge of one Knesset seat and created a bloc of sixty-two MKs together with Meretz, Hadash, and the Arab Democratic Party to oppose the right-wing and religious parties. Shas initially joined the coalition headed by Rabin, but subsequently bowed out, leaving the government largely reliant upon the quasi-coalition understandings reached with the five MKs of Hadash and the Arab Democratic Party.[33] This and the fact that the government did not have a stable majority in the Knesset and purportedly relied on "the Arab vote" was the context for the delegitimization campaign against the Rabin government in the early 1990s, a campaign that was exacerbated by the Oslo Process. Right-wing opposition members found many ways to repeat the claim that the Rabin government had "no mandate" because it did not have a "Jewish majority." In a demonstration against the government in Jerusalem on October 5, 1995, Benjamin Netanyahu, then head of the opposition, labeled the majority that had approved the Oslo Accords as "a non-Zionist majority that includes five representatives of Arab parties identified with the PLO" (Shragai 1995).

The delegitimization campaign continued after the 1996 election in which Netanyahu became prime minister. Defense Minister Yitzhak Mordechai said that "a formula must be found that will enable Israel's Arabs to preserve their rights and, on the other hand, will prevent a situation in which their vote will give a majority to the prime minister and thereby decide the fate of the nation and the state."[34] Such non-democratic expressions contribute to the delegitimacy of the Arab vote, as did planks in the Tzomet and Moledet platforms in 1996 that conditioned the voting right of Arab citizens of Israel on demands that no free citizen in a democracy should have to meet (such as a loyalty oath) or that Arabs in Israel were able to meet (such as compulsory military service):

> The Arabs in Israel must act loyally to the state of Israel and its laws. To be granted civil rights, they must meet all their civil obligations such as military service, payment of taxes, [and] construction in accordance with the planning and building laws. Arabs who do not wish to serve in the army shall do National Service, which shall be double the duration of

[33] On July 9, 1992, the Labor Party signed coalition agreements with Hadash and the Arab Democratic Party, both parties agreeing to support the Rabin government without being members of it. The agreement included commitments to Hadash and the Arab Democratic Party to establish the following entities: a joint committee to promote Arab equality that would include two representatives from the Arab Democratic Party, changes in the priorities for resource allocation, and equalizing the allocations for Arab and Jewish municipalities; a committee for matters concerning the Muslim trust that would deal with Waqf property defined as belonging to "absentees"; planning and building committees; a committee to ensure equal budgets and reduce gaps in consultation with Arab MKs; and enactment of a law ensuring equality for Druze citizens. From the Basic Principles of the Government and Coalition Agreements, 1992 (Galnoor and Hofnung 1993, 1047–56). The Arab Democratic Party was also integrated into the Labor list for the Histadrut election in 1994, and an Arab MK was added to the State Control Committee for the first time (Ettinger 2002).

[34] The article appeared in the *Kfar Habad* weekly in 1996, but the authors could not locate the issue.

> military service for them. Arab citizens of Israel who do not discharge their civil obligations shall be deemed residents and not enjoy civil rights such as voting or running for office, National Security allowances, etc. (Moledet platform, 1996 election)

The Yisrael Beitenu party placed the loyalty of Arab citizens at the center of its election campaign in 2009. Even though party leaders claimed that a law incorporating these elements would be directed at the entire population, the anti-democratic conditions in its platform resemble those from dark regimes:

> Every individual who wishes to receive Israeli citizenship has an obligation to be faithful to the state and its symbols and to swear loyalty to the state, its Declaration of Independence, its symbols – the flag and the anthem – and its sovereignty. Whoever refuses to take a loyalty oath shall have the status of permanent resident, but not be allowed to vote or run for office and will hold "lesser citizenship." (Yisrael Beitenu platform, 2009 election)

The "security net" provided by the Arab parties to the Rabin and Peres governments (1992–96) did not establish a precedent, nor did these parties become full coalition partners – delegitimizing the Arab vote also takes place on the left side of the political map. Nevertheless, this historical moment of cooperation opened the door to the possibility of productive political involvement of the Arab parties in Israeli policymaking. Beyond support for the government's foreign policy, the Arab representatives were involved in governmental changes on internal matters to increase equality for Arabs in Israel and reduce the economic, social, employment, and education gaps. The bloc of Arab parties in support of the government from the outside was in effect an informal but solid coalition resting on written agreements and a shared commitment to peace and equality (Neuberger 2000, 136). As noted, there was no sequel to it, even though the Basic Principles of the Sharon and Olmert governments included acceptable statements about ensuring equal rights for Arabs, while working to integrate them in civil society (Basic Principles of the Government, 2006, parags. 43–45, Knesset website).

There was also no sequel on the Arab side. Cooperation among Hadash, the Arab Democratic Party, and the Zionist left parties raised expectations that were not realized, and the trend toward political isolationism only deepened after the Rabin assassination. In the 1996 election, the Arab parties almost doubled their numbers – from five to nine Knesset seats – but the feeling grew among Arab voters that despite the special political status of Hadash and the Arab Democratic Party, gains were meager and hopes for more were in vain. Disappointment over unmet expectations pushed Arab political activists into new political frameworks that no longer strove for strategic cooperation with the Jewish parties (Osatzky-Lazar and Ghanem 1996).

In 2017 it was too early to gauge the political clout of the Joint List, which is the third-largest party in the Knesset. Some members of the Joint List had been unwilling to cooperate with Zionist parties, hence it had refused to sign a surplus votes agreement with Meretz prior to the election. The Jewish parties, led by the Zionist Camp, also showed no willingness to recognize the legitimacy of the Arab list. Following the 2015 election, for example, the parties composing the center-left bloc (the Zionist Camp, Meretz, and Yesh Atid) could have had fifty-three seats together with the Joint List, and a majority of sixty-three seats if Kulanu had added its MKs, which would have allowed them to form a coalition. This option was never seriously considered, however, because the parties – even on the left – refused to view the Joint List as a potential partner.

15.6 Participation on the Local Level

There were eighty Arab local authorities in Israel in 2013, of which thirteen were municipalities, sixty-four were local councils, and three were regional councils (Himeyn-Raisch 2008).[35] To these should be added thirty-three Arab localities within the jurisdiction of a regional council in which Jewish localities are the majority (e.g., five in the Jezreel Valley Regional Council and three in the Gilboa Regional Council). Most Arabs in Israel live in nationally homogeneous localities. In 2008, 94 percent lived in urban localities of over 2,000 residents, and 50 percent in cities of 20,000–50,000 residents, while the number of rural agricultural villages dwindled to thirty-one. Some 24 percent are residents of mixed cities (about half in East Jerusalem and the rest in Haifa, Tel Aviv-Jaffa, Acre, Lod, Ramla, Ma'alot-Tarshiha, and Nazareth Illit). In the 1980s there were only two Arab cities; in 2008 there were twelve, the largest being Nazareth (70,000), Umm al-Fahm (43,000), Tayibe (34,000), and Shfar'am (34,000).[36]

As of 2015, some Arab villages in Israel still have no recognized municipal status. Thus, an estimated 60,000–90,000 Arab citizens of Israel live in "unrecognized" villages with no basic services of water, education, health, or connection to the electricity grid. Most of these villages were founded early in Israel's history by refugees and "present absentees," who had left their homes during the war, and had their lands expropriated by the state. In a different category are the 40,000 Bedouin who today live in unrecognized villages in the Negev. Some of the unrecognized villages in the Galilee achieved recognition in the 1990s following pressure from the residents and the Association of Forty, founded in 1988 to advocate for the recognition of the unrecognized villages.[37]

A. Local Arab Government

Under Ottoman and British Mandate rule, Arab settlements preserved their traditional frameworks, placing authority in the hands of the village heads, family heads, and property owners. Most rural Arab villages were destroyed in 1948–49, and some in the aftermath (A. Golan 1992, 122–54). Following the war, approximately

[35] This includes Druze and Circassian local authorities, but not Arab residents of mixed towns, unrecognized villages, or predominantly Jewish regional councils. These numbers changed in the 2000s because of the merger and subsequent redivision of Arab local authorities. Counting all Arab localities (not just recognized Arab authorities) brings the number up to 107, with another few dozen Arab localities lacking all municipal status (Rekhess and Osatzky-Lazar 2005, 7; Manna and Gharrah 2008, 45).

[36] All figures above from CBS *Statistical Abstract* 2008, No. 59, table 11; CBS *The Arab Population of Israel* 2008.

[37] Data about the number of unrecognized villages and their population depend upon the definition. According to field surveys from the late 1990s conducted by the Association of Forty, there are some fifty unrecognized villages and another approximately sixty-four population clusters (Soen and Eisenkang-Kane 2004, 13–14, 65–72).

160,000 Arabs remained within Israel's borders in about a hundred locations, including two municipalities (Nazareth and Shfar'am) and one local council (Kafr Yasif). After the founding of Israel, Arab communities had little local governance as most of the Arab population was subject to military rule, which circumscribed their daily lives and interfered in their internal affairs. However, the central government sought to encourage local Arab government in order to create a reliable connection with the Arab population. Local government heads were carefully vetted and ostensibly represented the interests of the Arab population, but they also provided the government with control over a population that had been transformed overnight from the majority to a minority (J. Landau 1971, 217). Until martial law was lifted in 1966, thirty-seven Arab local authorities had been formed encompassing some 70 percent of the Arab populace, and another thirteen were added by 1975. Heading these authorities were the traditional local leaders, who worked together with the military rulers and central government, particularly Mapai, the ruling party, which was involved in the appointment of mukhtars (heads of extended families or villages) and the handing out of political favors to its supporters (A. Ghanem 2001).

Over time, however, the local authorities took on more importance to the Arab residents, certainly in comparison with the Jewish local authorities, for the reasons noted above. Indeed, even though the central government generally clipped the wings of the local authorities to ensure their weakness and dependence, the development of local governance in the Arab community contributed (even if not intentionally) to the political empowerment of the Arab citizenry. The elected municipal officials and local councils in Arab towns were forced to handle matters as best they could, which gradually fostered leadership, democratization, and modernization.

B. Local Elections

Mapai was not the only party engaged in forming local family lists in Arab localities. Other national parties were also maneuvering for influence, mobilizing support through traditional local leaders and forming affiliated party lists, for example Mapam (directly and via the Histadrut) and the NRP, the latter usually in control of the interior and religious ministries, which facilitated direct contact with the Arab population (Al-Haj and Rosenfeld 1990). Despite these efforts, the Communist Party (as Maki and, from 1965, as Rakah) was the most important national list for Arab citizens of Israel, allowing for expression of their national aspirations. The achievements of the Communist Party in the local authorities were limited, however, because of the traditional character of the voting and local dependence on the central government.

The first local elections in the Arab community were held in Nazareth in 1954. The following year, elections for local governments were held in five Arab towns (Shfar'am, Baqa al-Gharbiyye, Tayibe, Tira, and Fureidis), and voter turnout was particularly high – 94 percent on average. The lists identified with Mapai won a resounding majority, while the Communist Party was the only other list to win representation, which it did in three of five authorities. Over time, the number of towns holding local elections increased, but the results remained similar – copious support for the family lists affiliated with Mapai, followed by the Communist Party, whose representation gradually expanded. Even after military rule was lifted, election results changed little – major support, though ebbing, for lists affiliated with the Alignment (Labor), followed, in order, by the Communists (Rakah), the religious parties, Mapam, and Herut.

Change began in the mid-1970s with the appearance of independent Arab political parties on a national level, and this influenced the patterns of political organizing locally as well. Arab society was in transition and emerging political nationalism was trickling down to the local level. For example, the Ibnaa al-Balad (Sons of the Village) movement, founded in 1971 by Arab intellectuals, competed in the Umm al-Fahm election of 1973 on national issues, not just municipal matters (Al-Haj and Rosenfeld 1990). When direct election of the mayor was instituted in 1978, it stoked the rivalry between traditional leaders and a cadre of young, educated leaders who were intent on change. The new rivals for leadership, most of them white-collar professionals, drew legitimacy from independent sources in competition with the traditional leadership. At issue were the practical needs of housing, health, education, welfare, access roads, water, and sewerage; some voices called for setting aside the "big" national issues and concentrating on the daily hardship of the residents. Lurking on a deeper level, however, were issues of leadership in a changing Arab society and the legitimacy of the elected institutions. The traditional leaders fought to keep their grip on power locally, but they were willing to do this through the well-educated young men, on condition that they came from the right families.

Voting patterns during this period reveal that despite the weakening of the traditional family and religion in Arab society, local political representation remained largely in the hands of the family lists, which had adapted themselves to the changing rules of the game. The national parties also found ways to insinuate themselves, and the difference between party candidates and those chosen by families was often indistinguishable (*Kul al-Arab*, editorial, October 11, 2008).

The local lists declined until 1989, while the national Arab parties increased their constituencies, winning up to a third of the votes. The trend reversed in the 1993 election, however, and the traditional local lists have grown ever since (for data up to 2003 see Mustafa 2005, 18–24). The proliferation of lists relative to the number of residents reflects the intense ethnic-religious factionalism – not only between Muslims, Christians, and Druze, but also between families. The divisiveness of these internal rivalries is reflected in the number of lists competing in Arab towns, particularly in the cities – more, on average, than the number of lists competing in Jewish towns in the years 1978–98 (Goldberg 2001, 264; Mustafa 2005, 24). This remained true for the 2013 election (Rudnitzky 2014, 12). We have also noted that voter turnout for local elections in Arab towns was much higher – even reaching 90 percent – than turnout for local elections in Jewish towns, and even higher than Arab voter turnout for Knesset elections (Table 15.6).

Local government has been the arena where much of the political activity of Arabs in Israel played itself out. This stems from the failure of the national Arab parties to make headway on the "big issues," the critical importance of local issues (primarily land), and the fact that they are represented nationally by the relatively autonomous National Committee of Arab Local Authorities (see below). Local communities provide a sense of belonging to an organic collective framework, a dimension that is largely absent from national politics. Furthermore, local politics can serve as a channel for the ambition of educated Arabs and a springboard for national politics (Bishara 2000, 35–70; A. Ghanem 2001, 69–70).

Other arenas for political participation are the Arab umbrella organizations. Land Day on March 30, 1976 was a turning point in this collective organizing, reflected institutionally in the growth of the National Committee of Arab Local Authorities, which had been founded in 1974 based on the democratic representation of Arab localities. The aspiration of the National Committee to serve as the legitimate representative of Arab citizens and their needs has had its ups and downs, but mostly downs over the years. Present at its founding conference in 1974 were the secretary general of the Interior Ministry and the prime minister's adviser for Arab affairs, but this indirect recognition did not last long as the committee began taking on the issue of Arab land expropriation. When the Likud rose to power in 1977, the government cut off ties to the National Committee. This boycott was later retracted, but governments have taken various stances toward this body. Among Arabs, on the other hand, the National Committee carries considerable weight. Since the 1980s, it has expanded its political and national involvement, supporting activities such as the general strike of Arabs in Israel to protest the attempted assassination of Palestinian mayors in the West Bank, as well as organizing protest, solidarity, and aid activities for Palestinians in the territories (Reiter and Aharoni 1993, 32–33). Internally, the National Committee has sought to address a range of social and economic problems of the Arab community – development in education and culture, opportunities for youth, permits for homes illegally built, and agricultural development, as well as demands to allocate land for industry and housing, expand services to the religious, and release Waqf assets. In December 2006, the committee published *The Future Vision of the Palestinian Arabs in Israel* – an overview of the situation of the Arab minority in Israel. In parallel, the Islamic Movement has been growing, initially in the villages of the Triangle and later among the Negev Bedouin.

In addition to their work from within the National Committee, the mayors of local Arab authorities engage in other political organizing, most prominently as part of the Higher Monitoring Committee of Arab Citizens of Israel. This is the political umbrella of Arabs in Israel that was founded in 1982 (see the section on civil society below). This larger body includes members of the National Committee of Arab Local Authorities, the Arab MKs, members of the Histadrut leadership, student representatives, and others. In practice, the Higher Monitoring Committee is the representative of the Arab minority to government authorities, and it also voices its views on the Israeli–Palestinian conflict and other issues. Whether this body is recognized by the government and its ministries depends on the party in power and the issues then current.

C. The Crisis in Arab Local Authorities

Table 15.3 above provides data about the socioeconomic status of Arab municipalities and local councils, all ranked in the lower clusters by comparison with Jewish towns. The main contributing factor to this has been the long record of government discrimination. For most of Israel's history, Arab localities received an inequitable share of government transfers – allocations to the ongoing budget, special budgets, balance grants, and development grants (with the exception of construction grants from the Ministry of Education and the state lottery). From time to time, criteria would be set for allocating resources to disadvantaged areas, but these were irrelevant for Arab towns not on the list of National Priority Areas, or the towns were ineligible based on the number of new immigrants who live there. Another example was Project Renewal in the late 1970s to renovate disadvantaged neighborhoods, but the project was not offered to Arab localities (Al-Haj and Rosenfeld 1990, 38, 105). Jewish towns with similar profiles to Arab towns in terms of location and demographic characteristics enjoyed discounts, benefits, and grants for which the Arab towns were not eligible. As a result of the neglect by government ministries, conditions deteriorated in the Arab local authorities.

Although criteria for assistance were eventually set, discrimination continued against Arab towns by defining them, for example, as outside the National Priority Areas. Even when the definitions were changed in 1993 to include several Arab localities, some of these never received all the benefits to which they were entitled. Figure 15.2 shows that the general grant per capita to Arab towns in the 1970s and 1980s was approximately 25 percent of the general grant per capita to Jewish towns. This gap gradually narrowed and was even reversed in 1996 – when government development grants were transferred to Arab localities, particularly Druze and Circassian towns, and the government increased its share of the education and welfare budgets. This policy change happened during the premiership of Rabin (1992–95), who recognized the dire financial straits of the Arab local authorities, many of which needed economic recovery programs.

Nevertheless, these important changes could not reverse the cumulative effect on the Arab population of decades of neglect, as we saw in the clusters of Table 15.3, where most Arab municipalities are at the lowest socioeconomic level. In real terms, an Arab local authority receives a smaller general grant than a Jewish local authority with an identical profile (Razin 2002). The largest disparities are between Arab local authorities and "priority" Jewish local authorities in the north, the south, and the settlements in the occupied territories. But even in comparison with "non-priority" Jewish localities, for every one hundred shekel transferred on behalf of an Arab resident, 140 shekel are transferred on behalf of a Jewish resident (D. Ben-David 2005a).

The improved policy toward Arab localities did not last long. The 2003 cuts in government spending for local authorities severely harmed those already in financial distress, particularly the Arab authorities, whose ability to make up the difference from local income (taxes and licenses) was limited.[38] As a result, the Arab local authorities were plunged into an extended period of crisis, the starkest in their history. Khamaisi (2008, 414–15) lists four components of the crisis in Israeli local authorities, to which we add why it was particularly severe in the Arab community:

First, the division of labor between the central and local governments was not clearly defined, leading to a situation where some local authorities defaulted on obligations to the residents, sometimes even in violation of the law (State Comptroller *Annual Report* 2007). Wealthy and well-established towns

[38] The locally generated income in Arab local authorities constituted less than 40 percent of their budget, on average, compared with over 50 percent in the Jewish local authorities (Ben Bassat and Dahan 2008, 31).

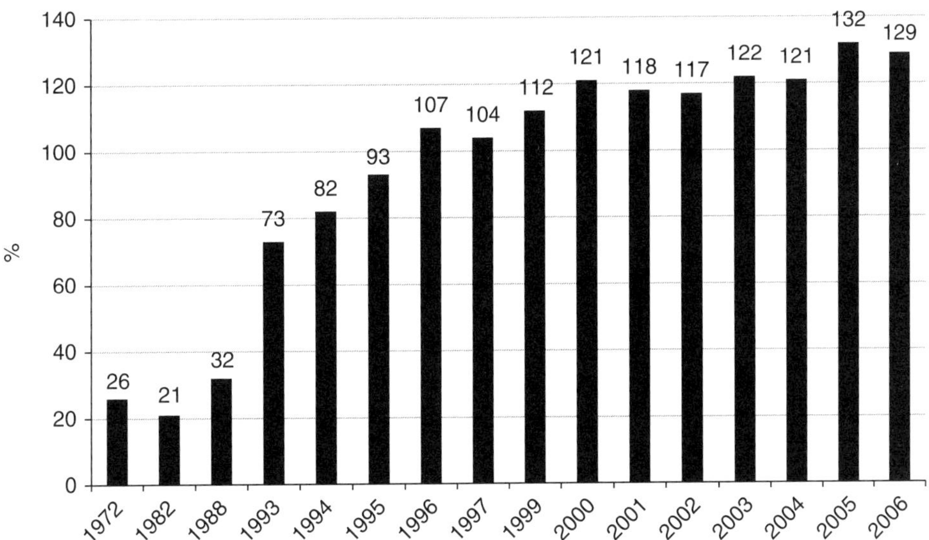

Figure 15.2 General government grants per capita: To Arab local authorities as a percentage of those to Jewish local authorities (1972–2006)
Sources: Ben Bassat and Dahan 2008, 31; Razin 1999. Data for 2000 are from Razin 2002.

managed to persuade the central government to allow them to finance services on their own (sometimes with loans). Disadvantaged towns – such as the Arab local authorities – were powerless to do this as their debt was already spiraling out of control.

Second, local authorities were unable to provide basic services – education, welfare, sewerage, sanitation, etc. – let alone community services or culture. Weak Jewish authorities had access to assistance from non-profits and philanthropies, only a few of which operated in Arab towns. The privatization of services also brought no relief because most Arab local authorities could not afford to make the payments.

Third, government budget cuts after 2003 hurt all the local authorities, but the effect in poorer Jewish and Arab authorities was to paralyze them – they were unable to pay suppliers, loan repayments had to be delayed, services were curtailed, and employee salaries were withheld.

Fourth, the local authority's inability to govern, particularly its ineffective collection of local taxes, led to a loss of confidence by the central government and the residents themselves, and appointment by the interior minister of a committee to run the municipal affairs until the subsequent election. Seventy percent of the committees appointed to govern localities after 2004 were in Arab communities. As a result, the poor public image is the result of both poor management and corruption combined with objective difficulties due to the Finance Ministry's decision to "starve" the local authorities (Razin and Hazan 2007, 177–94).

Thus a vicious cycle was created that was hard to interrupt: revenues of the Arab authorities were meager because of the low income of the residents; the low income is a reflection of the low socioeconomic ranking of the population, high unemployment, and the large proportion of families beneath the poverty line; as a result, factories are not attracted to Arab towns, which leads to the meager revenues from taxation and industry; and thus the cycle is perpetuated (Abu-Sharqiya 2005, 24; Sikkuy 1998). To this should be added the inefficiency at collecting property taxes, due partially to the unwillingness of mayors to enforce collection. Khamaisi sums it up by saying that the crisis in the Arab local authorities demands fundamental change in the rules of the game, and "a spatial redivision to add area to the Arab authorities for development and thereby enable them to increase their local income" (2008, 435).

D. Land and Town Planning

Another factor contributing to the difficulties of the Arab local authorities is the shortage of land and problematic town planning. Land expropriation is the most highly charged issue between Arab citizens and the state of Israel. Even after Israel's founding, Arab lands were frequently expropriated and transferred to the state and the Jewish National Fund, through which they were channeled to the Jewish population for establishing new towns or for use by kibbutzim, moshavim, and private entities. The land expropriation and transfer of ownership was executed legally in a variety of ways defined by the state as required for "public needs" or "security." As a result, the land area of Arab local authorities was reduced, as lands became part of the jurisdiction of Jewish local authorities. Having less space created an impossible situation for Arab farmers, who could no longer earn a livelihood from their land, and for Arab local authorities, which could not expand or develop by making use of the land for housing, industry, or business. Significant amounts of property that remained in Arab hands are privately owned, which does not enable planning for the general public.

Israeli bureaucracy dragged its feet in approving town plans for Arab localities, which compounded the difficulties and led to a plethora of illegal construction. For years, Arab locales, unlike their Jewish counterparts, did not have town plans, and when they were finally approved, they no longer met the changing needs of the Arab population, particularly the high rate of natural increase. Local representatives had not been brought into the decision-making about these town plans, so the distinctive needs of the Arab community were not reflected in them. By the 2000s, most recognized Arab localities already had valid town plans, but these have to be adjusted to existing conditions. Homes and businesses intermingle in Arab localities, for example, as they have evolved without planning for hundreds of years. Reorganizing based on a town plan would be prohibitively expensive for the Arab authorities, and the state does not contribute. Failure to address the shortage of land reserves for development and industrial construction to provide jobs means that the hardship of the Arab authorities will only worsen. Since 1948, some 600 Jewish localities were officially established, but not one new Arab locality, with the exception of townships created for the purpose of concentrating the Bedouin population in defined areas by promising them services in exchange for their renunciation of ancestral land.[39]

[39] In 2014, the National Council for Planning and Construction approved the establishment of a new Arab town adjacent to the existing Arab village Makr in the Western Galilee. As of 2016, planning of the new town is still underway. See Rinat 2014.

Arab local governments find themselves in dire straits – steering a course between difficult conditions (weak governance, tenuous management, and sparse resources) and the rising expectations of the residents who view local government as their main political arena. The disparity between weak execution and their political importance threatens the very stability of local government in Arab authorities.

15.7 Civil Society

In traditional societies with strong volunteer frameworks, civil society is configured differently than in the western world, as it is organized around the family, tribe, community, or religion. Arab society in Israel has a foot in both worlds, the traditional and the modern. The overview below does not represent the rich diversity of this social fabric.

A. The Appearance of Civil Society Organizations

Civil society organizations are a relatively new phenomenon in Arab society, certainly compared to their prevalence in Jewish society. In the past, the hubs of social and political power were the political parties elected to local government (primarily Maki and Hadash) and, to some extent, also the Histadrut; these served as organizing alternatives to parliamentary politics. In parallel, activism was extensive in informal frameworks and Christian philanthropic associations (Zeidan 2005). Thus, local government, local workers' councils, and several Histadrut groups provided channels for the intense activism of groups and movements in Arab society (Reiter and Aharoni 1993, 51). This duality – local government working side by side with volunteer organizations as an alternative to the state institutions – characterized the evolution of this sector in Arab society. As noted in Chapter 12, the surge of voluntarism in Arab society began in the 1980s: In 1998, one thousand Arab non-profits were registered (including Druze and Bedouin); in 2007, this had risen to almost 3,000. And yet the average number of active Arab organizations for every thousand Arab residents was still about a quarter that of the Jewish sector (Balbachan 2008a). Zeidan and Ghanem (2000) list several key factors to explain the proliferation of Arab civil society organizations:

- Higher education produced a cadre of young college graduates with honed political-social awareness, who founded non-profits to bring change to their communities.
- These organizations were intended to provide an alternative to – or to supplement – state services, which discriminated against Arab citizens.
- Arab college graduates faced obstacles in being hired for jobs in the Israeli work force, but the new or expanded non-profits provided employment and a source of income beyond the direct scrutiny of the state.
- The Nonprofit Associations Law (1980) made it easier to register Arab non-profits, and then High Court rulings safeguarded the right of Arab non-profits to organize.
- Intensification of the religious factor: The Islamic Movement founded religious and charitable trusts in Arab localities.

- Payes (2005) and Jamal (2008) cite additional factors: disappointment with the parties and parliamentary politics, and the perception of non-profits as more flexible channels for political activism.

The primary domains of Arab non-profit activity in 2007 were as follows: 31 percent in culture and recreation; 24 percent in social services, housing, and health; 19 percent in education and research; 12 percent in religion; 9 percent in civil rights and advocacy; and 5 percent other (Jamal 2008, 290; Even-Chorev 2008, 12). In comparison with the previous decade, there was a significant drop in religious non-profits and a rise in non-profits in the fields of culture, education, and research, as well as fostering Arab national identity (Rudnitzky 2014, 47). Research institutes were established in 2000 that had never previously existed for the Arab community of Israel, such as Mada al-Carmel: Arab Center for Applied Social Research; Ibn Khaldun: Arab Association for Research and Development; and Dirasat: Arab Center for Law and Policy.

Arab civil society has a higher proportion of social change organizations, including women's organizations, than Jewish civil society (Rekhess and Rudnitzky 2009, chapter 9, pages 11, 13). Many Arab non-profits are multi-purpose – they address a range of social issues, rather than specializing in just one. This testifies to the fact that Arab civil society in Israel is just evolving in terms of modernization and the division of function, and that many organizations still function in traditional patterns. This is also a product of the fact that civil society often provides social and cultural services in place of the central and local governments. Chapter 12 classifies civil society organizations into five categories: service providers; community organizations; organizations for political and social change; professional associations; and social enterprises. In general, the emphasis in Arab civil society is on community groups as well as political and social change organizations, and also on a hybrid that combines activities for social and political change together with communal work. Organizations that can be categorized as purely communal are rarer in Arab society because of the politicization of most of the civil society organizations.

B. Examples of Organizations in Arab Civil Society

Al-Ard ("the land"), founded in 1959, was an organization for social and political change, and would have become a political party had it not been disqualified by the High Court of Justice (*Yeredor v. Election Committee* 1965). Al-Ard supported the pan-Arabism of the Egyptian President Gamal Abdel Nasser, and sought to establish a national Arab movement independent of foreign bodies or commitment to the existence of Israel. The movement called for realization of the national rights of Palestinians in the entire land of Palestine; it opposed the positions of Maki, and challenged the traditional social-political structure of Arab society in Israel. These views were considered extreme at the time, not only by the Israeli government, but also by the Arab establishment. To sidestep these obstacles, al-Ard members – many of them students of law – came up with legal loopholes or borderline legal solutions such as registering a commercial company, founding an association based on still valid Ottoman law, and publishing single-issue newspapers under various names.

Disqualification of the al-Ard party by the Central Elections Committee and the High Court of Justice from running in the Knesset election of 1965 – and the subsequent outlawing of the movement – led to its decline. Some al-Ard leaders continued their efforts to promote these goals in other frameworks, but had limited influence over the public agenda. From the 1970s, the Abnaa al-Balad movement was considered inheritor of their mantle (see below).

Another example of an organization for social-political change was the action arm of the ***Association of Forty***. The association was founded in 1988 by representatives of unrecognized Arab villages in an effort to achieve official recognition and prevent the demolition of their homes, which government authorities alleged were built illegally. Most of the unrecognized villages existed before the founding of Israel, and some were established later by "internally displaced" Palestinians who had been uprooted from their homes during the war. The state seeks to exclude them from land surveys and planning on the grounds that the villages are small and lack infrastructure. The Association of Forty uses various strategies including the preparation and submission of town plans for thirty-five localities, and the prevention of evacuations, primarily of Bedouin settlements in the Galilee (Soen and Eisenkang-Kane 2005). According to the ***Arab Center for Alternative Planning*** (founded in 2000), there are ninety-five unrecognized Arab villages in Israel, of which fifty-nine are Bedouin; and by 2007, advocacy efforts had won official recognition of twenty-one such localities (see organization website). The Association of Forty is backed by the Higher Monitoring Committee and Arab political parties, and receives financial support from various bodies including the New Israel Fund.

Several legal organizations were founded to promote the human and civil rights of Arab citizens of Israel and to fight discrimination against them. ***Adalah*** ("justice") was founded in 1996 as an independent, non-partisan legal association that works to protect the human rights of Palestinian Arabs in Israel and the occupied territories. It seeks to achieve individual and collective rights in many fields: land, planning and housing, and civil, political, cultural, social, economic, and religious rights, as well as the rights of women and convicts. Adalah uses a range of strategies: litigation and other legal interventions before Israeli courts and state authorities; promotion of equal rights legislation; legal consultations to Arab individuals, NGOs, and institutions; appeals to international institutions and forums; reports and analyses of critical legal issues; and training of legal apprentices and new lawyers in human rights litigation and advocacy (see Adalah website). Another key rights organization is ***Mossawa*** ("equality"): ***The Advocacy Center for Arab Citizens in Israel***. Founded in 1997, Mossawa is an independent, non-partisan organization that promotes full civil rights for Arab citizens through advocacy and public campaigns. Mossawa also works to build political capacity in local communities and engages in social and economic research. Mossawa participated in the protests and demonstrations following the October 2000 events, and also the struggle for equal access to institutions of higher learning.[40] In response to the various constitution proposals

[40] See Mossawa website. Other litigation organizations: Karama Organization for Human Rights and Dirasat: Arab Center for Law and Policy.

that were published, Adalah and Mossawa both proposed constitutions of their own, claiming that the others did not protect the rights of Arab citizens.[41]

Joint Arab-Jewish civil society organizations view the elimination of anti-Arab discrimination in Israel as a shared civic goal. ***Sikkuy: The Association for the Advancement of Civic Equality*** was founded in 1991 as an Arab-Jewish organization working for civil equality in all areas. Among its activities: removing barriers that prevent the equal distribution of public resources to Arab citizens; creating cooperative frameworks in industry, tourism, and environment between neighboring Arab and Jewish communities; efforts to ensure the employment of Arabs in the civil service, government companies, universities, etc.; and programs for Jewish and Arab audiences to instill the value of equality and raise awareness about the need to eliminate discrimination. One signal contribution of Sikkuy is its annual Equality Index, which documents inequality in the fields of health, housing, education, employment, and social welfare (see Sikkuy website). ***Ta'ayush*** ("living together"): ***Arab-Jewish Partnership*** was founded in 2000 and works for civil and political equality between Jews and Arabs within Israel, and between Israelis and Palestinians, and to end Israeli control over the occupied territories. Examples of Ta'ayush activity: community empowerment and development projects, summer camps for youth, humanitarian assistance to Palestinians in the territories, and demonstrations and public campaigns against the route of the separation barrier and its humanitarian and political repercussions (see Ta'ayush website). Organizations important for Arab civil society are the ***New Israel Fund*** (founded in 1979) and ***Shatil*** (support and consulting to social change organizations, founded in 1982), which extend assistance to many educational, cultural, and social organizations (see organizational websites). The ***Abraham Fund Initiatives*** (named for Abraham/Ibrahim, the common forefather) was founded in 1989 and works to ensure equal opportunity for Arabs in planning, economics, and employment, and also supports educational and cultural initiatives (see organization website). The Abraham Fund together with other organizations founded the Coexistence Network in Israel, which coordinates activity among more than 150 coexistence organizations.[42]

Many organizations in Arab civil society merge community activity with political activism, as previously mentioned. The most important of these is the Higher Monitoring Committee of Arab Citizens of Israel (founded in 1982) in which all the Arab bodies and political movements are members. The Monitoring Committee has five professional subcommittees in the fields of education, welfare, sports, health, and agriculture. Another previously mentioned organization is the Islamic Movement, which wields considerable influence among the public and local authorities. In addition to its religious goals, the Islamic Movement is very active in welfare and education. It has preschools and informal religious training frameworks in the mosques, as well as

[41] Adalah published "The Democratic Constitution" and Mossawa published "An Equal Constitution for All? On a Constitution and Collective Rights for Arab Citizens in Israel." Both documents appear on the websites of these organizations.

[42] Examples of other Jewish-Arab organizations in Israel: Citizens' Accord Forum, Center for Jewish-Arab Economic Development, Negev Coexistence Forum. Organizations that combine community activism with work for social and political change: Bustan LeShalom (environment and environmental justice); Arab-Jewish Orchestra (culture); Sadaka-Re'ut: Arab-Jewish Youth Partnership; Shared Life: Partnership, Equality, Peace. Jewish-Arab schools: Hand-in-Hand, Hagar Association, Neve Shalom/Wahat al-Salam School for Peace. See www.coexnet.org.il (accessed October 11, 2017).

medical clinics, charitable trusts, and campaigns against the use of drugs. The Islamic Movement runs work camps for children and youth, art festivals in the spirit of Islam, and a separate, Islamic soccer league.

Civil society gave a new dimension to activism in Arab society in Israel. These organizations operate under trying circumstances – ongoing suspicion by state authorities and arbitrary limitations by the Registrar of Nonprofits.[43] They face funding complexities: Arabs accuse them of accepting support from Jewish and Zionist foundations, and Jews accuse them of accepting support from governments hostile to Israel. The foundations that do support them, such as the New Israel Fund, are attacked by the extreme right wing as being anti-Zionist and traitors.

Arab non-profits have a presence in Arab society – occasionally in society at large as well – and have a long list of accomplishments. Nevertheless, it is too early to say whether the non-traditional and politically unaligned organizations will survive in the long run. This is also true for the complex relationship between the organizations and the political parties. On the one hand, the social organizations express disappointment with the Arab parties – not only their parliamentary activity, but that the parties allegedly deal only with the bigger issues of the future of Palestine while neglecting the harsh daily lives of Arab citizens. On the other hand, Arab civil society is primarily a system that complements the political and business sectors (Y.T. Jabareen 2007), giving them public and intellectual support.

15.8 Policies toward Arab Citizens

During the pre-state period, there was virtually total separation between the Jewish and Arab communities economically, socially, culturally, and of course politically. The Jewish Yishuv was a well-organized political community having a strong collective consciousness, an urban base, and a developed economy. Its national institutions were absorbed into the state and provided a sturdy platform for majority rule. The Arab community that remained in Israel was disorganized, had a rather tenuous national consciousness, its Muslim majority was mostly rural, and its economy was comparatively not well developed (Grinberg 2001, 585–610). The founding of Israel created entirely new circumstances for the two communities: The indigenous Arab community was transformed from the majority into a small minority, with almost no political, economic, religious, or cultural elite (most of whom fled or were expelled from Israel), and it became entirely subservient to Jewish rule. What's more, the enmity between Israel and its neighbors adversely affected the Arab minority that remained, further eroding its status. Despite the weakness of the Arab community during the early years, the Jewish public and its leaders viewed it as a security threat, fearful about its loyalty to and identification with the state. The reality, however, was different: The large majority of Arab citizens of Israel were not involved in activity hostile to Israel, even during times of war, and the vast

[43] According to the Nonprofit Associations Law, the Registrar shall not register a non-profit "if any of its objectives negates the existence or democratic character of the state of Israel." A non-profit that does not receive certification of proper bookkeeping from the Registrar is prohibited from receiving government support. From 1988 to 2001, 60 percent of the non-profits not given this certification were Arab (Rekhess and Rudnitzky 2009, chapter 9, 18).

majority integrated into the Israeli work force in construction, agriculture, industry, and services (Benziman and Mansour 1992, 16, 21–24).

During Israel's first four decades, the policies toward Arab citizens were marked by suspicion, scrutinization, segmentation, dependence, and co-optation (Lustick 1980). It is sufficient to compare this with the policies of the "melting pot" or "ingathering of the exiles" toward Jewish citizens to see the profound difference. The policy toward Arabs had clear implications normatively and legally, as well as in the regulations and institutions, as we shall see below. The second, civic, stage, which began in the 1980s, was rooted in processes emerging in both Jewish and Arab societies, which forced the government to change its policies. Some of the Jewish public and leaders began to move gradually to a general civic approach, one that was more inclusive of non-Jewish citizens, manifested in legislation, government and ministry policies, and court decisions. In parallel, changes were beginning in Arab society – a demand to throw off the patron–client relationship.

A. In the Knesset

During the patronage stage, most interactions with Arabs in Israel did not take place in the Knesset or courts, but in government ministries. Labeling them a security threat rather than partners in a political community dictated how they were treated. Military rule was imposed without legislation, public discussion, or an opportunity to voice opposition, but decided in closed government deliberations based solely on a security perspective. And the government had no compunctions about passing laws in the Knesset that determined the fate of the Arab population (see Section 15.3 above), particularly laws regarding citizenship and land. Grim events for the Arab population – such as the Kafr Qasim (1956) and Land Day (1976) killings – were not substantively addressed in the Knesset. It was only the events of October 2000 that catalyzed the first Knesset discussion about Arab citizens and their status in Israel.

The presence of Arab representatives in affiliated Knesset party lists was not sufficient to engender change: Arabs were still not deemed equal representatives-partners, but rather intermediaries between their communities and government representatives. Arab MKs were generally unable to present comprehensive demands or raise sensitive issues in the Knesset. The effort to rescind military rule, for example, was led by Mapam and Rakah, not the affiliated Arab lists. The rise of independent Arab parties and the placement of Arabs in realistic places on Jewish party lists strengthened the ability of the Arab public to raise their concerns in the Knesset, but their political influence was still negligible compared to Jewish sectors, even those with fewer representatives, such as the ultra-Orthodox, the settlers, or "the Russians." Arab MKs remain unable to mobilize a majority for their bills, and are not equal partners to the Knesset work: Until formation of the Joint List in 2015, Arab MKs were generally appointed to the less important Knesset committees, and they are still not members of the powerful Foreign Affairs and Defense Committee.

B. Government Policy

Government policy toward the Arabs was formulated in closed meetings with the Advisor for Arab Affairs in the Office of the Prime Minister (Benziman and Mansour

1992, 52–53, 59–60). As far as can be determined, during the years 1948–67, only three discussions were held in the government plenary about what was called "the Arab sector": a decision in 1952 to equalize the wages of Arab and Jewish workers; a decision in 1954 to hold elections for the Nazareth municipality; and a decision in 1958 to develop an economic rehabilitation plan for the Arabs in Israel. After 1967, attention was diverted to the territories and the government conducted few discussions about Arab citizens, in retrospect all of them unproductive, such as the employment difficulties of Arab college graduates and Bedouin land issues in the Negev. At the initiative of Shmuel Toledano, then Advisor for Arab Affairs, the government began in 1973 to discuss its orientation toward Arabs in Israel, but no explicit decisions were taken.[44] Following Land Day in 1976, the government held two meetings that yielded decisions about arrangements for Bedouin land and promoting the integration of Arab citizens in the life of the country. In 1986, Ezer Weizman, then minister without portfolio with responsibility for Arab affairs, brought to the government a policy proposal concerning the Arab sector, but no decisions were made and no further deliberations were held; in 1987, the government made decisions intended to support the Druze population. In general, there is no evidence of any government discussion about the matter of principle – the existence of an Arab national minority in a Jewish state (as opposed to the security concerns about Arabs in Israel).

Thus, even after lifting military rule in 1966, the prime characteristic of Israeli government policies toward its Arab citizens was its avoidance of any clear, comprehensive policy. This ambiguity was convenient for those who dealt with the Arab population, as the practical repercussion was a combination of neglect, discrimination, and prioritizing security concerns. The failure to shape a policy is surprising because from a Jewish perspective, there were plenty of dramatic events with direct impact on the Arabs (the Six Day War, the first and second Intifadas, the Gulf War) that would call for a thorough examination of their status in Israel. The fact that successive Israeli governments felt no need to address the issues of principle related to the Arab public testifies to the short-sighted security approach that was adopted. Government dealings with Arabs were generally the product of the need to find an immediate solution to a specific problem (such as the October 2000 events). Indeed, in 2000–12, no fewer than ten government decisions were made to "develop Arab localities" and even a budgetary framework was allocated (see list in Rudnitzky 2014, 66). In 2007, the government established the Authority for Economic Development in the Arab, Druze, and Circassian Sector in response to stern directives by the OECD to increase the participation of Arabs (and ultra-Orthodox) in the work force prior to accepting Israel to this international body (Ministry of the Economy 2013).

These steps reflect change, both in words and the willingness to back them up with funding. Nevertheless, the amounts actually transferred were much smaller than what was promised, and the programs have been repeated and recycled over the years. Other practical decisions – improving municipal services, drafting Arabs

[44] Toledano reports that he recommended more liberal policies, and that the government began to treat Arabs as citizens with equal rights – "Respect him, but suspect him," rather than "Suspect him, but respect him." The authors express their thanks to Shmuel Toledano for providing this information based on a policy paper he wrote in 1974 as the Advisor for Arab Affairs.

to national service (see below), or building more housing – still attest to a significant gap between intent and implementation.[45]

C. Possible Types of Policy

Government policy toward the Arabs in Israel shifted from patronage to the civic stage because it was forced to, not because the government took the initiative or reconsidered its approach. Here we present a typology of the options that confronted Israeli governments over the years, some of which were partially applied: "transfer," coercion, coexistence, and full integration. Not one of these was formally adopted or consistently applied by any government, but none is entirely theoretical.

1 The underlying assumption that Arabs in Israel are an incorrigible fifth column leads to the immoral solution of "transfer" – expulsion from Israel. During the War of Independence, some Palestinian inhabitants were forcibly expelled (Morris 1988). Afterwards, the state authorities were responsible for planned acts of expulsion, such as the deportation of Majdal (Ashkelon) residents to the Gaza Strip in 1950, the forced relocation of Arab citizens from their homes to other places in Israel, or the deportation of refugees defined as "infiltrators." The use of transfer as a legitimate policy has greatly diminished since the 1960s, yet some political parties were elected to the Knesset on this platform – Moledet (1998–99) advocated transfer ("by choice") and Yisrael Beitenu impugns the loyalty of Arab citizens and advocates the handover of Arab towns from Israel to Palestine. The motivation is ostensibly security, which is a pretext for xenophobic nationalism (see Segev 2005, 548–63 and Arieli, Schwartz, and Tagari 2006 on proposals to transfer Palestinians out of the West Bank and Gaza Strip). Demanding "proof of loyalty" and the like might even be calculated moves to prevent Arabs from voting in the Knesset elections: Reducing Arab participation in elections would tilt the results in favor of right-wing parties.
2 A policy of coercion was adopted by Israeli governments after the founding of the state, and was based, as noted, on the presumption that the Arabs who remained in Israel were an imminent threat that must be neutralized, not equal partners in society or a political community. This was an extreme interpretation of the partition principle – that because the Jewish and Arab communities each preferred national independence, the two sides could not coexist or cooperate. Entrusting the treatment of Arabs in Israel to the security authorities gave license to the policy of coercion and military rule. It should be noted that another approach was advocated as early as 1948: A memorandum written by Bechor-Shalom Sheetrit, minister of minority affairs, expressed opposition to the security approach and military regime, and proposed tolerance toward the Arabs.

[45] The most ambitious program was launched by the Barak government in 2000 – a five-year plan for development that was budgeted at NIS 4 billion. In practice, only 70 percent was spent, and some of this came from ministry budget lines that already existed for these same objectives (Haider 2005, 19–41). Even the government's five-year plan 2010–14 "for the economic development of localities in the minority sector," approved upon Israel's acceptance to the OECD (2010), actually spent only 16.5 percent of the housing allocations (State Comptroller *Annual Report* 2013, 335–57).

The document recommended refraining from illegal land confiscation; arbitrary arrest; the uprooting of Arab citizens from their villages; demolition of homes; collecting taxes without the proper authority; destruction of Arab-owned property; forcing Arabs to work on military projects; forcing Arabs to abandon their homes in punishment for crimes (some fabricated); limiting Muslim access to mosques and Christian access to churches; expelling Bedouins from the Negev; imposing fees for work permits; evicting Arabs from sensitive areas without providing alternative housing; devising plans to concentrate Haifa Arabs in ghettos; and more (Korn 2008). In the 1960s, supporters and implementers of the coercion policy recognized its limitations because it was not practical – it did not achieve the goals and needlessly punished Arabs who were not a security risk. Ethical reasons were also given – a democratic state cannot behave this way toward its citizens. Intense parliamentary activity by Mapam and Rakah as well as public advocacy by Jewish-Arab intellectual organizations led to easements in the military regime, ultimately rescinded in 1966 by Levi Eshkol, prime minister and defense minister at the time.

3 The gradual decline of the coercion policy (though it has not yet disappeared entirely) yielded to an approach – or perhaps just a slogan – of coexistence. Whether out of understanding or in response to pressure, the state authorities came to realize that the arbitrary wielding of power that marginalizes and diminishes the Arab public cannot continue indefinitely (Jamal 2011). The change in policy was neither comprehensive nor calculated, but a collection of decisions that gradually coalesced into policy. The first step was removal of the administrative divisions between the minority and the majority accompanied by declarations about seeking "normalization" between Jews and Arabs. The second step was a set of decisions to improve the living conditions of Arab citizens to be implemented by all the government ministries. As noted, Shmuel Toledano, the Advisor for Arab Affairs (1965–77), proposed in 1974 comprehensive policy changes with respect to land, education, culture, and more. He called for a "gentlemen's agreement" between the state and its Arab citizens: The state would recognize its responsibility for the Arab citizens in exchange for the Arabs maintaining law and order. Although this has overtones of the patronage approach, the document avoids any demands for the Arabs to identify with the state, prove their loyalty to it, or commit to national service – civilian or military. The policy proposal even urged that sensitivity be shown about the nationalist feelings of the Arabs, and that Jewish symbols or ceremonies not be foisted upon them, nor the obligation to celebrate Independence Day. Toledano called for integrating "positive Arabs" in the state institutions, opening the Zionist parties to Arabs, ending the confiscation of lands, and encouraging urbanization in Arab society. The document was deliberated in the Ministerial Committee for Security Affairs in 1974, and though it was never official government policy, it had an influence on changing the previous policy assumptions. In critical areas, however, it had no effect whatsoever, as we shall see.

Implementation of the policy proposed by Toledano turned out to be impossible. The main obstacles were the need to uproot fundamental perceptions and foster awareness of the distress of the Arabs: It was hard to persuade the Jewish public and policymakers to show openness to the Arab public. Several examples: The refusal of many Jews to lease apartments to Arabs, which held back urbanization; the integration of Arabs into national service programs and public institutions began only in the 1990s; the call to improve the living conditions in Arab towns was not implemented; and so the gap only grew. The policy of land expropriation under the guise of security continued in plans such as "Judaizing the Galilee," which led to the Land Day events of 1976, ten years after military rule was rescinded. Land confiscation was a direct continuation of the coercion policies, in which the state allowed itself free rein vis-à-vis the Arab citizens. Land Day fractured relations and ended the declarations about coexistence. The response of the Arabs was that "existence precedes coexistence." The alienation between Arab citizens and the state (but not necessarily the Jewish citizens) continued.

4 Since the 1990s, conflicting trends have been evident in government policy, including declarations of policies designed to integrate Arabs into the life of the state. After Land Day, policy proposals about Israel's Arab citizens were presented to the government (Benziman and Mansour 1992, 98–100). The assumptions underlying these proposals were the demographic threat, trends toward "Palestinization," and expectations that Arab citizens could not identify with the state, hence Israel should make do with their loyalty on security matters and fulfilling their civic duties. At the same time, the proposals urged greater investment of economic resources to raise the standard of services for Arab citizens to equal that of the Jewish sector. It was said in the documents that no government had ever framed a coherent, long-term policy about the Arab sector, but rather reacted to crises with short-term solutions. This document, on the other hand, proposed that the way to integrate the Arab population was economic, and that equality of resource allocation and service provision would elicit greater support for the state. Despite the clarity of this instrumental goal, state authorities never implemented it, i.e., put it to the test.

In 1991, a decision was made by the Likud government to integrate Arab citizens, but this was never formulated as a plan. During its brief term in office (1992–95), the Rabin government – for ideological reasons that were reinforced by the peace process and the agreements with Arab political parties – adopted a policy designed to improve the situation of the Arab citizens, as we shall describe below. The Barak government (1999–2001) adopted a similar policy and even allocated funding to it, but implemented only some of the plans.[46] Two intifadas and the October 2000 events only worsened relations between the two communities, and reduced the willingness of the Israeli political system to promote equality and civil integration. Despite the declarations in the proposed Government Policy, the Sharon and Olmert governments (2001–9) did little on behalf of the Arab citizens. Prior to joining the OECD, as noted, Israel began to cite the importance of the Arab labor force for the state economy. The Netanyahu governments since 2009 have made important decisions, but no results are yet evident to change the socioeconomic situation described at the

[46] There are no accessible sources for the Likud government's 1991 multi-year development plan for the Arab sector. For decisions by the Barak government following deliberations of the Matan Vilnai Committee, see Ministry of Construction and Housing (2000).

beginning of this chapter.[47] One way or another, although slow winds of change can be discerned, these no longer satisfy segments of the Arab public for whom separatism and the demand for recognition as an autonomous national group have been growing.

D. Implementation of the Policy in the Ministries

We discussed above a range of policies that Israeli governments could have adopted, and did to some extent. In this section, we present the actions taken by government ministries, and focus on the "transition to civic thinking" from the mid-1990s (according to Reiter 2000).

So long as the basic security assumption was that the Arabs were a fifth column, government actions were designed to prevent this threat from being realized. We mentioned the main points: preventing the return to Israel of Palestinian refugees (or their immediate family members); expropriation of lands; reduced appropriations for services and development budgets; excluding Arab towns from national projects; and withholding construction permits. This was also true of civic projects such as the National Water Carrier (1965), which did not take into consideration the needs of Arab farmers; or Project Renewal (in the late 1970s), implemented primarily in Jewish neighborhoods. In addition to deliberate exclusion, there was also deliberate mistreatment, such as the settlement policy of "Judaizing the Galilee," which included the expropriation of lands from Arab citizens. In addition, the Arab exemption from military service served as the basis for discrimination in granting benefits to army veterans, later (1994) defined as illegal by the Supreme Court (see Section 15.3C in this chapter). Examples: housing assistance in Jewish development towns or when a government committee recommended in 1982 to lower tuition fees in institutions of higher learning.[48]

From the mid-1990s, there were harbingers of change in the government's policy toward Arabs and early signs of "civic thinking" from policymakers, administrators, and the public at large. Examples: cessation of the wholesale expropriation of lands; the reopening of Area 9 in the Galilee – a large tract of land that had been declared off limits to its Arab owners for use by the military; partial recognition of the illegal

[47] In late 2015, the government decided to launch an ambitious, five-year "Government Plan for Economic Development in the Arab Sector 2016–2020," promising to allocate NIS 15 billion for development of education, infrastructure, employment, health, and more in the Arab sector. See http://injaz.org.il/Public/files/תוכנית%20ממשלתית%20לפיתוח%20כלכלי%20בחברה%20הערבית-מצגת%20של%20אינגאז(1).pdf (accessed October 23, 2017) for a detailed overview of the plan. This was probably the most ambitious plan, given the approval of the Finance Ministry and the involvement of Arab representatives in its formulation. Initially, some conditions were made that rendered implementation difficult; however, as of early 2017 the plan is taking off.

[48] The Katzav Committee, headed by the deputy housing minister, recommended (in 1982) that tuition fees in institutions of higher learning be discounted for army veterans and residents of development towns or renewal neighborhoods. This would mean, for example, that a university student from a large family who receives a discharged soldier grant would pay only half the tuition. In response to public pressure, the government withdrew its approval for these recommendations. A proposed amendment to the Income Tax Ordinance stipulated that families of army veterans with three or more children would enjoy income tax benefits for which Arab families would not be eligible. It was later proposed that yeshiva students also enjoy reduced tuition rates – whether they were army veterans or not.

construction in Arab towns; narrowing the gap of Interior Ministry allocations to Jewish and Arab towns; rejection of proposals that openly discriminated against Arabs; invalidating discriminatory legislation such as the army veterans' grant of the National Security Institute; a decision by the Barak government to allocate some NIS 4 billion to develop Arab localities; and rescinding the government decision about National Priority Areas for education (March 2006), which had included only four Arab towns (Swirski and Dagan-Buzaglo 2009). (On the government decision in December 2015, see footnote 47 above.)

Another important initiative was the effort to bring college-educated Arabs into the civil service, which has continued intermittently since 1994. The defined goals of this project (Galnoor 2003, 441):

- Affirmative action to employ Arab and Druze college graduates in the civil service via special vacancy announcements.
- Signaling that the doors would be open: Arab and Druze college graduates were invited by the state to submit their candidacy not just for special vacancy announcements, but primarily for *ordinary* ones. For the first time, vacancies were also published in Arabic.
- Ensuring that all hirings of Arabs to civil service positions would be independent of political party influence; a training program to help new Arab employees succeed at their jobs.[49]

In 1994, the number of Arabs in the civil service was 1,369, which rose to 2,218 within two years when most of the new employees (85%) were hired via ordinary vacancy announcements. The number of Arab civil service employees increased to 3,883 in 2008, and their proportion rose from 2.5 percent of all civil service employees in 1994 to 6.7 percent in 2008 (Civil Service Commission 2009, 8). Nevertheless, despite repeated decisions of various governments, the proportion of Arabs remained minuscule in the civil service and on the directorates of government companies.[50] The employment situation of Arabs is not very different in other public institutions, mixed city municipalities, institutions of higher learning, and the commercial sector.

On a symbolic level, several changes occurred that were small, but significant. Examples: prizes to Arab authors, including the Israel Prize and the Speaker of the Knesset Award;[51] the inclusion of Arabs in peace-negotiating teams and, in another vein, in delegations to concentration camps; appointment of the first Arab justice to Israel's Supreme Court; the steady increase of Arab students in Israeli colleges and universities; the appointment of Arabs to Israeli embassies; Arab artists, writers, and athletes representing Israel abroad; and the 2007 law establishing the Academy of the Arabic Language in Israel. The fact that a list of "achievements" appears here is

[49] This policy became law in 2000 through an amendment to the Civil Service (Appointments) Law mandating the due representation of qualified Arabs, Druze, and Circassians through both special vacancy announcements and affirmative action.

[50] In 2004, the government decided that at least one Arab should serve on the directorate of every government company (Haider 2005).

[51] The Israel Prize was awarded in 1985 to Israel Television in Arabic for "its special contribution to society and the state"; in 1987 to Makram Khouri for acting; in 1990 to Sheikh Amin Tarif for "his special contribution to society and the state"; and in 1992 to Emil Habibi for Arabic literature.

an indication that such events are rare, and the time is still distant when there will be no need for indications and symbols, because no one will even notice that an Arab was chosen.[52]

E. Contribution of the Monitoring Mechanisms

Monitoring mechanisms do not make policy, but they play an important role in monitoring the implementation of policy: Only in the aftermath of the October 2000 events was an assessment made by a state institution of the status of Arabs in Israel: A state commission of inquiry (the "Or Report") and the State Comptroller Report from 2002 were the first to provide a comprehensive overview of the substandard infrastructure in Arab, Bedouin, Druze, and Circassian towns and villages. The latter report discusses three 4-year development plans initiated by Israeli governments since the 1980s.[53] It notes the extremely poor condition of the physical infrastructure in Arab local authorities, particularly the sewerage system, access to quality water, condition of the roads, and the development of industrial zones (that could provide local income for Arab municipalities and jobs for the residents). The report notes that the lack of locally generated income in Arab towns leads to overdependence on government support for development (State Comptroller *Annual Report* 2001, 128–29). It describes the gaps between the Jewish and Arab populations on various health indicators: the rates of mortality, infant mortality, death from cardiac diseases and cancer, congenital diseases, birth defects as a result of consanguineous marriages, and genetic diseases. Six years later, the State Comptroller's report of 2008 noted that state allocations to Arab localities and the dismal conditions in them had barely changed (Amsterdamski 2008; Kashti 2009).

The appointment in November 2000 of the "State commission of inquiry into the clashes between security forces and Israeli citizens in October 2000" ("the Or Commission") could have marked a turning point. For the first time in the history of Israel, an independent state body was established to investigate an issue that dealt entirely with the status of Arabs in Israel. The committee was appointed in response to strong public pressure, mostly, but not only, from Arab citizens and despite the initial opposition of the Barak-led government. It was headed by Supreme Court Justice Theodor Or and its other members were Justice Hashim Khatib and Professor Shimon Shamir. Although the letter of appointment called for investigating the events themselves, the committee chose not to ignore the historical, political, and economic context, and submitted a comprehensive analysis of the state of Israel's Arab citizens. Part one was devoted to an examination of the civil status of the Arab population, describing discrimination and inequity on a number of levels (Or Commission Final Report 2003, A, part 1, chapter 1):

- Resource allocation: to education, local councils and authorities, infrastructure, and police services.

52 On the disparity between the declared policies and reality of Israeli governments, see Shimon Shamir 2005.

53 The Development Plan for the Druze and Circassian Sectors 1995–99, ratified in 2000; the 1998 Development Plan for Bedouin in Northern Israel 1999–2003; the Multi-year Development Plan for the Arab Sector 2000–4 (the Vilnai Committee). From State Comptroller *Annual Report* 2001, 52B.

- Land and planning: land expropriations; the hemming in of Arab towns located in sensitive security zones, Jewish regional councils, or nature reserves to prevent their expansion; the absence of master plans and town planning schemes for construction; the problem of unrecognized settlements.
- The high levels of poverty and unemployment.

The committee's criticism of the ongoing discrimination against Arab citizens in Israel appeared together with personal recommendations on both the political and professional levels. For example, the report noted that Prime Minister Ehud Barak failed to address the problems evident in the Arab sector prior to eruption of the clashes, and did not meet to discuss them despite repeated requests by the security services; although Shlomo Ben-Ami, minister of internal security, worked to achieve calm and improve relations with the Arab sector, he did not ensure that the police force was prepared to deal with disruptions of public order and he was not aware of the use of live fire to disperse demonstrators; during the tenure of the northern district's chief of police, relations between Arab citizens and the police had deteriorated to the extent of a complete breakdown in communication, contributing to the severity of the clashes. The committee further stated that the harsh measures taken to disperse the demonstrations were not justified (Or Commission Final Report 2003, part 5, parags. 242, 257, 259, 272).

In its conclusions, the commission stressed the urgency of formulating an appropriate and responsible policy to address the situation of Arab citizens, because the issue can no longer be ignored and the state has the responsibility to take immediate action to reduce the gaps by setting clear objectives with timetables for their implementation. The commission stated that the prime minister must be personally involved and oversee the effort, "to erase the stain of discrimination against Arab citizens in all its various forms and expressions" (ibid., part 6, parag. 12). The committee criticized the lack of law enforcement in Arab localities and emphasized the need to initiate, develop, and allocate resources in order to close the gaps in education, housing, industry, employment, and services (particularly among the Bedouin). In the sensitive area of land, the state must adhere to the egalitarian principles of distributive justice, and formulate just and suitable planning policies to reduce the problem of illegal construction. The state is obligated to its Arab citizens not just in material matters, but must find ways and means to enable them to publicly express their culture and identity in Israel "in a proper and respectful manner" (ibid., part 6, parag. 13).

The Sharon-led government voted to accept the personal recommendations of the Or Commission report, and established a ministerial committee headed by Yosef (Tommy) Lapid to formulate a plan for implementing the other recommendations. Representatives of the Arab public refused to cooperate with the committee, however, as its members were extreme right-wingers. The Lapid Committee acknowledged the Israeli government's obligation to work toward civil equality – rights and responsibilities – of the Jewish and Arab citizens, and added several recommendations to improve relations between the communities. These included establishing a government authority to advance minorities, integrating Arab youth into the civilian national service program, and expediting the preparation of master plans and town planning schemes for Arab localities; several symbolic gestures were also recommended. The government adopted the conclusions of the Lapid Committee in May 2004 – and it became a decision added to the pile of decisions that have never been executed. On top of this, one year later, the state prosecutor accepted the recommendation of the Police Investigation Department to close the case against the accused police officers for lack of evidence.

Thus, the first comprehensive report by a serious, official body – a state commission of inquiry that investigated and recommended fundamental changes in state policy toward its Arab citizens – came to an end. Several recommendations were partially put into effect, such as halting the confiscation of lands, developing master plans and town planning schemes, reducing the allocation disparities to local authorities, establishing industrial zones, ongoing plans to achieve adequate representation, etc. On the other hand, the recommendations to conduct thorough, long-term planning, define objectives and priorities, and allocate the needed funds were not realized at all. And the recommendations to create a public atmosphere that would enable Arabs to feel a sense of belonging in Israeli society – such as taking them into consideration when preparing legislation – have been completely ignored.

15.9 Legal Rulings

Have the courts played a role in redressing the harm to Arab citizens? In the absence of a constitution and positive legislation on the status of minorities in Israel, and in view of the discriminatory laws enacted by the Knesset and the willful ignorance of Israeli governments, have the courts acted to set right the civil and collective status of Arabs in Israel? Opinions are mixed. We present below five court rulings related to the status of Arabs in Israel on key issues: political participation and representation; identity and status in a country defined as "Jewish and democratic"; distributive justice of material resources; and civil equality – collective, not just personal.

A. The Yeredor Ruling

A case came before the Supreme Court in 1965 on the question of whether the Central Elections Committee had the authority to disqualify the Arab Socialist List, a party founded by the al-Ard movement, from running in the Knesset election on the grounds that its platform negated the existence of the state of Israel. The court upheld the decision to disqualify the list (*Yeredor v. Central Elections Committee* 1965), noting that if the list were allowed to run for the Knesset, it would strive – as noted in its platform – to undermine the democratic foundations of the state. Writing for the majority, Supreme Court President Shimon Agranat stated that a list defined as "subversive" has no right to compete in an election on the grounds that no democratic government should give support and recognition to a movement that seeks its overthrow. This was the first time that the High Court related to the Jewish identity of the state (at the time not defined by the law as such), with Justice Agranat's assertion that a "sustainable Jewish state" must be a "fundamental, constitutional given" in every interpretation of the law. The minority position of Justice Haim Cohn held that there is full equivalence between a Jewish and an Arab party with regard to negating the existence of the state of Israel, and that the Arab identity of the petitioner neither strengthens nor weakens the case.

B. The Neiman Ruling

Prior to election of the eleventh Knesset in 1984, the Central Elections Committee disqualified the Kach Party from running because its political platform contained racist elements. The High Court of Justice accepted the Kach petition (*Neiman v. Central Elections Committee* 1984), stating that there were no grounds for disqualifying a racist list without an explicit statute to that effect. As a result of this ruling, the twelfth Knesset amended the Basic Law: The Knesset to explicitly cite three grounds for disqualification (in an attempt to appear balanced): A list of candidates is disqualified for running in the election if it negates the existence of Israel as a Jewish or democratic state, negates Israel's democratic character, or incites to racism. The legislative pronouncement that Israel is "Jewish" gave explicit constitutional primacy to the Jewish community in Israel. Although the vagueness of the phrase "Jewish and democratic" – and the conjunction that joins them – doubtfully contribute to the Jewishness or democracy of the state of Israel, they clearly reinforce the sense of alienation of its Arab citizens.

In that same election campaign, the Central Elections Committee had also disqualified the Progressive List for Peace on the grounds that elements in its platform identify with enemies of the state. In this case, too, the High Court overturned the decision of the Central Elections Committee (*Neiman v. Central Elections Committee* 1984).

C. The Ka'adan Ruling

In 1995, the Arab citizen Adel Ka'adan submitted an application to reside in the communal settlement of Katzir. After rejection of his application by the local council of Katzir, Ka'adan petitioned the High Court of Justice. In March 2000, the High Court issued a precedent-setting ruling that the state improperly discriminated between Jews and Arabs when it allocated lands to the Jewish Agency for establishing the community of Katzir for Jews only (*Ka'adan v. Israel Lands Administration* 2000).[54] The High Court anchored the principle of civil equality between Jews and Arabs in the right to land allocation, and invalidated the institutional discrimination practiced in Israel since its founding under the guise of "national institutions" that belong to the Jewish nation, rather than to Israeli citizens. Nonetheless, the Ka'adan case enforces the principle of equality in land allocation with respect to individuals only, not the collective land needs of Arab communities.

D. The Adalah Ruling

In June 1999, Adalah and the Association for Civil Rights in Israel petitioned the High Court of Justice against the municipalities in the mixed cities of Tel Aviv-Jaffa, Haifa, Lod, Ramla, Acre, and Nazareth Illit demanding that they add Arabic to all traffic, warning, and other signs within their jurisdictions in addition to the texts in Hebrew (and English). The petitioners claimed that the absence of Arabic text

[54] Despite this ruling, the local council did everything in its power to avoid carrying out the decision. In May 2004, prior to adjudication of a second petition, the Israel Lands Administration ordered that the family be allowed to acquire land in the settlement.

violates the Mandatory ordinance that Arabic is an official language, and thereby contravenes the principle of equality, which results in the discrimination of Arabic speakers in these cities. The attorney general argued on behalf of the respondents that the obligation to take Arabic into consideration as an official language was limited only to areas selected by the High Commissioner, and that the municipalities have the authority to set policies for their jurisdictions. The attorney general also argued that the definition of Israel as "Jewish and democratic" positions Hebrew as the principal official language of the state, while Arabic is a secondary official language.

In a majority opinion of two judges (High Court President Barak and Justice Dorner) versus one (Justice Cheshin), the High Court in July 2002 accepted the petition and instructed the municipalities to add Arabic text on outdoor signage within several years (*Adalah et al. v. Municipalities of Tel Aviv-Jaffa et al.* 2002). Nevertheless, the court accepted the contention of the respondents that the two languages are not equal in status, and that Hebrew has primacy over Arabic. In this ruling, the court was forced to grapple with the question of recognition by the state of the collective (in this case the cultural) rights of the Arab minority. The majority opinion chose to focus on specific arguments to justify its position, such as the need for an Arab citizen to understand city signs in order to access services, and it denied collective recognition of the language rights of the Arab minority. The court chose to avoid the issue, arguing that the authority to set policy on the more general subject is a matter for the political system:

> The subject of majority–minority relations by its very nature should be resolved between the majority and the minority using accepted democratic procedures. It is superfluous to state – we again emphasize – that we are not discussing the subject of individual rights, for which the arm of the court is long and is among the subjects we are involved with daily and hourly.

The question of communal equality for Arabs in Israel is a task for the political system, but it is our opinion that the state (in the attorney general's arguments) and the High Court (in this ruling) missed an opportunity to signal a willingness to view Arab citizens as a collective with cultural rights; after all, the issue was that of the Arabic language, not collective political rights.[55] Tel Aviv-Jaffa, and perhaps even towns in which Arabs do not reside, would lose nothing by having signage in Arabic, which invites Arabic language speakers to feel welcome unless this is not desired, or there is fear of setting a precedent; in reaction, Arab citizens have raised the demand for collective rights, as happened a few years later in the Vision Documents (below).

E. Higher Monitoring Committee of Arab Citizens of Israel

In this ruling, the High Court accepted Adalah's petition against a decision to define "National Priority Areas" in a way that discriminated against Arab settlements. The

[55] It could be argued that recognizing Arabic could serve as a bridge to court decisions and even legislation that would recognize additional collective rights. But beyond the question of whether cultural rights should be recognized or not, it should be noted that the status of Arabic is already enshrined in law (albeit Mandatory), but this has not led to the granting of other rights.

petition related to government decisions from 1998 and 2002 that gave education benefits to Jewish settlements located in National Priority Areas: exemption from preschool tuition, subsidies of some teaching expenses, longer school hours, scholarship priority to college or university students, funding of computer curricula in schools, etc. The petitioners argued that although there were low-income Arab settlements in proximity to the Jewish settlements, they were deliberately not included in the National Priority Areas. They also argued that the government decision was made without authority because this sort of decision should be a matter for legislation. In a ruling from March 2006, the High Court accepted the petitioner's arguments and ruled that the government decision is intrinsically discriminatory, and that policy decisions so broad in scope and impact have to be made by the legislative branch (*Higher Monitoring Committee v. Prime Minister* 2006).

The importance of this ruling is that it establishes that policy about the status of Arabs in Israel cannot be an administrative decision of one government or another, but requires statutory authorization of the Knesset. This ruling also has practical importance as it heralds change in the public status of Arabs: Previously, Arabs were excluded by Israeli governments from projects defined as "national"; now the court clarified that the (formal, at least) borders of Israeli nationalism could no longer be closed to the Arabs in Israel.

15.10 A National Minority and Israeli Democracy

Questions about the status of a national minority in a nation-state with a distinctive majority are not unique to Israel. Nevertheless, the historical circumstances of the protracted Israeli–Arab conflict and the shared national identity of the minority with an adversary across the border encumber the issue about the status of Arabs in Israel and complicate the finding of solutions or even the willingness to seek them. On most issues, the boundaries of Jewish consensus in Israel leave the Arabs on the outside. In general, Arab citizens are perceived as not belonging to Israeli society – a foreign body that can be ignored – and in the worst case, they are considered a hostile, scheming minority that must be monitored and controlled to ensure the security and existence of the Jewish state. In both cases, the result is the same, as we have seen: Arabs have been left outside the circles of influence over general Israeli policy, and even excluded from the discourse about "sectoral" subjects that affect Arab lives.

A. Changes

The gradual evolution of a more independent Arab community in Israel catalyzed organizing for political influence and power: It began with civil society organizations (action committees, media channels, groups unaffiliated with parties, rights organizations, etc.); then moved to vigorous and determined activism within the local authorities (including challenges to traditional Arab leadership); then independent parties; and, more recently, a joint list, which creates an opportunity for more political impact. As noted, Arab reactions to government activity swing between two poles – the aspiration for equality and integration in Israeli society and, on the other hand, separatist, isolationist tendencies. There is also an internal dilemma of the Arabs in

Israel – their identity among and within the traditional, religious, nationalist, and civil circles of the Arab community. And changes in these circles of identity are affected not only by internal Israeli processes and relations with Palestinians in the territories, but also, and with great intensity, by events in the Arab and Muslim world.

The approach of the Israeli-Jewish-Zionist political system toward Arabs in Israel has also seen change and flux. We noted the fear of Arab "disloyalty" as a central motif, but no comprehensive, systematic policy was ever put in place, despite the efforts and decisions of many governments. Ever since the coercive period of the military regime, governments have taken diverse and even contradictory policy positions, including attempts at coexistence between the communities and even stabs at an egalitarian civic approach and integration in the state and its economy. More egalitarian policies have become evident in several spheres, such as increased funding to Arab towns or more Arab employees in the civil service, the justice system, etc. The dynamic of "smaller government" and the emergence of a robust civil society may also contribute to improving the status of Arabs in Israel.

Has there been any change in the Jewish public's suspicion of and hostility toward Arabs in Israel? Surveys indicate some change in response to specific external events (Arian et al. 2005–10: 2008, 41; Smooha 2013). Along with improvements, however, there have also been manifestations of racism, primarily in legislation tabled by extremist parties in the Knesset. Paradoxically, it is possible that the very weakening of the Jewish-Zionist consensus and the rise of sectoralism in the political system may open the door to a new kind of consensus that is not just ethnic-communal, but also civic. In any event, the ongoing institutional discrimination, particularly with regard to lands and planning, the unilateral measures taken to address the severe problems in the Bedouin community, and insensitivity to Arab feelings and symbols, particularly in defining the state's "Jewish identity," all testify that Israel's Arab citizens are still not full partners to Israeli democracy in the twenty-first century.

B. The Vision Documents 2006–2007

A sense of alienation gave impetus to several Arab organizations to write the Vision Documents – a collective credo that had never previously been formulated.[56] These papers, written by academics and intellectuals not identified with the traditional frameworks of Arab society or political parties, reveal the desire of their authors to take initiative and have an impact on the Israeli agenda. And yet, a survey conducted in 2008 found that 85 percent of Arabs and 89 percent of Jews in Israel knew little or nothing about these documents (Smooha 2008, 3). Nevertheless, the demands they raised evoked vigorous public discussion in the media and among intellectuals of

[56] The term "Vision Documents" comes from the first of these: National Committee of the Arab Local Authorities in Israel, *The Future Vision of the Palestinian Arabs in Israel*, December 2006; Mossawa: Advocacy Center for Arab Citizens in Israel, a position paper by Yousef Jabareen, "An Equal Constitution for All? On a Constitution and Collective Rights for Arab Citizens in Israel," November 2006; Adalah: The Legal Center for Arab Minority Rights in Israel, "The Democratic Constitution," February 2007; Mada al-Carmel: Arab Center for Applied Social Research, "The Haifa Declaration," May 15, 2007. All have been published in Arabic, Hebrew, and English on the organization websites. Also see Rekhess 2008.

both communities, with the disappointment of the Jews expressed in an open letter to the writers of the documents by Professor Shimon Shamir, former Israeli ambassador to Egypt and Jordan (*Al-Sinara*, January 5, 2007):

> You begin the document with your own definition of the state of Israel: "Israel is the colonialist outcome initiated by the Zionist-Jewish elite in Europe and the west and realized by colonial countries contributing to it…" It is hard to shake off the feeling that the purpose of your one-sided definition is to strip away the identity of Jews in this land. In your document, the Arabs in Israel appear as a nation, while the Jews appear as a religious or ethnic group. In no place do you recognize the self-determination of the Jews as a nation.

The Vision Documents call for the state to take various measures, not all consistent, but all repeat the demand for full civil and national equality:

> This would require a change in the constitutional structure and a change in the definition of the State of Israel from a Jewish state to a democratic state established on national and civil equality between the two national groups, and enshrining the principles of banning discrimination and of equality between all of its citizens and residents. (Mada al-Carmel 2007, 16)[57]

In other words, in addition to calling for full individual equality for Arab citizens, the documents all carry a demand for recognizing the collective rights of the indigenous Palestinian minority in Israel. The components of these documents are summarized in Mossawa's legalistic one (Y.T. Jabareen 2006, 72–78), which we present here in brief:

- On the declarative level: Official recognition by Israel of the Arab community as a national minority and an indigenous population; appropriate expression in the state's symbols; official recognition of the Arab-Palestinian Nakba; recognition of the special relationship between Palestinian citizens of Israel and the Palestinian people and Arab nation.
- On the cultural level: Bilingualism in all areas of life; self-administration (autonomy) in education, culture, religion, communication, planning, and welfare.
- On the political level: Affirmative action in the allocation of material resources as compensation for the protracted period of discrimination; equality and fairness in immigration and citizenship; due representation in all public institutions; official recognition of the special status of the representative entities of the Arab minority.

The demands for change in resource allocation, citizenship laws, and due representation are also demands for individual civil rights. The collective rights, on the other hand, are reflected primarily in the demand for autonomy and recognition of representative Arab institutions. These appear in the other documents as a consociational democracy, i.e., arrangements that would give expression to the social-political uniqueness of the Arab national community, including forming their own national institutions and the direct election of Arab representatives to conduct their own distinctive affairs. Note that these documents do not carry the demand

[57] For example, MK Azmi Bishara's proposed Basic Law: The Arab Minority as a National Minority, January 3, 2000, P/2075.

for a binational state within the borders of Israel; the model that the writers had in mind was drawn from the arrangements used for some Jewish groups in Israel, primarily the autonomy of the ultra-Orthodox.[58] However, the proposed arrangements are not those commonly advocated by the Arab public in Israel. A public opinion survey showed that "a state of all its citizens" won the most support among Arabs (40%), followed by a Jewish and democratic state with full and equal rights for Arabs (26%), a binational state (9%), and a consociational democracy (8%) (Rekhess and Rudnitzky 2007, 9). A large majority of the Arab public, however, expressed general identification with the ideas presented in these documents (Smooha 2013, 125).

While the "future vision" of the mayors of Arab local authorities reflects a compromise among those who helped write it (including the Sons of the Village movement), and the other two are legal-constitutional papers, the Haifa Declaration is the most ideological and consistent. First, it fully recognizes the state of Israel and calls for historical reconciliation between the two nations based on Israel's recognition of the historic injustice done to the Palestinian nation, and recognition by the Palestinians and Arabs of "the right of the Jewish Israeli people to self-determination" (Mada al-Carmel 2007, 15). Second, the change required is in the constitutional structure of Israel – from a Jewish state to a democratic state founded on equality between the two national groups. Third, a salient part of the Haifa Declaration is devoted to acknowledging the responsibility borne by Arab society for the "social, family, sectarian, and local structures that curtail individual freedoms" and the "sectarian zeal" derived from them. Special emphasis is placed on eliminating the oppression of Arab women and the need to advance their status and equality.

The demands for political autonomy are the main minefield in these documents because they reinforce the fears of Jews who do not believe Arabs when they say they recognize the state of Israel, or those who fear that the Arabs want one and a half Palestinian states – one in the territories and another, binational half in Israel – leaving half a Jewish state only. Use of the term "colonialism" (harsher in the Hebrew version than in the English one), and the demand for political autonomy, play into the hands of extremist Jews, as does ignoring the right of the Jewish nation to self-determination. On the other hand, none of these documents delegitimizes the state of Israel, but rather they deny that the state should belong only to the Jews.

It is our view that the call for equality is in the interest of both Jews and Arabs, and that there is room for cultural autonomy as part of this. More importantly for the long term, there is a willingness to cooperate in shaping Israeli democracy. To that end, some Arab citizens must forego the demand for political-national autonomy, within Israel, with all this entails concerning a willingness to work together to strengthen the common democratic framework; and some Jewish citizens must give up their views that they are doing Arabs a favor by giving them rights, or that these rights are conditional upon good behavior. Citizens are citizens, and the rights of a

[58] Smooha (2008) believes that this is a smokescreen for "thin binationalism," disregarding the internal Jewish model; Yiftachel (2006) believes that this refers to cultural autonomy and self-government as part of a multi-cultural state, ignoring the demands for political autonomy.

minority are not bestowed by grace of the majority.[59] On the encouraging side are the mass protests in the summer of 2011, which showed signs of crossing the traditional barriers in Israeli society, to some extent also the barriers between Jews and Arabs; the success of the Joint List in the 2015 election; and the Netanyahu government's 2015 decision recognizing the need to divert resources to the Arab community.

The change that began to surface in the official state approach is the willingness to recognize Arabs as equal citizens in practice. The dominant view is that this refers to civil equality, particularly economic equality, but on an individual level only: The Arabs in Israel are deemed entitled to equal rights with Jews as individuals, but not as a separate and distinct community. In contrast, support has grown among Arabs in Israel for realizing their rights as a national collective by virtue of being an indigenous minority.

In our view, the state must recognize the Arabs as a separate community of Israeli citizens, but not its *political-national* rights. The dividing line is thin, but can be defined. Beyond their individual rights as citizens and full integration into the economy, Arabs in Israel should have collective rights in language, education, culture, religion, laws of personal status, and the like, and they should be entitled to conduct these affairs autonomously, not unlike the ultra-Orthodox in Israel, *mutatis mutandis* (including the problems of a core curriculum in schools and all the issues around the boundaries of intervention by the state). On the other hand, collective rights do not embrace the political realm; even though the Arabs in Israel are a distinct, indigenous, national minority, their national aspirations cannot be realized within the state of Israel. Therefore, elections to a separate representative "parliament" for Arabs in Israel should not be recognized, nor should a quota be set for the percentage of Arabs in the Knesset, nor should arrangements be made to prevent Arabs from voting for Jewish parties or Jews for Arab parties. The state should also not recognize separate national bodies (other than local authorities): Because this is a shared country, the political system is also shared, while the local and social frameworks can be integrated or not, at the discretion of each community.

Thus the question of the role of Arabs in Israel falls into our definition of an "open issue" or even a "wicked problem" – because of the difficulty of dealing with it and the internal contradictions woven into it over the years. Nevertheless, creating and putting in place a comprehensive, consistent, and fair policy remains within reach.

[59] On the right to be an Arab Knesset Member, Israeli literary icon Natan Alterman wrote a poem called "The Scolding of Tawfik Toubi," with the following lines: "So who is Tawfik Toubi? He is a Knesset Member / he is an Arab Communist. By right and not by grace does he sit in the parliament … / It may be time to remember that, friends" (November 1949).

16 Politics, Society, and Economics: How Did the State Provide for the Society?

16.1 Socioeconomic Policy

Israeli society has always been complex and heterogeneous. (We primarily discuss here Jewish society in Israel; for Arab society, see Chapter 15.) During the Yishuv period, Jewish society was already divided into camps that remained intact after the birth of the state. With the arrival of waves of immigrants, more groups joined the nascent Israeli state and the demographic balance shifted. Social and economic processes created new divisions, such as the formation of a socioeconomic class corresponding to country of origin, and the gulf between Jews and Arabs deepened. In the 1970s and 1990s, immigration from Ethiopia and the former Soviet Union added new elements to the mosaic of Israeli society. Our approach in this chapter is that the political system contended with the social complexity in different ways during each period in accordance with the dominant ideology, the results of previous policies, significant events (notably wars), and the prevailing trends in society.

The central characteristic of Israeli-Jewish society since the beginning of Zionism is that it is a society of immigrants. According to the Central Bureau of Statistics (CBS), about half a million immigrants arrived during the Yishuv period (1919–May 1948), followed by another 3.2 million after the founding of the state and through 2013 (CBS 2014a, table 2.12). Most of the pre-state immigrants came from Europe, while most of the immigrants from Asia and Africa came to the newly formed state, generating a demographic change. The concepts "immigrant"[1] and "veteran" Israeli are relative: New immigrants quickly became "veterans" when the next wave of immigration arrived. At the end of 2013, three-quarters of the Jews (75%) in the state were born in Israel, less than half (43%) had native-born fathers (CBS 2014a, table 2.9).

The challenge facing the political system was how to integrate the immigrants in a joint framework that would become a community (or a nation) capable of collective efforts and binding decision-making that transcends the cultural, religious,

[1] In this chapter, we refer to immigrants from Asia-Africa/Arab or Islamic countries as Mizrahim or Sephardim interchangeably; and to immigrants from Europe, North America, or other western countries as Ashkenazim. Studies use a variety of labels; official immigration data, for example, are by continent of origin. Year of publication also counts: initially, the use of "Sephardim" and "Eastern Jews" was more common, while "Mizrahim" has become more prevalent since the 1990s.

linguistic, and economic diversity of the immigrants. Initially, efforts were made to shape society and facilitate the integration of the immigrants via state mechanisms, such as the education system and the army, and also via social institutions, including political parties and the Histadrut Labor Federation.

However, the society in the newly created state was not a tabula rasa. The society and institutions that developed during the Yishuv period were dominated by immigrants from Eastern Europe, who were proponents of socialist Zionism, rejected the possibility of a sustainable Jewish future in the Diaspora, and sought to foster a pioneering spirit and forge a new society. Their challenge was how to integrate newcomers from a range of cultures and shape a society in accordance with their world view. Their aspiration was that this society would be molded by their own version of Zionist ideology, that of the central groups of the Yishuv period, so that the newcomers would adopt the template of the native-born Israeli Jew (after the Arabic name for a local cactus – *sabra*) and that this process would not be hindered by the "exilic" identities of the immigrants. The goal of this "all-embracing" policy in the early stage was captured by the slogan "from ingathering to integration of the exiles." The objective was to acclimatize the multitude of immigrants to the pioneering culture via an accelerated process of acculturation and have them assimilate the values of the pre-state society, particularly of the dominant labor movement. The aspiration was to throw everyone into a socio-political "melting pot" in which a variety of identities and groups would be melted into a new Hebrew society. This was an explicit policy to ignore the unique features, the diverse cultural heritages, and the different needs of the various groups of immigrants.

Was the challenge of integrating the exiles realized? After the birth pangs of the state's first two decades, it became clear to policymakers that the melting pot operates in its own way. Despite all the efforts at integration, dividing lines remained and were even sharpened, and new divisions emerged between different groups in society, particularly between immigrants from Asia-Africa (the "Mizrahim") and immigrants from Europe-America (the "Ashkenazim"). The processes of integration and adaptation were slow and led to alienation that peaked during the 1970s in light of the better absorption conditions offered to immigrants arriving from the Soviet Union (Ashkenazim). The policy failed to narrow the economic gaps, and the Mizrahim who lagged behind felt a growing sense of discrimination and hostility toward the establishment, which was expressed in political protest (see below). The political leadership was aware of the threat that the socio-ethnic rift posed to the collective framework and responded with a policy aimed at relieving the tension through efforts at integration in education and politics, and by allocating resources to the "underprivileged" immigrants – to support low-achieving pupils or improve physical conditions (Katz Committee 1971). These efforts were interrupted by the Yom Kippur War, which undermined confidence in the Labor-led political system and exposed hidden tensions within Israeli society. The political change – the upheaval of 1977 – soon followed.

In the 1980s and 1990s, two processes occurred that accelerated each other: In the political sphere, the helplessness of Israeli governments in setting socioeconomic policy became clear; the Likud governments declared their intention of strengthening the free market and diminishing the role of central planning in domestic policy. The retreat of state involvement has since been evident in all fields: in economics – the guiding hand and intensive involvement of the government was replaced by the "invisible hand" of the market and a policy of privatization (Galnoor et al. 2015); absorption of immigrants – the responsibility for immigrants in the 1990s was transferred from the ministries to local governments, non-governmental organizations, and the private sector; education – the aspiration to create a state education system with a uniform and comprehensive curriculum was replaced by an attempt to define shared "core" subjects for the separate school systems; and welfare – a gradual withdrawal of social services. Changes began even in the IDF, which remained the last declared stronghold of the social melting pot approach, such as divisions between religious and secular units, or proposals to cancel mandatory conscription (S.A. Cohen 1995; Sherer 1997).

In general, a sectoral and separatist group orientation gained strength in Israeli society, while social and cultural pluralism won greater legitimacy. Socioeconomic policy underwent far-reaching transformation – from an aspiration to "shape society" in pursuit of ideological-collective objectives, to a policy that "observes," reacts to changes, and retreats from involvement. As will be seen, this policy adopted a neoliberal ideology that places its trust in market forces, thus beneficent to the wealthy and increasing the inequality.

A. The Question of Equality

The most profound change in Israeli society is the growing inequality; Israel has one of the highest rates of income inequality in the west (OECD 2015). This can be attributed in part to processes of modernization and globalization. However, in Israel, where the political system has a major impact on society and the economy, inequality is directly linked to policy changes. The question, therefore, is how did Israel change during the course of four decades from a model egalitarian state to one of the leaders in poverty rates and income gaps among western countries? The widening gaps created new social divisions between rich and poor that cut across the previous divides in Israeli society; however, they also partially overlap with internal social divisions. This overlap accentuates the repercussions of inequality, particularly in the Arab population, where disparities exist on nearly every measure – education, income, social welfare, and unemployment (see Chapter 15).

Inequality not only poses a threat to economic stability and social cohesion, but also undermines the legitimacy of the political system and the willingness for political participation. In Chapter 8, we noted that political participation is directly influenced by variables such as income and education. The economically disadvantaged have limited access to higher education and, consequently, a lower chance of earning high income, hence their willingness to participate in the political process diminishes. Thus, alienation from the political system develops among the "have-nots," eroding its legitimacy. Those at the bottom of the socioeconomic scale do not trust the political system because they regard the government, quite justifiably, as responsible for their situation. Can a society in which there is profound inequality and widening gaps continue to be democratic? Inequality is the prism through which we observe Israeli society in this chapter. We will describe society through periods in the state's history, and examine the socioeconomic policies adopted in each.

B. A Portrait of the Society and its Boundaries

What are the boundaries of Israeli society? During Israel's first two decades, its Arab citizens lived under a military regime and were not considered an integral part of society. This exclusion of Arab citizens was reflected in land confiscation, limited rights, non-allocation of resources, and even being left out of statistical studies. However, the Arabs were not the only ones to be excluded. In those years, new immigrants – particularly from Asia and Africa – were not integrated into mainstream Israeli society. Many were sent to distant regions, and the geographic and cultural distance cut them off from the center of Israel's social and economic life. Consequently, a dichotomous definition of the society developed, reflecting the reality: a "first Israel" of Ashkenazim versus a "second Israel" of Mizrahim; immigrants from Europe-America versus immigrants from Asia-Africa. This definition is still accepted and unchallenged today in statistical data. Although based on country of origin, it is a closer reflection of the socioeconomic stratification during Israel's early years, though some of this class structure already existed in the Yishuv. When the state was founded, most of the Jews in Israel were of European origin, though important differences were associated with *place of origin*. There was a significant difference between professional and urban German Jews who fled from the Nazis and settled in Tel Aviv, and Jews from far-flung towns in Poland who joined a pioneer youth movement and settled on a kibbutz.

One fascinating expression of the diversity within the European groups can be found in the very categories used in research by the Institute of Applied Social Research in 1949: native-born immigrants from Romania, Poland, Russia, Germany, and Lithuania, or "immigrants from Yemen and other Eastern Jews" – without specifying the country (Weimann 2015, 67). Like the immigrants from the west, the post-1948 immigrants from the east were not all cut of the same cloth. There was a big difference between urban and village Jews from the same country, and between Jews from countries such as Yemen, Egypt, Iraq, and Morocco. Nonetheless, and despite the substantial differences between the groups of immigrants, several shared characteristics contributed to sharpening the distinction between immigrants by continent of origin and blurring the differences within each group: family size, level of education, attachment to tradition and religion, and fields of occupation, as well as the extent to which the group resembled veteran society in Israel. Thus, from the outset, there was already a gap between the collective self-image of a melting pot society and reality. The very diverse population that gathered in Israel not only included immigrants from different countries, but also from different cultures, social classes, professions, and levels of urbanism. Nonetheless, the Israeli ethos of the "*sabra*" was still identified with the pioneering Ashkenazi Jewish population, with the minority group of kibbutz members as its archetype (Blander 2004, 29–30). Moreover, the dichotomous division of the Jewish population by continent of origin gradually became entrenched – between "Sephardim" and "Ashkenazim" – and this was also expressed in economic and cultural gaps.

The 1970s marked a turning point in defining the boundaries of Israeli society – the Mizrahim, particularly those from northern Africa, formed a protest movement in 1971 (the "Black Panthers"; see below), while the Arab citizens of Israel rebelled against the injustice of land expropriation ("Land Day" in 1976). The changes in society and the weakening of the political mainstream (identified with the labor movement) enabled others to take center stage and redefine the boundaries of Israeli

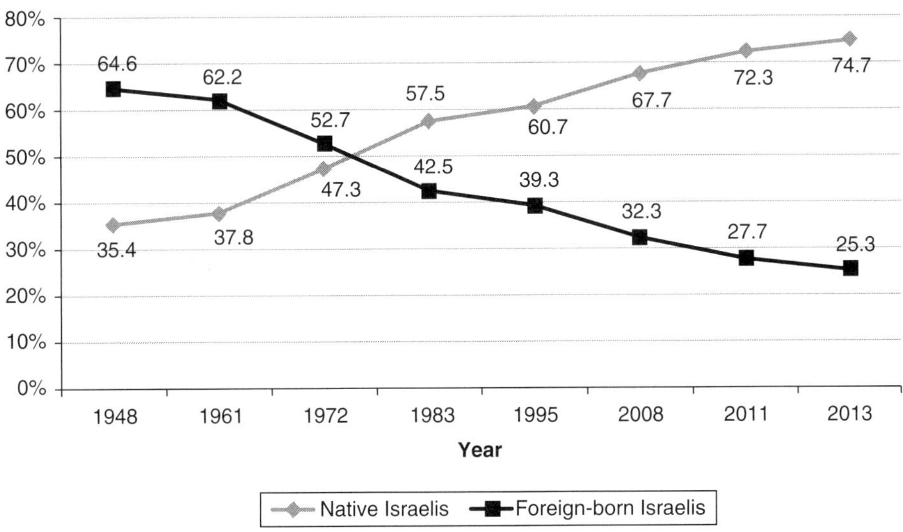

Figure 16.1 Percentage of native- and foreign-born Israelis in the Jewish population (1948–2013)
Note: Until 1995, the Jewish population included "others" (non-Arab Christians) and "no religious classification," usually immigrants from the former Soviet Union.
Source: CBS *Statistical Abstract* 2014, table 2.9.

society. In the 1980s and 1990s, there were again changes in the range of identities in society, particularly in the marginal groups – Arab citizens and some Mizrahim. After 1967, the Arabs saw themselves as Palestinians who were not only struggling for equal rights in the state, but also for the rights of the Palestinians in the territories; the Mizrahim, second- or third-generation Israelis, traditional ones in particular, united as a political force led by the Shas party and challenged the Ashkenazi hegemony in Israeli society and culture. At the same time, immigration from the former Soviet Union and Ethiopia introduced new groups of substantial weight (about 17% of the Jewish population) into the mosaic of Israeli society. Thus, Israel is still an immigrant society. While the percentage of foreign-born Israelis is decreasing gradually, they still constituted a high percentage (25%) in 2013 (Figure 16.1). Most non-native Israelis are from Europe and America, predominantly from the former Soviet Union. Only a minority of the state's Jewish population are second-generation Israelis (i.e., their father was also born in Israel). Thus, the division by group of origin still exists and is reinforced by the inequality in society.

16.2 The Yishuv Period: Inclusion and Separation

A. Description of the Society

The Jewish Yishuv was a minority group within a binational structure during the Mandate period, though its proportion of the population continually increased (Table 16.1). On the eve of Israel's birth, about 650,000 Jews lived in the Yishuv, constituting a third of the overall population (about 1.9 million) in Palestine (Eretz Israel). The differences between the Arab community, mostly rural, and the Jewish

Table 16.1 *The Arab and Jewish populations in the pre-state period (rounded)*

Year	Jews	Arabs and others	Arabs and others (%)	Total
1882	24,000	276,000	92	300,000
1918	60,000	600,000	91	660,000
1931	175,000	860,000	83	1,035,000
1936	384,000	983,000	72	1,367,000
1946	543,000	1,267,000	70	1,810,000

Source: Jewish Virtual Library N.d.

community, mostly urban, were evident throughout: disparities in wage levels, per capita income, and level of education. There was also a difference in the level of political institutionalization: The Jewish Yishuv developed elected representative bodies (Chapter 1), while Arab institutions were not developed (the primary political body was the Supreme Muslim Council). The two communities lived side by side – distinct geographically, culturally, religiously, economically, and politically.

Most of the immigrants prior to the establishment of Israel (about 89%) came from Europe. Until the 1930s, about 70 percent had immigrated from eastern Europe. After the Nazis rose to power and in the wake of World War II, the percentage of immigrants from central and western Europe increased. A small percentage of the immigrants (about 10%) came from countries in Asia and Africa. Until the Holocaust, the Diaspora in Europe was much larger than the Diaspora in Asia-Africa. Thus, relative to the size of their communities of origin, the percentage of immigrants from the east was roughly equal to the percentage of immigrants who arrived from the west until 1948 (Galnoor 1982, 56).

In the Jewish Yishuv, society and its political organizations developed concurrently, without sharp distinctions. It was a new society of immigrants that evolved without a residue of fixed political traditions or social classes, and this made it easier to shape the new institutions. Over time, components of status emerged that formed social strata: country of origin, years in the country, and professional identity. In the dominating socialist ideology, the pyramid of professional status was deliberately inverted, agriculture and manual labor as the most prestigious at the top, higher than the free professions and certainly above the Diaspora occupations of business, trade, and commerce. Amos Oz describes his admiration for the pioneers, and the scale of prestige in the "organized Yishuv," as opposed to the "dissidents" (members of the Irgun and Lehi), the ultra-Orthodox, Communists, Yemenites, Kurds, and Maghrabim – "all of them definitely our brothers … but what could you do, they would need a huge amount of patience and effort." And yet the social order was ambiguous:

> On the one hand, my father definitely belonged to the middle class … he was an educated man … while his interlocutor was a sweaty construction worker in overalls and heavy boots. On the other hand, this same worker was said to have some sort of degree in chemistry, and he was also a committed pioneer, the salt of the earth, a hero of the Hebrew Revolution, a manual laborer, while Father considered himself … to be a sort of rootless, shortsighted intellectual with two left hands. Something of a deserter from the battlefront where the homeland was being built. (Oz 2004)

Table 16.2 *Sources of Jewish immigration to Palestine/Eretz Israel from 1919 to May 1948*

Continent of origin	Immigrants	% of total
Asia	40,895	10
Africa	4,041	
Europe	377,381	89
America and Oceania	7,754	
Unknown	52,786	1
Total	482,857	100%

Source: CBS *Statistical Abstract* 2006, table 4.2.

Thus, the political and cultural elite of the Yishuv emerged from the agricultural settlements, who saw themselves as the ideological vanguard. Most of the political elite, like most of the Yishuv, were not native-born, and the majority came from eastern Europe (Table 16.2). As for the leaders of the Zionist institutions – only a minority were natives or immigrants from Yemen or Turkey (Horowitz and Lissak 1978, 47). Yishuv society was organized in political camps: the dominant workers' camp and the smaller and less organized citizens' camp and the religious camp. These formed the "organized Yishuv" and outside it were the Revisionist and the ultra-Orthodox camps. The institutional, party, and social structures were intertwined: Mapai was the dominant party in the workers' camp together with secondary centers, led by the Histadrut, and together they dominated all areas of life – employment, health, education, welfare, settlement, youth, sports, and defense. The citizens' camp, which was identified with the General Zionists Party, included part of the Revisionist movement. It did not develop a broad organizational umbrella on a similar level. It was a weaker federation of professional and local organizations, such as the Farmers' Association, but also included military organizations, an education system, youth movements, and the National Federation of Workers. The religious camp revolved around the Mizrahi and Hapoel Ha-Mizrahi parties, and it too had a religious education system, a workers' federation, a youth movement, and a settlement movement.

B. Policy

The Yishuv institutions were not sovereign, but were representative. A policy of integration, inclusion, consensus, and compromise characterized the political center during the Yishuv period. Various factors encouraged integration: the struggle against the British, the external threat from the Arabs, and the activity of institutions, the Histadrut in particular. The Yishuv leadership sprang from these institutions, which served as an agency for political recruitment. Furthermore, the need for monetary support from Diaspora Jewry required their participation in the political institutions and reinforced the representativeness of the entire system. The willingness to compromise, resolve conflicts, and generally abide by the rules of the game are part of the heritage that the Yishuv institutions bequeathed to the state (see Chapter 1). Another characteristic that had social repercussions was the intolerance and bitter struggle against those who were not part of the organized Yishuv – primarily the Revisionists and the Communists (Horowitz and Lissak 1978, 50–52, 89–114, 121–37).

The deep politicization was especially salient with regard to social and economic policy, and less prominent in foreign affairs and defense. Policies in areas such as immigration and absorption, education, and settlement were largely shaped by the parties and their battles for power. In education, partisanship was expressed in "streams," each affiliated with a particular party camp: the "general stream" of parties and organizations from the center and right, such as the General Zionists and the Revisionists; the "workers' stream" that was subordinate to the Histadrut and workers' parties; and the "religious stream" of Mizrahi and Hapoel Ha-Mizrahi. The immigration quotas were also filled in accordance with the relative strength of the parties, which were involved in the absorption process, or in referring children to youth movements – in exchange for political support. Most of the immigrants who arrived prior to World War II already had an ideological connection to the political camps in their countries of origin. Subsequently, immigrants arrived without a defined political identity, which stirred concern and aversion (D. Hacohen 1994, 7).

C. Socioeconomic Policy

The ethos of "pioneering" meant that policy sought to promote Zionist ideological objectives, rather than be shaped only by economic considerations. For example, the struggle for "Hebrew labor" was driven by Zionist considerations because the cost of employing a "Hebrew" (i.e., Jewish) laborer was higher and the skills inferior to those of an Arab laborer. The socioeconomic policy of the Jewish political center led by Mapai was designed to fulfill Zionist and socialist values through centralized control of the economy. The goals included land purchase, settlement, immigrant absorption, development, and defense. This required raising large sums of money from world Jewry, and development of an extensive philanthropic system (Jewish National Fund and United Israel Appeal), Zionist organizations (the Jewish federations, Hadassah, WIZO), and non-Zionist organizations (PICA [Palestine Jewish Colonization Association] and the JDC [the Joint Distribution Committee]). The private capital of wealthy immigrants gradually created a private sector alongside the public Histadrut one, and it was invested primarily in construction, industry, handcrafts, agriculture (citrus groves), transportation, and land purchases. The philanthropic and private sources of capital prevented public sector exclusivity in the economy and created a dual structure from the outset. However, despite the significant size of the private sector, which favored free enterprise, it did not gain much political power (Yaar and Shavit 2001). Economic and political power was in the hands of the workers' Histadrut camp, which included large companies as well as cooperatives, kibbutzim, and moshavim (Aharoni 1991).

The heritage of the Yishuv socioeconomic policy can be summarized in key characteristics that continued after the founding of the state. First, separation between the Jewish and Arab economies, and two sectors within the Jewish economy – public-Histadrut and private. Second, a centralized socioeconomic policy driven by ideological considerations. Third, a policy shaped by the power struggles between and within the political camps, and the allocation of resources (including political and administrative jobs, and immigration permits) determined by political arrangements among the parties.

16.3 The Statist Period: State = Society (Israel's Early Years)

A. Description of the Society

In 1948/49, the population of Israel was 873,000. Jews accounted for about 82 percent of this, of which 55 percent were from Europe, 10 percent from Asia-Africa, and 35 percent native-born (CBS *Statistical Abstract* 2006, table 4.2). Immigration during the first decade of the state changed the size, composition, and nature of Jewish society. Within less than three years, the Jewish population in Israel doubled with the arrival of some 700,000 immigrants, half from Europe (most Holocaust refugees) and half from Asia-Africa (Table 16.3). Subsequently, the proportion of immigrants from Asia-Africa gradually increased to over 70 percent. Fewer immigrants came in the 1960s (until 1968), and immigration came primarily from North Africa (Morocco, in particular) and Romania.

Many of the immigrants from the 1950s from both Europe and Asia-Africa arrived penniless, and struggled to adjust to life in Israel. Contrary to the claim that immigration from Europe was driven by Zionism while immigration from Asia and Africa was not, most of the immigrants from Europe starting from the 1930s came in response to distress in their countries of origin. Nonetheless, there were differences between the immigrants, which influenced the character of their absorption and integration into society. Many immigrants from Europe were at an advantage because of their affinity with the host society and because they had families or community networks in which to integrate. In contrast, the educational level of the non-urban immigrants from Asia-Africa was lower, their families were bigger, and their employment options, particularly for women, were limited. Most of the men were craftsmen, merchants, and community workers, and many (about 70%) had to change their occupation in Israel.

Within a short time, an employment hierarchy emerged: At the top were Israelis of European descent who arrived prior to 1948; at the bottom were new immigrants from Asia and Africa (D. Hacohen 1994, 318–22; Lissak 1999, 97). According to one approach, this division was not only a function of the objective characteristics of the immigrants from Asia-Africa, but also a result of the absorption policy during a period of accelerated economic development. The Mizrahim were a cheap labor force, mobile, and easy to manipulate due to their total dependence on the absorption institutions. Therefore, the Mizrahi labor force enabled the Ashkenazim – both newcomers and veterans – to climb the economic ladder (Swirski and Bernstein 1993). According to another approach, patterns of patronization did emerge, but as in other immigrant societies, the absorption processes are naturally advantageous to those who are equipped with tools that are accepted by the absorbing society. Israel underwent an accelerated process of modernization, and the expectation that the Mizrahi immigrants would quickly integrate into the structure of the veteran society was not realized during the initial decades. Subsequently, many climbed the social ladder, and yet, more than fifty years later, fewer Mizrahim are in the top income deciles or prestigious professions.

Table 16.3 *Immigration to Israel by continents of origin (1948–1968)*

Years	Total*	Asia	Africa	Europe	America and Oceania	% of total	
						Asia and Africa	Europe and America
1948–51	687,624	237,352	93,951	326,786	5,140	50	50
1952–54	54,676	13,238	27,897	9,748	2,971	76	24
1955–57	166,492	8,801	103,846	48,616	3,632	68	32
1958–60	75,970	13,247	13,921	44,595	3,625	36	64
1961–64	228,793	19,525	115,876	77,537	14,841	59	41
1965–68	82,244	15,018	25,394	31,638	9,247	50	50
Total	1,295,799	307,181	380,885	538,920	39,456	54	46

* The total is greater because it includes those for whom the continent of origin is unknown.
Source: CBS *Statistical Abstract* 2006, table 4.2.

B. Policy

The political leadership responded to the mass immigration by adopting an active and paternalistic policy toward all the immigrants, Mizrahim in particular. The policy was based on the melting pot approach, which sought to strip away the strangeness – the cloak of exile of the new immigrants – and eventually to erase the differences between the groups until they would resemble the preceding groups in every way, i.e., "detachment from the unique elements of ethnic traditions and creation of a cultural system that includes diverse cultural elements but is basically controlled by one dominant element – the Ashkenazi, west European culture" (Lissak 1999, 68).

The goal of the policy was to shape the immigrant to the *sabra* myth. Accordingly, there was no point in investing much in the adults, but rather to focus efforts on resocializing the younger generation, expecting them to internalize Israeli culture and its superiority to the cultures of their parents, especially Mizrahi culture (Lissak 1996, 78). Note, for example, Ben-Gurion's remarks in the Knesset on educating the children of immigrants from Yemen:

> It is not the intention of the government to freeze the Yemenite way of life of Yemenite immigrants. On the contrary, we want to accustom the Yemenite immigration to the Israeli way of life ... We want army commanders to emerge from Yemenite youth, just as they emerge from Ashkenazi youth ... as well as founders of farms, builders of settlements, and scientists. We want to erase any superfluous difference between them and other Jews. We don't want the attitude toward the woman, the boy, and the girl to remain what it was in Yemen ... we want to transform him as speedily as possible from a Yemenite to a Jew who has forgotten where he came from, just as I have forgotten that I am a Pole. (Knesset Records, February 14, 1951, 1102, in Lissak 1999, 69)

The active-patronizing policy toward the immigrants was implemented through institutions that encompassed all fields of life: the Jewish Agency, which was responsible for absorption; the Histadrut, on which most of the population depended for medical care, housing, and work; youth movements, in which young people fulfilled the goal of settlement; agricultural boarding schools where pioneering values were instilled in the children; and of course the IDF, in which mandatory conscription was considered a social melting pot. The policy was derived from ideological-collective considerations and aimed at a single objective – creating a unified society with shared content that works to fulfill common goals.

Immigration and Absorption – the "Ingathering of the Exiles"

The Law of Return of 1950 and the Citizenship Law of 1952 anchored the right of every Jew to immigrate to Israel and obtain citizenship. In those years, however, there was a debate on whether to limit the number of immigrants from North Africa by defining quotas, and whether to accept every Jew or filter out those who "are unable to help build the country," i.e., the infirm and the elderly. Selective immigration continued to be debated, but the immigration policy adopted in practice was eventually unlimited (D. Hacohen 1994, 54–122; Segev 1986). (On public opinion regarding immigration restrictions, see Blander 2004.) Immigrants who arrived empty-handed, such as those from the displaced persons camps in Europe, and those from Yemen and North Africa, were completely dependent on the absorption institutions and at the mercy of the patronizing policy that focused primarily on collective considerations. The government decided where they would live (at first in transit camps and later in immigrants' moshavim and development towns in frontier areas), and provided them public works jobs – planting trees, paving roads, or construction – because it was ideologically opposed to providing unemployment benefits.

Housing was a serious problem and the pace of construction could not keep up with the pace of the mass immigration; through May 1950, for example, some 390,000 immigrants arrived and only 50,000 housing units were built. Consequently, there was a need to create transit camps on the outskirts of cities. Living conditions were difficult and the immigrants, most of whom were unemployed, lived in tents and tin huts. This temporary solution lasted a long time, and more than half the immigrants remained in transit camps for over four years, a minority through the mid-1960s. These camps were usually built on the outskirts of urban areas to utilize existing infrastructure, allow the immigrants more independence, and enable direct contact with the veteran population. They were a failure: The immigrants did not become independent, but rather remained unemployed and dependent on the absorption institutions, which waged political battles at their expense. Contact with veteran Israelis engendered a sense of alienation among the new immigrants, and deepened the polarization. In retrospect, the transit camps became a symbol of the failure of the absorption policy of those years (D. Hacohen 1994, 79–86; D. Hacohen 2001, 423–26).

Ben-Gurion assigned the IDF a central role in the socialization of young immigrants, as well as their social and cultural absorption. Immigrant absorption was officially a civilian objective and included, for instance, female soldier-teachers in schools in the immigrants' communities – teaching them Hebrew and Israel's geography and history (D. Hacohen 1994, 157–76). Youth movements were also partners in the absorption and socialization efforts. Together with counselors from kibbutzim, they were active in transit camps and impoverished neighborhoods, teaching Hebrew and helping young Mizrahi immigrants acquire a profession; in doing so, they also tried to instill the "*sabra*" culture. The encounters between the immigrants and these "native" counselors were highly charged, to say the least (O. Almog 1997, 153–61).

The features of the absorption policy during this period did not fade away in subsequent years: challenges that placed an excessive burden on the political system, ad hoc solutions that became permanent, contradictions (i.e., trying to make the immigrants independent without providing employment), and politicization that made the immigrants a focus of power struggles between the parties and between institutions – as in education (see below). Yet, the absorption policy also reflected a deep commitment and high level of mobilization of the state's institutions and voluntary institutions to meet the challenge of immigration.

Education

Education policy in the 1950s is a good example of how the political system tried to realize statist principles (the description here and below follows Pasternak 2003). The goal of the state's education system was to turn the diverse multitude of immigrants into a cohesive, uniform society conforming to Zionist ideology and values. The first step was the Compulsory Education Law of 1949, which obligated parents to send their children to school. The infrastructure, of course, was not uniform because children were sent to one of three political "streams" that pre-dated the state. The education of new immigrant children became a battlefield between the streams, each seeking to educate the children in its own particular way. Initially, "uniform education" was instituted in the immigrant camps in an effort to imbue the children with a "new Israeliness." But some of the immigrants, particularly those from Yemen, supported by the religious parties, protested the attempt to instill the pupils with secular values and turn them away from religion. The crisis was not long in coming. The Frumkin Commission of Inquiry (established in 1950) harshly criticized the patronizing approach toward immigrants and the attempt to impose values on them that were contrary to their Jewish religion and tradition. The dispute over the education of immigrants led to a coalition crisis and the fall of the government in February 1951 (Zameret 1997, 123–36).

The compromise was the State Education Law (1953), designed to make the state education system non-partisan, but at the same time accommodate the religious and Orthodox parties. The party education streams were abolished, but the separate status in the Education Ministry of state-religious education was recognized, as was the independent, ultra-Orthodox education network. Together with the kibbutz and Arab school systems, we see that an all-inclusive ("state") education system was never really established.

The state education system instituted a policy of equal opportunity and a uniform curriculum. Within less than a decade, however, it became clear that the "equal opportunity" policy had failed and that education was only ostensibly egalitarian; it did not necessarily lead to equality in results because of social, economic, and cultural disparities. The curriculum was not adapted to the needs of the different population sectors or the socioeconomic environment in which they lived. The basic assumption was that the new Mizrahi immigrants would adjust, without taking into consideration their heritage and culture. Moreover, disparities developed between schools in different regions. Most immigrant children studied in schools where the pupils were all new immigrants, and these schools did not receive an equal allocation of resources: Their physical conditions and the quality of their teachers were inferior.

From the outset, there were signs of inequality, which continue into the twenty-first century. The representation of Mizrahim in education is pyramid-like: The higher the level of education, the lower the proportion of Mizrahim. Ethnic gaps existed in most fields: The level of scholastic achievement of Mizrahim was lower, their dropout rates were higher, the percentage of Mizrahim who matriculated was lower, and they were under-represented in higher education. The high dropout rates among Mizrahim were reflected in higher rates of juvenile delinquency.[2] In retrospect, there are different assessments of the education policy. Some claim that the policy in Israel's formative period was sincerely aimed at creating equality, as expressed by the minister of education at the time, Ben-Zion Dinur:

> This is the only way! A single and uniform program for all of the people, in all its strata. Our goal is to merge ethnic groups and individuals, merge values … [if] there is no uniform [education] program, we will create inequality and widen the ethnic divide. (Knesset Protocols 1950, 1143, cited in Pasternak 2003, 930)

Accordingly, the policy failure stems from mistakes made with good intentions due to the immaturity of the political system, not because of any hidden agenda (Lissak 1999, 134–36). Some critics of the education policy maintain that this notion of merging the ethnic groups served to camouflage an effort to turn the immigrants from Islamic countries into an inferior and unorganized class, differentiated from the Ashkenazi population, deprived of resources, and controlled by the state, i.e., that the policy of equality in education was, from the outset, only lip service and a means to impose the prevailing ideology on Mizrahi immigrants (Swirski 1995). In any case, this policy did not last long.

The failure of the equality in education policy and the concern about its social repercussions gave birth to the "policy of cultivation" in the 1960s. The idea was to institute a sort of affirmative action for pupils and institutions defined as disadvantaged. The change in policy was an acknowledgment of the gaps between the pupils, primarily between Mizrahim and Ashkenazim. However, the assumption remained that there should be a way to "adapt" the Mizrahi pupils to the existing system without changing it. The policy was accompanied by supplementary budget allocations for disadvantaged pupils and institutions, promoting immigrant pupils with high potential, placing them in boarding schools with high educational standards, and developing vocational education as an alternative to regular education. In retrospect, the compensatory education policy achieved little. It not only failed to narrow the gaps, but reinforced the trend of separation, while the vocational schools became, in practice, "tracks for Mizrahim" (Swirski 1990, 92–103; Pasternak 2003, 955–98).

Population Dispersion and Settlement

As in other areas, the policy in this field was subject to considerations of nation-building – the desire to extend Jewish population to outlying and unsettled regions

[2] In 1953, 75 percent of juvenile offenders were Mizrahi immigrants whose feelings of bitterness, alienation, and discrimination continued to simmer (Committee to Study Juvenile Delinquency 1956).

of the Negev and Galilee, and to change the Jewish Diaspora structure of employment by turning the immigrants into "producers," farmers in particular. Settlement in development towns and immigrant moshavim thus also served as a mechanism for social change. The policy of population dispersion had immigrants sent to agricultural settlements and development towns in northern and southern Israel. It was not consistent with the vision of "merging the exiles" because it created a separation between the veteran population, which lived mainly in cities in central Israel, and the immigrants, primarily Mizrahim, who were sent to live in the geographic, social, and cultural periphery (Gradus 2006, 77).

Despite the ideological dictates of mainstream Zionist ideology, a substantial number of immigrants chose to live in urban areas. In 1922, 35 percent of Israel's overall population lived in cities; by 1931, this had increased to 37 percent (McCarthy 1990, 155). In 1951, the overwhelming majority of Israeli Jews were city dwellers (71%, including six mixed cities) (CBS *Statistical Abstract* 1951–52, table 5). Public opinion supported the policy of population dispersion and dispatching immigrants to fulfill pioneering tasks: In 1949, 81 percent of the public were worried about the concentration of immigrants in the cities, and 98 percent believed that immigrants should be directed to agricultural settlements (Blander 2004, 17–18). In the 1950s, twenty-seven development towns were built, some of them on the foundations of pre-1948 Arab communities (Beersheba, Ashkelon, Jaffa) (Efrat 1997). In the early 1960s, about 275,000 people lived in development towns. Gradually, a homogeneous population of immigrants from Asia-Africa emerged in most of these towns as those of European origin gradually left them. Development towns were designed as urban centers that would serve rural communities in peripheral regions, but they had no suitable employment infrastructure, and the opposite ensued: Rural communities became providers of services and employment for the residents of development towns. In the 1960s, food and textile industries were established in development towns, but wages were low, and those employed in these industries were primarily unskilled and uneducated. Development towns were initially managed by government and Jewish Agency officials, which exacerbated tensions between the Ashkenazi officials and Mizrahi residents. By the early 1960s, however, residents began to take local politics into their own hands and political parties were forced to come to terms with this.

Another form of settlement was immigrant moshavim. About 150 were established throughout Israel in 1949–52 with the aim of integrating immigrants into the pioneering enterprise. Their population was homogeneous, primarily immigrants from Asia-Africa (65%). The assumption was that the semi-collective moshav, where each family owns a private farm and the infrastructure is shared, would be suitable for the extended families of the immigrants. However, most of the moshavim did not initially succeed due to objective economic factors as well as the immigrants' lack of agricultural experience. Nonetheless, the immigrant moshavim gradually began to find their place in Israeli agriculture (Lissak 1999, 33–36).

In 1948 and early 1949, about 120,000 immigrants were housed in neighborhoods and towns whose Arab residents had been expelled or fled during the war – in Jaffa, Lod, Ramle, Jerusalem, and Haifa (D. Hacohen 2001, 410). This provided a solution to the housing shortage for those immigrants, but there was also a political objective – to prevent the return of Arabs to their homes.

In sum, there was a contradiction between the policy of population dispersion and the slogans of integration of the immigrants. The geographic separation widened the gaps and created social enclaves in which the "second Israel" evolved.

C. Socioeconomic Policy

Economic policy in the first years of the state was influenced first of all by the security situation, the aspiration to create an economy that stands on its own ("economic independence"), and the challenge of absorbing the mass immigration. Intensive government involvement in the economy suited the urgent needs and was consistent with the socialist ideology of the leadership. The economic crisis and shortage of foreign currency led to adoption of an "austerity regime" on basic products from May 1949 to 1953, including food rationing to ensure an equal allocation of supplies. The austerity regime also preached solidarity and frugality, but public support quickly faded, mainly because of the black market that evolved, undermining the effectiveness of the rationing and stirring fierce public indignation. With the exception of the recession years 1952–53, Israel recorded impressive economic growth during its first decade. GDP rose by an average of about 10 percent annually, thanks to the growing work force, income of foreign capital (mainly reparations from Germany, but also donations), investment in infrastructure, construction, subsidies to encourage investment, and agricultural expansion (N. Gross 1997; Shalev 1993, 155). A policy of full employment was also instituted, which included public works projects. The unemployment rate gradually declined to 3.5 percent in 1961–65, until the recession of 1966 (Shalev 1993, 154). Agriculture was the principal economic branch in those early years, but there was already substantial industrial growth in the 1960s.

State involvement was manifested in the creation of a large public sector, consistent with the ideas of the welfare state. There was also an aspiration to provide social security, which was also designed to contribute to social integration. The policy was implemented by the Ministry of Welfare and local authorities, together with the Histadrut's health and other services. In 1953, the National Insurance Institute was established as a semi-autonomous entity responsible for the social security system. In the 1960s, the scope of the welfare policy expanded to include transfer payments for the elderly and children (Doron and Kramer 1991). Thus the policy that would continue through the 1980s had already appeared in the early days of the state: extensive state involvement in the economy and a firm effort to prevent unemployment and provide a safety net for the individual (Y. Ben-Porat 1989, 26).

Against the background of the accelerated economic development in Israel's early years, the underdevelopment of the Arab communities within Israel is even starker. The government's policy toward its Arab citizens included restrictions on movement imposed by martial law, land expropriation, and limitations on the employment of Arabs in the Jewish economy. All this hindered the development of both the Jewish and Arab economies. Gradually, after martial law was rescinded in the mid-1960s, Arab citizens began to participate in economic activity, initially as agricultural and construction laborers (see Chapter 15).

16.4 The Melting Pot Policy Fails, Cleavages Emerge

A. Description of the Society

From the late 1960s through the mid-1980s, the pace of immigration slowed and the number of immigrants in the 1970s totaled about 270,000, most from the Soviet Union (about 150,000), Argentina, and the United States (D. Hacohen 2001, 388). The challenge facing policymakers changed, and was now centered on absorbing veteran immigrants. The central characteristic of society during this period was the exacerbation of socioeconomic and cultural differences between Mizrahim and Ashkenazim. The term "cleavage" refers to the lines dividing a society into sectors and groups, usually with tension and polarization between them (Horowitz and Lissak 1989). In Israel, the cleavage lines are based on ethnic origin, but they also overlap with other variables: political (right-leaning versus left-leaning); economic (income gaps); and religious (traditional versus secular). During the Yishuv period, most of the Jewish population came from eastern Europe, but in the early 1970s, 47 percent of the Jews (foreign born or whose fathers were foreign born) were of Mizrahi origin and 44 percent were of European origin. Among native-born Israelis (second generation), 23 percent were Mizrahi and 16 percent were of European origin (CBS *Statistical Abstract* 2006, table 2.24). That is, a demographic change occurred during Israel's first two decades, accompanied by widening disparities between these two groups.

The disparities between newcomers and veterans were initially viewed as the consequence of migration itself. However, when substantial gaps remained in all fields among second-generation Israelis who were educated in Israel, these disparities became socially significant. In the 1970s, it became clear that the disadvantaged status of native-born, second-generation Mizrahim was not about to disappear (Smooha and Peres 1974, 12). While the overall standard of living rose from the mid-1950s, most of those who did not enjoy this improvement were of Mizrahi origin. In the late 1960s, the average income of a Mizrahi family was about 70 percent that of an Ashkenazi family. The disparity in per capita expenditure was 50 percent in the late 1960s, i.e., the average standard of living of an Ashkenazi was twice that of a Mizrahi. Nonetheless, there was also a significant narrowing of the gap in consumption patterns and ownership of household appliances during those years, and the improvement was greater among Mizrahim (Smooha and Peres 1974, 9–14).

The general level of education of the adult population rose only slightly during the 1950s and 1960s. The contribution of the Compulsory Education Law to narrowing the gap between the groups was most salient in elementary education, but diminished at the higher levels. This had a negative impact on the social mobility of the Mizrahim because job demands for an education were continually rising. In the early 1970s, the gap in elementary schools nearly disappeared, but significant disparities remained in secondary education, because most Mizrahim were channeled to vocational and agricultural schools, which lowered their access to higher education. In the late 1960s, the ratio of Ashkenazim to Mizrahim in universities was 7:1. However, among the second generation of Mizrahim, the overall gap began to narrow – except for professions of high status or income, such as medicine and engineering. In the short term, the smaller disparities in higher education were not immediately expressed in status and income, and the gap remained (Smooha and

Peres 1974, 20). In the long term, however, there is a trend of narrowing the gaps in the third generation. Moreover, Mizrahim also developed tracks of mobility that circumvent higher education, such as small and medium-sized businesses, which enabled some to join the middle class (Yaar 1986).

Another aspect of the rifts within Jewish society is reflected in the patterns of marriage – the wider the gaps, the fewer "mixed marriages" between Jews from different ethnic groups. The increase in such marriages indicates the lesser importance young people attribute to ethnic identity, which contributes to reducing the inequality perpetuated across generations. A study that compared marriage patterns in the 1970s and the early 1980s found that inter-ethnic marriages were generally on the rise (Shavit and Stier 1997). Within most groups from the same country, the tendency to marry within the group was lower. Ashkenazim increasingly married Mizrahim, while Mizrahim increasingly married Mizrahim from different countries. In other words, Mizrahim appeared to be forming an ethnic identity that was expressed in marrying within the Mizrahi bloc, while the ethnic boundaries of Ashkenazim appeared to be weakening. Among Ashkenazim, immigrants from the Soviet Union in the 1970s maintained the highest level of homogeneity: 60 percent married those of similar origin. Subsequently, the marriage pattern among those who immigrated from the former Soviet Union in the 1990s was similar, i.e., they act similarly to those from previous immigration waves from other countries.

Among Mizrahim, the likelihood of marriage between those of North African origin was 62 percent, while the likelihood of a woman of North African origin marrying a man of European origin was less than 2 percent. Among Israelis of Yemenite origin, about 50 percent married within this ethnic group. Therefore, the expectation that education level would eventually surpass ethnic origin as a predictor of choice of spouse remained unfulfilled in the early 1980s; ethnic origin was still a stronger predictor (Shavit and Stier 1997). The persistence of educational and economic disparities among second-generation Israelis preserved the pattern of ethnic marriages. Nevertheless, the trend was clear, and within a generation or two, almost half of all marriages would be "mixed," which means that ethnic origin was disregarded.

The challenge of social disparities during this period stood in the shadow of the security challenge – the Six Day War and the crisis of the Yom Kippur War – which heralded the weakening of the state, the end of Labor Party dominance, and the beginning of the "lost decade" in Israel's economy.

B. Policy

Domestic policy in this period was influenced by the threat posed by the ethnic gap and the feelings of alienation among Mizrahim. The political system, which until then had displayed paternalism toward Mizrahim, was forced to contend with the challenge created by the sense of discrimination. The policy adopted was designed to mitigate the gap through integration in education and involving Mizrahim in some of the institutions, for example political co-optation into the parties. At the same time, immigrants from the Soviet Union after 1967 were given better absorption conditions, which further exacerbated the sense of discrimination among deprived groups of veteran Mizrahim.

Absorption

The absorption policy in the 1970s changed due to the relative decline in immigration and because of significant improvement in the economic situation. The fact that most immigrants were "western" (from the Soviet Union or the United States), with higher education and professional-technological training, eased their absorption. They were also regarded as "Zionist" immigrants motivated by the 1967 victory, which boosted their status in society. Naturally, the Mizrahi immigrants from the 1950s did not look kindly upon the preferential treatment accorded the new Ashkenazim, compared to what they had received two decades earlier. The better material benefits, but also the fact that "seniority" among immigrants was no longer considered an advantage in the case of Mizrahim stirred resentment. These feelings were among the factors that engendered the Israeli "Black Panthers" movement (D. Hacohen 2001, 447–56).

Absorption policy continued to be centralized and controlled by the government and the Jewish Agency. At the same time, however, a new policy of liberalization was instituted, adapting absorption tracks to the needs and abilities of the immigrants. To this end, temporary absorption centers were established, and these provided reasonable services to the immigrants – housing and food, Hebrew-language instruction, cultural activity, and employment counseling – until permanent housing was found. The immigrants, especially those with academic training, could choose their place of residence, while others were directed to development towns. Many had to change professions and accept a much lower status. In the long run, however, their absorption was considered more successful compared to the immigrants of the 1950s.

Education

Israel instituted a policy of social and educational integration (1968) – ethnically heterogeneous classrooms aimed at breaking down barriers between the groups and encouraging weaker students to advance. In practice, despite the creation of junior high schools (grades 7–9) with children from various regions, many classrooms were not heterogeneous and separate tracks were formed for weaker pupils, most of them Mizrahim. The integration program was terminated in the 1980s because it failed to narrow the gap as hoped, though studies indicate slow improvement. It also clashed with the individualistic and achievement-focused orientation of the primarily Ashkenazi upper-middle class. Critics maintain that the program was a mere slogan and not implemented in practice. Moreover, circumventing arrangements such as ability groupings were developed, which reduced heterogeneity in the classrooms. In general, the integration policy had little positive impact on the achievements of Mizrahi pupils or on their self-image. The education policy changed again in the 1990s toward encouraging individualism, competitiveness, autonomy, and choice (Pasternak 2003, 959–70).

Project Renewal

This project, launched in the late 1970s, was one of the most important tangible attempts to institute a socioeconomic policy of affirmative action for those who lagged behind, and reflected the importance of social change in the Begin government elected in 1977. The program, a joint initiative of the government and Diaspora Jewry, allocated substantial resources (about $1.2 billion) to upgrade the housing conditions of residents of distressed neighborhoods and towns. In late 1982, the program included eighty-two Jewish neighborhoods having about 500,000 inhabitants. The program continued through the mid-1980s, and then fizzled out for various reasons – the Lebanon War, the economic crisis, and political power struggles, local and national, which disrupted it (S. Shapiro 1988). Residents included in the program were offered grants and low-interest loans, apartments were expanded, buildings were renovated or demolished and reconstructed, community centers and clubs were built, etc. By 2001, sixty-three neighborhoods had been renovated, about 63,000 apartments were expanded, and some 110,000 housing units were refurbished. In the 2000s, the project continued on a small scale (Tzadik 2006).

It is difficult to assess the success of the program due to its multiple objectives, but it can be said that the project was indeed implemented, albeit on a smaller scale than originally announced. Its main contribution was to improve housing infrastructure in poor neighborhoods. It led to an improvement in the surrounding conditions and neighborhood services (education, health, and culture). However, it failed to "put an end to poverty" as Menachem Begin had hoped (Shimshoni 2002, 262). Residents participated in some neighborhoods where steering committees were formed, which was definitely a new development. However, involvement in decision-making was limited and government officials gradually assumed greater control at the expense of the residents' ability to exert influence (Churchman 1988). The program did not succeed in encouraging social mobility nor did it generate real improvement in the social standing of the residents. Another significant shortcoming was that it included only Jewish neighborhoods during most of its lifetime, excluding the severely impoverished neighborhoods in Arab communities (Carmon 1988).

C. Socioeconomic Policy

From the mid-1950s, and except for the recession in 1966–67, GDP rose by about 10 percent yearly with an average 6–7 percent inflation annually. From the 1970s, economic developments were influenced by the steep increase in defense spending after the Yom Kippur War (nearly 30% of the GNP in 1974–80), the global energy crisis after 1973, the declining pace of immigration, and the increase in welfare outlays. In fact, after 1973, the economy never resumed the same growth rate, with an average 4 percent annually until 2010.

The social and political turmoil of the early 1970s refocused attention on domestic problems that had been neglected. Policymakers "discovered" inequality, poverty, and disparities between the wealthy and poor (primarily Mizrahim). The poverty of other groups such as Arab citizens was not yet noticed. The fear of a social rift compelled the government to allocate more resources for social services, guaranteed minimal income, disability benefits, and child allowances (Doron and Kramer 1991). State spending on social services from 1970 to 1980 rose substantially from 13 percent to 20 percent of the GNP. Indeed, by the first half of the 1970s, inequality had narrowed, with fewer respondents in both the lowest and highest income deciles. That was the lowest level of inequality recorded between 1967 and 2003 (Saporta, Abo-Zaid, and Leshem 2006, 9–10). However, after the 1973 war with the concomitant rise in defense spending, growth slowed, inflation accelerated, and the balance of payments deficit grew. The social commitments thus became a heavy burden

(Bruno 1989, 365). The Likud takeover in 1977 was accompanied by an expectation that policy would change. It declared it will create a new infrastructure for the Israeli economy: "The Likud will establish a free economy based on efficiency, initiative, and competition. The Likud will reduce government involvement in economic activity, and will strive to gradually reduce government supervision of economic activity" (Likud platform, 1977 election).

The first significant change was liberalization of the foreign currency market. The Likud platform in 1981 espoused "modern and advanced social liberalism." However, the finance minister, Yoram Aridor, championed a "correct economy" that aimed to benefit the public. There was an increase in real wages, taxes were lowered, the erosion of social security allowances was halted, and subsidies were reinstated. Consequently, there was a rise in disposable income and private consumption per capita. This policy led to a dramatic increase in inflation during the years of the Likud government, reaching triple digits in the early 1980s and over 400 percent in 1984 (Figure 16.2), while unemployment rose to 5 percent in 1981 (Bank of Israel 2006).

In 1981–84, the Israeli economy went into a tailspin – inflation soared, the growth rate dropped, and the balance of payments deficit ballooned (Y. Ben-Porat 1982). The economic situation further deteriorated with the surge in defense spending in the wake of the Lebanon War (1982), the allocation of large sums for settlements in the territories, and the funding of Project Renewal. Aborted projects such as the Lavi aircraft and the Mediterranean–Dead Sea Canal had been a further drain on public resources. The collapse of bank stocks in October 1983 threatened the stability of the economic system and led to a steep devaluation. Economic policy staggered during the crisis, with no fewer than four different finance ministers in six years (1977–83).

In 1985, the unity government adopted an emergency economic plan aimed at reining in inflation, reducing the budget deficit, implementing a steep cut in real wages and subsidies for basic commodities, and freezing prices and exchange rates. It was in effect an economic reform that changed the structure of the economy. Its main achievement was to lower inflation and stabilize prices (accompanied by a temporary rise in unemployment and an erosion of wages). The economic crisis and steep rise in defense spending changed the welfare policy (Bruno 1985). In the 1980s, the resources allocated to education, health, and welfare services were reduced. Nonetheless, the core of the previous welfare network remained intact and was somewhat strengthened with the new Income Support Law in 1980 (Doron and Kramer 1991).

During this period (1977–84), income inequality grew, in part due to the high inflation. The economic emergency plan slowed this trend and inequality in income distribution decreased in the years 1985–93. However, this was largely at the expense of the middle class, while the income of the top decile continued to increase (Saporta et al. 2006, 10). This inequality in Israeli society would continue to grow, reaching record levels in the 2000s. Another result of the political change of 1977 and the capitalist shift of economic policy in 1985 was the weakening of the powerful organizations that had symbolized the ethos of the labor movement – the Histadrut, Hevrat Ovdim, the kibbutzim, and the moshavim (Eisenstadt 2005, 22). In parallel, a consistent policy of privatization began, starting with government companies and later including social services (Galnoor et al. 2015).

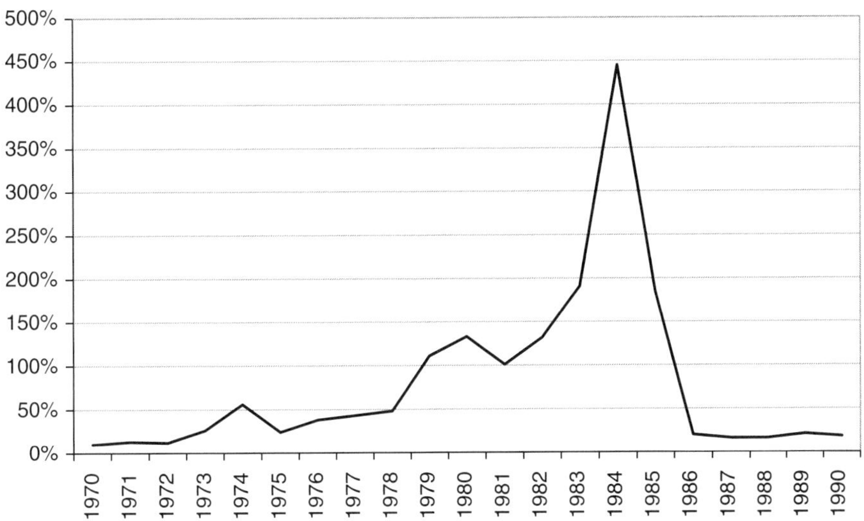

Figure 16.2 Inflation rates (1970–90) (%)
Sources: Bank of Israel, *Report 2003*, table 1.1 (2); Price Index 1965–2003 (Bank of Israel website).

The economic policy of the Likud government until 1984 was marked by internal contradictions: On the one hand, the rhetoric of privatization and measures to liberalize the economy and capital market; on the other hand, budgetary expansion, investments in the settlements, and also larger welfare programs "to benefit the people." This led to an inconsistent policy and a serious economic crisis.

16.5 State and Domestic Policy in the Pluralist Period

A. Description of the Society

The salient characteristics of Israeli society since the late 1980s are a changed social structure and increased inequality. The socioeconomic policy in the pluralistic period was influenced by the fact that the mosaic of Israeli society further split into internal parts composed of various groups, with weaker affinity between them. This process coincided with a general weakening of the state and, in particular, a weakening of political parties and other mediating institutions that had played an integral role in the past. The state's retreat from socioeconomic fields and the dwindling welfare state stemmed from an ideological approach that was directly influenced by a neo-liberal world view and globalization. Thus, in Israel, as in many western countries, privatization did not stop at selling government corporations, but was extended to placing responsibility for social service provision (e.g., education, health) into private hands. The weakness of state institutions contributed to the erosion of social cohesion and exacerbated the divide in society.

The changes in Israeli society made the melting pot policy impossible, even though efforts continued to forge a single, uniform society with shared values and symbols under the slogan of "a Jewish state" or "renewed Zionism." In practice, it became acceptable to maintain different identities and organize as separate groups in

Table 16.4 *Immigration to Israel from the former Soviet Union (1990–2015)*

Years	Immigrants
1990–2001	906,127
2002–15	121,136
Total	1,027,263

The former Soviet Union includes European and Asian republics.
Source: CBS *Statistical Abstract* 2007, table 4.4; from 2002 through June 2015, Ministry of Immigrant Absorption website.

all fields of life (Lissak 2000). Politically, this was expressed in parties based on ethnic identity, such as Shas and the parties of "Russian" immigrants. On a different plane, the state's retreat from many fields paved the way for the blossoming of civil society and the growth of independent voluntary organizations (see Chapter 12).

The arrival of about one million immigrants from the former Soviet Union after 1989 changed Israeli society demographically and culturally (Table 16.4). This wave of immigration was larger than the mass immigration of the 1950s (in 1948–51, about 690,000 immigrants arrived). However, it constituted only about 15 percent of the state's Jewish population, while the immigration in the 1950s had doubled it.

Some of these newcomers had Zionist motives for immigrating to Israel, while others came hoping that their lives would be better than in their lands of origin (Leshem and Sicron 1998, 446). Their large number, sociological characteristics, and arrival during the pluralist period enabled them to form a distinct community in Israeli society. The "Russian" community is concentrated in urban areas, primarily in outlying regions, and seeks to preserve its cultural and linguistic roots. The community networks of the first generation of immigrants are based on country of origin and differ from the veteran population in values, patterns of education, exposure to media in their own language, and more. Their group identity is stronger than their Israeli identity. They keep in contact with their lands of origin and many regard their original culture as superior to Israeli culture. They have separate civil society organizations and more than half draw their information from Russian-language media; this does not change over the years, even after they have become fluent in Hebrew. This inclination to maintain their language and community networks creates the feeling among veteran Israelis that "the Russians" seek to remain apart. Politically, the ability of immigrants to organize in separate ethnic parties reflects a model of "separative integration" – integration in the political system as a group that maintains its separate identity, and not as individuals who are liable to lose their unique characteristics (Leshem 2005). This group's identity as separate and different is evident in the first generation's sense of "Israeliness": Two decades after their immigration, only 60 percent feel a sense of belonging to the state, compared to 73 percent among veteran Israelis (Arian, Philippov, and Knafelman 2009). Nonetheless, this changes markedly with the Israeli-born second generation.

In the 1980s, about 17,000 Jews from Ethiopia immigrated to Israel, and another 40,000 arrived in the 1990s, primarily in Operation Moses (1984) and Operation

Table 16.5 *Immigrants to Israel from Ethiopia (1980–2015)*

Years	Immigrants
1980–89	16,965
1990–99	39,651
2000–15	36,532
Total	93,148

Source: CBS *Statistical Abstract* 2007, table 4.4; from 2002 through June 2015, Ministry of Immigrant Absorption website.

Solomon (1991). Immigration also continued intermittently in subsequent years, but in smaller numbers (Table 16.5). As of early 2014, first- and second-generation immigrants of Ethiopian origin totaled 124,300 (CBS 2014b, table 2.6). This group encountered serious and unique difficulties: In many cases, only part of the family arrived, while others remained in Ethiopia; many were in poor health; and they lacked formal education. Consequently, the absorption policy was different (see below), and unwittingly contributed to widening the geographic and social divide between them and the rest of the population, making their integration even more difficult (D. Hacohen 2001, 456–65). The religious establishment did not accept the Ethiopians as Jews and set strict conditions for their conversion. There were also blatant expressions of racism in Israeli society based on the color of their skin, which stirred violent demonstrations by Ethiopian youth, mostly native-born. These demonstrations peaked in 2015.

Within the Israeli mosaic of groups, one should not ignore the asylum seekers from Africa – the so-called "infiltrators" in government-inspired public discourse. Starting in the mid-1990s and through 2006, a relatively small number of asylum seekers (2,706) arrived in Israel via Egypt. The numbers began to rise, but the flow of asylum seekers came to an almost complete halt upon completion of Israel's southern border fence in December 2013. In 2016, there were an estimated 42,000 asylum seekers, most men of working age from Eritrea and Sudan. About 70 percent of the asylum seekers from Africa live in the neighborhoods of south Tel Aviv, and the rest in Eilat and other cities (Ministry of the Interior 2016).

The state of Israel has not formulated an official policy in regard to asylum seekers. They are not officially recognized as refugees, and most are not legally allowed to work. Consequently, the crime rate among them is high, and they are of public concern because a relatively high number of them are HIV-positive or infected with tuberculosis. Residents of neighborhoods with high concentrations of asylum seekers regard them as a threat to their daily lives, and protest the government's impotence in dealing with them. Israel's Prevention of Infiltration Law, enacted in 2012, allows for asylum seekers to be held in a detention facility for three years. The High Court declared the law unconstitutional and the Knesset enacted a more moderate amendment shortening the detention period to a maximum eighteen months. An open detention facility was built in southern Israel (Holot), which provides the asylum seekers with shelter and food, but requires them to register three times a day and prohibits them from working. After the High Court rejected the legislation for the second time, it was again amended in 2015, and the court approved the law, with the stipulation that the state may detain asylum seekers at the facility for up to twelve months. In parallel, the government adopted a policy of "voluntary departure," offering monetary incentives to asylum seekers to encourage them to leave Israel. The government does not address the living conditions of asylum seekers in Israel, and third-sector organizations have assumed primary responsibility for looking after them, protecting their rights, and trying to provide solutions for their distress.

Although the groups composing Israeli society are quite different from one another (Ashkenazim, Mizrahim, native-born, Russians, Ethiopians, religious, secular, Arabs, settlers, asylum seekers, etc.), they are not equal. Various indexes reveal the disparities between the groups in education, income, poverty, and unemployment. These gaps have grown over the years, but worsened in the 1990s and 2000s, leading to public discontent accompanied by a loss of confidence in the political leadership, a weakening of social cohesion and solidarity, and a lack of agreement on shared values. In light of the social goals of Zionism, one might have expected the disparities in Israeli society to narrow over the years, but the opposite has occurred. Since the 1990s, inequality, particularly in income and education, has rapidly grown. It can be seen between Arabs and Jews, between Mizrahim and Ashkenazim, among specific groups (ultra-Orthodox Jews, new immigrants, and the elderly), between men and women, and between central Israel and the periphery.

In the social protest of 2011, there was an important transition from the rhetoric of social "cleavages" and ethnic-based discrimination to (so far) the rhetoric of disparities between the few "haves," who enjoy economic growth, and the majority of "have-nots," who have been excluded and fallen behind. Of course, the "traditional cleavages" in society have not disappeared, but they are embodied in the gap between the socioeconomic deciles, and between the periphery and the center (D. Ben-David 2011, 14; Yonah 2015).

B. Education and Income Disparities in Israeli Society[3]

The data indicate that despite progress in education and income in the population as a whole, gaps persist between the strongest segments of the population (Ashkenazi, Jewish, secular men in central Israel) and others. (On the weakening of this hegemonic group, see Kimmerling 2001.) In regard to education and income, the hierarchy is clear: Ashkenazim are on the top rung, immigrants from the former Soviet Union are next, followed by the Mizrahim, with Arabs and ultra-Orthodox at the bottom.

Education

The policies adopted over the years have not led to a significant change in the educational disparities between groups in Israeli society. The gaps that existed after the 1950s have narrowed, but in the 2010s a large gap remains between Arabs and Jews

[3] Most of the data relate to Mizrahim compared to Ashkenazim because this is what most research on inequality examines. On inequality between Jews and Arabs, see Chapter 15.

and within Jewish Israeli society. Even in the second and third generation of pupils of Mizrahi origin, achievements are lower, the percentage of pupils getting vocational training is higher, dropout rates are higher, and the percentage of pupils who matriculate is lower. The higher the level of education, the wider the gap – and this negatively affects the chance of advancement by Mizrahim because the demands for education are rising over the years. In elementary education, there are no significant gaps, but disparities increase as pupils enter high school. Although the gaps have narrowed over the years, the pace is slow and there is no guarantee that closing the gap in the lower grades will engender a similar trend in the higher grades in the near future (Lavy 2003, 44–46). Similarly, the overall percentage of pupils eligible for matriculation has grown from under 50 percent in 2005 to 53 percent in 2014. However, studies still indicate significant differences in matriculation success between various groups in society. Arabs, especially Muslims, are at the bottom of the scale. Among Jews, teenagers from Ashkenazi origin are much more likely to matriculate than their Mizrahi counterparts; those of mixed Mizrahi-Ashkenazi origin are in the middle – more likely than Mizrahim and less likely than Ashkenazim to matriculate.

The percentage of Mizrahim studying for an undergraduate degree has gradually increased, but fewer Mizrahim (and residents of the periphery and Arabs) are in the universities; a higher proportion study at regional colleges and teachers' colleges (Ayalon 2006, 154). The differences are also salient in the subjects of study, with a particularly low percentage of Mizrahim studying subjects such as engineering, architecture, mathematics, and medicine. The gap is smaller among students of social sciences, humanities, and law (CBS 2008, table 8.52). Yet, the fact that a high percentage of students in high-status fields are of Israeli origin (their father too is native-born) indicates that ethnic origin becomes less significant over the years, as the percentage of second-generation, native-born Mizrahim continues to increase.

The education level of second-generation Ashkenazim is higher than that of Mizrahim and Arabs, but the gaps have gradually narrowed since 1975. In 1995, Ashkenazim aged twenty-five to twenty-nine (born in the 1960s and early 1970s) were still nearly four times more likely to have an academic degree than their Mizrahi counterparts. Thus, second-generation Mizrahim were unable to close the gap in acquiring an academic degree: only 29 percent in 2011, compared to 50 percent of second-generation Ashkenazim (Yinon Cohen 1998, 119–22; Dobrin 2015). However, ethnic origin in itself does not explain the disparity; there is a strong correlation with family background and, in particular, with the parents' education level and, to a lesser extent, income level. That is, given the same education level of the parents, there is no difference in achievement between the groups. Therefore, the gap today is a projection of the gaps in the 1950s and 1960s, not a result of discrimination. Nonetheless, the fact that most Mizrahim do not matriculate slows the process of narrowing the gap in the future. Among the third generation (born in 1960–77 to native-born parents), the education gap between Mizrahim and Ashkenazim is not lower than in the second generation (Yinon Cohen 2006, 339; D. Hacohen 2001, 446).

Therefore, the policies adopted by the state education system have generated gradual change that indicates a narrowing of the gaps. However, over the course of two generations, these policies have not been able to neutralize the impact of the initial advantage of higher levels of education and income, and significantly narrow the disparities in education.

Income

Since the 1970s, education disparities have narrowed, but income gaps between Ashkenazi men and other groups have widened. Wage gaps between second-generation Mizrahim and Ashkenazim are growing: The average income of Mizrahim dropped from 79 percent to 70 percent of the average income of Ashkenazim in the period from 1975 to 1982. The income gap also widened as careers advanced. A more troubling finding is that while in 1975 there was no income disparity among those with academic degrees, in 1995 the income of Mizrahim with an undergraduate degree was only 78 percent that of Ashkenazim with the same academic degree (D. Hacohen 1998, 122–24). Nonetheless, during the years 1988–2003, there was an improvement in the income of working-age (25–54), native-born, Mizrahi wage-earners, and many of them moved into the upper-middle class. This must also be qualified: Descendants of Asian-African origin are still over-represented among lowest income households, and second-generation Israelis of European-American origin are over-represented among highest income households (Kristal, Cohen, and Mundlak 2006, 24–25).

In regard to disparities in employment: Many Mizrahim are over-represented in the lowest levels, while Ashkenazim constitute a high percentage of white-collar workers; there are no significant differences between those born in Israel and those born abroad (first and second generation) (Nahon 1984, 89–92). As noted, the hierarchy in education is also reflected in income (Figure 16.3). At the bottom of the income rankings are Arabs, many of whom cannot extricate themselves from the cycle of poverty. In the middle are Mizrahim (first and second generation) whose relative situation has improved over the years, but who still lag behind Ashkenazim (first and second generation) in terms of income. There is a correlation between the widening income gaps between groups and the growing inequality between deciles, and this is because of the over-representation of Ashkenazim in the top deciles and Arabs and Mizrahim at the bottom. Nonetheless, one should not ignore the narrowing of income disparities between Ashkenazim and Mizrahim since the 1990s and early 2000s. In 2011, the income gap among second-generation Israelis was about 25 percent in favor of Ashkenazim, but this is significantly less than in the past. In particular, the disparity among third-generation Israelis narrowed to 19 percent. The relative representation of Mizrahim in the income deciles improved: In the top percentile, their representation is similar to that of the general population, and they are under-represented at the bottom (Momi Dahan 2013).

The gaps between Ashkenazim and Mizrahim in education and income have several salient characteristics. First, as noted, the inequality is a result of the lingering gaps that date back to the 1950s. Second, the trend of advancement in both education and income among Mizrahim is gradually narrowing these gaps (Momi Dahan 2013, 107–52). Third, the more "Israeli" one is, the better one's chances of higher income and education – regardless of whether one's roots are Ashkenazi or Mizrahi, i.e., the number of generations in Israel contributes to narrowing the gaps among Jews. Fourth, the data do not identify the "mixed" groups (whose parents originate from different continents) because the criterion used is father's continent of birth.

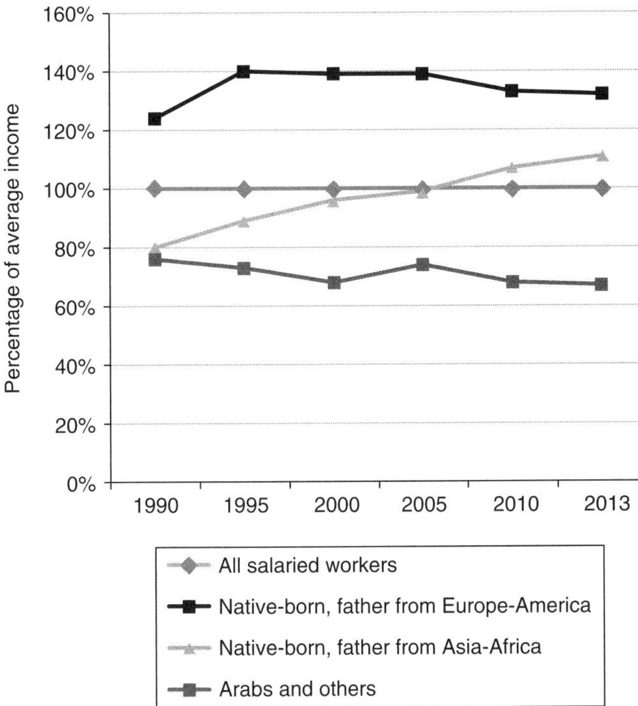

Figure 16.3 Monthly income of urban salaried workers among Ashkenazim, Mizrahim, and Arabs (1990–2013) (average income of salaried workers = 100%)
Sources: Swirski and Konor-Atias 2006; Swirski and Konor-Atias 2014.

However, the percentage of inter-ethnic marriages has steadily increased (Okun 2001), which indicates that education has replaced ethnic origin as the determining factor in the choice of a spouse.[4] The "mixed" Israelis succeed in narrowing the gap and their achievements in education and income are in the intermediate range between the Ashkenazim and Mizrahim. This group has the potential for making ethnic origin an irrelevant factor.

In summary, the gap remains between Ashkenazim and Mizrahim, but it is narrowing. Various factors explain this change: Second- and third-generation Mizrahim invested more in acquiring education, which boosted their standing in the job market. The rise in the level of higher education was made possible by the opening of new colleges, many in the periphery. Another explanation is the greater access to centers of political power, from which Mizrahim were excluded in the past (Momi Dahan 2013). At the same time, a Mizrahi middle class formed, some of whom integrated into the veteran Ashkenazi middle class (Birenbaum-Carmeli 2002), while others formed a distinct Mizrahi middle class, characterized by separate residential areas and by autonomous cultural and public spaces that emerged (Cohen and Leon

[4] However, since immigrants from the former Soviet Union tend to marry within their community, the arrival of this wave of immigration in the 1990s marked a decline in the percentage of inter-ethnic marriages (Ilany 2007; Okun and Khait-Marelly 2006).

2008). Other factors that may explain these changes are the participation of second-generation Mizrahi women in the work force, and the adoption of western family models of later marriages and fewer children (Momi Dahan 2013). Subjectively, however, 42 percent of the Mizrahim feel that there is discrimination against Mizrahim in Israel, compared to only 16 percent of Ashkenazim who feel this way (Hermann et al. 2011–15: 2015).

Disparities in Education and Income: Immigrants from the former Soviet Union and Ethiopia

Where are the immigrants from the former Soviet Union ("the Russians") on the socioeconomic scale? These immigrants are not a homogeneous group culturally, educationally, or vocationally. Many are concentrated in localities at the bottom of the socioeconomic scale, and a relatively large number live in southern Israel. Their average standard of living is lower, and the level of unemployment and poverty is higher than the rest of the Jewish population, as expected in the first generation of immigrants. In 2014, the (gross) income of new immigrants from the former Soviet Union was 70 percent the national average, and their level of expenditures was only 73 percent the national average. However, the gross income of older immigrants from three decades ago is now equal to the national average, and their expenditure is 92 percent (CBS *Statistical Abstract* 2015, 148).

Nonetheless, this wave of immigration is rich in human capital, and the average level of education exceeds that of the general population, indicating that the low employment level is temporary. Indeed, many of these Russian speakers initially engaged in work that did not match the potential of their education. However, they eventually integrated into the job market and began to gradually move up the scale of employment and income. Already in the 1990s, the employment of these immigrants began to reach the level of veteran Israelis with similar levels of education and experience (Eckstein and Weiss 2001), and this trend continued in the 2000s. Still, income disparities remain and Russian immigrants are over-represented in the lowest levels of income.

The picture is bleaker among immigrants from Ethiopia on every socioeconomic yardstick, and this is related to their education and employment characteristics, as well as to flaws in their absorption in Israel. Their matriculation rate is 50 percent, compared to the general rate of 63 percent (in 2013), and the gap is larger for the percentage of matriculating students who meet the entrance requirements for higher education (CBS 2014b). The Ethiopians are at the bottom of the income scale, and this is also true for those with a college education. The per capita income is about half that of the veteran population and, accordingly, the average expenditure in Ethiopian households is 35 percent lower. Poverty is particularly high (about 50%), and the unemployment rate is double the average in the total population (Bank of Israel 2007, 170–74).

Center versus Periphery

Despite its small size, Israel's geography reflects disparities. The socioeconomic situation of a person living in central Israel is better than that of someone living in the south, north, or Jerusalem on nearly every measure. Most of those living in the periphery are Arabs and low-income Jews – veteran Mizrahi immigrants and new

Russian and Ethiopian immigrants. The ultra-Orthodox are an exception to this overlap of groups of low socioeconomic status and geographic dispersion. Most live in the center of the country (Jerusalem, Bnei Brak, Elad, Beitar Illit), but the socio-economic situation of their communities resembles that of the geographic periphery.

Most local authorities in the lowest clusters are in the geographic periphery, including the populations cited above. For example, the lowest cluster comprises seven localities, five of them Bedouin in the south, and two ultra-Orthodox near Jerusalem (Table 5.5 in Chapter 5). Since the 1990s, the situation of the weaker population in the periphery has deteriorated further, due to the preference given to settlements in the territories, the state's cutbacks for social services, privatization, and outsourcing. There are also significant differences in the poverty rate. The percentage of poor families in the north and south is twice that of central Israel (with the exception of Jerusalem, which includes large, poor ultra-Orthodox and Arab families). Life expectancy and infant mortality in the periphery are also worse, primarily in areas with a large Arab population. Unemployment rates in the periphery have been continuously higher than the national average. In addition, the impact of economic prosperity was primarily felt in the center, because Israel's flourishing high-tech ventures operate mainly there. For example, 80 percent of those employed in the high-tech sector work in the Tel Aviv area.[5]

Gender Gaps in Education and Income

Surprisingly, the gender gaps in Israel are not consistently disappearing. In 1951, the Equal Rights for Women Law was enacted and women were conscripted into the IDF. Thus, the ethos of gender equality already existed when the state was born. However, the reality of disparities between women and men is more complex and, in areas like earnings, women and men have both advanced, but the original gap remains.

Over the years, women have made substantial progress in legislation and litigation, primarily in preventing discrimination and boosting the representation of women.[6] However, legislation alone does not change reality. Women have gained increasing political representation: From a low of seven MKs in the 1988 election, to a record thirty-two in the 2015 election, which is 27 percent of the legislature. This moved Israel into sixty-first place in an international ranking of women's representation in parliaments. Still, in the government elected in 2015, only three of the twenty ministers were women. In local government, which often serves as a springboard to national politics, only 2 percent of Israel's mayors are women.

Women constitute a majority at all levels of higher education (57% in 2014). They continue to account for a large percentage in schools of education and nursing, but women are increasingly entering other fields: More than 50 percent in schools of business and management, law, medicine, and biology. In engineering, architecture, and physics, the percentage of women is still low, but rising. Nonetheless, general employment rates are changing more slowly: For instance, there is a low percentage

[5] *Independent Cities Forum et al. v. Israel Lands Council* 2011. On the impact of suburbanization on housing and employment in Israel, see Czamanski 2003.

[6] For example, *Miller v. Minister of Defense* 1994, which allowed women to enter the IDF training course for pilots, and *Israel Women's Network v. Government of Israel* 1994, which mandated representation for women on the directorates of government companies.

of women in senior academic positions (26%), and only 13 percent of the most senior echelon are women (Council for Higher Education 2015).

The rate of women's participation in the work force is lower than that of men (about 58% compared to about 70% in 2012). It is low relative to western countries, in great part due to the low participation of Arab women. A number of other factors contribute to perpetuating the gender gap. First, the pattern of employment – the concentration of women in low-paying professions such as secretaries, child care, and teaching, and their low percentage in high-paying fields such as high-tech, where the ratio of men to women is 1.7 to 1. Second, women usually work part-time or fewer hours than men. Third, bias and discrimination – women in identical positions and with the same qualifications earn less than men. Fourth, norms such as the fact that women usually bear the burden of child care. Fifth, the rise in the birthrate among Jewish women (Tzameret-Kertcher 2014). The average monthly salary of women is about 68 percent of that of men (2013) because women work fewer hours, and the disparity in gross hourly income is about 15 percent (Swirski, Konor-Atias, and Rapoport 2015).

The participation rate of Arab women in the work force is relatively low (23% in 2013 compared to 60% among Jewish women), but rapidly rising. Interestingly, women entering the work force generally have an academic degree and earn more per hour than Arab men. The percentage of working, ultra-Orthodox women has been significantly growing too, and it is higher than that of ultra-Orthodox men, who generally devote their time to Torah study. Therefore, it is up to the woman to earn a livelihood. Within a decade, this rose from 51 percent (in 2003) to 71 percent (in 2014), compared to 45 percent for ultra-Orthodox men (Malach, Cohen, and Zicherman 2015).

C. Policy

Inequality, the absorption of immigrants from the former Soviet Union and Ethiopia, and the rifts within society are the principal policy challenges facing the political system in this period. Socioeconomic policy cannot be isolated from the "noisy" security environment – the many wars and military operations and the failures to make peace (see Tables 14.1–14.3 in Chapter 14). And, politically, the murder of Yitzhak Rabin (1995), direct election of the prime minister (1996–2003), the frequent government changes – all contributed to instability, boosted the power of the sectoral parties, and harmed the steering capacity of the political system, including the socioeconomic sphere.

Immigrant Absorption

The new policy toward immigrants from the former Soviet Union was called "direct absorption" – direct financial support to enable them to choose a place of residence and find a job. The state did not operate central absorption as in the past, though the Ministry of Immigrant Absorption and the Jewish Agency remained involved, either directly or through voluntary organizations. Most of the immigrants preferred to buy apartments in urban areas close to members of their family, resulting in geographic concentrations of Russian-speaking immigrants (D. Hacohen 2001, 467–71). The change from "collective absorption" of the immigrants, aimed at serving national objectives, to "private absorption" paralleled similar changes in the society. The melting pot approach had sought to disconnect immigrants from their past and integrate them into Israeli society and culture. In the 1990s and 2000s, veteran Israelis no longer expected the immigrants to assimilate, but rather to blend into a society that had become more pluralist – the "Israelization" of the culture and identity would occur naturally, and there was greater acceptance of groups with diverse identities.

The Ethiopian immigrants required a different policy. Unlike the 1950s, now there was recognition of the importance of preserving a group's tradition and culture, and of the fact that the wide gap between them and the absorbing society demanded a comprehensive approach to enable them to become part of modern life. In practice, however, the policy led to their segregation. Most children of Ethiopian immigrants were sent to schools and youth villages affiliated with the religious sector. Consequently, they made up 80 percent of the pupils in these institutions. Placing the immigrants in mobile homes or public housing among disadvantaged populations in peripheral cities (such as Afula, Kiryat Gat, Ashkelon, Ashdod, and Beersheba) created "Ethiopian neighborhoods." Even when offered the opportunity to purchase apartments, these immigrants preferred to live near their relatives. The absorption difficulties exacerbated the disparities between them and the rest of society on many socioeconomic indexes, even three decades after the wave of immigration and into the second and third generations (see above).

Education Policy

In the 1980s, there was a growing demand for pluralism and democratization of the education system. Accordingly, parents were offered wider choices, and unique and autonomous educational frameworks were established for various populations. Creeping privatization began at the primary school level (secondary education was already mostly independent), thus shifting more responsibility from the state to the individual (the pupils' parents). The guiding values were pluralism, choice, decentralization, self-management, and excellence (Yonah and Dahan 1999). This constituted a complete retreat not only from the uniformity envisioned by the melting pot approach, but also from the idea of integration. One example is the Kedma educational network created by Mizrahi intellectuals as an alternative to the education system (Pasternak 2003, 969). Another is El Hama'ayan, the separate school system of Shas geared for ultra-Orthodox and traditional Mizrahi pupils. The proliferation of democratic and experimental schools reflects the dissatisfaction with the education system and the trend toward establishing private schools that are largely funded by the state. The number of pupils in separate frameworks is growing: Of about 2.1 million pupils in 2014, nearly 500,000 (about 25%) were enrolled in the independent ultra-Orthodox schools (Aguda and El Hama'ayan), and other "recognized schools" that are not part of the state system (Knesset website, 2015).

Education policy was also directly affected by political instability – the frequent turnover of education ministers, who sought to leave their mark on the system by changing matriculation exam requirements, revising programs of study in accordance with their ideology, or instituting comprehensive reforms. One such attempt at reform was the Dovrat Committee (2005), which proposed sweeping pedagogical, structural, and organizational reform of the education system designed to strengthen public education, raise scholastic achievement, narrow disparities between sectors, create a high-quality pedagogical continuum from kindergarten through high school, extend the school day, grant pedagogical, administrative, and budgetary autonomy to school principals, add more depth to civic, social, and community education, improve the teaching profession and the status of teachers, and partner with the parents of the students (ibid., 1–17). This report was designed to generate a revolution in the education system, but was never implemented due to opposition from the teachers' unions, which contended, *inter alia*, that instead of aspiring toward an education system of solidarity and integration, it would intensify the trend of separation in education and encourage competitive education that is only interested in measuring achievement rather than content (Zelikovich 2004).

The Israeli education system is not a success story anymore. The task of policymakers is to create a shared core for the various educational institutions to ensure an educational common denominator that can connect the diverse parts of society, even if this connection is weak.

D. Socioeconomic Policy

While in the 1960s Israel was one of the world's most egalitarian societies, in the 2010s its level of inequality is among the most extreme of developed nations. The trend of prioritizing the market economy strengthened in light of globalization, the opening of the Israeli market to foreign investments, and the import of foreign workers to replace Palestinians who stopped working in Israel after the Intifada. Israel's neoliberal economic policy reduced state intervention in the economy, but in doing so it abandoned the principles of the welfare state and extended privatization to social services in education, health, and welfare. Government spending as a share of GDP plummeted from 70 percent in 1980 to 41.5 percent in 2013, and placed Israel below the OECD average and into twenty-second place among developed nations (OECD 2011).

The Israeli economy advanced from the 1990s, primarily thanks to technological developments that led to unprecedented growth in the high-tech industry. Immigrants from the former Soviet Union contributed to this growth, as did the peace process during the Rabin administration. This growth slowed in 1996–2000, and the year 2000 ended in recession due to the bursting of the "high-tech bubble" and the second Intifada, which harmed tourism-related businesses and the economy in general. The following years saw many ups and downs, especially after the global economic crisis in 2008, but the government adopted measures that prevented instability and succeeded in accelerating economic growth. In general, GDP per capita rose (from NIS 82,279 in 1995 to NIS 114,272 in 2010, and to NIS 133,942 in 2015 at 2010 prices) (CBS 2014a, table 14.2 and OECD Stat. 2015), though growth has slowed since 2011 and GDP per capita in Israel is slightly lower than the average in OECD countries. Since 2003, Israel's growth rate has been higher than other developed nations, but has slowed from nearly 5 percent in 2010 to 2.5 percent in 2015 (International Monetary Fund 2016). Thus, Israel's economy is growing at a moderate pace, but the fruits of this growth are not distributed equally.

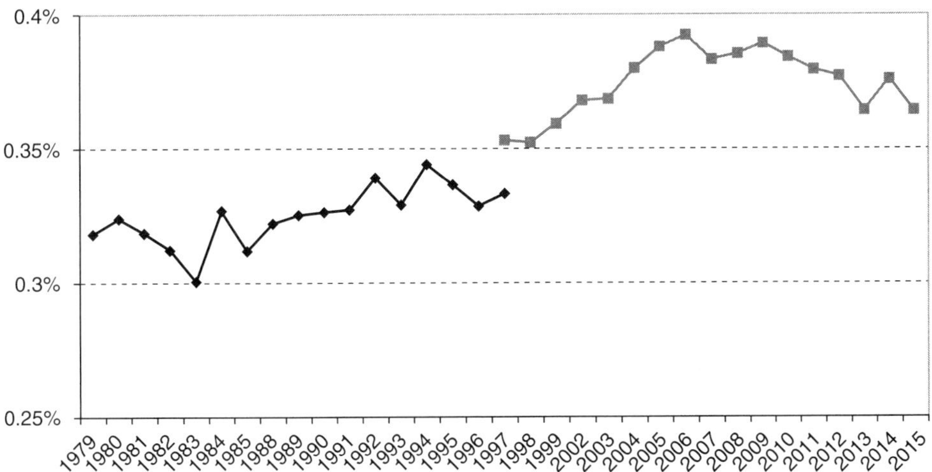

Figure 16.4 Gini index of inequality in the distribution of household disposable income after transfer payments and direct taxation (1979–2015)
Note: A new sample was introduced in 1997 that includes East Jerusalem, hence the different shades of the two lines plotted.
Source: National Insurance Institute *Annual Report* 2015, 37.

Inequality

The Gini index[7] of income inequality (Figure 16.4) shows a general trend of growth in income inequality, despite a slight decrease in the level of inequality since 2009: Accordingly, inequality as measured by the Gini index rose about 1.2 percent in the years 1999–2015 (after government intervention via transfer payments and direct taxation). Inequality is also on the rise in other countries, but what is unique to Israel is the rapid transition from a relatively egalitarian society to a society of wide disparities. While inequality grew by 5.3 percent on average in OECD countries from the mid-1980s through 2012, it grew by 13.8 percent in Israel (Swirski, Konor-Atias, and Rapoport 2015). In 2008, Israel was second only to the United States on inequality in a ranking of thirty western countries (OECD 2011), and in 2013 Israel was ranked fifth of thirty-four countries, with only Chile, Mexico, Turkey, and the United States ranked more unequal (ibid.).

Increased inequality is related to global economic trends, such as the globalization of merchandise and services, which exposes local production to competition from imports. It is also related to internal structural change in Israel toward a knowledge economy that favors those with higher education and creates income gaps between workers. Other more unique reasons for the growth in inequality in Israel include an increase in the most disadvantaged populations (the ultra-Orthodox and Arabs) and the immigration from the former Soviet Union, which initially increased the number of unskilled workers. Foreign workers also contributed to inequality because their employment led to a drop in wages in agriculture and construction, and pushed Israeli workers (primarily Arabs) out of these fields. In terms of policy initiatives, the

[7] The Gini index measures inequality in the hourly and monthly wages of salaried workers. The index ranges between 0 and 1, with 0 representing absolute equality and 1 absolute inequality.

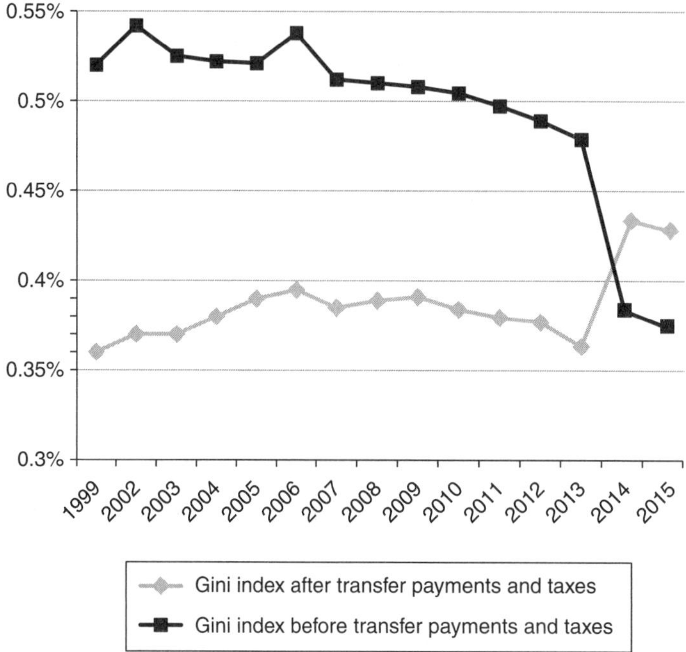

Figure 16.5 Gini index of income inequality before and after transfer payments and taxes (1999–2015)
Source: National Insurance Institute *Annual Report* 2015, 37.

rise in inequality after emerging from the recession in 2003 stemmed from cutbacks in welfare allowances (D. Ben-David 2010, 17–44) and increased regressive, indirect taxation. The Histadrut Labor Federation also weakened, resulting in less protection for the rights of low-paid workers (M. Dahan 2001, 630–31).

Progressive direct taxation and transfer payments help reduce inequality in Israel (Figure 16.5). However, inequality worsened even *after* state intervention, primarily due to cuts in welfare allowances and transfer payments and a reduction in the overall progressiveness of the tax system, which catered to Israelis with high incomes. In 1999, the mitigation of inequality (as measured by the Gini index) after transfer payments and taxes was about 30 percent in 2015

Inequality and Government Policy

INCOME GAPS. Since the 1990s, the general trend has clearly been one of socioeconomic polarization – the fruits of growth were divided in a way that created a very wealthy echelon, a very poor underclass, and a shrinking middle class. The blow to the middle class exacerbated inequality because the middle class is supposed to moderate disparities between the extremes (Swirski and Konor-Atias 2004). Polarization between rich and poor in Israel is one of the most extreme among western countries: The average income of the top decile in 2009 was about seven times higher than that of the lowest decile. Nearly half of Israel's income from capital and labor is in the hands of the top 20 percent, compared to 3 percent in the hands of the bottom 20 percent. That is, progressive income tax and transfer payments only slightly mitigate the disparity: The share of the top quintile in total income decreases by about 7 percent and the share of the bottom rises by about 3 percent (National Insurance Institute 2010, 39). In 2013, there was a slight decrease in inequality of income distribution, including a rise in the income of the lowest quintile without a parallel increase in the top quintile. However, disposable income per capita of the top 20 percent was still 7.1 times higher than that of the bottom 20 percent and 17.5 times higher when including income derived from market forces (work, pensions, and capital) (National Insurance Institute 2014, 62).

The policy adopted by Israeli governments in the 2000s, inspired by neoliberal ideas ("growth will benefit everyone"), launched a pincer movement of sharp cuts in both taxes and allowances, and this quickly worsened inequality. The wealthy were the main beneficiaries of the tax cuts, while cutbacks in allowances mainly harmed the poor. The reduction of total revenues from direct taxation (income tax, health tax, and social security tax) led the government to increase the share of indirect taxation (VAT, fuel excise tax, real estate purchase taxes). The ratio between indirect and direct taxation reached nearly 50 percent in 2011 and has remained so in 2015 (Bassok 2015), placing Israel among the five highest in the world on this measure (Sussman and Spivak 2011). This tax system imposes a heavy burden on the middle and lower classes, and increases inequality (Trajtenberg Committee 2011, 63–86).

POVERTY. The poverty line in Israel is defined as half the median disposal income per capita (Achdut 2009). This is a relative index that changes over time in accordance with market trends, therefore it is important to examine the rates of change. Figure 16.6 shows that, from the mid-1990s, the number of families living below the poverty line continually grew, and that the scope of poverty was stable from 2006 to 2008 at about 20 percent, followed by a moderate decline in poverty. Nonetheless, the poverty rate in Israel is much higher than the average in OECD countries (18.6% in 2013 versus 11.1%, respectively). The low support for the poor in Israel means that even according to the index of "economic income" (after direct taxes and transfer payments), the percentage of people lifted out of poverty is low in comparison to other countries. A disturbing finding is that, in the overall population, about 13 percent of the families with a working head of household are living under the poverty line (National Insurance Institute 2014).

The poverty rate in Israeli society is higher among particular groups and in the periphery. The ultra-Orthodox are poorest because of their high birthrate and scant participation in the work force; the Arabs are the next-poorest group, constituting about a third of impoverished families due to their high birthrate, unemployment, low levels of education and wages, and relatively low participation of women in the work force. In 2013, however, the poverty rate declined among Arab families primarily because more Arab women became employed (National Insurance Institute 2014). New immigrants who live in the periphery have the third-highest rate of poverty. As noted, poverty is also a matter of geography: Most of the poor are concentrated in Jerusalem (about a third of the families), in the north (close to a third), and in the south (about a quarter of the families). Thus, the poverty line largely overlaps demographics: Most of the ultra-Orthodox and Arabs live in these regions. Other groups with a high and persistent level of poverty are single-parent families and the elderly.

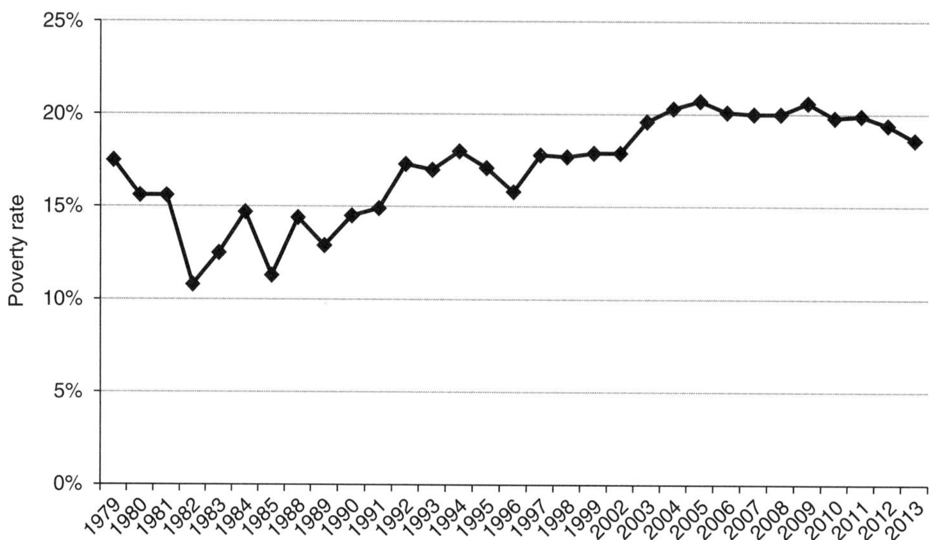

Figure 16.6 Poverty among all families in the population after transfer payments and direct taxes (1979–2013)
Note: A new sample was introduced in 1997 that includes East Jerusalem.
Source: National Insurance Institute 2014.

There are objective reasons for poverty in Israel, such as large family size and low employment rate among Arabs and the ultra-Orthodox. Although impoverished groups exist in all western countries, the number of families living below the poverty line in western countries is much lower than in Israel. Most support for the poor in Israel is low relative to other developed nations, and meager government assistance is one reason for the broad scope of poverty (M. Dahan 2007). The drastic and rapid changes in Israel were, therefore, the result of government policy.

UNEMPLOYMENT. There is a connection between unemployment rates and the levels of inequality and poverty. Figure 16.7 shows the fluctuations in unemployment rates – from about 4 percent in the 1970s to a peak of 11 percent in 2003. In recent years, unemployment rates have declined, dropping to 5.9 percent in 2014, despite a slower pace of economic growth. However, unemployment is still high among the weaker groups, including Arabs and residents of development towns. The allowances policy purports to encourage employment and, accordingly, the assistance provided to the unemployed is less than that of their European counterparts, primarily in terms of the eligibility period for unemployment benefits.

The issue of unemployment brings into sharp focus the tension between two opposing socioeconomic views. One contends that unemployment and need are symptoms of a socioeconomic policy that does not allow *certain* groups (such as single mothers, immigrants, the elderly, and residents of the periphery) to integrate into the work force, therefore a comprehensive and targeted policy is needed to improve their situation. The second contends that unemployment is a personal problem, and the solution must therefore be found by the individual. The latter approach prevailed in Israel during the 2000s; accordingly, the government pursued a "welfare-to-work"

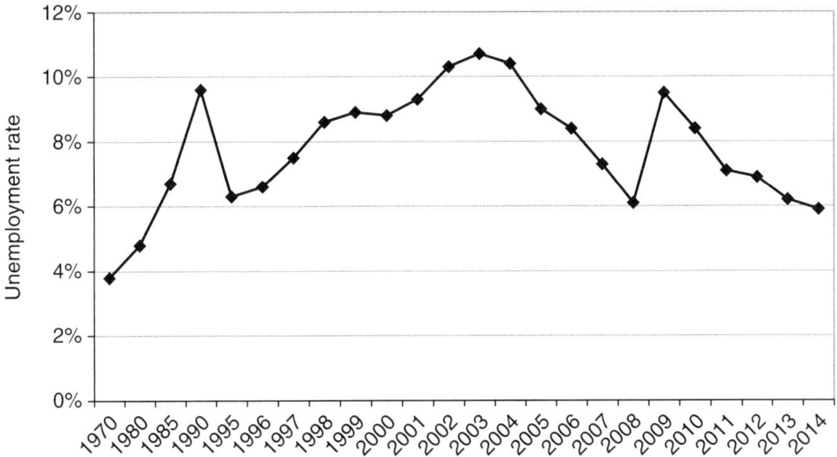

Figure 16.7 Unemployment rates (1970–2014) (%)
Sources: Bank of Israel 2006, Statistical Appendix; for 2007–11, Bank of Israel 2012; for 2012–14, Bank of Israel *Annual Report* 2015.

policy (the "Wisconsin Program") aimed at lowering the number of unemployed and pushing them into the work force through state-funded training programs. This policy of job placement instead of monetary assistance and transfer payments was contrary to the welfare policy of the 1960s and 1970s. Criticism against giving support to the unemployed intensified after the 1980s with the familiar (and unsubstantiated) contention that free handouts encourage people to prefer idleness and refrain from work. Accordingly, there was a large cut in transfer payments and stricter criteria were defined for receiving unemployment and income support benefits (Doron 2005).

E. The End of the Welfare State?

In Israel's first decades, the state (and the Histadrut) were involved in the economy and assumed responsibility for providing social services. To that end, the National Insurance Institute was created and the Compulsory Education Law was enacted; health, absorption, and housing services were provided; and a system of welfare services was developed for individuals in need. Since the 1980s, and especially during the 2000s, the policy changed and the state's commitment to its citizens' welfare has diminished significantly. Social spending as a percentage of all government expenditure rose during the 1990s, primarily due to the aging of the population, the immigration from Ethiopia and the former Soviet Union, and the rise in unemployment (Figure 16.8), though the level of public welfare spending as a percentage of GDP was still low relative to OECD countries. Since 2002, social spending has declined to an average of 37 percent. The level of allowances provided to weak populations in Israel is significantly lower than the norm in developed countries, far from that of France or Denmark, and even lower than in the United States, which does not purport to be a welfare state (M. Dahan 2009).

The fluctuations in social spending reflect opposing trends. On the one hand, there was a retreat from welfare policy inspired by neoliberal ideology, reflected

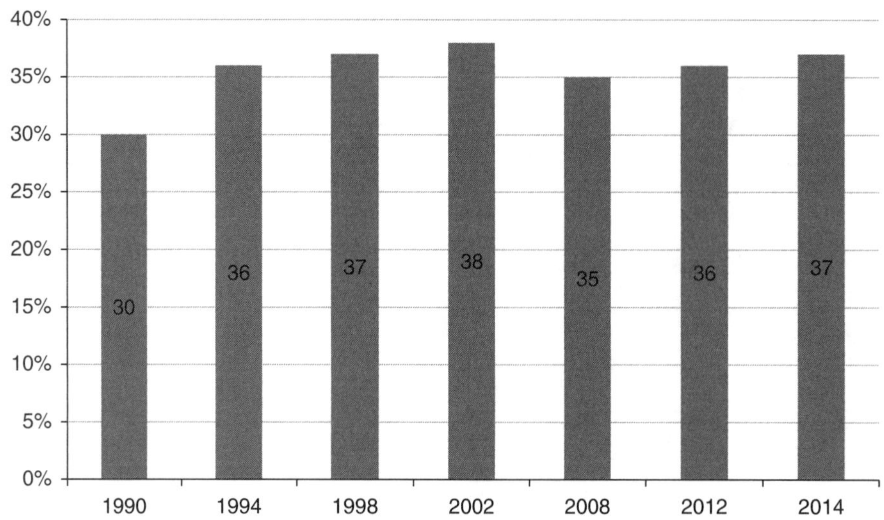

Figure 16.8 Social expenditures as a percentage of total government expenditure (1990–2014)
Sources: Horev and Kop 2009, 32; Ben-David 2014, 267.

in cutbacks to welfare allowances, smaller employer contributions to the National Insurance Institute, and creeping privatization of social services (Galnoor et al. 2015, 87–137). On the other hand, some social services expanded: The National Health Insurance Law (1994) mandated compulsory health insurance for the entire population; higher child allowances were extended to those who did not serve in the army; and partial funding of nursing services was provided via the National Insurance Institute (Rosenhek 2006, 239–40). However, even progressive social legislation such as the National Health Insurance Law, aimed at ensuring equal health service for all citizens regardless of their economic ability, was eroded by a "free market" policy. Over time, responsibility for a growing share of the payments was shifted to the citizens, the state-provided "health basket" shrank, and private supplementary insurance grew. The result was a gap between health services for different populations and an increase in the share of household spending on health services (Aviram, Gal, and Kattan 2007, 17–32; Shvartz and Davidovich 2005; Swirski, Konor-Atias, and Rapoport 2015).

The cumulative result was a retreat from the commitments of the welfare state, driven by a neoliberal ideology that derides state services (except security and police) and sanctifies the market. Since 1984, all the governments in Israel have adopted a consistent policy of privatization, even if not a systematic one. The underlying assumption of this policy is that the private-business market is more efficient and less corrupt than the public bureaucracy. Based on this assumption, privatization was implemented in a very broad range of public services (Galnoor et al. 2015, 480–505). These changes blurred the boundaries of responsibility of the private, social, and state sectors, as well as collaboration among the sectors, which is sometimes fruitful and other times problematic. The third sector (see Chapter 12) has also taken upon itself, either willingly or out of necessity, areas of responsibility that were previously within the purview of the state. For instance, during the second Lebanon War, when government ministries and the local governments barely functioned in the north, over two hundred social organizations swung into action to fill this void.

The policy of privatization also marked the transition from a society that had assigned many obligations to the state into a consumer society that emphasizes the role of citizens as individual "customers." Increased regulation has been presented as a way to ensure the quality of the privatized services, but the success of regulation in privatized fields such as education, welfare, public transportation, and pensions has been rather limited. Against this backdrop, the Ministry of Finance initiated an attempt to privatize a prison in 2004 – to transfer it from state responsibility to a private commercial company that won a tender. In response to a petition, the High Court restored state control over the prison, ruling that privatizing incarceration violates the prisoners' human rights (*Academic Center of Law and Business v. Minister of Finance* 2005; Barak-Erez 2011; Galnoor 2006; B. Sheleg 2006). The question of state control arose in a different way in 2014 in a fierce dispute over royalties from huge natural gas deposits in Israel's coastal waters. It turned out that in the concessions awarded to private companies that invested in drilling and discovered the gas after a long period, the state did not properly safeguard its citizens' greatest natural resource to date – *inter alia*, it failed to ensure competition and to demand a fair share of the royalties (B. Sheffer 2011).

In addition, there was increasing use of "contract workers" who do not enjoy the rights of salaried employees; labor organizations became less powerful; and the special needs of the growing elderly population and single-parent families were ignored. In these examples, government policy had a negative impact on the socioeconomic fabric of Israel, engendering a greater inequality and more widespread poverty. A policy that relies on exclusive market considerations tends to exclude long-term social repercussions, such as social solidarity, protection of rights, and concern for the needy and disadvantaged.

Inequality is not only a product of socioeconomic factors, but also a cause that creates a reality. It has an effect on political instability and democracy: The lower the socioeconomic level, the less political participation (Verba et al. 1995). The state's disavowal of responsibility for the individual's welfare and social security is liable to erode public confidence in the political system and undermine the democratic foundations. Indeed, as shown in Chapter 8, this occurred in Israel in the 2000s – a sharp decline in public trust in political institutions, as well as voting rates in local and Knesset elections. Inequality is also a reflection of the social and political situation.

16.6 The Newcomers and their Political Participation

The "newcomers" are those who arrived en masse after 1948. Here we present the patterns of and the barriers to their participation during the three time periods described above.

A. The Statist Period

Political participation in Israel's early days, in narrow terms of voting in elections, was certainly widespread. At the same time, not all the different groups of immigrants formed independent political organizations, and no immigrant party (whether from the east or west) had electoral success.[8] The mass immigration during the state's early years did not significantly change the balance of power among the parties. The general explanation for this is that new immigrants had no choice but to support the existing parties, the dominant party Mapai in particular, because they were dependent on the parties, the Histadrut, and the Jewish Agency for work, health services, housing, education, and the like. Resources were allocated according to the "party key" and this preserved the existing balance of power between the main parties. This also explains why Mapai was dominant, but its electoral strength remained rather stable over the years, and it never won an outright majority on its own.

The Mizrahi immigrants were much more dependent on the absorbing institutions, as Ephraim Kishon portrayed so effectively in his film *Salah Shabati*. Their traditional ethnic frameworks made it easier to mobilize them politically.

Already in 1949, there were demonstrations by unemployed immigrants in the transit camps, but they were quickly suppressed. In 1959, immigrants from Morocco rioted in Wadi Salib, an impoverished neighborhood in Haifa, and the unrest spread to other concentrations of immigrants from North Africa. During the riots, Mapai institutions were attacked, stores were looted, and demonstrators and policemen were injured. After the rapid and aggressive suppression of the protest, the government appointed a public commission of inquiry and announced new development programs. The transition from protest to party organization in the Knesset elections in 1959 was unsuccessful. In the short term, this spontaneous protest did not leave a mark on the political system. However, it illustrated the challenge posed by the deprived Mizrahi community. In retrospect, the Wadi Salib events symbolize the awakening of political consciousness among Mizrahim (Dahan Kalev 1999).

The immigrants in general, and the Mizrahim in particular, were largely unable to become autonomous citizens and gain access to political resources. Some of the western immigrants had an advantage in this area because of their political awareness (not necessarily democratic) or because it was easier for them to integrate into the existing socio-political fabric. In any case, the veteran party establishment regarded the immigrants as objects to be manipulated and recruited, not as citizens with independent preferences.

B. The Period of "Cleavages" (late 1960s to mid-1980s)

The two salient changes during this period were a fierce anti-establishment protest by a small group of activists who called themselves the Black Panthers, and a broad and gradual shift of voters from Mapai to a non-ethnic and long-established opposition party (Herut), ultimately bringing it to power. The main reasons for this include the maturation of the second generation of Mizrahi immigrants, and the growing sense of discrimination and resentment toward the absorbing institutions (led by

[8] Ethnic-based political organizations existed during the Yishuv period (the Yemenite Association and the Sephardic List), but even then this ran contrary to the prevailing norms, which favored ideological parties and rejected ethnic ones. These ethnic parties participated in the elections for the first three Knessets, but won little representation and were swallowed up by Mapai. Ethnic parties already participated in local elections in 1950, but they were sponsored by national parties, primarily Mapai and the National Religious Party.

Mapai). It should be noted that some of this occurred after the shock of the Yom Kippur War and the loss of faith in the political system.

The Black Panthers unleashed what is referred to in Hebrew as the "ethnic demon." They were a group of young people of North African heritage from poor and large families in the Musrara neighborhood of Jerusalem; many were school dropouts who did not serve in the army, and a few had a criminal record. The sense of Mizrahi discrimination intensified in light of the enthusiastic reception and improved absorption conditions given to the "Russian" immigrants in the 1970s. Inspired by street counselors and socially aware academics from Hebrew University, these young people demonstrated against the government, demanding equal allocation of resources, chanting: "We want our piece of the pie; if not, there will be no pie." Their demands, as defined when they registered as an association, included eliminating impoverished neighborhoods, free education and housing for the poor, shutting down institutions for juvenile delinquents and placement in agricultural boarding schools, and representation of Mizrahim in public institutions.

The response of the political system to the unconventional protest of the Black Panthers was predictable: disregard, astonishment, resentment, a sense of insult, disparagement of the activists, and their portrayal in the media as criminals who threaten society. An effort was also made to snuff out the protest by arresting the demonstrators. After the protest gained steam and won public sympathy, an effort was made to solve the individual problems of the leaders, as reflected in the meeting between Prime Minister Golda Meir and Black Panther leaders (Black Panthers 1971). The prime minister asked each of the participants about their personal lives (especially their place of work), and they tried to explain that it was not a matter of personal problems:

> We didn't come to talk about my personal job, because if this was only my problem, that would be great. There's a problem of the Sephardim, who comprise 65% of the population in Israel. The situation of this group is bad and they live on the poverty line. (Meir Abargil in Black Panthers 1971)

> We didn't come to tell our life story, we came to warn you. (Saadia Marciano in ibid.)

Another predictable response was co-optation of Black Panther leaders by existing parties. It took time before the leaders perceived it as a real problem; it was initially defined in terms of needed resources for welfare services and a problem of the Mizrahim rather than a general social issue. "It is true that there is poverty in Israel," noted Prime Minister Golda Meir, "but I don't agree that there is discrimination." The prime minister later formed a public committee to study the situation of children and teenagers in distress, and welfare budgets were increased (D. Bernstein 1979; Hofnung 2006).

The Black Panthers were active for only a short time and did not manage to leverage their support to gain parliamentary representation, primarily because of internal divisions. In the 1973 elections, two "Panthers" lists competed – had they run as a unified list, they would have won Knesset seats. The Black Panthers movement is recorded in the socio-political history of Israel as the instigator of a "formative confrontation" that highlighted the issue of the ethnic gap and the links among social change, political consciousness, and socioeconomic policy. The young people who organized the protest demonstrations in 2011, who were not yet born during the Panthers' time, invited a veteran Panther, Charlie Biton, to speak at their rally.

The development that changed Israeli politics was the groundswell of Mizrahi votes for the opposition party. An independent Mizrahi party did not arise, but the Likud – with its Ashkenazi leadership – became identified with the Mizrahi public. Already in the 1973 elections, more Mizrahim voted for the Likud than for Labor, and this trend continued, leading to the political "upheaval" in 1977. In these elections, 46 percent of first-generation Mizrahim (many of whom had previously voted for Mapai) and 65 percent of second-generation Mizrahim voted for the Likud. In 1981, two-thirds of the Likud's voters were Mizrahim (Arian and Shamir 1982, 93–97). The weakening hold of the party machinery on the Mizrahi immigrants, particularly those in development towns, and the maturation of a new and more critical generation, contributed to the change in voting patterns (Ben-Zadok and Goldberg 1983). Indeed, the policies of the Likud government in the years 1977–84 reflected changes in the support of Mizrahi voters – the neighborhood revitalization program (Project Renewal), the expansion of welfare services, and the policy of integration in education.

Mizrahi voting for the Likud was more than a protest vote, because these voters also identified with the Likud's hawkish positions. Thus, the ethnic issue converged with the party's views on foreign affairs and security. Ostensibly, the allocation of enormous resources for the construction of settlements in the territories conquered in 1967 should have aroused opposition among the disadvantaged Mizrahim, because this came at the expense of the development towns and poor neighborhoods. However, public opinion polls in the 1980s showed that first- and second-generation Israelis of Asian-African origin expressed more hawkish and militant views than their counterparts of European-American origin in regard to the occupied territories, the settlements, the peace process, and the Palestinians. What explains the overlap between hawkishness and Mizrahi origin? One possibility is that the frustration and alienation from the Labor Party drove Mizrahim to abandon its more dovish position, while the newfound support for the Likud engendered identification with the party's hawkishness. A second explanation emphasizes the contact that developed after 1967 between Jews from Arab countries and the Palestinians in the economic market. According to this approach, the negative attitude toward Palestinian Arabs derived from the fact that they posed a threat to the Mizrahim as competitors for jobs and social status. Some add a cultural threat, suggesting that hawkishness and intolerance toward the Arabs reflected an attempt to disassociate from the Arab characteristics of the Mizrahi identity. A third explanation is that Mizrahi origin in itself is not the determining factor in hawkishness; rather, the intervening variable is education: The higher the level of education among Mizrahim, the less inclined they are to support the Likud (Y. Peres 1971; Yishai 1985a).

Another political development was the gradual integration of Mizrahi immigrants in positions of political power that had previously been almost totally inaccessible to them. The change began in the local governments and the Histadrut, and in the 1960s and 1970s the number of Mizrahim also rose in the Knesset. In 1955, about 25 percent of the elected officials in local authorities were Mizrahim, and this climbed to 43 percent in 1965. Most were in development towns, not in the older cities, where "non-Ashkenazim" accounted for only about 20 percent of the elected officials (Weiss 1973, 69). While the representation of Mizrahim was growing, they were still under-represented on the highest rungs of political power (Smooha and

Peres 1974, 20–25), and those elected to the Knesset were not appointed to senior government positions before 1977 (Weiss 1977, 70).

C. Participation During the Pluralistic Period

Starting in the mid-1980s, the fragmentation of the party map – and the success of parties based on ethnic origin – reflected the changes in Israeli society. This was illustrated in the period of direct election of the prime minister in the 1990s: Many voters split their vote in these elections – voting for a major party candidate for prime minister and for a sectoral, "identity" party for the Knesset. This boosted the strength of Jewish ethnic parties (representing Mizrahim and Russian immigrants) and Arab separatist parties (in contrast to the Arab-Jewish Hadash party). As noted, Jewish ethnic parties were previously not accorded legitimacy and were unsuccessful in elections. The harbinger of change was the Tami (Movement for the Heritage of Israel) Party, which championed the link of religiosity and ethnicity, and most of its voters were of Moroccan origin. Tami won three seats in the 1981 elections and only one in 1984, and was assimilated into the Likud. Its presence was limited and short-lived, but Tami heralded the aspiration for political representation of the emerging Mizrahi middle class.

A different and larger Mizrahi public became a cohesive political power with the emergence of Shas (see Chapter 17). Shas was founded as a Sephardi, ultra-Orthodox party in protest of the discrimination of Mizrahim in Ashkenazi, ultra-Orthodox institutions. But Shas soon expressed the feelings of deprivation of a broad Mizrahi public, as well as the desire of its traditional members "to restore its glory of yore." Shas clearly stated its goal of restoring the lost dignity of Mizrahim, and insisted on referring to them as "Sephardim." It competed in the Knesset elections for the first time in 1984 and won four seats. Under the leadership of Aryeh Deri, it soared to a high of seventeen seats in the 1999 elections (making it the third-largest party in the parliament), in part as a response to the "Deri trial," which further kindled feelings of discrimination among the party's supporters (Deri was convicted of bribery and served a prison term). The strong support for a sectoral party such as Shas in the 1999 elections was also due to the split voting noted above. In subsequent Knesset elections, Shas won eleven or twelve seats, and was usually part of the coalition. In the 2015 election, Shas split and was reduced to only seven seats. Shas was unique in offering its voters not only a political-traditional home, but also essential services tailored to the needs of working-class Mizrahi families – an independent school network, religious institutions, and welfare services (Lehmann and Siebzehner 2006). Critics note that Shas has failed to narrow the gaps – for example, its schools do not teach universal content sufficiently.

A radical discourse of the "New Mizrahim" began in the 1990s, criticizing the "Ashkenazi hegemony" that turned the Mizrahim, alongside the Palestinians, into victims of the Zionist revolution. One expression was the formation of Keshet: The Mizrahi Democratic Rainbow – a group of Mizrahi intellectuals, second- and third-generation Israelis, who sought to bring "meaningful change in Israeli society and implement values of democracy, human rights, social justice, equality, and multi cultures" (www.ha-keshet.org.il). Keshet advocated a just distribution of resources and joined the struggle for the rights of public housing residents (Shalom Chetrit

2001, 330–31). It also initiated the demand for a redistribution of state lands held by the kibbutzim and moshavim. When the Israel Land Authority decided to rezone agricultural land for construction, allowing farmers to reap profits from state lands, Keshet petitioned the High Court, arguing that this violated the principle of equality in the allocation of state resources. The court concurred (*Mizrahi Democratic Rainbow v. Minister of National Infrastructure* 2000).

The emergence of sectoral parties was also reflected in initiatives by the immigrants from the former Soviet Union. Unlike newcomers from the 1950s, these immigrants came with political awareness and sought to ensure independent representation of their interests rather than integrating into existing parties. When they started to arrive in the late 1980s, the political system was already more open to ethnic group representation, and the separate political organization of the Russian immigrants fit into the new reality of Israeli society in which different groups were demanding their share of public resources. The immigrants from Russia were natural candidates for this in light of their number, their relatively high level of organization in civil society, their independent media outlets, and their lack of representation in the existing parties (T. Horowitz 2001). In the 1992 elections, there was still no separate ethnic party for about 250,000 Russian immigrants with the right to vote, and while their voting did not tip the scale in these elections, there was a clear tendency to vote for the left. The reasons for this vote were a protest against the absorption policy (the Likud government led by Yitzhak Shamir in the early 1990s) and the aspiration to change the public agenda from investing in settlements to absorbing immigration. In the 1996 elections, the Yisrael B'Aliyah party competed for the first time, led by Natan Sharansky. About 40 percent of the 400,000 Russian voters supported the party, giving it seven Knesset seats. The other 60 percent voted primarily for the Likud and right-wing parties. In the race for prime minister, most of the Russians preferred Benjamin Netanyahu to Shimon Peres, granting the former the victory (as they had done for Rabin in 1992 and as they would do for Barak in 1999 and Sharon in 2001). Again, the election system that enabled citizens to split their vote contributed to the coalescence of the Russian immigrants as an independent political force. It allowed them to express both their Russian sectoral preference in Knesset representation and a nationalist vote for prime minister (T. Horowitz 2001, 103–9, 118–20).

The Russians' political participation was evident already in the 1998 local elections – they managed to win about 15 percent of the officials elected, a percentage that exceeded their share of the population. In the 1999 Knesset election, over 50 percent of them voted for "Russian" parties: Yisrael B'Aliyah (36%), which won six seats, and Yisrael Beitenu led by Avigdor Lieberman (17%), which won four seats (Goldstein and Gitelman 2004). In the 2003 election, two continuous trends emerged: a decrease of independent Russian representation and a strengthening of support for the right. Over 80 percent of the Russians chose not to vote for Yisrael B'Aliyah, the only Russian party that competed in that election; it won only 16 percent of the votes and two Knesset seats, and later assimilated into the Likud. About a quarter of the immigrants voted for Yisrael Beitenu/National Union led by Avigdor Lieberman (three seats), a combination of an immigrant party and a far right-wing party. The rest of the Russian vote went to the Likud (25%), Shinui, which presented a secular platform (22%), and the Labor Party and Meretz (8%). In the 2006 election, the Russian vote enabled Avigdor Lieberman's party to win eleven seats, though many of them voted for Kadima, a centrist party. In the 2009 election, Yisrael Beitenu won fifteen seats and the National Union, four seats – about two-thirds of the votes came from Russian immigrants, who also awarded about five seats to the Likud and two to Kadima. In the 2013 election, Yisrael Beitenu aligned with the Likud (and won eleven seats as part of the Likud), but their combined strength declined relative to the previous Knesset.

In the 2015 election, Yisrael Beitenu competed on its own, but lost considerable power, dropping to only six seats; this was partly attributable to charges of major corruption involving senior party officials. Another reason was the party's emphasis on general right-wing, national, and anti-Arab themes, rather than issues closer to the immediate interests of the Russian immigrants. Consequently, there was also a decrease in voter turnout. In the absence of a "pure Russian" party, many Russian immigrants did not find a party with which they could identify: The other right-wing parties had a religious bent and therefore were not an attractive option for the secular immigrants, whose hawkish views prevented them from voting for leftist parties. Thus, it can be said that twenty-five years after the wave of immigration began, the immigrants' distinct political representation has weakened, especially among the second generation. Five MKs of Russian origin were elected on other party slates in the 2015 elections.

Polling data indicate that over 70 percent of Russian immigrants favor authoritarian characteristics of government, such as a strong leader and "a government of experts." A high percentage hold hawkish positions and negative views of the Arab minority in Israel. For example, 77 percent said the government should encourage Arabs to leave Israel (compared to 47% of the veteran Jewish public). In 2009, twenty years after the beginning of the large-scale immigration, many had a negative assessment of their integration into Israeli society: Many said they had yet to achieve the socioeconomic standing they had in their country of origin; only 60 percent felt a sense of belonging to the state and, among young people, only about 50 percent were sure they would like to live in Israel in the future (Arian, Philippov, and Knafelman 2009). Nonetheless, these immigrants have become more similar to the veteran population, with almost no differences between the general views of these two groups of Israelis. The Russian public, including its non-Jewish component, is undergoing a "sociological conversion" to mainstream Israeli society (Asher Cohen 2006).

Unlike the Russians, the immigrants from Ethiopia, many fewer in numbers, do not have separate political representation. There have been several MKs of Ethiopian origin, but their (weak) political presence has mainly been felt in waves of protest sparked by specific events, turning the spotlight on their distress, if only for a short time. In 1996, the Ethiopian public was enraged by the "blood donations" affair, when it was discovered that donations by Ethiopians were destroyed due to a fear of AIDS. This sparked violent demonstrations and led to the formation of a public committee to investigate the matter. In May 2015, there was a wave of protest by Ethiopians about police racism and violence, and about their discrimination in Israeli society. The demonstrations spilled into violence, and citizens and policemen were injured.

To summarize, new groups (Russians and Ethiopians, as well as asylum seekers) have recently joined Israeli society, and there has been a change in the political participation of the veteran group of traditional Mizrahim, who have become autonomous. Society has become more diverse and pluralistic, but also more polarized (Eisenstadt 2005, 7), and there is less willingness by various groups to cooperate on the basis of shared values and objectives. In parallel to the weakening of social cohesion, the inequality and socioeconomic disparities have widened due to government policy and the retreat from its commitments to welfare services (Bareli, Gutwein, and Friling 2005, 1). In the summer of 2011, a sweeping social protest erupted in Israel that largely transcended the old "cleavages" and expressed a demand for a different social ideology and policy (Feldhay, Yonah, and Galnoor 2012, 25–33).

16.7 Old Cleavages and New Inequality

The salient characteristic of Israeli society, dating back to the Yishuv period, is that it is sectoral, composed of various groups. However, the sectoral nature of the first four decades was different than that of the 2000s. In the early years, the aspiration was to turn society into a cohesive entity focused on shared content and objectives. Later, the society became more pluralistic and, with the exception of national mobilization during times of emergency, it seems to be a collection of groups, each with distinctive content, agendas, values, and aspirations. Some refer to this as "identity politics" because of the cultural, religious, national, geographic, and economic distinctions between the groups. Contrary to the ethos of inclusion and consensus that characterized Israeli society at its outset, the tendency toward conflict and separatism intensified (Eisenstadt 2005, 26–31) due to the weakness of integrative institutions, such as the Knesset and the inclusive political parties.

We noted the impact of neoliberalism that led to the state's retreat from responsibility and involvement – not only by selling government corporations, but also in welfare, education, and even the absorption of immigrants. Since the 1990s,[9] Israeli governments have implemented a consistent policy of privatization and outsourcing by transferring responsibility, ownership, service delivery, financing, and/or even regulation from the state to private commercial companies and third-sector organizations. This process has weakened the civil service and eroded yet another institution with integrative capacity. However, policy changes also reflect value transformations in the society – from collectivism to individualism (Ezrahi 1997). Thus, the state's retreat from excessive involvement in the lives of the individuals also boosted liberty, encouraged pluralism, and contributed to the growth of a dynamic and autonomous civil society.

Israeli society has been influenced by contrasting processes in the world, a phenomenon called "glocalization" – globalization and, sometimes in reaction, the strengthening of localism. Globalization has weakened the state and intensified the impact of international economic and technological developments. Concurrently, society has been eroded from below due to processes of coalescence and identification on an ethnic, religious, and cultural basis. The two processes may have conflicting

[9] In the past, the state and the Jewish Agency were involved in the absorption process; in the 1990s, immigrants were each given an "absorption basket" and expected to find housing and employment on their own. In the 2000s, encouraging immigration from North America was also privatized, transferred to the Nefesh B'Nefesh non-profit organization (Shpaizman 2011).

repercussions – an awareness of being "citizens of the world," together with a growing local multiculturalism – the mobility of ideas and people, together with a decline of solidarity and a widening of internal social gaps. (On glocalization, see Ram and Yiftachel 1999, 44–48.) The conflicting trends exist in Israel: openness and cosmopolitanism versus seclusion and xenophobia; a longing for solidarity versus splintering into hostile groups. Multicultural trends did not make the old cleavages disappear (Jews/Arabs, religious/secular, Ashkenazi/Mizrahi), but in the 2000s new "cleavages" emerged, engendered by the worsening inequality: poor versus rich; salaried workers versus tycoons; and periphery versus center. In part, these tensions overlap the old cleavages because there is a high percentage of Arabs and Mizrahim among the poor and residents of the periphery. Nonetheless, the neoliberal economic policy that sanctified market forces contributed to diverting the emphasis from a discourse of discrimination on an ethnic/national basis to a discourse of inequality in Israeli society.

The socioeconomic protest in the summer of 2011 epitomized these changes among significant parts of society, especially among young people. The "tent protest" was started by individuals who pitched tents on Rothschild Boulevard in Tel Aviv to protest the cost of housing. The scope and objectives of the protest soon widened under the slogan "The people demand social justice." Citizens from different sectors came together in mass demonstrations throughout the country, demanding that the government lower the cost of living with its onerous burden on the middle and lower classes; cut indirect taxation such as the tax on gasoline; and invest in public housing as well as education, health, and welfare services. Beyond specific demands, a call was sounded for returning to the welfare state, halting the policy of privatization, and instituting a policy based on social solidarity.

Pressured by the mass demonstrations, the government established the Committee for Socioeconomic Change (the "Trajtenberg Committee"), which proposed a long list of recommendations such as boosting the social services budget, increasing the progressiveness of the tax system, and expanding the supply of housing (2011). The government approved the report in October 2011. In parallel, the protest movement formed a committee of experts that proposed comprehensive and far-reaching solutions for social and economic reform in Israel – the "Spivak-Yonah Committee" (Yonah and Spivak 2012). By the end of 2015, only a few recommendations had been implemented (such as free education from age three), and the protest appears to have had no real significant results. However, it led to some changes in Israeli society and the public and political discourse:

- The protest placed socioeconomic issues at the top of the agenda in public discourse, including inequality, the cost of living, housing prices, privatization, and labor conditions. In the two election campaigns held since the protest (2013 and 2015), socioeconomic issues were accorded prominent space in the campaigns. However, the voters' ultimate decision was based on security and foreign relations issues, and the broad protest's demands were not reflected in the election results.
- Nonetheless, the protest served as a springboard for new parties that focused on socioeconomic issues, catering mainly to the Jewish middle class. In 2013, the Yesh Atid party led by Yair Lapid rode the waves of the protest and won nineteen

seats in the Knesset. In 2015, Yesh Atid weakened considerably (eleven seats), and the Kulanu party led by Moshe Kahlon emerged. The party's entry ticket to the Knesset (ten seats) was exclusively socioeconomic. In addition, three leaders of the protest entered the Knesset on the Labor Party slate.

- The protest reflected a change in the public's view of the state role and expressed opposition not only to the government's economic policy, but also to the underlying neoliberalism that had taken over the political agenda in Israel. The protest exposed the flaws of the system in which economic growth is not reflected in all segments of society, and expressed public longing for state involvement in providing welfare services. It called for reasserting its responsibility for areas such as education, health, and housing. All this ran contrary to the unbridled privatization pursued by Israeli governments, which abandoned important fields of life to market forces, transferring the state's roles to the business sector, under the assumption that it is more "efficient" and "not corrupt."
- The protest showed that embers of direct political participation are still burning in the Israeli public. What began as an exchange of messages and the mobilization of activists via the social channels quickly shifted to "traditional" patterns of participation, such as a continued presence in the street and mass demonstrations. After a long period of political apathy, a socioeconomic protest of unprecedented scope awakened on issues unrelated to security and foreign affairs. Protest tents were erected in cities throughout Israel and about half a million people participated in the demonstrations. However, while the protest spanned different political camps, key groups did not participate. Israelis from the poorest deciles in society viewed the protest as elitist and middle class, while the right-wing and national-religious public regarded it as a "left-wing," anti-government protest.

In light of these developments, the question again arises: Can the state shape the society? During the state's early years, the policy sought to mold society by direct intervention in all spheres of life. Gradually, the state stepped back and this trend accelerated in the early 1990s and stirred protest in the summer of 2011. The protestors argued that the government's economic policy was not simply "observing" free market forces and giving them free rein, but actually "intervening" on behalf of the rich and powerful in society. The immediate harvest of the protest was meager, but perhaps it marked a beginning of a new chapter in relations between state and society in Israel. To the question posed at the beginning of this chapter – whether inequality in society is a "malicious problem" that cannot be solved – the protesters responded with a resounding "no."

17 Religion and State: Between Social Conflict and Political Accommodation

17.1 The Challenge

> Despite the stipulations of Halakha [Jewish law] that normally restrict entry to the Temple Mount, in the current situation, when there is a fear of the loss of Jewish sovereignty on the Temple Mount, in this situation and for this purpose it is not only permitted but a sacred commandment to enter the Temple Mount. (Halakhic ruling by former Chief Rabbi Shlomo Goren, Davar, November 12, 1990)

Thus, some rabbis are willing to issue Halakhic rulings on political questions, and this can pose a dilemma for Orthodox Jews: Should they obey the religious ruling and violate the law of the state, or abide by the law and commit what has been represented as a religious transgression? The ruling suggests a willingness to mix the two worlds – commandments that are part of an individual's faith and commandments that are a political duty.[1] In this chapter, we address the question of how the state has contended with the challenge posed by Jewish religion.[2] We first present background data, followed by a political analysis of the issue, and conclude with policy decisions pertaining to relations between religion and the state.

According to Basic Law: Human Dignity and Liberty, the state of Israel is "Jewish and democratic." Numerous opinions have been expressed about this phrase, which seems to define the state's "identity." Ultra-Orthodox Jews do not recognize the state's "Jewishness" because it does not operate according to Torah law; religious Zionists recognize the secular state, but seek to infuse it with Jewish character (though not necessarily in accordance with Halakha); traditional Jews identify with the secular nature of the state, but also want public life to have religious Jewish characteristics; for secular Israelis, the state's connection to Judaism is primarily historical, national, cultural, and symbolic, and they oppose a state with religious identity whose laws dictate religious observance; immigrants from the former Soviet Union, most of them secular, emphasize the national character of the Jewish state and Israel

[1] Some try to resolve this by distinguishing between a "ruling" (*psak halakha*) and a "Torah opinion" (*da'at torah*) given by a religious sage, but not derived from Jewish law. In practice, the status of the rabbi is what determines the weight of the ruling or opinion in the eyes of the rabbi's followers.

[2] To that end, we distinguish between Jewish "religion" as a system of faith and observance of commandments, and "Judaism" as a mix of religion, tradition, culture, and nationalism.

as a place of refuge for those whose fate is bound up with the Jewish people, but they reject the imposition of religious law. For the Arab citizens of Israel, the term "Jewish state" means a state that is not democratic and, by definition, discriminates against non-Jewish citizens. When asked whether Israel can be both a democracy and a Jewish state, the majority of Jews in Israel say they believe it can be both, while most Arabs disagree. Although a majority of Jews (62%) think that democratic principles should take precedence over religious laws, 90 percent of the ultra-Orthodox and 65 percent of the religious think that if there is a contradiction between democratic principles and Halakha, the latter should prevail (Pew Research Center 2016).

These fundamentally different views reflect unbridgeable disagreements, and yet the political system is challenged to create a common denominator among the diverse groups. What Israel has, therefore, are political arrangements that inherently avoid making clear-cut decisions of principle and suffice with pragmatic measures. As discussed below, the effort to find a common denominator among the camps and to prevent the struggle over religion–state relations from becoming divisive and polarizing has led to deliberate ambiguity about the state's "identity" and complex, ad hoc arrangements that have not always been consistent. Compromises are a reflection of the "wickedness" of the problem, which has remained an open issue since the pre-state period. It has become clear that the political system lacks the strength to unequivocally resolve the religious question, while the indecision itself reinforces positions and makes the problem even more intractable. Changes in Israeli society and the balance of political power, as well as the divisions within the religious camp, indicate that the political system's handling of religious issues may have eased the short-term disputes, but yielded negative long-term results.

A. A Jewish State?

> Shall we end by having a theocracy? No, indeed. Faith unites us, science gives us freedom. We shall therefore prevent any theocratic tendencies from coming to the fore on the part of our priesthood. We shall keep our priests within the confines of their temples … they must not interfere in the administration of the state which confers distinction upon them, else they will conjure up difficulties without and within. (Herzl 1988, 147)

In Herzl's Jewish state, religion is within the purview of the individual and not a matter for the state to address. However, as Herzl himself soon learned, the bond between Jews and their religion is deep rooted, and secular Zionism could not ignore it. For many Jews, Judaism extended beyond the bounds of religion to encompass a national and personal identity. The UN decision on November 29, 1947 to form two states in the Land of Israel, Jewish and Arab, was copied to the Declaration of Independence that established "a Jewish State in the Land of Israel, to be known as the State of Israel." The "Jewishness" of the state in the Declaration bears several meanings: first, the historical and religious connection of Jews to the Land of Israel; second, the establishment of the "national home" according to Zionism, the national movement of the Jews, based on the right of the Jewish people to self-determination as expressed in the Balfour Declaration and recognized in the League of Nation's mandate and the UN resolution; third, the state as the aspiration of the Jewish nation – "This right is the natural right of the Jewish people to be masters of their own fate, like all other nations, in their own sovereign state." The "Jewishness" of Israel also appears in the statement of the Declaration of Independence that "the State of Israel will be open for Jewish immigration and for the ingathering of the exiles," expressing what would later become the Law of Return – granting automatic citizenship to every Jew who immigrates to Israel. This is the genesis of the complicated issue of "Who is a Jew?" – someone who defines him- or herself as a Jew? Or only if one is born to a Jewish mother? Or only if recognized as a Jew by the Orthodox movement of Judaism? Or also someone who underwent some form of conversion?

The Declaration of Independence also portends the potential future contradiction of the state being both "Jewish and democratic." The Declaration promises that the state will be based on freedom, justice, and peace; will ensure complete equality irrespective of religion, race, or sex; and will guarantee freedom of religion, conscience, language, education, and culture. This is not a formula for a theocratic state, but for a democratic one. Nonetheless, since Jewish nationality is also a religion, or is originally based on a religious definition, observant Jews can find numerous religious motifs in the Declaration. Thus, the diverse meanings of the term "Jewish state" date back to the beginnings of Zionism, and surfaced in a last-minute dispute between religious representatives who demanded that the Declaration of Independence include a reference to "the God of Israel," and some of the secular representatives who fiercely opposed this. The compromise that saved the day was the phrase "Rock of Israel" – both a name for God and an expression of the power of the people – and this was a harbinger of the political accommodations of the future. After Ben-Gurion read the Declaration, Rabbi Maimon, a representative of Agudat Yisrael, recited a traditional blessing as most of those present at the ceremony sat bareheaded, without the traditional head covering worn while reciting blessings (Segev 1986, 188; Asher Cohen 1997, 228). The extreme religious demand for a state governed by Jewish law poses a problem that cannot be resolved by the political system. However, most observant Jews do not share this demand, and politics has actually managed to establish arrangements that allow Israelis with conflicting world views to live together, while sidestepping fundamental decisions.

Since the enactment of the 1992 Basic Laws, which explicitly state that Israel is "Jewish and democratic," and additional legislation designed to ensure that the public sphere be Jewish, it has become customary to examine the question of state and religion in terms of "Jewish" versus "democratic." This tension, however, exposes only the tip of the iceberg, because there are also disagreements among the various groups – ultra-Orthodox, religious, traditional, and secular Jews; as well as among the movements (Orthodox, Conservative, and Reform) in Israel and overseas, and between Jews and members of other religions.

B. There Are Other Religions

In 2015, Jews accounted for 75 percent of Israel's population, 18 percent were Muslim (including those living in East Jerusalem and the Golan Heights), 2 percent were Christian (including non-Arab Christians), 2 percent were Druze, and 4 percent other (CBS *Statistical Abstract* 2015, table 2.2). Among the Arab population, 8 percent defined themselves as very religious, 47 percent as religious, 27 percent as not very religious, and 18 percent as non-religious (CBS 2010). In the past, nearly all the Christians in Israel were Arabs (see Chapter 15). Since the 1990s, some of the Christians are immigrants from the former Soviet Union who received citizenship under the amended Law of Return by virtue of their Jewish relatives. Most do not define themselves as religious (Sicron 1994). Accordingly, the complicated issue of personal status laws in Israel (as discussed below) is not confined to Jews; members of other religious groups also face this complication if they wish to marry in a civil procedure. The law in Israel does not provide an option of civil marriage for people who are not religious or for "mixed" marriages between members of different religions – and this applies equally to Jews and non-Jews. As of today, marriages conducted by a Reform or Conservative rabbi are also not recognized by the state. Similarly, Reform or Conservative conversions conducted in Israel are not recognized. However, in the wake of Supreme Court rulings (see below), the state recognizes conversions that are conducted entirely or in part outside Israel.

C. Judaism: Nationality, Culture, Religion

Despite the trend toward secularization in the modern era, religion remains a central factor in politics, including democratic countries. We present here models of state–religion relations and consider which are appropriate for Israel.

At the extreme is the *theocracy* operating under the laws of the only religion permitted in the state and led by clergy. There are no full theocracies today, though in Muslim states like post-1979 Iran, Islam dictates the affairs of state and public life, and legislation in conflict with the Quran is prohibited. At the other end of the spectrum is the *separation* model, which decrees the state's absolute neutrality vis-à-vis religion, and defines religion as a personal matter. The separation is designed to protect the freedom of religion, freedom from religion, and religious pluralism (United States), or to defend the state against religion (France).[3] Between these two poles lies the *official church* model applied in England, where the state recognizes one religion and one church as having special status. Another model is the *recognized communities*, as in Germany, where there is no official religion or church, but the state recognizes various religions, which receive government funding. This funding is derived from a special tax collected from consumers of religious services and is allocated to the communities in accordance with their relative size (Neuberger 1994, 7–11; Neuberger 2002).

Relations between the state and religion in Israel do not fit neatly into any of these models. Despite religious legislation, Israel is not a theocracy; and despite the privileged status of Judaism over other religions and the fact that personal status law is based on religious law (for other religions in Israel, as well), most Israeli citizens do not conduct their lives in accordance with religious commandments and are not coerced to do so. At the same time, there is no legal, institutional, or public separation between state and religion in Israel. Religious institutions, such as the chief rabbinate and the religious councils, are part of the national and local political systems, and the state finances religious institutions and religious education. The Orthodox version of Judaism reigns supreme in Israel, mandating a Jewish public sphere and

[3] France enacted a law in 2004 that prohibits the wearing of "religious signs and garb" such as veils and skullcaps in public places.

non-separation of state and religion. This Orthodox approach demands that the state enforce the observance of certain religious edicts in public life – Sabbath and dietary laws, for example. At the same time, characteristics of the "recognized communities" model exist in Israel – granting autonomy and partial state funding to non-Jewish communities, primarily for religious leaders and judicial institutions. In fact, the Israeli model is unique because it adds the component of nationality to state–religion relations. Identity cards in Israel used to include two fields where "Jewish" could be entered as both a religion and a nationality, identifying its holder as a member of both the Jewish religion and the Jewish people.

The political and public culture of Israel (a "civil religion" according to Liebman and Don-Yehiya 1983) is based on Jewish symbols like the flag and menorah, Jewish history, religious ceremonies, and seminal myths such as the Holocaust and the fall of Masada. The Jewish religion serves as a platform for Israeli nationality and shapes some of the shared content that lends legitimacy to the political system. One example of this "civil religion" is the Memorial Day ceremony for Israel's fallen soldiers. Memorial Day is a national day, but the ceremonies include religious motifs such as King David's biblical lament.[4] On the individual level, the combination of religion and nationality in Judaism creates contradictions in the views of Israeli Jews: 89 percent believe that someone can be a good Jew even if he or she does not observe religious tradition; in practice, the majority observe some commandments as they understand them: keep kosher at home; do not eat bread on Passover; and fast on Yom Kippur, light candles on the Sabbath, and eat a Sabbath meal (Arian and Keissar-Sugarman 2011, 33–35).

17.2 Who and What is a Jew?

The division into religious/secular, observant/non-observant is not dichotomous because there are different levels of affiliation as well as intermediate groups such as traditional or Reform Jews. Not only is there a continuum in the extent of religiosity or secularity, but the groups themselves are not distinct, exhaustive, or exclusive. It is impossible to define unequivocally who is ultra-Orthodox, or draw a line separating the ultra-Orthodox from the religious (the term *hardal* is used to describe someone who is both ultra-Orthodox and nationalist), or the religious from the traditional, or the traditional from the secular. Even secularism as a world view is not always unambiguous because the complexity of Jewish identity enables some people to define themselves as secular while also expressing support for public life in Israel having "Jewish character" or viewing themselves as national-religious (Hermann et al. 2015a, 19). An additional complication is that some of the labels are linked to other social categories. For example, Ha'edah Haharedit (an ultra-Orthodox anti-Zionist community) is Ashkenazi, while those referred to as "traditional" are usually identified with Jews of Mizrahi origin. The studies we cite below indicate the size of the groups according to one of two criteria: (1) self-definition of one's own religious observance; (2) positions on religious questions.

[4] In 2011, a typical dispute arose: The text used in IDF memorial ceremonies stating "the people of Israel will remember" was replaced by "God will remember" and then reinstated by order of the chief of staff upon the recommendation of a special committee.

Table 17.1 *Religiosity of Jews in Israel (self-defined) 1979–2016 (in rounded %)*

Year	Ultra-Orthodox	Religious	Traditional	Secular	Notes
2016	9	13	29	49	–
2013	10	10	36	43	"Traditional" includes traditional religious (13%) and traditional not very religious (23%).
2009	8	12	38	42	"Traditional" includes traditional religious (13%) and traditional not very religious (25%).
1999	5	12	35	48	"Secular" includes non-religious (43%) and anti-religious (5%).
1992	10	10	29	51	–
1986	–	15	38	47	"Religious" includes ultra-Orthodox and religious.
1979	7	10	41	42	–

Sources: CBS 2010; CBS 2013; Levy, Levinson, and Katz 2002; Gutmann 1996; Pew Research Center 2016.

A. The Self-Definition Continuum: From Ultra-Orthodox to Secular

Despite major changes in the composition of Jewish society, the distribution of self-defined religiosity has remained quite stable over the years (Table 17.1).[5]

If we combine the different categories in Table 17.1, we find that, in general, approximately 20 percent of Israeli Jews define themselves as religious (including the ultra-Orthodox), about 40 percent as traditional (in varying degrees), and about 40 percent as secular. The stability of self-defined religiosity can be explained by the fact that the growth in religiosity and traditionalism was offset by the arrival of non-religious immigrants from the former Soviet Union. Table 17.2 shows a different self-definition in reply to the question "To what extent do you observe religious tradition?" or "To what extent do you observe the commandments?"

The data in Table 17.2 also depict a stable percentage over the years of those who rigorously observe the commandments and those who observe them a little. The percentage increased, however, of those who observe commandments "to a great extent" as well as those who are completely non-observant. Both Tables 17.1 and 17.2 are based on self-reporting, but they reveal an interesting finding: Among those who define themselves as secular or not religious, many observe tradition to some extent. A survey conducted by the Guttman Institute (Arian and Keissar-Sugarman 2011) found that nearly a third of the public (the largest single group) defines itself as not religious and holds non-religious views such as support for open shopping centers on the Jewish Sabbath and civil marriage. However, this group also observes some

[5] A 2009 study found some decline in attachment to Jewish tradition and religion from 1991 to 1999, apparently due to immigration from the former Soviet Union. However, this attachment strengthened from 1999 to 2009, returning to the 1991 level (Arian and Keissar-Sugarman 2011, 10; Hermann et al. 2014, 250).

Table 17.2 *Self-reported keeping of tradition or observance of commandments – Jews in Israel (in rounded %)*

Year	Rigorously observant	Observe to a great extent	Observe a little	Completely non-observant
2016	39*		34	26
2008	13	22	48	17
1999	16	20	43	21
1991	14	24	41	21
1969	12	14	48	26
1962	15	15	46	24

* In the 2016 Pew survey, these two categories were combined: "Do you observe all or most of religious tradition?"

Sources: 1991, 1999, and 2008: Ventura and Philippov 2008; 1962 and 1969: A. Arian 1973; 2016: Pew Research Center 2016.

traditions (e.g., fasting on Yom Kippur or abstaining from bread on Passover), and attributes importance to Jewish ceremonies such as ritual circumcision and mourning practices. Among the Jewish-Israeli public, maintaining aspects of the tradition is regarded as part of their general Jewish identity, which is a broader self-definition than religiosity expressed in observing commandments (Levy et al. 2002). Overall, Israeli Jews are more observant than American Jews (Pew Research Center 2016).

B. The Positions Continuum: From the Extreme Ultra-Orthodox to the Completely Secular

In addition to the continuum of self-reported religiosity, Jewish groups also hold a range of views on the issue of state and religion (Neuberger 1994, 15–32). There is some overlap in the views of these groups, reflecting the complexity of Judaism as a nationality, religion, and/or culture and the various interpretations of the state's "identity." (Is it Jewish in the ethnic-national or Orthodox-religious sense? If so, is it still also civil-democratic?) At one end of the spectrum, a religious world view requires the state's Jewishness to be Orthodox-religious. According to this view, the principles of religion take precedence over the state laws and governmental authority. At the other end of the spectrum, a secular world view requires the liberal-democratic state to be free of religious identity. In between are views that combine various aspects of these polar positions. Moreover, the Jewish mosaic in Israel is part of the continuum of religious and other views of Diaspora Jewry – a very important topic, though not addressed in this chapter.

The Ultra-Orthodox (*Haredim*)

Ultra-Orthodox Jews, about 10 percent of the Jewish population in 2014, are at one end of the continuum. In their perspective, a Jew is one who observes the 613 commandments while a Jewish state should operate according to the laws of Halakha. The ultra-Orthodox originally rejected Zionism and the idea of establishing a state; despite some changes in their positions, they have yet to embrace state symbols and the shared content of "Israeliness." Most do not serve in the IDF and do not mark national days such as Independence Day and Holocaust Remembrance Day. The ultra-Orthodox are distinctive according to social, educational, economic, political, and geographic criteria, but they are not a monolithic group, and divided into different communities. While most cooperate with state agencies, isolationist minority groups like Eda Haredit (Neturei Karta) do not recognize the legitimacy of the state of Israel. They boycott the elections, do not recognize state laws and institutions, and refrain from receiving government services. Some declaratively act against the state and meet with hostile entities to demonstrate that not all Jews support the existence of a secular state of Israel.

The ultra-Orthodox live separately from the secular public, but most collaborate pragmatically in the political arena. At the time of the British Mandate, the ultra-Orthodox chose not to participate in the Jewish community's representative body; however, representatives of Agudat Yisrael signed the Declaration of Independence and have been partners in some government coalitions. Their approach to politics is entirely instrumental, aimed at serving their constituency – funding for ultra-Orthodox institutions and their independent education networks, and promoting religious legislation. Their political parties are identified as ultra-Orthodox in all respects – their platform, candidates, and voters. In the past, the Ashkenazi ultra-Orthodox were represented by the Aguda parties (Agudat Yisrael and Poalei Agudat Yisrael), and now by United Torah Judaism. Since 1984, Shas has represented ultra-Orthodox Jews of Mizrahi origin in the Knesset (see Chapter 9).

The ultra-Orthodox world is changing in the twenty-first century. Some changes are the result of external pressure on issues like army conscription, participation in the labor market, conversion to Judaism, and child allowances, while most changes derive from internal processes. Exposure to the modern world, though controlled (to the Internet, for example), and the proximity to Jews of different stripes (religious and secular), are having an impact. This is most prominently reflected in the growing demand for education among ultra-Orthodox young women and the rising employment rate of ultra-Orthodox men.[6] Today, more ultra-Orthodox youngsters are enrolling in institutions of higher education and serving in the army.[7] We can assume (though no data are available) that there is a substantial and relatively constant percentage who leave the ultra-Orthodox world, though some remain strictly observant. Despite the very high birthrate, the percentage of Ashkenazi ultra-Orthodox Jews in the population (Table 17.1) has not grown commensurately, nor has their representation in the Knesset.

The National-Religious

National-religious Jews accounted for about 10–11 percent of the Jewish population in 2014. From the outset, unlike the ultra-Orthodox community, they were an integral part of the Zionist movement and the efforts to establish a state. Core to

[6] See Ministry of Economy and Industry 2016.

[7] In 2014, 3,600 ultra-Orthodox men served in the army; 8,500 men and women engaged in academic studies; and 15,000 consulted career-counseling centers. The employment rate in the ultra-Orthodox population rose from 36 percent in 2003 to 45 percent in 2014 among men, and from 51 to 71 percent among women. The average employment rate of non-ultra-Orthodox Jews was 83 percent in 2014 (Malach et al. 2015, 45).

their views and lifestyle is the triad "the Torah of Israel for the people of Israel in the Land of Israel," i.e., religion, peoplehood, and state (or land). This group is not isolationist like the ultra-Orthodox, but is also distinct from a social and educational perspective, and sometimes also by area of residence. For them, the state of Israel, even if temporarily secular-mundane, has religious significance as the "dawn of redemption." National-religious Jews do not isolate themselves from secular Jews and do not renounce the modern world. They serve in the army, participate actively in the economy, and are full partners to the political system. In their view, the public sphere should be imbued with a religious Jewish spirit, and the state should be based on Halakha to the extent possible, or at least on the principles of Hebrew jurisprudence. They attribute a central role to the state and its laws in determining the religious character of the society, are opposed to the separation of religion and state, and seek to influence state activity. National-religious Jews are also not homogeneous in their views, and a small number favor separating religion from the state. According to this minority view, most prominently expressed by Yeshayahu Leibowitz, linking religious commandments to civil law not only violates individual liberty, but also detracts from religion by subjugating faith to the laws of the state. Consequently, politically engineered religious legislation entails compromises that are liable to harm the principles of faith, and should not be espoused by observant Jews (Leibowitz 1976).

Members of the national-religious camp are involved in the "secular world," but live in the "sacred world" and are committed to the religion's commandments and the values of Orthodox society. The parallel worlds create a complex identity with subidentities – for example, that of the religious kibbutz, or the *hesder* yeshivas, which combine military service with religious studies. In twenty-first-century Israel, one of the dominant identities of this camp is a hawkish-religious ("settler") one, an overlap between the national-religious identity and the Greater Israel ideology, which advocates the state's continued hold on the occupied territories. Plans for withdrawal from the territories and disengagement from the Gaza Strip in 2005 engendered a deep rift in the national-religious camp. From their perspective, loyalty to the state and obedience to its laws were challenged, and some (including rabbis) responded by declaring the primacy of an undivided Greater Land of Israel over state laws and government decisions (Paryente and Orr 2006). In the past, the National Religious Party (NRP) represented this camp, but the hawkish change in direction led some to vote for parties more to the right (Likud, Tehiya, National Union), while others, for different reasons, voted for Shas. As discussed below, some returned in 2013 to the NRP in its new incarnation (Jewish Home led by Naftali Bennett), but left again in 2015, primarily shifting their votes to the Likud. The number of MKs who define themselves as religious has increased in all parties in recent years, but with wide fluctuations: thirty-eight in the nineteenth Knesset and twenty-eight in the twentieth Knesset.

A study by Hermann et al. (2015a) attempted to isolate the national-religious public – to examine whether it constitutes a camp in itself, assess its size and components, and compare its views to the rest of Jewish society. In a national sample, 22 percent of Israeli Jews (about 1.2 million) responded affirmatively to the question, "Would you say that you belong to the national-religious sector, in terms of both your lifestyle and views?" This is a higher percentage than that published by the Central Bureau of Statistics (see Table 17.1) because of the broader definition of national-religious, which includes modern-liberal religious, ultra-Orthodox, non-religious traditional, nationalist ultra-Orthodox, and seculars (forty-five). Because of the mosaic composition of this group, those considered religious Zionists now account for only about half its members. Other key findings (ibid., 72–97):

- The national component is as strong as the religious; however, the ultra-Orthodox, nationalist component is gaining in strength and demanding that nationalism take a back seat to religiosity.
- A large majority (78%) vote for right-wing parties including Shas, which express hawkish views and attract non-religious, traditional, and even secular Israelis (some of whom voted for Jewish Home in 2013). Nonetheless, the percentage preferring a Jewish majority in Israel is considerably higher than the percentage preferring sovereignty over all the historical Land of Israel.
- The national-religious public has less trust than the secular public in the institutions of democracy – the Supreme Court, the government, and the Knesset. Approximately two-thirds prefer that fewer hours be devoted to the study of civics and democracy so that more hours could be spent studying Jewish history and instilling a love for the land.
- The majority (58%) attribute considerable importance to rabbinical rulings on political issues, and only 15 percent attribute no importance to them.
- A large majority (63%) responded that orders to evacuate Jewish settlements in the territories should be disobeyed or they "think" should be disobeyed (ibid., 145).

The growing representation of the national-religious in the Israeli elites, especially in the army, and the influence of religion have been described as the theocratization of the public sphere, which challenges the primacy of the rule of law over the rule of the rabbi and the Halakha (Y. Levy 2015).

The Traditional Public

This diverse conglomerate makes up over 30 percent of the Jewish population in Israel. In 2014, many of these (23%) identified as non-religious traditional, while others (13%) self-defined as religious-traditional. All stated that they are believers who observe religious commandments – some commandments or on occasion. A large percentage are Mizrahim (first and second generation). They are not fervently religious, but do not view themselves as secular. Their connection to tradition is part of their Jewish identity, without distinguishing between religion, nationalism, and culture. It is generally expressed in keeping kosher, going to the synagogue on holidays, and partial observance of the Sabbath. Their views on the question of state and religion are more complex than those of the ultra-Orthodox and national-religious; they do not advocate a clear-cut decision on this question. Since religious tradition is an important component of their personal lives and national identity, they do not want the state to be neutral about Judaism or devoid of religion, and they favor a tangible presence of (Jewish) tradition/religion in public life. At the same time, they do not support a religious presence that is excessively restrictive, such as the enforcement of Sabbath prohibitions on travel, cultural performances, or soccer games. Another example of this view: Many oppose civil marriage among Jews, but do not oppose civil marriage in Israel between a Jew and non-Jew. The traditional public is actually the majority in Israel because some of the secular public identifies with their views (Table 17.2). And this has a key moderating influence on the continuum of views, enabling the traditional public, at least potentially, to serve as a bridge between the secular and the religious.

The political representation of the traditional public has undergone far-reaching change over the years, hand in hand with the changes in ethnic identity. During Israel's first two decades, most traditional Mizrahim voted for Mapai and a few for the NRP. In the 1970s, they began to move to the Likud; and in the 1980s, a large number shifted their votes to the ethnic parties just emerging, like Tami and, in particular, Shas.

The Seculars

Seculars constituted about 45 percent of the Jewish public in the 2000s, with a high percentage of immigrants from the west and the former Soviet Union. Seculars are at the opposite end of the spectrum from the ultra-Orthodox in adopting a non-religious Jewish identity, with no commitment to faith or observance of religious commandments. Most recognize the state's connection to Judaism, but emphasize Jewish history, culture, and nationhood as seminal factors in their identity. Most of the secular public believe that Jewish religion is not relevant to the laws of the state or their private lives. Consequently, many favor separating religion from state. In their view, the religious lifestyle (not necessarily Orthodox) is just another legitimate alternative, alongside civil or non-religious lifestyles. Thus, someone who is not religious should not be subject to religious restrictions, especially in personal matters like marriage and divorce. For them, the state's role is only to ensure freedom of religion and freedom from religion. As noted, the secular outlook does not necessarily disclaim Jewish roots, and many secular Jewish Israelis accept the Sabbath as a day of rest without public transportation, but seek to give it a non-religious character. Many agree that kashrut (the Jewish dietary laws) should be observed in state institutions, but oppose any restrictions on the individual, for example prohibitions on the raising of pigs or selling of non-kosher meat (Barak-Erez 2007). Yet even among seculars, some observe religious tradition to some extent – a third say they keep kosher in their homes, nine out of ten attend a Passover seder, and only 60 percent never attend synagogue services.

The secular public, too, is not monolithic. For a minority, secularism is an inclusive world view – they define themselves as anti-religious and oppose any connection to Judaism. The League for the Prevention of Religious Coercion was active in the 1950s and 1960s. Its members, some of whom regarded themselves as "Cana'anites," sought to sever Israel's link to Judaism and the Jewish Diaspora, and establish a "Hebrew nation" based on ties to the Land of Israel and the Hebrew language (Ratosh 1982; Porath 1989; Horon 2000; A. Shapira 2002, 217–18).

Politically, the large parties – Mapai (Labor) and Herut (Likud) – adopted a moderate secular stance because they also sought to represent the traditional public and some of the national-religious. On the other hand, parties like Rakah and Mapam presented staunchly secular and even anti-religious positions. From the 1980s, parties such as Meretz on the left, Shinui and later Yesh Atid in the center, and Tzomet and Yisrael Beitenu on the right called for separating religion from the state, and waged campaigns against budget allocations for the ultra-Orthodox and conscription exemptions for yeshiva students. The "anti-religious" parties generally did not garner much support in Knesset elections with the brief exception of Shinui in 2003 and Yesh Atid in 2013, who won fifteen and nineteen seats, respectively, largely due to their aggressive anti-religious stance. However, anti-religious trends have moderated in recent years, and even members of parties with a secular platform express tolerance toward religious tradition.

C. Religiosity and Other Characteristics

Religiosity, as self-defined or based on the observance of commandments, is related to factors such as ethnicity, socioeconomic status, education, and views on security issues and foreign affairs. Thus views on the relationship between state and religion overlap with views on other issues. The connection between ethnicity and religiosity has weakened, but is still strong.[8] Thirty-six percent of Jews who define themselves as secular are from European-American origin, 23 percent are from the former Soviet Union and immigrated after 1990, 23 percent are native-born (at least second generation), and only about a fifth (19%) are of Asian-African origin. About half of traditional (54%) and religious (49%) Israeli Jews are of Asian-African origin. Only 27 percent of the religious and 19 percent of the traditional are of European-American origin; and only 11 percent of the traditional and 3 percent of the religious are immigrants from the former Soviet Union. Among the ultra-Orthodox, 40 percent are native-born (at least second generation), 9 percent are of European-American origin, and 29 percent are of Asian-African origin; immigrants from the former Soviet Union are absent from this group. The picture becomes clearer in the division by country of origin: About 60 percent of those born in Europe-America define themselves as secular, compared to only 14 percent of those born in Asia-Africa, most of whom (64%) define themselves as traditional. Among native-born Israelis, about 40 percent are secular and a similar number are traditional. This self-definition continues in the second generation: Most native-born Israelis whose parents came from Europe-America call themselves "secular," while most native-born Israelis whose parents came from Asia-Africa define themselves as traditional or religious.

Religiosity and education: Table 17.3 shows that secular and religious Israelis have the highest proportion of those with an academic education. The level of formal education is lowest among the ultra-Orthodox – only 15 percent say they have engaged in academic studies, as opposed to Torah study. In recent years, however, the number of ultra-Orthodox in academic studies has dramatically changed: from 2,000 in 2005 to 11,000 in 2015 (Bank of Israel 2012; Council for Higher Education 2015).

Religiosity and income: There is an inverse relationship between income and religiosity – the more religious, the lower the income, and vice versa. Among the ultra-Orthodox, there is a high proportion of households with no breadwinner (26%, compared to 17% among the non-religious and 19% in the Jewish population at large), or there is only one breadwinner (45%, versus 28% in the general population). The

[8] All the data that follow are from the Central Bureau of Statistics 2010.

Table 17.3 *Jewish Israelis with an academic education by religiosity – 2008 (%)*

	% with academic education
Ultra-Orthodox	15
Religious	43
Traditional, religious	19
Traditional, not very religious	32
Non-religious, secular	47
All Israeli Jews	36

Source: CBS, http://surveys.cbs.gov.il/Survey/survey.htm [in Hebrew] (accessed July 2, 2016).

percentage of ultra-Orthodox families with two breadwinners is about half that of secular families (22% versus 43%). The poverty rate among ultra-Orthodox families is the highest among Jews (54% in 2014 compared to 19% in the overall population); this can be attributed to the large number of children and the low rate of participation in the work force (CBS 2014a; National Insurance Institute 2015).

Religiosity and hawkishness: Since 1967, a clear overlap has emerged between religiosity and hawkish views on the issue of the territories. While in the past the ultra-Orthodox held moderate views on issues of security and foreign affairs, and were even opposed to settlements in the occupied territories, the idea of the Greater Land of Israel gradually became identified with religious commandments. Thus, about 80 percent of those who identify as national-religious say they are right-wing (Hermann et al. 2015a). Self-defined religiosity is the best predictor of views on security and foreign affairs: The ultra-Orthodox and religious are the most hawkish, and a relatively high percentage hold extreme right-wing positions; the secular have the most moderate views, while the traditional are in the middle, though closer to the secular (Ben Meir and Shaked 2007, 26). Religiosity is also linked to intolerant views of Arab citizens of Israel. For example, 71 percent of the religiously observant and 59 percent of the ultra-Orthodox agree that Arabs should be "transferred" or expelled from Israel (compared to 48% of all Jews) (Pew Research Center 2016). Similarly, 82 percent of the ultra-Orthodox and 67 percent of the religiously observant would not want an Arab neighbor, compared with 36–39 percent of traditional Jews (religious and non-religious) and 24 percent of secular Jews (Hermann et al. 2015a).

D. Public Opinion on State–Religion and Secular–Religious Relations

Surveys portray a complex and sometimes inconsistent picture of the Jewish public's views on questions of state and religion (based on Levy et al. 2002; Arian et al. 2005–10: 2007, 66; Arian and Keissar-Sugarman 2011, 52–55; Pew Research Center 2016). In any case, change has occurred – in 1969, 43 percent agreed that the state should have a Jewish character, though not necessarily a religious one. In 2000, 50 percent believed that the state should ensure that public life is conducted in a way that is consistent with the tradition, and in 2009, 61 percent supported this view. This strong support is dominated by the ultra-Orthodox and religious (up to 90%) and the traditional (76%). Nonetheless, 80 percent of the secular public believe that public institutions should serve only kosher food, and 60 percent favored more Jewish studies in the schools. On the other hand, among religious Israelis, particularly among the traditional, there is some support for civil marriage and opening places of entertainment and shopping centers on the Sabbath.

Since the late 1970s, the public consistently believes that the tension between religious and secular Jews in Israel is more severe than other tensions, such as those between Mizrahim and Ashkenazim, or between new immigrants and veteran Israelis, and that this rift is increasingly deep. There were shifts in this tension in 2015, however, as only 52 percent among the Jews believed that relations between the religious and the secular were good (Hermann et al. 2015a).

17.3 Political Arrangements: The "Status Quo" and its Gradual Erosion

A. The Yishuv Period

Under Ottoman rule and the British Mandate, religious communities were granted autonomy to conduct their internal affairs. In 1921, the office of the chief rabbinate was established and two rabbis were appointed, one Ashkenazi and the other Sephardic. In parallel, the Supreme Muslim Council was established. In accordance with the Religious Communities Ordinance (1926), the "Knesset Yisrael" institutions were established – the Elected Assembly, the National Council, the community councils, and the rabbinical court. Every Jew in Palestine (E.I.) automatically came under the purview of the Elected Assembly unless he or she renounced affiliation with it, as the ultra-Orthodox did, seeking recognition as a separate community. From the perspective of the Mandate authorities, the Jews were officially a religious community, and the Yishuv institutions were likewise religion-based entities. However, the overwhelming majority of the Zionist movement were not religious, and some Zionists held negative views of the religious lifestyle for ideological reasons. During that period, the lack of sovereignty made it possible for the Zionist movement and Yishuv institutions to avoid fundamental decisions on the status of religion, and the public accepted the fact that the religion-based autonomy of the community granted exclusive judicial authority over personal status (marriage and divorce) to the rabbinical court. The secular Jews also accepted this as part of the autonomy of Knesset Yisrael (see Chapters 1 and 2). In time, these arrangements and agreements from the Yishuv period, particularly the autonomy of religious and ultra-Orthodox education, would become the "status quo" arrangements after establishment of the state (see below).

B. The State Period

After the founding of Israel, the diverse Jewish groups were in broad consensus about the nascent state's main objectives. A willingness to compromise contributed to the status quo arrangements on the core issues of state and religion – personal status laws, education, military service, the Sabbath, and kashrut. The goal was to freeze the arrangements between the majority and the minority in order to avoid a rift between the camps. The status quo is an unwritten social convention that defines how it is possible to live together in the absence of theological and ideological agreement (Ravitzky 1997). It expresses the willingness of the secular majority to go a long way toward accommodating the religious minority on issues that are most sensitive to it, without making a constitutional decision on the status of religion in the state (Galnoor 1982, 52). It is a political arrangement based on understandings and compromises between elites that enables autonomy in certain areas, ensures everyone a piece of the government pie, and grants a mutual veto on important decisions (Don-Yehiya 1986). The status quo arrangements were gradually shaped in coalition agreements between Mapai and the national-religious parties, with the ultra-Orthodox in the background, outside the coalition, but setting the tone in matters of Jewish law. Mapai, as the dominant party, was the key to maintaining the status quo. Thus, the State Education Law (1953) recognized a separate state-religious stream and the independence of ultra-Orthodox education, promised allocations to religious institutions, and made ad hoc agreements, including a military draft exemption for yeshiva students and a prohibition on public transportation on the Sabbath, except for the city of Haifa.

Despite these arrangements, not everything went smoothly in the early years of the state. Many fierce struggles were waged on matters of state and religion, triggering demonstrations, protests, and political crises that sometimes toppled governments. These struggles, however, focus on expanding or narrowing the parameters of the status quo, and the crises were managed and resolved in negotiations between the parties. The political system was usually able to overcome the crises and reach compromises, which were quietly accepted by the secular majority. In general, issues pertaining to (the Jewish) religion were not settled at the community or local level. Instead, the national political system had to address them. The main stages of the status quo arrangements are outlined below.

Consensus and Formulation of the Status Quo Accords

A letter from David Ben-Gurion, then head of the Jewish Agency, to the leaders of Agudat Yisrael in 1947 is considered the seminal document of the status quo, but in fact some of the arrangements were in place earlier (Friedman 2005). Ben-Gurion's letter includes the outline of the status quo: On the one hand, it declares that Israel will not be a theocracy, will respect freedom of religion and conscience, and equal rights for non-Jews, and will prohibit coercion or discrimination on religious grounds. On the other hand, it defines the areas of compromise: Sabbath and the Jewish holidays as official days of rest, observance of kashrut in state institutions, and autonomous education for the various streams. Concerning laws of personal status, a general commitment was made to do everything "to avoid, heaven forbid, dividing Israel in two." The response of Agudat Yisrael's leaders reflects the religious perspective of the status quo as a line they would try to redraw: The agreement is important, "but still does not meet our demand." In the coalition agreement of the first government, which included the religious and ultra-Orthodox parties, the status quo was formulated as follows: "The government will provide for the public religious needs of its residents, but will refrain from involvement in religious matters. The Sabbath and Jewish holidays will be the days of rest in Israel."

During the War of Independence, the government adopted practical steps that had far-reaching repercussions – for example, exempting religious women and yeshiva students from army service, even though this was not included in the "status quo letter." Ben-Gurion declared that compromise on religious matters was designed "to prevent a religious war, a war for religion, and a war against religion, which could severely hinder the state's paramount mission of merging the exiles" (Bekerman 1983, 32). The status quo arrangements, despite their name, were subject to adjustments and changes. They reflected the tendency to rely on the political system to deal with conflicts in Israeli society through binding compromises achieved by political agreements between the elites. The principal method for resolving issues of religion and state was to include representatives of religious Jews in government coalitions. The "Religious Front" was part of the first government, and the NRP, later joined by ultra-Orthodox parties, was a partner in nearly all coalitions – even when they were not essential for securing a parliamentary majority (see below).

These arrangements were made at the national level, but friction was on the local level – in particular, vocal protest by the ultra-Orthodox against violating the Sabbath and disrupting their religious way of life. In the 1950s, a number of events in Jerusalem occurred that are recorded in the chronicles of battles between ultra-Orthodox and secular Israelis – protests against a mixed-gender swimming pool and against opening a movie theater before the end of the Sabbath, and violent demonstrations demanding the closure of roads on the Sabbath in religious neighborhoods. Unlike these local battles, changes in the status quo on key issues such as education, conscription of women, and the question of "Who is a Jew?" came in the wake of coalition crises.

New Linkages and the End of the "Historic Alliance"

Changes in Israeli society and politics since the 1960s have affected religious–secular relations. Israeli society has become more secular, and the religious public has become more hawkish and messianic since the 1967 war. The consensus weakened on many issues, along with the willingness to compromise, as various groups, both secular and religious, fervently clung to their world views, thus deepening the rifts in society. The formation of Gush Emunim (1974) signaled a convergence of religiosity and hawkishness – right-wing views on security and foreign affairs, particularly opposition to returning the territories. The NRP, which had been a partner in all the Mapai-led coalitions, severed this "historical alliance" and joined the coalition led by the Likud in 1977. Influenced by a "rebellion of the young people" (see below), the NRP adopted hawkish positions and its primary concern became the Greater Land of Israel. Thus, a division of labor emerged among the religious parties: The NRP focused on the territorial issue, while the ultra-Orthodox parties assumed responsibility for questions of religion in Israel.

The emergence of Shas in the 1984 election reinforced this trend. Despite its identity as an ultra-Orthodox party, Shas (unlike Agudat Yisrael) sought positions of power in the government and religious institutions, such as the chief rabbinate and religious councils. Shas created a new socio-political blend of religiosity and ethnicity, and also represented the burgeoning political power of the traditional Mizrahi population (Weissbrod 2009). In the early 1980s, the stalemate in the political system between the right and left boosted the power of the religious parties, enabling them to escalate their demands as the balancing player in coalitions (see below). Sweeping concessions made to the religious parties in coalition agreements were at odds with the secular public's unwillingness to accede to the religious minority's demands.

The surrender to what was termed the "political extortion" of the religious parties intensified the conflict between the camps and added to the disgust with politicians, especially those in the largest parties, who acceded to religious demands. The incongruence between the public mood and the political arrangements was a recipe for instability, which weakened the political system's steering capacity and reduced its ability to effectively manage the conflict over issues of religion and state. As a direct result, the decisions on these subjects landed in the court more frequently in the 1990s, though the court had occasionally ruled earlier on these issues (e.g., *Shalit v. Minister of the Interior* 1970 and other rulings on the Sabbath and kashrut). The political system no longer managed to resolve these issues, and referred the most burning ones to adjudication, for example the conscription of yeshiva students, the status of non-Orthodox conversion, and allowing travel on roads in religious neighborhoods on the Sabbath.

The Strengthening of Secular Awareness and the Crisis in Religious Zionism

As noted, the numerical balance between the large groups of "religious" versus "secular" Jews in Israel remained quite stable over the years. Conflicts, however, emerged: While the traditional, Sephardic ultra-Orthodox grew stronger politically (with the emergence of Shas), opposition was growing among the secular public in the 1990s to accommodation with the religious minority. Secularism was strengthened with the arrival of the immigrants from the former Soviet Union, which led to temporary surges of support for secular parties like Meretz and later Shinui and Yesh Atid, parties that sought to separate religion and state, prevent religious coercion, draft the ultra-Orthodox into the army, and eliminate special benefits. The religious parties, which had always represented a defined population, grew in power, thanks primarily to the emergence of the new formula that Shas embodied; the power of the Ashkenazi ultra-Orthodox remained stable; while the political clout of the NRP diminished. At the same time, immigrant parties emerged with specific demands on issues of state and religion (such as civil marriage and burial), as did parties with an anti-religious message.

The increasing polarization in the political system reflected societal changes, and marked a transition from the politics of accommodation to the politics of definitive decision-making, though such attempts usually resulted in indecision. Cohen and Susser (2003) emphasize a central theme in the politics of accommodation – the moderate forces in the rival camps sought to avoid clear-cut decisions and find a compromise they could accept. Crisis politics, on the other hand, emboldens the extreme voices in each camp, undermines the attempts at compromise, and aims to reach an unequivocal decision. Changes occurred in all areas of the status quo, but these were usually not the result of legislative amendments, policy revisions, or political decisions; the changes occurred on the ground due to the powerlessness of the political system. As noted, this weakness also created a vacuum into which the Supreme Court was drawn, yet it too was unable to resolve the disputes and only intervened on narrowly defined matters, referring questions of principle back to the Knesset. However, the court's intervention placed it in the eye of the storm, and marked it as the enemy of the religious public. The enactment of two Basic Laws in 1992 and the declaration of a "constitutional revolution" reinforced the fears of the religious public and intensified its demands to limit the power of the judiciary. The conviction of Shas head Aryeh Deri in 1999 and other Shas leaders was seen as further proof that "judicial activism" was designed to undermine the status quo in the name of liberal values.

With respect to foreign affairs, the national-religious public focused on the struggle against the Oslo Accords in the 1990s and against the disengagement from the Gaza Strip in the 2000s. Two events, more than anything else, mark the crisis in religious Zionism. The first was the assassination of Prime Minister Yitzhak Rabin in November 1995 by a young, religious man, who was educated in national-religious schools. Many Israelis viewed this murder as a reflection of the blind obedience paid to religious rulings issued by extremist rabbis, whose followers saw these rulings as not only superseding the laws of the state, but overriding the Jewish code of morality. The second event – the evacuation of settlements from the Gaza Strip in 2005 – shook the settlers' belief that the majority of Israelis ultimately supported them and viewed their actions as a pioneering mission similar to the pre-state settlement enterprise. The notion that they had become an unwanted burden on the state convinced many young people in the national-religious camp to pledge their first loyalty to the Greater Land of Israel rather than the state of Israel, much like the views of extremist ultra-Orthodox Jews in the past. Since in their view the state no longer represented "the dawn of redemption," they could stop obeying the law and the democratic decisions of the elected institutions. In the last decade or so, extremism has been unleashed in the religious camp, and Jewish terrorism has increased. Under the name "price tag," violent attacks were carried out on Arabs and their religious (Christian and Muslim) institutions (e.g., setting fire to churches). The most extreme was an attack in July 2015 in the Palestinian village of Duma, where Jewish terrorists set fire to a home, killing a baby and his parents, while another child was severely wounded. At first, the government and law enforcement agencies ignored these actions. Later, it was almost impossible to contend with the surging violence of extremist Jews in the territories.

As the national-religious camp increasingly focused on the settlement issue, and the hawk–dove divide displaced the previous quandaries of state and religion, questions about the limits of the status quo became less salient, and were placed in the more pragmatic hands of the ultra-Orthodox parties. The ultra-Orthodox realized that the effort to make the state more religious through legislation was impractical and sparked counterattacks from the secular public. Therefore, they took a different tack, preferring to defend what they considered most important – preventing the conscription of yeshiva students and securing funding for their educational institutions (Y. Sheleg 2004, 29). The formation of a right wing-religious coalition in May 2015 enabled the religious parties to advance both their religious interests and their national agenda more than ever before in the previous two decades.

17.4 The Institutional Infrastructure of Religious Affairs

Unlike countries where religious institutions are part of civil society, there are religious institutions in Israel whose status is anchored in legislation and whose activity is state funded. These institutions are ostensibly part of the executive branch. We address here a number of questions: How autonomous are the religious institutions? What is their relationship to other authorities (e.g., the status of rabbinical courts vis-à-vis the civil courts)? How representative are the religious institutions? To what extent do the political parties control institutions such as the religious councils? The array of Jewish religious institutions includes the Ministry of Religious Services, the chief rabbinate, and the rabbinical courts. On the local level, they include the local rabbinate and the religious councils.

A. Religious Institutions at the State Level

Ministry of Religious Services: Responsible for service provision and regulation of religious affairs, oversight of the holy places, and funding for religious institutions. The ministry also regulates 132 Jewish religious local councils and some 600 burial societies. The ministry was established under pressure from the religious parties (Fein 2009, 131) and, since 1955, nearly all its ministers have come from the NRP. A Shas minister headed the ministry from 1999 until it was abolished in 2003, when responsibility for religious services was transferred to the local authorities. The ministry was reestablished in 2008 under a Shas minister, and religious services for non-Jewish citizens remained within the purview of the Ministry of the Interior.

Chief Rabbinate: Established during the British Mandate period, its status was later defined in the Chief Rabbinate of Israel Law (1980). It is co-headed by a chief Ashkenazi rabbi and a chief Sephardic rabbi (the latter also known as Rishon Letzion), who are elected to a ten-year term by an assembly of 150 rabbis and representatives of the public. The Chief Rabbinate Council includes sixteen rabbis and serves as the top rabbinical body and High Rabbinical Court. The council publishes opinions on Halakhic issues, regulates religious affairs, oversees kashrut, and approves candidates to serve as rabbinical court judges, municipal rabbis, and marriage registrars. Until the 1980s, the chief rabbinate was identified with the NRP. However, the emergence of Shas and the growing involvement of Agudat Yisrael gave the ultra-Orthodox a foothold in this institution and its branches, and ultra-Orthodox rabbis (such as Rabbi Ovadia Yosef, the spiritual and political leader of Shas) were elected to the post. In 1964, following a High Court petition to examine whether the chief rabbinate was wrongfully denying kashrut certification, the court asserted its authority to scrutinize the chief rabbinate's judgment and stated that the latter did not have "immunity from the authority of the state courts" (*Southern Company Ltd. and Marbek Slaughter House v. Chief Rabbinate Council and Tel Aviv-Jaffa Religious Council* 1964). The Chief Rabbinate's authority is also controversial among the religious public regarding, for example, its exclusive control of kashrut certification and conversions.[9]

Rabbinical courts: In addition to the civil court system, there are parallel rabbinical courts that have exclusive authority over marriage and divorce between Israeli Jews. The regional rabbinical courts and the rabbinical appeals court operate by power of the

[9] As a result, well-known rabbis from the religious Zionist camp formed a separate network of conversion courts, independent of the chief rabbinate and without authorization from the state authorities (Ettinger 2015a).

Rabbinical Courts Jurisdiction (Marriage and Divorce) Law (1953). The Courts Law (1957) stipulates that the rabbinical courts are part of the court system. Religious court judges are sworn to remain faithful to the state of Israel, but unlike judges in other courts, they do not swear allegiance to "its laws" because they rule according to religious law. Nonetheless, Basic Law: The Judiciary states that the High Court of Justice is empowered to order religious courts to hear a specific case or to refrain from hearing a specific case that is not within its jurisdiction; and that the High Court may choose to examine whether the rabbinical courts have exceeded their authority, violated basic rules of justice, or acted contrary to the fundamental principles of the Israeli legal system (*Michal David v. High Rabbinical Court* 1997). When there is a clash between state law and Jewish law, the High Court's intervention as a court of appeal engenders criticism from the rabbinic institutions and religious public. For example, in *Bavli v. High Rabbinical Court* (1994), which weighed the property rights of women following divorce, the court subordinated rabbinical courts to the principles of civil law and ruled that they must act in accordance with civil law in all matters that do not pertain to personal status (see also Elon 1998). In another case, the High Court ruled that the rabbinical court is not authorized to hear matters outside its jurisdiction, even if the parties consent to this (*Amir v. High Rabbinical Court* 2006). So far, attempts to amend the law to circumvent the High Court and expand the authority of the rabbinical court have failed.[10] The administration of rabbinical courts was moved to the Ministry of Justice and then returned to the Ministry of Religious Services (under a Shas minister) in July 2015.

B. Religious Institutions at the Local Level

Local rabbinate: The local rabbis serve as religious leaders and marriage registrars. The religious councils pay their salary and their status is defined in the Regulations for Selecting Municipal Rabbis (1974), not in legislation.

Religious councils: These councils are responsible for providing Jewish religious services in accordance with the Jewish Religious Services (Consolidated Version) Law (1971). Their tasks: granting kashrut certificates, supervising kashrut, registering marriages and divorces, regulating kosher slaughter, ritual baths, and burial. The number of religious councils grew from 13 in 1948 to 180 in 1988, and decreased to about 130 in 2016.[11] According to the Jewish Religious Services Law (2008), funding for the religious councils comes from both the local authorities (60%) and the state budget (40%). Therefore, the ongoing budget crisis in the local authorities has hindered the operation of the religious councils.

The balance of power in the local authority determines the composition of the religious council. In the past, women were not allowed to be members of religious councils, but in 1987 Leah Shakdiel petitioned the High Court, demanding to serve on the religious council of Yeruham. The court ruled that women are entitled to serve on religious councils, and that appointments to the council are subject to the laws of the Knesset, not the laws of the Torah (*Shakdiel v. Minister of Religious*

[10] Such as the proposed Rabbinical Court Jurisdiction (Marriage and Divorce) Bill (Amendment – Jurisdictional Authority by Consent on a Civil Matter and Associated Authority) in 2006.

[11] See the Ministry of Religious Services' website: http://dat.gov.il/About/Pages/Default.aspx (accessed October 24, 2017).

Affairs 1988). The religious councils are an arena for power struggles between the religious parties. The NRP once wielded unchallenged control, but in the 1980s Shas gained power at its expense, and other parties, such as Meretz, sought representation in these bodies.

C. Institutions of Other Religions

The status of religions in Israel derives from the Ottoman "millet" system, which was adopted by the British Mandate. Under this system, each recognized faith community was accorded judicial autonomy on matters of personal status. Freedom of worship is generally protected in Israel, though the Jewish religion enjoys a privileged status, as reflected in budget allocations, for example. Non-Jewish religious institutions are not budgeted commensurate with their share of the population (Raday 2000). In addition, there have been repeated cases of arson and vandalism against non-Jewish religious institutions, perpetrated by Jewish religious extremists.[12]

The Muslim community: During the British Mandate period, the Supreme Muslim Council was established (1921) to manage the Muslim community's internal affairs. The council was authorized to oversee the finances of the Waqf (the Muslim charitable trust) and the Sharia courts. The Supreme Muslim Council ceased to operate in 1948 and the government did not establish any other institution to manage the Waqf funds, fearing it would become a center of political power. Responsibility for Waqf funds was assigned to the Custodian of Absentee Property, which transferred money to committees of trustees of the Muslim community for purposes of welfare, religion, and education. The Muslim population remained without religious institutions of its own, and the responsibility for 436 mosques, holy places, cemeteries, and about 300 imams and muezzins (Muslim clergymen who call to prayer) is now in the hands of the Ministry of the Interior. No Muslim religious councils or religious schools receive state funding. On matters of personal status, the legal authority of the Sharia courts was recognized in the Qadis Law (1961), which provides for the appointment of qadis (Islamic judges) by a Qadis Appointments Committee. Muslim members are a majority on the committee, which includes two government ministers, three MKs, and two members of the Bar Association.

The Druze community: The Religious Communities Ordinances (1957) recognize the Druze as a separate community. The community is led by the Druze Religious Council, which is appointed by the minister of interior in consultation with representatives of the Druze local authorities and religious leaders. The Religious Council (over 150 members) is responsible for overseeing holy sites and includes a wide representation of Druze clergy, leaders of the houses of prayers, local council representatives, and public leaders. The chair is appointed for a five-year term (Dana 2000, 31–32; Halabi 2002, 21). According to the Druze Courts Law (1962), the Druze community has its own courts, whose *qadi-madhab* (judges) must be qualified under Druze law. They rule on matters of marriage, divorce, and issues pertaining to the Druze Waqf.

[12] On June 18, 2015, the Church of the Loaves and Fishes in Tabgha, a sacred Christian site, was torched and a Hebrew prayer was spray-painted on the wall condemning idol worship.

Christian communities: These communities did not ask to organize under the Religious Community Ordinances, preferring to preserve their autonomy. Nonetheless, the government funds some of the Christian communities.

17.5 Religion: State, Community, and Individuals

A. State – Who is a Jew?

In Israel, the "Who is a Jew?" dispute has mainly revolved around application of the Law of Return (1950), which entitles every Jew to immigrate to Israel and receive automatic citizenship.[13] Therefore, since every Jew in the world has an inherent right to citizenship in the state of Israel, the answer to the "Who is a Jew?" question also determines eligibility for Israeli citizenship. In the discussion on the status of Arabs (Chapter 15), we noted that the law discriminates against non-Jews in acquiring citizenship. Here we address two "Jewish" aspects of the law: First, the law defines the gateway to citizenship in religious terms, thus bundling religious and national affiliation with the Jewish people, thereby creating an inseparable connection between religion, nationality, and state. Second, in addition to citizenship, the law establishes Orthodox Halakha (though not necessarily Orthodox conversion) as the determinant of whether a person belongs to the Jewish community.

In regard to the civil aspect, the original Law of Return did not define a Jew for purposes of registration as a citizen, and in the absence of a clear legal definition, Ministry of Interior officials registered immigrants at their own discretion. In practice, anyone who declared him-/herself a Jew was registered as such. The assumption was that only Jews would seek to immigrate to Israel, so if one regards oneself as a Jew and wishes to immigrate to Israel, the authorities have no reason to prevent this. In 1958, Minister of the Interior Yisrael Bar-Yehuda from the Ahdut Ha'avoda party issued directives to the registration clerks stating that a Jew is someone who declares in good faith that he is a Jew, or a child whose parents declare him to be a Jew, even if one of the parents is not Jewish. As long as this was conducted quietly, no one made an issue of it. However, these directives, which transformed a vague situation to official policy, sparked an outburst of rage among the religious public. From their perspective, the state was challenging Jewish law and its unequivocal biological definition of a Jew as someone who was born to a Jewish mother, or who underwent an Orthodox conversion.

In the midst of the coalition crisis, Ben-Gurion decided to solicit the opinions of fifty "Jewish sages" in Israel and abroad on the "Who is a Jew?" question. Most respondents supported the Orthodox position that Halakha is the basis for determining whether someone is a member of the Jewish people. As one of the rabbis explained, "For us, the religion is the same as our nationalism" (Galnoor and Hofnung 1993, 203–11). Consequently, the Ministry of the Interior revised the registration regulations to stipulate that a Jew is someone who was born to a Jewish mother, does not adhere to another religion, or has converted to Judaism in accordance with Halakha.

[13] More precisely, the Law of Return grants the right to settle in Israel, and the Citizenship Law awards automatic citizenship to anyone who immigrates under the Law of Return.

Two petitions were submitted to the Supreme Court to challenge the overlap of religion and nationality. In *Rufeisen v. Minister of the Interior* 1962, Brother Daniel, who was born a Jew and converted to Catholicism, argued that he was entitled to citizenship under the Law of Return because he still belonged to the Jewish nation, despite having left the Jewish religion. The court rejected his petition, stating, "a Jew who changed his religion cannot be considered a Jew in the sense that the Knesset intended in the Law of Return, and in the sense in which the term is commonly used" (Justice Berenson). In *Shalit v. Minister of the Interior* 1970, Major Shalit sought to register his children as Jews in the Population Registry under "nationality," despite the fact that their mother was not Jewish. The petition was based on his declaration that his children were living as Jews in Israel. The High Court accepted the petition, thereby approving the subjective test for defining Jewishness and distinguishing between the religious and the cultural-national definition of a Jew.

In the wake of the Shalit ruling, the religious parties succeeded in amending the Law of Return to explicitly define who is a Jew and set two paths for obtaining citizenship. The first affirms the religious definition of a Jew as "a person who was born to a Jewish mother or converted, and who does not belong to another religion." The second path circumvents the religious requirement and adds the possibility of a more national definition of a Jew, though still based on kinship – a child or grandchild of a Jew, the spouse of a Jew, or the spouse of a child or grandchild of a Jew. Under this clause, about a quarter of a million immigrants from the former Soviet Union arrived in Israel in the 1990s who were not Jews by religion, yet received citizenship based on family ties. The amendment includes another compromise: The definition adopts the biological definition of a Jew in accordance with the Orthodox interpretation of Halakha, but it does not specify which conversion would be considered acceptable. Thus, there is no invalidation of Reform or Conservative conversions, contrary to the position of the Orthodox movement. The Law of Return establishes an automatic connection between the right to immigrate to Israel and entitlement to citizenship. So far, the efforts to sever this connection and distinguish between the two have failed.[14]

How the political system has contended with the question of "Who is a Jew?" is typical of how the state addresses issues pertaining to the Jewish religion. After an initial period of vagueness, an effort was made to clarify the definition of a Jew through secondary legislation (registration directives); this led to a coalition crisis with the religious parties; and a compromise was reached after long negotiations and court rulings. However, this compromise (amendment of the Law of Return) was also equivocal and the political system continues to grapple with this issue.

B. Community: Who is Jew – The Boundaries of Affiliation to the Jewish Community

The argument over who belongs to the Jewish community was reflected in two main disputes: the status of the Reform and Conservative movements, and the conversions

[14] For example, the "Social Compact" (Gavison and Medan 2003; Artsieli 2004) proposed that those eligible to enter Israel under the Law of Return no longer be granted automatic citizenship. Instead, they would only receive citizenship after several years and after pledging allegiance to the state and showing some knowledge of the Hebrew language, Jewish heritage, and the history of the state and its institutions.

they conduct; and recognition of the Jewishness of remote communities (primarily in Africa and East Asia), whose members consider themselves Jewish.

Conversion

The dominant Orthodox movement controls religious institutions and religious parties in Israel. On the other hand, Jewish communities in the world are pluralistic: According to a 2016 survey, 90 percent of the Jews in the United States defined themselves as non-Orthodox. About half of Jewish Americans identify with the Reform (35%) and Conservative (18%) movements, while 10 percent identify as Orthodox (Lipka 2016). The question of conversion, therefore, extends beyond the borders of the Jewish community in Israel and stirs fierce disputes with Diaspora Jewry, primarily about Reform and Conservative conversion. Efforts by the religious parties to amend the Law of Return so it will recognize only those who "converted in accordance with Halakha" have failed to win Knesset approval. However, the wording of the proposed legislation created an opening for recognition of non-Orthodox conversion. The Alignment's refusal to change the Law of Return (and the status quo) was one reason the NRP initially refrained from joining the first Rabin government in June 1974 (Neuberger 1994, 92). At the time, a change in conversion was almost a theoretical question in light of the small number of Reform and Conservative Jews in Israel (Don-Yehiya and Liebman 1977, 377).

When the Likud rose to power and formed a coalition with the religious parties, amendment of the Law of Return became a key issue. Nonetheless, the legislation was not amended, in part due to strong opposition from American Jewish leaders, who viewed it as a serious blow to the Reform and Conservative movements and as an attempt by Israel to dictate the definition of their Jewishness. A series of High Court petitions starting in the 1980s addressed the status of non-Orthodox conversions conducted in Israel and abroad (*Miller v. Minister of the Interior* 1986; *Pesaro v. Minister of the Interior* 1995; *Na'amat v. Minister of the Interior* 2002; *Rodriguez-Tushbeim v. Minister of the Interior* 2005; *Shas v. Population Registry* 2006). The court ruled that for purposes of registration in the Population Registry, the state must recognize non-Orthodox conversions. Following these rulings, the "nationality" field was erased from Israeli identity cards in 2003, though it remained in the Population Registry. In short, for purposes of the Law of Return, there is no recognition of non-Orthodox conversion conducted in Israel, only for such conversions conducted overseas, either entirely or in part.

In 1997, the government formed the Ne'eman Committee on conversion with representatives of the various religious movements. The committee recommended that preparatory courses for conversion be taught at a proposed Institute for Jewish Studies to be operated by the Jewish Agency in conjunction with all of the movements. At the same time, to preserve Jewish unity, conversion would be "in accordance with Halakha" and take place in a conversion court to be established by the chief rabbis. This represented a partial compromise on the part of some Orthodox rabbis, but only in 2000 was the Joint Institute for Jewish Studies established (renamed in 2015 Nativ: National Center for Identity and Conversion). The website of the Center offers no data (www.nativhagiur.org.il), and it appears that only a few people have completed an Orthodox conversion process at these institutes. Hence, the previous situation remains unchanged, with the Orthodox rabbinical courts maintaining exclusive control over conversion. Nonetheless, reality has dictated a change in the status of the Reform and Conservative movements, and though the state does not recognize marriages conducted by their rabbis for purposes of registration at the Ministry of the Interior, many couples opt to marry in ceremonies conducted by non-Orthodox rabbis – in protest of the Orthodox establishment's coercion, or because of the gender inequality in the traditional marriage contract.

Recognition of "Remote" Jewish Communities

This subject arose in the past in the debate over the Jewishness of the Karaites, the Bene Israel (from India), and – in the late 1990s – the Beta Israel and Falash Mura (both from Ethiopia). The Orthodox stance, represented by the chief rabbinate, cast doubt upon their Jewishness. In the 1950s, about 7,000 Karaites immigrated to Israel from Egypt. They are unique in observing only the commandments of the Bible and not the Oral Law, unlike mainstream Judaism. The chief rabbinate does not recognize the Karaites as Jews, prohibits them from marrying Jews, and requires them to be buried in separate sections of the cemetery. Israel recognizes them as a distinct community.

During Israel's early years, 12,000 Jews from the Bene Israel community in India immigrated to Israel. The chief rabbinate recognized them as Jews, but recommended cautionary measures concerning marriage. Following a protest by members of the community, the government decided in 1964 to annul the rabbinate's recommendation.

For many years, the rabbinate would not recognize the Jewishness of Ethiopian Jews. In 1973, Chief Rabbi Ovadia Yosef recognized members of the Beta Israel community as Jews and supported bringing them to Israel, conditional upon their undergoing Orthodox conversion to dispel any doubts about their Jewishness. In Operation Moses (1984) and Operation Solomon (1991), many members of the community were brought to Israel. Israel did not, however, bring in the Falash Mura, descendants of the Beta Israel community who had converted to Christianity in the nineteenth century for economic and social reasons. Non-Jewish groups in Ethiopia had never fully accepted the Falash Mura, so intermarriage was rare, despite the conversion. Today, the Falash Mura view themselves as Jews in the process of returning to Judaism. Following the immigration of other Ethiopian Jews to Israel, among them members of Falash Mura families, they too sought to immigrate to Israel.

In 1993, a committee chaired by Minister of Immigrant Absorption Yair Tsaban recommended responding to each request of the Falash Mura on a case-by-case basis. Thus, approval to immigrate was granted to some for purposes of family unification or for humanitarian reasons. Meanwhile, the rabbinate began to support their immigration – they were considered Jews according to Halakha because they did not assimilate and were born to Jewish mothers (Y. Sheleg 2004, 49–53). However, the rabbinate limited the right of the *kessim*, the leaders of the Ethiopian community, to serve as rabbis and conduct marriages. In 2015, the government decided on a gradual process of immigration that would bring the remainder of the Falash Mura community to Israel.

C. Community – Education, the Sabbath, Kashrut, and Military Service

Education

During the Yishuv period, the schools of the religious stream taught both general and religious subjects, and the national institutions provided funding. In contrast, the ultra-Orthodox school system was independent, and their strictly religious study was funded by outside contributions. In 1949, Israel's Compulsory Education Law stipulated that parents must send their children to a school in one of the recognized education streams of the three political camps – labor, general, or religious. Arab children were to be sent to state Arab schools, with the exception of a few private schools (mainly Christian). This intensified the competition, primarily between the labor and religious streams, for the children of new immigrants. The religious complained of "anti-religious indoctrination" of the new immigrants, particularly with regard to immigrants from religious or traditional societies.

A commission of inquiry on the education of immigrant children (Frumkin Commission of Inquiry 1950) indeed found cases of anti-religious coercion. The education issue was so central in those days that these findings sparked the first government crisis and led to early elections in 1951 (Zameret 1997, 130–32; Don-Yehiya 1998). In 1953, the State Education Law was enacted, reinforcing the status quo arrangements in religious education. The law ostensibly eliminated the streams and created state education, but it left state-religious education intact as an autonomous enclave in the Ministry of Education (the Division for Religious Education and the Council for Religious Education), controlled by representatives of the NRP and funded by the government. The law also recognized the independence of the ultra-Orthodox school system, funded by the government but not under the supervision of the Ministry of Education, and subsequently the separate stream created by Shas – the Ma'ayan Hahinukh Hatorani network. These arrangements still existed in 2015, with some changes described below.

The public debate is not about the existence of separate educational frameworks for the secular, religious, and ultra-Orthodox. Rather, it hinges on the scope of state involvement in shaping the curriculum, government supervision of schools, and how they are funded. Secular Israelis complain in particular that ultra-Orthodox education is wholly devoted to religious studies and does not include general and civic education; they demand the introduction of a mandatory core curriculum in all state-funded institutions of learning. Moreover, all the decision-makers, functionaries, and teachers in the state-religious system are religious, many of whom are connected to religious parties, while both secular and religious people are involved in the general state education system. Furthermore, funding supplements for religious education have come in the wake of coalition negotiations, violating the principle of equal allocation for each pupil. For example, it was customary to fund educational institutions by the number of classrooms, not the number of pupils, which gave an advantage to religious and ultra-Orthodox institutions where there are fewer pupils per classroom.

The growth of Shas was accompanied by the formation in 1986 of Ma'ayan Hahinukh Hatorani, an independent stream of education with the status of an independent corporation funded by the state. The Shas school system is unique in providing an extended school day and meals, and it operates primarily in towns in the periphery, serving poor families. The network grew very rapidly – from 253 classes and institutions in 1993 to 846 in 2000. The total number of pupils in all types of Shas schools increased by about 50 percent in five years – from 21,750 in 1995 to 30,965 in 2000. (For the total number of ultra-Orthodox pupils since 2000, see Table 17.4.) The growth in the number of pupils in just the elementary schools continued in 2007–9, and reached about 26,500, including children in schools exempt from teaching non-religious subjects. In 2009, 10,843 pupils were enrolled in kindergartens operated by the Ma'ayan Hahinukh Hatorani network. Consequently, there was a huge increase in state funding for Shas educational institutions, which reflected not only the real growth in the number of pupils and scope of activity, but also Shas's power in coalition agreements.[15] Tables 17.4 and 17.5 show the steep increase in ultra-Orthodox education overall. In the 1980s, only about 6 percent of Israeli pupils attended institutions affiliated with the independent educational stream of Agudat Yisrael. As a result of the very high rate of natural increase, the creation of Shas educational institutions, and the inclusion of Talmud Torah institutions in the tally (since 2000), 27 percent of Jewish elementary school children and 21 percent of Jewish high school students were enrolled in ultra-Orthodox institutions in 2009.

Since the 1970s, the proportion of pupils in state elementary schools has dropped by 13 percent and in state-religious schools by 9 percent, while the percentage of children in ultra-Orthodox schools has risen by 23 percent (or 9% using the new definitions of institutional affiliation in effect since 2000). Enrollment in state high school education has dropped by 16 percent, in state-religious education by 5 percent, while ultra-Orthodox education grew by 20 percent (9% since 2000). These figures reveal a profound shift in the composition of the Jewish community in Israel – an increase in the overall number and percentage of ultra-Orthodox children (boys and, in particular, young women) enrolled in state-funded educational institutions.

A change of this magnitude can no longer be contained within the previous status quo arrangements in education (including the exemption of yeshiva students from army service). Hence the growing demands by the majority, whose children study in state schools and state-religious schools, that a core curriculum be required in all state-funded educational institutions in addition to religious studies (*Teachers Association v. Minister of Education* 2005).

The Sabbath

The new state of Israel decided to continue the Yishuv-era arrangements that defined the Jewish Sabbath and holidays as official days of rest, while offering non-Jews the option of choosing their own days of rest. Making Saturday an official day of rest met the social need of allowing each person a weekly day of rest, and combined it with the religious commandment of observing the Sabbath. A dispute arose from the outset, however, regarding the public character of the Sabbath: Secular Israelis who favored the social right to a day of rest had reservations about the restrictions on public transportation and the closing of entertainment sites, while observant Jews wanted the state to enforce the Sabbath in public places via the proposed Sabbath Law. Such legislation has not been enacted, despite repeated initiatives and coalition promises to the religious parties, due to strong opposition from the secular public. In addition, the religious parties feared that vague wording might be interpreted as condoning Sabbath violations and anchoring a porous status quo in legislation (Don-Yehiya 1997, 47–48). Some observant Jews are wary of Sabbath legislation that

[15] Despite our efforts, we were unable to obtain precise data on state funding for ultra-Orthodox institutions of education.

Table 17.4 *Jewish pupils in elementary schools by institutional affiliation (%)*

Year	Total pupils	State (%)	State-religious (%)	Ultra-Orthodox* (%)
1970	375,534	65.6	27.8	6.6
1980	424,173	74.2	20.1	5.7
1990	461,790	71.1	21.3	7.6
2000	549,558	60.4	19.2	20.4
2010	637,470	53.0	18.7	28.3
2014	698,415	52.2	18.5	29.3

* Ashkenazim and Sephardim; from 2000, includes Talmud Torah schools.
Source: CBS *Statistical Abstract* 2014, table 8.10.

Table 17.5 *Jewish pupils in secondary schools by institutional affiliation (%)*

Year	Total pupils	State (%)	State-religious (%)	Ultra-Orthodox* (%)
1970	129,436	74.4	21.9	3.7
1980	143,810	73.8	22.2	4.0
1990	205,139	75.9	18.4	5.7
2000	270,862	68.0	17.2	14.8
2010	283,527	60.7	16.9	22.4
2014	300,761	58.9	17.0	24.1

* Ultra-Orthodox secondary schools include the middle school level.
Source: CBS *Statistical Abstract* 2014, table 8.21.

would be repeatedly violated, while others emphasize the spiritual significance of the Sabbath and argue that this cannot be imposed through legislation. The compromise that emerged creates a distinction between two levels of Sabbath observance – state-wide arrangements that are broadly applied, or that apply to government bodies; and local arrangements that apply to vehicular traffic and the opening of stores and entertainment sites.

On the ***state level***, the Hours of Work and Rest Law (1951) establishes the Jewish Sabbath and holidays as the official days of rest, while also recognizing the equivalent of other religious communities. The legislation allows for exceptions, for example work on the Sabbath that is defined as essential by the labor minister. Some interpret this exception narrowly to allow only life-saving work, while others broadly interpret this to include any service the public needs on the Sabbath. In 1980, the law was amended to prevent discrimination in hiring observant Jews because of their refusal to work on the Sabbath. Enforcement of the law and sanctions for its violation depend largely on which minister is in office. In general, the trend is of decline in Sabbath observance. In the 1990s, many shopping centers began to operate on the Sabbath, despite protests by the religious parties, which argued that the local authorities were encouraging citizens to shop on the Sabbath. In 2009, most Israelis supported opening shopping centers on the Sabbath (68%), and only 16 percent said they do not shop on the Sabbath (Arian and Keissar-Sugarman 2011, 33, 52).

Many state arrangements are not anchored in law, but stem from government decisions or long-standing practices. For example, the government decided in 1982 that El Al planes would not fly on the Sabbath. Israel Railways and other public transport systems do not operate on the Sabbath. On the other hand, the High Court overturned a government decision that prohibited Israel Television from broadcasting on the Sabbath.[16] Kashrut is observed in the IDF, but there are different interpretations of what constitutes "life-saving work that overrides Shabbat" in the context of security needs. Refraining from such "life-saving work" is considered a grave violation of Jewish law (Yehoshuah Ben Meir 1983). There were also severe coalition crises over Sabbath violations: In 1976, F-15 aircraft that arrived from the United States after the onset of the Sabbath led the NRP ministers to quit the government; in 1999, the government permitted the Israel Electric Corp. to transport a large turbine on relatively empty roads on the Sabbath, and United Torah Judaism left the coalition in protest.

On the ***local level***, clashes usually focus on the opening of places of entertainment or travel on the Sabbath, and this primarily occurs in cities with mixed ultra-Orthodox and secular populations such as Jerusalem, Petah Tikva, and Beit Shemesh. The Municipalities Ordinance authorizes cities "to regulate the opening and closing of stores and factories, restaurants … and cinemas, theaters, and other places of public entertainment … and to supervise their opening and closing on a particular day." Thus, each municipality is entitled to enact bylaws to regulate the opening of such businesses in its jurisdiction. For example, Teddy Stadium was built in Jerusalem in 1990, despite a long fight by religious opponents concerned about Sabbath violation on a massive scale. In the 1980s, a fierce battle erupted after the mayor of Petah Tikva tried to enact a municipal bylaw that would allow the continued operation of cinemas on the Sabbath. In a precedent-setting ruling in 1987, related to the Jerusalem municipality's efforts to close cinemas on the Sabbath, the court ruled that a city bylaw could not prohibit the opening of places of entertainment on the Sabbath for religious reasons without the Knesset's explicit authorization (*State of Israel v. Kaplan et al.* 1988). The religious parties viewed this decision as a violation of the status quo, and set out to amend the Municipalities Ordinance (No. 40) (1990), known as the Authorization Law, to permit a city to exercise its authority to regulate places of entertainment "with regard to days of rest, taking into consideration reasons of religious tradition." Accordingly, there is no legal legitimacy for Sabbath violation, but in practice most cinemas, museums, and national parks, as well as many shopping centers and restaurants, are open on the Sabbath throughout Israel (Finkelstein 2016).

Nonetheless, there is broad consensus that in areas where most of the residents are religious, the Sabbath should not be publicly violated. However, this is difficult to implement with regard to travel on main roads on the Sabbath. In the 1950s, for example, there were violent confrontations between ultra-Orthodox residents of the Mea

[16] *Kaplan et al. v. State of Israel* 2006. A ruling in 1968 allowed gas stations to operate on the Sabbath: *Isramax v. State of Israel* 1968.

She'arim neighborhood in Jerusalem, who sought to protect their way of life and prevent violation of the Sabbath, and secular Israelis who needed to travel on the route known as "Kikar Shabbat." After a demonstrator was killed in one of the protests in 1956, a commission of inquiry was formed, which concluded that Mea She'arim Street should be closed to vehicular traffic on the Sabbath. Subsequently a bypass road was built to circumvent the ultra-Orthodox neighborhoods (Don-Yehiya 1997, 51). In the 1990s, battles were waged on two main arteries – Hashomer Street in Bnei Brak and Bar-Ilan Street in Jerusalem. In Bnei Brak, following a public committee's recommendation, Hashomer Street is closed during the entire Sabbath. In Jerusalem, two public committees and an appeal to the High Court failed to produce a solution acceptable to both sides. The committees recommended closing the street during times of prayer, but since Bar-Ilan Street is a major artery, and in light of the principle at stake, secular groups rejected the recommendations and the street remained open to traffic on the Sabbath by order of the High Court (*Horev v. Minister of Transportation* 1997). In practice, there is almost no traffic on Bar-Ilan Street on the Sabbath because a bypass road was built and also because cars driven on the street were subjected to harassment by ultra-Orthodox Jews.

In practice, the compromise is that if the restriction does not impose an intolerable burden on the secular public, there is room to consider the feelings of the religious public (see *Isramax v. State of Israel* 1968). The contradictions in public opinion reflect this intricate reality. In general, 70 percent of the Jewish public believes that the Sabbath atmosphere should be taken into consideration in the public domain, but the picture changes regarding specific issues: 72 percent of the Jewish public (including those who define themselves as religious) support the opening of cinemas, cafés, and restaurants on the Sabbath; 72 percent have no objection to holding sporting events on the Sabbath; 70 percent are in favor of opening shopping centers outside the cities (Levy et al. 2002, 92); and 63 percent are in favor of having public transportation (Pew Research Center 2016).[17] Therefore, the future of the status quo regarding Sabbath observance is uncertain, because of the gap between the legal prohibitions and a reality that allows Sabbath violation in practice.

Kashrut

Observance of Jewish dietary laws is more prevalent than Sabbath observance: 25 percent of the Jewish public do not keep kosher at all, 58 percent refrain from eating non-kosher meat, 44 percent keep kosher at home, and 68 percent do not eat bread on Passover (Pew Research Center 2016). Consequently, the status quo has been more closely maintained on this issue, and until recently there was no vehement dispute in this area. As noted, in 1947 it had been decided that kashrut would be observed in public institutions, and indeed only kosher food, under the supervision of the chief rabbinate, is served in the IDF, Israel Police, prisons, hospitals, educational institutions, government ministries, embassies, and so on. A number of laws mandate kashrut; the legislation pertaining to non-kosher meat is more controversial due to the

[17] A large majority of the national-religious public (not the ultra-Orthodox) are also opposed to public transportation on the Sabbath, even in areas where few religious Israelis live (Hermann et al. 2015a, 128).

demand for pork products among immigrants from the former Soviet Union, and to a lesser extent, the law prohibiting leavened food (*hametz*) on Passover.[18]

The prohibition on raising pigs was already disputed during the Mandate period, when local bylaws regulated the raising and marketing of pork. After the creation of Israel, government policy was to prohibit and restrict pig farming for religious reasons. The court ruled that it is not within the authority of officials or local councils to issue ordinances and bylaws restricting individual rights for religious reasons, and that this could only be done through legislation by the Knesset.[19] This led to enactment of the Local Authorities (Special Authorization) Law (1956), which authorized local authorities to set bylaws restricting or prohibiting pig farming or the sale of pork within its jurisdiction; and the Prohibition of Pig Farming Law (1962), which prohibited raising or keeping pigs, with the exception of Christian communities, scientific and research institutions, and zoos. Despite the religious parties' efforts and the promises they received, there is no sweeping prohibition on marketing or selling pork. Those who oppose extending the application of the Prohibition of Pig Farming Law to outlaw the sale of pork argue that such legislation would not only hurt people whose religion does not forbid them from eating pork, but would also impose religious commandments on those who do not believe in them. Since this does not involve a public act – buying and eating pork is a private matter – the claim that it hurts the sensibilities of the religious public is not relevant, and the legislature is not entitled to intervene (Barak-Erez 2007). Court rulings have also been in this spirit (Rubinstein and Medina 1996, 220).

The Basic Law: Freedom of Occupation (1992) opened an additional front in the battle over kashrut – the importation of non-kosher meat. Until that time, the government's Trade Administration imported kosher meat. However, the decision to privatize meat imports raised a coalition quandary because the Rabin government promised in its coalition agreement with Shas (1992) to preserve the status quo concerning meat imports and permit only kosher meat to be imported. In the Meatrael case, the High Court ruled that the importation of non-kosher meat does not violate the sensibilities of the religious public and that its prohibition contravenes the Basic Law: Freedom of Occupation. Therefore, the court granted the petitioner an import license (*Meatrael Ltd. v. Prime Minister* 1993). However, the opposition of the religious parties led to an amendment of the Basic Law: Freedom of Occupation – an "override clause" was added that enables the Knesset in special cases to enact legislation that is not subject to this Basic Law. The Meat and Meat Products Law (1994) was soon passed, which states that "a person may not import meat unless he has received a kashrut certificate for it," thus overriding the stipulations of the Basic Law: Freedom of Occupation.

The Prohibition of Fraud in Kashrut Law (1983) states that it is forbidden to advertise an eating place as kosher without receipt of a kashrut certificate from

[18] The Prohibition of Pig Farming Law (1962); Section 2 of the Meat and Meat Products Law (1994), which prohibits importing meat that lacks kashrut certification; the Festival of Matzot (Prohibition of Leavened Food) Law (1986), which forbids business owners from "publicly displaying a leavened food product for sale or consumption" on Passover.

[19] On this issue, see *Lazerovitz v. Food Products Comptroller* 1956, pertaining to the illegality of an order by the food comptroller; *Axel v. Mayor of Netanya* 1954, involving a butcher whose license was revoked because he refused to promise not to sell pork; *Freidi, Mendelson, et al. v. Tel Aviv Municipality* 1955.

the chief rabbinate. The rabbinate or a rabbi acting on its behalf determines what is kosher in accordance with Jewish dietary laws, and extraneous considerations must not influence their decision to award the certificate. In the Marbek case, the High Court ruled that the chief rabbinate abused its authority in stripping kashrut certification from the meat products of this slaughterhouse based on the fact that Marbek did not hire kashrut inspectors via the rabbinate (*Southern Company Ltd. and Marbek Slaughter House v. Chief Rabbinate Council and Tel Aviv-Jaffa Religious Council* 1964). In another case, the court ruled that the rabbinate could not condition kashrut certification upon the observance of other religious commandments that are not connected to food, such as "immodest" performances staged at the site (*Raskin v. Jerusalem Religious Council* 1990). However in a 2016 ruling the court retained the rabbinate monopoly on issuing kashrut certificates.

As in Sabbath observance, the reality concerning kashrut differs from the legal situation, especially after the arrival of the wave of immigration from the former Soviet Union, which led to a significant increase in the number of non-kosher stores. There are an estimated 600 such stores throughout Israel, as well as two food chains that sell non-kosher meat (Asher Cohen 2004, 41).

Military Service of Yeshiva Students

This issue has become the most incendiary of religion–state relations, intensifying polarization between the ultra-Orthodox and secular (Barak-Erez 2010). The fundamental debate pits the Jewish tradition of Torah study against the Zionist heritage of defending the homeland, and the value of equality versus freedom of religion. The reality, as usual, is more prosaic.

The ultra-Orthodox have always opposed military service by yeshiva students, claiming that Torah study is a supreme value, "equivalent to all other commandments." In the past, even some secular Jews shared the belief that yeshiva study keeps the embers of the Jewish people burning, and they were joined by some of the more Orthodox members of the national-religious public. However, opposition to military service is also a reflection of ultra-Orthodox reservations about the Zionist enterprise and the state of Israel – they do not think they should be compelled to defend a secular state that is not to their liking. Some assert that yeshiva students contribute more to sustain the state through their studies; as Rabbi Neria said, "The IDF protects the body and the yeshivas protect the soul. The IDF defends the Jews and the yeshivas defend Judaism." In addition, there is profound concern that military service would divert young ultra-Orthodox from the religious path (from testimony of ultra-Orthodox representatives appearing before the Tal Committee – see T. Tal 2005). Some also claim that the special religious lifestyle of yeshiva students would prevent them from acclimating to military service (e.g., the presence of young women on the bases), and others are skeptical about the utility of their military service.

Yet, the majority of the Jewish public (72%) support conscription to the army of ultra-Orthodox young men (Pew Research Center 2016, 16). Supporters of drafting yeshiva students argue that military service does not violate religious law, while evasion creates extreme inequality: "It's a strange partnership: I send a yeshiva boy to study for me and he sends me to be killed for him. This is infuriating!" (Brigadier General Nehemiah Dagan, former chief education officer, quoted in Neuberger

1994). The key argument pertains to the number of yeshiva students: While it is reasonable to grant an exemption to an elite minority of yeshiva students, the vast majority are not "Torah sages."

Military service by yeshiva students is currently deferred under Section 36 of the Defense Service (Consolidated Version) Law (1986), which enables the defense minister to exempt or defer military service "for reasons pertaining to needs of education, security-related settlement, or national economy, or for family or other reasons." Every yeshiva high school graduate and any other high school graduate who studied five matriculation units in Talmud is entitled to register in a yeshiva for students "whose vocation is Torah." Such students commit to devote all their time to Torah study and not engage in any other pursuit, and they receive a deferment that is periodically renewed upon submission of the required declaration and confirmation from the yeshiva director and the secretary of the Council of Yeshivas – until receipt of an exemption at age forty-one (or earlier, depending on their family situation). Those who stop attending yeshiva are required to perform full or abbreviated military service. This creates a vicious circle: Those who do not wish to study cannot enter the job market and are forced to remain in the yeshivas in order to receive an exemption from the army. This saga reflects a willingness to accommodate real needs of an ultra-Orthodox minority and a practice that spun out of control. In 1951, Defense Minister David Ben-Gurion announced in a letter, "I have released the yeshiva boys from regular service. This release only applies to yeshiva boys who actually engage in Torah study, and as long as they engage in Torah study at the yeshivas." In 1968, a ministerial committee decided to continue this arrangement, but limited the quota of exemptions to 800 per year.

The change of government in 1977 was a turning point in the arrangement for yeshiva students. In the coalition agreements between Begin's party and the ultra-Orthodox parties, the annual quota was eliminated and the criteria for receiving deferments were expanded to include, for example, yeshiva students who learn a vocation and "newly repentant" Jews. This led to a significant increase in the number of yeshiva students with a military exemption. Prior to 1977, about 2.5 percent of eligible conscripts received a deferment for yeshiva study. This grew to 6 percent in the 1980s and 8 percent in 1997, which, according to the IDF, was about 15 percent of the annual cohort (Mei-Ami 2007, 4). In 1986, a subcommittee of the Knesset Foreign Affairs and Defense Committee recommended narrowing the eligibility for this arrangement and setting a quota of 3 percent of potential conscripts each year. It also recommended a six-year deferral for all yeshiva students, to then be extended for only 200 outstanding students, and drafting the others for an abbreviated military service. These recommendations were rejected out of hand by the ultra-Orthodox leadership and never implemented. Figure 17.1 shows that the arrangement instituted in 1948 to defer the conscription of a handful of yeshiva students mushroomed to 53,000 in 2011.[20]

In 1970, and again in 1981, petitions were submitted to the High Court regarding the non-conscription of yeshiva students. The court rejected the petitions, ruling that

[20] The data only include ultra-Orthodox Jews who reported to the recruitment bureau and do not include those from the extremist communities like Neturei Karta and Satmar, which refuse to report to "this Zionist recruitment bureau."

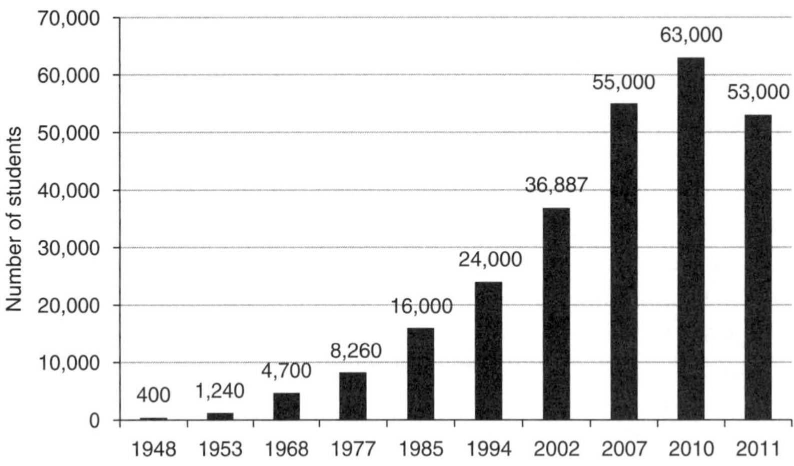

Figure 17.1 Number of yeshiva students who received deferrals (1948–2011)
Source: Plesner Committee 2012.

the petitioners lacked the requisite standing – i.e., they had failed to demonstrate that the non-conscription of yeshiva students caused them personal injury (*Becker v. Minister of Defense* 1970; *Ressler v. Minister of Defense* 1982). Later, the definition of the right of standing was expanded and, in the second Ressler case (*Ressler v. Minister of Defense* 1988), the court addressed the matter for the first time. The petition argued that deferral of conscription of yeshiva students should be based on legislation by the Knesset rather than an executive order from the defense minister, and that the religious grounds for the deferral are an extraneous consideration, discriminatory, and unreasonable. The court rejected the petition and ruled that the defense minister's considerations were reasonable. Nonetheless, the court noted that "quantity makes quality," i.e., that the sheer number of exemptions produced a qualitative change, and that the defense minister should reassess the situation in accordance with the changing circumstances and security needs.

In response to two additional petitions, the Supreme Court ruled, contrary to its previous stance, that the defense minister is not authorized to defer the service of yeshiva students and that "the decision on these questions should be made by the legislative branch" (*Rubinstein v. Minister of Defense* 1998). The court stated that this was not purely a legal matter, but entails socioeconomic issues, such as the economic distress of the yeshiva students, who live on allowances and contributions, and are not part of the work force. The change in the court's position is based on the remark in the second Ressler ruling that "quantity makes quality" – the greater number of exemptions (then about 25,000) required a reevaluation of the situation. The court refrained from ruling on the issue, and referred it to the legislature. In response, the Knesset formed a public committee chaired by former Supreme Court Justice Tsvi Tal. The Tal Committee concluded that it is impossible to achieve full equality because it is neither feasible nor desirable to impose army service on yeshiva students. The IDF is also aware of the difficulty of integrating yeshiva students into military frameworks. On the other hand, the current situation is a trap: Students remain in the yeshivas because they do not want to be conscripted, and this leaves them outside the labor force, engendering poverty and harming society at large.

The committee sought a way out – allowing the student a "year of decision" in which he could leave the yeshiva and try to become involved in public service in some way: military service, service in the IDF's Home Front Command, Fire and Rescue Brigades, or civilian services like those performed by religious young women in the National Service program. The committee believed that only those truly interested in religious studies would remain in the yeshivas, the number of draft dodgers would diminish, and those entering the job market would be able to provide for themselves and their families. The Knesset adopted the recommendations, and the Deferral of Service for Yeshiva Students Whose Vocation is Torah (2002), in brief the "Tal Law," was enacted as a temporary order for five years. In practice, next to nothing was done to implement the law – frameworks were not created for absorbing ultra-Orthodox yeshiva students in the army or civilian service, and it seemed that the IDF was not interested in those who chose a "year of decision" (T. Tal 2005). In 2006, the High Court rejected a petition that sought to overturn the Tal Law because it anchors inequality in legislation. The majority ruled that the law is proportional and had yet to be given a "proper chance" to realize its objectives. However, the court stated that its rejection of the petition was provisional (*Movement for Quality Government in Israel v. Knesset* 2006). In February 2012, the High Court overturned the Tal Law as unconstitutional because it anchors the exemption for yeshiva students and perpetuates inequality. Consequently, the government again formed several committees in 2012 and 2013 to address "equality in bearing the burden," but their recommendations were never implemented.

Conscription Law: In 2014, under the first Netanyahu government that did not include the ultra-Orthodox parties, the Knesset passed the Defense Service Law (Amendment 19) (2014), which regulates the integration of yeshiva students into regular army and civilian service. The legislation allowed for an "adjustment period" during which yeshiva students would be able to choose whether to enlist in regular army service, serve in a civilian framework, or continue in a yeshiva. Furthermore, those who were twenty-two years old at the time the law was enacted would receive an exemption from regular army service to allow them to enter the work force, while those aged eighteen to twenty-two would be able to defer their service until age twenty-four and receive an exemption. After the adjustment period, the government would set recruitment objectives on a sliding scale. If the recruitment objective in a given year is not met, mandatory conscription into military or civilian service would be instituted for all but 1,800 yeshiva students at age twenty-one. In the following Netanyahu government (2015), however, coalition agreements with the ultra-Orthodox parties stipulated that the 2014 amendment would be deferred and changed to eliminate the criminal sanctions on violations and extend the adjustment period. Meanwhile the number of Orthodox young men who enlist in army service (in special units) has increased slowly to several thousand in 2015.

The conscription of yeshiva students exemplifies the convoluted way in which the political system contends with issues of state and religion. The inability to decide on these matters due to their social and political sensitivity leads to escape strategies, such as ad hoc administrative decisions (an order by the defense minister), coalition agreements, referring it to the court or to parliamentary and public committees, and ultimately legislation, without the will or ability to implement it.

Exemption from Army Service for Religious Young Women

A large majority of Israelis (70%) are in favor of conscripting religious young women into the army. However, the exemption of these young women for religious reasons does not stir as much opposition as the exemptions given to yeshiva students (Levy et al. 2002, 124). The debate began with the founding of Israel, and a 1949 survey indicated that public opinion was split, with only 52 percent supporting the conscription of young women into the IDF or Sherut Leumi (national service) (Blander 2008). In 1952, the government's intention to draft religious young women into the Sherut Leumi program led Agudat Yisrael to quit the coalition. A year later, a new law mandated Sherut Leumi for young women who declare themselves religious. The ultra-Orthodox continue to oppose any service by young women, arguing that it is immoral and violates the Torah commandments. On the other hand, the national-religious public has always supported Sherut Leumi service for young women.

The Defense Service Law regulated exemption from army service for any young woman who declares in writing that "reasons of religious conviction" prevent her from serving in the IDF, and that she keeps kosher at home and outside it, and does not travel on the Sabbath. A young woman who requests an exemption had been required to appear before a committee and bring witnesses to testify to her religiosity. The coalition agreement between the NRP and Likud in 1977 led to changes in security service regulations: The candidate's general declaration of her religiosity became sufficient for obtaining an exemption from service.[21] Over the years, the percentage of young women not drafted into the army for religious reasons has grown. From 1997 to 2002, the percentage rose from 26 to 30 of the annual total of potential conscripts (Marciano and Greenberg 2004) (no confirmed hard data exist on the number of young women not conscripted). Ultra-Orthodox young women do not serve at all. Some national-religious young women serve in the army, and according to the IDF, their number rose from 935 in 2010 to 1,830 in 2015 (Ettinger 2015). Most volunteer for Sherut Leumi, and a minority do not serve at all.

The Sherut Leumi Law is not fully enforced, but is implemented on a voluntary basis by non-governmental organizations funded and supervised by the Ministry of Social Welfare. In 2006, about 9,000 young women (mostly religious) and a small number of young men volunteered for one to two years of the Sherut Leumi program. They served in educational frameworks (42%), health organizations (20%), non-profits (17%), social work (11%), or domestic security (4%) (G. Sheffer 2007). The primary and fundamental difference between women and men concerning exemptions is that women are entitled to exemptions for reasons of conscience and religion, while non-ultra-Orthodox men have neither option.

D. The Individual – Jewish Personal Status Laws and Other Issues

Personal Status Laws

The Rabbinical Courts Jurisdiction (Marriage and Divorce) Law (1953) states that matters of marriage and divorce are the purview of the rabbinical courts, and that Jews must be married in accordance with "Torah law" (Halakha). This requirement

[21] Defense Service Regulations (Exempting Women from Defense Service for Reasons of Religious Conviction) (1978). Regulations Publication 3895, September 28, 1978, 2176.

prevents marriage between members of different religions, those with no religion, or those "prohibited from marrying." The latter category includes marriage between a *kohen* (male member of the historically priestly class) and a divorcee, widow, or convert; marriage of a *mamzer* (someone born of an adulterous union) to a non-*mamzer*; and marriage of anyone to an *agunah* (a woman whose husband is missing or refuses to divorce her) or to a woman who has not been set free (*halitzah*) from the obligation of levirate marriage. Rabbinical law applies in Israel to all Jews – citizens, residents, and even foreigners. In matters of personal status, rabbinical law is the foundation of the status quo in religion–state relations.

Observant Jews – ultra-Orthodox, religious, and traditional as well – attribute great importance to adhering to Halakhicly prescribed marital laws because they believe it ensures the continuity of the Jewish people and protects from assimilation. They believe that if non-Orthodox marriages were conducted in Israel, this would cause a rift in the Jewish people, and it would be necessary to keep "lineage records" of those who marry in accordance with Halakha and exclude those violated the marriage prohibitions under Torah law. No data exist on public support for yielding personal status decisions to the rabbinical courts, but marriage by Halakhic rules seems to have enjoyed broad public support among Israeli Jews in the past (Don-Yehiya and Liebman 1977).

The attitude today has changed. Growing awareness of human and civil rights, including gender equality, and the influence of Reform and Conservative customs have changed the views of many Israelis toward the Orthodox marriage norms. Thus, while 80 percent of Israeli Jews say that it is important or very important to marry with a rabbi's blessing, about 50 percent do not dismiss the possibility of choosing to marry in a civil ceremony, and about 25 percent say they favorably consider the option of civil marriage (Arian and Keissar-Sugarman 2011, 37). These Israelis regard the requirement to marry according to Halakha as religious coercion. Moreover, those who oppose giving religion a monopoly over personal status law, without allowing for free choice, argue that this violates the basic values of democracy and contravenes the Universal Declaration of Human Rights, which states, "Men and women of full age, without any limitation due to race, nationality, or religion, have the right to marry and to found a family." Religious legislation stipulates that a person in Israel can only marry someone of the same religion. This not only violates the right to marry and freedom from religion, but also entails gender inequality – only men are empowered to grant a divorce and a woman is unable to divorce without her husband's consent.

Discontent in the secular public in Israel is expressed in the downward trend in the percentage of Israelis marrying in accordance with Orthodox Jewish law. Whether as an act of protest or for lack of choice (in the case of those "forbidden to marry"), about 5,000 people (7%) choose to marry annually in civil ceremonies outside Israel ("Cyprus weddings"), via the mail, or at consulates of foreign countries. More than half the Israelis marrying overseas were born in the former Soviet Union. Others choose to marry in Reform and Conservative ceremonies in Israel (which are not recognized by the Ministry of the Interior) and abroad. Such weddings have increased by 25 percent and a growing number of Israelis choose not to marry at all, preferring to live as common law couples or to enter into contractual marriage agreements (www.newfamily.org.il/rec/103 [accessed October 24, 2017]).

This trend signifies a departure from the status quo in matters of personal status. It has been incorporated into the platforms of secular parties such as Meretz, Shinui, and Yesh Atid and in legislative initiatives to introduce civil marriage in Israel for the entire public or, alternatively, for those who are forbidden to marry according to Halakha, who have no religion, or who wish to marry someone of a different religion. Already in the 1960s, eleven legislative proposals were submitted to revoke the Marriage and Divorce Law.[22] Immigrants from the former Soviet Union who arrived in the 1990s encouraged civil marriage initiatives, particularly in light of the doubts cast on the Jewishness of some of them. The religious and ultra-Orthodox parties recognized the need to address this population, which is not considered Jewish according to Halakha. Consequently, these parties did not object to legislation that would allow civil marriage for non-Jews, if this would not open the door to change in personal status laws vis-à-vis Jews. Thus far, however, none of the proposals to introduce civil arrangements have won Knesset approval (S. Lifshitz 2006).

In 2006, the High Rabbinical Court ruled that civil marriage conducted abroad will be deemed marriage and that the religious courts would not recognize the right of a person married in such ceremonies to marry someone else: "From the perspective of civil law, the parties married civilly, and are considered married throughout the world, including the state of Israel." Consequently, the High Court of Justice stated that "the recognition of the validity of the [civil] marriage is required under the rules of private international law, which constitute an integral part of Israeli law."[23] Therefore, it ruled that civil marriages conducted abroad are valid in form and substance. In 2010, the Knesset enacted the Spousal Agreements for Persons without a Religion Law (2010), which allows citizens who do not belong to a recognized religious community to marry in a spousal agreement. This law does not apply to any other marriage between citizens who are members of a religion – neither same-sex nor inter-religious marriages. As things stand now (2017), civil marriage in Israel seems unlikely.

The laws of personal status are another example of the dynamic nature of the status quo. The situation has changed and the laws have become irrelevant for some Israelis who choose not to marry in Orthodox ceremonies. The voluntary arrangements in civil society have slowly penetrated the political system, and this may lead to changes in the law.

22 In 1972, the Independent Liberals submitted a legislative proposal to permit civil marriage for those forbidden to marry under Halakha in the wake of a rabbinical court ruling in which the children of a Jewish mother from her second marriage to a Jew were declared *mamzerim* because her first marriage was to a convert – Jurisdiction on Matters of Marriage and Divorce Law (1972) (Knesset Records, seventh Knesset, session 319, June 21, 1972). Rabbi Goren eliminated the children's *maer* status in a ruling by a special rabbinical court (S. Goren 1973).

23 Justice Barak in *Jane Doe v. Tel Aviv-Jaffa Regional Rabbinical Court* 2003 noted the problematic situation:

> The recognition in Israel of civil marriage between Jews, citizens, or residents of Israel, which were conducted under the wings of foreign law, raises difficult questions. A situation in which thousands of Jewish couples, citizens or residents of the state, do not marry in Israel in accordance with Jewish law, but instead marry in civil marriages outside of Israel creates a reality that Israeli jurisprudence must address … The "outward" recognition given by the High Rabbinical Court to civil marriages between Jews in accordance with Hebrew law itself is very significant. Though it does not amount to recognizing the full status of civil marriage, it contributes toward preventing a rift between civil and religious law…

Abortions, Autopsies, Burial

Jewish law absolutely forbids abortion except in the case of saving the mother; it prohibits autopsies, which are viewed as violating the dignity of the deceased; and it permits Jewish burial only for those who are Jewish according to Halakha. These positions are not accepted by a large part of the secular public; enforcing them strictly would lead to clashes with other laws and not reflect the current Israeli reality. Disagreements on these issues have sparked demonstrations and acts of violence by the ultra-Orthodox and engendered coalition crises.

Abortions: Mandate-era law, which did not specify reasons or procedures for approving abortions, was followed in practice until 1977. The Penal Code (Aborting Pregnancy) Amendment (1977) defined the grounds for permitting abortions – cases of rape, incest, out-of-wedlock pregnancy, or young age. The law was enacted despite opposition by the religious parties, which were enraged above all by the clause permitting abortion when necessary for a woman's wellbeing. Pursuant to the coalition agreements following the 1977 election, the law was amended in 1979 and the social welfare clause was removed. Thus, legal abortions are only permitted for women who are older than forty or younger than seventeen, or who are single and pregnant, in the event of incest or rape, or if the medical committee is convinced that maintaining the pregnancy was likely to cause emotional or physical harm to the mother, or if a defect is found in the fetus. There are anti-abortion organizations in civil society that seek to persuade women against having abortions, and other organizations that work to expand the right of women to control their bodies and undergo abortions if they so choose without the need for the state's approval (see the websites of Efrat, Right to an Abortion, and New Family).

Autopsies: Jewish law ascribes great importance to the dignity of the dead. Autopsies are said to violate the sanctity of the dead body and the commandment to conduct a burial without delay; they violate prohibitions on mutilating and disrespecting the dead, or benefiting and stealing from the deceased. Nonetheless, in the pre-state period, the chief rabbinate agreed to autopsies when it was difficult to ascertain the cause of death or when the autopsy might save the lives of others, if the deceased was treated with respect and ultimately buried. The Anatomy and Pathology Law (1953) states that a corpse may be used for scientific purposes if the person agrees to it in writing before death, or if the body remains unclaimed. The law also permits autopsies when the cause of death is unknown or to help treat another person. The ultra-Orthodox fiercely opposed this legislation and demonstrated against it. There were also cases of corpse snatching to prevent an autopsy. Under an agreement with the ultra-Orthodox parties, the law was amended in 1980 to severely limit the performance of autopsies: Even if only one family member objects, an autopsy is prohibited, and unclaimed corpses can no longer be used for scientific purposes.

Organ donation: Jewish law tends to frown upon organ donation because of the debate about defining the moment of death. From a medical perspective, organs like the heart and lungs are harvested as a donation after brain death, but this definition is controversial in Jewish law. Some argue that a person's death is determined only when he or she completely and irreversibly ceases to breathe autonomously (this was the position of the chief rabbinate in the past). Others contend that a person is alive as long as his or her heart is beating, even with the help of a machine, so that it is forbidden to take organs in this condition. In either case, there is no clear Halakhic proscription on receiving donated organs – despite the prohibition on benefiting from the deceased and the concern that the donors will lack their donated organs when the dead are resurrected at the end of days. The Brain-Respiratory Death Law (2008) outlines a detailed medical procedure for determining brain death, aimed at enabling the religious and traditional public to donate organs. The law, which is consistent with both Halakhic views and medical procedures, stipulates that a person will be deemed dead the moment his brain stem dies. This enables the harvesting of organs before the heart stops beating, an essential condition for transplanting organs like the heart, lung, and liver. In 2009, the High Rabbinical Council decided to recognize brain death as the indicator of a person's death (S. Ilan 2008; Ettinger and Even 2009).

Violating the dignity of the dead: There is great sensitivity in the ultra-Orthodox community about ensuring the dignity of the dead when graves are discovered in the course of archeological excavations or construction. Work has often come to a halt after finding graves due to the ensuing demonstrations and protests by the ultra-Orthodox. For example, the construction of an emergency room at the Barzilai Hospital in Ashkelon was repeatedly delayed after human bones were discovered at the construction site (Ettinger 2009).

Burial: Jewish burial in Israel has always been subject to the laws of religion. Burial services are provided by private non-profit burial societies (*hevra kadisha*), whose activity is regulated by law – Jewish Religious Services Regulations (Burial Societies) (1966) – and supervised by the Ministry of Religious Services. They are required to act as a public trust, be non-discriminatory, and avoid extraneous considerations. Halakhic burial sometimes evokes disputes between the burial society and the family of the deceased, for example regarding the wording on the tombstone. The court ruled that there is no reason why the deceased's name cannot be written in non-Hebrew letters on the tombstone, despite the burial society's claim that this is forbidden by Jewish law (*Shavit v. Rishon Letzion Burial Society* 1999).

Another serious problem is the burial site of those not considered Jews according to Halakha, but who have no other religion and view themselves as Jewish in every respect. This problem became acute following the immigration wave from the former Soviet Union, particularly pertaining to the burial of immigrant soldiers defined as non-Jews, who were buried "outside the fence," meaning at a distance from the other graves. Ultimately, a decision was made to allocate special burial plots for immigrant soldiers who are not Jewish. This painful issue, together with growing secular consciousness, led to enactment of the Right to Alternative Civil Burial Law (1996), which permits the establishment of civil cemeteries and the assignment of non-religious burial plots in existing cemeteries. The Menuha Nekhona Association operates civil cemeteries in kibbutzim and several cities (M. Sela 2002, 29). However, due to opposition from the burial societies and the Ministry of Religious Services, civil cemeteries have not been established in recent years. The burial of members of other religions is assigned to their respective religious organizations.

17.6 Religious Parties in the Political System

A. The Religious Parties – Zionist and Ultra-Orthodox

Soon after the founding of the Zionist movement, the Mizrahi movement began to organize as a Zionist, religious party (1902). (*Mizrahi* in this instance is a Hebrew acronym for *merkaz ruhani*, meaning a "spiritual center.") A decade later, in 1912, anti-Zionist, ultra-Orthodox organizations banded together as Agudat Yisrael. These two parties operated during the Yishuv period and have continued to operate under various names:

- The national-religious Mizrahi and Ha-Mizrahi parties, which merged in 1955 into the National Religious Party (NRP), now named the Jewish Home.
- The ultra-Orthodox parties Agudat Yisrael and Poalei Agudat Yisrael, which merged and separated several times under the name Religious Torah Front, and called United Torah Judaism (UTJ) since 1992.
- Shas (Sephardic Association of Torah Guardians) first competed as a party in the 1984 election. This ultra-Orthodox, Sephardic party splintered from Agudat Yisrael and within a decade became the largest ultra-Orthodox party in the Knesset.

Over the years, other religious parties emerged and disappeared, including Tami (the Jewish Tradition Movement) in the 1981 election; Morasha in the 1984 election; and Degel Hatorah in 1988, which later joined UTJ. The total number of Knesset seats won by the three religious parties in the elections of 2009, 2013, and 2015 were nineteen, thirty, and twenty-one, respectively (Table 17.7 below). UTJ averaged six seats and Shas eleven (in 2015 they won only seven, plus nearly four for the splinter list headed by Eli Yishai, which did not pass the electoral threshold). The NRP (eight seats in 2015) exhibited the greatest fluctuations.

The NRP (Mizrahi and Ha-Mizrahi)

The Mizrahi movement, unlike the ultra-Orthodox world, did not view the Zionist aspiration to establish a Jewish state in the Land of Israel as "hastening the end" – a forbidden attempt to "induce redemption before its time" (Schwartz 2009). The movement leader, Rabbi Isaac Jacob Reines, believed that the Torah and the Land of Israel are two complementary sanctities, and that observance of the commandments in the Land of Israel would ensure the nation's existence. In 1920, Mizrahi established its headquarters in Jerusalem and became an active partner in the institutions of the Zionist movement and the Yishuv. It split into the Mizrahi movement, the party of the religious middle class whose slogan was "the Land of Israel for the people of Israel according to the Torah of Israel"; and Ha-Mizrahi, a workers' movement whose slogan was "Torah and labor," which joined the Histadrut labor federation and established religious kibbutzim and moshavim.

The two Mizrahi parties were represented in the pre-state Assembly of Representatives and the 1948 provisional government. During this early period, they formed the "historic alliance" with Mapai that continued until 1977. The Mizrahi parties controlled the religious institutions and the provision of religious services, and the chief rabbinate, and their representative, Rabbi Kook, served as the first

Ashkenazi chief rabbi (1921–35). Prior to the 1949 election, the religious parties united as the Religious Front, despite opposition from Ha-Mizrahi, which feared that the ultra-Orthodox would sequester observant Jews in a ghetto and limit their involvement in all areas of life. The Religious Front did not last long, and each of the religious parties competed separately in the 1951 election. In 1955, the two parties merged to form the NRP, which was a regular partner in coalitions with Mapai.

The ideological change in the NRP began after the Six Day War, and accelerated after the Yom Kippur War. The NRP shifted from being a party whose primary concerns were "religious," to one that gave top priority to the national ethos and Israel's hold on the territories captured in 1967. From the outset, the NRP was composed of factions, and at that time the young people's faction called for "change and renewal" (Asher Cohen 2004). This entailed an ideological shift – raising the flag of the Greater Land of Israel and championing the settlement enterprise; as well as political change – severing the historic alliance with Mapai and aligning with the hawkish side of Israeli politics. The young guard of the movement wanted to move beyond its narrow religious focus, to break down their isolation, and become a factor in Israel's national and social life (Liebman and Don-Yehiya 1984, 103–5). There were also strong messianic motifs (Aran 1987, 437–95). The young guard became the dominant force in the NRP, and after the Yom Kippur War it effectively became the voice of Gush Emunim in the party and the government. The NRP paid an electoral price for this – it lost half its strength in the 1981 elections, falling to six seats. Some of its voters sought more hawkish stances and preferred the Likud, Tehiya, or even the racist Kach movement. Others, primarily moderate religious Sephardim, voted for Tami.

The NRP became a regular coalition partner with the Likud (1977–84) and was given the education ministry for the first time. On the eve of the 1988 election, a group of religious and political moderates led by Rabbi Yehuda Amital quit the NRP and formed Meimad, which had no electoral success. In the 1988 election, the NRP won five seats and became a partner in the national unity government, and later in the narrow, Likud-led government. After the 1992 election, when it won six seats, the NRP remained in the opposition. Shas, which was a member of the Rabin-led coalition, managed to displace it from a number of religious institutions. In the 1996 election, the NRP won nine Knesset seats following the change in the electoral system, which encouraged voting for small parties, and in reaction to attacks against the national-religious public following the assassination of Prime Minister Yitzhak Rabin. The NRP became a key partner in the coalition led by Netanyahu. In the 1999 election, the NRP split: Some of its more hawkish members joined the National Union Party, and it dropped down to five seats. In 2001, the NRP did not join Sharon's coalition. In the 2003 election, the NRP, headed by the hawkish Effi Eitam, initially joined Sharon's coalition and later quit over the evacuation of the Gaza Strip. In the 2006 election, the NRP joined the National Union party, and for the first time since the establishment of Israel, no national-religious party competed in the Knesset election. The combined list won nine seats (three by ex-NRP members). In 2009, with a new name ("Jewish Home – The New NRP"), it won three seats and joined Netanyahu's coalition. In 2013, Jewish Home (NRP with National Union), led by Naftali Bennett, managed to draw support from traditional and even secular voters, and won twelve seats and senior ministries. Two years later in the

2015 elections, the party lost votes to the Likud and dropped to eight seats (six to ex-NRP members). It joined the coalition and was given the education, agriculture, and justice ministries.

The NRP's wide-ranging fluctuations since the 1980s (from three to twelve seats) indicate the diminished centrality of traditional religious Zionism. The moderate religious public has become integrated into Israeli society and does not feel the need for their own, sectoral political representation, but the NRP party moved toward extremism, both religiously and politically. A subculture of nationalist ultra-Orthodox Jews emerged who are ultra-Orthodox in their approach to Halakha, matters of modesty, and rabbinical authority, as well as nationalist and even ultra-nationalist in their commitment to the Greater Land of Israel. The roots of this group are in the Merkaz HaRav Yeshiva in Jerusalem, inspired by Rabbi Zvi Yehuda Kook. This yeshiva wields substantial political power and radicalized the party's positions. The NRP after 1967, led by Yosef Burg and Zevulun Hammer, was moderate on political and religious issues, but the twenty-first-century party has positioned itself on the far right of the political spectrum (Yehuda Ben Meir 2009) and is only one component of the new national-religious camp (Hermann et al. 2015a).

Agudat Yisrael and Poalei Agudat Yisrael (UTJ since 1992)

Established in 1912 in Katowice, Poland, as the ultra-Orthodox response to the nascent Zionist movement, Agudat Yisrael soon became active in Palestine too. From the outset until today, its leadership has been in the hands of rabbis of stature, referred to as the Council of Torah Sages, whose decisions guide the party's activity. Agudat Yisrael did not participate in the institutions of the Yishuv, preferring to remain separate. After the Holocaust, however, it adopted more moderate positions and engaged in pragmatic cooperation with the Yishuv institutions, primarily due to the leadership of the Gur Rebbe and his son-in-law, party leader Yitzhak Meir Levin. Consequently, extremist ultra-Orthodox movements such as Ha'edah Haharedit wanted no ties with heretical Zionism. Agudat Yisrael reflects the structure of ultra-Orthodox society, which is composed of different rabbinical communities, some of them dynasties, each representing a branch of ultra-Orthodoxy – the centrist Gur community, devotees of the Porush family, the Vizhnitz community, and the Lithuanian faction headed by Rabbi Shach, which quit the party in 1988 to form Degel Hatorah and returned in 1992 as part of UTJ.

Agudat Yisrael opposed the creation of a Jewish state in the historical Land of Israel and supported the continuation of the British Mandate. However, as the day of reckoning neared, it recognized the sovereignty of the national institutions and cooperated with them. Establishment of a secular state evoked great concern among them that "a Jew would not be able to live according to the Torah" (Friedman 2005, 68–77). On the other hand, they realized the need to have the interests of the ultra-Orthodox public represented in the new state and receive a share of resources. Consequently, Agudat Yisrael's leadership was willing to reach an accommodation that would enable coexistence with the secular majority. The aforementioned letter from Ben-Gurion to Agudat Yisrael's leader, Yitzhak Meir Levin, in 1947 was a key factor enabling a modus vivendi and allaying the concerns of the ultra-Orthodox. The promises offered in the letter paved the way for Agudat Yisrael's participation in 1948 in the Provisional State Council and in the coalition until 1952. Subsequently, by decision of the Council of Torah Sages, Agudat Yisrael was not represented in the government itself and did not bear direct ministerial responsibility in order to avoid taking part in the management of the affairs of a secular state. There were ways to work around this, however, and Agudat Yisrael (since 1992 as UTJ) has sometimes been a coalition partner. For example, UTJ joined the coalition formed after the 2015 election with two deputy ministers (health and education), as well as the chair of the Finance Committee, a prized parliamentary post.[24]

The Poalei Agudat Yisrael (PAY) party was initially part of Agudat Yisrael and accepted the authority of the Council of Torah Sages. Nevertheless, already in the Yishuv period, Agudat Yisrael leaders did not look favorably upon PAY's willingness to cooperate with the Zionist movement and Yishuv institutions. PAY was a partner in the Religious Front in 1949, which left the government in 1951 because of its opposition to mandatory conscription of women into the IDF or Sherut Leumi service. Since the 1961 election, PAY ran as a separate list and garnered one or two seats until 1981, when it failed to win representation. In 1984, Poalei Agudat Yisrael was a partner in the Morasha list that won two seats, and since the 1988 elections, it has been part of a joint list with Agudat Yisrael/UTJ.

Shas (Sephardic Association of Torah Guardians)

The success of the Mizrahi (Sephardic) ultra-Orthodox lists in the local elections in 1983 in Bnei Brak, Jerusalem, and Tiberias encouraged the formation of Shas prior to the 1984 election, with the slogan "restoring the glory of yore." The glory not only pertains to abiding by tradition and religious commandments; Shas also explicitly aims to enhance the stature of the traditional and ultra-Orthodox Mizrahi public. Shas grew out of a sense of continuous discrimination against ultra-Orthodox Mizrahim in Ashkenazi ultra-Orthodox society and in Agudat Yisrael. The desire to organize as a political power had existed for a long time, and the final push was provided by the spiritual leaders Rabbi Ovadia Yosef (1920–2013), a former Sephardi chief rabbi (the "Rishon Letzion"), and Rabbi Shach, who gave his blessing to the new party in the wake of a crisis in Agudat Yisrael. Shas is a party with interlocking and overlapping identities.

Although Shas is an ultra-Orthodox party, many of its voters are not ultra-Orthodox; Shas grew out of the Ashkenazi ultra-Orthodox world, but its voters are primarily Mizrahim; it regularly participates in coalitions and is part of the state establishment, but it regards itself as an "outsider" that represents the poor, the periphery, and parents who want a traditional education for their children. Shas voters earn less than the average salary, have a lower-than-average level of education among Jews, and include a high percentage of women and young people. Over the years, the Shas voter base has changed: In the 1990s, the percentage of ultra-Orthodox declined, while that of traditional and secular voters increased (Hermann and Yaar 2001, 355–68). In the 2000s, however, the decline of the party to eleven to twelve seats in the Knesset (only seven in 2015 due to a split) reflected another

[24] The UTJ deputy minister of health served with the power and authority of a full minister, while the prime minister held the titular post of health minister. In 2015, the High Court of Justice annulled this long-standing arrangement (*Yesh Atid v. Prime Minister et al.* 2015).

Table 17.6 *Shas voters: Religious self-definitions (%)*

Election year	Secular	Traditional	Religious	Ultra-Orthodox
2001	10	12	24	53
2003	6	17	25	52
2006	3	23	24	51
2009	0	24	21	55
2013	2	8	29	62
2015	0	7	29	64

Source: Israel National Election Studies 1999–2015.

major shift in the electoral base (Table 17.6). Its secular voters disappeared, the traditionals dwindled to 7–8 percent, and the ultra-Orthodox Mizrahi voters became the clear majority.

Shas is an ethnic party of Mizrahim according to the three criteria of messages, constituency, and leadership. Compared to earlier attempts to form ethnic parties, it is the most successful ethnic party and certainly the most successful Mizrahi party in Israel's history. For over thirty years, Shas has filled a vacuum in the political landscape when it transformed ethnic deprivation into a political resource, and the traditional-Mizrahi public into a distinct electoral force.

Unlike the Ashkenazi ultra-Orthodox parties, *Shas is a moderate ultra-Orthodox party*, more attuned to mainstream Israeli society. Nonetheless, the structure is similar – the rabbinical leadership in which a Council of Torah Sages chooses the party's leader and Knesset slate, and makes binding decisions for the party's MKs. Shas also declares the supremacy of Torah law and its desire to institute Halakhic law in Israel, but its approach is more conciliatory and for many years it has refrained from tabling religious legislation. Shas operates an independent education stream and a network of civil organizations, but unlike UTJ, its activity is not exclusively intended for the ultra-Orthodox public. Rather, it seeks to bring the traditional public closer to religion. Shas adopted a pragmatic approach to politics, which views coalition agreements as a legitimate means for obtaining support for its institutions. It has also not hesitated to accept responsibility for government ministries, and it exercises its political power to promote the interests of its constituency.

Shas is not an anti-Zionist party, but does not declare itself to be Zionist. Its statement of principles asserts that the movement "believes in the existence of the state of Israel as the state of the Jewish people, a state based on the values of democracy in accordance with the Torah of Israel." The "Zionism" of Shas is expressed in love for the Land of Israel, faith in the return to Zion, and willingness to live in Israel. When Zionism is identified with secular principles that clash with the Halakha – Shas rejects it.[25] Unlike religious Zionism, Shas does not view Israel as the harbinger of redemption, but has a positive attitude toward the state. Most Shas supporters serve in the IDF and cannot imagine boycotting Israel or isolating themselves from it.

25 See Baum-Banai 2001 for Zionist and anti-Zionist statements by Shas leaders.

Shas is not an emphatically hawkish party, and it sometimes seems to be a dovish party: Rabbi Ovadia Yosef spoke about returning territory because the preservation of human life overrides religious commandments (*pikuah nefesh*). The fact that Shas joined a coalition of leftist parties headed by Rabin (1992) can also be seen as a sign of dovish tendencies. However, a close look at the conduct of Shas MKs (including coalition members), and particularly an analysis of their voters' views, indicates that Shas is a moderate, not dovish, party with a pragmatic political line on foreign affairs and security, certainly compared to the hawkishness of the NRP (Hermann and Yaar 2001).

Shas is a *social movement* that operates from the "bottom up" with funding from the "top down" in order to promote a socioeconomic revolution in a religious spirit (Tesler 2001). The El Hama'ayan school system is designed to foster the traditional values of religious Judaism, educate the youth about Judaism and religious observance, and convey knowledge about Judaism to the general public, primarily the traditional one. Its cultural centers for Torah activity drew considerable response – they are funded by the state and provide services free of charge. In late 1992, less than a decade after it was founded, El Hama'ayan had about 350 branches, mainly in cities in the periphery. This activity yielded electoral results: Support for Shas grew impressively in places where El Hama'ayan was active. Over time, El Hama'ayan became an umbrella organization for women's associations, the Institute for Family Purity, a youth movement, organizations designed to persuade secular Jews to "return" to faith, and organizations for certifying kashrut. The Ma'ayan Hahinukh Hatorani education stream (see above) was initially funded by the Ministry of Religions and, as of 1990, by the Ministry of Education. It is notable for providing a long school day and meals for pupils. The network expanded rapidly and government funding grew commensurately. In the coalition agreements of 1992, the network was recognized as an independent body and a commitment was made to fund it according to the model of the independent ultra-Orthodox stream.

The fact that Shas repeatedly positioned itself in the role of coalition kingmaker enabled it to threaten a coalition crisis whenever its demands were not met, which usually culminated in increased funding for its institutions. It is estimated that, in the years 1991–98, funding for Shas educational institutions increased 600 percent beyond the rise in number of students and scope of activity (S. Ilan 2000b). Shas's methods of funding its activity frequently came under fire from the public and the state comptroller for improper management. Such methods included, for example, "double dipping" – accepting allocations for the same purposes from both the Ministry of Religion and the Ministry of Education; using multiple names for the same organization in order to access double funding; diverting funds to educational and religious organizations from budgets designed for other purposes; and falsely reporting the number of pupils and scope of activity. Aryeh Deri, the leader of Shas, was convicted of fraud and breach of trust for actions related to the transfer of funds while minister of the interior. Shas's campaign propaganda is unique in combining modern methods (new media, satellite television, video tapes, radio stations, and newspapers) with controversial religious symbols. In the 1996 elections, Rabbi Yosef and Rabbi Kedourie traveled throughout Israel distributing blessings and amulets in exchange for a promise to vote for Shas.[26] The rise of

[26] A 2000 amendment to the Knesset Election (Consolidated Version) Law (1969) prohibits the distribution of amulets.

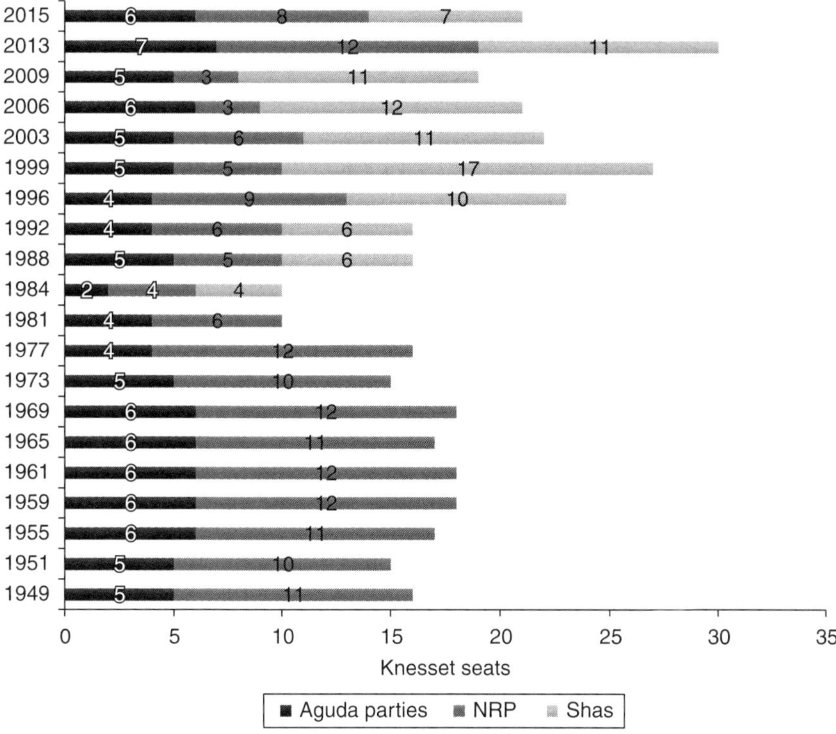

Figure 17.2 Representation of religious and ultra-Orthodox parties (Aguda parties; NRP/Jewish Home; and Shas) in the Knesset (1949–2015)
Note: The NRP in 1949 and 1951 includes both Mizrahi and Ha-Mizrahi. In 1981, the total includes Tami's three seats. In 1984, the total includes one Tami seat and Aguda includes two Morasha seats. In 1988, Aguda includes two seats of Degel Hatorah. In 2006 and 2009, the total includes six and four seats, respectively, of National Union, later absorbed by the NRP/Jewish Home.
Source: Knesset website.

Shas halted in the 2003 elections, but its strength in the Knesset has remained stable: eleven to twelve seats (Figure 17.2). Rabbi Ovadia Yosef died in October 2013 and the struggle for the leadership between Eli Yishai and Aryeh Deri split the party. Shas won seven seats in 2015, while Eli Yishai's Yahad did not pass the electoral threshold. Shas joined the coalition in 2015 with two ministers and two deputy ministers.

After more than three decades in politics, it can be said that Shas – unlike other parties with a meteoric rise to power (Rafi, Dash, Shinui, Kadima), and unlike other ethnic parties, none of which survived for long – has succeeded in establishing itself and coalescing a faithful constituency. The loyalty of Shas voters is rooted in a combination of religion, tradition, a sense of social discrimination, and services provided by the Shas network to poor populations. Shas also blurs some of the conventional boundaries in Israeli politics vis-à-vis religious parties: It is a religious party that has occasionally voiced dovish views; it is an ultra-Orthodox party that is not anti-Zionist; and it is a religious party whose voter base is ethnic and traditional, with a handful of secular supporters.

B. The Uniqueness of the Religious and Ultra-Orthodox Parties

A party can be characterized by three criteria: constituency, elected officials, and platform. In the past, NRP voters were primarily religious Zionists while Aguda voters were ultra-Orthodox. Shas began to change this because a large number of its voters are not ultra-Orthodox. However, the combined percentage of religious, ultra-Orthodox, and traditional Israelis is greater than 50 percent, while their electoral weight in the Knesset is 20–25 percent (21% in 2015 if Yahad headed by Yishai is included). In other words, not all religious, ultra-Orthodox, and traditional Israelis vote for religious parties. With regard to elected officials, the MKs chosen from these parties were ultra-Orthodox or religious (except for one or two secular MKs in Jewish Home in 2013 and in 2015). The platforms of these parties contain distinct religious messages – such as preserving and strengthening the Jewish character of Israel. Unlike UTJ, the NRP adds political messages, with an emphasis on settling the Greater Land of Israel and opposing the uprooting of settlements. The Shas platform is not exclusively religious; it also addresses social rights and the welfare state. Below we present additional characteristics that distinguish the religious and ultra-Orthodox parties, despite their differences, from the other parties.

The religious parties are "camp parties" – clearly identified with a specific public. Each of the religious parties has a separate school system, which indicates the central role played by these parties in shaping the identity of their members. They remain "catch-all" parties as Mapai had been in the past – maintaining separate institutions and providing services for their religious constituency from cradle to grave. The NRP, for example, provides kindergartens, state-religious schools, the Bnei Akiva youth movement, schools for young women, *hesder* yeshivas, the Emunah women's movement, the *Hazofe* newspaper (closed in 2008), the Religious Kibbutz Movement, and Ha-Mizrahi's Union of Moshavim.

The ultra-Orthodox parties are subject to the authority of religious leaders. In Agudat Yisrael and Shas, the rabbinical councils have the final say on all matters, including political issues. There are no democratic institutions or procedures in either party for electing candidates to local or Knesset elections. The list of candidates is determined by the party's Council of Torah Sages, and often by a single rabbi. The MKs in these parties have no independent discretion on most matters, particularly when it comes to joining or quitting a coalition, voting on proposed legislation, and decisions on the state budget or foreign affairs. They generally obey the decisions of the religious leadership. Indeed, Rabbis Shach and Ovadia Yosef became key political figures, with leaders from other parties lobbying them on the eve of elections or before important decisions. For example, Rabbi Ovadia Yosef's support for Yitzhak Rabin in 1992 paved the way for Shas participation in the coalition and approval of the Oslo Accords; Rabbi Shach's support for Benjamin Netanyahu in the 1996 election contributed to his victory. These rabbis also did not refrain from mixing rabbinical rulings with political matters. For example, a handwritten letter from Rabbi Ovadia Yosef on the eve of the 2006 election stated: "And I am making a ruling of Halakha! That everyone must vote and exercise influence for Shas. Be aware that voting for Shas strengthens the Torah and strengthens the yeshiva students, and strengthens the commandments of the holy Torah." After his death, religious authority waned in Shas.

The ultra-Orthodox parties do not operate according to democratic rules. They meet the minimum requirements under the Political Parties Law (a constitution, institutions, internal auditing, etc.) in order to participate in the election, and no more. Their undemocratic nature is particularly salient in the lack of representation for women; there is no female representation in their internal institutions, and certainly none in the Knesset or local government. The NRP, on the other hand, does not prohibit the participation of women. Over the years, several women have served as MKs from the NRP. Still, the representation of women is low in comparison to other parties (after the 2015 elections, one of eight).

The NRP is different than the ultra-Orthodox parties. The religious leadership and the political leadership are distinct. Thus, the NRP has never had a rabbinical body that serves as a supreme arbiter or a religious leader whose word is law on public issues. Moreover, the party operated in the past via democratic institutions. However, the phenomenon of obedience to rabbis among the settlers has influenced the NRP, and prior to the disengagement from the Gaza Strip (2005), some in the NRP called for submitting political decisions to the "test of Halakha" (Don-Yehiya 2005). Under the leadership of Naftali Bennett since 2013, the party has returned to the model of separating religion from state.

Electoral stability (Figure 17.2). The NRP had a loyal voter base in the past, and UTJ still does. This is because they are camp parties: Their voters identify with them and are willing to obey the parties' religious leaders. Agudat Yisrael in its various incarnations shows particular electoral stability – five to seven seats in every election since 1949 despite a high birthrate among its voters, indicating that the number of those who leave the UTJ fold or choose not to vote offsets the number of new voters. The electoral success of Shas has fluctuated greatly since its peak of seventeen seats in 1999 because its voter base is more diverse and dispersed, and includes traditional Jews who voted for the Likud and NRP in the past. In the 1999 election, the Shas Council of Torah Sages exhorted its public to vote for Shas and for Benjamin Netanyahu as prime minister (Aloush and Elituv 2004, 293). Continuous electoral stability – an average of eleven seats – also characterized the NRP until 1977. Since 1981, for the aforementioned reasons, the NRP lost votes to the right-wing and ultra-Orthodox parties, and its power dwindled. On the verge of disappearing, it merged with the National Union party, gaining twelve seats in 2013 and eight in 2015.

From a political perspective, the religious and ultra-Orthodox parties took upon themselves two main roles – struggling to infuse public space with Jewishness, and protecting the religious minority by representing its interests (Don-Yehiya and Liebman 1977). They did this primarily by preserving the status quo and simultaneously trying to expand it as much as possible. There was also a division of labor among the religious parties. The ultra-Orthodox focused less on affairs of state and more on protecting their minority rights and getting more funds for their institutions;

the NRP until 1977 controlled the religious establishment – the Ministry of Religion, the chief rabbinate, and the religious councils – and concentrated on strengthening religion in the lives of individuals, the community, and the public, with the backing of the ultra-Orthodox parties. After 1977, the NRP focused on retaining the Greater Land of Israel, promoting settlements, and resisting any territorial withdrawal. Indeed, in the past, the percentage of support for the NRP beyond the Green Line was threefold higher than the national average (Asher Cohen 2005). This support, however, subsequently diminished, and the NRP largely yielded the role of protecting the status quo to the ultra-Orthodox parties. The process of change in Shas was different. In its early days, it mainly raised the flag of ethnic discrimination, and later began to view itself as a social party that looks after the downtrodden in general, in addition to representing the Mizrahi ultra-Orthodox public.

Another change is that the three religious parties are now, in practice, part of the hawkish front. The ultra-Orthodox public and its leaders, who were moderate for many years on questions of foreign affairs and security, mobilized for the fight against the Oslo Accords, and from the mid-1990s have adopted positions close to those of the Likud. Direct election of the prime minister (1996–2003) brought to the surface the hawkish views of the ultra-Orthodox voters, which called for their leaders to take a clear stand for one candidate, and they adopted a position consistent with the right-wing inclinations of the ultra-Orthodox public (N. Horowitz 2002, 11). Likewise, the inclusion of all three religious parties in the 2015 Netanyahu coalition was assured.

C. Elections and Coalitions: The Power of the Religious Bloc and the "Balancing" Position

Figure 17.2 shows that the major change in the collective power of the religious parties was enhanced by the rising power of Shas, which won seventeen seats in the 1999 election, making it the third-largest party in the Knesset. Shas drew many new voters from the Mizrahi-traditional camp, thus the religious/ultra-Orthodox bloc in the Knesset gained considerable influence.

The electoral weight of the religious bloc does not necessarily indicate its real political power. The balance of power between the large parties is a better predictor of the religious bloc's power than its electoral strength. In the 1980s, despite their waning electoral strength, the religious parties increased their power because the stalemate between the two major parties turned them into the deciding factor. In fact, even when the religious bloc was at its electoral nadir (the elections in 1981 and 1984), it wielded great power because it was in a position to determine which big party would form the coalition. It is customary to say that since 1977 and the disappearance of the dominant party, the religious parties since have held the balancing position in the Knesset. The power of a balancing party derives from its ability to ally with a large party (or bloc) and determine who will hold the reins of government; or from the fact that their departure from the coalition would turn it into a minority coalition.

Table 17.7 presents a more complex picture of the religious parties' participation in coalitions. It shows that there was a tendency to invite them to join even when there was no coalition imperative. In 1955 and 1959, for example, the religious

Table 17.7 *Religious parties: Knesset seats, participation in first post-election coalitions, and coalition weight (1949–2015)*

Election	NRP (Jewish Home)	Agudat Yisrael (UTJ)	Poalei Agudat Yisrael	Other*	Weight in coalition	Balancing position?**	Ministries
1949	Religious Front – 16				16/73	Yes	3: Interior & Immigration; Welfare; Religion & War Injured
1951	10	3	2		15/65	Yes	4: Interior & Religion; Health; Transportation; Welfare
1955	11				11/80	No	2: Religion & Welfare; Postal Service
1959	12				12/86	No	2: Interior; Welfare***
1961	12		****		12/68	Yes	3: Interior & Health; Religion; Welfare
1965	11		2		13/75	No	3: Interior; Religion; Welfare
1969	12				12/102	No	3: Interior; Religion; Welfare
1973	10				10/68	Yes	3: Interior; Religion; Welfare
1977	12	4			16/62	Yes	3: Interior; Education & Culture; Religion
1981	6	4		3	13/61	Yes	4: Interior & Religion; Education & Culture; Labor & Welfare; Absorption
			Shas				
1984	4	2	4	2	12/97	No	3 ministers without portfolio
1988	5	5	6	–	16/95	No	4: Interior; Absorption; Religion; without portfolio
1992	–	–	6	–	6/62	Yes	1: Interior
1996	9	4	10	–	23/66	Yes	5: Interior; Labor & Welfare; Education & Culture; Transportation; Religion
1999	5	5	17	–	27/75	Yes	5: Health; Labor & Welfare; Infrastructure; Construction & Housing; Religion
2003	6	–	–	–	6/68	No	2: Welfare; Construction & Housing
2006	–	–	12	–	12/78	No	5: Industry, Commerce & Labor; Religion; Communications; 2 without portfolio
2009	3	5	11	–	19/74	Yes	4: Interior; Construction & Housing; Religion; 1 without portfolio
2013	12	–	–	–	12/68	Yes	3: Economy; Construction & Housing; Senior Citizens
2015	8	6	7	–	21/61	Yes	6: Education; Justice; Agriculture; Economy; Religion; Health

* Other: 1981 Tami (three MKs and one minister); 1984 Morasha (two MKs and one minister without portfolio); 2003 National Union (seven MKs).
** Balancing position: the government would lose its majority if the religious parties quit the coalition en bloc.
*** The Ministry of Religion was headed then by a non-partisan, Rabbi Ya'akov Toledano.
**** Poalei Agudat Yisrael joined the coalition (with two MKs) in 1963.

Note: An empty space means the party did not participate in the coalition, or did not exist at the time.
Source: Knesset website.

parties were not in a balancing position and Mapai could have formed a coalition without them, yet the NRP still joined. This was also the case after the 1965 election and in the National Unity Government of 1969. In the unity governments formed after the 1984 and 1988 elections, the two major parties had a majority coalition without the religious parties. However, the religious parties were essential because their decision to join one of the blocs could have determined which party formed the coalition.

The Zionist religious parties were coalition partners during the Yishuv period, so it was natural to bring them into the first government. In retrospect, however, this largely shaped the status quo and granted political power to the religious camp. Mapai viewed the religious public as comfortable allies and was willing to pay the price of compromise on matters of state and religion, while the Mizrahi parties (later the NRP) secured their control over the religious institutions and the state-religious education stream. After the "historical alliance" with Mapai was abandoned in 1977, the NRP continued to be a partner in Likud-led coalitions, and its political power increased as its position became more significant. It was a partner in the unity governments and continued to be a member of the ruling coalition until 1992. The NRP did not join the Rabin government in 1992 because of differences regarding the territories; after many years of coalition membership, it remained outside. The party returned to the coalition in 1996, this time headed by Netanyahu, and was a partner in the Barak coalition in 1999. However, it quit the coalition over disagreements on foreign affairs and security policies. In 2001, it initially refrained from joining the Sharon-led coalition, but returned to the coalition in 2002 and was a partner in the 2003 Sharon government until bolting in the wake of the disengagement plan. In 2006, the NRP-National Union remained outside the coalition because of its opposition to Prime Minister Olmert's plan to evacuate settlements, but later joined the coalition led by Netanyahu in 2009. In 2013, Jewish Home collaborated with Yesh Atid to impose a coalition without the participation of Shas and UTJ. In 2015, the three religious parties joined the coalition, forming a substantial third of the coalition members. In Israel's political history, the NRP has participated in more coalitions, of left and right, than any other party.

Agudat Yisrael was a partner in the first and second coalitions until it resigned in 1952 because of its opposition to compulsory national service for religious young women. Twenty-five years passed before it returned to the Likud-led coalition in 1977 and remained a coalition partner until 1992. It did not join Rabin's government in 1992, but returned to coalitions led by Netanyahu in 1996 and Barak in 1999. The party later quit Barak's coalition in protest over a Sabbath violation (the "turbine affair") by the Israel Electric Corporation. UTJ did not join the coalition formed after the 2006 elections, but returned in 2009 as a partner in the Netanyahu government. As noted, it remained outside the coalition in 2013 and returned in 2015 to the positions it had held in 2009.

Since the first foray of Shas into Knesset elections in 1984, it has been a regular coalition partner: in unity governments (1984, 1988), and governments led by Shamir (1990), Rabin (1992), Netanyahu (1996), and Barak (1999). For the first time in its history, Shas did not join the coalition in 2003, when Sharon formed the government. It was a coalition partner in the Olmert government (2006) and the Netanyahu government (2009), remained outside in 2013, and returned to the Netanyahu government in 2015.

The religious parties' participation in coalitions (Table 17.7) cannot be explained by coalition imperatives alone. During its dominant rule, Mapai preferred to have the NRP in the coalition even when the party's support was superfluous to achieve a Knesset majority. Similarly, the Likud brought Shas into the coalition even when its support was not essential. In Chapter 11, we observed that the presence of religious parties in coalitions also stems from the desire to include the camp of observant Jews in the government and thus ease tensions within Israeli society.

D. Coalition Agreements on Religious Issues

Study of the coalition agreements indicates the issues of greatest concern to the religious parties over the years, and reveals how the emphasis shifted from matters of state and religion (and preserving the status quo), to the issues discussed above. The scope of coalition demands, particularly the funding of educational and religious institutions, reflects the growing political power of the religious and ultra-Orthodox parties, and the willingness of the main coalition partners to meet their demands.

Coalition agreements with the Religious Front after the establishment of Israel shaped the parameters of the status quo, primarily with regard to the rabbinical courts and kashrut in public institutions. The conflict over education ended in a compromise – granting autonomy to the state-religious school system within the framework of the Ministry of Education. The coalition agreement in the third Knesset (1955) explicitly cites the status quo for the first time as the guiding principle for religious matters in Israel: "In the laws of marriage and divorce, public transportation, and all other religious matters, the status quo will be maintained during the term of this government."

A similar clause would appear in subsequent coalition agreements in the 1950s and 1960s. A change in the substance and scope of religious demands occurred in the first coalition formed by Menachem Begin, in 1977, when the NRP and Agudat Yisrael controlled the balancing position (16 of the 62-member coalition). In addition to obtaining three ministries, including for the first time the Ministry of Education and Culture, the agreement also met the NRP's demand to change the criteria for granting army exemptions to religious young women. Agudat Yisrael, which returned to the coalition after an absence of twenty-five years, made do with chair of the Knesset Finance Committee, consent to amend the Law of Return, and more funding for the ultra-Orthodox sector. Most of the sections in the 1981 coalition agreement between the Likud and the NRP, Agudat Yisrael, and Tami address issues pertaining to the status quo. Seventeen sections, for example, concern the Sabbath: reducing work, tightening supervision of Sabbath work permits, closing the ports, and halting El Al flights. Additional subjects included stricter enforcement of kashrut, ensuring the autonomous status of religious and ultra-Orthodox schools, halting excavations in areas where graves are found, and housing assistance for the religious and ultra-Orthodox public.

In the 1980s, "special funds" appeared in the coalition agreements – direct state funding for NGOs, primarily those of the religious and ultra-Orthodox parties. The special funds were transferred in two channels: via a list of names in the

Budget Law of institutions to be funded; and via the budgets of government ministries, usually those headed by a minister from the religious and ultra-Orthodox parties – Education, Religion, and the Interior. Reports from the state comptroller and public outrage were not sufficient to halt this system of special funds until the High Court forbade such grants without clear, relevant, and equal criteria (*Tomkhei Temimim Yeshiva v. State of Israel* 1983). Subsequently, a 1992 amendment to the Budget Principles Law prohibited the funding of special institutions via the Budget Law and stipulated that criteria must be formulated that meet standards of equality. Nonetheless, circuitous ways were found to transfer money to the favored institutions of the ultra-Orthodox parties, for example by making exceptions for the Center for Independent Education and Ma'ayan Hahinukh Haharedi, or by customizing criteria to particular institutions (De Hartog 1998).

There was also a status quo about importing kosher meat only, and exclusively by the state. The decision to privatize meat imports undermined this arrangement and, as noted, a change in Basic Law: Freedom of Occupation was required to restore the status quo ante. At the same time, the coalition agreements of the 1990s reflect the change in priorities of the religious parties. In the NRP's coalition agreement with the Barak government in 1999, for example, maintaining the status quo is mentioned only in a general way, and the other sections are devoted to matters of state and the roles and authority of the party's ministers. On the other hand, the coalition agreements with Shas and UTJ primarily deal with status quo issues – the conscription of yeshiva students and conversion. There was also a new topic of great importance to Shas – safeguarding the ultra-Orthodox sector's unique media channels. The agreement with UTJ aimed at maintaining the ultra-Orthodox way of life wherever they constitute a majority, preserving the independent status of ultra-Orthodox schooling, respecting the dignity of the dead, and observance of the Sabbath. The agreements also reflect the religious parties' fear that the courts would interpret Basic Laws in a way that contravenes religious law – in the name of values such as human dignity and equality. Thus, in the coalition agreements with Shas in 1992 and afterwards, a clause was inserted stating that any change in religious legislation would require the consent of all coalition partners. The 2006 coalition agreement with Shas also included demands pertaining to social welfare – raising child allowances and allocating resources for at-risk youth. In the coalition agreement between the Likud and the religious parties after the 2009 elections, the central topic was funding for Torah institutions and religious services. The coalition formed in 2013 excluded Shas and UTJ, primarily in order to facilitate legislative changes on conversion and the conscription of ultra-Orthodox Jews. These changes were not implemented during the short lifetime of that coalition. In the coalition agreements with the two ultra-Orthodox parties in 2015, the Likud promised to amend the legal changes made by the outgoing government and, in practice, return to the status quo ante.[27]

The coalition agreements show the change in emphases in the religious parties: NRP/Jewish Home – senior ministries and matters of state; Shas – ministries,

[27] See the coalition agreements of the thirty-fourth government between the Likud and the Shas and UTJ parties (April/May 2015), which included undertakings to amend the Defense Service Law of 2014 on the conscription of yeshiva students (Knesset website: http://main.knesset.gov.il/mk/government/Pages/CoalitionAgreements.aspx [in Hebrew] [accessed June 29, 2016]).

designated budgets, and social welfare; and Agudat Yisrael/UTJ (which participated in only some of the coalitions) – preserving the status quo, independence of ultra-Orthodox education, larger budgets, and, more recently, conscription, employment, and health. Many subjects are copied from one coalition agreement to the next, testifying to the fact that they were not implemented.

E. Coalition Crises due to Conflicts over Religion

The NRP was a partner in all the coalitions from 1949 to 1976, but these coalitions did not always operate smoothly. In fact, some of the most severe coalition crises, including some that led to the collapse of the government, revolved around religious issues. Particularly salient are the crises with the religious parties in the formative stage of the status quo agreement in the 1950s. The first coalition crisis was about education in the immigrant camps and occurred in February 1950, about a year after the formation of the government. Mapai, led by David Ben-Gurion, was forced to accept the demands of the religious parties: The immigrants from North Africa would be able to choose religious education, and in the camps of immigrants from Yemen, only religious education would be offered. A dispute over education arose again, even more intensely, at the end of 1950. This time, however, no compromise was reached; Ben-Gurion resigned and the government toppled. The second Knesset saw a controversy over the conscription of religious young women into military service and the Compulsory National Service for Women Law, and in September 1952, the ultra-Orthodox parties quit the government. The Mizrahi parties remained, however, enabling the government to continue.

In 1958, a dispute arose over the question "Who is a Jew?" (see Section 17.5A above), and the NRP left the government, returning only after the 1959 election when it was placed in charge of this issue (under the Ministry of the Interior). In the 1970s, a crisis again erupted in the wake of the Shalit case, and even though the NRP's departure would not have endangered the broad coalition, the Alignment (Mapai) acceded to its demand to amend the Law of Return and define a Jew in accordance with Halakha. The Alignment did not agree, however, to the NRP's demand to accept only Halakhic conversion as valid for defining a Jew (see above). After 1967, and especially after the formation of Gush Emunim (1974), the NRP also raised demands on issues of foreign affairs and security. Thus, for example, it joined the 1974 Rabin government only after receiving a promise that no territorial compromises would be made without holding a referendum.

The crisis that led to the breakup of the Rabin coalition in 1976 was the delivery of F-15 planes after the onset of the Sabbath. Agudat Yisrael, which was not a member of the coalition, submitted a no-confidence motion and the MKs from the NRP abstained from the vote, in violation of the principle of collective responsibility. Rabin decided, out of political calculations, to fire the three NRP ministers and resign, setting in motion early elections. The crisis also marks the end of the "historical alliance" between Mapai and the NRP. After the political upheaval in 1977, the religious parties (NRP and Agudat Yisrael) joined the coalition headed by the Likud. In November 1979, the NRP threatened to leave the government over an issue that was not directly related to religion or the status quo – the Supreme Court directive to evacuate the settlement in Elon Moreh. Maintaining the status quo became the province of Agudat Yisrael, which initiated a coalition crisis in 1979 by demanding modifications in the Abortion Law. In the 1980s, no coalition crises ensued over religious issues, but the religious parties played a key role in the crisis between the Likud and Labor in 1990, demonstrating their political muscle. At first, Shas and some of the Agudat Yisrael MKs joined forces with the Labor Party to bring down the unity government and form a coalition headed by Shimon Peres. However, a few MKs had second thoughts and did not show up for the Knesset vote to approve the coalition. Shas and Agudat Yisrael later joined a narrow government led by Yitzhak Shamir in exchange for special funding, laws to ban obscene advertisements, limiting public transportation on the Sabbath, and amendment of the Authorization Law.

The Deri trial that began in the 1990s diverted the emphasis from the religious to the ethnic sphere, and sharpened the resentment of the ultra-Orthodox public toward the justice system. The Rabin coalition formed after the 1992 election was crisis prone from the outset due to the combination of Shas and Meretz. The first crisis arose when Shas threatened to quit the coalition if Shulamit Aloni continued as minister of education, and she was replaced. A second crisis occurred in the wake of a High Court ruling on importing non-kosher meat (see above), and the government capitulated. Finally, Deri's indictment in 1993 prompted the departure of Shas from the government. From the mid-1990s, most of the crises have not been on issues that are directly religious. The NRP ministers voted in the Knesset against the Netanyahu government's Hebron Agreement in 1997, but the prime minister opted not to fire them. Shas quit the Barak coalition in 2000 on the eve of Barak's trip to Camp David for talks with Yasser Arafat. The NRP left the Sharon government in November 2004 in opposition to the disengagement from the Gaza Strip.

Among the religious parties, only Shas participated in the 2006 coalition headed by Olmert, but all three returned to the 2009 coalition headed by Netanyahu. However, a crisis developed (mainly on the issue of the conscription of yeshiva students), which forced the ultra-Orthodox parties to stay out of the 2013 coalition. Netanyahu conceded to the demands of Yesh Atid, a new party unexpectedly backed by the NRP, which was renamed the Jewish Home. This coalition did not last long, and in the 2015 Netanyahu coalition, all three parties were included.

F. The Positions of Non-Religious Parties on State and Religion

Mapai's position carried the most weight, and the predominant view in Mapai, led by Ben-Gurion, was that Judaism is both a nationality and a religion – in that order. Mapai choose the path of compromise to avoid sharp disagreement on matters of state and religion. This decision was manifested in forgoing a secular constitution, recognizing the religious streams of education, allowing the rabbinical court exclusive authority on personal matters, and consenting to religious legislation on some issues. Mapai's leaders, most of whom were secular, hoped the school system would gradually inculcate the image of the secular "new Jew." However, there was also a tendency to avoid head-on confrontation with traditional values, as represented by the religious parties. Mapai was inclined to secularize religious symbols and use them in a non-religious national context, for example "redemption of the land." There were some anti-religious voices in Mapai, but these were less dominant. Pinhas Lavon, for example, called for a separation of religion and state, and sought to liberate the new immigrants from the shackles of religion and "primitive tradition." However, there were other Mapai leaders with strong ties to tradition and religion, such as Bechor-Shalom Sheetrit and Yitzhak Ben-Zvi (Zameret 2002). The compromise adopted by Mapai stemmed from both pragmatism and empathy, and served as the foundation for its long-standing alliance with the NRP.

In the 1980s, after the Labor Party lost its dominance, it continued to adopt a moderate pragmatic stance on state and religion due to the balance of power in the Knesset and the need to meet the demands of the religious parties. In the 1990s, another reason was added – to win the support of parties like Shas in order to promote the peace process. During Ehud Barak's term as prime minister, a short and unsuccessful effort was made to declare a "civil revolution," change the status quo, and enact a constitution.

On the left side of the map, ***Mapam*** presented clearly secular positions, consistent with its Marxist-socialist ideology. Its youth movement Hashomer Hatzair and kibbutz movement spearheaded the struggle against religious domination, supported the activities of the League Against Religious Coercion, and were ready to openly confront the ultra-Orthodox. Mapam aspired to mold a secular society and viewed the separation of state and religion as a condition for socioeconomic development. For them, the days of religion as a social glue of the Jews were numbered, and thus efforts must be made to free Hebrew pioneers from the old religious and traditional characteristics. As an alternative to the religious identity and traditional ceremonies, the kibbutzim created and promoted secular ceremonies for Jewish festivals.

Mapam's hope and expectation that religion was transitory faded after the Six Day War and Yom Kippur War, when messianic elements strengthened and the power of right-wing and religious parties grew (E. Tzur 2002). Furthermore, the ultra-Orthodox have continued to regard the kibbutzim as the embodiment of secularism with its negative influence. Rabbi Shach, leader of the Lithuanian ultra-Orthodox faction, remarked in 1990, "There are kibbutzim where they don't know what Yom Kippur is, or the Sabbath, or the *mikveh* [ritual bath] – they have no knowledge, and they raise rabbits and pigs there. Do they have any connection at all with their ancestors?"

The Movement for Civil Rights and Peace – Ratz (Meretz) has raised the banner of separating religion from state since its founding (1973), and was the first party to call for civil marriage. Meretz, under the leadership of Shulamit Aloni, was uncompromising in opposing religion coercion, and waged a fierce battle against "special funds" for the religious parties and army exemptions for yeshiva students. Nonetheless, it joined the Rabin coalition in 1992 and the Barak coalition in 1999, though both coalitions included Shas. The original ***Shinui*** party, founded in 1974, aspired to ensure basic human rights and prevent religious coercion. In its later incarnation (1999–2005), it presented itself as a "secular movement" against religious coercion, the unequal military and taxation burden, and religious extortion. The anti-religious platform won Shinui six seats in 1999 and fifteen in the 2003 elections when anti-religious sentiment was on the rise among the secular public, making it the third-largest party in the Knesset. In the 2006 election, Shinui did not pass the electoral threshold. Its successor, which adopted similar positions, is ***Yesh Atid*** (2013, 2015).

The ***Revisionist*** movement was secular. Its leader, Ze'ev Jabotinsky, regarded himself as secular, and his vision of the Jewish state was far from religious, carrying negative overtones about religion and the exilic nature of the Jew. Nonetheless, Jabotinsky's national outlook was very Jewish in its historical roots, and he described his Zionist activity as "building a new Temple to one God – the people of Israel." The Revisionist movement he founded had a strong affinity with Judaism, unlike the socialist universalism of the labor movement. The values and symbols drawn from Jewish religion also sustained the aspiration for national liberation and the belief in the Greater Land of Israel (Liebman and Don-Yehiya 1983, 59–80). Unlike the movement founder Jabotinsky, Menachem Begin was raised in the spirit of Jewish tradition and driven by a deep connection to his religious heritage. He supported only Halakhic conversion and religious marriage, and the prohibition of work on the Sabbath. As prime minister, Begin brought the ultra-Orthodox into the coalition for the first time since the 1950s and agreed to ground El Al flights on the Sabbath and holidays. Begin implemented the agreements he made with them and the NRP, such as increasing the number of military exemptions for young women. "During his term, Israeli public space became much more Jewish than it had been before him" (A. Naor 2002).

During the Likud's nearly consecutive terms in office since 1977, the participation of the religious parties in the coalition was a given, including a willingness to go a long way toward accommodating their demands. As explained above, the short-lived government of 2013–15 was a notable exception.

17.7 Decisions

A. In the Government and the Knesset

During the Yishuv period and into the early state, the political system adopted what Lijphart (1984) called "the politics of accommodation" (or consensual politics) on matters of state and religion. Accommodation was based on channeling this conflict from society to politics; a major effort to include the religious groups via Knesset representation and participation in the coalition; and formulating solutions based on compromise. On the fundamental level of world views, it is impossible to bridge the gaping chasm between the extremes on the secular/ultra-Orthodox continuum. Thus, the advantage of politics is that decisive solutions are not always necessary. The political system searched and found ways to include both observant and non-observant Jews without employing harsh coercion and without making clear-cut decisions on questions of state and religion (Galnoor 1982, 52). The instruments used to achieve this were the politics of negotiation, bargaining, compromise, concessions, and pragmatic ad hoc solutions. Thus, the politics of accommodation often mean indecision and temporary arrangements that enable both sides to live together without having to surrender their world views or change their way of life. The central link was, as has been seen, inclusion in coalitions – the religious parties (the NRP and later Shas and recently UTJ too) were partners in nearly all of Israel's governments. The principle of inclusion did not include extreme ultra-Orthodox factions, extremist opponents of religion who were not interested in accommodation, or (for entirely different reasons) the Reform and Conservative movements in Judaism.[28] Accommodation

[28] In January 2016, the government finally decided to comply with an old court ruling, and allocated a separate place at the Western Wall for egalitarian prayer and mixed-gender ceremonies for non-Orthodox Jews. It remains to be seen if this compromise will be implemented.

required stability and hence preservation of the status quo and agreements on core questions (personal status law, the Sabbath, kashrut, and "Who is a Jew?"), as well as adaptation of these arrangements to new developments.

Another moderating aspect of the status quo was that it dealt with topics that the sides refrained from addressing, such as the constitutional status of religion in the state or legislation to prevent Sabbath violations. There was an occasional need to update the status quo, and as long as the political camps and parties controlled society, it was possible to adapt the status quo to the changing circumstances – sometimes, as we have seen, after coalition crises. Naturally, in a dynamic reality it was difficult to avoid political landmines, such as the question of kashrut on the state-owned ZIM line's first passenger ship, or registering Jewish nationality on identity cards. The status quo as a strategy of avoidance and postponing decisions gradually generated a gap between the reality and the arrangements, circumventing unresolved disagreements that continued to pile up, as we discuss below. In practice, beyond the commitment by the coalition parties to maintain the status quo, the agreements included explicit budgetary outlays, such as the transfer of special funds for religious institutions and services. This is an example of a "consociational" arrangement that engenders unsound governance. Another instrument of accommodation was the distribution of ministries among the coalition partners. Traditionally, the religious parties, including Shas since the 1980s, coveted ministries responsible for services and funding in the fields of greatest interest to their voters – religion, interior, welfare, and, alternately, the Ministry of Education.

On the other hand, perhaps surprisingly, religious legislation did not serve as the main channel for preserving the status quo, and it was not the preferred strategy of either the secular or the religious parties. The core issues of the status quo are anchored in legislation, but most of these laws were enacted during the state's first twenty years, and only a few laws on religious issues were passed in recent decades (see Appendix 1 at the end of this chapter). This is because of the informal character of the political arrangements in comparison with legislation, which is more definitive and not amenable to vague agreements and temporary compromises. Moreover, legislation does not always put an issue to rest, because sometimes lacunae remain that continue to stir dispute (such as the question of which conversions are recognized under the Law of Return). Sometimes a law intensifies the conflict when it is not enforced (such as the law prohibiting the display of *hametz* on Passover). What's more, the Sabbath Law was not enacted because the religious parties feared it would force them to agree to partial recognition of legal work on the Sabbath (Don-Yehiya 1997, 47–48).

Instead of new laws on matters of state and religion, there was a tendency to use secondary legislation, which provides a practical, technical, and administrative sphere: regulations, injunctions, and administrative orders. Ministers from religious parties adopt this method to implement policy and avoid disagreements, often circumventing or ignoring the government and Knesset, and sometimes with their quiet consent. Already in the first Knesset, Minister of Immigration Shapira from the Religious Front issued a regulation that "immigrants would not be allowed to disembark from ships on the Sabbath." During the gasoline shortage in Israel in the early 1950s, Transportation Minister David-Zvi Pinkas from Ha-Mizrahi issued emergency regulations that prohibited operation of a private vehicle on two days every week, one of them the

Sabbath. Even the registration of immigrants as Jews under the Law of Return was at the discretion of a Ministry of Interior official until a Mapam interior minister tried to change this in 1958 through regulations, which spawned an amendment to the law. As political agreements on state and religion became fewer and further between, it became less possible to introduce changes via regulations, let alone legislation.

Another method is the localization of arrangements by shifting responsibility to the local authorities, primarily on issues like kashrut and the Sabbath. The Authorization Law of 1990 states that the municipalities are entitled to exercise their authority to oversee the opening and closing of places of entertainment on days of rest, taking into consideration religious tradition (see discussion above). The advantage of shifting these disputes to the local level is that the national political leaders refrain from decisions of principle, and enable specific agreements via municipal bylaws that suit the character of the locale and community. Moreover, this allows the arrangements to differ from place to place.

In general, the political system tried to circumvent fundamental decisions on questions of state and religion. However, as its ability to establish binding arrangements waned, the tendency grew to appeal to external "apolitical" entities – public committees, monitoring bodies, and the courts – to propose solutions and reach agreements. Usually, these means were also of no avail, and the absence of arrangements has led in recent years to a flood of private bills on religious issues – almost none of which resulted in legislation.[29]

B. Court Rulings on Matters of State and Religion

On February 14, 1999, ultra-Orthodox Jews in Jerusalem demonstrated against the Supreme Court in a "mass prayer" rally. This followed the court's ruling against the Jerusalem religious council, compelling it to allow Meretz representatives to join the council, as required by law and commensurate with the balance of power on Jerusalem's city council. The demonstration, which drew tens of thousands into the streets, expressed the growing protest of the ultra-Orthodox (and other religious Jews) against the court's rulings on matters of religion and state (see Appendix 2 at the end of the chapter). These rulings sparked tempestuous statements by ultra-Orthodox leaders against what they called a "dictatorship of the High Court of Justice" (N. Horowitz 2002). The Supreme Court was portrayed as anti-religious, willing to undermine religion and Jewish law in the name of human and civil rights.

Is this a Kulturkampf? Is the Supreme Court indeed "anti-religious," its decisions exacerbating the rift between religious and secular Israelis? And how did this image take root among the ultra-Orthodox minority and other observant Jews? Below we present some concurrent processes that led to a change in the status of the Supreme Court and the role it plays in matters of state and religion.

[29] In the nineteenth Knesset (2013–15), 160 private bills were tabled on subjects such as civil union (marriage), conversion, equality of conscription, kashrut, the Sabbath, ritual baths, the Western Wall, military cemeteries, the appointment of women to committees for appointing religious court judges, and daylight saving time (the last two became law). See the Social Guard, "Social Index of the 19th Knesset," January 2015, http://hamishmar.org.il/category/madad-knesset-19/ (accessed August 15, 2016).

The weakening of the political system's steering capacity and the judicialization of politics. The weakness of the political system and the collapse of consensus on matters of state and religion, together with the status quo arrangements, reinforced the inclination to transfer more and more issues to the court to decide. Complex questions such as conversion, the conscription of yeshiva students, and "Who is a Jew?" – which were previously addressed through political accords – now found their way to the court. The judicialization of matters of state and religion placed the court in the eye of the storm: It was asked to rule on subjects of deep controversy that other authorities had been unable to resolve. In many cases, the court sought to refrain from ruling on these issues, preferring to refer them back to the elected authorities. For example, it did not intervene on the issue of military exemptions for yeshiva students (in 1970 and 1980 petitions), as long as it found the arrangement reasonable. However, the political leadership's inability to contend with the growing number of exemptions forced the court to revisit the issue. Even then, it refrained from issuing a decisive ruling and sent the matter back to the Knesset, until revocation of the Tal Law in 2012. Overall, the Supreme Court has made relatively few rulings on relations between state and religion, but the weakness of the political system has turned the court into a debating stage for this subject.

The rhetoric of a "constitutional revolution." In Chapter 6, we analyzed "judicial activism," including the court's judicial review of decisions made by other authorities. The interpretation of Basic Law: Human Dignity and Liberty and Basic Law: Freedom of Occupation, enacted in 1992, gave constitutional standing to certain fundamental rights, and established that regular legislation by the Knesset cannot contradict them (Mautner 1993). For example, the ruling in the Meatrael case (see section on kashrut above) generated a political storm because observant Jews viewed it as violating the status quo. It intensified the religious parties' resistance to Basic Laws and a constitution. In addition, broadening the right of legal standing expanded the range of subjects in High Court petitions. As noted, the court initially refrained from tackling the issue of conscripting yeshiva students (the petitioners were said to have no legal standing), but agreed to rule on an additional petition in 1986, rejected it, and expressed its view of the arrangements. In other cases, the court was inclined to maintain the status quo – for example, in regard to the status of the non-Orthodox movements in Judaism. And sometimes, it criticized the existing legal or normative situation, but deferred the decision to the political authorities (Raday 2000, 386). An examination of the number of rulings reveals a mixed picture. In some cases, the court took an activist approach and ruled on the basis of substantive argumentation, added comments of fundamental significance, and utilized the cases to establish judicial rules of broad character; in other cases, the High Court chose a narrow interpretation and was careful not to change the status quo (Cohn and Kremnitzer 2005).

Nonetheless, the rhetoric of a "constitutional revolution" became a hot-button issue to the religious public. The Supreme Court was perceived as leading an anti-religious revolution, without public debate or decision by the elected institutions. They argued that the court strayed beyond its role of resolving conflicts and had become an arbiter of values – liberal, anti-religious values. Another claim was that the composition of justices did not represent all of the groups in Israeli society.

Critics of the courts argued that the court should not express opinions on matters of state and religion, or even examine whether the existing arrangements are acceptable or appropriate, and certainly should not overturn them. Instead, it should continue in the role of "the old court" prior to the constitutional revolution, and adhere to the principle that issues of values and politics are not judiciable (Gavison 2000).

In our view, the arguments are one-sided and were never raised when the High Court ruled in favor of the religious minority or preserving the status quo. The High Court became increasingly involved in matters of state and religion because these subjects directly pertain to individual rights, and the court set out to protect fundamental rights – i.e., freedom of religion and freedom from religion, equality, freedom of occupation, and a woman's right to make decisions about her own health. It is the mandate of the court to examine the constitutionality of decisions made by the legislative and executive branches, partly because these decisions are sometimes arbitrary. In this way, the court protects the state's citizens, both secular and religious, from violations of their rights (Kremnitzer 2000).

Changes in society and increased awareness of human and civil rights. Israeli society is changing, becoming more pluralistic and more aware of human and civil rights, and equality. Some court decisions involve issues that are not seen as religious questions per se by the secular public, but interpreted by religious Jews as judicial intervention in matters of state and religion – for example, women's rights, homosexual rights, pornography, organ donation, and autopsy. Even a ruling on equal rights for Arabs (e.g., their right to purchase a home in the Jewish town Katzir) was interpreted as a blow to "the Jewish way of life."[30] In fact, many of the ostensibly "anti-religious" rulings are not actually "religious" or even delve deeply into questions of values. Rather, they are strictly legal and technical rulings, such as the decisions on daylight saving time, shutting down the settlers' pirate radio station Arutz Sheva, the rights of adoptive parents, non-Hebrew inscriptions on gravestones, and prohibition of corporal punishment of children in schools (Sternhell 1994; Cohn and Kremnitzer 2005).

Demands for transparency and sound governance. The court's involvement in cases of improper governance, corruption, and political appointments also contributed to its anti-religious image. Rulings on the allocation of special funds, improprieties in disbursements for ultra-Orthodox institutions, and the distribution of resources for religious educational institutions were interpreted as reflective of an anti-religious stance. One such example was the High Court ruling in 2004 that state funding would be withheld from ultra-Orthodox secondary schools after three years if they only teach religious studies and do not comply with the basic state core curriculum. Justice Edmund Levy wrote:

> Funding institutions that do not meet the conditions anchored in law and do not fulfill the objectives of state education constitutes a breach of authority and violates the obligation of trust the authority owes the public from which it draws its power. (*Association of Teachers v. Minister of Education* 2005)

[30] The Manof Center for Jewish Information presents the views of the ultra-Orthodox sector and attempts to show that the High Court's rulings are anti-religious. See Manof website: www.manof.org.il/index.php?option=com_content&view=frontpage&Itemid=94&lang=he [in Hebrew] (accessed June 30, 2016).

The overturning of improper political appointments made by ministers from religious parties was also labeled an anti-religious rather than an anti-corruption ruling (see *Women's Network v. Minister of Labor* 1998 on the issue of the appropriate representation of both genders). The conviction of politicians from religious parties in corruption cases created a feeling – primarily among ultra-Orthodox Mizrahim – that their leaders were singled out for persecution by the judicial system.[31] There is no factual basis to this claim. State comptroller reports on allocations to religious and ultra-Orthodox institutions from the budget of the Ministries of Welfare, Education, and Religion revealed the lack of equal criteria and transparency (e.g., State Comptroller *Annual Report* 1986A, 400).

Disagreement on authorities of rabbinical courts. One of the areas of fierce disagreement is whether the secular court has jurisdiction over rulings by the rabbinical court, the chief rabbinate, or the religious councils. The court's criticism of these institutions stirs great resentment in the religious public, and efforts have been made to enact "laws to circumvent the High Court" in order to change the legal situation set by court rulings. For example, some seek to expand the jurisdiction of the rabbinical courts and limit the High Court's oversight. There is still concern in the religious public about adoption of a "secular constitution," and bills have been submitted to establish a constitutional court, where representatives of the religious public could defend its interests (see Appendix 2 at the end of the chapter for important court decisions on religious matters).[32]

C. Public Committees

A recurring pattern appeared in the 1990s – formation of public committees on several core status quo issues, including conversion, conscription of yeshiva students, and Sabbath observance. An issue comes before the court, the court prefers not to rule and passes it on to the legislative branch, which forms a public committee to study the matter. It is interesting to note that the recommendations of many committees were adopted by the Knesset or the government, but not implemented in practice. Examples include the Zameret Committee on the question of travel on Bar-Ilan Street on the Sabbath; the Ne'eman Committee on the status of the non-Orthodox movements and the conversion process; and the Tal Committee on conscripting yeshiva students (see Zameret Committee Report 1996; Ne'eman Committee Report 1998; Tal Committee Report 2002). The recommendations of the Ne'eman Committee on conversion were approved by the government, including creation of an Institute for Jewish Studies to be jointly operated by the three movements. However, the institute was established only three years later, and only a few people have undergone conversion

[31] The main cases in which Shas leaders were involved: Rafael Pinhasi was convicted in 1997 of illegally transferring funds and received a suspended sentence of twelve months; Yair Levy was convicted in 1993 of embezzlement, forgery, fraud, and breach of trust, and was sentenced to four years in prison; Aryeh Deri was convicted in 1999 of bribery, fraud, and breach of trust and was sentenced to four years in prison; Shlomo Benizri was convicted in 2006 of bribery, breach of trust, obstruction of justice, and conspiring to commit a crime, for which he was sentenced to four years in prison.

[32] Protocol 189 of the March 14, 2004 session of the Knesset's Constitution, Law and Justice Committee: Proposed Basic Law: Adjudication. See also a background document on appointing judges: https://www.knesset.gov.il/mmm/data/pdf/m02731.pdf [in Hebrew] (accessed October 24, 2017).

under its auspices. The Plesner Committee (2012), the Peri Committee (2013), and the Shaked Committee (2014) addressed the question of yeshiva students bearing an "equal burden." With the exception of the last committee, whose recommendations became law but have also not been implemented (as of early 2016), the work of the public committees was at best educational, and at worst served as a fig leaf to conceal the government's lack of steering capacity.

17.8 Religion and Democracy

A. Daylight Savings Time as a Case in Point

As the Jewish High Holidays approach, and the autumn days in Israel become shorter, a brouhaha regularly ensues on the subject of daylight savings time. Some religious people want daylight to end even earlier by moving the clock back one hour, arguing that this would make it easier for those who get up early for morning prayers and for those fasting on Yom Kippur. Seculars, and many observant people too, would rather enjoy as many hours of daylight as possible. There is no other democratic country where the question of moving the clock hand is a religious one. Though the issue involves celestial bodies, the question is essentially technical: How many hours of sunlight should be exploited for work, leisure, transportation, etc.? This is a decision with social, economic, and safety ramifications. However, everything in Israel is religious, even daylight savings time. For many years, this was subject to the arbitrary decision of the interior minister, as the regulating authority: A religious/secular minister would move the clock back/forth to shorten/extend daylight savings time, and the days of winter would need to adapt themselves to whichever coalition was in power (Rothenberg 2009; Nachshoni 2007). There were even calls for civil disobedience and a refusal to move the clock according to the whims of the state authorities. Thus, a minor issue, which should have been left to a low-level official, was accorded a law of its own in 2005 (Amendment 1 of the Setting the Time Law 1992). The legislation reflects the political system's creativity in addressing religious issues, as well as willfully ignoring the secular majority: "Daylight savings time shall commence between the last Friday before the 2nd of April, and terminate on the last Sunday before the 10th of Tishrei." Thus, it was legislated that daylight savings time would start according to the civil calendar and end according to the Hebrew calendar, prior to the Yom Kippur fast.

But nothing lasts forever. When Shas was not in the coalition and the secular Gideon Sa'ar was minister of the interior in 2013, Amendment 3 of the aforementioned law was enacted. This sets daylight savings time for seven months, from the end of March through the end of October, similar to most European countries.

B. Religion as a Threat to Democracy

In fundamental Orthodox interpretation, Judaism represents an alternative system of values to that of the secular state. (We note that many observant Jews do not subscribe to this notion nor do they experience ongoing conflict between their faith and their citizenship.) According to this Orthodox analysis, to observe a commandment such as "you shall not murder" and other dictates of conscience, a person does not need a state; and to maintain democratic rule and the laws of the state, there is no need for the religious commandments. This sounds simple, but in Judaism, the boundaries between the individual and the community are ill defined. As long as there was no sovereign Jewish state, when a commandment of the religious community clashed with the laws of the state, it could be resolved by citing the Talmudic saying, "The law of the [foreign] kingdom is the binding law."

The establishment of Israel made this dilemma acute. Initially, as we have seen, the political system offered pragmatic solutions for conflicts that arose, and sidestepped fundamental decisions; and the religious partners in government did not demand the implementation of religious principles in all walks of life – not in foreign policy and matters of security, for example. By and large, the state in the early years did not threaten religion, and religion did not threaten democracy or the rule of law. The reality was less rosy, however, because already in 1948 a conflict emerged between supporters of a completely secular constitution and religious Jews who argued that "the constitution was given by God" (see Chapter 2). Nonetheless, the disagreement with most observant Jews was not then viewed as a clash of contradictory value systems – secular versus religious – because commonalities outweighed divisions, and there were other considerations.

The illegal activity of extremist ultra-Orthodox groups (such as Neturei Karta) was not considered a threat to democracy because it was a type of civil disobedience by marginal groups in society (and within ultra-Orthodox society). Their activity had no impact on the political system as a whole, and their disorderly conduct was usually treated with indulgence (Sprinzak 1986, 72–73, 122). On the other hand, the battles by the ultra-Orthodox against Sabbath violations, non-kosher meat sales, indecent advertisements, desecration of graves, and autopsies all directly affected the demands made by religious Zionist representatives in the government. But the ultra-Orthodox community at that time was not an ideological movement that threatened the rule of law, as it focused mainly on local issues (from the secular perspective). The occasional outbursts also served as a safety valve, which led to adaptations and ensured the continuation of the status quo.

Systematic violation of the law driven by a religious (faith-based) ideology first emerged in the activity of Gush Emunim. Members of this movement developed their own messianic interpretation of both the victory in the Six Day War and the trauma of the Yom Kippur War based on the "holiness of the land" (Aran 1987, 437–95; Feige 2009). Gush Emunim was founded in 1974 as an offshoot of the NRP and soon became an autonomous extra-parliamentary group. Its objective was to settle the territories captured in 1967 and thus dictate state policy toward them. This was a subversive call of a religious ideology, accompanied by illegal activity that challenged the model of a secular state that operates according to broader considerations. The method they chose was to present the government with facts on the ground by building settlements. For example, Gush Emunim built unauthorized settlements in Elon Moreh in the midst of the Palestinian population, contrary to the security approach taken by the Labor government at the time. After seven attempts to settle in the area that were thwarted by the army, the government relented in December 1975 and the settlement remained intact. The Elon Moreh case (*Duweikat v. Government of Israel* 1979) exposed the fact that Gush Emunim's arguments extended beyond the boundaries of democratic discourse. For them, the settlements were not for security purposes; rather, they expressed the eternal connection of the people of Israel with its land (Efrat 2014). Thus, according to Rabbi Shlomo Avineri, one of the leaders of Gush Emunim, "Any decision by a state agency to hand over parts of the Land of Israel to non-Jews is illegal and contrary to the laws of the Torah and the land" (Sprinzak 1986, 127).

The Camp David Accords and evacuation of Yamit in Sinai (1982) highlighted the threat posed by a group that did not accept the state's authority. There were also non-religious participants in the Stop the Withdrawal from Sinai Movement, but the messianic fervor of Gush Emunim activists and the religious ideology that led them to completely disregard decisions made by the democratic institutions transformed a legitimate political protest into a threat to democracy. In the early 1980s, the "Jewish Underground" was uncovered; it demonstrated how short the path was from religious fanaticism to acts of murder. Its members – most of them settlers – were convicted of committing acts of terrorism, attempts to assassinate three Palestinian mayors, an attempt to blow up a bus with Arab passengers, and a plan to blow up the Dome of the Rock mosque in Jerusalem. Never before had such an organization operated in Israel with an operational capacity that could have changed the course of the state's history. In addition, there was a growing tide of racism in the guise of Jewish religious faith, led by Meir Kahane and the Kach movement. Kahane was elected to the Knesset in 1981, but his movement's activities led the High Court to disqualify it from running in the 1984 elections. In this case, Israeli democracy was able to defend itself from a racist movement that declared the supremacy of the Jewish race in the name of religion. Since 1985, an amendment of Basic Law: The Knesset has prevented parties with racist platforms from participating in Knesset elections.

The Oslo Accords in the early 1990s again exposed the qualified allegiance to democracy of some religious Israelis. The opposition to agreements that were lawfully approved in the Knesset was violent and accompanied by incitement; and in the wake of this incitement, a young man wearing a skullcap, who was influenced by fanatical religious discourse, murdered Prime Minister Yitzhak Rabin on November 4, 1995. He justified his action by citing religious rulings that allowed for killing someone who "hands over parts of the Land of Israel to non-Jews."[33]

The evacuation of settlements from the Gaza Strip in 2005 again sparked a clash, pitting the state and a large group of religious Jews against each other. These groups place their faith in the holiness of the land and the rabbinical rulings that support

[33] In January 1995, ten months before the assassination of Rabin, a letter written by three rabbis was sent to forty Orthodox Jewish leaders in Israel and abroad. One of the writers was Eliezer Melamed, secretary of the West Bank Rabbinical Council. The following questions were posed in the letter:

> What is the law regarding this evil government and the one who heads it? Can they be considered accomplices to terrorist acts of murder? Does the Halakha call for their prosecution? And if they are accomplices to murder – what should their punishment be? Is the leadership obligated to warn them … that if, after the bitter experience with the agreement, they continue to apply it throughout Judea and Samaria … that [the leadership] will be obliged to apply the Torah Halakha law of a *moser* [an informer], who hands over Jewish souls and property to non-Jews?

Eleven rabbis responded, seven with an ambiguous response. Two confirmed that the law regarding a *moser* applied to Rabin (Karpin and Friedman 1998). Rabbi Nahum Rabinowitz warned the Rabin government that an attempt to force the people in Israel to cooperate with the Palestinians would be interpreted as an act of *moser* (ibid., 158). Also see Galnoor 1993.

this view above the laws of the state and the decisions of the elected democratic institutions. One member of the West Bank Rabbinical Council even ruled that it was prohibited to evacuate the illegal outposts and that it was a commandment to refuse orders to do so (Yedidia Stern 2009). This was not a rebellion against a specific law or government decision, but rather a denial of the right of the elected institutions to make decisions that contravene their view. This was not a legitimate political struggle conducted according to the rules of democracy. Rather, it was a Kulturkampf – religious-messianic versus democratic-constitutional.

As long as the latent threats to democracy were from resolute ultra-Orthodox Jews fighting for their version of a Jewish way of life in Israel, the concessions made by the secular majority were part of the rules of the game, and democracy can be said to have had the upper hand. However, when religion dictates foreign and security policy that determines the future of the state, the religious minority has gone beyond the boundaries of tolerance that a democracy can permit. This also had the tragic consequence of the murder of a prime minister.

C. Democratic Tolerance and its Boundaries

About seven decades after the founding of the state, the challenge of state–religion relations remains unresolved. The initial approach was not to make explicit decisions, but rather to develop consensual arrangements based on compromise, such as the status quo. The vagueness was designed to dodge the fundamental questions of the status of religion in Israel, the connection to the non-Orthodox Judaism of the majority of Jews outside Israel, and – as long as the state was not legally declared "Jewish" – the status of other religions (and other nations) within Israel.

Since the 1980s, for reasons discussed in this chapter, it has no longer been possible to manage issues of state and religion in the same way – by compromises and ad hoc solutions in reaction to crises and changes in public opinion. The previous model not only fails to provide a solution, it often exacerbates the problem and creates a negative cycle: A problem arises (such as the conscription of yeshiva students), a crisis flares, a temporary political compromise is reached (such as a coalition agreement), the arrangement does not work and is not accepted by either seculars or the religious (for differing reasons), the political system is powerless, the matter is referred to the courts, returned to the Knesset, handed over to a public committee, returned to the Knesset, which passes legislation that is not implemented by the executive branch – and so forth. In practice, the problem is left unresolved until the next crisis erupts.

Choosing the path of compromise was intended to prevent a rift in society and to ease tensions between secular and religious Jews. The changes that occurred in Israeli society and the radicalization of some of the religious public do not allow for this any longer.[34] All sides seem to feel that their way of life is threatened. In surveys conducted in 2012–14, 86 percent of the Jewish public said that the tension between secular and religious Israelis was "strong" (56%) or moderate (30%)

[34] The high birthrate among the ultra-Orthodox changed the balance of power, as did the change in the makeup of the society in Israel: One of every four people in Israel is not Jewish, including foreign workers (Asher Cohen 2004a).

(Hermann et al. 2011–15: 2014, 246). Many secular Israelis are disgusted with the status quo arrangements and argue that they violate the principle of equality and other basic rights such as freedom from religion and the right to marry. They oppose allocating resources to the ultra-Orthodox and believe that such funding perpetuates poverty, increases the birthrate, discriminates against women, and is a disincentive for engaging in productive work. A large portion of the religious public feel threatened by the erosion of the status quo (shops and places of entertainment that open on the Sabbath, the sale of non-kosher meat, civil marriages), court decisions, and the growth of anti-religious secularism. The ultra-Orthodox public, which is undergoing an accelerated process of change, is fearful of the impact of secularism on the young generation (in the army and elsewhere), and of modern technology, Sabbath violations, and harm to their way of life as the level of education and employment rises.

Has the time come to reach a decision once and for all on matters of state and religion in Israel? Does the harm caused by the existing partial arrangements outweigh the benefits? Can this be accomplished? We now briefly examine several options, starting with the more comprehensive ones.

Constitution. Thus far, the Basic Laws have avoided matters of religion and state, but a constitution requires an historic decision. Religious Jews, and certainly the ultra-Orthodox, would oppose this because their consent would be interpreted as formal recognition of the secularity of the state. Conversely, according special status to Judaism in the constitution would be opposed on principle by the secular, who would regard it as religious coercion. However, other options exist. One would be to anchor the status quo in the constitution. The difficulty is that there is no agreement on what constitutes the status quo, and currently both sides regard it as unsatisfactory. Even if it were possible to anchor the status quo in a constitution, this would remove the consensual and dynamic dimensions that sustained it.

A second option is to avoid matters of state and religion by granting them "immunity" – stating that the constitution does not apply to these matters and that they are regulated otherwise and defined in regular legislation. This option avoids one landmine – defining constitutionally the relations between religion and the state. However, it sets off another – the possibility that laws and arrangements might contravene the constitution. After all, nearly every basic right (such as equality and freedom of expression) touches upon matters of state and religion. In this situation, the court would be required to constantly determine whether a constitutional matter is at hand, and every decision would be anathema to one of the sides.

The third option would be for the constitution to articulate only a general principle – "freedom of religion and freedom from religion." This would allow observant Jews to defend their way of life and ensure secular Jews' protection from religious coercion in legislation or via coalition agreements. The difficulty is that such a general principle is open to interpretation and may reinstate the status quo through the back door, along with its constant tension between religious and secular Jews. It would also bring the subject back to the doorstep of the court.[35]

In Israel's current reality, instituting a Halakha-based constitution is not a possibility, and the likelihood of a liberal, democratic constitution that entrenches the

[35] The alternatives are based on Yedidia Stern 2001, 31–36.

separation of religion and state is remote. A constitution would need all sides to be willing to compromise and defer to the Supreme Court for authorized interpretations on matters of state and religion. Neither of these conditions obtains and, therefore, a constitutional solution is not on the horizon.

Regular laws and regulations. This possibility is limited because the political system finds it difficult to formulate laws on matters of state and religion that are acceptable to all sides. Furthermore, even when laws are passed, they are often not implemented – military conscription is an example of both situations. Knesset legislation is also liable to drag the court into the eye of the storm. In the past, legislation on questions of religion was the preferred method of the religious parties, but they now are reluctant to propose laws or new regulations that could actually limit their political gains.

Localization of the arrangements. Is it possible to transfer the responsibility for religious questions to the local authorities, or even to communities and neighborhoods? Secular Israelis who favor this approach believe that religious faith is not a matter for the state to address because of the polarization in society. Thus, they argue that it would be best to work out the arrangements and compromises, as well as the nature and scope of religious services, in accordance with local conditions and the residents' needs. For example, instead of central legislation in the Knesset, the sale of non-kosher meat could be limited to secular neighborhoods and prohibited in those with a religious majority. The same would apply to the Sabbath – the opening of businesses, closing of streets, billboard advertisements, and so on. Moderate religious Jews support this kind of solution, while extremist religious Jews are opposed because they see themselves as responsible for the entire public space. The religious parties fear that local authorities with a secular majority would not respect the needs of the religious communities, and they do not wish to weaken their bargaining power by removing religious matters from national politics.[36] Another difficulty is that the localization of religious matters would not resolve fundamental questions such as defining "Who is a Jew?," personal status law, conversion, or conscription of yeshiva students.

Understandings and accords in civil society. As in the localization approach, some of the disputes could be resolved outside the state framework via social covenants between secular and religious Israelis, and through civil society organizations that could mitigate the severity of conflicts and formulate possible compromises. Indeed, more and more civil society organizations have set out to strengthen coexistence between religious and secular Israelis.[37] These efforts demonstrate that channels still exist for resolving disputes and isolating the extremists. However, this approach to the tension between state and religion requires a stronger civil society than currently

[36] The Authorization Law (1990) is perhaps a precedent in this direction, but limits the municipality's authority to opening and closing places of entertainment in consideration of religious tradition.

[37] See for example the ***Gavison-Medan Covenant*** (http://en.idi.org.il/analysis/idi-press/publications/english-books/the-gavison-medan-covenant-main-points-and-principles/); ***Tzav Pius*** (www.tzav-pius.org.il/en); ***Gesher*** (www.gesherusa.org/what-is-gesher); ***Tzohar*** (www.tzohar.org.il/English/); ***Avi Chai*** (http://avichai.org/); ***Kinneret Covenant*** (www.netzerolami.org/Assets/kinneret_covenant_hinuch_booklet.pdf); and the "New Covenant on Religion and State," co-authored by MKs Lubotzky and Beilin and co-sponsored by the ***Meimad*** movement and ***Derakhim*** (Faust 1998, 23–28) (all accessed October 16, 2017).

exists in Israel. In addition, Israelis assume that "important decisions" can be made at the national level only.

Relations between state and religion in Israel are an open problem in search of a solution due to the erosion of the status quo arrangements, general public dissatisfaction, and the growing tension between the camps. First, there is a need to confront the threat against democracy by a religious group that challenges the state and its laws, and creates an artificial link (in the eyes of many secular and moderate religious Jews) between religious faith and political views. It will be difficult to find a reasonable compromise here, and the state must strictly apply the law to defend democracy. Second, in our opinion, a constitution or legislation will not resolve questions that pertain to the attributes of Israeli society, nor will an attempt to cling to status quo arrangements whose public validity has expired. Instead, we recommend a combination of the last two possibilities presented above – transferring responsibility to local communities and building understanding between the camps via civil society organizations.

Appendix 1: Main legislation on Jewish religious issues, by subject

Subject	Legislation (year enacted)	Explanations and notes
The individual and personal status	Age of Marriage Law (1950)	Prohibits underage marriage.
	Rabbinical Courts Jurisdiction (Marriage and Divorce) Law (1953)	Gives rabbinical courts exclusive authority over Jewish marriage and divorce.
	Amendment of Penal Code (Polygamy) Law (1959); Penal Code (1977), Article H, Sections 175–83	Prohibits polygamy; defines when polygamy is a felony and who bears criminal responsibility for it.
	Amendment of Family Law (Alimony) (1959)	Alimony to be set in accordance with religious law.
	Legal Capacity and Guardianship Law (1962)	A minor may only be converted to the religion of at least one of his parents. Minors require written consent of both parents to convert to another religion.
	Adoption of Children Law (1981)	Defines eligibility and conditions for adopting a child. No one may adopt a child of another religion, except international adoptions, when the court may authorize the adoption on condition that it is not deemed detrimental to the child's welfare.
Education	State Education Law (1953)	Ensures the existence of the state-religious education stream and the independence of ultra-Orthodox education.
	Unique Cultural Educational Institutions Law (2008)	Codifies the independence of both Aguda and Shas ultra-Orthodox education.
Conversion and "Who is a Jew?"	Law of Return (Amendment 2) (1970)	Defines the right of a Jew to immigrate to Israel. The Citizenship Law (1952) defines the rights of an immigrant. Immigration rights are extended to the child, grandchild, and spouse of a Jew, and to the spouse of a Jew's child and grandchild, except for someone who willingly converted from Judaism to another religion.
	Population Registry Law (1965), Sections 15 and 16	Defines conversion as an official act that obligates the authorities to inform the Population Registry; defines what is to be recorded in the registry; permits registration as a Jew only to those allowed to immigrate under the Law of Return.

(*continued*)

Appendix 1 *(continued)*

Subject	Legislation (year enacted)	Explanations and notes
Sabbath and Tisha B'Av	Hours of Work and Rest Law (1951)	Sets the Jewish Sabbath and holidays as official days of rest.
	Amendment of Municipalities Ordinance (No. 40) (1990) ("Authorization Law")	Authorizes local authorities to regulate the opening of businesses on rest days and affirms the continued validity of existing laws.
	Prohibition on Opening Entertainment Venues on Tisha B'Av (Special Authorization) Law (1997)	Permits local authorities to enact bylaws prohibiting the opening of entertainment venues on Tisha B'Av eve.
Kashrut	Prohibition of Pig Farming Law (1962)	Prohibits raising and keeping pigs, except in Christian communities, scientific and research institutions, or zoos.
	Prohibition of Kashrut Fraud Law (1983)	Defines who is entitled to a kashrut certificate and who is authorized to issue it. Prohibits defining a product as kosher without a valid certificate. Instructs the issuing rabbi to apply only criteria of kashrut.
	Festival of Matzot (Prohibition of Leavened Food) Law (1986)	Prohibits businesses from publicly displaying leavened products for sale or consumption during Passover.
	Meat and Meat Products Law (1994)	Makes mandatory a certificate of kashrut from the chief rabbinate to import meat to Israel.
State support for religious institutions	Religious Services Law (1949)	Ensures funding for religious services.
	Chief Rabbinate of Israel Law (1980)	Ensures religious services for the public.
IDF conscription	Defense Service Law (1959), Section 30	Exempts women from IDF conscription for reasons of conscience or religion.
	Defense Service (Consolidated Version) Law (1986), Sections 36–38 and 46–48	Defines the defense minister's authority and conditions for issuing exemptions, deferrals, and cancelations of military service; and the penalty for non-compliance.
	Deferral of Service for Yeshiva Students Whose Vocation is Torah Law (2002) ("Tal Law") (revoked)	Anchors in law the arrangements for deferring the service of yeshiva students.

Appendix 1 *(continued)*

Subject	Legislation (year enacted)	Explanations and notes
	Defense Service (Amendment 19) Law (2014); Defense Service (Amendment 19 – Extension of Validity of Transition Provision) Law (2015)	For an interim period, allows yeshiva students to choose army service, civilian activity, or continued yeshiva studies. If the government conscription targets are met, conscription will continue to be voluntary, and yeshiva students will be allowed to defer military service until age twenty-six, and receive an exemption. If not, compulsory conscription will be applied to all yeshiva students from age of twenty-one, except for 1,800 outstanding students. (The law has not been implemented.)
Burial and organ transplant	Jewish Religious Services (Consolidated Version) Law (1971)	Establishes religious councils and defines their authority to provide religious services and be responsible for Jewish burial.
	Anatomy and Pathology (Amendment) Law (1980)	Gives veto power to family of the deceased on conducting an autopsy.
	Brain-Respiratory Death Law (2008)	Establishes that brain death defines death.
	Organ Transplant Law (2008)	Enables organ transplants and gives donors priority to be organ recipients.
Abortion	Women's Equal Rights Law (1951)	Asserts a woman's right to make decisions about her health with the exception of what is prohibited in other laws, such as the Penal Code's prohibition on aborting pregnancy.
	Penal Code (1977)	Makes abortion a felony, except with committee approval, or when essential for saving the mother's life, or to prevent irreparable harm to the mother's health or wellbeing.
Harming religious sensibilities	Safeguarding of Holy Sites Law (1967)	Safeguards holy places and free access to them by members of all religions. Desecrating or damaging them is defined as a felony.
	Penal Code (1977)	Prohibits knowingly disturbing, scorning, insulting, or harming religious sensibilities, directly or indirectly.

(continued)

Appendix 1 *(continued)*

Subject	Legislation (year enacted)	Explanations and notes
Rabbinical courts	Women's Equal Rights Law (1951), Section 7	Equates the legal status of women and men and prohibits discrimination on the grounds of gender, with the exception of appointments to religious positions, including rabbis and rabbinical court judges.
	Rabbinical Court Judges Law (1955)*	Asserts the independence of rabbinical court judges; and their appointment by the minister of religious affairs.
	Civil Union Law for Persons with No Religion (2010)	Allows a civil union if both parties are registered as officially not belonging to any religion.
Miscellaneous	Prohibition on Discrimination in Products, Services, and Entry to Places of Entertainment and Public Places (2010)	Asserts equality and prohibits discrimination in entry to public places, with the exception of the separation of men and women in public places for reasons of religion and tradition.

* On Muslim and Druze religious courts, see Shari'a Courts (Approval of Appointments) Law (1953); Qadis Law (1961); and Druze Religious Courts Law (1962).

Appendix 2: Significant court rulings on issues of state and religion

Issue	Petition [year of ruling]	Ruling
"Who is a Jew?" and the Law of Return	*Rufeisen v. Minister of the Interior* [1962]	Petition to become a citizen under the Citizenship Law was rejected. The court ruled to separate religious from secular decisions.
	Shalit v. Ministry of the Interior [1970]	Although their mother was not Jewish, Shalit's children may be registered as being of Jewish *nationality*; state identity cards must separate nationality and religion.
	Ornan v. State of Israel [2013]	Petitioner's request to be recognized as a citizen by virtue of the Citizenship Law rather than his being Jewish and the Law of Return denied by the court.
Conversion (to Judaism)	*Pesaro v. Minister of the Interior* [1995]	For purposes of the Population Registry, the Religious Testimony Ordinance (Conversion) does not prevent recognition of non-Orthodox conversions conducted in Israel.
	Na'amat v. Ministry of the Interior [2002]	Conversion in a recognized Jewish community, including Conservative and Reform, in Israel or abroad, is recognized for purposes of registration in the Population Registry.

Appendix 2 *(continued)*

Issue	Petition [year of ruling]	Ruling
	Rodriguez-Tushbeim v. Minister of the Interior [2005]	A "stopover conversion" in an overseas Jewish community (including Reform and Conservative) by someone living in Israel is recognized for purposes of the Law of Return.
	Jane Doe v. Judge Rabbi Sherman et al. [2012]	This was an appeal to the High Court of a fifteen-year-old rabbinical court decision to not recognize a conversion. After the appeal was submitted, the rabbinical court annulled its earlier decision. The High Court severely criticized the rabbinical court.
Conversion from Judaism	*Gary Lee Beresford v. Ministry of the Interior* [1989]	The court ruled that the petitioners, who had converted to the Messianic Judaism movement, are members of another religion and therefore not entitled to rights under the Law of Return. On Jewish religious grounds, belief in Jesus constitutes being Christian, not Jewish; on secular-national grounds, Jews consider someone who believes Jesus was the messiah to belong to another religion.
Conscripting yeshiva students	*Ressler v. Minister of Defense* [1988]	Military duty is a public issue that should be left to political entities to resolve. Legally, it is reasonable for exemption decisions to fall within the purview of the defense minister.
	Rubinstein v. Minister of Defense [1998]	Given the significant increase in the number of those enjoying military deferrals, and because the issue is in fierce ideological dispute and entails a clash of human rights – the right to equality and the freedom of religion – there is a need for primary legislation and the defense minister is not authorized to continue to regulate it.
	Movement for Quality Government v. Knesset [2006]	The justices concurred that the Tal Law violates the principle of equality, but ruled that it should be given a chance to realize its objectives. Thus, the Supreme Court deferred a decision on the constitutionality of the Tal Law.
	Ressler et al. v. Knesset et al. [2012]	In a 6 to 3 vote, the court declared the Tal Law to be unconstitutional and that the Knesset cannot extend it in its current form.
	Movement for Quality Government v. Minister of Defense [2013]; *Ressler et al. v. Minister of Defense* [2013]	Petition demanded immediate recruitment of all ultra-Orthodox young men following invalidation of the Tal Law. Court issued order nisi, then canceled it following passage of the Equality in Sharing the Burden Law.

(continued)

Appendix 2 *(continued)*

Issue	Petition [year of ruling]	Ruling
Exemption from conscription for reasons of conscience	*Barzani v. Minister of Defense et al.* [1972]	Denial of the petition to exempt the daughter of a rabbi from military service for religious reasons. (The army had rejected the exemption request because of her immodest attire and lack of knowledge of Jewish holidays.) The court ruled that the exemption was based on the religiosity of the applicant, not that of her parents.
	Milo et al. v. Minister of Defense et al. [2004]	The exemption for reasons of conscience granted to women under Section 39 of the law applies only to reasons pertaining to tradition, religion, and ethnic customs.
Kashrut	*Raskin v. Jerusalem Religious Council* [1990]	The rabbinate has no authority to apply religious criteria other than kashrut criteria when granting or denying a kashrut certificate. Thus, the kashrut certificate of a wedding hall may not be revoked because of a performance by a belly dancer.
	Meatrael Ltd. v. Prime Minister [1993]	The state must not deny the petitioner a license to import non-kosher meat; to do so would contravene the Basic Law: Freedom of Occupation. Religious sensibilities are irrelevant for the granting of import licenses.
	Meatrael Ltd. v. Council of the Chief Rabbinate [1994]	Following amendment of the Basic Law: Freedom of Occupation, the court rejected the petition to allow the import of non-kosher meat. The new "override clause" in the Basic Law allows for limited violation of the freedom of occupation.
	Aviv Osoblanski Ltd. v. Council of the Chief Rabbinate [2001]	The rabbinate has no authority to apply criteria that do not directly pertain to the kashrut of food. The kashrut certificate may not be revoked from a factory that observes the rules of kashrut on the grounds that it also sells non-kosher meat.
	MK Solodkin v. Beit Shemesh Municipality [2004]	The sale of pork should be allowed in neighborhoods in which the majority of the consumers would purchase non-kosher meat.
Sabbath	*Isramax Ltd. v. State of Israel* [1968]	A local authority may consider religious sensibilities when enacting by-laws, if it is not a pretext for achieving a purely religious objective. Closing gas stations on the Sabbath is not within the municipality's authority.
	Baruch v. Transportation Supervisor, Tel Aviv and Central District [1978]	Petition rejected. Closing a segment of a street in Bnei Brak on the Jewish Sabbath and holidays to protect the ultra-Orthodox public's way of life does not constitute religious coercion. The constraint is limited and does not harm the sensibilities or conscience of secular Israelis, but merely causes them inconvenience.

Appendix 2 *(continued)*

Issue	Petition [year of ruling]	Ruling
	Horev v. Minister of Transportation [1997]	Preventing harm to religious sensibilities is a legitimate consideration, but must be balanced against the harm to basic rights. The court ruled that Bar-Ilan Street in Jerusalem should not be closed on the Sabbath.
Education	*Center for Religious Pluralism v. Ministry of Education et al.* [2008]	This petition sought to obligate the Education Ministry to enforce teaching of the core curriculum in ultra-Orthodox schools. The court noted that the core curriculum not only fosters common values, but is vital for realizing equality and the right to education of ultra-Orthodox students, and it criticized government policy for redefining ultra-Orthodox schools to allow them exemption from the core curriculum. In parallel with the litigation, the National Education Law was amended to entrench the exemption from core curriculum studies in "unique cultural education," i.e., ultra-Orthodox schools.
	No'ar KeHalakha v. Ministry of Education et al. [2009]	The court accepted the petition, ruling there was illegal ethnic discrimination of Mizrahi girls at the Beis Yaakov school in Emmanuel. The decision enraged the Ashkenazi ultra-Orthodox community.
Rabbinical courts (personal status laws) and religious institutions	*Schlesinger v. Minister of the Interior* [1963]	The registration official in the Ministry of the Interior has no authority to decide whether civil marriages are valid, but is obligated to register a couple as married based on a civil marriage certificate, regardless of its religious validity.
	Tsaban v. Minister of Religion [1986]	The law pertaining to civil court judges also applies to rabbinical court judges, hence they are prohibited from advising political entities.
	Shakdiel v. Minister of Religious Affairs [1988]	The Religious Services Law, which defines who is entitled to serve on the religious council, is a secular law. A woman is eligible to serve on a religious council, even if prohibited by the Halakha.
	Bavli v. High Rabbinical Court [1994]	The rabbinical court, as part of the Israeli judicial system, is obligated to apply civil law, including the principle of gender equality and individual rights, in all cases it adjudicates that are not matters of personal status. Hence, it must apply the rule of sharing assets established by the Supreme Court when dividing assets between a couple.
	Naot v. Haifa City Council [1996]	The court overturned the disqualification of appointments of representatives of non-Orthodox movements to religious councils. The local authority must allow representation on the religious council according to a political "party key" and may not disqualify candidates because of their world view.

(continued)

Appendix 2 *(continued)*

Issue	Petition [year of ruling]	Ruling
	Ben-Ari et al. v. Director, Population Administration, Ministry of the Interior [2006]	The registration official must register the petitioners (a same-sex couple) as married after they presented a valid certificate indicating they had been legally wed in Canada. The ruling does not constitute recognition of the validity of same-sex marriage by the authorities in Israel.
Status of non-Orthodox movements in Israel	*Peretz et al. v. Kfar Shmaryahu Local Council* [1962]	The court invalidated the local council's refusal to rent its hall to Reform Jews for prayer because this violates freedom of religion and conscience, and the principle of equality. The council is not permitted to discriminate against a particular group on the basis of religious belief.
	Association for Secular-Humanistic Judaism v. State of Israel [1997]	The Association's request to recognize it as a "religious community" was rejected because it lacks the institutional characteristics that make its members a community. The request to grant its members the right to form a secular court was also rejected.
Miscellaneous	*Universal City Studios v. Films and Plays Censorship Board* [1989]	The court overturned the board's decision to prohibit the screening of a film due to the religious sensibilities of Christians. It ruled that harm to religious sensibilities might serve as grounds for limiting freedom of expression only when there is near certainty that severe harm to sensibilities outweighs "the tolerance level" of a democratic society.
	Burial Society v. Kestenbaum [1992]	The court overturned the burial society's refusal to inscribe the name of the deceased on the tombstone in non-Hebrew letters.
	Adalah et al. v. Minister of Religious Affairs et al. [2000]	The Ministry of Religions engaged in unlawful discrimination by allocating only a negligible percentage of its budget to cemeteries of Arab religious communities. Hence, the ministry must allocate resources to cemeteries according to equal, clear, and transparent criteria.
	Hoffman v. Director-General, Office of the Prime Minister [2000]	The government must make arrangements to enable women to pray at the Western Wall (even if they are wearing a *tallit*), while minimizing harm to the sensibilities of other worshipers. Praying by women at the Western Wall may not be completely prohibited on the grounds of a fear of violence.
	Meshi-Zahav v. Jerusalem District Police Commander [2006]	In holding the Gay Pride march in Jerusalem, freedom of expression and the right to associate and demonstrate must be balanced against ensuring public safety and respecting the sensibilities of the religious public. The ruling affirmed the decision of the district police commander to approve the march in a limited format and far from ultra-Orthodox neighborhoods and crowded areas.

Appendix 2 *(continued)*

Issue	Petition [year of ruling]	Ruling
	Movement to Strengthen Tolerance in Religious Education et al. v. Attorney General et al. [2015]	The petition challenged the attorney general's decision not to indict for incitement the authors of the book *The King's Torah*, which calls for the killing of non-Jews as a Halakhic commandment. The court did not intervene in the attorney general's decision.

PART V

DEMOCRACY IN ISRAEL

In the first four parts of the book, we discussed characteristics of the political system. Now we can bring these parts together and ask what we have learned about democracy in Israel:

- To what extent is the heritage of the pre-state period and the development of the political system in its early years key to understanding the current reality, and one reason that several critical issues remain "open" for subsequent generations? In summarizing Part I, we cited the "constitution of 1949" as a framework that still exists, expressed over the years in the passage of the Basic Laws (most concerned with the rules of governance, with a few protecting human and civil rights). This heritage has had a profound impact on the political system, although enormous changes have taken place in all aspects of politics and society. Moreover, the political system was unable to overcome new problems that arose, particularly in the wake of the 1967 war and subsequent social divisions that emerged in Israeli society. Although the informal constitutional structure gave primacy to politics, contributing to the common denominator and stability in the nascent state, it subsequently provided a rather feeble defense against strong anti-democratic trends.
- The political institutions (the government, legislature, presidency, civil service, local government, and monitoring mechanisms) shape politics, but is Israel's crisis in steering capacity rooted in these institutions and their shortcomings? In summarizing Part II, we noted the erosion of public trust in these institutions and their diminished legitimacy in various parts of the political system itself. Israel's institutional structure has not changed substantially over the decades, except for the failed attempt to institute direct election of the prime minister. This stability is surprising in light of the many years in which the political system has been beset by a sense of crisis.
- Democracy assumes participation by citizens in the various channels (elections, political parties, third-sector organizations, and the media – both conventional and new). How can one explain, or at least define, the far-reaching changes in participation, including the decline in citizens' trust in the elected officials? The dearth of structural changes belies the major transformations within the political system – from well-organized, party-sponsored participation to autonomous

social and economic activity in civil society organizations and via social media, which are relatively independent. At the same time, many citizens are demanding more influence on policymaking between elections. This was the essence of the massive social justice protests in the summer of 2011.
- In Part IV, we addressed the "open issues" – fundamental problems that have accompanied Israeli democracy since its inception: security, the status of Arabs in Israel, economic inequality and social gaps, and religion–state relations. Can we attribute the inability to cope with these issues to objective difficulties (i.e., the "wickedness" of the problems themselves)? Or can they be explained by factors within the political system, including the nature and alleged weakness of democratic politics? Is democracy in Israel at risk?

In Chapter 18, we use the concept "political culture" to weave together the elements presented in the previous parts, and we raise questions about the nature of the political culture and the threats to democracy in Israel.

18 Political Culture in Israel

18.1 Political Heritage and Political Culture

A. Political Culture

The different definitions of political culture are a matter of emphasis.[1] One possibility is to see in political culture "the meanings attributed to politics"; this enables us to examine the shifting boundaries between the political and the apolitical, as discussed below.[2] The more common definition is that political culture refers to "the specifically political orientations – attitudes toward the political system and its various parts and attitudes toward the role of the self in the system" (Almond and Verba 1963, 12).[3] Accordingly, the focus is on examining the attitudes of citizens and the distribution of orientations toward politics within a particular community. For our purposes, we make do with a simple definition: *Political culture is the infrastructure of reciprocal relations between society and its political system* – i.e., shared content (such as consensus about having an election-based government) that facilitates the transition from relations among people and groups to joint and organized political action. This definition was designed to include the role of political culture in our discussion of the book's four subjects: the heritage of the Yishuv period and early years of the state, the institutionalization of political entities, civic behavior, and steering capacity. The discussion will primarily focus on the less formal components of political culture, the unwritten rules of joint political action. This is analogous to the "culture of driving" in the sense that, together with laws and regulations, it determines how traffic will actually flow. Traffic flows according to unwritten agreements among drivers, and they are the ones who create the driving culture (for better or worse). If only a small percentage of drivers stop obeying traffic signals, this is still enough to block traffic completely. The same applies to political culture – it is based on customs and determined by the percentage of people in society who are willing to comply with them over time. Thus, political culture in democracy is based on the

[1] We will not discuss here the fascinating topic of the interaction between "culture" and "politics" – concerning symbols, myths, collective memory, ideologies, and more. See Berezin 1997.

[2] "Political Culture." 2001.

[3] See a later elaboration in Almond and Verba 1980, 26–32.

extent to which citizens internalize the rules of the democratic game and elected officials internalize political ethics: "More than political agreements are agreements, they are political; more than they belong to the family of contracts, they belong to a broader and less defined family – to political culture" (Galnoor 1993a, 97).

B. Democratic Political Culture

The hidden yet most important component in democratic political culture is the unwritten contract between voters and elected officials, between citizens and leaders, and is based on the assumption that all sides will usually pursue shared objectives and at least adhere to the rules of the game. These rules determine the rule of law, the legality of government, and the possibility that all citizens will have equal rights and an opportunity to influence political action. These assumptions, considered naïve by ostensibly experienced people, are what largely determine the level of confidence in democracy itself, and thereby the firmness of the democratic political culture. This firmness is predicated upon a broad and solid consensus about the rules of the game (free elections, majority rule, an independent judiciary, multiple parties, etc.) and the values inherent in these rules. These values are, first and foremost, equality (otherwise, why allow everyone to vote?) and freedom (only free people can exercise their rights).

The experience of the twentieth century demonstrated that the more years of democracy a state accrues, the higher the probability that it will remain a democracy. What is the sequence of democratic development? One would assume that initially a society develops a strong collective belief in democratic values, such as freedom and equality, and then gradually moves on to instill democratic mechanisms – the so-called rules of the game – to attain these values. However, research on democracy does not provide a clear answer as to what the sequence has actually been. Historically, we find mixed paths: the gradual development of democracy in countries such as England, Sweden, and the United States; and the abrupt imposition of democracy upon countries such as Japan and Germany after World War II. Thus, democratic development can be a simultaneous, dual process that lasts a long time and is based on the mutual nurturing of values and the rules of the game. How many years are needed to sustain a democracy? It is difficult to say, but no states have abandoned democracy after a hundred years of it. When the unwritten contract between society and politics turns into a norm, faith in the primacy of democracy also evolves, including its ability to contend with emergencies and crises. In short, a democratic political culture develops, which contains a "democratic soul" that guides the actions of the individual or groups, and collective actions. The moral argument for democracy is that everyone has the right to shape one's own destiny; the practical argument is that a state that enjoys the trust of its citizens is much stronger, and an army of motivated citizens will better defend it than an army of mercenaries (Crick 2002, 12).

C. The Decline of Politics

In democratic states, politics does not need to be a grievous evil. On the contrary, politics is an excellent social instrument for bridging differences of opinion and an effective mechanism for reaching compromises and achieving agreements that enable joint action. To that end, only authorized representatives can enact laws; only independent judges administer justice; only authorized officials issue licenses; and freedom of expression and information and freedom of the media enable the public to monitor the public office holders. As noted in the introduction to this book, politics is a necessary glue in democracies not only for governance, but also for the apolitical parts of collective action. The economic market cannot be free without government regulation designed to prevent "market failures" or without the ability to intervene in a crisis. Civil society organizations also require government regulation to prevent, for example, the misuse of public contributions, or to encourage donations to them by granting tax benefits. Thus, democratic political culture means that the infrastructure of interaction between society and the political system is based on principles of equality and freedom, and the shared common contents are strong enough to overcome crises.

Politics, however – and politicians, in particular – have lost their luster in democratic states in recent decades. Confidence has waned in the political system's ability to cope with complex problems such as social disparities and poverty, violence, environmental dangers, and terrorism. Many feel that those who chose to be politicians are unworthy, solely interested in the trappings of power and personal gain. International institutes publish "corruption indexes" of states, while politics is perceived as "spin" built on disinformation and manipulation of the media. The abuse of social channels by unrestrained and anonymous talk-backers has exacerbated the situation. Accordingly, "anti-politics" expresses the citizens' sense of powerlessness, lowering voter turnout and preventing many good people from entering public service. This is also reflected in strong anti-democratic attitudes: Groups emerge that advocate "clean" politics devoid of politicians or a government of unelected "experts," and leaders preaching primitive populism, just short of authoritarian politics, magnify this. All this contributes to the delegitimization of democratic institutions even in states with a long democratic tradition, where citizens now recoil from politics or where political awareness seeks new, ostensibly "apolitical" channels of participation, such as protest movements (Stoker 2006; Hay 2007).

The paradox in this phenomenon is that the second half of the twentieth century was an era of victory for western democracy over all sorts of non-democratic regimes. Never before have there been so many democratic countries in the world. As of 2016, the UN has nearly 200 member-states, most with a democratic regime of one sort or another – including some that transitioned from communist regimes and dictatorships in Latin America, Africa, and Asia. Now there are signs of regression – was this an excessively sweeping success that exposed the limitations of the democratic system? Explanations abound: unfulfilled expectations regarding the state's ability to generate change, the collapse of the foundational institutions of modern democracy (parliaments, parties, free press, populism), and revulsion from the new cyber-politicians who are no more than polished facades rather than statespersons.[4]

Some propose alternatives – reduce the state by privatizing whatever is possible, thereby distancing tasks from government control and transferring them to business organizations, NGOs, or community associations. Some place their trust

[4] On "anti-politics" in Israel, see Hermann, Zaban, and Lebel 2008.

in trans-national frameworks – the global market, trade agreements, international courts. And some hope for a new participatory democracy via the social media. Without delving into the advantages and limitations of such alternatives, we note that in many states that have critical shared missions, Israel among them, the institution of state still has great (though no longer exclusive) importance. If a country like Israel seeks to function for the benefit of its citizens, it will not be able to do so without the infrastructure of a democratic political culture.

18.2 Political Culture in Israel

In Part I of this book, we noted a key component in the heritage of the Yishuv period and early state years – the preeminence of politics. This is shared by other new states-in-the-making, and even more so in Israel, whose society was not yet present at the formation of the state. Thus, Israeli political culture was largely shaped by the political leadership more than cultural and social norms. From the beginning, the political system enjoyed a preeminent position in society in areas that usually remain outside the grasp of politics in other countries: "It may be said that the polity 'invaded' society and not the other way around" (Galnoor 1982, 271). Some say there is no "political culture" in Israel, expressing their disappointment with the lack of civility and the unsound practices in Israeli politics. For better or worse, there is a political culture in Israel, and it has a democratic infrastructure that has held up, more or less, for nearly seventy years. We discuss below its features, contradictions, and shortcomings, as well as the questions regarding its durability.

A. Changes

Since Israel's founding, the cornerstone of the political system has been the primacy of politics – in society, economics, and even the fields of culture, communication, and more. Politics was almost entirely party-based, except for a few fields like security, the justice system, and higher education. The "Constitution of 1949" (see Chapter 2) was based on institutions inherited from the Yishuv period – a parliamentary system, a unicameral legislature, proportional elections, the centrality of political parties, coalitions (with a dominant pivot party), a centralized national bureaucracy, and weak local authorities. However, along with governmental and administrative centralization, there was also a distribution of tasks between the center and subcenters such as the Jewish Agency, the World Zionist Organization, and many party-affiliated organizations. Hence, the principle of proportionality (the "party key") was applied not only in the electoral system, but also in the allocation of resources and political appointments, with the aim of including in the political system most of the groups in the society. Internal politics sought to regulate, modulate, and manage conflicts through compromises and accommodations. This engendered flexibility that, as Ehud Sprinzak noted, bordered on illegalism regarded as functional, together with the worship of Mapai-style pragmatism, shortcuts, and improvisations (Sprinzak 1986, 77–92; Sprinzak 1993).

The political culture became established in the first nine Basic Laws (1958–88), which essentially codified the status quo, unlike the three later Basic Laws and the Parties Law (all enacted in 1992). Despite the enormous changes in all fields in

Israel, there have not been fundamental changes in the regime since 1949, except for the direct election of mayors in 1978 and direct election of the prime minister (1996–2003). At least until the late 1960s, the political system functioned, for better or worse, and was also quite stable despite the frequent crises. It could count on broad consensus among the Jewish citizens until the 1970s: a sense of shared destiny, national-religious identity, Zionism, and identification with the state (Galnoor 1982, 79–110). The tangible political expression of all this was reflected in the election results that preserved the division of power for over two decades: "The Israeli voter tends to use his vote as a symbolic expression of his identification with the state and with the political system" (A. Arian 1971, 8).

With the establishment of Israel "after two-thousand years in exile," as once was said, expectations were sky high – as if the state could solve all the problems of the Jewish people and also forge the masses of immigrants into a new Israeli society, homogeneous and exemplary. Most expectations could obviously not be fulfilled and, as in other western democracies, demands grew to end state intervention in the economy and society. However, Israel has been obliged to act on behalf of its citizens – perhaps more than in many other states – primarily to ensure security. There is also a high level of expectations: Israeli travelers overseas, for example, expect the Israeli embassies to look after their welfare and security.

As society evolved over time and the standard of living rose, it was inevitable that the strong identification of the Jewish citizens with the state would also change. Rising internal tensions in several areas affected the political culture. First, tension grew between ideology and pragmatism, and the centrality of ideology declined as the revolutionary fervor of the early years waned. Thus, for example, the one million immigrants from the former Soviet Union who arrived after the late 1980s – in the post-revolutionary era – identified less strongly with the state compared to their predecessors. Second, while the political leadership continued to emphasize the dominance of the state's missions – first and foremost, security – the ever present tension between the collective component and individualism intensified (Ezrahi 1997). This can be found in the disparity between textbooks in state schools, which continued to preach the duty of pioneering fulfillment, and the home and society, which encouraged children to fulfill their personal aspirations.[5] Third, there was no major change in the dominance of security considerations, but we noted greater transparency, increased civic involvement, more emphasis on domestic issues rather than foreign affairs in voters' considerations, and even demands to place social goals on par with security.

However, the most important change has been the transition from a consensual political culture of the early decades (characterized by a mechanism of informal arrangements, coalitions, compromises, etc.) to conflictual politics, which also became more open and pluralistic (see Chapter 8). Consequently, the political system was less able to employ mechanisms of self-legitimation and indoctrination as it had done in the past via the state and party media. And as the divide widened

[5] The tension is reflected in the attempts of education ministers from right-wing parties to infuse national and religious content into the education system at the expense of civic and individualistic content, and to emphasize the Jewish element in the citizenship program at the expense of other values. In early 2016, for instance, a crisis flared over a controversial high school textbook (Cotler and Hay 2016).

between society and the political system, social and economic "non-politics" grew stronger.

B. Interrupted Democratic Development

It is impossible to identify a "normal" sequence of democratic development (Galnoor 2015, 148–60). Therefore, we propose making do with partial tests, such as the stability of the institutions, increased representation, reduced use of coercive means, ability to overcome crises, internalization of the rules of the democratic game, and the like. On these criteria – and without presuming to have proof – the political system in Israel developed in a positive, democratic direction during the first two decades, notwithstanding many undemocratic occurrences during this period, usually in the name of security (Galnoor 1982, 352–64). Milestones in this development include the following:

- The "Lavon affair" in the early 1960s triggered a severe political crisis, but in retrospect it also marked the end of the era of the dominant leader (Ben-Gurion) and strengthened the norm of governance legality, including the need for civilian oversight on security.
- Transition to the moderate and non-revolutionary leadership of Levi Eshkol (1963–69) inaugurated a period of consolidation and bridge-building between the political camps, with an emphasis on domestic affairs (until 1967).
- In terms of democratic development, terminating the military government over the Arab population in 1966 signaled the first step toward equality for Israel's Arab citizens, though full equality is still far off.
- The 1965 election offered great potential for change in the political parties with the formation of two new political blocs (Alignment on the left and Gahal on the right) and the appearance of a centrist party (Rafi). The three lists won a total of eighty-three Knesset seats (70% of the total), and could have wrought major change in the political structure, which was a relic of the Yishuv period, but the 1967 war shifted political priorities in a new direction.
- In terms of the democratic rules of the game, the legitimacy of the parliament to legislate and the government to make binding decisions has not been tested since 1949, despite the crisis over reparations from Germany in 1951–52 and Ben-Gurion's disregard of the Knesset and government in his decision to launch the Sinai campaign in 1956. The six Knesset elections held through 1965 laid the foundation of a democratically elected, representative government. Despite the frequent coalition crises, the average Knesset term during that period was about three years. As discussed in Chapter 11, the coalitions have actually served as shock absorbers, contributing to government stability.
- By the mid-1960s, large-scale immigration had ended. From 1948 to 1968, about 55 percent of the immigrants came from North Africa and the Middle East, changing the ethnic composition of Jewish society in Israel (CBS *Statistical Abstract* 1981). The years of economic recession (1966–67) primarily hurt the poor, new immigrants, workers, and salaried employees. Compared to the euphoria of earlier years, the recession brought an atmosphere of desperation. It is difficult to assess how this crisis might have played out had it not abruptly ended with the 1967 war and the ensuing prosperity, including a new wave of

immigration. This new social-political configuration again turned in a different direction after the 1973 war.

- Were there also signs of an increasingly robust democracy? If we examine Israel during that period according to the conventional list of institutional characteristics essential for a functioning democracy, the answer is mostly yes. Examples include an elected leadership; fair, free, and regularly held elections; an independent judiciary; freedom of expression; freedom of association; civil rights; and a professional civil service (Dahl 2000).

The shocks of the 1967 and 1973 wars left a strong imprint on Israeli society and politics, and it is difficult to exaggerate their long-term impact. After the grand military victory of 1967, the previous political system, which had begun to change, seemed to be restored and reconstructed. The various labor parties, all of which coalesced in the "Alignment" headed by Prime Minister Golda Meir, won fifty-six Knesset seats in 1969, plus another four seats garnered by affiliated Arab parties. The euphoria of the 1967 triumph did not last long, however, as the reestablished old political system was shattered in the earthquake of the Yom Kippur War. In retrospect, the crisis was only deferred and unfolded over many years. Even worse, the 1973 war aroused a deep-rooted distrust of politics and political leaders, and this has continued. Moreover, arguments reawakened about the objectives of Zionism and how to meet them, and the broad consensus that served the stability of the political system dissipated. Terms such as "occupation," "redemption," "settlement," and "peace process" became fixtures in the political discourse and have remained so for nearly fifty years – with no solution in sight. Cracks appeared in other components too: the preeminence of politics in resolving internal disputes and coping with external challenges; and the strength of political institutions, such as the parties and the Histadrut Labor Federation. The mechanism of government coalitions for modulating conflicts was often transformed from shock absorber to shock generator. Many coalitions formed after 1967 have been too broad (unity governments), while others have been too narrow, even minority governments. And, as noted, faith in political institutions diminished.

C. Trust in Political Institutions

A study conducted in the mid-1990s found that a majority of Israelis still expressed trust in most of the state's institutions, except for political parties (Table 18.1). We added "still" to emphasize that despite the lack of comparable data from previous periods, there has been a decline in the citizens' trust in institutions, and as described below, this further declined in subsequent decades.

A democratic political culture needs institutions that not only function, but that also inspire trust. The deterioration in institutional trustworthiness raises concerns about the strength of Israeli democracy. In Table 18.2, the non-elected, non-representative institutions enjoy greater trust than the Knesset, the government, and, in particular, the political parties. In addition, the decline of public trust in the media in Israel, discussed in Chapter 13, is worrisome. Such distrust dissuades citizens from participating in elections, reinforces the inclination to disparage the rule of law, evokes longing for "strong leadership," and weakens democracy – all of this indeed occurred in Israel.

Table 18.1 *Trust in institutions in the 1990s*

High (+80%)	Medium (+40%)	Low (–40%)
IDF	Knesset	Political parties
Supreme Court	Government	

Source: Surveys (1991–95) in Peres and Yuchtman-Yaar 1998, 58–59.

Table 18.2 *Trust in institutions in the 2000s (%)*

	2003	2007	2011	2015
Supreme Court	70	58	69	62
IDF	83	73	86	85*
Knesset	51	32	52	35
Political parties	32	21	36	19
The government	55	30	51	36
The president	68	21**	78	70
The media	49	44	52	36

* In 2015, a wide disparity was recorded between the trust of Jewish and Arab citizens in the IDF – 93% and 37%, respectively.

** The year 2007 was when Moshe Katsav was president and his sexual offenses were revealed.

Source: Hermann et al. 2011–15: 2015, 85–89.

A study of voting patterns in the 1988 Knesset election identified a tendency among young people to vote for "lone horsemen" – personal lists of celebrity figures seen as daring individuals, or even saviors at the time. These lists, which were not political parties, received more young votes (mainly from soldiers) than from the national average of all voters (Galnoor 1984; Galnoor 1984a). This voting pattern resembles that of the 1984 election of Meir Kahane to the Knesset – a man barred from running in the 1988 election for violating the anti-racism law. Surveys show that such tendencies are not confined to young people, but that young people are likely to hold onto their distrust of democratic values for many years to come. The longing for strong leadership instead of "all these superfluous laws and arguments" has intensified over the years (A. Arian 1997, 347). It was reflected in the switch to direct election of the prime minister (1996–2003), which contributed to the personalization of politics. In Chapter 4, we noted the decline of the Knesset as an institution and its low status in the eyes of the public, as opposed to the strengthening of MKs as individuals. The parliament is the foremost political institution because it represents the sovereignty of the people. Erosion of its standing (and that of political parties) undermines the principle of representation, which is the foundation for democratic political culture, and encourages non-democratic populism.

D. Changes in Political Behavior

Israeli citizens are interested and well versed in politics. They say they follow events on a daily basis and discuss politics with friends (Hermann et al. 2011–15: 2011, 238).

Where does the political socialization of young people take place? In the Yishuv and Israel's early decades, the main agents of socialization were the youth movements, schools, and paramilitary organizations, followed by military service in the IDF. In the next decades, the influence of the family and party-based press grew, while for new immigrants the influential factors were the parties and their affiliated organization, the workplace, and the state bureaucracy (Galnoor 1982, 137). Today it is difficult to identify salient agents of socialization, and profound differences exist among the various groups in society. By the process of elimination, it can be said that the media in general and the social channels in particular have great influence, though it is early to define the exact nature of the new media impact and what political content it conveys. Studies indicate that the family has a strong effect on voting patterns, primarily with regard to the division into "blocs" – right (including the religious) versus left.[6] Voters in Israel are not inclined to rebel against their parents' parties, and are also loyal to the sectoral enclaves, especially the social networks of new immigrants, Arabs, and ultra-Orthodox. Political socialization and conservatism are particularly strong among observant Jews – settlers, national-religious, and ultra-Orthodox. On the other hand, the channels of "rebellion" that have strengthened are anti-politics, disengagement from politics, and non-participation in elections.

In Chapter 8, we analyzed the contradiction between the high voter turnout of Israeli citizens and their low sense of efficacy about political impact. This contradiction seems to have disappeared recently: In 2015, 78 percent of the citizens felt unable to influence government policy (Hermann et al. 2011–15: 2015, 62), and the percentage who felt this way correlates directly with the number of years of education. Accordingly, the voter turnout for Knesset and local elections has declined.

While previous patterns of political participation (political parties, elections) have declined, participation in third-sector organizations has flourished, with an average of about 1,500 new organizations registered annually since the 1980s (see Chapter 12). Many organizations emerged in response to the state's ineffectiveness, and they provide substitute services to the disabled, elderly, impoverished, and others. In contrast, many are extra-parliamentary organizations that mobilize public opinion to change government policies in the fields of security, society, and economics. These are non-partisan political organizations that provide a channel for spirited civil participation, a kind of alternative to parties and sometimes even to the Knesset as a public stage. The assumption that civil society can serve as an alternative to the political system constitutes a significant change in the political culture. Civil society is a positive addendum as a voluntary community forum for civil participation. However, it could become a negative outlet for vulgar populism or media brainwashing, which have found fertile ground in the social media channels.

As an illustration, let us examine the myths surrounding demonstrations in the Malkhei Yisrael (today Yitzhak Rabin) Square in Tel Aviv. Convention has it that to oppose or support the government, the masses must assemble in the city square or there will be no media coverage, i.e., no chance of having an impact. This myth was born with the Peace Now demonstration on September 24, 1982 calling for a state commission of inquiry and the government's resignation in the wake of the first

[6] In 1996, 81 percent of the respondents voted for the same political bloc – "right" or "left" – as had their fathers; 52 percent voted for the same party (A. Arian 1997, 335).

Lebanon War (Bar-On 1985, 60). Media reports estimated that 400,000 demonstrators gathered in the city square. Soon afterwards, a diligent engineer measured the human load of the square:

> If demonstrators were to stand packed like sardines on the entire square (which isn't reasonable), about four people could stand on each square meter, i.e., a total of 160,456 people. If we add 25% (a generous addition) for the crowd packed into the adjacent streets, we get to a theoretical number of 200,000 people. According to criteria for calculating crowd loads in large public buildings, it is reasonable to assume that the average density per meter was about 2.4 people, or about 120,000 people. In sum, the square's capacity ranges somewhere between 120,000 and 200,000 people. (Sofer 1983)

Politics based on participation that stems from a sense of obligation contributes to entrenching democracy; politics that is nothing more than media twittering could become destructive. Both patterns exist in Israel today and are changing the nature of the political culture as we defined it – the interaction between society and politics.

18.3 Ethical Conduct and a Robust Democracy

Ethical conduct and integrity are the opposite of corruption and mean that public office holders act on behalf of the public interest and do not use their position for personal gain (based on Galnoor 2010, 128–48). In a corrupt regime, individuals who control public resources derive personal or group benefit by virtue of their position (Heidenheimer 1970; Heidenheimer, Johnston, and LeVine 1989). Ethics is a system quality; anchored in the political culture, it reflects norms, not just laws. Accordingly, ethical conduct and its opposite, corruption, are largely based on subjective conjecture. Two prefatory remarks:

> First, ethical conduct must be fostered in both the political and administrative spheres – in the central government and local authorities. (It applies equally to the business sector, but that is not our focus here.) Public officials in Israel have been convicted of corruption offenses – bribery, fraud, forgery, double voting in the Knesset, and the like. Many of these offenses pertain to the exploitation of public resources – the misappropriation of public funds, graft, political appointments, preferential licensing, illegal contracts, misuse of public property, accepting funds fraudulently, and illegal gifts (V. Shiffer 1989; D. Navot 2010).
>
> Second, data on corruption are scarce except for cases that reach the courts. Acts of corruption are done surreptitiously, of course, which always leaves hanging the question of whether what has been uncovered is just the tip of an iceberg. International comparisons of corruption are based on surveys and subjective perceptions. These indices are culture dependent and have numerous biases. For example, some societies are traditionally more suspicious of their government authorities than others are. Nonetheless, corruption indicators point to the existence of similar characteristics in some countries and they measure change over time.[7] Beyond this, the subjective perceptions in a particular society ("our leaders

[7] Lederman, Loayza, and Soares 2005, 9. This article points to valid correlations that should still be approached with caution because they might also be biased.

are all corrupt") are important because democracy rests upon the presumption that public office holders serve the public and are not abusing their authority.

The line dividing democratic from undemocratic regimes is also the line that demarcates corrupt from uncorrupt regimes (Treisman 2000). In that sense, it makes no difference whether the corruption in an undemocratic country takes place in the king's court, the bureaucracy, the military, or the party, because the necessary condition that office holders are acting for the public good has not been met.

A. Changes in Ethical Norms in Israel

Politics in Israel was long dominated by one party, and many scholars have documented the political culture that evolved within this so-called "system" (*hashita*) and all its ramifications,[8] as well as the distortions it created between those in power and various groups in society (Galnoor 1991). As early as 1950, a report of the Jewish Agency auditor, Emil Shmorek, noted irregularities in the conduct of the organization's employees. The response of Levi Eshkol, then treasurer of the Jewish Agency, has entered the Israeli political lexicon: "Do not muzzle an ox [from eating] while it is treading out the grain" (Deuteronomy 25:4). An opposite example is the "Book of Taxpayers" published by the Income Tax Authority in 1953–56, listing individual taxpayers by name and their tax declarations – an attempt to apply public pressure on taxpayers whose standard of living was disproportionate to their tax declarations, in the opinion of the tax authorities.

How did "the system" undermine ethical norms? At first, benefits issued by public officials were not intended for personal gain, but for their parties, or for social and economic groups in their immediate circles. This practice, however, sowed the seeds for a political culture of "illegalism," which perhaps paved the way for the personal corruption that appeared later (Sprinzak 1986). Werner (1998, 143–46) noted the pattern of "self-circumvention" that can be traced to this period: distortions of wage arrangements, circumvention of budget regulations, and *protekzia* – knowing someone in power for an exchange of favors. Another example from the political-administrative folklore was the mythological "note" (*petek*) given to cronies applying for a job on which was written, "The bearer of this note is one of us." There was also the red Histadrut membership booklet, which members made sure to have peeking out of their pockets on visits to a government office; or the inflation of expenditures in public offices in order to transfer the balance to the party coffers. And despite all this, the general public in Israel did not view the bureaucracy as corrupt (Nachmias and Rosenbloom 1978, 56). Upon completing his term as attorney general in 1987, Yitzhak Zamir wrote:

> Criminal corruption manifested in bribery, stealing from the public coffers, or the like seems not to be prevalent among public officials in Israel. Cases of corruption that became public can still be regarded as exceptions from which no society is exempt. Nevertheless, one can learn from these that we are not immune from the spread of criminal corruption… (1987, 274)

[8] See D. Arian 1955; Akzin and Dror 1966; Caiden 1970; Sharkansky 1987; V. Shiffer 1989; Aharoni 1991, 109–24; Etzioni-Halevy 1993.

Zamir then warned against a decline in the ethical behavior of public officials that leads to criminal corruption. Transition from "the system" of benefits for the collective to benefits for personal gain was gradual, but sensitivity to public ethics began to grow in the 1970s together with the demand for applying the values of universalism and neutrality in service provision (Danet 1989). Several cases came to light following the 1967 war. Some were rumors, such as the rumblings about those getting rich on constructing fortifications along the Suez Canal (the "Bar-Lev Line"); some triggered the creation of state commissions of inquiry, such as the Netivei Neft oil company affair in 1972; some went to court – such as the cases of Avraham Ofer in 1976 and Yaakov Levinson in 1984; and some ended in convictions – Joshua Bension (1975), Asher Yadlin (1977), Michael Tzur (1977), Leah Rabin (1977), and Rafael Levi (1987).[9]

Since then the list has only lengthened, and citing individual cases is unnecessary because a former prime minister, a former finance minister, a number of MKs, mayors, and the head of the Tax Authority were convicted and sent to prison for various bribery offenses. We only note that strict adherence to the law and the rules aimed at preventing conflicts of interest does not mean there is no room for exercising discretion. However, discretion that is not exercised impartially could spawn corruption. In democratic regimes, public officials are subject to unique rules of conduct that include faithfulness to the law and impartiality – not to mention a public service ethic. The suspicion that all elected officials and civil servants are prone to corruption could deter honest people from filling these vital positions (Garment 1999, 9).

B. International Comparisons of Corruption

Recognizing that political and administrative corruption undermines development, business, and investments, international organizations started to publish comparative indexes of corruption. The World Bank publishes the Worldwide Governance Indicators in its World Development Report (WDR), while others survey expert opinions and public attitudes in different countries (see listing in Lederman, Loayza, and Soares 2005, 8–9). The World Bank defines corruption as "the abuse of public power for private gain" – when public officials demand or accept bribes in exchange for patronage, contracts, licenses, biased rulings, tax relief, etc. The index is based on the polling of experts as well as surveys conducted in democratic countries regarding the "control of corruption." The validity of these reports is controversial, and they should be viewed as indicators of the perception of corruption – and internal changes over time – in various countries.

Despite the limitations of the data, the indexes reinforce the feeling that corruption in Israel has grown and reached a high level compared to other western democracies. Israel was ranked twenty-two out of thirty-six states in the World Bank's index in 2006 (World Bank 2006); the Transparency International index ranked Israel eleven to twelve of twenty-eight states in 2014, just above the median

[9] Asher Yadlin of the Labor movement was the first senior public servant to be indicted. In October 1976, shortly before his appointment as Governor of the Bank of Israel, Yadlin was arrested and subsequently convicted of receiving bribes and benefits, and sentenced to five years. In his book *Testimony* (1981), Yadlin claims that he was the victim of a corrupt system that sacrificed him in order to save itself. For the full list, see Galnoor 2011, 130–33.

(www.transparency.org/cpi2014). The Jewish public in Israel ranked the state 2.4 on a 1–5 scale of corruption, and the Arab public ranked Israel at 2.0. Only 14 percent of Israel's citizens said that the leadership is not corrupt or not corrupt at all (Hermann et al. 2011–15: 2015, 89 and 178). Another interesting index is the *Bribe Payers Index*. Based on surveys of business professionals, the index examines the prevalence of bribery payments by companies in countries that export products. Israel was ranked nineteen out of thirty exporting nations, resembling Italy and Hong Kong (Transparency International 2007, 332). In short, the perception of corruption in Israel has worsened and the culture of corruption encompasses both the public and business sectors. Such widespread sentiments have a destructive impact on the faith of citizens in democracy.

C. Levels of Corruption

It is difficult to measure corruption, and even harder to examine its extent and grip on the political culture. Nonetheless, we will try to distinguish between different "levels" of corruption.

A *basic (personal) level* includes specific acts of petty corruption, such as a police officer accepting payment for ignoring an offense, an inspector granting a license to a business in exchange for services, or a clerk accepting a bribe to expedite a request. Some people believe that a certain amount of petty corruption is necessary, especially in developing countries, as a way to overcome bureaucratic red tape, or as a necessary supplement to the low wages of civil servants. Accordingly, it is tolerable because it creates an individual market of "supply and demand." The demand is from individuals who need licenses, permits, documents, or exemptions; or from businesses that need contracts, licenses, exclusive agency, priority status, special treatment, or a way to circumvent regulation. The supply is from officials in charge of granting licenses, construction permits, subsidies, or customs duty exemptions, who take advantage of the demand to line their pockets. The interface between the two yields the basic level of petty corruption in society – a specific and localized act.

The view that petty corruption by individuals is a necessary evil and even contributes to "oiling" the economy is no longer accepted. Studies carried out by the International Monetary Fund and the World Bank indicate that petty corruption is one of the main barriers to economic development because it directs investments to areas suffused with bribery, which are not necessarily worthy investments for the country (Mauro 1995). It also deters external investors who are not willing to play the game, and creates market failures that hinder opportunities for small businesses, whose ability to survive is jeopardized by bribes. This contrasts with big businesses, which can afford to give bribes, thereby creating monopolies and actually forcing small businesses out of competition.

A *systemic level* refers to wide-ranging corruption that – depending on the issue – is prevalent among elected officials and civil servants, and permeates business activity (whether legitimate or not, such as organized crime). An example would be an inspector who receives a bribe from a business firm and shares it with his political superior, a parliament member from that district, police officers, and – if necessary – also with judges. Licensing and tax authorities are generally crucial links in this chain.

Systemic corruption can strike deep roots in the culture of governance, particularly because of the interweaving of interests not just of the wealthy and powerful, but also of political figures and public administration authorities as well as the courts, the media, and social non-profits.[10] On the systemic level, chains are created whose links reinforce each other and allow for maintenance of a corrupt culture of governance. In democratic countries with systemic corruption, scandals sometimes erupt (such as those following an election), and then the differences are noticeable between:

- *a vertical chain*, in which there is collusion within an organization of politicians with officials, who cover for each other in supplying services for personal favors; and
- *a horizontal chain*, in which cross-institutional corruption permeates the bodies covering for each other – parliamentary committees, government ministries, local authorities, courts, the police, regulatory bodies, and even professionals such as lawyers, accountants, assessors, and engineers.

Systemic corruption might ensue when petty corruption expands into intermediary areas such as appointing cronies to jobs that control resources, funding candidates for election, circumventing procedures, turning a blind eye to borderline illegal activity, or ignoring offenses. Another practice is to refrain from delineating the line between the permissible and the prohibited in order to blur norms and advance the excuse known as "everybody does it."

What is the level of corruption in Israel and where is it manifested? This question cannot be reliably answered – facts are few, though impressions abound. At the basic, personal level – petty corruption by low-level officials – the situation in Israel seems relatively good. While offenses by low-level civil servants are occasionally discovered, especially during trying economic times, they do not add up to the deeply rooted, systemic corruption familiar from corrupt regimes in some other countries. The cases revealed in Israel so far occupy a kind of middle level of offense – bribes, political appointments to sensitive positions, conflicts of interest, sexual harassment, and breach of trust. Most offenders, by the way, are politicians and their political appointees, not professional civil servants.

According to surveys conducted in 2015 (Hermann et al. 2011–15: 2015, 89), most of the Jewish and Arab public believe that state leaders are quite or very corrupt, with an average score of 2.4 on a scale of 1 (not at all corrupt) to 5 (very corrupt). Comparative surveys on the public's feeling toward various institutions reinforce this impression.

Table 18.3 shows that in Israel, as in the other countries surveyed, there is a strong tendency to accuse institutions of corruption. In other countries, most institutions score above 3, on average, except for religious institutions, non-profits, the media, and the military. The same is true for Israel, with the exception of the military, the school system, and the courts. In Israel, the state-religious institutions, and

[10] In the example of Enron, the American energy conglomerate, corruption was manifest not just in the concealing of information from shareholders and the tax authorities, but also by contributing to the two political parties and both presidential candidates to ensure the long-term company interests regardless of who was elected. See Behn 2000; Sparrow 2000; Skrzycky 2003; Levi-Faur 2006, 363–66.

Table 18.3 *Perception of corruption in various institutions, Israel compared with the average of 107 states (2013)*

		Israel	Average of 107 states
General	Parties	4.2	3.8
	Religious	4.1	2.6
	Media	3.5	2.7
	Business	3.5	3.6
	Parliament	3.5	3.4
	Non-profits	3.2	2.7
	The courts	2.9	3.6
Public administration	Civil servants	3.7	3.6
	Police	3.5	3.7
	Health system	3.1	3.3
	Education system	2.7	3.2
	The military	2.3	2.9

1 = no corruption at all; 5 = completely corrupt.

Source: Transparency International 2013, 24.

political parties in particular, are considered very corrupt, even more than in other countries. However, the (low) standing of the Knesset is similar to that of other parliaments. Israel does not fare well in a comparative assessment of corruption in the media and non-profit organizations. On the other hand, its court system, school system, and military are relatively more highly regarded, while the perception of other institutions, such as the business sector, are held in similar regard to other countries. Compared to the 2003 survey, the Israeli civil service was ranked more favorably than other institutions, and more favorably relative to other countries. The IDF, school and health systems, business sector, and the police were also considered less corrupt (Transparency International 2004).

In general, institutions are perceived as more corrupt than in previous years, and – in the eyes of the public – corruption has already risen to the systemic level. The concern is that the lack of clear ethical norms will spread to the systemic level, creating horizontal and vertical chains of corruption that will be hard to dismantle. There are already many signs, especially in the bonds forged between the wealthy and the politically powerful, and despite the efforts of the legal system, there are still no signs of strong antibodies to prevent a slide down this slippery slope.

Countries with an extended history of democracy have generally elevated their public service ethic, and usually grow stronger in terms of integrity, while the situation is paradoxically reversed in Israel. On the one hand, Israel does well on the general indicators of democracy – political competition, orderly regime change, high citizen involvement, and freedom of the press. All these should rank Israel (minus the occupied territories) high on the scale of integrity and democratic strength, but this did not happen. One proposed explanation is that the increased corruption is the result of governmental instability, as in "eat and be merry because tomorrow we may no longer be in power." But this is a partial explanation at best, because the decline in ethical conduct began when the government was relatively stable. In place of an explanation, a description may be useful: In the past, corruption clustered in benefits for one's party or sector – not for direct personal gain. Once this type of corruption subsided, it did not yield the anticipated ethic based on universal rules of politics and administration. The weakening of the central governance capacity was not accompanied by a change in the rules of the game, nor were sufficient resources allocated to it. Indeed, the perception that ethical norms are less important than economic or political gain seems to continue. Thus, no efforts were made to develop a governance culture – with the exception of the Supreme Court rulings until the 2000s – and from there the path to using public office for personal gain is short.

Three examples illustrate this point.[11] In the "Bar-On-Hebron affair" of 1997, there were already clear signs of systemic corruption (Negbi 2004, 13–29). The Talia Sasson Report in 2005 revealed that the government itself was flagrantly circumventing basic principles of democratic culture. And in the Holyland affair (2012–16), these signs turned into full-blown systemic corruption, which ultimately landed a prime minister in prison.

D. Examples of Corruption and the Lack of a Culture of Ethics

The Bar-On-Hebron Affair

In January 1997, Roni Bar-On was appointed Israel's attorney general by the government headed by Benjamin Netanyahu. In a news report on the state television channel, a reporter raised suspicions of criminal activity around this appointment, including a disturbing allegation that it was part of a deal: the appointment was designed to help MK Aryeh Deri in his trial in exchange for the support of Shas, Deri's party, in evacuating the Israeli settlers from Hebron. Elyakim Rubinstein, the attorney general appointed to replace Bar-On, wrote in a legal opinion in April 1997:

> The police investigation raised suspicions of crimes related to the appointment of Atty. Bar-On to the post of attorney general. The materials suggest that MK Deri, Atty. Hoter-Ishai, and businessman David Appel – all linked in friendship and business – had an interest in the appointment of Atty. Bar-On to the post of attorney general ... The evidence suggests that individuals indicted for criminal activity conspired out of personal interests to determine who would become the attorney general, and – through connections and political power – they even succeeded. (E. Rubinstein 1997)

During the investigation, evidence was also found that ministers and the director-general of the Office of Prime Minister did not provide the government with accurate information about the appointment. Following a public outcry, Bar-On resigned two days after his appointment.

The case revealed a level of systemic corruption in the nexus of political and business interests conspiring to appoint a crony to the most senior legal position in the civil service – seemingly to influence a criminal case. The breach discovered in this appointment – thanks to the alertness of the media and the public response – was

[11] There were, of course, earlier corruption scandals, such as the oil company Netivei Neft affair in 1972, which exposed a culture of "getting things done" – prioritizing the ability to achieve results at the price of corruption and shortcutting the law. Ethics and integrity were perceived in this context as small obstacles that could and should be circumvented. See summary in Galnoor 2011, 137–38.

closed with creation of a special Appointments Committee to screen candidates for the position of attorney general. But this did not end the systemic corruption, manifested in inappropriate political appointees, including subsequent attorney generals, and the willingness of the most senior officials, including the prime minister and other ministers, to use their power to pursue extraneous goals and personal gain.

The Report of Attorney Talia Sasson

The Sasson Report (Sasson 2005) revealed severe flaws in the culture of governance – the state intentionally conniving, fraudulently and knowingly engaging in self-deception (ibid.). The report documents violations of the law and the rules of proper administration in the construction of illegal settlements in the occupied territories. This policy was carried out by politicians and senior civil servants in several government ministries in collaboration with settler leaders. The report calls it "a policy of turning a blind eye," a patently unethical culture of winking at wrongdoers. The violations took place with the full knowledge of these authorities over a long period of time, and revealed deliberate efforts to blur the differences between the legal and illegal "political" settlements and "security" settlements, "authorized" and "unauthorized" settlements, new settlements and the expansion of existing settlements, settlements and outposts – and other invented terms designed to legalize and obfuscate:

> Unauthorized outposts were established in violation of proper procedures and rules of administration, and especially in gross and ongoing violation of the law. Furthermore, the state authorities speak in two voices. Sometimes they authorize and sometimes they prevent. The rules have become flexible. One hand works to build outposts while the other invests resources and forces in evacuating them … It is state and public authorities who are violating the law, the very rules and procedures established by the state for itself. (ibid., 42)

Of particular note is the fact that the government of Israel and the prime minister who ordered this investigation probably knew it would implicate them in illegal activity. In terms of ethics, therefore, the report itself is part of the deception because the government treated it like a passing incident intended to placate international public opinion and had no intention of implementing its recommendations.

The fraudulent conduct exposed in the Sasson Report reveals governmental corruption involving many organizations and designed to favor one particular group in society. Government authorities that act in crooked ways pave the way for systemic corruption.

The Holyland Affair[12]

In the 1990s, word got out that a massive construction project was planned for one of the high and beautiful hilltops in southwest Jerusalem, a project that would disfigure the city's unique skyline. Despite numerous objections, the project was quickly approved by the Jerusalem municipality under then mayor Ehud Olmert. The head of the local committee for planning and construction that approved the project was Uri Lupolianski, who later succeeded Olmert as mayor of Jerusalem. The scope of

[12] Partially based on Amram 2014.

approved construction – ten apartment towers (twelve to eighteen floors) plus a tower at the top of the hill (thirty-two floors) – was highly unusual. But despite raised eyebrows, criticism in the media, and professional objections, the project was approved and construction commenced. Suspicion of criminal actions only began to surface in 2008 – namely, that the real estate developers had bribed the mayor and top city officials in exchange for the approvals and extensive construction.

The full extent of the systemic corruption was revealed in January 2012, when the state attorney filed an indictment against thirteen defendants and three companies for paying or accepting bribes. The primary defendants among the public officials were former mayor (and later prime minister) Ehud Olmert, former Jerusalem mayor Uri Lupolianski, the city engineer, Olmert's bureau chief, and the head of the Israel Lands Authority. The business entities charged were the developers of the Holyland apartment complex along with several intermediaries and emissaries who had unlimited access to municipal officials, negotiated the kickbacks, and passed them from one to another. The district court convicted Olmert and gave him a six-year sentence. Nine other defendants and three companies were also convicted of accepting and paying bribes. In the ruling, the judge called for a change in legislation to create transparency in the activity of "fixers"[13] in the corridors of power and to prevent illegal lobbying that may entail bribery (*State of Israel v. Hillel Charney et al.* 2014).

In an appeal to the Supreme Court, an expanded panel of five justices voted by majority decision to acquit Ehud Olmert of receiving kickbacks in the Holyland affair, citing reasonable doubt. However, they did not overturn his conviction on accepting bribes in a related case. His prison term was reduced to one and a half years. The sentences of the other defendants convicted in the affair were revised and in some cases reduced, but the bribery charges remained. Supreme Court Justice Salim Jubran pointed out the damage of bribery to social values:

> The war against corruption requires a relentless battle. If he who became the prime minister of Israel committed the crime of accepting a bribe – what will an ordinary citizen think of his leaders; if they were caught up in this, how can he [the citizen] be held to a higher standard? The loftier the role of the public figure – the more egregious the breach of trust. Accepting bribes undermines sound government institutions and harms the running of a life-seeking state, hence the need to act fearlessly and with determination to wipe out such phenomena. (*Olmert v. State of Israel* 2015)

Construction of the Holyland project – the so-called "Jerusalem real estate monstrosity" – was halted, but it became a symbol of blatant corruption of public officials, businessmen, and fixers, who left behind a scar for generations to come.

Is the political system in Israel corrupt? The evidence is troubling. In the course of the sixteenth Knesset (February 2003 to April 2006), for example, the police conducted twenty-eight criminal investigations against members of the Knesset. Ten resulted in indictments and most of the MKs were convicted.[14] Ten years later, one might have expected

[13] See Halkin 2010. The article was written in connection with the Holyland scandal.

[14] See "List of all Israeli public officials convicted of a crime or misdemeanor." https://en.wikipedia.org/wiki/List_of_Israeli_public_officials_convicted_of_crimes_or_misdemeanors#Public_officials (accessed August 12, 2016).

these sentences to have a deterrent effect on public officials, but more cases of corruption followed, for example the convictions of former Minister of Finance Avraham Hirschson, President Moshe Katsav, and Prime Minister Ehud Olmert. The list includes more than ten mayors, several senior personnel in government ministries and government corporations, the chair of Israel's largest bank, a former district court judge – all sent to prison. Thus, the justice system works well and does not discriminate between the powerful and ordinary citizens, but its deterrent capability is far from effective.

E. Public Attitudes

In surveys of the citizens' perception of corruption (2003–10), 90 percent on average said there is substantial corruption in Israel, and 84 percent on average thought that this resembled or was higher than in other countries. In a 2010 survey, 50 percent of the respondents said that to reach the top political echelon in Israel, one has to be corrupt (Arian et al. 2005–10: 2008, 52; Arian et al. 2005–10: 2010, 70). In 2015, only 24 percent said that the leadership in Israel is "not corrupt" or "not corrupt at all," while 32 percent said that it is "a bit corrupt" and 48 percent chose the "corrupt" or "very corrupt" categories (Hermann et al. 2011–15: 2015, 90). Corruption in Israel is different from corruption in countries like India (Jalan 2005, 8–9, 26), but despite the angry and resentful mood, public vigilance is minimal, which leads to the incorrect notion that government and public ethics cannot go hand in hand.[15] In a survey conducted prior to the 2006 Knesset election, for example, voters were asked, "What determines which party you vote for?" The ranking of responses was as follows: foreign affairs and security, social issues, economic issues, party leadership, and – in last place (13%) – the fight against corruption (*Yediot Aharonot*, February 17, 2006). To the question "Would you vote for a party list that included people convicted or suspected of corruption?," 25 percent responded "never," 35 percent said "depending on the charges," 23 percent allowed that "It would bother me, but I'd vote for it," and 15 percent stated it would not bother them.

These replies reflect the problem: the acceptance of corruption as inevitable, bound to happen. The vast majority of those surveyed in this poll (73%) have a relativist ethic of governance – citizens who are reconciled to the notion that public officials are corrupt, citizens who will not use their civic power to deter and punish. Consequently, the most severe sanction of political corruption – withholding support at the ballot box – is not part of the democratic toolbox. This threatens the dike holding back systemic corruption in the political-administrative culture and allows corruption to become a "normal" part of the relations between society and the political system. What's more, corrupt behavior filters down to individuals and groups in society in a kind of "Do as I do."

F. Hazardous Zones

To understand the systemic problem caused by the lack of a public ethic in Israel, let us look at the problematic areas. Although the following list is based on impressions,

[15] Retired Judge Amnon Strashnov wrote, "Politics is a dirty, power-driven business with a pinch of moral decadence. I guess it's built in" (*Haaretz*, December 29, 2005).

these areas are not surprising, as they are hazardous zones in other countries as well, and often appear in the Israeli media chronicles and courts.

- ***Land:*** This area is distinctive in Israel because the state and the Jewish National Fund control most of the land in the country. It is an area with many opportunities for corrupt deals and misconduct by giving preferential treatment to specific groups or business interests. Symptomatic of this are the pitched battles between ministers over who will be responsible for the Israel Land Administration. Furthermore, the continued efforts to privatize state lands in Israel have opened new opportunities for corrupt circular transactions. Closely related is the area of planning and construction licensing, which is vulnerable to bribery and conflicts of interests at the local and national levels, as demonstrated in the Holyland affair (discussed above).
- ***Taxation, licensing, inspection, regulation, and approval of grants and exemptions:*** Opportunities for corruption come up primarily around tax evasion, construction permits, and business licenses. Misconduct in this vast zone may remain at what we called the basic (personal) level, i.e., localized economic corruption, but the involvement of large business interests and the weakness of the local authorities are liable to make this corruption systemic. For example, the director of the Income Tax Authority was convicted in 2010 of accepting bribes and conflict of interest. In corrupt countries, the field of taxation is particularly problematic, deeply affecting public perceptions. In general, how the authorities manage services such as licensing, inspection, etc. plays a significant role in subjective attitudes among the public about the existence of systemic corruption.
- ***The occupied territories:*** Control over several million Palestinians who have lacked political and civil rights for fifty years has an inherently corruptive influence. The apartheid regime in South Africa was corrupt. Instances of petty corruption have appeared among Israelis serving in the civil administration of the occupied territories, and there have also been cases of power abuse by military commanders. Systemic corruption, however, relates to the settlements, whose construction and public finances have never reached a minimal level of public transparency. To this day, aggregate data cannot be found in the state budget about the amount of state investment in the territories. Israeli citizens have never been informed about the economic cost of the settlement project.

  There are back channels for transferring funds from the state budget to the settlement enterprise – via the Settlement Division of the World Zionist Organization, for example, which is external to the government.[16] The establishment of a shadow system in the occupied territories, parallel to the government, is a sure recipe for lack of control, contempt for the law, and ultimately

[16] In an official legal opinion, Deputy Attorney General Dina Silber wrote, "The legal directive to restore discretionary authority to the government in this field [i.e., and take it away from the Settlement Division] is consistent with the trend of strengthening the government's capacity to execute its policy. That is governance" (Ministry of Justice, document 408-22-9092-099998, February 26, 2015). See also Galnoor 2015a. Subsequently, Amendment 2 to the World Zionist Organization-Jewish Agency (Status) Law (1952) was enacted in late 2015 to legitimize the transfer of funds through the Settlement Division.

corruption (see the Talia Sasson Report above). It also raises questions about democracy in Israel in light of the lack of democracy in the occupied territories.[17]

- ***The money-power nexus:*** This is a relatively new domain that emerged full blown in Israel rather recently. It has aspects of petty, personal corruption, such as a building contractor supporting a candidate for mayor in exchange for licenses; and symptoms of systemic corruption, as revealed in the Bar-On-Hebron affair; or support for then President Ezer Weizman from a wealthy businessman; or illegal contributions to the election campaigns of candidates for prime minister and the Knesset. The concentration of wealth in a small number of families and the centralized ownership of the media are part of the phenomenon (T. Goldstein 2006; Matskin 2012, 114). Suffice it to say that most of the present-day wealthy people in Israel made their fortune in financial transactions – there were no such "tycoons" in Israel two decades ago.
- ***Privatization policies:*** Since the 1980s, various Israeli governments have pursued a policy of downsizing the public sector, selling off government corporations, and privatizing and outsourcing many social services. Privatization is a neoliberal ideology advanced in the name of free markets, globalization, economic efficiency, and fostering competition (Galnoor et al. 2015). In the context of corrupting the political culture, several questions arise: Are there clear and transparent criteria for reducing state responsibilities and transferring public assets to private hands? Does privatization indeed stimulate real competition? Is privatization driven by calculation of the public good or by business interests? Negative answers to these questions may indicate corruption, particularly the emergence of the "tycoons" mentioned above, who handle public funds, and prosper on money-power relations.
  In November 2009, the Israeli High Court of Justice prohibited the operation of a private prison in Israel because it harms the basic rights of prisoners for the sake of a private company's business interests (*Academic Center of Law and Business v. Minister of Finance* 2005; Galnoor 2006).[18] Government activities, commercial and non-commercial, are subject to public and parliamentary oversight, but there is no oversight of the power wielded by private interests.

G. Corruption in Israel in the Twenty-First Century

While most democratic countries have over the years moved in the direction of greater concern about a public ethic – though corruption has not entirely disappeared – Israel seems to be moving in the opposite direction. According to indicators of governmental

17 In 2011, MK Miri Regev and nineteen other MKs submitted a bill to legalize outposts in the territories considered illegal by Israel, which had stated, "An outpost built on private Palestinian land that was not marked as such cannot be evacuated if the person claiming ownership does not submit a claim in court or present evidence of ownership within four years" (www.inn.co.il/News/News.aspx/230353 [accessed October 24, 2017]). Although this bill exhibits profound contempt for the rule of law as it abrogates property laws for political reasons, it was supported by a majority of MKs. Ultimately, domestic and international pressure forced the prime minister to oppose them and see them voted down in the Knesset (Association for Civil Rights in Israel 2012).

18 In a case nicknamed "Kids for Cash," two judges in Pennsylvania were convicted in 2008 of having accepted $2.6 million in bribes from private prison companies in exchange for imprisoning teenagers (Ecenbarger 2009).

corruption, Israel ranks poorly among western democracies, and somewhere in the middle of democratic countries in general, which includes states that have introduced democracy within the past few decades. The examples presented above illustrate that in the political system of Israel, a corrupt marketplace of supply and demand seems to have developed between those in power who are willing to accept favors and private people or business enterprises eager to offer them. This is new, compared with the party and sectoral corruption that characterized Israel's early years. Ongoing media exposure, stepped-up litigation, and resolute law enforcement have not managed to eradicate this problem.

The courts are perhaps the last bastion against the spread of corruption, but a significant gap exists between addressing specific cases of corruption and dealing with systemic unethical conduct. Closing this gap is not within the power of the judiciary, particularly since the public appears unwilling to use its clout to penalize politicians who took this path. Israel could not be described as riddled with the corruption of a third world country, certainly not at the level of petty corruption (bribing clerks and police officers). However, an increasing number of corruption cases have been uncovered among very high-ranking officials in various fields, including campaign finance, and signs of systemic corruption have begun to appear as the interests of senior echelons in the government and public administration dovetail with private interests. If this trend continues, it is a matter of time before Israel graduates to the next level.

Honesty in government is a value rooted in political culture. Remedy will require major efforts of financial oversight and judicial enforcement, but these are not enough. In the long run, the political culture must change because this is what corrupts or cleanses the relationship between government and its citizens (for a similar conclusion, see Lederman et al. 2005, 27). In order to foster honesty, a richer menu is needed in addition to legislation and litigation. It would require instilling democratic values and educating for democracy, rebuilding faith in political institutions, reforming the civil service, reducing centralization, strengthening the parties as viable institutions, recognizing the contribution of civil society and the media, strengthening the local authorities, and more.

18.4 Steering Capacity and Policy

The principal mission of the state is to enable its citizens to achieve common goals. Accordingly, governance needs to develop "steering capacity," i.e., the capability of coping with external challenges (security, foreign affairs) and internal challenges that stem in part from social and cultural differences. An essential question arises: Is there a shared political language that enables the different segments of society to collaborate, creating a widely accepted foundation for political discourse and political action? And, further, does it enable the steering of the collective ship – setting policy, making decisions, and implementing them? We will also try to respond to the question of whether Israel is a "politically developed" country.

A. One State, Several Societies, Many Cultures

From a governance perspective, a homogeneous society – uni-national, with no significant religious, linguistic, geographic, or economic differences – is easier to steer.

The assumption here is that the state is a "neutral" institution, not an instrument for guarding the interests of a particular group or groups. Homogeneity might be easier, but it does not preclude disagreements, as many homogeneous societies can attest. After all, politics is designed to bridge differences and conflicting interests, and these exist even among people working toward a common objective. How does a democratic political system cope with acute internal disagreements in order to avoid fragmentation or anarchy? Let us pose the question differently: Assuming we have a democratic regime and that homogeneity makes steering "easier" for a state, does the state threaten the unique and diverse identities within it, or do such identities threaten the state? This is a familiar dilemma for democracies: how to reconcile the legitimate demands for unity and diversity; how to achieve political unity without cultural unity; and how to foster the citizens' sense of belonging and at the same time respect profound cultural differences (Parekh 1999).

Of course, we need to know how deep the internal divisions are and what the incentives are for bridging them without the use of coercion. Israeli society has always been heterogeneous (see Chapter 16). However, in the "statism" period of Israel's early years – despite the mosaic of an immigrant society, the rivalry between political camps, and disparities between veterans and new immigrants – there was a consensus among Jewish citizens concerning the overall objectives for which the state was established. This included tacit agreement about democratic politics as a means of achieving these objectives. The combination of the state's power and the Mapai hegemony led by Ben-Gurion's "statist" policy (Kedar 2009, 76–89) sustained the common denominator of the diverse groups in Jewish society until the late 1960s. And it also encompassed exclusion of the Arab citizens of Israel.

Following the 1967 and 1973 wars with their shocks and changes to the political system, confrontations over the character of society and objectives of the state were renewed. The political upheaval of 1977 was a reflection of demographic changes in society and the growing strength of the second and third generation of Mizrahi immigrants, who were previously in the political periphery. In the 1980s and 1990s, political parties appeared in both the Jewish and Arab sectors that were identified exclusively with distinct groups in the society – Shas (Sephardic Jews), Yisrael B'Aliyah (Russian immigrants), and the Arab Democratic Party. The discourse on rights was adopted not only by liberal groups (usually educated Jews of western origin), but also by groups considered peripheral who now expressed their demands in the new social language of this discourse (Mautner, Sagi, and Shamir 1998, 68–69). These processes changed both the reality and perception of the status of groups in Israeli society – from a temporary situation characteristic of an immigrant society ("from ingathering to assimilating the exiles") to a new fluid situation, which raises substantive questions about the shared identity, the future of the society, and the role of politics. Is society in Israel composed of an assortment of tribes?[19]

In retrospect, the vision of the melting pot that inspired the state's policy of intervention faded in the 1970s. Although it had been successful in some areas, such as military service as a socialization mechanism for Jewish citizens, it is now considered

[19] In a speech on June 7, 2015, President Rivlin listed four "tribes" – three Jewish (ultra-Orthodox, national-religious, and secular) and one Arab. www.president.gov.il/English/ThePresident/Speeches/Pages/news_070615_01.aspx (accessed August 12, 2016).

a failure in the cultural and personal context by most Mizrahi immigrants. Among veterans, too, belief declined in the idea of acculturating immigrants, i.e., assimilating them into the existing culture without changing it. The melting pot vision seems to have been designed only for those outside the veteran elite who had dominated Israel since its establishment, not for forging a "new Israeli" using the identities of all the immigrant groups. Nonetheless, the melting pot as *an autonomous social-cultural process*, as opposed to deliberate state policy, contributed to the collective goals of shared life and common concerns. These processes continue today in full force, because Israel is still mostly an immigrant Jewish society: 26 percent were born abroad and another 46 percent are second generation (CBS *Statistical Abstract* 2013, table 2.6).

In the wake of the changes described above, two outlooks or predictions have emerged about the future of Israeli society. First, the divisions in society are deep and increasingly discordant; with disparities growing and difficult to bridge, the shared framework is in danger of collapsing. Hence, the chance of a shared political culture is slim. Second – and this outlook is more elaborate – the internal divisions in Israeli society indicate a process that will eventually create a shared culture, which some call a "multicultural society" (Nachtomy 2003). There will be a (thin or thick) layer of shared identity in which each group has a right to its unique culture, while respecting the separate identities of the other groups. Now the question is, what would be the essence and content of the shared part of the culture? Some aspire to a primarily civic culture – shared and agreed citizenship content – that is inclusive of all the participating subcultures and identities. Others aspire to an exclusively Jewish shared content and identity. The former see a civic political culture as the foundation for the shared vision and the state's political action. The latter would like the political culture to be ethno-Jewish, inclusive of all the Jewish subcommunities within Israel, and perhaps the Jewish Diaspora as well.

It should be noted that politics plays a different role in each outlook. According to the ***deep division*** outlook, electoral politics exacerbates tensions and reinforces the trend of separatism. The parties do not bridge or converge interests; on the contrary, they actually represent the interests of the separate identities (the so-called "sectors" or "tribes"). The parties and their client organizations operate in the Knesset solely on behalf of their supporters, without concern for the general public good. Some, particularly among the religious, even try to impose their culture and way of life on the other groups. Under these circumstances, it is not just politics, but civil society as well that is not a unifying factor contributing to mutual trust, but rather a collection of interest groups that lacks a mandate from and is not accountable to the general public.

And for the ***eventually shared culture*** outlook, politics is a crucial instrument. For the civic aspirants, the current divisions can lead to an inclusive citizenship that is unafraid of separate identities; at which point politics will serve its classic function – as an arena for ideological competition and a mechanism for resolving conflicts and reaching compromises. The political system will bestow legitimacy upon the separate culture of each group, including those that are very different – such as Arabs and ultra-Orthodox Jews – on condition that each group respects the democratic way of life, recognizes the shared civic identity, and compromises on some of its demands in order to allow others to maintain their culture and preserve their identity. Under such circumstances, the political parties and civil society organizations will not only seek to meet separate objectives, but will also strive to promote the general public weal.

A Deep Divide

Eisenstadt analyzed the dynamic changes in Israeli society and concluded that even though the framework was preserved and a thin layer of shared "mass culture" emerged, the gap has widened between the "sectoral creation" and the all-inclusive "social creation." In his view, the rift between the sectors has grown worse, and a struggle has begun over the symbols of collective identity and the shaping of the institutional system (Eisenstadt 1996). Lissak similarly noted a deepening of the cleavages and an intensification of the internal disputes in society, so much so that it reminded him of the sectoral pattern of the political culture in the Yishuv period (Lissak 1998, 132; Yatziv 1999). Kimmerling, on the other hand, predicted the end of the hegemony of the *ahusalim* (a Hebrew acronym for Ashkenazi, secular, veteran, socialist, and nationalist) – the elite who dominated the state since its establishment. For Kimmerling, the struggle is being waged among the diverse cultures in Israel over definition of the collective identity, access to resources, and the political rules of the game: "Each group feels threatened by the others, and as the sense of threat intensifies … its willingness to engage in verbal and physical violence, both internally and externally, intensifies" (2001, 14–15). He later added that the separate sectors among the Jews in Israel are united only in a "culture of security" – an amalgamation of religion, ultra-nationalism, and militarism.[20]

The "deep divide" outlook was presented earlier by Smooha (1997), who defined Israel as an "ethnic democracy" in which the state and the democratic rules of the game were designed to primarily serve the Jewish citizens, the veteran Ashkenazi Jews in particular.[21] Scholars of Israeli society disagree on the character of the social structure in the past, the lines of division today, and the outcomes of the melting pot policy. However, their common conclusion seems to be that the shared political culture is weak and perhaps non-existent. In terms of steering capacity, this could mean that except for the shared security anxiety, there is no common content. When each sector looks only after itself, an all-out struggle for public resources is waged among the sectors (e.g., most articles in Rosenthal 2001). As noted, politics in such circumstances, especially a proportional election system, exacerbates the divisions. This mood is reflected in surveys on relations among groups in Israeli society.

In Table 18.4 the national divide (Jewish–Arab) tops the list of both Arabs and Jews. However, a substantially higher percentage of Arabs than Jews perceive this to be the greatest source of tension. The ethnic divide appears at the bottom of the list – only an average of 24 percent – but it ranks higher among Mizrahi Jews (31%) than Ashkenazi Jews (21%). The ideological divide on the territorial issue between right and left has intensified since 2009 during the Netanyahu governments. The average is 60 percent, but more predominant among the left (72%) than among the right (63%) or center (56%). A majority perceive greater tension between the rich

[20] Personal communication with Itzhak Galnoor.

[21] For a different version, which portrays Israel as an "ethnocracy" and thus undemocratic, see Yiftachel 2000.

Table 18.4 *Perception of strong tension between groups in Israel (%, 2015)*

Groups	Total	Jews	Arabs
		Define the tension as the strongest	
Jews v. Arabs	67	44	64
Right v. Left	60	10	8
Rich v. Poor	51	14	7
Secular v. Religious	48	21	12
Mizrahim v. Ashkenazim	24	4	1

Source: Hermann et al. 2011–15: 2015, 101–3.

and poor, giving it third place on the list, above the "conventional" tensions based on religion or ethnic origin. This is relatively new, and reflects the growing economic disparity in Israeli society.

Table 18.4 shows that while Israel is one state (disregarding the controversial territories and about 3–4% of its citizens who live there as settlers), it contains at least two very distinct societies (Jews and Arabs) and powerful tensions based on ideology, economics, and religion. Diverse identities are in motion within Israeli society, but they do not yet constitute multicultural pluralism (Yonah 1998; Yonah 2001).

Steering capacity requires a minimal level of national or civic solidarity. Otherwise, it is impossible to put in place a general policy that extends beyond the sector, ethnic group, religion, or culture. Without this minimum in the political culture, policies unrelated to security issues fall short of general legitimacy, especially on social and economic affairs.

A Shared Political Culture – Civic with Various Identities, or Something Else?

Since the 1970s, the internal divisions have intensified, to the point of depicting Israeli society as a federation of five sectors, partly overlapping, and nearly equal in size, separated by cultural rifts and conflicting interests: Arab and – among the Jews – religious, Mizrahi, Ashkenazi, and Russian (Peres and Ben Rafael 2006, 270–72). Israel seems to be a mosaic of cultures, each with its own identity (and subdivisions), values, and language. Moreover, since the 1980s, when the state ceased to function as a preeminent agent seeking to shape a common identity, these processes have been overtaken by "social market forces," enabling the separate cultures to grow in the civil society and political arena.

Therefore, is it possible to have a significant common identity in Israel that both binds yet also recognizes diversity and accepts the various cultures? The notion of "citizenship with separate identities" in its radical version aspires to almost completely eliminate the state's "republican" educational activism, indirectly asserting that there is no need to invest in a shared culture.[22] This view represents a type of anarchism that rejects the state as a source of evil and, unlike classic liberalism, which advocated a weak state based on individual liberty, it emphasizes the autonomy of group identity. In this approach, the state interferes with various identities and hinders them from expressing themselves and flourishing. The objection is not

22 For a general review, see Yonah and Shenhav 2005.

only to the dominance of the majority culture, but to any pretension of shaping and developing a shared culture.

Regarding the state as merely a mechanism of regulation, devoid of any mission of its own – certainly lacking in a "culture" – is not new, of course. However, within the state, is there a need for society to share a culture, at least a political culture? More moderate versions of multiculturalism recognize that for a culture to be truly pluralistic, there must be a shared common denominator, valued by all the components, and enabling them to engage in otherwise impossible creative interaction. Accordingly, the shared culture of a particular society within a state or any other political community fosters a sense of belonging among the citizens, beyond their group affiliation. It also entails a readiness for joint action. This sense of belonging is political, a genuine sense of citizenship, and begets a commitment to the shared political community – its existence, sustenance, continuity, and vitality.[23]

Is it feasible to envisage in Israel a "thin" civic state, based primarily on shared citizenship?

- Among many Jews, particularly those who are religious or traditional, there is a longing for a strong "Jewish State" with a specific, uniform identity, and without divisive disagreements. For them, shared citizenship is not the common denominator.
- In practice, the different groups are opponents and some are even hostile to each other – some reject the values and beliefs of the others, denounce their cultures, or display enmity and suspicion toward them. For example, the ultra-Orthodox do not accept secular culture as equally valid with a right to exist; many Jews harbor such attitudes toward the culture of the Arab citizens of Israel.[24] Such absolute rejection of "others" also exists in the attitudes of the extreme right.
- Inequality and relations of control and dominance constitute an impediment to multiculturalism. Moreover, when the Israeli state started to retreat from its economic and social commitments, its reduced involvement was not neutral, but strengthened the dominant majority cultures. Hence the proposal that the state adopt a sort of "affirmative action" policy for cultural minorities – special rights to enable them to preserve and nurture their culture (Margalit and Halbertal 1998). Diminished state involvement has also benefited the upper class, and decreased the incentive of the other classes to expand their citizenship commitment.
- In Israel, tolerance of diverse cultures faces difficult tests. Should the state fund groups that reject its right to exist, or that oppose its legal definition as a Jewish state, or that do not recognize its secular authority?

Acceptance of a shared civic political culture as the common denominator does not currently seem imminent in Israel. As long as security threats exist, it is doubtful that

[23] Parekh 1999 also emphasizes what the political commitment does *not* include: shared objectives, a uniform view of history, support for the existing system of government, and the dominant cultural ethos.

[24] The good will of the diverse groups and a willingness to recognize and tolerate others is crucial for maintaining multiculturalism. However, an accord of multiculturalism is possible among liberal and non-liberal groups based on interests, when it is accepted as the lesser evil by the non-liberal groups, especially if they are minority groups (Y. Tamir 1998, 90–91).

Israelis will develop the tolerance required to maintain a society that comfortably includes a range of other cultures.[25] For this and other reasons too, the alternative – Israel as synonymous with a Jewish state and society – is more plausible. The amendments to the Basic Law: The Knesset and to the Knesset Elections Law – stipulating that party lists and candidates cannot run for office if they reject the existence of Israel as a Jewish and democratic state, support armed struggle against it, or incite to racism – have set a tenuous border for democratic tolerance in Israel. But the line was crossed in 2016 with an amendment to the Basic Law: The Knesset that allows a special majority of MKs to impeach an elected MK for allegedly violating one of these clauses.[26] The very fact that this anti-democratic law was enacted shows that parties and groups are no longer tolerant of those who are different from them, and are prepared to use a temporary majority against them.

The position we present below is not a middle path, but rather an attempt to suggest a different approach to the relations between a shared identity and separate identities, and to point to the role of politics in this context.

B. Is There an Israeli Society?

We posit that Israeli society is complex, dynamic, and interesting. Rifts that were considered impossible to mend have moderated over time, such as the divisions between groups based on country of origin, regarded now as the weakest tension in Israeli society (Table 18.4). Even the schism between "left" and "right" on the occupied territories, security, etc. – which was a focal point of tension from the 1970s – has been subject to pendulum swings. It eased during the period of the unity governments (1984–90); peaked with the Oslo Accords and the assassination of Yitzhak Rabin in 1995; lessened with the emergence of the Kadima party led by Sharon, Olmert, and Livni (2005); and again worsened following the elections of Netanyahu from 2009 onwards. Despite the fluctuations, the *ideological* gaps narrowed on this central issue. The distance between the extreme positions remains unchanged, but there is broad agreement – unprecedented, even during the Labor governments until 1977 – on establishment of a Palestinian state alongside Israel. The arguments are still over the specific terms, the borders, and the timing. In addition, a new rift emerged, noted in Table 18.4 – the growing resentment in Israeli society about wealth disparities, which peaked in the 2011 protest movement.

The previous political culture lost its hegemonic status, and based on this premise, we consider two questions: First, has the escalation of internal divisions destroyed the foundation for proper interaction between the society and its political system? That is, is there still a shared language for political action? Second, is Israel on a course that would leave the state only the roles of maintenance (e.g., law and order) vis-à-vis a society with separate identities?

Katz and Sela examined identities only indirectly, but focused on the cultural demands of various groups in society (Arabs, religious Jews, Mizrahi Jews, Russian

[25] We can present another approach – a multicultural society as an interim stage leading to a gradual blurring of separate identities in a natural, dynamic way, and formation of an Israeli identity that includes traces of all the associated cultures. Thus, after the stage of separatism, there will be a blending of groups by virtue of the shared life and joint political action.

[26] Basic Law: The Knesset (Amendment 45 – Impeachment of an MK) (July 20, 2016).

immigrants, and young people) and presented illuminating findings (1999, 28–35, 50–56). These groups had many demands from the state, and every group demanded a culture policy that would recognize their distinctiveness. However, no explicit demands were made for a separate or isolated culture, surprisingly not even among the Arabs or Russian immigrants, who came close to this, but stopped short of rejecting a (civil) "Israeli" identity that includes, or should include, them as well. Immigrants from Russia, for example, expressed a desire to make their unique contribution to Israeli culture; the Mizrahi group vigorously demanded full representation of their deprived culture – but as part of the general culture; Arab citizens demanded state recognition of their difference and uniqueness as well as cultural autonomy, but not beyond this. Their opposition to a state defined as "Jewish" did not entail negation of the state itself or the culture of its Jewish majority. Jewish groups, too, sought recognition of their separate identity, rejected the idea of being swallowed up in the melting pot, and demanded state resources for preserving their culture. The research identified a distinct thirst for "authentic" cultural uniqueness, but also for commonality – crystallization of a new "Israeliness" in which diverse groups would find a comfortable place. As noted above, for many but not all Jews, this means a Jewish Israel. As for practical expectations from government policy, the groups expressed support for cultural autonomy (but not social or political autonomy), along with a desire to contribute to "Israeliness" in general.

The gradual disappearance of the previous consociational structure, the dwindling consensus, and the instability of the political system engendered predictable responses in the Jewish public. The first was to converge under the umbrella of the security threat (see Chapter 14), though this could not always cover up disagreements over the question of a Palestinian state, disengagement from the Gaza Strip, construction of a separation barrier, the second Lebanon War, and the like. And the second response was an attempt to forge a common (Jewish) denominator through the education system.[27]

Citizenship Education

The debates over the core curriculum in the education system reflect the tension between the state's aspiration to mold a unifying framework for the different groups in society (even if artificially) and, on the other hand, the opposition of minority groups, which regard such efforts as attempts to erase their identities on the pretext of a pluralistic education system.

In September 2003, then education minister Limor Livnat presented a core curriculum for elementary schools (Yaacov J. Katz 2006). Two years later, the Dovrat Committee regarded the core curriculum as one of the pillars of the comprehensive reform it proposed for the education system. It recommended that implementation of the core curriculum in elementary schools would be a condition for receipt of public funds. The motivation for launching a core curriculum was fear "of the disintegration of Israeli society due to the cleavages that characterize it" and the desire

[27] Arab intellectuals in Israel responded with their own "vision documents" aimed at redefining their standing as an autonomous, native community in the state (see Chapter 15). Interestingly, some of these documents demand recognition of the autonomy of Arab citizens as part of a consociational arrangement (National Committee of Arab Local Authorities 2006).

"to introduce a core curriculum in the schools that will serve as an educational common denominator for all of pupils in society … and a social glue to prevent the complete dissolution of society" (Dovrat Committee 2005).[28]

These declarations expose the trap in the part of the core curriculum that seeks to foster social solidarity:

> It will serve as a foundation for promoting collective understanding and fruitful cooperation in Israeli society, and will also enable various social groups to fulfill their specific social objectives. The core curriculum will lay the infrastructure for promoting social understanding and *public unanimity* on basic issues, despite the different goals on the agenda of the various sectors of society. (Ministry of Education 2003 [emphasis added])

The declaration ostensibly offers equal participation to all groups in society, but anchors the core curriculum in "Jewish and universal values" and sets prerequisites for this participation – recognition of Israel as a Jewish and democratic state (Yaacov J. Katz 2006, 189). Parts of the curriculum stirred fierce criticism. Arab educators were not partners in shaping it and complained that the curriculum set unacceptable conditions. While the Dovrat Committee report recognized a separate, collective Arab identity, it called for recognition of the basic premises of Jewish-Zionist nationalism; furthermore, Arabic was not recognized as a mandatory language for all pupils (Amara 2006). The ultra-Orthodox objected to the core curriculum not only because of its Zionist content, but also because of its espousal of universal values and the unacceptable pedagogical methods it sought to instill in their education network (Yonah 2006, 208). Liberal opponents were not against the idea of a core curriculum, but strongly objected the proposed shared contents with its nationalistic tenor, as a guise for imbuing the "correct identity" in different groups in Israeli society. They argued that certain assertions presented as "truths" – for example, the "Jewishness" of the state – are not accepted by all the citizens, and that the curriculum was designed to instill an ethno-national version of democracy (ibid., 212).

The first step taken to create a common denominator reflected the curriculum's nationalist objectives, indeed bordering on disrespect for democratic values. In 2003, the Ministry of Education published the booklet *100 Basic Concepts on Heritage, Zionism, and Democracy*, which became a mandatory list for all pupils to memorize and be tested on (Rapel and Levin 2003). The substantive criticism of the booklet was its pedagogical shallowness – the superficial memorizing of complex concepts, instead of learning about and understanding their meaning. Furthermore, the booklet had tunnel vision of the world, focusing on Jewish-Zionist exclusivity. It showed disrespect for universal democratic values and the culture of non-Jewish citizens. The Ministry of Education's promise to publish a separate booklet for Arab schools was never carried out. In October 2006, the Ministry canceled the *100 Basic Concepts* booklet. Yet, the danger of indoctrination via a "national" curriculum – ignoring the complexity of Israeli society and straying from the worthy aim of finding shared values for all pupils – was not internalized. In early 2016, another attempt was made by the Ministry of Education to infuse national and religious content into the citizenship curriculum in high schools (see below).

[28] Also see Yaacov J. Katz 2006, 189; Ministry of Education 2003; Ministry of Education 2003a.

The core curriculum was supposed to be implemented in all elementary schools, and the Ministry of Education conditioned government funding for its adoption. This requirement also applied, in part, to the ultra-Orthodox schools of Agudat Yisrael and Shas. The matter reached the High Court, which ruled that implementation of the core curriculum as a condition for funding is not only reasonable, but promotes equality in society (*Center for Religious Pluralism et al. v. Ministry of Education* 2009). In practice, however, ultra-Orthodox schools did not incorporate the core curriculum and the Knesset enacted a law in 2008 that granted 260 ultra-Orthodox high school-yeshivas an exemption (Gavison 2008). Finally, the 2015 coalition agreement between the Likud and the ultra-Orthodox parties states that the core curriculum will not be mandatory.

Does the experience to date suggest there is no chance of agreement on formulating a core curriculum that would meet the needs of society and be acceptable to the diverse groups (or at least to most of them)? In our opinion, the difficulty is not the content or the teaching of good citizenship and democracy – as long as there is no attempt to exploit them for unsuitable purposes. However, a curriculum exclusively and unilaterally imposed by the Education Ministry is doomed to fail. It may even have a detrimental effect on developing a common denominator. The education process has an element of coercion, but it should not be abused. The makeup of Israeli society in the twenty-first century requires that the idea of pluralism be part of the education system and the shared culture.

Education ministers come and go, and eventually they realize that it is no longer possible to coerce their social and cultural values on the population. Shared content exists and, if left alone, can gradually evolve into an educational program that is partly shared and partly pluralistic; it will grow from civil society and its diverse cultures, rather than from state institutions. Such a curriculum should focus on educating good citizens. The objectives were aptly presented in the Kremnitzer Committee report (1995, 10) as

> imparting knowledge, understanding, and an ability to analyze, judge, and make decisions on social and political questions; internalizing the values of the state; generating a commitment to a democratic system and a willingness to defend it; instilling the capability and desire to become an active, involved, and responsible citizen.

Education should seek to impart shared citizenship and not create a shared Jewish identity. This principle has not driven the policy of the Ministry of Education under the leadership of Minister Naftali Bennett (2015–) from the religious Jewish Home party. In yet another attempt to convert citizenship education in high schools into Jewish-Zionist exhortation, the ministry sought to impose a mandatory rewritten citizenship textbook designed to strengthen the national Jewish character of Israel at the expense of its democratic values.[29] Even more egregious is the attempt to turn the matriculation examination in citizenship into a tool for tendentious learning. In

[29] The book was harshly criticized by experts who questioned not only its indoctrination objectives, but also its quality. For example, an early version of the book seen by the authors stated, "A democratic political culture does not exist to an equal extent in all democracies, and is not a necessary condition for defining a state as democratic." See also the discussion of this book by the Knesset Education Committee (December 22, 2015). http://main.knesset.gov.il/Activity/committees/Education/News/Pages/22122015.aspx [in Hebrew] (accessed August 16, 2016).

the school text prepared by the ministry, the universal values of democracy or good citizenship are not to be found. The first chapters concern the history of the state of Israel; Israel as a Jewish and democratic state; justification for a democratic nation-state; and the like.[30]

The Mysteries of Israeliness

What "Israeliness" could perhaps serve as a common denominator for all parts of society in Israel? After several generations, it is already clear that it is not the new Hebrew identity that would sprout from the soil of the homeland, disconnected from the exilic diaspora past, as many movements in Zionism once believed. For most Jews in Israel, "Israeliness" nowadays is expressly Jewish – national, religious, cultural, and/or historical – and not just territorial state citizenship. Some Jews in the Diaspora also share this view. For Jews in Israel, the state is the embodiment of Zionism and, to a large extent, also an expression of their Jewish identity, or their Judaism. Many (not all) are unwilling to consider non-Jewish citizens of Israel as part of the "Israeli" nation. Yet the substance is not clear, even for Jewish Israelis, and certainly not obvious: The elements of Judaism, Jewish identity, Zionism, and Israeliness are still jostling among themselves (Galnoor 1982, 87).

Nonetheless, given all the reservations mentioned above, is there a foundation of "Israeliness," perhaps even a shared culture, that enables some solidarity, or at least the ability to act together politically to achieve common goals? The answer is obviously influenced by the internal divisions within society, and we will return to this later. Among Jewish citizens, the answer is by and large affirmative – certainly with regard to the mission of preserving the state's existence and security, but also in terms of Jewish-Israeli identity (in this order, among the majority). Israeliness exists in the culture, the attachment to the homeland, the lifestyle, the identity of most Jews, and the desire to live in Israel.[31] Still, this connection continually faces challenges stemming from existential insecurity about the state's survival and dissatisfaction with its actions. It is difficult to find a comparable case in another country, where citizens threaten the state as if it were a real entity – to boycott it, emigrate from it, or not "recognize" it. These are not individuals pursuing personal gain or economic careers elsewhere, but (Jewish) groups that declare conditional loyalty to the state – the ultra-Orthodox, for example, or settlers after their evacuation from the Gaza Strip, or liberals who fear that the ruling majority is non-democratic.

Let us turn now to the internal divisions, the social rifts. Those divided by the Jewish–Arab cleavage have fewer overlapping loyalties than Jews divided by other rifts. Shas, for example, represents a Mizrahi/ultra-Orthodox/traditional group, but it also partly overlaps with Ashkenazi ultra-Orthodox Jews, and traditional or secular Mizrahi Jews. New immigrants from the former Soviet Union are perceived

[30] Ministry of Education, Basic Concepts for the Teacher (Citizenship), 2015. http://citizenship.cet.ac.il/ShowItem.aspx?ItemID=c700351b-de32-4849-a71b-166c654330b0&lang=HEB [in Hebrew] (accessed August 16, 2016).

[31] "Do you want to live in Israel in the distant future?" The general average of positive responses from 1986 to 2010 was 73 percent (Arian et al. 2005–10: 2010, 81). "To what extent do you feel yourself part of the state of Israel and its problems?" There were 88 percent positive responses among Jews and 32 percent among Arabs. As to the desire to remain in Israel, there was no difference between Jews and Arabs: 83–85 percent (Hermann et al. 2015, 32, 35).

to be a separate group that added a new division to Israeli society, but members of this group connect with secular Ashkenazi Jews, partly with nationalist groups, and even with the remnant "Russian" culture of the early veteran immigrants. And, as expected, survey research shows that the second generation is already quite Israeli, as had been true of previous immigrant groups. The absence of "Israeliness" on the part of Arabs in Israel is largely a reaction to having been rejected by the majority, i.e., the unwillingness of Jewish Israelis to share the state with them in partnership. Nevertheless, Arab citizens express a willingness for a true, equal partnership in a civic state. From this perspective, their loyalty to Israeli democracy is no weaker than that of the Jews (see Chapter 15).

The mosaic-like nature of Israeli society is not an obstacle in itself, assuming that the various groups have a strong and explicit interest in preserving the joint framework and that they do not challenge the state's very existence, the law of the land, or the need for institutions. That said, all citizens and groups still have the legitimate right to actively seek changes in their country, to make it more democratic and amend its laws and institutions. According to these general criteria, Israel is clearly one state (with the exception of the occupied territories) that has a robust common denominator. This does not mean there is no intense competition among the sectors, to the point of willingness to exclude entire population groups, and thus undermine the common shared interests. The struggles have usually been over political dominance and resource allocation with the exception of extreme groups that aspired to impose their identity on the entire society. Indeed, as noted above, attempts to impose one version of a Jewish/Zionist identity have been made recently by the majority in the Knesset, posing a tangible threat to democracy.[32] Similarly, efforts to exclude Arabs from the Knesset, or the law enacted to restrain opposing civil society organizations, or the recurring attempts to tame the independent media, undermine the validity of an inclusive Israeliness.

Still, steering the political system toward common goals and the general public interest can stumble, but it is not an impossible endeavor. Fortunately, each of the groups challenges a *different* facet of the state: the ultra-Orthodox object to the secular (and Zionist) character; the Arabs oppose the exclusionary Jewishness; the Mizrahi Jews contest the Ashkenazi dominance; the new Russian immigrants condescend to the native ethos; and so on. From the perspective of the political system, although a homogeneous society is easier to steer (though perhaps a bit boring), multiple cultures and social separation are not necessarily an insurmountable obstacle for defining shared objectives and striving to reach them. Israel's achievements indicate that this was and still is possible. The requirements include a pluralistic democracy ready to recognize and tolerate moderate multiculturalism, and diverse groups prepared to give up some of their demands for the sake of solidarity. A state like this, regardless of its internal social and cultural differences, does not threaten the unique identities within it. And the unique identities do not threaten the state, which serves as a democratic steering mechanism acting for the shared common good.

[32] Two examples: Basic Law: The Knesset (Amendment 45 – Impeachment of an MK) (enacted July 20, 2016); and the Disclosure of Support from a Foreign Political Entity (Amendment) Law, 2016 (enacted July 11, 2016).

C. Political Discourse and Political Action

For someone peering into Israel from the outside, the political system is enviable in its energy, vitality, and the interest it evokes. For those living in Israel, they are more likely to feel helplessness, opposition, anger, and even revulsion. Israelis have high expectations from their state in general and from their leaders in particular, and have felt dissatisfied for a long time. "They're all corrupt," many say, especially after political leaders including a former president, prime minister, and finance minister were sent to prison on various charges of corruption. "This is not the state we longed for," many told the media on Israel's 67th Independence Day (2015). "The system does not function well," others say – even the IDF did not function well, stated the Winograd Committee report (2008) on the second Lebanon War.

How Does Politics Work in Israel?

In the early years of the state, the channels of political communication were the political parties, the public bureaucracy, and the mass media (most affiliated with the state and the parties), as well as a few independent newspapers that sometimes strayed beyond the consensus (Galnoor 1982, 246–49). The steering capacity of the political system was sustained by the strong identification of the Jewish citizens with the political system. However, one should not exaggerate the level of consensus that prevailed then; it is enough to recall the Lavon affair in the 1960s. Nevertheless, the assumption in those years was that the role of the state was to shape society. This placed politics in high standing, which allowed the political system to be centralized, dominant, and quite stable. The steering capacity of the political system demonstrated tangible results – the founding of the state, absorption of immigrants, overcoming the economic crisis, and the military victories from 1948 through 1967.

That early period was also turbulent, but the political system was able to overcome a long series of crises and shocks, internal and external (see list in Galnoor 1982, 266–67). As explained in Chapter 2, the unwritten "1949 constitution" served as an agreed upon framework for political action. And this action – despite all the well-known reservations about Mapai's rule – was democratic. In this context, mechanisms such as the government coalitions, or the "party key" for allocating resources, were stabilizing factors because they linked the separate interests in society (primarily of the strong groups) with the steering capacity. Here, again, it is important to emphasize the role of the parties, which filled the classic role of aggregating and representing interests despite the rifts in society. The political culture during that period was primarily party based, and the starting point for describing what has changed in Israeli politics since the 1970s is the transformed role of the parties and media channels (Galnoor 1998, 199).

The changed role of the parties also stemmed from the changes in society, of course, and brought with it changes in the steering capacity – erosion of the political system's ability to regulate conflicts and overcome crises. For example, when we compared the decision-making process for the withdrawal from the Sinai Peninsula in 1957 with the partial withdrawal from Lebanon in 1982, we pointed out how difficult it was for the political system in the later event to forge agreement about the policy (Galnoor 1996). Moreover, there are disagreements about the democratic rules of the game: During the debate over disengagement from the Gaza Strip (summer

2005), some MKs did not recognize the authority of the Knesset and the government to order a withdrawal from territories occupied in 1967 (N. Tzur 2006). In another example, after discovering large reserves of natural gas in the economic waters of Israel, a fierce public dispute arose over the agreements the government signed with private gas companies. When the High Court (in 2016) rejected one section of the agreement because it limited the legislative authority of the Knesset in the future (*Labor Party et al. v. Government of Israel*), Justice Minister Ayelet Shaked not only expressed her dissatisfaction, but attacked the court's judgment and challenged its very authority to exercise judicial review of the government's actions.[33]

In Chapter 11, we explained why steering capacity was severely constrained by the weakening of the institution of government coalition. Since 1984, most of the coalitions have been too large (unity governments) or too small, "minimal," meaning that the departure of a single party would topple it or result in a minority government. Thus, the coalitions themselves became a source of instability in the political system. One indication of this is the growing futility of political agreements (Israeli Association for Parliamentary Issues 1991). In the past, democracy in Israel was based on agreements, mainly secret and informal, between the national parties. The agreements were usually honored and thus contributed to stability and steering capacity. The Supreme Court was assigned primarily a corrective role and rarely had to exercise judicial review. When the unity government was dismantled in March 1990, the full ugliness of the change was exposed: Political agreements and understandings were no longer respected, and a danger arose of forming a government coalition in exchange for payments (M. Ben-Porat 2005, 6). Trust was at such a low level that one of the negotiators demanded a financial guarantee to ensure the validity of the coalition agreement. As a result, a vital component of democratic political culture eroded – the ability to make binding agreements. Instead, politics required the High Court to rule on the legality, transparency, and even the "contractual" validity of political agreements (*Levy v. Prime Minister Shamir* [1990]; *Shalit v. Prime Minister Peres* [1990]). Thus, there is no good answer to the above question: How does politics work in Israel today?

Policymaking, Decisions, and Steering Capacity

The foregoing description might give the impression that the political system in Israel does not function at all. This is not the case: Elections are held, power is turned over, coalitions are formed, the Knesset enacts laws, and the government makes decisions. The intriguing questions are, first, what is the new agora of politics in Israel – where understandings are forged and decisions shaped? And, second, are there important areas in which decisions are not made, or where decisions made have lacked validity and are not implemented?

As for the first question, the preeminence of politics in Israel's early years could not be sustained because socioeconomic development created new centers of power and the missions of the state changed. The new players – the business sector, civil

[33] "Once again the Supreme Court has turned itself into a venue for arbitrating on purely political and macroeconomic questions. We have reached an absurd situation in which the petitioners against the [natural gas] plan are NGOs and political entities that act via the justice system instead of the public arena. There is no justification for the High Court to intervene" (Gorali 2016).

society organizations, and the new media – not only took over some of the state's roles, but also sought to influence its policies. In security and foreign affairs, the government still holds exclusive sway. The second Lebanon War, for example, was launched by rapid decision of the government (in fact, by a narrow forum within the government) without involving external entities. However, the war and its outcomes were part of a trenchant public discourse in all the arenas listed above. While the government still has a monopoly on security issues, there is considerable openness on domestic affairs and the executive branch finds it difficult to make unilateral decisions and sometimes to carry them out. The government headed by Rabin, for example, decided to tax capital gains, and the Knesset passed legislation to this effect in December 1994. The decision was made, however, without consulting the business sector, labor federation, or the banks (which were charged with collecting the new tax), and elicited insurmountable opposition. The government was forced to back down and the law was revoked. Only after several committees was a new capital gains law passed in 2003, following nine years of consultations and public debate (Galnoor, Oser, and Gadot-Perez 2012, 23–41).

The public arena took on greater importance despite the consistent feeling of Israeli citizens that they are not efficacious and unable to influence the government. Contributing to this attitude is the politics-as-happening syndrome – an arena that is shallow in content, sensational, personal, raucous, and violent. If Israeli politics were to operate entirely in the media, it would become a soap opera, and sometimes it seems to have already reached that point. Equally troubling are the economic data showing that not all groups in society are present in this new agora (see Chapter 16). The new link between money and power has augmented the impact of wealthy people (local and foreign) on leaders, election campaigns, and politics in general.

As for the second question, the political system has become more open, and from this perspective even more democratic. However, the delicate balance between participation and steering capacity was disrupted (usually in favor of the strong groups), and one consequence is that decisions are taken but not implemented. We have cited Knesset laws that remained on the books only, and government decisions that were not executed – most famously, the decision to evacuate "illegal outposts" in the West Bank (Sasson 2005). On a higher level of weak steering capacity are the open issues discussed in Chapters 14–17. These have been on the agenda continuously for decades, and the governments of Israel have been unable to resolve them. Instead, governments have usually decided not to decide; and when a government decided to decide, it was unable to implement the decision.

The precis of the four main areas and the unresolved issues in each are:
Security and foreign affairs – the future borders of the state.
Arab citizens of Israel – ensuring full equality in all fields.
Socioeconomic policy – bridging the deep gaps in society.
Status of religion in the state – boundaries of religious legislation concerning personal and community rights.

And what about cases when an attempt was made to resolve an open issue? In September 1993, the Oslo agreement was signed and approved in the Knesset by a slight majority. Two years later, on November 4, 1995, Yitzhak Rabin was murdered for political-religious motives in an effort to undermine the agreement. Hillel Halkin, who noted that he opposed the Oslo Accords, wrote after the murder (1996):

> [Yigal Amir] was what is known in Hebrew as a *sh'liah avera*, a messenger of sin, for a large body of Israelis who would not have dreamed of doing what he did. This public, heavily represented in what is known as the "national-religious camp" and in the settlements of Judea and Samaria that are the most threatened by the Oslo pact, owes itself and the nation a reckoning for having allowed elements in its midst to be swept away by inflammatory rhetoric and bizarre rabbinical rulings that could have encouraged a Yigal Amir to think he was acting on its behalf.

Political murder is the end of the road because the intricate questions of decision-making in democracy become meaningless. A political assassin's sword drawn from its scabbard, even once, continues to threaten, symbolizing contempt for any kind of democratic political culture. Political violence did not start in Israel in 1995, but the murder of a prime minister because of his views intensified the violence in society and in politics too. This is the horrifying answer to the question posed above: What has changed in Israeli politics?

18.5 Is the Political Culture in Israel Democratic?

A. Paradoxes and Dilemmas

Diamond (1993) suggests four paradoxes of a democratic system, and these provide a general framework for summarizing the state of democracy in Israel, adding several dilemmas that are unique to Israel's situation.

First, democracy literally means "rule by the people," but it depends, especially at the outset, on the behavior of the political elite; democracy requires broad and intensive participation by the citizens, but is very dependent on the commitment to democracy of the leaders.

In Israel's early years, despite the internal divisions and lack of a party with a Knesset majority, the level of public trust in the leadership was high. Were the leaders committed to democracy? By and large the answer is affirmative, at least as far as adherence to the democratic rules of the game is concerned. From this narrow perspective, democracy in Israel met Schumpeter's minimum requirements (1944): The role of citizens is to elect their leaders and allow them to govern, until the next election. Over the years, however, breaches emerged in relations between the citizens and their leaders, and it is doubtful that the behavior of the political elite contributed to instilling democracy in Israel.

Second, democracy institutionalizes and regulates the struggle for power. But if the conflicts become too acute and the society too divided, there is a danger of dissolving the shared framework, which leads to political instability.

Democracy in Israel did institutionalize and regulate the internal power struggles, albeit at the expense of the weaker groups in society. The political system was stable and had proven steering capacity, particularly in the area of security. Later, the internal conflicts indeed intensified, and they threaten the very capacity for shared political action.

Third, democratic regimes have an inherent internal tension: representativeness versus governability – or, in our term, versus steering capacity. Representativeness means that the citizen can influence the government and sometimes even be involved in the policymaking; steering capacity requires the government to act not only according to the legitimate interests of individuals and groups, but also to mediate among interests and pursue the common good. That is, when the government turns the steering wheel, the entire ship must turn.

In the past, the balance in Israel clearly tilted toward the requirements of governability and, despite the high proportion of representation because of the electoral system, the citizens' influence on steering the ship of state was strictly demarcated and exerted indirectly via powerful party intermediaries. From this perspective, democracy in Israel later became more representative because of new and diverse options that became available to citizens – especially through civil society organizations and media channels – as well as more direct representativeness in the political parties. The prevailing assumption is that the scale tipped in favor of representativeness at the expense of governability, hence the attempts to strengthen the executive branch. However, as we argued in Chapter 8 on political participation, this assumption is rather misleading.

Fourth, democracy is based on the ongoing consent of the citizens to conditionally empower their representatives. This consent must be renewed from time to time, and its steadiness depends on public legitimacy – an unwritten pact that is conditional, in part, on the government's effectiveness. Citizens expect the government to cope with security, social issues, and economic problems and to enforce law and order. Consent and legitimacy depend on steering capacity, and sometimes this means that the representatives need to act decisively and quickly, and face the judgment of the public only after the fact. This tension makes it difficult for democratic governments to make unpopular decisions, or to act on the basis of long-term considerations.

In Israel, the crisis in the government's legitimacy looms as a tangible threat to democracy. In surveys cited in this book, Israeli citizens feel that the unwritten pact with them has been violated time and again, and that they cannot trust the leaders' motives or the effectiveness of the government, even on security matters. This is expressed in a growing mood of "anti-politics" – frustration and revulsion from the political system, and the loss of the previous Israeli passion to debate political issues. Apathy among the citizens is also a dangerous enemy of democracy. Above all, there is not a sufficiently robust majority expressing satisfaction with democracy in Israel.[34] Table 18.5 shows that defining the state as "Jewish and democratic" did not contribute to strengthening democracy in Israel.

In addition to the above four general paradoxes of democratic regimes, there are unique dilemmas in Israel discussed in the previous chapters.

- The centrality of security considerations had an emphatic effect on democracy. Many in Israel presume that the principles of democracy and the rigorous protection of human and civil rights, in particular, "hinder" the security mission and give an advantage to its non-democratic rivals.[35] In Chapter 14 we explained

[34] In 2003–10, the percentage of Israeli citizens expressing satisfaction with the functioning of democracy ranged from 49 to 66 percent, with an average of 55 percent (Arian et al. 2005–10: 2008, 42, 102; Arian, Philippov, and Knafelman 2009, 95).

[35] Yitzhak Rabin said on Channel 1 television in 1994 that the advantage of the Palestinian Authority was its ability to operate in the territories "without a High Court of Justice and without B'Tselem [a human rights organization]."

Table 18.5 *Israel is defined as both a Jewish state and a democratic state. Personally, which part of the definition is more important for you? (Jews, %)*

The Jewish part	37 (71% among religious Jews)
The democratic part	35 (53% among secular Jews)
Both are equally important	27 (64% among traditional Jews)
Neither are important/don't know	1
Total	100%

Source: Hermann et al. 2011–15: 2015, 68–69.

why this presumption is unfounded – democracies have proven time and again their ability to defeat non-democratic rivals. On the other hand, security considerations in Israel apparently do "hinder" the internalization of democracy, whenever it is a primary and often exclusive criterion for gauging the state's success. For some reason, democratic constraints are held responsible for military failures, inability to deal with terrorism, and a public sense of insecurity. Such presumptions have been fostered by political and military leaders.

- In Israel, the advantages of democracy are not yet perceived as axiomatic. In fact, the word "democracy" does not appear in Israel's Declaration of Independence or the Basic Laws until 1985. How can we explain this "oversight," which lasted for nearly forty years? In Chapter 1, we suggested that the omission actually indicated strength because a democratic regime was perceived as self-evident by the Zionist movement – an exception among the states established after World War II. Moreover, there were strong non-democratic, European influences on the Zionist movement and many autocratic leaders, as well as shrill anti-democratic tones and tendencies. Nonetheless, a robust democratic regime was instituted in the state of Israel in 1948.

  In 1985, the Basic Law: The Knesset was amended to state, "a list of candidates will not participate in the Knesset elections if its objectives or actions include … negation of the state's democratic character." The Basic Law: Human Dignity and Liberty, enacted in 1992, cites the "values of the state of Israel as a Jewish and democratic state."

  Labeling the state "Jewish and democratic" reveals insecurity regarding both. It adds nothing to the democratic character of the regime in Israel, just as defining the state as "Jewish" adds nothing to its "Jewishness." The label did manage, however, to alienate non-Jewish citizens from their state. Excluding Arab citizens from the legal definition of the state is one of the gravest problems of Israeli democracy, and the hyphenated "Jewish-democratic" formulation does not alleviate the problem, but further inflames it. Legally defining the state as "Jewish and democratic" unnecessarily contributes to confusion, a misleading contradiction between the two, a Jewish majority that prefers the first of the two, and polarization within Jewish society.
- In the 2010s, Israel finds itself ranked as one of the democracies with the highest level of inequality (see Chapter 16; also, D. Ben-David 2011, 102–4). The economic disparities widened over a relatively short period starting from the 1980s, the direct result of policy by successive governments. Under slogans of

abolishing the previous socialist system, responding to the dictates of globalization, developing a free market, and privatization, the disparities grew, eroding the solidarity that was part of the ethos of Israeli (Jewish) society. Indeed, there are indications that this process might also undermine the willingness to mobilize for security missions (Y. Levy 2003; Y. Levy 2007). In democracies, socioeconomic inequality breeds political inequality. Accordingly, the political participation of citizens with higher income, more years of education, and greater employment opportunities carries more weight and has a stronger impact on policy. Political participation in Israel points toward these trends, but the lack of data on the distribution of participation among different groups makes it impossible to draw unequivocal conclusions. We already said, however, that the division between rich and poor poses a relatively new, but very tangible, threat to democracy in Israel.

B. Democratic Political Development

The prevailing assumption is that the longer the democratic experience of a state, the greater the prospect of remaining democratic. Does this rule apply to Israel?

The start was promising, not only on the declarative level, but also in practice. In January 1949, before the end of the war, elections were held for the Constituent Assembly followed by elections for the Histadrut Labor Federation and, in 1950, for local governments. Thus, the principle of general elections was realized and suffrage was universal over the age of eighteen, despite calls to withhold this right from new immigrants (because they were still unfamiliar with Israel), from Arabs remaining in Israel (because they should be defined as enemies), from women (a demand by some ultra-Orthodox groups), and even from "shirkers" (those who did not mobilize for the war effort). The elections in Israel's early years did not comply with all the criteria of equal political franchise, but the leaders at the time did not succumb to the non-democratic temptation to exclude groups and laid a solid foundation for the future. Furthermore, unlike other national movements at a similar stage of state-building, the bitter rivalries of the Yishuv period were channeled into the parliamentary arena (see Chapter 1) – from violent confrontations to democratic voting – and this should not be taken for granted.

The political system enjoyed legitimacy and support, primarily due to the accomplishment of establishing the state and the military victories, despite the enormous challenge of absorbing the new immigrants, the austerity period of the 1950s, the economic recession of the 1960s, and the various political crises, including the fury of many at accepting reparations from Germany and the Lavon affair. Without exaggerating the attributes of the nascent state, one can say that it was a good start in terms of democratic development, and anticipation was high that the democratic rules of the game would indeed strike roots and be internalized: the rule of law and the lawfulness of the government; regular and fair elections; a choice among political parties representing diverse ideologies and interests; respect for majority rule; the separation of powers, including an independent judiciary; and, over time, rigorous safeguarding of human, civil, and minority rights; freedom of conscience, expression, assembly, and so on.

However, democracy is more than just the rules of the game. A citizen in a democracy should not only understand the game, but also identify with what these rules signify, i.e., their purpose. Merely following the democratic rules would be like assuming that the purpose of driving is to obey traffic laws, without asking about the destination. The democratic traffic laws have a distinct purpose, and one that is not easy to fulfill: to aspire toward political equality.

The political equality underlying the rules of the political game represents a general and basic human value that was stated with clarity in the American Declaration of Independence in 1776: "all men are created equal … endowed by their Creator with certain unalienable rights." This is the foundation stone from which the others arise: from "natural rights" to "human dignity and liberty." The political expressions of this value are equality before the law, equal votes, equal rights, and human and civil liberties. Hence the prohibition on preventing any person – through legislation or majority vote – from enjoying his or her equal rights: praying or not praying is their own business. Similarly, this is why opponents have the infuriating right to say whatever they wish, as long as they do not harm others, and why a wicked person such as Yigal Amir, who assassinated Prime Minister Rabin, has the right to vote in elections because other prisoners are so entitled. Moreover, if the cornerstone of democracy is the value that human beings are free and equal, then democracy itself – the aggregation of all the rights and freedoms – must necessarily respect other values. Beyond the value of equality, democracy strives to be neutral because its compelling *raison d'être* is to enable all the other (non-violent) values to coexist.

Therefore, democracy does not need hybrid supplemental titles such as "popular democracy," "class-based democracy," "post-colonial democracy," or, in Israel, "Zionist democracy," "Jewish democracy," "national-based democracy," or "secular democracy." Such supplements are actually designed to subtract or exclude someone – a person or group – from the community of free and equal citizens. As noted, we do not know if democratic political development begins with the belief in the value that all people are equal, or that this belief derives from observing the democratic rules. It could also progress simultaneously. Living with the democratic rules is surely a learning experience, which may at least boost the legitimacy of democracy among individuals and groups, and hopefully also recognition of its advantages.

In Israeli society, however, this process did not occur, and it is unclear whether Israel's citizens have greater faith in democracy after nearly seventy years of experience. Public opinion surveys raise doubts about this question. Some may, of course, question our assumption that the democratic rules of the game have been generally observed in Israel, given the deprivation of certain groups, the inequality of the Arab citizens, and the non-application of democracy in the occupied territories. For our purposes, it is enough to agree that at least the formal democratic rules have been maintained, and their implementation in Israel (not including the territories) is not inferior compared to the average democratic regime in the west. If so, what does the skepticism of Israeli citizens express? Why do many feel that they derive no benefit from democracy? According to surveys (Hermann et al. 2011–15: 2013, 103), the aggregate average figures for 2009–13 indicate a gradually decreasing majority for the following democratic values:

- 85 percent support democracy in general;
- 75 percent support freedom of expression;
- 70 percent support the right of all citizens to vote;
- 60 percent support equal rights for Arab citizens.

However, the following replies indicate that there is a small, or no, majority in support of specific democratic rights:

- 55 percent would limit some rights of Orthodox Jews or Arab citizens of Israel;
- 52 percent would avoid criticizing the state publicly;
- 50 percent would maintain freedom of the press;
- 14 percent would enable Arab citizens to participate in critical decisions regarding the future of the state.

Thus, in response to generalizations about democracy, there is a solid majority, but in response to specific questions that examine "the democratic soul" of Israeli citizens, support is shrinking; indeed, the majority disappears on freedom of the press and the rights of Arab citizens. This contradiction reflects a failure to internalize democratic values. The picture was even gloomier among young people, either because they are more truthful and less "politically correct," simply telling the pollsters openly what their elders learned to conceal, or because they are less democratic. Either way, these indicate that the democratic future may not be rosier than the present. And there is another concern: Without internalized democratic values, adherence to the rules of the game will continue to decline, including the rule of law and the rights of minorities, organizations, and individuals. Legislative acts and proposals submitted to the Knesset in recent years confirm the fear of non-democratic exploitation of majority rule.[36]

C. Roots of the Democracy Crisis in Israel

Is it possible to identify the reasons for the interrupted development of Israeli democracy? We suggest in this book that the political system in Israel functions, though Israeli citizens are not satisfied with how it functions. Despite the recent

[36] The following is a selection of the laws and bills (2009–15) that raise concerns about non-democratic exploitation of majority rule. ***General:*** a proposal by a Kadima MK to subordinate the democratic aspect of Israel's regime to its being the nation-state of the Jewish people, and to lower the status of the Arabic language; the "Boycott Law," which allows for the suit of anyone who calls for a boycott of Israel (or an area under its control), without requiring that damages be proven, and allows for sanctions on NGOs convicted of calling for a boycott. ***Curbing the High Court:*** bills submitted by Likud MKs that would change the composition of the Judicial Appointments Committee in order to strengthen the hand of the justice minister on this committee, and would have mandated a hearing before the Knesset's Constitution Committee for candidates for the Supreme Court and the president of Israel. ***Loyalty and citizenship:*** bills submitted by Yisrael Beitenu MKs that would require a loyalty oath to Israel as a "Jewish, Zionist, and democratic state, and to its symbols and values" as a condition for naturalized citizenship; stripping the citizenship of any person who acts against the Jewish people or Israel as the state of the Jewish people; mandating the playing of the national anthem at events in institutions of higher learning; allowing a special majority in the Knesset to impeach MKs (passed in 2016). ***Restricting civil society:*** a bill by Likud MKs to amend the Defamation Law to permit libel suits against anyone who speaks ill of Israel or its entities, including claims for civil damages – aimed primarily against organizations that publish information on rights violations by the IDF in the territories; a bill sponsored by a Yisrael Beitenu MK to tax organizations that receive donations from a foreign political entity; the Disclosure of Support from a Foreign Political Entity (Amendment) Law (enacted July 11, 2016). ***Discrimination against women:*** ever increasing exclusion of women from public space – in the IDF, bus seating rules, on billboards and in publications of institutions, in singing performances, and more. For an extensive discussion, see *Haaretz Magazine* 2011.

decline in adherence to the democratic rules of the game, these rules are still generally observed, and democratization has grown over the years as far as openness of the system is concerned as well as broader access and participation by citizens. Note also the substantial (85%) declared support for democracy among Israelis, which may contribute to bridging disagreements in society. Furthermore, citizens' dissatisfaction that breeds distrust for democracy is not unique to Israel. Globalization and the end of the Cold War stirred unmet expectations for world peace and economic prosperity, which the democratic countries failed to deliver, and disappointed those who saw that the agenda did not change. Moreover, the narrowing of disparities has not been regarded as an objective; indeed, worldwide inequality has escalated. Israel is part of this global agenda in which politics in democratic countries has been dethroned. But there are also internal reasons that expedited this process in Israel.

During the first two decades, democratic development in Israel combined steering capacity to overcome crises with the maintenance of political equality, growing openness, and a greater responsiveness to citizens' demands (Galnoor 1982, 368–79). This general assessment does not gloss over the inequality that existed at the outset or the severe flaws in the political system that surfaced in the Lavon affair. Similarly, Smooha (2000) regards Israel as a "non-civic democracy, of low quality, but stable" and calls this regime "a non-Western model of ethnic democracy."[37] He points out that Israel is a democracy with emphasis on the rules of the game ("the procedural minimum"), but he does not explain the decline in the legitimacy of democratic values.

In our view, the main threats to Israeli democracy derive from the rather consistent inability to resolve the four main challenges, or "open issues": security and the continuous occupation since 1967; the status of Arab citizens in Israel; the growing socioeconomic gaps; and the unresolved issue of state and religion. The fact that these have remained on the agenda so long has contributed to weakening the political system and to doubts about the advantages of democratic regimes. Citizens are entitled to assume that democratic leaders are elected to provide solutions, not just to contain or manage difficult problems. Leaving them "open" tends to diminish the moral infrastructure of democratic systems. Perhaps the expectations of citizens are exaggerated, but, in practice, a political system that does not "solve" the most pressing problems will be regarded as disconnected and incapable of fulfilling its mission. Moreover, the common denominator that the ethnic democracy offers to the Jews in Israel, which according to Smooha unifies the divided parts of Jewish society, is inadequate.

Topping the list of unresolved problems is the security issue, which in our opinion constitutes the primary factor underlying the weakness of democracy in Israel. As noted in Chapter 14, security in Israel has not improved since 1967, and all wars and military operations since then have been internally disputed. Even the excuse that "our foes are not democratic" rings hollow. Moreover, vagueness surrounding the "decision not to decide" about the future of the occupied territories undermines trust in the efficacy of democracy. There is, of course, also a moral issue: democracy requires popular belief in the justifiability of state actions. This is how democracies win wars.

37 Ethnic democracy: "a democratic regime in which civil rights are granted to all permanent residents interested in receiving citizenship, while giving preferred status to the majority group" (Smooha 2000, 579).

The gradual development of democracy in Israel was interrupted during the pre-war "waiting period" in May 1967, and more directly because of the combined outcome of the Six Day War, the War of Attrition in 1969–70, and particularly the Yom Kippur War. These events taken together generated a sense of distrust vis-à-vis the leadership and doubts about the ability of the democratic political system to successfully meet the most critical test of all – defending the existence of the state and the security of its citizens. The victory in 1967 led to soaring expectations, and frustration soon followed. Some fifty years later, not only is the security issue constantly on the agenda, but rivals seem to come and go while hopes for a solution dwindle. For the citizens of Israel, the most important problem for the government to tackle, far above all others, is security. Security remains the paramount consideration when Israelis vote, though internal issues have risen in importance over the years. If the Israeli public appraises democracy according to its achievements in maintaining security, and if the appraisal is that since 1967 security has not improved and even declined, it is no wonder that the internalization of democratic values is interrupted. In our view, this is the dominant factor, though dissatisfaction about the handling of social, religious, and economic problems is also profound.

The crisis in Israeli democracy was stoked by additional factors – institutional (the decline of political parties and the fragile coalitions); the behavior of leaders (flawed policymaking and corruption); and anti-political sentiment. Jointly they contribute to instability and the feeling that democracy is not functioning well. The crisis is surprising from another perspective because the latter part of the twentieth century was a time of victory for democracy. The values and rules of democracy proved themselves to be not "the worst form of government, except for all the others," as the saying goes, but effective and preferable to non-democratic systems. Democracy proved its effectiveness in the toughest external tests of war against non-democratic regimes and outlasted most of them. Subsequently, despite the enormous challenge that terrorism poses and the increasing internal threats from non-democratic parties and groups, democratic regimes have so far been able to contend with emergencies, to restrain the temporary restrictions imposed on human rights, and to revoke these restrictions to restore normal life. The citizens of Israel may keep this lesson in mind, rather than envying the supposed "effectiveness" of non-democratic rivals.

18.6 Threats to Democracy in Israel

Democracy requires constant attention and pulse monitoring by alert and politically attentive citizens. Monitoring is needed to remove and replace rapacious leaders and non-democratic groups – those who condition freedom of expression on loyalty or patriotism, for example. No less dangerous are proponents of "temporary" measures, ready to suspend democracy until the crisis passes. Democracy once suspended is very difficult to restore because its "working tools" – such as free elections to change the leadership – are incapacitated. Democracy functions on delicate balances, and thus could be vulnerable. Halting is easier than restarting. The essence of democracy is not fragile, however, so long as the citizens trust it and accept with understanding the complexity of the decision-making process, designed in part to enable them to participate and exert influence. Therefore, every citizen holds the magic potion for the continuation of democracy. The appreciation of the citizens is the reason why an extended democratic political culture indeed strengthens democracy. States that have accrued a century or more of continuous democracy may worry about erosion, but not annulment. (This assessment is based on the experience of western democracies and is not a prediction.)

Compared to new democracies, Israeli democracy is not in its infancy; democratic institutions existed in the Yishuv period in Palestine. Nonetheless, despite this accumulated experience, democracy in Israel is at risk, though not from a military coup or apocalyptic, demographic calculations that predict a takeover by a non-democratic majority (ultra-Orthodox Jews, Arabs, or a combination of both). The threat is that ongoing instability in the political system will gradually unravel the delicate balance of democratic values, rules of the game, and citizens, trust. A democracy is at risk of collapse when many citizens and social groups (the number is difficult to assess) lose faith in its values, its superiority (compared to other systems of governance), and the benefit they derive from it.[38] Democracy is liable to collapse when leaders exploit it to enact laws and make decisions that are essentially non-democratic (see footnote 36 above). This is the threat that exists in Israel.

A. The Sense of Danger and the Primacy of Security Considerations

Most Israeli Jews feel that the state's very existence is threatened (usually coupled with the belief that "the whole world is against us"). Such beliefs are subjective, but can lead to a longing for a different type of regime – or to so-called "strong leadership."

In a workshop conducted in Jerusalem high schools in the mid-1980s, the pupils, parents, and teachers were presented with a frightening scenario about Israel:[39]

> **Scenario:** The agreement between the state of Israel and the state of Palestine collapsed and the situation has reverted to the dark days of violent confrontation, with hundreds killed on each side. The IDF demands that the government approve a call-up of reserve soldiers for extended periods. The economic situation in Israel has severely deteriorated because of inflation, the flight of capital, the European Union boycott, and collapse of the artificial-heart, high-tech industry that had flourished in recent years. Riots erupt because of unemployment, a housing shortage, the deterioration of social services, and air pollution. The riots are reaching the stage of widespread civil disobedience.
>
> The Syrian government is exploiting the situation to activate Hezbollah forces, which are shelling northern communities and inflicting heavy losses. The Syrian and Egyptian armies are conducting wide-scale maneuvers along the Israeli borders. Jordan and Iraq are also threatening. The new US president announces that his country will not intervene in the Middle East conflict, and will halt economic and military support for Israel.

[38] Sixty percent of Israel's citizens agreed that "a few strong leaders can be better for the state than all the discussions and laws." Agreement with this statement was higher among immigrants from the former Soviet Union (78%) and lower among Arab citizens (34%) (Arian et al. 2005–10: 2010, 67).

[39] The data are from the original exercise conducted by Itzhak Galnoor in a Jerusalem high school. The wording of the scenario was not retained, but this is an updated version used in the 2000s for a graduate workshop in citizenship education and democracy at the Hebrew University of Jerusalem.

Government Response: Following a series of marathon discussions and based on the opinion of the attorney general, the government of Israel declares a state of emergency and the following temporary measures:

- Dissolve the Knesset; suspend the Basic Laws and the High Court's authority.
- Delegate all legislative, executive, and judicial powers to the "Senior Steering Team" composed of the prime minister, the defense minister, and the finance minister.
- Prohibit all party activity, strikes, demonstrations, and public assemblies during the state of emergency; monitor all the media channels and strictly enforce the restrictions on them.
- Declare the state of emergency to be limited to one year, after which the Senior Steering Team will decide whether to extend it.

Questionnaire: Participants were asked to assume that they are aware of the emergency situation and threats against Israel. Given this scenario, two questions were posed:

1. As citizens, would you accept the government's decisions – with full consent; with partial consent; with indifference; with acquiescence for lack of an alternative; or with fierce opposition?
2. As citizens, how would you act?
   ✓ Volunteer for activities aimed at strengthening the work of the Senior Steering Team during the emergency period.
   ✓ Support the Senior Steering Team so that it can fulfill the difficult mission it faces.
   ✓ Wait for the end of the year and try to continue with my regular life routine.
   ✓ Oppose with all legal means that are still available (petitions, private communication, etc.).
   ✓ Actively oppose in every possible way, including illegal non-violent activities (such as joining an underground organization).

Responses to Question 1: A minority (about 20%) opted for the first and second possibilities, i.e., full or partial consent. A low number of respondents (about 5%) said they would be "indifferent"; and a large majority (about 75%) opted for the fourth and fifth possibilities – that they would acquiesce to the emergency decision for lack of an alternative or would oppose it. This breakdown was expected – in structured exercises about general *attitudes* toward democracy, respondents tend to opt for the "right" answer. The only significant difference was between the pupils and the parent/teacher respondents – the percentage of pupils at the two extremes was much higher: The younger pupils were more inclined to either conform or oppose. By and large, respondents were opposed to a unilateral revocation of democracy by the government.

Responses to Question 2: This question asked the respondents to shift from a general stance to practical action, and presented them with a difficult dilemma. Few said that they would act to strengthen or support the Senior Steering Team (about 20%), while the great majority of pupils, parents, and teachers converged in the middle – they would continue with their life routines or resist through legal means that remained available (about 70%). A minority of all respondents (about 10%), including the pupils, chose the extreme option of active struggle, including illegal activity, to defend suspended democracy.

The limitations of this workshop are evident – they are context and events dependent, and we don't know what the result would have been had the events really taken place. Nonetheless, we suggest that the responses reflect a general acceptance among many Jewish citizens in Israel of the need to suspend democracy in an emergency. They are personally prepared to sacrifice a great deal for security, and in difficult moments they are also collectively willing to surrender democracy itself.[40] For example, a Jewish majority (59%) agreed with the following statement: "To protect security, the state is permitted to monitor what its citizens write on the Internet" (Hermann et al. 2011–15: 2015, 78). The historical experience of democratic regimes successfully coping with emergencies through democratic procedures, and the lessons from other countries that "temporarily" suspended democracy and failed to restore it, have not been internalized and are far from self-evident in Israel.

As for the workshop above, the scenario was rather clear that the government acted illegally (despite the attorney general's opinion, deliberately inserted) when it stopped playing according to the democratic rules. In the concluding session of the workshop, we presented our view that the only way to prevent the revocation of democracy is a clear, a priori message sent by the citizens to the elected officials, that if the officials violate the rules, these rules cease to be binding upon the public too, who will no longer be required to obey them. When the unwritten agreement behind the delegation of authority from the citizens to the government is unilaterally broken, citizens are entitled to actively resist in every possible way (non-violently, we would stipulate). This is the most effective deterrent in a democracy to prevent revocation of the rule of law.

The dominance of security "hinders" democracy in Israel in other areas. A democratic political system that is incapable of deciding on the most critical problem for fifty years – the future of territories captured in 1967 – loses trust and raises doubts about the effectiveness of democracy. In this case, ambiguity has not opened up new alternatives; on the contrary, it has invited pressure from strong groups, i.e., the settlers and their supporters, who have relentlessly pursued a clear and definitive agenda. One may argue that the lack of political decision over the territories stems from divided public opinion, namely the lack of a clear majority in one direction or another. However, a representative democratic regime is not just a mirror positioned to reflect. The role of democratic leaders is also to speak truth to the public on whether it is possible to continue the occupation forever. Leadership means formulating alternatives, explaining them to the public, and obtaining authorization to decide among them.[41] A political system that refrains from doing so for such an extended period ultimately damages its own legitimacy.

[40] On the socialization of the conflict and its security aspects, see Rachamim and Bar-Tal 2006.

[41] Examples of difficult territorial decisions made and implemented by the Israeli government: return of the Sinai Peninsula to Egypt (Prime Minister Begin); peace treaty with Jordan (Prime Minister Rabin); withdrawal from south Lebanon (Prime Minister Barak); withdrawal from the Gaza Strip (Prime Minister Sharon).

B. The Threat to Solidarity

Is it possible to have a strong economy and a weak society? Theoretically, it is possible, and there are many democracies with deep socioeconomic gaps. Can democracy survive, or at least remain stable over time, with deep rifts in society? In principle, if the regime is based on the assumption that "all people are born equal," it is obligated to pursue this value to prevent a situation in which people are born equal, but die less equal. Backing away from some level of solidarity among members of a democratic community undermines the rationale of the rules of the game and ultimately weakens trust in democracy. Moreover, political equality is difficult to maintain without social equality, even though there are examples of democracies that survive despite the inequality in their midst.

In Israel, given the external threats, the secret of Israeli existence is solidarity, not just security. The relatively new development since the 1990s of growing disparities, and the ensuing internal rifts in society, pose a threat to democracy. The OECD data presented in Chapter 16 show that Israel was second only to the United States in 2008 on a ranking of inequality among thirty western countries, and that by 2013 the situation had worsened, as measured by the Gini index of inequality in disposable income. Because the state demands a supreme effort from its citizens in light of the security challenges, citizens have high expectations of the state, often expressed as: "What does the state do for me?" Even if these expectations are exaggerated, a fair democratic system does not humiliate or ignore the weaker groups, or those who depend on it – Arabs, ultra-Orthodox Jews, women, new immigrants, the elderly, or foreign workers. This is why the tax mechanism is used in all democracies, in varying degrees, to advance equality through progressive taxation; most democracies have instituted affirmative action for particular groups, while others have laws and policies that ensure social rights in education, housing, employment, and health.

Another practical argument for striving for more equality in Israel is that groups that feel unfairly treated by the political system (especially Arab citizens) are liable to opt out of it. In that case, democracy would become more limited and threatened from within by an alienated public or group that does not obey the law, pay taxes, or participate in elections. When many citizens, or important groups, lose faith in the value or supremacy of democracy and the benefits it offers, democracy becomes partial or non-existent. The 2011 social protest was a non-violent effort, primarily of young people, to democratically change how the state functions and institute a policy based on social solidarity. It highlighted the link between the growing gaps and the weakening of democracy. The lack of a continuous positive response by the government to such mass political participation further lowered public trust in democracy.

C. The Remedy: A Democratic Political Culture

The vacuum that developed in the Israeli political system accorded the Supreme Court a critical role in defending democracy, particularly in safeguarding human rights corresponding to the new Basic Laws of 1992. To this category we can add the determined and consistent battle of law enforcement authorities against political and administrative corruption. At the same time, efforts were made to strengthen the executive branch by forming broad coalitions ("unity governments") and the defunct experiment of direct election of the prime minister in 1996–2003 (see Chapter 5). In addition, attempts were made to "strengthen governance" via a written constitution, as well as legislation designed to regulate political party activity and campaign finances. All these are important, but the danger for democracy in Israel lies in the combination of ongoing instability in the political system and the lack of confidence by the citizens in its ability to cope with the external and internal challenges. Attacks against the Supreme Court, human rights organizations, free media, the universities, the school curriculum, cultural organization, the "intellectuals," etc. reflect the weakness of democracy in Israel.

The remedy can be found, as always, in educating for citizenship. The experience in democratic countries indicates that the higher the educational stock per capita in a particular society, the higher the prospects for equality, including political equality. More years of education translates into a stronger sense of efficacy, more skills for active participation, higher capacity to link specific needs and government policy, and a greater likelihood of belonging to networks of political activity (Verba 2003, 668–69). Of course, the distribution of the educational stock must include all groups in society. In democratic states, the declared aspiration is equal education; in many countries, however, including Israel, this is not the case. The first step, therefore, is to define education – from kindergarten to higher education – as the prime public investment, i.e., a public good for which the state is responsible and which should not be left in the hands of market forces or private organizations (Galnoor et al. 2015). The second step is conscious investment in democracy development. The question was raised long ago by Jean-Jacques Rousseau: Is it possible to educate for democratic citizenship? A report published in 1995 on citizenship education in Israel presented this goal:

> To enable the individual to fulfill himself, accompanied by a connection and commitment to the society in which he lives. The strength and quality of the democratic regime are commensurate with the citizens' commitment to the democratic idea and to their ability and readiness to be active and responsible citizens. (Kremnitzer Committee 1995)

The Kremnitzer Committee report recommended a process spanning all the years of schooling, as part of all fields of study, while developing a civic climate in the school. A task force was appointed at the Ministry of Education to implement the recommendations, and citizenship studies were somewhat expanded. Since then, however, these recommendations have long been shelved, and ministry policy is not aimed at strengthening democratic citizenship (see footnote 29 above). In 1998, an advisory group to the education secretary in England, headed by Bernard Crick, published its conclusions. The objectives were similar, and even more ambitious:

> We aim at no less than a change in the political culture of this country, both nationally and locally; for people to think of themselves as active citizens, willing, able, and equipped to have an influence in public life and with the critical capacities to weigh evidence before speaking and acting; to build on and to extend radically to young people the best in existing traditions of community involvement and public service, and to make them individually confident in finding new forms of involvement and action among themselves.[42]

[42] Advisory Group on Citizenship 1998. *Education for 2015 and for Teaching of Democracy in Schools*, Qualifications and Curriculum Authority (quoted in Crick 2002, 114).

The report was adopted as a mandatory program in all the high schools in England, consciously aiming at changing the formalistic citizenship studies and turning them into an instrument for acquiring political skills, exposure to cultural differences, discussions on controversial issues, acquiring skills for community advocacy, and active participation in school and community affairs.

Hence, the remedy: Economists place their trust in the free market, jurists look to the law and judicial rulings, and political scientists focus on political culture. A political culture that reinforces democratic values is the crucial foundation for the proper functioning of democracy, a system of governance that, as noted, prefers wordy political discourse and cumbersome decision-making in order to facilitate citizen participation. The current situation in Israel calls for a richer menu than perfect market competition, or legislation and court rulings designed to punish leaders and institutions that stray, or a political process. To instill the values of democracy, restore trust in the political institutions, and inculcate the democratic rules of the game, enormous efforts must be devoted to political education for democratic citizenship. This is the one and only sphere of effective action.

Unstable democracy has a breaking point, with anarchy lurking behind it. We need to return to the schools – to educating for democracy and good citizenship.

Bibliography

OFFICIAL ISRAELI DOCUMENTS

"Agranat Commission." 1962. *Report of the Commission of Jurists on the Power of the Attorney General* [in Hebrew].

1975. *Report of the Commission of Inquiry on the Yom Kippur War*. Tel-Aviv: Am Oved [in Hebrew].

"Brodet Committee." 2007. *Report of the Committee for Examining the Defense Budget*, May [in Hebrew].

Civil Service Commission. 2009. *Report on Appropriate Representation of the Arab Population, Including Druze and Circassians, in the Civil Service – 2008*. Jerusalem [in Hebrew].

Committee to Study Juvenile Delinquency. 1956. *Report submitted to the Minister of Justice* [in Hebrew].

Constitution Committee ("Warhaftig Committee"). 1949. The Provisional State Council. *On the Problems of a Constitution for Israel*. Booklet 1–5. Jerusalem: Government Printer.

Council for Higher Education. 2015. Planning and Budgeting Committee. *System of Higher Education in Israel 2014*, May. Jerusalem [in Hebrew].

"Dinur Committee." 2003. *Report of the Committee for Reform of Public Broadcasting*. Ministry of Commerce and Industry [in Hebrew].

"Dovrat Committee." 2005. *Report of the National Task Force to Advance Education in Israel: The National Plan for Education*. Ministry of Education [in Hebrew].

"Frumkin Commission of Inquiry." 1950. *Report of the Commission of Inquiry Concerning Education in the Immigrant Camps* [in Hebrew].

"Galnoor Committee." 2000. *Report of the Public Committee to Examine the Working Conditions of Knesset Members* [in Hebrew].

2003. *Report of the Committee to Examine the Roles of the Third Sector in Israel, and Policy Regarding It*, June. Beersheva: Israeli Center for Third Sector Research [in Hebrew].

Income Tax Authority. 1995. *Regulations for Tax Year 1995, updated to 15 March 1995*. Jerusalem: Ronen Missim Publications and Income Tax Commission [in Hebrew].

Israel Defense Forces. 1994. *The Spirit of the IDF: Values and Fundamental Principles* [in Hebrew].

Israeli Judiciary. 2007. *Report of the Committee to Examine Labor Tribunals* [in Hebrew].

2013. *Courts Administration in Israel, Semi-annual Report, First Half of 2013*. http://elyon1.court.gov.il/heb/haba/dochot/doc/fitst2013.pdf [in Hebrew] (accessed February 18, 2016).

2014. Ombudsman's Office. *Annual Report 2013*, March [in Hebrew].

"Kahan Commission." 1983. *Report of the Commission of Inquiry into the Events at the Refugee Camps in Beirut*. www.mfa.gov.il/mfa/foreignpolicy/mfadocuments/yearbook6/pages/104%20report%20of%20the%20commission%20of%20inquiry%20into%20the%20e.aspx (accessed May 5, 2016).

Karp, Yehudit. 1984. *Report on the Investigation of Suspicions against Israelis in Judea and Samaria*. Jerusalem: Ministry of Justice [in Hebrew].

"Katz Committee." 1971. *Report of the Prime Minister's Committee on Children and Youth in Distress* [in Hebrew].

Knesset Constitution, Law and Justice Committee. 2006. *A Constitution in Broad Consensus*. Report on the Proposed Constitution for Israel, February. http://main.knesset.gov.il/Activity/committees/Huka/Pages/default.aspx (accessed October 18, 2017).

Knesset Records.

Knesset. Foreign Affairs and Defense Committee. 2004. *Report of the Committee for Investigating the Intelligence Services following the Iraq War*, March [in Hebrew].

"Kremnitzer Committee." 1995. *Report of the Committee on Civic Education,* "On Being Citizens: Educating all Israeli Pupils for Citizenship" [in Hebrew].

"Landau Committee." 1980. *Report of the Committee to Examine the Structure and Authority of Courts*, November [in Hebrew].

"Landes Committee." 2014. *Report of the Committee to Study the Plans for Future Public Broadcasting in Israel*, March [in Hebrew].

"Levine Committee." 2000. *Report of the Public Committee to Examine the Financing of Political Activity*.

"Locker Committee." 2015. *Report of the Committee for Examining the Defense Budget*. June 26. www.pmo.gov.il/Documents/duach%20(2).pdf [in Hebrew].

Ministry of Construction and Housing. 2000. *Multi-year Plan for Development of Settlements in the Arab Sector*, October 22. www.moch.gov.il/Gov_Decisions/Pages/GovDecision.aspx?ListID=f33e0a4b-aa35-4b12-912e-d271a6476a11&WebId=fe384cf7-21cd-49eb-8bbb-71ed64f47de0&ItemID=155 [in Hebrew] (accessed June 7, 2016).

Ministry of Economy and Industry. 2016. *Master Plan for Ultra-Orthodox Employment in Israel*, March. http://economy.gov.il/Employment/UniquePopulation/Orthodox/Pages/ProfessionalTraining.aspx [in Hebrew] (accessed August 14, 2016).

Ministry of Education. 2003. "The Core Curriculum." Pedagogical Secretariat, March [in Hebrew].

2003a. "The Core Curriculum for Elementary School Education in Israel." Pedagogical Secretariat, April [in Hebrew].

Ministry of Finance. 2014. *Proposed State Budget for Fiscal Year 2015*. November, Jerusalem. http://mof.gov.il/BudgetSite/statebudget/BUDGET2015/Documents/MainBudgetFull_2015.pdf [in Hebrew] (accessed May 3, 2016).

Ministry of Foreign Affairs. N.d. *The 2014 Gaza Conflict: Factual and Legal Aspects*. http://mfa.gov.il/ProtectiveEdge/Pages/default.aspx (accessed May 5, 2016).

Ministry of Justice. Various years. *Report Submitted in Compliance with the Freedom of Information Law 1998*.

2006. *Report of the Committee to Examine Ways to Increase the Use of Mediation in the Courts*, July [in Hebrew].

Ministry of the Economy. 2013. *Employment of Arab College Graduates in Israel – A Survey*, Report 2.

Ministry of the Interior. 2016. Population and Immigration Authority. *Data on Foreigners in Israel*, April. www.piba.gov.il [in Hebrew] (accessed June 15, 2016).

National Insurance Institute. Various years. *Annual Report: Poverty and Social Disparities* [in Hebrew].

"Ne'eman Committee." 1998. *Report and Recommendations of the Committee to Formulate Ideas and Proposals Regarding Conversion in Israel*. www.knesset.gov.il/docs/heb/neeman.htm [in Hebrew] (accessed June 24, 2016).

Office of the Prime Minister. 2008. *Civil Society and the Business Community: Partnership, Empowerment, and Transparency*. Division of Policy Planning, February [in Hebrew].

2015. *Government Plan for Economic Development in the Arab Sector 2016– 2020*, Decision 922 from December 30, 2015. http://injaz.org.il/Public/files/תוכנית%20ממשלתית%20לפיתוח%20כלכלי%20בחברה%20ערבית-מצגת%20של%20אינגאז(1).pdf [in Hebrew] (accessed June 7, 2016).

Official Gazette. See *State Records*.

Ombudsman's Office. Various years. *Annual Report*.

"Or Commission Final Report." 2003. *Report of the State Commission of Inquiry into the Events of October 2000*, September [in Hebrew].

"Or Committee." 1997. *Report of the Committee to Examine the Structure of the Regular Courts in Israel* [in Hebrew].

"Ostrovsky-Cohen Committee." 1995. *Report of the Public Committee on Freedom of Information*, July [in Hebrew].

"Plesner Committee." 2012. *Report of the Committee for Equality in Sharing the Burden*. Jerusalem.

President's Commission to Examine the Structure of Governance in Israel. 2007. "Parties in an Era of Electronic Media." Jerusalem: Center for Civil Empowerment, no. 2 [in Hebrew].

"Rosen-Zvi Committee." 1995. *Report of the Committee to Examine Wages, Pension, and Benefits of Members of the Knesset*, February [in Hebrew].

"Rubinstein Committee." 2004. *Report of the Public Committee to Examine Parliamentary Supervision over the Defense Establishment and How to Improve It*," December. www.knesset.gov.il/committees/heb/docs/defense16-1.pdf [in Hebrew] (accessed April 12, 2016).

"Sanbar Committee." 1981. *Report of the Committee regarding Local Government in Israel* [in Hebrew].

Sasson, Talia. 2005. *Interim Report on Unauthorized Outposts*. Prepared for the Office of the Prime Minister, March. English summary: www.mfa.gov.il/NR/rdonlyres/5AD2CBB2-851D-4917-89B2-CFF60C83C16C/0/SummaryoftheOpinionConcerningUnauthorizedOutposts.doc (accessed August 3, 2010).

"Shahar Committee." 1998. *Report of the Committee to Merge Local Authorities* [in Hebrew].

"Shamgar Committee." 1998. *Report of the Public Committee to Examine the Method of Appointment of the Attorney General and Subjects Related to his Position*. Ministry of Justice.

"Sheshinski Committee." 2011–15. Reports 1 and 2 of the Committee to Examine the Fiscal Policy on Oil and Gas Resources in Israel [in Hebrew].

"Spivak-Yonah Committee." 2011. *Recommendations of the Committee on Housing, Transportation, Land, and Spatial Policy Planning for Social Justice*.

State Comptroller. Various years. *Annual Report*.

1992 and 2000. *Report on Audit of the Local Authority*.

2005. *The Decision-making Process Prior to the Return of Elhanan Tennenbaum from Lebanon. Statement of State Comptroller Eliezer Goldberg* (July 3) [in Hebrew].

2006. *Annual Report 57B: The Disengagement Plan* [in Hebrew].

2014. *Audited Report of Financing of Candidate Parties and Lists during the Period of Election of the 19th Knesset*. www.mevaker.gov.il/he/Reports/Report_237/febdc193-047e-4078-9dd1-a8901bc4b832/2014-Bchirot-Din.pdf [in Hebrew] (accessed April 13, 2016).

State Records [previously termed *Official Gazette*], containing the legal codex, bills tabled, amendments, and government publications. Jerusalem: Government Printer.

"Tal Committee." 2002. *Report of the Committee to Propose an Arrangement on the Matter of Conscripting Yeshiva Students*. www.knesset.gov.il/docs/heb/tal.htm [in Hebrew] (accessed June 25, 2016).

The People's Council: The Provisional State Council. 1948. Fifth Session, vol. 1, June 22–23. Jerusalem: Government Printer [in Hebrew].

"Trajtenberg Committee." 2011. *Report of the Committee for Socioeconomic Change*. www.teammanuel2011.org.il/general/fullreport [in Hebrew] (accessed October 24, 2017).

"Turkel Commission." 2011. *Report of the Public Commission to Examine the Maritime Incident of 31 May 2010*. www.turkel-committee.gov.il/index-eng.html (accessed May 5, 2016).

"Winograd Commission." 2007. *Interim Report of the Commission to Examine the Military Campaign in Lebanon in 2006*, April [in Hebrew].

2008. *Final Report of the Commission to Examine the Military Campaign in Lebanon 2006*, April [in Hebrew]. Official English summary: http://online.wsj.com/public/resources/documents/winogradreport-04302007.pdf (accessed April 12, 2016).
"Witkon Committee." 1972. *Report of the Committee to Investigate the Matter of Netivei Neft* [in Hebrew].
"Zameret Committee." 1996. *Report of the Public Committee to Formulate Recommendations regarding Traffic on Shabbat on Bar-Ilan Street, in Jerusalem, and outside Jerusalem* [in Hebrew].
"Zamir Committee." 1995. *Report of the Committee on Municipal Courts: Conclusions and Recommendations*, September [in Hebrew].
2001. *Report of the Committee on the Procedure for Appointment of Judges*, April [in Hebrew].
"Zeiler Commission of Inquiry." 2007. *Report of the Commission of Inquiry into Law Enforcement in the Case of Parinyan and the Policeman Tzahi Ben Or*, February [in Hebrew].

COURT CASES

(Listed chronologically by date of filing within each category[1])

HCJ 7/48 *Karbutli v. Minister of Defense*, PD 2, 5 [1949].
HCJ 10/48 *Ziv v. Gubernick*, PD 1, 85, 89 [1948].
HCJ 1/49 *Bejerano v. Minister of Police.*
HCJ 59/49 *Diamant v. Minister of Finance*, PD 4, 164.
HCJ 95/49 *al-Khuri v. Chief of Staff.*
HCJ 144/50 *Sheib v. Minister of Defense* [1951].
HCJ 64/51 *Daoud et al. v. Minister of Defense et al.*, PD 1117, 5.
HCJ 65/51 *Jabotinsky v. Weizmann*, PD 5, 801.
HCJ 25/53 *Kol Ha'am v. Minister of the Interior*, PD 165, 7 (1) [1953].
HCJ 73/53 *Kol Ha'am v. Minister of the Interior*, PD 7, 871 [1953].
HCJ 115/53 *Kaufman v. Minister of the Interior et al.*, PD 7, 534.
HCJ 105/54 *Lazerowitz v. Food Products Comptroller*, PD 10, 40 [1956].
HCJ 122/54 *Axel v. Mayor of Netanya et al.*, PD 8, 524.1 [1954].
HCJ 72/55 *Freidi, Mendelson, et al. v. Tel Aviv Municipality et al.*, PD 10, 734 [1955].
HCJ – Further Hearing 13/60 *Attorney General v. Matana*, PD 16, 430.
HCJ 311/60 *Miller et al. v. Minister of Transportation*, PD 15, 1989, 1996.
HCJ 72/62 *Rufeisen v. Minister of the Interior*, PD 16 (4), 2428.
HCJ 143/62 *Schlesinger v. Minister of the Interior*, PD 17 (1), 225 [1963].
HCJ 243/62 *Israel Film Studios v. Geri*, PD 16, 2407 [1962].
HCJ 262/62 *Peretz et al. v. Kfar Shmaryahu Local Council*, PD 16, 2101 [1962].
HCJ 195/64 *Southern Company Ltd. and Marbek Slaughter House v. Chief Rabbinate Council and Tel Aviv-Jaffa Religious Council*, PD 18 (2), 324, 334–35 [1964].
HCJ 253/64 *G'eris v. Haifa District Supervisor*, PD 673, 18 (4) [1964].
HCJ 58/68 *Shalit v. Minister of the Interior*, PD 477, 23 (2), 477.
HCJ 222/68 *National Groups v. Minister of the Police*, PD 24 (2), 141.
HCJ 98/69 *Bergman v. Minister of Finance*, PD 693, 23 (1).
HCJ 281/69 *Adi Kaplan v. Prime Minister and Broadcasting Authority*, PD 23 (2), 394.
HCJ 283/69 *Ravidi and Maches v. Hebron District Military Court, IDF, et al.*, PD 419, 24 (2).
HCJ 40/70 *Becker v. Minister of Defense*, PD 24 (1), 238 [1970].
HCJ 456/71 *Sarah Barzani v. Minister of Defense et al.*, PD 26 (2), 543 [1972].
HCJ 302/72 *abu Hilu et al. v. Government of Israel*, PD 169, 27 (2).
HCJ 394/72 *French Hill Hotel Corporation Ltd. v. Local Committee for Planning and Construction, Jerusalem et al.*, PD 27 (2) [1973].
HCJ 623/76 *State of Israel v. Moshe Kol*, PD 31 (2), 3.

[1] HCJ = High Court of Justice.

HCJ 531/77 *Baruch v. Transportation Supervisor, Tel Aviv and Central District*, PD 160, 32 (2) [1978].
HCJ 606/78 *Ayub et al. v. Minister of Defense et al.*, PD 33 (2), 113.
HCJ 660/78, 610/78 *Ayoub et al. v. Minister of Defense et al.*, PD 113, 33 (2).
HCJ 148/79 *Saar v. Minister of the Interior and the Police*, PD 169, 34 (2).
HCJ 390/79 *Duweikat v. Government of Israel*, PD 34 (1), 1 [1979] ("the Elon Moreh case").
HCJ – Further Hearing 13/80 *Hendeles v. Kupat Am et al.*, PD 35 (2), 788.
HCJ 1/81 *Shiran et al. v. Broadcast Authority*, PD 35 (3), 365, 274.
HCJ 246/81 *Derekh Eretz v. Broadcasting Authority*, PD 35 (4), 1.
HCJ 448/81 *Ressler et al. v. Minister of Defense Ariel Sharon*, PD 36 (1), 1981.
HCJ 512/81 *Archeological Institute v. Minister of Education*, PD 35 (4), 53 [1981].
HCJ 652/81 *Sarid v. Speaker of the Knesset*, PD 36 (2), 197.
HCJ – Further Hearing 2/82 *Ressler v. Minister of Defense Ariel Sharon*, PD 36 (1), 708.
HCJ 141/82 *Rubinstein v. Speaker of the Knesset*, PD 141, 37 (3).
HCJ 179/82 *Ressler v. Minister of Defense*, PD 36 (4), 421.
HCJ 243/82 *Zichroni v. IBA Executive Committee*, PD 37 (1), 757 [1982].
HCJ 153/83 *Levy et al. v. CO Southern District*, Israel Police, PD 38 (2), 393.
HCJ 780/83 *Tomkhei Temimim Yeshiva v. State of Israel*, PD 34 (2), 273 [1983].
HCJ 2/84 *Neiman v. Central Elections Committee to the 11th Knesset*, PD 39 (2), 225.
HCJ 234/84 *Hadashot v. Minister of Defense*, PD 38 (2), 77 [1984].
HCJ 731/84 *Kariv v. Knesset House Committee*, PD 39 (3), 337.
HCJ 732/84 *Tsaban v. Minister of Religion*, 40 (4), PD 141 [1986].
HCJ 742/84 *MK Kahane v. Speaker and Deputy Speakers of the Knesset*, PD 39 (4), 85.
HCJ 73/85 *Kach Faction v. Speaker of the Knesset*, PD 141 (3), 39.
HCJ 381/85 *Bank Leumi et al. v. Commission of Inquiry on Bank Share Regulation et al.*, PD 39 (4), 225 [1985].
HCJ 399/85 *Kahane v. Executive Committee of the Israel Broadcast Authority*, PD 41 (3) [1985].
HCJ 620/85 *MK Miari v. Speaker of the Knesset et al.*, PD 41 (4), 169.
HCJ 669/85 *MK Kahane v. Speaker and Deputy Speakers of the Knesset*, PD 40 (4), 393.
HCJ 14/86 *Laor v. Israeli Film Censorship Council*, PD 41 (1), 421 [1986].
HCJ 44/86 *Association of Butchers v. Chief Rabbinate*, PD 40 (4), 1.
HCJ 230/86 *Shoshana (Susan) Miller v. Minister of the Interior*, PD 40 (4), 436 [1986].
HCJ 428/86 *Barzilai v. State of Israel*, PD 40 (3), 505.
HCJ 910/86 *Ressler v. Minister of Defense*, PD 441, 42 (2) [1988].
HCJ 153/87 *Shakdiel v. Minister of Religious Affairs et al.*, PD 221, 42 (2) [1988].
HCJ 59/88 *MK Yair Tzaban v. Minister of Finance*, PD 42 (4), 705 [1988].
HCJ 482/88 *Reisser v. Speaker of the Knesset*, PD 42 (3), 142.
HCJ 680/88 *Schnitzer v. Chief Military Censor*, PD 42 (4), 617 [1988].
HCJ 806/88 *Universal City Studios v. Films and Plays Censorship Board*, PD 43 (2), 22 [1989].
HCJ 142/89 *L.A.O.R. Movement v. Speaker of the Knesset*, PD 529, 44 (3).
HCJ 465/89 *Raskin v. Jerusalem Religious Council*, PD 673, 44 (2) [1990].
HCJ 1179/90 *Ratz Party: Movement for Civil Rights and Peace v. Acting Speaker of the Knesset*, PD 44 (2), 31.
HCJ 1523/90 *Levy v. Prime Minister Shamir*, PD 44 (2), 213.
HCJ 1601/90 *Shalit v. Prime Minister Peres*, PD 44 (3), 353.
HCJ 1635/90 *Jerzhevski v. Prime Minister Yitzhak Shamir et al.*, PD 45 (1), 37.
HCJ 168/91 *Morcus v. Minister of Defense et al.*, PD 45 (1), 467.
HCJ 4481/91 *Bargil et al. v. Government of Israel*, PD 210, 47 (4).
HCJ 5711/91 *Poraz v. Speaker of the Knesset*, PD 44 (3), 317.
HCJ 1000/92 *Bavli v. High Rabbinical Court*, PD 48 (2), 221 [1994].
HCJ 4354/92 *Faithful of the Temple Mount and the Land of Israel Movement v. Prime Minister*, PD 47 (1) [1993].
HCJ 5871/92 *Meatrael Ltd. v. Minister of Commerce and Industry*, PD 48 (2), 844 [1993].
HCJ 5973/92 *Association for Civil Rights in Israel v. Minister of Defense*, PD 47 (1), 471.
HCJ 6163/92 *Eisenberg v. Minister of Housing and Construction*, PD 47 (2), 229.

HCJ 6168/92 *Association for Secular Humanistic Judaism v. State of Israel*, PD 51 (4), 289, 302 [1997].
HCJ 1031/93 *Pesero (Goldstein) v. Ministry of the Interior*, PD 49 (4), 661 [1995].
HCJ 1843/93 *Pinchasi v. Israel Knesset*, PD 49 (1), 661 [1995].
HCJ 2918/93 *Kiryat Gat Municipality v. State of Israel*, PD 54 (3), 637.
HCJ – Further Hearing 3299/93 *Wechselbaum v. Minister of Defense*, PD 49 (2), 195.
HCJ 3872/93 *Meatrael Ltd. v. Prime Minister et al.*, PD 485, 47 (5) [1993].
HCJ 4267/93 *Amitai et al. v. Rabin et al.*, PD 47 (5), 441.
HCJ 453/94 *Israel Women's Network v. Government of Israel*, PD 48 (5), 501 [1994].
HCJ 706/94 *Ronen v. Prof. Amnon Rubinstein* [unpublished, 1999].
HCJ 4541/94 *Miller v. Minister of Defense et al.*, PD 49 (4), 94 [1994].
HCJ 4733/94 *Yehudit Naot v. Haifa City Council*, PD 49 (5), 111, 119 [1996].
HCJ 4914/94 *Turner v. State Comptroller and State Control Committee*, PD 49 (3), 771 [1995].
HCJ 5009/94 *Meatrael Ltd. v. Council of the Chief Rabbinate of Israel*, PD 617, 48 (5) [1994].
HCJ 5364/94 *Velner v. Rabin et al.*, PD 758, 49 (1).
HCJ 3358/95 *Hoffman v. Director-General, Office of the Prime Minister*, PD 345, 54 (2) [2000].
HCJ 6055/95 *Tzemah v. Minister of Defense*, PD 50, 3 (5), 241.
HCJ 6698/95 *Ka'adan v. Israel Land Administration et al.*, PD 258, 54 (1) [1995].
HCJ 3434/96 *Hofnung v. Speaker of the Knesset*, PD 50 (3), 68.
HCJ 5016/96 *Horev v. Minister of Transportation*, PD 51 (4), 1 [1997].
HCJ 1715/97 *Israel Investment Managers Association v. Minister of Finance*, PD 50, 1 (4), 367.
HCJ 2624/97 *Yedid Ronel v. Government of Israel*, PD 51 (3), 71.
HCJ 3267/97 *Rubinstein v. Minister of Defense*, PD 55 (2), 255 [1998].
HCJ 5227/97 *Michal David v. High Rabbinical Court in Jerusalem*, Tak-El 98 (3), 443.
HCJ 240/98 *Adalah v. Minister of Religious Affairs et al.*, PD 52 (5), 167 [2000].
HCJ 2671/98 *Israel Women's Network v. Minister of Labor and Welfare*, PD 52 (3), 630 [1998].
HCJ 5933/98 *Documentary Filmmakers Forum v. President of the State et al.*, PD 54 (3), 496 [1998].
HCJ 403/99 *MK Ran Cohen et al. v. Prime Minister B. Netanyahu et al.* [unpublished, 1999].
HCJ 1030/99 *Oron v. Speaker of the Knesset*, PD 56 (3), 640 [1999].
HCJ 4112/99 *Adalah and the Association for Civil Rights in Israel v. Municipality of Tel Aviv-Jaffa*, PD 393, 56 (5) [2002].
HCJ 244/00 *New Discourse: The Mizrahi Democratic Rainbow v. Minister of National Infrastructure, Israel Lands Authority, et al.*, PD 56 (6), 25 [2000].
HCJ 4124/00 *Ornan Yekutieli v. Minister of Religious Affairs* [unpublished, 2010].
HCJ 5167/00 *Weiss v. Prime Minister*, PD 55 (2), 455.
HCJ 7203/00 *Aviv Osoblanski Ltd. v. Council of the Chief Rabbinate of Israel*, 56 (2), PD 196 [2001].
HCJ 24/01 *Ressler v. Israeli Knesset*, PD 699, 56 (2).
HCJ 953/01 *MK Solodkin v. Beit Shemesh Municipality*, PD 595, 58 (5) [2004].
HCJ 6427/02 *Movement for Quality Government v. the Knesset* [2006].
HCJ 10296/02 *Association of Teachers in Secondary Schools, Seminars, and Colleges v. Minister of Education et al.*, PD 59 (3), 224 [2005].
HCJ 316/03 *Bakri v. Israel Film Council* [2003].
HCJ 2232/03 *Jane Doe v. Tel Aviv-Jaffa Regional Rabbinical Court* [unpublished, 2006]. www.nevo.co.il (accessed October 16, 2017).
HCJ – Further Hearing 6354/03 *Sabit v. Government of Israel*, Tak-El 2004 (2), 3006.
HCJ 6973/03 *Marciano et al. v. Minister of Finance*, PD 270, 58 (2).
HCJ 8638/03 *Amir v. High Rabbinical Court in Jerusalem* [2006].
HCJ 11163/03 *Supreme Monitoring Committee for Arab Affairs in Israel v. Prime Minister of Israel* [unpublished, 2006].
HCJ 11225/03 *MK Bishara v. Attorney General* [unpublished, 2006].
HCJ 11298/03 *Movement for Quality Government v. Knesset House Committee*, PD 59 (5), 865.
HCJ 1027/04 *Independent Cities Forum et al. v. Israel Lands Council* [2011].
HCJ 2056/04 *Beit Sourik Village Council v. Government of Israel*, PD 58 (5), 807.

HCJ – Further Hearing 2309/04 *Eichenstein et al. v. Sharon et al.* [unpublished].
HCJ 5261/04 *Fuchs v. Prime Minister of Israel*, PD 59 (2), 446, 7.
HCJ – Further Hearing 7802/04 *Leora Milo v. Minister of Defense et al.*, Tak-El 2004 (4), 719 [2004].
HCJ 8600/04 *Shimoni v. the Prime Minister*, Tak-El 2005 (1), 995.
HCJ 1661/05 *Gaza Coast Regional Council et al. v. Israeli Knesset et al.*, Tak-El 2005 (1), 2461.
HCJ 2605/05 *Academic Center of Law and Business et al. v. Minister of Finance et al.* [2009].
HCJ 3045/05 *Ben-Ari v. Director, Population Administration, Ministry of the Interior* [unpublished, 2006].
HCJ 5372/05 *Movement for Quality Government v. Knesset House Committee*, Tak-El 2005 (4), 80.
HCJ 6893/05 *Levy v. Government of Israel et al.*, Tak-El 2005 (3), 1417.
HCJ 7710/05 *Bar Hen et al. v. Prime Minister Ariel Sharon et al.*, Tak-El 2005 (3), 2400.
HCJ 8276/05 *Adalah v. Minister of Defense*, Tak-El 2006 (4), 3675.
HCJ 4585/06 *Families of the Victims of October 2000 et al. v. Public Security Minister and Cmdr. Bentzi Sao* [unpublished, 2006].
HCJ 8988/06 *Meshi-Zahav v. Jerusalem District Police Commander* [unpublished, 2006].
HCJ – Further Hearing 10030/06 *Movement for Quality Government v. Prime Minister et al.* [2007].
HCJ 258/07 *Galon v. Governmental Commission of Inquiry to Investigate Events of the 2006 Lebanon Campaign* [unpublished, 2007].
HCJ 466/07 *MK Galon et al. v. Attorney General et al.* [unpublished, 2012].
HCJ 1999/07 *Galon v. Governmental Commission of Inquiry to Investigate Events of the 2006 Lebanon Campaign 2007* [unpublished, 2007].
HCJ 4805/07 *Center for Religious Pluralism, Movement for Progressive Judaism in Israel v. Ministry of Education et al.* [2008].
HCJ 6298/07 *Ressler v. Israeli Knesset* [2012].
HCJ 1067/08 *No'ar KeHalakha v. Ministry of Education et al.*, PD 63 (2), 398 [2009].
HCJ 5551/08 *Shalit v. State of Israel* [unpublished, 2008].
HCJ 6063/08 *Shahar v. State of Israel* [unpublished, 2008].
HCJ 3002/09 *Israel Medical Association et al. v. Prime Minister Benjamin Netanyahu* [unpublished, 2009].
HCJ 2684/12 *Movement to Strengthen Tolerance in Religious Education et al. v. Attorney General et al.* [2015].
HCJ 6704/12 *Ressler et al. v. Minister of Defense* [2012].
HCJ 7146/12 *Adam et al. v. Knesset* [2013].
HCJ 7385/13 *Eitan: Israeli Immigration Policy Center v. Government of Israel* [2014].
HCJ 8425/13 *Eitan: Israeli Immigration Policy Center v. Government of Israel* [2014].
HCJ 2266/14 *Roi Yellin et al. v. Im Tirtsu* [2015].
HCJ 3132/15 *Yesh Atid Party v. Prime Minister* [2015].
HCJ 4374/15 *Movement for Quality Government v. Prime Minister* [2015].
HCJ 262/16 *Labor Party et al. v. Government of Israel* [2016].
Civil Appeal 65/57 *Haetzni v. Ben-Gurion*, PD 11, 403.
Civil Appeal 294/91 *Burial Society v. Kestenbaum*, PD 46, 464 (2) [1992].
Civil Appeal 6821/93 *United Mizrahi Bank Ltd. v. Migdal Cooperative Village et al.*, PD 49 (4) [1995].
Civil Appeal 6024/97 *Frederika Shavit v. Rishon Letzion Burial Society*, PD 53 (3), 600 [1999].
Civil Appeal 751/10, CA 1236/10, CA 1237/10 *John Doe v. Ilana Dayan-Orbach and Telad Jerusalem Studios Inc.* [unpublished, 2010].
Civil Appeals Authority 1863/90 *Ravitz et al. v. Dayan et al.*, PD 45 (2), 309 [1991].
Civil Appeals Authority 4905/98 *Gamzu v. Yeshayahu et al.*
Civil Case 818/93 *Ariel Sharon v. Uzi Benziman* [unpublished, 1997].
Civil Case 42868-05-10 (Jerusalem) *Im Tirtsu v. Roi Yellin et al.* [2013].
Court-Marshal MR 3/57 *Military Prosecutor v. Shmuel Malinki et al.* [1957].
Criminal Appeal 125/50 *Yakobowitz v. Attorney General*, PD 6, 514.

Criminal Appeal 217/68 *Isramax v. State of Israel*, PD 343, 22 (2).
Criminal Appeal 5270/14 *Olmert v. State of Israel* [2015].
Criminal Case (Jerusalem) 3471/87 *Israel v. Kaplan et al.*, PD 24 (1), 337.
Criminal Case (Jerusalem) 305/93 *State of Israel v. Aryeh Deri.*
Criminal Case (Tel Aviv) 5880/95 *State of Israel v. Ofer Nimrodi and David Ronen.*
Criminal Case (Tel Aviv) 8074/96 *Israel v. Rafael Pinchasi* [unpublished].
Criminal Case (Jerusalem) 4830/98 *State of Israel v. Katz et al.* [2003].
Criminal Case (Tel Aviv) 10291-01/12 *State of Israel v. Hillel Charney et al.* [2014].
Criminal Miscellaneous Petition 1339/00 *Nimrodi v. State of Israel* [2000].
Election Appeal 1/65 *Yardor v. Central Elections Committee to the 6th Knesset*, PD 19 (3), 396.
Election Appeal 2/84 *Neiman v. Chair, Central Elections Committee*, PD 39 (2).
Election Appeal 1/88 *Neiman v. Central Elections Committee to the 12th Knesset*, PD 42 (4), 177.
Election Appeal 55/03 *MK O. Pines-Paz v. Baruch Marzel* [2003].
Election Appeal 131/03 *Balad v. Central Elections Committee to the 16th Knesset* [2003].
Election Appeal 561/09 *Balad et al. v. Central Elections Committee to the 18th Knesset et al.* [2009].
Election Approval 11280/02 *Central Elections Committee for the 16th Knesset v. Ahmad Tibi* [unpublished, 2003].
Election Approval 50/03 *Central Elections Committee v. Bishara* [unpublished, 2003].
Election Approval 2013, *Central Elections Committee for the 19th Knesset v. MK Hanin Zuabi.*
Election Approval 2015, *Central Elections Committee for the 20th Knesset v. MK Hanin Zuabi.*
Election Approval 2015, *Central Elections Committee for the 20th Knesset v. Baruch Marzel.*
International Court of Justice. 2004. *Legal Consequences of the Construction of a Wall in the Occupied Palestinian Territory*. July 9. www.icj-cij.org/docket/files/131/1677.pdf (accessed March 31, 2016).

ARTICLES AND BOOKS

A Constitution for Israel. 1987. *A Constitution for Israel.* A publication of the Constitution for Israel Movement [in Hebrew] [booklet].
Abu-Asba, Khaled. 2006. "The Arab Education System." In *Barriers to Equality*, eds. Shlomo Hasson and Michael M. Karayyani. Jerusalem: Floersheimer Institute for Policy Studies, 183–94 [in Hebrew].
Abu-Sharqiya, Naif. 2005. "Obstacles to Managing an Arab Local Authority." In *Municipal Elections in the Arab and Druze Sector 2003*, eds. Elie Rekhess and Sara Osatzky-Lazar. Tel-Aviv: The Dayan Center, Tel-Aviv University [in Hebrew].
Achdut, Leah. 2009. "On the Absolute and the Relative in the Definition of the Poverty Line." In *Disputes in Economics*, eds. Arie Arnon and Moshe Justman. Jerusalem and Tel-Aviv: Van Leer Jerusalem Institute and Hakibbutz Hameuchad, 122–58 [in Hebrew].
Adoni, Hanna, Dan Caspi, and Akiba A. Cohen. 2006. *Media, Minorities and Hybrid Identities: The Arab and Russian Communities in Israel.* Cresskill, NJ: Hampton Press.
Aharoni, Yair. 1991. *Israeli Economy: Dreams and Realities*. London: Routledge.
Akzin, Benjamin. 1955. "The Role of Parties in Israel Democracy." *Journal of Democracy* 17: 509–33.
1956. "On the Stability and Reality of Constitutions." In *Studies in Economic and Social Sciences: Scripta Hierosolymitana*, ed. R. Bachi. Jerusalem: Magnes Press, vol. 3, 318–39.
1965. *Proposal for a Constitution for the State of Israel.* Tel-Aviv: Bnai Brith [in Hebrew].
1966. *Issues in Law and Politics*. Jerusalem: Magnes Press [in Hebrew].
1967. *Theory of Government*. Jerusalem: Akademon, Hebrew University [in Hebrew].
Akzin, Benjamin, and Yehezkel Dror. 1966. *National Planning in Israel.* Tel-Aviv: Hamidrasha Leminhal [in Hebrew].
Al-Haj, Majid. 1996. *Education among Arabs in Israel: Control and Social Change.* Jerusalem: Magnes Press [in Hebrew].

1997. "Identity and Orientation among Arabs in Israel: Being a Double Periphery." *Medina, Mimshal Veyahasim Beinleumiyim* 41–42: 103–22 [in Hebrew].
Al-Haj, Majid, and Henry Rosenfeld. 1990. *Arab Local Government in Israel*. Westview Studies on the Middle East. Boulder, CO: Westview Press.
Alimi, Eitan Y. 2008. "Naming a Child: On the Similarities and Dissimilarities between Social Movements and Interest Groups." *Civil Society and the Third Sector in Israel* 2 (2): 29–52 [in Hebrew].
Allon, Yigal. 1960. *A Mask of Sand*. Tel-Aviv: Hakibbutz Hameuchad [in Hebrew].
Almog, Eytan. 2003. "The Beginning of Radio Broadcasting in Palestine during the Mandate Period: A Yishuv-Zionist or Mandate-Colonial Interest?" In *Jerusalem under the Mandate: Achievements and Heritage*, ed. Yehoshua Ben-Arieh. Jerusalem: Yitzhak Ben-Zvi Institute, 217–50 [in Hebrew].
Almog, Oz. 1993. "War Memorials in Israel: A Semiotic Analysis." *Megamot* 34: 179–210 [in Hebrew].
1997. *The Sabra: A Profile*. Tel-Aviv: Am Oved [in Hebrew].
Almond, Gabriel Abraham, and G. Bingham Powell. 1978. *Comparative Politics: Systems Processes and Policy*, 2nd edn. Boston, MA: Little, Brown.
Almond, Gabriel Abraham, and Sidney Verba. 1963. *The Civic Culture*. Princeton, NJ: Princeton University Press.
1980. *The Civic Culture Revisited*. Boston, MA: Little, Brown.
Alon, Gideon. 1995. *Direct Election*. Tel-Aviv: Bitan [in Hebrew].
2001. "Proponents of Direct Election: It's Not the System that Failed, but the Knesset." *Haaretz* March 9 [in Hebrew].
2003. "Rivlin: The Knesset is Being Treated like a Doormat by its Members." *Haaretz* December 23 [in Hebrew].
2003a. "The Likud and NRP Gained a Seat; Hadash and One Nation Dropped to Three Seats." *Haaretz* January 30 [in Hebrew].
2003b. "Why, for Example, Do We Have to Ask the MKs for Approval to Prosecute an MK Who Hunted Partridges without a License?" *Haaretz* April 27 [in Hebrew].
2004. "The Authority that Doesn't Stop Making Laws, and the Authority that Doesn't Bother Implementing Them." *Haaretz* June 20 [in Hebrew].
2009. "Thus We Formed a Coalition: An Interview with David Libai who Headed Barak's Negotiation Team." *Haaretz* July 5 [in Hebrew].
Aloni, Shulamit. 1997. *I Can Do No Other: Shulamit Aloni Converses with Idith Zertal*. Or Yehuda: Maariv-Hed Artzi [in Hebrew].
Aloush, Zvi, and Yossi Elituv. 2004. *Ben Porat Yosef: His Life, Doctrine, and the Political Moves of Rabbi Ovadia Yosef*. Tel-Aviv: Kinneret [in Hebrew].
Amara, Mohamed. 1998. "The Clan in Arab Politics: Adjusting to Changing Patterns." In *The Arabs in Israeli Politics*, ed. Elie Rekhess. Tel-Aviv: Tel-Aviv University [in Hebrew].
2006. "A True Core Curriculum or No Core at All?" In *Towards an Educational Revolution*, ed. Dan Inbar. Jerusalem and Tel-Aviv: Van Leer Jerusalem Institute and Hakibbutz Hameuchad, 195–202 [in Hebrew].
Amram, Azri. 2014. "The Complete Guide to the Holyland Affair." *Mako* May 13. www.mako.co.il/news-law/legal/Article-712eb06a872f541004.htm [in Hebrew] (accessed August 11, 2016).
Amsterdamski, Shaul. 2008. "The Knesset Approved the Public Housing Law." *Calcalist* July 30. www.calcalist.co.il/real_estate/articles/0,7340,L-3097609,00.html [in Hebrew] (accessed March 31, 2016).
Aran, Gideon. 1987. "Religious Messianism for a Zionist Religion: The Roots and Culture of Gush Emunim." Ph.D. dissertation, Hebrew University of Jerusalem [in Hebrew].
2013. *Kookism: The Roots of Gush Emunim*. Jerusalem: Carmel [in Hebrew].
Arbel, Yonatan, and Tehilla Shwartz-Altshuler. 2008. *Information Wants to be Free*. Jerusalem: Israel Democracy Institute [in Hebrew].
Arian, Asher. 1971. *Consensus in Israel*. New York: General Learning Press.
1973. *The Choosing People*. Cleveland, OH: Case Western Reserve University Press.

1990. "Israel's National Unity Governments and Domestic Politics." In *The Elections in Israel – 1988*, eds. Asher Arian and Michal Shamir. Boulder, CO: Westview Press, 205–21.

1997. *The Second Israeli Republic*. Haifa and Tel-Aviv: Haifa University and Zmora-Bitan [in Hebrew].

1999. *Security Threatened*. Tel-Aviv: Papyrus, Tel-Aviv University [in Hebrew].

2001. "Israeli Public Opinion in the Wake of the 2000–2001 Intifada." *Strategic Assessment* 4 (2). Tel-Aviv: Institute for National Security Studies. www.inss.org.il/uploadImages/systemFiles/Israeli%20Public%20Opinion%20in%20the%20Wake%20of%20the%202000–2001%20Intifada.pdf (accessed November 13, 2015).

Arian, Asher, and Tamar Hermann. 2010. *Israeli Democracy Index*. Jerusalem: Israel Democracy Institute [in Hebrew].

Arian, Asher, and Ayala Keissar-Sugarman. 2011. *A Portrait of Israeli Jews: Beliefs, Observance, and Values of Israeli Jews, 2009*. Jerusalem: Israel Democracy Institute and Avi Chai Israel Foundation. http://avichai.org/knowledge_base/beliefs-observances-and-social-interaction-among-israeli-jews-2009-abstract/ (accessed June 21, 2016).

Arian, Asher, and Michal Shamir. 1982. "Ethnic Voting in the 1981 Election." *State, Government and International Relations* 19–20: 88–104 [in Hebrew].

eds. 1990. *The Elections in Israel – 1988*. Boulder, CO: Westview Press, 155–71.

eds. 1995. *The Elections in Israel – 1992*. Albany, NY: SUNY Press.

eds. 2002. *The Elections in Israel – 2001*. Jerusalem: Israel Democracy Institute [in Hebrew].

2004. "On Mistaking a Dominant Party in a Dealigning System." In *The Elections in Israel – 2003*, eds. Asher Arian and Michal Shamir. New Brunswick, NJ: Transaction Publishers, 13–32.

eds. 2005. *The Elections in Israel – 2003*. New Brunswick, NJ: Transaction Publishers.

eds. 2011. *The Elections in Israel – 2009*. New Brunswick, NJ: Transaction Publishers.

Arian, Asher, et al. 2005–10. *Israeli Democracy Index*. Jerusalem: Israel Democracy Institute [in Hebrew].

Arian, Asher, David Nachmias, and Ruth Amir. 2002. *Executive Governance in Israel*. Jerusalem: Israel Democracy Institute [in Hebrew].

Arian, Asher, David Nachmias, Doron Navot, and Danielle Shani. 2003. *The 2003 Israel Democracy Index: Measuring Israeli Democracy*. Jerusalem: Israel Democracy Institute and The Guttman Center for Public Opinion and Policy Research [in Hebrew].

Arian, Asher, Michael Philippov, and Anna Knafelman. 2009. *Democracy Index 2009: Marking Twenty Years since the Immigration from the FSU*. Jerusalem: Israel Democracy Institute.

Arian, Asher, Gabriel Weimann, Gadi Wolfsfeld, Dan Caspi, Charles S. Liebman, and Yoram Peri. 2003a. *Media During Elections: Lessons and Changes*. Tel Aviv: Herzog Institute for Media, Politics, and Society, Tel-Aviv University, January [in Hebrew].

Arian, David. 1955. "The First Five Years of the Israel Civil Service." *Scripta Hierosolymitana* III: 340–77.

Ariel, Yaron, and Ofer Carmel. 2011. *Survey of News Consumption*. Jezreel Valley: Department of Communications, College of Jezreel Valley [in Hebrew].

Arieli, Shaul. 2011. *People and Borders: About the Israeli Palestinian Conflict*, 2nd edn. Tel-Aviv: Kapaim.

Arieli, Shaul, and Michael Sfard. 2006. *The Wall of Folly*. Tel-Aviv: Yediot Aharonot [in Hebrew].

Arieli, Shaul, Doubi Schwartz, and Hadas Tagari. 2006. *On Injustice and Folly: On the Proposals to Cede Arab Localities from Israel to Palestine*. Jerusalem: Floersheimer Institute for Policy Studies. http://fips.huji.ac.il/sites/default/files/floersheimer/files/arieli_schwartz_injustice_and_folly_english.pdf (accessed April 1, 2016).

Arieli-Horowitz, Dana, ed. 2006. *Phantom in Politics: Referenda in Israel*. Jerusalem: Magnes Press and the Israel Democracy Institute [in Hebrew].

Arnon, Arie, and Moshe Justman, eds. 2009. *Disputes in Economics*. Jerusalem and Tel-Aviv: Van Leer Jerusalem Institute and Hakibbutz Hameuchad [in Hebrew].

Aronson, Shlomo. 1998. "A Constitution for Israel: The British Model of David Ben-Gurion." *Politika* 2: 9–30 [in Hebrew].

Arrow, K. [1951] 1963. *Social Choice and Individual Values*. New Haven, CT: Yale University Press.
Artsieli, Yoav. 2004. *The Gavison-Medan Covenant: Main Points and Principles*. Jerusalem: Israel Democracy Institute and Avi Chai Israel Foundation.
Ashkenazi, Moty, Baruch Nevo, and Nurit Ashkenazi. 2003. *This Evening at 6, the War will Break Out*. Tel-Aviv: Hakibbutz Hameuchad [in Hebrew].
Association for Civil Rights in Israel. 2012. *Situation Report: The State of Human Rights in Israel and the OPT*. December. http://reliefweb.int/sites/reliefweb.int/files/resources/ACRI-Situation-Report-2012-ENG.pdf (accessed August 22, 2016).
Atmor, Nir. 2008. "The Race for the Internet: Parties and an Online Campaign in the 2006 Election." In *The Elections in Israel 2006*, eds. Asher Arian and Michal Shamir. Albany, NY: SUNY Press, 365–400 [in Hebrew].
2009. "Online Campaigns in the 2009 Election." Jerusalem: Israel Democracy Institute. www.idi.org.il/articles/5480 [in Hebrew] (accessed October 25, 2017).
2013. "Voter Turnout in the 2013 Election from a Local Perspective." *Parliament* 75. Jerusalem: Israel Democracy Institute. www.idi.org.il/parliaments/3461/3462 [in Hebrew] (accessed October 18, 2017).
Atmor, Nir, and Yael Hadar. 2008. "Election Participation and the Decline of Voter Turnout in Israel." Israel Democracy Institute. www.idi.org.il/BreakingNews/Pages/Breaking_the_News_80.aspx [in Hebrew] (accessed March 31, 2016).
Atmor, Nir, Itzhak Benenson, Abraham Diskin, and Vald Kharbash. 2009. *Regional Elections in Israel*. Jerusalem: Van Leer Jerusalem Institute and Merkaz Metzila [in Hebrew].
Averbach, Lior. 2015. "Some 2 Million People Are Exposed to the TV Election Campaign." *Globes* March 10. www.globes.co.il/news/article.aspx?did=1001017292 [in Hebrew] (accessed April 11, 2016).
2016. "TGI Survey for 2015: Yisrael Hayom Leads, Yediot Records a Rise." *Globes* January 27. www.globes.co.il/news/article.aspx?did=1001098512 [in Hebrew] (accessed March 24, 2016).
Aviram, Uri, John Gal, and Yosef Kattan, eds. 2007. *Formulating Social Policies in Israel: Trends and Issues*. Jerusalem: Taub Center [in Hebrew].
Avizohar, Meir, and Avi Bareli, eds. 1989. *Now or Never: Mapai's Deliberations during the Final Year of the British Mandate*. Beit Berl: Aynot [in Hebrew].
Avnon, Dan. 1996. "The 'Enlightened Public': Jewish and Democratic or Liberal and Democratic." *Mishpat Umimshal* 2 (July): 417–51 [in Hebrew].
1998. "The Nondemocratic Aspect of the Basic Laws with Regard to Human Rights." *Politika* 5: 53–70 [in Hebrew].
Avraham, David. 2014. "Masses of Readers Complained of the Lack of Balance in Reporting of Protective Edge Campaign." *Walla News* September 4. http://b.walla.co.il/item/2782354 [in Hebrew] (accessed May 6, 2016).
Axford, Barrie, and Richard Huggins, eds. 2001. *New Media and Politics*. London: Sage Publications.
Ayalon, Hanna. 2006. "Inequality in Higher Education." In *In/Equality*, eds. Uri Ram and Nitza Berkowitz. Beersheva: Ben-Gurion University of the Negev, 148–55 [in Hebrew].
Azulai, Liron, Galit Widerman-Eliassy, and Vardit Dameri-Madar. 2009. *Change of Jurisdiction: Just a Matter of Economics?* Policy Paper. Jerusalem: Van Leer Jerusalem Institute [in Hebrew].
Azulai, Yuval. 2007. "Zecharia Baumel's Father: 'My Son is in Syria.'" *Haaretz* October 18 [in Hebrew].
Azulay, Ariella, and Adi Ophir. 2008. *This Regime Which Is Not One: Occupation and Democracy between the Sea and the River*. Tel-Aviv: Resling [in Hebrew].
Azulay, Moran, Itamar Eichner, and Omri Efraim. 2015. "Ministers' Committee Approved Left-wing NGO Law." *YNet* December 27. www.ynet.co.il/articles/0,7340,L-4744692,00.html [in Hebrew] (accessed June 5, 2016).
Bader, Yohanan. 1950 (?). *A Proposal by the Herut Movement for a Basic Constitution for the State of Israel*. Herut Movement Publication [in Hebrew].

Bagehot, Walter. 1867. *The English Constitution*. Available online at www.gutenberg.org/ebooks/4351 (accessed April 8, 2016).

Bagno, Olena. 2011. "The Price of Fear: Israel Beitenu in 2009." In *The Elections in Israel – 2009*, eds. Asher Arian and Michal Shamir. New Brunswick, NJ: Transaction Publishers, 19–40.

Bagno-Moldavsky, Olena, and Yehuda Ben Meir. 2014. "Who in Israel is Ready for a Peace Agreement with the Palestinians?" *Strategic Assessment* 17 (1, April): 47–56. www.inss.org.il/uploadImages/systemFiles/Bagno-Moldavsky%20and%20Ben%20Meir_adkan17_1ENG5.pdf (accessed May 7, 2016).

Balbachan, Yoel. 2008. "The Ethiopian Community in Israel from a 'Slightly Different' Angle: Database Findings." Presented at the Eleventh Spring Conference of the Israeli Center for Third Sector Research [in Hebrew].

2008a. "Trends in the Registration of New Third-Sector Organizations in 2007." Newsletter. Beersheva: Israeli Center for Third Sector Research, Ben-Gurion University of the Negev.

Baltatzis, Patrick. 2006. "Is Blogging Innovating Journalism?" *Innovation Journalism* 3 (2, May): 1–11.

Bana, Jalal, Baruch Kra, and *Haaretz* correspondents. 2002. "Amos Baranes Acquitted of 1974 Rachel Heller Murder." *Haaretz* December 11.

Bank of Israel. Various years. *Annual Report* [in Hebrew].

2006. "Statistical Appendix: Unemployment Rates 1969–2006." *Annual Report*.

2007. *Integration of Immigrants from Ethiopia in Israel: Situation Report Summary 2006*. April [in Hebrew].

2012. *Key Data on the Israeli Economy*. March [in Hebrew].

Bar, Aliza. 1996. *Primaries and Other Methods of Candidate Selection*. Jerusalem and Tel-Aviv: Israel Democracy Institute and Hakibbutz Hameuchad [in Hebrew].

Barak, Aharon. 1987. "The American Constitution and Israeli Jurisprudence." *Zmanim* 26: 12–19 [in Hebrew].

1988. "The Foundations of Law Act and the Heritage of Israel." *Shenaton Hamishpat Ha'Ivri* 13: 227–56 [in Hebrew].

1990. "Forty Years of Israeli Law." *Mishpatim* 19 (4): 631–46. Jerusalem: Hebrew University [in Hebrew].

1992. "The Constitutional Revolution: Basic Rights Protected." *Mishpat Umimshal* 1 (August) [in Hebrew].

1993. "The Essence of Judicial Activism." *Iyunei Mishpat* 17 (3) [in Hebrew].

1996. "Judicial Review of Administrative Decisions and Administrative Discretion." Presented at the Annual Public Administration Conference, February 5 [in Hebrew].

1997. "The Constitutionalization of the Israeli Legal System as a Result of the Basic Laws and its Effect on Procedural and Substantive Criminal Law." *Israel Law Review* 31 (3).

1999. "The Role of the Supreme Court in a Democratic Society." In *Fundamental Issues in a Democratic Society*, ed. Raphael Cohen-Almagor. Tel-Aviv: Sifriyat Hapoalim [in Hebrew].

2002. "The Press as Public Servant." *Alei Mishpat* 2 (1–2): 293–96 [in Hebrew].

2004. "The Constitutional Revolution – a Bat-Mitzva." *Mishpat Ve'asakim* 1 [in Hebrew].

2006. *The Judge in a Democracy*. Princeton, NJ: Princeton University Press.

Barak, Aharon, and Haim Berenson, eds. 2000. *Berenson Book*. Jerusalem: Nevo [in Hebrew].

Barak, Ehud. 2003. "Leaving Lebanon: A Test Case in Inter-echelon Relations." In *Civil–Military Relations in Israel: Influences and Restraints*, ed. Ram Erez. Tel-Aviv: Jaffee Center for Strategic Studies, Tel-Aviv University, 29–37 [in Hebrew].

Barak, Oren, and Gabriel Sheffer. 2006. "Israel's 'Security Network' and its Impact." *International Journal of Middle East Studies* 38 (2): 235–61.

Barak-Erez, Daphne, ed. 1999. *First Judgments: Reflections upon Decisions of the Israeli Supreme Court during the First Year of Israel's Independence*. Tel-Aviv: Hakibbutz Hameuchad [in Hebrew].

2000. "The Judiciability of Politics." *Plilim* 8: 369–87 [in Hebrew].

2007. *Outlawed Pigs: Law, Religion and Culture in Israel*. Madison, WI: University of Wisconsin Press.

2010. "The Drafting of Yeshiva Students: From Compromise to Controversy." In *Crossroads of Decisions in Israel*, eds. Dvora Hacohen and Moshe Lissak. Sede Boqer: Ben-Gurion Research Institute [in Hebrew].

2011. "The Private Prison Controversy and the Privatization Continuum." *Law & Ethics of Human Rights* 5 (1): 138–57.

Barber, Benjamin R. 2003. *Strong Democracy*. Berkeley, CA: California University Press.

Barda, Moshe. 2007. "Multiyear Data on IDF Recruitment." Jerusalem: Knesset Research and Information Center.

Barel, Zvi. 2005. "Present-Absentee Press." *Haaretz* December 11 [in Hebrew].

Bareli, Avi. 2014. *Authority and Participation in a New Democracy: Political Struggles in Mapai, Israel's Ruling Party, 1948–1953*. Boston: Academic Studies Press.

Bareli, Avi, Daniel Gutwein, and Tuvia Friling, eds. 2005. *Society and Economy in Israel: Historical and Contemporary Perspectives*. Beersheva: Ben-Gurion Institute, Ben-Gurion University of the Negev [in Hebrew].

Bar-Gil, Orit. 2008. "Israel is an Expert in Stopping Development." *Globes* 27 July. www.globes.co.il/news/article.aspx?fid=724anddid=1000365691andnextArticleId=724 [in Hebrew].

Barkai, Haim. 1983. *The Early Days of the Israeli Economy*. Jerusalem: Falk Institute, Hebrew University [in Hebrew].

Bar-Mor, Hadara. 1999. *Nonprofit Organizations – The Legal Situation: Third Sector Research*. Israeli Center for Third Sector Research. Beersheva: Ben-Gurion University of the Negev.

Bar-On, Mordechai. 1985. *Peace Now: Profile of a Movement*. Tel-Aviv: Hakibbutz Hameuchad [in Hebrew].

1997. "The Struggle over the 1948 Achievements – Israel's Security Policy." In *The First Decade 1948–1958*, eds. Zvi Zameret and Hanna Yablonka. Jerusalem: Ben-Zvi Institute, 12–26 [in Hebrew].

Bar-On, Mordechai, and Zvi Zameret, eds. 2002. *On Both Sides of the Bridge: State and Religion in the Early Years of Israel*. Jerusalem: Ben-Zvi Institute [in Hebrew].

Bar-Or, Amir. 1998. "The Development of the Interrelationship between the Yishuv's Political Institutions and Early State Institutions with the Haganah and the Early IDF (1920–49)." Ph.D. dissertation, Hebrew University of Jerusalem [in Hebrew].

2003. "The Development of Reciprocal Relationship between the Yishuv Institutions and the Hagana and IDF." Doctoral dissertation, The Hebrew University.

Barsela, Anat. 2007. *Ground to a Halt: Denial of Palestinians' Freedom of Movement in the West Bank*. Jerusalem: B'Tselem, August.

Bar-Siman-Tov, Yaacov. 1994. *Israel and the Peace Process, 1977–1982*. Albany, NY: SUNY Press.

2005. *The Israeli–Palestinian Conflict: From a Peace Process to a Violent Confrontation 2000–2005*. Jerusalem: Jerusalem Institute for Israel Studies [in Hebrew].

Bar-Tal, Daniel. 2007. *Living with the Conflict: Sociopsychological Analysis of Israeli-Jewish Society*. Jerusalem: Carmel [in Hebrew].

Barzilai, Gad. 1991. "Mass Media and Wars." *Kesher* 10 (November) [in Hebrew].

1998. "Judicial Hegemony, Party Polarization, and Social Change." *Politika* (December): 31–51 [in Hebrew].

1999. "Center against Periphery: Politics and Laws of 'Prevention of Terrorism Acts.'" *Plilim* 8: 229–49 [in Hebrew].

2006. "Parliamentarism in Decline: Referenda from a Political Constitutional Perspective." In *Phantom in Politics: Referenda in Israel*, ed. Dana Arieli-Horowitz. Jerusalem: Magnes Press, 193–206 [in Hebrew].

Barzilai, Gad, and Efraim Inbar. 1996. "The Use of Force: Israeli Public Opinion on Military Options." *Armed Forces and Society* 23 (1): 19–50.

Barzilai, Gad, and David Nachmias. 1997. *Accountability: The Attorney General*. Policy Paper No. 6. Jerusalem: Israel Democracy Institute [in Hebrew].

Barzilai, Gad, Ephraim Yuchtman-Yaar, and Zeev Segal. 1994. *The Israeli Supreme Court and the Israeli Public*. Tel-Aviv: Papyrus, Tel-Aviv University Press [in Hebrew].

Bashir, Bashir. 2011. "A Binational State is a Moral and Feasible Solution." *Falastin* 10 (February 19) [in Arabic].

Bassok, Moti. 2015. "Israel's Tax Revenues Hit Record High in January 2015." *Haaretz* March 2. www.haaretz.com/israel-news/business/1.645033 (accessed October 17, 2017).
Baum-Banai, R. 2001. "An Ultra-Orthodox-Zionist Movement?" In *Shas: The Challenge to Israeliness*, ed. Yoav Peled. Tel-Aviv: Yediot Aharonot, 102–25 [in Hebrew].
Bavly, Michael, Frances Raday, Avi Dabush, and Hadas Eytan. 2007. *Civilians on the Frontline: Citizens' Views of Home Front Failures during the Second Lebanon War*. Jerusalem: Shatil [in Hebrew].
Bechor, Guy. 1996. *A Constitution for Israel: The Story of a Struggle*. Jerusalem: Keter Publishing House [in Hebrew].
Behn, Robert D. 2000. *Rethinking Democratic Accountability*. Washington, DC: Brookings Institution Press.
Beilin, Yossi. 1985. *The Price of Unity: The Labor Party up to the Yom Kippur War*. Tel-Aviv: Revivim [in Hebrew].
Bekerman, Zvi, ed. 1983. *The State of Israel as a Jewish State*. Jerusalem: Ministry of Education [in Hebrew].
Ben Bassat, Avi, and Momi Dahan. 2003. *Social Rights in the Constitution and in Practice*. Jerusalem: Hebrew University, School of Public Policy, August, 1–38 [in Hebrew].
2006. *The Balance of Power in the Budgeting Process*. Jerusalem: Israel Democracy Institute [in Hebrew].
2008. *The Crisis in Local Government: Efficiency Versus Representativeness*. Jerusalem: Israel Democracy Institute [in Hebrew].
2009. "Social Identity and Local Elections." In *The Political Economics of the Municipalities.* Jerusalem: Israel Democracy Institute [in Hebrew].
Ben Bassat, Avraham, ed. 2001. *From Government Intervention to Market Economics: The Israeli Economy 1985–98*. Tel-Aviv: Am Oved [in Hebrew].
Ben Eliezer, Uri. 2003. "Civil Society and Military Society in Israel." In *In the Name of Security: The Sociology of War and Peace in Israel in Changing Times*, eds. Majid al-Haj and Uri Ben Eliezer. Haifa: Haifa University, 29–76 [in Hebrew].
Ben Meir, Yehoshua. 1983. "The Validity of IDF Safety Directives." *Tehumin* 4: 248–53 [in Hebrew].
Ben Meir, Yehuda. 1995. *Civil–Military Relations in Israel*. New York: Columbia University Press.
2006. "Changes in Civil–Military Relations." In *Relations between the Civilian and Military Echelons in Israel: Against the Backdrop of Military Conflicts*, ed. Ram Erez. Tel-Aviv: Jaffee Center for Strategic Studies, Tel-Aviv University, 17–21 [in Hebrew].
2009. "The Rise and Fall of the NRP." December 9. Jerusalem: Israel Democracy Institute. https://www.idi.org.il/articles/8112 [in Hebrew] (accessed October 18, 2017).
Ben Meir, Yehuda, and Olena Bagno-Moldavsky. 2013. *The Voice of the People: Israeli Public Opinion on National Security*. Tel-Aviv: Institute for National Security Studies.
Ben Meir, Yehuda, and Omer Einav. 2015. "Public Opinion Survey of the Institute for National Security Studies: The Public Remains Divided about the Results of the Protective Edge Campaign." http://heb.inss.org.il/index.aspx?id=4354&articleid=8843 [in Hebrew] (accessed May 5, 2016).
Ben Meir, Yehuda, and Dafna Shaked. 2007. *The People Speak: Israeli Public Opinion on National Security 2005–2007*. Tel-Aviv: Institute of National Security Studies, Tel-Aviv University.
Ben Ze'ev, Moshe. 1989. "The 'Political Echelon Facing Commissions of Inquiry: The Conflict, Tensions, and Fears." In *The Yitzhak Kahan Book*, eds. Menachem Elon, Moshe Ben-Ze'ev, Aharon Barak, N. Lifschitz, and Moshe Landau. Tel-Aviv: Papyrus [in Hebrew].
Ben-Aharon, Yitzhak. 1977. *In the Eye of the Storm*. Tel-Aviv: Hakibbutz Hameuchad [in Hebrew].
Ben-Ami, Shlomo. 2005. *Scars of War, Wounds of Peace: The Israeli-Arab Tragedy*. London: Weidenfeld and Nicolson.
Ben-Arieh, Asher. 2001. "The Making of Social Policy in Israel: The Perceived Influence of Members of the 13th Knesset." *Review of Policy Research* 20 (2): 311–30.

Ben-Arieh, Yehoshua, ed. 2003. *Jerusalem under the Mandate: Achievements and Heritage*. Jerusalem: Yitzhak Ben-Zvi Institute [in Hebrew].

Ben-David, Dan. 2005. "One Hand Takes While the Other Hand Gives." *Haaretz* 28 January [in Hebrew].

ed. 2005a. *State of the Nation: Society, Economy and Policy in Israel*. Jerusalem: Taub Center for Social Policy Studies in Israel.

ed. 2010. *State of the Nation: Society, Economy and Policy in Israel 2009*. Jerusalem: Taub Center for Social Policy Studies in Israel.

ed. 2011. *State of the Nation: Society, Economy and Policy in Israel 2010*. Jerusalem: Taub Center for Social Policy Studies in Israel.

Ben-David, Mishka. 1990. *From Pleshet to Ziklag: Studies in the Novels of the War for Independence*. Tel-Aviv: Sifriat Tarmil, Defense Ministry Publishing House [in Hebrew].

Bender, Arik. 2005. "63 Refuseniks during the Disengagement." *NRG* September 7. www.nrg.co.il/online/1/ART/980/911.html [in Hebrew] (accessed April 1, 2016).

Bendor, Ariel. 1995. "Flaws in Enacting Basic Laws." *Mishpat Umimshal* 2: 443–54 [in Hebrew].

1999. "The Basic Laws as the Basis for a Constitution." *Mishpat Umimshal* 5: 15–48 [in Hebrew].

Ben-Dor, Gabriel. 1977. "Politics and the Military in Israel in the 1970s." In *The Political System in Israel*, eds. Moshe Lissak and Emanuel Gutmann. Tel-Aviv: Am Oved, 411–32 [in Hebrew].

Ben-Elia, Nahum. 2004. *The Fourth Generation: New Local Government in Israel*. Jerusalem: Floersheimer Institute for Policy Studies [in Hebrew].

Ben-Eliezer, Uri. 1993. "The Meaning of Political Participation in a Non-Liberal Democracy: The Israeli Experience." *Comparative Politics* 25 (4): 397–412.

1998. *The Making of Israeli Militarism*. Bloomington, IN: Indiana University Press.

Ben-Gurion, David. 1955. *The Military and Security*. Tel-Aviv: Ma'arkhot [in Hebrew].

1969. *The State of Israel Renewed*. Tel-Aviv: Am Oved, vol. 1, 179–91 [in Hebrew].

1976–87. *Memoirs*, 6 volumes. Tel-Aviv: Am Oved [in Hebrew].

1983. *War Diary*, 3 volumes, eds. Gershon Rivlin and Elhanan Oren. Tel-Aviv: Am Oved [in Hebrew].

Benhabib, Seyla. 1994. "Deliberative Rationality and Models of Democratic Legitimacy." *Constellations* 1 (1): 26–52.

Benjamini, Haim. 1983. "The Six Day War, Israel 1967." *Journal of Strategic Studies* 6 (3, September): 56–69.

Ben-Menachem, Hanina. 1988. "The Foundations of Law Act 1980: Duty or Consultation?" *Shenaton Hamishpat Ha'Ivri* 13 [in Hebrew].

Ben-Porat, Dafna. 2002. *Setting Regulations by Virtue of the Laws Passed in the Fifteenth Knesset*. Jerusalem: Knesset Research and Information Center, December [in Hebrew].

Ben-Porat, Miriam. 2005. *Basic Law: State Comptroller*. Jerusalem: Institute for Comparative Research on Legislation and Law, Faculty of Law, Hebrew University of Jerusalem [in Hebrew].

Ben-Porat, Yoram. 1982. "The Revolution that Never Happened: Ideology and Economic Policy 1977–81." *Economics Quarterly*, Falk Institute, 115: 325–33 [in Hebrew].

1989. "The Israeli Economy: Growing Pains." In *The Israeli Economy: Growing Pains*, ed. Yoram Ben-Porat. Tel-Aviv: Am Oved, 9–28 [in Hebrew].

ed. 1989a. *The Israeli Economy: Growing Pains*. Tel-Aviv: Am Oved [in Hebrew].

Ben-Rafael, Eliezer, and Yitzhak Sternberg, eds. 2007. *New Elites in Israel*. Jerusalem: Bialik Institute [in Hebrew].

Bensimhon-Peleg, Sarit. 2008. *Jewish Philanthropy and the Israeli Third Sector: The Case of Israeli Think Tanks*. Tel-Aviv: Hartog School of Government and Public Policy, Tel-Aviv University.

Benvenisti, Eyal. 1993. "Deportations without Prior Hearing." *Mishpat Umimshal* 1 (2): 441–70 [in Hebrew].

Ben-Zadok, Efraim, and Giora Goldberg. 1983. "A Sociopolitical Change in the Israeli Development Towns." *Plural Societies* 14 (1–2): 49–65.

Benziman, Uzi. 2005. "The Media do not Disengage from the Authorities." *The Seventh Eye* 56 (May) [in Hebrew].

2005a. "Sudoku without Shame." *The Seventh Eye* 57 (July) [in Hebrew].

Benziman, Uzi, and Atallah Mansour. 1992. *Subtenants*. Jerusalem: Keter Publishing House.

Benziman, Yuval. 2010. "Contradictory Representation of the IDF in Cultural Texts of the 1980s." In *Militarism and Israeli Society*, eds. Gabriel Sheffer and Oren Barak. Bloomington, IN: Indiana University Press, 329–45.

Berezin, Mabel. 1997. "Politics and Culture: A Less Fissured Terrain." *Annual Review of Sociology* 23: 361–83.

Bernstein, Deborah. 1979. "The Black Panthers: Conflict and Protest in Israeli Society." *Megamot* 25: 65–81 [in Hebrew].

Bernstein, Marver H. 1959. "Israel's Capacity to Govern." *World Politics* 11: 399–417.

Bialer, Uri. 1990. *Between East and West: Israel's Foreign Policy Orientation 1948–1956*. Cambridge: Cambridge University Press.

Bilski Ben-Hur, Raphaella. 1993. *Every Individual, a King: The Social and Political Thought of Ze'ev Vladimir Jabotinsky*. Washington, DC: B'nai B'rith Books.

Binder, Leonard, James S. Coleman, Joseph LaPalombara, Lucian W. Pye, Sidney Verba, and Myron Weiner, eds. 1971. *Crises and Sequences in Political Development*. Princeton, NJ: Princeton University Press.

Birenbaum-Carmeli, Daphna. 2002. *Tel Aviv North: The Making of the New Israeli Middle Class*. Jerusalem: Magnes Press, Hebrew University [in Hebrew].

Bishara, Azmi. 1993. "On the Palestinian Minority in Israel." In *Israeli Society: Critical Perspectives*, ed. Uri Ram. Tel-Aviv: Breirot, 203–21 [in Hebrew].

2000. "The Israeli Arab: Analysis of a Divided Political Discourse." In *The Jewish–Arab Rift in Israel: A Reader*, eds. Ruth Gavison and Dafna Hacker. Jerusalem: Israel Democracy Institute, 35–70 [in Hebrew].

Black Panthers. 1971. Minutes. Stenograph from a Meeting of the Prime Minister with the Black Panthers. Jerusalem, April 13.

Blander, Dana. 2004. "Nation-building from the Perspective of Public Opinion." *Israeli Sociology* 6 (1) [in Hebrew].

2008. "Public Opinion in the First Years of the State." Jerusalem: Israel Democracy Institute. www.idi.org.il/GuttmanCenter/SurveyArticle/Pages/Surveys_Articles_5.aspx [in Hebrew] (accessed August 15, 2016).

2011. "Not Immune Forever: On Denying Rights under the Law of Immunity to MK Hanin Zoabi." *Parliament* 70. Jerusalem: Israel Democracy Institute [in Hebrew].

Blander, Dana, and Eran Klein. 2002. *Private Members' Bills: Comparative Analysis and Recommendations*. Jerusalem: Israel Democracy Institute [in Hebrew].

Blander, Dana, and Gideon Rahat. 2000. "Referendum: Myth and Reality." Policy Paper No. 20. Jerusalem: Israel Democracy Institute [in Hebrew].

Blander, Dana, and Efrat Waksman. 2002. *Patterns of Civic Involvement*. Jerusalem: Israel Democracy Institute [in Hebrew].

2004. "Nation-building from the Perspective of Public Opinion." *Israeli Sociology* 6: 9–37 [in Hebrew].

Blum, Yehuda Zvi. 1971. "Zion was Redeemed in International Law." *HaPraklit* 27: 315 [in Hebrew].

Bogdanor, Vernon, ed. 1988. *Constitutions in Democratic Politics*. Aldershot, UK: Gower.

ed. 2005. *Joined Up Government*. Oxford: British Academy and Oxford University Press.

Bondi, Ruth. 1990. *Felix: Pinchas Rosen and His Times*. Tel-Aviv: Zmora Bitan [in Hebrew].

Borochov, Eliahu. 2004. *Economics and Local Government*. Unit 7. Ra'anana: Open University [in Hebrew].

Bourdieu, Pierre. 1996. *Sur la télévision*. Paris: Liber-Raisons d'agir [in French].

Bracha, Baruch. 1984. "Racism and the Foundations of Immunity." *Haaretz* September 9 [in Hebrew].

Bradbury, J. 2003. "Royal Commissions." In *The Concise Oxford Dictionary of Politics*, eds. Iain McLean and Alistair McMillan. New York: Oxford University Press.

Brandman Institute Research. 2006. *"Caviar in Pita" Survey: Sense of Belonging and Differentiation of Immigrants from the Commonwealth of Independent States*. December. www.brandman.co.il/articles.php?articleid=194 (accessed March 28, 2016).

Brauner, Eliezer. 2003. "Structural, Behavior, and Environmental Characteristics of Third-sector Organizations in Israel that Commit Crimes related to Exploitation of their Preferred Status." Ph.D. dissertation, Ben-Gurion University of the Negev [in Hebrew].

Brenner, Uri. 1978. *Altalena*. Tel-Aviv: Hakibbutz Hameuchad [in Hebrew].

Brichta, Avraham. 2001. "The Knesset as the Representative of the Public." In *The Parliament in Israeli Democracy*, ed. Efraim Torgovnik. Tel-Aviv: Tel-Aviv University and the Israeli Association for Parliamentary Issues, 45–51 [in Hebrew].

2005. "The 2003 Election to the Local Authorities in Israel." *Medina Vehevra* 5 (1): 977–84 [in Hebrew].

2007. "The Reform Needed in the Israeli Electoral System." *Medina Vehevra* 6 (1): 7–17 [in Hebrew].

Brichta, Avraham, and Ami Pedahzur, eds. 2001. *Elections to the Local Authorities in Israel – 1998: Continuity or Change*? Tel-Aviv: University of Tel-Aviv [in Hebrew].

Brichta, Avraham, Eran Vigoda-Gadot, and Guy Pade, eds. 2010. *City and State in Israel: Local Government on the Eve of the Seventh Decade*. Jerusalem: Carmel [in Hebrew].

Britain. 1957. "Report of the Committee on Administrative Tribunals and Inquiries." Cmnd. 218, 1957.

1958. Tribunals and Inquiries Act.

Bruno, Michael. 1985. "Economic Stabilization: The Emergency Plan in its Early Phase." *The Economic Quarterly* 31 (124, March): 207–23 [in Hebrew].

1989. "External Shocks and Domestic Responses: Israel's Macro-economic Performance 1965–82." In *The Israeli Economy: Growing Pains*, ed. Yoram Ben-Porat. Tel-Aviv: Am Oved, 365–92 [in Hebrew].

Buchbut, Amir. 2015. "Chief of Staff Appointed Team to Study the Military Option against Iran." *Walla* June 29. http://news.walla.co.il/item/2868071 [in Hebrew] (accessed May 31, 2016).

Butler, David, and Austin Ranney, eds. 1994. *Referendums around the World*. London: Macmillan.

Byman, Daniel, and Natan Sachs. 2012. "The Rise of Settler Terrorism: The West Bank's Other Violent Extremists." *Foreign Affairs* (August 14).

Byrne, Janet, ed. 2012. *The Occupy Handbook*. New York: Back Bay Books.

Byrnes, Rita M., ed. 1990. *A Country Study*. Washington, DC: Library of Congress, Federal Research Division.

ed. 1996. *A Country Study: South Africa*. Library of Congress, Federal Research Division, May.

Caiden, Gerald E. 1970. *Israel's Administrative Culture*. Berkeley, CA: Institute of Governmental Studies, University of California.

Caplan, Kimmy. 2006. "Profiles in the Haredi Press in Israel: History, Development, and Characteristics." *Segmental Media in Israel* 3: 1–47.

Carmel, Amos. 2001. *Everything is Political*. Tel-Aviv: Dvir Publications [in Hebrew].

Carmon, Naomi. 1988. "Planned Social Change: An Evaluation." *Megamot* 31 (3–4): 299–321 [in Hebrew].

Caspi, Dan. 1986. "Electoral Rhetoric and Political Polarization: The Begin–Peres Debates." *European Journal of Communication* 1: 447–62.

1990. *Government and Politics / Mass Media and Politics*. Unit 10. Ra'anana: Open University [in Hebrew].

1996. "American-Style Electioneering in Israel: Americanization Versus Modernization." In *Politics, Media and Modern Democracy*, eds. David L. Swanson and Paolo Mancini. Westport, CT: Praeger, 173–92.

1998. "The Agenda-setting Function of the Mass Media in the Knesset." In *The Mass Media in Israel*, eds. Dan Caspi and Yehiel Limor. Ra'anana: Open University, 507–20 [in Hebrew].

1998a. "Decentralizing the Media in a Centralized System." In *The Mass Media in Israel*, eds. Dan Caspi and Yehiel Limor. Ra'anana: Open University, 207–17 [in Hebrew].

2005. *Due to Technical Difficulties: The Fall of the Israeli Broadcasting Authority*. Tel-Aviv: Tzivonim [in Hebrew].
ed. 2007. *Communication and Politics in Israel*. Jerusalem and Tel-Aviv: Van Leer Jerusalem Institute and Hakibbutz Hameuchad [in Hebrew].
2007a. "On Elites in the Media." In *New Elites in Israel*, eds. Eliezer Ben-Rafael and Yitzhak Sternberg. Jerusalem: Bialik Institute, 137–57 [in Hebrew].
Caspi, Dan, and Nelly Elias. 2000. "Being Here but Feeling There: The Case of Russian Media in Israel." *Israeli Sociology: A Journal for the Study of Israeli Society* 2 (2): 415–55 [in Hebrew].
Caspi, Dan, and Mustafa Kabha. 2001. "From Holy Jerusalem to the Wellspring: Competing Trends in Israel's Arabic Press." *Panim* 16: 44–55 [in Hebrew].
Caspi, Dan, and Baruch Leshem. 2007. "From Electoral Propaganda to Political Advertising: On Changes in the Election Campaigns and the Study of Them." In *Communication and Politics in Israel*, ed. Dan Caspi. Jerusalem and Tel-Aviv: Van Leer Jerusalem Institute and Hakibbutz Hameuchad, 110–33 [in Hebrew].
Caspi, Dan, and Eleanor Lev. 2009. "Fast Americanization: The Adoption of New Media in the 2009 Knesset Electoral Campaign." *Kesher* 39: 6–16 [in Hebrew].
Caspi, Dan, and Yehiel Limor. 1992. *The Mediators: The Mass Media in Israel, 1948–1990*. Tel-Aviv: Am Oved [in Hebrew].
eds. 1998. *The Mass Media in Israel*. Ra'anana: Open University [in Hebrew].
1999. *The In/Outsiders: The Media in Israel*. Cresskill, NJ: Hampton Press.
Caspit, Ben, and Ilan Kfir. 1997. *Netanyahu: The Road to Power*. Tel-Aviv: Maariv [in Hebrew].
Central Bureau of Statistics (CBS). Various years. *Statistical Abstract of Israel*.
1998. "Daily Newspapers and Periodicals Published in Israel, 1995." *Current Briefings in Statistics* No. 4, Jerusalem.
2003. *Survey of Household Expenditures 2001*. www.cbs.gov.il/hodaot2004/19_04_253e.htm (accessed August 3, 2016).
2004. "Characterizing and Categorizing the Local Authorities by Socioeconomic Level of the Population 2001." Publication 1222.
2008. *Social Survey 2007*. June [in Hebrew].
2008a. *The Local Authorities in Israel 2006*. Publication 1315. Jerusalem.
2010. *Social Survey 2009: Religiosity in Israel – Characteristics of Different Groups*. www.cbs.gov.il/reader/newhodaot/hodaa_template.html?hodaa=201019101 [in Hebrew] (accessed June 21, 2016).
2010a. *The Arab Population of Israel 2008* [in Hebrew].
2011. *Defense Expenditures in Israel 1950–2009*. Publication 1449. Jerusalem. www.cbs.gov.il/webpub/pub/text_page.html?publ=7&CYear=2009&CMonth=1 [in Hebrew] (accessed August 8, 2016).
2012. "Monthly Income and Consumption Expenditure per Household, Population Group, and Number of Persons in Household." www.cbs.gov.il/publications15/1593/pdf/t06.pdf (accessed June 7, 2016).
2013. "Report of the Demographic Situation of Israel in 2011." July. www.cbs.gov.il/population/demo_skira.pdf [in Hebrew] (accessed May 4, 2016).
2013a. "Survey of Household Expenditures." www.cbs.gov.il/publications15/1613/pdf/t15.pdf (accessed June 7, 2016).
2014. "Paid Income of Employees" from the 2014 Household Expenditure Survey. www.cbs.gov.il/reader/newhodaot/hodaa_template.html?hodaa=201515276 [in Hebrew] (accessed June 7, 2016).
2014a. *Social Survey Data Generator*. http://surveys.cbs.gov.il/Survey/survey.htm [in Hebrew] (accessed June 22, 2016).
2014b. *The Ethiopian Population of Israel*. November [in Hebrew].
2014c. "Expenditures and Income of Non-Profit Institutions: 2011–2013." Media Release August 18. www.cbs.gov.il/hodaot2014n/08_14_217e.pdf (accessed June 28, 2016).
2016. "Israel's Foreign Trade 2015." January 13. www.cbs.gov.il/reader/newhodaot/hodaa_template.html?hodaa=201616009 [in Hebrew] (accessed May 5, 2016).

Chazan, Naomi. 2005. "A Constitution? Not So Fast." *Haaretz* December 27 [in Hebrew].
Chester, Daniel Norman, and Nona Bowring. 1962. *Questions in Parliament*. Oxford: Clarendon Press.
Churchman, Arza. 1967. "Editorial." *Management Science* 14 (4): 141–46.
1988. "Resident Involvement in Project Renewal: Goals and Achievements." *Megamot* 31 (3–4): 342–62 [in Hebrew].
Cohen, Amichai, and Stuart Cohen. 2014. *Israel's National Security Law*. Tel-Aviv: Yediot Aharonot [in Hebrew].
Cohen, Asher. 1997. "State and Religion: Seculars, Religious, and Ultra-Orthodox." In *The First Decade 1948–1958*, eds. Zvi Zameret and Hanna Yablonka. Jerusalem: Ben-Zvi Institute, 227–42 [in Hebrew].
1999. "Idol worship." *The Seventh Eye* 19 (March) [in Hebrew].
2004. *Israeli Assimilation: The Absorption of Non-Jews into Israeli Society and its Influence on the Collective Identity*. Tel-Aviv: The Rappaport Center for Assimilation Research and Strengthening Jewish Vitality [in Hebrew].
ed. 2004a. *Religious Zionism: A Collection of Articles in Memory of Zevulun Hammer*. Jerusalem: Bialik Institute [in Hebrew].
2005. "Religious Zionism and the National Religious Party in the 2003 Elections: An Attempt to Respond to the Challenges of Religious, Ethnic, and Political Schism." In *The Elections in Israel 2003*, eds. Asher Arian and Michal Shamir. New Brunswick, NJ: Transaction Publishers, 187–213.
2006. *Non-Jewish Jews in Israel: Jewish and Israeli Identity and the Challenge of Expanding the Jewish Nationality in Israel*. Jerusalem: Shalom Hartman Institute and Keter Publishing House [in Hebrew].
2011. "Parties of the Scattering Camp: Religious Zionism and its Parties in the 2009 Elections." In *The Elections in Israel 2009*, eds. Asher Arian and Michal Shamir. New Brunswick, NJ: Transaction Publishers, 101–29.
Cohen, Asher, and Jonathan Rynhold. 2006. "Direct Democracy in a Deeply Divided Society: Will a Referendum Prevent a Rift in the Nation?" In *Phantom in Politics: Referenda in Israel*, ed. Dana Arieli-Horowitz. Jerusalem: Magnes Press, 139–64 [in Hebrew].
Cohen, Asher, and Bernard Susser. 2003. *From Accommodation to Escalation: Secular-Religious Conflict in Israel*. Jerusalem: Schocken [in Hebrew].
Cohen, Avner. 1998. *Israel and the Bomb*. New York: Columbia University Press.
Cohen, Ayelet, and Motti Neiger. 2007. "To Talk and to Talkback: Analyzing the Rhetoric of Talkbacks in Local Newspapers." In *Journalism. Dot. Com: Online Journalism in Israel*, ed. Tehilla Shwartz-Altshuler. Jerusalem: Israel Democracy Institute, 321–50 [in Hebrew].
Cohen, Bernard C. 1963. *The Press and Foreign Policy*. Princeton, NJ: Princeton University Press.
Cohen, Eli. 2015. "The Big Winners of TGI: *Hamevaser* and *Merkaz Ha'inyanim*; Record for *Yated* on Tuesdays." *Behadrei Haredim* March 31 [in Hebrew].
Cohen, Gili. 2015. "Defense Exports from Israel in 2014: 5.6 Billion; Sales to Africa Rose by 40%." *Haaretz* May 21. www.haaretz.co.il/news/politics/1.2642295 [in Hebrew] (accessed May 5, 2016).
Cohen, Hillel. 2000. *Present Absentees: Palestinian Refugees in Israel since 1948*. Jerusalem: Institute for Israeli Arab Studies.
Cohen, Jean L., and Andrew Arato. 1992. *Civil Society and Political Theory*. Cambridge, MA: MIT Press.
Cohen, Jonathan, Yariv Tsfati, and Tamir Sheafer. 2008. "The Influence of Presumed Media Influence in Politics." *Public Opinion Quarterly* 72 (2): 331–44.
Cohen, Joshua, and Joel Rogers. 1993. "Associations and Democracy." *Social Philosophy and Policy* 10 (2): 282–312.
Cohen, Ran. 2008. *The Battle for One's Home: Getting to the Public Housing Law*. Tel-Aviv: Hemed and Yediot Aharonot.
Cohen, Stuart A. 1995. "The Israeli Defense Forces (IDF): From a 'People's Army' to a 'Professional Army': Causes and Implications." *Armed Forces and Society* 21 (2): 237–54.

2006. "Changing Civil–Military Relations in Israel: Towards an Over-subordinate IDF?" *Israel Affairs* 12 (4, October): 769–88.

Cohen, Stuart A., and Eliezer Don-Yehiya, eds. 1986. *Comparative Jewish Politics*, vol. 2, *Conflict and Consensus in Jewish Political Life*. Tel-Aviv: Bar-Ilan University Press.

Cohen, Uri, and Nissim Leon. 2008. "Concerning the Question of the Mizrahi Middle Class." *Alpayim* 32: 83–101 [in Hebrew].

Cohen, Yeroham. 1973. *The Allon Plan*. Tel-Aviv: Hakibbutz Hameuchad [in Hebrew].

Cohen, Yinon. 1998. "Socioeconomic Gaps between Mizrahim and Ashkenazim 1975–95." *Israeli Sociology* 1 (1): 115–33 [in Hebrew].

2006. "National, Gender, and Ethnic Wage Gaps." In *In/Equality*, eds. Uri Ram and Nitza Berkowitz. Beersheva: Ben-Gurion University of the Negev, 339–47 [in Hebrew].

Cohen-Almagor, Raphael. 2007. *The Democratic Catch: Free Speech and its Limits*. Tel-Aviv: Maariv [in Hebrew].

Cohn, Haim, ed. 1962. *Law in a Developing State: Jubilee Book for Pinchas Rosen*. Jerusalem: Hebrew University [in Hebrew].

1985. "Symposium on Judicial Pardons." *Mishpatim* 15 [in Hebrew].

Cohn, Margit, and Mordechai Kremnitzer. 2005. "Judicial Activism: A Multi-Dimensional Model." *Canadian Journal of Law and Jurisprudence* 18: 333–56.

Condorcet, Nicolas de. 1785. *Essai sur l'application de l'analyse à la probabilité des décisions rendues à la pluralité des voix*. Paris: Imprimerie Royale [in French].

Conference in memory of Moshe Shani, "Local and Central Government in Israel." Haifa: Haifa University.

Conference on "The Gender Gap in Voting Patterns in Israel." 2014. Jerusalem: Center for Advancement of Women in the Public Sphere and Van Leer Jerusalem Institute, October 23.

Cotler, Amit, and Shahar Hay. 2016. "Storm over Citizenship Book: Not the Democracy We Were Raised on." *Haaretz* January 6 [in Hebrew].

Crick, Bernard, ed. 2001. *Citizens: Towards a Citizenship Culture*. Oxford: Blackwell.

2002. *Democracy: A Very Short Introduction*. Oxford: Oxford University Press.

Crozier, Michel J., Samuel P. Huntington, and Joji Watanuki. 1975. *The Crisis of Democracy: Report on the Governability of Democracies to the Trilateral Commission*. New York: New York University Press.

Czamanski, Daniel. 2003. "On the Impact of Suburbanization on Housing and Employment in Israel." Expert Opinion submitted to High Court of Justice. www.admati.org.il/Portals/0/Documents/articles/dc1.doc [in Hebrew] (accessed April 11, 2016).

Dahan, Michael. 1999. "National Security and Democracy on the Internet in Israel." *Javnost – The Public* 6 (4): 67–78.

Dahan, Momi. 2001. "The Rise of Economic Inequality." In *From Government Intervention to Market Economics: The Israeli Economy 1985–98*, ed. Avraham Ben Bassat. Tel-Aviv: Am Oved, 610–56 [in Hebrew].

2007. *Why is Poverty Widespread in Israel?* Jerusalem: Israel Democracy Institute [in Hebrew].

2009. *Third Generation Poverty*. Jerusalem: Israel Democracy Institute [in Hebrew].

2013. "Did the Melting Pot Succeed in the Economic Field?" *Economics Quarterly*: 107–52 [in Hebrew].

Dahan, Tal. 2008. *The State of Human Rights in Israel and the Occupied Territories: 2008 Report*. Jerusalem: Association for Civil Rights in Israel.

Dahan Kalev, Henriette. 1999. "The Wadi Salib Events." *Teoriya Uvikoret* 12–13: 149–58 [in Hebrew].

Dahl, Robert A. 1971. *Polyarchy*. New Haven, CT: Yale University Press.

2000. *On Democracy*. New Haven, CT: Yale University Press.

Dahlgren, Peter. 2004. "Mass Media: Introduction and Schools of Thought." In *The International Encyclopedia of the Social and Behavioral Sciences*, eds. Neil J. Smelser and Paul B. Baltes. Philadelphia, PA: Elsevier.

Dahrendorf, Ralf. 1997. *After 1989: Morals, Revolution and Civil Society*. London: Macmillan.

Dalton, Russell J. 1996. *Citizen Politics*, 2nd edn. London: Chatham House.

Dalton, Russell J., and Martin P. Wattenberg, eds. 2000. *Parties Without Partisans*. New York: Oxford University Press.

Dana, Nissim. 2000. *The Druze in Israel: Between Tradition of the Past and Challenge of the Future*. Jerusalem: Ministry of Education [in Hebrew].

Danet, Brenda. 1989. *Pulling Strings: Biculturalism in Israeli Bureaucracy*. Albany, NY: SUNY Press.

Darom, Naomi. 2015. "Thus the PR Army of the IDF Spokesperson Promotes the Top Brand in the Country." *Haaretz* February 25 [in Hebrew].

Dattel, Lior. 2014. "755,000 Children in Food Insecurity: Eight Facts about Poverty in Israel." *The Marker* June 23 [in Hebrew].

Dayan, Daniel, and Elihu Katz. 1992. *Media Events: The Live Broadcasting of History*. Cambridge, MA: Harvard University Press.

De Hartog, Amnon. 1998. "State Support for Public Institutions: The Emergence of Special Allocations." *Mishpatim* 29 (1): 75–107 [in Hebrew].

1999. *State Support for Public Institutions: Legislation Versus Reality*. Jerusalem: Floersheimer Institute for Policy Studies [in Hebrew].

De Swaan, Abram. 1973. *Coalition Theories and Cabinet Formations*. Philadelphia: Elsevier.

De Tocqueville, Alexis. [1835] 2003. *Democracy in America*. New York: Penguin Classics.

Dery, David. 1994. *Who Governs Local Government?* Jerusalem and Tel-Aviv: Israel Democracy Institute and Hakibbutz Hameuchad [in Hebrew].

1999. "Local Government: De Facto Decentralization." In *Public Policy in Israel*, eds. David Nachmias and Gila Menahem. Jerusalem: Israel Democracy Institute, 159–73 [in Hebrew].

2000. "Agenda Setting and Problem Definition." *Policy Studies* 21 (1): 37–47.

2005. *Controlling Government: Norms and Sayings*. Jerusalem: Hebrew University, School of Public Policy [in Hebrew].

Deutsch, Karl W. 1963. *The Nerves of Government: Models of Political Communication and Control*. Glencoe, IL: Free Press.

Deutsch, Sinai. 1987–88. "Jewish Law in Court Rulings." *Mehkarei Mishpat* 6: 7–37 [in Hebrew].

Diamond, Larry. 1993. "Democracy as Paradox." In *Israeli Democracy under Stress*, eds. Ehud Sprinzak and Larry Diamond. Boulder, CO: Lynne Rienner Publishers, 21–43.

Diamond, Larry, and Richard Gunther, eds. 2001. *Political Parties and Democracy*. Baltimore: Johns Hopkins University.

Dinstein, Yoram. 1971. "Zion Shall Be Redeemed in International Law." *HaPraklit* 27: 5 [in Hebrew].

Diskin, Avraham. 2000. "Rethinking De Swaan (1973): A Note on Closed Coalitions, Uni-Dimensionality and the Role of Sectarian Political Parties." In *Parties, Elections and Cleavages – Israel in Comparative and Theoretical Perspective*, eds. Reuven Y. Hazan and Moshe Maor. London: Frank Cass, 141–47.

Diskin, Abraham, and Hanna Diskin. 1988. *How to Choose: Voting Systems in Parliamentary Elections*. Jerusalem: Jerusalem Institute of Israel Studies [in Hebrew].

Diskin, Avraham, and Avi Eden. 1999. *The Rational Voter in the Municipal Elections in Israel*. Jerusalem: Floersheimer Institute for Policy Studies [in Hebrew].

Diskin, Avraham, and Itzhak Galnoor. 1990. "Political Distances between Knesset Members and Coalition Behaviour: The Peace Agreements with Egypt." *Political Studies* 38: 710–17.

Dobrin, Nurit. 2015. *Equal Opportunities in Education: Demographic and Socioeconomic Barriers*. Working Paper Series 19, January. Jerusalem: Central Bureau of Statistics [in Hebrew].

Dolev, Talal, Rachel Szabo-Lael, Hillel Schmid, and Dorit Bar-Nir. 2008. *"Towards the Community" Policy: Evaluation Study*. Jerusalem: Myers, JDC, Brookdale Institute, and the Ministry of Social Affairs and Services, September.

Don-Yehiya, Eliezer. 1986. "Conflict and Consensus in Jewish Political Life." In *Comparative Jewish Politics*, vol. 2, *Conflict and Consensus in Jewish Political Life*, eds. Stuart A. Cohen and Eliezer Don-Yehiya. Tel-Aviv: Bar-Ilan University Press.

1997. *The Politics of Accommodation: Conflict Resolution on Matters of Religion in Israel*. Jerusalem: Floersheimer Institute for Policy Studies [in Hebrew].

1998. "Religious Zionism and Questions of Immigration and Absorption." In *Ingathering of the Exiles: Aliyah to the Land of Israel, Myth and Reality*, ed. Dvora Hacohen. Jerusalem: Zalman Shazar Center [in Hebrew].

ed. 2005. *The Disengagement Plan: Halakha versus Democracy?* Tel-Aviv: Bar-Ilan University [in Hebrew].

Don-Yehiya, Eliezer, and Charles Liebman. 1977. "Separation between Religion and State: Slogan and Content." In *The Political System in Israel*, eds. Moshe Lissak and Emanuel Gutmann. Tel-Aviv: Am Oved, 376–83 [in Hebrew].

Dor, Gal, and Menachem Hofnung. 2006. "Litigation as Political Participation." *Israel Studies* 11 (2, Summer): 131–57.

Dor, Ofir. 2015. "Channel 10 CEO to Employees: We Did It, the Ownership Agreement was Signed with the RGE Group." *Calcalist* June 2 [in Hebrew].

Dorner, Dalia. 1999. "Does Israel Have a Constitution?" *St. Louis Law Journal* 43: 1325–35.

Doron, Abraham. 2005. "'From Welfare to Work' Programs: Historical and Intellectual Sources." In *Society and Economy in Israel: Historical and Contemporary Perspectives*, eds. Avi Bareli, Daniel Gutwein, and Tuvia Friling. Beersheva: Ben-Gurion Institute, Ben-Gurion University of the Negev, 519–40 [in Hebrew].

Doron, Abraham, and Ralph Kramer. 1991. *The Welfare State in Israel: The Evolution of Social Security Policy and Practice*. Boulder, CO: Westview.

Doron, Gideon, and Giora Goldberg. 1990. "No Big Deal: Democratization and the Nomination Process." In *The Elections in Israel – 1988*, eds. Asher Arian and Michal Shamir. Boulder, CO: Westview Press, 155–71.

Dotan, Yoav. 2000. "Does Israel Need a Constitutional Court?" *Mishpat Umimshal* 5: 120–24 [in Hebrew].

Dotan, Yoav, and Menachem Hofnung. 2001. "Interest Groups in the Israeli High Court of Justice." *Law and Policy* 23 (1): 1–27.

2005. "Legal Defeats – Political Wins. Why Do Elected Representatives Go to Court?" *Comparative Political Studies* 38 (1): 75–103.

Dowty, Alan. 1998. The Jewish State: A Century Later. University of California. Press.

2001. "Establishing a State and Nation Building." In *Israel in the First Decade*, Unit 1, ed. Benyamin Neuberger. Ra'anana: Open University [in Hebrew].

Dromi, Uri, ed. 2005. *Brethren Dwelling Together: Orthodoxy and Non-Orthodoxy in Israel: Positions, Propositions, and Accords*. Jerusalem: Israel Democracy Institute [in Hebrew].

Dror, Yehezkel. 1989. *Memorandum to the Prime Minister*. Jerusalem: Akademon [in Hebrew].

Dror, Yuval. 2009. "The Actual is not Reality on the Internet." *The Seventh Eye* March 15. www.the7eye.org.il/17026 [in Hebrew] (accessed August 30, 2016).

2009a. "The Frenzy for Now." *Panim* 48: 7–14 [in Hebrew].

Drory, Ze'ev. 2005. *The Israel Defense Force and the Foundation of Israel: Utopia in Uniform*. London and New York: Routledge and Curzon.

Druckman, James N. 2003. "The Power of Television Images: The First Kennedy–Nixon Debate Revisited." *Journal of Politics* 65 (2, May): 559–71.

Duverger, Maurice. 1955. *Political Parties*. Edison, NJ: John Wiley.

1972. *Political Parties*. London: Methuen.

Dvori, Nir. 2015. "Orders from Ya'alon: Administrative Detention for Jews Too." *Mako* August 2. www.mako.co.il/news-military/security-q3_2015/Article-444ef92768cee41004.htm [in Hebrew] (accessed May 3, 2016).

Easton, David. 1965. *A Framework for Political Analysis*. Englewood Cliffs, NJ: Prentice Hall.

Ecenbarger, W. 2009. "Luzerne's Youth Court Scandal: How? Why?" *Philadelphia Inquirer*, October 25.

Eckstein, Zvi, and Yoram Weiss. 2001. "Integration of Immigrants from the Soviet Union in the Israeli Job Market." In *From Government Intervention to Market Economics: The Israeli Economy 1985–98*, ed. Avraham Ben Bassat. Tel-Aviv: Am Oved, 435–59 [in Hebrew].

Economist. 1998. "The New-Look BBC: The BBC is Remodeling Itself to Ape the Big American Media Companies." August 29.

Efrat, Elisha. 1997. "Development Towns." In *The First Decade 1948–1958*, eds. Zvi Zameret and Hanna Yablonka. Jerusalem: Ben-Zvi Institute, 103–12 [in Hebrew].

2014. *The Burden of the Jewish Settlements: Geopolitical Settlement in an Occupied Region.* Tel-Aviv: Sifrei Tzameret [in Hebrew].

Efrati, Herzliya, ed. 2003. *Introduction to National Security*. Tel-Aviv: Defense Ministry Publications [in Hebrew].

Eilam, Uzi. 2007. "Defense Export Control in 2007: State of Affairs." *Strategic Assessment* 9 (4, March). Tel-Aviv: Institute for National Security Studies. www.inss.org.il/uploadImages/systemFiles/AdkanEng9_4_Eilam.pdf (accessed April 9, 2016).

Eilam, Yigal. 1991. *Complying with Orders*. Jerusalem: Keter Publishing House [in Hebrew].

Eisenstadt, Shmuel N. 1996. "The Struggle over Symbols of Collective Identity and their Boundaries in Post-Revolutionary Israeli Society." In *Zionism: A Contemporary Controversy*, eds. Pinhas Ginossar and Avi Bareli. Beersheva: Ben-Gurion Institute, Ben-Gurion University of the Negev, 1–29 [in Hebrew].

2005. "Israeli Society between Sectarianism and Integration." In *Society and Economy in Israel: Historical and Contemporary Perspectives*, eds. Avi Bareli, Daniel Gutwein, and Tuvia Friling. Beersheva: Ben-Gurion Institute, Ben-Gurion University of the Negev, vol. 1, 7–31 [in Hebrew].

Elazar, Daniel, ed. 1981. *Kinship and Consent: The Jewish Political Tradition and its Contemporary Manifestations*. Lanham, MD: University Press of America.

1988. *Introduction to the Constitution of the State of Israel*. Jerusalem: Jerusalem Center for Public Affairs.

2001. "The Local Dimension of Government and Politics in Israel." In *Local Government in Israel*, eds. Daniel Elazar and Chaim Kalchheim. Jerusalem: Jerusalem Center for Public Affairs [in Hebrew].

Elbaz, Sagi, and Daniel Bar-Tal. 2016. "Dissemination of Culture of Conflict in the Israeli Mass Media: The Wars in Lebanon as a Case Study." *The Communication Review* 19 (1): 1–34.

Eldar, Akiva, and Idith Zertal. 2007. *Lords of the Land: The War over Israel's Settlements in the Occupied Territories 1967–2007*. New York: Nation Books.

Elizur, Yuval, and Eliahu Salpeter. 1973. *Who Rules Israel*. New York: Harper & Row.

Ellul, Jacques. 1973. *Propaganda: The Formation of Men's Attitudes*. Trans. Konrad Kellen and Jean Lerner. New York: Vintage Books.

Elon, Menachem. 1987. "More about the Foundations of Law Act." *Shenaton Hamishpat Ha'Ivri* 13: 227–56 [in Hebrew].

1988. *Jewish Law*, 3rd edn. Jerusalem: Magnes Press [in Hebrew].

1998. "These Are Obiter Dicta…Based on a False Premise and Should Be Reversed: Demurrals and Musings about the Bavli and Lev Affairs." In *Multiculturalism in a Democratic and Jewish State*, eds. Menachem Mautner, Avi Sagi, and Ronen Shamir. Tel-Aviv: Ramat Publishers, 361–407 [in Hebrew].

Elran, Meir, and Altshuler, Alex. 2014. "Operation Protective Edge: Lessons from the Civilian Front." *INSS Insight*, 581. Tel-Aviv: Institute for National Security Studies, July 31. www.inss.org.il/publication/operation-protective-edge-lessons-from-the-civilian-front-interim-summary/ (accessed October 18, 2017).

Elster, Jon. 1998. "Introduction." In *Deliberative Democracy*, ed. Jon Elster. Cambridge, UK: Cambridge University Press, 1–18.

Emerson, Kirk, Nabatchi, Tina, and Balogh, Stephen. 2012. "An Integrative Framework for Collaborative Governance." *Journal of Public Administration Research and Theory* 22 (1): 1–29.

Endeweld, Miri, Alex Fruman, and Daniel Gottlieb. 2008. *Poverty and Social Gaps in 2007 – Annual Report*, National Insurance Institute. www.btl.gov.il/English%20Homepage/Publications/Poverty_Report/Documents/oni2007-E.pdf (accessed September 16, 2015).

Enoch, David, Iddo Porat, Re'em Segev, and Mordechai Kremnitzer. 2007. *Collateral Damage: The Harming of Innocents in the War against Terror*. Jerusalem: Israel Democracy Institute.

Epstein, Alek D. 1999. "In Search of Legitimacy: Development of Conscientious Objection in Israel from the Founding of the State to the Lebanon Campaign." *Israeli Sociology* 1 (2): 319–54 [in Hebrew].

2003. "On the Collapse of the Normative Framework of Citizens' Commitment to the Army in the 1990s." In *In the Name of Security: The Sociology of War and Peace in Israel in Changing Times*, eds. Majid al-Haj and Uri Ben Eliezer. Haifa: Haifa University, 215–39 [in Hebrew].

2006. "The Impact of the Arab–Israeli Conflict on the Political Behavior of the 'Russian' Israelis." *Social Issues in Israel* 2: 94–115 [in Hebrew].

Erez, Ram, ed. 2006. *Relations between the Civilian and Military Echelons in Israel: Against the Backdrop of Military Conflicts*. Tel-Aviv: Jaffee Center for Strategic Studies, Tel-Aviv University [in Hebrew].

Ettinger, Yair. 2002. "Fond Memories of Days Gone By." *Haaretz* October 17 [in Hebrew].

2009. "Rabbinate Stalls on Protected Hospital Wing." *Haaretz* January 22. www.haaretz.com/rabbinate-stalls-on-protected-hospital-wing-1.268605 (accessed June 28, 2016).

2015. "A Quiet Coup: Young Religious Women Are Flocking to the Israeli Army." *Haaretz* November 25. www.haaretz.com/israel-news/1.677390 (accessed October 16, 2017).

2015a. "Defying Chief Rabbinate, Prominent Rabbis Form Alternative Conversion Court." *Haaretz* August 10.

Ettinger, Yair, and Dan Even. 2009. "Rabbinate Accepts Bill Equating Brain Death with End of Life." *Haaretz* September 24. www.haaretz.com/rabbinate-accepts-bill-equating-brain-death-with-the-end-of-life-1.7358 (accessed June 28, 2016).

Etzioni, Amitai. 1959. "Alternative Ways to Democracy: The Example of Israel." *Political Science Quarterly* 74: 196–214.

Etzioni-Halevy, Eva. 1975. "Protest Politics in the Israeli Democracy." *Political Science Quarterly* 90 (3): 497–520.

1993. *The Elite Connection and Democracy in Israel*. Tel-Aviv: Sifriyat Hapoalim [in Hebrew].

Etzioni-Halevy, Eva, and Rina Shapiro. 1977. *Political Culture in Israel*. Westport, CT: Praeger.

European Social Survey. 2010 and 2012. www.europeansocialsurvey.org/ (accessed September 27, 2017).

Even, Shmuel. 2015. "The Cost of Defense in Israel: Security Expenditures and Recommendations for Setting the Security Budget." Memorandum 146. Tel-Aviv: Institute for National Security Studies. www.inss.org.il/he/wp-content/uploads/sites/2/systemfiles/memo146_7%20(3).pdf (accessed October 18, 2017).

Even, Shmuel, and Zvia Gross. 2008. *Proposed Legislation on the IDF: Authority, Responsibility, and Civil-Military Relations*. Tel-Aviv: Institute for National Security Studies.

Even-Chorev, Nadav. 2008. *Arab NGOs for Civil and Social Change in Israel*. Jerusalem: Van Leer Jerusalem Institute.

Ezrahi, Yaron. 1997. *Rubber Bullets: Power and Conscience in Modern Israel*. New York: Farrar, Straus and Giroux.

2006. "On Wearing Out." *The Seventh Eye* 60 (January). www.the7eye.org.il/23978 [in Hebrew] (accessed July 16, 2016).

2007. "The Threat to the Future of Public Broadcasting in Israel." *Media Frameworks: An Israeli Periodical for the Media* December 1: 204–7 [in Hebrew].

Ezrahi, Yaron, Omri Ben-Shachar, and Rachel La'el. 1997. *Reforms in Public Broadcasting*. Jerusalem: Israel Democracy Institute [in Hebrew].

Ezrahi, Yaron, Zohar Goshen, and Shmuel Leshem. 2003. *Cross Ownership: Control and Competition in the Israeli Media*. Jerusalem: Israel Democracy Institute [in Hebrew].

Faust, Shmuel, ed. 1998. *Peace within Israel: Towards a Covenant*. Jerusalem: Beit Morasha [in Hebrew].

Feige, Michael. 2002. *One Space, Two Places: Gush Emunim, Peace Now and the Construction of Israeli Space*. Jerusalem: Magnes Press [in Hebrew].

2009. *Settling in the Hearts: Jewish Fundamentalism in the Occupied Territories*. Detroit: Wayne State University Press.

Fein, Y. 2009. *Thus It Was Born: Establishment of Israeli Governance 1947–1951.* Jerusalem: Carmel [in Hebrew].

Feldhay, Rivka, Yossi Yonah, and Itzhak Galnoor. 2012. "The Protest of Summer 2011: Social Activism and Deliberative Democracy." In *To Do Things Differently: A Model for a Well-Ordered Society*, eds. Yossi Yonah and Avia Spivak. Tel-Aviv: Hakibbutz Hameuchad, 25–48 [in Hebrew].

Feller, S.Z. 1987. *Fundamentals of Penal Code B*. Jerusalem: The Center for Interdisciplinary Legal Research, Hebrew University [in Hebrew].

Felsenthal, Dan. 1979. "Aspects of Coalition Payoffs: The Case of Israel." *Comparative Political Studies* 12 (2, July): 151–68.

Felsenthal, Dan, and Moshe Machover. 1995. "Is This the Way to Elect a Prime Minister? The Paradoxical Properties of an Electoral Procedure Used in Israel." *Medina, Mimshal Veyahasim Beinleumiyim* 40: 57–68 [in Hebrew].

Finer, Samuel E. 1962. *The Man on Horseback: The Role of the Military in Politics*. London: Pall Mall Press.

Finer, Samuel E., Vernon Bogdanor, and Bernard Rudden. 1995. *Comparing Constitutions*. Oxford: Clarendon Press.

Finkelstein, Ariel. 2016. *The Sabbath in Israel: A Survey*. Jerusalem: Institute for Zionist Strategies.

Fischer, Claude S. 2005. "Bowling Alone: What's the Score?" *Social Networks* 27 (2): 155–67.

Fischer, Louise, ed. 1996. "Letter to Meir Weisgal." *Chaim Weizmann – The First President: Letters and Papers*. Israel State Archives.

Fishman, Herzl. N.d. (195–?). *Israeli Civics*. Tel-Aviv: Chechik [in Hebrew].

Friedberg, Asher. 2005. "Election Financing in Local Authorities in Israel: State Audit Perspectives." *Medina Vehevra* 5 (1) [in Hebrew].

Friedman, Menachem. 1991. *Haredi Ultra-Orthodox Society: Sources, Trends, and Processes*. Jerusalem: The Jerusalem Institute for Israel Studies [in Hebrew].

2005. "And These are the Chronicles of the Status Quo: State and Religion in Israel." In *Brethren Dwelling Together: Orthodoxy and Non-Orthodoxy in Israel: Positions, Propositions, and Accords*, ed. Uri Dromi. Jerusalem: Israel Democracy Institute [in Hebrew].

Friedrich, Carl. 1949. "On the Constitution of Israel." *Molad* 2 (10): 137–40 [in Hebrew].

Frish, Felix, and Efrat Weiss. 2002. "An Explosives Belt Found in a Palestinian Ambulance." *YNet* March 27. www.ynet.co.il/articles/0,7340,L-1795050,FF.html [in Hebrew] (accessed November 11, 2015).

Fukuyama, Francis. 2004. *State Building*. Ithaca, NY: Cornell University Press.

Galili, Yehudit. 2005. "The State Comptroller: A Comparative Survey." Submitted to the Knesset State Control Committee. Jerusalem: Knesset Research and Information Center.

Gallagher, Michael. 1991. "Proportionality, Disproportionality, and Electoral Systems." *Electoral Studies* 10: 33–51.

Galnoor, Itzhak. 1961. "Coalition Negotiations after Election of the Fifth Knesset." Seminar paper. Jerusalem: The Hebrew University of Jerusalem [in Hebrew].

1973. "Inquiry Commissions as a Government Decision-Making Mechanism." *Netivei Irgun Uminhal* 1: 3–11 [in Hebrew].

1975. "Government Secrecy: Exchanges, Intermediaries and Middlemen." *Public Administration Review* 35: 32–42.

1975a. "Politics and Leaks." *Molad* 35–36: 67–76 [in Hebrew].

ed. 1977. *Government Secrecy in Democracies*. New York: Harper & Row and New York University Press.

1977a. "Transformation in the Israeli Political System since the Yom Kippur War." *Medina Umimshal* 11 [in Hebrew].

1980. "The Style and the Pose." *Haaretz* November 4 [in Hebrew].

1982. *Steering the Polity: Communication and Politics in Israel*. London and Beverly Hills, CA: Sage Publications.

1982a. "Israeli Democracy and Citizen Participation." *Molad* 41: 71–87 [in Hebrew].

1984. "A Trend of Extremism." *Haaretz* September 6 [in Hebrew].
1984a. "The Voices of the Soldiers in Search of a Leader." *Haaretz* September 2 [in Hebrew].
1987. "Introduction." In *Interest Groups in Israel*, ed. Yael Yishai. Tel-Aviv: Am Oved and the Eshkol Institute, 1–10 [in Hebrew].
1989. "Consensus and Dissension in Israel after the War of Independence." In *Israeli Society*, ed. Shmuel Stempler. Tel-Aviv: Ministry of Defense Publication [in Hebrew].
1989a. "Secrecy." *International Encyclopedia of Communications*. Oxford: Oxford University Press, vol. 4, 34–37.
1991. "Introduction." In *The Political Economy of Israel*, Yair Aharoni. Tel-Aviv: Am Oved and the Eshkol Institute, i–iii.
1992. "A Rollercoaster." *Haaretz* January 1 [in Hebrew].
1992a. "Assumptions without Proof." *Maariv* January 1 [in Hebrew].
1993. "Orwell's Ministry of Propaganda." *Maariv* March 3 [in Hebrew].
1993a. "Political Agreements." *Medina Umimshal* 38: 97–105 [in Hebrew].
1995. *The Partition of Palestine: Decision Crossroads in the Zionist Movement*. Albany, NY: SUNY Press.
1996. "The Crisis in the Israeli Political System." In *Israel Approaching 2000*, eds. Moshe Lissak and Baruch Knei-Paz. Jerusalem: Magnes Press, 144–75 [in Hebrew].
1998. "Parties, Communications and Israeli Democracy." In *The Demise of Political Parties: Israeli Democracy in Crisis*, ed. Dan Koren. Tel-Aviv: Hakibbutz Hameuchad, 195–214 [in Hebrew].
1998a. "Lights Out." *The Seventh Eye* 15 (July) [in Hebrew].
1999. "Foreword." In *The In/Outsiders: The Media in Israel*, eds. Dan Caspi and Yehiel Limor. Cresskill, NJ: Hampton Press, xv–xvi.
2001. "Civil Service." In *The International Encyclopedia of the Social and Behavioral Sciences*, eds. Neil J. Smelser and Paul B. Baltes. Philadelphia, PA: Elsevier, vol. 3, 1886–91.
2003. *No Mr. Commissioner: Behind the Scenes of Israeli Politics and Administration*. Tel-Aviv and Jerusalem: Yediot Aharonot and the Jerusalem Institute for Israel Studies [in Hebrew].
2004. "The Judicialization of the Public Sphere in Israel." *Israel Law Review* 37 (2–3): 500–42 [in Hebrew].
2006. "And Maybe We Should Also Privatize the Courts?" *Haaretz* June 18 [in Hebrew].
2008. "The Conception Underlying the Conception: The Yom Kippur War and the Lessons Not Learned." In *National Trauma: The Yom Kippur War after Thirty Years*, eds. Moshe Shemesh and Ze'ev Drori. Beersheva: Ben-Gurion University [in Hebrew].
2009. "Academic Freedom under Political Duress: Israel." *Social Research* 76 (2): 541–60.
2011. *Public Management in Israel: Development, Structure, Functions, and Reforms*. London: Routledge.
2015. "Israel: Interrupted Democratic Development?" *Turkish Policy Quarterly (TPQ)* 14 (1), May: 148–60.
2015a. "The Settlement Division." *The Marker* April 28 [in Hebrew].

Galnoor, Itzhak, and Menachem Hofnung, eds. 1993. *The Government of Israel*, Anthology of Documents. Jerusalem: Nevo [in Hebrew].

Galnoor, Itzhak, Jennifer Oser, and Alma Gadot-Perez. 2012. *The Political Environment of Policy Making in Israel*. Jerusalem: Magnes [in Hebrew].

Galnoor, Itzhak, Amir Paz-Fuchs, and Nomika Zion, eds. 2015. *Privatization Policy in Israel: State Responsibility and the Boundaries between the Public and the Private*. Jerusalem: Van Leer Jerusalem Institute [in Hebrew]. To be published in English by Palgrave Macmillan in 2018.

Ganayem, Asmaa, Sheizaf Rafaeli, and Faisal Azaiza. 2009. "Digital Divide: Internet Usage within Arab Society in Israel." *Megamot* 46 (1–2): 164–96 [in Hebrew].

Gaoni, Yael. 2009. "The First Day of Election Propaganda: Cumulative Rating of 20.8% for the Various Channels." *Globes* January 28 [in Hebrew].

Garment, Suzanne. 1999. *Scandal: The Culture of Mistrust in American Politics*. New York: Times Books/Random House.

Gavison, Ruth. 1976. "On the Correct Interpretation of Parag. 15 of the Commissions of Inquiry Law 1968 and the Involvement of the High Court of Justice." *Mishpatim* 6: 548–61 [in Hebrew].

1985. "The Controversy over Israel's Bill of Rights." *Israel Yearbook of Human Rights* 15: 113–54.

1998. *The Constitutional Revolution: Reality or Self-Fulfilling Prophecy?* Jerusalem: Israel Democracy Institute [in Hebrew].

2000. "Public Involvement of the High Court of Justice: A Critical Perspective." In *Judicial Activism For and Against: The Role of the Supreme Court in Israeli Society*, eds. Ruth Gavison, Mordechai Kremnitzer, and Yoav Dotan. Jerusalem: Magnes Press, 106–12 [in Hebrew].

2003. "Constitutions and Political Reconstruction? Israel's Quest for a Constitution." *International Sociology* 18 (1, March): 53–70.

2008. "Core Curriculum Bypass Legislation." *Haaretz* July 3 [in Hebrew].

Gavison, Ruth, and Dafna Hacker, eds. 2000. *The Jewish–Arab Rift in Israel: A Reader.* Jerusalem: Israel Democracy Institute [in Hebrew].

Gavison, Ruth, and Yaacov Medan. 2003. *The Basis for a New Social Compact between Observant and Secular Jews in Israel.* Jerusalem: Israel Democracy Institute and Avi Chai Israel Foundation [in Hebrew].

Gavison, Ruth, and Hagai Shneidor, eds. 1991. *Human Rights and Civil Liberties in Israel: A Reader.* 3 volumes. Tel-Aviv: Frizer Communication [in Hebrew].

Gavison, Ruth, Mordechai Kremnitzer, and Yoav Dotan. 2000. *Judicial Activism For and Against: The Role of the Supreme Court in Israeli Society*. Jerusalem: Magnes Press [in Hebrew].

Gazit, Shlomo. 1995. *The Carrot and the Stick: Israel's Policy in Judea and Samaria 1967–8.* Washington, DC: Bnai Brith.

2003. *Trapped Fools: Thirty Years of Israeli Policy in the Territories*. London: Frank Cass.

2006. "Steps toward the Yom Kippur War." In *Relations between the Civilian and Military Echelons in Israel: Against the Backdrop of Military Conflicts*, ed. Ram Erez. Tel-Aviv: Jaffee Center for Strategic Studies, Tel-Aviv University, 35–40 [in Hebrew].

Gedalya, Einat, Hanna Herzog, and Michal Shamir. 2009. "Tzip(p)ing through the Elections: Gender in the 2009 Elections." In *The Elections in Israel – 2009*, eds. Asher Arian and Michal Shamir. New Brunswick, NJ: Transaction Publishers, 165–93.

Geertz, Clifford, ed. 1963. *Old Societies and New States*. New York: Free Press.

Gelber, Yoav. 1986. *Why Did They Disband the Palmach?* Jerusalem: Schocken [in Hebrew].

Ghanem, As'ad. 2001. "Elections to the Arab Local Authorities." In *Elections to the Local Authorities in Israel – 1998: Continuity or Change?*, eds. Avraham Brichta and Ami Pedahzur. Tel-Aviv: University of Tel-Aviv [in Hebrew].

2004. "About the Situation of the Arab-Palestinian Minority in Israel." *Medina Vehevra*: Special volume on the Arab minority in Israel, 4 (1): 933–52. Haifa: University of Haifa, Department of Government and Political Philosophy [in Hebrew].

2009. "The Bi-National State Solution." *Israel Studies* 14 (2).

Ghanem, Honeida. 2009. *Reinventing a Nation: Palestinian Intellectuals in Israel.* Jerusalem: Eshkol Institute and Magnes Press [in Hebrew].

Gharrah, Ramsees, ed. 2013. *Arab Society in Israel (5): Population, Society, Economy.* Jerusalem: Van Leer Jerusalem Institute.

ed. 2015. *Arab Society in Israel (7): Population, Society, Economy*. Jerusalem: Van Leer Jerusalem Institute.

Gidron, Benjamin. 2009. "Between Gaza and Beersheva – the Center and the War in the South." *Newsletter of the Israeli Center for Third Sector Research* 31 (February) [in Hebrew].

Gidron, Benjamin, and Inbal Abbou. 2014. *Social Businesses in Israel: From Exclusion to Social and Economic Inclusion.* Jerusalem: Ahvah Publishers [in Hebrew].

Gidron, Benjamin, and Yael Alon. 2007. *Database Report 2007: Patterns and Changes in the Israeli Third Sector in the Last Twenty Years.* Beersheva: Israeli Center for Third Sector Research, Ben-Gurion University of the Negev [in Hebrew].

Gidron, Benjamin, and Dikla Yogev. 2010. *Business Ventures by NPOs, Social Businesses, Social Cooperatives – Different Forms of Hybrid Organizations Combining Social and Business Goals: Some Insights from a Survey in Israel*. Istanbul Abstracts, International Society for Third-Sector Research.

Gidron, Benjamin, Yael Alon, and Rinat Ben-Nun. 2004. *Report on the Database of Israel's Third Sector: Salaries in Third Sector Organizations*. Beersheva: Israeli Center for Third Sector Research, Ben-Gurion University of the Negev [in Hebrew].

Gidron, Benjamin, Michal Bar, and Hagai Katz. 2003. *The Third Sector in Israel: Between Civil Society and the Welfare State*. Tel-Aviv: Hakibbutz Hameuchad [in Hebrew].

Gilead, Zerubavel, ed. 1963. *The Palmach Book*, 2 vols. Tel-Aviv: Hakibbutz Hameuchad [in Hebrew].

Ginossar, Pinhas, and Avi Bareli, eds. 1996. *Zionism: A Contemporary Controversy: Research Trends and Ideological Approaches*. Beersheva: Ben-Gurion Institute, Ben-Gurion University of the Negev [in Hebrew].

Gluska, Ami. 2007. "Israel's Decision to Go to War." *Middle East Review of International Affairs* 11 (June).

Golan, Arnon. 1992. "The Transfer of Abandoned Rural Arab Lands to Jews During Israel's War of Independence." *Cathedra* 63: 122–54 [in Hebrew].

Golan, Galia. 2015. *Israeli Peacemaking Since 1967: Factors Behind the Breakthroughs and Failures*. London: Routledge.

Goldberg, G. 1981. "Religious Parties in Opposition 1965–1977." In *Comparative Jewish Politics*, eds. Sam Lehman-Wilzig and Bernard Susser. Tel-Aviv: Bar-Ilan University Press, 138–57.

1992. *Political Parties in Israel: From Mass Parties to Electoral Parties*. Tel-Aviv: Tel-Aviv University [in Hebrew].

1993. "You Don't Need a Constitution to Plant Trees." *Medina, Mimshal Veyahasim Beinleumiyim* 38: 29–48 [in Hebrew].

2001. *Changes in Israeli Voter Behavior in Elections for Local Government*. Jerusalem: Jerusalem Center for Public Affairs, 249–76.

2005. "The Rise of Mizrahi Power in Local Government." *Medina Vehevra* 5 (1): 1061–70 [in Hebrew].

2006. "The Growing Militarization of the Israeli Political System." *Israel Affairs* 12 (3, July): 377–94.

Goldstein, Ken, and Zvi Gitelman. 2004. "From 'Russians' to Israelis?" In *The Elections in Israel – 2003*, eds. Asher Arian and Michal Shamir. New Brunswick, NJ: Transaction Publishers.

Goldstein, Tani. 2006. "BDI: Centralization Increases; 18 Families Control the Economy." *YNet* February 13. www.ynet.co.il/articles/0,7340,L-3215359,00.html [in Hebrew] (accessed August 12, 2016).

Gorali, Moshe. 2016. "Shaked v. High Court Natural Gas Decision: 'Wielding Authority Irresponsibly.' Mandelblit: 'The Judiciary Must not be Harmed.'" *Calcalist* April 4. www.calcalist.co.il/local/articles/0,7340,L-3685195,00.html#:g9 [in Hebrew] (accessed August 16, 2016).

Gordon, Evelyn. 1998. "How the Government's Attorney Became Its General." *Azure* 5758 (4): 75–116.

Goren, Biranit, and Noah Harnick. 1996. "Three Years, Thirty Quotes." *Kol Ha'ir* May 31 [in Hebrew].

Goren, Shlomo. 1973. *[Rabbinical] Ruling on the Brother and Sister*. Chief Rabbinate of Israel.

Gozansky, Tamar. 2008. "Kol Ha'am, the Newspaper of the Communist Party in Israel." *Tamar Gozansky Website*. http://gozansky.co.il/?p=331 [in Hebrew] (accessed March 27, 2016).

Grabelsky-Lichtman, Tsfira, Shoshana Blum-Kulka, and Jacob Shamir. 2009. "Success and Failure in Televised Political Debates." *Megamot* 46 (1–2): 7–37 [in Hebrew].

Gradus, Yehuda. 2006. "The Geography of Center and Periphery." In *In/Equality*, eds. Uri Ram and Nitza Berkowitz. Beersheva: Ben-Gurion University of the Negev, 73–81 [in Hebrew].

Grant, August E., and Jeffrey S. Wilkinson, eds. 2008. *Understanding Media Convergence: The State of the Field*. New York: Oxford University Press.
Gratch, Haya, ed. 1973. *Twenty-five Years of Social Research in Israel*. Jerusalem: Jerusalem Academic Press.
Greenberg, Hanan. 2005. "The National Service Revolution Takes Off." *YNet* February 7. www.ynet.co.il/articles/1,7340,L-3042150,00.html [in Hebrew] (accessed April 4, 2016).
Greenberg, Hanan, and Ali Waked. 2009. "IDF Checks: Only 250 of Gaza Casualties Were Civilians." *YNet* January 26. www.ynet.co.il/articles/0,7340,L-3661844,00.html [in Hebrew] (accessed April 4, 2016).
Greenberg, Yitzhak. 1991. "National Security and Military Strength: Between Statesman and Military Commander." *Documents and Research on the History of the Defense Establishment*, 40–41 [in Hebrew].
Grinberg, Lev. 1989. "Public Activists of the Histadrut and Local Authorities: The Ethnic Dimension." Jerusalem: The Jerusalem Institute for Israel Studies, no. 33 [in Hebrew].
2000. "Why Didn't We Continue in His Path?" In *Disputed Memory: Myth, Nationalism and Democracy – Essays following the Rabin Assassination*, ed. Lev Grinberg. Beersheva: Ben-Gurion University, 123–51 [in Hebrew].
2001. "Social and Political Economics." In *Trends in Israeli Society*, 2 vols., eds. Ephraim Yaar and Zeev Shavit. Ra'anana: Open University, 585–610 [in Hebrew].
2009. *Politics and Violence in Israel: Democracy Versus Military Rule*. Trans. Gila Svirsky. London: Routledge.
Gross, Eyal. 2016. "The Suspension Law: Majority Tyranny Instead of Democracy." *Haaretz* February 9.
Gross, Nachum. 1997. "Israel's Economy." In *The First Decade 1948–1958*, eds. Zvi Zameret and Hanna Yablonka. Jerusalem: Ben-Zvi Institute, 137–50 [in Hebrew].
Grossman, David. 1994. *Sleeping on a Wire*. Trans. Haim Watzman. New York: Picador.
Gurevitch, Michael, and Jay E. Blumler. 1995. *The Crisis of Public Communication*. London: Routledge.
Gutman, Yechiel. 1981. *The Attorney General Versus the Government*. Jerusalem: Idanim [in Hebrew].
Gutmann, Amy, and Dennis Thompson. 2004. *Why Deliberative Democracy?* Princeton: Princeton University Press.
Gutmann, Emanuel. 1961. "Some Observations of Politics and Parties in Israel." *Indian Quarterly* 17: 12–29.
1975. "On Personal Responsibility and Responsible Persons." *Medina Umimshal* (September): 167 [in Hebrew].
1988. "Israel: Democracy Without a Constitution." In *Constitutions in Democratic Politics*, ed. Vernon Bogdanor. Aldershot, UK: Gower, 290–308.
1996. "The Religious Cleavage." In *Israel Approaching 2000*, eds. Moshe Lissak and Baruch Knei-Paz. Jerusalem: Magnes Press, 61–73 [in Hebrew].
Guttman, Eliyahu. 1978. "The Impact of Sadat in Jerusalem on Israeli Jews." *Jerusalem: Israel Institute of Applied Social Research Newsletter* 46 [in Hebrew].
Haaretz. 1950. "Basic Laws on the Way to the Constitution." Editorial, June 15.
2003. "The Cost of the Settlements." Supplement for Rosh Hashanah 5764. September 26.
Haaretz Magazine. 2011. "Black Flag: The Attack on Democracy." November 18. www.haaretz.co.il/magazine/democracy-under-attack [in Hebrew] (accessed August 18, 2016).
Habermas, Jürgen. 2006. "Why Europe Needs a Constitution." In *The Shape of the New Europe*, eds. Ralf Rogowski and Charles Turner. Cambridge, UK: Cambridge University Press, 25–45.
Hacohen, Dvora. 1994. *Immigrants in a Storm: The Great Aliya and its Absorption in Israel 1948–1953*. Jerusalem: Ben-Zvi Institute [in Hebrew].
ed. 1998. *Ingathering of the Exiles: Aliyah to the Land of Israel, Myth and Reality*. Jerusalem: Zalman Shazar Center [in Hebrew].
2001. "Immigration and Absorption in Israel 1948–1998." In *Trends in Israeli Society*, 2 vols., eds. Ephraim Yaar and Zeev Shavit. Ra'anana: Open University, 365–486 [in Hebrew].

Hacohen, Eli. 2004. "How the Internet Weakened Military Censorship." *YNet* October 24 [in Hebrew].

Haidar, Aziz, ed. 2005. *Arab Society in Israel. Volume 1: Population, Society, Economy*. Jerusalem and Tel-Aviv: Van Leer Jerusalem Institute and Hakibbutz Hameuchad [in Hebrew].

ed. 2010. *The Collapse of Arab Local Authorities: Suggestions for Restructuring*. Jerusalem and Tel-Aviv: Van Leer Jerusalem Institute and Hakibbutz Hameuchad [in Hebrew].

Haider, Ali. 2005. *Government Policy toward Arab Citizens: Two Years since the Or Report*. Jerusalem: Sikkuy, 68–75 [in Hebrew].

ed. 2005–10. *The Equality Index of Jewish and Arab Citizens in Israel*. Jerusalem: Sikkuy.

Halabi, Musbah. 2002. *The Druze Community*. Daliat al-Carmel: Asia Publications [in Hebrew].

Haleva-Amir, Sharon. 2014. "Political Communication: Online Campaigns in the Election of the 19th Knesset." In *Annual Report: The Media in Israel 2013, Priorities, Usage and Trends*, eds. Rafi Mann and Azi Lev-On. Ariel: Institute for New Media Research, 79–90 [in Hebrew].

Halevy, Efraim. 2006. *Man in the Shadow: Inside the Middle East Crisis with a Man Who Led the Mossad*. New York: St. Martin's Press.

Halkin, Hillel. 1996. "Israel and the Assassination: A Reckoning." *Commentary* January: 27.

2010. "What Makes a Macher?" *Forward* June 9. http://forward.com/articles/128641/what-makes-a-macher (accessed August 31, 2016).

Hall, Peter A., and Rosemary C.R. Taylor. 1996. "Political Science and the Three New Institutionalisms." *Political Studies* 44: 936–57.

Handelman, Don, and Lea Shamgar Handelman. 1991. "The Presence of the Death: Memorials of National Death in Israel." *Suomen Antropogi* 4: 3–17.

Harel, Amos, and Avi Issacharoff. 2004. *The Seventh War: How We Won and Why We Lost the War with the Palestinians*. Tel-Aviv: Yediot Aharonot [in Hebrew].

Haski-Leventhal, Debbie, Hila Yogev-Keren, and Hagai Katz. 2011. *Philanthropy in Israel 2008: Patterns of Volunteering, Donations and Organ Donations*. Beersheva: Israeli Center for Third Sector Research [in Hebrew].

Hasson, Shlomo, and Michael M. Karayyani, eds. 2006. *Barriers to Equality*. Jerusalem: Floersheimer Institute for Policy Studies [in Hebrew].

Havens, Harry S. 2005. "The Evolution of the General Accounting Office: From Voucher Audits to Program Evaluations." A paper prepared for the 1989 conference of the Association for Public Policy Analysis and Management, translated into Hebrew and submitted to the Knesset's State Control Committee in 2005.

Hay, Colin. 2007. *Why We Hate Politics*. Cambridge, UK: Polity Press.

Hazan, Reuven Y. 1996. "Presidential Parliamentarism: Direct Popular Election of the Prime Minister, Israel's New Electoral and Political System." *Electoral Studies* 15 (1, February): 21–37.

1998. "Thy Destroyers and Devastators Shall Go Forth from Thee: The Effect of the Primaries on Parties." In *The Demise of Political Parties: Israeli Democracy in Crisis*, ed. Dan Koren. Tel-Aviv: Hakibbutz Hameuchad, 78–84 [in Hebrew].

1998a. "Neither Parliamentary nor Presidential: Change in the Electoral System and the Form of Government in Israel." *Politika* 2: 97–111.

2001. *Reforming Parliamentary Committees*. Columbus, OH: Ohio State University Press.

Hebrew University. 2012. "Survey: Today's Palestinians Tend More Towards Hamas than Abu Mazen." Division of Marketing and Communication. December 27. www.huji.ac.il/cgi-bin/dovrut/dovrut_search.pl?mesge135659364905872560 [in Hebrew] (accessed May 5, 2016).

Hegel, Georg Wilhelm Friedrich. [1821] 1969. *Hegel's Philosophy of Right*. Trans. T.M. Knox. New York: Oxford University Press.

Heidenheimer, Arnold J., ed. 1970. *Political Corruption*. New York: Holt, Rinehart and Winston.

Heidenheimer, Arnold J., Michael Johnston, and Victor T. LeVine, eds. 1989. *Political Corruption: A Handbook*. New Brunswick, NJ: Transaction Publishers.

Heller, H. 1933. "Political Power." In *Encyclopedia of the Social Sciences*. New York: Macmillan, vols. 11–12, 300–5.

Hermann, Tamar. 1995. "New Challenges to New Authority: Israeli Grassroots Activism in the 1950s." In *Israel: The First Decade of Independence*, eds. S. Ilan Troen and Noah Lucas. Albany, NY: SUNY Press, 105–22.

1996. *From the Bottom to Top: Social Movements and Political Protest*, Vol. 1. Ra'anana: Open University [in Hebrew].

2005. "Changes in Official Security Policy and Jewish-Israeli Attitudes toward Handling of the Israeli-Palestinian Conflict 2000–2004." In *The Israeli-Palestinian Conflict: From a Peace Process to a Violent Confrontation 2000–2005*, ed. Yaacov Bar-Siman-Tov. Jerusalem: Jerusalem Institute for Israel Studies, 194–96 [in Hebrew].

Hermann, Tamar, and Ephraim Yaar. 2001. "The 'Dovishness' of Shas – Image and Reality." In *Shas: The Challenge to Israeliness*, ed. Yoav Peled. Tel-Aviv: Yediot Aharonot, 343–89 [in Hebrew].

Hermann, Tamar, and Ephraim Yuchtman-Yaar. 1997. "Is There a Mandate for Peace? Israeli Public Opinion and the Peace Process." In *Communications and Democracy in Israel*, ed. Dan Caspi. Jerusalem and Tel-Aviv: Van Leer Jerusalem Institute and Hakibbutz Hameuchad, 191–222 [in Hebrew].

Hermann, Tamar, et al. 2011–15. *Israeli Democracy Index*. Jerusalem: Israel Democracy Institute. [The Hebrew text has more detail.]

Hermann, Tamar, Gilad Be'ery, Ella Heller, Chanan Cohen, Yuval Lebel, Hanan Mozes, and Kalman Neuman. 2015a. *The National-Religious Sector in Israel 2014*. Jerusalem: Israel Democracy Institute [in Hebrew].

Hermann, Tamar, Hila Zaban, and Yuval Lebel. 2008. "What is Anti-Politics?" Jerusalem: Israel Democracy Institute. http://en.idi.org.il/analysis/articles/anti-politics/ (accessed August 9, 2016).

Herzl, Theodor. [1896] 1988. *The Jewish State*. New York: Dover Publications.

Herzog, Hanna. 1986. *Political Ethnicity: The Image and the Reality*. Tel-Aviv: Hakibbutz Hameuchad [in Hebrew].

1999. *Gendering Politics: Women in Israel*. Ann Arbor, MI: University of Michigan Press.

2001. "Women the Rising Power: Elections 1998." In *Elections to the Local Authorities in Israel – 1998: Continuity or Change?,* eds. Avraham Brichta and Ami Pedahzur. Tel-Aviv: University of Tel-Aviv, 133–58 [in Hebrew].

Herzog Institute. 2004. "Does Society Hurt the Economy? Coverage of Social and Economic Issues in the Media." *Study Day*. Tel-Aviv: Tel-Aviv University, December 22 [in Hebrew].

Himeyn-Raisch, Naomi. 2008. "Changes in the Status of the Local Government." *Parliament* 60. Jerusalem: Israel Democracy Institute. www.idi.org.il/parliaments/4503/4508 [in Hebrew] (accessed October 18, 2017).

Hirschauge, Orr. 2009. "Bill for Electronic Ballots Expected to be Tabled in the Knesset Next Week." *The Marker* May 13 [in Hebrew].

History of the Haganah. 1954. Tel-Aviv: Ma'arkhot (an updated four-volume edition was published in 1972) [in Hebrew].

Hofnung, Menachem. 1991. *Security Needs Versus the Rule of Law 1948–1991*. Jerusalem: Nevo [in Hebrew].

1996. "Civilian Supervision over the Defense Establishment." In *Israel Approaching 2000*, eds. Moshe Lissak and Baruch Knei-Paz. Jerusalem: Magnes Press, 233–53 [in Hebrew].

1996a. *Democracy, Law and National Security in Israel*. Aldershot, UK: Dartmouth Publishing Co.

1997. "Authority, Influence, and the Separation of Powers: Judicial Review in Israel in a Comparative Perspective." *Mishpatim* 28: 212–14 [in Hebrew].

2004. "Fat Parties – Lean Candidates: Funding Israeli Internal Party Contests." In *The Elections in Israel – 2003*, eds. Asher Arian and Michal Shamir. New Brunswick, NJ: Transaction Publishers, 63–85.

2006. *Protest and Butter: The Black Panthers Demonstrations and Allocations for Social Needs*. Jerusalem: Nevo [in Hebrew].

Holtzman, Avner. 2002. *Image before My Eyes*. Tel-Aviv: Am Oved [in Hebrew].

Horev, Tuvia, and Yaakov Kop, eds. 2009. *Allocation of Resources to Social Services 2008*. Jerusalem: Taub Center for Social Policy Studies in Israel [in Hebrew].

Horne, Ron. 2008. *Differences among Local Authorities in the Property Tax for Residential Units*. Jerusalem: Floersheimer Institute for Policy Studies [in Hebrew].

Horon, Adia G. 2000. *East and Arabs, Canaan: History of the Land of the Hebrews*. Tel-Aviv: Dvir Publications [in Hebrew].

Horowitz, D. 1982. "The Israel Defence Forces: A Civilianized Military in a Partially Militarized Society." In *Soldiers, Peasants & Bureaucrats*, eds. R. Kolkowitz and A. Korbonski. London: Allen & Unwin, 77–106.

Horowitz, Dan, and Moshe Lissak. 1989. *Trouble in Utopia: The Overburdened Polity in Israel*. Albany, NY: SUNY Press.

Horowitz, Donald. 1990. "Politics of Mutual Veto: The Israeli National Coalition." In *The Elections in Israel – 1988*, eds. Asher Arian and Michal Shamir. Boulder, CO: Westview Press, 223–34.

Horowitz, Neri. 2002. *Jews – The Town is Burning! Torah Judaism between the 1999 and 2001 Elections*. Jerusalem: Floersheimer Institute for Policy Studies [in Hebrew].

Horowitz, Tamar. 1999. "Determining Factors of the Vote Among Immigrants from the Former Soviet Union." In *The Elections in Israel – 1996*, eds. Asher Arian and Michal Shamir. Albany, NY: SUNY Press, 149–70.

2001. "From Center to Periphery: The Russian Vote in the Municipal Elections." In *Elections to the Local Authorities in Israel – 1998: Continuity or Change?*, eds. Avraham Brichta and Ami Pedahzur. Tel-Aviv: Tel-Aviv University, 119–31 [in Hebrew].

2001a. "Increasing Political Power of Immigrants from the FSU in Israel: From Passive Citizenship to Active Citizenship." In *From Russia to Israel: Identity and Culture in Transition*, eds. Moshe Lissak and Elazar Leshem. Tel-Aviv: Hakibbutz Hameuchad [in Hebrew].

Hoverman, Hagai. 2008. *Against All Odds: Forty Years of Settlements in Judea and Samaria*. Jerusalem: Sifriyat Netsarim [in Hebrew].

Howard, Marc Morjé, and Leah Gilbert. 2008. "A Cross-National Comparison of the Internal Effects of Participation in Voluntary Organizations." *Political Studies* 56: 12–32.

Ilan, Amitzur. 1983. "The Political Struggle over the Establishment of the State of Israel and its Sovereignty." In *The War of Independence 1947–49*, ed. Yehoshua Ben-Arieh. Jerusalem: Keter Publishing House, vol. 10, 48–72 [in Hebrew].

1989. *Bernadotte in Palestine*. London: Macmillan.

Ilan, Shahar. 2000. "A Sectoral Knesset." *Haaretz Report: State of the Knesset* (November 2000–March 2001), November 14 [in Hebrew].

2000a. "The Knesset Enacts, the Government Ignores." *Haaretz* December 26 [in Hebrew].

2000b. *The Ultra-Orthodox Inc.: The Budgets, Evasions, and Trampling the Law*. Jerusalem: Keter Publishing House [in Hebrew].

2008. "Mitzvah, not Murder." *Haaretz* April 3. www.haaretz.com/mitzvah-not-murder-1.243229 (accessed June 28, 2016).

Ilany, Ofri. 2007. "Ashkenazi-Mizrahi Marriages Have Not Narrowed Ethnic Gap." *Haaretz* January 21.

Inglehart, Ronald F. 1989. "Political Value Orientations." In *Continuities in Political Action*, eds. M. Kent Jennings and Jan W. Van Deth. Berlin: Walter de Gruyter, 67–102.

1999. "Postmodernization Erodes Respect for Authority, but Increases Support for Democracy." In *Critical Citizens*, ed. Pippa Norris. Oxford: Oxford University Press, 250–56.

Inglehart, Ronald F., and Pippa Norris. 2003. *Rising Tide: Gender, Equality and Cultural Change around the World*. Cambridge: Cambridge University Press.

International Comparative Social Enterprise Models – ICSEM, Liege, Belgium, University of Liege. www.ces.ulg.ac.be/en_GB/research-2/International-Comparative-Social-Enterprise-Models-ICSEM-Project (accessed April 10, 2016).

International Constitutional Law. www.servat.unibe.ch/icl/ (accessed April 13, 2016).

The International Encyclopedia of the Social and Behavioral Sciences. 2001. Eds. Neil J. Smelser and Paul B. Baltes. Philadelphia, PA: Elsevier.

International Monetary Fund. 2016. *World Economic Outlook: Too Slow for Too Long*. World Economic and Financial Surveys. April. www.imf.org/external/pubs/ft/weo/2016/01/pdf/text.pdf (accessed June 23, 2016).

International Telecommunication Union. 2009. *Measuring the Information Society Report 2009: ICT Development Index*. www.itu.int/ITU-D/ict/publications/idi/material/2009/MIS2009_w5.pdf (accessed August 25, 2016).

Internet World Stats. 2015. "Internet Users in the World by Regions: November 2015." www.internetworldstats.com/stats.htm (accessed June 6, 2016).

N.d. Usage and Population Statistics. www.internetworldstats.com/stats.htm (accessed September 27, 2017).

Islamoglu, Huricihan. 2001. "Civil Society." In *The International Encyclopedia of the Social and Behavioral Sciences*, eds. Neil J. Smelser and Paul B. Baltes. Philadelphia, PA: Elsevier, 1891–97.

Israel Democracy Institute. 1997. "A Discussion about the Institution of President." Jerusalem, February 25 [in Hebrew].

1999. *Roundtable on Polls in the Era of Elections*, May 6 [in Hebrew].

2007. *Constitution by Consensus*. Jerusalem: Israel Democracy Institute. www.idi.org.il/media/4569/constitution-by-consensus.pdf [in Hebrew] (accessed October 18, 2017).

2008. "World View: Comparative Forms of Governments." *Newsletter* November 18. Jerusalem [in Hebrew].

N.d. *IDI Resources on the 2015 Elections*. http://en.idi.org.il/tools-and-data/links-to-idi-resources/the-2015-knesset-elections/idi-resources-on-the-2015-elections/ (accessed June 11, 2016).

Israel Institute of Applied Social Research. 1949. *Public Opinion on Dismissals of Government Officials, Number of Newspapers in Israel, the Yiddish and Foreign Language Press*, Publication 1. Jerusalem, April [in Hebrew].

1949a. *Public Opinion on the Number of Newspapers in Israel, the Yiddish and Foreign Language Press*. Jerusalem, April [in Hebrew].

1970. "The Continuing Survey." No. 8, June, 14.

Israel National Election Studies (INES). 1999–2015. www.ines.tau.ac.il/2013.html (accessed April 10, 2016).

Israeli Association for Parliamentary Issues. 1988. *The Justiciability of Knesset Decisions*, Colloquium at the Knesset, July 5.

1991. *Political Agreements*. Jerusalem: The Knesset.

Israeli Audience Research Board. 2013. Ratings. February. http://data.isoc.org.il/sites/default/files/mtsgt_tspyyt_vydv_btry_vvdt_hmdrvg-_ynvr_2013_1.pdf [in Hebrew] (accessed March 22, 2016).

Israeli Center for Third Sector Research. 2005. *A Quick Look at the Third Sector in Israel: Size, Sources of Funding, and Distribution of Third Sector Organizations in Israel*. Beersheva: Israeli Center for Third Sector Research, June [in Hebrew].

Israeli Press Council. 2007. *Report of the Committee to Establish Rules of Professional Ethics in Times of Conflict*. April 18 [in Hebrew].

Izikovich, Gili. 2009. "Does the Knesset Channel, Marking a Fifth Year Anniversary, Operate Independently?" *Haaretz* November 20 [in Hebrew]. www.haaretz.co.il/1.1291041 (accessed March 22, 2016).

Jabareen, Hassan. 2005. "Collective Rights and Reconciliation in the Constitutional Process: The Case of Israel." *Adalah Newsletter*, vol. 12 (April) [in Hebrew].

Jabareen, Yousef T. 2006. *An Equal Constitution for All? On a Constitution and Collective Rights of Arab Citizens in Israel*. Haifa: Mossawa Center.

2007. "NGOs as a Political Alternative: A Critical Perspective." In *The Arab Minority in Israel and Election of the 17th Knesset: Start of a New Era?*, ed. Elie Rekhess. Tel-Aviv: University of Tel-Aviv, 93–99 [in Hebrew].

Jalan, Bimal. 2005. *The Future of India: Politics, Economics and Governance*. New York: Penguin/Viking.

Jamal, Amal. 2002. "Abstention as Participation: The Labyrinth of Arab Politics in Israel." In *The Elections in Israel – 2001*, eds. Asher Arian and Michal Shamir. Jerusalem: Israel Democracy Institute, 57–98 [in Hebrew].

2006. "Referenda as Decision-Making Mechanism in Rigid Ethno-National States: Israel as Example." In *Phantom in Politics: Referenda in Israel*, ed. Dana Ariele-Horowitz. Jerusalem: Magnes Press, 165–91.

2008. "The Counter-hegemonic Role of Civil Society: Palestinian-Arab NGOs in Israel." *Citizenship Studies* 12 (3, June): 283–306.

2011. *Arab Minority in Israel: The Politics of Indigeneity*. London: Routledge.

Jamal, Amal, and Samah Bsoul. 2014. *The Palestinian Nakba in the Israeli Public Sphere: Formations of Denial and Responsibility*. Nazareth: I'lam Media Center [in Hebrew].

Jerusalem Post. 2008. "Arab Leaders Demand Government Reopen Probe into October 2000 Deaths." October 4. www.jpost.com/Israel/Arab-leaders-demand-government-reopen-probe-into-October-2000-deaths (accessed June 9, 2016).

Jewish Virtual Library. N.d. "Demographics of Israel: Jewish and Non-Jewish Population of Israel-Palestine (1517–Present)." www.jewishvirtuallibrary.org/jsource/Society_&_Culture/israel_palestine_pop.html (accessed June 17, 2016).

Johnson, Thomas J., and Barbara K. Kaye. 2004. "Wag The Blog: How Reliance on Traditional Media and the Internet Influence Credibility Perceptions of Weblogs Among Blog Users." *Journalism and Mass Communication Quarterly* 81 (3): 622–42.

Kabha, Mustafa. 2006. *The Arab Press in Israel 1948–2006 as an Apparatus in the Identity-building Process*. Tel-Aviv: Herzog Institute for Media, Politics and Society, Tel-Aviv University [in Hebrew].

Kabha, Mustafa, and Ronit Barzilai. 1996. *Refugees in their Own Country*. Givat Haviva Publication [in Hebrew].

Kabir, Omer. 2012. "The Social Knesset: Our Politicians Still Don't Understand Facebook." *Calcalist* December 9 [in Hebrew].

Kadish, Alon. 1996. "A Professional or a People's Army: The IDF at the End of the War of Independence." *Ma'arkhot* 349: 53. Tel-Aviv: Israel Ministry of Defense Publications [in Hebrew].

Kalb, Marvin, and Carol Saivetz. 2007. "The Israeli–Hezbollah War of 2006: The Media as a Weapon in Asymmetrical Conflict." *The International Journal of Press/Politics* 12 (3).

Karniel, Yuval. 1999. "Freedom of Expression on the Internet." *Alei Mishpat* 1: 163–92 [in Hebrew].

Karp, Yehudit. 1993. "Basic Law: Human Dignity and Liberty: The Biography of a Power Struggle." *Mishpat Umimshal* 1: 333–37 [in Hebrew].

Karpin, Michael, and Ina Friedman. 1998. *Murder in the Name of God: The Plot to Kill Yitzhak Rabin*. New York: Henry Holt and Company.

Kashti, Or. 2009. "State Comptroller Report 2009: Ministry of Education – Failures in Dealing with Disadvantaged Populations." *Haaretz* May 6. www.haaretz.co.il/news/education/1.1259286 [in Hebrew] (accessed April 7, 2016).

Katz, Elihu. 1969. "Mass Media in Election Campaigns." *Molad* 11–12: 551–62 [in Hebrew].

Katz, Elihu, and Hadassah Haas. 1995. "Twenty Years of Television in Israel: Are there Long-term Effects?" *Zmanim* 52: 80–91 [in Hebrew].

Katz, Elihu, and Hed Sela. 1999. *Culture Policy in Israel* (a Beracha Report). Jerusalem: Van Leer Jerusalem Institute [in Hebrew].

Katz, Hagai, and Hila Yogev. 2009. *The Third Sector's Coping with the Economic Crisis: A Glance at the Israeli Third Sector*. Beersheva: Israeli Center for the Study of the Third Sector, Ben-Gurion University of the Negev [in Hebrew].

Katz, Hagai, Esther Levinson, and Benjamin Gidron. 2007. *Philanthropy in Israel, 2006: Patterns of Giving and Volunteering of the Adult Jewish Population*. Beersheva: Israeli Center for Third Sector Research, Ben-Gurion University [in Hebrew and English].

Katz, Richard S. 1996. "Party Organizations and Finance." In *Comparing Democracies: Elections and Voting in Global Perspective*, eds. Lawrence LeDuc, Richard G. Niemi, and Pippa Norris. Thousand Oaks, CA: Sage, 107–33.

Katz, Richard S., and Peter Mair. 1992. "The Membership of Political Parties in European Democracies." *European Journal of Political Research* 22 (3, October): 329–45.

Katz, Yaacov J. 2006. "The Core Curriculum in Israel: An Educational Common Denominator for all Population Sectors." In *Towards an Educational Revolution*, ed. Dan Inbar. Jerusalem and Tel-Aviv: Van Leer Jerusalem Institute and Hakibbutz Hameuchad, 186–94 [in Hebrew].

Katz, Yossi. 2014. *The Tombstone in Israel's Military Cemetery Since 1948: Israel's Transition from Collectivism to Individualism*. Jerusalem: Magnes Press.

Kaufman, Ilana, and Rachel Israeli. 1999. "The Odd Group Out: The Arab-Palestinian Vote in the 1996 Election." In *The Elections in Israel – 1996*, eds. Asher Arian and Michal Shamir. Albany, NY: SUNY Press.

Kedar, Nir. 2009. *Mamlakhtiyut: David Ben-Gurion's Civic Thought*. Beersheva and Jerusalem: Ben-Gurion University of the Negev and Ben-Zvi Institute.

Kelsen, Hans. 1929. *Vom Wesen und Wert der Demokratie, Mohr Tübingen*, revised and expanded edition [in German]. Tübingen, Germany: J.C.B. Mohr Siebeck Verlag.

Kenig, Ofer. 2004. "A Comparative Analysis of Arab Parties in Israel." *Tarbut Demokratit* 8: 109–43 [in Hebrew].

2007. *Raising the Election Threshold*. Jerusalem: Israel Democracy Institute [in Hebrew].

2012. *Between Shamir and Ben-Gurion*. Jerusalem: Israel Democracy Institute [in Hebrew].

2014. *The Primaries System in Israel: An Interim Evaluation*. Jerusalem: Israel Democracy Institute [in Hebrew].

2015. *The Electoral Threshold, Wasted Votes, and Proportionality*. Jerusalem: Israel Democracy Institute [in Hebrew].

Kenig, Ofer, and Shlomit Barnea. 2009. "The Selection of Ministers in Israel: Is the Prime Minister 'a Master of his Domain'?" *Israel Affairs* 15 (3, July): 261–78.

Kenig, Ofer, Gideon Rahat, and Reuven Y. Hazan. 2004. "The Political Consequences of the Introduction and Repeal of the Direct Elections for the Prime Minister." In *The Elections in Israel – 2003*, eds. Asher Arian and Michal Shamir. New Brunswick, NJ: Transaction Publishers, 33–61.

Keshev: Center for the Protection of Democracy in Israel. 1999. "A Look at the News: News Coverage on Two Television Channels in Israel." January [in Hebrew].

2001. "Jewish Media or Israeli Media?" www.keshev.info/images/stories/PDF/civil_or_ethnic_media_full_text_heb.pdf [in Hebrew] (accessed October 4, 2017).

2009. March. www.keshev.org.il/siteEn/FullNews.asp?NewsID=134andCategoryID=9 (accessed July 20, 2010).

Key, V.O. 1959. "Legislative Control." In *Elements of Public Administration*, ed. Fritz Morstein-Marx. Englewood Cliffs, NJ: Prentice Hall, 312–36.

Kfir, Aharon, ed. 2005. *Local and Central Government in Israel*. Haifa: Haifa University.

Kfir, Aharon, and Jacob Reuveny, eds. *Public Administration in Israel towards the 2000s*. Tel-Aviv: Tcherikover [in Hebrew].

Kfir, Ilan, and Danny Dor. 2015. *Barak: The Wars of My Life*. Tel-Aviv: Kinneret, Zmora Bitan [in Hebrew].

Khamaisi, Rassem. 2008. "Arab Local Authorities in Temporary or Structural Crisis." In *Arab Society in Israel*, eds. Adel Manna and Ramsees Gharrah. Jerusalem: Van Leer Jerusalem Institute, vol. 2, 409–38 [in Hebrew].

ed. 2009. *Arab Society in Israel. Volume 3: Population, Society, Economy*. Jerusalem and Tel-Aviv: Van Leer Jerusalem Institute and Hakibbutz Hameuchad [in Hebrew].

2010. "Between the Hammer and the Anvil: Spatial and Structural Barriers in Outline Planning of Arab Localities in Israel." In *The Collapse of Arab Local Authorities: Suggestions for Restructuring*, ed. Aziz Haidar. Jerusalem and Tel-Aviv: Van Leer Jerusalem Institute and Hakibbutz Hameuchad, 47–75 [in Hebrew].

ed. 2011. *Arab Society in Israel (4): Population, Society, Economy*. Jerusalem and Tel-Aviv: Van Leer Jerusalem Institute and Hakibbutz Hameuchad [in Hebrew].

Khoury, Jack. 2015. "Israeli Islamic Movement Leader Sentenced to 11 Months for Incitement." *Haaretz* March 26.

Kies, Naomi. 1975. "The Effect of Policy on Public Opinion in Israel 1967–74." *Medina, Mimshal Veyahasim Beinleumiyim* 8: 36–61 [in Hebrew].

Kimche, Yigal. 1992. "Just Honor and Refreshments." *Haaretz* October 8 [in Hebrew].

Kimmerling, Baruch. 1993. "Militarism in Israeli Society." *Teorya Uvikoret* 4: 123–40 [in Hebrew].

2001. *End of the Ashkenazi Hegemony*. Jerusalem: Keter Publishing House [in Hebrew].

2004. *Immigrants, Settlers, Natives: Israel Between Plurality of Cultures and Cultural Wars*. Tel-Aviv: Am Oved [in Hebrew].

Kimmerling, Baruch, and Joel S. Migdal. 2003. *The Palestinian People: A History*. Cambridge, MA: Harvard University Press.

King, Anthony, ed. 2002. *Leaders' Personalities and the Outcomes of Democratic Elections*. Oxford: Oxford University Press.

Kirchheimer, Otto. 1966. "The Transformation of the West European Party System." In *Political Parties and Political Development*, eds. Joseph La Palombara and Myron Weiner. Princeton, NJ: Princeton University Press, 177–200.

Kishon, Ephraim. 1989. "Sallah Shabati." In *Seven Comedies of Ephraim Kishon*. Tel-Aviv: Maariv Books [in Hebrew].

Klagsbald, Avigdor. 2001. *State Commissions of Inquiry*. Jerusalem: Nevo [in Hebrew].

Klein, Claude. 2003. "A Constitutional Court: Not So Alarming." *Mehkarei Mishpat* 19 (2): 497–513 [in Hebrew].

Klinghoffer, Yitzhak. 1964. "A Declaration of Basic Human Rights (Proposed Bill)." Tel-Aviv: Liberal Party Publications [in Hebrew].

Knesset. 2015. "The Knesset in the Government System: Knesset Election Results." www.knesset.gov.il/description/eng/eng_mimshal_res.htm (accessed October 1, 2017).

Knesset Communications and Public Relations Division. 2016. "Suspension Law Approved in First Reading." Press Release, March 28. http://main.knesset.gov.il/News/PressReleases/Pages/press280316-mr.aspx [in Hebrew] (accessed June 5, 2016).

Kohn, Yehuda Pinchas. 1949. *A Constitution for Israel: A Proposal and Commentary*. State of Israel, Provisional State Council [in Hebrew].

Konstantinov, Vlacheslav. 2008. "The 'Russian' Immigration and the Elections from 1992 to 2006 – 'Formation of a Third Israel'?" In *The Elections in Israel – 2006*, eds. Asher Arian and Michal Shamir. Albany, NY: SUNY Press, 139–68 [in Hebrew].

Kop, Yaakov, ed. 2000. *Pluralism in Israel, from a Melting Pot to a Mixed Grill*. Jerusalem: Center for Social Policy Studies [in Hebrew].

Koren, Dan, ed. 1998. *The Demise of Political Parties: Israeli Democracy in Crisis*. Tel-Aviv: Hakibbutz Hameuchad [in Hebrew].

Koren, Dan, and Boaz Shapira. 1997. *Coalition Politics in Israel*. Tel-Aviv: Zmora-Bitan [in Hebrew].

Korn, Alina. 2008. "Good Intentions: The Short History of the Minority Affairs Ministry (May 1948–July 1949)." *Cathedra* 127: 113–40 [in Hebrew].

Kotev, Guy. 1999. "The End of the Censorship Era." *The Seventh Eye* 20 (September) [in Hebrew].

Kraines, Oscar. 1961. *Government and Politics in Israel*. Boston: Houghton Mifflin.

Kremnitzer, Mordechai. 1987. "The General Security Services Pardon: Did the High Court of Justice Meet the Test?" *Iyunei Mishpat* 12 (3): 595–620 [in Hebrew].

2000. "A Broad Perspective of the Role of the High Court of Justice: A Statement of Defense." In *Judicial Activism For and Against: The Role of the Supreme Court in Israeli Society*, eds. Ruth Gavison, Mordechai Kremnitzer, and Yoav Dotan. Jerusalem: Magnes Press, 235–39 [in Hebrew].

2001. "Preliminary Judicial Review at the Legislative Stage." *Models of Judicial Review, Public Council – Fifth Assembly*, November 1–2. Jerusalem: Israel Democracy Institute [in Hebrew].

Kremnitzer, Mordechai, and Ariel Bendor. 2000. *Basic Law: The Military – A Commentary*. Jerusalem: Sacher Institute, Hebrew University [in Hebrew].
Kretzmer, David. 1990. *The Legal Status of the Arabs in Israel*. Boulder, CO: Westview Press.
1990a. "The Supreme Court and the 4th Geneva Convention: Domestic Enforcement and Interpretation." *Mishpatim* 26: 49–96 [in Hebrew].
2002. *The Occupation of Justice: The Supreme Court of Israel and the Occupied Territories*. Albany, NY: SUNY Press.
Kristal, Tali, Yinon Cohen, and Guy Mundlak. 2006. *Rising Inequality and Trade Unions in Israel*. Policy Study No. 1, Program on Economy and Society. Jerusalem: Van Leer Institute [in Hebrew].
Laakso, Markku, and Rein Taagepera. 1979. "'Effective' Number of Parties: A Measure with Application to West Europe." *Comparative Political Studies* 12: 3–27.
Lachmann-Messer, Davida. 1998. "Map of the New Media: Structure and Ownership – Challenges and Dangers." In *The Mass Media in Israel*, eds. Dan Caspi and Yehiel Limor. Ra'anana: Open University, 183–91 [in Hebrew].
Lahav, Pnina. 1988. "A Barrel without Hoops: The Impact of Counterterrorism on Israel's Legal Culture." *Cardoza Law Review* 10: 529–60.
1993. "The Press and National Security." In *National Security and Democracy in Israel*, ed. Avner Yaniv. Boulder, CO: Lynne Rienner Publishers.
1997. *Judgment in Jerusalem: Chief Justice Simon Agranat and the Zionist Century*. Berkeley and Los Angeles: California University Press.
Lahav, Pnina, and David Kretzmer. 1985. "A Declaration of Human and Civil Rights in Israel." *Mishpatim* 7: 154–72 [in Hebrew].
Landau, Jacob M. 1971. *Arabs in Israel: Political Studies*. Tel-Aviv: Department of Defense [in Hebrew].
1993. *The Arab Minority in Israel 1967–1991: Political Aspects*. Oxford: Clarendon Press.
Landau, Moshe. 1989. "On Justiciability and Reasonableness in Administrative Law." *Iyunei Mishpat* 14 [in Hebrew].
1994. "Basic Law: The President." Law Faculty, Hebrew University of Jerusalem [in Hebrew].
1996. "Bestowing a Constitution on Israel by Way of Court Rulings." *Mishpat Umimshal* 3: 697 [in Hebrew].
Lankin, Eliyahu. 1974. *The Story of the Commander of the Altalena*. Tel-Aviv: Hadar [in Hebrew].
Lasswell, Harold. 1941. "The Garrison State." *American Journal of Sociology* 46: 455–68.
Laver, Michael, and Norman Schofield. 1990. *Multiparty Government: The Politics of Coalition in Europe*. New York: Oxford University Press.
Lavi, Zvi. 1998. "The 'Editors' Committee' – Myth and Reality." In *The Mass Media in Israel*, eds. Dan Caspi and Yehiel Limor. Ra'anana: Open University, 320–56 [in Hebrew].
Lavie, Ephraim, and Arik Rudnitzky. 2009. *Arab Politics in Israel and the 18th Knesset Elections*. Election Update No. 1. Tel-Aviv: Moshe Dayan Center, Konrad Adenauer Program for Jewish – Arab Cooperation, Tel-Aviv University.
eds. 2010. *Politics, Elections and Local Government in the Arab Municipalities in Israel*. Tel-Aviv: The Konrad Adenauer Program for Jewish–Arab Cooperation, Tel-Aviv University [in Hebrew].
Lavon, Pinchas. 1986. *On Values and Assets*. Tel-Aviv: Hakibbutz Hameuchad [in Hebrew].
Lavy, Victor. 2003. "Education in Recent Decades and its Effect on Social Gaps." In *Education and Social Justice in Israel: On Equality of Opportunity*, eds. Samuel Shye and Nomika Zion. Jerusalem: Van Leer Jerusalem Institute, 44–64 [in Hebrew].
Lazarsfeld, Paul, and Robert K. Merton. 1948. "Mass Communication, Popular Taste and Organized Social Action." In *The Communication of Ideas: A Series of Addresses*, ed. Lyman Bryson. New York: Institute for Religious and Social Studies, distributed by Harper.
Lebeau, Eran. 2005. "The Disengagement File: Hold Your Nose." *The Seventh Eye* 56 (May) [in Hebrew].
Lederman, Daniel, Norman V. Loayza, and Rodrigo Soares. 2005. "Accountability and Corruption: Political Institutions Matter." *Economics and Politics* 17 (1): 1–35.

Lehmann, David, and Batia Siebzehner. 2006. *Remaking Israeli Judaism: The Challenge of Shas*. London and New York: Hurst and Oxford University Press.

Lehman-Wilzig, Sam N. 1992. *Israeli Public Protest 1949–1992*. Tel-Aviv: Bar-Ilan University Press [in Hebrew].

1992a. *Wildfire: Grassroots Revolts in Israel in the Post-Socialist Era*. Albany, NY: SUNY Press.

2004. "Worth an Agora? 2003 E-lection Party Sites and Public Discourse." *Israel Affairs* 10 (4): 242–62.

Leibowitz, Yeshayahu. 1976. *Judaism, Jewish People, and the State of Israel*. Jerusalem: Schocken [in Hebrew].

Lerner, Hanna. 2004. "Democracy, Constitutionalism, and Identity: The Anomaly of the Israeli Case." *Constellations* 11 (2): 237–57.

Leshem, Elazar. 2005. "Immigrants from the FSU between Isolationism and Integration into Israeli Society." In *Society and Economy in Israel: Historical and Contemporary Perspectives*, eds. Avi Bareli, Daniel Gutwein, and Tuvia Friling. Beersheva: Ben-Gurion Institute, Ben-Gurion University of the Negev, 541–80 [in Hebrew].

Leshem, Elazar, and Moshe Sicron. 1998. "The Absorption Process of FSU Immigrants 1990–95: Main Findings." In *Portrait of an Immigration Wave: Absorption Processes of FSCU Immigrants 1990–1995*, eds. Elazar Leshem and Moshe Sicron. Jerusalem: Magnes Press, 442–64 [in Hebrew].

eds. 1998a. *Portrait of an Immigration Wave: Absorption Processes of FSCU Immigrants 1990–1995*. Jerusalem: Magnes Press [in Hebrew].

Levi, Omri. 2009. "Strictly Kosher Cell Phones: The Story of the Telephone for the Ultra-Orthodox." *YNet* January 16 [in Hebrew].

Levi-Faur, David. 1999. "More Competition, More Regulation." *Politika* 4: 27–44 [in Hebrew].

2006. "Varieties of Regulatory Capitalism: Sectors and Nations in the Making of a New Global Order." *Governance* 19: 363–66.

Levin, Hanoch. 1988. *Schitz, Heffetz, and Others: Plays*. Tel-Aviv: Hakibbutz Hameuchad [in Hebrew].

Levinger, Esther. 1993. *War Memorials in Israel*. Tel-Aviv: Hakibbutz Hameuchad [in Hebrew].

Levinson, Chaim. 2009. "IDF: More than 300,000 Settlers Live in West Bank." *Haaretz* July 27. www.haaretz.com/idf-more-than-300-000-settlers-live-in-west-bank-1.280778 (accessed May 4, 2016).

Levy, Shlomit, Hanna Levinson, and Elihu Katz. 2002. *A Portrait of Israeli Jews: Beliefs, Observance, and Values of Israeli Jews, 2000*. Jerusalem: Israel Democracy Institute and Avi Chai Israel Foundation.

Levy, Yagil. 2003. *A Different Army for Israel*. Tel-Aviv: Yediot Aharonot [in Hebrew].

2005. "Local Crisis." *The Seventh Eye* 54 (January) [in Hebrew].

2007. *From the People's Army to the Army of the Peripheries*. Jerusalem: Carmel [in Hebrew].

ed. 2015. *Mandatory Service or the Duty to Serve?* Ra'anana: Open University [in Hebrew].

2015a. *The Theocratization of the Israeli Military*. Tel-Aviv: Am Oved [in Hebrew].

Levy, Yagil, and Eti Sarig, eds. 2014. *Local Government: Between the State, the Community and the Market Economy*. Ra'anana: Open University [in Hebrew].

Liebes, Tamar, and Elihu Katz. 1986. "Patterns of Involvement in Television Fiction: A Comparative Analysis." *European Journal of Communication* 1: 151–71.

Liebman, Charles S., and Eliezer Don-Yehiya. 1983. *Civil Religion in Israel*. Berkeley, CA: University of California Press.

1984. *Religion and Politics in Israel*. Bloomington, IN: Indiana University Press.

Lifshitz, Shahar. 2006. *The Spousal Registry*. Jerusalem: Israel Democracy Institute.

Lifshitz, Yaakov. 2007. *The Economics of Producing Defense*. New York: Springer-Verlag.

Lijphart, Arend. 1984. *Democracies: Patterns of Majoritarian and Consensus Government in Twenty-one Countries*. New Haven, CT: Yale University Press.

1997. "Unequal Participation: Democracy's Unresolved Dilemma." *American Political Science Review* 91 (1): 1–14.

1999. *Patterns of Democracy: Government Forms and Performance in 36 Countries*. New Haven, CT: Yale University Press.

Limor, Nissan. 2005. *Supervision of Nonprofits*. Tel-Aviv: Globes, Library of Professional Publications, Voluntary and Nonprofit Organizations Sector [in Hebrew].

2008. "Proposal to Regulate Philanthropical Foundations in Israel." Beersheva and Tel-Aviv: Israeli Center for Third Sector Research, Ben-Gurion University of the Negev, and School of Management, Tel-Aviv University [in Hebrew].

2010. "Civil Society and the Third Sector in Israel." Presented at the Caesarea Economic Policy Planning Forum 2010. Jerusalem: Israel Democracy Institute.

ed. 2014. *Yearbook of Non-Profit Organizations in Israel: Summary of Data*. NPTech. http://nptech.org.il/wp-content/uploads/2014/08/ShnatonGiudestarDigitalFinal.pdf [in Hebrew] (accessed March 3, 2016).

Limor, Nissan, and Noy Brindt. 2014. *Legislative Principles for a New Law of Associations*. Jerusalem: Van Leer Jerusalem Institute [in Hebrew].

Limor, Yehiel. 1997. "'Le petit prince' and 'Big Brother' or the Media Industry in Israel in an Age of Change." In *Communications and Democracy in Israel*, ed. Dan Caspi. Jerusalem and Tel-Aviv: Van Leer Jerusalem Institute and Hakibbutz Hameuchad, 29–46 [in Hebrew].

2003. "Mass Media in Israel." In *Trends in Israeli Society*, 2 vols., eds. Ephraim Yaar and Zeev Shavit. Ra'anana: Open University, 1103–17 [in Hebrew].

Limor, Yehiel, and Chanan Naveh. 2007. *Pirate Radio in Israel*. Haifa: Pardes [in Hebrew].

Lindell, Geoffrey. 2003. "British Tribunals of Inquiry: Legislative and Judicial Control of the Inquisitorial Process – Relevance to Australian Royal Commissions." Research Paper No. 5, 2002–3. Melbourne: Department of the Parliamentary Library.

Lipka, Michael. 2016. "Unlike U.S., Few Jews in Israel Identify as Reform or Conservative." Pew Research Center, March 15. www.pewresearch.org/fact-tank/2016/03/15/unlike-u-s-few-jews-in-israel-identify-as-reform-or-conservative/ (accessed June 24, 2016).

Lipset, Seymour Martin. 1960. *Political Man: The Social Basis of Politics*. Garden City, NY: Doubleday.

Lissak, Moshe. 1971. "The Israeli Defense Forces as an Agent of Socialization and Education in a Democratic Society." In *The Perceived Role of the Military*, ed. M.R. Van Giles. Rotterdam: Rotterdam University Press, 325–40.

1983. "Army, Society, and Government in Israel: Paradoxes in Israeli Civil–Military Relations." *Skirah Hodshit* February–March [in Hebrew].

1996. "Ethnicity in Israel in an Historical Perspective." In *Israel Approaching 2000*, eds. Moshe Lissak and Baruch Knei-Paz. Jerusalem: Magnes Press, 74–89 [in Hebrew].

1998. "The Decline of Political Parties and Rise of Sectoral Politics." In *The Political System in Israel*, eds. Moshe Lissak and Emanuel Gutmann. Tel-Aviv: Am Oved [in Hebrew].

1999. *The Mass Immigration in the Fifties: The Failure of the Melting Pot Policy*. Jerusalem: Bialik Institute [in Hebrew].

2000. "Major Cleavages in Israeli Society." In *Pluralism in Israel, from a Melting Pot to a Mixed Grill*, ed. Yaakov Kop. Jerusalem: Center for Social Policy Studies, 27–54 [in Hebrew].

Lissak, Moshe, and Emanuel Gutmann, eds. 1977. *The Political System in Israel*. Tel-Aviv: Am Oved [in Hebrew].

Lissak, Moshe, and Baruch Kimmerling, eds. 1984. *Armed Forces and Security: A Reader*. Jerusalem: Department of Sociology and Social Anthropology, Hebrew University [in Hebrew].

Lissak, Moshe, and Elazar Leshem, eds. 2001. *From Russia to Israel: Identity and Culture in Transition*. Tel-Aviv: Hakibbutz Hameuchad [in Hebrew].

Lomsky-Feder, Edna. 2003. "From Agent of National Memory to Local Mneumonic Community: Memorial Ceremonies in Israeli Schools." *Megamot* 42 (3): 366–68 [in Hebrew].

Lomsky-Feder, Edna, and Eyal Ben-Ari, eds. 1999. *The Military and Militarism in Israeli Society*. Albany, NY: SUNY Press.

Lowrey, Wilson. 2006. "Mapping the Journalism–Blogging Relationship." *Journalism* 7 (4): 477–500.

Lubitsch, Vered. 2005. "Glatt-Berkowitz's Punishment: Suspended Sentence and a Fine." *YNet* March 16. www.ynet.co.il/articles/0,7340,L-3059058,00.html [in Hebrew] (accessed March 23, 2016).

Lustick, Ian. 1980. *Arabs in the Jewish State: Israel's Control of a National Minority*. Austin: University of Texas Press.

Mada al-Carmel. 2007. *The Haifa Declaration*. May 15, Haifa.

Mair, Peter. 1998. "Western Europe: Indifference and its Dangers." In *The Demise of Political Parties: Israeli Democracy in Crisis*, ed. Dan Koren. Tel-Aviv: Hakibbutz Hameuchad, 23–44 [in Hebrew].

Mair, Peter, and Ingrid Van Biezen. 2001. "Party Membership in Twenty European Democracies, 1980–2000." *Party Politics* 7 (1): 5–22.

Mako. 2014. "Survey: 47% Oppose Ground Offensive in Gaza." July 10. http://www.mako.co.il/news-military/security/Article-812624f87c00b31004.htm (accessed May 5, 2016) [in Hebrew].

2015. "The Last Poll Before the Election: A Difference of 4 Seats between the Zionist Camp and Likud." March 13. www.mako.co.il/news-israel-elections/elections-2015-polls/q1_2015/Article-c446c18f3931c41004.htm [in Hebrew] (accessed March 29, 2016).

Malach, Gilad, Doron Cohen, and Haim Zicherman. 2015. *A Master Plan for Ultra-Orthodox Employment in Israel*. June. Jerusalem: Israel Democracy Institute [in Hebrew].

Mann, Rafi, and Azi Lev-On. 2014. *Annual Report: The Israeli Media in 2013: Agendas, Uses and Trends*. Ariel: Institute of New Media Research [in Hebrew].

2015. *Annual Report: The Israeli Media in 2014: Agendas, Uses and Trends*. Ariel: Institute of New Media Research [in Hebrew].

2016. *Annual Report: The Israeli Media in 2016*. Ariel: The Institute for New Media Research.

Manna, Adel, and Ramsees Gharrah, eds. 2008. *Arab Society in Israel*, 2 vols. Jerusalem: Van Leer Jerusalem Institute [in Hebrew].

Maor, Anat. 2008. "The Dramatic Growth of Private Legislation in Israel, 1992–2006." *Israel Studies Forum* 23 (1): 84–103.

Maoz, Asher. 1999. "The Boundaries of Justiciability: Knesset, Government, Law Court." *Plilim* 8 (389): 435–44 [in Hebrew].

Maoz, Moshe. 1962. "Local Governance in Arab Settlements in Israel." *Hamizrah Hahadash* 14 [in Hebrew].

Marciano, Ilan, and Hanan Greenberg. 2004. "Deputy Chief of Staff: Many Girls Are Not Drafted 'Because It's Not Challenging.'" *YNet* July 13. www.ynet.co.il/articles/0,7340,L-2946559,00.html [in Hebrew] (accessed June 27, 2016).

Margalit, Avishai, and Moshe Halbertal. 1998. "Liberalism and the Right to Culture." In *Multiculturalism in a Democratic and Jewish State*, eds. Menachem Mautner, Avi Sagi, and Ronen Shamir. Tel-Aviv: Ramat Publishers, 93–105 [in Hebrew].

Margalit, Avishai, and Michael Walzer. 2009. "This is Not the Way to Conduct a Just War." *Haaretz* April 8 [in Hebrew].

Marmor, Galit, and Gabriel Weimann. 2001. "Measuring Emotional Appeals in Israeli Election Campaigns." *Politika* 7: 63–78 [in Hebrew].

Maschler, Michael, Eilon Solan, and Shmuel Zamir. 2013. *Game Theory*. Cambridge, UK: Cambridge University Press.

Matsik, Ilan. 2009. "Between Ronny Daniel and Khader Shahin." *NRG* October 8 [in Hebrew].

Matskin, Asaf. 2012. *Too Close to the Edge: The Story of Corruption in Israel*. Tel-Aviv: Hakibbutz Hameuchad [in Hebrew].

Mauro, Paolo. 1995. "Corruption and Growth." *Quarterly Journal of Economics* 110 (3): 681–712.

Mautner, Menachem. 1993. "The Decline of Formalism and the Rise of Value-laden Jurisprudence in Israeli Law." In *Judicial Activism*, ed. Ariel Porat. Tel-Aviv: Ramot, 126–33 [in Hebrew].

Mautner, Menachem, Avi Sagi, and Ronen Shamir, eds. 1998. *Multiculturalism in a Democratic and Jewish State*. Tel-Aviv: Ramat Publishers [in Hebrew].

McCarthy, Justin. 1990. *The Population of Palestine: Population History and Statistics of the Late Ottoman Period and the Mandate*. New York: Columbia University Press.

McCombs, Maxwell E., and Donald L. Shaw. 1972. "The Agenda-Setting Function of the Mass Media." *Public Opinion Quarterly* 36: 176–87.

McGann, James G. 2015. *2014 Global Go To Think Tank Index Report*. Think Tank and Civil Societies Program, The Lauder Institute, The University of Pennsylvania. www.kas.de/wf/doc/kas_40212-544-1-30.pdf?150123124359 (accessed October 6, 2017).

McLuhan, Marshall. 1966. *Understanding Media: The Extensions of Man*. New York: McGraw-Hill.

McLuhan, Marshall, and Bruce R. Powers. 1989. *The Global Village: Transformations in World Life and Media in the 21st Century*. New York: Oxford University Press.

McQuail, Denis. 1977. "The Influence and Effects of Mass Media." In *Mass Communication and Society*, eds. James Curran, Michael Gurevitch, and Janet Woolacott. London and Ra'anana: Edward Arnold and Open University Press, 70–93.

Medding, Peter Y. 1972. *Mapai in Israel: Political Organization and Government in a New Society*. London: Cambridge University Press.

1990. *The Founding of Israeli Democracy 1948–1967*. Cambridge: Cambridge University Press.

Mei-Ami, Naomi. 2007. *Drafting Yeshiva Students to the IDF and the Law Exempting Yeshiva Students Whose Service is their Faith (the Tal Law)*. Jerusalem: Knesset Research and Information Center, February 28 [in Hebrew].

Mendelevitch, Yosef. 1985. *Operation Wedding: The Struggle, Arrest and Release of a Prisoner of Zion*. Jerusalem: Keter Publishing House [in Hebrew].

Menuchin, Ishai, ed. 1999. "Who's Afraid of Freedom (of Information)?" Coalition for Freedom of Information, Shatil [in Hebrew].

2003. "Freedom of Information: A Necessary Condition for Public Participation." In *Participation: Your Way to Make a Difference*, eds. Arza Churchman and Elisheva Sadan. Tel-Aviv: Hakibbutz Hameuchad, 40–54 [in Hebrew].

Menuchin, Ishai, and Dina Menuchin, eds. 1985. *The Limits of Obedience*. Tel-Aviv: Yesh Gvul Movement and Siman Kria Books [in Hebrew].

Menuhin, Nezer. 2004. "Local Government in the Contemporary World." In *Principles of Local Government*, Unit 2. Ra'anana: Open University [in Hebrew].

Meridor, Dan. 1993. "Principles of the Proposed Basic Law: Legislation." *Mishpat Umimshal* 1 (2): 387–93 [in Hebrew].

Mezey, M. 1979. *Comparative Legislatures*. Durham, NC: Duke University Press.

Michels, Robert. [1911] 1962. *Political Parties: A Sociological Study of the Oligarchical Tendencies of Modern Democracy*. New York: Collier Books.

Michelson, Menachem. 1998. "The Ultra-Orthodox Press in Israel." In *The Mass Media in Israel*, eds. Dan Caspi and Yehiel Limor. Ra'anana: Open University, 213–32 [in Hebrew].

Milbrath, Lester W., and M. Lal Goel. 1977. *Political Participation: How and Why Do People Get Involved in Politics?*, 2nd edn. Chicago: Rand McNally.

"Militarism." 1970. *Oxford English Dictionary*. Oxford: Clarendon Press, vol. VI, 438.

Mill, John Stuart. [1859] 2002. *On Liberty*. Mineola, NY: Dover Publications.

Mintz, Alex. 1985. "The Military-Industrial Complex: American Concepts and Israeli Reality." *Journal of Conflict Resolution* 29: 623–39.

Miron, Dan. 1992. *Facing the Silent Brother: Essays on the Poetry of the War of Independence*. Jerusalem: Keter Publishing House [in Hebrew].

Misgav, Haim, and Udi Label, eds. 2008. *In the Shadow of the Disengagement: Strategic Dialogue in Crisis*. Jerusalem: Carmel [in Hebrew].

Mishal, Nissim. 1978. "Broadcasting Authority: Political Dynamics." M.A. dissertation, Bar-Ilan University [in Hebrew].

Mitzna, Amram. 2006. "Inter-echelon Relations during the First Intifada." In *Relations between the Civilian and Military Echelons in Israel: Against the Backdrop of Military Conflicts*, ed. Ram Erez. Tel-Aviv: Jaffee Center for Strategic Studies, Tel-Aviv University, 55–60 [in Hebrew].

Montevideo Convention on the Rights and Duties of States. 1933. www.ilsa.org/jessup/jessup15/Montevideo%20Convention.pdf htm (accessed October 25, 2017).

Morris, Benny. 1988. *The Birth of the Palestinain Refugee Problem 1947–1949*. Cambridge: Cambridge University Press.

1996. "The Israeli Press in the Qibya Events, October–November 1953." *Teoriya Uvikoret* 8: 33–46 [in Hebrew].

Mughan, Anthony, and Richard Gunther. 2000. "The Media in Democratic and Nondemocratic Regimes: A Multilevel Perspective." In *Democracy and the Media*, eds. Richard Gunther and Anthony Mughan. Cambridge: Cambridge University Press, 1–27.

Mustafa, Mohanad. 2005. "Local Elections in the Arab Palestinian Minority in Israel: The Rise of the Hamula and Decline of the Parties." In *Municipal Elections in the Arab and Druze Sector 2003*, eds. Elie Rekhess and Sara Osatzky-Lazar. Tel-Aviv: The Dayan Center, Tel-Aviv University, 18–24 [in Hebrew].

2008. *Local Politics: Characteristics and Repercussions*. Jerusalem: Israel Democracy Institute Bulletin [in Hebrew].

Nachmias, David, and Ori Arbel-Ganz. 2005. "The Crisis of Governance." *Israel Affairs* 11 (2, April): 293–96.

Nachmias, David, and David H. Rosenbloom. 1978. *Bureaucratic Culture*. London: Croom Helm.

Nachshoni, Kobi. 2007. "Rabbi Rothenberg: Religious People, Say 'Yes' to Daylight Savings Time." *YNet* July 25. www.ynet.co.il/articles/1,7340,L-3429758,00.html [in Hebrew] (accessed June 30, 2016).

Nachtomy, Ohad, ed. 2003. *Examining Multiculturalism in the Israeli Context*. Jerusalem: Magnes Press [in Hebrew].

Nadel, Baruch. 1968. *Assassination of Bernadotte*. Tel-Aviv: Guttman [in Hebrew].

Nahas, Dunia Habib. 1976. *The Israeli Communist Party*. London: Croom Helm.

Nahon, Yaakov. 1984. *Trends in Occupational Status: The Ethnic Dimension*. Jerusalem: Jerusalem Institute of Israel Studies [in Hebrew].

Nakdimon, Shlomo. 1978. *Altalena*. Jerusalem: Idanim [in Hebrew].

1987. *First Strike: The Exclusive Story of How Israel Foiled Iraq's Attempt to Get the Bomb*. New York: Summit Books.

Naor, Arye. 1986. *A Government at War: The Functioning of the Israeli Government in the Lebanon War*. Tel-Aviv: Yediot Aharonot [in Hebrew].

2002. "Begin as Prime Minister: Policymaking as an Ideological Issue." *Hayarden* 212: 52–54 [in Hebrew].

2006. "The Lebanon War: From Grand Plan to Limited Plan and Back." In *Relations between the Civilian and Military Echelons in Israel: Against the Backdrop of Military Conflicts*, ed. Ram Erez. Tel-Aviv: Jaffee Center for Strategic Studies, Tel-Aviv University, 41–48 [in Hebrew].

Naor, Mordecai. 1997. "The Press in the 1950s." In *The First Decade 1948–1958*, eds. Zvi Zameret and Hanna Yablonka. Jerusalem: Ben-Zvi Institute, 215–26 [in Hebrew].

National Committee of Arab Local Authorities. 2006. *The Future Vision of the Palestinian Arabs in Israel*. Nazareth.

Navot, Doron. 2010. "Corruption in Local Government in Israel." In *City and State in Israel: Local Government on the Eve of the Seventh Decade*, eds. Avraham Brichta, Eran Vigoda-Gadot, and Guy Pade. Jerusalem: Carmel, 131–51 [in Hebrew].

Navot, Suzie. 1998. "An Act within the Scope of a Knesset Member's Function: New Criteria in the Supreme Court Judgments." *Hamishpat* 4: 61–99 [in Hebrew].

2007. "Double Voting and the Price of Errors in the Wake of HCJ 11298/03 *Movement for Quality Government v. the Knesset House Committee*." *He'arat Din: Electronic Law Journal of the Haifa Law Faculty* 3 (1): 20–38.

Negbi, Moshe. 1985. *Paper Tiger*. Tel-Aviv: Sifriyat HaPoalim [in Hebrew].

1987. *Above the Law: The Constitutional Crisis in Israel*. Tel-Aviv: Am Oved [in Hebrew].

1991. "Self-censorship." In *Human Rights and Civil Liberties in Israel: A Reader*, eds. Ruth Gavison and Hagai Shneidor. Tel-Aviv: Frizer Communication, 81–85 [in Hebrew].

1995. *Freedom of the Press in Israel: The Legal Aspect*. Jerusalem: Jerusalem Institute for Israel Studies [in Hebrew].

2004. *We Were like Sodom: On the Slope from a Law-abiding State to a Banana Republic*. Jerusalem: Keter Publishing House [in Hebrew].

Netzer, Shraga. 1980. *Writings from my Notebook*. Tel-Aviv: Am Oved [in Hebrew].

Neuberger, Benyamin. 1990. "Constitutional Issues in Israel." In *Government and Politics in Israel*, Unit 3, ed. Benyamin Neuberger. Ra'anana: Open University.

ed. 1994. "Religion, State, and Politics." In *Government and Politics in Israel*, Unit 6. Ra'anana: Open University.

1997. *Political Parties in Israel*. Ra'anana: Open University [in Hebrew].

1998. *The Arab Minority in Israeli Politics: National Alienation and Political Integration*. Ra'anana: Open University [in Hebrew].

2000. "The Arab Voice: Between Integration and Delegitimization." In *The Jewish–Arab Rift in Israel: A Reader*, eds. Ruth Gavison and Dafna Hacker. Jerusalem: Israel Democracy Institute, 133–43 [in Hebrew].

2002. "State and Religion: Arrangements and Trends in Democratic States." In *On Both Sides of the Bridge: State and Religion in the Early Years of Israel*, eds. Mordechai Bar-On and Zvi Zameret. Jerusalem: Ben-Zvi Institute, 3–20 [in Hebrew].

2007. "National Security and Democracy: Tension and Dilemmas." In *National Security and Democracy*, eds. Benyamin Neuberger, Ilan Ben Ami, and Ariela Gross Rophe. Ra'anana: Open University, 5–10 (Hebrew-English edition).

Neuberger, Benyamin, Ilan Ben Ami, and Ariela Gross Rophe, eds. 2007. *National Security and Democracy*. Ra'anana: Open University (Hebrew-English edition).

New Profile: Movement for the Civilization of Israeli Society. 2007. www.newprofile.org/english/?p=21 (accessed April 8, 2016).

Newton, Kenneth, and Heiko Giebler. 2008. *Patterns of Participation: Political and Social Participations in 22 Nations*. Discussion Paper SP IV 2008–201. Berlin: Wissenschaftszentrum Berlin für Sozialforschung (WZB).

Niv, David. 1965–76. *Battles of the Irgun Zvai Leumi*. Tel-Aviv: Mossad Klausner, vol. 6, 259–78 [in Hebrew].

Nollert, Michael, and Monica Budowski. 2009. "Government Policy and the Nonprofit Sector: Switzerland." The Johns Hopkins Comparative Nonprofit Sector Project, Working Paper 48. Baltimore, MD: Johns Hopkins University Press.

Norris, Pippa. 1997. "Choosing Electoral System: Proportional, Majoritarian and Mixed Systems." *International Political Science Review* 18 (3): 297–312.

2003. "Preaching to the Converted? Pluralism, Participation and Party Web Sites." *Party Politics* 9 (1): 21–45.

Norris, Pippa, and James Davis. 2007. "A Continental Divide? Social Capital in the US and Europe." In *Measuring Attitudes Cross Nationally: Lessons from the European Social Survey*, eds. Roger Jowell, Caroline Roberts, Rory Fitzgerald, and Gillian Eva. London: Sage Publications, 239–65.

Nossek, Hillel, ed. 2002. *Israel at the Beginning of the 21st Century: Society, Law, Economics and Communication*. Tel-Aviv: Gomeh-Cherikover [in Hebrew].

Nossek, Hillel, and Yehiel Limor. 2001. "Fifty Years in a 'Marriage of Convenience': News Media and Military Censorship in Israel." *Communication, Law and Policy* 6 (1, January): 1–35.

2002. "Normalization of an Anomaly: Military Censorship in Israel." In *Israel at the Beginning of the 21st Century: Society, Law, Economics and Communication*, ed. Hillel Nossek. Tel-Aviv: Gomeh-Cherikover, 65–96 [in Hebrew].

2006. "The Military and the Media in the Twenty-first Century: Towards a New Model of Relations." *Israel Affairs* 12 (3, July): 484–510.

NP Tech. 2012. *Yearbook of Israeli Nonprofits, Selected Data*. http://index.justice.gov.il/Pubilcations/Articles/Documents/NPTech_Bookletfinal1.pdf (accessed April 8, 2016).

NRG. 2005. "Sweeties, Homos, and Real Men Become Pilots." April 24. www.nrg.co.il/online/1/ART/925/973.html [in Hebrew] (accessed February 7, 2016).

O'Loughlin, Toni. 2008. "Truth after 42 Years: Beatles Banned for Fear of Influence on Youth." *Guardian* September 21.

"Occupy Movement." *Wikipedia*. https://en.wikipedia.org/wiki/Occupy_movement (accessed April 8, 2016).
OECD. 2011. *Society at a Glance: Social Indicators*. www.oecd-ilibrary.org/social-issues-migration-health/society-at-a-glance-2014_soc_glance-2014-en;jsessionid=1b0pfngkf9f8.x-oecd-live-03 (accessed April 8, 2016).
2015. *In It Together: Why Less Inequality Benefits All*, May 21. www.oecd.org/social/in-it-together-why-less-inequality-benefits-all-9789264235120-en.htm (accessed April 8, 2016).
Stat. 2015. *Level of GDP Per Capita and Productivity*. https://stats.oecd.org/Index.aspx?DataSetCode=PDB_LV (accessed June 16, 2016).
Okun, Barbara S. 2001. "The Effects of Ethnicity and Educational Attainment on Jewish Marriage Patterns: Changes in Israel 1957–1995." *Population Studies* 55 (1): 49–64.
Okun, Barbara S., and Orna Khait-Marelly. 2006. "Socioeconomic Status and Demographic Behavior of Adult Multiethnics: Jews in Israel." Working Paper Series. Jerusalem: Department of Sociology, Hebrew University, 1–82.
Olshan, Yitzhak. 1978. *Discussions*. Jerusalem: Schocken [in Hebrew].
Osatzky-Lazar, Sara. 2006. *Israel in the First Decade: The Arabs in the First Decade*. Tel-Aviv: Open University [in Hebrew].
Osatzky-Lazar, Sara, and As'ad Ghanem. 1996. *Arab Voting Patterns in the Fourteenth Knesset Election*. Givat Haviva: Center for Peace Research [in Hebrew].
1999. *Arab Voting Patterns in the Fifteenth Knesset Election*. Givat Haviva: Center for Peace Research [in Hebrew].
Oz, Amos. 2004. *Tale of Love and Darkness*. Trans. Nicholas de Lange. Orlando, FL: Harcourt.
Pa'il, Meir. 1979. *From the Haganah to the IDF*. Tel-Aviv: Zmora-Bitan-Modan [in Hebrew].
Palestinian Center for Human Rights. 2014. *Annual Report 2014*. www.pchrgaza.org/files/2015/annual_pchr_eng_2014.pdf (accessed May 5, 2016).
Panim. 2009. Special Issue: Journalism 2010: Where now? 48 (Winter) [in Hebrew].
Parekh, Bhikhu. 1999. "What is Multiculturalism?" *India Seminar*. New Delhi: Seminar Publications. www.india-seminar.com/1999/484/484%20parekh.htm (accessed August 12, 2016).
Paryente, Bilha, and Emda Orr. 2006. "Religious-Zionist Society in Israel: Identities in Conflict? In What Sense?" *Megamot* 44 (2): 247–76 [in Hebrew].
Pasternak, Rachel. 2003. "Education in Israeli Society." In *Trends in Israeli Society*, eds. Ephraim Yaar and Zeev Shavit. Ra'anana: Open University, vol. 2, 989–1015 [in Hebrew].
Patinkin, Don. 1959. *The Israel Economy: The First Decade*. Jerusalem: Maurice Falk Institute for Economic Research in Israel.
Payes, Shany. 2005. *Palestinian NGOs in Israel: The Politics of Civil Society*. New York: I.B. Tauris.
Pedatzur, Reuven. 2003. "The Israeli Culture of Security." *Politika* 10: 87–117 [in Hebrew].
2007. "The Iranian Nuclear Threat and the Israeli Options." *Contemporary Security Policy* 28 (3): 513–41.
Pedersen, Mogens. 1979. "The Dynamics of European Party Systems: Changing Patterns of Electoral Volatility." *European Journal of Political Research* 7 (1): 1–26.
Peled, Elad, ed. 1999. *Fifty Years of the Israeli Educational System*. Jerusalem: Ministry of Defense in cooperation with the Ministry of Education, 249–69 [in Hebrew].
Peled, Yoav, ed. 2001. *Shas: The Challenge to Israeliness*. Tel-Aviv: Yediot Aharonot Books [in Hebrew].
Peled, Yoav, and Adi Ophir, eds. 2001. *Israel: From a Mobilized to a Civil Society*. Jerusalem and Tel-Aviv: Van Leer Jerusalem Institute and Hakibbutz Hameuchad [in Hebrew].
Peleg, Israel. 1981. "Objectivity in Television News." Ph.D. dissertation, Hebrew University of Jerusalem [in Hebrew].
Pereg, Noa. 2009. "TIM Survey: Some 76% of the Israeli Population Surfs the Internet." *Globes* January 14 [in Hebrew].
Peres, Shimon. 1998. *A New Beginning*. Tel-Aviv: Zmora Bitan [in Hebrew].
Peres, Yochanan. 1971. "Ethnic Relations in Israel." *American Journal of Sociology* 6: 1021–47.

Peres, Yohanan, and Eliezer Ben-Rafael. 2006. *Cleavages in Israeli Society*. Tel-Aviv: Am Oved [in Hebrew].

Peres, Yohanan, and Ephraim Yuchtman-Yaar. 1998. *Between Consent and Dissent: Peace and Democracy in the Israeli Mind*. Jerusalem: Israel Democracy Institute [in Hebrew].

2000. *Between Consent and Dissent: Peace and Democracy in the Israeli Mind*. Lanham, MD: Rowman & Littlefield.

Peri, Yoram. 1983. *Between Battles and Ballots: Israeli Military in Politics*. Cambridge and New York: Cambridge University Press.

1984. "The Study of Civil–Military Relations in Israel." In *Armed Forces and Security: A Reader*, eds. Moshe Lissak and Baruch Kimmerling. Jerusalem: Department of Sociology and Social Anthropology, Hebrew University, 209–31 [in Hebrew].

1996. "Is Israeli Society Truly Militaristic?" *Zmanim* 56: 94–112 [in Hebrew].

2001. "Changes in Security Discourse in the Media, and Transformation of the Perception of Citizenship in Israel." *Tarbut VeDemokratiya* 4–5: 233–65 [in Hebrew].

2003. "The Democratic Election Putsch." In *In the Name of Security: The Sociology of War and Peace in Israel in Changing Times*, eds. Majid al-Haj and Uri Ben Eliezer. Haifa: Haifa University, 125–44 [in Hebrew].

2004. *Tele-Populism: Media and Politics in Israel in the 1990s*. Stanford: Stanford University Press.

2006. *Generals in the Cabinet Room: How the Military Shapes Israeli Policy*. Washington, DC: United States Institute of Peace.

2009. "Do the Israeli Media Criticize the Military and the Culture of Security?" In *An Army that Has a State?*, eds. Gabriel Sheffer, Oren Barak, and Amiram Oren. Jerusalem: Carmel, 195–217 [in Hebrew].

Peri, Yoram, and Yariv Tsfati. 2007. "Seeing is Believing? Distrust of the Centrist Media and News Consumption of Sectoral and Non-Israeli Channels." In *Communication and Politics in Israel*, ed. Dan Caspi. Jerusalem and Tel-Aviv: Van Leer Jerusalem Institute and Hakibbutz Hameuchad, 162–84 [in Hebrew].

Perlmutter, Amos. 1969. *Military and Politics in Israel*. London: Frank Cass.

Pesso, Rotem. 2013. "The November 2013 Draft – All the Data." IDF Blog, November 7. www.idf.il/1133-19841-he/Dover.aspx [in Hebrew] (accessed May 5, 2016).

Pew Research Center. 2016. *Israel's Religiously Divided Society*. www.pewforum.org/files/2016/03/Israel-Survey-Full-Report.pdf (accessed June 21, 2016).

Pilovski, Varda, ed. 1990. *The Transition from Yishuv to State 1947–49: Continuity and Changes*. Haifa: Herzl Institute, University of Haifa [in Hebrew].

Pipa, Tony. 2006. "Weathering the Storm: The Role of Local Nonprofits in the Hurricane Katrina Relief Effort." Working Paper, Nonprofit Sector Research Fund. Washington, DC: The Aspen Institute.

Poguntke, Thomas, and Paul Webb, eds. 2005. *The Presidentialization of Democracy: A Study in Comparative Politics*. Oxford: Oxford University Press.

Polas, Yisrael. 1992. "The President – a Superfluous Job." *Haaretz* September 25 [in Hebrew].

"Political Culture." 2001. *The International Encyclopedia of the Social and Behavioral Sciences*, eds. Neil J. Smelser and Paul B. Baltes. Philadelphia, PA: Elsevier, vol. 17, 114640–44.

Porath, Yehoshua. 1974. *The Emergence of the Arab-Palestinian National Movement 1918–1929*. London: Frank Cass.

1989. *Carrying a Pen: The Biography of Uriel Shelakh (Yonatan Ratosh)*. Tel-Aviv: Zmora, Makhbarot Lesifrut [in Hebrew].

Porath, Yehoshua, and Atallah Mansour. 1990. "The Arabic Press in Israel." *Kesher* 7: 71–77 [in Hebrew].

President's Commission to Examine the Structure of Governance in Israel. 2007. "Parties in the Age of Electronic Communications." Center for Citizens' Empowerment [in Hebrew].

Putnam, Robert D. 1993. *Making Democracy Work: Civic Traditions in Modern Italy*. Princeton, NJ: Princeton University Press.

1995. "Bowling Alone: America's Declining Social Capital." *Journal of Democracy* 6: 65–78.

Rabin, Yitzhak. 1979. *Service Notebook*. Tel-Aviv: Maariv [in Hebrew].

1990. Interview with Rabin in the weekend supplement of *Yediot Aharonot*, June 15 [in Hebrew].

Rabinowitz, Dan. 2001. "De Tocqueville in Umm al-Fahim." In *Israel: From a Mobilized to a Civil Society*, eds. Yoav Peled and Adi Ophir. Jerusalem and Tel-Aviv: Van Leer Jerusalem Institute and Hakibbutz Hameuchad, 350–60 [in Hebrew].

Rabinowitz, Dan, and Khawla Abu-Baker. 2002. *The Stand-Tall Generation*. Jerusalem: Keter Publishing House [in Hebrew].

Rachamim, Yehezkel, and Daniel Bar-Tal, eds. 2006. *Socialization into Conflict in Israeli-Jewish Society*. Tel-Aviv: Walter Lebach Institute for Jewish-Arab Coexistence through Education, Tel-Aviv University [in Hebrew].

Rackman, Emanuel. 1955. *Israel's Emerging Constitution 1948–1951*. New York: Columbia University Press.

Raday, Frances. 2000. "Religion and Equality through the Perspective of Jurisprudence." In *Berenson Book*, eds. Aharon Barak and Haim Berenson. Jerusalem: Nevo, 341–91 [in Hebrew].

Raday, Itamar, and Arik Rudnitzky, eds. 2015. *The 20th Knesset Election Results in the Arab Sector*. Bayan 5 (May). Tel-Aviv: Adenauer Program, Tel-Aviv University [in Hebrew].

Radzyner, Amihai. 2010. "A Constitution for Israel: The Design of the Leo Kohn Proposal, 1948." *Israel Studies* 15 (1): 16.

Rahat, Gideon. 2000. "The Politics of Regime Structure Reform in Israel." Ph.D. dissertation, Hebrew University of Jerusalem.

2001. "The Electoral System 1948–1959: From Default to an Entrenched System." In *Iyunim Bitkumat Israel: Studies in Zionism, the Yishuv, and the State of Israel 11*. The Ben-Gurion Research Center, Ben-Gurion University of the Negev, 369–446 [in Hebrew].

Rahat, Gideon, and R.Y. Hazan. 2001. "Candidate Selection Methods: An Analytical Framework." *Party Politics* 7 (3): 297–322.

2003. "Political Participation in Party Primaries: Increase in Quantity, Decrease in Quality." Presented at a workshop of the European Consortium for Political Research, March–April, Edinburgh, Scotland.

Rahat, Gideon, and Ofer Kenig. *From Party Politics to Personalized Politics? Party Change and Political Personalization in Democracies*. Oxford: Oxford University Press (forthcoming).

Rahat, Gideon, and Neta Sher-Hadar. 1999. "The 1996 Party Primaries and their Political Consequences." In *The Elections in Israel – 1996*, eds. Asher Arian and Michal Shamir. Albany, NY: SUNY Press, 241–68.

Ram, Uri, ed. 1993. *Israeli Society: Critical Perspectives*. Tel-Aviv: Breirot Press [in Hebrew].

Ram, Uri, and Nitza Berkowitz, eds. 2006. *In/Equality*. Beersheva: Ben-Gurion University of the Negev [in Hebrew].

Ram, Uri, and Oren Yiftachel, eds. 1999. *Ethnocracy and Glocalization: New Approaches to the Study of Society and Space in Israel*. Beersheva: Negev Center for Regional Development, Ben-Gurion University of the Negev [in Hebrew].

Rapel, Yo'el, and Itamar Levin. 2003. *Heritage, Zionism, and Democracy: 100 Basic Concepts*. Tel-Aviv: Yediot Aharonot [in Hebrew].

Ratosh, Yonatan. 1982. *The Beginning of Days: The Development of Hebraism*. Tel-Aviv: Hadar [in Hebrew].

Ravitzky, Aviezer. 1997. *Religious and Secular Jews in Israel: A Kulturkampf?* Jerusalem: Israel Democracy Institute [in Hebrew].

Razin, Eran. 1998. *Fiscal Disparities between Arab and Jewish Local Authorities*. Jerusalem: Floersheimer Institute for Policy Studies [in Hebrew].

1999. *Fiscal Disparities between Arab and Jewish Local Authorities. Is the Gap Narrowing? A Policy Paper*. Jerusalem: Floersheimer Institute for Policy Studies [in Hebrew].

2002. *Fiscal Disparities between Local Authorities in Israel in 2000: Continuity and Change in a Period of Political Instability*. Jerusalem: Floersheimer Institute for Policy Studies [in Hebrew].

2004. "Needs and Impediments for Local Government Reform: Lessons from Israel." *Journal of Urban Affairs* 26: 623–40.

Razin, Eran, and Anna Hazan. 2007. "Local Government Amalgamation in Israel." In *Local Government Reforms in Countries in Transition, a Global Perspective*, eds. Fred Lazin, Matt Evans, Vincent Hoffmann-Martinot, and Hellmut Wollmann. Lanham, MD: Rowman & Littlefield Publishers, 177–94.

Reiter, Yitzhak. 2000. "The Status of Arabs in Israel in an Era of Peace." In *The Jewish–Arab Rift in Israel: A Reader*, eds. Ruth Gavison and Dafna Hacker. Jerusalem: Israel Democracy Institute, 245–70 [in Hebrew].

Reiter, Yitzhak, and Reuven Aharoni. 1993. *The Political Life of Arabs in Israel.* Beit Berl: The Institute for Israeli Arab Studies [in Hebrew].

Reiter, Yitzhak, and Orna Cohen, eds. 2013. *Arab Society in Israel: An Information Manual*, 2nd edn. Jerusalem: Abraham Fund.

Rekhess, Elie, ed. 1998. *The Arabs in Israeli Politics*. Tel-Aviv: Tel-Aviv University [in Hebrew].

ed. 2007. *The Arab Minority in Israel and Election of the 17th Knesset: Start of a New Era?* Tel-Aviv: Tel-Aviv University [in Hebrew].

ed. 2007a. *The Arabs in Israel Three Years after Publication of the Or Commission Report*. Tel-Aviv: Moshe Dayan Center, Konrad Adenauer Program for Jewish–Arab Cooperation, Tel-Aviv University [in Hebrew].

2008. *The Arab Minority in Israel: An Analysis of the "Future Vision" Documents.* New York: American Jewish Committee.

Rekhess, Elie, and Arik Rudnitzky, eds. 2007. *The Future Vision of the Palestinian Arabs in Israel*. Tel-Aviv: Konrad Adenauer Program, Tel-Aviv University.

eds. 2009. *Arab Society in Israel: Information Dossier*. Jerusalem: Abraham Fund Initiatives [in Hebrew].

Rekhess, Elie, and Sara Osatzky-Lazar, eds. 2005. *Municipal Elections in the Arab and Druze Sector 2003*. Tel-Aviv: The Dayan Center, Tel-Aviv University [in Hebrew].

Reshef, Tzali. 1996. *Peace Now: From the Officers' Letter to Peace Now*. Jerusalem: Keter Publishing House [in Hebrew].

Reznik, Shlomo. 2003. "Taking the Law into Your Hands from Right and Left." In *In the Name of Security: The Sociology of War and Peace in Israel in Changing Times*, eds. Majid al-Haj and Uri Ben Eliezer. Haifa: Haifa University, 520–29 [in Hebrew].

Rhodes, Rod A.W. 2012. "Waves of Governance." In *The Oxford Handbook of Governance*, ed. David Levi-Faur. Oxford: Oxford University Press, 33–48.

Riker, William H. 1962. *The Theory of Political Coalition*. New Haven, CT: Yale University Press.

Rinat, Zafrir. 2014. "Israel's First New Arab City on its Way to Becoming a Reality." *Haaretz* November 5. www.haaretz.com/israel-news/.premium-1.624707 (accessed June 7, 2016).

Rittel, Horst W.J., and Melvin M. Webber. 1973. "Dilemmas in a General Theory of Planning." *Policy Sciences* 4. Philadelphia, PA: Elsevier, 155–69.

Roberts, Nancy. 2000. "Wicked Problems and Network Approaches to Resolutions." *International Public Management Review* 1 (1): 38–57.

Robinson, Piers. 2001. "Theorizing the Influence of the Media on Politics: Models of Media Influence on Foreign Policy." *European Journal of Communication* 16 (4): 523–44.

Rolnik, Guy. 2009. "Don't Subsidize Print Journalism." *The Marker Week* September 24 [in Hebrew].

Rosen, Ayelet. 2015. "Election Campaign Broadcasts: Who Needs Them Anyway?" *Mako* March 9. www.mako.co.il/culture-tv/local/Article-f0f7e589ad9fb41006.htm [in Hebrew] (accessed August 4, 2016).

Rosenberg, Gerald N. 1993. *The Hollow Hope: Can Courts Bring About Social Change?* Chicago, IL: The University of Chicago Press.

Rosenbloom, David H., and Richard D. Schwartz, eds. 1994. *Handbook of Regulation and Administrative Law*. New York: Marcel Dekker.

Rosenhek, Zeev. 2006. "The Welfare State in Israel." In *In/Equality*, eds. Uri Ram and Nitza Berkowitz. Beersheva: Ben-Gurion University of the Negev, 234–41 [in Hebrew].

Rosenthal, Ruvik. 2000. *Kafr Qasim: Events and Myth*. Tel-Aviv: Hakibbutz Hameuchad [in Hebrew].

ed. 2001. *The Great Divide: Israeli Society Between Rift and Repair*. Tel-Aviv: Yediot Aharonot [in Hebrew].

ed. 2009. "Survey of Media Consumption Habits." *Panim* 48: 29–32 [in Hebrew].

Rosman-Stollman, Elisheva, and Aharon Kampinsky, eds. 2014. *Civil–Military Relations in Israel*. Lanham, MD: Lexington Books.

Rosner, Rivka. 2008. "It's all Money… Stupid." Interview with Hanoch Marmari. *Eretz Aheret* 45: 16–22 [in Hebrew].

Rosner, Tal. 2006. "High Court: Israel Discriminates Against Arabs." *YNet* February 27. www.ynetnews.com/articles/0,7340,L-3221512,00.html (accessed April 7, 2016).

Roth, Nurit. 2007. "The Judge: Under the Cloak of Anonymity, Freedom of Expression Becomes Freedom to Denigrate and Incite." *The Marker* April 25 [in Hebrew].

Rothenberg, Naftali. 2009. "They Darkened our World." *YNet* September 29. www.ynet.co.il/articles/0,7340,L-3782538,00.html [in Hebrew] (accessed June 30, 2016).

Rott, Anat. 2014. *Not at Any Price: The Story Behind the Struggle over the Land of Israel*. Jerusalem: Begin Center [in Hebrew].

Rouhana, Nadim, Nabil Saleh, and Nimer Sultany. 2004. "Voting Without Voice: About the Vote of the Palestinian Minority in the 16th Knesset Elections." In *The Elections in Israel – 2003*, eds. Asher Arian and Michal Shamir. New Brunswick, NJ: Transaction Publishers.

Rouhana, Nadim, Mtanes Shihadeh, and Areej Sabbagh-Khoury. 2010. "Turning Points in Palestinian Politics in Israel: The 2009 Elections." In *The Elections in Israel – 2009*, eds. Asher Arian and Michal Shamir. New Brunswick and London: Transaction, 131–69.

Rozin, Orit. 2002. "From 'We' to 'I': Individualism in Israeli Society in the Early 1950s." Ph.D. dissertation, Tel-Aviv University [in Hebrew].

2011. *The Rise of the Individual in 1950s Israel: A Challenge to Collectivism*. Waltham, MA: Brandeis University Press.

Rubinstein, Alon. 2004. *The Local Authorities: Key Problems and Options for Solving Them*. Jerusalem: Knesset Research and Information Center [in Hebrew].

Rubinstein, Amnon. 1982. *A Certain Political Experience*. Jerusalem: Idanim [in Hebrew].

1991. *Constitutional Law in the State of Israel*, 4th edn. Jerusalem and Tel-Aviv: Schocken [in Hebrew].

1992. "Help, the House is on Fire." *Maariv* January 1 [in Hebrew].

Rubinstein, Amnon, and Barak Medina. 1996. *Constitutional Law in the State of Israel*, 5th edn. Jerusalem: Schocken [in Hebrew].

2005. *Constitutional Law in the State of Israel*, 6th edn. Jerusalem and Tel-Aviv: Schocken [in Hebrew].

Rubinstein, Amnon, and Liav Orgad. 2005. "The Legal Status of the Constitutional Preamble: The Case of Israel." *Hamishpat* 20: 38–53 [in Hebrew].

Rubinstein, Elyakim. 1976. "From a Yishuv to a State: Institutions and Parties." In *The Jewish Community at the Time of the National Home 1917–1948*, ed. B. Eliav. Jerusalem: Keter Publishing House, 129–232 [in Hebrew].

1980. *Judges of the Land: The Origin and Character of the Israel Supreme Court*. Jerusalem: Schocken [in Hebrew].

1997. "Opinion Regarding the Appointment of Atty. Bar-On to the Post of Attorney General." Ministry of Justice, April 18 [in Hebrew].

Rudnitzky, Arik, ed. 2013. *Arab Politics in Israel and the 19th Knesset Election*. Konrad Adenauer Program for Jewish–Arab Cooperation 3 (7, March). Tel-Aviv: Moshe Dayan Center for Middle East and African Studies, Tel-Aviv University. www.kas.de/wf/doc/kas_33718-1522-2-30.pdf?130308100452 (accessed September 7, 2015).

2014. *The Arab Population in Israel: Basic Data*. Tel-Aviv: Institute for National Security Studies [in Hebrew].

Saban, Ilan. 2000. "The Legal Status of Minorities in Deeply Divided Democratic Societies." Ph.D. dissertation, Hebrew University of Jerusalem.

Sa'di, Ahmed. 2001. "The 'Shrinking of the State' in Israel and its Implications for the Palestinian Minority." In *Israel: From a Mobilized to a Civil Society*, eds. Yoav Peled and Adi Ophir. Jerusalem and Tel-Aviv: Van Leer Jerusalem Institute and Hakibbutz Hameuchad, 337–49 [in Hebrew].
Sager, Samuel. 1971. "Pre-state Influences on Israel's Parliamentary System." *Parliamentary Affairs* 25 (1): 29–49.
Saidov, Yossi. 2009. "Speak in Numbers, Ma'am." *The Seventh Eye* 10 (February) quoting *Haaretz* poll of January 15, 2009 [in Hebrew].
Salamon, Lester M., S. Wojciech Sokolowski, and Regina List. 2003. "Global Civil Society: An Overview." Center for Civil Society Studies. Baltimore, MD: The Johns Hopkins Comparative Nonprofit Sector Project, Johns Hopkins University, Institute for Policy Studies. http://ccss.jhu.edu/wp-content/uploads/downloads/2011/09/Book_GCSOverview_2003.pdf (accessed October 18, 2017).
Salzberger, Eli, and Fania Oz-Salzberger. 2006. "The Tradition of Freedom of Expression in Israel." In *Be Quiet, Someone is Speaking! The Judicial Culture of Freedom of Speech in Israel*, ed. Michael D. Birnhack. Tel-Aviv: Tel-Aviv University Press, 27–70 [in Hebrew].
Samuel-Azran, Tal, Moran Yarchi, and Gadi Wolfsfeld. 2015. "Aristotelian Rhetoric and Facebook Success in Israel's 2013 Election Campaign." *Online Information Review*http://vanatteveldt.com/wp-content/uploads/Aristotelian-rhetoric-and-Facebook-success-in-Israels-2013-election-campaign-published.pdf (accessed October 18, 2017).
Saporta, Ishak, Salem Abo-Zaid, and Dotan Leshem. 2006. *Inequality in the Distribution of Income among Households and Wage-Earners of Israel: 1967–2003*. Jerusalem: Van Leer Jerusalem Institute [in Hebrew].
Sartori, Giovanni. 1976. *Parties and Party Systems: A Framework for Analysis*. Cambridge: Cambridge University Press.
Sasson, Talia. 2015. *On the Brink of the Abyss: Is the Triumph of the Settlements the End of Israeli Democracy?* Jerusalem: Keter Publishing House [in Hebrew].
Scarrow, Susan. 2000. "Parties without Members? Party Organization in a Changing Electoral Environment." In *Parties without Partisans: Political Change in Advanced Industrial Democracies*, eds. Russell J. Dalton and Martin P. Wattenberg. Oxford: Oxford University Press, 79–101.
Schafferman, Karin Tamar. 2009. "Participation, Abstention and Boycott: Trends in Arab Voter Turnout in Israeli Elections." *Parliament* 61. Jerusalem: Israel Democracy Institute [in Hebrew].
Schattschneider, Elmer E. 1942. *Party Government*. New York: Holt, Rinehart and Winston.
Schiff, Ze'ev, and Ehud Ya'ari. 1984. *Israel's Lebanon War*. New York: Simon & Schuster.
1990. *Intifada: Palestinian Uprising – Israel's Third Front*. New York: Simon & Schuster.
Schmid, Hillel, and Avishag Rudich. 2008. *Public Opinion Survey on Philanthropy in Israel*. Jerusalem: Center for the Study of Philanthropy in Israel, Hebrew University [in Hebrew].
2009. *Philanthropy in Israel: A Compilation of Numbers and Statistics*. Jerusalem: Hebrew University [in Hebrew].
Schmitter, Philippe C. 1989. "Corporatism is Dead! Long Live Corporatism!" *Government and Opposition* 24 (1): 54–73.
Schnell, Izhak, Gideon Biger, and Anda Rosenberg, eds. 2013. *Land Policies in the Zionist and Democratic State of Israel*. Tel-Aviv: Walter Lebach Institute, Tel-Aviv University [in Hebrew].
Schultz, Julianne. 1998. *Reviving the Fourth Estate*. Cambridge, UK: Cambridge University Press.
Schumpeter, Joseph A. 1944. *Capitalism, Socialism and Democracy*. London: George Allen and Unwin.
Schwartz, Dov. 2009. *Religious Zionism: History and Ideology*. Boston: Academic Studies Press.
Schwartz, R. 2005. "State Control in Developed Democracies." Submitted to the Knesset State Control Committee. Jerusalem: Knesset Research and Information Center.
Schweitzer, Avram. 1986. "We Should Not Allow the Internal Democracy to Go Crazy." *Haaretz* May 18 [in Hebrew].
Sebba, Leslie. 1977. "The Pardoning Power: A World Survey." *Journal of Criminal Law and Criminology* 68 (1, March): 83–121.

Segal, Zeev. 1984. "Commission of Inquiry Pursuant to the Commissions of Inquiry Law: Its Constitutional Status and Legitimate Area of Activity." *Mehkarei Mishpat* 3: 199–246 [in Hebrew].

Segev, Tom. 1986. *1949: The First Israelis*. Trans. Arlen N. Weinstein. New York: Free Press.

2005. *Israel in 1967: And the Land Changed its Visage*. Jerusalem: Keter Publishing House [in Hebrew].

Sela, Avraham. 2007. "Civil Society, the Military, and National Security: The Case of Israel's Security Zone in South Lebanon." In *An Army that has a State?*, ed. Gabriel Sheffer. Jerusalem: Van Leer Jerusalem Institute, 21–34 [in Hebrew].

Sela, Michal. 2002. *State and Religion in Israel: A Review of Legislation, Court Rulings, and Policy*. Jerusalem: Religious Action Center and the Movement for Progressive Judaism.

Shachar, Yoram, Meron Gross, and Chanan Goldschmidt. 2004. "The Hundred Leading Precedents of the Supreme Court: A Quantitative Analysis." *Mishpat Umimshal* 7 (1): 243–303 [in Hebrew].

Shafat, Gershon. 1995. *Gush Emunim: The Story Behind the Scenes*. Jerusalem: Beit El Library [in Hebrew].

Shahar, Yoram. 2002. "The Early Drafts of the Declaration of Independence." *Iyunei Mishpat* 26 (2): 523–600 [in Hebrew].

Shai, Aaron. 2002. "The Fate of Abandoned Arab Villages in Israel on the Eve of the Six Day War and its Immediate Aftermath." *Cathedra* 105: 151 [in Hebrew].

Shalata, Bilal. 2001. "Connected to an IV." *The Seventh Eye* 34 [in Hebrew].

Shalev, Michael. 1993. "Workers, State, and Crisis: Economics and Diplomacy in Israel." In *Israeli Society: Critical Perspectives*, ed. Uri Ram. Tel-Aviv: Breirot Press, 148–71 [in Hebrew].

Shalev, Michael, and Gal Levy. 2004. "The Winners and Losers of 2003: Ideology, Social Structure, and Political Change." In *The Elections in Israel – 2003*, eds. Asher Arian and Michal Shamir. New Brunswick, NJ: Transaction Publishers, 247–76.

Shalom, Zaki. 2009. "Defining the Enemy in an Asymmetrical Confrontation: The Case of the Second Lebanon War." *Strategic Assessment* 12 (3, November). Tel-Aviv: Institute for National Security Studies. www.inss.org.il/uploadimages/Import/(FILE)1259664194.pdf (accessed November 13, 2015).

Shalom Chetrit, Sami. 2001. "Mizrahi Politics in Israel: Between Identification and Integration to Protest and Alternative." Ph.D. dissertation, Hebrew University of Jerusalem [in Hebrew].

Shamgar, Meir. 1971. "The Observance of International Law in the Administered Territories." *Israel Yearbook of Human Rights*, 1.

Shamgar Handelman, Lea. 1986. *Israeli War Widows: Beyond the Glory of Heroism*. South Hadley, MA: Bergin and Garvey.

Shamir, Jacob, Neta Ziskind, and Shoshana Blum-Kulka. 1999. "What's in a Question? A Content Analysis of Survey Questions." *The Communication Review* 3 (4).

Shamir, Michal, ed. 2015. *The Elections in Israel*. Jerusalem: Israel Democracy Institute [in Hebrew].

Shamir, Ronen. 1990. "Landmark Cases and the Reproduction of Legitimacy: The Case of Israel's High Court of Justice." *Law and Society Review* 24.

Shamir, Shimon. 2005. *Arabs in Israel: Two Years after the Or Commission Report*. Tel-Aviv: Tel-Aviv University and Konrad Adenauer Foundation [in Hebrew].

2007. "An Open Letter." *al-Sinara* January 5 [in Arabic].

2009. "Advancing and Integrating the Arab Sector: Objectives and Obstacles." In *Arab Society in Israel: Information Dossier*, eds. Elie Rekhess and Arik Rudnitzky. Jerusalem: Abraham Fund Initiatives [in Hebrew].

Shamir, Yitzhak. 1994. *Summing Up: An Autobiography*. London: Weidenfeld and Nicolson.

Shapira, Anita. 1985. *From the Dismissal of the Head of the National Command to the Disbanding of the Palmach*. Tel-Aviv: Hakibbutz Hameuchad [in Hebrew].

2002. "Judaism and Israeliness: A Historical Perspective." In *Religion and Nationalism in Israel and the Middle East*, ed. Neri Horowitz. Tel-Aviv: Am Oved, 205–25 [in Hebrew].

2004. *The Spring of His Life.* Tel-Aviv: Hakibbutz Hameuchad [in Hebrew].
Shapira, Boaz. 2005. "National Leap, Local Climb: Thoughts about Elections to the Local Authorities." *Medina Vehevra* 5 (1): 1183–94 [in Hebrew].
Shapira, Jonathan. 1977. *Democracy in Israel.* Ramat Gan: Massada [in Hebrew].
1996. *A Society Captive to Politicians.* Tel-Aviv: Sifriyat Hapoalim [in Hebrew].
Shapiro, Shimon. 1988. "Issues in Evaluating Programs for Deliberate Social Change: Project Renewal." *Megamot* 31 (3–4): 269–85 [in Hebrew].
Sharett, Moshe. 1955. "Socialism in Israel – in What Way?" *Molad* 13: 47–58 [in Hebrew].
1978. *Personal Diary*, 9 vols., ed. Yaakov Sharett. Tel-Aviv: Maariv [in Hebrew].
Sharkansky, Ira. 1987. *The Political Economy of Israel.* New Brunswick, NJ: Transaction Publishers.
1995. "Expanding the Frontiers of State Audit: Israel's Auditor as Critic of Political Morals." In *Studies in State Audit*, eds. A. Friedberg, B. Geist, N. Mizrahi, and I. Sharkansky. Jerusalem: State of Israel, State Comptroller's Office, 95–103.
Shavit, Yossi, and Haya Stier. 1997. "Ethnicity and Education in Marriage Patterns in Israel: Changes over Time." *Megamot* 38 (2): 207–25 [in Hebrew].
Sheafer, Tamir. 2001. "Charismatic Skill, Political Communication, and Politics." Ph.D. dissertation, Hebrew University of Jerusalem.
Shefet, Avraham, and Shmuel Shefet. 2001. "The Legal Framework of Local Government." In *Local Government in Israel*, eds. Daniel Elazar and Chaim Kalchheim. Jerusalem: Jerusalem Center for Public Affairs [in Hebrew].
2004. "Law and the Courts in Local Government." In *Principles of Local Government*, Unit 6. Ra'anana: Open University [in Hebrew].
Sheffer, Brenda. 2011. "Israel: New Natural Gas Producer in the Mediterranean." *Energy Policy* 39: 5379–87. https://en.wikipedia.org/wiki/Leviathan_gas_field (accessed November 11, 2015).
Sheffer, Gabriel, ed. 2007. *An Army that Has a State? A New Look at the Role of Security and the Defense System in Israel.* Jerusalem: Van Leer Jerusalem Institute [in Hebrew].
Sheffer, Gabriel, and Oren Barak. 2013. *Israel's Security Networks.* Cambridge, UK: Cambridge University Press.
Shefi, Smadar. 1997. "New Horizons – Ten Years of Art." In *The First Decade 1948–1958*, eds. Zvi Zameret and Hanna Yablonka. Jerusalem: Ben-Zvi Institute, 281–99 [in Hebrew].
Shelah, Ofer. 2006. "Inter-echelon Relations in the al-Aqsa Intifada: What Changed?" In *Relations between the Civilian and Military Echelons in Israel: Against the Backdrop of Military Conflicts*, ed. Ram Erez. Tel-Aviv: Jaffee Center for Strategic Studies, Tel-Aviv University, 69–74 [in Hebrew].
Sheleff, Leon. 1989. *The Voice of Honor: Civil Disobedience and Civil Loyalty.* Tel-Aviv: Tel-Aviv University [in Hebrew].
1993. "The Green Line is the Border of Activism: Queries about the Supreme Court Judgments in the Territories." *Iyunei Mishpat* 17: 757–809 [in Hebrew].
1996. *The Bitterness of Law and the Essence of Government: On the Rule of Law, Method of Government, and Legacy of Israel.* Tel-Aviv: Papyrus, Tel-Aviv University [in Hebrew].
Sheleg, Bambi, ed. 2006. "Constitutional or Unconstitutional? On Privatizing the Prisons." *Eretz Aheret* 33 (April–May) [in Hebrew].
Sheleg, Yair. 2004. *Not Halakhicly Jewish: The Dilemma of Non-Jewish Immigrants in Israel.* Jerusalem: Israel Democracy Institute [in Hebrew].
Shenhav, Shaul. 2003. "The Voice of the State: The Israeli Government's Shaping of the Narrative of the State in the Early Years." Ph.D. dissertation, Hebrew University of Jerusalem [in Hebrew].
Shenhav, Yehouda. 2001. "The Red Line of the Green Line." In *Real Time: The al-Aqsa Intifada and the Israeli Left*, ed. Adi Ophir. Jerusalem: Keter Publishing House, 205–12 [in Hebrew].
Sherer, Moshe. 1997. "Full Service, Partial Service, or Exemption from the Israel Defense Force: Problems and Consequences." *Hevra Urevakha* 17 (1): 7–31 [in Hebrew].
Sherf, Ze'ev. 1959. *Three Days.* Tel-Aviv: Am Oved [in Hebrew].

Shetreet, Shimon. 1977. "The Commission Investigating the Yom Kippur War: A Favorable Overall Balance." *Mishpatim* 8: 74–90 [in Hebrew].

1985–86. "The Role of the Knesset in Treaty Making." *Hapraklit* 36: 360–61 [in Hebrew].

2004. *On Adjudication: Justice on Trial*. Jerusalem and Tel-Aviv: Israel Democracy Institute and Yediot Aharonot [in Hebrew].

2006. *The Court at a Crossroads: Report on the Relationship among the Branches of Government*. President's Commission to Examine the Structure of Governance in Israel [in Hebrew].

2006a. "Legal Aspects of the Peace Process and the Approval of Peace Agreements." In *Phantom in Politics: Referenda in Israel*, ed. Dana Arieli-Horowitz. Jerusalem: Magnes Press, 193–206 [in Hebrew].

Shiffer, Varda, ed. 1989. *Moral Integrity in the Civil Service*. Jerusalem: Office of the State Comptroller [in Hebrew].

2003. "Civil Society and Redistribution of Power and Authority among Governmental Bodies." Ph.D. dissertation, Hebrew University of Jerusalem [in Hebrew].

Shiffer, Zalman. 2007. "The Debate over the Defense Budget in Israel." *Israel Studies* 12 (1, Spring): 193–214.

Shimshoni, Daniel. 1982. *Israeli Democracy*. New York: The Free Press.

2002. *Project Renewal: The Politics of Change*. Tel-Aviv: Hakibbutz Hameuchad [in Hebrew].

Shpaizman, Ilana. 2011. *Privatizing the Encouragement of Immigration to Israel*. Jerusalem: Van Leer Jerusalem Institute [in Hebrew].

Shragai, Nadav. 1995. "Tens of Thousands Demonstrate in Jerusalem against the Accords, Damage Cars of Rabin and Ministers, and Refuse to Disperse." *Haaretz* October 6 [in Hebrew].

Shtrasnov, Amnon. 2005. "Verbal Corruption." *Haaretz* December 29 [in Hebrew].

Shvartz, Shifra, and Nadav Davidovich. 2005. "Medicine, Society, and Politics: The National Health Insurance Law as a Case Study." In *Society and Economy in Israel: Historical and Contemporary Perspectives*, eds. Avi Bareli, Daniel Gutwein, and Tuvia Friling. Beersheva: Ben-Gurion Institute, Ben-Gurion University of the Negev, vol. 2, 431–76 [in Hebrew].

Shwartz-Altshuler, Tehilla. 2002. "Concentrated Ownership of the Print Media: Theoretical and Practical Aspects." Ph.D. dissertation, Hebrew University of Jerusalem.

ed. 2007. *Journalism. Dot. Com: Online Journalism in Israel*. Jerusalem: Israel Democracy Institute [in Hebrew].

2014. "Freedom of the Press: Issues and Events, Israel 2013." In *Annual Report: The Israeli Media in 2013: Agendas, Uses and Trends*, eds. Rafi Mann and Azi Lev-On. Ariel: Institute of New Media Research, 53–78 [in Hebrew].

Shye, Samuel, and Nomika Zion, eds. 2003. *Education and Social Justice in Israel: On Equality of Opportunity*. Jerusalem: Van Leer Jerusalem Institute [in Hebrew].

Shye, Samuel, Alon Lazar, Rivka Duchin, and Benjamin Gidron. 1999. *Philanthropy in Israel: Monetary Donations and Volunteering Patterns of the Public*. Beersheva: Israeli Center for Research into the Third Sector, Ben-Gurion University of the Negev [in Hebrew].

Sicron, Moshe. 1994. *Demography: The Israeli Population – Characteristics and Trends*. Jerusalem: Carmel [in Hebrew].

Sikkuy. 1998. "Toward Quality Local Authorities in the Arab Sector." A joint program with Sikkuy, the Ministry of the Interior, and JDC-Israel, December [in Hebrew].

Silber, Ilana, and Zeev Rosenhek. 1999. *The Historical Development of the Israeli Third Sector*. Beersheva: Israeli Center for Third Sector Research, Ben-Gurion University.

Silver, Ilana. 2008. "The Age of Philanthropists? The Israeli Case." *Civil Society and the Third Sector in Israel*, 2 (1): 9–32 [in Hebrew].

Singer, Jane B., David Domingo, Ari Heinonen, Alfred Hermida, Steve Paulussen, Thorsten Quandt, Zvi Reich, and Marina Vujnovic. 2011. *Participatory Journalism: Guarding Open Gates at Online Newspapers*. Hoboken, NJ: Wiley-Blackwell.

Sivan, Emanuel. 1991. *The 1948 Generation: Myth, Profile and Memory*. Tel-Aviv: Ministry of Defense [in Hebrew].
Skorbianski, Aaron. 1972. "The Story of the Plane Hijacking in the Soviet Union: Coverage by the Israeli Press." Seminar paper for the course, "Secrecy and Publicity in Public Administration." Hebrew University of Jerusalem [in Hebrew].
Skrzycky, Cindy. 2003. *The Regulators: Anonymous Power Brokers in American Politics*. Lanham, MD: Rowman & Littlefield.
Small, Melvin, and Joel David Singer. 1982. *Resort to Arms: International and Civil Wars 1816–1980*. London: Sage Publications.
Smolsky, Raz. 2008. "City Property Tax in Israel Does Not Reflect the Differential Value of the Property." *The Marker* December 12 [in Hebrew].
Smooha, Sammy. 1997. "Ethnic Democracy: Israel as an Archetype." *Israel Studies* 2 (2): 198–241.
2000. "The Regime of the State of Israel: Civil Democracy, Non-Democracy, or Ethnic Democracy?" *Sotziologia Yisraelit* 2 (2): 565–630 [in Hebrew].
2008. *Index of Arab–Jewish Relations in Israel 2007: Attitudes toward the Arab Vision Papers*. Haifa University, April [in Hebrew].
2009. "The Israeli Palestinian-Arab Vision of Transforming Israel into a Binational Democracy." *Constellations* 16 (3): 509–22. http://soc.haifa.ac.il/~s.smooha/uploads/editor_uploads/files/VisionTransformingIsraelIintoBinationalDemocracy_pdf.pdf (accessed December 9, 2015).
2013. *Still Playing by the Rules: Index of Arab–Jewish Relations in Israel 2012*. Haifa: Haifa University [in Hebrew].
Smooha, Sammy, and Yochanan Peres. 1974. "The Ethnic Gap in Israel." *Megamot* 20 (1, January): 5–42 [in Hebrew].
Social Media Branding. N.d. "Election 2015 Research." www.mitoog.com/#!elections-israel-2015/ctzx [in Hebrew] (accessed March 29, 2016).
Soen, Dan, and Perla Eisenkang-Kane. 2004. "Local Government in the Arab Sector." *Principles of Local Government*, Unit 5. Ra'anana: Open University [in Hebrew].
2005. "The Unrecognized Villages." *Principles of Local Government*, Unit 5. Ra'anana: Open University [in Hebrew].
Sofer, Y. 1983. "The Mysteries of Kings of Israel Square." *Maariv* January 31 [in Hebrew].
Solomon, Gil. 2006. "Blumenthal is not Alone: The Full Parade of Convicts." *NRG* March 13. www.nrg.co.il/online/1/ART1/059/569.html [in Hebrew] (accessed April 11, 2016).
Spanier, John. 1959. *The Truman–MacArthur Controversy and the Korean War*. Cambridge, MA: Belknap Press.
Sparrow, Malcolm K. 2000. *The Regulatory Craft*. Washington, DC: Brookings Institution Press.
Sprinzak, Ehud. 1979. "Altalena." *Medina, Mimshal Veyahasim Beinleumiyim* 14: 88–96 [in Hebrew].
1986. *What is Just in His Eyes: Illegalism in Israeli Society*. Tel-Aviv: Sifriyat Hapoalim [in Hebrew].
1993. "Elite Illegalism in Israel and the Question of Democracy." In *Israel Democracy under Stress*, eds. Ehud Sprinzak and Larry Diamond. Boulder, CO: Lynne Rienner Publishers, 173–98.
1995. *Between Extra-Parliamentary Protest and Terror: Political Violence in Israel*. Jerusalem: Jerusalem Institute for Israel Studies [in Hebrew].
Stein, Yehoyakim. 1990. "The Unconscious: Eyes Right!" *Haaretz* January 12 [in Hebrew].
Stern, Yedidia. 2001. *Toward Resolving the Constitutional Aspect of State – Religion Relations*. Jerusalem: Israel Democracy Institute [in Hebrew].
2009. *Between Halakha and Politics*. Jerusalem: Israel Democracy Institute [in Hebrew].
Stern, Yoav. 2007. "Appeal to the Attorney General: Tell the GSS to Stop Impeding Legitimate Political Activity." *Haaretz* March 22 [in Hebrew].
Sternhell, Zeev. 1994. "Two Conceptions of Individual, Nation, and Society." *Mishpat Umimshal* 2: 167–72 [in Hebrew].

Stoker, Gerry. 2006. *Why Politics Matter: Making Politics Work*. Basingstoke, UK: Palgrave Macmillan.

Strøm, Kaare. 1998. "Parliamentary Committees in European Democracies." *Journal of Legislative Studies* 4 (1): 21–59.

Strøm, Kaare, and Wolfgang C. Muller. 1999. "The Keys to Togetherness: Coalition Agreements in Parliamentary Democracies." *Journal of Legislative Studies* 5 (3–4): 255–82.

Sulitzeanu-Kenan, Raanan, Amnon Reichman, and Eran Vigoda-Gadot. 2007. "Judicial Workload: A Comparative Study of 17 Countries." Summary Report (May). Haifa: Center for Public Management and Policy [in Hebrew].

Susser, Bernard, and Asher Cohen. 1999. "From a Consociational to a Crisis-ridden Democracy." *Politika* 3: 9–30 [in Hebrew].

Sussman, Nathan, and Avia Spivak. 2011. "The New Fiscal Rule and Tax Policy." Symposium on the State Budget and the New Fiscal Rule. Jerusalem: Van Leer Jerusalem Institute. www.vanleer.org.il/sites/files/atttachment_field/TheFiscalRule2011-Sussman-and-Spivak.pdf [in Hebrew] (accessed March 16, 2016).

Swirski, Shlomo. 1990. *Education in Israel: Schooling for Inequality*. Tel-Aviv: Breirot [in Hebrew].

1995. *Seeds of Inequality*. Tel-Aviv: Breirot [in Hebrew].

Swirski, Shlomo, and Deborah Bernstein. 1993. "Who Did What Work, for Whom, and for How Much? Israel's Economic Development and the Emergence of the Ethnic Division of Labor." In *Israeli Society: Critical Perspectives*, ed. Uri Ram. Tel-Aviv: Breirot, 120–47 [in Hebrew].

Swirski, Shlomo, and Noga Dagan-Buzaglo. 2009. *Separation, Inequality, and Faltering Leadership: Education in Israel*. Tel-Aviv: Adva Center.

Swirski, Shlomo, and Etty Konor-Atias. 2004. *The Shrinking of the Middle Class in Israel 1988–2002*. Tel-Aviv: Adva Center [in Hebrew].

2006. *A Social Report 2006*. Tel-Aviv: Adva Center [in Hebrew].

2014. *A Social Report 2013*. Tel-Aviv: Adva Center [in Hebrew].

Swirski, Shlomo, Etty Konor-Atias, and Emma Rapoport. 2015. *A Social Report 2014*. Tel-Aviv: Adva Center.

Symposium. 1995. "Judicial Review of the Criminal Process: Decisions about Indictments and Pardons." *Hamishpat* 5: 4–10 [in Hebrew].

Szuster, Amir. 2014. *Political Considerations in Determining Grant Allocations for Local Authorities in Israel*. Jerusalem: Van Leer Jerusalem Institute [in Hebrew].

Tal, Ori. 2008. *Data about the Investigation of Heads of Local Authorities by Enforcement Arms of the Ministry of Environmental Protection*. Jerusalem: Knesset Research and Information Center [in Hebrew].

Tal, Tsvi. 2005. "On the Problem of Conscripting Yeshiva Students." In *Brethren Dwelling Together: Orthodoxy and Non-Orthodoxy in Israel: Positions, Propositions, and Accords*, ed. Uri Dromi. Jerusalem: Israel Democracy Institute, 342–55 [in Hebrew].

Tamir, Josef. 2002. "Despite the Obstacles: Milestones in the Establishment of an Ombudsman." *Iyunim Bevikoret Hamedina* 59: 27–66 [in Hebrew].

Tamir, Michal. 2009. *The State Comptroller: A Critical Look*. Police Paper No. 81, Jerusalem: Israel Democracy Institute [in Hebrew].

Tamir, Yael. 1998. "Two Concepts of Multiculturalism." In *Multiculturalism in a Democratic and Jewish State*, eds. Menachem Mautner, Avi Sagi, and Ronen Shamir. Tel-Aviv: Ramat Publishers, 79–92 [in Hebrew].

Tannenbaum, Avraham. 2003–4. "On the Proper Status of Jewish Law." *Sha'arei Mishpat* 3: 393–423 [in Hebrew].

Taylor, Charles. 1985. *Philosophy and the Human Sciences: Philosophical Papers 2*. Cambridge, UK: Cambridge University Press.

Tesler, Riki. 2001. "The Price of Revolution." In *Shas: The Challenge to Israeliness*, ed. Yoav Peled. Tel-Aviv: Yediot Aharonot, 210–78 [in Hebrew].

2005. "The Gush Emuni Bloc in Municipal Elections 2003: Formation, Penetration and Effect." *Medina Vehevrah* 5 (1).

Thompson, Mark R. 2000. "Whatever Happened to Democratic Revolutions?" *Democratization* 7 (4): 1–20.
Tishler, Asher, and Yoad Shefi. 2005. *The Optimal Structure of the Israeli Defense Industry*. Tel-Aviv: Jaffee Center for Strategic Studies, Tel-Aviv University [in Hebrew].
Tov, Imri. 2003. "The Supervision of the IDF: Economic Aspects." In *Civil–Military Relations in Israel: Influences and Restraints*, ed. Ram Erez. Tel-Aviv: Jaffee Center for Strategic Studies, Tel-Aviv University [in Hebrew].
2005. "The Defense Budget Debate, Yet Once More." *Strategic Assessment* 8 (3), November. Tel-Aviv: Institute for National Security Studies. www.inss.org.il/uploadImages/system Files/adkanENG8_3_Tov_budget.pdf (accessed November 13, 2015).
Transparency International. Various years. Annual reports. *Global Corruption Report*. www.transparency.org (accessed April 13, 2016). Comparison with Israel in www.ti-israel.org [in Hebrew] (accessed August 20, 2016).
Treisman, Daniel. 2000. "The Causes of Corruption: A Cross-National Study." *Journal of Public Economics* 76: 399–457.
Tsibel, Natalia, and Luisa Burck. 2013. *Characterization and Classification of Geographic Units by the Socioeconomic Level of the Population in 2008*. Publication 1530. Jerusalem: Central Bureau of Statistics.
Tsidon, Asher. 1964. *The House of Representatives: A Guide to the Knesset, Legislation, and Governance*. Jerusalem: Ahiasaf [in Hebrew].
Tucker, Nati. 2013. "Elections 2013: The Money, the Campaigns, and the Battles Move from the Street to the Internet." *The Marker* January 10 [in Hebrew].
Tushnet, Mark. 1999. *Taking the Constitution Away from the Courts*. Princeton, NJ: Princeton University Press.
Tuttnauer, Or. 2013. *The Role of the Opposition in the Knesset*. Jerusalem: Israel Democracy Institute [in Hebrew].
Tzadik, Ami. 2006. "Status Report: Project Renewal." Jerusalem: Knesset Research and Information Center [in Hebrew].
Tzameret-Kertcher, Hagar. 2014. *Gender Index 2014*. Jerusalem: Van Leer Jerusalem Institute.
Tzur, Eli. 2002. "Mapam and its Attitude toward Religion in the Second Decade: From a Fighting Socialism to Liberal Secularism." In *On Both Sides of the Bridge: State and Religion in the Early Years of Israel*, eds. Mordechai Bar-On and Zvi Zameret. Jerusalem: Ben-Zvi Institute, 246–72 [in Hebrew].
Tzur, Nadir. 2006. *The Man Who Freed the Strip: Ariel Sharon and the Story of the Disengagement*. Tel-Aviv: Tzivonim [in Hebrew].
UK. 2010. House of Commons Information Office on "Parliamentary Questions" – Factsheet P1, revised August 2010. www.parliament.uk/documents/commons-information-office/p01.pdf (accessed June 6, 2016).
UK, National Council for Voluntary Organizations. 1996. "Meeting the Challenge of Change: Voluntary Action into the 21st Century." Report of the Commission on the Future of the Voluntary Sector. London: National Council for Voluntary Organizations.
UN Human Rights Council. 2009. *Report of the United Nations Fact-Finding Mission on the Gaza Conflict* ("the Goldstone Report"), September 15.
UN Security Council. 2006. *Report of the Secretary-General on Implementation of Security Council Resolution 1701* S/2006/730. www.un.org/en/ga/search/view_doc.asp?symbol=S/2006/670 (accessed April 13, 2016).
United States, National Commission on Terrorist Attacks upon the United States. 2003. *The 9/11 Commission Report*. New York: W.W. Norton.
Urian, Dan. 2004. "Patriotism in Israeli Theater." In *Patriotism – We Love You Homeland*, eds. Avner Ben-Amos and Daniel Bar-Tal. Tel-Aviv: Hakibbutz Hameuchad [in Hebrew].
Urieli, Nahman, and Amnon Barzilai. 1982. *The Rise and Fall of Dash*. Tel-Aviv: Reshafim [in Hebrew].
Vaaknin-Gil, Sima. 2015. "Censorship in Israel." *Mishpat VeTsava* [Law and the Military], July [in Hebrew].
Van Deth, Jan W., and Martin Elff. 2004. "Politicization, Economic Development and Political Interest in Europe." *European Journal of Political Research* 43 (3): 475–506.

Ventura, Raphael. 1997. "The Influence of the Close Family Circle on the Voting Patterns of the Individual in Israel." Ph.D. dissertation, Tel-Aviv University [in Hebrew].

Ventura, Raphael, and Michael Philippov. 2008. *Israeli Secularism in the Surveys of the Guttman Institute 1990–2008*. Jerusalem: Israel Democracy Institute [in Hebrew].

Verba, Sidney. 2003. "Would the Dream of Political Equality Turn out to be a Nightmare?" *Perspectives on Politics* 1 (4, December): 663–79.

Verba, Sidney, Kay Lehman-Schlozman, and Henry E. Brady. 1995. *Voice and Equality – Civic Voluntarism in American Politics*. Cambridge, MA: Harvard University Press.

Verba, Sidney, et al. 2000. "Rational Action and Political Participation." *Journal of Theoretical Politics* 12: 243–68.

Vermeer, Jan Pons. 2003. "Bureaucracy and the Media." In *Media Power, Media Politics*, ed. Mark J. Rozell. Lanham, MD: Rowman & Littlefield, 97–118.

Wald, Emanuel. 1992. *The Gordian Knot: Myths and Dilemmas of Israeli National Security*. Tel-Aviv: Yediot Aharonot Books [in Hebrew].

Walzer, Michael. 1967. "The Obligation to Disobey." *Ethics* 77 (3, April).

1977. *Just and Unjust Wars*. New York: Basic Books.

1989. "Citizenship." In *Political Innovation and Conceptual Change*, eds. Terence Ball, James Farr, and Russell L. Hanson. Cambridge, UK: Cambridge University Press, 211–19.

Walzer, Yael. 2015. "This Year We Watched the News More: A Round-up of 2014 in Television." *YNet* January 4. www.ynet.co.il/articles/0,7340,L-4611055,00.html [in Hebrew] (accessed March 24, 2016).

Warhaftig, Zerach. 1988. *A Constitution for Israel*. Jerusalem: Mesilot [in Hebrew].

Waxman, Efrat, and Dana Blander. 2002. *Patterns of Civic Involvement*, Policy Paper No. 26. Jerusalem: Israel Democracy Institute [in Hebrew].

Webb, Paul, David M. Farrell, and Ian Holliday, eds. 2002. *Political Parties in Advanced Industrial Democracies*. Oxford, UK: Oxford University Press.

Weimann, Gabriel. 1996. "From Polls Shall You Distance Yourself?" *The Seventh Eye* 2 (March) [in Hebrew].

2007. *Public Criticism of the Media in the Second Lebanon War 2006*. Tel-Aviv: Department of Communications, Tel-Aviv University [in Hebrew].

2008. "The Media, Propaganda, and the Election Campaign in Israel." *Basha'ar Bareshet*. www.bashaar.org.il/News.asp?id=91 [in Hebrew] (accessed March 29, 2016).

2015. *The Pioneering Study of Public Opinion Research in Israel: The Israel Institute of Applied Social Research*. Tel-Aviv: Tzivonim [in Hebrew].

Weimann, Gabriel, and Gadi Wolfsfeld. 2002. "The 2001 Election: The Campaign that Changed Nothing." In *The Elections in Israel – 2001*, eds. Asher Arian and Michal Shamir. Jerusalem: Israel Democracy Institute, 101–26 [in Hebrew].

Weimann, Gabriel, Yariv Tsfati, and Rebeka Tukachinsky. 2006. *The Media Coverage of the Israeli 2006 Election*. Tel-Aviv: Herzog Institute for Media, Politics and Society, University of Tel-Aviv [in Hebrew].

Weinstein, Joshua I., ed. 1998. *Disobedience and Democracy*. Jerusalem: Shalem Center [in Hebrew].

Weiss, Shevach. 1970. *A Typology of Local Representatives and the Problem of the Stability of Local Government*. Jerusalem: Akademon [in Hebrew].

1973. *The Politicians in Israel*. Netanya: Achiasaf [in Hebrew].

1977. *The Knesset*. Netanya: Achiasaf [in Hebrew].

1996. "Analysis of Election Results to the 14th Knesset and Prime Ministership." Labor Party [in Hebrew].

1998. *Speaker's Time*. Jerusalem: [no publisher], [in Hebrew].

Weissbrod, Lilly. 2009. "Shas: An Ethnic Religious Party." *Israel Affairs* 9 (4), June 20.

Weitz, Yechiam. 1996. "A Party Struggles with its Failure." *Cathedra* 77: 129 [in Hebrew].

1999. "The Revolution that Didn't Happen." *Panim* 9 [in Hebrew].

ed. 2001. *Israel in the First Decade*. Ra'anana: Open University [in Hebrew].

2002. "The Robbed Cossack." *The Seventh Eye* 40 (September) [in Hebrew].

Werner, Simcha. 1998. "Ethics and Morality in Public Administration in Israel." In *Public Administration in Israel towards the 2000s*, eds. Aharon Kfir and Jacob Reuveny. Tel-Aviv: Tcherikover, 131–65 [in Hebrew].

Witkon, Alfred. 1962. "Law in a Developing State." In *Jubilee Book for Pinchas Rosen*, ed. Haim Cohn. Jerusalem: Hebrew University [in Hebrew].

Woldendorp, Jaap, Hans E. Keman, and Ian Budge. 2000. *Party Government in 48 Democracies, 1945–1998*. Dordrecht: Kluwer Academic Publishers.

Wolfowicz, Nathan. 2004. "Hershele Ostropoler in Court." *Haaretz: Passover Supplement* based on an article in 1951 [in Hebrew].

Wolfsfeld, Gadi. 1988. *The Politics of Provocation: Participation and Protest in Israel*. Albany, NY: SUNY Press.

1991. "Media, Protest and Political Violence." *Journalism Monographs* 127: 1–61.

1995. "Voters as Consumers: Audience Perspectives on the Election Broadcasts." In *The Elections in Israel – 1992*, eds. Asher Arian and Michal Shamir. Albany, NY: SUNY Press, 235–54.

Wolfsfeld, Gadi, and Gabriel Weimann. 1999. "The Battle for the Agenda in the Election Campaign of 1996." *Politika* 4: 9–25 [in Hebrew].

Workshop for Public Knowledge. N.d. www.obudget.org/g2/main/#main//2014/main (accessed April 10, 2016).

World Bank. 2005. "Political Stability in 61 Democracies." www1.worldbank.org/publicsector/indicators/htm

2006. "Worldwide Governance Indicators: Israel." http://info.worldbank.org/governance/wgi/index.aspx#reports (accessed February 17, 2016).

N.d. World Bank. IBRD. IDA. Development Indicators. http://data.worldbank.org/country/israel (accessed May 6, 2016).

Yaacobi, Gad. 1980. *The Government*. Tel-Aviv: Am Oved [in Hebrew].

Yaacobi, Gad, and Ehud Gera. 1975. *The Freedom to Choose*. Tel-Aviv: Am Oved [in Hebrew].

Ya'alon, Moshe. 2006. "Dialogue between the Civilian and Military Echelons: The Actual and the Desirable." In *Relations between the Civilian and Military Echelons in Israel: Against the Backdrop of Military Conflicts*, ed. Ram Erez. Tel-Aviv: Jaffee Center for Strategic Studies, Tel-Aviv University, 15–18 [in Hebrew].

2008. *The Long Short Road*. Tel-Aviv: Yediot Aharonot [in Hebrew].

Yaar, Ephraim. 1986. "Private Entrepreneurship as a Path to Socioeconomic Mobility: An Additional Look at Ethnic Stratification in Israel." *Megamot* 29 (4): 393–412 [in Hebrew].

Yaar, Ephraim, and Zeev Shavit, eds. 2001–3. *Trends in Israeli Society*, 2 vols. Ra'anana: Open University [in Hebrew].

Yaari, Aviezer. 2004. *Civilian Supervision of the Army in Israel*. Tel-Aviv: Jaffee Center for Strategic Studies [in Hebrew].

2006. *Who Does the Council Advise?* Tel-Aviv: Jaffee Center for Strategic Studies, Tel-Aviv University, September [in Hebrew].

Yadgar, Yaacov. 2002. "National Identity in Crisis: The National Narrative in the Israeli Press in the Context of the Lebanon War." In *The Lebanon War and its Effect on Israeli Society and Politics*, ed. Eliezer Don-Yehiya. Ramat Gan: Argov Center, Bar-Ilan University, 18–30 [in Hebrew].

Yanai, Nathan. 1981. *Party Leadership in Israel: Maintenance and Change*. Ramat Gan: Turtledove Publishing.

1982. *Political Crises in Israel*. Jerusalem: Keter Publishing [in Hebrew].

1987. "Ben-Gurion's Concept of *Mamlahtiut*." *Cathedra* 45: 169–89 [in Hebrew].

1990. "The Resumption of a Communal Coalition Tradition." In *Israel's Odd Couple: The 1984 Knesset Elections and the National Unity Government*, eds. Daniel J. Elazar and Shmuel Sandler. Detroit, MI: Wayne State University Press, 169–92.

1990a. "The Transition to a State without a Constitution." In *The Transition from Yishuv to State 1947–49: Continuity and Changes*, ed. Varda Pilovski. Haifa: Herzl Institute, University of Haifa, 23–35 [in Hebrew].

Yaniv, Avner, and Fabian Pascal. 1980. "Doves, Hawks and Other Birds of a Feather: The Distribution of Israeli Parliamentary Opinion on the Future of the Occupied Territories, 1967–1977." *British Journal of Political Science* 10 (2): 260–67.

Yaron, Reuven. 1973. "The President's Powers Should be Expanded." *Maariv* April 3 [in Hebrew].

Yatziv, Gadi. 1999. *The Sectoral Society*. Jerusalem: Bialik Institute [in Hebrew].

Yiftachel, Oren. 2000. "Ethnocracy, Geography, and Democracy: The Politics of Judaizing Israel/Palestine." *Alpayim* 19: 78–105 [in Hebrew].

2006. "The Vision Documents: Look at the Example from Slovakia." *Haaretz* December 21 [in Hebrew].

Yishai, Yael. 1985. "The Israeli Labor Party and the Lebanon War." *Armed Forces and Society* 11 (3): 379–97.

1985a. "Hawkish Proletariat: The Case of Israel." *Journal of Political and Military Sociology* 13: 53–73.

1987. *Interest Groups in Israel*. Tel-Aviv: Am Oved and the Eshkol Institute [in Hebrew].

1997. *Between the Flag and the Banner: Women in Israeli Politics*. Albany, NY: SUNY Press.

1998. "Civil Society in Transition: Interest Politics in Israel." *Annals of the American Academy of Political and Social Science* 555: 147–62.

1998a. "Political Parties and Social Movements: Integration or Separation?" In *The Demise of Political Parties: Israeli Democracy in Crisis*, ed. Dan Koren. Tel-Aviv: Hakibbutz Hameuchad, 155–66 [in Hebrew].

1999. "'Old' Versus 'New' Politics in the 1996 Election." In *The Election in Israel – 1996*, eds. Asher Arian and Michal Shamir. Albany, NY: SUNY Press, 171–201.

2001. "Bringing Society Back In: Post-Cartel Parties in Israel." *Party Politics* 7 (November): 667–87.

2003. *Between Recruitment and Rapprochement: Civil Society in Israel*. Jerusalem: Carmel [in Hebrew].

2008. "Civil Society Disintegrating? Some Comments on the Current Situation." *Civil Society and the Third Sector in Israel* 2 (2): 7–27 [in Hebrew].

YNet. 2009. "IDF and the Palestinians: Casualty Numbers Were Not Exaggerated." January 22. www.ynet.co.il/articles/0,7340,L-3660395,00.html [in Hebrew] (accessed May 5, 2016).

Yoaz, Yuval, and David Ratner. 2004. "ILA to Allow Israeli Arab Family to Build in Jewish Town." *Haaretz* May 10.

Yonah, Yossi. 1998. "Constitutional Citizenship, a Nation State, or a Multicultural Democracy? Israel and the Limits of Liberal Democracy." *Alpayim* 16 (April): 238–63 [in Hebrew].

2001. "The Third Arrangement." In *The Great Divide: Israeli Society Between Rift and Repair*, ed. Ruvik Rosenthal. Tel-Aviv: Yediot Aharonot, 322–34 [in Hebrew].

2006. "A Common Core: A Recipe for Social Control?" In *Towards an Educational Revolution*, ed. Dan Inbar. Jerusalem and Tel-Aviv: Van Leer Jerusalem Institute and Hakibbutz Hameuchad, 203–13 [in Hebrew].

2015. *Cracks in the Wall: The Israeli Social Protest of 2011*. Jerusalem: Keter Publishing House.

Yonah, Yossi, and Yossi Dahan. 1999. "The Education System in Transition: From Collectivism to Civil Individualism – Parental Choice as a Case Study." In *Fifty Years of the Israeli Educational System*, ed. Elad Peled. Jerusalem: Ministry of Defense in cooperation with the Ministry of Education, 163–79 [in Hebrew].

Yonah, Yossi, and Yehouda Shenhav. 2005. *What is Multiculturalism? On the Politics of Identity in Israel*. Tel-Aviv: Bavel [in Hebrew].

Yonah, Yossi, and Avia Spivak. 2012. *To Do Things Differently: A Model for a Well-Ordered Society. The Social Protest of 2011–2012*. Tel-Aviv: Hakibbutz Hameuchad [in Hebrew].

Young, D. 2012. "The State of Theory and Research on Social Enterprises." In *Social Enterprises: An Organizational Perspective*, eds. Benjamin Gidron and Yeheskel Hasenfeld. London: Palgrave Macmillan, 19–46.

Yuran, Noam. 2001. *Channel 2: The New Etatism*. Tel-Aviv: Resling [in Hebrew].

Zadok, Haim. 1974. "A Legal Opinion about Ministerial Responsibility." In *The Israeli Political System*, eds. Itzhak Galnoor and Menachem Hofnung. Jerusalem: Akademon, 511–14 [in Hebrew].

Zahor, Ze'ev. 1997. "The First Election and the Political Map." In *The First Decade 1948–1958*, eds. Zvi Zameret and Hanna Yablonka. Jerusalem: Ben-Zvi Institute, 27–40 [in Hebrew].

Zameret, Zvi. 1988. "The Affair of Count Folke Bernadotte's Mediation." *First Year of Independence 1948–1949*, ed. Mordechai Naor. Jerusalem: Ben-Zvi Institute, 143–56 [in Hebrew].

1997. "Ten Years of Education." In *The First Decade 1948–1958*, eds. Zvi Zameret and Hanna Yablonka. Jerusalem: Ben-Zvi Institute, 123–36 [in Hebrew].

2002. "'A Jewish State – Yes; A Clerical State – No.' The Attitude of Mapai Leadership to Religion and the Religious Public." In *On Both Sides of the Bridge: State and Religion in the Early Years of Israel*, eds. Mordechai Bar-On and Zvi Zameret. Jerusalem: Ben-Zvi Institute, 175–245 [in Hebrew].

Zameret, Zvi, and Hanna Yablonka, eds. 1997. *The First Decade 1948–1958*. Jerusalem: Ben-Zvi Institute [in Hebrew].

Zamir, Yitzhak. 1983. "Legal Aspects of a Commission of Inquiry." *Hapraklit* 35 (3): 323–32 [in Hebrew].

1987. "Ethics in Politics." *Mishpatim* 17 (2): 250–83 [in Hebrew].

1989. "Human Rights and State Security." *Mishpatim* 19: 17–39 [in Hebrew].

1993. "Judicial Activism: The Decision to Decide." *Iyunei Mishpat* 17 (3): 647–58 [in Hebrew].

ed. 1993–94. *Interpretation of the Basic Laws*. Jerusalem: Hebrew University [in Hebrew].

1999. "Administrative Tribunals: Their Establishment, Composition and Administration." In *The Tamir Book*, eds. Yosef Tamir and Ora Hirsch. Tel-Aviv: Bursi, 81–95 [in Hebrew].

Zarhia, Zvi. 2014. "Party Debts Revealed: Fearful of Banks, Borrowing from the State." *The Marker* August 12. www.themarker.com/news/1.2506331 [in Hebrew] (accessed August 4, 2016).

Zarkawy, Nihad, and Idit Blit-Cohen. 2008. "An Online Nonprofit Association: Israeli Nonprofit Associations' Usage of the Internet." *Society and the Third Sector in Israel* 2 (2) [in Hebrew].

Zeidan, Elias. 2005. *Volunteering, Giving, and Attitudes toward Organizations in Arab-Palestinian Society in Israel*. Beersheva: Israeli Center for Third Sector Research, Ben-Gurion University of the Negev [in Hebrew].

Zeidan, Elias, and As'ad Ghanem. 2000. *Giving and Volunteering in Palestinian Arab Society in Israel*. Beersheva: Israeli Center for Third Sector Research, Ben-Gurion University of the Negev [in Hebrew].

2000a. "Donation and Voluntarism in Arab-Palestinian Society in Israel." Beersheva: Israeli Center for Third Sector Research, Ben-Gurion University of the Negev [in Hebrew].

Zelikovich, Moran. 2004. "Experts: Dovrat Report Will Turn Schools into Machines for Grades." *YNet* July 4. www.ynet.co.il/articles/0,7340,L-2942029,00.html [in Hebrew] (accessed March 16, 2016).

Zrahiya, Zvi. 2015. "Israel Passes 2015–2016 Budget in Late Night Vote." *Haaretz* November 19. www.haaretz.com/israel-news/.premium-1.687018 (accessed June 6, 2016).

2015a. "The Secret Deals of the Finance Ministry." *The Marker* February 8 [in Hebrew].

Index